D1713261

HANDBOOK OF LATIN AMERICAN STUDIES: No. 56

A Selective and Annotated Guide to Recent Publications in Art, History, Literature, Music, Philosophy, and Electronic Resources

VOLUME 57 WILL BE DEVOTED TO THE SOCIAL SCIENCES: ANTHROPOLOGY, ECONOMICS, GEOGRAPHY, GOVERNMENT AND POLITICS, INTERNATIONAL RELATIONS, AND SOCIOLOGY

EDITORIAL NOTE: Comments concerning the *Handbook of Latin American Studies* should be sent directly to the Editor, *Handbook of Latin American Studies*, Hispanic Division, Library of Congress, Washington, D.C. 20540.

HANDBOOK OF LATIN AMERICAN STUDIES: NO. 56

HUMANITIES

Prepared by a Number of Scholars
for the Hispanic Division of The Library of Congress

DOLORES MOYANO MARTIN, *Editor*
P. SUE MUNDELL, *Assistant Editor*

1999

UNIVERSITY OF TEXAS PRESS   *Austin*

International Standard Book Number 0-292-75231-8
International Standard Serial Number 0072-9833
Library of Congress Catalog Card Number 36-32633
Copyright © 1999 by the University of Texas Press
Printed in the United States of America

Requests for permission to reproduce material
from this work should be sent to
Permissions, University of Texas Press,
Box 7819, Austin, Texas 78713-7819.

First Edition, 1999

The paper used in this publication meets
the minimum requirements of American National
Standard for Information Sciences—Permanence
of Paper for Printed Library Materials,
ANSI Z39.48-1984. ∞

CONTRIBUTING EDITORS

HUMANITIES

Edna Acosta-Belén, *State University of New York-Albany*, LITERATURE
Maureen Ahern, *The Ohio State University*, TRANSLATIONS
Severino João Albuquerque, *University of Wisconsin-Madison*, LITERATURE
Félix Angel, *Inter-American Development Bank*, ART
Uva de Aragón, *Florida International University*, LITERATURE
Barbara von Barghahn, *George Washington University*, ART
María Luisa Bastos, *Lehman College-CUNY*, LITERATURE
Alvaro Félix Bolaños, *University of Florida*, LITERATURE
Dain Borges, *University of California-San Diego*, HISTORY
John Britton, *Frances Marion University*, HISTORY
Francisco Cabanillas, *Bowling Green State University*, LITERATURE
Sara Castro-Klarén, *The Johns Hopkins University*, LITERATURE
Don M. Coerver, *Texas Christian University*, HISTORY
Edith B. Couturier, *National Endowment for the Humanities*, HISTORY
Edward Cox, *Rice University*, HISTORY
Joseph T. Criscenti, *Professor Emeritus, Boston College*, HISTORY
César Ferreira, *University of Oklahoma*, LITERATURE
Francisco J. Fonseca, *Princeton University*, ELECTRONIC RESOURCES
José Manuel García García, *New Mexico State University*, LITERATURE
Magdalena García Pinto, *University of Missouri, Columbia*, LITERATURE
John D. Garrigus, *Jacksonville University*, HISTORY
Miguel Gomes, *University of Connecticut*, LITERATURE
Lance R. Grahn, *Marquette University*, HISTORY
María Cristina Guiñazú, *Lehman College-CUNY*, LITERATURE
Michael T. Hamerly, *Independent Consultant, Seattle, Washington*, HISTORY
Robert Haskett, *University of Oregon*, HISTORY
José M. Hernández, *Professor Emeritus, Georgetown University*, HISTORY
Rosemarijn Hoefte, *Royal Institute of Linguistics and Anthropology, The Netherlands*, HISTORY
Joel Horowitz, *Saint Bonaventure University*, HISTORY
Regina Igel, *University of Maryland*, LITERATURE
Nils P. Jacobsen, *University of Illinois*, HISTORY
Peter T. Johnson, *Princeton University*, ELECTRONIC RESOURCES
Erick Langer, *Carnegie Mellon University*, HISTORY
Pedro Lastra, *State University of New York at Stony Brook*, LITERATURE
Asunción Lavrin, *Arizona State University at Tempe*, HISTORY
Peter S. Linder, *New Mexico Highlands University*, HISTORY
Maria Angélica Guimarães Lopes, *University of South Carolina*, LITERATURE
Carol Maier, *Kent State University*, TRANSLATIONS

Teresita Martínez-Vergne, *Macalester College*, HISTORY
David McCreery, *Georgia State University*, HISTORY
Joan E. Meznar, *Westmont College*, HISTORY
Molly Molloy, *New Mexico State University*, INTERNET RESOURCES
Elizabeth Monasterios, *State University of New York-Stony Brook*, LITERATURE
Naomi Hoki Moniz, *Georgetown University*, LITERATURE
José M. Neistein, *Brazilian-American Cultural Institute, Washington*, ART
José Miguel Oviedo, *University of Pennsylvania*, LITERATURE
Suzanne B. Pasztor, *University of the Pacific*, HISTORY
Daphne Patai, *University of Massachusetts-Amherst*, TRANSLATIONS
Anne Pérotin-Dumon, *Pontificia Universidad Católica de Chile*, HISTORY
Charles A. Perrone, *University of Florida*, LITERATURE
René Prieto, *Southern Methodist University*, LITERATURE
José Promis, *University of Arizona*, LITERATURE
Inés Quintero, *Universidad Central de Venezuela*, HISTORY
Susan E. Ramírez, *DePaul University*, HISTORY
Jane M. Rausch, *University of Massachusetts-Amherst*, HISTORY
Oscar Rivera-Rodas, *University of Tennessee, Knoxville*, LITERATURE
Humberto Rodríguez-Camilloni, *Virginia Polytechnic Institute*, ART
Mario A. Rojas, *Catholic University of America*, LITERATURE
Kathleen Ross, *New York University*, TRANSLATIONS
William F. Sater, *California State University, Long Beach*, HISTORY
Jacobo Sefamí, *University of California-Irvine*, LITERATURE
Susan M. Socolow, *Emory University*, HISTORY
Robert Stevenson, *University of California, Los Angeles*, MUSIC
Barbara A. Tenenbaum, *Hispanic Division, The Library of Congress*, HISTORY
Juan Carlos Torchia Estrada, *Consultant, Hispanic Division, The Library of Congress*, PHILOSOPHY
Lilián Uribe, *Central Connecticut State University*, LITERATURE
Stephen Webre, *Louisiana Tech University*, HISTORY
Raymond L. Williams, *University of California, Riverside*, LITERATURE
Stephanie Wood, *University of Oregon*, HISTORY

SOCIAL SCIENCES

Juan M. del Aguila, *Emory University*, GOVERNMENT AND POLITICS
Benigno E. Aguirre-López, *Texas A&M University*, SOCIOLOGY
Amalia M. Alberti, *Independent Consultant, San Salvador*, SOCIOLOGY
G. Pope Atkins, *University of Texas at Austin*, INTERNATIONAL RELATIONS
Melissa H. Birch, *University of Kansas*, ECONOMICS
Eduardo Borensztein, *International Monetary Fund*, ECONOMICS
Jacqueline Braveboy-Wagner, *The City College-CUNY*, INTERNATIONAL RELATIONS
Roderic A. Camp, *Tulane University*, GOVERNMENT AND POLITICS
William L. Canak, *Middle Tennessee State University*, SOCIOLOGY
Gustavo Cañonero, *IMF*, ECONOMICS
César Caviedes, *University of Florida*, GEOGRAPHY
Marc Chernick, *Georgetown University*, GOVERNMENT AND POLITICS
Jeffrey Cohen, *Texas A&M University*, ANTHROPOLOGY
Harold Colson, *University of California, San Diego*, ELECTRONIC RESOURCES

Foreign Corresponding Editors

Special Contributing Editors

CONTENTS

HISTORY

EDITOR'S NOTE

I. GENERAL AND REGIONAL TRENDS

THE FIELD OF LATIN AMERICAN history continues to evolve in unpredictable and original ways. A new generation of scholars is replacing the "aficionados and autodidacts" of the "Old Guard" exemplified by the Ecuadorian Jorge Salvador Lara (b. 1926, p. 317). In contrast to their predecessors, these new men and women have been professionally trained in their national universities or abroad, their research objectives are more specialized and focused, their investigations more rigorous, their methodologies more innovative, and their conclusions less generalized. This hemisphere-wide development, underway for the last two to three decades, is especially evident in the works reviewed for *HLAS 56* from four countries: Colombia, Ecuador, Bolivia, and Argentina. One contributor observes that new Colombian historians are "posing new questions, experimenting with methodologies, and exploring untapped archives"—a transformation reflected in articles edited since 1963 and published in the *Anuario Colombiano de Historia Social y de la Cultura.* A ground breaking work, consisting of articles by Colombian and foreign historians evaluating the state of their art, is *La historia al fin del milenio* (item **2691**). These essays "attest to the enormous strides made in historiography in recent years and to the vigor of Colombian intellectual life in spite of the country's political travails." (pp. 379–380). In Ecuador, the Pontificia Universidad Católica and the Facultad Latinoamericana de Ciencias Sociales (FLACSO), both in Quito, have trained a remarkable group of young men and women, authors of several original theses, now published, on the protectorate of Indians (item **2317**), the development of the Chota River Valley (item **2327**), and the nature of the cinchona trade (item **2353** and p. 337). Another remarkable Ecuadorian work is Tobar Donoso's "examination of the legal status of Indians with regard to tithing, debt peonage, and agrarian reform" (item **2750** and p. 390). In Bolivia, a number of well-trained younger scholars are producing local and regional history, some focusing at last on the long-neglected eastern lowlands (see item **2829** and p. 406 and item **2861** and p. 409). On the other hand, the colonial history of Bolivia, or Upper Peru as it was then known, continues to attract "at least as many, if not more, North Americans and Europeans" as it does Bolivians (p. 318). In Argentina, the more than "ten years since the restoration of democracy have permitted a flourishing of the historical profession." While the decline of the publishing industry in Argentina has reduced the historical output to journal articles and short books, the level of writing remains extremely high (p. 422).

This biennium has also seen a shift in the theoretical underpinnings of Latin American historiography. Economic determinism is losing its hold as a leading explanation for the forces driving Latin American history, while interest in culture or how "ethnic practices . . . shape . . . behavior" continues to climb (p. 393). In their studies of cultural history, researchers are delving further into the use of nontraditional sources of information, such as visual materials, while also exploring the rituals, traditions, and practices that bind a society together. Examples of the latter in

HLAS 56 include studies of the rituals of death and examinations of the bureaucracy. One historian emphasizes how "visual images are gaining in importance for our understanding of history." He points to three beautiful volumes that illustrate his point: "Mould de Pease and Longhi have assembled extraordinary photos and paintings in an upbeat nationalist volume showing how Peru became the diverse nation it is today" (item **2798**). Likewise, The Smithsonian Institution's exemplary edition of selected photos by Peru's outstanding photographer Martín Chambi (item **2765**) shows, better than any text, the complexity of Cusco regional society during the mid-20th century (p. 393). In Mexico, historians are tapping the nation's photographic archives in order "to provide extraordinary insights into the Mexican soul," a trend exemplified by a notable volume of portraits of dead children from Ameca, Jalisco (item **1364**) that illuminates a neglected area of the national experience, that "other-wordly aspect of Mexican cosmology" (p. 195). The examination of death and its changing rituals is also evident in Peru, where Tamayo Herrera provides preliminary insights into a new terrain of cultural inquiry (item **2809** and p. 402). In the River Plate region numerous works reveal a strong interest "in the history of bureaucrats and bureaucracy" as a distinct group with its own practices, traditions, and beliefs (items **2469, 2515, 2544, 2545, 2613, 2618, 2625, 2634** and **2635** and pp. 352–372).

Demographic history continues to attract scholars interested in exploring the complexity and richness of Latin America's populations. Nancie L. González (item **1723**) and Darío Euraque (item **1716**) explore the previously neglected subject of Palestinian emigration to Central America (p. 236). A "magisterial study" of the importation of Asian workers to the Caribbean and their working conditions is found in the pages of Walton Look Lai's *Indentured labor* (item **2041** and p. 292). Kartick has published a worthwhile analysis of the "unsuccessful attempt of Chinese immigrants to achieve self-sufficiency in British Guiana" (item **2037** and p. 291). Robert Levine is the author of a scholarly and well-written history of the Jewish experience in Cuba (item **1838** and p. 267). Jarach and Smolensky provide a noteworthy assessment of the fate of two thousand Italian Jews who fled to Argentina between 1938–42 to escape from fascism (item **3050**). And well-known female author Marjorie Agosin's *The cross and the star* (item **2868**) provides a poignant memoir of a Jewish childhood in southern Chile, a region dominated by Nazis during World War II (p. 411).

The study of Afro-Latin American populations is another powerful trend that continues to thrive in works reviewed for this volume. Brazilians, as usual, lead the way in the quantity and quality of their works on Afro-Brazilian history. Recent studies offer fascinating new insights into slavery and urban life in the 19th century (items **3360** and **3368**), and race and politics in the 20th century (items **3310** and **3223**). Ecuadorians held a third historical congress entirely devoted to the study of the nation's African roots (item **2736**). And in literature, there has been a remarkable increase of interest in the works of Afro-Ecuadorian writers, such as Antonio Preciado (item **4066**) and Nelson Estupiñán Bass (item **3978**), and female poet Luz Argentina Chiriboga (item **3959**). One outstanding study annotated in this volume, singled out as a truly unparalleled work, is the "Herculean investigation" of the Cuban slave market written by Bergad, Iglesias and Barcia (item **1985** and p. 285). Another excellent cultural history by González Pérez examines the "whitening" of black memory, or how the desire for cultural and social assimilation on the part of Puerto Rico's Africans caused their disappearance from the island's abolitionist and folkloric literature (item **2024** and p. 290). Finally, several articles on civil unrest in the late 18th century "delineate the unique combination of slave rebelliousness, class conflict, French revolutionary ideology, and international commercial relationships that fostered Venezuelan nationhood" (items **2275, 2246, 2270, 2271,** and **2253** and pp. 323–326).

Imaginative new approaches to the history of indigenous populations and further explorations of "indigenous thought" continue in *HLAS 56*. An example of the former is an innovative study of "frontiers" by Catherine Julien (item **600**), and histories of less well-known indigenous populations such as the following: "the Pijaos (item **563**), the Cazuetíos (item **584**), Pakaxe (item **571**), Muiscas (item **629** and **591**), Tomuza (item **620**), Soito (item **572**), Puelches (item **576**), Guaikuru (item **666**), Mojos (item **587**), and Churumatas (item **574** and **631**)" (p. 105). Moreover, "indigenous thought is the centerpiece of an extremely significant group of studies" exploring the "meanings of history, myth, and visions of the past, present, and future" as gleaned from a variety of indigenous records (items **542, 438, 455, 491,** and **551** and p. 77). Other works recognize "that indigenous people and Spaniards had a shared cultural experience—some have used the term 'dialogue'—in which both sides contributed to the formation of a kind of indigenous Catholicism," a far more complex phenomenon than "earlier treatments of 'syncretism'" would indicate (p. 76).

The history of women in Latin America continues as a leading trend in this *HLAS*. Since *HLAS 54* there has been a steadily increasing number of examinations of indigenous women before and after the Spanish conquest. Good illustrations of this work are the special issue of the journal *Ethnohistory* devoted to "Women, Power and Resistance in Colonial Mesoamerica" (item **434**); Frances Karttunen's "revisionist assessment of La Malinche," Hernán Cortés' indigenous female companion and informant (item **474**); and Stephanie Wood's exceptionally fine investigation of rural Nahua women of the Toluca Valley (item **549** and p. 104). The plight of Latin American women in general is skillfully examined by Asunción Lavrin in her excellent study of the "female ideal" as envisioned by the Catholic Church (item **903** and p. 148). Historians of Mexico have used oral history, prosopography, and biography to shed light on the history of the nation's women during the Revolution (p. 196). Marie-Antoinette Menier has documented a little-known and fascinating case of female self-assertion in the 19th-century Caribbean when Guadeloupe's first qualified midwives confronted the male establishment (item **2056** and p. 294). In Brazil, the study of women continues to flourish, especially in works concerning the meaning of marriage in a patriarchal society (items **3241, 3247, 3357, 3262,** and **3230**), and in rigorous analyses of female prostitution (items **3362** and **3365**).

The centennial of the Spanish American War of 1898 is beginning to generate the anticipated publications, especially in Spain where historians have issued works such as *Ramón La Sagra y Cuba* (item **2074**) and half a dozen serious studies of the conflict (p. 263). Undoubtedly, many more works on the topic will be featured in the next humanities volume, *HLAS 58*.

II. OBITUARIES

GEORGE A. KUBLER (1912–1996)

We deeply regret the death of George A. Kubler, founding father of the field of Latin American art history in the United States, and the first to prepare our chapter on the art history of Spanish America, participating as contributing editor from *HLAS 8* (1943) through *HLAS 10* (1947). Kubler, a native of Los Angeles, entered Yale University in 1929 and, after completing his doctorate, remained there the rest of his life. He was a splendid mentor who trained numerous students who went on to become outstanding scholars. He also produced a number of seminal studies such as *The Quechua in the colonial world* (1946), *The Tovar Calendar* (1951) and *The shape of time* (1960), the latter turning into one of the most influential works of its day. Like Lewis Hanke, Kubler was a multidisciplinary pioneer who explored the interactions and relationships of art with economics, linguistics, demography, anthropology, and, towards the end of his life, the impact of art and visual imagery on evolutionary biology.

IRVING A. LEONARD (1896–1995)

Another Yale alumnus and a native of New Haven, Leonard was one of our first contributors. He died in Washington, DC at age 99, a loss deeply felt by the *HLAS* family. Leonard earned a doctorate in Latin American history from the University of California at Berkeley. He worked for the Rockefeller Foundation and taught at Brown University and the University of Michigan where he became chair of the Romance Languages Department. Leonard inaugurated our chapter on "Spanish American Colonial Literature," promising to rescue it from a "neglect" which he attributed to the prevalence of the "Black Legend" about Spain in the English-speaking world. And rescue it he did, devoting his entire life and scholarship to the subject of the colonial literature and history of Spanish America. He was the first to single out the importance and significance of the Spanish chronicles of discovery and conquest as keys towards understanding the Latin American character, history, and destiny. Leonard served as our contributor for 28 years, from our first volume in 1936 through *HLAS 26* (1964). Now, more than 60 years later, one can still read his early introductory essays in the *Handbook* with astonishment and delight for they have lost none of their originality, power, and acuity. Shortly before his death, Leonard was awarded the Order of the Aztec Eagle by the government of Mexico for his outstanding contribution to the study of that country.

ROBERT J. MULLEN (1917–1997)

We note with sadness the passing of a third devoted and talented contributor. A native of Milwaukee, Wisconsin, Mullen was raised in Texas, and graduated from the University of Notre Dame. After 30 years of service as a Navy captain and government employee, Mullen embarked on a third career. In 1971, he was awarded the first PhD in Latin American art history by the University of Maryland where his mentor was another *HLAS* contributor, the art historian James A. Lynch. From 1975 until his retirement in 1996, Mullen served with distinction as professor of art history at the University of Texas in San Antonio. He is the author of numerous books on the art and architecture of Oaxaca, Mexico. He served as our contributor for the chapter on the colonial art of Middle America from *HLAS 38* (1976) through *HLAS 48* (1986).

III. CLOSING DATE

The closing date for works annotated in this volume was early 1996. Publications received and cataloged at the Library of Congress after that date will be annotated in the next humanities volume, *HLAS 58*.

IV. ELECTRONIC ACCESS TO THE *HANDBOOK*

The *HLAS* staff continues to maintain, update, and improve its World Wide Web site, *HLAS Online*, which is available at **http://lcweb2.loc.gov/hlas/**. As of August 1998, all bibliographic records corresponding to *HLAS* volumes 1–56, plus available in-process records for volumes 57–60, are accessible at no charge to those with graphical browsers such as Netscape, WebExplorer, etc., as well those using the non-graphical browser LYNX. Version 2.0 of the *Handbook of Latin American Studies CD-ROM* or *HLAS/CD*, containing all bibliographic records and chapter essays for volumes 1–55, is scheduled to be released early in 1999 by its publisher, the Fundación Histórica Tavera (for further information on purchasing the *HLAS/CD*, please write to the Fundación Histórica Tavera, Claudio Coello No. 123, 28006 Madrid, Spain or send a fax to 34-91-581-1932). In addition to including the data from two new volumes of the *Handbook* print edition, the new CD-ROM interface was redesigned to make it more user-friendly.

V. CHANGES IN VOLUME

Changes in Coverage

Because of budgetary constraints, and in line with changes recommended by the *Handbook*'s Advisory Board at their November 1992 meeting, the chapter on Spanish-American literature before modernism was eliminated.

Electronic Resources

The Electronic Resources chapter was prepared jointly by Molly Molloy from New Mexico State University, Peter Johnson from Princeton University, and Francisco Fonseca, also of Princeton.

Art

Félix Angel, curator of the Inter-American Development Bank's Cultural Center, annotated works on the 19th- and 20th-century art of Spanish America.

History

Susan Ramírez of DePaul University assumed responsibility for canvassing the materials on the ethnohistory of South America. Lance Grahn, Marquette University, covered the colonial history of Colombia and Venezuela. John Garrigus of Jacksonville University assisted Anne Pérotin-Dumon by annotating works on Haiti. Suzanne Pasztor, University of the Pacific, collaborated on the revolution and post-revolution period of Mexican history. Erick Langer of Carnegie Mellon University covered the 19th- and 20th-century history of Bolivia. Peter Linder of New Mexico Highlands University and Inés Quintero of Universidad Central de Venezuela annotated materials on the national history of Venezuela. Joel Horowitz of Saint Bonaventure University assisted Joseph Criscenti in covering the national history of Argentina, Paraguay, and Uruguay. Brazilian history was covered by Dain Borges, University of California at San Diego, and Joan Meznar, Westmont College.

Literature

César Ferreira of the University of North Texas covered prose fiction for Bolivia, Ecuador, and Peru. José Manuel García García of New Mexico State University prepared the chapter on Mexican prose fiction. Edna Acosta-Belén of the State University of New York at Albany and Uva de Aragón of Florida International University covered the prose fiction of the Hispanic Caribbean. Two new contributors joined the group collaborating on poetry: Miguel Gomes of the University of Connecticut, who reviewed works from Chile, and Jacobo Sefamí of the University of California at Irvine, who covered Mexico. Charles Perrone of the University of Florida annotated Brazilian *crônicas*, and Severino João Albuquerque of the University of Wisconsin-Madison covered Brazilian drama. Maureen Ahern of The Ohio State University joined the group of contributors working on literature in translation.

Subject Index

The *Handbook* uses *Library of Congress Subject Headings (LCSH)* when they are consistent with usage among Latin Americanists. Differences in practice, however, make adaptation of LCSH headings necessary: 1) the *Handbook* index uses only two levels, while LC headings usually contain more; and 2) *Handbook* practice is to prefer a "subject-place" pattern, while LC practice generally uses a "place-subject" pattern. Automation of the *Handbook* has required that the subject index be compiled with two audiences in mind: users of the print edition and users of the online database. It has also demanded that index terms, once established, remain as stable as possible. Work has begun towards a complete thesaurus of *Handbook* subject index terms. In the meantime, cross references are included from subject terms used in *HLAS 48-HLAS 55* to new terms in this volume. (A list of the subject headings used in indexing *HLAS 50-HLAS 60* is available from the *Handbook's* World Wide Web site at **http://lcweb2.loc.gov/hlas/subjects.html**.) Finally, since the *Handbook* is arranged by discipline, readers are encouraged to consult the table of contents for broad subject coverage.

Other Changes

In line with the Library of Congress' recent decision to romanize Chinese-language materials using the pinyin rather than the Wade-Giles system (to take effect in the year 2000 or soon therafter), with this volume the *Handbook* will begin using pinyin to cite materials in that language.

VI. EDITOR'S FAREWELL

It is with a heavy heart that I bid farewell to the *Handbook of Latin American Studies* after 29 years of service, 22 as Editor and seven as Assistant Editor. These have been among the most challenging and exciting years of my professional life. In the course of it, there have been disappointments and achievements but, above all, extraordinary challenges that helped me to grow and mature both as an individual and as a professional. As I look back over all these years, I perceive my editorship as an exceptional journey that illuminated the richness, complexity, and creativity of Latin American culture in its infinite mutations. This revealing trajectory also exposed me to the fine scholarship that seeks to explore and understand this wondrous Latin American universe which, no longer exotic and remote, is now a vibrant component of the United States.

Dolores Moyano Martin

HANDBOOK OF
LATIN AMERICAN STUDIES:
No. 56

ELECTRONIC RESOURCES

PETER T. JOHNSON, *Bibliographer for Latin America, Spain, and Portugal, Princeton University*
MOLLY MOLLOY, *Assistant Professor, New Mexico State University, Las Cruces*
FRANCISCO J. FONSECA, *Assistant to the Bibliographer for Latin America, Spain, and Portugal, Princeton University*

THIS SECTION OFFERS a highly selective listing of electronic resources available on CD-ROM, diskette, or through the Internet. Materials included here cover the humanities; some are exclusively Latin American in content, while others have significant portions devoted to Latin America. Consultation of *HLAS 54*, pp. 3–22, and *HLAS 55*, pp. 1–12, will yield additional citations appropriate for many humanities topics. Given the dynamic qualities involved in developing and marketing electronic resources, researchers are advised to identify different strategies for keeping abreast of the various forms in which electronic information appears. Increasingly, such resources receive notice in scholarly and professional journals and many are also displayed in "live" interactive demonstrations at national and international conferences. In addition, libraries customarily provide links on their Internet home pages to various electronic resources, some of which are accessible only by use of a password due to licensing agreement restrictions. The Research Libraries Information Network or RLIN's subscription-based electronic resources file (Machine-Readable Data File or MDF) reveals many general as well as highly specialized resources, an indication of the continuing electronic publishing boom. As new resources are developed, many of the better-funded university and research libraries acquire them.

By providing ready access to vast amounts of information, the development of electronic resources is rapidly changing research possibilities. As with print information, identifying and searching appropriate resources requires knowledge and tenacity because of the considerable range of quality and user-friendliness demonstrated by these products. Developing and maintaining basic searching skills is indispensable as software changes, data is reconfigured, and availability and access methods evolve. Above all, the ability to mediate between print and electronic resources remains paramount, for not all materials of current or historical importance are accessible exclusively from electronic resources. Furthermore, economic realities suggest that certain areas of the humanities, including most of its important texts, will not be electronically available for many years to come. This is not to diminish the valuable contributions that the electronic resources cited below have made and continue to make to Latin American area research. Indeed, these resources signal the creative strength and vigor of many countries' public and private sectors, all working to provide improved access to information, thereby enhancing research prospects. [PTJ and FJF]

CD-ROM AND DISKETTE RESOURCES

For inclusion in this subsection, a title must provide qualitatively important material as well as easy access from initial installation through actual use. Some titles reviewed achieved the first standard, but proved nearly impossible to install or use because of product or software design defects; these titles the contributing editors chose to exclude. The process of reviewing titles for over a year revealed certain patterns worth remembering as these formats gain increasing application.

Specialized databases extend broadly across the humanities. At one level are national book publisher association trade lists formatted into a kind of *Books in Print.* Book dealers also are beginning to offer access to their bibliographic files; these generally are more complete than the publishers' trade listings because they include government documents and non-commercial imprints. While originally intended as marketing tools for books and serials, these products may provide annotations and other information about the publisher or author, while their selectivity and scholarly focus offer added value.

Libraries' general and specialized catalogs are increasingly being placed on CD-ROMs and often are concurrently accessible through the Internet. Because of the need to acquire updated CD-ROMs to maintain currency with new accessions, bibliographic databases of this type are best used through the Internet whenever available. Among the more specialized databases appearing are those providing access to dissertations and theses, special collections, and library holdings for a specific time period, such as the *Epistolario* (item **11**), which contains the Nicolás Guillén epistolary in the Fondos de la Biblioteca Fernando Ortiz.

Serials in different configurations now figure commonly among the bibliographic materials available on CD-ROMs and diskettes. Ranging from the complete texts of an entire collection of a serial title, to just indexes for one or more serials, resources of this kind can be expected to multiply rapidly in the coming years. As more serial titles become accessible electronically, either through online services or as single stand-alone databases, greater use of these resources will occur, provided that search engines are appropriate and user instructions uncomplicated. Nonetheless, for a variety of economic and technological reasons, the digitization of many major Latin American humanities titles, regardless of whether or not they are still actively being published, will not occur for some time.

Increasingly, electronic resources include both images and written text, as does *Cultura cubana* from Cuba's Biblioteca Nacional José Martí (item **8**). Useful for didactic purposes as well as for research, such databases advance access to scarce or unique resources while contextualizing them through provision of bibliographies and explanatory texts. Such resources allow the creation of interactive works based upon the combination of moving images, sound clips, text, and user-controlled, non-linear navigation.

Researchers should be aware that access to electronic resources held by libraries other than one's own can be difficult, in part because many interlibrary loan departments do not handle such materials due to licensing agreement restrictions. The problem of accessing and/or sharing electronic resources is sometimes compounded by incompatible system requirements and/or peculiar installation procedures. Difficulties such as these led us to request assistance from our colleagues at several different institutions so that we might have a more representative sampling of current electronic materials. We are grateful to Paul Bary of Tulane University, Nicolás Rossi of Libros Argentinos, and Mark. L. Grover of Brigham Young University for their assistance in reviewing materials that were unavailable to us at the Princeton University Library. In such cases, we have included the reviewer's names at the end of the annotation. [PTJ and FJF]

INTERNET RESOURCES

I first began to compile lists of Latin American Internet resources in 1993. In the intervening five years, the quantity of information products and modes of access have exploded. Recent surveys suggest that the number of Internet hosts increases by about 50 percent per year.[1] It is tricky to compile valid Internet statistics, but the effort to count "hosts" and estimate the actual number of users based on that figure has been taking place since the early 1980s, so there is at least some consistency in the process. Network Wizards defines a "host" as a computer system connected to the Internet, either full or part-time, via direct or dialup connections. Yet a single host may also provide Internet access to a large number of individual users.[2] Given its structure, it is best to describe Internet growth in terms of trends, rather than absolute numbers.

As in most of the world, in Latin America the Internet evolved from a restricted academic/research network subsidized by universities, governments, and international agencies, to a broad-based network open to businesses as well as to individuals able to afford access through a commercial provider. The Jan. 1998 *Network Wizards Domain Survey*, which attempts to discover every host on the Internet by doing a complete search of the Domain Name System, reports about 29.7 million hosts worldwide; the commercial sector (the ".com" domain) outnumbers all others, with 8.2 million hosts. According to the International Telecommunications Union, the US and Canada account for about 66% of the world's Internet users while Latin America and the Caribbean account for only about 1 percent.[3] Nonetheless, Latin America has shown some of the fastest rates of Internet *growth* since 1994. In fact, by the end of 1996, nearly all Latin American and Caribbean countries had established Internet connections.

The tremendous expansion of Internet access in Latin America provides new opportunities for south-north and south-south information transfers, although it will take time for this new communication potential to be realized. Yet Internet enthusiasts, especially those from technical and business fields, are often unaware of the huge gaps in economics and education that must be bridged in order to integrate networking into peoples' everyday lives. Even in the privileged world of North American academia, many scholars in the humanities and social sciences do not have access to the equipment, software, and specialized training required to become full participants in the "Internet culture." This situation is even more acute in Latin America, where there are greater economic disparities between public and private educational sectors. Furthermore, as researchers in the region overcome technological obstacles to electronic information access and networking, the human and organizational difficulties of working in a new kind of information culture become apparent. Language is another important factor that currently hinders full Internet participation and development in Latin America: English is by far the dominant language on the Internet, and non-English-speakers may question whether the net has anything to offer them. This situation can change, but it will require that Internet users in Latin America create their own unique information resources rather than simply adopt the commercial products offered by North American and European companies.

Many pioneering networking efforts by NGOs and others in the non-profit sector in Latin America have been fueled by international development and research funds and outside expertise. To make access a reality for significant numbers of people in the region, governments must make major commitments to the development of their telecommunications infrastructure. This is currently happening through privatization, rather than public-sector investment, and the benefits of Internet development are thus accruing to the business classes, but not to those in the public-education, labor, or grassroots sectors. As commercial use of the Internet expands, it becomes harder to maintain the proportion of online space available to educational, non-profit, local, and independent information providers, especially in less-developed regions such as Latin America. To date, the Internet has done little to alleviate basic economic inequalities in Latin America or elsewhere and this situation will doubtless continue into the near future.

When I began using the Internet in 1990, I found that it could provide access to certain information not readily available from traditional published sources. For Latin Americanists, the Internet now serves as a welcome tool to access current and detailed information from the region. Since 1995, it has been possible to read current news from major media in many Latin American countries. Even before traditional published sources appeared on the Internet, scholars, activists, journalists, and others were creating and disseminating unique information from and about the region to the rest of the world. As established bibliographic, reference, and news sources create online sites, the potential for information exchange grows exponentially. For example, although both *HLAS* and the *Hispanic American Periodicals Index (HAPI)* have been accessible online and/or on CD-ROM (items **15** and **14**) for several years, their advent onto the World Wide Web (items **28** and **27**) has the potential to greatly expand access for Latin American researchers. As the Internet becomes more available to academics in Latin America, bibliographic research tools like *HLAS* and *HAPI* will be used for the first time by many in the region. In my recent experience providing Internet training to Latin American academics, I learned that many of the region's researchers are unaware of the kinds of research databases and bibliographic tools traditionally available in US academic libraries. Latin American scholars are often surprised to find that their articles and books are cited in databases such as *HAPI* and *HLAS*, and that their books are more likely to be held by US libraries than by those of their own regional universities.

The primary value of the Internet has been and still is communication. The Internet is a "network of networks" of people keeping each other informed of events and sharing information to solve problems, to publicize situations requiring action, and to facilitate the creation of new knowledge. The Internet can create communities of affinity without geographic limitations by providing the space and the means whereby vast amounts of current information can be accessed and manipulated quickly across great distances. The Internet can provide gigabytes of information on the latest hot story, but its value as an archival resource for future researchers remains more potential than real. The current challenge for librarians and scholars is to assist in the evolution of the Internet from a communications tool into a functioning virtual library.

Since the advent of the World Wide Web, the hypertext capabilities of the Internet have made it possible for each person to chart an individual path through the available information, "jumping" electronically to the highlighted connections that make sense to them for a particular inquiry. Nevertheless, the web has not lived up to its popular image as a virtual library. The Internet does not (yet?) provide the kind of controlled subject access and the bibliographic or inventory control that exists in a research library. In the past three years, however, the combined effect of automated search engines and human-organized subject guides and indexes have made it much easier to find specific information on the Internet. Another recent and significant development for academic researchers is the availability of bibliographic, statistical, and full-text databases via the web. Many high-quality information products—the *Handbook of Latin American Studies* is a prime example—now exist in multiple formats (print, CD-ROM, and web) and are accessible to large numbers of users outside of major research libraries in the US and Europe.

The sites described below represent a very selective list of Internet resources of use to Latin American humanities researchers. I often use the modern English fable of the "Blind Men and the Elephant" as a metaphor for the Internet.[4] Each person who ventures onto the Internet with an information need will have a unique experience colored by how he approaches the Internet, where he happens to look, and/or by what previous knowledge and experience he brings to the search. Each person will thus form an individual and incomplete perception of the Internet. My selections of sites for this article are informed by years of experience as an academic librarian and my own curiosity about the development of the Internet as a research tool. The following are some questions I considered when choosing Internet resources to highlight for Latin American humanities researchers: 1) Is it *functional?* Does it do what it says it does? Do I use it? Does it work for me? Have others reported successfully using the resource? 2) Is it *unique?* Does it provide information not available elsewhere, or does it compile and present the information in a way that makes it uniquely useful? 3) Is it *representative?* I have tried to include at least one Internet resource representing each of the major subject areas covered in the *HLAS* humanities volume.

I have organized the Internet resources reviewed below into the following categories: 1) Directories and Organizational Sites; 2) Database Sites; and 3) Subject Specific Sites. These categories are not mutually exclusive and because of the hypertext nature of the web, almost all sites provide links to other sites. *Directories and Organizational Sites* exist for the main purpose of organizing and providing links to large numbers of other Internet sites in particular subject areas. Some of these sites have already been described in previous issues of *HLAS*, but my focus here will be to highlight their value to humanities scholars. Also, the sheer volume of Internet information, especially web-based resources, has increased dramatically in the past two years, so these sites include many new links and features. I have selected the directory sites with the most academic content, but there are also many commercial Latin American directories available, such as *Directorio GlobalNet* [http:// www.dirglobal.net/] and *Mundo Latino* [http://www.mundolatino.org]. An extensive list of Latin American directories and search engines can be found on the University of Texas at Austin's LANIC Search page [http://www.lanic.utexas.edu/ world/search/].

The resources listed under *Database Sites* provide access to organized, electronically searchable bodies of data useful for Latin American humanities research. They may provide full-text articles, statistical information, or bibliographic citations. Most academic libraries have access to scholarly humanities databases that include significant Latin American content. The Modern Language Association's *MLA Bibliography*, for example, includes bibliographic citations to materials in linguistics, literary criticism, folklore, theater and related subjects, and is now available in print, CD-ROM (item **17**) and on the web via OCLC's Firstsearch. When discussing "web resources," it is important to distinguish between public domain databases, which do not charge for access, and proprietary databases, which require subscription fees and provide Internet access via passwords or some other validation process. For more Internet-accessible databases, see the "Databases" section of my guide to "Internet Resources for Latin America" (item **21,** or see http://lib.nmsu.edu/subject/bord/laguia/index.html#data). In the section below on *Subject-Specific Sites* I have included Internet resources grouped according to the subject areas covered in the humanities volumes of the *HLAS:* Art, History, Literature, Music, and Philosophy. Although I cannot claim that these are the best, and they are certainly not the only sites on the Internet for these topics, I have included them as representative samples of the kinds of information available on the Internet of potential use to humanities researchers.

I will offer the reader a general caveat regarding the search for and use of Internet resources. Each researcher should be curious and willing to spend some time exploring and critically evaluating what they find. New resources appear daily. Many are the work of individual scholars and may be buried in the departmental pages of a university or research center but have extraordinary value to others working in the same field, while others may be heavily promoted in directories and indexes but offer only very superficial treatment of a topic. In some cases, Internet sites might be most valuable as primary research materials, for example, the texts of Zapatista communiques, 1994–1998, archived on the *Ya Basta!* website [http://www.ezln.org/].

The Internet information included here is accurate as of Jan. 1999. Although the site's stability was a consideration for its inclusion, the mercurial nature of the Internet guarantees that addresses may change, sites may disappear or move, and new sites will continue to be added. [MM]

Notes:

1 Glave, James. "Dramatic Internet Growth Continues," in *Wired News* [online], Feb 16, 1998, http://www.wired.com/news/news/technology/story/10323.html.

2 For more information on how Internet growth is measured, see *Network Wizards Internet Domain Survey,* http://www.nw.com/zone/WWW/top.html; and, Press, Larry. "Tracking the Global Diffusion of the Internet," in *Association for Computing Machinery. Communications of the ACM,* Vol. 40, No. 11, Nov. 1997, pp. 11–17. A Latin American source for Internet statistics is *Nodos y Servidores WWW de América Latina y el Caribe,* compiled by the Costa Rican National Research Network, http://www.cr/latstat/.

3 Capdevila, Gustavo. "Liberalization of Information Sector Excludes South," in *Inter Press Service,* Sept. 30, 1997 [retrieved online via *Global NewsBank,* Feb. 26, 1998].

4 See "Groping for Our Piece of the Elephant: Latin American Information on the Internet," in *Technology, the Environment, and Social Change: Papers of the 38th Annual Meeting of the Seminar on the Acquisition of Latin American Library Materials (SALALM),* edited by Pat Noble. Albuquerque: SALALM Secretariat, 1995, pp. 193–209.

CD-ROM AND DISKETTE RESOURCES

1   **ARGENA II.** México: Archivo General de la Nación, 1995. 1 computer laser optical disc.

Indexes, in Spanish, of the groups into which the Mexican National Archive organizes its collections of colonial documents. ARGENA II contains records of all 22 groups indexed in the first edition (*Argena,* 1991) and records of 76 additional groups (of 115 groups of colonial documents in the Archive). Includes bibliographical references, illustrations, tables, and appendices about Mexican rulers, and maps and tables about the collections. Early versions were difficult to install and use, but ongoing efforts have resulted in improvements. System requirements: IBM-compatible PC/MS-DOS. [P. Bary]

2 Bibliografía en CD-ROM de la *Nueva Revista de Filología Hispánica.* México: Consejo Nacional de Ciencia y Tecnología de México, 1993. 1 computer laser optical disc.

Contains all the bibliographic references (more than 150,000) to the journal's contents from 1947–91. Covers literature, linguistics, philological theory and methodology, and book and journal reviews for Spain and Latin America. Provides several search indexes, including title, author, editor/translator, and date of publication. Menus and toolbars are available in both English and Spanish. System requirements: IBM-compatible PC/MS-DOS 3.3+.

3 Bibliografía para la historia de las artes visuales en la Argentina. Buenos Aires: Fondo Nacional de las Artes, 1994. Four 3.5-inch diskettes.

Comprehensive collection of bibliographies on the visual arts, including architecture, drawing, cinematography, photography, and engraving ranging from precolumbian times to 1992. Includes monographic histories and surveys as well as articles from journals and catalogs, organized by period, topics, techniques, and type of document. Menu-based program, in Spanish, is easy to operate. System Requirements: IBM-compatible PC/MS-DOS 3.1. [N. Rossi]

4 Brasil. Coordinação de Leonardo Antonio Dantas Silva. Madrid: Fundación Histórica Tavera, Publicaciones Electrónicas DIGIBIS; Assessoria de Comunicação Social do Ministério das Relações Exteriores; Ministério da Cultura; Embaixada do Brasil en Madrid, 1997. Computer laser optical disc (4¾ in.) (Clásicos Tavera: Serie I, Iberoamérica en la Historia; 3)

Compilation of more than 20 classic works on Brazilian history includes: João Capistrano de Abreu, *O descobrimento do Brasil* and *Capítulos de história colonial (1500–1800)*; André João Antonil, *Cultura e opuléncia do Brazil, por suas drogas e minas*; John Armitage, *The history of Brazil, from the period of the arrival of the Braganza family in 1808 . . .* (v. 1–2); Ambrósio Fernandes Brandão, *Diálogos das grandezas do Brasil*; Frei Manoel Calado, *O valeroso lucideno e triunfo da liberdade* (v. 1–2); Vicente Licínio Cardoso, *Á Margem da história do Brazil* and *Á margem da história da República* (v. 1–2);

Antonio da Silva Jardim, *A república no Brazil*; Henry Koster, *Travels in Brazil*; Manoel de Oliveira Lima, *Dom João VI no Brazil, Formação histórica da nacionalidade brasileira, O império brasileiro*, and *Pernambuco, seu desenvolvimento histórico*; José Antônio Gonsalves de Mello, *Gente da nação* and *Tempos dos flamengos: influencia da ocupação holandesa no vida e na cultura do Norte do Brasil*; Joaquim Aurélio Barreto Nabuco, *O abolicionismo*; Eduardo da Silva Prado, *A ilusão americana*; Gabriel Soares Souza, *Tratado descriptivo do Brasil em 1587*; Francisco Adolpho Varnhagen, *História geral do Brasil*; and José Francisco Oliveira, *O occaso do Império*. [Ed.]

5 Ciencia y cultura en Chile. Colima, Mexico: CENEDIC, Univ. de Colima, 1994. 1 computer laser optical disc.

Contains 18 assorted databases including a bibliography of Chilean imprints (1982–93); two databases covering Chilean popular and classical music from the 19th and 20th centuries; and one database containing information from Chilean periodicals by and about Chilean and other Latin American authors. To be updated irregularly. Relatively easy to use via a "guided search" system. System requirements: IBM-compatible PC/MS-DOS 3.0+.

6 El cine argentino. Buenos Aires?: Fundación Cinemática, 1995. 1 computer laser optical disc.

Database of 1,850 Argentine movies produced between 1933–95, including 200 that were not commercially screened. Searchable by title, biography (actors, producers, directors, cinematographers, etc.) prizes, images, and musical themes. A few sound and video clips are included. The first menu is blurry and includes only minimal searching instructions. A bit confusing for first-time users. In Spanish. System requirements: IBM-compatible PC/Windows 3.1+/sound card.

7 Congreso de la Asociación de Historiadores Latinoamericanistas Europeos, *10th, s.l., 1993.* Las transformaciones hacia la sociedad moderna en América Latina: causas y condiciones de la economía, la política y en las mentalidades. Leipzig/Köln, Germany: Asociación de Historiadores Latinoamericanistas Europeos, 1996. 1 computer laser optical disc.

Contains papers presented at the conference as well as the first two issues of the Association's publication, *Cuadernos de Historia Latinoamericana*. Straightforward presentation of document files with no search engine; only quirk is that papers are in WordPerfect as well as ASCII format, while the *Cuadernos* are in Pagemaker and Word. System requirements: IBM-compatible PC or MAC/WordPerfect 5.1; Pagemaker and Word 6.0 or any compatible word processing program.

8   Cultura cubana: una aproximación bibliográfica. La Habana: Biblioteca Nacional José Martí, 1996. 1 computer laser optical disc.

Divided into two main sections. The first is dedicated to all matters concerning the Biblioteca Nacional: history, services offered, specialized collections, general bibliographic holdings, and catalog and reference capacity. The second covers Cuban culture as represented in approximately 1,300 of the most relevant works of the 19th and 20th centuries. The second section is searchable by author, title, publisher, and year. A logical and clear arrangement make this database very user-friendly. English and Spanish menu options. Includes sound clips. System requirements: IBM-compatible PC/Windows 3.11+/ compatible sound blaster card.

9   Diccionario bio-bibliográfico de escritores de México, 1920–1970. Colima, Mexico: Centro Nacional Editor de Discos Compactos, Univ. de Colima; Provo, Utah: Brigham Young Univ., 1995. 1 computer laser optical disc.

Primarily an information manual of national and international writers who have written at least one published book of literature (i.e., novel, short story, poetry, theater, literary criticism). Also provides photos and voice record. Fine presentation and good search system. System requirements: IBM-compatible PC/MS-DOS 3.3+/High Sierra format CD-ROM drive.

10   Dicionário eletrónico Aurélio para Windows. Rio de Janeiro: Lexikon Informática Ltda., 1993. 9 computer laser optical discs.

The second edition (1986) of the *Novo Dicionário da Lingua Portuguesa* by Aurélio Buarque de Holanda Ferreira is the most comprehensive Brazilian Portuguese dictionary

available. This Windows version provides access to definitions, synonyms, and examples of usage. The program works with Word 2.0 to 7.0, Word Perfect 6.0 to 7.0, Ami Pro, Word Pad, and Write. Easy to use, with appropriate instructions and help screens. System requirements: IBM-compatible PC/Windows. [M.L. Grover]

11   Epistolario: catálogo electrónico del epistolario de Nicolás Guillén. La Habana: Centersoft; Instituto de Literatura y Linguística; 1994–95. Two 3.5-inch diskettes.

Bibliographic entries of the epistolary in the Fondos de la Biblioteca Fernando Ortiz. Includes sender, recipient, description, date, and geographic location, as well as searching index. Pull-down menus are also in English, but help text is in Spanish only. Fairly easy to use via buttons. System requirements: IBM-compatible PC/Windows 3.1.

12   Fondo documental y bibliográfico del Museo Naval: catálogos. Madrid: Fundación Histórica Tavera, Publicaciones Electrónicas DIGIBIS; Museo Naval, 1997. 1 computer laser optical disc (4¾ in.)

Includes 11 databases containing the catalogs and/or indexes from the following collections of the Museo Naval de Madrid and the Archivo General de Marina Alvaro de Bazán. From the Museo Naval: "Colección Antonio de Mazarredo;" "Colección de Documentos de Vargas Ponce;" "Colección de Documentos de Fernández Navarrete;" "Catálogo de Documentos de la Expedición Malaspina;" "Real Companía de Guardias Marinas: Probanzas;" and "Catálogo de Publicaciones Seriadas." From the Archivo: "Independencia de América: Expediciones de Indias, 1818–1839;" "Documentos de la Sección de Corsos y Persas, 1784–1838;" "Documentos de la Independencia de Colombia;" "Documentos de la Campaña del Pacífico: 1863–1867;" and "Cuba, Puerto Rico y Filipinas, 1868–1898." [Ed.]

13   Guía preliminar de fuentes documentales etnográficas para el estudio de los pueblos indígenas de Iberoamérica. Madrid: Fundación Histórica Tavera, 1996. One 3.5-inch diskette.

Lists over 270 archives and collections, with a general index organized by country. Although not all Latin American countries are listed, it does include material in European and North American collections. Emphasizes 16th-19th centuries, with some material on 20th century. Searchable by index. Relatively easy to use though presentation of search results is cumbersome as search term is not highlighted. Instructions in English. System requirements: IBM-compatible PC. For a review of the web version of the database see item **35.**

14 *Handbook of Latin American Studies CD-ROM: HLAS/CD, Vols. 1–53, 1936–1994.* Edited by the Hispanic Division, The Library of Congress. Madrid: Fundación MAPFRE América; Washington, D.C.: The Library of Congress, 1995.

The fundamental annotated bibliography for research materials on Latin America is now searchable in English and Spanish with easily understood directions. Published in 1995, version 1.0 of *HLAS/CD* covers vols. 1–53 (1936–1994) of the print version. Humanities disciplines covered include art, cinema, history, language, literature, music, philosophy, and bibliography. Also covers the social sciences. Can be searched by keyword, author, title, and subject. Contains approximately 250,000 citations. Version 2.0, scheduled to be released in early 1999, will cover vols. 1–55 (1936–1997). System requirements: IBM-compatible PC/DOS 5.0+/Windows 3.1+. See item **37** for the review of *HLAS Online*, the web version of the *Handbook.*

15 *Hispanic American Periodicals Index: HAPI [CD-ROM].* Compiled by UCLA Latin American Center. Edited by Barbara G. Valk. Baltimore: National Information Services Corp.

Includes approximately 210,000 citations to over 400 journals published since 1970, approximately 50 percent of which are humanities related. Updated quarterly. System requirements: IBM-compatible PC. See item **28** for review of *HAPI Online*, the web version of the index.

16 *Historia y sociedad peruanas: fondo bibliográfico de la Pontificia Universidad Católica del Perú;* Madrid: Fundación Histórica Tavera, Publicaciones Electrónicas DIGIBIS, 1997. 1 Computer laser optical disc (4¾ in.)

Electronic compilation of 35 important monographs, some otherwise out of print, covering anthropology, art, economics, history, international relations, law, politics, so-

ciology, including issues of migration, the military, religion, and utopias. Includes the following works: Carlos Aguirre, *Agentes de su propia libertad;* Rolena Adorno, *Cronista y Príncipe;* Quintín Aldea V, *El indio peruano y la defensa de sus derechos;* Teófilo Altamirano, *Los que se fueron: peruanos en Estados Unidos* and *Exodo: peruanos en el exterior;* Antonio del Busto D., *San Martín de Porres;* Luis Jaime Castillo, *Personajes míticos, escenas y narraciones de la iconografía mochica;* Adolfo Figueroa, *La economía campesina en la Sierra del Perú;* Ricardo González Vigil, *El Perú es todas las sangres;* Jorge A. Guevara Gil, *Propiedad agraria y derecho colonial;* Teodoro Hampe-Martínez, *Don Pedro de la Gasca;* Ana Marie Hocquenghem, *Iconografía mochica;* Jeffery Klaiber, *La Iglesia en el Perú;* Armando Nieto Vélez, *Francisco del Castillo;* Juan Ossio Acuña, *Parentesco, reciprocidad y jerarquía en los Andes;* José Antonio Payet, *La responsabilidad por productos defectuosos: biblioteca para leer el Código Civil . . . ;* Liliana Regalado de H., *Religión y evangelización en Vilcabamba, 1572–1602, Sucesión incaica,* and *Instrucción al Licenciado Lope García de Castro;* Lucila Castro de Trelles, *Relación de la religión y ritos del Perú hecha por los padres agustinos;* Denis Sulmont and Marcel Valcárcel, *Vetas de futuro;* Jan Szeminsky, *La utopía tupamarista;* F. de Trazegnies G., *La idea del derecho en el Perú Republicano del siglo XIX* and *Ciriaco de Urtecho;* Efraín Trelles, *Lucas Martínez Vegazo;* Adolfo Winternitz, *Itinerario hacia el arte;* Celia Wu B., *Generales y diplomáticos;* Manuel Marzal F., *Estudios sobre religión campesina, Historia de la antropología indigenista, La transformación religiosa peruana, El sincretismo iberoamericano, Los caminos religiosos de los inmigrantes de la Gran Lima,* and *La utopía posible;* Enrique Rojas Z., *Los asháninkas: un pueblo tras el bosque;* and Anita Cook, *Wari Tiwanaku.* [Ed.]

17 *MLA International Bibliography [CD-ROM].* New York: H.W. Wilson.

Bibliographic records covering over 3,000 publications (1963-present), including journals and series, newspapers, working papers, proceedings, and bibliographies with an emphasis on literature, linguistics, and folklore. Includes a keyword index as well as a thesaurus. Can be networked and includes help screens. Extremely easy to use. System requirements: IBM-compatible PC.

18 Nexos. México: Nexos, 1996. 1 computer laser optical disc.

Full text of the journal *Nexos* (1978–95) on Mexican politics, culture, and history. Searchable by author, title, notes, and keyword. Also includes *Nexos TV*—the transcripts of the TV program of the same name, 1989–95. Has help manual as a separate database. Perplexing initially, but fairly easy after a short exposure. Menu driven. No help screens. In Spanish. System requirements: IBM-compatible PC/MS-DOS.

19 Obras completas de José Martí: iconografía, cronología. Canada: Centro de Estudio de Tecnologías Avanzadas, 1995? 1 computer laser optical disc.

Includes four searchable databases: chronology, complete works, iconography (51 photos and sketches) and "sistema José Martí," which includes categories such as themes/subjects, places (listed by country), poetry, biographical notes, and quotes from other authors. Very user-friendly with iconographic desktop. Includes online help. In Spanish. System requirements: IBM-compatible PC/Windows 3.1+.

20 Series retrospectivas do Paraná. Curitiba, Brazil: Instituto Paranaense de Desenvolvimento Econômico e Social, 1994. One 3.5-inch diskette.

Through tables, presents historic data (1940–80) on the population and industry of Paraná. Offers useful statistical information, but lack of overall inventory or listing of included tables requires users to examine each table individually to determine if the desired data is provided. In Portuguese. Very straightforward and easy to use. Provides simple index to search for data by *municipio.* System requirements: IBM-compatible PC/MS-DOS 3.1+/Windows 3.1.

Thouvenot, Marc. TEMOA: outil de consultation et de recherche sur les textes; programme. See item **538.**

INTERNET RESOURCES
Directories and Organizational Sites

21 Internet resources for Latin America. Compiled by Molly Molloy. [URL: http://lib.nmsu.edu/subject/bord/laguia]

This guide has been available on the Internet since 1994. It does not attempt to cover the region comprehensively, but rather, to provide some context for understanding the development of the Internet in Latin America. An introductory essay provides some background and links for further information on Latin American networking. The guide includes web sites, electronic mail lists, and Usenet groups; most resources listed include brief annotations. The guide also includes the URLs (Internet addresses) for all sites in the text so that it can be used in print format as well as online.

22 LANIC: Latin American Network Information Center. Compiled by The University of Texas at Austin, Institute for Latin American Studies. [URL: http://www.lanic.utexas.edu/]

Provided by The University of Texas at Austin's Institute for Latin American Studies (ILAS) since 1992, LANIC serves as the primary gateway for Latin American information on the Internet and is the official Latin American Studies site for the W3 Consortium Virtual Library. The LANIC homepage provides access to resources in lists by country and by subject. LANIC has worked with other Latin American studies and bibliographic organizations to provide Internet access to specialized databases. Within each subject, links are arranged by region and by country or into subcategories as appropriate. LANIC subject pages are compiled and maintained by subject specialists at The University of Texas and elsewhere who work cooperatively to maintain the accuracy of the listings. The LANIC subject index under http://www.lanic.utexas.edu/la/region contains many categories of interest to humanities researchers including Art, Cinema and Video, History, Journalism, Languages, Libraries and Archives, Literature, Music, Performing Arts, Publishers, and Radio and Television. The Libraries and Archives page provides links to dozens of online library catalogs in the region and elsewhere, while the Publishers page provides links, not only to publishers, but also to Latin American booksellers and full-text online books. The Languages section is one of the most extensive, with over 160 links to pages on languages spoken in Latin America, teaching materials, language schools in the region, and general linguistic resources. Over 170 links to Literature sites include many online resources for popular literary figures; for example four sites are devoted exclusively to Pablo Neruda. The Art resources page includes more than 120 links to art museums in the region, online periodicals, pages devoted to individual artists, and more. Finally, for those seeking information on Latin American music, the Internet provides excellent access pages describing many popular musical styles. The LANIC Music page includes over 130 links; Brazil and Cuba unsurprisingly account for the largest number. Some sites are academically oriented, while many others are devoted to popular artists. The rapid growth of Internet commerce in recent years has made it possible to locate and buy Latin American and other "world music" that is otherwise very difficult to find in retail stores.

23   Latin American Library, Tulane University. Compiled by Paul Bary. [URL: http://www.tulane.edu/~ latinlib/ lalhome.html]

Provides access to some original materials (photographs, ancient Middle American texts, and art) from one of the premiere Latin American collections in the world. Also provides links to many electronic journals relating to Latin America [http://www.tulane. edu/~ latinlib/revistas.html]. Some subscription resources are restricted to Tulane users.

24   Seminar on the Acquisition of Latin American Library Materials (SALALM). Compiled by David Block. [URL: http:// latino.lib.cornell.edu/salalmhome.html]

The SALALM homepage is notable as a resource for learning about the Latin American book trade and the acquisition of Latin American books, journals, and other information by academic libraries. Scholars will find especially useful the links to more than 20 sites for Latin American book dealers, book fairs, and other book trade information.

DATABASES

25   ALAT: América Latina/Latin American database [y] ALPE: América Latina en la prensa española (ALPE)/Latin America in Spanish newspapers. (Recopilación de Centro de Información y Documentación Científica (CINDOC), Area de América Latina, Consejo Superior de Investigaciones Científicas (CSIC), España. [URLs: http:// www.eurosur.org/CINDOC/alat.htm; http:// www.eurosur.org/CINDOC/alpe.htm]

ALAT is a bibliographic database containing over 20,000 records on Latin American humanities and social sciences topics from Spanish research sources (books, journals, theses, conference proceedings, etc.) from 1975 to the present. Access is via telnet and requires a password, although the web site offers trial searches free of charge by emailing alatina@cindoc.csic.es. ALPE includes over 26,000 references to articles from the Spanish press concerning Latin America from 1993 to the present. Newspapers covered include *El País, ABC, El Mundo, Diario 16, La Vanguardia, El Periódico* and *La Gaceta de los Negocios.* Database is searchable for free via the web and provides very complete bibliographic citations. More information about these databases and other information services provided by CINDOC can be found at its web address [http://www. eurosur.org/CINDOC/arealat.htm].

26   ARL: Latin Americanist Research Resources Pilot Project. Compiled by Association of Research Libraries and The Univ. of Texas at Austin's Latin American Network Information Center, UT-LANIC. [URL http:// lanic.utexas.edu/project/arl/]

Thirty-seven members of ARL participate in this pilot project to provide distributed access to over 350 Latin American journals from Mexico, Brazil, and Argentina. Participating libraries maintain subscriptions to a list of titles, scan the tables of contents into the database, and provide free interlibrary loan of articles from the database to other participating libraries. Journal coverage varies considerably, although for most titles at least three years are included. Many of the titles covered are not included in other bibliographic works (such as HAPI). The Mellon Foundation and the participating libraries provide funding for the project and UT-LANIC provides technical support and access to the database. Searching the database is slow, but it contains unique information that has no other bibliographic access. Non-member libraries may access the database, but must pay for interlibrary loan of articles. LANIC also provides access to a test version of the next phase of the ARL project: distributed access to Latin American research resources—20th-century presidential messages from Argentina and Mexico [http://www.lanic.utexas. edu/project/arl/pm/sample2/index.html]. The presidential documents are available as scanned images (obtained from the published sources, often preserved on microfilm) that must be downloaded from the web, page by page as graphics files. This database contains a great deal of information—currently over 75,000 pages of speeches—that previously was accessible in only the most extensive Latin American collections. The graphics format of the files makes the database tedious to use and the texts of the documents are not searchable. However, for serious students of the political figures included, these online documents may provide new research possibilities. The introductory pages include detailed instructions for accessing and downloading the files from the web and the contents screens provide a good outline of the available documents by name, date, and title of the particular speech.

27   **Handbook of Latin American Studies: HLAS Online.** Compiled by the Hispanic Division, The Library of Congress. [URL: http://lcweb2.loc.gov/hlas/]
HLAS Online provides annotations and complete bibliographic information from published materials from and about Latin America on a wide range of topics in the humanities and the social sciences. *HLAS Online* is unique among Internet-accessible databases for the time-span and depth of its coverage (over 60 years), and its reviews of many different kinds of materials: books, journal articles, conference proceedings, dissertations and theses, electronic resources, etc. The materials, published in many countries and in several languages, are chosen by specialists in each discipline covered. The web site contains the bibliographic citations, annotations, and most of the introductory essays included in the print *HLAS* since 1935, as well as entries that will appear in future published volumes, over 300,000 records in all. The web search interface, available in English and Spanish with a Portuguese version to be released soon, is powerful. It offers simple and advanced features that serve the needs of researchers at many different levels. Hypertext features allow searchers to easily refine keyword searches by jumping to a listing of all records containing a particular subject heading. (See also item **14** for a review of *HLAS* on CD-ROM.)

28   **Hispanic American Periodicals Index (HAPI) Online.** Compiled by UCLA Latin American Center. [URL: http://hapi.gseis.ucla.edu]

HAPI Online combines current information about Latin America with complete coverage spanning more than 25 years, from 1970 to the present. The database contains over 200,000 citations from 400 humanities and social science journals published worldwide. Most of the journals covered by *HAPI* are not comprehensively indexed elsewhere, although many articles from these journals are selectively included in *HLAS. HAPI* does not include annotations, abstracts, or full texts, but fee-based document delivery is offered for many articles. The web interface allows users to quickly check cross-references using hypertext links embedded in the database. Access to *HAPI* is by subscription, with various pricing options available depending on search needs.

29   **REDIAL: Base de Datos Redial-Tesis.** Recopilación de Red Europea de Información y Documentación sobre América Latina (REDIAL). [URL: http://www.eurosur.org/REDIAL/producto.htm]
Redial-Tesis contains bibliographic information on 5,300 Latin American studies theses and dissertations in the humanities and social sciences disciplines completed at many European universities between 1980–96. The database uses Microisis software and can be consulted by title, author, subject, or country and university where the thesis was written. This database provides access to a unique body of scholarly information (unpublished European dissertations) that may not be included in larger databases, such as OCLC's WorldCat or RLIN's Union Catalog. REDIAL provides other information services to the European Latin Americanist community. The general REDIAL website [http://www.eurosur.org/REDIAL/red_que.html] provides contact information for member libraries and information centers in Spain, Germany, Austria, Belgium, Poland, England, Sweden, and Switzerland.

SUBJECT SPECIFIC SITES
Art

30   **Cuba Poster Project/Proyecto de Afiches Cubanos.** Compiled by Cuba Poster Project. [URL: http://www.zpub.com/cp]
The Cuba Poster Project (CPP) is dedicated to documenting and disseminating the poster art of post-revolutionary Cuba. The CPP has completed photo-documentation

of the OSPAAAL (Organization in Solidarity with the People of Asia, Africa, and Latin America), and is in the process of doing the same for Editora Política (the publishing department of the Cuban Communist Party). The CPP is also researching background information, cataloging images, and building an electronic archive. The dozens of images and commentaries available via this web site provide a new level of access to primary materials for the study of art and politics in Latin America.

31   Diego Rivera Museo Virtual/Virtual Museum. Compiled by Javier A. Rivera. [URL: http://www.diegorivera.com/]
Provides hundreds of images of Diego Rivera's paintings, murals, and illustrations. While browsing, the user can click on "thumbnail" images in order to get a larger version that can be saved in various graphic formats. Also includes biographical information about the artist, but site's main value is in the high quality of the images.

32   Latin American cinema. Compiled by Gayle Williams, Univ. of Georgia. [URL: http://www.libs.uga.edu/humaniti/ltamcine.html]
Provides links to many cinema pages in the region, biographical information on important personalities, as well as links to film organizations and research centers.

33   The original Frida Kahlo homepage. Compiled by Cascade Internet Development (personal page created by "Carrie"). [URL: http://www.cascade.net/kahlo.html]
This page appeared on the web in 1995 and claims to be the "original and official" Frida Kahlo home page. It seems to be the work of an admirer and dedicated student of the artist and her work, although the complete identity of the compiler is not provided without making an inquiry via email. The level of information is appropriate for students of all ages. The extensive pages of links refer the user to many more sites for information on Frida and other Mexican artists of the period.

34   Webmuseo de Latinoamérica. Recopilación de Arnulfo Zepeda, *et al.* [URL: http://museos.web.com.mx]
Webmuseo is a project of the Mexico City chapter of SIGGRAPH, the computer graphics special interest group of the Association for Computing Machinery (ACM). This "work-in-progress" provides a detailed look at five different museums located in Mexico and Venezuela: Museo Franz Mayer, Museo Etnológico del Territorio Federal de Amazonas, Conventos de Morelos, Museo de Barquisimeto, and Museo de Arte de Coro. The project looks at the museum collections in the historical context of the European conquest of the Americas. The site is graphically pleasing and easy to navigate; essays by museum curators provide a narrative context for the images. This experiment in using Internet technology to create an "interactive community" presents a "fragment of Latin American reality" (quoted from the "Sala de Introducción").

History

35   Guía preliminar de fuentes documentales etnográficas para el estudio de los pueblos indígenas de Iberoamérica. Recopilación de Daniel Restrepo Manrique *et al.*, Fundación Histórica Tavera, Spain. [URL: http://www.lanic.utexas.edu/project/tavera]
A detailed bibliographic guide and directory of archival resources for the study of indigenous peoples of the Americas produced by the Fundación Histórica Tavera and provided in electronic form by UT-LANIC. The guide reviews ethnohistorical sources in libraries and archives in the US and eleven Latin American and five European countries. This guide offers an excellent starting point for any student of Latin American ethnohistory. All texts in the guide are in Spanish. For a review of the diskette version of this database, see item **13**.

36   H-LatAm: Latin American history forum. Compiled and edited by H-Net Humanities & Social Sciences Online. [URL: http://h-net2.msu.edu/~latam]
H-LatAm is an international forum for the scholarly discussion of Latin American history. It is a member of the H-Net Humanities & Social Sciences Online initiative and affiliated with the Conference on Latin American History (CLAH) [http://www.h-net.msu.edu/~clah/]. Includes archives of several discussion lists, book and journal reviews, professional announcements, and other resources.

37   Historical Text Archive: Latin America and Mexico. Compiled by Don F. Mabry, Mississippi State University. [URLs:

http://www.msstate.edu/Archives/History/
Latin_America/latam.html; http://www.
msstate.edu/Archives/History/Latin_
America/Mexico/mexico.html]

The Historical Text Archive (HTA) began in 1990 as a place to store and make available via FTP electronic documents related to the study and teaching of history. It now covers many areas of world history, including Latin America, with a separate section on Mexico. HTA provides the full texts of many reviews, essays, articles, government documents, and online books useful for the study of history, government, and politics in Latin America. The Mexico page includes a complete electronic book (Donald J. Mabry and Robert J. Shafer's *Neighbors, Mexico and the United States: Wetbacks and Oil*, HTA Edition, 1997), as well as several collections of photographs. The site contains much original material, but it may be difficult to determine the authenticity of some of the documents. Some links jump to internal pages at other sites so navigation can be tricky. Many people contribute to the site and it lacks some editorial coherence, but overall, the HTA (especially the Mexico page) is a valuable effort to provide a wide range of materials in a very accessible format.

Languages and Literature

38   Comp-jugador. Compiled by Daniel German, Margaret Lashua, and Alex López-Ortíz. [URL: http://csgwww.uwaterloo.ca/~dmg/lando/verbos/con-jugador.html]

Language reference tools such as interactive bilingual and multilingual dictionaries, thesauri, automatic translation sites, and so forth abound on the Internet. Daniel German's Comp-jugador is an excellent example of a working tool that has become very popular with Spanish teachers and students. The database contains complete conjugations for more than 10,000 Spanish verbs: the user types a verb into the search box and the complete conjugation is returned.

39   Instituto Cervantes/Centro Virtual Cervantes. Recopilación del Instituto Cervantes, Madrid. [URLs: http://www.cervantes.es; http://cvc.cervantes.es/portada.htm]

Instituto Cervantes exists to promote and teach the Spanish language worldwide.

This site offers teaching materials and detailed descriptions of language courses sponsored by its centers. It also provides search access via the Internet to many of the library catalogs in the "Red de Bibliotecas del Instituto Cervantes" in the different countries [http://www.cervantes.es/rbic.html]. Site uses frames and is slow and somewhat difficult to navigate.

40   Latbook: libros y revistas argentinas en Internet. Recopilación de Librería Fernando García-Cambeiro. [URL: http://www.latbook.com]

Primarily a commercial site for selling new Argentine literature, but the size of this bibliographic database of over 30,000 Argentine books and periodicals makes it useful as an academic research tool. The book database includes full bibliographic and ordering information (if available); the periodical database includes tables of contents and some articles from current issues. Created by Librería Fernando García-Cambeiro. For more access to current Latin American literature, see the lists of publishers and booksellers on UT-LANIC [http://www.lanic.utexas.edu:80/la/region/publish/] and on the SALALM website [http://latino.lib.cornell.edu/salalmhome.html].

41   Latino literature web page. Compiled by Lisette Blanco-Cerda, Our Lady of the Lake University, San Antonio, Texas. [URL: http://www.ollusa.edu/alumni/alumni/latino/latinoh1.htm]

Presents a personal tour through major figures and movements of Latin American literature. This site has been available since 1996, but at this writing (March 1998) many of the pages are still "under construction" and contain little information. Provides brief biographical and critical information on many writers, with a special focus on modern Mexican-American authors.

42   Mundo latino: rincón literario. Recopilación de Red Mundo Latino. [URL: http://www.mundolatino.org/cultura/litera/]

An excellent site for links to many Spanish language and literary pages on the web. Although it can be slow to navigate and it is difficult to determine who is responsible for the pages, it does provide a good selection of sites arranged by genre—poetry, novels, theater, etc.

43   Sor Juana Inés de la Cruz Project.
Compiled by Luis M. Villar, Dartmouth College, Dept. of Spanish and Portuguese. [URL: http://www.dartmouth.edu/~sorjuana]

The Sor Juana project provides a hypertext interface to a large body of electronic texts representing the complete plays, poetry, and prose of this famous literary and religious figure of colonial Mexico. In addition to the texts, the web site provides a brief outline of the poet's life, essays by Sor Juana scholars, bibliographies and more. This site is unique for its well-organized compilation of a complete body of literary work.

Music

44   Iberian and Latin American Music Online. Compiled by the Dept. of Music, Royal Holloway College, Univ. of London. [URL: http://www.sun.rhbnc.ac.uk/~vhwm002/ILM/]

Iberian and Latin American Music Online (ILA) began in 1994 as an electronic mailing list for scholars of Iberian and Latin American music to exchange information. It has developed into a web site that provides an online journal, *Iberian Discoveries*; academic announcements; archives of mailing lists; and links to other Internet resources. ILA also provides access to a unique online database, the International Inventory of Villancico Texts (IIVT), compiled by Paul Laird and maintained on the web by Alvaro Torrente [http://www.sun.rhbnc.ac.uk/~vhwm002/ILM/IIVT/index.html]. The database currently includes records for nearly 8,000 manuscripts and over 13,000 imprints. The goal of the IIVT is to provide bibliographic control for all villancico sources, especially the manuscripts currently found in Iberian and Latin American archives and libraries.

45   Latin American Music Center, Indiana Univ. Compiled by the School of Music, Indiana Univ. [URL: http://www.music.indiana.edu/som/lamc/]

The LAMC is devoted to the study of Latin American art music. The web site provides full-text access to the LAMC newsletter, *LAMúsiCa*. The "Online Resources" page [http://www.music.indiana.edu/som/lamc/links/] includes links to other sites for Latin American art music information, including pages on famous composers, colonial music, electronic music, and online discussion lists.

46   Latin Music Online. Compiled by "Little Judy" *et al.* [URL: http://www.lamusica.com]

Latin Music Online began in 1995 as an outgrowth of the rec.music.afro-latin Usenet group. Participants in that group, led by "Little Judy" (a computer professional and Latin music enthusiast in New York), established the web page which grew into a commercial site for access to record and concert reviews, concert and club schedules, musician biographies and interviews, discographies, CDs and videos, and much more. The evolution of Latin Music Online is representative of many Internet efforts (especially in cultural fields): started by devoted volunteers, the sites gain popularity and morph into successful commercial ventures. This site does not intend to cover the entire Latin American music scene; its focus is *música tropical,* Latin jazz, and other urban music, primarily in New York, but it does provide links to pages representing a wider range of Latin American styles. As a commercial venture, Latin Music Online provides advertising space and has many shopping links, but this does not interfere with its quality content. It is unlikely that such an effort could exist without advertising. Also, the convenience of reading a review and immediately being able to make an online purchase of a hard-to-find CD is very appealing.

Philosophy

47   Página latinoamericana de filosofía, Montevideo, Uruguay. Recopilación de Agustín Courtoisie. [URL: http://www.ngweb.com/latinofil/]

Three issues of this quarterly online journal devoted to Latin American cultural analysis and criticism are available on the web site. In addition to articles, original drawings by various artists are included as illustrations. Linked pages include details on contributing writers and artists and an annotated list of other philosophy information on the Internet.

48   Paulo Freire Institute/Instituto Paulo Freire. Recopilação de Moacir Gadotti,

Director, Instituto Paulo Freire. [URL: http://www.ppbr.com/ipf]

The Paulo Freire Institute is an international network of people and institutions with members in 18 countries worldwide. Its main purpose is to research, organize, and gather data, thoughts, and information in the fields of education, culture, and communication. The site is a work-in-progress devoted to the thought and practice of this famous Brazilian educator. It currently contains online biographies, bibliographies of Freire's writings and of published works about Freire, and links to organizations in related fields.

49 Proyecto Filosofía en Español. Recopilación de Univ. de Oviedo, España, revista *El Basílico.* [URL: http://www3.uniovi.es/~filesp/]

On the web since 1996, the Proyecto Filosofía en Español provides access to databases, electronic texts, electronic discussion archives, online journals, professional and scholarly associations, Spanish academic publishers, book reviews, etc. devoted to Spanish and Latin American philosophy. The effort is supported by the journal *El Basílico* and is located at the Univ. de Oviedo. The site contains extensive full-text documents covering several historical periods and written by many authors. This site would be worthwhile to any student of Spanish or Latin American philosophy.

50 Seminario Latinoamericano de Filosofía e Historia de las Ideas. Recopilación de Fernando Flores, Depto. de Historia de las Ciencias y las Ideas, Univ. of Lund, Sweden. [URL: http://www.ldc.lu.se/~latinam/indexe.htm]

The information on this site is provided in Spanish, English, Swedish, Portuguese, and French by a team of scholars at the Univ. of Lund, Institution för Kulturvetenskaper. Includes many online academic papers contributed by scholars, links to online journals and related Internet sites, book reviews, etc.

JOURNAL ABBREVIATIONS

HAPI/CD. Hispanic American Periodicals Index: HAPI (CD-ROM). UCLA Latin American Center. Los Angeles; National Information Services Corporation (NISC). Baltimore, Md.

HLAS/CD. Handbook of Latin American Studies CD-ROM: HLAS/CD. Fundación MAPFRE América, Madrid. Hispanic Division, Library of Congress, Washington.

MLA Int. Bibliogr./CD. MLA International Bibliography. H.W. Wilson. New York.

ART

SPANISH AMERICA
Colonial
General, Middle America, and the Caribbean

BARBARA VON BARGHAHN, *Professor of Art History, George Washington University*

INVESTIGATIONS IN ARCHITECTURAL HISTORY have featured prominently in recent scholarship in the realm of Mexican art history. It is gratifying to observe that after a prolonged period of attention paid to 18th-century and Baroque monuments, the pendulum has begun to swing back toward the provocative *inmuebles* of the 16th century. Recent scholarship on that century has been groundbreaking indeed. While, for a time, the monumental works of Toussaint, Kubler, and McAndrew seemed to have exhausted all paths of fruitful inquiry, new research has incorporated archaeological data, secular structures, previously remote sites, and issues of conservation (items **99, 101, 128, 72,** and **65**). These new considerations have contributed to updated methodologies and have effectively challenged some of the canonical accounts of 16th-century architecture codified in the 1950s-60s (items **104, 88,** and **87**). New examinations of social and economic histories have broadened the avenues of architectural study to produce accounts far more compelling than those limited to strict formal analysis (items **96** and **111**). In particular, the function of liturgy as a formative structural principle continues to be explored (item **85**).

In other areas of art historical research, the inexhaustible field of Mexican iconography continues to receive much attention. Iconographic studies of retablos, vernacular traditions, and sub-genres such as allegorical painting are among the most intriguing contributions.

Familiar controversies continue, of course, to smolder. Most notably, the question of precolumbian continuity and synchronism remains current in exhibitions and monographs. While the issue remains as divisive as ever, new methodologies incorporating cultural analysis have been brought to bear on the subject and will surely broaden the debate.

Among recent publications from which scholars will surely benefit are the republications of classic texts by pioneers in the field of Mexican art history. Most notable among these are *Historia de la pintura en Puebla*, by Francisco Pérez Salazar (item **123**) and the *Obras escogidas* of Francisco de la Maza, edited by Elisa Vargas Lugo (item **105**). De la Maza's observations continue to be fresh and insightful after more than half a century and his formative influence in the field will be noted by historiographers for years to come.

One of the outstanding texts included in this section is *El patrimonio cultural de México*, edited by Enrique Florescano (item **86**). This collection of essays has ushered Mexican art history and cultural criticism firmly into the postmodern era of interdisciplinary study. By employing new sociological approaches and methods and addressing issues such as cultural hegemony, nationalism, and the legal issues surrounding patrimony, this book may raise eyebrows, but its impact will surely be felt.

Historical studies concerning the role of prominent religious orders are welcome scholarly texts (items **120, 116,** and **68**), yet much more work remains to be done with respect to advocational images and ideas. Knowledge about military architecture and fortress monasteries also has advanced (items **118** and **124**). There is, however, a critical need for serious monographs on major masters. Encyclopedic clusterings of painters and sculptors produce stunning picture books, but with regard to individual artists, discussions about stylistic evolution and the completion of their workshops are too abbreviated. Equally meager has been the iconographical analysis of monumental works and pictorial programs. The late Santiago Sebastián López was one of the few specialists who addressed "symbolical content." His erudite approach to the examination of art will be greatly missed.

The publication of survey texts continues to fill important gaps in the art historical bibliography. Books highlighting the decorative arts and individual architectural sites play an important role in laying the foundations for future monographs and detailed studies. An additional benefit of these surveys—and, indeed, of most of the works reviewed here—is their contribution to the rapid improvement of the photographic record of Mexican art history. Chandeliers, jamb sculptures and retablos need no longer suffer from dismal b/w reproductions. Colonial painting has perhaps profited the most from the improved quality of reproductions: the catalog of the *Juegos de ingenio* exhibition (item **100**) and Juan Miguel Serrera Contreras' monograph on Alonso Vázquez (item **130**) feature particularly sumptuous plates.

As usual, the reference items this year are broad in scope, covering a plethora of topics, all of which reveal the diversity of Mexico's artistic heritage. The plentiful corpus of new books should continue to inspire further important contributions to the field. A note of appreciation is given to Graham Mayer, an M.A. candidate in Latin American architecture at George Washington University, for his collaboration in the preparation of this chapter.

GENERAL

51 Aguilar, María Dolores *et al*. Mudéjar iberoamericano: una expresión cultural de dos mundos. Edición de Ignacio L. Henares Cuéllar y Rafael J. López Guzmán. Granada, Spain: Univ. de Granada, 1993. 334 p.: bibl., ill.

The persistence of the various manifestations of *mudéjar* culture in Spain and Latin America is the subject of this collection of fine papers originally presented at the Seminario Internacional sobre el Mudéjar sponsored by the Univ. de Granada, Spain in Dec. 1991. This event marked the culmination of a series of international symposia initiated in Teruel in 1975 that have considerably advanced the scholarship on *mudéjar* art. Eight of the 18 papers address topics related to Latin America, beginning with the theoretical essay by Enrique Nuere, "La Carpintería en España y América a través de los Tratados" (p. 173–187). Decorative and structural aspects of South American *mudéjar* architecture are covered by: Jaime Salcedo Salcedo, "La Presencia Mudéjar en la Arquitectura del Nuevo Reino de Granada" (p. 257–263); Alfonso Ortiz Crespo, "Techumbres y Cubiertas Mudéjares en el Ecuador" (p. 265–286); and Rodolfo Vallín, "Las Armaduras Mudéjares en Colombia" (p. 307–324). Suggestive comparisons of evangelical work in Indian communities and town-planning in Mexico and Peru are treated by Ramón Gutiérrez, "Parroquias de Indios y Reorganización Urbana en la Evangelización Americana" (p. 213–232). See also item **60**. [H. Rodríguez-Camilloni]

52   **Artigas H., Juan B.** *et al.* Centros históricos: América Latina. Coordinación
de Ramón Gutiérrez. Bogotá: Junta de Andalucía, Consejería de Obras Públicas y Transportes, 1990. 282 p.: ill. (some col.), maps.
(Col. SomoSur; 10)

This volume is an important anthology
of 17 case studies of historic centers in capital
cities and some smaller towns in several
countries. The authors—distinguished architects specializing in the protection and preservation of their countries' cultural property—
offer an historic overview of the growth of
each city, followed by an analysis of factors
affecting conservation of their respective
historic centers today. Beyond identifying
patterns of unity and diversity across Latin
America, valuable recommendations for immediate action are submitted in the hope that
they will lead to a redefinition of preservation
policies. The illustrations, reproductions of
historic documents, and contemporary photographs are an excellent complement to the
texts. [H. Rodríguez-Camilloni]

**Bibliografía para la historia de las artes
visuales en la Argentina.** See item **3.**

53   **Exposición Barroco Latinoamericano.**
Buenos Aires: Facultad de Arquitectura
y Urbanismo, Instituto de Arte Americano e
Investigaciones Estéticas Mario J. Buschiazzo:
Museo Nacional de Bellas Artes, 1989? 116 p.:
ill.

Popular edition in Spanish of selected
papers dealing with Spanish colonial architecture and urbanism originally presented at the
International Symposium on Latin American
Baroque Art held in Rome in April 1980 under the auspices of UNESCO and the Istituto
Italo-Latino Americano. The lack of illustrations is a major drawback, and some of the
essays do not have footnotes. Most authors
argue for a broader definition of the term
"baroque" when applied to Spanish colonial
architecture: one that looks beyond formal
and decorative aspects and acknowledges special conditions that characterized the social
milieu in which those works were created.
Specific South American topics are addressed
by Ramón Gutiérrez, "Reflexiones para una
Metodología de Análisis del Barroco Americano;" José García Bryce, "El Barocco en
la Arquitectura del Perú;" Antonio Bonet
Correa, "El Convento de Santa Catalina de
Arequipa y la Arquitectura de los Conventos

de Monjas en Hispanoamérica;" and Ricardo
Jesse Alexander, "El Barroco Guaraní (la Estructura del Espacio Arquitectónico)." For a
fully illustrated edition, the reader should
consult Istituto Italo-Latino Americano, *Mos-
tra Barrocco Latino Americano* (Rome, 1980).
[H. Rodríguez-Camilloni]

54   **Fernández, Alejandro; Rafael Munoa**
and **Jorge Rabasco.** Marcas de la plata
española y virreinal. Madrid: Antiquaria,
1992. 366 p.: ill., indexes. (Diccionarios Antiquaria; 8)

Indispensable reference work for identification of seals and inscriptions used by
16th–19th-century silversmiths in Spain and
the Spanish-American colonies. The catalog
consists of 2,200 markings reproduced in
drawings and photographs to facilitate their
reading, arranged by geographic location and
corresponding date. The South American examples listed belong to production centers in
Bogotá, Lima, Arequipa, and Buenos Aires.
[H. Rodríguez-Camilloni]

55   **Gasparini, Graziano.** El amanecer del
Renacimiento en América: una apreciación arquitectónica = The dawning of the
Renaissance in the Americas. New York: Research Institute for the Study of Man, 1995.
31 p.: appendix, bibl., ill.

Short but elegant companion catalog to
the exhibition with the same title held at the
Research Institute for the Study of Man in
1995. The text and photographs by renowned
architect and architectural historian Graziano Gasparini focus on the cultural transmission of the Italian Renaissance from the
Old World to the New World during the colonial period. The author is quick to point out
that the "Renaissance [was] not merely identified with the artistic manifestations of a
specific culture and period; it [was] a phenomenon that extend[ed] to literary, philosophical, scientific, and political expressions, and
even to a way of being and doing . . . The Renaissance was not just a prerogative of Italian
culture, for from Italy it radiated to the rest of
the European countries, determining very diverse phases of cultural renovation that persisted even beyond the seventeenth century."
(p. 13) [H. Rodríguez-Camilloni]

56   **Gasparini, Graziano.** The pre-Hispanic
grid system: the urban shape of conquest and territorial organization. (*in* Settle-

ments in the Americas: cross-cultural perspectives. Edited by Ralph Bennett. Newark, Del.: Univ. of Delaware Press, 1993, p. 78–109, maps, photos)

Author looks at examples of orthogonal town planning in precolumbian Mexico and Peru and concludes that early urban design patterns in the New World that exhibit regular grid systems occurred in the same formal way and that they appeared in situations accompanied by attitudes very similar to those that motivated their use in the Old World. The opinion is therefore advanced that the precolumbian contribution to the territorial organization of towns during the Spanish colonial period merits a closer examination. [H. Rodríguez-Camilloni]

57   González Hernández, Vicente. Presencia de Aragón en el arte de América. Zaragoza, Spain: Comisión Aragonesa V Centenario; Diputación General de Aragón, 1990. 120 p.: bibl., ill., index. (Col. Aragón y América; 17)

Small book published for the Biblioteca Quinto Centenario looks at the artistic influences wielded by political administrators, religious dignitaries, architects, and artists from Aragon in the Spanish American colonies. Notable examples of Aragonese artists include painter Pedro García Ferrer, who worked on the dome of the Cathedral of Puebla, Mexico in the 17th century, and architect Marcos Ibáñez, who designed the new Cathedral of Guatemala City in 1782. Other aspects of Aragonese-South American relations are explored in chap. 4, "El Arte de los Capuchinos Aragoneses en Venezuela;" chap. 5, "Un Recuerdo a Aragón en Colombia;" chap. 7, "Paraguay y el Oscense D. Félix de Azara;" chap. 8, "Argentina y Chile: Religión y Arte;" and chap. 9, "El Perú Durante el Virreinato del Aragonés Melchor Navarra y Rocafull." [H. Rodríguez-Camilloni]

58   Heredia Moreno, María del Carmen; Mercedes de Orbe Sivatte; and **Asunción de Orbe Sivatte.** Arte hispanoamericano en Navarra: plata, pintura, y escultura. Pamplona, Spain: Gobierno de Navarra, Depto. de Educación y Cultura, 1992. 270 p.: bibl., ill. (some col.), index, maps. (Arte; 26)

Model study of little-known examples of 16th- to 19th-century Latin American colonial art preserved in churches and monasteries in Spain's Navarra prov. yields important

new findings concerning patronage in the viceroyalties of Mexico and Peru that benefited many Iberian religious institutions. Problems of chronology, provenance, attribution, iconography, materials, and techniques are addressed in the well-written introduction, followed by a detailed catalogue raisonné featuring 139 gold and silver pieces, 28 paintings, and five sculptures. Close reading of documentary records and inscriptions has permitted the attribution of some works to individual silversmiths like Rodallega, Peña Roja, and Lezana or painters like fray Alonso de Herrera. Most works are reproduced in excellent full color plates, often complemented by close-up details. Indispensable source for future studies on the subject. [H. Rodríguez-Camilloni]

Latin American Library, Tulane University. See item **23.**

59   Magna Mater: el sincretismo hispanomericano en algunas imágenes marianas. Trabajo concebido y dirigido por Anna Gradowska *et al.* Caracas: Museo de Bellas Artes, 1992. 196 p.: bibl., ill. (some col.).

The thorny problem of theological synchronism in Latin American art is addressed again in this catalog of the 1992 Caracas exhibition. While this issue will remain controversial, contributors have made provocative headway in developing an updated methodology for such comparative art historical questions. By adopting Manuel Marzal's model of dialectical interaction between cultures to justify synchronic interpretation, the exhibition escapes the limitations implicit in formal iconographic analysis.

Milbrath, Susan. Representations of Caribbean and Latin American Indians in sixteenth-century European art. See *HLAS 55:510.*

60   El mudéjar iberoamericano: del Islam al Nuevo Mundo. Granada, Spain: El Legado Andalusí, 1995? 319 p.: bibl., col. ill.

Splendid multiauthored deluxe volume served as companion catalog to 1995 traveling exhibition of same title mounted in Granada and other Spanish cities under the auspices of the Junta de Andalucía's Consejería de Cultura, Granada's El Legado Andalusí, UNESCO, and other organizations. The main text is a collection of fine essays by leading art historians and is dedicated to the memory of María Dolores Aguilar García and Santiago

Sebastián López, scholars well-known for lifetime contributions to the study of mudéjar art and Iberoamerican culture. It is perhaps the most complete volume on the subject to date, with well-documented and beautifully illustrated studies on *mudéjar* art and architecture in the Iberian Peninsula and Latin America. Articles dealing specifically with Spanish South America include Rodolfo Vallín Magaña, "Lo Mudéjar en la Nueva Granada y Venezuela;" Alfonso Ortiz Crespo, "Influencias Mudéjares en Quito;" Ramón Gutiérrez, "Presencia Mudéjar en la Arquitectura del Perú;" Pedro Querejazu, "El Mudéjar como Expresión Cultural Ibérica, y su Manifestación en las Tierras Altas de la Audiencia de Charcas, Hoy Bolivia;" Alberto Nicolini, "El Mudéjar en la Argentina;" Juan Benavides, "El Mudéjar en la Capitanía General de Chile;" and Alberto Nicolini, "El Mudéjar en el Paraguay." Volume concludes with exhaustive bibliography by locality and fully illustrated catalogue raisonné of the exhibition. See also item **51**. [H. Rodríguez-Camilloni]

61   Nuestras raíces: muestra de arte ibero-americano. México: Consejo Nacional para la Cultura y las Artes, Organización de las Naciones Unidas para la Educación, la Ciencia y la Cultura; Instituto Nacional de Antropología e Historia 1991. 143 p.: col. ill.

Contains primarily high-quality photographs to show the beauty of art from Spanish and Portuguese-speaking countries. Pt. 1 is devoted to precolumbian art, notably fine ceramics and objects made of gold, jade and stone. Pt. 2 examines painting and sculpture from Portugal, Spain, and Latin America.

62   Palm, Erwin Walter. Heimkehr ins Exil: Schriften zu Literatur und Kunst. Auftrag der Heidelberger Akademie der Wissenschaften herausgegeben von Helga von Kügelgen und Arnold Rothe. Köln, Germany: Böhlau Verlag, 1992. 486 p., 59 p. of plates: bibl., ill. (Forum Ibero-Americanum; 6)

Anthology makes available in a single volume seminal essays on the history of colonial Latin American art and architecture by renowned German scholar Erwin Walter Palm (1910–88). Though best known throughout Latin America for his pioneer research on colonial architecture of Santo Domingo and his classic 1955 work, *Los monumentos arquitectónicos de La Española* (see item **154**), Palm's interests in art history were vast; he

contributed many essays on theory and methods applicable to the analysis and interpretation of Spanish colonial art and architecture in general. Arranged thematically, this anthology includes summary English translations of essays originally written in German or Spanish. Many of Palm's recommendations for advancing scholarship in the field remain valid. For example, he insisted that the history of Spanish American architecture should encompass national American history, national European (Spanish) history, and the history of artistic ideas; and that studies in iconology and in anthropological analysis should be intensified. Scholars will find most useful the complete bibliography of his writings. [H. Rodríguez-Camilloni]

63   Reframing the Renaissance: visual culture in Europe and Latin America, **1450–1650.** Edited with an introduction by Claire Farago. New Haven, Conn.: Yale Univ. Press, 1995. 394 p.: bibl., ill., index.

Book resulted from conference session titled "Reevaluating the Eurocentrism of Italian Renaissance Art History" organized by the editor and Gail Geiger for the College Art Association Annual Meeting in Chicago in Feb. 1992. Revised and expanded papers presented in that session by Eloise Quiñones Keber and Cecilia Klein are complemented with new contributions by other distinguished Renaissance art historians. Explores how the extensive cultural exchange that took place between the Old and New Worlds in the 16th century affected artistic practice and discussions. Offers many new methodological approaches for the analysis and interpretation of European and Latin American art of the same period. All essays are illustrated with excellent b/w photographs and fully documented with expanded footnotes. Concludes with an exhaustive consolidated bibliography. [H. Rodríguez-Camilloni]

64   Schenone, Héctor H. Iconografía del arte colonial. v. 1–2. 1. ed. argentina. Buenos Aires?: Fundación Tarea, 1992. 2 v.: bibl., ill.

Monumental work by renowned Argentinian art historian is a major contribution to the field. Represents an exhaustive study of iconography of the Christian saints as depicted in Latin American colonial art. Organization closely follows the classic study by Louis Réau, *Iconographie de l'art chrétien*

(Paris, Presses universitaires de France, 1955–59), with detailed information on the lives of the saints and their attributes, and history of the religious orders active in Latin America. The alphabetical classification with listing of each saint's feast day and most common representations in art, including references to specific examples, makes this an indispensable research tool that will greatly facilitate future iconographic studies. The few b/w reproductions, often poorly cropped, are of only referential value, but a wealth of additional information is contained in the footnotes, general bibliography, and fully illustrated glossary of religious signs and symbols, including liturgical vestments, objects, and artifacts. [H. Rodríguez-Camilloni]

Webmuseo de Latinoamérica. See item **34.**

MEXICO

65 **Aguilar Marco, José Luis** *et al.* Misiones en la península de Baja California. México: Instituto Nacional de Antropología e Historia, 1991. 327 p.: bibl., ill., maps. (Col. científica; 226. Serie Historia)

The peninsula of Baja California is poorly represented in scholarship on the architectural history of Mexico. Issued by the Faculty of Architecture of the Univ. Autónoma de Baja California, this study provides a welcome introduction to the state's 16th- and 17th-century missions. The architectural studies of individual monuments are prefaced by excellent chapters on the demographics and the history of evangelization of the region. Photographs of these often ignored structures are supplemented by well drafted elevations and plans. Also voices the faculty's concerns about issues of historic preservation.

66 **Alarcón Cedillo, Roberto M.** and **Armida Alonso Lutteroth.** Tecnología de la obra de arte en la época colonial: pintura mural y de caballete, escultura y orfebrería. México: Univ. Iberoamericana, 1993. 119 p.: bibl., ill. (some col.).

Short analysis of techniques of artistic production in colonial New Spain, divided into four chapters dealing with mural and easel painting, sculpture, and metalworking. Excellent introduction to the subject in the tradition of Abelardo Carrillo y Gariel's

monumental *Técnica de la pintura de Nueva España.* The book offers very good photographic documentation throughout, especially the chapter on sculpture.

67 **Alcalá y Mendiola, Miguel de.** Descripción en bosquejo de la Imperial Cesar[e]a, muy noble y muy leal ciudad de Puebla de los Angeles. Recopilación e investigación del Lic. Ramón Sánchez Flores. Puebla: Junta de Mejoramiento Moral, Cívico y Material del Municipio de Puebla, 1992. 206 p.: ill. (some col.).

This manuscript, written between 1696–1746, provides invaluable documentation concerning churches, convents, and monasteries of Puebla. Despite the lack of visual materials, the historical material is an important complement to chronicles of viceregal New Spain.

68 **Arroyo González, Esteban** and **María de Cristo Santos Morales.** Monasterio de Santa Rosa de Lima, Puebla de los Angeles, MDCCXL. México: Provincia de Santiago de México; Instituto Dominicano de Investigaciones Históricas, 1992. 80 p.: bibl., col. ill.

In 1677 the Dominicans of the province of San Miguel y Santos Angeles petitioned Pope Clement XI, Bourbon king Charles II, and Bishop of Puebla Monsignor Manuel Fernández de Santa Cruz to build a monastery devoted to St. Rose of Lima (1587–1617). The Dominican tertiary was the first canonized saint of the Americas (April 12, 1671). A Cédula Real was issued on June 7, 1678. Begun under the authority of Viceroy Don José de Monclova, the institution founded by Padre Bernardo de Andia was begun by Don Miguel de Rabozo on April 8, 1690. This superlative volume concerns the building's construction, which took several years to complete, and the decoration of the Church of Santa Rosa de Santa María, the heart of the complex. Of additional value is the concluding chapter containing biographies of nuns whose portraits appear in the Convent of Santa Rosa.

69 **Aubry, Andrés.** La restauración de la Iglesia de San Nicolás en San Cristóbal de las Casas, Chiapas. Tuxtla Gutiérrez, Mexico: Tall. Gráf. del Estado, 1992. 19 p.

A brief chronology of issues confronting the conservation effort at the 16th-century Church of San Nicolás in San Cristóbal de las Casas.

70 Basílica Catedral de Puebla. Introducción y notas de Julio Espinosa Martínez. Puebla, Mexico: s.n., 1994. 33 p.: bibl., ill.

Short, descriptive account of the Cathedral of Puebla includes sketches of the facade and interior details, and is prefaced by a brief history of the city.

71 Bengoechea Izaguirre, Ismael. El gaditano Fray Andrés de San Miguel, arquitecto de la Nueva España: discurso de recepción como Académico de Número . . . Discurso de contestación por don Pablo Antón Solé. Cádiz, Spain: Real Academia Hispanoamericana, 1992. 96 p.: bibl., ill.

The text of the author's oral dissertation presented to the Real Academia Hispanoamericana. Explores the life and theoretical contributions of the architect Fray Andrés de San Miguel (1577–1652), who travelled from Cadíz to New Spain in 1597. Several of Andrés de San Miguel's major achievements such as the Church of San Angel de Coyoacán and the draining of the Valley of México are discussed in detail. A section on architectural style highlights the influence of Vitruvius and Leon Battista Alberti on the designs of Fray Andrés. Includes a favorable response to the dissertation by Pablo Antón Solé.

Boils Morales, Guillermo. Arquitectura y sociedad en Querétaro, siglo XVIII. See item **1123.**

72 Bretos, Miguel A. Iglesias de Yucatán. Portafolio fotográfico de Christian Rasmussen. Mérida, Mexico: Producción Editorial Dante, 1992. 162 p.: bibl., ill.

Uses the monumental *Catálogo de construcciones religiosas del estado de Yucatán,* compiled between 1929–33, as a springboard for further investigation. Bretos examines major Yucatecan monuments such as Mérida's Convento Mayor, the Cathedral of San Idelfonso, and San Antonio de Padua Izamal as repositories of complex iconographic programs. The theme of religious synchronism between Spanish Catholicism and native Yucatecan religion is observed in the use and history of the monuments, particularly those in the vernacular tradition. Valuable contributions include studies of remote monuments such as Ichmul, inaccessible to the compilers of the *Catálogo.* Bretos' text is accompanied by remarkable b/w photographs by Christian Rasmussen.

Bretos, Miguel A. La provincia de San Joseph de Yucatán: conversión y arquitectura religiosa en el país de los Mayas. See item **1127.**

73 Cabral, Ignacio. Arquitectura religiosa en San Pedro, Cholula, Puebla. Santa Catarina Mártir, Mexico: Univ. de las Américas—Puebla, 1994. 38 p.: col. ill.

Collection of color photographs of religious architecture in the municipality of San Pedro in Cholula. Photographs are accompanied by short descriptive texts.

74 Cabrera, Francisco J. El coleccionismo en Puebla. México: F.J. Cabrera, 1988. 251 p.: bibl., ill.

Short history of art and antiquity collections in Puebla beginning in the 17th century with the library of Bishop Juan de Palafox y Mendoza. Concentrates on the collection of 19th-century textile magnate Francisco Cabrera Ferrando. Includes facsimile of inventory of Cabrera's collection and extensive excerpts from Cabrera's European travel diaries.

75 Cabrera Siles, Esperanza and **Patricia Escandón.** Historia del Nacional Monte de Piedad, 1775–1993. México: Nacional Monte de Piedad, 1993. 348 p.: bibl., ill.

Compact historical volume about El Sacro y Real Monte de Piedad inaugurated on Feb. 25, 1775 under the aegis of Don Pedro, the Count of Santa María de Regla, to replicate an archetype in Madrid.

76 Carrasco Franco, Germán. Tepotzotlán: joya del México colonial; libro de fotografías. México: Ayuntamiento de Tepotzotlán, 1993. 120 p.: col. ill.

A pictorial album of 17th- and 18th-century architecture, sculpture, and paintings, with special concentration on Jesuit artistic heritage. Through stunning photographs, reveals the multiple facets of Tepotzotlan, a colonial "diamond" of New Spain.

77 Castelló Yturbide, Teresa *et al.* El arte plumaria en México. México: Fomento Cultural Banamex; BANAMEX-ACCIVAL, 1993. 250 p.: bibl., col. ill.

A stunning volume with a copious number of color plates. The well-documented text begins with the Aztecs and their use of feathers, and concludes with a discussion of the indigenous Mexican art known as *plumaria.* The heart of the book is devoted to examples of *plumaria* that survive from the viceregal period. The all-encompassing scope of the art works ranges from Christian devotional subjects to liturgical vestments, etc. Several plates detail concerns about the conservation of the rare works of art, and the bibliography is valuable for further investigation. Also of interest is the glossary of native birds indicating specific feathers used in the art of *plumaria*.

78   Castrejón Díez, Jaime and **Ruby Nickel de Castrejón.** Santa Prisca, Taxco.
13. ed. México: Editorial Santa Prisca, 1992. 64 p.: bibl., ill. (some col.).

Largely descriptive account of the church of Santa Prisca in Taxco. The authors explicitly recognize that the book is an appreciative work and not a scholarly undertaking. Nonetheless, some color plates are helpful additions to the bibliography on this important Mexican monument, especially those of the Altar of Santa Cecilia and the Capilla de los Indios.

79   Castro Morales, Efraín. El arte de la herrería en México. Introducción de Guillermo Tovar de Teresa. Fotografías de José Ignacio González Manterola. México: Grupo Financiero Bancomer, 1994. 228 p.: ill. (some col.).

This book represents another beautiful photographic study from the Fundación Cultural Bancomer. Mexican ironworking, incorporating locks, decorative railings, ecclesiastical furnishings, and tools, is treated as a fine art in its own right. An introduction by Guillermo Tovar de Teresa traces the history of Mexican ironworking from the 16th century to its 19th-century heyday.

80   Catedrales de México. Dirección y coordinación general de Carmen Valles Septién. México: CVS, 1993. 267 p.: bibl., ill. (some col.).

This very fine survey of the major churches of Mexico covers a range of decorative elements, architecture, sculpture, and paintings. An impressive roster of art historians compiled the documented text entries. Despite the number of contributors, the text provides an organized journey into the world of Baroque Mexico. The illustrations are of exceptional quality.

81   Chanfón Olmos, Carlos. Wilars de Honecort: su manuscrito. México: Univ. Nacional Autónoma de México, Facultad de Arquitectura, 1994. 308 p.: bibl., ill., maps. (Col. Mexicana de tratadistas)

This facsimile of Villard de Honnecourt's Bibliothèque Nationale manuscript will prove invaluable to Spanish-speaking students of Gothic art.

82   Chessal, Luis. San Luis Potosí: estampas de mi ciudad; 400 cuatro siglos de esfuerzo, San Luis Potosí, S.L.P., Mex., 1592–1992. San Luis Potosí, Mexico: s.n., 1992. 1 v. (unpaged): ill.

A collection of 23 engravings of architectural details from San Luis Potosí, with brief descriptive captions.

83   Ciudades mexicanas en la época colonial: exposición temporal, Museo Nacional de Historia, Castillo de Chapultepec. México: INAH-SEP, 1988. 48 p.: bibl., ill.

This exhibition at Chapultepec Castle employed evidence from Mexican material culture to illustrate development of the city from the 16th to the last half of the 18th century. The catalog is divided into chapters on each of the three centuries featuring historical issues such as city planning, cultural diffusion, and migration from rural areas. Period maps are particularly effective in illustrating processes of historical change.

84   Colección de documentos en torno a la Iglesia de San Gabriel Tlacopan. Recopilación de Emma Pérez-Rocha. México: Instituto Nacional de Antropología e Historia, Depto. de Etnohistoria, 1988. 156 p.: ill. (Cuaderno de trabajo; 3)

Collection of historical documents concerning the church of San Gabriel Tlacopan features extensive 18th-century inventories of church and parish holdings (1751, 1767) and selected correspondence of Fray Alonso González.

85   Cómez Ramos, Rafael. Andalucía y México en el Renacimiento y Barroco: estudios de arte y arquitectura. Sevilla, Spain: Ediciones Guadalquivir, 1991. 118 p.: bibl., ill. (Biblioteca Guadalquivir; 10)

Proposes a formative relationship between Andalusian artistic tradition and the generation of 16th-century *mudéjar* and *tequitqui* styles in Mexico. Includes an excellent chapter on the influence of Andalusian liturgy on the architecture of New Spain.

86   Consejo Nacional para la Cultura y las Artes (Mexico). El patrimonio cultural de México. Recopilación de Enrique Florescano. México: Consejo Nacional para la Cultura y las Artes, 1993. 424 p.: bibl. (Sección de obras de historia)

Collection of essays concerning the impact of cultural hegemony on cultural preservation. Most selections discuss Mexico and its culture. Topics addressed include nationalism and historic preservation, television and cultural identity, and Mexican film as national patrimony. The influence of Marx and the Annales School is evident in several selections, particularly Enrique Nalda's excellent essay "Elementos para la Elaboración de una Política de Conservación del Patrimonio Arqueológico."

87 Conventos coloniales de Morelos.
México: Instituto de Cultura de Morelos, 1994. 282 p.: bibl., ill. (some col.).

Several well-known scholars revisit and question the conclusions of the first phase of Mexican architectural historiography (1926–65). Most notably, reexamines the question of the military role played by the first 16th-century *conventos* and the functions of the open chapels and atria. These new perspectives are employed in analyses of individual *conventos* such as Santo Domingo Oaxtepec, San Diego Cuatla, and the monastery of Tepotztlán.

88 Córdova Tello, Mario. El convento de San Miguel de Huejotzingo, Puebla. México: Instituto Nacional de Antropología e Historia, 1992. 124 p.: bibl., ill., maps. (Col. científica; 243. Serie Arqueología)

The famous *convento* at Huejotzingo is perhaps Mexico's most important 16th-century architectural monument. It is therefore gratifying to see new scholarship on the structure continue to emerge, building on the foundations laid down by Kubler, McAndrew, and Toussaint. Córdova's noteworthy contributions include a chronicle of Huejotzingo's early history and evangelization. His account of the three distinct building phases between 1524–80 employs archaeological data to reinforce and clarify Kubler's earlier conclusions on the composite nature of the structure.

89 Cortina Portilla, Manuel. Algo de lo nuestro. México: CONSA, 1990. 66 p.: bibl., col. ill.

Ninth work in the annual CONSA series on the economic history of Mexico City. Six thematic chapters examine topics such as the history of toolmaking, the Mexi-

can system of *castas*, the emergence of the Churrigueresque pilaster and the dawn of the Mexican railroad. A single, full page plate illustrates each chapter.

90 Cortina Portilla, Manuel. Sucedió en el valle. México: CONSA, 1991. 68 p.: ill. (some col.), map.

The tenth CONSA annual has the early history of Mexico City as its theme and is organized around five full-page color plates.

91 Curiel, Gustavo. Tlalmanalco: historia e iconología del conjunto conventual. México: Univ. Nacional Autónoma de México, 1988. 233 p., 111 p. of plates: bibl., ill. (some col.). (Monografías de arte; 17)

Proposes a new iconographic reading of the murals and sculpture of the much studied *convento* of Tlalmanalco. The numerous didactic programs can be read as allegorical psychomachy, symbolizing the struggle between evangelization and "idolatry" in 16th-century Mexico. Such allegories reflect the equation of native religious traditions with idolatry by early mendicants such as Jerónimo de Mendieta. The discussion of the use of classical pagan motifs in these moralizing compositions, and the theological tensions implicit in such inclusions, is particularly fascinating. Curiel's investigations in this area are the most insightful since Francisco de la Maza's *Mitología clásica en el arte colonial* (see *HLAS 32:396*).

92 Escalada, Xavier. Guadalupe, arte y esplendor. 2. ed. México: Enciclopedia Guadalupana, 1991. 178 p.: col. ill.

A richly illustrated volume about the advocation of the famous "Virgin of Guadalupe." One of the most intriguing plates in the book is the sacred *tilma* with the constellations identified on Mary's blue mantle. The stars depicted accord with the appearance of the sky at the winter solstice of 1531. The volume concludes with a comparative examination of narrations based on the original Nahuatl treatise of Guadalupe, *Nican Mopohua*, by Antonio Valeriano (1520–1605). Reproduces the oldest literal version by Luis Becerra Tanco (1666).

93 Fernández García, Martha *et al.* El Palacio de la Escuela de Medicina. México: Facultad de Medicina, Univ. Nacional Autónoma de México, 1994. 172 p.: bibl., ill. (some col.).

This lavishly illustrated study places

the Palace of the School of Medicine (formerly the Palace of the Inquisition) within the context of the Baroque *oeuvre* of the architect Pedro de Arrieta. His formative influence on the architectural landscape of Mexico City is discussed in the first section, while the second is devoted to a formal analysis of the Palace. A wealth of illustrations, including detailed floor plans, archival photographs, and several of Arrieta's sketches and elevations, complement beautiful contemporary photographs.

94 Giffords, Gloria Fraser. Mexican folk retablos. Photographs by Jerry D. Ferrin. Rev. ed. Albuquerque: Univ. of New Mexico Press, 1992. 192 p.: bibl., col. ill., index.

This study characterizes retablo images as a folk tradition which retained a "naive" Baroque vocabulary free of the stylistic metamorphoses of the Academy of San Carlos. Popular saints commonly found in retablos are each illustrated by a single outstanding example. The identification of a group of retablos united by their use of red bole underpainting is an important advance in retablo conoisseurship.

95 González Cosío D., Bertha. Los Sepulcros de Santo Domingo y Cocheras: una casa en el centro histórico de la Ciudad de México. México: Consejo Nacional para la Cultura y las Artes; Instituto Nacional de Bellas Artes, 1993. 79 p.: bibl., ill.

Descriptive and historical account of an early-16th-century Mexico City house on the corner of Los Sepulcros de Santo Domingo and Cocheras streets. Includes brief histories of several of the house's famous residents such as Leona Vicario, Andrés Quintana Roo, and painter Juan Cordero. Gives short stylistic description of the house as an architectural monument and provides recommendations for its historic preservation.

96 Guzmán Pérez, Moisés *et al.* Arquitectura, comercio, ilustración y poder en Valladolid de Michoacán, siglo XVIII. México: Instituto Nacional de Antropología e Historia, 1993. 241 p.: bibl., ill., maps. (Col. Regiones de México)

A study of the political and economic factors that shaped the urban and architectural configuration of 18th-century Valladolid

(now Morelia.) Focuses on careers of architect Diego Durán and Basque merchant Juan Manuel de Michelena e Ibarra.

97 Hernández Pons, Elsa C. El Convento Dominico de Chapultenango, Chiapas. Tuxtla Gutiérrez, Mexico: Gobierno del Estado de Chiapas, Consejo Estatal de Fomento a la Investigación y Difusión de la Cultura, Instituto Chiapaneco de Cultura, 1994. 71 p.: bibl., ill. (Cuadernos ocasionales)

Very short history of the Dominican *convento* at Chapultenango, Chiapas. The text, while cursory, is well illustrated and includes some unpublished photographs.

98 Jalisco, su Palacio de Gobierno: crónica de un recinto con belleza y con historia. Edición preparada y dirigida por Fernando Martínez Réding. Guadalajara, Mexico: Gobierno del Estado de Jalisco, 1977. 138 p.: ill. (some col.), maps.

A good investigation of the Governor's Palace in Jalisco from the Spanish conquest to the 19th century. While the quality of photographs could be better, the text provides critical information concerning the importance of the structure during the colonial epoch.

99 Jiménez M., Víctor and **Rogelio González Medina.** El ex-obispado de Oaxaca: un caso singular en la arquitectura colonial mexicana; con algunas notas sobre Inquisición y evangelización. México?: Tule, 1992. 265 p.: bibl., ill., index.

Architectural history of the Federal Palace of Oaxaca, formerly the bishopric of Oaxaca. Engaging and well-documented study contends that the Palace dates from the second half of the 16th century, much earlier than the 17th or 18th century dates that have been advanced elsewhere. Conclusion is based on stylistic analysis of the original facade, which the authors believe corresponds to Kubler's "European Renaissance" category of 16th-century civic architecture in Mexico. Provides accounts of the building's various stages of renovation and expansion. The inclusion of previously unpublished 19th-century photographs and records of chroniclers such as Eduard Mühlenpfordt, is particularly interesting.

100 Juegos de ingenio y agudeza: la pintura emblemática de la Nueva España. México: Banamex-Accival, 1994. 426 p.: bibl., ill. (some col.).

Catalog of the 1994 exhibition on Mexican allegorical painting provides a gold mine for students of iconography. With sections on Marian imagery, *memento morii*, and emblematic representations of the Virgin of Guadalupe, the catalog is exhaustively documented and exquisitely illustrated. This is surely one of the most provocative and ambitious exhibitions of recent memory in the field, and the catalog itself is a magnificent work of scholarship.

Klaren, Peter F. Spain in America: the Viceroyalties of New Spain and Peru, 1521–1825. See item **898.**

101   Loera y Chávez de Esteinou, Margarita and **Guadalupe Gómez y Domínguez.** Murmullos de antiguos muros: los inmuebles del siglo XVI que se conservan en el Estado de México. Toluca, Mexico: Instituto Mexiquense de Cultura, 1994. 233 p.: bibl., ill., maps. (Documentos y testimonios)

As a catalog of extant 16th-century structures in the state of Mexico, this study is invaluable in its broad scope. Eschewing the prevalent bias toward religious architecture, Loera y Chávez gives equal consideration to important monuments of civic and residential architecture such as aqueducts, fountains, and bridges.

102   Mangino Tazzer, Alejandro. Influencias artístico-culturales entre América y Europa. México: Univ. Autónoma Metropolitana, Unidad Azcapotzalco, 1994. 199 p.: bibl., ill.

Posits that Mexican Baroque architecture shares a stylistic and functional affinity with the precolumbian traditions it replaced. This concept of artistic continuity is also extended to musical and literary traditions in Mexico.

103   Manrique, Jorge Alberto; Alfonso Morales; and **Servando Aréchiga.** Guillermo Kahlo: fotógrafo oficial de monumentos. México: Casa de las Imágenes, 1992. 174 p.: ill.

An important artistic study of the late-19th- and early-20th-century Mexican photographer Guillermo Kahlo. The b/w photographs of diverse churches in the city and state of Mexico, the states of Guanajato and Puebla, and the cities of Guadalajara, Oaxaca, Querétaro, San Luis Potosí, and Tlaxcala are significant pictorial documents.

104   Manrique, Jorge Alberto. Manierismo en México. México: Textos Dispersos Ediciones, 1993. 61 p.: bibl., ill.

Treatise on Mexican architecture of the late-16th century challenges the problematic attempt to place monuments of the 1570s–80s into the stylistic categories of "pure Renaissance" or "sober Baroque." Proposes instead a new consideration of mannerism in Mexican art. By understanding monuments of these decades as products of a mannerist sensibility, their forced categorization into stylistic extremes can be avoided. Divided into sections on mannerist historiography and stylistic analysis of individual buildings.

105   Maza, Francisco de la. Obras escogidas. Prólogo y selección de Elisa Vargas Lugo de Bosch. México: Comité Organizador San Luis 400; Instituto de Investigaciones Estéticas, Univ. Nacional Autónoma de México, 1992. 740 p.: ill. (Col. Cuatro siglos. Serie Obras escogidas de autores potosinos; 2)

Selection of 33 papers published in the *Anales* of the Instituto de Investigaciones Estéticas between 1940–72. The field of Mexican art history has rapidly gained momentum in recent decades, making recognition of pioneers, such as Francisco de la Maza, increasingly appropriate. The gathering into a single compendium of many of De la Maza's groundbreaking shorter works, several of which are difficult to find outside of Mexico, will prove invaluable to scholars worldwide. Several essays included here, such as "Fray Diego Valadés: escritor y grabador franciscano del siglo XVI," have provided the critical foundations for much subsequent scholarship in the field. Although controversial, De la Maza's lifelong interest in Mexican art's participation in the European classical tradition will continue to elicit scholarly attention.

106   Merlo Juárez, Eduardo; Miguel Pavón Rivero; and **José Antonio Quintana Fernández.** La Basílica Catedral de la Puebla de los Angeles. Puebla, Mexico: Litografía Alai, 1991. 385 p.: bibl., ill. (some col.).

One of the most handsome volumes on the Cathedral to appear in recent years. The exquisitely illustrated text studies not only the architecture of the Cathedral, but also the interior decoration beginning with the *altar mayor* and concluding with the diverse chapels, each of which is distinguished by important paintings by renowned masters such as Pedro García Ferrer, Juan Tinoco, Jose de Ibarra, Miguel de Cabrera, Cristóbal de Villalpando, Juan Rodríguez Juárez, José de Ibarra, Luis Berruecos, etc.

107 México y La Real Fábrica de Cristales de la Granja. México: Museo Franz Mayer, 1994. 116 p.: bibl., ill.

Catalog of an exhibition on fine Mexican crystal and glassware. Focuses on production of the 18th-century La Granja Factory.

108 The missions of Northern Sonora: a 1935 field documentation. Historical and archaeological aspects by Arthur Woodward. Integrated with the architecture, text and measured drawings by Scofield DeLong and Leffler B. Miller. Photographs by George Alexander Grant. Edited with preface, notes, appendices, and references by Buford Pickens. Tucson: Univ. of Arizona Press, 1993. 230 p.: bibl., ill., index, maps. (The Southwest Center series)

Well-illustrated study of mission churches of the Sonoran Desert and Arizona founded in the late 17th century by the Jesuit friar Eusebio Francisco Kino (d. 1711) and occupied by the Franciscans after the expulsion of the Jesuits (1767) by edict of Charles III. The publication of the 1935 report of the National Park Service field expedition constitutes a significant record of the remains of 12 missions.

109 Monterrosa Prado, Mariano and Leticia Talavera Solórzano. Catálogo de bienes muebles de la Parroquia de San José de la Cuidad de Puebla. México: Gobierno del Estado de Puebla, 1991. 200 p.: ill.

This exhaustive catalog of the furniture, sculpture, and paintings held by the parish of San José in Puebla provides data on the date, size, material, attribution, and state of preservation for each entry. A singular and very useful feature of the catalog is the inclusion of maps indicating the location of each object within the church.

110 Morales García, Rogelio. Crónica de un palacio. 2a. ed. Morelia, Mexico: Gobierno del Estado de Michoacán, 1989. 114 p.: bibl., ill.

History of the Government Palace in Morelia concentrates on its previous role as the Tridentine Seminary (1545–1861). Provides accounts of some of the Seminary's

more famous students such as Melchor Ocampo and Dr. José Sixto Verduzco. Photographs and descriptions of the early 20th-century murals by Alfredo Zalce are also included.

111 Muchas moradas hay en México. México: Univ. Nacional Autónoma de México, Coordinación de Humanidades; Instituto del Fondo Nacional de la Vivienda para los Trabajadores, 1993. 157 p.: bibl., ill. (some col.).

Survey of the history of residential architecture in Mexico spans the centuries between Maya ruins and the high rise developments of Abraham Zabludofsky. Emphasizes history of the marginal and often ignored residences of Mexican workers. Includes critical analysis of the influence of class and social stratification on residential architecture.

112 Museo Franz Mayer (Mexico). La platería del Museo Franz Mayer: obras escogidas, siglos XVI–XIX. Recopilación de Cristina Esteras Martín. México: Museo Franz Mayer, 1992. 347 p.: bibl., ill. (some col.), indexes.

Valuable resource for the study of sacred and secular silver in viceregal Mexico, with an array of fine objects from the Franz Mayer Museum, all codified with good illustrations of hallmarks and stamps.

113 Museo Nacional de Arte (Mexico). Museo Nacional de Arte: una ventana al arte mexicano de cuatro siglos; Museo Nacional de Arte, noviembre de 1994. México: Consejo Nacional para la Cultura y las Artes, 1994. 192 p.: bibl., col. ill.

Sumptuous photographs embellish this selection from the permanent collection of the Museo Nacional. Particularly outstanding are chapters on 19th- and 20th-century Mexican painting and sculpture. Reproductions of portraits by Hermengilio Bustos and several landscapes by José María Velasco receive important attention. Brief introductions by Juana Gutiérrez Haces, Jaime Cuadriello, Fausto Ramírez, and Karen Cordero Reiman accompany the chapters.

114 Museo Nacional del Virreinato (Mexico). Pintura novohispana: Museo Nacional del Virreinato, Tepotzotlán. t. 2, Siglos XVIII, XIX y XX, primera parte. Texto de Roberto M. Alarcón Cedillo, María del Rosario García de Toxqui. Colaboración de Ana

Joaquina Montalvo de Morales *et al.* Tepotzo-tlán, Mexico: Asociación de Amigos del Museo Nacional del Virreinato, 1994. 1 v.: bibl., ill. (some col.).

Vol. two of the collection catalog of the Museo del Virreinato in Tepotzlán offers a stunning array of high-quality reproductions. Concentrates on the Museum's holdings of 19th- and 20th-century oil paintings. Works are divided into iconographic categories such as the life of Christ, Marian themes, depictions of the Trinity and hagiographies. This organizing principle is extremely effective in highlighting the distinctive iconography of Central Mexican painting. Also important is a chapter on the Museum's fine collection of ex-voto retablos.

115 Museo Nacional del Virreinato (Mexico). Tepotzlán: la vida y la obra en la Nueva España. México: Sociedad de Amigos del Museo Nacional de Virreinato; Bancomer, 1988. 270 p.: bibl., ill. (some col.), maps.

A spectacular monograph about the artistic legacy of Tepotzlán, with historical analysis of the colonial epoch that culminates in an overview of the collections of the Museo Nacional del Virreinato. The magnificent illustrations of architecture, painting, sculpture, and the decorative arts (including rare photographs of 18th-century apparel), are complemented by fine details of major works.

116 Oratorios de San Felipe Neri en México y un testimonio vivo, la fundación del Oratorio de San Felipe Neri en la villa de Orizaba. Prólogo de R.P. Francisco Aguilera. Investigación de Mariano Monterrosa. Fotografía de Bob Schalkwijk. México: Centro de Asistencia y Promoción, A.C., 1992. 96, civ p.: bibl., col. ill.

A scholarly book about St. Philip Neri (1515–95), founder of the Congregation of Oratorians in Rome (1575), and the Oratorian institutions in New Spain. This well-organized volume begins with two chapters about the Counter-Reformation period and the spiritual mission of the Congregation of St. Philip Neri in Italy and Mexico. Chap. 3 concerns the Houses of the Oratorians in Mexico. Chap. 4 focuses on the Oratorio of San Felipe Neri in Orizaba established in the Sanctuary of Our Lady of Guadalupe in 1775. Numerous color plates and a select bibliography accompany the superb text.

117 Ortiz Lajous, Jaime. San Luis Potosí: una veta de cuatrocientos años. Fotografía de Ignacio Urquiza. San Luis Potosí, Mexico: Grupo Azabache, 1992. 189 p.: bibl., col. ill.

Superb color illustrations of San Luis Potosí capture the vibrant architecture and sculpture of this important colonial center of New Spain from the Spanish Conquest to the 19th century. Commentaries concern the historical foundation of the city, Baroque and Neoclassical ecclesiastical and civil monuments, as well as major haciendas.

118 Ortiz Lanz, José Enrique. Arquitectura militar de México. Fotografías de Lourdes Grobet. México: Secretaría de la Defensa Nacional, 1993. 292 p.: bibl., col. ill.

Extensive study of 16th- to 18th-century defense forts in New Spain contains lavish color illustrations with numerous project plans. The superbly organized text covers not only the purpose of diverse fortifications, but also their historical context. The material includes an analysis of the earliest structures of the Conquest, the defense of Mexican territory, the diffusion of design from Spain to Mexico, and an analysis of specific monuments.

119 Ortiz Macedo, Luis. La Hacienda de San Agustín de las Cuevas. México: Afianzadora Insurgentes, 1990. 125 p.: ill. (chiefly col.).

The sanctuary of San Agustín de las Cuevas at Tlalpan originated in 1532, according to a plan in the Archivo General de la Nación reproduced in this book. Although this volume concentrates on the architecture and gardens of the haciendas of Tlalpan that flourished until the beginning of the 20th century, it also contains information about the old Parish Church of San Agustín, which was consecrated in 1637 and placed under the authority of the Franciscans by Urban VIII. The Church was transferred later to the Dominican order.

120 Ortiz Macedo, Luis *et al.* La Merced: tradición renovada. Coordinación de Luis Ignacio Sáinz. México: Banco Nacional de Comercio Interior, 1992. 217 p.: bibl., ill.

Excellent study of La Merced in Mexico City from the arrival in 1530 of 12 Mercedarian friars under the aegis of Fray Juan de Leguizamo to the 20th century. An informative book about Mexican society when the

Mercedarian order flourished as one of the richest institutions in New Spain. The *mercado* of La Merced also is discussed from the colonial period to the advent of the Mexican muralists.

121 Palacio de Iturbide (México). Pasado y presente del centro histórico: Palacio de Iturbide, marzo-mayo 1993. México?: Banamex; Fomento Cultural Banamex, 1993. 164 p.: bibl., col. ill.

This exhibition catalog for the Palace of Iturbide centers on the evolution of Mexico City from the Spanish Conquest to the 20th century. The myriad art works not only present a compelling glimpse of the city's growth over five centuries, but also capture the essence of the social factions which shaped its destiny.

122 Peralta Flores, Araceli and **Jorge Rojas Ramírez.** Xochimilco y sus monumentos históricos. México: Pórtico de la Ciudad de México; Instituto Nacional de Antropología e Historia, 1992. 116 p.: bibl., ill.

Architectural survey of the suburb of Xochimilco with emphasis on the area's precolumbian and colonial monuments. Based on an analysis of Xochimilco's history, topography, and urban growth patterns, the authors propose that the area's architectural monuments share a stylistic continuity that unites each major period of building activity. Analysis of the monuments is divided by typology, featuring discussions of religious, civil, and residential architecture.

123 Pérez Salazar, Francisco. Historia de la pintura en Puebla y otras investigaciones sobre historia y arte. México: Perpal, 1990. 868 p.: bibl., ill. (some col.), index.

This republication of the important 1923 *Historia de la pintura en Puebla* retains much of its value for modern historians as a compact source of Vasari-like biographical information on Poblano painters from the colonial period to the 20th century. Accompanied by extensive selections of the author's shorter writings on various subjects including 16th-century Mexican literature, the history of engraving in Puebla, and 18th-century Poblano historiography. A short biography of Pérez Salazar introduces this edition.

124 Perry, Richard D. Mexico's fortress monasteries. Illustrations by the author. Santa Barbara, Calif.: Espadaña Press, 1992. 223 p.: bibl., ill., index.

Analyzes Mexican architecture in five chapters: 1) monasteries of the Valley of Mexico; 2) buildings in Hidalgo; 3) monuments of Puebla and Tlaxcala; 4) monasteries of Cuernavaca and Morelos; and 5) structures of Oaxaca. The author examines the variety of open-air churches, atria, open chapels, convents, churches, murals, and altarpieces that comprise the artistic heritage of colonial Mexico. Contains many drawings and plans.

125 La platería mexicana. México: Instituto Nacional de Antropología e Historia, 1994. 143 p.: bibl., col. ill.

Catalog of the exhibition on Mexican silver spanning precolumbian production and the 20th century. The essay on the history of the technology of silversmithing by María Teresa Martínez Peñaloza is particularly instructive.

126 Platería novohispana, 1600–1830: noviembre de 1994. México: Arte Europeo, 1994? 63 p.: col. ill.

With a brief introduction by Dr. Cristina Esteras Martín, this simple catalog, the companion to the Nov. 1994 exhibition held at the Centro de Cultura Casa Lamm (Mexico City), is valuable primarily for its fine annotated color reproductions of colonial silver objects from Mexico and Central America. It is not necessary to be an expert in art history to enjoy and understand its content. Perfect for high school level to introduce students to silvermaking in the Americas. [F. Angel]

127 Ramírez Romero, Esperanza. Arquitectura religiosa en Morelia. Morelia, Mexico: Instituto Michoacano de Cultura, 1994. 21 p., 62 leaves of plates (some folded): bibl., ill.

Collection of unbound plates featuring elevations, floor plans, and maps of Morelia's Baroque churches. Includes short introductory text.

128 Rivas Manzano, Ana Carolina and **Arnulfo Irigoyen Coria.** Joyas arquitectónicas de la Sierra Mazateca = TsoMni chji si tjin i'nde tsan i'nde nasin sroba: edición bilingüe español-mazateco. Traducción al Mazateco de R.P. Heriberto Prado Pereda. México: Patronato Pro-Rescate de los Tesoros Culturales Indígenas de la Sierra Mazateca A.C., 1992. 76 p.: bibl., ill. (Patrimonio próximo a desaparecer)

Study of the architectural patrimony of the Sierra Mazateca region of northern Oaxaca focuses on churches of San José Tenango, San Juan Coatzospan, and San Francisco Huehuetlan. Monuments are placed within the context of the history of the area's evangelization. Extensive excerpts from the correspondence of the 16th-century *corregidor* Francisco de Castañeda provide valuable insights on the monuments.

129   Sánchez Lara, Rosa María. Los retablos populares: exvotos pintados. México: Univ. Nacional Autónoma de México, Instituto de Investigaciones Estéticas, 1990. 85 p.: bibl., ill. (some col.). (Monografías de arte, 0185–1799; 18)

Among the many recent additions to the bibliography on Mexican *retablos*, Sánchez Lara's account stands out as transcending purely formal analysis by incorporating social and economic contexts. Particularly helpful are the sections on *retablo* production in the states of Guanajuato and Zacatecas that highlight the importance of regional exvoto traditions. Also includes a study of some iconographic elements common to Mexican *retablos*, such as El Niño de Atocha.

130   Serrera Contreras, Juan Miguel. Alonso Vázquez en México. Prólogo de Guillermo Tovar de Teresa. México: Pinacoteca Virreinal de San Diego-INBA, 1991. 63 p.: bibl., ill. (some col.).

Monographic study on works that Alonso Vázquez produced during his stay in New Spain between 1603–08. Discusses the importance of Vázquez's Sevillian background and his later influence on 17th-century Mexican painting. Also includes detailed accounts of his Mexican patronage. Features beautiful color plates and an introduction by Guillermo Tovar de Teresa.

131   Sodi Miranda, Federica. La cerámica novohispana vidriada y con decoración sellada del siglo XVI. México: Instituto Nacional de Antropología e Historia, 1995. 150 p.: bibl., ill., map. (Col. científica; 291. Serie Arqueología)

The archaeological site at Complejo Hidalgo, discovered during the extension of the subway system, has yielded a rich deposit of 16th-century glazed ceramics. This study is divided into three sections: 1) urban transformations of the site during subsequent centuries; 2) a study of the social and economic milieu of 16th-century ceramicists; and 3) archaeological analysis of the finds. Develop-

ment of typologies for these ceramics and detailed materials analysis in the last section are particularly interesting.

132   Tamez, Enrique *et al*. Catedral Metropolitana: corrección geométrica, informe técnica. México: Asociación Amigos de la Catedral Metropolitana de México, 1995. 383 p.: bibl., ill. (some col.) plans.

Highly technical series of architectural analyses of the preservation of the National Cathedral of Mexico. Includes information on previous structural work, theory, experimental excavations, and results of current restoration project.

133   Terán, Silvia. La platería en Yucatán. Coordinación de Luz Elena Arroyo. Diseño e ilustraciones de Patricia Etcharren. Fotografías de Javier Amezquita *et al*. Curador, Donald Rohan. 2. ed., revisada e ilustrada. Merida, Mexico: Dirección General de Culturas Populares, 1994. 110 p.: bibl., ill. (some col.).

This survey of silver and gold jewelry from the Yucatán concentrates on historical metallurgical techniques and traditional jewelry morphologies. Includes history of Yucatecan metalworking and excellent archival photographs.

134   Terán Bonilla, José Antonio. La extraña casa de San Luis Tehuiloyocan: un caso de magia y religión. Puebla, Mexico: Gobierno del Estado de Puebla, Comisión Puebla V Centenario, 1991. 76 p.: bibl., ill. (some col.), maps. (Col. V centenario)

Iconographic study of decorations in a house in San Luis Tehuiloyocan dating from the last quarter of the 18th century. The author believes that various inscriptions and *opus sectile* friezes display an occult or "magical" theme uniting the interior decorative scheme. While the theological and historical contexts of such iconography are not fully explored, the publication of such a decidedly unusual example of vernacular architectural ornamentation will surely elicit further attention.

135   Torres, Louis. San Antonio missions. Photography by George H.H. Huey. Tucson, Ariz.: Southwest Parks and Monuments Assn., 1993. 48 p.: bibl., ill. (some col.).

A guide to the missions of the San Antonio region intended for popular audiences. Short texts on the Viceroyalty and the apostolic Franciscans introduce beautifully illustrated studies of each mission.

136 **Tovar de Teresa, Guillermo.** The city of palaces: chronicle of a lost heritage. Introductory texts by Enrique Krauze and José E. Iturriaga. Mexico: Vuelta, 1990. 2 v.: ill., indexes, maps.

Survey of major non-extant Mexico City architectural monuments explores transformations that major streets such as Madero, Empedradillo, and 5 de Mayo have undergone since the 16th-century founding of the city. Archival prints, photographs, and historical descriptions underscore the changing character of Mexico City's historic district.

137 **Tovar de Teresa, Guillermo.** Los escultores mestizos del barroco novohispano: Tomás Xuárez y Salvador de Ocampo, 1673–1724. Introducción de Julián Meza. Textos sobre la sillería de San Agustín de Abundio Tomás Parra. México: Banca Serfín, 1990. 175 p.: bibl., col. ill.

Well-documented study of Tomás Xuárez (ca. 1650–1724), a *cacique* from Coatepec (Chimalhuacan Atengo) and his son and disciple, Salvador de Ocampo (ca. 1665–1732). The exhaustive examination of major altarpieces and decorative reliefs constitutes a major contribution to knowledge about these colonial specialists in wood carving. The lucid text is enhanced by quality color plates.

138 **Tovar de Teresa, Guillermo.** México barroco. Realización y diseño de Beatrice Trueblood. México: SAHOP, 1981. 332 p.: bibl., ill. (some col.), index.

A sumptuously illustrated survey of the Baroque in colonial Mexico contains abundant examples of architecture, sculpture, and paintings. The text dissects the stylistic complexities of Baroque Mexico in a clear and riveting manner. The design and organization of the work, as well as the selection of major structures, enhance this study, raising it to the level of a classic.

139 **Treib, Marc.** Sanctuaries of Spanish New Mexico. Drawings by Dorotheé Imbert. Foreword by J.B. Jackson. Berkeley: Univ. of California Press, 1993. 352 p.: bibl., ill. (some col.), index.

Comprehensive volume about the colonial churches of New Mexico, with valuable insight into the social and economic circumstances under which adobe structures were built to serve the growing population.

Effectively combines a sense of history with a cogent and well-organized discussion about diverse types of village churches. The text has many good illustrations accompanied by excellent plans.

140 **Valdés Leal, Juan de.** Juan de Valdés Leal y el arte sevillano del barroco. Coordinación, investigación, revisión, edición y cuidado de la publicación de Lucía García-Noriega y Nieto *et al.* México: Centro Cultural Arte Contemporáneo, A.C.; Fundación Cultural Televisa, A.C., 1993. 340 p.: bibl., ill. (some col.).

This impressively illustrated exhibition catalog focuses on stylistic crosscurrents between Seville and viceregal New Spain. Its primary contributors are Antonio de la Banda y Vargas, Enrique Pareja López, Elisa Vargas Lugo, and Duncan Kinkead. Among the subjects investigated are the culture in Seville during the epoch of Valdés Leal; Sevillian painting; Valdés Leal's influences on Juan Correa and Cristóbal de Villalpando; Sevillian sculpture of the 16th-18th centuries; and Valdés Leal and his work, including his series, "The Life of St. Ignatius Loyola" (San Pedro, Lima).

141 **Vargas Lugo de Bosch, Elisa; José Guadalupe Victoria;** and **Gustavo Curiel.** Juan Correa: su vida y su obra. t. 3, Cuerpo de documentos. México: Univ. Nacional Autónoma de México, 1985–1994. 1 v.: appendix, bibl., ill. (some col.).

Valuable addition to the bibiliography on Juan Correa. José Guadalupe Victoria's entry on Franciscan imagery in Correa's painting represents an important advance in Correa scholarship. Of particular interest is the appendix detailing recent attributions.

142 **Vargas Lugo de Bosch, Elisa.** México barroco. México: Hachette Latinoamérica; Salvat; Grolier, 1993. 168 p.: bibl., col. ill.

Volume investigates art, religion, society and economy in Baroque Mexico. Pt. 1 of this scholarly work provides substantial information about the cultural legacy of *criollismo*. Pt. 2 discusses civil architecture, focusing on Mexico City, regional styles, and 18th-century palaces of singular distinction. Pt. 3 is devoted to religious architecture including altarpieces with paintings and sculpture of incredible beauty. This section also contains a useful discussion about materials and techniques of *estofado*. The didactic analysis of painting is particularly impressive. Pt. 4 concerns the diverse types of ornamentation that characterize Baroque interiors. The text contains an excellent glossary and high-quality color photographs.

143   Vasconcelos Beltrán, Rubén. Con el alma en la tierra. Oaxaca, Mexico: Gobierno del Estado de Oaxaca, 1992. 2 v. (469 p.): ill. (some col.). (Col. Glifo)

Vasconcelos' account of the current state of cultural policy in Oaxaca praises the stewardship of Governor Heladio Ramírez López as fundamental to the newfound support of the arts in the state. The Governor's active participation in cultural initiatives ranges from the archaeological preservation of Monte Albán and Cerro de las Minas to the foundation of youth orchestras and museums of modern art. While such an overtly partisan tone in a scholarly publication may be disconcerting to readers, it should be noted that Vasconcelos is writing in his capacity as Director General of the State Council for Culture and the Arts.

Los vascos en México y su Colegio de las Vizcaínas. See item **1247.**

144   Velásquez Thierry, Luz de Lourdes. El azulejo y su aplicación en la arquitectura poblana. Puebla, Mexico: Gobierno del Estado de Puebla, Comisión Puebla V Centenario, 1991. 111 p.: bibl., col. ill. (Col. V Centenario)

The critical role of decorative tiles in the distinctive architectural style of Puebla has been frequently addressed by scholars. Previous studies, however, often have lacked adequate color photographs. This short volume takes steps to remedy this deficiency. An introduction examining tile-making techniques and their history in Puebla complements the architectural study.

145   Yampolsky, Mariana and **Chloë Sayer.** The traditional architecture of Mexico. New York: Thames and Hudson, 1993. 208 p.: bibl., ill. (some col.), index, maps.

Primarily a picture book of fine photographs of rural houses, village plazas, haciendas, and town residences with a useful glossary and bibliography on tradition and change in Mexican secular architecture.

146   Yoneda, Keiko. Los mapas de Cuauhtinchan y la historia cartográfica prehispánica. 2. ed. México: CIESAS; Puebla, Mexico: Estado de Puebla; México: Fondo de Cultura Económica, 1992. 204 p.: bibl., ill., maps (some col.). (Col. Puebla)

Author states that the intent of this study is to analyze the maps "as history rather than as art." The main focus is on the *Mapa de Cuautinchan No. 1 (Mapa de las conquistas chichimeca); Mapa de Cuauhtinchan No. 2 (Mapa de la ruta Chicomoztoc-Cuauhtinchan); Mapa de Cuauhtinchan No. 3 (Mapa de las migraciones Uexotzinco-Tepaneca); Mapa de Cuautinchan No. 4 (Mapa de los linderos de Cuauhtinchan, año 1563)*; and, to a somewhat lesser and comparative extent, the *Mapa pintado en papel europeo y aforrado en el indiano (Mapa de los linderos de Cuauhtinchan y Totomihuacan).* [R. Haskett]

CENTRAL AMERICA AND THE CARIBBEAN

147   Arellano, Jorge Eduardo. Granada, aldea señorial. Managua: Municipalidad de Granada; Instituto Nicaragüense de Cultura Hispánica, 1989. 32 p.

Small, elegiac pamphlet covers history of the Nicaraguan city of Granada from the 16th to the 19th centuries. Contains previously unpublished photographs of architectural monuments from the late 19th and early 20th centuries.

148   Bernal Ponce, Juan. Ciudades del Caribe y Centroamérica: del siglo XV al siglo XIX. Cartago: Editorial Tecnológica de Costa Rica, 1993. 463 p.: bibl., ill., maps.

Excellent comparative analysis of Spanish, English, French, and Dutch urbanism in the colonial Caribbean. Discusses the impact of various colonial economic enterprises on the formation of urban spaces. The section on Spanish fortifications is particularly outstanding. Includes rich visual documentation, which provides for invaluable site analyses.

Delgado Mercado, Osiris. Historia general de las artes plásticas en Puerto Rico. v. 1. See item **288.**

149   Gutiérrez, Samuel A. Taboga: redescubrimiento de la isla y de su arquitectura. Panamá: Academia Panameña de la Historia, 1993. 107 p.: bibl., ill. (some col.), maps.

Photographic essay on the island of Taboga features architecture amid panoramic landscape settings. A brief history of the island accompanies the images.

150 Llamazares Martín, Vicente. Santo Domingo. Fotografías de Vicente Llamazares Martín. Madrid: Ediciones de Cultura Hispánica, 1990. 244 p.: bibl., chiefly col. ill. (Col. Ciudades iberoamericanas)

A pictorial survey of architecture of Santo Domingo includes several excellent photographs of colonial buildings. The text by Tirso Mejía Ricart and Luis Eduardo Delgado provides a useful history and analysis of the city's development from the Spanish conquest to the 20th century.

151 Martínez Castillo, Mario Felipe. Cuatro centros de arte colonial provinciano hispano criollo en Honduras. Tegucigalpa: Editorial Universitaria, 1992. 145 p.: bibl., ill. (Col. Arte hondureño)

Survey of four major centers of colonial art production in Honduras emphasizes architecture and architectural sculpture of Tegucigalpa and Comayagua.

152 Mejía-Ricart Guzmán, Tirso. Santo Domingo: ciudad primada; sus orígenes y evolución histórica. Santo Domingo: Fundación Mejía-Ricart-Guzmán Boom, 1992. 49 p.: bibl., col. ill., map. (Col. Temas históricos; 3)

Short commemorative history of Santo Domingo in honor of the Quincentennial. Intended for popular audiences, chapters on each of the city's four centuries are illustrated by color photographs.

153 Monte Urraca, Manuel E. del. Memorias de la ciudad de Santo Domingo: origen, decadencia y rescate de su patrimonio cultural. Santo Domingo: Empresas Unidas, 1992. 258 p.: bibl., ill. (some col.).

Lucid examination of architecture of Santo Domingo, from the 16th to the 20th centuries. Very good illustrations and useful documents are quoted. Considerably augments knowledge about the important center of the Dominican Republic.

154 Palm, Erwin Walter. Los monumentos arquitectónicos de La Española. 2. ed. ampliada. Santo Domingo: Editora de Santo Domingo, 1984. 1 v. (various pagings): bibl., ill., index. (Col. de cultura dominicana; 53)

The reprinting of material from Palm's classic two-volume work *Los monumentos arquitectónicos de La Española* (1955) constitutes a major contribution to study of colonial architecture in the Dominican Republic. Pt. 1 (vol. 1 of 1955 edition) focuses on the phases of architectural style, defined as Gothic, Mudejar, Plateresque, classical Roman, Manneristic, Imperial, Baroque, and Plain (Neoclassical). Pt. two (vol. 2 of the earlier edition) is dedicated to the study of religious and civil monuments of the colonial period.

Platería novohispana, 1600–1830: noviembre de 1994. See item **126.**

155 500 años de historia monumental: una recopilación de los calendarios Bermúdez, Serie Quinto centenario. Dominican Republic: Descendientes de las familias Bermúdez y Rochet, 1992. 136 p.: bibl., col. ill.

A pictorial survey with color plates of historic buildings of the Dominican Republic and very good descriptive texts about the religious and civil structures built from the 16th to the 18th centuries.

156 Staackmann Alvarez, Carmen Patricia. Catorce plazas cercanas a antigua Guatemala. Guatemala: Univ. Rafael Landivar, Facultad de Arquitectura, 1989. 236 leaves: bibl., ill.

Author's thesis analyzes 14 Guatemalan plazas. The premise that historical development of the Guatemalan plaza is closely linked to colonial economic patterns is placed in the context of a short history of Old World urban organization. Studies of building materials and patterns of use are applied to each case study. Analysis of damage caused by earthquakes and deterioration is also addressed.

South America

HUMBERTO RODRIGUEZ-CAMILLONI, *Professor and Director, Henry H. Wiss Center for Theory and History of Art and Architecture, College of Architecture and Urban Studies, Virginia Polytechnic Institute and State University*

WORKS REVIEWED FOR THIS VOLUME of *HLAS* reflect significant advances in scholarship on the history of art and architecture of Latin America. More and more titles are published every year that stress comparative views of the Old and New Worlds, and across the American continent. Even though essential surveys containing factual information continue to be completed in various countries, by region, province, or city, there is also an unprecedented increase in studies that apply new methods of analysis and interpretation. As a result, Spanish American colonial art and architecture can now be appreciated more within the context of the history of ideas, which, in turn, will lead to an even wider recognition of their unique qualities.

Outstanding examples reviewed during this biennium include *Reframing the Renaissance: visual culture in Europe and Latin America* (item **63**), a collection of high quality essays that attempt to reevaluate the Eurocentrism of Italian Renaissance art history; Héctor H. Schenone's *Iconografía del arte colonial* (item **64**), a monumental reference work on the iconography of the Christian saints depicted in Latin American colonial art; and *Las misiones jesuíticas del Guayrá* (item **160**), the second volume in ICOMOS-UNESCO's "La Herencia de la Humanidad" series that documents some of the problems affecting the conservation of historic monuments on the World's Heritage List.

Important studies on iconography and iconology of South American colonial art and architecture include Ramón Mujica Pinilla's *Angeles apócrifos en la América virreinal* (item **198**); Jorge A. Flores Ochoa's *El Cvzco: resistencia y continuidad* (item **188**); and Rafael Ramos Sosa's *Arte festivo en Lima virreinal* (item **205**). These well-documented studies suggest new approaches for the analysis and interpretation of art from this period. The identification and discussion of little-known sources and the special emphasis on the relationships between art and ritual are of vital importance.

The largest number of titles are fairly evenly distributed among architecture, painting, and sculpture, but urban history, historic preservation, and the decorative arts are also represented. The continuing support of several financial institutions—such as Banco de la República in Colombia, Banco de los Andes in Ecuador, and Banco Latino in Peru—has again made possible the publication of deluxe editions with excellent illustrations that are contributing to a new international appreciation of the rich artistic heritage of the Spanish colonial period. Fine examples of this type of publication are Gustavo Mateus Cortés' *Tunja: el arte de los siglos XVI, XVII, XVIII* (item **173**); Ximena Escudero de Terán's *América y España en la escultura colonial quiteña: historia de un sincretismo* (item **186**); and *Museo de Arte de Lima: 100 obras maestras* (item **199**).

The Banco de Crédito del Perú has also released Jorge A. Flores Ochoa, Elizabeth Kuon Arce, and Roberto Samanez Argumedo's groundbreaking *Pintura mural en el sur andino* (item **189**) as part of the celebrated "Colección Arte y Tesoros del Perú." This monumental work and Pablo Macera's *La pintura mural andina, siglos XVI–XIX* (item **194**) have opened a new chapter in the history of Spanish American colonial art by uncovering a significant corpus of virtually unknown mural paintings that rival contemporary examples from Mexico and Colombia.

The relatively recent inclusion of a number of historic monuments and sites from South American countries in the UNESCO World's Heritage List has served as the impetus for the publication of major books documenting the histories of the sites and restoration works performed to date, thus offering a wealth of enormously valuable information for future comparative studies. Such is the case with the work on the Jesuit missions of Paraguay mentioned above (item **160**), to which should be added Antonio Eduardo Bösl's *Una joya en la selva boliviana: la restauración del templo colonial de Concepción* (item **181**) and Alcides J. Parejas Moreno and Virgilio Suárez Salas' *Chiquitos: historia de una utopía* (item **202**). Similarly, the city of Quito has been the subject of various studies concerning problems of conservation of the historic center and its momuments. Potosí is also elegantly documented by Daniel Gluckmann in another volume of the series "Colección Ciudades Ibero-americanas" (item **190**).

The decorative arts are mostly represented by studies on silverwork, a subject that has received increasing attention in recent years. Most valuable here is the new monumental reference work by Alejandro Fernández, *Marcas de la plata española y virreinal* (item **54**), which will greatly facilitate the identification of marks and inscriptions used by silversmiths in Spain and Spanish America. *Arte hispanoameri-cano en Navarra: plata, pintura, y escultura* (item **58**), by María del Carmen Heredia Moreno, exemplifies a model survey of Spanish American colonial art in Spain; and patient archival work by the same author provides useful data on legislation govern-ing the work of Peruvian silversmiths (item **192**).

Publications associated with special symposia and exhibitions merit separate mention. Several of these events were organized as part of the celebration of the Quincentennial of the discovery of the Americas, which offered a unique opportu-nity to give maximum visibility to the artistic heritage of Spanish America. Two of these publications stand out as major contributions to the study and interpretation of Mudejar art: *Mudéjar iberoamericano: una expresión cultural de dos mundos* (item **51**) and *El mudéjar iberoamericano: del Islam al Nuevo Mundo* (item **60**). Containing original research by leading scholars in the field, both works should be indispensable references for years to come. Although much more modest in scope, also belonging to this category are Ramón Mujica Pinilla's *Los Cristos de Lima: esculturas en madera y marfil, s. XVI–XVIII* (item **185**) and Rolena Adorno *et. al.'s Guamán Poma de Ayala: the colonial art of an Andean author* (item **176**).

Proceedings from the Coloquio Internacional de Historia del Arte (17th, Zaca-tecas, Mexico, 1993) were published a year later in three volumes by the Instituto de Investigaciones Estéticas, Univ. Nacional Autónoma de México. Although not restricted to South American colonial topics, the collected essays represent a healthy cross-section of current state-of-the-art research in the field. A paper this author devoted to the study of *quincha* architecture in Peru is reviewed below (item **206**).

Also worthy of note is the international conference on "Cultural Transmission and Transformation in the Ibero-American World, 1200–1800," which was held at Virginia Polytechnic Institute and State University, Blacksburg, Virginia, in October 1995, with the participation of a distinguished group of scholars. It is anticipated that the papers, dealing with various aspects of transmission and transformation of European and Mesoamerican architecture and sacred art, will be published in elec-tronic form in the near future by the Inter-American Institute for Advanced Studies in Cultural History, under the direction of Dr. James B. Kiracofe.

In addition, on March 1, 1996, New York's Brooklyn Museum opened the spectacular exhibition "Converging Cultures: Art and Identity in Spanish America," which explores the evolution of the Spanish American Viceroyalties of New Spain (modern-day Mexico) and Peru through 250 works, including painting, sculpture, costumes, textiles, domestic and religious objects, as well as illustrated manuscripts. The exhibition consists mainly of works from the Brooklyn Museum's permanent collection of Spanish colonial materials, one of the largest in the US. According to its handsome companion catalog, the exhibit aims to examine issues of identity as they were expressed and reflected in a wide range of objects and images, studying both native contributions and examples of European imported culture. The exhibition also traveled to the Phoenix Art Museum (Dec. 1996-Feb. 1997) and the Los Angeles County Museum of Art (Mar. 30-June 8, 1997).

Finally, it is with deep sorrow that I have to report on the recent deaths of three distinguished colleagues and personal friends, Damián Bayón, Santiago Sebastián López, and María Dolores Aguilar García. Their lifelong contributions to the study of Iberoamerican art and architecture have been chronicled in several volumes of *HLAS* and many other publications. Their passing has left a great void in the field, and they will always be remembered with respect and admiration. With affection and gratitude, this chapter is dedicated to their memory.

CHILE, ARGENTINA, PARAGUAY, AND URUGUAY

157   Academia Nacional de Bellas Artes (Argentina). Patrimonio artístico nacional: inventario de bienes muebles. v. 3, Provincia de Jujuy. Buenos Aires: Academia Nacional de Bellas Artes, 1991. 1 v.: bibl., ill. (some col.), indexes.

Third volume in a series follows the format of previous volumes on the Corrientes (see *HLAS 48:365*) and Salta provinces (see *HLAS 54:190*). Fieldwork conducted by Iris Gori and Sergio D. Barbieri under the direction of Héctor H. Schenone in 33 localities led to the identification of 705 works of painting, sculpture, furniture, and decorative arts pertaining to religious monuments and private collections. This resulting high quality catalogue raisonné, illustrated with b/w and color photographs, significantly expands the corpus of Spanish colonial art available to the general readership and scholarly community. The bibliography includes a comprehensive list of published works and manuscript archival sources.

158   El Arca de tres llaves: crónica del Monasterio de Carmelitas Descalzas de San José, 1690–1990. Santiago: Cochrane S.A., 1989. 316 p.: bibl., ill.

History of the Carmelitas Descalzas de San José nunnery in Santiago from its foundation in 1690 to the present deals primarily with the lives of the individuals in the religious community. Art and architecture are mentioned only in a parenthetic way and illustrated with a few b/w photographs of uneven quality.

159   Bárcena, J. Roberto and Daniel Schávelzon. El Cabildo de Mendoza: arqueología e historia para su recuperación. Mendoza, Argentina: Municipalidad de Mendoza, 1991. 174 p., 25 leaves of plates: appendix, bibl., ill. (some col.), maps.

Well-documented report discusses the meticulous work of historical archaeology undertaken to locate and excavate the foundations of the 1749 Cabildo de Mendoza, destroyed by an earthquake in 1861. Findings reveal data pertaining to the material fabric of the building and artifacts from the time when it was in use. Measured planimetric and section drawings and b/w and color photographs with detailed captions accompany the text. An appendix of selected transcribed manuscript sources follows the comprehensive bibliography.

160   Cabral, Salvador et al. Las misiones jesuíticas del Guayrá. Dirección editorial de Manrique Zago. Fotografías de Carlos Mordo. Buenos Aires: Manrique Zago Ediciones, 1993. 222 p.: appendices, bibl., ill. (some col.). (La Herencia de la humanidad; 2)

Splendid multiauthored volume is second in the ICOMOS-UNESCO series "La Herencia de la Humanidad" documenting monuments and sites on the World's Heritage List. Focus is the extant architectural remains and religious sculpture from 30 Jesuit mission towns known as the "Paraguay Reductions," founded during the 17th–18th centuries to protect the Guaraní Indians from the Portuguese slave trade and depredations of Spanish colonists, and to teach them the arts of Christian town life. Of special interest are chap. 4, "La Arquitectura de las Misiones del Guayrá" by Alberto de Paula, and chap. 5, "Imaginería y Patrimonio Mueble" by Bozidar Darko Sustersic. Problems affecting conservation of the ruins are discussed in chap. 6 by Roberto Di Stefano. A useful second appendix describes the technique of photogrammetry used for recording the historic monuments. The texts are complemented with full color reproductions of historic documents, spectacular aerial photographs and close-up views of the ruins and works of art.

161 Chiappero, Rubén Osvaldo. La Capilla de San José del Rincón: texto y contexto de una obra de arquitectura popular santafesina. Santa Fe de la Vera Cruz, Argentina: Amaltea, 1990. 65 p.: bibl., ill.

Original research on an important example of regional religious architecture in the province of Santa Fe dating from the first half of the 19th century. The building is placed in its historical context and the formal analysis is enhanced by a set of handsome measured drawings. The text is also complemented with pen-and-ink drawings by well-known genre artist Juan Arancio. Also includes b/w photographs, which have not reproduced well due to the poor quality of the printed paper.

162 Espejo Tapia, Juan Luis. Solares y casas de la Villa de San Felipe el Real. Introducción de Eduardo Cavieres F. Santiago: Depto. de Ciencias Históricas, Facultad de Filosofía, Humanidades y Educación, Univ. de Chile, 1988. 103 p.: bibl., ill., index, maps. (Serie Nuevo Mundo; 2)

Posthumous publication of study by noted historian Juan Luis Espejo T. (1888–1983) is an important contribution to the history of colonial town planning in South America. New introduction provides essential historical background on the founding of the city of San Felipe in 1740 and its growth

during the next decade. The main text is a block-by-block and lot-by-lot survey of the colonial town, including the names of the successive landowners. This painstaking chain-of-title research offers unique insights into settlement patterns during the colonial period.

163 Muñoz González, Eduardo. Reseña de proyectos de restauración monumental. Texto y dibujos de Eduardo Muñoz González. Antofagasta, Chile: Univ. de Antofagasta, Facultad de Educación y Ciencias Humanas, Instituto de Investigaciones Antropológicas, 1986? 1 v. (unpaged): ill.

Pamphlet printed on poor quality paper briefly describes 15 restoration and conservation projects of prehistoric and historic monuments and sites in northern Chile. Information is limited to identification of each monument by name, location, and approximate date, followed by a general description and indication of the technical intervention. Monuments are illustrated with only a single architectural drawing, mainly of referential value.

164 Páez de la Torre, Carlos; Celia Terán; and Carlos Ricardo Viola. Iglesias de Tucumán: historia, arquitectura, arte. Buenos Aires: Fundación Banco de Boston, 1993. 250 p.: bibl., ill.

This book on the churches of the city and province of Tucumán is organized according to five travel itineraries written as separate chapters. In them, the text reads as a series of catalog entries rather than as a continuous narrative. Nowhere is an attempt made to provide a thematic overview that would help tie the material together. The small b/w illustrations, mostly of poor quality, are only of referential value.

165 Parsons, Anna María and Anna María Martins. El espejo salvaje: imaginería franciscana en la mirada indígena = The savage mirror: Franciscan imagery in colonial Paraguay. Fotografía de Fernando Allen. Asunción: Edición Fotosíntesis, 1992. 128 p.: col. ill.

Short general introduction opens this handsome photographic album devoted to colonial sculpture from the Franciscan mission churches in Paraguay at Atyrá, Caazapá, Capiatá, Tobatí, and Yaguarón. With the exception of the main altarpiece of the church of

San Buenaventura at Yaguarón, carved by the Portuguese artist José de Souza Cavadas between 1752–59, the fine examples of polychromed and gilded wood sculpture reveal the hand of indigenous artisans who reinterpreted the European forms in their own original ways.

166 Ponte, Jorge Ricardo. Mendoza, aquella ciudad de barro: historia de una ciudad andina desde el siglo XVI hasta nuestros días. Mendoza, Argentina: Municipalidad de la Ciudad de Mendoza, 1987. 588 p.: bibl., ill., maps.

Comprehensive urban history of the city of Mendoza from its foundation in 1561 up to the present is divided into seven major periods: 1) the first years (1561–1761); 2) the city of adobe (1761–1861); 3) reconstruction after the earthquake (1861–83); 4) the idea of progress and hygienic urbanism (1884–1911); 5) the presumptuous city (1912–30); 6) the preeminence of urban life (1931–51); and 7) from capital city to Great Mendoza (1952–82). The analysis relies heavily on historic descriptions and plans showing the street layouts during different periods. Statistical data and municipal ordinances are discussed in some length, including 20th-century master plans for land use and urban growth. Unfortunately, the poor quality of the paper used severely affects the illustrations, particularly the b/w photographs and line drawings.

167 Ribera, Adolfo L. Esculturas españolas en Buenos Aires. (*in* Estudios en homenaje a Don Claudio Sánchez-Albornoz en sus 90 años: anexos de *Cuadernos de historia de España.* Buenos Aires: Instituto de Historia de España, 1990, v. 6, p. 223–237, bibl., photos)

Brief study highlights examples of Spanish religious sculpture dating from the 16th-18th centuries in public and private collections in Buenos Aires. Even though an extant historic document shows that an important shipment of paintings and sculpture was made in 1649 by Zurbarán to Buenos Aires, no records appear to have survived that would firmly place the origin of contemporary works of sculpture there as belonging to any well-known artistic shops in Andalusia or Castile. The works described here were acquired during the present century, but may be thought of as representative of Spanish pieces that could have been exported to the American colonies during the colonial period.

Rojas Abrigo, Alicia. Historia de la pintura en Chile: libro audio visión. v. 1. See item **305.**

168 Schávelzon, Daniel. La arqueología urbana en la Argentina. Buenos Aires: Centro Editor de América Latina, 1992. 115 p.: bibl., ill. (Los Fundamentos de las ciencias del hombre; 39)

Popular pocket-size edition meant as a general introduction to historic archaeology in Argentina. Introductory chapter offers an historic overview of the discipline from the pioneer work of Juan B. Ambrosetti in 1905 to the present. Of special interest is the technical report on the excavation of Parque Lezama in Buenos Aires carried out in 1988–89 by the author with the collaboration of Ana María Lorandi.

169 Urgell, Guiomar de *et al.* El mate de plata. Buenos Aires: Asociación Amigos del Museo Municipal de Arte Hispanoamericano Isaac Fernández Blanco, 1988. 177 p.: bibl., ill. (some col.).

Original study traces the history behind the decorative silver gourd known as the *mate,* a name used in Spanish to designate both the aromatic beverage and the container used to hold it. A quintessential Argentine tradition, the use of the *mate* is also widespread elsewhere in South America, particularly in Paraguay, Uruguay, and parts of Brazil, Chile, and Peru. Drawing largely from the rich collection of silver *mates* in the Museo Municipal de Arte Hispanoamericano Isaac Fernández Blanco in Buenos Aires, the authors propose a typological classification according to morphology and date that should prove useful for future studies. The larger portion of the text consists of a fully illustrated catalogue raisonné of 123 items that show the high level of artistic achievement reached by colonial silversmiths.

COLOMBIA AND VENEZUELA

170 Cabellos Barreiro, Enrique. Cartagena de Yndias: mágica acrópolis de América. Madrid: CEDEX-CEHOPU; Colegio de Caminos, Canales y Puertos; Quinto Centenario, 1991. 237 p.: appendix, bibl., col. ill., maps. (Col. de ciencias, humanidades e ingeniería; 38)

Readable history of Cartagena de Indias from the 16th century to Independence gives a good account of various military engineering projects aimed at protecting the city with a formidable system of fortification walls. The narrative begins with a clear explanation of military architecture terminology and strategic considerations and follows a strict chronological order in the subsequent chapters. Illustrations include full color reproductions of historic documents and contemporary photographs. Extant and demolished bastions and gateways of Cartagena with the names of the engineers who designed them and dates of construction are conveniently listed in an appendix.

171 Duque Gómez, Luis. Rescate del patrimonio arquitectónico de Colombia. Bogotá: Fundación para la Conservación y Restauración del Patrimonio Cultural Colombiano, Banco de la República, 1991. 158 p.: bibl., ill. (chiefly col.).

Very fine publication considers the major restoration and conservation projects carried out by the Fundación para la Conservación y Restauración del Patrimonio Cultural Colombiano during the last two decades. The projects include religious and secular monuments in Santa Fe de Bogotá, Sopo, Tunja, Monguí, Tópaga, Chiquinquirá, Villa de Leiva, Popayán, Cartagena, Pamplona, Manizales, and Medellín. For each monument, a brief history is followed by a description of the technical interventions. The visual material selected, including excellent b/w and color photographs as well as as detailed architectural drawings, constitutes an impressive record worthy of emulation for similar projects.

172 Lecciones barrocas: pinturas sobre la vida de la Virgen de la Ermita de Egipto. Coordinación de Yvonne López. Investigación, guión, y curaduría de José Hernán Aguilar. Bogotá: Banco de la República, Museo de Arte Religioso, 1990. 98 p.: ill. (some col.).

Exhibition catalog documents the restoration of 23 Flemish paintings from the Ermita de Egipto in Bogotá undertaken by the Museo de Arte Religioso. The paintings, believed to be works from the shop of Peter Paul Rubens, depict scenes from the life of the Virgin Mary that were copied and reinterpreted many times in the Spanish American colonies. The actual technical interventions are fully described and illustrated with color photographs that should be valuable as a reference for other restoration projects.

173 Mateus Cortés, Gustavo. Tunja: el arte de los siglos XVI, XVII, XVIII. Bogotá: Litografía Arco, 1989. 1 v.: bibl., 290 col. ill.

Deluxe edition on Spanish colonial religious art in Tunja celebrates the 450th anniversary of the founding of the city. Most impressive are the handsome color plates with detailed captions documenting the wooden gilded altarpieces, sculpture, painting, and gold and silverwork from the 14 extant churches of the period: the Cathedral, San Laureano, Santo Domingo, San Francisco, Las Nieves, Santa Bárbara, San Agustín, San Juan de Dios, Santa Lucía and Santa Clara (16th c.); San Ignacio, San Lázaro and La Concepción (17th c.); and El Topo (18th c.). The text, divided into sections corresponding to the different artistic media, is much too short, however, and provides only an historic and descriptive introduction to the subject. Includes selected bibliography and glossary of technical terms.

174 Montenegro, Juan Ernesto. Los siete relojes de la catedral. Caracas: La Bodoniana, 1991. 240 p.: ill.

Not an art historical text per se, but a collection of short literary essays describing Caracas during the Spanish colonial period: its streets, monuments, and people. Title refers to the first chapter, which tells the story of the seven clocks of the Cathedral.

175 Reynal, Vicente. Fray Domingo de Petrés: arquitecto capuchino valenciano en Nueva Granada, Colombia. Valencia, Spain: V. Reynal, 1992. 262 p.: bibl., ill.

Comprehensive monograph on the Spanish architect Fray Domingo de Petrés (1759–1811), whose life and work in the Nuevo Reino de Granada was first documented by the same author (writing as Fray Antonio de Alcácer) in an earlier study, *Fray Domingo de Petrés, arquitecto capuchino* (see *HLAS 23 : 1426*). Petrés' arrival in Bogotá in 1792 marked the beginning of a prolific professional career that included the design of the present Cathedral of Bogotá (1806) and several other important churches. Emphasizes factual biographical information rather than stylistic analyisis or interpretation of the buildings.

Rueda, Marta Fajardo de; Alexandra Kennedy; and **Santiago Sebastián.** Barroco de la Nueva Granada: colonial art from Colombia and Ecuador. See item **208.**

PERU, ECUADOR, AND BOLIVIA

176 **Adorno, Rolena** *et al.* Guamán Poma de Ayala: the colonial art of an Andean author. New York: Americas Society, 1992. 114 p.: ill.

Handsome companion catalog to the exhibition organized by the Visual Arts Dept. of the Americas Society in New York between Jan.–March 1992. The exhibition consisted of 80 reproductions of designs by Guamán Poma from the *Nueva corónica i buen gobierno,* c. 1615, and a selection of precolumbian and colonial art and historic publications of related interest. The erudite texts provide a solid art historical appreciation of the famous drawings by the Indian *cronista,* who left behind a rare visual record of the colonial world as seen through the eyes of the dominated culture.

177 **Albornoz, César** *et al.* Centro histórico de Quito: sociedad y espacio urbano. Quito: Dirección de Planificación, I. Municipio de Quito, Ecuador; Sevilla, Spain: Consejería de Obras Públicas y Transporte, Junta de Andalucía; Ministerio de Asuntos Exteriores de España, 1990. 237 p.: ill. (some col.), maps. (Serie Quito; 2)

Vol. 2 of the *Serie Quito* follows the format of the previous publication. Examines the historic center as a social setting. Also considers major socioeconomic parameters, such as rural-urban migration, demographic distribution, urban transportation, social organization, and labor force. Pt. 6, which deals with preservation and development, includes the outline of a rehabilitation plan with specific recommendations for immediate action that could be relevant to other Latin American cities.

178 **Andrade, Roberto** *et al.* Centro histórico de Quito: la vivienda. Quito: Dirección de Planificación, I. Municipio de Quito, Ecuador; Sevilla, Spain: Consejería de Obras Públicas y Transporte, Junta de Andalucía; Ministerio de Asuntos Exteriores de España, 1991. 237 p.: bibl., ill. (some col.). (Serie Quito; 5)

Vol. 5 in the *Serie Quito* follows same format of previous volumes. The six-part text discusses different aspects of the problems of contemporary housing in the historic center of Quito: housing and the historic center, housing deterioration, housing typology, construction methods, housing interventions, and proposals for new solutions.

179 **Arellano López, Luis.** Caquiaviri: reliquia del altiplano. (*Rev. UNITAS,* 12, enero 1994, p. 105–110, facsims.)

General description of rural church in the Altiplano region of Bolivia, near lake Titicaca, after its restoration in 1988. Original Franciscan structure dating from the 16th century includes later works through the 18th century. Of special interest was the discovery of remnants of mural painting, including a large representation of Saint Christopher bearing the inscription "Año de 1699 Cura, El Comisario Diego Vásques."

180 **Bacacorzo, Gustavo.** Tres muestras arquitectónicas de Arequipa. (*Bol. Inst. Riva-Agüero,* 16, 1989, p. 191–196, bibl.)

Uneven and somewhat disjointed article discusses the chronology of the Cathedral of Arequipa, the lives of some of the nuns associated with Santa Catalina, and two colonial buildings the author regards as examples of *mudéjar* architecture in the city.

181 **Bösl, Antonio Eduardo.** Una joya en la selva boliviana: la restauración del templo colonial de Concepción. Bolivia: Vicariato Apostólico de Ñuflo de Chávez, 1987. 175 p.: bibl., ill. (some col.), maps.

Detailed account of major restoration project of the Jesuit mission church of Concepción in the province of Chiquitos carried out under the direction of Swiss architect Hans Roth between 1975–78. The original 1753–56 edifice, built by the famous Jesuit missionary Martin Schmid, had fallen into bad disrepair and threatened to totally collapse in 1974. The project entailed reconstruction of large portions of the church and nearby structures. The monumental effort was facilitated by the skill of local craftsmen, who in the process trained a new generation of artisans for similar restoration work. Readable text intended for professionals and the general public is complemented with invaluable photographic record.

182 Carrión, Fernando *et al.* Centro histórico de Quito. Problemática y perspectivas. Quito: Dirección de Planificación, I. Municipio de Quito, Ecuador; Sevilla, Spain: Consejería de Obras Públicas y Transporte, Junta de Andalucía; Ministerio de Asuntos Exteriores de España, 1990. 239 p.: ill. (some col.), maps. (Serie Quito; 1)

Multidisciplinary study of the historic center of Quito is first of a 12-volume series. Motivated by the inclusion of the city in the World's Heritage List, this *Serie Quito* follows the model established by Jorge Enrique Hardoy, *et al.* in *El centro histórico de Quito: introducción al problema de su preservación y desarrollo* (see *HLAS 50:246*). The text is divided into six parts covering the following topics: urban policies, archaeology and history, cultural heritage and society, architectural heritage, urban change and conservation, and planning and rehabilitation. A few color plates alternate with b/w photographs of uneven quality. Primarily useful for its information on historic preservation planning.

183 Castelli G., Amalia. Angelino Medoro y el tríptico de la anteportería de San Francisco. (*Hist. Cult./Lima,* 21, 1991/92, p. 289–302, bibl., photos)

Analyzes famous triptych in the *anteportería* of the Franciscan monastery in Lima following its 1988 restoration. The traditional attribution of the whole work to the Italian painter Angelino Medoro (active in Lima during the beginning of the 17th century) is open to question in view of significant stylistic discrepancies between the central Crucifixion and the side paintings. While the two largest paintings from outside and inside of the triptych—representing Christ entering Jerusalem and the Crucifixion, respectively—reveal Medoro's hand, the other representations appear to have been executed by lesser, unknown artists.

184 Colonial Quito. Editorial direction by Gabriel Iriarte, Marcela García. Text by Iván Cruz. Photographs and layout by Santiago Montes. Translation by Cathy de Guáqueta and Pegi Dromgold. Map by Daniel García G. Quito: Mayr & Cabal; Ediciones Libri Mundi, 1991. 49 p.: bibl., col. ill., map.

Short, descriptive traveller's guide to the city's historic monuments and major museums. The text relies on early research by noted art historians José Gabriel Navarro and

José María Vargas. Fully illustrated with fine color plates.

185 Los Cristos de Lima: esculturas en madera y marfil, s. XVI–XVIII; Lima, Perú, noviembre–diciembre 1991, Catedral Metropolitana. Textos de Ramón Mujica Pinilla. Fotografía de Daniel Giannoni. Lima: Fondo Pro-Recuperación del Patrimonio Cultural de la Nación; Banco de Crédito del Perú, 1991? 77 p.: bibl., ill. (some col.).

Fine catalog of rare exhibition of polychromed wood and ivory crucifixes held at the Cathedral of Lima from Nov.–Dec. 1991. Introductory essay, "El Culto al Crucificado en la Cultura y en la Escultura del Virreinato Peruano" by Mujica Pinilla provides a good art historical background, with essential references to the origin of the popular iconographic theme in Europe and the Viceroyalty of Peru. Crucifixes belonging to various Lima churches and monastic institutions underwent careful conservation by a team of specialists working under the patronage of the Fondo Pro-Recuperación del Patrimonio de la Nación in celebration of the Quincentenary. The catalogue raisonné, fully illustrated with excellent color plates, permits a unique comparative analysis of exceptional-quality sculpture from Europe and the colonies, assembled together for the first time.

186 Escudero de Terán, Ximena. América y España en la escultura colonial quiteña: historia de un sincretismo. Quito: Ediciones del Banco de los Andes, 1992. 287 p.: bibl., ill. (some col.).

Beautifully illustrated monograph on colonial sculpture in Quito covers much more ground than Gabrielle G. Palmer's *Sculpture in the Kingdom of Quito* (see *HLAS 50:250*). The general text, consisting of 64 pages, does a good job of presenting a general history of the Quito school and the work of sculptors like Bernardo Legarda, Manuel Chili, and Caspicara, who represent a high point in the development of this art during the 18th century. Unfortunately, however, author relies on European stylistic labels from Renaissance to Rococo, which confuse rather than clarify the definition of the unique qualities of colonial art. Nevertheless, the superb color plates offer an unparalleled tour de force and an indispensable reference for future research. Excerpts of important documents related to the artists Diego de Robles,

Bernardo Legarda, and Caspicara are transcribed in the appendix, followed by a glossary of technical terms and a useful bibliography of primary and secondary sources.

187 Exposición Universal de 1991 (Sevilla, Spain). Pabellón del Perú. Perú, presencia milenaria. Arequipa, Perú: Cuzzi y Cia., 1992. 132 p.: ill. (some col.).

Companion catalog to exhibition with the same title held at the Peruvian Pavilion in the World's Fair of Seville, 1992 features handsome portfolio of b/w and color plates mostly of precolumbian art. Only chap. 4, "Principales Manifestaciones Artísticas en el Período Virreynal" by Cecilia Bákula briefly describes general aspects of colonial painting and silverwork.

Fernández Rueda, Sonia. Historiografía de la arquitectura en la época colonial: algunas consideraciones. See item **2329.**

188 Flores Ochoa, Jorge A. El Cvzco: resistencia y continuidad. Cusco, Peru: Editorial Andina, 1990. 158 p.: bibl., ill. (some col.). (Serie Arqueología, etnohistoria y etnología de la ciudad del Cuzco y su región; 1)

This modest publication contains three important but separate iconographic studies on art and ritual in the city of Cuzco from the 17th century to the present: "Arte de Resistencia en Vasos Ceremoniales Inca. Siglos XVII–XVIII;" "Taytacha Qoylluriti. El Cristo de la Nieve Resplandeciente;" and "La Fiesta de los Cuzqueños: La Procesión del Corpus Christi." Well-researched and full of insights, the essays emphasize iconology and anthropological analysis. Unfortunately, the illustrations have not reproduced well due to the poor quality of the paper.

189 Flores Ochoa, Jorge A.; Elizabeth Kuon Arce; and Roberto Samanez Argumedo. Pintura mural en el sur andino. Lima: Banco de Crédito del Perú, 1993. 359 p.: bibl., ill. (some col.), index. (Col. Arte y tesoros del Perú)

Book lives up to the high standard set by previous volumes in the "Colección Arte y Tesoros del Perú" series. This monumental, ground-breaking work fills a significant void in the literature of Latin American colonial art. Years of painstaking fieldwork conducted in the departments of Cuzco and Puno have uncovered an impressive corpus of pictoral material that is published here for the first

time in all of its splendor. Exquisite color plates depict not only the mural paintings, but also the settings where they are found. An excellent text discusses the form and meaning of the works revealing a wide range of iconographic subjects predominantly but not exclusively of religious nature. Good bibliography complements the footnotes in the individual chapters. Recent restoration and conservation work undertaken on some of the monuments has also yielded important information on materials and techniques used. This will undoubtedly become the standard work on the subject for years to come.

190 Gluckmann, Daniel. Potosí. Fotografías de Daniel Gluckmann. Textos de Teresa Gisbert, José de Mesa, Valentín Abecia Baldivieso. Madrid: Agencia Española de Cooperación Internacional, Ediciones de Cultura Hispánica, 1990 226 p.: ill. (some col.). (Col. Ciudades iberoamericanas)

Another volume in the handsome series devoted to Spanish American cities, which is part of the Biblioteca Quinto Centenario (see *HLAS 52:271*). Far more general than *Potosí, patrimonio cultural de la humanidad* (see *HLAS 54:232*), this publication is intended for the general public. Two introductory chapters provide an overview of the political and cultural history of the city, with an emphasis on its art, architecture, and urbanism. The photographic essay in stunning color that follows takes the reader on a visual tour of the surrounding landscapes, streets, historic monuments, works of art, and human activities that give the city its distinct character.

191 Gutiérrez, Ramón. Evolución histórica urbana de Arequipa, 1540–1990. Edición de Pedro Belaúnde M. y Elias Mujica B. Lima: Facultad de Arquitectura, Urbanismo, y Artes, Univ. Nacional de Ingeniería; Epígrafe Editores, 1992. 249 p.: bibl., ill. (Ciudades peruanas; 1)

Comprehensive urban history of Arequipa by distinguished architectural historian celebrates the 450th anniversary of the founding of the city. Well-documented and well-illustrated monograph is the most complete publication available on the subject. Also of value for the wealth of information it provides on religious and secular architecture in the city from the 16th-20th centuries. Even though no separate bibliography is included, major primary and secondary sources are found in the footnotes.

192 Heredia Moreno, María del Carmen. Ordenanzas de la platería limeña del año 1778. (*Lab. Arte*, 5, 1992, p. 57–76, appendix, photo)

Article continues earlier research on the subject by same author (see *HLAS 54: 222*). Discusses ordinances drawn by viceroy Don Manuel de Guirior in 1778 for the regulation of the silversmiths working in Lima and other cities of the Viceroyalty of Peru. This important document, consisting of 31 articles, superseded earlier ordinances of 1633. Comparisons are also made with the 1776 Guatemala ordinances and those issued by Charles III in 1771.

193 Jurado Noboa, Fernando; Rocío Aguilar; and Vicente Moreno. Casas del Quito viejo. v. 1. Quito: s.n., 1992? 1 v.: bibl., ill. (Col. Medio milenio; 6)

Popular edition printed on poor quality paper documents 50 historic houses in Quito dating from the 17th-20th centuries. The text deals mainly with the history of the families associated with the houses and the shifting functions that the houses accommodated across the years. Little attention is given to any morphological analysis of the buildings themselves, and the b/w photographs provide a partial visual image at best. Authors indicate that a forthcoming second volume will be devoted to houses in the historic neighborhood of La Ronda.

Klaren, Peter F. Spain in America: the Viceroyalties of New Spain and Peru, 1521–1825. See item **898.**

194 Macera, Pablo. La pintura mural andina siglos XVI-XIX. Fotografía de Alberto Rojas Alva. Edición y producción de Carlos Milla Batres. Lima: Editorial Milla Batres, 1993. 190 p.: ill. (some col.), map. (Colección Perú artístico)

Long-awaited publication by eminent historian Pablo Macera is a fine complement to *Pintura mural en el sur andino* (see item **189**). The text is the result of several years of fieldwork and original research in Lima, Arequipa, and Cuzco initiated in 1974–75. Even though described by the author himself as a "history of Andean culture," this book provides good descriptive information and analysis of an important corpus of colonial mural painting (with material not covered in the

publication mentioned above). The magnificent color plates by leading photographers Alberto Rojas Alvas, Wilfredo Loayza, and others are an invaluable record of unique murals shown in their state of conservation of 20 years ago.

195 Mariazza F., Jaime. Antecedentes hispanos de estructuras funerarias en el Virreinato del Perú. (*Bol. Inst. Riva-Agüero*, 16, 1989, p. 181–190, bibl., photos)

Brief study identifies selected examples of Spanish catafalques dating from the 16th century, representatives of a European tradition that was transmitted to the New World during the colonial period. Author observes that the iconographic themes associated with several of these monuments included references to classical mythology frequently found in Italian Renaissance sources.

196 Mesa, José de and Teresa Gisbert. Monumentos de Bolivia. 3. ed. rev. La Paz: Embajada de España en Bolivia; Comisión del V Centenario; Madrid?: Agromán S.A.; La Paz?: Fundación B.H.N., 1992. 328 p.: bibl., ill. (some col.), maps.

Totally revised and expanded edition of *Bolivia: monumentos históricos y arqueológicos* (see *HLAS 30:251*) by leading Bolivian art historians is greatly enhanced with a wealth of new illustrations and high-quality printing. The text reflects advancements in scholarship made in recent years, and incorporates discussion of new discoveries such as the mural paintings in the Oruro churches of Copacabana de Andamarca and Belén de Huachacalla. Separate chapters are also devoted to precolumbian architecture and the Jesuit missions in Moxos and Chiquitos. In an opening chapter, authors explain their choice of stylistic labels applicable to the viceregal period, which very closely follows European classification.

197 Mesa, José de and Teresa Gisbert. Pervivencia del estilo virreinal en la pintura boliviana del siglo XIX. (*Lab. Arte*, 5, 1992, p. 143–157, map, plates)

Noted Bolivian art historians discuss the continuity of stylistic traits of colonial painting in examples of 19th-century Bolivian painting. This is true not only of religious representations such as the Virgen de Guadalupe, Virgen de Copacabana, and Virgen de los Remedios, but also of satiric portraits that were very popular after Independence.

198 **Mujica Pinilla, Ramón.** Angeles apócrifos en la América virreinal. Lima: Fondo de Cultura Económica, Instituto de Estudios Tradicionales, 1992. 293 p., 16 leaves of plates: bibl., ill. (some col.). (Sección obras de historia)

Exhaustive, multidisciplinary study sheds new light on the meaning of the celebrated *ángeles arcabuceros* (archangels with muskets) commonly depicted in paintings from the Cuzco School. Close reading of several theological texts such as Andrés Serrano's *Feliz memoria de los siete príncipes de los asistentes del trono de Dios, y estímulo a su utilísima devoción: Miguel, Gabriel, Rafael, Uriel, Sealthiel, Jehudiel, Barachiel* (Mexico, 1699) reveals that the theme had its origins in medieval apocalyptic traditions surrounding mystery cults and drew inspiration from various apocryphal sources. The author further speculates on how these representations could have played a key role as instruments for the transmission of the Christian faith and how in turn they may have been perceived by the indigenous populations for whom they were intended. By far the most complete study on the subject to date, this work will serve as the basis for future research.

199 **Museo de Arte de Lima.** Museo de Arte de Lima: 100 obras maestras = Art Museum of Lima: 100 masterpieces. Lima: Asociación Museo de Arte de Lima; Banco Latino, 1992. 209 p.: col. ill., maps.

Handsome catalog of the Museo de Arte de Lima makes available for the first time a selection of masterpieces from its rich holdings covering 3,000 years of cultural achievement. Erudite bilingual texts cover each of the major periods of the development of Peruvian art: Federico Kauffman Doig, "Pre-Columbian Art;" Mariano Paz Soldán, "Viceregal Art;" Juan Manuel Ugarte Eléspuru, "Republican Art;" and Elida Román, "Contemporary Art." Works representative of the viceregal period include painting, sculpture, and silverwork shown to best advantage in full-page color plates by artist-photographer José Casals.

200 **Navarro, José Gabriel.** La pintura en el Ecuador del XVI al XIX. Quito: Dinediciones, 1991. 260 p.: bibl., col. ill.

Elegant posthumous publication by well-known historian and art critic José Gabriel Navarro Enríquez (1881–1965) makes available for the first time an important pioneering work on the history of painting in Ecuador from the 16th-19th centuries. The first three chapters present a coherent narrative dealing with the history of colonial painting in Quito during the 16th–17th centuries. The remaining eight chapters are organized by groups of artists and read more like a series of biographical sketches with an emphasis on factual and descriptive information. Among these, by far the most developed are chapters 4–6, devoted to Miguel de Santiago, Nicolás Javier de Goríbar, and Bernardo Rodríguez and Manuel Samaniego, respectively. The 150 fine quality color reproductions permit a good appreciation of the works discussed. A complete bibliography of publications by the author is also provided.

201 **Oruro: catálogo de su patrimonio arquitectónico urbano y rural.** Coordinación general de Teresa Gisbert C., Juan Carlos Jemio S. y Nelson Mostacedo D. Arquitectos responsables, Elizabeth Torres *et al.* La Paz: Instituto Boliviano de Cultura, 1993. 200 p.: bibl., ill. (some col.)., maps.

Comprehensive catalog of historic monuments of Oruro follows same format of previous survey *Potosí: catalogación de su patrimonio urbano y arquitectónico* (see *HLAS 54:231*). Descriptive information, architectural plans, and b/w photographs are included, with the actual inventory forms reproduced in the text. Also includes a few color plates of varying quality and fold-out plans of the town's historic center.

202 **Parejas Moreno, Alcides J.** and **Virgilio Suárez Salas.** Chiquitos: historia de una utopía. Santa Cruz, Bolivia?: Cordecruz; Univ. Privada de Santa Cruz de la Sierra, 1992. 332 p.: bibl., ill. (some col.), maps.

Comprehensive study of the eastern province of Chiquitos in the department of Santa Cruz is divided into two parts, written by historian Alcides Parejas Moreno and architect Virgilio Suárez Salas, respectively. Pt. 1 focuses on the geographic setting and the socioeconomic, political and religious history of the region during the colonial period. Pt. 2 is a detailed account of the urban and architectural history of the ten Jesuit missions (reducciones) founded between 1691–1760. The missions have survived as living towns and bear witness to the success of the evangelical enterprise that inspired the creation of artistic works of high quality and exceptional beauty. For this reason, the Chiquitos Jesuit missions of San Francisco Javier, San Rafael, San José, San Juan Bautista, Concepción, San Miguel, San Ignacio, Santiago, Santa Ana, and Santo Corazón were entered into the UNESCO World's Heritage List in 1990. Profusely illustrated with photographs, this work is an important contribution. While some scholars will question the use of the unfortunate stylistic label *barroco mestizo selvático*, the historic data is backed by primary and secondary sources mentioned in the footnotes and bibliography.

203   Plan distrito metropolitano Quito.
v. 5, Diagnóstico del centro histórico. Quito: Ilustre Municipio de Quito, Dirección de Planificación, 1992? 1 v. bibl., ill.

Vol. 5 in the popular series *Plan Distrito Metropolitano* is intended to document the studies, projects, and public works undertaken by the municipal government during 1988–92. An attempt is made to assess the historic development of the city and its present conditions in terms of demographic, socioeconomic, and political parameters. Historic surveys conducted to date and mapping of urban areas for future interventions are discussed in some detail.

204   Plan distrito metropolitano Quito.
v. 27, Planes parciales de áreas históricas. Quito: Ilustre Municipio de Quito, Dirección de Planificación, 1992? 1 v.: bibl., ill.

Vol. 27 in the series *Plan Distrito Metropolitano* discusses plans for intervention in the historic districts of Quito. Planning policies reveal some of the problems inherent in regulating urban growth in historic centers. Proposes recommendations for action according to the specific needs of each neighborhood. Beyond the urban districts, some of the targets include the surrounding rural areas with their haciendas. The b/w photographs suffer from the poor quality paper.

205   Ramos Sosa, Rafael. Arte festivo en Lima Virreinal, siglos XVI–XVII. Sevilla, Spain: Junta de Andalucía, Consejería de Cultura y Medio Ambiente, Asesoría Quinto Centenario, 1992. 294 p.: bibl., ill. (some col.), index.

Considerably expands earlier study by Lorene Pouncey, "Túmulos of Colonial Peru" (see *HLAS 50:251*), examining in detail the iconography of festive monuments erected

in Lima to commemorate political and religious events such as the entries of newly appointed viceroys, births or deaths of Spanish monarchs and religious holidays. The well-documented and well-illustrated text provides important insights into the relationship of art and ritual during the viceregal period. Comparative information on similar practices in Europe and the Viceroyalty of Mexico is also provided. Excellent reference for future research on the subject.

206   Rodríguez Camilloni, Humberto. Tradición e innovación en la arquitectura del Virreinato del Perú: Constantino de Vasconcelos y la invención de la arquitectura de quincha en Lima durante el siglo XVII. (*in* Coloquio Internacional de Historia del Arte, *17th, Zacatecas, Mexico, 1993.* Arte, historia e identidad en América: visiones comparativas. México: Univ. Nacional Autónoma de México, Instituto de Investigaciones Estéticas, 1994, t. II, p. 387–403, appendix, ill., photos)

First in-depth study devoted to the antiseismic construction system devised by the Portuguese architect Constantino de Vasconcelos (d. 1668) for the reconstruction of the San Francisco de Lima church in 1657–74. Shows his originality in adapting precolumbian *quincha* architecture in the construction of the complex forms of roofing structures of the Franciscan church, including the dome above the transept and a variety of vault types as well. These monumental forms, consisting of plaster-coated webs of bundled and matted reeds on timber frames or brick ribs, were reinforced by strong cane bent to produce the desired curvilinear shapes. Light, yet elastic enough to survive the severe earthquakes, *quincha* roofing allowed for flexibility of formal and spatial design; and it was adopted almost universally on the Peruvian coast thereafter. Unpublished documentary evidence is also presented showing that collaboration between Vasconcelos and his assistant, Manuel de Escobar, extended to other works in Lima at the time.

207   Rodríguez Camilloni, Humberto. Utopia realized in the New World: form and symbol of the City of Kings. (*in* Settlements in the Americas: cross-cultural perspectives. Edited by Ralph Bennett. Newark, Del.: Univ. of Delaware Press, 1993, p. 28–52, facsims., maps, photos)

Revised and expanded English version of study dealing with the iconography of the gridiron plan of Lima. First published in Spanish in 1986 (see *HLAS 50:253*).

208   Rueda, Marta Fajardo de; Alexandra Kennedy; and Santiago Sebastián.
Barroco de la Nueva Granada: colonial art from Colombia and Ecuador. New York: Americas Society, 1992. 80 p.: ill.

Nicely illustrated catalog prepared in conjuction with the exhibition of the same title held at the Americas Society in New York in 1992 to celebrate the Quincentennial of the discovery of the Americas. Featured in the exhibition were 68 works of colonial art on loan from public and private collections and religious institutions in Colombia and Ecuador. Comparative visions of the Old World and the New World are discussed in Santiago Sebastián's opening essay, "European Models in the Art of the Viceroyalty of New Granada," followed by critical overviews of colonial art in Colombia and Ecuador, respectively, by Marta Fajardo de Rueda and Alexandra Kennedy, who also curated the exhibition.

209   San Cristóbal Sebastián, Antonio. La Escuela de los Retablos de Trujillo. (*Hist. Cult./Lima*, 21, 1991/92, p. 247–288)

Detailed study of colonial altarpieces in Trujillo refutes undocumented claims about possible activity of sculptor Luis de Espíndola in that city from 1649–70. Proposes a new classification for the celebrated wooden retablos of the Trujillo churches based on morphological analysis and attention to methods of construction. Unlike cities such as Lima and Cuzco, Trujillo was the center of development of the fine art of *retablos* totally independent from those on church portals. During the 18th century, the documented work of sculptor Fernando Collado is recognized as a high point.

210   San Cristóbal Sebastián, Antonio.
Lima: estudios de la arquitectura virreinal. Lima: Epígrafe Editores, 1992. 238 p.: bibl., ill.

Important contribution to the study of colonial architecture in Lima offers a more scholarly approach than author's previous book, *Arquitectura virreinal religiosa de Lima* (see *HLAS 52:273*). For example, specific sources of documentation in the Archivo General de la Nación in Lima are given here

in footnotes. Major chapters are devoted to analysis and interpretation of individual monuments, urban spaces, and architectural details. Author argues for a pluralism of styles present in colonial architecture in Lima, but insists on the use of European stylistic labels that are often problematic.

211   Sanz, María Jesús. Platería peruana en Sevilla y su provincia. (*Lab. Arte*, 5, 1992, p. 101–121, facsim., photos)

Study examines a selection of silverwork from religious institutions and private collections in Seville believed to be imported pieces from the Viceroyalty of Peru. Even though identification is made difficult by the absence of any inscriptions or marks, formal and stylistic comparative analysis strongly suggests a Peruvian provenance for several objects.

212   Silva Santisteban, Fernando *et al.* Patrimonio monumental de Cajamarca. Cajamarca, Peru: INC Editores, 1986. 129 p.: bibl., ill.

Popular edition of proceedings from the Seminario-Taller de Restauración y Conservación de Monumentos Históricos de Cajamarca held in that city under the auspices of the Instituto Nacional de Cultura in Aug. 1987. Essays vary considerably in quality, ranging from a general social and political history of Cajamarca by Silva Santisteban to personal accounts of life in the city by Zevallos de La Puente. More specifically related to the topic of the seminar are the criteria and recommendations for the restoration of historic monuments of adobe and stone offered by Samanez Argumedo and Morales.

213   Terán Najas, Rosemarie. La ciudad colonial y sus símbolos: una aproximación a la historia de Quito en el siglo XVI. (*Nariz Diablo*, 19, enero 1994, p. 60–69, photos)

Study examines social history and religious traditions in 17th-century Quito that contributed to the definition of the "colonial city and her symbols." A large portion of the text is devoted to the biography of Santa Mariana de Jesús (1618–45), whose pious life in Quito served as an inspiration for religious fervor.

214   La toma simbólica del centro de Quito. Recopilación de Jorge Benavides Solís. Quito: Bananapub, 1988. 125 p.: bibl., ill.

Small popular publication focuses on problems affecting the conservation of the historic center of Quito, such as public administration mechanisms, traffic congestion, and street vendors. Newspaper articles by different authors addressing these issues are transcribed in the final chapter. Useful only as a measure of public reaction to the inclusion of Quito in the World's Heritage list.

19th and 20th Centuries

FELIX ANGEL, *Curator, Cultural Center, Inter-American Development Bank*

THE ECONOMICS OF THE ART WORLD have changed dramatically in the last few years, as have the motivations for producing and publishing art books. The uncertainties of the world's economic markets have translated into diverse possibilities for financial speculation and related activities in the art world; Latin America has not been impervious to this trend.

There has been a noticeable increase in the number of publications dedicated to individual artists in mid-career or younger. Such publications, however, rarely contain more than a tributary essay in praise of the artist's work and some biographical information, while offering little of scholarly or research value. When well illustrated, these books are worthwhile primarily for the visual references they provide for those planning further studies of a particular artist. Nevertheless, it is frequently difficult to discern any relevant scholarly information in this type of work.

Still scarce in Latin America are art publications that demonstrate significant scholarly dedication and research. It is, however, possible to find some satisfactory publications, mostly in the area of art history. Among those reviewed this biennium, the following three works merit particular attention: Osiris Delgado's *Historia general de las artes plásticas en Puerto Rico, vol. 1* (item **288**), Alicia Rojas' *Historia de la pintura en Chile* (item **305**), and the catalogue raisonné of Remedios Varo by Ricardo Ovalle (item **266**).

An outstanding example of books dedicated to criticism is Marta Traba's *Art of Latin America, 1900–1980* (item **219**). This book, published ten years after the author's death, is probably her best edited work.

In the essay category, an area of very few new publications, older texts are rather more interesting than the recent ones. The first volume of Octavio Paz's collection entitled *Los privilegios de la vista* (item **218**) and Jorge Romero Brest's *¿Qué es una obra de arte?* (item **299**) continue to command attention.

As far as monographs on artists, especially those on living artists, it is difficult to find a solid work not devoted to a specific agenda, namely, promoting the artist. A few, such as *Tábara* by Carlos Areán (item **311**), deserve recognition as serious works, however.

There are some pleasant surprises found among works devoted to a special theme, such as *La cera en México* by María José Esparza Liberal and Isabel Fernández de García (item **243**) and the *Diccionario crítico de artistas plásticos del Ecuador del siglo XX* by Hernán Rodríguez Castelo (item **312**).

Finally, it is important to single out institutions whose publications consistently exhibit a high degree of professionalism in both technical standards and documentation. A fine example of such an institution is the Galería de Arte Nacional, in Caracas, which has produced a number of excellent works reviewed below (items **328, 325,** and **320.**)

GENERAL

215 Agramunt Lacruz, Francisco. Un arte valenciano en América: exiliados y emigrados. Valencia, Spain: Generalitat Valenciana, Consell Valencià de Cultura, 1992. 356 p.: bibl., ill., index.

Fascinating, unique study of more than 100 artists from Valencia, Spain who, at the time of the Republican defeat by Franco's forces in 1939, emigrated to the New World, settling mostly in Mexico but also in Argentina, the Dominican Republic, Cuba, Colombia, Venezuela, and the US. Since the only selection criterion for inclusion in this work is birth in Valencia, a wide range of artists are discussed (e.g., painters, sculptors, architects, graphic artists, stage designers, etc.). Charming, if somewhat limited, publication includes a good bibliography and profuse illustrations.

Bibliografía para la historia de las artes visuales en la Argentina. See item **3.**

216 Colle Corcuera, Marie-Pierre. Artistas latinoamericanos en su estudio. Introducción de Carlos Fuentes. México: Editorial Limusa, 1994. 237 p.: bibl., ill. (some col.).

Handsome coffee-table book in the style of *Architectural Digest,* perfect as a gift but of little academic use. Includes erudite and enthusiastic introduction by Carlos Fuentes and beautiful, but somewhat artificially staged, photographs of Latin American artists. Unfortunately, Colle Corcuera's text is more anecdotal than interpretive or conceptual and sheds little light on the artists or their work.

217 Latin American artists of the twentieth century. Edited by Waldo Rasmussen with Fatima Bercht and Elizabeth Ferrer. New York: The Museum of Modern Art, 1993. 424 p.: bibl., col. ill., index.

Impressive, well-produced publication by MOMA honoring the Quincenntenial may appease critics who complain that the museum rarely and condescendingly exhibits Latin American art despite its large holdings.

For decades the institution has failed to recognize the importance and historic role of many Latin American artists. Unfortunately, this work's rather outdated view fails to validate Latin America's contribution to the arts in the 20th century, which it presents more as a regional phenomenon subject to outside influences rather than as a strong, original force capable of influencing others. In the Introduction, Waldo Rasmussen suggests that in the future more works by Latin American artists will join the MOMA collection. Edward J. Sullivan's essay, "Notes on the Birth of Modernity in Latin American Art," represents a well-intentioned but failed attempt to address the subject. Despite much research and documentation conducted by the oldest museum of modern art, the book does not rescue Latin American art from its assigned second-class status.

218 Paz, Octavio. Los privilegios de la vista. v. 1, Arte moderno universal. Ed. del autor, 2. ed. Barcelona: Círculo de Lectores; México: Fondo de Cultura Económica, 1994. 1 v.: bibl., ill. (some col.), index. (Letras mexicanas. Obras completas de Octavio Paz; 6)

First volume of essays on the visual arts written by Mexican poet and Nobel laureate Octavio Paz is preceded by a preliminary note or *Aviso,* meaning both "warning" and "notice." Paz states that he has not written about art as a professional critic but as an *aficionado.* Covers heterogeneous topics such as Paz's famous essay "Apariencia Desnuda" on Marcel Duchamp; "El Grabado Latinoamericano;" and "Arte e Identidad: los Hispanos de los Estados Unidos," which Paz wrote for the exhibition catalog of *Hispanic-American artists in the United States* (Corcoran Gallery of Art, 1986). Despite Paz's *Aviso,* the collection is a superb exercise in erudition that requires the reader to have an acquaintance with the history of culture, philosophy, literature, and the arts in general.

219 Traba, Marta. Art of Latin America, 1900–1980. Washington: Inter-American Development Bank; Baltimore, Md.:

Johns Hopkins Univ. Press, 1994. 178 p.: bibl., col. ill., index.

Published by the Inter-American Development Bank in English and Spanish, and profusely illustrated in full color (with 106 reproductions), Marta Traba's last book, finished shortly before her death, was printed 10 years after it was originally drafted. Having frequently expressed her desire to write this type of book, it is rather poignant to note that she never saw the completed work. Nearly 20 persons at the IDB's Publications Unit and Cultural Center worked carefully on the book, supplementing the original manuscript with updated information. Ralph Dimmick has provided a superb translation; however, Traba's style was carefully maintained, and this is probably the best written and edited of her books. After so long, the work remains the most complete, comprehensive, and fresh view of the panorama of the 20th-century art of Latin American and the Caribbean.

MEXICO

220   Altamirano Piolle, María Elena. Homenaje nacional, José María Velasco. Introducción de Fausto Ramírez. Prólogo de Xavier Moyssén. México: Amigos del Museo Nacional de Arte, 1993. 2 v. (555 p.): bibl., ill. (some col.).

Most complete catalog to date includes overview of Velasco's life and work analyzing his impact on Mexican art. Excellent reproductions.

221   La arquitectura mexicana del siglo XX. Coordinación y prólogo de Fernando González Gortázar. México: Consejo Nacional para la Cultura y las Artes, 1994. 339 p.: bibl., ill. (some col.), index. (Cultura contemporánea de México)

Ambitious study, an impressive academic work, summarizes the complexity of 20th-century Mexican architecture. Covers works from the famous 1910 Centennial celebration to the beginning of the 1990s, and encompasses urban works as well as private houses. Nearly 27 contributors set the context and offer balanced views of individual figures and their ideas while also discussing the influence of national events, international trends, and Mexico's precolumbian past, all of which make Mexican architecture one of the most dynamic and innovative in the world. Includes

annotated bibliography, index with more than 650 names, and hundreds of illustrations, most in b/w. Strongly recommended for Spanish-speaking architecture students, given the wide use of technical terms.

222   El arte francés del siglo XIX en México: Museo de San Carlos, noviembre 89-febrero 90. México: Instituto Nacional de Bellas Artes, 1989. 65 p.: bibl., ill. (some col.).

Catalog of French art works collected by Mexico City's Real Academica de Bellas Artes de San Carlos (oldest art academy in Spanish America, founded 1781) gives clear picture of artistic climate during second half of 19th century, and French cultural influence on Mexico. Interesting and curious examples, by Ingres, Delacroix, Fantin-Latour, Fragonard, Rodin, etc. Texts are brief and precise, but photography is poor.

223   Arte y coerción: primer coloquio del Comité Mexicano de Historia del Arte. México: Univ. Nacional Autónoma de México, Instituto de Investigaciones Estéticas, 1992. 264 p.: bibl.

Collection of history of art papers presented and discussed at a symposium (Mexico City, 1990). Main topic was the relationship and interplay between art and power, and the effects of controls exerted upon and issuing from art.

224   Aurrecoechea, Juan Manuel and **Armando Bartra.** Puros cuentos: la historia de la historieta en México. v. 2, 1934–1950. México: Consejo Nacional para la Cultura y las Artes, Dirección General de Publicaciones; Dirección General de Culturas Populares, Museo Nacional de Culturas Populares; Grijalbo, 1993. 1 v.: bibl., ill. (some col.), indexes.

Vol. 2 consists of very good compilation of information and astute observations on the history of cartoons in Mexico. Written in accessible, easy-to-read prose.

225   Azaceta, Luis Cruz. Luis Cruz Azaceta. Concepto de catálogo y cuidado de la edición, Alberto Ibarra Dorado. Garza García, Mexico: Galería Ramis Barquet, 1993. 1 v. (unpaged): chiefly ill. (some col.).

Catalog of Azaceta's work from 1993 (including a few from 1992). Excellent color reproductions and bilingual texts, the best of which is a very *à propos* article by Gerardo Mosquera.

226 **Báez Macías, Eduardo; Graciela Romandía de Cantú;** and **Elia Espinosa.** El caballo en el arte mexicano. México: Fomento Cultural Banamex, 1994. 206 p.: bibl., col. ill.

Unusual book, packed with illustrations, addresses importance of the horse (imported to the Americas by the Spaniards) within Mexican art. The animal is depicted as a central or secondary subject associated with various situations, both real and imaginary. Based on exhibition held at Palacio Iturbide in 1994. Essays by Eduardo Báez, Graciel Romandía de Cantú, and Elia Espinosa explain historical significance of the horse in art in general and Mexican art in particular.

227 **Bartra, Eli.** Frida Kahlo: mujer, ideología, arte. 2. ed. ampliada y rev. Barcelona: Icaria, 1994. 121 p.: bibl., ill. (some col.).

Worthwhile but not entirely successful attempt to clarify the relationship between ideology and sexism in art. Asserts that their interplay determines the methodology for analysis as well as the perception of the artistic object itself. Uses some aspects of Frida Kahlo's work to make the point.

228 **Bonifaz Nuño, Rubén.** Ricardo Martínez. México: Instituto Nacional de Bellas Artes, 1994. 205 p.: bibl., ill. (some col.).

Book-catalog published by Mexico's Institute of Fine Arts on the occasion of Martínez's 1994 exhibition. Excellent color reproductions illustrate the consistent development of Martínez's painting and formalistic style through five decades. Helpful text explains the nature, meaning, lyric context, and structural aspects of Martínez's work.

229 **Chadwick, Whitney.** Leonora Carrington: la realidad de la imaginación. México: Consejo Nacional para la Cultura y las Artes, Dirección General de Publicaciones, 1994. 165 p.: bibl., ill. (some col.). (Galería. Col. de arte mexicano)

Carrington's extraordinary life, a mixture of fantasy and madness, has lent her work a unique quality that enhances and transcends its intrinsic worth. Like the New York School that claimed successful European immigrants to New York as its own, Mexico claims the British Carrington and thus her connection to Europe's avant-garde, Surrealism in particular. The relationship between Mexican art and Leonora Carrington has never been convincingly established. This book, published under the sponsorship of Mexico's National Council for Culture and Arts, also fails to establish it. Rather it portrays the artist as a tireless and adventurous wanderer very fortunate in her life and more-than-generous friends. See also item **241.**

230 **Charlot, Jean.** México en la obra de Jean Charlot. México: Consejo Nacional para la Cultura y las Artes, 1994. 222 p.: bibl., ill. (some col.).

Accurate portrait of early 20th-century European intellectual interested in the fascinating cultural milieu of the New World. Monograph concerns French-born artist who joined the Mexican Renaissance as historian, critic, painter, sculptor, and theoretician, and who claims the honor of having painted the first mural of the Mexican Mural Movement along the stairs of Colegio de San Idelfonso.

231 **100 pintores mexicanos.** Monterrey, Mexico: Museo de Arte Contemporáneo de Monterrey, 1993. lxxxvi, 160 p.: bibl., ill. (some col.).

Essay by Luis Carlos Emerich tracing the evolution of Mexican art from José María Velásquez through the contemporary scene precedes this well-printed catalog of the exhibition. Could serve as a dictionary or guide for laymen interested in a chronological narrative of Mexican art, and its most important figures.

232 **Cimet Shoijet, Esther.** Movimiento muralista mexicano: ideología y producción. México: División de Ciencias y Artes para el Diseño, 1992. 183 p.: bibl. (Libros de la telaraña; 1)

Interesting short essay based on author's 1979 PhD dissertation in art history discusses issues not frequently taken into consideration when analyzing the Mexican Mural Movement, especially its ideological contradictions. Includes selected writings by prestigious critics and historians, as well as manifestos and documents from the period.

233 **Conde, Teresa del; Enrique Franco Calvo;** and **Tessa Corona del Conde.** Fernando Castro Pacheco: color e imagen de Yucatán. Fotografía de Gabriel Figueroa Flores y Ricardo Garibay Ruiz. Mérida, Mexico: Univ. Autónoma de Yucatán, Dirección General de Extensión, 1994. 254 p.: bibl., ill. (some col.). (Yucatán, raíces y expresión de su identidad)

Comprehensive book with bilingual texts on the multifaceted work of Mexican artist Fernando Castro Pacheco depicts his excursions into painting (oils, watercolors, and *temple*), drawing (at which he excels), printmaking, sculpture, and pastel. Nevertheless, Castro Pacheco's work appears to be somewhat derivative of the Mexican muralists towards the end of their movement, especially Zúñiga and Martínez.

234 Conde, Teresa del. Frida Kahlo: la pintora y el mito. México: Instituto de Investigaciones Estéticas, Univ. Nacional Autónoma de México, 1992. 144 p.: bibl., ill. (Monografías de arte/Instituto de Investigaciones Estéticas; 20)

New book by first author to write a monograph (México: UNAM, 1976) exploring the life of Frida Kahlo. Shares insights, primarily from a psychological viewpoint, about this colorful character as woman and artist.

235 Conde, Teresa del *et al.* Pintura mexicana, 1950–1980: Gilberto Aceves Navarro, Raúl Anguiano . . . = Mexican painting. México: Consejo Nacional para la Cultura y las Artes; Instituto Nacional de Bellas Artes; IBM México, 1990. 119 p.: bibl., ill.

Short and informative texts by several authors, including Teresa del Conde and Fernando Gamboa in one of his last contributions. They examine 46 artists representing different currents in Mexican art. According to the catalog, these artists were exhibited "together for the first time," as part of *México: una obra de arte,* in New York, 1990–91.

Consejo Nacional para la Cultura y las Artes (Mexico). El patrimonio cultural de México. See item **86.**

236 Coronel, Pedro. Pedro Coronel. México: Grupo Financiero, 1993. 191 p.: bibl., ill. (some col.).

Introductory text by Jorge Alberto Manrique offers biographical profile of the artist within the context of Mexican art. The rest of the texts are interviews and articles about Coronel's painting and sculpture over a 25-year period (1923–85). Impressive roster of contributors includes well-known Mexican and foreign historians, art critics, and poets such as Octavio Paz, Juan García Ponce, Justino Fernández, Raquel Tibol, and Juan Acha. Excellent reproductions.

237 44 años del Salón de la Plástica Mexicana. México: Instituto Nacional de Bellas Artes, 1994. 208 p.: ill. (some col.).

Chronology of the *Salón de la Plástica Mexicana,* a national, annual art exhibition established with government support in 1949 and organized by Fernando Gamboa to stimulate the plastic arts in Mexico. Throughout the years, the Salón has served as a national forum to discuss the arts, promote new talent, and recognize veterans in the field. Good reference work.

238 Cuevas, José Luis. Gato macho. México: Fondo de Cultura Económica, 1994. 728 p.: index. (Col. Tierra firme)

Dense and thick volume consists of articles previously published in *Excélsior* and other books, written throughout author's lifetime. Texts are witty, intense, and filled with detail. In this autobiography, Cuevas addresses what he thinks is important for the public to know about his work and him. Includes onomastic index but lacks illustrations.

Diego Rivera Museo Virtual/Virtual Museum. See item **31.**

239 Directorio de las artes plásticas. 2. ed. Ciudad Satélite, Mexico: J. Porrua, 1994. 204 p.: bibl., ill. (some col.).

Incomplete guide to art museums, art schools, associations, publications, etc., includes data on Mexican artists (alive and dead). Unclear selection of artists suggests a commercial, rather than scholarly, intent. Lacks elementary information on artists such as dates of birth. Best section lists cultural institutions and museums with addresses and phone numbers.

240 Eder, Rita. Gunther Gerzso: el esplendor de la muralla. México: Consejo Nacional para la Cultura y las Artes, Dirección General de Publicaciones, 1994. 187 p.: bibl., ill. (some col.). (Galería. Col. de arte mexicano)

With simple words and clear methodology, Eder deciphers Gerzso: the man, the artist, and his work. Explains the artist's work from his early years as a set designer for the Mexican movie industry to his "imaginary cities," tracing relationships and affinities with Mexican precolumbian art, art history, fellow Latin American artists and, above all, Surrealism. Rigorous and objective text proves its points. Illustrations are as effective as the text.

241 Emerich, Luis Carlos and **Lourdes Andrade.** Leonora Carrington: una retrospectiva. Monterrey, Mexico: Museo de Arte Contemporáneo de Monterrey, 1994. 152 p.: ill. (some col.).

Excellent bilingual (English-Spanish), illustrated catalog of this British artist's retrospective (Monterrey Museum of Art, Sept.–Nov. 1994). It appears as if Carrington's surrealistic painting and Mexican art (e.g., Siqueiros) both require much explanatory literature. Luis Carlos Emerich, however, adopts the opposite approach by stating that Carrington's paintings would not be enigmatic if they were explained. He perceives them as being closely associated with the artist's colorful life, as if driven more by her personal struggle than an artistic vision. See also item **229.**

242 Encuentros con Diego Rivera. Coordinación de Guadalupe Rivera Marín y Juan Coronel Rivera. Prólogo de Jaime Labastida. Cronología de Manuel Reyero. Investigación, iconografía y montaje de Luis Cortés Bargalló *et al.* México: BNCI; Siglo Veintiuno Editores; Colegio Nacional, 1993. 399 p.: bibl., ill. (some col.).

Very well-documented publication on the life and times of Diego Rivera, from his childhood to his religious polemics and love affairs. Good addition to any Rivera library collection.

243 Esparza Liberal, María José and **Isabel Fernández de García Lascurain.** La cera en México: arte e historia. Prólogo de Teresa Castelló Yturbide. México: Fomento Cultural Banamex, 1994. 253 p.: bibl., ill. (some col.).

Lavishly illustrated book traces the history of wax image-making from colonial times to present. Covers its use in creating religious imagery, and the importance of this craft in determining and promoting Mexican popular culture.

244 Etcharren, Patricia. El bordado en Yucatán. Mérida, Mexico: Casa de las Artesanías del Gobierno del Estado de Yucatán, 1993. 127 p.: bibl., ill. (some col.).

Enlightening but basic work could serve as textbook for those interested in the evolution of fashion and costume in the Americas. Part of research project on the history

and development of embroidery in the Yucatán peninsula sponsored by the local government. Covers native and Spanish traditions as well as older ones such as Moorish influences. Includes charming illustrations.

245 Exposiciones, 1989–1994. México: Secretaría de Comercio y Fomento Industrial, 1994. 180 p.: ill. (chiefly col.).

Unattributed volume sponsored by Mexico's Secretaría de Comercio y Fomento Industrial (SECOFI) gathers biographical and visual information on three dozen artists who exhibited at SECOFI's gallery from 1989–94. Useful publication because it includes lesser-known artists, some of them very young.

246 Ezquerra de la Colina, José Luis. Ezquerra y la arquitectura lejanista. Puebla, México: Univ. Popular Autónoma del Estado de Puebla, 1994. 251 p.: bibl., ill. (some col.).

Stylized, romantic style of popular Mexican architect José Luis Ezquerra de la Colina is featured in this book presented by Fernando Rodríguez Concha (Director of the School of Architecture of the Popular Univ. of the State of Puebla). This portfolio of Ezquerra's prolific architectural work, often described as *lejanismo* (defined as "cultural emotions and passions from the past"), describes work strongly reminiscent of picturesque and popular Mediterranean architecture (e.g., postcards, travel brochures, etc.).

247 Fabrés y su tiempo, 1854–1938. México: INBA, Museo de San Carlos, 1994. 175 p.: bibl., ill. (some col.).

Well-respected teacher and Catalonian artist Antonio Fabrés taught at the Art Academy of San Carlos, Mexico City (1902–07), where his students included Diego Rivera and José Clemente Orozco. A well-respected teacher, he was another foreign artist who steered and promoted art education in Mexico towards the end of Porfirio Díaz's regime (1880–1911). This well-documented study features Fabrés' exhibit at the San Carlos Museum and includes many works on loan from private collections and Barcelona museums. By no means an innovator, Fabrés was a realist and allegorical painter with noted drawing ability and good knowledge of fin-de-siècle decorative arts fashionable in pre-revolutionary Mexico.

248 Fernández Ruiz, Consuelo; Leticia Gámez Ludgar; and **María de los Angeles Sobrino Figueroa.** El paisaje mexicano en la pintura del siglo XIX y principios del XX. Fotografía de Enrique Salazar e Hijar. México: Banamex, Fomento Cultural Banamex, 1991. 93 p.: bibl., col. ill.

Catalog of exhibition at Palacio de Iturbide in Mexico is worthwhile mainly for the authors' time charts identifying dates for works of many traveling artists, as well as those of the great landscape painter José María Velasco and his disciples. Charts are followed by different interpretations of the subject of landscape in first decades of the 20th century.

249 Flores, Leopoldo. Leopoldo Flores 2000 D.C. México: Univ. Nacional Autónoma de México, 1994. 168 p.: col. ill.

Mexico state's Museo Universitario Contemporáneo de Arte (formerly the Museo Universitario de Ciencias y Artes) initiated its program of activities with an exhibition and book on Flores. The artist is partly responsible for the creation of the Museo de Arte Moderno del Estado de México. The exhibit entitled "2.000 D.C." was organized to honor Flores. The stained-glass work he executed for the city of Toluca (called "Cosmovitral") is by far his greatest achievement. In English and Spanish, with many color illustrations.

250 Foley, Martin. El recogedor de soles: la vida y obra de Feliciano Béjar. Fotografías de Bob Schalkwijk. Mexico: Centro Cultural San Angel, 1992. 165 p.: bibl., ill. (some col.).

Biography of this Mexican artist, written in cooperation with Béjar's friends and family, devotes much space to his special interest in the relationship among architecture, metal and glass sculpture, and landscape design.

251 García Ponce, Juan. Las formas de la imaginación: Vicente Rojo en su pintura. Selección y nota de Alejandro Katz. México: Fondo de Cultura Económica, 1992. 75 p.: col. ill. (Tezontle)

Katz has selected these somewhat speculative, critical essays written by García Ponce from 1963–84 on Rojo, a Spanish painter who settled in Mexico. They provide step-by-step observations of the painter's development. For specialists and connoisseurs of post-1950s Mexican art.

252 Garrido, Esperanza *et al.* Felipe Santiago Gutiérrez: pasión y destino. Toluca, Mexico: Instituto Mexiquense de Cultura, 1993. 191 p.: ill. (some col.).

Very informative, though awkwardly written, biography sheds light on 19th-century Mexican painter whose extensive travels in the Americas are reflected in his uneven body of work. Provides realistic portrait of the life and times of a Latin American artist who tried to make a living from his craft.

253 International Biennial of the Poster in Mexico, *3rd, Mexico City?, 1994.*
3a. Bienal Internacional del Cartel en México, '94 = Third International Biennial of the Poster in Mexico. México: Fondo Nacional para la Cultura y las Artes, 1994. 165 p.: ill. (chiefly col.).

Very rarely does one see a publication like this catalog of a 1994 Mexican poster exhibit. Provides international view of the craft of graphic design and includes Latin American artists from throughout the world. Posters highlight contemporary social issues ranging from violence to AIDS. Good reference work for professionals and those interested in graphic design.

254 Introducción a la cultura artística de México: siglo XX. México: SEP, SESIC; Consejo Nacional para la Cultura y las Artes, 1994. 147 p.: bibl., ill. (some col.).

Useful, well-produced volume serves as layman's introduction to Mexican visual arts, literature, dance, architecture, and other cultural manifestations. Although not a research tool, it is a reliable reference work.

255 Jalisco: genio y maestría. Monterrey, Mexico: Museo de Arte Contemporáneo de Monterrey, 1994. 177 p.: bibl., col. ill.

José María Estrada, Carlos Villaseñor, Dr. Atl, and José Clemente Orozco are four of many great painters from Jalisco. Book is based on an exhibition of the region's artists from Independence to present. Includes lavish color illustrations of impressive works. Inexplicably, provides no biographical information on the artists.

256 Kaminer, Saúl. Kaminer: las cuatro tierras = the four lands. México: Museo del Palacio de Bellas Artes, 1994. 119 p.: col. ill.

A member of the young generation of Mexican artists who lived and worked in

Paris, Kaminer achieved considerable success as a professional and consistent painter. Hard-cover, bilingual catalog of a traveling exhibit of his work to be shown in Mexico and Washington also contains enthusiastic and unconditional praise by writers who recognize his talent, as does the Mexican art establishment.

257 Luna Arroyo, Antonio. Dr. Atl. México: Salvat, 1992. 176 p., 16 p. of plates: bibl., col. ill. (Col. Biografías. Serie Pintores. Artistas latinoamericanos)

Author, a personal friend of Dr. Atl (pseud. for Gerardo Murillo), presents a firsthand account of the life and interests—artistic and otherwise—of one of the most fascinating personalities in Mexican art. Includes the few autobiographical notes left by the artist and excerpts from writings by personalities such as Siqueiros.

258 Méndez, Leopoldo. Leopoldo Méndez: artista de un pueblo en lucha. México: Centro de Estudios Económicos y Sociales del Tercer Mundo, A.C.; Instituto de Investigaciones Estéticas, UNAM, 1981. 127 p.: bibl., ill.

Various authors, including Elena Poniatowska and Ida Rodríguez Prampolini, write, with personal affection, about different aspects of Méndez's life as a man and as an artist. They also explore his connection with the *Taller Editorial de Gráfica Popular.* Good introduction to the artist and his work.

259 Mendiola, María Luisa. Vicente Mendiola: un hombre con espíritu del Renacimiento que vivió en el siglo XX. Toluca de Lerdo, Mexico: Instituto Mexiquense de Cultura, 1993. 159 p.: bibl., ill. (some col.).

Architect Mendiola was active during the Mexican Renaissance years (1920s). This work is a labor of love by his daughter, also an architect. Consists of valuable information on his architectural work, watercolors, and other drawings. Carlos Chanfón Olmos provides good summary of Mendiola's accomplishments and description of his personality (p. vii, par. 4).

260 Moreno Villarreal, Jaime. Lilia Carrillo: la constelación secreta. México: Consejo Nacional para la Cultura y las Artes; Ediciones Era, 1993. 141 p.: bibl., ill. (some col.). (Galería. Col. de arte mexicano)

Posthumous book-catalog about Carrillo (d. 1974), an influential artist whose work,

first noted in 1956, was described as "lyric abstraction." She helped move painting beyond the outdated and rigid principles of the Mexican School. Includes text by Moreno Villarreal, articles by other authors, and a chronology of her life by her husband, longtime friend, and inspirational force, Manuel Felguérez.

261 Moyssén Echeverría, Xavier. David Alfaro Siqueiros: pintura de caballete. México: Fondo Editorial de la Plástica Mexicana, 1994. 132 p.: bibl., ill. (chiefly col.).

Best known for his monumental murals, his rhetoric, and even his graphics, Siqueiros' easel works have not received much attention. He frequently used the easel scale to investigate and research new possibilities to expand and enhance his painting. They included the use of photography in which he posed to study foreshortening of images and difficult angles. By no means exhaustive, Moyssén's text is balanced and adequately covers the selection of mostly color illustrations.

Muchas moradas hay en México. See item **111.**

262 Museo Dolores Olmedo Patiño. Textos de José Juárez *et al.* Xochimilco, Mexico: Museo Dolores Olmedo Patiño, 1994. 175 p.: ill. (some col.).

Olmedo, a collector and participant in the Mexican art movement during the second quarter of the 20th century, is known not so much as an artist but as a character whose passion for the arts—and occasionally for the artists—allowed her to be an intimate member of artistic circles (e.g., Diego Rivera and Frida Kalho). Olmedo amassed one of the most important collections of Mexican art in existence today and housed it in Xochimilco. Book includes major works by Rivera and Kahlo. Valuable catalog of the collection, including reproductions, appears at the end of the work. Also useful for biographical information and description of the museum and its collection.

263 Navarrete, Sylvia. Miguel Covarrubias: artista y explorador. México: Dirección General de Publicaciones del Consejo Nacional para la Cultura y las Artes, 1993. 139 p.: bibl., ill. (some col.). (Galería. Col. de arte mexicano)

Simple and unpretentious biographical study of Covarrubias focuses on various facets of the artist's career, from caricature and painting to dance and anthropology. Includes well-selected reproductions.

264 Nelken, Margarita. Carlos Orozco Romero. 2a. ed. México: Univ. Nacional Autónoma de México, Coordinación de Humanidades, 1994. 208 p.: bibl., ill. (some col.). (Col. de arte/Univ. Nacional Autónoma de México; 7)

Author perceives artist Orozco Romero as one of the most original and outstanding innovators of the Mexican School, notwithstanding the fact that the accompanying illustrations, which cover almost 50 years of activity, reveal Rouault's strong influences in artist's early works, Dr. Atl's in his landscapes, Diego Rivera's in his portraits, Siqueiros' in his surreal compositions and Tamayo's in his fantastic depictions. Although author's thesis is unconvincing, book is well organized and printed.

The original Frida Kahlo homepage. See item 33.

265 Ortiz Gaitán, Julieta. Entre dos mundos: los murales de Roberto Montenegro. México: Instituto de Investigaciones Estéticas, Univ. Nacional Autónoma de México, 1994. 220 p.: bibl., ill. (some col.), index. (Serie especial)

Dispassionate and accurate study of the mural work of Mexican artist Roberto Montenegro (d. 1968). Author clearly delineates influences that shaped the style of this first-generation muralist, and four stages undergone by Montenegro's work. Describes his struggle to come to terms with changes in the political and economic spheres of Mexican society (from an early decorative style influenced by Art Nouveau to the eclecticism of his final years). Well-illustrated example of rigorous research. Includes documented addendum and bibliography.

266 Ovalle, Ricardo et al. Remedios Varo: catálogo razonado = catalogue raisonné. México: Ediciones Era, 1994. 342 p.: bibl., ill. (some col.).

This "catalogue raisonné," an addition to the abundant bibliography on the Spanish-born, Mexican-adopted Remedios Varo, is a priority for any art collector or scholar interested in the surrealist painter. The introductory texts by Alberto Blanco, Teresa del Conde, Salomon Grimberg, and Janet A. Kaplan are written with enthusiasm. The texts

provide a good counterbalance to the "catalogue" section, and include a biographical sketch by Walter Gruen, comments on several of Varo's works by her brother Rodrigo, as well as the obligatory technical data, photographs—mostly in color, and other information typical of a "catalogue raisonné."

267 Paalen, Wolfgang. Wolfgang Paalen: retrospectiva. México: Museo de Arte Contemporáneo Alvar y Carmen T. de Carrillo Gil, 1994. 277 p.: bibl., ill. (some col.).

Superbly crafted book concerns Paalen's retrospective held at Carrillo Gil Museum (México, 1994). Includes articles by Octavio Paz, André Breton, and others who discuss the plastic and literary work of this elusive artist of the 1930s Abstraction, Creation, and Surrealist movements who emigrated to Mexico in 1939. Wonderful biographical material is scattered throughout this volume emphasizing Paalen's contradictions and his many approaches, all of which result in a challenging labyrinth of ideas and visual interpretations.

268 Paisaje, imagen, palabra: la expresión artística del México regional de fin de milenio. Coordinación de Mónica Lavín. Mexico: Danés Edicions d'Art, 1993. 204 p.: col. ill.

Coffee-table book more interesting than most because it offers a rigorous attempt to convey the art of provincial Mexico, its geographical diversity and complex cultural past and present. Includes short essays on topics such as the black and Indian roots of Tabasco's literature and art exemplified by poems, photographs, and reproductions of artwork. Very good guide for those interested in the country's cultural milieu.

269 Palacio de Bellas Artes (México). Palacio de Bellas Artes México. Ensayo de Xavier Moyssén.Textos de Adamo Boari y Federico Mariscal. Fotografías de Marc Mogilner. México: Aeroméxico; Milán: Franco Maria Ricci, 1993. 199 p.: ill. (some col.).

Mexico City's Palacio de Bellas Artes is an eclectic and accomplished building. Designed in the tradition of the 19th-century beaux arts style, it integrates neoclassical forms with art nouveau and art deco architecture, sculpture, painting, and decorative arts, executed by some of the fashionable artists of the period. Begun in 1904 as part of the celebration of the nation's centennial (1910), the

Palacio represents the final years of the Porfiriato. Includes excellent essay by Xavier Moyssén tracing the building's history as well as equally good photographs of dozens of architectural and artistic details. Recommended for scholars and students of art or architecture.

270 Prignitz-Poda, Helga. El Taller de Gráfica Popular en México, 1937–1977. Traducción de Elizabeth Siefer. México: Instituto Nacional de Bellas Artes, 1992. 448 p.: bibl., ill.

Taller de Gráfica Popular or TGP was created in Mexico in 1937 as an alternative to mural and easel painting. Based on a clear socio-political agenda, TGP was, along with muralism, a unique event in the history of Latin American art and a forerunner of similar workshops in other regions of the Americas, such as Puerto Rico. Excellent, well-illustrated, and in-depth study that contains valuable information. Author traces and analyzes TGP's origins, development, and outcome in an attempt to decipher its complex political and aesthetic ideology, stylistic traits, and philosophical differences among its members.

271 Ramírez, Fausto. Crónica de las artes plásticas en los años de López Velarde, 1914–1921. México: Univ. Nacional Autónoma de México, Instituto de Investigaciones Estéticas, 1990. 218 p.: bibl., ill., index. (Cuadernos de historia del arte; 53)

Analyzes the state of Mexican arts during the years the poet spent in Mexico City, beginning with the election of Victoriano Huerta and ending with that of Alvaro Obregón. These were the post-Díaz years before the radical regime that followed stimulated a Mexican renaissance in the arts.

272 Rivera, Arturo. Arturo Rivera. México: Grupo Financiero Serfin, 1994. 105 p.: ill. (some col.). (Col. Abside)

Arturo Rivera's drawings are a mixture of Renaissance-like scientific endeavors, academic dexterity, and surrealistic sensibility. Unfortunately, an oeuvre as visually complex as his requires a simpler format and better organized layout that that provided here. Even the artist's biography is complicated needlessly by the use of difficult-to-understand euphemisms. Furthermore, essays by José Manuel Orozco and Luis Carlos Emerich fail to illuminate the artist's motivations, which are actually much better perceived through the illustrations of his work. Indeed, these provide the best reference on Rivera's work and are the book's most valuable component.

273 Rivera, Diego. Diego Rivera: retrospectiva. Madrid: Ministerio de Cultura, Dirección General de Bellas Artes y Archivos, Centro Nacional de Exposiciones, 1992. 385 p.: bibl., ill. (some col.), index.

Retrospective of Rivera celebrates the 100th anniversary of his birth and the 50th anniversary of his Detroit murals. Includes extraordinary collection of essays on the artist, some of them more worthwhile than others, but still of value to all Rivera scholars. Originally published in English.

274 Romandía de Cantú, Graciela and **Román Piña Chán.** Adela Breton: una artista británica en México, 1894–1908. Edición de Mario de la Torre. México: Smurfit Cartón y Papel de México, 1993. 147 p.: bibl., ill. (some col.).

Breton, who emigrated to the New World relatively late in the 19th century, was not a great artistic innovator, but through her journal (deposited at the Museum and Art Gallery, Bristol, England) she provided a valuable document of the period. In it, she describes the Mexican landscape and, most importantly, many precolumbian structures that have since been destroyed or are in ruins. Bilingual edition includes a fair translation into English.

275 Salazar, Ignacio. Ignacio Salazar. México: Grupo Financiero Serfin, 1994. 103 p.: col. ill. (Col. Abside)

Includes a quite valuable interview by Teresa del Conde with the artist. Otherwise, a somewhat promotional publication.

276 Siqueiros, David Alfaro. Siqueiros: el lugar de la utopía. México: Instituto Nacional de Bellas Artes; Sala de Arte Público Siqueiros, 1994? 173 p.: bibl., ill. (some col.).

Beautifully designed catalog includes excellent graphics, reproductions, and good quality printing. Splendid effort by the Instituto Nacional de Bellas Artes de México to present the Sala de Arte Público Siqueiros in Mexico City. These art works together with their Chapultepec house were donated by Siqueiros and his wife to the Mexican people. Work consists primarily of the artist's personal archives and library, both of which contain important documentation (1927–74).

Miscellaneous essays accompany the text which is also complemented by an abbreviated but concise chronology and detailed bibliography.

277 Universidad Nacional Autónoma de México. Museo Universitario de Ciencias y Arte. Tres décadas de expresión plástica. México: Museo Universitario de Ciencias y Arte, 1993. 396 p.: ill. (some col.).

Illustrated catalog of exhibition celebrates 33 years of the University Museum of Arts and Sciences (MUCA) and features the permanent collection and recently donated artworks by Mexican artists. Covers 216 artworks and 118 artists and contains several essays that trace the history of the museum. High-quality production and useful research tool.

278 Vargas, Ismael. Ismael Vargas. México: Grupo Financiero Serfin, 1994. 111 p.: ill. (some col.). (Col. Abside)

Elena Poniatowska's text on Ismael Vargas' work intentionally replicates the chaotic visual structure of Vargas' paintings but fails to explore their deceptive decorative quality, religious allusions, hidden irony, and the persistent use of patterned images. This interesting approach to the artist sheds little light on his work.

279 28 artistas guanajuatenses en apoyo al campo. Guanajuato, Mexico: Gobierno del Estado de Guanajuato, Instituto de la Cultura del Estado; Desarrollo Rural de Guanajuato, 1994. 1 v. (unpaged): ill. (some col.).

According to Carlos Medina Plascencia, Governor of the state of Guanajuato, the exhibition that led to this catalog had two goals: 1) to promote the artists of the region; and 2) to help, via the sale of artworks, the peasant community of the state. Includes a few Guanajuato artists whose works are worth disseminating. Additional articles add little to the publication, and most are promotional.

Webmuseo de Latinoamérica. See item **34.**

CENTRAL AMERICA

280 Flores, Juan Carlos. Magic and realism: Central American contemporary art = Magia y realismo: arte contemporáneo centroamericano. Tegucigalpa: Galeria Trio's, 1992. 294 p.: bibl., ill. (some col.).

Six countries (Guatemala, Nicaragua, El Salvador, Honduras, Costa Rica, and Panama) are represented by 37 artists in this rare compilation of recent Central American art. Eccentric and eclectic selection criteria leaves out international figures such as Armando Morales of Nicaragua (see item **283**), Benjamín Cañas of El Salvador, and Carlos Mérida of Guatemala. The book, nevertheless, gives an idea of the work of several lesser known artists from the region. Incomplete bibliography.

281 Kunzle, David. The murals of revolutionary Nicaragua, 1979–1992. Berkeley: Univ. of California Press, 1995. 203 p.: bibl., ill. (some col.), index, map.

Remarkable book on the relatively unknown Sandinista revolutionary muralist movement that developed after the fall of Somoza in 1979. Despite the book's overt political stance ("impassioned" according to Eva Cockcroft), it illustrates an important period in Nicaragua's history. Unfortunately, this particular mural movement lacked originality and was very derivative of the worst experiments of the Mexican Mural Movement (i.e., propaganda art).

282 Méndez Dávila, Lionel. Elmar Rojas. Estudio introductorio por Edward J. Sullivan. Guatemala: Armitano Editores; Galería Ambiente Ediciones, 1993? 230 p.: ill. (some col.).

The best paintings by Guatemalan Elmar Rojas are probably those belonging to the decade 1980–90. This book by Dávila, with introduction by Edward J. Sullivan, seems to prove this assertion, more for the illustrations included than for the critical analysis, which is less than satisfactory. The book also makes obvious the always present decorative inclinations of Rojas' painting, which dominate, for better or worse, his past and present production. Unfortunately, this long, well printed and illustrated promotional book is void of context.

283 Morales, Armando. Armando Morales, pintura: abril-septiembre, 1990, México. México: Museo Rufino Tamayo; Museo de Monterrey, 1991? 103 p.: ill. (some col.).

Good quality catalog published for Morales' exhibit held at both the Rufino Tamayo and Monterey museums in 1990. Includes texts by major art critics (e.g., Ashton, Bayón, Messer, Tibol, etc.) and does justice to the work of this extraordinary painter and his equally extraordinary career. Excellent quality and selection of reproductions. Biographical addendum is informative and enlightening.

284   Zúñiga, Francisco. Francisco Zúñiga. México: El Equilibrista; Madrid: Turner Libros, 1994. 206 p.: bibl., ill. (some col.).

With this publication, which obviously the sculptor himself directed in great part, Costa Rican-born Zúñiga develops a comprehensive guide to his mature work that even reaches back to his pertinent earlier works, including some sensible woodcuts. Not a comprehensive book, however, despite the claim that it covers his sculpture, painting, and drawing from 1928–92. The informative data and the mostly b/w visual material selected are didactic; nevertheless, a more complete book on this artist, including an evaluation of his contribution to 20th-century sculpture, is still necessary.

THE CARIBBEAN AND THE GUIANAS

285   Las artes visuales puertorriqueñas a finales del siglo XX. Edición de Adlín Ríos Rigua. Santurce, P.R.: s.n., 1992 240 p.: ill. (some col.).

Anthology of texts on Puerto Rican art gives partial view of artistic developments during post-1980s. Covers painting, sculpture, printmaking, photography, filmmaking, and architecture. Also includes short sociological essay about art, society, and communication. Presents broad picture with little in-depth analysis.

286   Bazán de Huerta, Moisés. La escultura monumental en La Habana. Cáceres, Spain: Univ. de Extremadura, 1994. 165 p.: bibl., ill.

Provides useful information, but says much less than expected about the artistic significance of Havana monuments. [J.M. Hernández]

287   Binnendijk, Chandra van and **Paul Faber.** Twintig jaar beeldende kunst in Suriname, 1975–1995 = Twenty years of visual art in Suriname, 1975–1995. Paramaribo: Stichting Surinaams Museum; Amsterdam: Koninklijk Instituut voor de Tropen;

Rotterdam: Museum voor Volkenkunde, 1995. 111 p.: bibl.

Presents overview of Suriname paintings, sculptures, and works on paper in 100 color plates and text. Introductory essay in both Dutch and English introduces artists, art schools, and organizations, and places these in an international context. Includes short biographies of featured artists. [R. Hoefte]

Cuba Poster Project/Proyecto de Afiches Cubanos. See item **30.**

288   Delgado Mercado, Osiris. Historia general de las artes plásticas en Puerto Rico. v. 1. Santo Domingo: Editora Corripio, 1994. 1 v.: bibl., ill. (some col.), index.

Vol. 1 of first comprehensive, well-documented, and user-friendly history of Puerto Rican plastic arts published to date (i.e., Quincentennial of Columbus' arrival in Puerto Rico). Provides very good account of evolution of the arts on the island, from pre-columbian times to the 17th century (except for gold and silver crafts covered through the 20th century). Includes examples of native Puerto Rican art, Spanish colonial architecture—mainly religious and military—painting and sculpture. First complete study of the subject includes about 240 illustrations, but only eight in color. Satisfactory bibliography and numerous notes complement this excellent teaching tool.

289   García, Domingo. Domingo García: cuatro décadas de pintura; Convento de los Domínicos, Instituto de Cultura Puertorriqueña, 3 de diciembre de 1987 al 28 de febrero de 1988, San Juan, Puerto Rico = four decades of painting. Translations by Lilliana Ramos Collado. San Juan, P.R.: Instituto de Cultura Puertorriqueña, 1988? 96 p.: ill. (some col.).

García can be called "expressionist" because of the raw qualities of his painting which may explain its apparent uneveness. Informative catalog-book celebrates 40 years of professional work and places in perspective the artist and development of Puerto Rican art, especially in terms of its differences from and similarities with contemporaneous US painting.

290   Gerón, Cándido. Obras maestras de la pintura dominicana = Masterpieces of Dominican painting, 1844–1993. Santo Domingo: s.n., 1994. 2 v.: ill. (some col.).

Two large bilingual volumes on Dominican art from 1844–1993 consist of uneven and overgenerous selections of paintings and superficial texts lacking accurate information and historical context. Still useful for libraries given that there is so little published material on Dominican art.

291 Henríquez, Nicole and **Jacqueline Römer-de Vreese.** Ocalia paints Curaçao. Zutphen, Netherlands: Walburg Pers, 1995. 128 p.: photos.

Impressive hommage to Curaçao's naïve artist Hipólito Ocalia (1916–84). Three-part essay covers life, philosophy, and works of Ocalia. Contains some 60 beautiful color reproductions of his paintings and art works. Also includes listing of exhibitions, biography, and list of works. Summaries in Papiamentu, French, and Spanish. [R. Hoefte]

292 *The Journal of Decorative and Propaganda Arts.* Vol. 22, 1996, Cuba Theme Issue. Edited by Narciso Menocal. Miami: Wolfson Foundation of Decorative and Propaganda Arts.

Another exceptionally fine issue of this journal devoted to Cuba (1875–1945, 291 p.). For first issue entirely devoted to a Latin American country (Argentina, 1875–1945), see *HLAS 54:320*; for second Latin American issue (Brazil, 1875–1945), see Vol. 25, 1995, of *The Journal of Decorative and Propaganda Arts.* Cuban issue includes splendid photographs, illustrations, reproductions, and maps in b/w and color. Edited and organized by Narciso Menocal, Univ. of Wisconsin. Consists of 14 articles on: Cuban culture by Menocal; Havana between two centuries by C. Venegas Fornias; Etienne-Sulpice Hallet and Espada Cemetery by Menocal; the architecture of American sugar mills and the United Fruit Co. by F. Préstamo; imaging Cuba under the American flag and Charles Edward Dotty in Havana, 1899–1902 by M.A. Bretos; the years of the journal *Social* by M.L. Lobo Montalvo and Z. Lapique Becali; American architects in Cuba, 1900–30 by J.A. Gelabert-Navia; the city as landscape, Jean Claude Nicolas Forestier and the great urban works of Havana, 1925–30 by J.F. Lejeune; the quest for a national identity in painting by Menocal; Amelia Peláez by J.A. Molina; Enrique Riverón and the Cuban *vanguardia* by G.V. Blanc; avant-garde architecture, from art deco to modern regionalism by E.L. Rodrí-

guez; and Cuban connections among Key West, Tampa and Miami, 1870–1945 by P. Harper. [Ed.]

293 Lezama Lima, José. La visualidad infinita. Introducción, estudio crítico, selección y notas de Leonel Capote. La Habana: Editorial Letras Cubanas, 1994. 344 p.: bibl., index.

Antología de ensayos de crítica de pintura cubana, además de poemas dedicados por el autor a sus amigos pintores. En la obra de Lezama Lima, la expresión plástica ocupó un lugar relevante, especialmente la pintura cubana que lo acompañó por igual en su hogar y en la soledad de su estudio. Estos textos delatan su pasión por las artes plásticas y su contribución renovadora en el género de la crítica de arte. [U. de Aragón]

Monte Urraca, Manuel E. del. Memorias de la ciudad de Santo Domingo: origen, decadencia y rescate de su patrimonio cultural. See item **153.**

294 Núñez Jiménez, Antonio. El libro del tabaco. Nuevo León, Mexico: Pulsar, 1994. 284 p.: bibl., col. ill.

Fascinating book on the use of tobacco in Cuba and Hispanic America covers its long-lasting cultural presence from ancient times through the colonial period to today. Also examines impact of this American product on the Old World. But its chief concern is tobacco's impact on the visual arts, which is examined in several worthwhile and well-documented short texts such as "El Tabaco en la Plástica," "El Tabaco en la Historia de Cuba," etc. Also includes reproductions of the delightful "marquillas" which illuminate these texts. Recommended for those interested in the history of Latin American art, especially lithographs and the role they played among engravers and artists towards the end of the 19th century.

SOUTH AMERICA
Argentina

El cine argentino. See item **6.**

295 Galerie Jutta Wiegert (Buenos Aires).
Panorama de la pintura argentina contemporánea = a prospect of contemporary Argentine painting. Buenos Aires: Galerie Jutta Wiegert, 1991. 885 p.: col. ill. (Artistas plásticos contemporáneos; 1)

Useful as a panoramic and comprehensive view of Buenos Aires' contemporary art scene. As texts were written by artists themselves, work lacks overall critical analysis, but illustrations are good and well selected.

296 Gené, Enrique H. Leopoldo Presas, el amor en todos sus formas: meditación en torno de un humanista de nuestra plástica. Buenos Aires: Editorial Club de Estudio, 1993. 208 p.: ill. (some col.).

Exquisitely printed book illustrates Presas' exceptional art. Text by Gené sheds little light. More of a promotional than a research work.

Gutman, Margarita and **Jorge Enrique Hardoy.** Buenos Aires: historia urbana del área metropolitana. See item **3037.**

297 Roca, Miguel Angel. Obras, proyectos, escritos 1965–1990. Prefacio, artículos y descripción de las obras por Miguel Angel Roca. Textos de Giancarlo de Carlo *et al.* Buenos Aires: G. Gili, 1990. 220 p.: bibl., ill. (some col.).

Roca is undoubtedly one of the most brilliant Argentine architects and, as with most serious architects, every project reflects not only his personal interpretation of particular problems, but his sensitivity to the realities and demands of the present. His designs reveal his understanding of the interaction between private and public space. Projects commissioned by Córdoba City reflect the sensitivity, intelligence, and pragmatism of this fine architect. Includes several articles on Roca's work, good illustrations, chronology, biography, and bibliography.

298 Romero Brest, Jorge. Arte visual en el Di Tella: aventura memorable en los años 60. Buenos Aires: Emecé, 1992. 213 p.: ill.

The Visual Arts Center (CAV), a dependency of the Torcuato Di Tella Institute, was the most influential artistic group and leading art think tank in Argentina during 1963–70. Its director, Jorge Romero Brest, was the "grey eminence" of the Buenos Aires art scene. Most—if not all—major figures in Argentine plastic arts went from CAV into the national and international art worlds. Romero Brest himself recalls his CAV experience here, a basic source for understanding the development of the visual arts in Argentina during those crucial years.

299 Romero Brest, Jorge. ¿Qué es una obra de arte? Buenos Aires: Emecé, 1992. 153 p.

Ambitious title and six chapters in which Romero Brest attempts to define "What is a work of art?" Published four years after his death, one wonders whether the author would have approved the publication of this draft. An erudite theoretician of art with vast cultural knowledge, especially philosophy, Romero Brest was most influential during the 1960s.

300 Xul Solar, Alejandro. Xul Solar: collection of the art works in the museum. Texts by Jorge Luis Borges *et al.* Edited by Mario H. Gradowczyk. Buenos Aires: Pan Klub Foundation; Xul Solar Museum, 1990. 119 p.: bibl., col. ill.

Includes essay by Jorge Luis Borges, prologue by Jacques Lasagne, text by art critic Aldo Pellegrini, and writings by Xul Solar. Highlights collection at Buenos Aires museum that bears his name. Presents convincing picture of the personality and artistic dimension of this Argentine artist (1887–1963), one of the most original innovators of the early 20th-century avant-garde movements.

Bolivia

301 Iturralde L., Luis. Medio siglo de obra arquitectónica, 1931–1981: historia ilustrada del inicio y desarrollo de la arquitectura contemporánea en Bolivia. La Paz: Servicio Gráfico Quipus, 1994. 104 p.: ill. (some col.).

Partial and personal account of beginnings and development of modern architecture in Bolivia, told by one of its more productive architects. Useful for any future, more extensive and complete history of the subject. Includes mostly colored illustrations.

Mercado, Melchor María. Album de paisajes, tipos humanos y costumbres de Bolivia, 1841–1869. See item **2849.**

Chile

302 Bravo, Claudio. Claudio Bravo: visionario de la realidad. Edward J. Sullivan, curador. Santiago: Museo Nacional de Bellas Artes, 1994. 117 p.: bibl., ill. (some col.).

Book-catalog documents Bravo's first exhibit in Chile, which covered the years the artist lived abroad (1961–93). Text by Edward Sullivan. Exceptionally fine printing with simple layout and many color illustrations. Splendid reference on this artist's work.

303 Matta Echaurren, Roberto Sebastián. Matta. Buenos Aires: Der Brücke Ediciones, 1990. 111 p.: bibl., ill. (some col.). (Col. Cuadernos de arte; 9)

Interesting and eccentric compilation in an odd format somewhat reminiscent of Matta's own witty paintings. Consists of several writings by the artist related to ideas that inspired several graphic portfolios (e.g., *Hom'mére IV-Point Dáppui, 1983;* and *Hom'mére V-N'oús, 1985*). Includes color illustrations and Matta's autobiography as well as other texts about him by Marcel Duchamp, André Breton, and Octavio Paz.

304 Pereira Salas, Eugenio. Estudios sobre la historia del arte en Chile republicano. Edición de Regina Claro Tocornal. Santiago: Ediciones de la Univ. de Chile, 1992. 344 p.: bibl., ill. (some col.), index.

Covers the history of Chilean art (1810–1910). Despite author's death in 1979, editor Regina Claro Tocornal and team completed and corrected the original manuscript. The editor warns that work is not exhaustive and chapters are missing. Nevertheless, a commendable attempt to cover a large topic.

305 Rojas Abrigo, Alicia. Historia de la pintura en Chile: libro audio visión. v. 1. Santiago: Impresos Vicuña, 1981- . 1 v.: bibl., ill., slides.

Valuable history of Chilean painting published by the Banco Español-Chile. Vol. 1 covers several centuries, from the foundation of the city of Santiago in 1541 to the influence of the Peruvian Cuzco School of painting through the 1843 arrival in Santiago of influential French painter Raymond August Quinsec Monvoisin. After the establishment of his "academy," he became the official painter of the so-called *Generation of 1842*. Useful work for course use written in simple prose. All illustrations are in b/w, but includes 100 color slides. Excellent addenda consists of notes, slide index, and bibliography.

306 Tacla, Jorge. Jorge Tacla. Edición de Alberto Ibarra Dorado. Garza García, Mexico: Galería Ramis Barquet, 1994. 132 p.: bibl., ill. (some col.).

Consists of work produced from 1990–

93 by Chilean-born artist who lives in New York City. Promotional publication was printed for a show entitled "Internal Biology" held at Ramis Barquet Gallery, Mexico City. Includes biography, bibliography, many color reproductions, and a useful short essay by Dan Cameron.

Colombia

307 Groot, José Manuel. José Manuel Groot, 1800–1878: Biblioteca Luis-Angel Arango, Santa Fe de Bogotá, octubre 1991. Investigación de Beatriz González y Martha Segura. Bogotá: Banco de la República, 1991. 91 p.: bibl., ill. (some col.). (Historia de la caricatura en Colombia; 8)

Well-documented catalog published for exhibition of Groot's paintings, drawings, caricatures, landscapes, and portraits held at Bogotá's Luis Angel Arango Library. An artist of many interests, Groot is also a writer whose collected articles are included as well. Moreover, he is recognized as one of the initiators of the *costumbrista* current in Colombian art. Includes b/w and color reproductions.

308 Le Corbusier en Colombia. Recopilación de Hernando Vargas Caicedo. Bogotá: Cementos Boyacá, 1987. 157 p.: bibl., ill. (some col.).

Well-documented compilation of articles about French architect Le Corbusier's influence on Colombian architecture, urban planning, and Santafé de Bogotá (1945–58). His ideas were far more influential than the actual work he was commissioned to perform in Colombia. Essays place Le Corbusier in context by comparing his work with other architectual projects comissioned by post-1958 Colombian administrations.

309 Obregón, Alejandro. Alejandro Obregón: obras maestras, 1941–1991. Caracas: Centro Cultural Consolidado, 1991. 110 p.: ill. (some col.). (Exposición; 5. Catálogo; 5)

Better than the selection of Obregón's paintings is the professional analysis by José María Salvador who documents this exhibit/catalog. Especially worthwhile is Salvador's own excellent bibliography of his articles about the artist (1944–90s). Illustrated in color.

310 Rubiano Caballero, Germán; Federica Palomero; and María Clara Martínez Rivera. Antonio Barrera: paisajista colombiano. Bogotá: Amazonas Editores, 1993. 158 p.: bibl., ill. (some col.).

Barrera was a Colombian painter whose work became more conventional with the years and thus more commercial and successful among his loyal followers before his death at age 42. This unpretentious study is so well-balanced, organized, and illustrated, one wishes more important Colombian artists could be subjected to the same approach. Rubiano's text and Martínez's careful biography and bibliography should be noted, especially because of the use made of the artist's extensive and detailed personal archive. Provides an accurate perspective on Barrera's contribution to landscape interpretation, a tradition well established in Colombian art since the 19th century.

Ecuador

311 Areán González, Carlos Antonio. Tábara. Quito: Doble O Producciones, 1990. 271 p.: ill. (some col.).

Readable, illuminating study about one of the best painters and strongest personalities in Ecuadorean art. Areán, who is well acquainted with the artist, places Tábara in context of precolumbian art, the Catalonian art scene, 20th-century modernists, and many other influences and experiences that affected Tábara's oeuvre. Color and layout are not up to the standards of Areán's text.

312 Rodríguez Castelo, Hernán. Diccionario crítico de artistas plásticos del Ecuador del siglo XX. Quito: Casa de la Cultura Ecuatoriana Benjamín Carrión, 1992. 419 p.: bibl., ill.

Excellent reference, in a practical softcover format, for those interested in "who's who" in Ecuadorean art. Contains excellent descriptive and biographical notes on works of artists listed despite a few omissions. Should serve as a model for other Latin American countries to produce similar references. Although artists are listed alphabetically, an additional index of all artists mentioned at the end would have further enhanced this valuable work.

313 Rodríguez Castelo, Hernán and **Ramiro Jácome Durango.** Iza, Jácome, Román, Unda: los cuatro mosqueteros. Quito: Fundación Cultural Exedra, 1993. 175 p.: bibl., ill. (some col.).

Four Ecuadorian artists whose work began to appear in 1969 are the subject of this well printed book, which despite its capricious title is interesting for many reasons. One is the account of the activity of the artists and their relation to the art scene in the city of Guayaquil, traditionally an active center for the visual arts in Ecuador, that they helped revitalize. The excessively detailed information (sometimes on the verge of gossip), intertwined with the narration of the artistic life and times of the four artists (provided by Jácome) and the parallels the book establishes with everything that happened in Latin America at the time, makes the book somewhat disorganized; yet it holds the reader's attention. The generous reproductions are good; in the end it is these that provide unity to the work, while differentiating the uneven talent of the four.

Peru

314 Gutiérrez L., Julio G. Sesenta años de arte en el Qosqo, 1927–1988: ensayos, articulos y comentarios. Cusco, Peru: Municipalidad del Qosqo, 1994. 325 p.: ill. (some col.).

Anthology encompasses 100 articles on Cusco's art, mainly of local and regional interest, written by Gutiérrez over the course of his life. Although articles are dated and arranged by subject, the organization is too loose to cover specific subjects, as in the case of six pieces dedicated to José Sabogal, all of which shed little light on an important Peruvian artist. Some articles are too casual and routine and their inclusion does not enhance the book. Few illustrations.

Museo de Arte de Lima. Museo de Arte de Lima: 100 obras maestras = Art Museum of Lima: 100 masterpieces. See item **199.**

Nolte Maldonado, Rosa María Josefa. Qellcay, arte y vida de Sarhua: comunidades campesinas andinas. See *HLAS 55:1044.*

315 Paternosto, César. The stone and the thread: Andean roots of abstract art. Translated by Esther Allen. Austin: Univ. of Texas Press, 1996. 272 p.: bibl., ill., index, map.

Excellent collection of sophisticated

essays for specialists concerning connections and mutual influences among North American, Latin American, and ancient American art. For example, analyzes the significance of precolumbian stone works, geometrical design, and weaving as metaphors. Paternosto's individualistic approach succeeds in illuminating the complex pattern of influences that underlie art and culture. Excellent b/w illustrations.

316 Pintura peruana: década de los 90; homenaje a Juan Acha. México: Museo José Luis Cuevas; Lima: Museo de Arte, 1996. 61 p.: col. ill.

Not a comprehensive catalog of contemporary (i.e., 1990s) Peruvian artists given the editors' preferences and selection criteria. Pays tribute to Acha, the Peruvian critic and historian. Well illustrated in color.

317 Vargas Llosa, Mario; Ana María Escallón; Ricardo Pau-Llosa; and **Judith Alanis.** Fernando De Szyszlo. Edición y recopilación de Ana María Escallón. Bogotá: Ediciones Alfred Wild, 1991. 236 p.: ill., photos.

For those researching De Szyszlo, this book consists of two very useful components: 1) illustrations covering almost 50 years and a veritable visual journey through the work of this prolific Peruvian painter; and 2) a chronology by Judith Alanis that explains, even more accurately than De Szyszlo's words, the motivations behind the painter's images. Edited and compiled by Ana María Escallón, Director of the OAS Museum of the Americas in Washington.

Uruguay

318 Abbondanza, Jorge. Manuel Espínola Gómez. Montevideo: Edición Galería Latina, 1991. 224 p.: ill. (some col.).

Covers Espínola Gómez's multifaceted career of more than 50 years as a painter, draftsman, graphic designer, interior decorator, set designer, etc. Addressed to laymen, not scholars, and published by a commercial gallery.

319 Laroche, Walter E. Pintores uruguayos en España, 1900–1930. Montevideo: Galería de la Matriz, Artes Plásticas, 1992. 192 p.: ill. (some col.).

Montevideo's active commercial art trade is stimulated by its proximity to Buenos Aires. Early modernist movements in both cities share strong links with early 20th-century Spanish painters such as Rusiñol, Sorolla, Anglada Camarasa, Joaquín Mir, etc. Features many Uruguayan artists such as Blanes Viale, Carlos María Herrera, Carmelo de Arzadun, Rafael Barradas, and of course, Torres García. Contains good selection of illustrations (without documentation) to help establish similarities and differences between the Uruguayans and their Spanish counterparts. For specialists.

Venezuela

320 Artistas y cronistas extranjeros en Venezuela, 1825–1899. Caracas: Fundación Galería de Arte Nacional, 1993. 76 p.: bibl., ill. (some col.).

Informative document on exhibition held at Caracas' Fundación Galería de Arte Nacional (March-May 1993) that brought together oils, watercolors, drawings, photographs, and books written by artists of the time (e.g., Camille Pisarro who traveled throughout Venezuela). Introductory texts by Yasminy Pérez Silva and Elías Pino Iturrieta on circumstances and intellectual attitudes of the period are concise, clear, and illuminating.

321 Barroso Alfaro, Manuel. Manuel A. González, 1851–1880, el escultor de Guzmán Blanco. Caracas: Ediciones de la Presidencia de la República, 1993. 154 p.: bibl., ill. (some col.).

Venezuelan presidents have on occasion been great supporters of the arts (e.g., Vicente Gómez, 1920s and Marcos Pérez Jiménez, 1950s). In 1870–77, President Antonio Guzmán Blanco, an admirer of Napoleon III, promoted his favorite sculptor, Manuel González. Between the two, they transformed the face of Caracas. Author's well-documented study describes how the president and sculptor changed the city.

322 Bellermann, Ferdinand Konrad. Ferdinand Bellermann en Venezuela: memoria del paisaje, 1842–1845; diciembre 1991–febrero 1992. Caracas: Consejo Nacional de la Cultura; Embajada de la República Federal de Alemania en Venezuela, 1991. 101 p.: ill. (some col.).

Bellermann visited Venezuela in 1842 as did other German artists stimulated by the scientific writings of explorer Alexander von

Humboldt. Fascinated by the tropics, Beller-mann devoted his three-year visit to painting. This 1991 exhibit, organized by the Fundación Galería de Arte Nacional of Caracas, features more than 100 splendid works on loan from German museums. The tradition of landscape painting in Latin America owes a large debt to Europeans such as Bellermann. Catalog also includes several letters written by Bellermann to a female correspondent, Friederike Moller, which are as revealing as his paintings.

323   **La construcción de la mirada: XX años del Museo de Arte Moderno Jesús Soto, 1973–1993.** Ciudad Bolívar, Venezuela: Fundación Museo de Arte Moderno Jesús Soto; Caracas: Monte Avila Editores, 1993. 159 p.: ill. (some col.).

In 1959, Venezuelan artist Jesús Soto decided to donate a museum in his name to his hometown, Ciudad Bolívar, chiefly because of the national government's lack of support for art in the provinces. In 1973, this exemplary museum was established, designed by architect Carlos Raúl Villanueva and filled with Soto's personal collection (much of it geometric, hard-edged, color field, and kinetic art). Excellent reference source includes valuable illustrations and texts by different contributors.

324   **Diehl, Gaston.** Oswaldo Vigas. Versión libre al español de Juan Liscano. Caracas?: Armitano, 1990? 299 p.: bibl., ill. (some col.), index.

Picasso, Wifredo Lam, and Matta (to a lesser extent) have been great influences on the work of this Venezuelan artist. Vigas' unconditional admiration for them in his youth is corroborated by many photos of all three painters included in the biographical notes. Although like other Venezuelan artists, he briefly followed the 1960s informalist trend, he was inspired by these idols of his adolescence throughout his life. Includes very good color reproductions, but overall this is a work designed for promotion rather than scholarly analysis.

325   **Galería de Arte Nacional (Venezuela).** Donación Miguel Otero Silva: arte venezolano en las colecciones de la Galería de Arte Nacional y el Museo de Anzoátegui. Textos de Manuel Espinoza y Susana Benko. Caracas: Fundación Galeria de Arte Nacional, 1993. 164 p.: bibl., ill. (some col.), index.

Catalog of the Miguel Otero Silva Collection of Venezuelan art from the Galería de Arte Nacional (Caracas) and Museo de Anzoátegui consists mostly of paintings by the most important Venezuelan artists from the 1890s-1970s. Otero Silva was a writer and intellectual devoted to the Venezuelan visual arts. Includes illustrations, clear texts, footnotes, bibliography, and a chronology of Otero Silva's life that reveals his tastes and interests in art collecting.

326   **Lovera, Juan.** Juan Lovera y su tiempo. Venezuela: Ediciones Petróleos de Venezuela, 1981. 111 p.: bibl., ill. (some col.).

Well-focused and balanced work about Juan Lovera (1776–1841), a Venezuelan artist active during the pre- and post-independence periods, a time when most painting in Venezuela was confined to foreigners. Despite Lovera's somewhat rough style, the historical significance of his work and its lack of sophistication imbue his paintings with a certain appeal and validity. This is especially true of his historic canvases.

327   **Los 80: panorama de las artes visuales en Venezuela.** Caracas: Galería de Arte Nacional, 1993? 200 p.: ill. (some col.).

Useful work, sponsored and published by the Galería de Arte Nacional (GAN), covers the Venezuelan art scene of the 1980s. Includes painting, sculpture, video, photography, and ceramics. Also provides month-by-month and year-by-year chronology of events, all of which present a good panorama of Venezuelan art from a domestic and international perspective.

328   **Reverón, Armando.** Armando Reverón, 1889–1954: exposición antológica. Caracas: Fundación Galería de Arte Nacional, 1992. 188 p.: bibl., ill. (some col.).

Excellent catalog exemplifies the professionalism characteristic of most official art institutions in Venezuela, a professionalism attained through staging of exhibitions at home and abroad that promote national artistic values. Well-organized and presented publication consists of various worthy essays and superb photographs that illustrate different and disparate aspects of Reverón's art and life. Includes biographical note and bibliography.

329   **Silva, Carlos.** La obra pictorica de Marcos Castillo. Caracas: Armitano Editores, 1992. 250 p.: bibl., ill. (some col.).

Good book on this Venezuelan Modernist, well documented and illustrated, is the kind of book needed to understand in part the origins of Modernist trends in Venezuela's visual arts. In Castillo's case, one wonders why his ealiest work seems to be much more interesting than that of more recent years. The reason may be the fact that Castillo was one of those artists that, while assimilating new ways in his formative period, became trapped in his own potential and efforts, which at the end did not allow him to evolve with originality. While the book explains very well the development of Castillo's painting from many angles, and includes quotations about his ideas and articles written by himself, for those not well versed in Venezuelan art the book would have been better if it had contained more historic references to his time and his contemporaries, in Venezuela as well as abroad.

330   **Soto, Jesús Rafael.** Jesús Soto: la física, lo inmaterial; Museo de Bellas Artes, Caracas, del 17 de noviembre de 1992 al 14 de febrero de 1993, Museo de Arte Moderno Jesús Soto, Ciudad Bolívar, del 14 de marzo al 16 de mayo de 1993. Caracas: Museo de Bellas Artes; Ciudad Bolívar: Museo de Arte Moderno Jesús Soto, 1992. 124 p.: ill. (some col.).

Soto was one of the leading exponents of Op Art, which, like Kineticism, went through classical and mannerist phases. Soto's contributions are among the most ingenious. This retrospective exhibit covers 40 years (1952–92) of works on "immaterial" elements that exemplify Soto's optical perception and visual interpretations of space, movement, and virtual reality. Useful contribution to the story of Soto, but bound in a difficult-to-handle volume.

Webmuseo de Latinoamérica. See item **34.**

BRAZIL

JOSE M. NEISTEIN, *Executive Director, Brazilian-American Cultural Institute, Washington*

THE OVERWHELMING MAJORITY OF WORKS selected for this volume of the *Handbook,* some 80 percent, focus on the 20th century, including painting, sculpture, printmaking, architecture, photography, caricature, and comic strips. This emphasis reflects the predominant interest of Brazilian art scholars. There are, nonetheless, some remarkable and enlightening works on other periods.

Among theoretical and reference publications worthy of note are a study of the seminal art critic Sergio Milliet (item **332**), a pioneering monograph on Porto Alegre's statues (item **331**), and Ferreira Gullar's challenging and provocative essays (item **333**).

For the colonial period, the encompassing chronicle of the São Bento Monastery in Rio de Janeiro deserves attention (item **338**). Rediscovered essays by Mário de Andrade on religious art in Brazil are perceptive both historically and aesthetically (item **335**). The monograph on the contribution of the Jesuits to the colonial architecture of Rio de Janeiro greatly enriches the bibliography of that particular creative period in Brazilian architecture (item **367**).

Attention is called to the 19th century thanks to a rich book on the Imperial Museum of Petrópolis (item **339**) and several essays on architectural iron structures dating from the 1860s-1920s (item **368**); otherwise the 19th century is not well represented.

The 20th century sparkles with a variety of subjects. The monographs on painter Guignard (item **347**), sculptor Amilcar de Castro (item **351**), and painter Cícero Dias (item **346**) deserve special attention. Aracy Amaral's reappraisal of the "Week of Modern Art of 1922" broadens our critical views of that movement (item **340**). Anésia Pacheco e Chaves' *Cadernos* are a stimulating contribution (item **344**). The book on Krajcberg updates the topic of art and ecological preservation (item **348**). The Washington exhibition of Brazilian Women in the Arts and its catalog (item **341**) were landmark productions. The study of rural native architecture resulted in a groundbreaking work (item **363**). The Contemporary Art Museum of the University of São Paulo shows up as the sole iconographic memory of the São Paulo Biennial (item **381**).

Elise Grunspan's exploration of photographic identity—as seen by both the photographed subject and the photographing power—takes an intellectually fresh, albeit disquieting sociological approach (item **362**). Sebastião Salgado is by now an icon among photographers all over the world (item **361**).

REFERENCE AND THEORETICAL WORKS

331 Doberstein, Arnoldo Walter. Porto Alegre, 1900–1920: estatuária e ideologia. Porto Alegre, Brazil: SMC, 1992. 105 p.: bibl., ill. (Cadernos da memória; 2)

Analyzes the wealth of public statuary produced in Porto Alegre between 1900–20, considering influence of patrons' ideologies on aesthetic themes. Examines impact of positivism on both politics and artistic taste. Also takes into account importance of capitalism and the immigrant work ethic in the development of artistic values in Rio Grande do Sul. Long overdue and welcome addition to the literature.

332 Gonçalves, Lisbeth Rebollo. Sérgio Milliet, crítico de arte. São Paulo: EDUSP; Editora Perspectiva, 1992. 198 p.: bibl., ill. (Col. Estudos; 132. Crítica)

Sérgio Milliet (1898–1966) was one of the finest, most cultured, and most profound art critics Brazil ever produced. His texts on painting, and his *Diário crítico* (see *HLAS 10: 3848, HLAS 11:3383, HLAS 17:2590, HLAS 20:4333,* and *HLAS 48:6366*), were the barometer of the São Paulo Biennial and of Brazilian creativity for decades, especially during the 1950s-60s. This sociological biography underscores his vivid interest in art and society. As an intellectual, he bridged the gap between European and Brazilian society.

333 Gullar, Ferreira. Argumentação contra a morte da arte. Rio de Janeiro: Editora Revan, 1993. 135 p.: ill. (some col.).

A series of essays published mostly in the *Jornal do Brasil* between 1991–92 are even more compelling thanks to their compilation in one volume. Discusses seminal questions of contemporary art. Offers a reappraisal of the values destroyed by the avantgarde movement, while providing a historical perspective and overview of key points of contention. This original contribution includes a variety of topics.

334 Souza, Alcídio Mafra de. Guia dos bens tombados, Santa Catarina. Florianópolis, Brazil: Fundação Catarinense de Cultura; Rio de Janeiro: Expressão e Cultura, 1992. 152 p.: bibl., ill., maps.

Santa Catarina state has a rich cultural patrimony (e.g., churches, chapels, public buildings, military architecture, plantations, and colonial cities from 1500s onward) that is a reminder of the strategic effort to expand the Luso-Brazilian borders to the Río de la Plata. In the 20th century an influx of immigrants from around the world added its imprint to the state's Portuguese heritage. This book looks at the whole picture. Pen-and-ink drawings, descriptions, historical introductions, and bibliography round out this edition.

COLONIAL PERIOD

335 Andrade, Mário de. A arte religiosa no Brasil: crônicas publicadas na *Revista do Brasil* em 1920. Estabelecimento do texto crítico por Claudéte Kronbauer. São Paulo: Experimento; Editora Giordano, 1993. 98 p.: bibl., ill.

Rediscovered essays, first published in 1920, point to some basic historical and artistic issues that gave Catholic art in Brazil its originality. Explores the Portuguese Catholic heritage and the variations that developed in

Bahia, Rio de Janeiro, and Minas Gerais. Perceptive observations. Kronbauer establishes critical text.

336 Arte do marfim: do sagrado e da história na Coleção Souza Lima do Museu Histórico Nacional. Curadoria de Lucila Morais Santos. Rio de Janeiro: Centro Cultural Banco do Brasil, 1993. 83 p.: bibl., col. ill.

Ivory from the Orient first appeared in Brazilian religious carvings in the 18th century. In the begining, ivory was used only to make hands, feet, and faces for images otherwise made of wood. Bahia was the center of Brazilian art production from ivory. The most important Portuguese colonial ivory works, however, were produced in India and Ceylon as a result of missionary activity. This wideranging catalog of an exhibition of over 200 pieces is a fine source for research, study, and comparisons.

337 Carvalho Júnior, Dagoberto Ferreira de. A talha de retábulos no Piauí. Recife, Brazil: Comitê Norte Nordeste de História da Arte, 1990. 115 p.: bibl., ill., maps.

The contributions of the state of Piauí to the history of colonial carved altars and *santos* are virtually unknown even in Brazil. Hence the importance of this mongraph. Departing from the Portuguese models, Carvalho points to some of the sober original features created in Piauí in the 18th and early 19th centuries.

338 Rocha, Mateus Ramalho. O Mosteiro de São Bento do Rio de Janeiro, 1590/1990. Rio de Janeiro: Studio HMF, 1991. 405 p.: bibl., ill. (some col)., index, col. map.

Chronicle of architecture and artistic patrimony of São Bento Monastery in Rio de Janeiro, one of the finest works of architecture in Brazil. Often called "The Anchor of Rio de Janeiro," the church and monastery proper are one of the glorious architectural complexes of Brazil. This scholarly, meticulous book does justice to the beauty of the architecture. A wealth of illustrations depict the main features of Benedictine life.

19TH CENTURY

339 O Museu Imperial. São Paulo: Banco Safra, 1992. 337 p.: bibl., ill. (some col.).

Housed in the former summer residence of Emperor Dom Pedro II in Petrópolis, the Museu Imperial was opened to the public in 1943. Primarily a pictorial work, book also provides a brief history of the palace and a description of the museum. Short explanations accompany excellent photographs of the museum's collections. Of particular interest to researchers are the descriptions of the museum's archival and library holdings that emphasize the First and Second Empires and the initial stages of the Republic. Available resources include textual documents, as well as maps, photographs, and engravings.

20TH CENTURY

340 Amaral, Aracy A. Artes plásticas na Semana de 22. São Paulo: Bovespa, 1992. 254 p.: bibl., ill. (some col.), index.

Written to celebrate 70th anniversary of the Semana de Arte Moderna of 1922, book reappraises that seminal event by focusing on the destructive role of the *modernista* movement. Emphasizes movement's rejection of the superseded past, especially traditionalism and internationalism, and its embrace of the new. A wealth of visual material, rich bibliography, insightful details, and many photographs.

341 Amaral, Aracy A. and **Paulo Herkenhoff.** Ultramodern: the art of contemporary Brazil. Washington: National Museum of Women in the Arts, 1993. 128 p.: bibl., ill. (some col.).

The seminal artistic and intellectual role played by women artists in 20th century Brazil was brought to bear in this remarkable exhibition. Catalog includes excellent essays by Aracy A. Amaral and Paulo Herkenhoff, and a good number of b/w and color reproductions. A variety of aesthetic trends are represented. Works by four generations of artists were assembled.

Barros, Manoel de. O encantador de palavras: poemas escolhidos de Manoel de Barros. See item **3932.**

342 Bracher, Carlos. Do ouro ao aço. Textos de Francisco Iglésias e Angelo Oswaldo de Araújo Santos. Fotos de Rômulo Fialdini. Belo Horizonte, Brazil?: Empresas Belgo-Mineira; Rio de Janeiro?: Salamandra, 1992. 103 p.: ill. (some col.).

Generally considered the great heir

of the landscape painting tradition of Minas Gerais (Guignard, Macier, Inimá), Bracher makes his home in Ouro Preto. His paintings are expressionistic blends of architecture and mountains. Excellent color reproductions of works related to the subject of this book: gold and steel produced in Minas. Includes insightful texts by Francisco Iglésias and Angelo Oswaldo de Araújo Santos and excellent photographs by Rômulo Fialdini.

343   Campos, Jorge Lucio de. A vertigem da maneira: pintura e vanguarda nos anos 80. Rio de Janeiro: Diadorim; Univ. do Estado do Rio de Janeiro, 1993. 125 p.: bibl., ill.

Consideration of Italian *transavanguardia*, Anglo-Saxon "bad painting," German *Neue Wilden*, yuppies as patrons of the arts, and the labyrinth of the postmodern form the core of this book. Loss of power and control is one of the main themes of the author, an incisive cultural analyst and polemicist. The most incisive pages examine the minimalist and conceptual destruction of the fetichist value of the art object. Extensive bibliography.

344   Chaves, Anésia Pacheco e. Cadernos. São Paulo: Árvore da Terra Editora, 1993. 1 v.: ill. (some col.).

In her philosophical text that runs parallel with the photographic iconography of the book, author says: "*Cadernos* makes it posssible to play with the written text and, at the same time, with the image." Book records Anésia's creative itinerary, focusing on her notebooks as aesthetic objects and as a statement of cultural philosophy. An original contribution.

345   DaSilva, Orlando. Viaro: uma permanente descoberta. Curitiba, Brazil: Prefeitura Municipal, Fundação Cultural, 1992. 340 p.: bibl., ill.

Paraná artist Guido Viaro left behind a large and varied expressionistic production of b/w woodblock prints and etchings, both as book illustrations and separate art works. Book is a compilation of almost 200 reproductions with introductions. A good research source for future studies. Includes chronology and bibliography.

346   Dias, Cícero. Cícero Dias: anos 20 = les années 20. Texto de Luis Olavo Fontes. Rio de Janeiro: Editora Index, 1993. 95 p.: ill. (some col.).

Cícero Dias was a prominent Brazilian artist of the 1920s-30s, whose work blended Pernambucan patriarchal life and surrealistic fantasy. Text and reproductions focus on those themes, on Dias' ties to folk art, and on the Brazilian art context of those decades. A fine contribution.

347   Guignard, Alberto da Veiga. Guignard: uma seleção da obra do artista. São Paulo: Museu Lasar Segall, 1992. 70 p.: ill. (some col.).

After studies in Germany, France, Italy, and Switzerland, Guignard reestablished himself in Brazil in 1930 and became one of the finest Brazilian artists ever. An eccentric and reclusive painter, he displayed an orientation somewhat between timid nationalism and Odilon Redon's symbolism, his works turning the mountains of Minas Gerais into an elusive, somewhat fantastic place. This catalog does him justice.

348   Krajcberg, Frans. Imagens do fogo. Rio de Janeiro?: Banco Multiplic, 1992. 67 p.: ill. (some col.).

A naturalized Brazilian citizen born in Poland, Krajcberg works in southern Bahia. In 40 years he has built an artistic universe of forms and materials extracted directly from nature. In his works, beauty and protest walk side by side. He has become a national and international emblem of conservation. Includes chronology, critical evaluation, and reproductions.

349   Locatelli, Aldo. Aldo Locatelli. Redação de Véra Stedile Zattera. Caxias do Sul, Brazil: VSZ Arte e Cultura, 1990. 179 p.: bibl., col. ill.

Aldo Locatelli was born in 1915 in Bergamo, Italy, where he trained as an easel painter and muralist. He emigrated to Brazil shortly after World War II, establishing himself in Porto Alegre where he was influenced by Brazilian academic traditions. This book accuately reflects his highly personal vision, represented in both religious and secular subjects.

350   Martins, Aldemir. Aldemir Martins. São Paulo: Eletricidade de São Paulo S.A., 1992. 93 p.: ill. (some col.).

Born in Ceará in 1922, Martins has lived in São Paulo since 1946. However, he has never ceased to be a *nordestino*, and his paintings, drawings, and prints are filled with *cangaceiros*, animals, and cacti from that region. This small, well-done publication includes a short biography, some critical evaluations, and excellent color reproductions. His works have become an emblem of Brazilian iconography.

351   Naves, Rodrigo *et al.* Amilcar de Castro. Fotografias de Pedro Franciosi. Organização de Alberto Tassinari. São Paulo: Editora Tangente, 1991. 175 p.: bibl., ill. (Col. Goeldi)

The output and significance of Amilcar de Castro is far greater than revealed in previous studies. This book, the most complete monograph to date and an important addition to the Brazilian avant-garde bibliography, contains extensive, excellent b/w documentation on artist's sculptures, drawings, and prints by Pedro Franciosi and seminal essays by Ferreira Gullar, Hélio Oiticica, Rodrigo Naves, and Ronaldo Brito. Clear, conceptual organization by Alberto Tassinari.

352   Portinari, Cândido. Portinari 90 anos. Prefácio de Antonio Callado. Apresentação de Ralph Camargo. Rio de Janeiro: Salamandra Consultoria Editorial, 1993. 167 p.: bibl., ill. (some col.).

This miniretrospective designed to celebrate Portinari's 90th birthday gathered lesser-known paintings, drawings, and watercolors from various periods. Each work selected is described, with references added. Not all selected works were reproduced. Lacks scholarly or even proper critical text.

353   Quirino Campofiorito: exposição retrospectiva comemorativa dos 90 anos do artista. Rio de Janeiro: Museu Nacional de Belas Artes; Niterói, Brazil: Museu Antônio Parreiras, 1992. 69 p.: ill. (some col.).

On Campofiorito's 90th birthday, the Museu Nacional de Belas Artes in Rio put on a retrospective of this Italo-Brazilian artist, from his realistic paintings produced in Rome in early 1930s to 1992, including his metaphysical interlude. Includes chronology, self statement, excerpts of reviews, and introductions. No bibliography.

354   Ribeiro, Angela Brant. 15 pintores contemporâneos brasileiros = 15 Brazilian contemporary painters. Texto e versão inglês de Angela Brant Ribeiro. Edição especial. Rio de Janeiro: Spala Editora, 1991. 207 p.: col. ill.

Color reproductions and introductions to works by a number of contemporary Brazilian painters of various aesthetic representational backgrounds. Includes biographical data and some general artistic evaluations.

355   Rito, Lucia and **Wilson Coutinho.** Coca-Cola: 50 anos com arte = Coca-Cola: 50 years of art. São Paulo?: Coca-Cola, 1992? 54 p.: ill. (some col.).

Twenty-five Brazilian artists reinterpret the Coca-Cola image. Some of the most imaginative artists of the century collaborated on this Brazilian answer to Pop Art. Excellent color reproductions. Insightful essays.

356   Wakabayashi, Kazuo. Wakabayashi. Apresentação de Jayme Mauricio. Rio de Janeiro?: Salamandra, 1992. 143 p.: ill. (some col.).

Born in Japan in 1931, Wakabayashi emigrated in 1961 to Brazil where he became one of the foremost Japanese-Brazilian artists. He has come a long way, from his representational beginnings in Japan to his current pattern paintings that integrate his Japanese traditional background and his Brazilian abstract experience. Sharp color reproductions, biography, and critical contributions by both Jayme Mauricio and Paulo Mendes de Almeida.

FOLK ART

357   Arte no trabalho. São Paulo: Prêmio Editorial, 1991. 95 p.: bibl., col. ill. (Biblioteca EUCATEX de cultura brasileira)

Eclectic work documents Brazilian artistic achievements as reflected in the country's accumulated cultural experience. Reveals a strong syncretism through generations of woodcarvers, potters, knitters, embroiders, metal craftsmen, weavers, basket makers, etc. A wealth of color photographs. Simple, effective introductory texts.

358   Museu de Arte Moderna do Rio de Janeiro. Viva o povo brasileiro: artesanato e arte popular. Rio de Janeiro: Editora Nova Fronteira, 1992. 111 p.: col. ill.

Catalog, enriched by essays by Clarival do Prado Valladares and Marcus Lontra/Mário Jardim, provides color reproductions of the exhibit's main pieces, primarily works in clay and wood. A good source for the study of Brazilian folk art. Exhibition included works by some of the most expressive folk artists of Brazil.

PHOTOGRAPHY

359 Eletricidade de São Paulo S.A. (ELE-TROPAULO). São Paulo: registros 1899–1940 = São Paulo: records 1899–1940. Pesquisa e textos de Benedito Lima de Toledo e José Alfredo Otero Vidigal Pontes. Ed. bilíngüe português-inglês. São Paulo: ELETROPAULO, 1992. 143 p.: ill. (Col. Memóri livros; 3)

ELECTROPAULO has one of the richest available collections of photographs of São Paulo. Approximately 120 selected images depict the development of the megalopolis. Collection could aid those intending to do in-depth research on the period; otherwise, it's a piece of nostalgia.

360 Marques, João Avelino. Os sete dias. Texto de Mário Cláudio. Direcção gráfica de Armando Alves. Porto, Portugal: Figueirinhas, 1992. 1 v.: col. ill.

Photographer Marques says that "Photography is a trilogy for me: the inside of things, the inside of people, and the inside of myself." This unusually beautiful, expressive color photography book captures the core of that trilogy in a tour around the world and inside the artist's soul.

361 Salgado, Sebastião. As melhores fotos = The best photos. São Paulo: Boccato Editores, 1992. 89 p.: bibl., ill. (Col. As melhores fotos; 5)

Today Sebastião Salgado is generally accepted not only as Brazil's best photographer, but as one whose work is among the most profound and meaningful in the world. Pain, guilt, and visual pleasure merge in his work. Book brings together some of his most striking b/w shots in several countries, including Brazil.

362 O sujeito em perigo: identidade foto-gráfica e alteridade no Brasil; do século XIX até 1940. Projeto e pesquisa de Elise Grunspan. Recife, Brazil: Fundação Joaquim Nabuco, Editora Massangana, 1992. 1 v.: ill.

Exhibition questions photographic identity from the viewpoints of both photographed subject and power. Exemplified are the system of poses and their codifications.

Special emphasis on black slaves and photography, and on *cangaceiros* and photography. Elise Grunspan's texts are short but sharp. Special chapter on judiciary photographs.

CITY PLANNING, ARCHITECTURE, AND LANDSCAPE ARCHITECTURE

363 Ferraz, Marcelo Carvalho. Arquitetura rural na Serra da Mantiqueira. Apresentação de Lina Bo Bardi, Antônio Cândido, e Agostinho da Silva. São Paulo?: Quadrante, 1992. 93 p.: col. ill., maps. (Pontos sobre o Brasil)

Very special monograph on Brazilian indigenous architecture includes splendid, eloquent color photographs. In his introduction, Antônio Cândido points out the articulation of landscape, housing, everyday life, habits, games: humanized beauty.

364 Indice de arquitetura brasileira, 1981–1983. Pesquisa e coordenação de Eunice R. Ribeiro Costa. Revisão e colaboração de Emily Ann Labaki Agostinho. São Paulo: Univ. de São Paulo, Faculdade de Arquitetura e Urbanismo, Serviço de Biblioteca e Informação, 1992. 126 p.

Source of bibliographical references from 1981–83 not only for Brazilian architecture but also for city planning, museum exhibitions, and other architecture-related projects during the same period. Entries are arranged in alphabetical order.

365 Katinsky, Júlio Roberto. Brasília em três tempos: a arquitetura de Oscar Niemeyer na capital. Rio de Janeiro: Editora Revan, 1991. 79 p.: ill. (some col.).

Overview of Niemeyer's creative process in Brasília is divided into sections: "Tempos de Juscelino;" "Tempos de Ditadura (1964–1984)" and "Tempos de José Aparecido." Blends history, aesthetics, and technology. Adequate b/w photos and sketches. See also item **366.**

366 Niemeyer, Oscar. Meu sósia e eu. Versão para o inglês de Dina Laver e Adriana Reiche. Rio de Janeiro: Editora Revan, 1992. 121 p.: bibl., ill. (some col.).

Niemeyer gives a report on his architectural output. He also elaborates on city planning, sculpture, design, and drawing. He reminisces about his political activities and elaborates on his ties to the Partido Comunista Brasileiro. Bibliography, photographs, and plans complete this excellent source of research. See also item **365**.

367 Pontifícia Universidade Católica do Rio de Janeiro. A forma e a imagem: arte e arquitetura jesuítica no Rio de Janeiro colonial. Rio de Janeiro: Pontifícia Univ. Católica do Rio de Janeiro, s.d. 218 p.: bibl., ill., photos, maps.

In-depth monograph on contributions of the Jesuits to colonial architecture of Rio de Janeiro state. Of special interest to this section are the chapters "O Solar do Colégio," "A Espacialidade Missioneira Jesuítica no Brasil Colonial," and "As Igrejas Jesuíticas Fluminenses." Includes bibliography, b/w photos, drawings, and plans.

368 Seminário Arquitetura do Ferro, *Belém, Brazil, 1992.* Arquitetura do ferro: memória e questionamento. Organização de Jussara da Silveira Derenji. Belém, Brazil: Univ. Federal do Pará; Edições CEJUP, 1993? 184 p.: bibl., ill. (some col.), map.

Essays are from *Anais* of the Seminário Arquitetura do Ferro sponsored by the Univ. Federal do Pará. In addition to essays on past and present iron architectural structures in Brazil, includes studies of similar structures in Chile, Costa Rica, US, and some European countries. Blends technology and aesthetics. Many photographs in color and b/w illustrate the diversity.

369 Seminário Natureza e Prioridades de Pesquisa em Arquitetura e Urbanismo, *São Paulo, 1990.* Anais. São Paulo: USP/FAU/ Comissão de Pesquisa; FUPAM; FAPESP, 1990. 258 p.: ill.

Essays are grouped under following topics: 1) "A Interdisciplinidade na Pesquisa em Arquitetura e Urbanismo;" 2) "Pesquisa Básica, Pesquisa Aplicada e Metodologia de Pesquisa em Arquitetura e Urbanismo;" and 3) "Prioridades de Pesquisa e Problemas Estruturais da Sociedade Brasileira." Excellent research source.

AFRO-BRAZILIAN AND INDIAN TRADITIONS

370 Siqueira Júnior, Jaime Garcia. Arte e técnicas kadiwéu. São Paulo: Secretaria Municipal de Cultura, Prefeitura do Municí-pio de São Paulo, 1993? 125 p.: bibl., ill. (some col.), maps (some col.).

The Caduveo have always made ceramics. Their art has been collected, studied, and displayed for over a century by scholars such as Guido Boggiani (1890s) and Levi-Strauss (1935). Both studied the patterns of Kadiwéu body paintings. This monograph discusses social and historical aspects of Kadiwéu art, and includes drawings, photographs, reproductions, a bibliography, and some learned essays.

371 Varela Torrecilla, Carmen. Catálogo de arte plumario amazónico del Museo de América. Madrid: Dirección General de Bellas Artes y Archivos, Ministerio de Cultura, 1993?. 173 p.: bibl., ill. (some col.).

Because many of the pieces displayed in this catalog belong to extinct tribes, identification was often difficult and sometimes impossible. Catalog is a first-rate source for the study of featherwork artifacts from the Amazon Basin. Includes excellent color photographs, detailed texts, technical descriptions, and sketched illustrations.

MISCELLANEOUS

372 Banco Sudameris Brasil. A metrópole e arte. São Paulo: Prêmio Editorial, 1992. 127 p.: bibl., ill. (some col.). (Arte e cultura; 13)

Focuses on art works inspired by and made for the big Brazilian cities. Records the most relevant modern, stimulating, provocative works found in the streets and plazas of Rio, São Paulo, and other urban centers, from the turn of the century to present day. Analytical texts, interviews, and visually rich images make this publication unique. Includes chronology.

373 Bardi, Pietro Maria. História do MASP. São Paulo: Instituto Quadrante, 1992. 175 p.: ill. (some col.). (Pontos sobre o Brasil)

The Museu de Arte de São Paulo has the finest collection of old masters and impressionist and post-impressionist painters in South America, as well as an excellent 20th-century collection. Also supportive of performing arts, the museum is one of Brazil's main cultural centers. In this book, one of the museum's founders discusses its history.

374 **Belluzzo, Ana Maria de Moraes.** Voltolino e as raízes do modernismo. São
Paulo: Editora Marco Zero; Programa Nacional do Centenário da República e Bicentenário da Inconfidência Mineira, MCT/CNPq;
Secretaria de Estado da Cultura de São Paulo,
1992. 278 p.: ill.

Voltolino was a character created by
Lemmo Lemmi, a significant caricaturist of the
Old Republic and very popular in São Paulo.
Art and daily life, and art and history, are the
themes of artist's work, which was published
by *O Pirralho* and *Revista Ilustrada* from
1880s-early 1900s. Excellent research places
drawings in the general context of society.

375 **Costa, Janete.** Interiores. Fotos de
Mário Grisolli. Rio de Janeiro: Editora
Index, 1993. 116 p.: col. ill.

By blending the highest international
standards and Brazil's unique visual taste,
Janete Costa has made a name for herself as
one of Brazil's most imaginative interior designers. This book is the best reference to her
work of the past 30 years, thanks to the quality color photographs by Mário Grisolli and
texts by Clarival do Prado Valladares, Roberto
Burle Marx *et al.*

376 **O desejo na Academia: 1847–1916.** São
Paulo: Secretaria de Estado da Cultura,
Pinacoteca, 1991. 130 p.: bibl., ill. (some col.).

Contains illustrations of works by Brazilian artists schooled in the 19th-century
tradition in Rio de Janeiro and eventually
abroad. Exhibition focused on the nude and
eroticism. Broad variety of essays, a bibliography, and many color reproductions place
the catalog in an unusual niche among Brazilian art history sources.

377 **Morais, Frederico.** Azulejaria contemporânea no Brasil. v. 2. São Paulo: Editoração, Publicações e Comunicações, 1990.
1 v.: bibl., col. ill.

The enduring Portuguese tile tradition
is alive and well in Brazil, as is a more contemporary Brazilian azulejos style. Chapter
titles are: "Bahia: o Artista como Herói;"
"Pernambuco: a História como Tema;" "Paraíba;" "Integração com a Arquitetura;" and
"Uma Estética Kitsch." Includes many illustrations and an English abstract.

378 **Nery, João Elias.** Humor gráfico brasileiro nas décadas de 70 e 80. (*Comun.
Soc.*, 12:20, dez. 1993, p. 49–60)

The comic books of Henfil and Angeli
are considered here as models of Brazilian
comic book production in those decades.
While in the 1970s resistance to the dictatorship was the main subject, in the 1980s common sense and individual behavior were the
focus. Graphic humor, and political and be-
havioral critique.

379 **Silva, José Antonio da.** J.A. Silva: José
Antonio da Silva; 5 décadas de arte
brasileira = J.A. Silva: José Antonio da Silva;
5 decades of Brazilian art. São Paulo: Lloyds
Bank, 1992. 72 p.: col. ill.

José Antonio da Silva ranks among the
best Brazilian naive painters. Fifty years'
worth of his work is reproduced here. These
texts, however, serve only as general introductions; J.A. da Silva still awaits a scholarly
appraisal.

380 **Silveira, Nise da.** O mundo das imagens. São Paulo: Editora Ática, 1992.
165 p.: bibl., ill. (some col.).

Of special interest are the essays and
reports on the relationship between art and
schizophrenia. Includes bibliography and
many appropriate illustrations.

381 **Universidade de São Paulo. Museu
de Arte Contemporânea.** O Museu de
Arte Contemporânea da Universidade de São
Paulo. São Paulo: Banco Safra, 1990. 319 p.:
ill. (some col.).

The Museu de Arte Contemporânea of
the Univ. de São Paulo has one of the most diversified national and international art collections in Brazil. Texts demonstrate, among
other things, that this unique collection is
the sole iconographic memory of the São
Paulo Biennial. The Zanini and Pfeifer administrations are exhaustively studied and major
works are highlighted. Chronology and name
index are included, but no bibliography.

JOURNAL ABBREVIATIONS

Bol. Inst. Riva-Agüero.   Boletín del Instituto
Riva-Agüero. Pontificia Univ. Católica del
Perú. Lima.

Comun. Soc.   Comunicação e Sociedade. Instituto Metodista do Ensino Superior. São
Paulo.

Hist. Cult./Lima.   Historia y Cultura. Museo Nacional de Historia. Lima.

J. Decor. Propag. Arts. The Journal of Decorative and Propaganda Arts. Wolfson Foundation of Decorative and Propaganda Arts. Miami, Fla.

Lab. Arte. Laboratorio de Arte: Revista de Departmento de Historia del Arte. Univ. de Sevilla. Sevilla, Spain.

Nariz Diablo. Nariz del Diablo. Centro de Investigaciones y Estudios Socio-Económicos. Quito.

Rev. UNITAS. Revista UNITAS. Unión Nacional de Instituciones para el Trabajo de Acción Social. La Paz.

HISTORY

ETHNOHISTORY
Mesoamerica

ROBERT HASKETT, *Associate Professor of History, University of Oregon*
STEPHANIE WOOD, *Assistant Professor of History, University of Oregon*

THE FLOW OF HIGH QUALITY ethnohistorical literature continues unabated, much of it still energized by the marshalling of funds and the influence of debates responding to the 1992 Columbian Quincentenary. In seeking more nuanced interpretations of indigenous voices and visions of the past, the scholars represented below continue to persevere in the expansion of intellectual horizons, ranging ever more widely in terms of questions asked, topics investigated, methodologies employed, and geographic areas covered.

This is apparent, first, in a solid body of investigations devoted to peoples and places that have received scant or only episodic attention until recent years. The inhabitants of western and northern Mexico are featured in several scholarly treatments, studies which consciously or implicitly establish links with cultures inhabiting regions more traditionally considered to be part of Mesoamerica; Charlotte M. Gradie's "Discovering the Chichimecas" (item **452**) and José Luis Mirafuentes Galván's "Augustín Aschuhul" (item **499**) are excellent examples. Looking south to the Soconusco region, Sandra L. Orellana's *Ethnohistory of the Pacific Coast* (item **504**) alerts us to the importance of this pivotal region in the overall Mesoamerican socioeconomic scheme. Cultural exchange is an explicit theme in several other works that explore the implications of the colonial-era colonization of sedentary indigenous people from the center in areas such as the Bajío, seen most notably in David Wright's "La Conquista del Bajío (item **550**), and in Andrea Martínez Baracs' "Colonizaciones Tlaxcaltecas" (item **493**).

Having said this, we must hasten to add that the great bulk of scholarship reviewed for this issue remains oriented towards the peoples of central and southeastern Mesoamerica such as the Maya, but above all the Nahuas (and within this group the Mexica/Aztecs), both before and after the conquest. Yet there is a perceptible shift in focus away from imperial capitals, ceremonial centers, and ruling elites toward inquiries whose goal is to arrive at a better understanding of life in the appendages of empire, away from the center, and gauging not only the influence of state systems on these places, but the impact of the "periphery" on the "core." For the Nahuas, articles noted below in *Economies and polities of the Aztec realm* (item **431**) and *Prehispanic domestic units in western Mesoamerica* (see *HLAS 55:146*) are important examples of this trend. Susan Kellogg's several contributions examine more thoroughly "domestic" issues for the imperial capital itself (items **476** and **477**). Among Maya scholars, too, we observe a tendency to move away from a preoccupation with elites and ceremonial centers to look more closely at hinterlands and more diverse layers of society; here, archaeological studies with true ethnohistorical significance that were carried out by Nancy Gonlin (item **450**), Anncorinne Freter (item **441**), Thomas R. Hester and Harry J. Shafer (item **462**), and Eleanor King and Daniel Potter (item **478**) are worthy of special attention.

Interest in the complex nature and meanings of prehispanic deities has not waned; readers will find references to two different encyclopedic dictionaries devoted to this topic below (items **498** and **494**). Jacques Lafaye's insights into the cultural implications of the hispanized Aztec deity Quetzalcoatl and the Indianized Virgin of Guadalupe captured international attention two decades ago and continue to leave their mark on more recent scholarship. The full meaning of both of these key concepts in Mesoamerican ethnohistory may forever elude definitive interpretations, since the documentary record is frustratingly incomplete. Yet the debates are rich and informative, and have spawned some very meticulous research efforts, most notably those by Florescano (items **439** and **440**), Stenzel (item **531**), Poole (item **510**), and Noguez (item **502**).

Attempts to decipher the coded messages sent by Quetzalcoatl and Guadalupe can be situated in a persistent stream of inquiries into Mesoamerican belief systems. Carrasco's anthology, *The imagination of matter* (item **470**), and his intriguingly entitled article "Give Me Some Skin" (item **409**) are indicative of revisionist, multidisciplinary approaches asking new questions of well-known sources. And just as we find Poole probing the real meaning of "Tonantzin" and Poole and Jeanette Peterson exploring postconquest native responses to the Virgin of Guadalupe (item **509**), we see a variety of studies about what became of native practices after the Spaniards introduced Christianity and how indigenous peoples interpreted Catholicism.

Two notable themes have emerged in a number of recent works on colonial religiosity. One is the recognition that indigenous people and Spaniards had a shared cultural experience—some have used the term "dialogue"—in which both sides contributed to the formation of a kind of indigenous Catholicism; Jacques Lafaye spoke to this topic in his presentation for the 47th International Congress of Americanists (see also Peterson's essay in the conference proceedings, *Five Hundred Years after Columbus,* item **437**). William B. Taylor made a similar argument in a Quincentenary talk he gave that was later published by Robert Dash (item **535**). This first theme leads logically to the second, that indigenous Christianity was/is more complex than earlier treatments of "syncretism" indicate. George Baudot spoke in the tradition of Louise Burkhart's *The slippery earth* at the 47th International Congress of Americanists on Nahuatl usage and terminology for Christian demons (see Baudot's article in *Five Hundred Years after Columbus,* item **437**), which is carried over to his article "Nahuas y Españoles" (item **391**), while Fernando Cervantes elsewhere has undertaken similar studies (items **412** and **413**). Scholars will find related articles in the valuable compilation entitled *Chipping away on earth* (item **416**).

The persistence of indigenous ritual in the colonial context is explored in studies by Richard Greenleaf (item **454**), Ana Luisa Izquierdo (item **472**), Serge Gruzinski (item **455**), and Nancy Farriss (item **436**). S.L. Cline (item **418**) provides a rare glimpse of the process of religious indoctrination at the local level, revealing the sluggishness with which baptism and Christian marriage took hold in Morelos in the late 1530s. Robert Haskett's study of the same region in a much later period (item **460**) uncovers revealing tensions in relations between Spanish priests and indigenous parishioners.

Indigenous thought is the centerpiece of an extremely significant group of studies, both in terms of number and worth, dedicated to the publication and analysis of codices and native language records, both precontact and colonial. Some are excellent new entries in the venerable body of high quality facsimiles of codices with commentary (e.g., Bruce Love's edition of the *Paris Codex,* (item **490**); a stunning new edition of the *Matrícula de tributos,* (item **496**); and Constanza Vega's rendering of the *Códice Azoyú 1,* (item **545**)). Yet we are most struck by a cluster of innovative inquiries into the meanings of history, myth, and visions of the past, present, and future extrapolated from a variety of records in the indigenous tradition. Studies of Quetzalcoatl and Tula, such as the valuable piece by Emily Umberger (item **542**), have contributed much. Sure to be influential are Enrique Florescano's *Memory, myth, and time in Mexico* (item **438**, an updated English translation of his earlier *Memoria mexicana*), Serge Gruzinski's *Conquest of Mexico* (item **455**), Joyce Marcus' *Mesoamerican writing systems* (item **491**), Elizabeth Boone and Walter Mignolo's *Writing without words* (item **551**), and Bruce Byland and John Pohl's skillful application of the techniques of epigraphy, art history, ethnohistory, archaeology, and ethnology in their study of Mixtec codices, *In the realm of 8 deer* (item **405**). James Lockhart's *We people here* (item **547**) is the most sophisticated reading yet of major indigenous texts connected with the Spanish conquest of the Mexica.

Moving beyond the codices and into the evolving Spanish era are notable new studies of indigenous language records, sometimes accompanied with transcriptions and translations of the originals and often seeking indigenous views of the past. Useful examples include Jorge Klor de Alva's "El Discurso Nuahua" (item **479**), a special issue of the *UCLA Historical Journal* entitled "Indigenous Writing in the Spanish Indies" (item **541**), Gordon Brotherston's *Book of the Fourth World* (item **401**), S.L. Cline's *Book of tributes* (item **396**), and *Xalisco, la voz de un pueblo* (item **407**). A hint of the rich future of computer-borne publication and analysis is given by Marc Thouvenot's fascinating new analytical computer database program *TEMOA* (item **538**), which is coupled with the transcription of a growing number of indigenous language records. We expect that many scholars will be excited by the possibilities for detailed and comprehensive searching for terms, phrases, and content offered by this tool. Also promising, in the electronic vein, are the Internet listservs AZTLAN (to subscribe, write listserv@ulkyvm.louisville.edu) and NAHUAT-L (listproc@listserv.umt.edu), with book reviews, meeting reports, and a great variety of discussion related to Mesoamerican ethnohistory.

We note as well a range of other studies focused on various topics connected to the indigenous experience with colonialism in Mesoamerica, such as a cluster of investigations centered around the analysis of the Canek Manuscript, a description of an encounter between Spanish priests and the resurgent Itzá "kingdom" of the Petén (items **458, 473**, and **508**). Durable topics such as the conquest of Mexico (items **417** and **428**), epidemic disease (items **400** and **497**), and land and agrarian issues (items **444** and **445**) are given interesting new twists. Susan Kellogg's "Hegemony out of Conquest" (item **475**) and *Law and the transformation of Aztec culture* (item **476**) trace the contours of cultural contact, conflict, and change as the central Mexican Nahuas faced the emerging colonial system.

During the last biennium, we noted a rise in the number of treatments of indigenous women before and after the Spanish conquest. Our present sample includes several studies in this genre of real worth, especially the contributions in a special issue of the journal *Ethnohistory* entitled "Women, Power, and Resistance in Colonial Mesoamerica" (item **434**), but also Frances Karttunen's revisionist assessment of La Malinche (item **474**) and Stephanie Wood's investigation of rural Nahua women of the Toluca Valley (item **549**). Nonetheless, there is a discernible, and quite welcome, tendency in the body of books and articles we have reviewed for this issue to find more authors putting women's history into ethnohistory, by considering issues of gender, sexuality, and even rape as integral elements in broader sorts of inquiries; this can be seen in much of Kellogg's work (e.g., item **476**), as well as in Restall (item **514**), Mirafuentes Galván (item **499**), and Haskett (item **460**), to name a few of the more obvious examples.

We have every confidence that the trends and tendencies we have discussed here will persist over the next few years, and that we will be able to report in *HLAS 58* on many fresh new insights offered by these and other scholars.

382 Alcina Franch, José. Calendario y religión entre los zapotecos. México: Univ. Nacional Autónoma de México, Instituto de Investigaciones Históricas, 1993. 457 p., 35 p. of plates: appendix, bibl., ill. (Serie de culturas mesoamericanas; 3)

Compilation of author's important work on Zapotec ritual and calendar, based on nearly 100 17th-century Zapotec-language calendrical documents (some of which are transcribed without commentary in a lengthy appendix) associated with a 1704 anti-idolatry investigation staged in the Villa Alta region. Using these documents, witness testimony, and other sources, the author presents a comprehensive treatment which, though dated in some ways, will still be of interest to ethnohistorians.

383 Anawalt, Patricia Rieff. Riddle of the emperor's cloak. (*Archaeology/New York*, 46:3, May/June 1993, p. 30–36, facsims., ill., map, photo)

Enlightening though brief analysis of the meaning of the blue tie-dye design of the imperial cloak of Aztec rulers. The author carefully explains how she arrived at her conclusions, using techniques ranging from the analysis of Nahuatl terms, pictorial representations, and historical texts to the replication of Aztec techniques by modern-day dyers. She believes that the resulting design signaled links between the ruling elite and Toltec forebears.

384 Anderson, Arthur J.O. and **Wayne Ruwet.** Sahagún's *Manual del Christiano*: history and identification. (*Estud. Cult. Náhuatl*, 23, 1993, p. 17–45)

Commentary on four folios of text identified as a fragment of the *Manual* (c. 1578) conveying lessons on proper comportment of men and women in marriage. Some echoes of indigenous traditions are evident, as is Sahagún's effort to undermine them with Catholic mores. This important text is presented in transcription and English translation.

385 Armillas, Pedro. Pedro Armillas: vida y obra. Edición de Teresa Rojas Rabiela. México: Instituto Nacional de Antropología e Historia; Centro de Investigaciones y Estudios Superiores en Antropología Social, 1991. 2 v.

Pays homage to the late archaeologist with biographical and career sketches, and an anthology of major articles, the bulk dating from 1944–69, several originally in English, most from very diverse organizations. Includes studies of archaeology (Teotihuacán, Tula), deities (Quetzalcoatl, Tlaloc), the "ecology of colonialism," and, especially, Mesoamerican cultural development.

386 Arzápalo Marín, Ramón. The esoteric and literary language of Don Joan Canul in the *Ritual of the Bacabs*. (*New Sch.*, 10, 1986, p. 145–158, bibl.)

Preliminary linguistic discussion of this lengthy and important Maya manuscript. Important, too, for the careful establishment of an appropriate methodology of analysis.

387 Aztec imperial strategies. Frances F. Berdan et al. Washington, D.C. : Dumbarton Oaks Research Library and Collection, 1996. viii, 392 p. : ill., maps.

Important collection of articles by well-known scholars which in combination stress the importance of "place oriented studies" as correctives to the more typical homogenized, urban-oriented, and Valley of Mexico-centered depiction of the Aztec empire. The impressive work contained in this excellent volume, which includes a series of detailed appendices centered on provincial description and organization, presents new interpretations of the extent of the Aztecs domains, imperial strategies, economic relations between core and provinces, and the significance of artistic expression and writing systems in the socio-political ideology of the empire. Here it is worth listing the contents of the anthology, which is divided into three main sections: Forward by Elizabeth Hill Boone, Introduction by Michael E. Smith and Frances F. Berdan; Part I: The Empire's Center; "Political Organization of the Central Provinces," by Mary G. Hodge; "The Basin of Mexico Market System and the Growth of Empire," by Richard E. Blanton; "Art and Imperial Strategy," by Emily Umberger. Part II: The Outer Provinces: "The Tributary Provinces," by Frances F. Berdan; "The Strategic Provinces," by Michael E. Smith; "Aztec Presence and Material Remains in the Outer Provinces," by Emily Umberger; "Manuscript Painting in Service of Imperial Policy," by Elizabeth Hill Boone. Part III: Imperial Strategies: "Imperial Strategies and Core-Periphery Relations," by Frances F. Berdan and Michael E. Smith; "A Consideration of Causality in the Growth of Empire: A Comparative Perspective," by Richard E. Blanton; "Appendix 1, Data on Political Organization of the Aztec Empire's Central Provinces," by Mary G. Hodge and Richard E. Blanton; "Appendix 2: Data on Market Activities and Production Specializations of Tlatoani Centers," by Richard E. Blanton and Mary G. Hodge; "Appendix 3: Material Remains in the Central Provinces," by Emily Umberger; and "Appendix 4: Province Descriptions," by Michael E. Smith and Frances F. Berdan.

388 Baquedano, Elizabeth and **Michel Graulich.** Decapitation among the Aztecs: mythology, agriculture and politics, and hunting. (*Estud. Cult. Náhuatl*, 23, 1993, p. 163–177, bibl., ill., photo)

Using ethnohistorical and archaeological records, the authors reconstruct the important role of decapitation in rituals designed among other things to guarantee the fertility of the earth and, hence, abundant agricultural harvests, as well as the fertility of the animals which will be hunted. For archaeologist's comment see *HLAS* 55:77.

389 Batalla Rosado, Juan José. El Códice Tudela: análisis histórico y formal de su primera sección. (*An. Mus. Am.*, 1, 1993, p. 121–142, bibl., graph, photos, tables)

Preliminary study of the first 10 folios of this important 16th-century codex, intended as the first of a projected series of articles. Here the author is most interested in

establishing the true pagination of the text, which has been confused over the years.

390 Batalla Rosado, Juan José. Los *tlacuiloque* del Códice Borbónico: análisis iconográfico de los signos calendáricos. (*Estud. Hist. Soc. Econ. Am.*, 10, 1993, p. 9–24, ill., tables)

Analysis of calendrical symbols in the codex, the style of which suggests that three scribes participated in their creation.

391 Baudot, Georges. Nahuas y españoles: dioses, demonios y niños. (*in* De palabra y obra en el Nuevo Mundo. v. 1, Imágenes interétnicas. Edición de Miguel León-Portilla *et al.* Madrid: Siglo Veintiuno Editores, 1992, p. 87–113)

Densely argued analysis of Nahua and Spanish concepts of the "other" as they operated in the initial cultural encounter that was part of the conquest of Mexico. Author adds fuel to the debate on whether or not the Mexica believed the Spaniards were gods by arguing that the Iberians were so radically beyond any prior indigenous experience or conceptualization that they were situated in the sacred, rather than the secular, world.

392 Bechtloff, Dagmar. La formación de una sociedad intercultural: las cofradías en el Michoacán colonial. (*Hist. Mex.*, 43:2, oct./dic. 1993, p. 251–263, bibl.)

Brief, but well-developed, look at how indigenous *cofradías* in Pátzcuaro served to acculturate and, at the same time, to preserve indigenous society in the face of external pressures. Argues that in Pátzcuaro *cofradías* played a vital intermediary role between indigenous elites, Spanish society, and the colonial economy.

393 Berdan, Frances F. Trauma and transition in sixteenth-century central Mexico. (*in* The meeting of two worlds: Europe and the Americas, 1492–1650. Edited by Warwick Bray. Oxford, England: Oxford Univ. Press; The British Academy, 1993, p. 163–195, bibl., ill., maps)

Comprehensive synthetic overview based on recent ethnohistorical work by Berdan and other important authors explains how central Mexican indigenous societies weathered the Spanish conquest. Author demonstrates that despite a certain amount of trauma, indigenous peoples were able gradually to create a new colonial culture which continued to preserve many traits drawn from the past.

394 Berlin, Heinrich; Gonzalo de Balsalobre; and Diego de Hevia y Valdés. Idolatría y superstición entre los indios de Oaxaca. 2. ed. corr. y augm. México: Ediciones Toledo, 1988. 153 p.

Superior 2nd ed. of 17th-century curate's account of indigenous religious practices, plus the bishop's recommendations regarding future investigation and prosecution of "idolatry." Berlin ably expands Balsalobre's revelations with rich Inquisition material (AGN Mexico) about the same Oaxacan community. Contains fascinating incidental information on indigenous literacy and book possession.

395 Bonaccorsi V., Nélida. El trabajo obligatorio indígena en Chiapas, siglo XVI: Los Altos y Soconusco. México: Univ. Nacional Autónoma de México, Centro de Investigaciones Humanísticas de Mesoamérica y el Estado de Chiapas, 1990. 72 p.: bibl.

An informed synthesis of published secondary studies and archival records (largely royal orders now in Guatemala City) on the institutions of slavery, encomienda, and repartimiento as they applied to Highland and Lowland indigenous communities of what is now Chiapas.

396 The book of tributes: early sixteenth-century Nahuatl censuses from Morelos (Museo de Antropología e Historia, Archivo Histórico, Colección antigua, vol. 549). Edited and translated by S.L. Cline. Los Angeles: UCLA Latin American Center Publications, Univ. of California, 1993. 313 p.: bibl. (Nahuatl studies series; 4. UCLA Latin American studies; 81)

Painstaking transcription and translation of detailed censuses from the communities of Huitzillan and Quauhchichinollan in the Cuernavaca region. Author's informative commentary elucidates the very rich contents of these documents and significantly expands our understanding of Nahua social and familial structure, household size and composition, mechanisms of land tenure, and gendered ordering of labor.

397 Boone, Elizabeth Hill. Aztec pictorial histories: records without words. (*in* Writing without words: alternative literacies in Mesoamerica and the Andes. Durham, N.C.: Duke Univ. Press, 1994, p. 50–76, bibl., facsims.)

Careful discussion of the main genres of late-precontact Mexica historical texts. Author demonstrates that there was no single method used to retell events and that the particular form of discourse used was directly related to the kind of history being recorded. A work of considerable interpretive significance.

398 Boone, Elizabeth Hill. The painting styles of the manuscripts of the Borgia Group. (*in* Circumpacifica: Festschrift für Thomas S. Barthel. Frankfurt am Main: P. Lang, 1990, p. 35–54, bibl., facsims., ill.)

Thoughtfully executed analysis of several features of the group of codices long know as the "Borgia Group." By studying the human figures and day signs, as well as larger iconographic elements, the author demonstrates that the group should not be regarded as a single unit, but can rather be broken into two stylistically related groups. This realization has important implications for the continuing study of the provenance of these documents.

Bretos, Miguel A. La provincia de San Joseph de Yucatán: conversión y arquitectura religiosa en el país de los Mayas. See item **1127.**

399 Brooks, Francis J. Motecuzoma Xocoyotl, Hernán Cortés, and Bernal Díaz del Castillo: the construction of an arrest. (*HAHR,* 75:2, May 1995, p. 149–183)

Deconstruction of key Spanish and indigenous accounts offers an aggressively revisionist interpretation of the "arrest" of Montezuma by Cortés.

400 Brooks, Francis J. Revising the conquest of Mexico: smallpox, sources, and populations. (*J. Interdiscip. Hist.,* 24:1, Summer 1993, p. 1–29, graphs, tables)

Determinedly critical reevaluation of the 1520 smallpox pandemic which is believed to have facilitated the Spanish defeat of the Mexica. The author questions the validity of earlier interpretations of available primary sources, concluding that mortality was not as severe as is usually assumed. See item **497** for a critique of Brook's position.

401 Brotherston, Gordon. Book of the fourth world: reading the Native Americas through their literature. Cambridge; New

York: Cambridge Univ. Press, 1992. 478 p., 24 p. of plates: bibl., ill. (some col.), index, maps.

Significant addition to ethnohistorical literature explores often ephemeral boundaries between "history" and "myth" in native-language records. While the book does not deal exclusively with Mesoamerica, the analysis of Nahuatl and Maya texts forcefully demonstrates the fallacy of applying uncritically "western" definitions of these concepts. Author is especially concerned with discussing how European stories (such as Aesop's fables) came to be translated into indigenous languages and how European culture entered into the pre-existing indigenous literary systems. For literary critic's comment see *HLAS 54:3462.*

402 Brotherston, Gordon. Tula: touchstone of the Mesoamerican era. (*New Sch.,* 10, 1986, p. 19–39, bibl., ill., map)

Intriguing and well-supported argument against taking Tula, Hidalgo too literally as the sole geographic location of the cultural wellspring "Tollan." Brotherston posits the existence of other "Tulas" which contributed to the cultural evolution of Mesoamerica, a process that was collapsed in time and space by later central Mexican chroniclers.

403 Brumfiel, Elizabeth M. Factional competition in complex society. (*in* Domination and resistance. Boston: Allen & Unwin, 1989, p. 127–139)

Excellent article demonstrates how precontact central Mesoamerican elites negotiated the past to legitimate and display their present status and to form factional coalitions by manipulating an array of symbols and ritual display.

404 Burkhart, Louise M. The voyage of Saint Amaro: a Spanish legend in Nahuatl literature. (*Colon. Lat. Am. Rev.,* 4:1, 1995, p. 29–57)

Penetrating interpretation of two Nahuatl versions of the life of a minor saint uncovers transformation of a thoroughly Christian message into a "hybrid" text permeated with indigenous cultural values. Includes composite English-language translation of both manuscripts.

Butzer, Karl W. and **Barbara J. Williams.** Addendum: three indigenous maps from New Spain dated ca. 1580. See *HLAS 55:2362.*

405 Byland, Bruce E. and **John M.D. Pohl.** In the realm of 8 Deer: the archaeology of the Mixtec codices. Norman: Univ. of Oklahoma Press, 1994. 292 p.: bibl., ill. (some col.), index, maps.

Fascinating analysis of the corpus of Mixtec codices interweaves ethnohistorical, epigraphic, archaeological, and ethnographic research. By linking people and ritualized events pictured in the codices with real archaeological remains and surviving local lore, the authors show how factionalized ruling elites of the Tilantongo and Jaltepec areas established their legitimacy during the Postclassic period. This superb book makes an important contribution by helping us to consider precontact indigenous "history" on its own terms as well as to grasp the full significance of the Mixtec codices.

406 Caciques and their people: a volume in honor of Ronald Spores. Edited by Joyce Marcus and Judith Francis Zeitlin. Ann Arbor: Museum of Anthropology, Univ. of Michigan, 1994. 300 p.: bibl., ill., maps. (Anthropological papers; 89)

Celebratory volume in honor of Ronald Spores' retirement contains articles from scholars trained or influenced by him. Contributions of ethnohistorical interest ranging from the preconquest through colonial periods can be grouped into several categories. Sociopolitical characteristics of *cacicazgos* and their rulers are examined in: 1) Hicks' reconstruction of the organization of Xaltocán, in the northern Valley of Mexico, and its relationships with Tlatelolco and Tenochtitlán in the 15th century; 2) Redmond and Spencer's comparison of Taino and Oaxacán *cacicazgo* organization; 3) Marcus' comparative analysis of rituals of inauguration; 4) Zeitlin's compilation of archaeological and historical data to arrive at a model of barrio structure in Tehuantepec; and 5) Chance's reasoned examination of the persistence into the 18th century of indigenous ruling elites in central New Spain. The meanings of indigenous pictorial records are explored by Lind, who posits the extent of the precontact *altepetl* of Cholula on the basis of the obverse of the 16th-century *Codex of Cholula,* and by M.E. Smith, who suggests that the visible materials on the *Codex Selden* were painted to be submitted as evidence in a 16th-century court case. Ecological orientations of *cacicaz-*

gos are extrapolated by Monaghan, who identifies a system of ecological verticality in pre-contact Oaxaca, and by Hunt, who suggests reasons for an apparent lack of irrigation drawn from the Rio Grande in Cuicatlán until the 20th century. Romero Frizzi interprets the role of indigenous attitudes toward rulers, alliance, and outsiders as they affected the course of the Spanish conquest and the emergence of the colonial state in Oaxaca.

407 Calvo, Thomas *et al.* Xalisco, la voz de un pueblo en el siglo XVI. México: CIESAS; Centro de Estudios Mexicanos y Centroamericanos, 1993. 213 p.: bibl., map.

This worthwhile book can be situated within the growing genre of published, locally-focused Nahuatl language documents written in Latin script. What makes the present volume different is its connection with what is now the state of Nayarit. The records, dating from the 1570s-90s and arranged into four thematic sections, deal with community finance, indigenous interaction with Franciscans, Spanish conquerors and the local *encomendero*, and the local native ruling elite.

408 Carmack, Robert M. La conquista de Mesoamérica desde la perspectiva de una teoría mundial. (*Rev. Hist./Heredia*, 28, julio/dic. 1993, p. 9–40)

Reasoned essay argues for applicability of world systems theory (with some modifications) to pre-contact and conquest-era Mesoamerica. The author frames his ideas with a theoretical discussion of the Spanish conquest and the ways in which indigenous socio-political organization, aid, and opposition shaped its outcome.

409 Carrasco, David. Give me some skin: the charisma of the Aztec warrior. (*Hist. Relig.*, 35:1, Aug. 1995, p. 1–26)

Innovative analysis of the Xipe-centered festival of Tlacaxipeualiztli sees it as a ritual metaphor of power linked to warfare that brought the battlefield into controlled ceremonies staged in the imperial capital. Article analyzes several distinct components of the month-long festival, including recreation of battles during gladitorial sacrifice, and mock combat between participants wearing flayed skins of captives and young Mexica warriors attempting to grab pieces of those skins.

410 Carrasco, David. Quetzalcoatl and the irony of empire: myths and prophecies in the Aztec tradition. Pbk. ed. Chicago: Univ. of Chicago Press, 1992. 233 p.: bibl., ill., index.

Reprint of the 1982 edition with a new three-page preface that touches on the historiographical debates about indigenous expectation of Quetzalcoatl's return and its coincidence with Cortes' arrival.

411 Carrillo y Ancona, Crescencio and **Juan Francisco Molina Solís.** Historia antigua de Yucatán. Suplemento. Estudio preliminar, recopilación y notas de Hernán R. Menéndez Rodríguez. Mexico: ICY; Consejo Nacional para la Cultura y las Artes: Programa Cultural de las Fronteras, 1989. 131 p.

Photographic reproductions and transcriptions of the Maya-speaking bishop-historian's previously unpublished manuscript, a supplement to his better-known volumes of Yucatecan history. Also includes responses from another 19th-century historian with whom he had heated debates over themes contained herein: the ruins of Uxmal, the foundation of Maní, and the original name for Yucatán.

412 Cervantes, Fernando. Christianity and the Indians in early modern Mexico: the native response to the Devil. (*Hist. Res./Oxford*, 66:160, June 1993, p. 177–196)

Thoughtful and intricate evaluation of how indigenous peoples incorporated the Devil and other Christian concepts into their own belief systems and how the resulting indigenous version of Christianity evolved over time and space.

413 Cervantes, Fernando. The Devil in the New World: the impact of diabolism in New Spain. New Haven, Conn.: Yale Univ. Press, 1994. 182 p.: bibl., facsims., ill., index, map.

Exacting investigation of Spanish perceptions of demonism in indigenous religious practices as well as the real and imagined role of devil imagery and belief in native practices. Author ably charts evolution of Spanish attitudes, identifying a gradual shift from a linkage of the agency of the devil to "idolatrous" practices as a matter of course in the 16th century to identification of other causes in the 18th century.

414   Chase, Diane Z. Postclassic Maya elites: ethnohistory and archaeology. (*in* Mesoamerican elites: an archaeological assessment. Norman: Univ. of Oklahoma Press, 1992, p. 118–134)

Persuasive comparison of ethnohistorical and archaeological sources centered on the Postclassic sites of Santa Rita Corozal (Belize) and Mayapán. Focusing on distribution of elite residences and identification of a kind of "middle" level of society, author creates vivid tapestry of social complexity, spatial organization, and temporal evolution. For a different view of the class issue see item **414.**

415   Chimalpahin Cuauhtlehuanitzin, Domingo Francisco de San Antón Munón. Memorial breve acerca de la fundación de la ciudad de Culhuacan. Estudio, paleografía, traducción, notas e índice analítico por Víctor M. Castillo Farreras. México: Univ. Nacional Autónoma de México, Instituto de Investigaciones Históricas, 1991. lxviii, 157 p.: bibl., index, map. (Serie de cultura náhuatl. Fuentes; 9)

Nahuatl transcription with Spanish translation of the *Memorial Breve* covers the period 670-1299 and comprises part of Mexican Manuscript 74 of the National Library in Paris. Work benefits from the collaboration of the Nahuatl Texts Workshop at UNAM. Introduction explores relationships between and the contexts of Chimalpahin's various extant works.

416   Chipping away on earth: studies in prehispanic and colonial Mexico in honor of Arthur J.O. Anderson and Charles E. Dibble. Edited by Eloise Quiñones Keber with the assistance of Susan Schroeder and Frederic Hicks. Lancaster, Calif.: Labyrinthos, 1994. 266 p.: bibl., ill.

Collection of 27 articles derived from papers presented at sessions in honor of Anderson and Dibble given at the 1992 meeting of the American Society of Ethnohistory. Articles are divided into five sections: 1) in "Producing the Florentine Codex," Anderson, Dibble, and their editor, Norma B. Mikkelsen provide recollections of their work; 2) in "Bernardino de Sahagún: Ethnography and Evangelization in Sixteenth-Century Mexico," León-Portilla, Thouvenot, Hanson, Sell, and Keber discuss various aspects of the friar's ca-

reer, production, and goals; 3) in "Other Places, Other Texts," Noguez, Carrasco, Schroeder, Schwaller, Terraciano, Restall, and López Austin examine issues related to translation, interpretation, the nature of texts, and the development of colonial traditions of alphabetic writing among the Nahua, Mixtec, and Maya; 4) in "Re/Constructing the Nahua World before and after the Conquest," Heyden, Berdan, Kaufman, Durand-Forest, Wilkerson, Favrot Peterson, and Poole undertake sometimes dense analysis of the ethnohistorical record; and 5) in "Recovering Texcoco: History and Archaeology," Mohar Betancourt, Hicks, T. Charlton, C. Otis Charlton, Valle, and Harvey provide insights into precontact and colonial organization of an area of special interest to Dibble. Collectively these many pieces provide an important sampling of cutting-edge work inspired and aided by pioneering efforts of the honorees.

417   Clendinnen, Inga. "Fierce and unnatural cruelty:" Cortés and the conquest of Mexico. (*in* New World encounters. Edited by Stephen Greenblatt. Berkeley: Univ. of Calif. Press, 1993, p. 12–41)

Beautifully written contemplation of competing Spanish and Nahua versions of the conquest. Although the author views them in some sense as "fiction" in that they are informed by a number of distinct agendas, she nonetheless extracts a revisionist, nuanced narrative of the conquest dynamics and the evolution of the attitudes of one group of combatants towards the other.

418   Cline, S.L. The spiritual conquest reexamined: baptism and Christian marriage in early sixteenth-century Mexico. (*HAHR*, 73:3, Aug. 1993, p. 453–480)

Detailed analysis is based on Nahuatl-language household censuses from Morelos (1535–40). Author demonstrates that even in this period many people remained unbaptized and were not yet married by Catholic ritual. Taking social status, age, and gender into account, her findings suggest that previous older ideas about the speed and completeness of Christianization in the early colonial years need to be reexamined.

419   Codex Madrid: tro-cortesiano, cuyo original se encuentra en el Museo de América de Madrid. Madrid: Testimonio, 1991. 112 p.

Color facsimile replete with simulated worm holes. Companion volume contains valuable analysis by Manuel Ballesteros Gaibrois that considers the dating of this precolumbian Maya codex, its place of origin, stylistics, calendrical information, writing structure, epigraphy, phonetic readings, portraits of divinities, unique scenes, and year-end ceremonies.

420 Códice Boturini, o Tira de la Peregrinación. México: Taller de Artes Gráficas, Grupo Gisma, 1991. 80 p.

Excellent facsimile of this important document.

421 Códice Techialoyan de Huixquilucan: Estado de México. Estudio introductorio de Herbert R. Harvey. Toluca, Mexico: Gobierno del Estado de México, Secretaría de Finanzas y Planeación; El Colegio Mexiquense, 1993. 105 p., 20 leaves of plates: bibl., ill., maps, col. facsims.

Another beautiful facsimile from the Techialoyan group, with a preliminary contextual study of the times, places, and personages illuminated in this Codex Hemenway. A tribute is owed to the Colegio Mexiquense for paving the way to a greater understanding of these unusual colonial manuscripts with this series.

422 Códices de Cuernavaca y unos títulos de sus pueblos. Textos y recopilación de Juan Dubernard Chauveau. México: Grupo Editorial M.A. Porrúa, 1991. 396 p., 4 folded leaves of plates: ill. (some col.), maps.

Handsome presentation of facsimiles and transcriptions of a series of primordial titles and related documents written by indigenous citizens of Cuernavaca during the Spanish era. Also includes Spanish translations, principally dating from the 18th century. Features full Spanish and partial Nahuatl text of the "Municipal Codex of Cuernavaca," drawn from the Pichardo copy held by the Bibliothèque Nationale in Paris.

423 Códices y documentos sobre México: primer simposio. Recopilación de Constanza Vega Sosa. México: Instituto Nacional de Antropología e Historia, 1994. 344 p.: bibl., ill. (Col. científica. Serie Historia)

This work was part of the 47th International Congress of Americanists in New Orleans, but has been followed by meetings in Mexico with the same title and ethnohistori-

cal focus. Contributors here include Miriam, Bricker, Wulfing, Vail, Paxton, Fahmel Bever, Parmenter, Johnson, Haley, Cederstrøm, Merlo, Troike, Vega Sosa, Heyden, Baus Czitrom, Odena Güemes, Brambila, Rousseau, Durand-Forest, Berger, Tena, Baños Ramos, Oliver Vega, Islas Jiménez, and Piana. Among other documents and codices, the following are highlighted: the *Chilam Balam de Kaua*, *La relación de las cosas de Yucatán*, the *Códices Madrid, Borbonicus, Azoyú, Kingsborough*, and the *Humboldt Fragment 1*; the *Fifth Relation* of Chimalpahin, and the *Lienzos de Ihuitlan; Tlapiltepec, Metlatoyuca, Itzquintepec*, and *San Bernabé Ocotepec* (the latter of the Techialoyan group).

424 Colección de documentos del Archivo General de la Nación para la etnohistoria de la Mixteca de Oaxaca en el siglo XVI. Recopilación de Ronald Spores. Nashville, Tenn.: Vanderbilt Univ., 1992. 104 p.: bibl. (Vanderbilt University publications in anthropology; 41)

Very useful transcriptions of 238 documents from three different collections in the *Archivo General de la Nación* (Mexico City) on a variety of subjects such as *cabildo* office-holding, cacique privileges, tributes, markets, land issues, stockraising, fiesta expenditures, and Catholic masses.

425 El contacto entre los españoles e indígenas en el norte de la Nueva España. Coordinación de Ysla Campbell. Ciudad Juárez, Mexico: Univ. Autónoma de Ciudad Juárez, 1992. 215 p.: bibl. (Col. Conmemorativa quinto centenario del encuentro de dos mundos; 4)

Anthology in Spanish with several contributions of special note for ethnohistorians: 1) Deeds' investigation of 17th-century rebellions of the Tepehuanes and Tarahumaras of Nueva Vizcaya; 2) Griffen's comparison of European relations with different northern indigenous groups, 16th-19th centuries; 3) Adam's examination of documentary and archaeological evidence of Spanish impact on the Pueblo peoples, 1520–1700; 4) González Rodríguez's exploration of the 16th-century Fransiscan presence and their accounts from the North; 5) Merrill's study of the evolution of a new variant of Catholicism among the Tarahumara over four centuries; and 6) Castañeda's summary of 16th-century efforts to introduce the Spanish language in Nueva Galicia.

426 Contribuciones a la arqueología y et-
nohistoria del Occidente de México.
Edición de Eduardo Williams. Zamora, Mexico: El Colegio de Michoacán, 1994. 411 p.:
bibl., ill. (Col. Memorias)

Four concluding studies in this anthology are welcome additions to the ethnohistorical coverage of western Mesoamerica: 1) encompassing Schöndube's reflections on the
limited accounts of Sayula; 2) Soto de Are-
chavaleta's analysis of the unusually early
record of an expedition into what became part
of Nueva Galicia (the *Treslado de una*
Vesitación . . . de 1525); 3) Ruiz Medrano's
fresh look at the Mixtón War (drawing on a
previously unstudied questionnaire of 1544 in
the Archivo General de Indias, Seville); and 4)
Wright's interesting examination of Otomíco-
lonization of Guanajuato and Querétaro in
the 16th century.

427 Dakin, Karen and **Christopher H. Lutz.**
Nuestro pesar, nuestra aflicción: tune-
tuliniliz, tucucuca; memorias en lengua náhuatl enviadas a Felipe II por indígenas del
Valle de Guatemala hacia 1572. México:
Univ. Nacional Autónoma de México, Centro
de Investigaciones Regionales de Mesoamérica, 1996. 209 p.: bibl., facsims., maps, tables.

Excellent presentation of 22 Nahuatl-
language *memorias* sent to the Crown by citizens of indigenous communities of Santiago
de Guatemala and its region in 1572. Lutz's
introductory essay provides valuable historical information about the region, its peoples,
and the issues raised in the documents, while
Dakin, who transcribed and translated them,
contributes a careful grammar and paleography. Facsimiles of the *memorias* are included,
followed by Dakin's transcriptions (with
Spanish loan words in italics, a great addition)
and translations. Of significant use to interested scholars, in their own right these *me-*
morias are an excellent example of Nahuatl
records from beyond the Nahua heartland.

428 Damrosch, David. The aesthetics of
conquest: Aztec poetry before and after
Cortés. (*in* New World encounters. Edited by
Stephen Greenblatt. Berkeley: Univ. of Calif.
Press, 1993, p. 139–158)

Insightful interpretation of poems from
the *Cantares mexicanos* and *Romances de*
los señores de la Nueva España, arguing how
even the most idyllic-seeming poetry functioned as a literary arm of Mexica imperial

strategy, and how the genre was modified by
post-conquest poets trying to make sense of
changes wrought by the Spanish conquest and
the process of Christianization.

Daniel, Douglas A. Tactical factors in the
Spanish conquest of the Aztecs. See item
1139.

429 Dehouve, Danièle. Entre el caimán y el
jaguar: los pueblos indios de Guerrero.
México: Centro de Investigaciones y Estudios
Superiores en Antropología Social, 1994. 210
p.: appendix, bibl., ill. (some col.). (Historia de
los pueblos indígenas de México)

Careful overview of this region in preconquest and colonial times pays close attention to changes taking place within the indigenous world after the Spanish conquest,
especially in relation to development of silver
mining and to Asian trade passing to and
from Acapulco. Includes a discussion of survival of native ritual, as well as attempts to
suppress it, and a useful documentary appendix with two translated Nahuatl records.

430 Durán, Diego. The history of the Indies
of New Spain. Translated, annotated,
and introduced by Doris Heyden. Norman:
Univ. of Oklahoma Press, 1993. 642 p.: bibl.,
ill. (some col.), index, map. (Civilization of
the American Indian series; 210)

Excellent new unabridged English
translation—made from the original held in
Madrid—of this crucial source for ethnohistorians of Mesoamerica. Heyden provides an
informative introduction as well as helpful
notations in the text itself. B/w reproductions
of the original illustrations are included.

431 Economies and polities in the Aztec
realm. Edited by Mary G. Hodge and
Michael E. Smith. Albany: Institute for Mesoamerican Studies, Univ. at Albany, State
Univ. of New York; Austin: Univ. of Texas
Press, 1994. 478 p.: bibl., ill., index. (Studies
on culture and society; 6)

Scholarly anthology draws much from
archaeological investigation but also intensive interdisciplinary work with ethnohistorical manuscripts, resulting in many significant historical assessments regarding
political geography, social stratification, demography, diet and subsistence, agriculture,
land distribution, labor, craft production, and
trade. Besides the editors, authors of the more
ethnohistorical pieces include Williams,

Hicks, Berdan, Barbosa-Cano, and Rojas. Also noteworthy is an article by Smith (see item 527) and another by Smith and Heath-Smith (see item 529) convincingly show how employment of archaeological and ethnohistorical records leads to more comprehensive conclusions about the shape of past societies.

432 Escalante Hernández, Roberto. Códice Madrid: Tro-Cortesiano. Puebla, Mexico: Centro de Investigaciones Históricas y Culturales, Museo Amparo, 1992. 83 p.: bibl., ill.

Inexpensive reproductions and an introductory study for the non-specialist. See also item 419, which contains a superior facsimile and analytical study.

433 La escritura pictográfica en Tlaxcala: dos mil años de experiencia mesoamericana. Recopilación de Luis Reyes García. Dibujos de los códices tlaxcaltecas por César J. Meléndez Aguilar. Tlaxcala, Mexico: Univ. Autónoma de Tlaxcala, Secretaría de Extensión Universitaria y Difusión Cultural: Centro de Investigaciones y Estudios Superiores en Antropología Social, 1993. 341 p.: bibl., ill. (Col. Historia de Tlaxcala; 1)

Extremely valuable recuperation of the indigenous historical record for the Tlaxcala area, in the form of an anthology with information on numerous codices, documents, and paintings from the 16th-18th centuries. Extensive drawings and photographic reproductions.

434 *Ethnohistory: the Bulletin of the Ohio Valley Historic Indian Conference.* Vol. 42, No. 4, Fall 1995. Women, power, and resistance in Colonial Mesoamerica. Edited by Kevin Gosner and Deborah E. Kanter. Columbus, Ohio: Ohio Valley Historic Indian Conference.

This impressive volume of new scholarship grew out of a meeting of the American Society for Ethnohistory in Bloomington, Indiana in 1993. It highlights diversity of indigenous (and culturally mixed) women's experiences in the colonial context, except for one paper on the precolumbian era. Includes: 1) Kellogg's examination of gender and social differentiation in Tenochtitlan in the late prehispanic period; 2) Restall's study of two incidents of attempted rape against Maya women of colonial Yucatán, their responses, and larger issues of subordination and resistance; 3) Dunn's exploration of a response by a group of Ixil-Maya women to a plague in 1795, as evidence of their role in guarding custom; 4) Kanter's analysis of the decline of native women's land ownership, 1750–1900, in the Toluca Valley; 5) Pescador's inquiry into cultural effects of migration by indigenous women to Mexico City in the late 18th century; 6) Few's comparison of two women's differing experiences with the Inquisition in 17th-century Guatemala and their implications for understanding the "gendered discourses of colonial women;" and 7) Silverblatt's critical examination of all these contributions, raising common themes, future directions for analysis, and theoretical questions for both ethnohistory and feminist studies.

435 Evans, Susan T. Aztec household organization and village administration. (*in* Prehispanic domestic units in Western Mesoamerica: studies of the household, compound, and residence. Boca Raton, Fla.: CRC Press, 1993, p. 173–189)

New installment in this author's ongoing study of rural *calpulli* organization in the Aztec era. Building on her examination of the *tecpan*, structure six at Cihuatecpan, Teotihuacan Valley (see *HLAS 54:644*), Evans here pays close attention to household composition and its relationship to demands of a maguey-based agriculture. In so doing, she is able to extend our general knowledge of residence patterns, household size, and social stratification, as well as the implications of an expanding noble class.

436 Farriss, Nancy. Sacred power in colonial Mexico: the case of sixteenth-century Yucatán. (*in* The meeting of two worlds: Europe and the Americas, 1492–1650. Edited by Warwick Bray. Oxford, England: Oxford Univ. Press; The British Academy, 1993, p. 145–162, bibl.)

Excellent interpretation of incorporation of Christian elements into persistent Maya ritual by colonial indigenous elites. Author argues that adopted practices were thought to give access to the "sacred power" of the conquerors, a mechanism which would aid Maya elites in the maintenance of their own political authority.

437 Five hundred years after Columbus: proceedings. Compiled by E. Wyllys Andrews and Elizabeth Oster Mozzillo. New Orleans, La.: Middle American Research Institute, Tulane Univ., 1993. 293 p.: bibl., index. (Publication; 63)

Reports on conference sessions—including descriptions of individual papers—provide an indication of recent directions in research. Sample panels worth perusing for Mesoamerican ethnohistorical content are: Anthropology 01 (two papers on Aztec religion); Anthropology 04 (a paper on Aztec weaving); Anthropology 06 (several papers on precontact and colonial Mayan cultural history); Archaeology 07 (several papers on 16th-century Highland indigenous society); Culture 10 (with several papers on indigenous Christianity that reassess older views of syncretism); General 01 (with a notable paper on 16th-18th century records, many in Nahuatl, from an indigenous *caja de comunidad* in the Puebla region); History 11 (with two papers on Horacio Carochi, nahuatlato, and one on another Jesuit linguist in 17th-century Sonora, among the Opata); History 12 (on codices, Techialoyans, and primordial titles); Linguistics 02 (on the decipherment, reading, and preservation of central Mexican maps and codices); and Linguistics 09 (Mayan epigraphy).

438 Florescano, Enrique. Memory, myth, and time in Mexico: from the Aztecs to Independence. Translated by Albert G. Bork with the assistance of Kathryn R. Bork. Austin: Univ. of Texas Press, 1994. 282 p.: bibl., ill., index, map. (Translations from Latin America series)

Sophisticated ruminations on construction and uses of history in precolumbian, colonial, and national periods. Of interest to ethnohistorians studying indigenous forms of historical discourse, their evolution, and their contributions to the emerging mestizo memory of the past.

439 Florescano, Enrique. El mito de Quetzalcóatl. (*Allpanchis/Cusco*, 23:40, segundo semestre 1992, p. 11–93, bibl, ill.)

Interpretation of context and meaning of the Quetzalcoatl "myth," following diverse strands of its evolution over time and space. See also item **440.**

440 Florescano, Enrique. El mito de Quetzalcóatl. México: Fondo de Cultura Económica, 1993. 182 p.: bibl., ill. (Cuadernos de La Gaceta; 83)

Careful synthesis and thoughtful reflections on recent discoveries and new ideas seeking a clearer understanding of Quetzal-coatl (as Plumed Serpent, Venus, Wind/Creator God, and "culture hero" Ce Acatl Topiltzin) and the elaboration of his multidimensional "myth" from pre- to post-classic times across Mesoamerica. See also item **439.**

441 Freter, Anncorinne. The classic Maya collapse at Copan, Honduras: an analysis of Maya rural settlement trends. (*in* Archaeological views from the countryside: village communities in early complex societies. Edited by Glenn M. Schwartz and Steven E. Falconer. Washington: Smithsonian Institution Press, 1994, p. 160–176, bibl., ill., maps)

Compelling synthesis of recent investigations at Copán that reveal the important role of overpopulation and environmental degradation in the site's gradual abandonment. Features the roles of rural out-migration, social class, and access to resources.

442 Frye, David. Telling histories: a late-colonial encounter of "Spanish" and "Indian" in rural Mexico and in the archives. (*Colon. Lat. Am. Rev.*, 3:1/2, 1994, p. 115–138)

Author questions worth of the "positivist" view of history by centering his focus around the analysis of a suit brought by a Spanish traveller against several indigenous people in the San Luis Potosí area in the late 18th century. Author deftly shows how witnesses' personal agendas, social rank, and gender affected how their stories were told to the magistrate presiding over the case and how he interpreted their stories based on the same factors.

443 Furst, Jill Leslie. Rulership and ritual: myth and the origin of political authority in Mixtec pictorial manuscripts. (*in* Circumpacifica: Festschrift für Thomas S. Barthel. Frankfurt am Main: P. Lang, 1990, p. 123–141, bibl., facsims.)

By examining representations of rulers' succession in the Bodley, Selden, and Vindobonensis Mexicanus I codices, author is able to establish clear links between rituals performed by creator deities in the past and by those destined to rule on earth in the present. In this way, divine sanction for legitimacy of temporal rulers was asserted.

444 García Bernal, Manuela Cristina. Desarrollos indígena y ganadero en Yucatán. (*Hist. Mex.*, 43:3, enero/marzo 1994, p. 373–400, appendix, map, table)

Study of the internal dispersion of the Maya in colonial era based on a 1688 Yucatecan *matrícula* and a number of recent secondary works. Author argues that one powerful motor of this movement was the rise of labor-hungry livestock haciendas, to which growing numbers of people relocated. Geographic patterns of the movement, specific motives, and consequences are all discussed. An appendix presents demographic data from selected communities appearing in the 1688 census.

445 García Martínez, Bernardo. Jurisdicción y propiedad: una distinción fundamental en la historia de los pueblos de indios del México colonial. (*Rev. Eur.*, 53, Dec. 1992, p. 47–60, bibl.)

Thoughtful discussion maintains that indigenous ideas of "space" drew a distinction between political jurisdiction and properties being cultivated by the community and its citizens. Focusing on 16th-century central Mexico, author examines localized case studies from indigenous communities such as Tepeaca and Coyoacán. Some attention is paid to Iberian concepts and how they affected indigenous attitudes and procedures.

446 García Zambrano, Angel J. El poblamiento de México en la época del contacto, 1520–1540. (*Mesoamérica/Antigua*, 13:24, dic. 1992, p. 239–296, facsims.)

Solid study reconstructs how prehispanic urban ordering and foundation rituals entered into Spanish efforts to impose Iberian forms of urbanization during the first century of contact. Author makes interesting use of data from a number of Mesoamerican primordial titles, *relaciones geográficas*, and other colonial documents in the indigenous tradition.

447 Giesing, Kornelia. Die Herren der zwanzig Tageszeichen Codex Borgia 9–13: Gedanken zu einer indo-mexikanistischen Hypothese. (*in* Circumpacifica: Festschrift für Thomas S. Barthel. Frankfurt am Main: P. Lang, 1990, p. 143–164, bibl., facsims., tables)

Discusses improbability of Hindu-Sanskrit influence on Codex Borgia, but allows for a possible residual effect of oral history on the Mixteca Puebla culture's pictographs. [C.K. Converse]

448 Gil, Fernando. Primeras "doctrinas" del nuevo mundo: estudio histórico-teológico de las obras de Fray Juan de Zumárraga, 1548. Buenos Aires: Publicaciones de la Facultad de Teología de la Pontificia Univ. Católica Argentina Santa María de los Buenos Aires, 1993. 750 p.: bibl., ill., index, map.

Included in the abundant information about this first bishop of Mexico (who bore for a time the title, "Protector of Indians") is some previously unpublished material illuminating Zumárraga's perspectives on indigenous peoples and Church and State policies toward them. A very brief section analyzes the depiction of Zumárraga in the codices.

449 Gingerich, Willard. Quetzalcoatl and the agon of time: a literary reading of the *Anales de Cuauhtitlan*. (*New Sch.*, 10, 1986, p. 41–60)

Compelling examination of what the author regards as the important "symbolic structure and myth" of the *Anales*, and by extension the broader body of texts in the native tradition. The *Anales* are seen as a vision of the past created from an indigenous author's unique perspective (situated in a specific context and trying to make sense of the present as well as the past) rather than a strictly "factual" historical narrative in the western tradition.

450 Gonlin, Nancy. Rural household diversity in late classic Copán, Honduras. (*in* Archaeological views from the countryside: village communities in early complex societies. Edited by Glenn M. Schwartz and Steven E. Falconer. Washington: Smithsonian Institution Press, 1994, p. 177–197, bibl., ill., maps)

Basing her conclusions on a variety of archaeological data, author finds levels of wealth varied widely in the rural hinterland of Copán, even within the commoner class. Article adds to the stream of work finding much greater societal complexity among the classic Maya than was once thought to have existed. Of fundamental ethnohistorical interest.

451 González Dávila, Gil. Guerra de los Chichimecas. Presentación de Juan Gil Florez. Ed. facsimilar. Guadalajara, Mexico: Gobierno del Estado de Jalisco; Univ. de Guadalajara, Instituto Jalisciense de Antropología e Historia, 1994. 27 p. (Col. Histórica de obras facsimilares; 9)

Facsimile of a copy of a manuscript earlier attributed to Gil González Dávila, but actually written by the Spaniard Gonzalo de las Casas in Mexico sometime before 1585. Contains ethnohistorical information on the Pames, Guamares, Guachichiles, and Zacatecas peoples.

452 Gradie, Charlotte M. Discovering the Chichimecas. (*Americas/Francisc.*, 51: 1, July 1994, p. 67–88)

Thoughtful, well-supported inquiry into socio-cultural underpinnings and implications of the designation "Chichimeca" as it was applied to the peoples of northern Mexico. Author is careful to explain different meanings of this term for the Mexica and for Spaniards, juxtaposed against cultural realities of the region inhabited by the "Chichimeca."

453 Graulich, Michel. Afterlife in ancient Mexican thought. (*in* Circumpacifica: Festschrift für Thomas S. Barthel. Frankfurt am Main: P. Lang, 1990, p. 165–187, bibl., tables)

Careful examination of central Mexican beliefs of various possible fates after death puts forward an intriguing revisionist interpretation.

454 Greenleaf, Richard E. Persistence of native values: the Inquisition and the Indians of colonial Mexico. (*Americas/Francisc.*, 50: 3, Jan. 1994, p. 351–376)

Were accused idolators of Texcoco, Oaxaca, the Yucatán, and other areas guilty as charged or victims of indigenous (or even Spanish Catholic) power struggles? This is but one of the issues raised by the author as he details patterns of persistent indigenous religious practices through the early-17th century as evidenced in Inquisition records. Author maintains that while such sources must be read with circumspection, they are valuable for ethnohistorians. For a different view on the veracity of these kinds of records see item **536.** For historian's comments see item **1162.**

Grigsby, Thomas L. and **Carmen Cook de Leonard.** Xilonen in Tepoztlán: a comparison of Tepoztecan and Aztec agrarian ritual schedules. See *HLAS 55:739.*

455 Gruzinski, Serge. The conquest of Mexico: the incorporation of Indian societies into the Western world, 16th-18th centuries. Translated by Eileen Corrigan. Cambridge, England: Polity Press; Cambridge, Mass.: Blackwell Publishers, 1993. 336 p.: bibl., ill., index, map.

Excellent English translation of this author's valuable *La colonisation de l'imaginaire*, originally published in France in 1988 (see *HLAS 50:1066*). Gruzinski deftly examines dynamics of cultural continuity and change, especially as they were played out in the transition from pictographic to alphabetic writing, in evolving indigenous concepts of the past and the consequences of conquest, and of religion.

456 Gubler, Ruth. Epocas de padecimiento y dispersión para los Mayas de Yucatán. (*Estud. Cult. Maya*, 19, 1992, p. 269–289, bibl.)

Examination of the nature and causes of mainly Postclassic migrations connected with such sites as Chichén Itzá and Mayapán in the Yucatán is based on correlating information found in such sources as the *Chilam Balam of Chumayel, Maní*, and *Tizimín* with the *Relaciones de Yucatán*. Links the conflicts associated with at least some of this migration to conquest-era strife between Xiu and Cocom peoples.

457 Guevara Hernández, Jorge. El Lienzo de Tiltepec: extinción de un señorío zapoteco. México: Instituto Nacional de Antropología e Historia, 1991. 101 p.: bibl., ill., map. (Col. científica; 234. Serie Etnohistoria)

Reproduction and analysis of early 18th-century *lienzo* from the jurisdiction of Villa Alta, Oaxaca comprises 36 pictorial scenes with Zapotec glosses and brief texts containing local history, genealogy, and assertions about a Netzichu cacique's rights to tribute and personal service. Offers some revisions of a study from 1956.

Guía preliminar de fuentes documentales etnográficas para el estudio de los pueblos indígenas de Iberoamérica. See item **35.**

458 Hanks, William F. The language of the Canek Manuscript. (*Anc. Mesoam.*, 3: 2, Fall 1992, p. 269–279, appendix, bibl., tables)

Well-crafted analytical reading of this colonial-era Spanish-language manuscript from the Yucatán, recounting Franciscan efforts to missionize the resisting Itzá and their ruler, Canek. Hanks employs careful analysis of the sometimes ambivalent language of the text to suggest the identity, viewpoint, and purpose of the author. Of interest to those struggling to unlock the secrets of many forms of colonial texts. For related articles see items **473** and **508.**

459 Harris, Max. The dialogical theatre: dramatizations of the conquest of Mexico and the question of the other. New York: St. Martin's Press, 1993. 211 p.: bibl., ill., index.

Thought-provoking interpretation of early postconquest evangelical plays sponsored by the Franciscans, above all *The Conquest of Jerusalem* performed in Tlaxcala in 1539, as vehicles for dialogue between conquerors and the conquered. Author aims to establish the ways in which the indigenous voice entered the performance; a later discussion of this same theme surrounds a critique of the work of Sahagún and Durán. All of this is set within an analytical context, at least partially informed by canons of literary criticism, related to broader questions of "otherness," and how cultural difference has been and continues to be approached in both Christian and non-Christian reflection. Not everyone will agree with this approach, or with specific conclusions made in the book, but the author provides nourishing intellectual food for thought.

460 Haskett, Robert. "Not a pastor, but a wolf:" indigenous-clergy relations in early Cuernavaca and Taxco. (*Americas/Francisc.*, 50:3, Jan. 1994, p. 293–336)

Study of often-tense relationships between parish priests and their indigenous parishioners from the later 16th-18th centuries. At the core of the source base are a series of Nahuatl petitions which give evidence for power negotiations between representatives of the two groups. Issues of religiosity, material support, racism, sexuality, rape, and mistreatment are raised.

461 Haskett, Robert. Visión nahua de los conquistadores españoles en la región colonial de Cuernavaca= Nahua views of the Spanish conquerors in the colonial Cuernavaca region. (*in* Mesoamerican and Chicano art, culture, and identity = El arte, la cultura y la identidad mesoamericana y chicana. Salem, Ore.: Willamette Univ., 1994, p. 50–75)

Exploration of how indigenous peoples negotiated power in the colonial context, as evidenced in conventions of their own Nahuatl-language written records, in their local self-governance, in elaboration of their material culture, in litigation over land, labor, and tributes, and finally, in manipulation of their own community histories.

462 Hester, Thomas R. and **Harry J. Shafer.** The ancient Maya craft community at Colha, Belize, and its external relationships. (*in* Archaeological views from the countryside: village communities in early complex societies. Edited by Glenn M. Schwartz and Steven E. Falconer. Washington: Smithsonian Institution Press, 1994, p. 48–63, bibl., ill., map)

Straightforward summary of many years of archaeological sleuthing demonstrates that Colha served as a significant source of utilitarian and ritual chert tools for a wide region over a sweep of as many as 2000 years. In the process, the important economic role played by a small site such as Colha is delineated, suggesting once again that the precontact Maya world was one of much greater complexity than once believed.

463 Heyden, Doris. El árbol en el mito y el símbolo. (*Estud. Cult. Náhuatl*, 23, 1993, p. 201–219)

Analysis of a number of important pictorials and chronicles from the Nahua, Mixtec/Zapotec, and Maya traditions. Heyden fashions a synthetic discussion of the importance of certain trees in religious thought, ritual, and festivities during the precontact era.

464 Heyden, Doris. The eagle, the cactus, the rock: the roots of Mexico-Tenochtitlán's foundation myth and symbol. Oxford: B.A.R., 1989. 163 p.: ill., maps. (BAR international series; 484)

Well-drawn study of the Mexica uses of symbols—most importantly the "eagle and cactus" emblem of Tenochtitlán—to support their own self-validating historical memory in a process called "visual education." Book makes important contribution to our understanding of the meanings of such concepts as "myth" and "history" when applied to nonwestern visions of the past, a contribution which in turn has wider implications for the more general debate about what is "fact" and what is "fiction."

465 Hillerkuss, Thomas. Ecología, economía y orden social de los tarahumaras en la época prehispánica y colonial. (*Estud. Hist. Novohisp.*, 12, 1992, p. 9–62, bibl., maps)

Detailed overview postulates late preconquest and early colonial structure of Tarahumara society. Extrapolating from a large number of 17th- and 18th-century records and accounts, author analyzes indigenous economic and social ordering within its distinctive ecological context. Lengthy bibliography of primary sources is a useful addition.

466 Hillerkuss, Thomas. Los méritos y servicios de un maya yucateco principal del siglo XVI y la historia de sus probanzas y mercedes. (*Estud. Hist. Novohisp.*, 13, 1993, p. 9–39, bibl.)

Critical biographical reading of a series of *probanzas de méritos* drawn up on behalf of Gaspar Antonio Chi, of the Xiu of Maní, a multi-lingual noble who served secular and religious authorities as interpreter, *maestro de capilla*, teacher, and a notary for Fray Diego de Landa. Excellent example of the career of an archtypical indigenous ally of the Spanish which shows how difficult it was for such a person to gain meaningful recognition from the authorities in Spain.

467 Hirth, Kenneth G. Identifying rank and socioeconomic status in domestic contexts: an example from Central Mexico. (*in* Prehispanic domestic units in western Mesoamerica: studies of the household, compound, and residence. Boca Raton, Fla.; Ann Arbor, Mich.: CRC Press, 1993, p. 121–146)

Suggestive study of *Gobernador*-phase Xochicalco, Morelos, focused on households rather than individuals or larger groups. Socioeconomic status is inferred from a complex set of archaeological data, including architectural elaboration, residence size, and the amount and type of artifacts present. Points the way for further attention on what may turn out to be a more realistic method of delineating social status and societal organization.

468 Historia general de Centroamérica. t. 1., Historia antigua. Edición de Robert M. Carmack. Coordinación general de Edelberto Torres-Rivas. Madrid: Comunidades Europeas; Sociedad Estatal Quinto Centenario; FLACSO, 1993. 1 v.: bibl., ill., index, maps.

First of six projected volumes seeking to create a historical panorama of Central America includes chapters by Carmack, Henderson, Hasemann, Lara Pinto, Fonseca, and Cooke. Authors examine archaeology, history, historiography, geography and culture of the region in the precontact period. For historian's comment on all six vols., see item **1633**.

469 Los huicholes: documentos históricos. Recopilación de Beatriz Rojas. México?: INI; CIESAS, 1992. 272 p.: bibl., map. (Biblioteca Gonzalo Aguirre Beltrán. Palabra antigua)

Skillfully compiles scarce records on a people whose history has received relatively little attention. Informed introductions and helpful maps bracket these 16th- to 20th-century documents that illuminate missionary activities, indigenous uprisings, *presidio* conditions, land struggles, and national wars at the local level.

470 The imagination of matter: religion and ecology in Mesoamerican traditions. Edited by David Carrasco. Oxford, England: B.A.R., 1989. 224 p.: bibl., ill. (BAR international series; 515)

Collection of 11 articles utilizes both archaeological and written records to identify and interpret Mexica concepts of the fundamental interrelationship of the natural and supernatural worlds. The collection is in some ways a forerunner of editor Carrasco's later *To Change Place* (see *HLAS 54:577*). The present book includes Aguilera's interpretation of the Templo Mayor as an observatory; Aveni's engaging look at the astronomical orientation of ceremonial sites; Boone's penetrating inquiry into the shifting images of the deity Huitzilopochtli; Broda's discussion of Aztec science; Heyden's interpretation of the importance of plants in the thought, ritual, and even social ordering of the Mexica; Klor de Alva's study of ways in which the dialogue between Sahagún and his informants affected the representation of Mexica culture; Milbrath's proposal of the centrality of Venus in the calendrics of the Mixteca-Puebla area; Ortiz Montellano's treatment of Aztec linkages of the body with the supernatural world; Townsend's analysis of form and function of the Templo Mayor; and Van der Loo's revisionist examination of certain elements of the Borgia group.

471 Indian women of early Mexico. Edited by Susan Schroeder, Stephanie Wood, and Robert Haskett. Norman: Univ. of Oklahoma Press, 1997. 496 p.: bibl., ill., index, maps.

Important, innovative compilation of investigations into the histories of indigenous women in early Mexico reveals richness and complexity of the lives of indigenous peoples. Topics include housework, Aztec wives, early Spanish-indigenous marriages, naming patterns, *cacicas* (ruling class women), crime, and rebellion. The studies, based on native language sources, cover the Aztecs-Nahuas-Mexicas, the Mixtecas, and the Mayas and the peoples of northern New Spain. Aside from introductory and concluding essays provided by the editors, specific contributions are as follows: "Mexica Women on the Home Front: Housework and Religion in Aztec Mexico," by Louise M. Burkhart; "Aztec Wives," by Arthur J.O. Anderson; "Indian-Spanish Marriages in the First Century of the Colony," by Pedro Carrasco; "Gender and Social Identity: Nahua Naming Patterns in Postconquest Central Mexico," by Rebecca Horn; "From Parallel and Equivalent to Separate but Unequal: Tenochca Mexica Women, 1500–1700," by Susan Kellogg, "Activist or Adulteress? The Life and Struggle of Doña Josefa María of Tepoztlan," by Robert Haskett; "Matters of Life at Death: Nahuatl Testaments of Rural Women, 1589–1801," by Stephanie Wood; "Mixteca *Cacicas*: Status, Wealth, and the Political Accommodation of Native Elite Women in Early Colonial Oaxaca," by Ronald Spores; "Women and Crime in Colonial Oaxaca: Evidence of Complementary Gender Roles in Mixtec and Zapotec Societies," by Lisa Mary Sousa; "Women, Rebellion, and the Moral Economy of Maya Peasants in Colonial Mexico," by Kevin Gosner; "Work, Marriage, and Status: Maya Women of Colonial Yucatan," by Marta Espejo-Ponce Hunt and Matthew Restall; "Double Jeopardy: Indian Women in Jesuit Missions of Nueva Vizcaya," by Susan M. Deeds; "Women's Voices from the Frontier: San Esteban de Nueva Tlaxcala in the Late Eighteenth Century," by Leslie S. Offutt; and "Rethinking Malinche," by Frances Karttunen. [S. Ramírez]

472 Izquierdo, Ana Luisa. Un documento novohispano del siglo XVII como fuente para el estudio de la religion maya. (*Estud. Cult. Maya,* 19, 1992, p. 321–334, bibl.)

Intriguing analysis of an Inquisition case in Mérida from 1673–82. While the defendant was considered a mulatto, he and others ran afoul of the Holy Office because groups of mulattoes and Maya were jointly carrying out "pagan" rites at various locations. Author demonstrates how many of these rites were linked to known Maya ritual practices. Shows how Inquisition cases can be used to reconstruct colonial indigenous religious practices, even if defendants were not themselves Indians.

473 Jones, Grant D. The Canek manuscript in ethnohistorical perspective. (*Anc. Mesoam.,* 3:2. Fall 1992, p. 243–268)

Well-reasoned study of this key Spanish-language manuscript discovered in private hands in 1988. Jones reveals strong internal and contextual evidence to date the manuscript and to suggest the identity of its author. He also demonstrates how important it is as a source for reconstruction of Spanish attitudes and activities toward the independent State of the Itzá in the late 17th century. Article includes a facsimile of the document as well as a transcription and English translation. For related articles see items **458** and **508.**

474 Karttunen, Frances E. Between worlds: interpreters, guides, and survivors. New Brunswick, N.J.: Rutgers Univ. Press, 1994. 364 p.: bibl., ill., index.

Contains a sensitive and informed biography of the often misunderstood conquest-era Doña Marina, or "La Malinche," among 15 other cultural intermediaries whose experiences collectively represent various nations and span several centuries.

475 Kellogg, Susan. Hegemony out of conquest: the first two centuries of Spanish rule in central Mexico. (*Radic. Hist. Rev.,* 53, Spring 1992, p. 27–46)

Identification and analysis of patterns of adaptation in indigenous responses to the imposition of the Spanish legal and religious systems, primarily as they affected traditional structures of family and gender. While this process led to persistence of a distinctly indigenous culture, it also fostered solidification of the Spanish system as the "normal and natural" status quo and resulted in the transformation of indigenous society.

476 Kellogg, Susan. Law and the transformation of Aztec culture, 1500–1700. Norman: Univ. of Oklahoma Press, 1995. 318 p.: bibl., ill., index.

Well-drawn analysis of legal records and wills in Nahuatl and Spanish from the Nahua community of 16th- and 17th-century Mexico City. Through deep textual interpretations, author uncovers shifting cultural patterns (especially among indigenous women) in landholding, gender relations, family and kin, and inheritance. Book suggests that Spanish legal and religious practices interacted with indigenous ways in a gradual process of "mutual accommodation" which resulted in the significant alteration of Nahua customs by 1700.

477 Kellogg, Susan. The social organization of households among the Tenochca Mexica before and after the Conquest. (*in* Prehispanic domestic units in western Mesoamerica: studies of the household, compound and residence. Boca Raton, Fla.: CRC Press, 1993, p. 207–224)

Careful investigation of the family and household among the indigenous people of Tenochtitlán/Mexico City employs an array of ethnohistorical records, above all early colonial Nahuatl testaments and related materials. Author finds a distinct, though not immediate, shift from multifamily households to nuclear ones as a result of the Spanish conquest. Clearly lays out reasons for this shift, as well as changing relationship between families and the state.

478 King, Eleanor and **Daniel Potter.** Small sites in prehistoric Maya socioeconomic organization: a perspective from Colha, Belize. (*in* Archaeological views from the countryside: village communities in early complex societies. Edited by Glenn M. Schwartz and Steven E. Falconer. Washington: Smithsonian Institution Press, 1994, p. 64–90, bibl., ill., maps)

Careful revisionist study arguing against the notion that socioeconomic complexity increases in direct proportion to the size of the site under study. Instead, by focusing on chert-working craft specialization at the small site of Colha, authors uncover a complex, evolving system of status and production ranging from the late preclassic through the late classic eras. Another study broadening our knowledge of the Lowland Maya by moving away from an exclusive preoccupation with large sites and elites.

479 Klor de Alva, José Jorge. El discurso nahua y la apropiación de lo europeo. (*in* De palabra y obra en el Nuevo Mundo. v. 1,

Imágenes interétnicas. Edición de Miguel León-Portilla *et al.* Madrid: Siglo Veintiuno Editores, 1992, p. 339–368)

Compelling discussion of how the Nahuas appropriated certain European modes of expression, above all the use of alphabetic writing in their own language, to come to terms with and survive under Spanish colonial hegemony. Shows how efforts by Spanish secular and religious authorities to foster the spread and standardization of alphabetic Nahuatl aided—sometimes inadvertently—this survival.

480 Kobayashi, Munehiro. Tres estudios sobre el sistema tributario de los mexicas. México: Centro de Investigaciones y Estudios Superiores en Antropología Social; Kobe, Japan: Kobe City Univ. of Foreign Studies, 1993. 171 p.: bibl., ill., maps.

Three useful articles, drawing from a considerable number of primary sources, illuminate Aztec food acquisition and consumption, tameme transportation, chinampa agriculture, the political-territorial structure of the empire, composition of and relations between individual tlatocayotl, and the material culture of the elite, its elaboration, exchange, and redistribution.

481 Krippner-Martínez, James. The vision of the victors: power and colonial justice. (*Colon. Lat. Am. Rev.,* 4:1, 1995, p. 3–28)

Insightful analysis of records of the 1530 trial, torture, and execution of the Tarascan Cazconzi at the hands of Nuño de Guzmán. Sees the documents and the acts they recorded as efforts to signify Spanish power at the expense of a vilified "other," while stressing the importance of seeking indigenous perspectives in what seem at first sight to be thoroughly Spanish records.

Kurtz, Donald V. and **Mary Christopher-Nunley.** Ideology and work at Teotihuacan: a hermeneutic interpretation. See *HLAS 55:126.*

482 Landa Abrego, María Elena. Historia de un pueblo: Nauzontla. Puebla, Mexico: Gobierno del Estado de Puebla, Comisión Puebla V Centenario, 1992. 185 p.: bibl., map. (Col. V centenario)

This slim volume presents a number of transcribed court cases centered around recognition and defense of a *cacicazgo* in this Totonac town, said to have been granted by

Cortés in 1519, as well as related land issues extending to 1824. The documents are valuable for insights they provide into the development of indigenous lore about the origins of their landbase in the colonial setting, and how they went about legitimizing and protecting their possession.

Latin American Library, Tulane University. See item **23.**

483   Leibsohn, Dana. Primers for memory: cartographic histories and Nahua identity. (*in* Writing without words: alternative literacies in Mesoamerica and the Andes. Durham, N.C.: Duke Univ. Press, 1994, p. 161–187)

Examines *Mapas de Cuauhtinchan 1–2* and classes them as historical texts enshrining concepts of the *altepetl*, its origins and nature, and its relations to both external and internal sociopolitical entities.

484   Lenkersdorf, Gudrun. La fundación del Convento de Comitán: testimonios de los tojolabales. (*Estud. Cult. Maya*, 19, 1992, p. 291–319, bibl.)

Well-researched study, based on litigation records from the early 1580s held by the Archivo General de Indias in Seville, presents an indigenous-centered view of relations between members of the Dominican order and the people of this town in Chiapas. Aside from detailing the kinds of material and labor support expected by and given to the friars, author also provides important information about the sociocultural state of the community in the late 16th century.

485   León Cázares, María del Carmen. Un levantamiento en nombre del Rey Nuestro Señor: testimonios indígenas relacionados con el visitador Francisco Gómez de Lamadriz. México: Univ. Nacional Autónoma de México, Instituto de Investigaciones Filológicas, Centro de Estudios Mayas, 1988. 130 p.: bibl., 1 folded map. (Serie Cuadernos/Centro de Estudios Mayas; 18)

Thirty-seven communications in Spanish from indigenous communities of Chiapas and Guatemala in 1701 illuminate native views of colonial authority and efforts to secure local interests in a Crown-vs.-Audiencia power struggle. Protests center on excessive demands, abuses of authority, and unusual conditions rather than on the overall Spanish presence.

486   León-Portilla, Miguel. Imágenes de los otros en Mesoamérica antes del encuentro. (*in* De palabra y obra en el Nuevo Mundo. v. 1, Imágenes interétnicas. Edición de Miguel León-Portilla *et al.* Madrid: Siglo Veintiuno Editores, 1992, p. 35–56)

Intriguing essay based on the Florentine Codex and other similar sources illuminates the images the Mexica held of other peoples and cultures prior to the Spanish conquest. The author, who features Nahua views of the Otomí, Huastecos, Tarascans, Chichimecas, and time-distant Toltecs, also suggests how traditional ways of viewing "others" may have affected interpretations of Cortés and his followers. See items **487, 452,** and **479** for related articles.

487   León-Portilla, Miguel. Las profecías del encuentro: una apropiación mesoamericana del otro. (*in* De palabra y obra en el Nuevo Mundo. v. 2, Encuentros interétnicos. Edición de Miguel León-Portilla *et al.* Madrid: Siglo Veintiuno Editores, 1992, p. 225–248)

Based on a critical reading of such sources as the books of the Chilam Balam and the Florentine Codex, author suggests the ways in which the by now familiar Maya and Nahua prophecies associated with the Spanish conquest can be situated within indigenous belief systems.

488   Lockhart, James. A double tradition: editing book twelve of the Florentine Codex. (*in* Critical issues in editing exploration texts: papers given at the 28th Annual Conference on Editorial Problems, Univ. of Toronto, 6–7 November 1992. Toronto: Univ. of Toronto Press, 1995, p. 125–147)

Shares much with the introduction to *We people here* (item **547**), but with some additional details and nuances.

489   López-Austin, Alfredo. Tamoanchan y Tlalocan. México: Fondo de Cultura Económica, 1994. 261 p.: bibl., ill. (Sección de obras de antropología)

Thought-provoking consideration of complex meanings of Tamoanchan and Tlalocan for preconquest central Mexicans. Author deftly interweaves discussions of intricacies of beliefs in both concepts to arrive at stimulating conclusions about these key ideologies.

490   Love, Bruce. The Paris codex: handbook for a Maya priest. Introduction by George E. Stuart. Austin: Univ. of Texas Press, 1994. 124 p.: bibl., ill., index, maps.

One of four surviving preconquest Maya codices, probably from Mayapan ca. 1450. This serious study compares the Paris codex with the Dresden one, the Books of Chilam Balam, and modern ethnography in an effort to understand how Lowland Maya priests probably read this rare and valuable precolumbian manuscript with its multiple, interwoven calendrical-ritual cycles. Author prefers "signs of the night" over a zodiacal reading of the constellation pages. For anthropologist's comment, see *HLAS 55:433*.

491 Marcus, Joyce. Mesoamerican writing systems: propaganda, myth, and history in four ancient civilizations. Princeton, N.J.: Princeton Univ. Press, 1992. 495 p.: bibl., ill., index, maps.

Challenging analysis of uses of what is usually termed propaganda, myth, and history to legitimate social stratification and political legitimacy among the precontact Mexica, Mixtec, Zapotec, and Maya. Author offers probing interpretations of various literary strategies, making significant observations about how our own concepts need to be modified in the context of the four target cultures. For anthropologist's comment see *HLAS 55: 435*.

492 Marcus, Joyce. Royal families, royal texts: examples from the Zapotec and Maya. (*in* Mesoamerican elites: an archaeological assessment. Norman: Univ. of Oklahoma Press, 1992, p. 221–241)

Using evidence of literacy, which she maintains was the exclusive domain of elites, Marcus argues against those who are developing multi-class models of precontact societies. Instead, the author sees only two major classes (elite and commoner), however internally ranked, which were consciously kept separate on the basis of the ideology of origin (divine vs. temporal) and the elite manipulation of written history. For a different view of the class issue see item **414.**

493 Martínez Baracs, Andrea. Colonizaciones tlaxcaltecas. (*Hist. Mex.*, 43:2, oct./dic. 1993, p. 195–250, bibl.)

Lengthy, well-researched article outlines timing and spread of post-conquest Tlaxcalan colonies beyond the core of Mesoamerica. While some mention is made of a Tlaxcalan presence in Central America, author concentrates mainly on the process and results of colonization in the Mexican north.

Treats late 16th-century internal Tlaxcalan acceptance of, as well as resistance to, the colonization scheme and its consequences in the mid to late colonial era. Author suggests that the Tlaxcalan colonies absorbed indigenous peoples of the north while at the same time maintaining a privileged position that was not distributed evenly between the new "Tlaxcalans" and those descending from original colonists.

494 Mateos Higuera, Salvador. Enciclopedia gráfica del México antiguo. v. 1, Los dioses supremos. v. 2, Los dioses creadores. v. 3, Los dioses creados. v. 4, Los dioses menores. México: Secretaría de Hacienda y Crédito Público, 1994. 4 v.: bibl., ill. (some col.).

Multi-volume reference work has useful summaries of attributes, beliefs, and rituals associated with deities venerated by the Mexica and affiliated central Mexicans. Handsomely illustrated, each entry includes a bibliography, mainly concerned with pertinent published primary accounts in Spanish. While this encyclopedia offers little innovative research on these deities, it provides a helpful summary of them that could serve as a point of departure for further study.

495 Matos Moctezuma, Eduardo. La piedra del sol: calendario azteca. México: Grupo Impresa, 1992. 1 v. (unpaged): bibl., ill. (some col.).

Beautifully executed celebration of the so-called "Aztec Calendar Stone," complete with stunning illustrations and a color overlay of the monument. Commentary traces its history from discovery in Mexico City's main plaza in 1790, as well as the uncovering of the statue of Coatlicue. Also includes historiographical discussion. Matos adds his own interpretation of the meaning of the symbols, and appends a facsimile of the first study of the stone written by Antonio de León y Gama in 1792.

496 Matrícula de tributos: nuevos estudios. México: Secretaría de Hacienda y Crédito Público, 1991. 154 p.: col. ill., maps.

Beautiful reproduction of the codex, arranged folio by folio, is accompanied by clear descriptive commentary by Víctor M. Castillo. Also makes comparisons with the Codex Mendoza, the pertinent folio of which is also pictured. A series of seven excellent maps show regional origins of various products involved in the tribute system.

497 McCaa, Robert. Spanish and Nahuatl views on smallpox and demographic catastrophe in Mexico. (*J. Interdiscip. Hist.*, 25:3, Winter 1995, p. 397–431, table)

Meticulously-researched rejoinder to Brook's revision of the impact of smallpox on the Mexica in 1520 (item **400**). Fielding an array of Spanish and Nahuatl texts, McCaa argues that there is very strong evidence that smallpox caused widespread death. Comparisons with Europe and the Caribbean islands are made, and details of 16th-century Spanish medical beliefs and practices are given to help explain why natives struck down by unfamiliar diseases were unable to give care to victims and thus probably experienced much higher mortality than Europeans. For historian's comment see item **1189**.

Mejías López, William. Hernán Cortés y su intolerancia hacia la religión azteca en el contexto de la situación de los conversos y moriscos. See item **1190**.

498 Miller, Mary Ellen and **Karl A. Taube.** The gods and symbols of ancient Mexico and the Maya: an illustrated dictionary of Mesoamerican religion. New York: Thames and Hudson, 1993. 216 p.: bibl., ill., index, maps.

Concise and valuable descriptions of deities, objects, places, and concepts are punctuated with eye-catching illustrations. Includes an overview of Mesoamerican culture and chronology, an essay on the conceptual underpinning of Mesoamerican theology, a guide to sources, and a discussion of 20th-century research and writing on Mesoamerican religion.

499 Mirafuentes Galván, José Luis. Agustín Ascuhul, el profeta de Moctezuma: milenarismo y aculturación en Sonora; Guaymas, 1737. (*Estud. Hist. Novohisp.*, 12, 1992, p. 123–141)

Intriguing investigation tracing events back into the 17th century suggests how and why the Pima of lower Sonora came to revere Moctezuma I as a deity who would overturn the existing order and return the land to the indigenous people. Well supported by primary accounts, article links the aborted teachings of the "prophet" Aschuhul in 1737 with a belief connecting Moctezuma I with the foundation of Casa Grande, and with the realities of life in the later colonial period which included periodic outbreaks of epidemic disease, abuse and rape by Spaniards, and struggles of both Spanish lay and missionary societies to control Pima resources.

500 Monaghan, John. The text in the body, the body in the text: the embodied sign in Mixtec writing. (*in* Writing without words: alternative literacies in Mesoamerica and the Andes. Durham, N.C.: Duke Univ. Press, 1994, p. 87–101)

Absorbing essay in which author suggests, following such people as Eric Thompson, that Mixtec codices served as "scripts" for songs and chants in which participants acted out elite-centered genealogical and historical material. The analytical method and conclusions reached here have wider applicability for Mesoamerican native literature as a whole.

501 Muriá, José María. Conceptos europeos en la descripción de la sociedad nahua. (*in* De palabra y obra en el Nuevo Mundo. v. 1, Imágenes interétnicas. Edición de Miguel León-Portilla *et al.* Madrid: Siglo Veintiuno Editores, 1992, p. 319–338, ill., plate)

Penetrating evaluation of how European concepts of governmental and social organization colored their descriptions of the Nahua. Beginning with the *Letters* of Cortés, author demonstrates how shifting European ideologies led to evolving, and sometimes misleading, interpretations by authors writing in Mexico, Spain, and elsewhere into the 19th century.

Newson, Linda A. The demographic collapse of native peoples of the Americas, 1492–1650. See item **1201**.

502 Noguez, Xavier. Documentos guadalupanos: un estudio sobre las fuentes de información tempranas en torno a las mariofanías en el Tepeyac. Toluca, Mexico: El Colegio Mexiquense; México: Fondo de Cultura Económica, 1993. 280 p.: appendices, bibl., ill. (Sección de obras de historia)

Another serious, detailed historical investigation into the original sources that touch on the apparition and the cult of the Virgin of Guadalupe, with appendices of selected documents in Nahuatl and Spanish. Revision of author's doctoral dissertation at Tulane Univ. For historian's comment see item **1202**.

Olmstead, Andrea. Montezuma. See item **4784**.

503 Orellana, Sandra Lee. Estrategias k'iche's de conquista en la costa sur de Guatemala, 1375–1524. (*Mesoamérica/Antigua*, 14:25, junio 1993, p. 27–38)

Using a variety of ethnohistorical sources, author analyzes several principle strategies of the Quiché in conquering and then controlling territory on the southern coast of Guatemala. In this expansion—which began in the 14th century—Quiché rulers used marital ties, resettlement, and tribute to forge and maintain control.

504 Orellana, Sandra Lee. Ethnohistory of the Pacific Coast. Illustrations by Fred Folger. Lancaster, Calif.: Labyrinthos, 1995. 161 p.: bibl., ill., index.

Capably synthesizes information from archival and published sources for a history of the lesser-known Mesoamerican coastline provinces of Suchitepéquez, Soconusco, and Escuintla. Examines geo-political boundaries, indigenous settlement patterns, linguistic history, and economic organization from pre-contact times through the 18th century.

505 Oudijk, Michel R. The second conquest: an ethnohistory of a Cajonos Zapotec village & the Lienzo of Tabaá I. (*Wampum/Leiden*, 13, 1995, p. 3–157, appendix, bibl., ill., maps, tables)

Continuation of Chance's *Conquest of the Sierra: Spaniards and Indians in colonial Oaxaca* (see *HLAS 52:1004*) describes history of the Sierra Zapoteca up to present. Offers new insights on historical processes and developments. Looks at Zapotec society from within rather than from without. Includes analysis of and commentary on the Lienzo de Tabaá I. [R. Hoefte]

506 Paredes Martínez, Carlos S. Los tributos de Michoacán en los *Códices de Cutzio y Arao.* (*Yumtzilob/Leiden*, 5:2, 1993, p. 155–171)

Competent treatment of two similar *amatl* manuscripts from 1542, held at Princeton and the Univ. of Texas at Austin, detailing tributes and efforts of indigenous peoples of the indicated communities to ease *encomienda* demands.

507 Parmenter, Ross. The lienzo of Tulancingo, Oaxaca: an introductory study of a ninth painted sheet from the Coixtlahuaca Valley. Philadelphia, Penn.: The American Philosophical Society, 1993. 86 p.: bibl., ill., index, maps. (Transactions of the American Philosophical Society, 0065–9746; v. 83, pt. 7)

Comparative and authoritative treatment of the most recently uncovered Coixtlahuaca Valley *lienzo* from San Miguel Tulancingo in the Mixteca Alta. Of late 16th-century origin, this cloth pictorial combines cartography and political history, highlighting churches, palaces, and ten couples (a "ruler list") bearing glyphic names.

508 Pendergast, David M. and **Grant D. Jones.** Poor beds of sticks and rings of pure gold: material culture in the Canek Manuscript. (*Anc. Mesoam.*, 3:2, Fall 1992, p. 281–290, bibl.)

Combining descriptions from the manuscript with other ethnohistorical data and archaeological material, the authors reconstruct at least partially some of the material cultural of the Itzá Maya, including domestic items, jewelry and clothing, canoes, buildings, and religious articles. For related article see items **458.**

Pendergast, David M. Worlds in collision: the Maya/Spanish encounter in sixteenth and seventeenth century Belize. See *HLAS 55: 350.*

509 Peterson, Jeanette Favrot. The Virgin of Guadalupe: symbol of conquest or liberation? (*Art J.*, 51:4, Winter 1992, p. 39–47)

Innovative work explores iconography in search of the meaning of the Virgin held by different groups of Mexicans, including the indigenous, "disenfranchised population."

510 Poole, Stafford. Our Lady of Guadalupe: the origins and sources of a Mexican national symbol, 1531–1797. Tuscon: Univ. of Arizona Press, 1995. 336 p.: bibl., facsim., index.

Revisionist, even-handed exploration of development of devotion to this unique virgin and her strong, if often misunderstood, associations with *indianismo* and *criollismo.* If some early Internet debates are any indicator, this work will stimulate considerable discussion. However, the author is meticulous in his use of primary sources and attention to historical accuracy. For historian's comment see item **1214.**

511 Poole, Stafford. Some observations on mission methods and native reactions in sixteenth-century New Spain. (*Americas/Francisc.*, 50:3, Jan, 1994, p. 335–349)

Lucid exploration of a few complex issues relating to 16th-century Mexican evangelization aims, methods, and results, with some attention on the Virgin of Guadalupe. Recognizes recent analysis of indigenous Christianity and continues the discussion of "syncretism," calling for further research into actual religious practice in daily life and at the community level. For historian's comment see item **1215**.

Pueblos y culturas indígenas. See item **632**.

512   Quiñones Keber, Eloise. Codex Telleriano-Remensis: ritual, divination, and history in a pictorial Aztec manuscript. Foreword by Emmanuel Le Roy Ladurie. Illustrations by Michel Besson Austin: Univ. of Texas Press, 1995. 365 p.: bibl., ill. (some col.), index, maps.

Full-scale facsimile in beautiful color reproduction, with the most detailed description and study yet published. This fascinating manuscript is a mid-16th composite of different precontact book-like traditions, encompassing information about calendrical rituals, annalistic historical events, a migration account, and a dynastic chronicle, covering several centuries and concluding in 1563.

513   Read, Kay. Sacred commoners: the motion of cosmic powers in Mexica rulership. (*Hist. Relig.*, 34:1, Aug. 1994, p. 39–69)

The author is attempting to create a new model of what rulership and power meant to the Mexica by focusing heavily on the rule of Ahuitzotl as it is described in Durán, and by comparing it to some concepts of rule and rulers drawn from Book 6 of the Florentine Codex. These, in turn, are discussed in relation to ideas about power expressed by more modern writers, such as Foucault. Some interpretations will cause debate, but are valuable for this reason.

514   Restall, Matthew. Life and death in a Maya community: the Ixil testaments of the 1760s. Lancaster, Calif.: Labyrinthos, 1994. 194 p.: bibl., ill.

Commentary, transcription, and translation of 65 Maya-language wills. The author, especially interested in ferreting out elements of cultural continuity and change in the testaments, identifies said elements in the excellent discussions introducing each document. Worthy addition to the growing body of high-quality, analytical publications of native-language records.

515   Reyes García, Cayetano. Los centinelas del mar del sur. (*Relaciones/Zamora*, 14:55, verano 1993, p. 139–161, table)

Presentation with informative commentary of a late 18th-century document that contains important ethnohistorical information about settlements on the Pacific coast of what are now the states of Michoacán and Colima of Nahuatl-speaking archers and their families who kept watch on shipping and possible activities of pirates. Significant source on the nature of indigenous colonization sponsored by the State in frontier or strategic areas.

516   Reyes Retana, Oscar. Códice de Jilotepec. Jilotepec, Mexico: H. Ayuntamiento de Jilotepec, 1990. 86 p.: bibl., ill.

Description, analysis, and facsimile presentation of a document in the Ayuntamiento of Jilotepec that concerns dynastic history of an Otomí lineage of that community and its experiences from 1430–1589 with Mexica and Spanish conquest as well as with the arrival of the Catholic faith. Somewhat in the tradition of annals, its colonial section may have served as a kind of *probanza de méritos* for a colonial-era cacique. A more thoroughly revisionist study of this manuscript is forthcoming from historian David Wright.

517   Robertson, Donald. Mexican manuscript painting of the early colonial period: the metropolitan schools. Foreword by Elizabeth Hill Boone. Norman: Univ. of Oklahoma Press, 1994. 234 p., 88 p. of plates: bibl., ill., index, maps.

New edition of this seminal work by a pioneer in the classification and interpretation of indigenous pictorial manuscripts. Many of Robertson's ideas seem fresh today, and the book remains a major resource for ethnohistorians. Boone's insightful preface places the book in the contemporary scholarly context.

518   Rodas, Isabel. Relaciones de los grupos de poder en el cabildo de Patzicía, 1564–1811. (*Estudios/Guatemala*, 3, enero 1993, p. 50–72, bibl.)

Well-researched study of the basis of power of those who controlled town government in this Cakchiquel town in Guatemala. By examining a variety of archival material, the author is able to demonstrate that an indigenous elite, basing their power on access to land, labor, and the right to collect tribute, dominated local government into the mid-18th century, when their authority began to be challenged by mestizos and ladinos who assumed growing internal influence.

519 Romero Conde, Paulino. La milpa y el origen del calendario maya. Mérida, Mexico: Gobierno del Estado de Yucatán; Univ. Autónoma de Yucatán, Dirección General de Extensión, 1994. 137 p.: bibl., ill.

Methodologically innovative study that proposes a detailed modern Maya farmers' almanac (4/93–4/94) that draws from the Haab calendar and ancient cosmology and proposes a zodiac with animals identified in the constellations. Bears a vague resemblance to the newer, interdisciplinary fields of archaeoastronomy and ethnoastronomy.

520 Rubí Alarcón, Rafael. Comunidades indígenas, siglos XVI y XVII del centro y la montaña de Guerrero. (*Estud. Cult. Náhuatl*, 23, 1993, p. 297–341)

Careful reconstruction of the political organization of indigenous communities of the *alcaldía mayor* of the Minas de Zumpango and of the Tlapa region during the first two colonial centuries. Of note is a section detailing Chilpancingo's early involvement with the supply of travelers along the Acapulco-Mexico City road, and its eventual split from the jurisdiction of Zumpango.

521 Rubí Alarcón, Rafael. Tributo prehispánico en el actual Guerrero. Guerrero, Mexico?: Colegio de Bachilleres del Estado de Guerrero, 1992. 104 p.: bibl. (Serie Orígenes)

Intended for teaching the history of the state of Guerrero, but useful for scholars working on this region because of its synthesis of primary (although all are published) and secondary sources on a topic with political, economic, and social significance and also because it illuminates a lesser-studied region.

Ruz, Mario Humberto. Los linderos del agua: Francisco de Montejo y los orígenes del Tabasco colonial. See item **1230.**

522 Sahagún, Bernardino de. Adiciones, Apéndice a la postilla; y Ejercicio cotidiano. Edición facsimilar, paleografía, versión española y notas de Arthur J.O. Anderson. Prólogo de Miguel León-Portilla. México: Univ. Nacional Autónoma de México, Instituto de Investigaciones Históricas, 1993. ccxv, 203 p.: bibl. (Facsímiles de lingüística y filología nahuas; 6)

Previously unpublished Nahuatl manuscripts, originally produced ca. 1563–79, designed to assist Catholic priests with the doctrinal instruction of indigenous peoples. Introduction briefly mentions some prehispanic traditions the manuscripts illuminate (e.g., references to Tlaloc, Quetzalcoatl, Tezcatlipoca, the calmecac and telpochcalli).

523 Schele, Linda. Apuntes sobre Copán No. 8: los fundadores del linaje de Copán y otros sitios mayas. (*Yaxkin/Tegucigalpa*, 12:2, julio/dic. 1989, p. 107–138, ill.)

Analyzes glyphic inscriptions to arrive at the origins of lineages at Copán, Yaxchilán, Tikal, and Naranjo. Includes many illustrations of the glyphic phrases.

524 Sepúlveda y Herrera, María Teresa. Catálogo de la colección de documentos históricos de Faustino Galicia Chimalpopoca. México: Instituto Nacional de Antropología e Historia, 1992. 133 p.: appendices, bibl., ill. (Col. Fuentes)

Essential research guide to Nahuatl manuscripts from the 16th and 17th centuries, compiled and hand copied in the mid-19th, that form a collection in the Biblioteca Nacional de Antropología e Historia (Mexico City). Lessons for studying Nahuatl comprise one of several interesting appendices.

525 The sky in Mayan literature. Edited by Anthony F. Aveni. New York: Oxford Univ. Press, 1992. 297 p.: bibl., ill., index.

The Dresden Codex naturally figures prominently in this anthology exploring astronomy and calendrics. Other important sources include the Paris Codex, the Madrid Codex, the Books of Chilam Balam, the Popol Vuh, and monumental inscriptions. Contributions by Aveni, B. Tedlock, V. Bricker, H. Bricker, Hofling, O'Neil, Closs, Lounsbury, Paxton, D. Tedlock, and Frake.

526 Sluyter, Andrew. Long-distance staple transport in western Mesoamerica: insights through quantitative modeling. (*Anc. Mesoam.*, 4:2, Fall 1993, p. 193–199, bibl., graph, maps, table)

Proposal of an alternative model to the now standard one conceived by Robert D. Drennan shows that it would have been energetically possible for Mesoamericans to engage in long distance trade in staples. Evidence for shipment of maize between Zempoala and Tenochtitlán during famine is used to test the model, which has suggestive results for ethnohistorians.

527 **Smith, Michael E.** Economies and polities in Aztec-period Morelos: ethnohistoric overview. (*in* Economies and polities in the Aztec realm. Albany: Institute for Mesoamerican Studies, State Univ. of New York at Albany, 1994, p. 313–348)

Excellent synthesis of archaeological and ethnohistorical data to create a socioeconomic profile of late-postclassic Morelos, and above all, the important *altepetl* of Cuauhnahuac (modern Cuernavaca) and Huaxtepec. Author's discussion is ably situated within the broader context of the Mexican heartland, and makes important contributions in the areas of tribute and trade.

528 **Smith, Michael E.** Houses and the settlement hierarchy in late postclassic Morelos: a comparison of archaeology and ethnohistory. (*in* Prehispanic domestic units in western Mesoamerica: studies of the household, compound, and residence. Boca Raton, Fla.; Ann Arbor, Mich.: CRC Press, 1993, p. 191–206)

Careful correlation of archaeological data, mainly from the late post-classic site of Cuexcomate in western Morelos, with early colonial Nahuatl-language census data from the same region (see also item **396**). The sum of these parts is highly suggestive and has much to say about the persistence of a prehispanic system of social ordering as expressed in settlement and household organization in the countryside.

529 **Smith, Michael E.** and **Cynthia Heath-Smith.** Rural economy in late postclassic Morelos. (*in* Economies and polities in the Aztec realm. Albany: Institute for Mesoamerican Studies, State Univ. of New York at Albany, 1994, p. 349–376)

Straightforward and informative study that seeks to recover the texture of life in late-postclassic western Morelos. Focusing on the sites of Cuexcomate and Capilco, authors assess evolving socioeconomic impact of such things as population growth, shifts in agricultural production, and conquests by Cuauhnahuac and the Aztec empire in the 1420s and 1430s. For related articles see items **527** and **431**.

530 **Smith, Michael E.** Social complexity in the Aztec countryside. (*in* Archaeological views from the countryside: village communities in early complex societies. Edited by Glenn M. Schwartz and Steven E. Falconer. Washington: Smithsonian Institution Press, 1994, p. 143–159, bibl., graphs, ill., map)

By focusing on the archaeological record, bolstered by a judicious use of ethnohistorical sources from two communities of rural late postclassic western Morelos (Cuexcomate and Capilco), author is able to delineate the existence of true social complexity outside of urban areas. A solid addition to a growing body of work on central Mexico which is revising the older notion that complex societies existed primarily in an urban setting.

531 **Stenzel, Werner.** Quetzalcoatl de Tula: mitogénesis de una leyenda postcortesiana. San Nicolás de los Garza, Mexico: Univ. Autónoma de Nuevo León, Facultad de Filosofía y Letras, 1991. 118 p.: bibl. (Cuadernos del unicornio; 13)

An important contribution to a favored topic, this translation from German surveys dozens of ethnohistorical sources and their references to Quetzalcoatl, tracing the evolution of this historical-mythical figure from the wind god to the white god expected to return.

532 **Stone, Cynthia Leigh.** Rewriting indigenous traditions: the burial ceremony of the *cazonci*. (*Colon. Lat. Am. Rev.*, 3:1/2, 1994, p. 87–114)

Absorbing examination of the evolving Spanish description of this rite, from the heavily indigenous influenced *Relación de Michoacán* of the 1530s to the late 18th-century *Crónica de Michoacán* of Pablo Beaumont. In a process with important implications for ethnohistorians, the Tarascan voice was replaced by Spanish interpretations, the character of which was determined by biases and agendas of individual chroniclers.

533 **Stresser-Péan, Guy.** El Códice de Xicotepec: estudio e interpretación. Traducción del manuscrito original de Araceli Méndez. Dibujos de Françoise Bagot. Fotografías del códice de Georges-Yves Massart. Presentación de Charles E. Dibble. 1ra. edición en español. México: Centro Francés de Estudios Mexicanos y Centroamericanos; Fondo de Cultura Económica; Puebla: Gobierno del Estado de Puebla, 1995. 209 p.: bibl., facsims., ill., map, photos, tables.

Handsome critical edition of recently discovered pictographic annals from an *altepetl* incorporated into the Texcocan domain in the 15th century. Spanning the years 1431–1533, the codex is significant in that it presents a provincial historical vision from a community in which Totonac and Nahuatl-speaking Acolhua coexisted. Stresser-Péan's excellent study is divided into three parts: 1) general description of the codex, analysis of glyphs, dates, and other pictorial elements, and their comparison with similar representations in other central Mexican codices; 2) detailed section-by-section discussion of the document; and 3) broad history of the time and place of the document's production. Beautiful facsimile of the codex is included.

Suárez Roca, José Luis. Lingüística misionera española. See item **778.**

534 Suma y epíloga de toda la descripción de Tlaxcala. Paleografía, presentación y notas de Andrea Martínez Baracs y Carlos Sempat Assadourian. Prólogo de Wayne Ruwet. Tlaxcala, Mexico: Univ. Autónoma de Tlaxcala, Secretaría de Extensión Universitaria y Difusión Cultural; México: Centro de Investigaciones y Estudios Superiores en Antropología Social, 1994. 257 p.: bibl., ill., index. (Col. Historia. Serie Historia de Tlaxcala; 3)

Transcription of a 69-folio document, attributed by the editors to Diego Muñoz Camargo, that was recently discovered in the holdings of the Bible Society in Great Britain. In an informative introductory essay, the present text is compared to another found in the same repository, the *Descripción de la ciudad y provincia de Tlaxcala . . .* , also linked to Muñoz Camargo. Editors suggest that in both the author was responding to the call for *relaciones geográficas,* with the *Suma* (ca. 1585–99), bearing a much closer resemblance to that documentary genre than the *Descripción.* Extremely valuable publication of a crucial source for the history of 16th-century indigenous central Mexico.

535 Taylor, William B. La religión colonial y las metáforas del Quinto Centenario: los Santiagos mejicanos y los Cristos de Caña = Colonial religion and Quincentennial metaphors: Mexican Santiagos and *Cristos de Caña.* (*in* Mesoamerican and Chicano art, culture, and identity = El arte, la cultura y la identidad mesoamericana y chicana. Salem, Oregon: Willamette Univ., 1994, p. 26–69)

Reexamines interpretations given religious images that held prominent places in Quincentenary museum exhibitions. Argues against a narrow "history-as-conquest" view of early Mexico as well as the other extreme of over-emphasizing resistance. Explores religious change as a window into "colonialism as a shared culture," drawing from Ashis Nandy.

536 Tedlock, Dennis. Torture in the archives: Mayans meet Europeans. (*Am. Anthropol.,* 95:1, 1993, p. 139–152, bibl., ill.)

Reinterpretation of early colonial records in Maya and Spanish—including testimony from Landa's idolatry investigations—that suggests alternative readings of both Spanish actions and apparent human sacrifice and crucifixion allegedly practiced by so-called "idolators." For another view see also item **436.** For anthropologist's comment see *HLAS 55:454.*

Testimonios, cartas y manifiestos indígenas: desde la conquista hasta comienzos del siglo XX. See item **662.**

537 Thiemer-Sachse, Ursula. Die Zapoteken: indianische Lebensweise und Kultur zur Zeit der spanischen Eroberung. Drawings by Anna Gröszer. Berlin: Gebr. Mann Verlag, 1995. 547 p., 39 p. of plates: bibl., ill., maps. (Indiana. Beiheft: 0341–8642; 13)

Detailed ethnohistorical study examines Zapotec socioeconomic conditions and culture on eve of Spanish conquest. Based on archaeological, ethnographical, sociological, and linguistic sources. Author's dialectical analysis provides a unique perspective. [C.K. Converse]

538 Thouvenot, Marc. TEMOA: outil de consultation et de recherche sur les textes; programme. Paris: Editions SUP-INFOR, 1994? 1 computer program, version 3.1.

A computer program designed to assist complex research in colonial Nahuatl documents, particularly in searching for one or more strings of letters, with an ingenious built-in feature that accounts for Nahuatl orthographic variation. The following is a list of encrypted texts that are consulted only through *TEMOA* and are also published by SUP-INFOR on diskettes (with paleography and trilingual—French, Spanish, and English—introductory studies all written by Thouvenot, unless otherwise indicated): *CASTILLO: Escrits de Cristobal de Castillo* (1990); *303PBN: BN303 ou Anales Mexicanos* (1990); Durand-Forest and Thouvenot, *3CHIMAL: Troisiéme Relation de Chimalpahin* (1990); *Poo1A: Annotations du Codex Xolotl* (1992); *Po11A: Annotations de la Mapa Quinatzin* (1992); *Po22B: Annales de Tlatelolco* (1992); *Po40A: Histoire mexicaine depuis 1221 jusqu'en 1594* (1992); *Po85A: Fragment de l'histoire des anciens mexicains* (1992); *P217A: Fragment d'histoire de Mexique* (1992); *P311A: Crónica Mexicayotl* (1992); *P312A: Codex Chimalpopoca: Annales de Cucuhtitlan* (1992); *P312B: Codex Chimalpopoca: Leyenda de los Soles* (1992); *P373A: Annotations de la Mapa Tlotzin* (1992); *Po10B: Lienzo de Tetlama* (1994); *Po13A: Mapa de Tepechpan* (1994); *Po15A: Annotations du Codex en Croix* (1994); *Po23A: Codex Mexicanus 23–24* (1994); *Po25A: Plan topographique de Hueyapan* (1994); *Po26A: Amecameca: cédula de diligencia* (1994); *Po28A: Tlaxinican, Tlayolotlacan Tecpanpa . . .* (1994); *Po30A: Chalco: Reçus présentés par le capitaine Jorge Ceron y Carabajal* (1994); *Po33A: Xochimilco: Plan e titre d'une propriété sise a Huexocolco* (1994); *Po34A: Xochimilco: Plan de plusieurs propriétés* (1994); *Po37A: Codex Vergara* (1994); *Po59A: Codex Azcatitlan* (1994); *Po72A: Príncipes Mexicanos* (1994); *Po73A: Confirmation des élections de Calpan* (1994); *Po77A: Manuscrit Testeriano No. 77* (1994); *PO78A: Manuscrit Testeriano No. 78* (1994); *Po94A: Santa Isabel Tola: Títulos de tierras* (1994); Romero Galván, *Po41A: Codex Cozcatzin* (1995); Quiñones Keber and Besson, *P385A: Codex Telleriano-Remensis* (1995); *Po86A: Fragment d'un Proces* (1995); *Po91A: Mapa de Sigüenza* (1995); *Po93A: Codex Boturini* (1995); *Po98A: Lienzo de Tetlama* (1995); *P101A: Lienzo de Tetlama* (also 1995); *P102A: Mapa de Coatlan del Río* (1995); *P103A: Plan topographique de Santa María Ixcatlan* (1995); *P104A: Genealogie de Citlalpopoca* (1995); *P106A: Plan du Tianquiztli* (1995); *P107A: Plan topographique de Texcoco* (1995); *P108A: Tributs de Tlaxmican, Tlaylotlacan, Tecpanpa, etc.* (1995); *P111A: Temascaltepec: Pieces d'un proces criminel* (1995); *P112A: México-Tenochtitlan: Proces, 1593* (1995); *P115A: Testament de Don Antonio Totoquihuaztli* (1995); Galarza with Thouvenot, *TECHIA: Corpus Techialoyan: Textes en caractères latins* (1990); Eisinger, *CF INDEX: Index lexical du texte nahuatl du Codex de Florence* (1994). A special dimension of *TEMOA* is the provision for "reeling in" additional documents of one's own transcription, so that they might be combined with these others for ever-more effective searching. SUP-INFOR recently began adding Otomí texts, as well: Wright, *GARCIA: Traduction d'un manuscrit en otomi et espagnol faite par Diego García de Mendoza Motecsuma (AGN de México)* (1995), and, Wright, *MARTIN: Manuscrit en otomi et espagnol de Francisco Martín de la Puente (AGN de México)* (1995). Also available are a database called *XOLOTL* (1990) and an analysis based on that codex and database (*Codex Xolotl. Etude d'une des composantes de son écriture: les glyphes. Dictionnaire des éléments constitutifs des glyphes*) (1990). Finally, Thouvenot has invented a program, *POHUA* (1990), that provides for the creation of a database centered on any Nahua codex to assist with the recording and analysis of textual descriptions of pictorial images. As this body of materials continues to grow at a rapid pace, its value increases dramatically. System requirements: IBM PC XT, AT, PS/2 or compatible; DOS 2.1 or higher; 512k ram; disk drive.

539 Tonda, Juan and **Francisco Noreña.** Los señores del cero: el conocimiento matemático en Mesoamérica. Ilustraciones de Ignacio Pérez-Duarte. México: Pangea; Consejo Nacional para la Cultura y las Artes, Dirección General de Publicaciones, 1991. 59 p.: ill. (Col. Los Señores—)

Brief book looks at nature of Maya vigesimal counting system, and especially at their concept of zero. Comparisons are made with ancient old world systems.

540 Toriz Proenza, Martha. La fiesta prehispánica: un espectáculo teatral; comparación de las descripciones de cuatro fiestas hechas por Sahagún y Durán. México: Instituto Nacional de Bellas Artes, 1993. 161 p.: bibl., ill.

Collects and compares passages from key ethnohistorical sources that describe precolumbian Nahua ritual, highlighting theatrical elements. Research was slow in getting published and therefore does not refer to other recent work on theater, but makes a useful contribution nonetheless.

541 UCLA Historical Journal. Vol. 12, 1992, Indigenous Writing in the Spanish Indies. Edited by Lisa Sousa. Los Angeles: Dept. of History, Univ. of California.

High-quality collection of cutting-edge research on the interpretation of colonial records in Nahuatl, Mixtec, and Yucatec Maya. Terraciano and Restall review the main documentary types and conventions in these three languages, while Terraciano and Sousa examine Oaxacan primordial titles in Nahuatl and Mixtec. Restall and Sigal examine such sources as litigation against alleged sexual abuse of Maya women by Catholic priests and the *Chilam Balam* to gain insights into colonial Maya sexuality. Sell uncovers sometimes surprisingly positive attitudes towards precontact Nahua society in Nahuatl-language Catholic sermonaries, confessionals, and the like.

542 Umberger, Emily. Antiques, revivals, and references to the past in Aztec art. (*Res/Harvard*, 13, Spring 1987, p. 62–105)

Splendid study that slipped through the cracks of earlier *HLAS* contributions. Explores indigenous historical consciousness by analyzing artistic evidence of the appreciation of the Mexica accorded ancient cities (especially Tula, Teotihuacán, and Xochicalco) and objects from ancient cultures, even to the point of making "archaizing copies."

543 Valero de García Lascuráin, Ana Rita. La ciudad de México-Tenochtitlán: su primera traza, 1524–1534. México: Editorial Jus, 1991. 133 p.: bibl., map. (Col. Medio milenio)

Although one of the principal interests here is the distribution of houselots to Spanish conquerors (including a marvelously detailed map), there is a reasonably informative precontact background section that draws from published primary and secondary sources. One interested in the work of Kellogg or García Zambrano, or in studying the distribution (or dislocation) of the indigenous population might find this context useful.

544 Valle P., Perla. Memorial de los indios de Tepetlaóztoc ó Códice Kingsborough: "—a cuatrocientos cuarenta años—."

México: Instituto Nacional de Antropología e Historia, 1992. 166 p.: ill. (some col.), maps. (Col. científica; 263. Serie Etnohistoria)

Careful pictographic reading of this four-part central Mexican codex painted in 1554. The manuscript contains some precolumbian history (including the town founding 440 years earlier by Chichimecas, hence the subtitle) but emphasizes colonial tribute demands. Author includes a paleographic transcription of the Spanish text.

545 Vega Sosa, Constanza. Códice Azoyú 1: el reino de Tlachinollan. México: Fondo de Cultura Económica, 1991. 139 p.: bibl., ill. (some col.), maps.

Study and excellent facsimile reproduction of an annals-like codex from the Tlapa region, in the Sierra Madre del Sur, of what is now the state of Guerrero. The codex, covering from 1300–1565, shows evidence of Teotihuacán, Mixtec, and Nahua influence on Tlapaneca culture, and also contains information about the impact of the Spanish conquest. An article by the same author (see *HLAS 55:458*) contains commentary highlighting tribute and festivals in the *Códice Azoyu 2* and the *Humboldt Fragment 1* from the same area, documents which are also mentioned comparatively in the book.

546 Vos, Jan de. La comunidad recreada: respuestas de los indios de Chiapas a la conquista. (*Rev. Hist./Heredia*, 28, julio/dic. 1993, p. 41–58)

Story of Juan López, an oral tradition collected in six versions from three different Chiapas towns, is interpreted as an alternative account of Tzeltal revolt (1712), with added elements from subsequent episodes of local resistance to outside exploitation (1838, 1855, and 1916). Author questions ability of the Western academic method to comprehend peasant realities on peasant terms. Challenging thesis merits attention. [S. Webre]

547 We people here: Nahuatl accounts of the conquest of Mexico. Edited and translated by James Lockhart. Berkeley: Univ. of California Press, 1993. 335 p.: bibl., ill., index. (Repertorium Columbianum)

Book Twelve of the Florentine Codex and fragments of other relevant texts provide 16th-century indigenous perspectives on the Spanish conquest. The informants' Nahuatl,

Sahagún's Spanish, and parallel English translations of both allow for comparisons. Besides examining specific features of each text, the introduction deftly explores more general cultural attitudes and concepts. A paperback edition would make this a serious classroom rival of *The broken spears* (see *HLAS 54:438*). For related work see item **488**.

548 Weeks, John M. Maya civilization. New York: Garland Pub., 1993. lxvi, 369 p.: ill., indexes. (Garland reference library of the humanities; 1796. Research guides to ancient civilizations; 1)

A guide for the general reader and useful to undergraduate students as a quick reference or introduction. Surveys museums and research institutions, Mayanists' biographies and writings, cultural and social histories, indigenous pictorial and written sources, and, primarily, archaeological site reports.

549 Wood, Stephanie. La mujer nahua rural bajo la colonización española: el valle de Toluca durante la época colonial tardía = Rural Nahua women under Spanish colonization: the late colonial Toluca valley. (*in* Mesoamerican and Chicano art, culture, and identity = El arte, la cultura, y la identidad mesoamericana y chicana. Salem, Ore.: Willamette Univ., 1994, p. 78–103)

Searches 108 Nahuatl testaments by men and women from 1589–1801 (but the bulk after 1750) for evidence of the impact of Spanish patriarchal forms on indigenous structures. Concludes that the indications of significant change were not as considerable as had been expected, and calls for further research.

550 Wright Carr, David Charles. La conquista del Bajío y los orígenes de San Miguel de Allende. (*Mem. Acad. Mex. Hist.,* 36, 1993, p. 251–293)

Detailed, thoroughly-researched study of the Otomí roots of San Miguel de Allende and other settlements in the Bajío. Wright discusses first the precontact cultural landscape, followed by a reconstruction of the phases of Otomí and then Spanish penetration. Author also discusses the area's development in the context of mission expansion and the Chichimec war.

551 Writing without words: alternative literacies in Mesoamerica and the Andes. Edited by Elizabeth Hill Boone and Walter

Mignolo. Durham, N.C.: Duke Univ. Press, 1994. 322 p.: bibl., ill., index.

Series of sophisticated essays identifies and discusses important media of expression among the Nahua, Mixtec, Zapotec, Maya, and Inca. Boone provides an enlightening introduction which raises the need to redefine the concept of "writing" in light of indigenous conventions and cultures and in opposition to more traditional western, often ethnocentric definitions, and posits a broader and more flexible meaning. Mignolo concludes the volume with a challenging commentary that follows indigenous literacy into the colonial era and beyond, identifying the tensions and results of the campaign to teach Castillian to make the Nahua, Maya, Inca, and others better vassals and citizens. Chapters with special significance for ethnohistorians are annotated separately (see items **397, 483,** and **500**).

Yoneda, Keiko. Los mapas de Cuauhtinchan y la historia cartográfica prehispánica. See item **146.**

552 Zantwijk, Rudolf van. The image of Tenochtitlán in the Aztec literary tradition. (*New Sch.,* 10, 1986, p. 61–84, bibl.)

Perceptive interpretation of *difrasismo* in early colonial ethnohistoric texts (including the *Florentine Codex* and the *Cantares Mexicanos*). Author analyzes how the authority of Tenochtitlán was validated by casting it as a uniquely chosen holy place, a center of supreme government, the locus of ultimate military force, and a preeminent cultural center, among other images. Pertinent sections of Nahuatl texts and English translations are presented in parallel columns.

553 Zorita, Alonso de. Life and labor in ancient Mexico: the brief and summary relation of the lords of New Spain. Translated and with an introduction by Benjamin Keen. Norman: Univ. of Oklahoma Press, 1994. 328 p.: bibl., index.

Paperback reissue of Keen's earlier translation includes a new preface that discusses Zorita's place in the European current of social humanism and surveys some of the past 30 years' revisionism regarding Zorita's information on Aztec social organization and land tenure, highlighting the *calpulli,* for example.

South America

SUSAN E. RAMIREZ, *Professor of History, DePaul University*

THE FIELD OF ETHNOHISTORY as manifested in the publications reviewed here continues to develop and advance. The books and monographs can be divided into several, overlapping categories. The most basic are three items that will facilitate research, including two guides to archives. One is a wide-ranging primer on manuscript references on native life in colonial Paraguay found in the archives of that country and in those of Argentina and Spain (item **656**). The second is a truly superb catalog of the "Caciques e Indios" section of the National Archive of Colombia, which has recently moved to more spacious quarters in an ultra-modern new building near the presidential palace (item **565**). The catalog's four indexes (toponyms, personal names, years, and themes) make it a model for investigative efficiency. It should be noted, too, that this archive is a leader in the microfilming of colonial sources, and all of the papers in this section can be obtained on film. The third item is a short overview of the field in the Southern Cone by Kristine Jones that will prove of interest not only to those focused on southern South America, but perhaps, too, to those looking for information to compare and contrast with their own findings elsewhere (item **599**).

To these research aids can be added published primary sources. The transcription and editing of unpublished sources is now a long-established practice that we hope continues. Such work, whether it be of standard works, such as the reedition of the *Relación de la religión y ritos del Perú hecha por los padres agustinos* (item **638**) or *El Tercer Concilio Limense* (item **605**), or of "new finds," such as the Toledo-ordered Visita of Tiquipaya (item **585**) or a court case over land involving Felipe Guamán Poma de Ayala (item **588**), gives many home-bound investigators access to materials necessary to carry out their work.

By far the largest category of works deals with local histories, defined either by territorial boundaries or by ethnic group. Most studies concentrate on indigenous groups in a given territory during various historical epochs. We find here examples about different areas of Peru (Cusco, Piura, Juliaca, Lima, and Southern Peru), Chile, Ecuador, Colombia, Argentina, Venezuela, Brazil, Paraguay, and French Guiana. Other studies disregard the modern frontiers of nation-states and smaller administrative districts to study indigenous groups wherever they lived. To the already well-studied Tiwanaku (item **601**), Chankas (item **583**), Aymara (item **609**), and Guarani (items **568** and **604**), we here add studies of the less well-known peoples identified as the Pijaos (item **563**), Cazuetíos (item **584**), Pakaxe (item **571**), Muiscas (items **629** and **591**), Tomuza (item **620**), Soito (item **572**), Puelches (item **576**), Guaikuru (item **666**), Mojos (item **587**), and Churumatas (items **574** and **631**).

Interest in the Inca has not diminished. To the recent book-length reinterpretations of the empire (e.g., Bauer, Geoffrey Conrad, etc.), we add two more: one by Gustavo Valcárcel (item **664**) and one by Martti Pärssinen (item **627**). Other works include an imaginative study on frontiers by Catherine Julien (item **600**); the Inca use of space (item **616**); and three articles on irrigation by Jeanette Sherbondy (items **651**, **652**, and **653**).

Although these local histories offer a grab-bag of foci and methodologies, they indicate significant ethnohistorical progress, helping correct the almost total neglect in surveys of the native side of the story. Studies of the history of peoples who never had contact with the Inca, who may have lived in the lowlands and jungle regions far from the highland Inca administrative center or Spanish population centers, give readers some understanding of the diversity and range of indigenous cultures that existed. They also remind us that the so-called "conquest" and/or "invasion" of the Spanish, Portuguese, and other European powers (the French in Guyana) did not take place in two years (at Tenochtitlán), or an afternoon (at Cajamarca), but was gradual. Decades and centuries passed before some native groups experienced the full weight of colonial domination.

These realizations and other ethnohistorical perspectives (as opposed to strictly European views) are just beginning to be reflected in "national" history textbooks (e.g., those by María Rostworowski and Waldemar Espinoza Soriano). These local histories will help diversify and balance the "centralized" (i.e., Lima- or Cusco-centered) and "Western" biases of many colonial and national overviews. The study of the various ethnic groups living under Inca hegemony will also help readers counter the Cusco-centered, top-down, imperial biases of many chroniclers. We can hope that the future authors of US textbooks will find more space than that currently dedicated to an overview of the Aztecs and the Incas (usually in an initial chapter) to add these findings and undo the "history written by the victors" slant of many such works.

Another large group of monographs and articles is thematically organized. The numerous studies of indigenous resistance and rebellion, following the lead of such scholars as Scarlett O'Phelan and Steve Stern, mark the death knoll of the myth of the passive peasant, should there still be any lingering doubt. Several of the studies, most notably Ward Stavig's article (item **654**), use violence and revolt as a way to recover and understand the values and mindset of the actors. With or without the Jesuit missions, the Guarani and cross-cultural contact continue to attract scholarly attention.

Themes underrepresented here include women (items **566** and **624**); huacas and looting (item **673,** although Rostworowski is planning a text on the same topic); kuracas (item **628**); Inca succession (item **637**); and *mitmaq* (item **608**). Only one item dealt with medical practices (item **639**), although one can hope that other authors will be attracted to the theme, given the world-wide interest in the medicinal properties of plants native to the fast-disappearing rainforests. Trade and exchange relationships (items **618** and **649**) need more attention to more fully describe the contacts between highland and lowland peoples (item **669**). The scant attention to migration (item **581**) was another surprise given recent interest in the topic by Nicolás Sánchez Albornoz, Ann Whitman, David Robinson, and Karen Powers, whose book on colonial Ecuador deals, in part, with the topic (item **2363**).

The one disappointment is the absence of work from a comparative approach. Although such studies bring unique perspectives to scholarship, their funding can be problematic. Nonetheless, they often prove valuable not only to ethnohistorians of Latin America, but also to specialists of other disciplines with other regional and temporal interests. Some works in this broad category were, from my perspective, "most memorable" either for methodological or thematic reasons. Included here are works calling attention to hitherto relatively neglected themes, such as the anthologies on drinking (item **644**) or the mestizo (item **633**), both of which are so ubiquitous as to escape particular notice, until now. The psychohistory of Garcilaso de la Vega (item **589**) relates well to studies of indigenous memory, identity, and mindset (items **636**, **596**, and **658**), illustrating how new insights can be coaxed out of standard sources. Catherine Julien's book on the boundaries of Condesuyo represents a topic that has rarely been systematically and closely studied; it is based on both archaeological and historical analysis (item 600). A study of toponyms as indicators of the economic resources used by native peoples during their seasonal itineraries offers a model for the study of place names elsewhere (item 618). Finally, Golte's monograph (item 582) on Moche iconography promises to prove helpful in understanding the ritual role of important native officials in early colonial times, perhaps thus confirming strong continuities between the Moche and the Chimu (the latter under Inca rule).

Finally, some of the items reviewed here were published to commemorate the Quincentenary. These range in focus and scholarly appeal. These and other, more popular, publications are of note, because they help maintain interest in the past by making professional efforts accessible to the general public.

In sum, new data, new interpretations, and new topics combine to make the field of ethnohistory an exciting one to read.

554 **Adelaar, Willem F.H.** La procedencia dialectal del manuscrito de Huarochirí en base a sus características lingüísticas. (*Rev. Andin.*, 12:1, julio 1994, p. 137–154, bibl.)

Good study of the Quechua of the Huarochirí manuscript, which tries to classify language of the text among various Quechua dialects by using its phonological, morphological, and syntactic characteristics.

555 **Aldana Rivera, Susana** and **Alejandro Diez Hurtado.** Balsillas, piajenos y algodón: procesos históricos en el extremo norte. Lima: CIPCA; TAREA, 1994. 162 p.: bibl., ill. (some col.), index, maps.

Well-written book synthesizes geographical and historical information to place the northern-most region of modern Peru in a wider context. The title refers to: 1) rafts that native fishermen and traders used in the 16th century; 2) burros and mules that have moved people and goods overland since colonial times; and 3) cotton, one of the traditional products of the area. These three themes link the story of Piura from prehispanic and colonial to modern times.

556 **Amat Olazábal, Hernán** *et al.* V centenario, 1492–1992: analísis y debate. Lima: Centro de Estudios Histórico-Militares del Perú, 1992. 328 p.: bibl., ill.

Another compilation of articles to commemorate the Quincentennial. Contributions treat the prehispanic period (Amat Olazábal), the "discovery" (Vega), demographic consequences of "discovery" (Bueno Mendoza), the Inca elite and state (Espinoza Soriano and Guzmán Palomino), the conquest (Guillén Guillén), the juridical aspects of encounter (Solar Rojas), the resistance of jungle peoples (Chávez Valenzuela) and the chronicler Salinas y Córdova (Barrantes Arrese).

557 **Andrade Reimers, Luis.** El siglo heroico. Quito: Banco Central del Ecuador, 1992. 281 p.: bibl. (Col. histórica; 22)

Summary of the Inca conquest of its empire and its subsequent conquest by the Spanish, written with a slight emphasis on events that happened in what is today Ecuador. Based mostly on chronicles and other published sources, both primary and secondary.

558 **Ayca Gallegos, Oscar Raúl.** Los orígenes de Juliaca: 8,000 años de historia. Tacna, Peru: Instituto de Estudios Andinos, 1992. 133 p.: bibl., ill. (Serie cultura andina)

Little book on prehispanic history of Juliaca, Peru from the Formative Period through its incorporation by the Inca into the Tawantinsuyo. Includes a map, illustrations, and a bibliography.

559 **Balée, William L.** Footprints of the forest: Ka'apor ethnobotany; the historical ecology of plant utilization by an Amazonian people. New York: Columbia Univ. Press, 1994. 396 p.: bibl., ill., index. (Biology and resource management in the tropics series)

Focuses on historical ecology as a powerful paradigm for comprehending interrelationships between Amazonian environments and associated indigenous societies. Examines interpenetration of culture and environment rather than just the adaptation of human beings to the environment. Author studied the Ka'apor people of the eastern state of Maranhão and their use and management of forest resources. Book contains extensive appendices summarizing author's scientific findings.

560   **Bechis, Martha.** Matrimonio y política en la génesis de dos parcialidades mapuche durante el siglo XIX. (*Mem. Am.*, 3. 1994, p. 41–62, bibl., graphs)

Suggestive study on the unusual marriage pattern of Mapuche and Arucanian peoples living in 19th-century Argentina. Author hypothesizes that multiple marriages were a means to ally and bind persons to a *parcialidad.*

561   **Bejder, Peter.** Solgudens Rige: inkaernes historie og kultur. Herning, Denmark: Forlaget Systime, 1993. 112 p.: bibl.

General historical account of the Inca empire. Unfortunately, author does not take into account the latest ethnohistorical research for a better understanding and interpretation of the Inca empire. Includes several factual errors. [I. Schjellerup]

562   **Beltrán Acosta, Luis.** La verdadera resistencia indígena contra la Corona española. Caracas: Ediciones Los Heraldos Negros, 1993. 189 p.: bibl., ill.

Book written to examine native reaction and resistance to Spanish contact and colonization in what are today Venezuelan territories, akin to previously published works by Miguel León-Portilla on the Aztecs and Guillermo Guillén-Guillén on the Incas. Chapters highlight prehispanic society, Columbus' voyages, native American slavery, and the various forms of native resistance.

563   **Bernal Andrade, Leovigildo.** Los heróicos pijaos y el Chaparral de los Reyes. Bogotá: Litho Imagen, 1993. 370 p.: ill., map (1 folded).

Dense but sparsely footnoted book on the Pijaos (an indigenous group which inhabited the north of the Dept. of Huila and the south of Tolima in modern Colombia at the time of contact) and the Chaparral de los Reyes, complete with transcribed primary sources. Based on chroniclers' accounts and other records, author details the long history of Pijaos resistance to colonial rule, and subsequent settlement of their territory around the town and fort of Medina de las Torres de los Pijaos del Chaparral de los Reyes.

564   **Bernand, Carmen.** The Incas: people of the sun. Translated from the French by Paul G. Bahn. New York: Harry N. Abrams, 1994. 191 p.: ill. (some col.), photos. (Discoveries)

Popular book on the Incas of Peru highlights the Hiram Bingham expedition that found the "lost city" of the Incas, Machu Picchu; the conquest at Cajamarca; everyday life and work of native Peruvians; and religious beliefs. Contains excerpts from primary sources in a documentary section and numerous line drawings and color photographs.

Block, David. Mission culture on the upper Amazon: native tradition, Jesuit enterprise & secular policy in Moxos, 1660–1880. See item **2473.**

Brotherston, Gordon. Book of the fourth world: reading the Native Americas through their literature. See item **401.**

565   **Caciques e indios: catálogo e índices.** Bogotá: Archivo General de la Nación, Ministerio de Gobierno, 1992. 679 p.

Long-awaited index to the "Caciques e Indios" collection of the colonial section of the Archivo Nacional of Colombia. Indices to toponyms, names, years, and themes make this an easy resource to consult and use.

566   **Cajías de la Vega, Magdalena *et al.*** La mujer en las sociedades prehispánicas de Bolivia. La Paz: Investigaciones Históricas, Identidad y Memoria, Centro de Información y Desarrollo de la Mujer, 1994. 87 p.: bibl., maps.

Short book based on secondary sources covers role of women in prehispanic society. To understand this topic, authors necessarily discuss social-familial, political, and economic structures of the Aymara and the Tawantinsuyo in general.

567   **Cañedo-Argüelles Fabrega, Teresa.** El poder religioso como cauce y obstáculo de la transculturación andina: la integración alterada; Valle de Moquegua, siglos XVI-XVIII. (*in* Memoria, creación e historia: luchar contra el olvido. Coordinación de Pilar García Jordán, Miguel Izard y Javier Laviña. Barcelona: Univ. de Barcelona, 1993, p. 179–192)

Densely written, well-documented article on the failure of the Catholic Church to achieve effective conversion among the natives of southern Peru. Author argues that, especially after independence, native customs and traditions reappeared and displaced Church-imposed norms and rules.

568 Carbonell de Masy, Rafael; Teresa Blumers; and Ernesto J.A. Maeder. Estrategias de desarrollo rural en los pueblos guaraníes, 1609–1767. Barcelona: A. Bosch; Sociedad Estatal Quinto Centenario; Instituto de Estudios Fiscales; Instituto de Cooperación Iberoamericana, 1992. 512 p.: bibl., ill. (some col.), index, maps. (Monografías Economía quinto centenario)

Serious study of the history of Jesuit missions among the Guaraní centers on their economic development. Years of archival research in approximately 12 countries has resulted in a readable, detailed exposition on several aspects of the economic (and to a lesser extent, religious and social) life of the missions. Includes thorough indexes, extensive notes, and a long bibliography.

569 Cárdenas Ayaipoma, Mario. La población aborigen del Valle de Lima en el siglo XVI. Lima: Univ. Nacional Mayor de San Marcos; CONCYTEC, 1989. 124 p.: bibl., ill., map.

Short book delivers much more than the title might indicate. Transcends study of indigenous demographic trends to analyze and describe political and economic organization and social structure of the inhabitants of a region made up of the valleys along the Rimac, Lurín, and Chillón Rivers. Last chapter reconstructs history of the school for the sons of *curacas*.

570 Carrera, Manuel Mesías and Frank Salomon. Historia y cultura popular de Zámbiza. Quito: Centro Ecuatoriano para el Desarrollo de la Communidad, 1990. 201 p.: bibl., ill. (Serie Historia social e identidad nacional)

Local history of San Miguel de Zámbiza (Ecuador), from 1583. After a brief historical sketch, Salomon presents a discussion of one ethnic lord, Don Pedro de Zámbiza. Book ends with a description of popular culture, including festivities, traditions, music, and poetry.

571 Choque Canqui, Roberto. Sociedad y economía colonial en el sur andino. La Paz: Hisbol, 1993. 180 p.: bibl. (Biblioteca andina; 17)

Book unites various conference papers

given by the author on the *señorío* of Pakaxe. Section one discusses the *mita*, tribute, and education. Section two focuses on native production and commerce. All chapters are based on primary sources and copiously footnoted.

572 Civrieux, Marc de. Watunna, un ciclo de creación en el Orinoco. 2a ed. Caracas: Monte Avila Editores, 1992. 273 p.: bibl., ill. (Estudios)

Book attempts to fix the oral tradition of the Soito or Makiritares of the Upper Orinoco (Venezuela). Legends refer to the "Gente Antigua" or the heavenly ancestors and convey tribal law and modes of conduct. Long introduction places legends in their historical context. Includes helpful glossary and bibliography.

573 Cronistas indios y mestizos. v. 2, Guamán Poma de Ayala. Recopilación de Francisco Carrillo. Lima: Editorial Horizonte, 1991–1992. 1 v.: bibl., ill. (Enciclopedia histórica de la literatura peruana; 7)

Volume dedicated to the long letter written by Felipe Guamán Poma de Ayala to the king of Spain. Lengthy introduction is followed by excerpts organized under such topics as the governing Incas, customs, Spanish conquest, viceregal life, and exploitation of the Indian.

574 Doucet, Gastón Gabriel. Acerca de los Churumatas, con particular referencia al antiguo Tucumán. (*Histórica/Lima*, 17:1, julio 1993, p. 21–91, bibl.)

Close and questioning examination of some generally accepted statements on the Churumatas from the 16th and 17th centuries. Author's analysis of quotes from known primary sources thus summarizes what is known about this ethnic group and to what degree each piece of information is reliable and verifiable. Complements item **631.**

575 Dueñas de Anhalzer, Carmen. Soberanía e insurrección en Manabí. Quito: Facultad Latinoamericana de Ciencias Sociales; Abya-Yala, 1991. 146 p.: bibl. (Col. Tesis; 3)

Short book on 19th-century history of the province of Manabí (Ecuador), based on primary research in the archives of Quito and Guayaquil. Analyzes land conflicts and the commercial economy to explain social and political trends.

576 Durán, Víctor. Las poblaciones indígenas del sur mendocino durante los siglos XVI y XVII. (*An. Arqueol. Etnol.*, 46/47, 1991/92, p. 9–40, bibl, graphs)

Reexamines primary and secondary sources on 16th- and 17th-century ethnohistory of native peoples of southern Mendoza, especially those called "Puelches." Author includes extensive quotes from documentary materials. Much of the information relates to material culture.

577 Estrella, Eduardo. La función social del beber en los pueblos andinos prehispánicos. (*Anu. Estud. Am.*, 50:2, 1993, p. 45–58)

Short study of consumption of *chicha* (maize beer) in the Andes, and particularly in Ecuador. Based theoretically on Cassirer and Lévi-Strauss, article categorizes uses of *chicha* in different cultural contexts. Author's evidence mainly comes from chronicles and 16th-century Spanish accounts.

578 Fedorova, I.K. Ostrov Paskhi: ocherki kul'tury XVIII-XIX vv [Easter Island: essays in XVIII-XIX century culture]. Saint Petersburg, Russia: Nauka, 1993. 284 p.: bibl., ill.

In her third published study of the inhabitants of Easter Island, author draws on ethnographic evidence and folklore to illuminate several complex areas of Rapa Nui culture and ethnohistory, including social structure, religion, and language. Two extensive bibliographies of Russian and Western sources support the original research in this study published for the Museum of Anthropology and Ethnography in Saint Petersburg. Some illustrations. [B. Dash]

579 Fernández, Juan Patricio. Relación histtorial de las misiones de indios chiquitos que en el Paraguay tienen los padres de la Compañía de Jesús. Presentación y notas por Daniel J. Santamaría. San Salvador de Jujuy, Argentina: Centro de Estudios Indígenas y Coloniales, Depto. Editorial, 1994. 229 p.: bibl. (Biblioteca de historia y antropología; 2)

Reedition of 19th-century study by the Jesuit Juan Patricio Fernández of the Chiquitos missions of Paraguay. (See also item **613**). Account is valuable for its ethnographic material and its literary style. Author's ideas illustrate the transition between the heroic and the Baroque and the rationalization of the Enlightenment.

580 Figueiras, Miguel Angel. Cacique y coronel del Ejército Argentino, Y. Coliqueo y su tribu: 130 años de evolución, 1860–1990; Los Toldos-Prov. Bs. As. Buenos Aires?: s.n., 1991. 134 p.: bibl., ill., maps.

Local history of the Argentine town of Los Toldos (Buenos Aires Prov.) summarizes biography of Ignacio Coliqueo (1796–1871). Book includes some primary sources and discusses the history of the town up to 1990.

581 Galdós Rodríguez, Guillermo. Migración y estructuralismo en la etnohistoria de Arequipa. Arequipa, Peru: Centro de Publicaciones de la Facultad de Ciencias Histórico Sociales de la UNSA, 1992. 162 p.: ill., maps.

Hypothesizes that migration of Andean peoples determined socioeconomic structures of native communities in the circum-Arequipa area of southern Peru. Also includes information on the etymology of the toponym "Arequipa," mitmaqs, guano, and technology.

582 Golte, Jürgen. Iconos y narraciones: la reconstrucción de una secuencia de imágenes moche. Lima: IEP, 1994. 144 p.: bibl., ill. (Fuentes e investigaciones para la historia del Perú, 1019–4487; 10)

Innovative attempt to systematically understand the atypical and extraordinary productivity and artistic creativity of the Moche culture. Author searches for answers to questions about exchange of products and politico-religious power from an analysis of paintings and effigy pottery.

583 González Carré, Enrique. Los señorios chankas. Lima: Univ. Nacional de San Cristóbal de Huamanga: Instituto Andino de Estudios Arqueológicos, 1992. 153 p.: bibl., ill., maps.

Dense volume, based on archaeological remains and documentary evidence, presents the history from the Lithic through Inca times of the Chanca peoples, who lived in Ayacucho, Apurímac, and part of the Huancavelica.

584 González Segovia, Armando José. Ibeandí maendurí = Nuestra historia. Versión corr. y aum. Venezuela: Asociación de Escritores de Venezuela, Seccional Cojedes; Consejo Nacional de la Cultura, 1990? 60 p.: bibl., ill., two maps.

Short contribution to history of the Caquetíos peoples of Venezuela from prehispanic times to the 18th century. Second half of the book covers efforts by missionaries to convert and hispanicize native peoples, and the subsequent transition to towns and parishes (pueblos de doctrina) with a duly constituted native *cabildo* or council.

585   Gordillo, José M. and **Mercedes del Río.** La visita de Tiquipaya, 1573: análisis etno-demográfico de un padrón toledano. Cochabamba, Bolivia: UMSS; CERES; ODEC/FRE, 1993. 271 p.: appendix, bibl.

Detailed scholarly analysis of the Toledo-ordered *visita* of Tiquipaya in 1573 (a copy of which is transcribed and included in the appendix). Authors use statistical tools and demographic and anthropological concepts to study this local census and arrive at conclusions about the nature of Spanish rule vis-à-vis that of the Incas. Study complements the seminal study of Nathan Wachtel on the social organization and political reforms of the Inca Huayna Capac in the same geographical setting.

586   Groot de Mahecha, Ana María and **Eva María Hooykaas.** Intento de delimitación del territorio de los grupos étnicos pastos y quillacingas en el altiplano nariñense. Bogotá: Fundación de Investigaciones Arqueológicas Nacionales, Banco de la República, 1991. 166 p.: appendices, bibl., ill., maps. (Publicación de la Fundación de Investigaciones Arqueológicas Nacionales; 48)

Interdisciplinary study based on archaeological, historical, and linguistic evidence that attempts to document native history of the highlands *(altiplano)* immediately prior to the Spanish invasion and during the first few years of colonization. Authors identify ethnic groups involved (Pastos and Quillacingas), indigenous settlement patterns, migrations, and types of inter-group contacts. Charts are included in two appendices.

587   Grupo de Estudios del Noroeste Boliviano Amazónico. Agricultores prehispánicos en la fertilización de la tierra en pampas estériles en la Amazonía boliviana: práctica de una cultura desaparecida. (*in* Memoria, creación e historia: luchar contra el olvido. Coordinación de Pilar García Jordán, Miguel Izard y Javier Laviña. Barcelona: Univ. de Barcelona, 1993, p. 29–40)

Brief, popular unfootnoted essay on the prehispanic Mojos of northeastern Bolivia. Much bibliography on the topic is overlooked.

588   Guamán Poma de Ayala, Felipe. Y no ay remedio—. Edición de Elías Prado Tello y Alfredo Prado Prado. Lima: Centro de Investigación y Promoción Amazónica, 1991. 410 p.: 2 folded ill.

Exciting contribution to our knowledge about Felipe Guamán Poma de Ayala, author of *Nueva Corónica y Buen Gobierno*, a long letter to the King of Spain on the history and 17th-century conditions of the native inhabitants of the Andes. This book is based on and includes the transcription of a court case about land ownership in the Valle of Chupas (Ayacucho) to which Guamán Poma was a party. Careful reading of the manuscript provides information on rural villages of early-17th-century Chupas, as well as on slavery and the foundation of Huamanga. Includes lengthy introductory essay by well-known historian Pablo Macera.

Guía preliminar de fuentes documentales etnográficas para el estudio de los pueblos indígenas de Iberoamérica. See item 35.

Guía preliminar de fuentes documentales etnográficas para el estudio de los pueblos indígenas de Iberoamérica. See item 13.

589   Hernández, Max. Memoria del bien perdido: conflicto, identidad y nostalgia en el Inca Garcilaso de la Vega. 1ra. ed. peruana, corr. y aum. por el autor. Lima: Instituto de Estudios Peruanos; Biblioteca Peruana de Psicoanálisis, 1993. 236 p.: bibl. (Col. Biblioteca peruana de psicoanálisis; 15. Perú problema, 0079–1075; 22)

Psychoanalytic analysis of the life and work of Inca Garcilaso de la Vega. Author hypothesizes that Garcilaso wrote to "restore the identity to his soul . . ." (p. 22) Living in a society that valued "pure blood" (*pureza de sangre*), Garcilaso, who was a mestizo, bastard, and expatriate, strove to be recognized as an equal in Spanish society. Keeping these factors in mind helps understand Garcilaso's interpretation of Inca society and empire.

590   Hernández, Max; Alberto Péndola and **María Rostworowski de Diez Canseco.** El umbral de los dioses. Edición de Moisés Lemlij y Luis Millones, Lima: Biblioteca Peruana de Psicoanálisis, Seminario Interdisciplinario de Estudios Andinos, 1991. 281 p.: bibl. (Biblioteca peruana de psicoanálisis; 6)

A product of history and psychoanalysis, this book unites innovative chapters by several authors on various aspects of the Andean mind set. Analysis of myths, Santa Rosa's dreams, and the Taki Onqoy are some of the subjects covered.

591 Herrera Angel, Marta. Autoridades indígenas en la provincia de Santafé, siglo XVIII. (*Rev. Colomb. Antropol.*, 30, 1993, p. 7–35, bibl.)

Examines political structure of Muisca indigenous communities in 18th-century New Granada. Author argues that the Spanish used indigenous officials to serve the ends of the colonial state.

592 Hinojosa C., Iván. El nudo colonial: la violencia en el movimiento tupamarista. (*in* Congreso Nacional de Investigaciones en Historia, *1st, Lima, 1984.* Actas. Lima, CONCYTEC, 1991, v. 1, p. 61–75, bibl.)

Short article examines the role violence played in the Túpac Amaru rebellion. Author concludes that the violence of the rebels was surpassed by the violence of a coalition of whites, mestizos, and even some Indians. His references to the secondary literature contribute to this informative article.

Hirschkind, Lynn. History of the Indian population of Cañar. See item **2334.**

593 L'histoire de la Guyane française. Cayenne: C.D.D.P. de Cayenne, 1990? 1 v.

Historical anthology on French Guiana covers precolumbian times, slavery, social structure, and economy in the 18th century.

594 Hocquenghem, Anne-Marie. Los guayacundos de Caxas y la Sierra Piurana: siglos XV y XVI. Lima?: Centro de Investigación y Promoción del Campesinado; Instituto Francés de Estudios Andinos, 1990? 200 p.: bibl., ill., maps. (Col. Travaux de l'IFEA; 48)

Regional history by long-time resident and serious scholar of the area traces cultural evolution of a people during the 15th and 16th centuries. Concludes that in prehispanic times the modern Piura region of Peru was inhabited by Yungas on the coast, Guayacundos (of Jivaro extraction) in the highlands of Ayabaca, and other Amazonic groups in the highlands of Huancabamba. Inca domination of the Guayacundos was short and, therefore,

weak. Author bases her findings on archaeology as well as documentary sources and ethnographic observation.

595 Huellas en la tierra: indios, agricultores y hacendados en la pampa bonaerense. Recopilación de Raúl J. Mandrini y Andrea Reguera. Tandil, Argentina: Instituto de Estudios Histórico Sociales, 1993. 355 p.: bibl., ill.

Compilation of articles on agrarian history of the pampas of Buenos Aires from prehispanic times to the 20th century. Some chapters cover smallholders and renters as well as Indians and *hacendados.* Several contributions are good examples of quantitative history. Others discuss the importance of the environment and ecological systems.

596 Huhle, Rainer. El terremoto de Cajamarca: la derrota del Inca en la memoria colectiva; elementos para un análisis de la resistencia cultural de los pueblos andinos. (*Ibero-Am. Arch.*, 18:3/4, 1992, p. 384–427)

Interesting discussion of the first encounter between Pizarro, Valverde, and other Spanish invaders and the Inca Atahualpa at Cajamarca in 1532 and of how the event is recalled and portrayed in popular drama, rituals, and ceremonies.

597 Hux, Meinrado. Caciques borogas y araucanos. Buenos Aires: Ediciones Marymar, 1992. 187 p.: ill., maps. (Col. Patagonia)

Over 50 biographical sketches of caciques and native leaders who lived in the late 18th and 19th centuries, by an author who has published four other works on the same or similar themes. Book lacks introduction or conclusion that places these biographies in historical perspective, that discusses how and why these individuals were selected, that underscores their similarities and/or differences, or that discusses the individuals' roles in the history of Argentina and Chile. Nonetheless, could provide some scholar a beginning for a prosopography of native leaders.

598 Izko Gastón, Xavier. La doble frontera: ecología, política y ritual en el altiplano central. La Paz: Hisbol/Ceres, 1992. 131 p.: bibl., ill., maps. (Biblioteca andina; 11)

Solidly researched book presents two studies. The first analyzes an 1894 court case about inter-ethnic land conflict (between the *ayllus* Sakaka and Kirkyawi), begun in 1646, with evidence dating to 1591. The second part discusses conflict between ethnic groups and the State or other forces external to the indigenous organization.

Jaguar no sokuseki: Andesu, Amezon no shū-kyo to girei [Jaguar's trace: religion and ritual in the Andes and the Amazon]. See *HLAS 55: 859.*

599 Jones, Kristine L. Comparative ethno-history and the Southern Cone. (*LARR*, 29:1, 1994, p. 107–118, bibl.)

Short overview of ethnohistory traces the field's development and advances in North American research and then reviews studies by scholars of the Southern Cone, especially those on Argentina and Chile. Author ends with good suggestions for future research.

600 Julien, Catherine J. Condesuyo: the political division of territory under Inca and Spanish rule. Bonn, Germany: Seminar für Völkerkunde, Univ. Bonn, 1991. 173 p.: bibl., ill., maps. (Bonner amerikanistische Studien = Estudios americanistas de Bonn, 0176–6546; 19)

Slim volume designed to create an image of the 16th-century economy across a large territory (Condesuyo) and therefore, to put regions in a comparative framework. In particular, author analyzes territorial organization under both Spanish and Inca rule. Study begins with the reconstruction of the Spanish political division of the 1570s and then looks backward to the political division of territory under an earlier, Andean central authority.

601 Kolata, Alan L. The Tiwanaku: portrait of an Andean civilization. Cambridge, Mass.: Blackwell, 1993. 317 p.: bibl., ill., index, maps. (The Peoples of America)

First published history of the Tiwanakan peoples from their origins to the present day based on historical documents, accounts and legends of contemporary inhabitants, and results of archaeological excavations. Author discusses origins of their massive architecture, the nature of their sophisticated hydraulically-engineered agriculture, their obsession with decapitation and the display of severed heads, and reasons for their sudden decline at the end of the 10th century.

602 Kurella, Doris. Handel und soziale Organisation im vorspanischen nördlichen Andenraum: zur politischen Ökonomie subandiner Häuptlingstümer im Gebiet des ehemaligen Nuevo Reino de Granada vor der Eroberung durch die Spanier im frühen 16. Jahrhundert. Bonn: Holos, 1993. 352 p.: bibl., maps. (Mundus Reihe Alt-Amerikanistik; 9)

Based on a wealth of primary sources, illustrates diversity of social organization and economic activities of precolumbian multi-ethnic groups of the northern Andes. Author's findings deviate from those of others by emphasizing that large, dominant groups were socially and economically more dependent on small communities than hitherto recognized. [C.K. Converse]

603 Langebaek Rueda, Carl Henrik. Noticias de caciques muy mayores: orígen y desarrollo de sociedades complejas en el nororiente de Colombia y norte de Venezuela. Bogotá: Univ. de los Andes, 1992. 256 p.: bibl., maps.

Thoughtful book on the evolution of peoples and cultures in what today is northeastern Colombia and northern Venezuela from the prehispanic period to the 16th century. Author assesses effects of social, technological, and environmental factors on the development of complex societies and discusses relationships between indigenous societies in the 16th century. Based on archaeological and ethnohistorical sources.

604 Levinton, Norberto. La tapiización de los Ava. (*in* Historia de los argentinos. Argentina: Asociación de Fabricantes Argentinos de Coca-Cola, 1990, p. 151–173, bibl.)

Thought-provoking, innovative study of the Guaranis before and after contact with the Spanish, especially the Jesuit order. Author focuses on transformation of identity.

605 Lisi, Francesco Leonardo. El tercer concilio limense y la aculturación de los indígenas sudamericanos: estudio crítico con edición, traducción y comentario de las actas del concilio provincial celebrado en Lima entre 1582 y 1583. Salamanca, Spain: Univ. de Salamanca, 1990. 382 p.: bibl. (Acta Salmanticensia. Estudios filológicos; 233)

This new edition of 1586 text of the third Concilio de Lima found in the Biblioteca Universitaria de Salamanca includes a study of the evangelization policy of the Catholic Church at the end of the 16th century and a lengthy discussion of José de Acosta. Extensive footnotes, a good bibliography, and both the Latin text and its Spanish translation should prove helpful to all scholars of 16th-century religion in Peru.

606   Lorandi, Ana María and **Mercedes del Río.** La etnohistoria: etnogénesis y transformaciones sociales andinas. Buenos Aires: Centro Editor de América Latina, 1992. 204 p.: bibl. (Los Fundamentos de las ciencias del hombre; 69)

Volume written to succinctly describe various theories that underpin the field of ethnohistory. Focused on the Andes, it analyzes in detail the hegemony of the Inca and Spanish empires over various ethnic groups. Different chapters reviewing theories, sources, the Inca empire, the Spanish empire, and indigenous social movements give the reader a basic overview of the development of the field in the last few decades.

607   Lorier, Eduardo. La Capataza: probanza de la desaparición de un pueblo de indios; San Borja del Yi. Montevideo: Ediciones de la Banda Oriental, 1992. 117 p.: map. (Lectores de Banda Oriental; 5. ser., 31)

History of the Guaranis in the 19th century and their quest for a permanent home in San Borja del Yi (Uruguay). The story revolves around the figure of Doña Luisa Tiraparé, the widow of the *cacique* Fernando Tiraparé; the struggle for land; and the hispanization of a resistant native culture. Based on primary sources in local archives and in the Archivo General de la Nación.

608   Mallma Cortéz, Arturo Luis. Los mitmaq yauyos en el reino wanka. Lima: Univ. Nacional Mayor de San Marcos, Seminario de Historia Rural Andina, 1989. 74 p.: bibl., ill.

Summary of longer thesis on the same subject that covers prehispanic history of the Kingdom of the Wankas and their subjugation and control by the Incas, and the role of the *mitmaq* in the "destructuration" of the Tawantinsuyo. Conclusions are based on analysis of material remains, toponyms, iconography, and ethnography. Waldemar Espinoza Soriano has published similar studies of *mitmaq* elsewhere.

609   Mamani Condori, Carlos B. Los aymaras frente a la historia: dos ensayos metodológicos. Chukiyawu: Aruwiyiri, 1992. 24 p.: bibl., ill. (Serie Cuadernos de debate; 2)

Short publication of two interpretive essays: 1) methodology of history and archaeology, arguing that the past is not "dead" and must be resurrected and brought to life to orient the future of indigenous peoples; and 2) use of oral narratives as historical sources. Author argues that stories can reveal the past of indigenous peoples and show them the path to the future.

610   Mandrini, Raúl J. Las transformaciones de la economía indígena bonaerense: ca. 1600–1820. (*in* Huellas en la tierra: indios, agricultores y hacendados en la pampa bonaerense. Recopilación de Raúl J. Mandrini y Andrea Reguera. Tandil, Argentina: Univ. Nacional del Centro, IEHS, 1993, p. 45–74)

Excellent study of evolution of the "ecosistema agrário pastoril indígena bonaerense" in the 18th and 19th centuries. Among other things concludes that the lands claimed by the *porteño* state after 1820 were not virgin or vacant lands, but densely populated areas used for specialized economic activity.

611   Mariño Blanco, Tomás Antonio. Akuhena: historia documental y testimonial del Territorio Federal Amazonas. Caracas: Gráficas Lithocom, 1992. 207 p.: bibl., ill. (some col.), maps.

Administrative or political history of the federal territory of Amazonas (Venezuela) from 12,000 BC to 1991. The title *Akuhena* comes from a Makiritare word meaning "sacred celestial lake of eternity." Author tells a story of an isolated part of Venezuela and attempts to incorporate it into the effective national life of the country. Chapters often contain texts of laws establishing various administrative jurisdictions and maps of the same.

612   Martins, Gilson Rodolfo. Breve painel etno-histórico do Mato Grosso do Sul. Campo Grande, Brazil: Ministério da Educação, Univ. Federal de Mato Grosso do Sul, Pró-Reitoria de Extensão e Assuntos Estudantis, 1992. 75 p.: bibl., ill., maps (some col.).

Brief book on native peoples of Mato Grosso do Sul, written for a popular audience. One important theme is how indigenous peoples used the complex eco-system to subsist and reproduce their way of life.

613   Menacho, Antonio. Por tierras de Chiquitos: los jesuitas en Santa Cruz y en las misiones de Chiquitos en los siglos 16 a 18. San Javier, Bolivia: Vicariato Apostólico de Nuflo de Chávez, 1991. 142 p.: bibl., col. ill.

Book written to commemorate the 300th anniversary (Dec. 31, 1691) of the establishment of the *reducción* or settlement mission of San Javier de Chiquitos. Narrative retells history of Jesuit evangelization of the inhabitants of Chiquitos up to Jesuit expulsion in 1767–68.

614   Méndez Beltrán, Luz María. La población indígena, su distribución espacial y el proceso de aculturación en La Araucanía, siglos XVII y XVIII: el recuento de 1796. (*Mem. Am.*, 3, 1994, p. 9–40, map, tables)

Interesting, well-documented article re-examines demographic data for the native population of southern Chile during the 18th century. Lengthy discussion of organization and geographical distribution of native peoples on the land. Author concludes that the native population was more acculturated and peaceful than the general literature suggests.

615   Mendizábal Losack, Emilio. Estructura y función en la cultura andina: fase inka. Lima: Univ. Nacional Mayor de San Marcos, Editorial de la Univ., 1989. 304 p.: bibl., ill.

Book, published posthumously, is divided into six parts: 1) computations; 2) the *tupu* as a measure of land; 3) sacred numbers; 4) the *pachaka*; 5) the *ayllu*; and 6) succession. Based on writings of the Spanish chroniclers and author's ethnographic experiences.

616   Miño Garcés, Leonardo. El manejo del espacio en el imperio inca. Quito: Facultad Latino Americana de Ciencias Sociales, Sede Ecuador, 1994. 158 p.: bibl., maps. (Serie Tesis-historia)

Analysis that approaches the use of space, the environment, and the natural resources of the region around Cuzco as a manifestation and product of Inca civilization. Author suggests that the physical and organizational structure of the region mirrored the dominant imperial cosmology.

617   Mugica, Martín Joseph de. Abusos de varias clases de mitas y carácter perezoso del yndio representados para su remedio al Rey Nro. Señor por el ex-diputado de Guamanga: edición de la versión original de 1813 con dos apéndices. Lima: Editorial Los Pinos, 1992. 38 p.: appendices. (Documentos para la historia y geografía del Perú)

Short publication of original proposal for the native labor draft in the Andes made to the Cortes de Cadiz and reactions of various delegates. According to R. Ravines, proposal is the best source of understanding the *mita* (forced draft labor of native people) for Andean people under Spanish colonial rule. In appendix two, Salvador Palomino describes how communal labor built and maintained bridges ca. 1971, attesting to primacy and durability of certain native American forms of organization.

618   Nacuzzi, Lidia R. and **Cecilia B. Pérez de Micou.** Rutas indígenas y obtención de recursos económicos en Patagonia. (*Mem. Am.*, 3, 1994, p. 91–103, bibl., map, table)

Study of indigenous routes in the second half of the 19th century in Patagonia emphasizes use of toponyms as a means to describe places where indigenous people camped and secured various types of natural resources. Offers a model for analysis.

619   La naturaleza en la América Austral: Alberto María de Agostini, un piemontese (i.e., piamontese) al "Fin del Mundo." Torino, Italia: Museo nazionale della montagna Duca degli Abruzzi; Club alpino italiano, Sezione di Torino, 1994. 69 p.: chiefly ill. (Cahier museomontagna; 97)

This exceptional collection of 50 exquisite photographs of Tierra del Fuego, taken during 1910–29, is printed on excellent paper. Of special interest are many photos of the region's extinct Indians (e.g., Ona, Selknam, Alacaluf, Tehuelche, etc.). Photographer was Father De Agostini (1883–1950), Italian Salesian priest, probably the first Catholic missionary to befriend and live among these Indians. [Ed.]

620   Nieves, Fulvia. Cúpira, su pasado y su presente: interpretación arqueológica y etnohistórica de la etnia tomuza. Caracas: Univ. Central de Venezuela, Consejo de Desarrollo Científico y Humanístico, 1992. 286 p.: bibl., ill., maps. (Col. Estudios)

Study of prehistoric and colonial populations of a region on the east central coast of Venezuela based in part on excavations at Cúpira and Chupaquire. Material remains provide a cultural sequence of the inhabitants and document relations between peoples of this region and others.

621 Orellana Rodríguez, Mario. Historia y antropología de la isla de La Laja. Santiago: Editorial Universitaria, 1992. 117 p.: bibl., ill., maps. (Col. Imagen de Chile)

Case study of Spanish colonization of the province of La Laja (Chile) reminds readers that the "conquest" of Peru did not end with the capture of Atahualpa in 1532. Underscores the gradual nature of "conquest" and settlement and the moving frontier that spread out from these and other centers. Combines classical historical analysis of primary and secondary sources with archaeological excavation of forts and ethnographic field work amongst the contemporary Pehuenches in 1990.

622 Ossio A., Juan M. Los indios del Perú. Madrid: Editorial MAPFRE, 1992. 304 p.: bibl., ill., indexes. (Col. MAPFRE 1492. Col. Indios de América)

Three-part book on the Andean Indians. Pt. 1 describes prehispanic cultures with an emphasis on the Incas. Pt. 2, on the colonial era, centers on the themes of resistance and adaptation of native peoples to European and creole pressures. In pt. 3, author describes the organization of native communities and their relationship to the State.

623 Palermo, Miguel Angel. La compleja integración hispano-indígena del sur argentino y chileno durante el período colonial. (*Am. Indíg.*, 51:1, enero/marzo 1991, p. 153–192, bibl., map)

Excellent article on cross-cultural contact between five indigenous groups and the Spaniards in Chile and Argentina. Author describes a poly-ethnic and poly-centric society, maintained via economic exchanges, marriage, alliances, and other means, but often marked by tension and friction.

624 Palermo, Miguel Angel. El revés de la trama: apuntes sobre el papel económico de la mujer en las sociedades indígenas tradicionales del sur argentino. (*Mem. Am.*, 3, 1994, p. 63–90, bibl.)

Good statement of historical context of acculturation and hispanization as a prelude to the overview of the roles of women in Pampas and Patagonian society. Based on original research and primary sources.

625 Palomino, Enrique. Qosqo, centro del mundo: a 500 años de su frustrada desaparición. Lima: Municipalidad provincial del Qosqo, 1993. 154 p.: bibl., ill.

Little volume retells history of the Tawantinsuyu, written for a popular audience to commemorate the Quincentennial.

626 Palomino Díaz, Julio. Intiwatanas y números: ciencia del pasado andino. Qosqo, Peru: Municipalidad del Qosqo, 1994. 114 p.: bibl., ill. (some col.).

Short study of units of measure used by the Incas also covers astronomy and architecture. Important chapters discuss the astronomical observatory of Suchuna (Saqsay waman) and the Intiwatana (solar dial).

627 Pärssinen, Martti. Tawantinsuyu: the Inca state and its political organization. Helsinki: SHS, 1992. 462 p.: bibl., ill., index, maps. (Studia historica, 0081–6493; 43)

Up-to-date synthesis of the history of the Inca State and its political organization, based not only on standard chronicles and secondary sources, but also on primary sources and the most recent research. Author provides critical analysis of sources and interpretations uncommon to most syntheses of this type. Tackles questions and debates openly, presenting possible answers and interpretations.

628 Pease G.Y., Franklin. Curacas, reciprocidad y riqueza. Lima: Pontificia Univ. Católica del Perú, Fondo Editorial, 1992. 208 p.: bibl.

Serious and well-footnoted book on political and economic relations between Andean leaders and their followers written by one of the foremost authorities on Peruvian ethnohistory. Pease reviews secondary literature and adds results of his own research in various archives to formulate his interpretation of the role of the *curaca* in several aspects of exchange both before 1532 and thereafter.

629 Pérez Correa, Hernán. Indios muiscas: 500 años, 1492–1992; real historia. Bogotá: Penitenciaria Central de Colombia, 1992. 199 p.: ill., indexes, maps.

Work details history of the Muiscas and the Spaniards who passed through or settled the territory of present-day Colombia from prehispanic times to 1992. Probably written with the Quincentenial in mind; loosely organized and unfootnoted chapters cover diverse topics such as the discovery of America and Columbus' first voyage, Chibcha marriage rituals, and native participation in the 1992 Congress of Colombia.

630 Porro, Antonio. As crônicas do Rio Amazonas: tradução, introdução e notas etno-históricas sobre as antigas populações indígenas da Amazônia. Petrópolis, Brazil: Vozes, 1993. 221 p.: bibl., ill., map. (Publicações CID. História; 14)

Useful collection of extracts from primary sources that describe the Amazon River and its inhabitants includes an introduction and ethnohistoric notes to each selection. Covers the 16th through the late 18th centuries and includes such observers as Gaspar de Carvajal, Pedro de la Gasca, and José Chantre y Herrera.

631 Presta, Ana María and **Mercedes del Río.** Reflexiones sobre los churumatas del sur de Bolivia, siglos XVI-XVII. (*Histórica/Lima*, 17:2, dic. 1993, p. 223–237, bibl.)

This short examination of available records regarding the Churumatas complements and expands upon item **574.** Concludes that Churumata groups were *mitmakuna*; that some left the Tarija valleys because of pressure from Chiriguanos; and that they relocated close to kin to gain access to land.

632 Pueblos y culturas indígenas. Edición de Jorge Núñez Sánchez. Quito: Editora Nacional; Asociación de Historiadores Latinoamericanos y del Caribe, 1991. 258 p.: bibl., facsims. (Col. Nuestra patria es America; 4)

Work compiled and edited for 500th anniversary of the "discovery" of America discusses indigenous culture under European rule. Ten essays focus on idolatry and the Church, historiography (including a critical analysis of some chronicles), and resistance.

633 500 años de mestizaje en los Andes. Edición de Hiroyasu Tomoeda y Luis Millones. Osaka, Japan: National Museum of Ethnology; Lima: Biblioteca Peruana de Psicoanálisis; Seminario Interdisciplinario de Estudios Andinos, 1992. 279 p.: bibl,, ill. (Biblioteca peruana de psicoanálisis; 11)

Edited book of studies deals with the mestizo, a subject that rarely gets the in-depth attention it deserves. Unlike many ethnohistorical studies that deal with indigenous alone or with interaction between groups of natives and Spaniards, this work carries the story forward by detailing the creation of a new social group. Studies cover Peru, Chine, and Argentina in colonial and modern times.

634 Ramírez, Susan E. The world upside down: cross-cultural contact and conflict in sixteenth-century Peru. Stanford, Calif.: Stanford Univ. Press, 1996. 234 p.: bibl., ill., index, maps.

Excellent study, rooted in a variety of rich resources, on the impact of Spanish colonialism on indigenous leadership, land, tribute, and religious beliefs and practices in northern Peru. Covering the five decades before and after contact, delves into native structures, functions, concepts, and perspectives and shows how life was changed dramatically in a short span of time. [S. Wood]

635 Ramón Valarezo, Galo. La resistencia andina: Cayambe, 1500–1800. Quito: Centro Andino de Acción Popular, 1987. 284 p.: bibl., ill. (Cuaderno de discusión popular; 14)

Well-documented history of the *cacicazgo* Cayambe (Ecuador) and its transformations during colonial times. Based on primary documentation in various Ecuadorian and Spanish archives, author explores changes in distribution and utilization of natural resources under Inca and Spanish domination; the establishment of the *encomienda* and the hacienda; demographic consequences of contact between 1550 and 1720; and native responses to accommodation and resistance. The history of one hacienda, Guachalá, is featured.

636 Rappaport, Joanne. Cumbe reborn: an Andean ethnography of history. Chicago: Univ. of Chicago Press, 1994. 261 p.: bibl., ill., index, map.

The book examines "experiences turned-stories" that were told, sung, written, and performed by the people of the indigenous community of Cumbal in the highlands of southern Colombia. These stories, especially those about the loss of aboriginal lands, are told and retold "to stand as evidence of the need for militant action in the present"

(p. 5) and to spur people into action. In studying these narratives, the author explores the nature and purpose of popular historical memory, indigenous identity, and ethnic militancy. For anthropologist's comment see *HLAS 55:999.*

637 Regalado de Hurtado, Liliana. La sucesión incaica: aproximación al mando y poder entre los incas a partir de la crónica de Betanzos. Lima: Pontificia Univ. Cátolica del Perú, Fondo Editorial, 1993. 124 p.: bibl.

Book adds to our knowledge of Inca succession based on the chronicle of Juan Diez de Betanzos. Author considers the *ayllu,* kinship, curacal succession, and mythology to seek a paradigm for the structure of power under the Inca. She advances a hypothesis on the dual nature of imperial power.

638 Relación de la religión y ritos del Perú hecha por los padres agustinos. Edición, estudio preliminar y notas de Lucila Castro de Trelles. Lima: Pontificia Univ. Católica del Perú; Fondo Editorial, 1992. xci, 75 p.: bibl., ill., indexes, map. (Clásicos peruanos; 8)

One of the first lengthy texts to relate evangelization experiences in colonial Peru. This chronicle, written by an Agustinian priest living in Huamachuco, contains detailed ethnographic observations that help reconstruct and understand multiple facets of the Andean religious mentality. Another valuable text for the study of the extirpation of idolatry.

639 Rodríguez Rivas, Julio. Médicos y brujos en el Alto Perú: datos y meditaciones sobre la medicina colonial. La Paz: Editorial Los Amigos del Libro, 1989. 371 p.: bibl. (Enciclopedia boliviana)

Medical history of what is now Bolivia during colonial times. Author discusses diseases, wars, epidemics, and wounds as well as what priests, curers, charlatans, witches, and a few physicians did to cure them. Author quotes extensively from Felipe Guamán Poma de Ayala, Garcilaso de la Vega, Bartolomé de Arzáns de Orzúa y Vela, and Roberto Querejazu Calvo, and supplements and explains their observations with information from other, mostly secondary, sources.

640 Rostworowski de Diez Canseco, María. Ensayos de historia andina: elites, etnías, recursos. Lima: IEP; BCRP, 1993. 460 p.: bibl. (Historia andina; 20)

This volume by one of the foremost contributors to Peruvian ethnohistory reproduces 15 previously published articles from widely scattered and sometimes difficult-to-find sources. Articles are arranged in four categories: 1) elites and genealogy; 2) land tenure and administration of natural resources; 3) ethnic groups and Andean space; and 4) ethnic groups under Spanish colonialism. The last category includes important articles on tribute and *visitas.*

641 Ruiz-Esquide Figueroa, Andrea. Los indios amigos en la frontera araucana. Santiago: Dirección de Bibliotecas, Archivos y Museos; Centro de Investigaciones Diego Barros Arana, 1993. 116 p.: bibl., ill. (Col. Sociedad y cultura; 4)

Study reexamines the War of Arauco and life on the Chilean frontier in the 17th century, specifically focusing on a group of "friendly Indians" who allied with the Spanish and Creoles during both periods of peace and confrontation. Two questions orient the research: 1) why did this group of "friendly Indians" form? and 2) what was its significance? Author concludes that without these collaborations Spanish-Creole society may not have been able to resist native attacks.

642 Ruiz-Peinado Alonso, José Luis. Hijos del río: negros del Trombetas. (*in* Memoria, creación e historia: luchar contra el olvido. Coordinación de Pilar García Jordán, Miguel Izard y Javier Laviña. Barcelona: Univ. de Barcelona, 1993, p. 349–357, bibl.)

Very short, concise overview of the *mocambo* or *quilombo* (run-away slave settlements) of Brazil, from the 18th century to modern times, is based mostly on secondary sources. Author limits article to the population living along the Trompetas River and emphasizes culture of resistance that was able to survive there.

643 Saitō, Akira. Tamashii no seifuku: Andesu ni okeru kaishū no seijigaku = La conquista espiritual de America. Shohan. Tokyo: Heibonsha, 1991. 397 p.: bibl., ill.

From an anthropological perspective, author analyzes the indigenous peoples' response to the extermination of their native religion and the process of conversion in Peru of the Inca Empire since the beginning of the 16th century. Placing special emphasis on the concept of "a representation of others" in the adaptation (or rejection) of different cultures, describes this representation of others as a political bargaining tool among Indians and Spanish priests, and shows how their own images of "others" have affected the process and outcome of their political negotiation. Tentative but provocative study. [K. Horisaka]

644 Salazar-Soler, Carmen *et al.* Borrachera y memoria: la experiencia de lo sagrado en los Andes. Recopilación de Thierry Saignes. La Paz: Hisbol; Lima: Instituto Francés de Estudios Andinos, 1993. 202 p.: bibl. (Biblioteca andina; 16. Travaux de l'Institut français d'études andines; 69)

Important book on a familiar custom from uncommon perspectives. Contributing authors place the custom of drinking alcohol in a cultural context, reminding readers of the larger relationship between drinking and social, political, and religious structures.

645 San Félix, Alvaro. Testamentos y mortuorias registrados en el asiento de San Luis de Otavalo en los siglos XVI y XVII. (*Sarance/Otavalo*, 18, oct. 1993, p. 145–199)

Analysis of wills and related documents from Otavalo between 1689–1851 emphasizes religious customs, inheritance patterns, funeral rites, ceremonies, and bequests. Includes some price information. Fails to systematically analyze patterns of accumulation of wealth or what these manuscripts tell us about material culture.

646 Santa Cruz Pachacuti Yamqui Salcamayhua, Juan de. Relación de antigüedades deste reyno del Piru. Estudio etnohistórico y lingüístico de Pierre Duviols y César Itier. Lima: Institut français d'études andines; Cusco: Centro de Estudios Regionales Andinos Bartolomé de Las Casas, 1993. 276 p.: bibl., ill. (Archivos de historia andina, 1022–0879; 17. Travaux de l'Institut français d'études andines; 74)

Long-awaited book that publishes text of well-known, early-17th-century chronicle, written by a native resident of the circum-Cuzco region. Besides providing a facsimile of the actual hand-written text (from the Biblioteca Nacional in Madrid) and a transcription, also includes associated critical analyses of the text and its language.

647 Santamaría, Daniel J. El campesinado indígena de Jujuy en el siglo XVII: un estudio sobre las formas de integración étnica en situación colonial. (*Am. Indíg.*, 52:1/2, enero/junio 1992, p. 223–250, map)

Using census lists and other information, author addresses problem of ethnicity of native groups of Jujuy in the 17th century. Provocative analysis of personal names will surely stimulate further research and discussion.

648 Santamaría, Daniel J. and Jaime Peire. ¿Guerra o comercio pacífico?: la problemática interétnica del Chaco centro-occidental en el siglo XVIII. (*Anu. Estud. Am.*, 50: 2, 1993, p. 93–127)

Article based on extensive archival research reviews 18th-century plans to put natives to work on haciendas or to stimulate trade as a way of pacifying and transforming the Chaco into a useful territory between Alto Peru and the coast.

649 Santamaría, Daniel J. La puerta amazónica: los circuitos mercantiles de los ríos Madeira y Guaporé en la segunda mitad del siglo XVIII. (*Mem. Am.*, 2, 1993, p. 51–61, bibl., tables)

Short history of settlement and riverborne mercantile expansion on the frontier between Spanish and Portuguese territories, beginning in the 16th century but emphasizing activities after 1750, is based primarily on secondary sources and travelers' accounts.

Scatamacchia, Maria Cristina Mineiro and **Francisco Moscoso.** Análise do padrão de estabelecimentos Tupi-Guarani: fontes etno-históricas e arqueológicas. See *HLAS 55:592*.

650 Sepúlveda Escobar, Carlos Humberto and **José Eduardo Rueda Enciso.** Ensayos de historia araucana. v. 1. Bogotá: Editorial Gente Nueva, 1992. 1 v.: bibl., ill., map.

Book explores social, political, and economic history of the Llanos (plains) of Arauca and Casanare, particularly the region between the Arduca and Casanare Rivers, in present-day Dept. of Arauca (Colombia). This local history begins with a study of the native groups that existed at the time of the Spanish arrival, and proceeds to discuss their conquest; the settlement of the land by the Spanish; and the establishment of Jesuit missions at the beginning of the 17th century. History continues with the Jesuit expulsion and its consequences into the 18th and early-19th centuries. Besides secondary material, chapter footnotes include references to primary sources from Colombia's Archivo Nacional, Spain's Archivo General de Indias (Sevilla), and Italy's Archivo Romana de la Compañía de Jesus.

651 Sherbondy, Jeanette E. El agua: ideología y poder de los Incas. (*in* El agua: mitos, ritos y realidades; coloquio internacional, Granada. Edición de José A. González Alcantud y Antonio Malpica Cuello. Granada, Spain: Centro de Investigaciones Etnológicas Angel Ganivet; Diputación de Granada; Barcelona, Spain: Anthropos, Editorial del Hombre, 1995, p. 87–102)

Good article on the role of water in Inca cosmology, based on participant observation, plus linguistic and historical data.

652 Sherbondy, Jeanette E. Irrigation and Inca cosmology. (*in* Univ. of Calgary Archaeological Association, *24th, Calgary, 1991.* Culture and environment, a fragile coexistence. Calgary, Alberta: Archaeological Association, Univ. of Calgary, 1993, p. 343–351)

Author demonstrates how the Incas replicated the universe through ritual, myth-history, construction of temples and sacred sites, and distribution of land rights and irrigation waters. Concludes that the Inca kings and queens placed themselves at the center of an earthly cycle of waters, that they kept in balance through prayers, offerings, and ceremonies.

653 Sherbondy, Jeanette E. Water and power: the role of irrigation districts in the transition from Inca to Spanish Cuzco. (*in* Irrigation at high altitudes: the social organization of water control systems in the Andes. Arlington, Va.: Society for Latin American Anthropology, American Anthropological Association, 1993, p. 69–97)

Clear look at the first 50 years of Spanish occupation of Cuzco centers on control over lands and irrigation canals by *panacas* and *ayllus.* Author uses structural analysis of the 16th-century works of the Incas, ethnographic inquiries into farming and irrigation practices, field surveys of Inca canals, and analysis of colonial manuscripts to reach her conclusions.

654 Stavig, Ward A. Violencia cotidiana de los naturales de Quispicanchis y Canas y Canchis en el siglo XVIII. (*in* Congreso Nacional de Investigaciónes en Historia, *1st, Lima, 1984.* Actas. Lima, CONCYTEC, 1991, v. 1, p. 77–99, tables)

Well-written and insightful survey of violence involving the peoples of the Vilcanota River valley during the late 17th and 18th centuries. Author analyzes revolts, conflicts over lands and resources, and inter-group and inter-personal conflict as a means to understand Andean society and culture more intimately.

655 Stern, Steve J. Peru's Indian peoples and the challenge of Spanish conquest: Huamanga to 1640. 2nd ed. Madison: Univ. of Wisconsin Press, 1993. 295 p.: bibl., ill., index, map.

Now classic work on early colonial history of inhabitants of Ayacucho (or Huamanga) stresses their resistance to the imposed order. Chap. 3 is a readable study of the Taki Onqoy.

656 Sušnik, Branislava. Introducción a las fuentes documentales referentes al indio colonial del Paraguay. Asunción: Museo Etnográfico Andrés Barbero, 1992. 46 p.

Required guide to documentary references to native life of colonial Paraguay. Lists manuscripts and guides to manuscripts in the Archivo Nacional de Asunción, the Archivo General de la Nación (Buenos Aires), the Archivo del Museo Mitre (Buenos Aires), and the Archivo General de Indias (Sevilla), among others. Also includes lists of chronicles, 19th-century ethnographic and archaeological studies, and documents on specific ethnic groups.

657 Sušnik, Branislava. Una visión socio-antropológica del Paraguay, XVI-1/2 XVII. Asunción: Museo Etnográfico Andres Barbero, 1993. 149 p.: bibl.

Welcome addition to literature on early colonial history of Paraguay to ca. 1680 focuses on Spanish-Guarani encounter and the process of accommodation. Unlike more popular studies on the same subject, this one is copiously footnoted and based on primary sources in archives in Asunción, Buenos Aires, and Sevilla.

658 Szemiński, Jan. Un buen español es un español muerto: maten a los españoles. (*in* Congreso Nacional de Investigaciones en Historia, *1st, Lima, 1984.* Actas. Lima, CONCYTEC, 1991, v. 1, p. 15–60, bibl., table)

Analysis goes beyond answering the question of why Spaniards were killed during the Túpac Amaru rebellion to consider the Andean native population's image of God and the King of Spain, as well as the Andean understanding of a need for the Catholic religion and its practitioners. Interesting interpretation of the 18th-century Andean mind-set.

659 Szemiński, Jan. La utopía tupamarista. 2. ed. Lima: Pontificia Univ. Católica del Perú, Fondo Editorial, 1993. 363 p.: bibl., ill.

Interesting contribution to the study of the Túpac Amaru rebellion in Southern Peru between 1780–84. In the innovative first two chapters, author discusses definitions of common terms used in the documentation. He then proceeds to describe participants' thinking and insurrection's revolutionary objectives.

660 Tamayo Herrera, José. Historia general del Qosqo: una historia regional desde el período lítico hasta el año 2000. v. 1–3. Qosqo, Peru: Municipalidad del Qosqo, 1992. 3 v. (951 p.): bibl., ill. (some col.).

Commissioned by the Concejo Provincial del Qosqo in 1990, this three-volume set presents basic synthesis of the regional history of Qosqo (Cusco) from the pre-agricultural age to 1992. In separate sections, it covers region's geography; pre-Inca archeology; the Inca empire; colonial times; the Independence movement; and republican history of the area. Vol. 3 ends with a bibliography of published sources on the city and its hinterland.

661 Teruel, Ana A. Zenta y San Ignacio de los Tobas: el trabajo en dos misiones del Chaco occidental a fines de la colonia. (*Anu. IEHS*, 9, 1994, p. 227–252, graph, map, tables)

Good article comparing two missions in the Chaco region is based on original research. Contains map and several tables summarizing economic data, especially concerning labor.

662 Testimonios, cartas y manifiestos indígenas: desde la conquista hasta comienzos del siglo XX. Selección, prólogo, notas, glosario y bibliografía de Martin Lienhard. Caracas: Biblioteca Ayacucho, 1992. 396 p.: bibl., ill. (Biblioteca Ayacucho; 178)

Collection of writings and testimonies by native Americans that illustrates the diplomatic and negotiating dialogue between the

colonized and the colonizer. Organized by cultural areas (Mesoamerica, Andes, Tupi-Guarani area, Continental Caribe area, and the Pampa of Argentina) and historical moments, material permits the reader to trace various political and cultural strategies employed by native Americans against the European invaders and their descendants. Some material has been previously published elsewhere.

663 Torre y López, Arturo Enrique de la. Juan Santos: ¿el invencible? (*Histórica/Lima*, 17:2, dic. 1993, p. 239–266, bibl., maps)

Well-organized survey of the viceregal campaigns against the rebellion of Juan Santos Atahualpa, with a clear emphasis on tactics and military strategy. Four helpful maps are appended. This article should be read before item **672** if the reader lacks a clear chronology of events.

664 Valcárcel, Gustavo. Perú, mural de un pueblo: apuntes marxistas sobre el Perú incaico; el modo de producción andino. 2a ed. Lima: Consejo Nacional de Ciencia y Tecnología, 1988. 334 p.: bibl., ill., index.

Updated re-edition of a book that first appeared in 1965. This example of history written with a theoretical model in mind is based on chronicle literature and secondary sources.

665 Valcárcel, Luis Eduardo. Antología. v. 1–2. Lima: Municipalidad del Qosqo, 1991. 2 v.

Two-volume compilation of Valcárcel's writings about Cusco. Introduction to Vol. 1 by poet Angel Avendaño puts author's life and work in historical perspective. Excerpts from some of his 17 books and 3,000 articles are included under such headings as "The Land," "Indigenismo," and "Personages." Vol. 2 is largely dedicated to reproducing a long chapter from Valcárcel's memoirs on Cusco in the early 20th century, previously published by the Instituto de Estudios Peruanos.

666 Vangelista, Chiara. Los guaikurú, españoles y portugueses en una región de frontera: Mato Grosso, 1770–1830. (*Bol. Inst. Hist. Ravignani*, 8, segundo semestre 1993, p. 55–76)

Interesting article on inter- and intra-ethnic relations on the frontier between territory claimed by both Spanish and Portuguese colonials. Focuses on how the Guaycuru responded to new developments and modified their policy toward "others." Based both on primary and secondary sources, outlines changes in traditional Guaycuru social organizations as they jockeyed for an advantageous role and position between two colonial powers. Ultimately, the Guaycuru allied with the Portuguese against the Spanish as a means of maintaining a greater measure of autonomy.

667 **Vega, Juan José.** Los incas frente a España: las guerras de la resistencia, 1531–1544. Lima: Peisa, 1992. 300 p.: bibl., ill., col. map.

This work by a historian known for such studies focuses on Inca resistance to Spanish invasion, especially before 1544. One of the book's most important contributions is the author's discussion of political tensions within native society ca. 1532: there was a struggle for power among the *panacas* of Cuzco; the generals of commoner origin distrusted the Cuzco nobility; and some ethnic groups, which had been conquered by the Inca, strained to regain their independence. These factors plus Spanish arms and ambition, and the short-lived native belief that the Spaniards were divine, contributed to disintegration of the once mighty Inca empire. Analysis parallels and overlaps, in part, classic studies of Miguel León-Portilla on the Aztecs or Nahua of central Mexico.

668 **Villar, Daniel.** Ocupación y control del espacio por las sociedades indígenas de la frontera sur de Argentina, siglo XIX: un aporte al conocimiento etnohistórico de la región pampeana. Bahía Blanca, Argentina: Univ. Nacional del Sur, Depto. de Humanidades, 1993. 27 leaves: bibl.

Another short study of the Pampeana region of Argentina in the 19th century. Study of resource use and territorial occupation and how these were gradually transformed to fit European colonial demands as a result of native-European interaction along a frontier. Simultaneously provides another example of the "destructuration" suffered by native peoples here and elsewhere in America.

669 **Viola Recasens, Andreu.** La cara oculta de los Andes: notas para una redefinición de la relación histórica entre Sierra y Selva. (*Bol. Am.*, 33:42/43, 1992/93, p. 7–22)

Short article reexamines highland-lowland jungle contacts using archaeological and ethnohistorical evidence for the area of present-day Peru and Bolivia. Research supports multi-faceted contacts between the peoples of the two eco-zones, at least to the time of the Inca conquest.

670 **Whitehead, Neil L.** Native American cultures along the Atlantic littoral of South America, 1499–1650. (*in* The meeting of two worlds: Europe and the Americas, 1492–1650. Edited by Warwick Bray. Oxford, England: Oxford Univ. Press; The British Academy, 1993, p. 197–231, bibl., ill.)

Well-written overview of cross-cultural contact along the Atlantic littoral from 1499–1650 provides detailed history of development of European colonial activity and Amerindian reactions. Aftershock of European impacts is evaluated based on ethnological material from the period of first contact. Final section considers problems and limitations of analyzing cultural change in anthropological contexts.

671 **Whitehead, Neil L.** Recent research on the native history of Amazonia and Guayana. (*Homme/Paris*, 33:126/128, avril/déc. 1993, p. 495–505, bibl.)

Short summary overview of lowland indigenous history notes relative underdevelopment of historical study of native Amazonia. Also mentions debates on "myth" and "history," European images of the Amerindian, hyphenated histories, and the theoretical impact of the study of political and economic evolution. Includes extensive bibliography.

Writing without words: alternative literacies in Mesoamerica and the Andes. See item **551.**

672 **Zarzar, Alonso.** Conquista y Utopía en la rebelión de Juan Santos Atahualpa. (*Nariz Diablo*, 19, enero 1994, p. 51–59, bibl., photo, tables)

Short analysis of goals and designs of Juan Santos Atahualpa, highlighting his utopian dreams. Uses the rebel's few statements. The testimonies of others are used to retrieve outlines of his thought.

673 **Zevallos Quiñones, Jorge.** Huacas y huaqueros en Trujillo durante el virreinato, 1535–1835. Trujillo, Peru: Editora Normas Legales, 1994. 115 p.: ill.

Book destined to be a valuable resource for historians, ethnohistorians, and archaeologists alike treats the practice of colonial treasure hunting in native burials and shrines on the north coast of Peru. Includes separate chapters on the Valleys of the Moche, Chimu, Chicama, and Virú, as well as a section with documentary transcriptions. Commentary by the author, a long-time student of the north coast history and archaeology, is based mostly on research in the local archives of Trujillo.

GENERAL HISTORY

JOHN BRITTON, *Professor of History, Francis Marion University*

ALTHOUGH THE FLOOD OF QUINCENTENNIAL-RELATED PUBLICATIONS reached its high-water mark in the 1992–93 biennium, discussions of the historical role of Columbus and the nature of the conquest continued to have prominence in the current group of books and articles. New themes emerged, however, that reflected a growing concern among academics about the need to examine the historical roots of contemporary issues. Some critics might complain that this exercise constitutes a form of presentism, but there is also a strong case to be made for these shifts of interest as a normal and healthy part of the academic process. In particular, the publications under study here revealed a focus on the economic evolution of Latin America, perhaps as a reflection of interest in the North American Free Trade Agreement (NAFTA) and the overall push toward privatization throughout the hemisphere. A second theme involved studies of the left, perhaps as an outgrowth of the wave of crises that afflicted leftist governments and political parties in the region.

Studies of the colonial period continued to dominate. The Quincentennial emphasis on Columbus and the conquest era remained heavy, but some scholars combined these familiar themes with innovative approaches. Ares Queija's examination of native American reenactments of the conquest in the colonial period provided a valuable perspective on this topic (item **798**). Amidst the loud polemics surrounding the actions of the Spanish conquistadores, Morales Padrón wrote a less strident study of the struggles not only for wealth and power, but also for food, health, and survival (item **934**). Las Casas scholarship was also an active arena, and Gutiérrez's new biography of the defender of native Americans effectively evoked the troubled times of the 16th century (item **877**). Perhaps in response to the condemnatory tone of much of the recent writing on the role of the Spanish and their ethnic descendants in Latin America, Carrera Damas brought forth a collection of essays that examined the sociocultural identity of the criollo population from the colonial period to the modern era (item **693**).

Economic history was an important theme across all historical epochs. The colonial roots of economic and technological innovation were the subjects of two important books: Bernal's broad study of credit and finance (item **805**) and García Tapia's examination of the application of industrial technology from the 1500s-1800s (item **709**). Cortés-Conde presented an incisive analysis of export-driven economic growth from 1880–1930 (item **1007**). Guillén examined the larger questions surrounding the event that brought the growth era to an end—the world-wide economic crisis of 1929 (item **1061**). With his comprehensive examination of Latin American economic history since the 1820s, Bulmer-Thomas contributed a major work of synthesis; incorporating both international and national trends, the text strikes a sensible balance of narrative, analysis, and quantification (item **1052**).

As the Latin American left suffered through severe problems in the 1990s, historians examined some of its crucial episodes in the 19th and 20th centuries. Chasteen's article analyzed leftist rebels' use of broad public appeals to collective identity and self-sacrifice in 1890s Brazil and Uruguay (item **696**). Cruz Capote discussed the first international conference of communist parties in Latin America, held in Buenos Aires in 1929 (item **1054**). The migration of Spanish leftists to Latin America in the wake of Franco's fascist victory in the late 1930s is the subject of an interpretive article by Olmos Sánchez (item **1072**). The impact of anarchism, the often-forgotten leftist rival to communism, is examined in-depth in a volume of carefully selected writings prefaced by an excellent introductory essay from the pen of Angel Cappelletti.

Publications in social history provided some acute insights on vital topics. Practitioners of women's history were particularly prolific. Lavrin adroitly explored the image of the female ideal within the institutional ambience of the colonial Catholic Church (item **903**). Bermúdez's quartet of essays examined the position of women in late 19th-century Colombia, while providing a broader perspective on the challenges confronting women's history throughout the region (item **687**). Kuznesof reviewed the life-course patterns of women caught up in the initial stages of industrialization (item **729**). Arrom and Guy took the long view in assessing future directions for research in gender history (item **677** and **713**). The study of religion in the modern era benefited from three exemplary works. Pazos used Vatican archives to buttress his overview of the Catholic Church in Latin America in the 1890s (item **1032**), while Bastian wrote a pair of penetrating articles on the 20th-century surge of Protestantism in the region (items **681** and **682**). Taylor and Pease assembled an exceptionally well organized book of thematically linked essays on native American perceptions of and strategies for dealing with the presence of powerful foreign institutions in their societies (item **784**). Taussig's concluding essay punctuates this volume with the disturbing notion that historical/anthropological studies often fail to grasp the nature of these types of power relationships.

The writing of textbooks constitutes one of the most important tasks confronting the professional academician. This biennium saw the appearance of five exceptional entries in this field, each one of which had notable strengths. Pérez Herrero placed the Spanish and Portuguese empires in the broader context of European imperialism (item **951**) while Maza Zavala explained the contrasting colonial efforts of Spain and Great Britain in America in a stimulating study in comparative history (item **744**). Halperín Donghi's survey of Latin America since independence, long a popular and influential textbook in Spanish, is available in English at last in a very readable translation by Chasteen (item **714**). Fuentes and Winn authored two highly literate, interpretive texts linked to their respective video documentaries with the obvious intention of pairing the printed page with the television image in the classroom (items **706** and **788**).

GENERAL

674 Alperovič, Moisej S. Sobre la exposición de algunos problemas de la historia no sólo de América. (*Estud. Latinoam./Poland*, 15, 1992, p. 267–279)

"Think piece" offers interesting interpretation of Marx's view of Bolívar, and also discusses other issues in Marxist theory and historiography.

675 Andrés Gallego, José. De lo inglés a lo hispánico: las relaciones de poder entre España y América. (*An. Hist. Contemp.*, 8, 1990/91, p. 13–25)

Author applies Bernard Bailyn's concepts on "latent events" and their larger meaning to several themes in Latin America including legal-administrative history and role of indigenismo in the political and social history of the region.

676 Anguita Galán, Eduardo and **Jesús Moreno Gómez.** Malagueños en América: del orto al ocaso. Málaga, Spain: Servicio de Publicaciones, Diputación Provincial de Málaga, 1992? 491 p.: bibl., ill., maps.

Ten biographical sketches ranging from 16th to 20th century include early colonial explorer and soldier Gonzalo Suárez Rendón, military officers José Lachambre Seguí and Luis Molina (who were active in the late colonial wars in Cuba), and leading modern Mexican historian Juan Antonio Ortega y Medina.

ARL: Latin Americanist Research Resources Pilot Project. See item 26.

677 Arrom, Silva Marina. Historia de la mujer y de la familia latinoamericanas. (*Hist. Mex.*, 42:2, oct./dic. 1992, p. 379–418, bibl.)

A much-needed and well-executed historiographical work examines recent publications on women's history and family history. Particularly helpful in pointing out areas in need of more research.

678 Ballesteros Gaibrois, Manuel. Pueblos, lenguas y evangelización en Méjico, América Central y Area Meridional. (*Hisp. Sacra*, 40, julio/dic. 1988, p. 675–690)

Interpretive essay examines work of missionaries with native American languages.

679 Baquero, Gastón. Indios, blancos y negros en el caldero de América. Madrid: Ediciones de Cultura Hispánica, 1991. 289 p. (Literatura)

Fast-paced survey focuses on the conquest and the opinions of major literary figures on issues relating to ethnic conflict in the Americas. Includes unexpected selections—Faulkner, Conan Doyle, Arciniegas, Borges, among others—but is weakened by absence of footnotes and bibliography.

680 Bastian, Jean Pierre. América Latina, 1492–1992: conquista, resistencia y emancipación. México: Univ. Nacional Autónoma de México, Instituto de Investigaciones Jurídicas; Guatemala: Corte de Constitucionalidad de Guatemala, 1992. 88 p.: bibl. (Cuadernos constitucionales México-Centroamérica; 4)

General interpretation of dynamics of Latin America's struggles to deal with impact of the conquest emphasizes social and religious dimensions of the conflict between elites and masses.

681 Bastian, Jean Pierre. The metamorphosis of Latin American Protestant groups: a sociohistorical perspective. (*LARR*, 28:2, 1993, p. 33–61, bibl., table)

Stimulating interpretation of sociological and ideological meaning of Protestantism in Latin America includes contrasts of 19th-century emphasis on literacy, education, and democracy with more recent movements that emphasize oral experiences and "caudillo-style models of religious and social control."

682 Bastian, Jean Pierre. Protestantism in Latin America. (*in* The Church in Latin America, 1492–1992. Edited by Enrique Dussel. Kent, England: Burns & Oats; Maryknoll, N.Y.: Orbis Books 1992, p. 313–350, bibl., map)

This bold evaluation of changing historical role of Protestantism encompasses politics and sociology as well as religion. Bastian connects Protestantism to early 20th-century opposition to oligarchies and also examines its corporatist tendencies since 1960.

683 Batllori, Miguel. L'americanisme entre els jesuïtes catalans exiliats a Itàlia per Carles III. (*in* Jornades d'Estudis Catalano-Americans, 4th, Barcelona, 1990. Actes. Barcelona: Generalitat de Catalunya, Comissió América i Catalunya, 1992, p. 11–16)

Brief study examines Jesuits' defense of their missionary work in America.

684 Baud, Michiel. Families and migration: towards an historical analysis of family networks. (*Econ. Soc. Hist. Neth.*, 6, 1994, p. 83–107)

Presents conceptual framework to analyze migrant families, based mainly on literature on Latin America and the Caribbean. Author focuses on organization of migration within households and its consequences for cohesion and internal power relations within families. Argues that redistribution of resources and income reveals logic and viability of migrant households. [R. Hoefte]

685 Becerra, Irma. La América encubierta, 1492–1992. Tegucigalpa: Baktún, 1992. 167 p.: bibl., ill., maps. (Col. América Latina; 1)

This short but broadly-based assessment of impact of the conquest expands on author's view of distortions of previous historical studies and on roles of violence, racism, and machismo in sociological and philosophical dimensions of the European *encubierta* of America. First of a projected five-volume series on broad themes in Latin American history.

686 Berlinguer, Giovanni. The interchange of disease and health between the Old and the New World. (*in* International Congress on the Great Maritime Discoveries and World Health, *1st, Lisboa, 1990.* Proceedings. Lisboa: Escola Nacional de Saúde Pública; Ordem dos Médicos; Instituto de Sintra, 1991, p. 125–137)

Gives broad overview of several areas for further research in medical and environmental history.

687 Bermúdez Q., Suzy. Hijas, esposas y amantes: género, clase, etnia y edad en la historia de América Latina. Bogotá: Ediciones Uniandes, Univ. de los Andes, 1992. 186 p.: bibl., ill.

Presents valuable pioneering overview of feminist studies in Latin American history. First essay examines historiographical and theoretical issues. The next two cover colonial period and emergent bourgeois society (1850–1930) in Latin America in general, and fourth deals specifically with women and the family in Colombia (1850–86).

688 Block, David. Quincentennial publishing: an ocean of print. (*LARR,* 29:3, 1994, p. 101–128, appendices)

Gives helpful overview of publications associated with the Quincentennial. Block uses both qualitative and quantitative approaches, and provides even-handed commentary on a broad selection of works.

689 Bosch García, Carlos. El descubrimiento y la integración iberoamericana. México: Univ. Nacional Autónoma de México, 1991. 329 p.: bibl., maps. (500 años después; 5)

Publication contains 31 articles and essays on a variety of topics ranging from conquest era to 19th-century foreign relations of Mexico. Convenient collection of writings by eminent Mexican historian.

690 Caillavet, Chantal and **Martin Minchom.** Le métis imaginaire: idéaux classificatoires et stratégies socio-raciales en Amérique latine, XVIe-XXe siècle. (*Homme/*

Paris, 32:122/124, avril/déc. 1992, p. 115–132, bibl.)

Sociology, semantics, and history are combined in this synthesis of recent studies of ethnic classifications. Authors focus on the importance and the ambiguous status of the mestizo.

Canedo, Lino Gómez. Evangelización, cultura y promoción social: ensayos y estudios críticos sobre la contribución franciscana a los orígenes cristianos de México, siglos XVI-XVIII. See item **1131.**

691 Cárcel Ortí, Vicente. Una fuente para la historia de España y de Hispanoamérica: el Archivo de la Nunciatura de Madrid. (*Hispania/Madrid,* 52:181, mayo/agosto 1992, p. 585–608)

Provides informative discussion of archive that contains the papers of the papal representative in Spain from early 1600s to 1922, including documents relevant to the Catholic Church in Latin America.

692 Cárcel Ortí, Vicente. La Iglesia en España e Hispanoamérica: estudios recientes en el Archivo Secreto Vaticano sobre las épocas moderna y contemporánea. (*An. Valent.,* 18:35, 1992, p. 27–53)

Detailed description of archival documents, but only last four pages concern Latin America.

693 Carrera Damas, Germán. De la dificultad de ser criollo. Caracas?: Grijalbo, 1993. 248 p.: bibl. (Col. Tierra nuestra)

Exceptional collection of essays ponders place of the criollo in Latin American history in light of polemics surrounding the conquest and its cultural, social, and political implications. Also includes author's essay on impact of the French Revolution in Latin America.

694 Caulfield, Sueann. Women of vice, virtue, and rebellion: new studies of representation of the female in Latin America. (*LARR,* 28:2, 1993, p. 163–174)

Review essay deals with recent publications on tensions between established authority and various dissident responses by women in Brazil, Mexico and Argentina.

695 Céspedes del Castillo, Guillermo. La exploración del Atlántico. Madrid: Editorial MAPFRE, 1991. 341 p.: bibl., ill., index, maps. (Col. América 92; 3. Col. MAPFRE 1492)

Sweeping survey examines exploration of the Atlantic from Phoenicians of 5th century BC to 20th-century submarine and space satellite. The Portuguese and Spanish expeditions figure prominently through the middle portions of the text. An admirable synthesis.

696 Chasteen, John Charles. Fighting words: the discourse of insurgency in Latin American history. (*LARR*, 28:3, 1993, p. 83–111, bibl., photos)

Drawn mainly from 1890s Brazil and Uruguay, Chasteen's essay presents several stimulating insights on the value of serious study of published pronouncements and symbolic actions of revolutionaries.

697 Checa Godoy, Antonio. Historia de la prensa en Iberoamérica. Sevilla: Ediciones Alfar, 1993. 541 p.: bibl., ill. (Col. Alfar/universidad; 74. Serie Ediciones, textos y documentos)

Encyclopedic and descriptive rather than interpretive and analytical, volume is an important preliminary step in historical assessment of the press in Latin America. Well organized on the basis of specific periods in histories of individual nations. Brief bibliography but no footnotes.

698 Ciencia, vida y espacio en Iberoamérica: trabajos del Programa Movilizador del C.S.I.C., "relaciones científicas y culturales entre España y América." Coordinación de José Luis Peset Reig. Madrid: Consejo Superior de Investigaciones Científicas, 1989. 3 v.: bibl., ill. (some col.). (Estudios sobre la ciencia; 10)

Collection of 81 essays is organized in five categories: medical history, social sciences in general (including philosophy and linguistics), engineering and technology, the social sciences as applied to urban life, and geography and navigation. The 13 studies on engineering and technology provide much groundbreaking work in an often neglected area.

699 Coffee, society, and power in Latin America. Edited by William Roseberry, Lowell Gudmundson, and Mario Samper K. Baltimore, Md.: Johns Hopkins Univ. Press, 1995. 304 p.: bibl., ill., index, maps. (Johns Hopkins studies in Atlantic history and culture)

Exceptionally well-focused collection of scholarly articles explores the wealth of diversity in history of coffee production and consumption in the Western Hemisphere. Studies cover a geographical and structural range from large plantations of Brazil to smallholdings of Costa Rica, and include important findings on labor systems.

700 Confronting change, challenging tradition: women in Latin American history. Edited by Gertrude Matyoka Yeager. Wilmington, Del.: Scholarly Resources Inc., 1994. 242 p.: bibl. (Jaguar books on Latin America; 7)

These carefully selected articles and documents provide wide range of coverage of women's history from early 19th to late 20th century. Includes succinct, thought-provoking introduction by editor Yeager, and classic essay on *Marianismo* by Evelyn Stevens. Articles are reprinted with original footnotes.

701 Congrés Internacional d'Estudis Històrics "Les Illes Balears i Amèrica," Palma, Spain, 1992. Congrés Internacional d'Estudis Històrics "Les Illes Balears i Amèrica." Coordinació de Román Piña Homs. Palma, Spain: Institut d'Estudis Baleàrics, 1992. 3 v.: bibl., ill.

Contains wide range of articles and documents, some based on archival research.

702 Conquista y resistencia en la historia de América = Conquesta i resistència en la història d'Amèrica. Coordinación de Pilar García Jordán y Miquel Izard. Barcelona: Publicacions Univ. de Barcelona, 1992. 485 p.: bibl.

As title indicates, volume contains selection of essays that portray process of conquest from the perspective of those who opposed it. Chronology runs from precolumbian conflicts among native Americans to early resistance to Columbus expeditions to struggles of Bolivian campesinos against US interventions.

703 Deiros, Pablo Alberto. Historia del cristianismo en América Latina. Buenos Aires: Fraternidad Teológica Latinoamericana, 1992. 847 p.: bibl., ill., maps.

Extensive survey covers Catholic Church in colonial and national periods in the first 584 p., and devotes final 200 p. to rise of Protestantism. Author is on the faculty of Seminario Internacional Teológico Bautista of

Buenos Aires. Valuable as a Protestant evangelical interpretation of religious history of Latin America.

704   Eiras Roel, Antonio and **Ofelia Rey Castelao.** Los gallegos y América. Madrid: Editorial MAPFRE, 1992. 354 p.: bibl., indexes. (Col. Las Españas y América; 11. Col. MAPFRE 1492)

Usually when talking about Galicians and America, focus is on massive 19th-century Galician immigration to the New World. This work, on the other hand, examines less-studied Galician participation in discovery, conquest, and colonization, and Galicians' contribution to religious, political, economic, and intellectual life in the New World. [J.M. Pérez]

705   Encuentro Internacional Quinto Centenario, *San Juan, 1990.* Impacto y futuro de la civilización española en el Nuevo Mundo: actas. Madrid, Spain?: s.n., 1991. 660 p.: bibl. (Col. Encuentros. Serie Seminarios)

Includes 72 papers on themes ranging from Columbus and his times to literature, science, and a section entitled "Otros Temas." Authors' approaches vary from literary criticism, to historical studies based on archival research, to essays of opinion.

706   Fuentes, Carlos. El espejo enterrado. México: Fondo de Cultura Económica, 1992. 440 p.: bibl., ill. (some col.), index, maps. (Col. Tierra firme)

Author's stimulating interpretive synthesis of Latin American history emphasizes cultural, social, and biographical factors. This work is tied to Fuentes' video documentary of the same name and is intended for classroom use.

707   Fuster Ruiz, Francisco. América y el Archivo General de la Marina. (*An. Hist. Contemp.*, 8, 1990/91, p. 75–93, table)

Valuable guide includes Archive's history and organization, and also possible topics for research in Latin American history in the colonial and national periods.

708   Galíndez, Jesús de. Presencia vasca en América: recopilación de trabajos de Jesús de Galíndez publicados en la prensa vasca del exilio. Vitoria, Spain: Servicio Central de Publicaciones del Gobierno Vasco, 1984. 201 p.: ill. (some col.).

Biographical emphasis is reinforced by photographs.

709   García Tapia, Nicolás. Del dios del fuego a la máquina de vapor: la introducción de la técnica industrial en Hispanoamérica. Valladolid, Spain: Ambito Ediciones; Instituto de Ingenieros Técnicos de España, 1992. 364 p.: bibl., ill., indexes.

Valuable synthesis of history of industrial technology covers early colonial period to early 19th century. Author combines his own archival research with findings of historical monographs. Book is illustrated with relevant reproductions of drawings of machinery. Discusses textile manufacturing, sugar mills, mining, metallurgy, and development of pumps to remove water from mines.

710   González Cembellín, Juan Manuel. América en el País Vasco: inventario de elementos patrimoniales de origen americano en la comunidad autónoma vasca. Vitoria, Spain: Servicio Central de Publicaciones del Gobierno Vasco, 1993. 231 p.: bibl., ill. (some col.). (Amerika eta euskaldunak = América y los vascos; 16)

Catalog describes donations and gifts made by Basque immigrants in America back to their homeland in Spain. Churches, convents, hospitals, schools, and furniture dominate the listings. The introduction includes useful commentary and statistical charts.

711   Guerra, Francisco. Las cátedras de medicina en las universidades españolas de América y Filipinas, 1538–1898. (*Estud. Hist. Soc. Econ. Am.*, 9, 1992, p. 253–260)

Very brief survey of an important topic is mainly a chronological listing of the founding of medical schools and programs.

712   Guerra Vilaboy, Sergio. La revolución en la historia de América Latina: los aportes de Manfred Kossok. (*Jahrb. Gesch.*, 31, 1994, p. 361–372)

Useful analysis examines works of the German historian who applied Marxist interpretations in his wide-ranging studies.

713   Guy, Donna J. Future directions in Latin American gender history. (*Americas/Francisc.*, 51:1, July 1994, p. 1–9)

Stimulating review surveys recent publications in gender history and suggestions for further research, including importance of Catholic traditions and significance of industrial modernization for women and for gender relations.

H-LatAm: Latin American history forum. See item **36.**

714 Halperín Donghi, Tulio. The contemporary history of Latin America. Edited and translated by John Charles Chasteen. Durham, N.C.: Duke Univ. Press, 1993. 426 p.: bibl., ill., index. (Latin America in translation/en traducción/em tradução)

Overdue English translation of a textbook that appeared in its original form in Spanish in 1967 and which has enjoyed wide readership and influence in Latin America since then. Chasteen's translation is based on 13th edition (1990). Donghi organizes his text in periods of 10 to 50 years, and achieves coherence within each section through development of certain themes. This interpretive approach has much to offer the professoriate as well as students.

715 Halperín Donghi, Tulio. Hispanoamérica en el espejo: reflexiones hispanoamericanas sobre Hispanoamérica, de Simón Bolívar a Hernando de Soto. (*Hist. Mex.*, 42:3, enero/marzo 1993, p. 745–787, bibl.)

Author explores writings of Bolívar, Sarmiento, Martí, Mariátegui, Prebisch, Véliz, De Soto and other intellectuals for their views of major political and economic problems confronting Spanish America since 1820s. Halperín Donghi's focus is on historical themes rather than ideologies.

716 Hilton, Sylvia L. and **Ignacio González Casasnovas.** Fuentes manuscritas para la historia de Iberoamérica: guía de instrumentos de investigación. Madrid: Fundación MAPFRE América, Instituto Histórico Tavera, 1995. xliii, 617 p.: indexes.

This exceptionally valuable research tool consists of a listing of guides to manuscript collections located in the Latin American nations, the US, Canada and other non-Latin nations of the Americas, Europe, Australia, and the Philippines. The chronological coverage extends from the late 15th century to the early 20th century. This publication is organized by country, further subdivided by city, and is strengthened by six indexes.

717 Historia general de la emigración española a Iberoamérica. Madrid: Historia 16, 1992. 2 v.: bibl., ill.

Vol. 1 consists of 20 studies of Spanish immigration to America from colonial period to the Spanish Civil War and years after World War II. Vol. 2 contains 17 essays on regional origins of the Spanish emigrants to America. Balanced blend of narrative, analysis, and statistics.

718 El historiador frente a la historia: corrientes historiográficas actuales. México: Univ. Nacional Autónoma de México, Instituto de Investigaciones Históricas, 1992. 129 p.: bibl. (Serie Divulgación; 1)

Eleven brief, often provocative essays by leading Mexican historians examine important recent trends in historiography. Some topics included are regional studies, gender history, quantitative approaches, and economic history.

Historical Text Archive: Latin America and Mexico. See item **37.**

719 Horia, Vintilă. Reconquista del descubrimiento. Madrid: Veintiuno, 1992. 288 p.: bibl. (Col. Veintiuno)

Extensive commentary moves from the Europe of Columbus to the Mexico of the Cristeros to the Argentina of Borges. A serious effort to synthesize literature, philosophy, and politics not only of the first encounter but also of five centuries of Hispanic-American history.

720 La Iglesia en América: siglos XVI-XX; Sevilla, 1992. Madrid: Editorial Deimos, 1992. 285 p.: bibl., ill.

Evangelism is central theme in this set of 14 essays that run from early colonial missionary work to evangelization drives of late 20th century. Introduction by José Carlos Martín de la Hoz provides a sensible conceptual framework.

721 The Indian in Latin American history: resistance, resilience, and acculturation. Edited by John E. Kicza. Wilmington, Del: Scholarly Resources, 1993. 240 p.: bibl. (Jaguar books on Latin America; 1)

Book of selected readings is intended for the college classroom. Ten articles range from preconquest Inca to 20th-century struggles for land reform and ethnic identity. Kizca's introductory essay gives a valuable overview. These reprinted articles include all original footnotes.

722 Inikori, Joseph E. and **Stanley L. Engerman.** Gainers and losers in the Atlantic slave trade. (*in* The Atlantic slave trade: effects on economies, societies, and peoples in

Africa, the Americas, and Europe. Edited by Joseph E. Inikori and Stanley L. Engerman. Durham, N.C.: Duke Univ. Press, 1992, p. 1–21, bibl.)

This introduction to a volume of selected essays on the slave trade addresses several general questions including social costs of the slave trade in Africa, role of slavery in the rise of the Western world, and the enduring legacy of slavery in the Atlantic region.

723 La interminable conquista, 1492–1992.
Buenos Aires: Ediciones AYLLU; Movimiento Argentino de Emancipación e Identidad de América Latina, 1992. 153 p.: bibl., ill. (Col. Perspectivas)

Contains highly charged collection of writings critical of the conquest. Authors include Enrique Dussel, Tomás Borge, Rubén Dri, and Rigoberta Menchú (two poems and an interview).

724 The Jesuit tradition in education and missions: a 450-year perspective. Edited by Christopher Chapple. Scranton, Pa.: Univ. of Scranton Press; London: Associated University Presses, 1993. 290 p.: bibl., ill., index.

Ten essays in this collection focus on history of Jesuit educational ideas and institutions, while six others examine Jesuit missionary contacts with non-European peoples. Four of the essays deal specifically with Latin American themes: missionaries in Peru and Paraguay, the work of Eusebio Kino, and Jesuit education and modernity in Latin America. Based on secondary works.

725 Jornadas de Andalucía y América, 11th, Univ. de Santa María de la Rábida, Sevilla, Spain, 1992. Huelva y América: actas. Edición de Bibiano Torres Ramírez. Huelva, Spain: Diputación Provincial de Huelva, 1993. 2 v.: bibl., ill., maps.

Extremely focused study has a heavily biographical emphasis.

726 Jornadas de Estudios Históricos, 3rd, Salamanca, Spain, 1991. Problemas actuales de la historia. Salamanca, Spain: Univ. de Salamanca, 1993. 257 p.: bibl. (Acta Salmanticensia. Estudios históricos y geográficos; 84)

Collection of 14 articles is concerned with a wide range of historiographical issues, many of which pertain to Latin America. Of special interest are Pérez Ledesma's essay on

social movements and Fernández Buey's observations on contemporary Marxism.

727 Kieniewicz, Jan. Situation, colonialism, backwardness: on the possibilities of comparative studies of Eastern Europe and Latin America. (*Estud. Latinoam./Poland*, 14:1, 1992, p. 81–85)

Provides brief exploration of suggested themes in comparative history.

728 Knight, Franklin W. Columbus and slavery in the New World and Africa. (*Rev. Rev. Interam.*, 22:1/2, primavera 1992, p. 18–35, bibl.)

In a clearly written provocative essay, author reminds us of imprecision in transmittance of Columbus' words, making it difficult to understand today precisely what he thought in 1492. Rather than debating his role in introducing slavery to the Americas, we should view his actions as precipitating the modern global village by inadvertently linking a new Atlantic world consisting of Europe, Africa, and the Americas. [E.L. Cox]

Kollokvium istorikov SSSR i Meksiki, 1st, Moscow, 1988. I kollokvium istorikov SSSR i Meksiki [1st Colloquim of Soviet and Mexican Historians]. See item **1099.**

729 Kuznesof, Elizabeth Anne. Women, work and the family in Latin America: a life course perspective on the impact of changes in mode of production on women's lives and productive roles. (*in* El poblamiento de las Américas, *Veracruz, 1992.* Actas. Liège, Belgium: International Union for the Scientific Study of Population, 1992, v. 2, p. 71–113, bibl.)

Important synthesis focuses on recent studies on adaptations of women to rapidly changing work and family situations in the transition to industrial society.

730 Ladin meizhou Lishi Cidian [Historical Dictionary of Latin America]. Edited by the Institute of Latin American Studies, Chinese Academy of Social Sciences. Shanghai, China: Shanghai Lexicographical Press, 1993. 576 p.: appendices, chronology, maps, plates, tables.

First and only medium-sized dictionary of Latin American history ever published in China contains 4,880 entries on pre-columbian, conquest, colonial, independence, and national history. Work of concerted effort by more than 60 Institute researchers over 10 years. [Mao Xianglin]

731 Die Lateinamerikanistik in der Schweiz. Edited by Walther L. Bernecker, José Manuel López de Abiada, and Linda Shepard. Frankfurt am Main: Vervuert, 1993. 343 p.: bibl. (Lateinamerika-Studien; 31)

Interdisciplinary team presents historiographical essays and bibliographies of Swiss contributions and publications covering Latin American research (1827–1991). Includes information on status of specific Latin American studies in Swiss universities. Indispensable for studies of Swiss immigration and the Swiss perspective on Latin America. [C.K. Converse]

732 Latin America: conflict and creation; a historical reader. Edited by E. Bradford Burns. Englewood Cliffs, N.J.: Prentice-Hall, 1993. 336 p.: bibl., ill.

Volume of selected readings intended for the college classroom has strength of Burns' succinct introduction for each selection. Emphasis on social and economic history and "the revolutionary option."

733 Latin American urbanization: historical profiles of major cities. Edited by Gerald Michael Greenfield. Westport, Conn.: Greenwood Press, 1994. 536 p.: bibl., index, maps.

Volume uses an encyclopedic approach. Each of its 21 chapters is devoted to urban history of one nation, including succinct overviews of the main urban centers in that country.

734 Lazcano González, Rafael. Bibliographia missionalia Augustiniana: América Latina, 1533–1993. Madrid: Editorial Revista Agustiniana, 1993. 647 p.: ill., indexes. (Col. Guía bibliográfica; 3)

Listing of 4,427 books and articles on Augustinian missionary history is organized by nations and by biographies, with emphasis on the latter. The last 15 pages provide a bibliography of *hermanas agustinas*. Includes useful indexes.

735 León-Portilla, Miguel. The New World, 1492–1992: an endless debate? (*Diogenes/Philosophy*, 157, Spring 1992, p. 1–21)

Author concludes that the debate is "endless" but also makes some astute observations concerning the need to bring native American pre-encounter experiences into the mainstream of world history texts. His comments on Edmundo O'Gorman's view of the "discovery" are stimulating and provocative.

736 Lian, Yunshan. Shei Xian Daoda Meichou [Who first arrived in America?] Beijing: China Social Sciences Press, 1992. 158 p.: appendices, ill., maps, plates.

Supported with ample evidence, asserts that Fa Xian (a Chinese Buddhist Monk, 337–422) first arrived in America in the early 5th century, long before Christopher Columbus, analyzing why the Chinese could have arrived there earlier than Columbus. Disagrees with the viewpoint that the latter achieved this discovery while the former did not. Concludes that both arrivals contributed greatly to the development of human civilization. A valuable and representative work on this more than 200-year-long dispute in world history. See *HLAS 52:730* for a related book by another Chinese scholar who refutes the assertion that the Americas were first discovered by a Chinese monk. [Mao Xianglin]

737 Loureiro, Celso. Fons americans en arxius de Catalunya. Barcelona: Generalitat de Catalunya, Comissió Amèrica i Catalunya, 1992. 148 p. (Col. Joan Orpí)

Listing of archives is accompanied by brief descriptions of their contents. The most extensive holdings deal with 19th and 20th centuries. Many of the archives are located in Barcelona but several are scattered throughout other municipalities.

738 Luna, Lola G. Movimientos de mujeres, Estado y participación política en América Latina: una propuesta de análisis histórico. (*Bol. Am.*, 33:42/43, 1992/93, p. 255–266, bibl.)

Author attempts to formulate a conceptual framework for women's political participation history that is based largely on the patriarchal/oligarchical nature of Latin American society.

739 Luo, Rong-qu. 15 shi Zhong qi hang hai fa zhan qu xiang de duibi yu si suo [A comparison between the orientations of the development of navigation in fifteenth-century China and the West]. (*Li Shi Yan Jiu* 1, 1992, p. 3–19)

This study of Columbus and the great Chinese navigator Zheng He is the best article on the subject published in China. Based on numerous historical materials, article offers well-founded explanations for the tremendous impact of the travels of Columbus and Vasco da Gama compared to the relatively minimal impact of those of Zheng He. The author, a noted historian in China, is Chairman of the Chinese Society of Latin American History Studies. [Mao Xianglin]

740 Macías Hernández, Antonio M. La migración canaria, 1500–1980. Oviedo, Spain: Ediciones Júcar, 1992. 242 p.: bibl., ill. (Cruzar el charco; 4)

General synthesis of immigration patterns from Canary Islands to the Americas is based on extensive archival research and a broad knowledge of published monographs. Author provides effective combination of narrative, analytical explication, and demographic statistics. Discussion of troubled economic conditions of the islands that stimulated much of the migration in 1700s and 1800s is especially impressive.

741 Malamud, Carlos. El espejo quebrado: la imagen de España en América de la independencia a la transición democrática. (*Rev. Occident.*, 131, abril 1992, p. 180–198)

Broad generalizations characterize this brief essay as it moves from negative image of Spain in 19th century to the more positive image of late 20th century.

742 Martínez Carreras, José Urbano. Historia del colonialismo y la descolonización: siglos XV-XX. Madrid: Editorial Complutense, 1992. 183 p.: bibl., maps.

Succinct, sometimes terse textbook survey examines rise and fall of European colonialism in the Americas, Asia, the Pacific, Africa, and the Middle East.

743 Martínez Sanz, José Luis. Relaciones científicas entre España y América. Madrid: Editorial MAPFRE, 1992. 377 p.: bibl., indexes. (Col. Relaciones entre España y América; 13. Col. MAPFRE 1492)

General study examines transfer of European scientific knowledge and practices to America from 1500s to early 20th century. Text is well organized. Each chapter begins with a survey of advancements in Europe and then traces movement of these theories and their applications through Spain to America. Includes helpful bibliography.

744 Maza Zavala, Domingo Felipe. Hispanoamérica Angloamérica: causas y factores de su diferente evolución. Madrid: Edi-

torial MAPFRE, 1992. 298 p.: bibl., indexes, maps. (Col. Realidades americanas; 1. Col. MAPFRE 1492)

Essay in comparative history extend from early colonial period to late 20th century. Author emphasizes colonial period in which economic drive of the British colonies contrasted with restrictive policies of the Spanish empire. Well organized, stimulating study of a large and important topic.

745 Meier, Johannes. The religious orders in Latin America: a historical survey. (*in* The Church in Latin America, 1492–1992. Edited by Enrique Dussel. Kent, England: Burns & Oats; Maryknoll, N.Y.: Orbis Books, 1992, p. 375–390, tables)

Sweeping synthesis covers both colonial and national periods. Supported by extensive footnotes.

746 Mémoires en devenir: Amérique latine XVIe-XXe siècle; colloque international de Paris, 1er-3 décembre 1992. Edition de François-Xavier Guerra. Bordeaux: Maison des Pays ibériques, 1994. 377 p. (Col. de la Maison des Pays ibériques: 0296–7588; 62)

In a brilliant introduction Sorbonne professor Guerra discusses meaning and projections of 21 papers submitted at an international colloquium (Paris, Dec. 1992) held under auspices of Association française des sciences sociales sur l'Amérique latine (AFSAL). Overall, volume is a reassessment of historical memory in Latin America. Six contributions deal with the colonial period, eight with 19th-century nationalism, and seven with contemporary problems and models. [T. Hampe-Martínez]

747 Menard, Russell R. and Stuart B. Schwartz. Why African slavery?: labor force transitions in Brazil, Mexico, and the Carolina lowcountry. (*in* Slavery in the Americas. Edited by Wolfgang Binder. Würzburg, Germany: Königshausen and Neumann, 1993, p. 89–114)

Essay in comparative history examines reasons for plantation owners' option for African slavery as a source of labor. Impressive, refined set of generalizations emphasizes market forces while allowing for circumstantial differences in each locality.

748 Míguez, Eduardo José. Capitalismo y migraciones en la formación de las sociedades iberoamericanas. (*Rev. Occident.*, 131, abril 1992, p. 37–50)

Explores paradoxical relationship between European migration to Latin America and development of capitalism on both sides of the Atlantic. No footnotes or bibliography.

749 Morales Padrón, Francisco. Andalucía y América. Málaga, Spain: Editorial Arguval, 1992. 317 p.: bibl., ill., indexes, maps. (Col. Tres culturas; 1. Col. MAPFRE 1492)

Convenient synthesis of Andalucía's contribution to Latin American history has sensible combination of social, economic, political, cultural, and biographical factors. Contains an especially interesting chapter on Andalucía's continuing scholarly interest in the Americas into 19th and 20th centuries.

750 Morales Saro, María Cruz. Archivo de Indianos, Colombres, Asturias. Fotografía de Antonio Alonso. Asturias, Spain: Archivo de Indianos; Principado de Asturias, 1992? 82 p.: bibl., ill. (some col.).

Commemorative booklet concerns founding of the archive and museum. Numerous photographs accompany a discussion of the purposes and physical facilities.

751 Mörner, Magnus. African slavery in Spanish and Portuguese America: some remarks on historiography and the present state of research. (*in* Slavery in the Americas. Edited by Wolfgang Binder. Würzburg, Germany: Königshausen and Neumann, 1993, p. 57–87, bibl.)

Succinct assessment of studies of African slavery moves from Tannenbaum's and Freyre's theses to more recent findings of 1970s-80s. Insights on national and regional differences.

752 Mörner, Magnus. The Americanist Congresses and the Swedes. (*Ibero-Am./Stockholm*, 24:1, 1994, p. 3–17, bibl.)

Succinct, informative account of Swedish participation in the Americanist Congresses from 1894 meeting in Stockholm to 1991 meeting in New Orleans includes interesting observations on changes in thematic emphases over the years.

753 Mörner, Magnus. En torno al uso de la comparación en el análisis histórico de América Latina. (*Jahrb. Gesch.*, 31, 1994, p. 373–390)

Reflective survey of comparative history is based on careful reading of previous scholarly efforts. Mörner concludes that middle-level, regional comparative studies offer best potential for meaningful generalizations.

754 Mörner, Magnus. Historia social hispanoamericana de los siglos XVIII y XIX: algunas reflexiones en torno a la historiografía reciente. (*Hist. Mex.*, 42:2, oct./dic. 1992, p. 419–471, bibl.)

Extensive, penetrating review focuses on monographs published since 1950s. Topics involve demography, social classes, *mentalidades*, and social movements.

755 Mörner, Magnus. Local communities and actors in Latin America's past. Stockholm: Stockholm Univ., Institute of Latin American Studies, 1994. 231 p.: bibl., index, maps, photos, tables. (Monograph series; 25)

Mörner analyzes histories of four localities giving particular attention to roles of community leaders: Concepción, at one time a Jesuit mission; Obera, a Swedish settlement (both in northern Argentina); Paucartambo in the Peruvian Andes; and Ocumare de la Costa in Venezuela.

756 Murcia y América: VII Curso de Aproximación a la España Contemporánea, febrero-marzo, 1991. Edición de Juan Bautista Vilar. Murcia, Spain: V Centenario, Comisión de Murcia, 1992. 290 p.: bibl., ill. (Col. Carabelas. Ensayo; 5)

Ten essays on various topics span period from late-16th-century trade to exiles from Spanish Civil War of 1930s. Five of the essays focus on port of Cartagena in 17th and 18th centuries and include research from archival sources.

757 Navarros en América: cinco crónicas. Pamplona, Spain: Gobierno de Navarra, 1992. 315 p.: bibl., col. ill., maps.

Quincentennial celebratory publication contains five historical sketches: a brief history of Pamplona, Colombia; Cipriano Barace's missionary work in Bolivia; the Aycinena family of Guatemala; Iturbide of Mexico; and immigrants to Argentina. Lacks footnotes.

Ortega y Medina, Juan Antonio. Reflexiones históricas. See item **1107.**

758 Parsons, Lee Allen. Columbus to Catherwood, 1494–1844: 350 years of historic book graphics depicting the islands, Indians, and archaeology of the West Indies, Florida, and Mexico = De Colón a Catherwood, 1494–1844: 350 años de gráficas de libros históricos; descripción de las islas, indios y arqueología de las Indias, Flórida y México. Miami Lakes, Fla.: Jay I. Kislak Foundation Inc., 1993. 121 p.: bibl., ill. (Kislak bibliographic series; 1)

Publication features b/w reproductions of illustrations from books about the New World based on holdings of Kislak Collection. Each of the 44 illustrations is accompanied by a commentary by Parsons. Includes De Bry, Humboldt, Del Río, Waldeck, and others.

759 Peralta Agudelo, Jaime Andrés. En busca de América. Bogotá: Tercer Mundo Editores, 1992. 276 p. (Temas de actualidad)

Assessment of varieties in Latin American society and culture ranges from conquest to late 20th century. Interesting subjective judgments on contemporary problems. Lacks scholarly apparatus.

760 Piel, Jean. Développement historique de duex frontières: en expansion de l'Europe jusqu'au XXe siècle; l'Amérique latine et l'Europe de l'Est. (*Estud. Latinoam./Poland*, 14:1, 1992, p. 87–106)

Senior French historian with extensive knowledge of histories of Eastern Europe and Latin America employs center-periphery framework to compare how the two regions experienced Christianization, colonization, and ethnic miscegenation as a result of the expansion of Western Europe. Careful descriptions of similarities and differences for 19th and 20th centuries; less convincing for 18th. Nevertheless abounds in sophisticated insights. [A. Pérotin-Dumon]

761 Prat, José. Medio milenio del Nuevo Mundo. Albacete, Spain: Excma. Diputación Provincial de Albacete, 1992. 223 p.: ill. (Ediciones de la Diputación de Albacete. Biblioteca José Prat)

Attempts a sweeping synthesis of five centuries of Latin American history. More commentary on literary and intellectual themes than on social, economic, and political matters.

762 Problems in modern Latin American history: a reader. Edited by John Charles Chasteen and Joseph S. Tulchin. Wilmington, Del.: SR Books, 1994. 339 p.: bibl. (Latin American silhouettes)

Intended for Latin American survey courses in college, this reader begins with independence movements and strikes a healthy balance of social, cultural, economic, and political history including caudillismo, populism, revolution, and women's history. Includes a mixture of contemporary documents with historical articles.

763 Proyección y presencia de Segovia en América. Dirección y edición de Mariano Cuesta Domingo. Segovia, Spain: Deimos, 1992. 602 p.: bibl.

Collection includes 36 historical studies, some of which are product of archival research while others are mainly "think pieces." Strong biographical emphasis, especially for sketches of Domingo de Soto and Antonio de Herrera.

764 Quesada Camacho, Juan Rafael. América Latina: memoria e identidad, 1492–1992. San José: Editorial Respuesta, 1993. 163 p.: bibl.

Conceptual study of image of Latin American society is contained within historiography of events of 1492, the fourth centennial (1892), and the fifth (1992).

765 500 anos de invasão, 500 anos de resistência. Organização de Roberto Zwetsch. Rio de Janeiro: Centro Ecumênico de Documentação e Informação; São Paulo: Edições Paulinas, 1992. 321 p.: bibl., map.

Collection of 16 essays generally views history from perspective of native Americans, Africans, and other peoples on the margins of society. Authors represent a leftist ecumenicalism drawn from Catholic, Methodist, and Lutheran churches.

766 Ramón, Armando de; Juan Ricardo Couyoumdjian; and Samuel Vial. Ruptura del viejo orden hispanoamericano. Santiago: Editorial Andrés Bello, 1993. 412 p.: bibl., ill., maps. (Historia de América; 2)

Survey text in Latin American history begins with Bourbon Reforms of 1700s, covers independence period, and includes first half-century of independence to 1875. Much of discussion of independence period centers on biographical portraits and military history. Last section provides interesting overview of the colonial legacy of politics of instability and *caudillismo* and of the beginnings of economic modernization.

767 Rank and privilege: the military and society in Latin America. Edited by Linda Alexander Rodríguez. Wilmington, Del.: Scholarly Resources, 1994. 239 p.: bibl. (Jaguar books on Latin America; 8)

Ten scholarly articles and editor's introduction are focused on varied connections between broad social changes and role of the military. Useful collection includes original footnotes for each article.

768 Reunión Iberoamericana para la Recuperación y Conservación de Archivos y Documentación de los Trabajadores y los Movimientos Sociales, 1st, Buenos Aires, 1992. Documentos. Edición de Aurelio Martín Nájera y Agustín Garrigós Fernández. Madrid: Editorial Pablo Iglesias, 1992. 588 p.: bibl.

Contains country-by-country reports on status of labor history archives, with the most extensive reports from Brazil and Mexico. Publication could become a landmark if organization's efforts continue to expand.

769 Robinson, John L. Anti-Hispanic bias in British historiography. (*Hisp. Sacra*, 44:89, enero/junio 1992, p. 21–46)

Close examination of reading lists for British pre-university students concludes that much anti-Hispanic bias appears in books published in 1970s-80s. Robinson's analysis is penetrating and his conclusions are disturbing.

770 Rodríguez Sáenz, Eugenia. Historia de la familia en América Latina: balance de las principales tendencias. (*Rev. Hist./Heredia*, 26, julio/dic. 1992, p. 145–183, bibl.)

Well-informed synthesis focuses on recent research on the family, including elite families, demographic and structural trends, and tension between patriarchy and individualism. Gives close examination to research on Costa Rica. Includes bibliography (11 p.).

771 Romano, Ruggiero. Consideraciones: siete estudios de historia. Lima: Fomciencias; Instituto Italiano de Cultura, 1992. 290 p.: bibl., ill., maps. (Grandes estudios andinos; 2)

Seven of author's previously published essays are presented here to give the reader a convenient compilation. Romano tends to concentrate on economic history, from which he moves into abstractions regarding the im-

balances between "center" and "periphery" and the often conflicting roles of the nation and the State.

772 Shijie huaren Jingying Zhuanlue: Nanmeichou yu Jialada juan [Biographies of overseas Chinese elites in the world: volume on South America and Canada. Edited by Zhuang Yianlin and Deng Guangdon. Nanchang, China: Hundred Flowers Literature and Art Press, 1994. 328 p.: appendices.

Contains 10 biographies of overseas Chinese elites in South America, prominent figures in all walks of life, ranging from president of a country to industrialists. An appendix entitled "Overseas Chinese and Latin America" provides a general survey of their situation in that region. [Mao Xianglin]

773 Silver, John. The myth of El Dorado. (*Hist. Workshop*, 34, Autumn 1992, p. 1–15)

Intelligent exploration of European intellectual response to the myth of El Dorado ranges from flights of fantasy to efforts at realism. Includes Raleigh, Humboldt, Burton, and Conrad.

774 Simposio América V Centenario, 1492–1992, Murcia, Spain, 1990. De la América española a la América americana: actas. Edición de F.V. Sánchez Gil y F. Martínez Fresneda. Murcia, Spain: Instituto Teológico de Murcia O.F.M., 1991. 196 p.: bibl., ill. (PITM. Serie mayor; 4. CAM cultural)

First four essays deal with religious and ethical issues surrounding erection of the Spanish Empire. Fifth and final essay concerns role of Murcia in Spanish America through colonial period into the 20th century.

775 Sizonenko, Aleksandr Ivanovich. Russkie otkryvaiut Latinskuiu Ameriku. [The Russians discover Latin America.] Moscow: Russian Academy of Sciences, Institute of Latin Amrrican Studies, 1992. 113 p.

Well-known Russian historian reviews experiences of Russian explorers, scientists, diplomats, architects, and artists in Latin America since 18th century. Based on primary sources that combine vignettes on singer Shaliapin in Buenos Aires, ballet dancer Pavlova and composer-pianist Rachmaninov in Cuba, and poet Mayakovsky in Mexico. [B. Dash]

776 **Smith, Peter H.** The State and development in historical perspective. (*in* Americas: new interpretive essays. New York: Oxford Univ. Press, 1992, p. 30–56)

Smith assesses role of the State in economic development, from colonial-period mercantilism to 19th-century liberalism and 20th-century industrial developmentalism. He also includes a well-reasoned comparative analysis of Latin America with the Pacific Rim nations.

777 **Stannard, David E.** American holocaust: Columbus and the conquest of the New World. New York: Oxford Univ. Press, 1992. 358 p.: bibl., ill., index.

Disturbing and challenging synthesis examines European defeat and destruction of native American polities and societies beginning with the Spanish conquistadores in the Caribbean in 1490s and early 1500s and ending with US gold-seekers in 1850s California. Author's philosophical/ideological analysis indicts Christian teachings as a motive force behind the conquest.

778 **Suárez Roca, José Luis.** Lingüística misionera española. Oviedo, Spain: Pentalfa Ediciones, 1992. 324 p.: bibl. (Col. El Basilisco)

Systematic examination of work of Spanish missionaries with native American languages is based on missionaries' grammar books and dictionaries. The most intensive analysis (a chapter of 138 p. comprising nearly half of the text) focuses on work with Nahuatl.

779 **Symposium Internacional de Historia de la Masonería Española, 5th, Cáceres, Spain, 1991.** Masonería española y América. Coordinación de José Antonio Ferrer Benimeli. Zaragoza, Spain: Centro de Estudios Históricos de la Masonería Española, 1993. 2 v.: bibl., ill., maps.

Unusually strong collection of essays offers important insights and some valuable research in history of Spanish Masonry in the Americas from colonial period into the 20th century. Themes include Masonic influences in Brazilian abolitionism and various movements for independence throughout the hemisphere. Coverage of Argentina and Cuba is especially prominent.

780 **Testimonios: cinco siglos del libro en Iberoamérica; Caracas-Madrid 1992.** Barcelona: Lunwerg, 1992. 340 p.: bibl., ill., index. (Col. Encuentros. Serie Catálogos)

Annotated guide was prepared to accompany the international exposition of books, manuscripts, maps, and other documents from pre-colonial period to independence.

781 **Tres levantamientos populares: Pugachóv, Túpac Amaru, Hidalgo.** Coordinación de Jean A. Meyer. México: CEMCA; Consejo Nacional para la Cultura y las Artes, 1992. 195 p.: bibl., ill., maps.

Relatively small volume brings together some leading historians engaged in an important exercise: comparative history. Their well-researched examinations of uprisings in Russia, Peru, and Mexico yield some valuable insights, which are summarized effectively in concluding chapter by Enrique Florescano.

782 **Turley, David.** Slavery in the Americas: resistance, liberation, emancipation. (*Slavery Abolit.*, 14:2, Aug. 1993, p. 109–116)

Interesting "think piece" surveys recent publications on origins and process of emancipation. Covers US and British West Indies as well as Cuba and Brazil.

783 **Villechenon, Florence Pinot de.** L'Amérique latine dans les expositions universelles. (*Rev. hist./Paris*, 586, avril/juin 1993, p. 511–601, bibl.)

Short wonderful summary of how Latin America presented itself to the world in various "world's fairs" in the 19th and 20th centuries. Recommended. [B. Tenenbaum]

784 **Violence, resistance, and survival in the Americas: Native Americans and the legacy of conquest.** Edited by William B. Taylor and Franklin Pease G.Y. Washington: Smithsonian Institution Press, 1994. 296 p.: bibl., ill., index.

History and anthropology intersect in these 10 articles that span period from 1500s to 20th century with focus on native American responses to external domination in both North and South America. Michael Taussig's "Coda" is a bold essay advocating a reorientation of academic perspectives on the plight of the powerless.

785 **Wang, Jia-feng** and **Guei Qi-peng.**
Zheng He Gelumbu Shi zhong xi zhi
minde zhui qiu [Pursuits of Chinese and
Western inhabitants in the times of Zheng He
and Columbus]. (*La Mei Shi Yan Jiu Tong
Xun*, 23/24, 1991, p. 24–40)
Argues that Columbus' voyage, rather
than Zheng He's, marked a new time for man-
kind not because of different levels of productive forces between China and Western Europe, but because of different historical
environments in these two lands. The great
European explorations were a product of a
common pursuit by all social classes and
strata, while Zheng He's voyage was not im-
pelled by economic expansion. [Mao Xian-
glin]

786 **Where cultures meet: frontiers in Latin
American history.** Edited by David J.
Weber and Jane M. Rausch. Wilmington, Del.:
SR Books, 1994. 233 p.: bibl. (Jaguar books on
Latin America; 6)
Impressive array of articles and essays
explores this important topic with a strong
emphasis on comparative history. Authorities
range from Sarmiento, Turner, and Webb to
Slatta and Vianna Moog.

787 **Wilson, Richard.** Shifting frontiers: his-
torical transformations of identities in
Latin America. (*Bull. Lat. Am. Res.*, 14 : 1,
Jan. 1995, p. 1–7)
Brief but challenging "think piece" fo-
cuses on complex and subtle interaction of
European and native American cultures and
cultural identities.

788 **Winn, Peter.** Americas: the changing
face of Latin America and the Caribbean. New York: Pantheon Books, 1992. 639
p., 24 p. of plates: bibl., ill. (some col.), index,
maps.
College text was written to coordinate
with PBS series "Americas." Organization is
more topical than in most texts, with much
attention given to economics, immigration,
ethnicity, role of women, religion, art, and
Latin Americans in the US. An important innovation in the field of Latin American history texts published in the US.

789 **Zhou, Shixiu** and **Corcino Medeiros
dos Santos.** O descobrimento da
América pelos chineses. Porto Alegre, Brazil:
EDIPUCRS; Centro de Estudos Ibero-Americanos, IFCH/PUC-RS, 1992. 104 p.: ill., maps.

First book published by a Chinese
scholar in Portuguese in Brazil. Consists of
five chapters on: 1) the development of Chinese history; 2) ancient Chinese shipbuilding
and navigation; 3) historical records of
America in ancient Chinese books; 4) similarities between the ancient cultures of China
and America; and 5) Chinese scholars' debate
on whether the Chinese discovered America.
Author serves as professor of Latin American
history, specializing in Brazilian studies, at
Hubei Univ. [Mao Xianglin]

COLONIAL

790 **Academia Argentina de Letras.** España
y el Nuevo Mundo: un diálogo de quinientos años. Prólogo de Federico Peltzer.
Buenos Aires: Academia Argentina de Letras,
1992. 2 v.: bibl., ill., index. (Biblioteca de la
Academia Argentina de Letras. Serie Estudios
académicos; 30)
Over 80 contributors focus on broad
cultural and historical themes as well as
more specialized areas in literature and linguistics. Highly diverse collection includes
some valuable interpretive essays. Unfortunately, the breadth of topics defies convenient
summation.

791 **Alvarez Gutiérrez, Jaime.** Carta a su
Alteza, el Micer de Aragón, Señor de
Castilla y Don de Parte del Mundo, Juan Carlos Alfonso Víctor María de Todos los Santos,
Rey de España . . . Colombia: Editorial Cabra
Mocha, 1992. 270 p.
Lengthy letter to the King of Spain
serves as a literary device to express author's
judgments on the conquest and its consequences. Last portion deals with history of
modern Colombia.

792 **Alvear Acevedo, Carlos** and **María del
Consuelo García y Stahl.** El español
ante el amerindio: un caso de conciencia.
México: Editoral Jus, 1993. 358 p.: bibl. (Col.
de historia. Nueva historia)
Useful synthesis on Spanish-Native
American interactions in 16th century is
based on scholarly monographs. Extensively
footnoted and nicely organized.

793 **América em tempo de conquista.** Or-
ganização de Ronaldo Vainfas. Rio de
Janeiro: J. Zahar Editor, 1992. 210 p.: bibl., ill.
(Col. Jubileu)

This group of 11 essays covers wide range of topics on preconquest, conquest, and colonial eras, including analyses of Amazon sexuality, writings of Cieza de León, and role of women in early colonial period.

794 Añeses de Gaztambide, Miriam. Tras las huellas de Cristóbal Colón. Panama?: Cultural Panamericana, 1991. 135 p.: bibl., ill., maps.

Brief biographical essay includes maps and illustrations but has few footnotes and a limited bibliography.

795 Arcelus-Ulibarrena, Juana Mary. La profecía de Joaquín de Fiore en el "Floreto de Sant Francisco" y su presencia en el Nuevo Mundo. (*Arch. Francisc. Hist.*, 85:1/4, Dec. 1992, p. 5–38)

Presents revisionist interpretation of impact of medieval religious thought in early years of the conquest—especially among the Franciscans in New Spain.

796 Archivo General de Indias (Spain). Catálogo de las consultas del Consejo de Indias. v. 10–11. Introducción y dirección de Antonia Heredia Herrera. Sevilla, Spain: Diputación Provincial, 1993–94. 2 v.: index. (V centenario del descubrimiento de América)

Lists documents in the Archivo General de Indias by date, giving brief description of contents. Extensive index is of value for researchers.

797 Arenas Frutos, Isabel. Expediciones franciscanas a Indias, 1700–1725 (*Arch. Ibero-Am.*, 52:205/208, 1992, p. 158–185, tables)

Listing of documents for 16 Franciscan expeditions to Spanish America includes citations from Archivo General de Indias, and names and brief descriptions of the members of the expeditions along with an analytical introduction.

798 Ares Queija, Berta. Representaciones dramáticas de la conquista: el pasado al servicio del presente. (*Rev. Indias*, 52:195/196, mayo/dic. 1992, p. 231–250)

Sophisticated study views colonial period reenactments of the conquest as indications of Native American efforts to deal with their contemporary circumstances as well as with the traumatic events from their past.

799 Arias González, Luis and **Agustín Vivas Moreno.** Los manuales de confesión para indígenas del siglo XVI: hacia un nuevo modelo de formación de la conciencia. (*Stud. Hist. Hist. Mod.*, 10/11, 1992/1993, p. 245–259)

Close examination of these confession manuals reveals much about nature of the interaction of priests and native Americans and the mind sets of both groups. An interesting approach to the mentalities of the colonial period.

800 Arranz Márquez, Luis. Don Diego Colón, almirante, virrey y gobernador de las Indias. v. 1. Madrid: Consejo Superior de Investigaciones Científicas, Instituto Gonzalo Fernández de Oviedo, 1982. 1 v: bibl. (Col. Tierra nueva e cielo nuevo; 5)

Lengthy biographical-historigraphical essay precedes 230 p. of documents concerning life of Diego Colón to 1512. Author's archival research is evident in the introductory essay as well as in the documentary section.

801 Assadourian, Carlos Sempat. La economía colonial: la transferencia del sistema productivo europeo en Nueva España y el Perú. (*Anu. IEHS*, 9, 1994, p. 19–31)

Spanish version of previously published article (see *HLAS 54:1060*).

802 Ayala, Manuel José de. Diccionario de gobierno y legislación de Indias. v. 11, De oro a preferencia. Edición y estudios de Marta Milagros del Vas Mingo. Madrid: Instituto de Cooperación Iberoamericana; Ediciones de Cultura Hispánica, 1995? 1 v.

Vol. 11 in republication of 1936 edition (see *HLAS 52:760*).

803 Barajas Salas, Eduardo. Cronistas extremeños de Indias. Badajoz, Spain: s.n., 1992. 448 p.: bibl.

Volume of considerable biographical and historiographical value is based on work in archives as well as secondary sources.

804 Beauperthuy de Benedetti, Rosario. Colón y la primera ordenanza médico-naval. Paris: Editions Hervas, 1991. 45 p.: bibl., ill., maps.

Brief account examines medical history of the four voyages of Columbus.

805 Bernal, Antonio-Miguel. La financiación de la carrera de Indias, 1492–1824: dinero y crédito en el comercio colonial español con América. Sevilla, Spain: Fundación El Monte, 1992. 763 p.: bibl., col. ill.

Volume is not a narrow monograph on

money and credit, but a panoramic study of fiscal and monetary aspects of Spanish colonial economy. Combines narrative and statistical approaches to provide interesting material on interplay of government and entrepreneurs. Detailed footnotes include primary sources and secondary works.

806 Bernal Rodríguez, Manuel. Nota sobre el influjo de la espiritualidad renacentista en la reprobación moral de la emigración a Indias: el camino del infierno. (*Anu. Estud. Am.*, 49:2, 1992, p. 3–9)

Brief but thoughtful commentary focuses on writings of humanist Juan de Mal Lara.

807 Bertrand, Michel. Los cargos de los oidores dentro de la Real Hacienda indiana: siglos XVII y XVIII. (*Estud. Hist. Soc. Econ. Am.*, 9, 1992, p. 37–51)

Based on archival research, this interpretive study deals with resistance of American *audiencias* to Spanish financial reforms of late 1600s and 1700s.

808 La Biblioteca Colombina y Capitular. Sevilla, Spain: Junta de Andalucía, Consejería de Cultura y Medio Ambiente, Asesoría Quinto Centenario; Cabildo Catedral de Sevilla, Biblioteca Capitular Colombina, 1991. 103 p.: bibl.

Includes biographical sketch of Fernando Colón and description of current condition of his library.

809 Bidegain, Ana María. The Church in the emancipation process, 1750–1830. (*in* The Church in Latin America, 1492–1992. Edited by Enrique Dussel. Kent, England: Burns & Oats; Maryknoll, N.Y.: Orbis Books, 1992, p. 81–104, bibl., maps)

Synthesis emphasizes interplay of Enlightenment ideas with international and imperial politics as context for clerical activism in the independence movements.

810 Bono, Juan Angel del. Peripecias y enfermedades en la conquista de América. Buenos Aires: Editorial Plus Ultra, 1993. 172 p.: bibl., ill.

Brief but suggestive study focuses on physical and medical problems confronting the conquistadores, in particular illnesses such as syphilis, tuberculosis, and influenza. Author relies on published sources including several of the standard chronicles.

811 Borobio, Dionisio; Federico Rafael Aznar Gil; and Antonio García y García. Evangelización en América. Salamanca, Spain: Caja de Ahorros y Monte de Piedad de Salamanca, 1988. 352 p.: bibl. (Col. Salamanca en el descubrimiento de América; 2)

Three extended, well-documented essays deal with Church's perspective on process of conversion of Native Americans in early colonial period. Emphasizes role of Univ. of Salamanca.

812 Brübach, Nils. "Seefahrt und Handel sind die fürnembsten Säulen eines Estats:" Brandenburg-Preußen und der transatlantische Sklavenhandel im 17. und 18 Jahrhundert. (*in* Amerikaner wider Willen: Beträge zur Sklaverei in Latinamerika und ihren Folgen. Frankfurt: Vervuert Verlag, 1994, p. 11–42, map)

Brandenburg-Prussia, the last state in Europe and only German territory to participate in the trans-Atlantic slave trade, was involved in the trade between 1682–1731. Although of minor importance, the Prussian trade transported 18,000 slaves on 52 voyages. Prussians had one of the lowest slave mortality rates among the traders. [C.K. Converse]

813 Bruno, Cayetano. Las órdenes religiosas en la evangelización de las Indias. Rosario, Argentina: Ediciones Didascalia, 1992. 212 p.: bibl. (Col. 500 años; 10)

Brief survey examines role of religious orders in conversion of Native Americans utilizing institutional and biographical approaches. Draws from archival research along with standard published sources.

814 Bruno, Cayetano. La presencia de España en Indias: acción política y religiosa. Rosario, Argentina: Ediciones Didascalia, 1991. 204 p.: bibl. (Obras para la evangelización y la catequesis; 29)

Compact overview of social structure of the colonial period is punctuated with author's rejection of view that the conquest amounted to a holocaust. Both archival and secondary sources.

815 Camargo Pérez, Gabriel. Misterio y hallazgo del Nuevo Mundo. Bogotá: Editorial Grijalbo, 1992. 384 p.: bibl., ill., maps.

History and geography come together in this cursory survey of European explorations of the Americas. Based on secondary works.

816 Camorlinga Alcaraz, José María. El choque de dos culturas: dos religiones. México: Plaza y Valdés Editores, 1993. 116 p.: bibl.

In a theological study of religions of the Aztecs and the Spanish, author emphasizes emergence and continued relevance of ideas of Las Casas.

817 Campillo y Cosío, José del. Nuevo sistema de gobierno económico para América. Edición, introducción y notas de Manuel Ballesteros Gaibrois. Oviedo, Spain: Grupo Editorial Asturiano, 1993. 321 p.: bibl., ill. (Anaquel cultural asturiano; 25)

Republication of 1789 book by the reform-minded Spanish economist and government official includes a perceptive introduction and helpful footnotes by Manuel Ballesteros Gaibrois.

818 Camus Ibacache, Misael. La visita *ad limina* desde las iglesias de América Latina en 1585–1800. (*Hisp. Sacra*, 46:93, enero/junio 1994, p. 159–189, bibl., tables)

Research in Vatican archives is basis for this examination of Church's requirement for bishops to make periodic visits to Rome and the special burdens that it imposed (as a result of distance and cost) on the Latin American bishops.

819 Canclini, Arnoldo. La fé del descubridor: aspectos religiosos de Cristóbal Colón. Buenos Aires: Editorial Plus Ultra, 1992. 344 p.: bibl., index.

Book concentrates on religious outlook and values of Columbus, relying on published scholarly studies. Canclini argues that Columbus was of the traditional Catholic faith and did not believe in superstitions or other heterodoxy.

820 Canclini, Arnoldo. La partida final del Almirante: luces y sombras en la muerte de Cristóbal Colón. Buenos Aires: Editorial Plus Ultra, 1992. 147 p.: bibl.

Brief study of the last years and death of Columbus is based mainly on published sources.

821 Canedo, Lino Gómez. Los gallegos en los descubrimientos y las exploraciones. La Coruña, Spain: Xunta de Galicia, Consellería de Relacións Institucionais e Por-

tavoz do Gobeirno, Comisionado Director do V Centenario, 1991. 163 p.: bibl., ill. (some col.), index. (Col. Galicia e América)

Compact study documents Galician presence on the frontiers of exploration, from Columbus voyages into the 18th century. Incorporates archival research. Includes onomastic index and extensive bibliography.

822 Casado Arboniés, Manuel. Bajo el signo de la militarización: las primeras expediciones científicas ilustradas a América, 1735–1761. (*in* Jornadas sobre "España y las expediciones científicas en América y Filipinas," 1st, Madrid, 1991. La ciencia española en ultramar: actas. Madrid: Doce Calles, 1991, p. 18–47, bibl., ill.)

Article explores purposes and outcomes of major expeditions and emphasizes not only their military character but also their mix of astronomical, navigational, cartographical, and biological investigations that responded to a variety of imperial interests.

823 Casas, Bartolomé de las. Apologética historia sumaria. Edición de Vidal Abril Castelló *et al.* Madrid: Alianza, 1992. 3 v.: bibl., indexes. (Obras completas / Bartolomé de las Casas; 6–8)

Includes useful preliminary study by Vidal Abril Castelló that gives historical and biographical background and five introductory essays by Las Casas scholars that explore in depth the context, content, and writing of *Apologética historia.*

824 Casas, Bartolomé de las. Brevíssima relación de la destruyción de las Indias. Edición de Andrés Moreno Mengíbar. Sevilla, Spain: Er Revista de Filosofía; Napoli, Italy: Istituto italiano per gli studi filosofici, 1991. 205 p.: bibl., ill. (some col.). (Col. Er textos clásicos)

New edition of the classic work includes several contemporary illustrations and brief excerpts from later writers influenced by Las Casas, including Montaigne, Kant, and Diderot.

825 Casas, Bartolomé de las. Obras completas. v. 11.2, Doce dudas. Edición de Juan Bautista Lassegue Moleres. Estudio preliminar, índices y bibliografía de J. Denglos. Dirección de Paulino Castañeda Delgado. Madrid: Alianza, 1994? 1 v.

This thoughtfully edited volume of Las Casas' response to the conquest of Peru includes brief introduction to establish the historical setting, extensive comparative analyses of manuscripts, and useful indices and bibliography.

826 Castilla Urbano, Francisco. Juan Ginés de Sepúlveda: en torno a una idea de civilización. (*Rev. Indias,* 52:195/196, mayo/dic. 1992, p. 329–348)

Examines Sepúlveda's social and political views of Native Americans and their status in the Spanish Empire as somewhere between slaves and citizens.

827 Castilla y León en América. Spain: Caja España, 1991. 3 v.: bibl., ill. (some col.), maps (some col.).

Fifty-seven articles cover three centuries of colonial history with an emphasis on immigration, the Church, government officials, and economic relations between Castile and America. The articles on economic history incorporate a large amount of archival research.

828 Castillo Meléndez, Francisco; Luisa J. Figallo Pérez; and **Ramón María Serrera Contreras.** Las Cortes de Cádiz y la imagen de América: la visión etnográfica y geográfica del nuevo mundo. Cádiz, Spain: Servicio de Publicaciones, Univ. de Cádiz, 1994. 504 p.: bibl., ill.

Publishes results of last of the great geographic *relaciones* requested in 1812. Responses from Peru, Venezuela, and New Spain's Guadalajara proved to be very strong on cultural aspects of peoples surveyed. [E.B. Couturier]

829 Catz, Rebecca. Christopher Columbus and the Portuguese, 1476–1498. Westport, Conn.: Greenwood Press, 1993. 133 p.: bibl., index. (Contributions to the study of world history; 0885–9159; 39)

Examines life of Columbus in Portugal (1476–88) and his return to that nation in later years. Catz emphasizes Columbus' opportunities for learning about the Atlantic from experienced Portuguese sailors in the years before his epic voyage.

830 Cebrián González, María del Carmen. Expediciones franciscanas a Indias, 1725–1750. (*Arch. Ibero-Am.,* 52:205/208, 1992, p. 187–207, tables)

List of the documents for 24 Franciscan expeditions to Spanish America includes citations for the Archivo General de Indias and the names and brief descriptions of expedition members. Includes analytical introduction.

831 Chocano Higueras, Guadalupe; Ignacio Fernández Vial; and **Consuelo Varela.** La Santa María, la Pinta y la Niña. = The Niña, the Pinta, and the Santa María. Translated by Paul A. Isbell. Madrid?: Empresa Constructora, 1991. 130 p.: ill. (some col.). (Biblioteca Quinto Centenario)

Nicely illustrated book has explanatory text in Spanish and English.

832 Ciencia colonial en América. Edición de Antonio Lafuente y José Sala Catalá. Madrid: Alianza, 1992. 433 p.: bibl. (Alianza universidad)

Wide-ranging collection includes articles on medicine, botany, and mining engineering and also philosophy and politico-bureaucratic studies.

833 Ciencia y técnica entre viejo y nuevo mundo: siglos XV-XVIII. Edición de Jaime Vilchis y Victoria Arias. Madrid: Lunwerg Editores, 1992. 291 p.: col. ill., col. maps.

Elaborate color illustrations are accompanied by brief text with limited scholarly apparatus. Sources of photographs and maps are identified in detail.

834 Columbus, Christopher. La carta de Colón: anunciando el descubrimiento. Edición de Juan José Antequera Luengo. Madrid: Alianza Editorial, 1992. 75 p.: bibl., ill.

Reproduction of an important document.

835 Columbus, Christopher. Libro de las profecías. Preparación de Juan Fernández Valverde. Madrid: Alianza Editorial, 1992. 138 p.: bibl. (Biblioteca de Colón; 4)

Thoughtful introduction and extensive editorial footnotes enhance value of this publication of Columbus' quest for a Biblical explanation for the significance of his voyages.

836 Comellas, José Luis. Sevilla, Cádiz y América: el trasiego y el tráfico. Málaga, Spain: Editorial Arguval, 1992. 336 p.: bibl., ill., index. (Col. Tres culturas; 3. Col. MAPFRE 1492)

Survey of cycles of transatlantic trade in the Spanish Empire also gives considerable attention to social history. Four-page bibliographical essay provides valuable introduction to secondary sources.

837 Congreso de Historia del Descubrimiento 1492–1556, Madrid y Sevilla, 1991. Actas. Madrid: Real Academia de la Historia: Confederación Española de Cajas de Ahorros, 1992. 4 v.: bibl., ill., maps.

Large collection of essays on the exploratory voyages has a good balance of Native American and European topics. Focus of these volumes is on Mesoamerica.

838 Congreso Internacional El Monacato Femenino en el Imperio Español, 2nd, México, 1995. El monacato femenino en el imperio español: monasterios, beaterios, recogimientos y colegios; memoria. Coordinación de Manuel Ramos Medina. México: Centro de Estudios de Historia de México, 1995. 596 p: bibl.

Papers from international conference of scholars studying female monastic institutions in the Spanish-speaking world. There are 43 essays on education, culture, conventual life, foundation, spirituality, and monastic writing, to cite a few themes. Comprehensive sampler of cutting-edge research and fresh interpretations. Highly recommended for its wide scope. [A. Lavrin]

839 Connaughton, Brian F. América Latina, 1700–1850: entre el pacto colonial y el imperialismo moderno. (*Cuad. Am.*, 7:38, marzo/abril 1993, p. 38–66)

Gives broad overview of transformation of Latin American economic structures from the Hapsburgs through the Bourbons and the independence movements to early stages of "modern imperialism."

840 A conquista espiritual da América espanhola: 200 documentos, século XVI. Organização de Paulo Suess. Petrópolis, Brazil: Vozes, 1992. 1028 p.: bibl., ill., indexes. (Publicações CID. História; 13)

Collection of readings spans centuries from preconquest Teotihuacán to late 16th-century controversies about clerical treatment of Native Americans. Includes a 34-p. bibliography.

841 Los conquistados: 1492 y la población indígena de las Américas. Recopilación de Heraclio Bonilla. Bogotá: Tercer Mundo Editores; Quito: Facultad Latinoamericana de Ciencias Sociales, Sede Ecuador; Ediciones Libri Mundi, 1992. 450 p.: bibl. (Historia)

Most of these essays, written by leading authorities of the colonial period, are syntheses with extensive footnotes that provide useful historiographical background. Robin Blackburn's extended essay on capitalism and slavery is especially stimulating.

842 Cremades Griñán, Carmen María. Reformismo, comercio y relación entre América y Cartagena. (*An. Hist. Contemp.*, 8, 1990/91, p. 203–214)

Political-social analysis of debate concerning liberalization of Spain's commercial policy in late 1700s includes some archival documentation.

843 Crouch, Dora P. Roman and Spanish colonization. (*in* Settlements in the Americas: cross-cultural perspectives. Edited by Ralph Bennett. Newark, Del.: Univ. of Delaware Press, 1993, p. 197–209, facsim., maps)

Author concentrates on the founding of cities and sees similarities between Roman settlements and Spanish colonies in America.

844 Cubero Sebastián, Pedro. Peregrinación del mundo del doctor D. Pedro Cubero Sebastián, misionero apostólico. Madrid: Miraguano Ediciones; Ediciones Polifemo, 1993. 436 p.: port. (Biblioteca de viajeros hispánicos; 10)

Republication of 1682 edition of account of around-the-world journey including a voyage from the Philippines to New Spain on the Manila Galleon.

845 Cuesta Domingo, Mariano. Descubrimientos geográficos durante el siglo XVIII: acción franciscana en la ampliación de fronteras. (*Arch. Ibero-Am.*, 52:205/208, 1992, p. 293–342, ill., maps)

Describes geographic work of selected missionaries on all frontiers and includes copies of their maps. [E.B. Couturier]

846 Cuesta Domingo, Mariano. Rumbo a lo desconocido: navegantes y descubridores. Madrid: Anaya, 1992. 239 p.: bibl., col. ill., index.

Commemorative book includes pictures with explanatory text.

847 Díaz-Jove, Santiago. Gijoneses en Indias: notas sobre emigración e índice geobiográfico, 1700–1825. Gijón, Spain: Editorial Auseva, 1992. 228 p.: bibl., ill., maps. (Monumenta histórica asturiensia; 29)

Alphabetical listing of brief biographical sketches of immigrants from Asturias to America is drawn from Archivo Histórico Municipal de Gijón. The 40-p. introductory essay provides some historical and demographic context.

848   Elkin, Judith Laikin. Imagining idolatry: missionaries, Indians, and Jews. (*in* Religion and the authority of the past. Ann Arbor: Univ. of Michigan Press, 1993, p. 75–99, bibl.)

Examines reasons for Inquisition's prosecution of *Judeo-conversos* in the New World and concludes that one reason was to provide recently converted Native Americans with examples of punishment for idolatry.

849   Elliott, John Huxtable. The rediscovery of America. (*N.Y. Rev. Books*, 40:12, June 24, 1993, p. 36–41, facsim., plates)

Extended, thought-provoking review essay deals with issues surrounding the Columbian encounter, from assertions that a holocaust took place to studies of colonial institutions and cultural intermediaries between native Americans and Europeans.

Eltis, David and **Stanley L. Engerman.** Was the slave trade dominated by men? See item **1010.**

850   Errasti, Mariano. América franciscana. v. 1, Evangelizadores e indigenistas en el siglo XVI. Santiago: CEFEPAL, 1986. 1 v: bibl., ill.

Biographical sketches of 23 Franciscans is based on secondary sources. Section entitled "Los Oscuros Pioneros del Caribe" is an interesting attempt at synthesis.

851   Eslava Galán, Juan. El enigma de Colón y los descubrimientos de América. Barcelona: Planeta, 1992. 247 p.: bibl., ill., index. (Memoria de la historia; 63. Personajes)

Often speculative and sometimes stimulating volume brings together the outstanding unanswered questions about Columbus and his voyages. Based on secondary sources.

852   España y América al encuentro: textos y documentos desde los cronistas de Indias a los escritores contemporáneos, 1492–1992. Edición de María Enriqueta Soriano Pérez-Villamil, Pilar Maícas y Mercedes Gómez del Manzano. Madrid: Biblioteca de Autores Cristianos, 1992. 430 p.: bibl., ill. (Biblioteca de autores cristianos; 522)

Collection of brief selections mostly from Columbus, Vespucci, and members of the generation of the encounter also includes Borges, Paz, García Márquez, and other 20th-century writers. Emphasis on religion and culture.

853   Esteve Barba, Francisco. Historiografía indiana. 2a ed., rev. y aum. Madrid: Gredos, 1992. 754 p.: bibl., indexes. (Manuales)

Revision of 1964 version (see *HLAS 28:422*) incorporates more recent research in this area.

854   La Expedición Malaspina, 1789–1794. v. 3, Diarios y trabajos botánicos de Luis Nee. Estudio de Félix Múñoz Garmendia. Madrid: Ministerio de Defensa, Museo Naval; Barcelona: Lunwerg, 1989. 1 v.

This volume of the oversized edition includes informative introductory essay and relevant color illustrations.

855   La Expedición Malaspina, 1789–1794. v. 4, Trabajos científicos y correspondencia de Tadeo Haenke. Estudio de María Victoria Ibáñez Montoya. Madrid: Ministerio de Defensa, Museo Naval; Barcelona: Lunwerg, 1987? 1 v.

This volume has interesting biographical sketch of Haenke and also many b/w and color illustrations.

856   La explotación del éxito colombino: con el sistema de viajes de "descubrimiento y rescate." Introducción, estudio histórico y edición de textos de Demetrio Ramos Pérez. Madrid: Ministerio de Cultura V Centenario; Testimonio, 1992. 298 p. (Tabula Americae; 17)

Commemorative collection of documents includes short introduction.

857   Fernández Buey, Francisco. La controversia entre Ginés de Sepúlveda y Bartolomé de las Casas: una revisión. (*Bol. Am.*, 33:42/43, 1992/93, p. 301–347, bibl.)

Synthesizes recent publications on this much-studied debate. Author emphasizes historical context, philosophical and political orientations of the antagonists, and long-term relevance of this confrontation between European and native American interests.

858   Fisher, John Robert. Relaciones económicas entre España y América hasta la independencia. Madrid: Editorial MAPFRE, 1992. 280 p : bibl., ill., index. (Col. América 92; 6. Col. MAPFRE 1492)

Synthesizes economic history of Spanish-American empire from arrival of Columbus to independence period. Although a solid survey of first two centuries of the empire, attention is focused on dynamics of free trade in 1700s. Also has brief but insightful bibliographical essay.

859 Flórez Miguel, Marcelino. Ambición y muerte en la conquista de América. Valladolid, Spain: ÁMBITO, 1992. 93 p.: bibl.

Short history of the conquest is written for a popular audience from perspective of the Native Americans.

860 La formación de América Latina: la época colonial. Introducción y selección de Manuel Miño Grijalva. México: Colegio de México, Centro de Estudios Históricos, 1992. 250 p.: bibl., ill., maps. (Lecturas de historia mexicana; 8)

Collection of nine articles has broad geographical coverage from New Spain to Puerto Rico, Guatemala, and Peru. Articles are printed with footnotes and bibliographies intact. Authors include Zavala, Boyd-Bowman, Durand, and Assadourian.

861 Fuentenebro Zamarro, Francisco. Segovianos en el descubrimiento de América, 1492–1577. Madrid: Impr. Fareso, 1991. 302 p.: bibl.

Contains brief biographical sketches of 16 Segovians who were active in the period of the conquest and exploration, from Diego Velázquez to Pedrarias to Juan de Medina Rincón.

862 Fuentes Gómez de Salazar, Eduardo de. Estrategias de la implantación española en América. Madrid: Editorial MAPFRE, 1992. 322 p.: bibl., index. (Col. Armas y América; 2. Col. MAPFRE 1492)

Interesting analytical approach gives this study a special value. Author analyzes strategies in exploration and military engagement employed by Columbus, Cortés, Pizarro, and other leading figures of the conquest era.

863 Gajardo, Félix. Colón en la ruta de fenicios y cartagineses. Santiago: Red Internacional del Libro, 1992. 244 p.: ill., index, maps.

Attempts to trace roots of Columbus' plans for his historic voyage to the Phoenicians, Carthagenians, and the Old Testament.

864 Gandía, Enrique de. La ruta de Colón. (*Invest. Ens.*, 43, enero/dic. 1993, p. 15–63)

Lengthy discourse takes issue with earlier studies to argue that Columbus sailed further to the north in 1492 and touched on Florida. Lacks footnotes and bibliography.

865 Garavaglia, Juan Carlos. Human beings and the environment in America: on "determinism" and "possibilism." (*Int. Soc. Sci. J.*, 134, Nov. 1992, p. 269–577, photo)

Garavaglia uses relationship between humans and the environment in the Valley of Mexico in prehispanic and colonial periods to generalize about variety and fragility of ecosystems.

866 García, Juan Andreo and Lucía Provencio Garrigós. Pasajeros a América: aportación al estudio de la emigración del Reino de Murcia durante el siglo XVI. (*An. Hist. Contemp.*, 8, 1990/91, p. 97–130, appendix, graphs, map, tables)

Quantitative study is based on archival research and includes an appendix listing names of, and some biographical information on, 225 immigrants.

867 García, Sebastián. La Rábida, pórtico del Nuevo Mundo: síntesis histórico-artística. Madrid?: Comunidad Franciscana del Convento de Santa María de La Rábida, 1992. 222 p.: col. ill.

Profusely illustrated work includes some explanatory text.

868 García-Baquero González, Antonio. La carrera de Indias: suma de la contratación y océano de negocios. Sevilla, Spain: Algaida; Sociedad Estatal para la Exposición Universal Sevilla 92, 1992. 348 p.: bibl.

Well-organized synthesis of history of ocean-going trade in Spanish American empire is based on published secondary sources. Concluding chapter contains author's analysis of the impact of economic cycles on colonial trade.

869 García-Baquero González, Antonio. Comercio y burguesía mercantil en el Cádiz de la carrera de Indias. Huelva, Spain: Diputación Provincial de Huelva, 1991. 188 p.: appendices, bibl. (Historia; 11)

Volume of nine scholarly essays complement author's previous work *Cádiz y el Atlántico* (see *HLAS 42:1846a*). Four of the essays appear for the first time. Based on archival research and published with footnotes and appendices.

870 **García Oro, José.** Prehistoria y primeros capítulos de la evangelización de América. Caracas: Ediciones Trípode, 1988. 431 p.: bibl. (Col. Evangelizadores de América; 17)

Detailed study examines work of the Catholic Church with emphasis on its formative missionary efforts in the Canary Islands and the role of Cardinal Francisco Jiménez de Cisneros in the early missionary drive in the Antilles. Includes archival research and is heavily footnoted.

871 **García Sánchez, Francisco.** El Medellín extremeño en América. Medellín, Spain: Sánchez Trejo, 1992. 374 p.: bibl., ill. (some col.).

Largely biographical approach includes some illustrations.

872 **Garrain Villa, Luis José.** Llerena en el siglo XVI : la emigración a Indias. Mérida, Spain: Junta de Extremadura, 1991. 390 p.: bibl., ill., indexes, maps. (Extremadura enclave 92)

Detailed study examines immigration of 361 natives of the town of Llerena in Extremadura to Spanish America in late 1500s. Historical account is followed by a section of brief biographical sketches of the immigrants (with extensive footnotes) and another section listing archival sources.

873 **Gómez Ruiz, Manuel** and **Vicente Alonso Juanola.** El ejército de los Borbones: organización, uniformidad, divisas, armamento. v. 3, pts. 1–2, Tropas de Ultramar, siglo XVIII. Madrid: Servicio Histórico Militar; Museo del Ejército, 1993? 2 v.: bibl.

These oversized volumes provide documentation from Spanish archives, including statistics on personnel and weapons along with maps and illustrations. Vol. 3 covers the Spanish Empire in America from Cuba and Louisiana to Río de la Plata and Chile.

874 **González-Ripoll Navarro, María Dolores.** La expedición del Atlas de la América septentrional, 1792–1810: orígenes y recursos. (*Rev. Indias,* 50:190, sept./dic. 1990, p. 767–788)

Study provides in-depth examination of intentions, plans, and personnel of the cartographic expedition. Author's research includes documentation from Archivo Museo D. Alvaro de Bazán.

875 **Guillamón Alvarez, Francisco Javier.** Algunos reflexiones sobre el cabildo colonial como institución. (*An. Hist. Contemp.,* 8, 1990/91, p. 151–161)

Based on narrow sample of published monographs, attempts to develop some generalizations about functioning of the cabildo within the colonial system.

876 **Gutiérrez, Gustavo.** Dios o el oro en las Indias. San Salvador: UCA Editores, 1991. 162 p.: bibl. (Col. La Iglesia en América Latina; 15)

Explication of theology of Las Casas includes some biographical information based on well-known sources. Extensive footnotes add depth to the explication.

877 **Gutiérrez, Gustavo.** Las Casas: in search of the poor of Jesus Christ. Translated by Robert R. Barr. Maryknoll, N.Y.: Orbis Books, 1993. 682 p.: bibl., index.

Extensive biography gives emphasis to theology. Although clearly sympathetic to Las Casas, Gutiérrez is careful to place him in his turbulent times and give appropriate attention to his opponents. Research is based on impressive array of archival records as well as secondary sources.

878 **Gutiérrez Lorenzo, María Pilar.** Expediciones en tiempos de Carlos IV. (*in* Jornadas sobre "España y las expediciones científicas en América y Filipinas," 1st, Madrid, 1991. La ciencia española en ultramar: actas. Madrid: Doce Calles, 1991, p. 64–77, ill.)

Well-organized article places scientific expeditions to America in 1770s-80s in their political and imperial framework.

879 **Gutiérrez Lorenzo, María Pilar** and **Javier Casado Arboniés.** La formación universitaria de Manuel del Castillo y Negrete y su carrera administrativa en América, 1750–1812. (*Estud. Hist. Soc. Econ. Am.,* 9, 1992, p. 213–222)

Biographical sketch of Spanish colonial official who served on *audiencias* in Guadalajara, Bogotá, Mexico City, and Guatemala is based on archival research.

880 **Hampe Martínez, Teodoro.** Los funcionarios de la monarquía española en América. (*Histórica/Lima,* 16:1, junio 1992, bibl.)

Sociology and history are combined in

this study of internal workings and class origins of the Spanish bureaucracy in the Hapsburg period. A scholarly synthesis based on published monographs.

Harley, J. Brian. Rereading the maps of the Columbian encounter. See *HLAS 55:2249.*

881 Harris, Olivia. "The coming of the white people:" reflections on the mythologisation of history in Latin America. (*Bull. Lat. Am. Res.*, 14:1, Jan. 1995, p. 9–24)

Anthropologist author argues that both historians and anthropologists have placed too much emphasis on periodization and, especially in Latin America, on the year 1492. Harris shows how Native Americans have a variety of ways of conceptualizing the arrival of the Europeans.

882 Hennessy, Alistair. The nature of the conquest and the conquistadors. (*in* The meeting of two worlds: Europe and the Americas, 1492–1650. Edited by Warwick Bray. Oxford, England: Oxford Univ. Press; The British Academy, 1993, p. 5–36, bibl.)

Broadly-based comparative study focuses on differences among the Spanish, Portuguese, and British conquests, with stimulating commentary on the "culture heroes" who emerged in these three empires: the Spanish *conquistador*, the Portuguese *bandeirante*, and the British farmer.

883 Hera, Alberto de la. Iglesia y Corona en la América española. Madrid: Editorial MAPFRE, 1992. 512 p.: bibl. (Col. Iglesia católica en el Nuevo Mundo; 12. Col. MAPFRE 1492)

Synthesis draws together missionary work, theology, and political-institutional history to provide overview of relations between the Church and native Americans in Spanish America from late 1400s to late 1700s. There are no footnotes, but main primary and secondary sources are mentioned in the text.

884 Hernández de Torres, Eduardo. Los Agustinos en la evangelización americana: aportaciones al V centenario. (*Relig. Cult.*, 35:170, junio/sept. 1989, p. 363–384)

Celebratory essay is a broad survey based mainly on secondary works.

885 Hernández Sánchez-Barba, Mario. El americanismo del Conde de Floridablanca. (*An. Hist. Contemp.*, 8, 1990/91, p. 45–57)

This analysis of Floridablanca's ideas on the Americas and Spanish foreign policy is essentially an essay in intellectual history.

886 Hurtado, Publio. Los extremeños en América. Introducción, cronologías, índices y mapas de Alfonso Artero Hurtado. Sevilla, Spain: Gráficas Mirte, 1992. 356 p.: maps.

Biographical sketches of Extremadurans in the conquest has some historiographic value.

887 Ille, Hans-Jürgen. Censura y diálogo de las culturas de Europa e Hispanoamérica en el período colonial. (*in* Diálogo y conflicto de culturas: estudios comparativos de procesos transculturales entre Europa y América Latina. Frankfurt: Vervuert Verlag, 1993, p. 37–46)

Interpretive essay on the transatlantic book trade and process and politics of imperial censorship is based largely on published monographs and collections of documents.

888 Inikori, Joseph E. Slavery and Atlantic commerce, 1650–1800. (*Am. Econ. Rev.*, 82:2, May 1992, p. 151–157, bibl., tables)

Inikori applies his historical model of a "world economic order" to the Atlantic region to present a perspective on the role of African slavery in the overall economic development of this area (including South and North America, Africa, and Europe).

889 Izard, Miquel. Elegir lo posible y escoger lo mejor. (*Bol. Am.*, 33:42/43, 1992/93, p. 141–158, bibl.)

Sharply critical evaluation of the Spanish colonial effort is a potent mixture of scholarship and polemic.

890 Izard, Miquel. Poca subordinación y menos ambición. (*Bol. Am.*, 33:42/43, 1992/93, p. 159–182, bibl., table)

Pointed assessment of Spanish-Native American relations in northern New Spain/Mexico and the Caribbean coast of Central America emphasizes violence and disruption.

891 Jacobs, Auke P. Migraciones laborales entre España y América: la procedencia de marineros en la carrera de Indias, 1598–1610. (*Rev. Indias*, 51:193, sept./dic. 1991, p. 523–543, tables)

Demographic study focuses on the 9,524 sailors identified in ships' registers. Author discusses their origins, ages, and working conditions as well as desertions to remain in America.

892 **Jarcho, Saul.** Quinine's predecessor: Francesco Torti and the early history of cinchona. Baltimore, Md.: Johns Hopkins Univ. Press, 1993. 354 p.: bibl., ill., index, maps. (The Henry E. Sigerist series in the history of medicine)

Highly specialized study focuses on spread of the use of cinchona (or Peruvian bark) from west coast of South America throughout Europe in 1600s and 1700s as a treatment for malaria. Emphasizes the work of Jesuits and of Torti. Slight attention to Native American origins of the use of this medication. Based on extensive reading of contemporary medical texts.

893 **Jornadas de Historia Marítima, *1st, Madrid, 1987.*** España y el ultramar hispánico hasta la Ilustración. Madrid: Instituto de Historia y Cultura Naval, 1989. 150 p.: bibl., ill. (some col.), maps. (Cuadernos monográficos del Instituto de Historia y Cultura Naval, 0212–467X; 1)

These seven studies on Spanish maritime history are based largely on previously published secondary studies. Angel Guirao de Vierna's "El Profesional del Mar: Reclutamiento, Nivel Social, Formación" is an interesting study of the preparation and background of Spanish naval officers.

894 **Jornadas sobre el V Centenario del Descubrimiento de América, *Ubeda, Spain, 1992.*** Colonización y evangelización en la América Española. Ubeda, Spain: Centro Asociado a la U.N.E.D. de Jaén, 1992. 166 p.: bibl., ill.

Seven scholarly essays cover various aspects of colonial history: mining, social position, immigration, evangelization, art, the clergy of New Spain, and literature.

895 **Jornadas sobre Zamora, su Entorno y América, *Zamora, Spain, 1991.*** Zamora y América: actos. Zamora, Spain: I.E.Z. Florián de Ocampo; Diputación de Zamora; Caja Rural de Zamora, 1992. 594 p.: bibl., ill., maps.

Wide-ranging collection of articles on role of Spanish province of Zamora in the conquest and colonial period gives emphasis to the Church, including career of Toribio de Benavente (Motolinía).

896 **Juan Vidal, Josep.** Mallorca en tiempos del descubrimiento de América. Prólogo de Antonio Domínguez Ortiz. Mallorca, Spain: El Tall Editorial, 1991. 121 p.: bibl., ill. (El Tall del temps; 6)

Economic, social, and political history of Mallorca based on archival research provides in-depth study of the island during difficult transition from medieval times to early modernity.

897 **Kiple, Kenneth F.** and **Brian T. Higgins.** Mortality caused by dehydration during the Middle Passage. (*in* The Atlantic slave trade: effects on economies, societies, and peoples in Africa, the Americas, and Europe. Edited by Joseph E. Inikori and Stanley L. Engerman. Durham, N.C.: Duke Univ. Press, 1992, p. 321–337, bibl.)

Fine essay in medical history stresses fatal combination of tropical heat, sweating, sea sickness, dysentery and inadequate medical treatment for slaves in transit from Africa.

898 **Klaren, Peter F.** Spain in America: the Viceroyalties of New Spain and Peru, 1521–1825. (*in* Temples of gold, crowns of silver: reflections of majesty in the Viceregal Americas. Washington: George Washington Univ., 1991, p. 1–15, facsims., plates, photos)

Sprightly essay on art and architecture of the colonial era includes interesting explanations of the political, religious, and social contexts.

899 **Klein, Herbert S.** Las características demográficas del comercio atlántico de esclavos hacia Latinoamérica. (*Bol. Inst. Hist. Ravignani*, 8, 1993, p. 7–27, graphs, tables)

Overview of slave trade utilizes both quantification and prose analysis. Examines population patterns based on sex, age, and destination; also provides data on mortality during the Atlantic crossing.

900 **Kubler, George.** Cities of Latin America since Discovery. (*in* Settlements in the Americas: cross-cultural perspectives. Edited by Ralph Bennett. Newark, Del.: Univ. of Delaware Press, 1993, p. 17–27, bibl.)

General overview surveys urban history of the colonial period.

901 **Landers, Jane.** New research on the African experience in Spanish America and the Caribbean. (*CLAHR/Albuquerque*, 3: 2, Spring 1994, p. 215–219)

Interesting book review essay focuses on Patrick Carroll's 1991 study of Africans in colonial Veracruz (see *HLAS 52:857*) and Gwendolyn Hall's *Africans in colonial Louisiana: the development of Afro-Creole culture in the eighteenth century*, (Baton Rouge: 1992). Good historiographical depth.

902 Langue, Frédérique. Las élites en América española: actitudes y mentalidades. (*Bol. Am.*, 33:42/43, 1992/93, p. 123–139, bibl.)

Drawing on thorough research in secondary sources dating from 1970s-80s, author nonetheless posits rudimentary foundations for elite identity in 18th-century Spanish America, such as pluralism, wealth, aristocratic ethos, and social networks. Includes section focusing specifically on Venezuela. More useful for its bibliography than for its conclusions. [L.R. Grahn]

903 Lavrin, Asunción. La vida femenina como experiencia religiosa: biografía y hagiografía en Hispanoamérica colonial. (*Colon. Lat. Am. Rev.*, 2:1/2, 1993, p. 27–51, bibl.)

Intelligent, imaginative interpretation discusses image of the female within the Catholic Church. Lavrin argues that this image also reflected male-female relations and other issues in the larger social environment outside the Church.

904 León Pinelo, Antonio de. Recopilación de las Indias. Edición y estudio preliminar de Ismael Sánchez Bella. México: M.A. Porrúa, 1992. 3 v.: bibl. (Serie A—Fuentes. b, Textos y estudios legislativos)

Massive new edition in large print of this historic document includes 47-p. preliminary study by Sánchez Bella giving biographical background and historical context.

905 Levaggi, Abelardo. Los tratados entre la Corona y los indios, y el plan de conquista pacífica. (*Rev. Complut. Hist. Am.*, 19, 1993, p. 81–91)

Study in legal history concentrates more on the law and theory than on their practical application in the Americas.

906 Libro de los privilegios del Almirante Don Cristóbal Colón, 1498: originales conservados en el Archivo General de Indias. Estudio preliminar, edición, notas y transcripción de Ciriaco Pérez Bustamante. Madrid:

Testimonio Compañía Editorial, 1992. 178 p.: bibl. (Tabula Americae ; 20)

A 57-p. introduction greatly strengthens the value of this publication of Columbus' claims to power.

907 Linares Maza, Antonio. Bartolomé de Las Casas, un andaluz en el Nuevo Mundo: desagravio psiquiátrico al primer anticolonialista, precursor de los derechos humanos. Málaga, Spain: Editorial Arguval, 1993. 171 p.: bibl.

Interpretive psychological biography of Las Casas includes examination of Menéndez Pidal's historiographical dispute. Unfortunately lacks detailed footnotes and slights the work of Hanke and Pagden.

908 Lobo Cabrera, Manuel. Canarias y el Atlántico esclavista: condición del esclavo y la respuesta social. (*in* Coloquio Internacional Sobre Abolición de la Esclavitud, *Madrid, 1986.* Esclavitud y derechos humanos: la lucha por la libertad del negro en el siglo XIX; actas. Edición de Francisco de Solano y Agustín Guimerá. Madrid: Consejo Superior de Investigaciones Científicas, Centro de Estudios Históricos, Depto. de Historia de América, 1990, p. 51–60, bibl.)

Study of the Canary Islands as a way station in the Atlantic slave trade is based on published monographs.

909 Lockward, J. Alfonso. "Algunas cruces altas" con el *Libro de las profecías* de Cristóbal Colón. Miami: Editorial Unilit, 1991. 298 p.: bibl., ill., index.

Contains some speculations on the mysticism and prophecies of Columbus.

910 López Medel, Tomás. Colonización de América: informes e testimonios, 1549–1572, por L. Pereña, C. Baciero, F. Maseda. Madrid: Consejo Superior de Investigaciones Científicas, 1990. 378 p.: indexes. (Corpus hispanorum de pace; 28)

Volume contains documents on Guatemala and New Grenada, and "Meditación sobre las Indias Occidentales." Also includes useful indexes.

911 López-Ríos Fernández, Fernando. Medicina naval española en la época de los descubrimientos. Barcelona: Editorial Labor, 1993. 215 p.: bibl., ill. (some col.), indexes, col. maps.

Useful synthesis includes not only specialized medical history but also an examination of living conditions and diet aboard ship. The numerous illustrations are relevant to the text. Book also includes a helpful glossary of medical terms and extensive footnotes.

912 **Luca de Tena, Torcuato.** América y sus enigmas (y otras americanerías). Barcelona: Planeta, 1992. 218 p.: bibl., index. (Memoria de la historia. Episodios)

Suggestive, speculative volume on the conquest era focuses especially on Columbus and Cortés. Often interesting but lacks scholarly apparatus.

913 **Lucena Salmoral, Manuel.** Las expediciones científicas en la época de Carlos III, 1759–88. (*in* Jornadas sobre España y las expediciones científicas en América y Filipinas, *1st, Madrid, 1991*. La ciencia española en ultramar: actas. Madrid: Doce Calles, 1991, p. 48–63, ill., tables)

Overview of the 20 major scientific expeditions covers their origins, purposes, and results. Direct prose style and useful charts make for efficient presentation of this descriptive material.

914 **Luque Colombres, Carlos A.** Los aborígenes americanos en la época del descubrimiento: su concepto de la moralidad a través de usos y costumbres regionales. (*Invest. Ens.*, 43, enero/dic. 1993, p. 237–257)

Survey of the Spanish and Portuguese chroniclers' evaluations of the morality of the native Americans is based on published sources.

915 **Manrique, Nelson.** Vinieron los sarracenos—: el universo mental de la conquista de América. Lima: DESCO, 1993. 609 p.: bibl.

Provocative examination focuses on attitudes and ideologies of late medieval Spain and their roles in the conquest and colonization of America. Manrique emphasizes resilience of Catholic religion and ethnocentric attitudes and their impact on Jewish, Islamic, and Native American peoples.

916 **Manzano Manzano, Juan.** Historia de las recopilaciones de Indias. 3. ed. Madrid: Instituto de Cooperación Iberoamericana, Ediciones de Cultura Hispánica, 1991. 2 v.: bibl., ill.

Vol. 1 surveys work of *recopiladores* from Vasco de Puga to Diego de Encinas. Vol. 2 focuses on the work of Antonio de León Pinelo and *recopilación* work in post-Pinelo period. For review of first edition, see *HLAS 19: 3164* and *HLAS 21:2444*.

917 **Marchena Fernández, Juan.** Reformas borbónicas y poder popular en la América de las Luces: el temor al pueblo en armas a fines del período colonial. (*An. Hist. Contemp.*, 8, 1990/91, p. 187–199)

Author concentrates on problems that confronted the Spanish Army in the Americas. Concerned about possibility of a foreign invasion, Spanish officers were also troubled that soldiers recruited from popular classes posed a threat to political and social stability. Combines archival research with published monographs.

918 **Márquez, Rosario.** La emigración española a América en la época del comercio libre, 1765–1824. (*Rev. Complut. Hist. Am.*, 19, 1993, p. 233–247, graphs, tables)

Largely statistical study of Andalusian immigration emphasizes fluctuations during years of war and other dislocations.

919 **Martín Hernández, Francisco.** La influencia de los colegios mayores españoles en la fundación y primer desarrollo de los americanos. (*Estud. Hist. Soc. Econ. Am.*, 9, 1992, p. 9–22)

Institutional study focuses on founding and operation of the *colegios mayores* in Peru, New Spain, and Chile in 16th and 17th centuries.

920 **Martínez Martínez, María del Carmen.** La emigración castellana y leonesa al Nuevo Mundo, 1517–1700. Valladolid, Spain: Junta de Castilla y León, Consejería de Cultura y Turismo, 1993. 2 v.: bibl., ill., indexes. (Estudios de historia)

Vol. 1 of this thorough study includes a discussion of evolution of the Crown's immigration policies and a balanced prose and statistical examination of immigrants' origins and destinations. Vol. 2 contains over 400 p. of alphabetical listings of immigrants including in many cases place of origin in Spain and destination in America. Work is based on archival research and an impressive command of relevant published monographs.

921 **Martínez Riaza, Ascensión.** Las diputaciones provinciales americanas en el sistema liberal español. (*Rev. Indias*, 52:195/196, mayo/dic. 1992, p. 647–691)

Detailed examination of the varied levels of participation of American delegates to the Spanish Cortes (1810–23) is based on a close reading of the records of the Cortes.

922   Martini, Mónica Patricia. El indio y los sacramentos en Hispanoamérica colonial: circunstancias adversas y malas interpretaciones. Buenos Aires: PRHISCO-CONICET, 1993. 300 p.: bibl., ill.

Thoughtful, carefully focused account of a sensitive subject draws from primary documents as well as historical monographs. Using a topical analysis of the sacraments from Baptism through Extreme Unction to Holy Orders, Martini considers singular events and individual circumstances but generally concentrates on the middle ground where native and European traditions interacted.

923   Marzal, Manuel María. Daily life in the Indies: seventeenth and early eighteenth centuries. (*in* The Church in Latin America, 1492–1992. Edited by Enrique Dussel. Kent, England: Burns & Oats; Maryknoll, N.Y.: Orbis Books, 1992, p. 69–80)

Brief but insightful work discusses daily life of Native Americans as seen through their participation in Catholic religious festivals and pilgrimages.

924   Matilla Tascón, Antonio. Americanos en la documentación notarial de Madrid. Madrid: Fundación Matritense del Notariado, 1990. 472 p.: index. (Estudios históricos notariales; 3)

Alphabetical listing of names in notarial archives, ranging from early 1500s to 19th century, includes brief description of each document.

925   Maura, Juan F. Esclavas españolas en el nuevo mundo: una nota histórica. (*CLAHR/Albuquerque*, 2:2, Spring 1993, p. 185–194)

Very brief but interesting essay on a seldom-studied subject draws from some archival research.

926   McFarlane, Anthony. Challenges from the periphery: rebellion in colonial Spanish America. (*in* Rebelión y resistencia en el mundo hispánico del siglo XVII, *Lovaina, Belgium, 20–23 de noviembre de 1991.* Actas del coloquio internacional. Edición de Werner Thomas. Colaboración de Bart de Groof. Leuven, Belgium: Leuven Univ. Press, 1992, p. 250–269)

Thoughtful comparative analysis of causes of rebellions in 17th- and 18th-century Spanish colonies emphasizes reign of Charles III. Based on published monographs.

927   La medicina en el descubrimiento. Coordinación de Juan Riera. Valladolid, Spain: Univ. de Valladolid, Secretariado de Publicaciones, 1991. 114 p.: bibl. (Acta histórico-médica vallisoletana; 34. Monografías)

Six scholarly articles focus on history of medicine in early colonial period. Footnoted articles on importation of American medicinal substances to Castile, medical libraries in America, and surgical practices are based on some archival research.

928   Memoria del Nuevo Mundo: Castilla-La Mancha y América en el Quinto Centenario. Coordinación de Pedro Miguel Ibáñez Martínez. Ciudad Real, Spain: Ediciones de la Univ. de Castilla-La Mancha, 1992. 307 p.: bibl. (Col. Estudios; 12)

Varieties in approach characterize these 19 historical studies that range from Castilian immigration to a biographical portrait of Gutiérrez de la Pena (victor over Lope de Aguirre) to Pedro Pizarro's Peruvian possessions.

929   Miguel López, Isabel. El comercio hispanoamericano a través de Gijón, Santander y Pasajes, 1778–1795. Valladolid, Spain: Secretariado de Publicaciones, Univ. de Valladolid, 1992. 364 p.: bibl., ill., maps. (Serie Historia y sociedad; 22)

Study of trade between northern Spain and the American colonies includes larger economic and institutional contexts as well as specialized discussion of the commerce itself. Well-organized and based on archival research.

930   Miño Grijalva, Manuel. La protoindustria colonial hispanoamericana. México: El Colegio de México, 1993. 227 p.: bibl., ill. (Serie Ensayos / Fideicomiso Historia de las Américas. Sección de obras de historia)

Solid balance of author's own archival research and inclusion of published monographs characterize this significant synthesis of history of textile manufacturing in the Spanish American empire from 1500s-1700s. Includes extensive footnotes and an annotated bibliography.

931   Mira Caballos, Esteban. Las licencias de esclavos negros a Hispanoamérica, 1544–1550. (*Rev. Indias*, 54:201, mayo/agosto 1994, p. 273–297, tables)

Archival documentation forms basis for this close examination of slave shipments to the Spanish colonies. Qualitative and quantitative analysis reveals names of license-holders, destination of slaves, and numbers of slaves in each shipment. Thorough explication of valuable documents.

932   Mires, Fernando. Tesis en torno a la Iglesia colonial en Hispanoamérica. (*in* International Congress of Americanists, *45th, Bogotá, 1985.* Historia. Bogotá: Ediciones Uniandes, 1988, p. 183–197)

Author proposes 17 theses regarding complex struggle with the Catholic Church concerning protection of the Native American peoples during the conquest and the colonial period.

933   Morales Padrón, Francisco. Canarias en los cronistas de Indias. Las Palmas, Spain: Ediciones del Cabildo Insular de Gran Canaria, 1991. 109 p.: bibl., ill. (Col. Alisios; 3)

Brief commemorative work has some biographical and historiographical merit.

934   Morales Padrón, Francisco. Vida cotidiana de los conquistadores españoles. Madrid: Temas de Hoy, 1992. 268 p.: bibl., ill. (Historia de la España sorprendente)

Author draws from standard chronicles and some insightful archival research to cover topics such as: conflict between conquistadors and imperial law; medical problems caused by diseases and wounds; weapons and battle tactics; relations with native women; reactions to native religious practices; and petitions to the Crown by famous, marginal, and forgotten conquistadors.

935   Morazzani de Pérez Enciso, Gisela. El manejo doloso de los fondos reales: la crisis del siglo XVIII y los Oficiales Reales de Hacienda. (*An. Univ. Chile*, 20, agosto 1989, p. 351–371, bibl.)

Based on archival research, analytical work discusses financial crises and budgetary reforms in 18th-century Spanish Empire.

936   Mörner, Magnus. Die sozialen Strukturen im Wandel. (*in* Handbuch der Geschichte Lateinamerikas. Stuttgart, Germany: Klett-Cotta, 1994, v. 1, p. 454–504)

Concise work analyzes sociohistorical development of colonial Hispanic America (1550–1760) and current status of research on the topic. Covers geographical, social, and economic distribution of the population; State and society; social stratification; urban-rural dichotomy; and geographic diversity. Mörner suggests further research to document development of specific social and economic aspects at local and regional levels. [C.K. Converse]

937   Mota Murillo, Rafael. Fuentes para la historia franciscano-americana del siglo XVIII. (*Arch. Ibero-Am.*, 52:205/208, 1992, p. 1–80)

Bibliography of 989 entries is organized mainly by regions and provinces, from the Antilles and California to the Río de la Plata. Includes both older and more recent monographs as well as published collections of documents and other bibliographies.

938   Moyano Bazzani, Eduardo L. Aportaciones de la historiografía portuguesa a la problemática fronteriza luso-española en América meridional, 1750–1778. (*Rev. Indias*, 52:195/196, mayo/dic. 1992, p. 723–747, maps)

Provides concise overview of author's larger study of historical and historiographical debates concerning the Portuguese-Spanish boundaries in South America.

939   Muldoon, James. The Americas in the Spanish world order: the justification for conquest in the seventeenth century. Philadelphia: Univ. of Pennsylvania Press, 1994. 239 p.: bibl., index.

Intellectual and political history intersect in this impressive study of Juan de Solórzano Pereira, the Spanish scholar-bureaucrat who examined and explained nature of imperial power as applied in the Americas. Muldoon combines broad reading of scholarly studies with a thorough command of Solórzano's writings to reveal how lingering medieval influences had an impact on 17th-century debates about power and religion in the relations between Europeans and Native Americans.

940   Murillo Velarde, Pedro. Geographía de América. Prólogo de Antonio Domínguez Ortiz. Estudio preliminar de Ramón María Serrera Contreras. Ed. facsím. Granada,

Spain: Univ. de Granada, 1990. 391 p.: bibl. (Archivum; 14)

Facs. ed. of 1752 primary source on geography and history of New Spain and several other sections of America. Includes impressive prologue by Ramón Serrera that recovers one of the works of an important Spanish historian, juridical scholar, and theologian. Should join José Antonio Villaseñor y Sánchez as a contemporary description of 18th-century New Spain. [E.B. Couturier]

941 Nacher Malvaioli, Giancarlo V. Don Cristóbal Colón. Guadalajara, Mexico: Editorial Font, 1990. 187 p.: bibl., ill., index, maps.

Brief work is mainly a commemorative biographical sketch.

942 Newson, Linda A. Los sistemas de trabajo y la demografía en América española durante la colonia: patrones de mortalidad y fecundidad. (*in* Congresso sobre a História da População da América Latina, *1st, Ouro Preto, Brazil, 1989*. Actas. São Paulo: Fundação SEADE, 1990, p. 289–297, bibl.)

Interpretive study of relationships among labor systems, mortality, and fertility is based on combination of a broad survey of published monographs and some archival research.

943 Olmo Pintado, Margarita del. La historia natural en la *Historia del Nuevo Mundo* de B. Cobo. (*Rev. Indias,* 52:195/196, mayo/dic. 1992, p. 795–823, graphs, ill., map, tables)

Intensive textual analysis of Cobo's work focuses on its philosophical and cultural assumptions.

944 Ordóñez de Ceballos, Pedro. Viaje del mundo. Madrid: Miraguano Ediciones, 1993. 491 p. (Biblioteca de viajeros hispánicos; 8)

Republication of the early 17th-century account includes brief introduction and prologue.

945 El Otro Occidente: los orígenes de Hispanoamérica. México: Teléfonos de México, 1992. 355 p.: bibl., ill. (some col.), maps.

High-quality illustrations are accompanied by explanatory text.

946 Pardo Tomás, José and María Luz López Terrada. Las primeras noticias sobre plantas americanas en las relaciones de viajes y crónicas de Indias, 1493–1553. Valencia, Spain: Instituto de Estudios Documentales e Históricos sobre la Ciencia, Univ. de València, C.S.I.C., 1993. 364 p.: bibl., indexes. (Cuadernos valencianos de historia de la medicina y de la ciencia; 40. Serie A, monografías)

Well-organized study examines Spanish perceptions and use of American plants in early colonial era. First section discusses depiction of plant life in writings of leading chroniclers; second section explains foods, medicines, textiles, dyes, and other practical applications. Includes a 64-p. descriptive listing of plants discussed by the chroniclers.

947 Parrón Salas, Carmen. Cartagena y el comercio libre, 1765–1796. (*An. Hist. Contemp.,* 8, 1990/91, p. 215–224, tables)

Article explores problems of free trade policy and trade with the American colonies from Spanish port of Cartagena.

Parrón Salas, Carmen. La dislocación del comercio americano y las últimas tentativas normalizadoras: 1808–1818. See item **1031.**

948 Patronato Provincial del V Centenario del Descubrimiento de América (Huelva, Spain). Los lugares colombinos y su entorno. Dirección de Diego Ropero-Regidor. Madrid: Fundación Ramón Areces, 1992. 301 p.: bibl., ill. (some col.).

Volume of glossy color photographs includes supportive text.

949 Penyak, Lee. Más que sólo la destrucción de la Leyenda Negra: un vistazo a los estudios actuales sobre la Inquisición española. (*CHELA,* 4, 1989, p. 77–88)

Review of recent publications places Spanish Inquisition in its European context.

950 People and issues in Latin American history: the colonial experience; sources and interpretations. Edited by Lewis Hanke and Jane M. Rausch. New York: M. Wiener Pub., 1993. 356 p.: bibl., ill.

Book of readings is intended for the college classroom. Utilizes thematic organization to focus on issues such as nature of Inca rule and Native American-Spanish relations.

Pereña, Luciano. La idea de justicia en la conquista de América. See item **4892.**

951 Pérez Herrero, Pedro. América Latina y el colonialismo europeo, siglos XVI-XVIII. Madrid: Editorial Síntesis, 1992. 280 p.: bibl., maps. (Historia universal; 14. Moderna)

Well-organized textbook on Spanish, Portuguese, French, Dutch, and British Empires is based on impressive grasp of leading scholarly monographs. Develops appropriate balance between intentions and policies of the European metropolises and varied histories of their American colonies. Heaviest coverage on the Spanish Empire.

952 Pérez Tomás, Eduardo E. De columbina haereditate, 1492–1810. v. 1. México: Instituto Panamericano de Geografía e Historia, 1993. 350 p. (Instituto Panamericano de Geografía e Historia; 457)

Broad survey of Latin American history is contained in a highly selective mixture of brief descriptive and interpretive chapters.

953 Petrocelli, Héctor B. Lo que a veces no se dice de la conquista de América: encuentro de dos mundos. 2a. ed. corr. y aum. Rosario, Argentina: Ediciones DIDASCALIA, 1992. 174 p.: bibl. (Obras para la evangelización y la catequesis; 39)

Response to recent critics of the Spanish conquest gives a dim view of preconquest Native American cultures and emphasizes strengths of Spanish rule and missionary and educational work of the Catholic Church. Interesting as a part of the recent polemical historiography of the conquest. Numerous footnotes and textual passages identify many of the protagonists in this debate.

954 Pinto Rodríguez, Jorge. La fuerza de la palabra, evangelización y resistencia indígena: siglos XVI y XVII (*Rev. Indias,* 53: 199, sept./dic. 1993, p. 677–698)

Study of linguistics of missionary work in the Americas includes examinations of native responses and limits of the impact of language on conversion process.

955 Prien, Hans-Jürgen. Lenguas y evangelización en la época colonial: ¿adaptación o dominación? (*Jahrb. Gesch.,* 30, 1993, p. 55–73)

Author explores use of Spanish and Native American languages in evangelization. Based on selected published works.

956 Queirós, Pedro Fernandes de. Memoriales de las Indias Australes. Edición de Oscar Pinochet de la Barra. Madrid: Historia 16, 1990. 444 p. (Crónicas de América; 64)

The 54 memorials written by Queirós cover years 1597–1615, including his voyages to the South Pacific for Spain. Oscar Pinochet's introduction nicely summarizes the limited biographical material available on Queirós.

957 Ramos Pérez, Demetrio. Los últimos días de Cristóbal Colón y sus testamentos: con estudio y transcripción de los documentos. Madrid: Ministerio de Cultura V Centenario; Testimonio Compañía Editorial, 1992. 231 p.: bibl. (Tabulae americanae; 16)

Close account of the last words, death, burial, and will of Columbus is accompanied by relevant documents.

958 Real Díaz, José Joaquín. Estudio diplomático del documento indiano. Madrid: Dirección de Archivos Estatales, 1991. 243 p.: bibl., ill. . (Publicaciones de la Escuela de Estudios Hispano-Americanos; 190)

Republication of original 1970 work (see *HLAS 34:1393*).

959 Remesal, Agustín. Un banquete para los dioses: comidas, ritos y hambres en el Nuevo Mundo. Madrid: Alianza Editorial, 1993. 229 p., 24 p. of plates: bibl., ill. (some col.). (Libro de bolsillo; 1625. Sección Libros útiles)

Convenient summary of conquistadors' responses to Native American food, drink, and other consumables such as tobacco is based largely on published contemporary accounts. Lacks footnotes and references to modern scholarship.

960 Reunión de Historiadores de la Minería Latinoamericana, *1st, Zacatecas, Mexico, 1990.* Primera Reunión de Historiadores de la Minería Latinoamericana. v. 1, Minería colonial latinoamericana. Recopilación de Dolores Avila Herrera, Inés Herrera Canales y Rina Ortiz. México: Instituto Nacional de Antropología e Historia, 1992. 1 v.: bibl., ill. (Col. científica; 258. Serie Histórica)

Seven papers concentrate on economics of colonial mining. Worthy of special note is one by Carlos Contreras on financing of a Peruvian mining district and another by Kendall Brown on distribution of mercury. [E.B. Couturier]

961 Reyes Ramírez, Rocío de los. Expediciones y viajes de franciscanos en los libros registros del Archivo General de Indias, siglo XVIII. (*Arch. Ibero-Am.*, 52:205/208, 1992, p. 811–832, table)

Provides listing and brief description of 234 documents pertaining to Franciscan travel between Spain and the American colonies. Includes a helpful introduction.

962 Rivera Pagán, Luis N. Libertad y servidumbre indígena en la conquista española de América. (*in* Descubrimiento, conquista y colonización de América: mito y realidad. Santo Domingo: Centro para la Investigación y Acción Social en el Caribe (CIASCA), 1992, p. 41–70)

Explores origins of enslavement of Native Americans from arrival of Columbus to establishment of the encomienda. Based on secondary works and published documents.

963 Rodríguez, Ligia. El controvertido papel de los misioneros en Indias. (*CLAHR/Albuquerque*, 3:4, Fall 1994, p. 459–467)

General appraisal of impact of missionaries on Native Americans in early colonial era is drawn from published sources.

964 Rodríguez León, Mario A. Invasion and evangelization in the sixteenth century. (*in* The Church in Latin America, 1492–1992. Edited by Enrique Dussel. Kent, England: Burns & Oats; Maryknoll, N.Y.: Orbis Books, 1992, p. 43–54)

Interpretive essay discusses the defeat of the Dominicans' methods for peaceful evangelization by the Crown's push for "colonial Christendom" among the Native Americans.

965 Romano, Ruggiero. Coyunturas opuestas: la crisis del siglo XVII en Europa e Hispanoamérica. México: El Colegio de México; Fideicomiso Historia de las Américas; Fondo de Cultura Económica, 1993. 171 p.: bibl., ill. (Serie Ensayos. Sección de obras de historia)

Challenging comparative examination of economic histories of Spanish America, Spain, and other European nations reveals

less conjunction and more divergence and autonomy. Romano uses both quantitative and qualitative analysis and draws heavily from published scholarly monographs.

966 Rueda Iturrate, Carlos José de. Financiación de la Orden de San Francisco en los Cedularios del Archivo General de Indias. (*Arch. Ibero-Am.*, 52:205/208, 1992, p. 833–848)

Lists 151 18th-century documents concerning finances of the Order. Includes brief description of each document.

967 Ruíz C., Nydia M. Los catecismos políticos en España y América, 1793–1814. (*in* Memoria, creación e historia: luchar contra el olvido. Coordinación de Pilar García Jordán, Miguel Izard y Javier Laviña. Barcelona: Univ. de Barcelona, 1993, p. 211–277)

Provides textual explication of instructional publications intended to build support for the Spanish government during these crisis years.

968 Ruiz Martín, Felipe. Los destinos de la plata americana, siglos XVI y XVII. Madrid: Ediciones de la Univ. Autónoma de Madrid, 1991? 57 p.: bibl.

Brief work traces path of Spanish-American silver into Europe and Asia. Based on a wide range of monographs, including publications in Italian, French, Dutch, and German.

Sachsen und Lateinamerika: Begegnungen in vier Jahrhunderten. See item 1038.

969 Salinas, Maximiliano. Christianity, colonialism and women in Latin America in the 16th, 17th and 18th centuries. (*Soc. Compass*, 39:4, Dec. 1992, p. 525–542)

Interpretive analysis examines Catholic Church's symbolic depiction of women. While central theme is the subordination of women, Salinas also discusses assertion of more positive images of females, including the presence of the "subversive woman: a popular, festive and cosmic reinterpretation of Mary."

970 Sánchez, Joseph P. African freedmen and the *fuero militar:* a historical overview of *pardo* and *moreno* militiamen in the late Spanish empire. (*CLAHR/Albuquerque*, 3:2, Spring 1994, p. 165–183, ill.)

Concise study examines legal status and privileges of free blacks in the Spanish colonial militia. Based on archival research and reinforced by numerous illustrations.

971   Sánchez Bella, Ismael. Documentos vaticanos sobre la *Recopilación de Indias* de 1680. (*Historiogr. Bibliogr. Am.*, 31:1, 1987, p. 63–80, appendix, bibl.)
Publication of the documents is accompanied by a five-page explanatory introduction.

972   Sastre Santos, Eutimio. Ensayo de una periodización de la construcción de la Iglesia en las Indias, 1492–1648. (*Hisp. Sacra*, 45:91, enero/junio 1993, p. 187–219)
Broadly interpretive article deals with problem of periodization in New World church history and opts for space-time determinants for the period under study.

973   Sebastián, Santiago. Iconografía del indio americano, siglos XVI-XVII. Prólogo de Dietrich Briesemeister. Madrid: Ediciones Tuero, 1992. 150 p.: bibl., ill., index. (Col. Investigación y crítica; 9)
Study examines evolution of European image of Native Americans through the work of contemporary chroniclers and artists. Several small-sized reproductions of artists' renderings are included. Author connects image of Native Americans to rise of *leyenda negra* in other European nations. An interesting angle on continuing debate about meaning of the conquest.

974   Spain, Europe, and the Atlantic world: essays in honour of John H. Elliott. Edited by Richard L. Kagan and Geoffrey Parker. Cambridge, England; New York: Cambridge Univ. Press, 1995. 359 p.: bibl., ill., index, port.
Collection of essays deals mainly with Spanish and European history but includes three interpretive essays on Spanish America: 1) Peter Bakewell on institutional bases of Spanish domination in America; 2) Anthony Pagden on 16th-century warnings about Spain's overextension of its empire; and 3) Josep Fradera on Spanish colonial policy in 19th century.

975   Starke, Klaus-Peter. Der spanisch-amerikanische Kolonialhandel: die Entwicklung der neueren Historiographie und küngtige Forschungsperspektiven. Münster & Hamburg: Lit, 1995. 146 p. (Hamburger Ibero-Amerika Studien, 8.)
Useful "state-of-the-art" essay concerning the large Atlantic Hispanic-American trade from 16th-18th centuries. Author emphasizes the provenance of trading goods, the structure of trade, capital distribution, and the role of the merchant elites. His revised bibliography includes such "classical" authors as Braudel, Chaunu, Hamilton, Lapeyre, Smith, and Vilar as well as more recent investigators like Gracía, Baquero, García Fuentes, Morineau, and Moutoukias. [T. Hampe-Martínez]

976   Subirats, Eduardo. El continente vacío: la conquista del Nuevo Mundo y la conciencia moderna. Madrid: ANAYA & Mario Muchnik, 1994. 524 p.: bibl., ill., index, map. (Actas)
Provocative philosophical analysis of meaning of the conquest emphasizes author's views on ambiguities in Las Casas' defense of the Native Americans. Subirats turns to Inca Garcilaso de la Vega as early exponent of comprehensive anti-imperialist thought, and places 16th-century and early 17th-century ideas in a modern context.

977   Szaszdi Nagy, Adam. La legua y la milla de Colón. Valladolid, Spain: Casa-Museo de Colón; Seminario Americanista de la Univ. de Valladolid, 1991. 77 p.: bibl. (Cuadernos colombinos; 17)
Very brief and highly specialized work deals with often-covered territory.

978   Tanzi, Héctor José. El concepto geográfico del mundo antes de Colón. (*Rev. Hist. Am.*, 114, julio/dic. 1992, p. 91–140, ill., maps)
Author places Columbus in the context of European geographical perceptions of the world in late 1400s in order to assess his frame of reference at the time of the first voyage. Based on extensive reading of monographs and published documents.

979   Tardieu, Jean-Pierre. Las vistas de un arbitrista sobre la aparición de un hombre nuevo en las Indias occidentales, mitad del siglo XVII. (*Anu. Estud. Am.*, 50:1, 1993, p. 235–249)
Provides explication of Cristóbal de Lorenzana's proposal for a gradual integration of Africans into Latin American society.

980   Thornton, John K. The role of Africans in the Atlantic economy, 1450–1650: modern Africanist historiography and the world-systems paradigm. (*CLAHR/Albuquerque*, 3:2, Spring 1994, p. 125–140)

Thornton takes issue with assumptions of the world systems paradigm regarding Africa's relative "backwardness" when compared to Europe. He argues that Africa played an active role in its relations with European nations. He cites recently published historical research that indicates significant African advancements in production of military weapons, textiles, and steel to support his conclusions.

981 Tornero Tinajero, Pablo. Los pueblos de Huelva y América: la proyección atlántica del litoral onubense. Huelva, Spain?: Energía e Industrias Aragonesas, S.A., 1990. 168 p.: bibl., ill. (some col.), maps.

Color illustrations accompany account of role of the seaport of Huelva in Columbus expedition of 1492. Based on published monographs and general studies.

982 Torre Villar, Ernesto de la. Descubrimiento y conquista de América: temas para su estudio. México: Univ. Nacional Autónoma de México, 1992. 177 p.: bibl. (500 años después; 9)

Examines impact of law and religion on establishment of the colonial system in New Spain. In contrast to many recent considerations of the conquest, this book emphasizes work of religious leaders such as Sahagún and Quiroga in conversion of the Native Americans.

983 Torres Ballesteros, Pedro. Universitarios alcalaínos en las audiencias americanas: siglo XVIII. (*Estud. Hist. Soc. Econ. Am.*, 9, 1992, p. 191–212, graph)

Well-documented study offers valuable insights into connections between university education and service in the colonial bureaucracy.

984 Trueba, Eduardo. Sevilla, tribunal de océanos: siglo XVI. Sevilla: E. Trueba, 1988. 202 p.: bibl., ill.

Brief account focuses on emergence of Seville as a legal center of the Spanish Empire, especially through the Casa de Contratación. Based on archival research. More descriptive than analytical.

985 Universidad Pontificia de Salamanca (Spain). Centro de Estudios Orientales y Ecuménicos Juan XXIII. La primera evangelización de América: contexto y claves de interpretación. Edición de Dionisio Borobio. Salamanca, Spain: Centro de Estudios Orientales y Ecuménicos Juan XXIII, Univ. Pontificia de Salamanca, 1992. 249 p.: bibl., indexes. (Bibliotheca oecumenica Salmanticensis; 18)

Collection of seven articles includes both carefully documented studies and essays of opinion. An important contribution is Adolfo González Montes' historiographical survey of Protestant views of the conquest and evangelization.

986 Utopía y realidad indiana. Salamanca, Spain: Univ. Pontificia de Salamanca, 1992. 237 p.: bibl., ill. (Cátedra V centenario; 6)

Well-focused collection of seven historical essays analyzes theme of utopian thought in the 16th-century Spanish response to questions involving the place of Native Americans in Spanish America.

987 Varela, Consuelo. Cristóbal Colón: retrato de un hombre. Madrid: Alianza Editorial, 1992. 204 p.: bibl., ill. (some col.).

Portrait of Columbus includes his youth, education, friends, and public image at the time of his voyages. Written in a popular style and based on published sources.

988 Vargas Machuca, Bernardo de. Apologías y discursos de las conquistas occidentales. Edición y estudio preliminar de María Luisa Martínez de Salinas. Valladolid, Spain: Junta de Castilla y León, Consejería de Cultura y Turismo, 1993. 148 p.: bibl. (Estudios de historia)

Publication of Vargas Machuca's attack on Las Casas is accompanied by well-researched introduction.

989 Vidart, Daniel. Los muertos y sus sombras: cinco siglos de América. Montevideo: Ediciones de la Banda Oriental, 1993. 314 p.: bibl., ill., maps.

Sharply critical analysis of Spanish conquest makes use of terminology of genocide in explaining events from 1492 to about 1600. Vidart relies on published sources and includes critiques of reactions of contemporary observers such as Columbus, Oviedo, and Las Casas.

990 Vila Vilar, Enriqueta. Los Corzo y los Mañara: tipos y arquetipos del mercader con Indias. Sevilla, Spain: Escuela de Estudios Hispano-Americanos, 1991. 321 p.: bibl., ill. (Publicaciones de la Escuela de Estudios Hispano-Americanos de Sevilla; 361)

Ground-breaking work examines 16th-and 17th-century Sevilla and its relations with Spain's colonies. Focuses on two families of Corsican origin who surpassed other merchants in wealth and influence. Part of continuing study of commercial structure and power in first period of colonization, work is based on private and public archives. Links Spain with Indies in original and stimulating ways, and emphasizes art, social relations, and piety as they affected commercial activities and family history. See also item **2431.** [E.B. Couturier]

991 Vila Vilar, Enriqueta. La postura de la Iglesia frente a la esclavitud, siglos XVI y XVII. (*in* Coloquio Internacional sobre Abolición de la Esclavitud, *Madrid, 1986.* Esclavitud y derechos humanos: la lucha por la libertad del negro en el siglo XIX; actas. Edición de Francisco de Solano y Agustín Guimerá. Madrid: Consejo Superior de Investigaciones Científicas, Centro de Estudios Históricos, Depto. de Historia de América, 1990, p. 25–31)

Surveys clerical expressions of opposition to slavery. Suggestive, coherent essay.

992 Villegas, Silvio. Aspectos de la Inquisición en la América Hispana: una aproximación al tema. (*Bol. Acad. Nac. Hist./Caracas,* 77:305, enero/marzo 1994, p. 49–62, bibl.)

Institutional study is drawn from selected published works. Good organization but little breadth in research.

993 Vitoria, Francisco de. *Relectio de Indis = Carta magna de los indios;* 450 aniversario, 1539–1989. Estudios de Luciano Pereña. Traducción de Carlos Baciero. Madrid: Consejo Superior de Investigaciones Científicas, 1989. 132 p., 6 p. of plates: ill.

Commemorative republication of this classic work.

994 Walton, Timothy R. The Spanish treasure fleets. Sarasota, Fla.: Pineapple Press, 1994. 256 p.: bibl., ill., index, maps.

Popular history is based on secondary sources and is nicely illustrated with 60 b/w pictures including several photographs of coins. Last chapter summarizes modern efforts to locate and recover remains of sunken treasure-bearing vessels. Work's main flaw, as stated in author's preface, is absence of research in Spanish archives.

995 Wright, A.D. The institutional relations of Church and State in the overseas Iberian territories. (*Hisp. Sacra,* 40, julio/dic. 1988, p. 693–699)

Very brief general study of authority of imperial officials in Church affairs combines archival research with selected published monographs.

996 Zamora, Hermenegildo. Escritos franciscanos americanos del siglo XVIII. (*Arch. Ibero-Am.,* 52:205/208, 1992, p. 691–766)

Extensive alphabetical listing of Franciscan writers whose works fall into 16 categories including sermons, theology, law, philosophy, and history. Author gives brief biographical sketch of most of the writers.

997 Zavala, Silvio Arturo. El mundo americano en la época colonial. Suplemento bibliográfico, 1967–1991. México: Instituto Panamericano de Geografía e Historia, 1992. 245 p.: index. (Pub.; 456)

Extensive bibliography is organized topically and includes index of authors. In addition to customary subjects (geography, Native American civilizations, colonization, etc.), volume includes chapters on contacts with Africa, Asia, and the Pacific. Supplement to 1969 publication (see *HLAS 32:993*).

INDEPENDENCE AND 19TH CENTURY

998 Acevedo, Edberto Oscar. Manual de historiografía hispanoamericana contemporánea. Mendoza, Argentina: Univ. Nacional de Cuyo, Facultad de Filosofía y Letras, 1992. 316 p.: bibl.

Important contribution to historiography of modern Latin America employs both a country-by-country approach and general analyses of three schools: romanticism and liberalism, liberal positivism, and *renovación crítica*. Concentrates on 19th and early 20th centuries. Influenced by and revises Bradford Burns' 1978 article (see *HLAS 42:1899* and *7626*).

El anarquismo en América Latina. See item **1046.**

999 Anes Alvarez, Rafael. La emigración de asturianos a América. Colombres, Spain: Archivo de Indianos, 1993. 174 p.: bibl. (Cruzar el charco; 10)

Provides competent overview of causes and consequences of immigration, mainly to Cuba and Argentina, from mid-1800s into first decades of 20th century. Includes statistical information and several helpful charts.

1000 Ardao, Arturo. España en el origen del nombre *América Latina.* Montevideo: Biblioteca de Marcha; Facultad de Humanidades y Ciencias de la Educación; Facultad de Ciencias Sociales, 1992. 121 p.: bibl., index.

Thorough examination of origins of the term *América Latina* in mid-19th-century Spain is based on extensive reading in Spanish journals and books of the day. Ardao emphasizes influence of Francisco Muñoz del Monte and Emilio Castelar.

1001 Arrieta, Angel Mari. La emigración alavesa a América en el siglo XIX (1800–1900). Vitoria, Spain: Servicio Central de Publicaciones del Gobierno Vasco, 1992. 517 p.: bibl., ill. (some col.), index, maps. (Amerika eta euskaldunak = América y los vascos; 15)

Highly focused study of causes and consequences of immigration from Alava to America (mainly Argentina) is based on archival research. Includes statistics, maps, immigration lists, and analytical discussions.

1002 Barbier, Jacques A. *Comercio neutral* in Bolivarian America: La Guaira, Cartagena, Callao and Buenos Aires. (*in* América Latina en la época de Simón Bolívar: la formación de las economías nacionales y los intereses económicos europeos, 1800–1850. Edición de Reinhard Liehr. Berlin: Colloquium Verlag, 1989, p. 363–377, tables)

Presents analytical/speculative estimate of impact of Spain's flawed and putatively disruptive neutral trade policy during Napoleonic wars. Barbier gets maximum use from available sources.

Beozzo, José Oscar. The Church and the liberal states, 1880–1930. See item **1048.**

1003 Bernecker, Walther L. Las relaciones entre Europa y Latinoamérica durante el siglo XIX: ofensivas comerciales e intereses económicos. (*Hispania/Madrid,* 53 : 183, enero/abril 1993, p. 177–212, bibl.)

Important synthesis is based on published monographs (many in German) on policies of European nations toward Latin America and policies of Latin American governments toward Europe, including immigration as well as trade and investment.

Bulmer-Thomas, Victor. The economic history of Latin America since independence. See item **1052.**

1004 Bushnell, David and **Neill Macaulay.** The emergence of Latin America in the nineteenth century. 2nd ed. New York: Oxford Univ. Press, 1994. 341 p.: bibl., index, map.

Second edition of this exceptionally well-written college text (see *HLAS 52:873*) offers new material on Peru and an updated bibliographical essay.

1005 Carron, Alexandre and **Christophe Carron.** Nos cousins d'Amérique: histoire de l'émigration valaisanne au XIXe siècle. v. 1–2. 2. éd. Sierre, Switzerland: Editions Monographic, 1990. 2 v.: bibl., ill., photos.

Largely narrative, sometimes anecdotal account focuses on immigrants from Swiss Canton of Valais who settled in Argentina, Chile, and Brazil in mid- to late 19th century. Some archival sources and private letters. Numerous photographs.

Claro Tocornal, Regina. La Revolución Francesa y la independencia hispanoamericana. See item **4848.**

Connaughton, Brian F. América Latina, 1700–1850: entre el pacto colonial y el imperialismo moderno. See item **839.**

1006 Cortés Alonso, Vicenta. La manumisión y la sociedad hispanoamericana. (*in* Coloquio Internacional sobre Abolición de la Esclavitud, *Madrid, 1986.* Esclavitud y derechos humanos: la lucha por la libertad del negro en el siglo XIX; actas. Edición de Francisco de Solano y Agustín Guimerá. Madrid: Consejo Superior de Investigaciones Científicas, Centro de Estudios Históricos, Depto. de Historia de América, 1990, p. 33–41, tables)

Brief general study of manumission in Latin America includes some comparisons with US. Sources are published scholarly monographs.

1007 Cortés Conde, Roberto. El crecimiento de las economías latinoamericanas, 1800–1930. (*Hist. Mex.,* 42 : 3, enero/marzo 1993, p. 633–647, bibl., tables)

Incisive analysis examines export-driven growth (using Chilean, Brazilian, Mexican and Argentine economies as examples), and post-1930 debate concerning long-term effects of this type of growth.

Cultura e identidad nacional. See item **1308.**

1008 Deive, Carlos Esteban. Los restos de Colón: defensa del hallazgo dominicano de 1877. Santo Domingo: Ediciones Fundación García Arévalo, 1993. 191 p.: bibl. (Serie Investigaciones; 17)

Author defends thesis concerning location of remains of Columbus in the Dominican Republic.

1009 Demélas-Bohy, Marie-Danielle and **François-Xavier Guerra.** Un processus révolutionnaire méconnu: l'adoption des formes représéntatives modernes en Espagne et en Amérique, 1808–1810. (*Caravelle/Toulouse*, 60, 1993, p. 5–57)

Well-researched study focuses on Spanish-American deputies in the Cortes assembled in Cádiz from 1808–13 who initiated some basic mechanisms of modern democracy. *Suplentes* were more radical than deputies elected in America and reinforced a Liberal majority in the Cortes. Authors' claim that the Cortes "set in motion the independence process" is controversial given its limited legitimacy in America. [A. Pérotin-Dumon]

1010 Eltis, David and **Stanley L. Engerman.** Was the slave trade dominated by men? (*J. Interdiscip. Hist.*, 23:2, Autumn 1992, p. 237–257, graphs, tables)

Quantitative study focuses on gender and age composition of slave population transported to the Americas. Although adult males were largest single category, authors find significant fluctuations in percentages of adult females and children.

1011 Emancipación y nacionalidades americanas. Coordinación de Demetrio Ramos Pérez. Madrid: Ediciones Rialp, 1992? 629 p.: bibl., ill. (some col.), maps. (Historia general de España y América; 13)

Work of broad synthesis draws from monographs and other secondary sources and strikes a good balance of political, military, economic, and social history. Each chapter has a helpful bibliographic essay. Numerous illustrations and maps.

1012 Ezquerra Abadia, Ramón. Las causas de la emancipación hispanoamericana. (*Rev. Indias*, 54:200, enero/abril 1994, p. 21–31)

"Think piece" on origins of the independence movements emphasizes multiple causation.

1013 Federalismos latinoamericanos: México, Brasil, Argentina. Coordinación de Marcello Carmagnani. México: El Colegio de México; Fideicomiso Historia de las Américas; Fondo de Cultura Económica, 1993. 416 p.: bibl. (Serie Estudios / Fideicomiso Historia de las Américas. Sección de obras de historia)

Volume contains 10 analytical essays that explore the important and often neglected subject of federalism not only in its technical meaning as division of power in a country between national government and the states, but also in a larger sense as a source of democratic practices and values. Essays cover 19th and 20th centuries in all three countries.

1014 Fernández de Pinedo, Emiliano. La emigración vasca a América, siglos XIX y XX. Colombres, Spain: Ediciones Jucar, 1993. 232 p.: bibl., maps. (Cruzar el charco; 6)

Study in historical demography is based on archival research and wide range of published government reports and historical monographs. Author divides this work into two periods: 1830–80 and 1880–1936. Migration to Cuba is preeminent in the first period; migration to Argentina in the second.

1015 Fernández González, Francisco. Toledo en el IV centenario del descubrimiento de América. Toledo, Spain: Instituto Provincial de Investigaciones y Estudios Toledanos, 1991. 89 p.: bibl., ill. (Publicaciones del Instituto Provincial de Investigaciones y Estudios Toledanos. Serie I, Monografías; 25)

Brief account of political and physical arrangements for Toledo's participation in 4th centenary includes description of the celebration itself.

1016 Filippi, Alberto. Instituciones e ideologías en la independencia hispanoamericana. Prólogo de José Aricó. Buenos Aires: Alianza Editorial, 1988. 307 p.: bibl. (Alianza estudio; 5)

Contains collection of Filippi's critical essays on European intellectuals' responses to the emerging Latin American nations, particularly Venezuela and Colombia. One essay analyzes Marx's view of the Americas; another explores interpretations of Bolívar as a fascist. Valuable for insights into European historiography of Latin America.

1017 Flórez Estrada, Alvaro. Examen imparcial de las disensiones de la América con la España. Madrid: Dirección de Estudios y Documentación, Servicio de Publicaciones, Secretaría General del Senado, 1991. 1 v.: bibl., ill.

Reprint of 1812 examination of causes of the rift between Spain and its American colonies is accompanied by a 54-p. introduction by José Manuel Pérez-Prendes y Muñoz de Arracó that gives helpful biographical and historical background.

1018 García López, José Ramón. Las remesas de los emigrantes españoles en América, siglos XIX y XX. Oviedo, Spain: Ediciones Jucar, 1992. 211 p.: bibl., ill. (Cruzar el charco; 3)

Pioneering study examines an obscure but important subject—the return of money and of wealth in general from America to Spain by Spanish immigrants who lived in the Western Hemisphere. Based on research in the records of Spanish banks.

1019 Glade, William P. Commercial policy in early republican Latin America: a reassessment from the standpoint of global perspective. (in América Latina en la época de Simón Bolívar: la formación de las economías nacionales y los intereses económicos europeos, 1800–1850. Edición de Reinhard Liehr. Berlin: Colloquium Verlag, 1989, p. 379–396)

Glade uses a broad perspective based on the policy debates concerning international trade to deal with problems of economic and technological development in Latin America. A valuable synthesis based on scholarly monographs.

1020 González Pizarro, José Antonio. Imagen e impresiones de América de los integrantes de la Armada y de la Comisión de Naturalistas Españoles, 1862–1866. (Jahrb. Gesch., 29, 1992, p. 279–307)

Impressive account relates emergence of a favorable image of Spanish America in the writings of members of the 1862–66 expedition. This study utilizes the archives of the Museo Naval and the Museo Nacional de Ciencias Naturales.

1021 Güenaga de Silva, Rosario and **Adriana Rodríguez.** La comunicación interoceánica y el juego de los intereses económicos internacionales sobre Magallanes y el Istmo centroamericano. (Estud. Hist. Soc. Econ. Am., 10, 1993, p. 233–243, table)

Article deals mainly with effects of transisthmian commerce on Chilean trade via the Straits of Magellan, 1840s-80s. Includes some archival research.

1022 Hermann, Christian. La diplomatie de la France en Amérique latine au lendemain des indépendances. (Mélanges/Paris, 28:3, 1992, p. 79–95, bibl.)

Reviews existing literature and sets agenda for much-needed revisionist research on French diplomacy in newly independent Latin American nations. [A. Pérotin-Dumon]

1023 La independencia americana: consecuencias económicas. Edición de Leandro Prados de la Escosura y Samuel Amaral. Madrid: Alianza Editorial, 1993. 329 p.: bibl., ill. (Alianza universidad; 745)

Eleven papers presented at a seminar at the Univ. Carlos III in July 1991 are published here, along with a 29-p. bibliography of recent scholarly work in this area. This important collection includes country-by-country surveys for Mexico, Cuba, Colombia, Peru, Brazil, Paraguay, and Argentina. The fragmenting of Central America and the impact of independence on Spain and Portugal are also discussed. John Coatsworth provides an incisive general essay.

1024 Kellenbenz, Hermann. Südamerikafahrer am Kap der Guten Hoffnung. (in Amerikaner wider Willen: Beiträge zur Sklaverei in Latinamerika und ihren Folgen. Frankfurt: Vervuert Verlag, 1994, p. 43–124, tables)

Consists of meticulously recorded statistical data on South American-African maritime traffic around the Cape of Good Hope (1807–50). Lists names of ships and their captains, flags under which ships sailed, arrivals, departures, destinations, and cargoes. Author elaborates on archival material by describing observed changes in nationalities involved in the slave trade, and the fate of some of their ships. [C.K. Converse]

1025 Kinsbruner, Jay. Independence in Spanish America: civil wars, revolutions, and underdevelopment. Albuquerque: Univ.

of New Mexico Press, 1994. 178 p.: bibl., ill., index, maps. (Diálogos)

In this considerably revised version of 1973 ed. of this textbook (see *HLAS 36:1655*), Kinsbruner now argues that movements for independence were quite varied and included several examples of efforts to carry out significant social revolutions and not simply changes in governing elites. Stimulating study based on intelligent survey of recently published scholarly monographs.

1026 Latin American revolutions, 1808–1826: Old and New World origins. Edited and with an introduction by John Lynch. Norman: Univ. of Oklahoma Press, 1994. 409 p.: bibl., ill., index.

Thoroughly updates 1965 book of readings on the independence era by Lynch and R.A. Humphries (see *HLAS 28:457a*). Lynch provides valuable synthesis in his introduction. Most of the new articles appeared originally in the 1970s and 1980s.

1027 Lynch, John. Caudillos in Spanish America, 1800–1850. Oxford, England: Clarendon Press; New York: Oxford Univ. Press, 1992. 468 p.: bibl., index, maps.

Comparative study of caudillos is also a major interpretation of a crucial period in Spanish-American political history. In his synthesis that draws from published monographs, Lynch also includes some of his own primary research. Biographical studies of Rosas, Páez, Santa Anna, and Carrera form the foundation for a carefully reasoned analysis of this politico-cultural phenomenon.

1028 Mateo Avilés, Elías de. La emigración andaluza a América, 1850–1936. Málaga, Spain: Editorial Arguval, 1993. 331 p.: bibl. (Col. Tres culturas; 5)

Well-organized, comprehensive study of Andalusian immigration is based on government reports and monographic studies. Includes informative footnotes.

1029 Mathew, W.M. Britain and the Bolivarian republics, 1820–1850: interimperium and the tariff. (*in* América Latina en la época de Simón Bolívar: la formación de las economías nacionales y los intereses económicos europeos, 1800–1850. Edición de Reinhard Liehr. Berlin: Colloquium Verlag, 1989, p. 397–421, table)

Careful examination of tariff policies in trade between Great Britain and the Boli-

varian nations concludes that nations of northern and western South America exercised more independence in their commercial policies than previous studies had indicated, and that the tariff itself had limited effects on trade.

1030 Núñez Seixas, Xosé M. Actitudes del nacionalismo gallego frente al problema de la emigración gallega a América, 1856–1936. (*Stud. Emigr.*, 28:102, giugno 1991, p. 190–217, bibl.)

Analyzes responses of Galician intellectual and political leaders to overseas migration from mid-19th century to 1920s. Includes commentary from Galician residents of Buenos Aires and Havana.

1031 Parrón Salas, Carmen. La dislocación del comercio americano y las últimas tentativas normalizadoras: 1808–1818. (*Jahrb. Gesch.*, 30, 1993, p. 153–182, map, tables)

Author traces disruption and decline of trade within the Spanish Empire during the wars for independence utilizing primary sources from Spain, New Spain, and Panama.

1032 Pazos, Antón M. La Iglesia en la América del IV centenario. Madrid: Editorial MAPFRE, 1992. 429 p.: bibl., indexes. (Col. Iglesia Católica en el Nuevo Mundo; 13. Col. MAPFRE 1492)

Important historical analysis examines situation of the Catholic Church in Latin America in late 19th century. Topics include Church finances, external pressures from liberal reformers and Protestants, internal divisions, and reform movements. Pazos makes good use of Vatican archives as indicated in his extensive footnotes.

1033 Pereira Castañares, Juan Carlos. España e Iberoamérica: un siglo de relaciones, 1836–1936. (*Mélanges/Paris*, 28:3, 1992, p. 97–127)

Useful study that includes cultural and political as well as diplomatic relations is based mainly on published secondary works with some archival documentation.

1034 Pietschmann, Horst. Hamburgo y la América Latina en la primera mitad del siglo XIX. (*in* Congreso Internacional de Historia Económica y Social de la Cuenca del Caribe, 1763–1898, *1st, San Juan, 1987. Actas.* San Juan: Centro de Estudios Avanzados de Puerto Rico y el Caribe, 1992, p. 455–487, bibl., tables)

In-depth portrait of trade between this German port and Latin America includes statistical analyses and examination of the manuscript of Hamburg merchant Georg Degetau.

1035 Richmond, Douglas W. Comparative elite systems in Latin America and the United States, 1870–1914. (*Rev. Hist. Am.*, 114, julio/dic. 1992, p. 61–89)

Exemplary essay in comparative history stresses role of elites in industrialization and social reform. Covers Argentina, Mexico, Chile, Peru, and Brazil.

1036 Ríos, María del Carmen. Aculturación de América Latina en el último tercio del siglo XIX. (*Hisp. Sacra*, 40, julio/dic. 1988, p. 637–651)

"Think piece" attempts a study of Latin American cultural values in which theme of modernization is a central factor. Author concentrates on Argentina's Generation of 1880.

1037 Rodríguez O., Jaime E. La independencia de la América española: una reinterpretación. (*Hist. Mex.*, 42:3, enero/marzo 1993, p. 571–620)

Extensive and stimulating review of recently published scholarship forms basis for author's reinterpretation of independence period as a time of broader and deeper social movements, which in many regions were authentic social revolutions or, at least, the early stages of such revolutions.

1038 Sachsen und Lateinamerika: Begegnungen in vier Jahrhunderten. Edited by Michael Zeuske, Bernd Schröter, and Jörg Ludwig. Frankfurt am Main: Vervuert Verlag, 1995. 290 p.: bibl. (Bibliotheca Ibero-Americana; 52)

Collection of research papers traces business, scientific, and cultural contacts between Saxony and Latin America (1750–1850). Uses many local, State, and business archives. Interesting data and studies illustrate economic efforts of small German state (1820–30). [C.K. Converse]

1039 Sagredo B., Rafael. Ciencia, viajes e independencia. (*Mem. Acad. Mex. Hist.*, 37, 1994, p. 29–64, bibl., tables)

Interpretive study examines impact of scientific expeditions to America (especially

those led by purveyors of Enlightenment thought), and consequent stimulus to science in Latin America. Also discusses the tenuously related sense of creole nationalism that emerged in the same era. Based on published studies and some archival material.

1040 Schneider, Jürgen. Sinopsis sobre el comercio exterior en Latinoamérica, 1810–1850. (*in* América Latina en la época de Simón Bolívar: la formación de las economías nacionales y los intereses económicos europeos, 1800–1850. Edición de Reinhard Liehr. Berlin: Colloquium Verlag, 1989, p. 489–502, tables)

Incisive survey of recent scholarship in economic history rejects dependency theory and affirms conceptual approaches of "staple theory" as pioneered by Canadian Harold Innes.

1041 Schneider, Jürgen. Trade relations between France and Latin America, 1810–1850. (*in* América Latina en la época de Simón Bolívar: la formación de las economías nacionales y los intereses económicos europeos, 1800–1850. Edición de Reinhard Liehr. Berlin: Colloquium Verlag, 1989, p. 423–437, graph, tables)

Balanced prose explanations and statistical analyses support Schneider's view that Latin America in general benefited from its trade with France, although the French lost ground to the highly competitive British merchants.

1042 Simmons, Merle Edwin. La revolución norteamericana en la independencia de Hispanoamérica. Madrid: Editorial MAPFRE, 1992. 372 p.: bibl., index. (Col. España y Estados Unidos; 5. Col. MAPFRE 1492)

Intellectual history focuses on impact of North American Revolution against the British Empire on precursors and leaders of movements for independence in Spanish America. This much-needed study examines international interaction of ideas and personalities in half-century from 1775–1825.

Spain, Europe, and the Atlantic world: essays in honour of John H. Elliott. See item **974.**

1043 Vargas Martínez, Gustavo. Bolívar y el poder: orígenes de la revolución en las repúblicas entecas de América. México: Univ. Nacional Autónoma de México, Coordinación de Humanidades, Centro Coordinador y

Difusor de Estudios Latinoamericanos, 1991. 197 p.: bibl., index. (500 años después; 2)

Offers interesting interpretation of Bolívar as a revolutionary. Author argues that Bolívar led a broad social revolution (not simply a political revolution) to expel the Spanish Empire and to create a cohesive nation in Spanish South America. Vargas Martínez integrates Bolívar's ideas with his administrative actions and political failures.

1044 Vázquez Franco, Guillermo and **Juan Manuel Casal.** Historia política y social de Iberoamérica: investigaciones y ensayos. Montevideo: Fundación de Cultura Universitaria, 1992. 2 v.: bibl.

Group of essays deals mainly with Uruguayan economic and political history from early 1800s to 1930s, with some coverage of Argentina, Brazil, Peru, and Paraguay. Considerable emphasis on British economic influence. Based mainly on secondary sources.

1045 Xin Shijiede Zhendang: Lading Meichou Duli Yundong [New World tremblings: the Independence Movement of Latin America]. Edited by Lu Guojun and Hao Mingwei. Shanghai, China: Shanghai Academy of Social Sciences Press, 1991. 274 p.

The first and only academic work ever published in China on the Latin American independence movement. Analyzes movement's causes, leadership, nature, path, and achievements, from Chinese perspective. One of the nine chapters contains an interesting section on the contributions of Chinese laborers to the Cuban independence movement. Authors are senior research fellows from Institute of World History, Chinese Academy of Social Sciences. [Mao Xianglin]

20TH CENTURY

Acevedo, Edberto Oscar. Manual de historiografía hispanoamericana contemporánea. See item **998.**

1046 El anarquismo en América Latina. Selección y notas de Carlos M. Rama y Angel J. Cappelletti. Prólogo y cronología de Angel J. Cappelletti. Caracas: Biblioteca Ayacucho, 1990. 698 p.: bibl. (Biblioteca Ayacucho; 155)

Valuable work contains a 200-p. introductory essay by Angel Cappelletti concentrating on 1870–1930 period in Argentina, Brazil, Peru, and Mexico. The 450 p. of documents include the writings of Diego Abad de Santillán, Emilio López Arango, Rodolfo González Pacheco, and Ricardo Flores Magón.

Anes Alvarez, Rafael. La emigración de asturianos a América. See item **999.**

1047 Angell, Alan. The left in Latin America since 1930: a bibliographical essay. (*Historia/Santiago*, 26, 1991/92, p. 61–70)

Succinct commentary covers broad cross-section of writing by and about leftists and analyzes the organizations they formed. Offers intelligent, dispassionate observations.

1048 Beozzo, José Oscar. The Church and the liberal states, 1880–1930. (*in* The Church in Latin America, 1492–1992. Edited by Enrique Dussel. Kent, England: Burns & Oats; Maryknoll, N.Y.: Orbis, 1992, p. 117–138, table)

Overview of Catholic Church's responses to the social, political, and economic transformation of Latin America includes trenchant observations on tensions between Latin American and European Catholicisms.

1049 Bergquist, Charles. Labor history and its challenges: confessions of a Latin Americanist. (*Am. Hist. Rev.*, 98:3, June 1993, p. 757–764)

Well-conceived consideration of recent developments in labor history includes traditional issue of worker-mamagement conflicts and newer issues centering on gender, internationalism, and postmodernist critique of historical sources.

1050 Bethell, Leslie and **Ian Roxborough.** The postwar conjucture in Latin America: democracy, labor, and the Left. (*in* Latin America between the Second World War and the Cold War, 1944–1948. Edited by Leslie Bethell and Ian Roxborough. New York: Cambridge Univ. Press, 1992, p. 1–32)

Essay defines internal and external factors that pushed most Latin American nations toward democracy and reform from 1944–46, and the sudden shifts that contained and eventually defeated these tendencies in most nations (except Guatemala and Argentina) by 1946–48.

1051 Bethell, Leslie and **Ian Roxborough.**
The postwar conjuncture in Latin
America and its consequences. (*in* Latin
America between the Second World War and
the Cold War, 1944–1948. Edited by Leslie Bethell and Ian Roxborough. New York: Cambridge Univ. Press, 1992, p. 327–334)
    Authors argue that conjuncture of do-
mestic and international circumstances after
World War II that created an opening for
emergence of social democracy in Latin
America quickly succumbed to conservative
consolidation in the early years of the Cold
War.

1052 Bulmer-Thomas, Victor. The economic history of Latin America since
independence. Cambridge, England: Cambridge Univ. Press, 1994. 495 p.: bibl., ill., index, maps. (Cambridge Latin American studies; 77)
    In this impressive work of synthesis,
approximately three-fourths of the text deals
with 20th century. Organization centers
around several basic approaches in economic
policy including export-led growth, import-
substitution industrialization, export promotion, and debt-led growth. Text is clearly written; work avoids arcane jargon and can benefit the generalist as well as the specialist.

1053 Collier, Ruth Berins and **David Collier.**
Shaping the political arena: critical
junctures, the labor movement, and regime
dynamics in Latin America. Princeton, N.J.:
Princeton Univ. Press, 1991. 877 p.: bibl., index.
    Excellent comparative-historical anal-
ysis of eight countries (Argentina, Brazil,
Chile, Colombia, Mexico, Peru, Uruguay, and
Venezuela) focuses on emergence of different
forms of control and mobilization of the labor
movement. By concentrating on alternative
strategies of the State in shaping the labor
movement, authors are able to explain different trajectories of national political change in
countries with longest history of urban, commercial, and industrial development. Important and valuable work includes glossary of
terms and extensive index (general and by
country).

**Congreso de la Asociación de Historiadores
Latinoamericanistas Europeos, *10th, s.l.,
1993*.** Las transformaciones hacia la sociedad
moderna en América Latina: causas y condi-

ciones de la economía, la política y en las
mentalidades. See item **7.**

Cortés Conde, Roberto. El crecimiento de las
economías latinoamericanas, 1800–1930. See
item **1007.**

1054 Cruz Capote, Orlando. La primera conferencia de los comunistas latinoamericanos. (*Santiago/Cuba*, 75, junio 1993,
p. 45–76)
    Penetrating analysis focuses on the
meeting of Latin American Communist Party
representatives in Buenos Aires in 1928. Author stresses influence of Latin American perspectives in the discussions of theory and
practice—especially the impact of José
Carlos Mariátegui.

1055 Dietl, Ralph. USA und Mittelamerika:
die Aussenpolitik von William J.
Bryan, 1913–1915. Stuttgart, Germany: Franz
Steiner, 1996. 496 p.: bibl., index. (Beiträge
zur Kolonial- und Überseegeschichte: 0522–
6848; 67)
    Argues that in his short term as US
Secretary of State, Bryan designed a hemi-
spheric policy very different from that of his
predecessors. Bryan's policy was based on
moral principles, settlement of conflicts by
arbitration, and stabilizing loans, rather than
US jingoism and influence of "special interests" in the Caribbean region. Using Nicaragua, Haiti, Santo Domingo, and Mexico as examples, author describes shaping of that good
neighborly policy which was eliminated after
Bryan's resignation. Contains abundant information obtained from archives in US, UK,
and Mexico. [H.M. Meding]

**1056 Drugs in the Western Hemisphere: an
odyssey of cultures in conflict.** Edited
by William O. Walker, III. Wilmington, Del.:
Scholarly Resources, 1996. 262 p.: bibl. (Jaguar books on Latin America; 12)
    Useful collection of essays includes
primary sources (many from US Dept. of
State), press accounts, and scholarly analyses.
Walker's introduction, conclusion, and bibliographical essay give collection a coherence
that will be appreciated by both specialists
and students.

1057 Dussel, Enrique. The Church in populist regimes, 1930–59. (*in* The Church
in Latin America, 1492–1992. Edited by Enrique Dussel. Kent, England: Burns & Oats;

Maryknoll, N.Y.: Orbis Books, 1992, p. 139–152, bibl.)

Effective synthesis of Church's responses to rise of populist governments includes its appeals to the middle class and working class and its tentative alliances with several populist regimes.

1058 Egea Bruno, Pedro María. Cartagena en el comercio exterior con el continente americano, 1909–1919. (*An. Hist. Contemp.*, 8, 1990/91, p. 239–255, graphs, tables)

Quantitative case study of impact of World War I on trade through Cartagena (Spain) contains useful charts and tables. Clearly-written prose discussion.

Federalismos latinoamericanos: México, Brasil, Argentina. See item **1013.**

Fernández de Pinedo, Emiliano. La emigración vasca a América, siglos XIX y XX. See item **1014.**

1059 La formación de la imagen de América Latina en España, 1898–1989. Coordinación de Montserrat Huguet Santos, Antonio Niño Rodríguez y Pedro Pérez Herrero. Madrid: Organización de Estados Iberoamericanos para la Educación, la Ciencia y la Cultura (OEI), 1992. 437 p.: bibl., ill. (Cuadernos de cultura iberoamericana)

The product of a 1989 conference held by the Facultad de Geografía e Historia de la Univ. Complutense de Madrid, this collection of essays embodies an impressive level of scholarly work in Latin American studies in Spain. Most essays are based on research in important archives and reading in professional monographs and journals.

García López, José Ramón. Las remesas de los emigrantes españoles en América, siglos XIX y XX. See item **1018.**

1060 Garrigos Meseguer, Antonio. Evangelizadores de América: historia de la OCSHA. Prólogo de Eduardo Pironio. Madrid: Biblioteca de Autores Cristianos, 1992. 812 p.: bibl., index. (Biblioteca de autores cristianos; 524)

Traces history of Obra de Cooperación Sacerdotal Hispano-Americana (OCSHA) from its origins in Spain in 1948 through its expansion into individual Latin American nations and the state of Florida in US. Since author was a participant in the movement he describes, book often takes on the quality of a primary source.

1061 Guillén, Diana. América Latina frente a la crisis de 1929. (*Secuencia/México*, 16 enero/abril 1990, p. 123–136, photo)

Guillén's stimulating reinterpretation of economic and political events of early 1930s turns attention to long-term trends as the fundamental historical factors, rather than to immediate, dramatic impact of the stock market crash and onset of the depression.

1062 Historia política del siglo XX. Edición de Jorge Núñez Sánchez. Quito: Editora Nacional; Asociación de Historiadores Latinoamericanos y del Caribe, 1992. 279 p.: bibl. (Col. Nuestra patria es América; 3)

Seven contributions to this collection of nine essays focus on 20th-century liberal and far left trends in Ecuador, Argentina, Uruguay, Venezuela, and Brazil. Remaining two essays deal with general trends throughout Latin America: Manuel Caballero discusses revolutionary armed struggle and Maria Helena Capelato examines populism and propaganda.

1063 El impacto político de la crisis del 29 en América Latina. México: Alianza Editorial Mexicana; Consejo Nacional para la Cultura y las Artes, 1990. 181 p.: bibl. (Los Noventa; 30)

Insightful interpretive essays are based mainly on secondary sources. Nations included are Argentina, Bolivia, Brazil, Chile, Mexico, Peru, and Uruguay.

1064 Klaiber, Jeffrey. Iglesia, dictaduras y democracia en América Latina. Lima: Pontificia Univ. Católica del Perú, Fondo Editorial, 1997. 502 p.: bibl., index.

Klaiber, a talented historian, has written a thought-provoking synthesis of the impact of the Catholic Church on political and social change in Latin America since middle years of the 20th century. Text is organized country-by-country, and author's frames of reference range from Argentina's "Dirty War" to the uprising in Chiapas. The 27-p. bibliography is of considerable value for both specialists and generalists.

1065 Kołodziej, Edward and **Rafał Mrowiec.** Ameryka Łacińska, Hiszpania i Portugalia: w źródłach Archiwum Akt Nowych do roku 1945 [Latin America, Spain, and Portugual in the collections of the Archives of New Records up to 1945]. Warszawa, Poland: Uniwersytet Warszawski, Centrum Studiów Latynoamerykańskich; Naczelna Dyrekcja Archiwów Państwowych, Archiwum Akt Nowych, 1996. 224 p.: indexes. (Seria "Informatory")

Lists some 2,072 Polish documents dating from 1918–45 concerning Latin America, Spain, and Portugal preserved in the Archives of New Records in Warsaw. Documents are grouped by archival collection. Four indexes are included: 1) geographical/ethnic; 2) name; 3) subject; and 4) organization/office/institution/company/press. [Z. Kantorosinski]

1066 Latin America in the 1940s: war and postwar transitions. Edited by David Rock. Berkeley: Univ. of California Press, 1994. 302 p.: bibl., index.

Important collection of thoughtful essays focuses on political-economic history of Latin America within international framework of World War II and onset of the Cold War. Gives much attention to labor politics, populism and democratization, and economic policies.

1067 Latin America since 1930: economy, society, and politics. pt. 2, Politics and society. Edited by Leslie Bethell. Cambridge, England; New York: Cambridge Univ. Press, 1994. 1 v.: bibl., index. (The Cambridge history of Latin America; 6, pt. 2)

This installment of the *Cambridge History of Latin America* series presents nine well-informed, interpretive studies on the following topics: State organization, democracy, the Left, the military, the urban labor movement, rural mobilization, women, and religion. Each study is accompanied by a wide-ranging, annotated bibliographical essay.

1068 Lavrin, Asunción. Unfolding feminism: Spanish-American women's writing, 1970–1990. (*in* Feminisms in the academy. Ann Arbor: Univ. of Michigan Press, 1995, p. 248–273, bibl.)

This conceptually sophisticated essay covers a challenging period in women's history. Lavrin examines the *machismo-marianismo* dyad and patriarchal theory. She also discusses specific movements, including Argentina's Madres de la Plaza de Mayo. Last section analyzes individual writers such as

Chilean Julieta Kirkwood and use of testimonial texts or *protagonismo.*

Mateo Avilés, Elías de. La emigración andaluza a América, 1850–1936. See item **1028.**

1069 Mestre Vives, Tomás. Los apóstatas del "Destino Manifiesto": viaje de ida y vuelta. (*Razón Fe,* 226 : 1127/1128, sept./oct. 1992, p. 147–158, bibl.)

"Think piece" on travails of the left in 1980s Latin America includes commentary on Nicaragua, Cuba, and Mexico.

1070 Müller, Jürgen. Nationalsozialismus in Lateinamerika: die Auslandsorganisation der NSDAP in Argentinien, Brasilien, Chile und Mexiko, 1931–1945. Stuttgart, Germany: Heinz, 1997. 566 p.: bibl. (Historamericana; 3)

Well-documented, comprehensive study of activity of foreign branch of Hitler's National Socialist Party in Latin America. Drawing on extensive research in German and Latin American archives, author examines and compares origins, development, membership, propaganda, and influence of this organization in the various nations. Emphasizes differences between German diplomats and party leaders over political actions, exertion of influence, and ideological proselytizing in Latin American German communities. [H.M. Meding]

Núñez Seixas, Xosé M. Actitudes del nacionalismo gallego frente al problema de la emigración gallega a América, 1856–1936. See item **1030.**

1071 O'Brien, Thomas F. The revolutionary mission: American enterprise in Latin America, 1900–1945. New York: Cambridge Univ. Press, 1996. 356 p.: bibl., ill., index. (Cambridge Latin American studies; 81)

Excellent study examines impact of US corporate enterprises—especially their cultural values—on Latin American society at level of both elites and lower-class peasants and workers. Especially provocative combination of economic, cultural, and international history provides penetrating insights into interaction of multinational corporations with frequently exploited, sometimes resistant, native communities. Case studies in Central America, Peru, Chile, Cuba, and Mexico draw heavily from records of US corporations.

1072 Olmos Sánchez, Isabel. América y el exilio español republicano. (*An. Hist. Contemp.*, 8, 1990/91, p. 131–147)

Well-organized work studies efforts to settle refugees from the Spanish Republic in Latin America. Author concentrates on ideological and institutional rivalries within the left that often made this process difficult. Based on published monographs and some archival research.

Pereira Castañares, Juan Carlos. España e Iberoamérica: un siglo de relaciones, 1836–1936. See item **1033.**

1073 Piel, Jean. Vingt ans d'histoire contemporaine de l'Amérique Latine en France: 1968–1987. (*Cah. Am. lat.*, 9, 1990, p. 111–130)

Overview of French historical studies on Latin America covers institutions, graduate research, and historiographical trends in scholarly research and published works.

1074 Pike, Fredrick B. FDR's Good Neighbor Policy: sixty years of generally gentle chaos. Austin: Univ. of Texas Press, 1995. 394 p.: bibl., ill., index.

Exploration of sources, conceptualizations, and implementation of the Good Neighbor Policy is a tour de force by a veteran Latin American historian. Although Roosevelt is the central figure in his study, Pike incorporates evidence from popular culture, high culture, diplomacy, politics, and ideology from several Western Hemisphere nations to provide a sweeping analysis of essence of the Good Neighbor Policy and its relevance to last years of the 20th century. The 14-p. preface contains a valuable autobiographical sketch by the author.

Richmond, Douglas W. Comparative elite systems in Latin America and the United States, 1870–1914. See item **1035.**

1075 Rinke, Stefan H. "Der letzte freie Kontinent": deutsche Lateinamerikapolitik im Zeichen transnationaler Beziehungen, 1918–1933. Stuttgart: Heinz, 1996. 2 v.: bibl., ill., index. (Historamericana; 1)

Well-researched, extensively documented examination of German diplomatic, economic, and cultural relations with Latin America based on unexploited archival material (1918–33). Concludes that Weimar Republic's Latin American foreign policy, recognizing US hegemony, was cautious and motivated primarily by economic interests. Therefore, Germans, being neither centrally directed nor well coordinated, relied on private initiative and propagandized functional elites of ethnic German communities to facilitate capital investment and retention of Latin American countries as source of raw materials and markets. After 1933, author observes, anti-Weimar sentiment and cultural propaganda aided Nazi influence. [C.K. Converse]

1076 Rock, David. War and postwar intersections. (*in* Latin America in the 1940s: war and postwar transitions. Edited by David Rock. Berkeley: Univ. of California Press, 1994, p. 15–40)

Rock provides effective set of generalizations on shifting relationships between US and Latin America from World War II to early Cold War, and also devotes considerable attention to political and economic issues within Latin American nations.

1077 Rolland, Denis. Les perceptions de la France en Amérique latine: structures et évolution, 1918–1945. (*Mélanges/Paris*, 28:3, 1992, p. 161–189)

Study in cultural history traces decline of France's influence in 20th-century Latin America in the intellectual, educational, and technological realms, a process that culminated during World War II when the Vichy regime was perceived as betraying the heritage of 1789. [A. Pérotin-Dumon]

1078 Skidmore, Thomas E. and **Peter H. Smith.** Modern Latin America. 3rd ed. New York: Oxford Univ. Press, 1992. 449 p.: bibl., ill., index, maps.

Authors focus on economic and political factors in history of individual nations and of region as a whole. Most of this sophisticated text consists of chapters on individual countries covering period from 1880s to early 1990s.

1079 Stemplowski, Ryszard. Towards comparative history of Eastern Europe and Latin America, 20th century. (*Estud. Latinoam./Poland*, 14:1, 1992, p. 15–22)

General and largely theoretical work examines a potentially important topic.

Vázquez Franco, Guillermo and **Juan Manuel Casal.** Historia política y social de Iberoamérica: investigaciones y ensayos. See item **1044.**

MEXICO
General and Colonial Period

ASUNCION LAVRIN, *Professor of History, Arizona State University at Tempe*
EDITH B. COUTURIER, *National Endowment for the Humanities*

SINCE THE MID 1970s, when the Archivo General de la Nación, under the direction of Alejandra Moreno Toscano, began a systematic recovery of local and provincial archives, the publication of guides to collections or documentary sources has become increasingly important in Mexico. Thus, we can point to the significant number of such materials reviewed this biennium as the expression of a trend that has reached full maturity. It is also worth noting that the proceedings of several international and regional conferences on Mexican history have been published, allowing scholars to assess the new crop of revisionist works usually presented at these events (items **1136, 1091,** and **1092**).

Regional history, a trend that began taking shape during the last decade, is now, with the arrival of the late 1990s, well-grounded in the field. In this volume, we note the predominance of studies on western Mexico, especially Jalisco and Michoacán, and also the appearance of Chiapas as a subject of local history, possibly a result of its current political notoriety (items **1126, 1199, 1250,** and **1129**). The strength of central Mexican historiography has not diminished, but it is now better matched by work on other regions. Complementary to this trend are the microstudies of several towns; one of the best reviewed here is Juan Carlos Garavaglia and Juan Carlos Grosso's monograph on Tepeaca (item **1150**).

Colonial historians are not exploring the multiple meanings of popular and elite religion to the extent that would be desirable to match similar developments in early modern European history. We do, however, have some serious works on the historical mystique of the Virgin of Guadalupe and her worship that may trigger more critical readings of religion as culture and as history (items **1214** and **1202**). The study of Church credit is the other topic that seems to be gathering momentum, especially among economic historians. An international conference organized by Gisela von Wobeser and UNAM's Instituto de Investigaciones Históricas in 1994 will stimulate this subject and connect it with ongoing research on the 19th century. Two works are particularly deserving of mention: one is the first thorough study of 16th-century credit (not exclusively ecclesiastic) by Martínez (item **1187**) and the other is a synthesis of 18th-century credit by von Wobeser (item **1253**).

Some important contributions to social history were made this biennium. The heterodox nature of this branch of history foils any attempt at classification. Suffice it to say that an interdisciplinary methodology makes some of these works significant, while the strength of others derives from an astute use of the sources to extract information on people's daily lives, attitudes, and group mentality, as well as to determine the influence of State and religious policies on personal behavior. The studies by Alberro, Boyer, Calvo, Cope, González Muñoz, Pescador, Stern, and Patch shed light on the special dimensions of acculturation, gender and race relations; family structure, strategies, and networks; and the dialogue of power between elite and non-elite groups. Elinor Melville's work on sheep is an innovative venture into environmental history (item **1191**). We would also like to highlight the latest work by the indefatigable Woodrow W. Borah on price trends of royal tribute, a remarkable synthesis in the field of economic history (item **1124**), and the study by Richard Garner of economic growth in Bourbon Mexico (see *HLAS 54:1159*).

Other topics that drew our attention were demographic surveys and their connection with family formation (items **1104** and **1160**) and the study of elite local groups (items **1173**), among which that of González Muñoz merits special mention (item **1158**). Also important are revisionist visitations to late-colonial institutions (item **1171**). The reissue of works by two notable historians, Jean-Pierre Berthe and Silvio Zavala, pays due homage to their sustained labors in colonial historiography (see item **1122** and *HLAS 54:1195*).

In 1995 Mexicans observed the tricentennial of the death of Sor Juana Inés de la Cruz; several conferences commemorated this event. Their proceedings will broaden the corpus of works on the poet and the culture of her century, as well as on female convent life (items **1236** and **1134**).

For the northern regions, two significant works reviewed here concern the California missions and native populations; Crosby focuses on the 18th century (item **1262**) and Phillip on the 19th (item **1275**). Questions raised by the Quincentenary of the encounter continue to influence the most analytical research on the north, which explains, evaluates, and sometimes condemns the missionary enterprise (items **1259, 1265, 1269, 1280, 1282,** and **3229**). Research on the non-missionary populations would be welcome in the future.

In order to better serve our readers, the colonial portion of this chapter has been reorganized into two subsections instead of the previous three. As of *HLAS 56*, colonial Mexican materials will be subdivided as follows: 1) General, Central, and South; and 2) North and Borderlands.

We acknowledge the assistance of José Maldonado, doctoral candidate at Arizona State University, in the review of materials for this section. Works reviewed by him are identified by his initials.

GENERAL

1080 Aguilar Camín, Héctor. Subversiones silenciosas: ensayos de historia y política de México. México: Aguilar, 1993. 215 p.: bibl. (Nuevo siglo)

Interpretation of Mexico's history by a well-known essayist is of interest to specialists. This collection of essays measures the impact of history on the mind of a much-read and popular author of contemporary Mexico. Of interest to historians of culture. [AL]

1081 Alonso Gutiérrez, José Félix; Silvia Ávila Flores; and **José Villalbazo Reyes.** Guía del fondo Convento de Jesús María. México: Secretaría de Salud, Oficialía Mayor, Unidad de Información y Documentación Institucional, 1989. vii, 143 leaves: bibl. (Serie Guías/Unidad de Información y Documentación Institucional; 14)

Very useful guide to the rich archives of the Convent of Jesús María, which has the most complete collection of account books among the nunneries of the capital. Materials range from the late 16th- to the mid-19th centuries. [AL]

1082 Alvarado Gómez, Armando *et al.* La participación del Estado en la vida económica y social mexicana, 1767–1910. Prólogo de Cuauhtémoc Velasco Avila. México: Instituto Nacional de Antropología e Historia, 1993. 472 p.: bibl., ill. (Col. científica; 273. Serie Historia)

Collection of nine essays deal with the intervention of the State in the design of policies on key social, legal, and economic issues from 1763–1910. Largely pithy and informative, but lacks overarching interpretation or unifying conclusion. [AL]

1083 Archivo General de la Nación (México): guía general. Coordinación general de Juan Manuel Herrera Huerta y Victoria San Vicente Tello. México: Secretaría de Gobernación, 1990. 525 p.: bibl., ill., index, maps.

General guide to all the collections in the Mexican National Archives. Brief descriptions of each section give information on general context of the series, sections, and detailed guides to the collections. Well-printed and illustrated, this guide is an excellent introduction to the resources of one of the best archives in the Americas. [AL]

ARGENA II. See item **1.**

1084 Beltrán Bernal, Trinidad and **Elvia Montes de Oca Navas.** Bibliografía histórica del Estado de México. v. 1–2. Toluca de Lerdo, Mexico: Colegio Mexiquense, 1989–1990. 2 v.: bibl., index.

Excellent annotated bibliography of the state of Mexico covers its history since precolumbian times. Citations are organized chronologically and thematically, including a variety of themes such as land tenure, literature, statistics, history, mining, and education. Cites the libraries where the works are found. [AL]

1085 Biosca Sáiz, Dolores *et al.* Tabasco en Chiapas: documentos para la historia tabasqueña en el Archivo Diocesano de San Cristóbal de Las Casas. Coordinación de Mario Humberto Ruz. México: Univ. Nacional Autónoma de México, Instituto de Investigaciones Filológicas, Centro de Estudios Mayas, 1994. 158 p.: bibl., ill., index. (Cuaderno; 23)

Guide to Tabascan documents in the diocesan archive of San Cristóbal de las Casas, primarily its "Civil section" and documents on the late 19th century. Most of the documents deal with ecclesiastical affairs. Sources are rich in socioeconomic data. [AL]

1086 Boletín de Fuentes para la Historia Económica de México. 1990–1992. México: Centro de Estudios Históricos, El Colegio de México.

Publication of economic essays in a short series designed to acquaint historians with numerous archival sources for economic history. The *Boletín* was not designed to become a permanent journal and published less than ten numbers between 1990–92. Articles by well-known historians are informative and very useful guides to resources. [AL]

1087 Caldera Robles, Manuel *et al.* Capítulos de historia de la ciudad de Guadalajara. Coordinación de Lina Rendón García.

Guadalajara, Mexico: Ayuntamiento de Guadalajara, 1992. 2 v.: bibl., ill., maps. (Col. Guadalajara 450 años; 14–15)

Eighteen essays on the history of the city of Guadalajara from its foundation to the 20th century. Covers a variety of topics such as labor, education, female workers, the Church, and water usage. Rich source of urban history. [AL]

1088 Colegio Mexiquense. Temas de historia mexiquense. Coordinación de María Teresa Jarquín O. Toluca de Lerdo, Mexico: El Colegio Mexiquense; H. Ayuntamiento de Toluca, 1988. 290 p.: bibl.

Collection of essays on history of the state of Mexico demonstrates diversity of themes under research and study in the late 1980s. [AL]

1089 Coloquio de Antropología e Historia Regionales, *12th, Zamora, Mexico, 1990.* Herencia española en la cultura material de las regiones de México: casa, vestido y sustento. Edición de Rafael Diego-Fernández Sotelo. México: El Colegio de Michoacán, 1993. 541 p.: bibl., ill. (Col. Memorias)

Papers include many works based on original documentation, some of which have already been published in slightly different form. A summary of topics and research on material culture, with special emphasis on the colonial period, provides a vision of the topic and illustrates various methods of describing and analyzing this theme. [EBC]

1090 Compañía Real del Monte y Pachuca. Archivo Histórico. Guía general del Archivo Histórico de la Compañía de Minas de Real del Monte y Pachuca. Coordinación general de Belem Oviedo Gámez. México: Archivo General de la Nación; Pachuca, Mexico: AHCRMyP, 1993. 223 p.: bibl., ill.

Guide to one of the richest archival collections on Spanish American mining. Comprises public and private documents from the 18th century to the 1980s, and all activities connected to these well-known mines: labor and personnel, union administration, taxation, engineering works, etc. [AL]

1091 Conference of Mexican and United States Historians, *6th, Chicago, 1981.* Los intelectuales y el poder en México = Intellectuals and power in Mexico: memorias de la VI Conferencia de Historiadores Mexicanos y Estadounidenses = papers presented at the VI Conference of Mexican and United States Historians. Edited by Roderic Ai Camp, Charles A. Hale, and Josefina Zoraida Vázquez. México: El Colegio de México; Los Angeles: UCLA Latin American Center Publications, Univ. of California, Los Angeles, 1991. 841 p.: bibl. (UCLA Latin American studies; 75)

Belated but still welcome publication of valuable papers from a 1981 conference. The theme, "Intellectuals and the State," receives particular emphasis in papers exploring the 20th century. [EBC]

1092 Conference of Mexican and United States Historians, 7th, Oaxaca, Mexico, 1985. La ciudad y el campo en la historia de México: memoria. Edición de Ricardo Sánchez, Eric Van Young y Gisela von Wobeser. México: Univ. Nacional Autónomo de México, Instituto de Investigaciones Históricas, 1992. 2 v.: bibl., ill., maps.

Selected conference papers on city and countryside are divided into following categories: precolumbian societies; politics of center and periphery; politics in urban society; city and countryside; frontier society; industrialization problems; and intellectual life, education, and art. This "must read" for Mexicanists is nicely edited by Ricardo Sánchez, Eric Van Young, and Gisela von Wobeser.

Cortina Portilla, Manuel. Algo de lo nuestro. See item **89.**

Cortina Portilla, Manuel. Sucedió en el valle. See item **90.**

1093 Entre lagos y volcanes: Chalco Amecameca, pasado y presente. v. 1–2. Coordinación de Alejandro Tortolero. Zinacantepec, Mexico: Colegio Méxiquense; Chalco de Díaz Covarrubias; H. Ayuntamiento Constitucional Chalco, 1993. 2 v.: bibl., ill., maps.

Commendable effort to collect a series of studies on the history of Chalco. Based on archival research, Vol. 1 highlights demographic, economic, and social topics of the area from the precolumbian period to the present in 16 essays. Vol. 2 contains a broad interdisciplinary bibliography. [AL]

Estadísticas históricas de México. See *HLAS* 55:23.

1094 Las formas y las políticas del dominio agrario: homenaje a François Chevalier. Coordinación de Ricardo Palafox Avila,

Carlos R. Martínez Assad y Jean A. Meyer. Guadalajara, Mexico: Editorial Univ. de Guadalajara, 1992. 319 p.: bibl. (Col. Fundamentos. Serie Laboratorio de Antropología)

Papers from a 1990 conference emphasize the 19th and 20th centuries in this *homenaje* to Chevalier. Papers tend to be cumulative rather than based on extensive new research. Some major themes first articulated by Chevalier can be found here as research has proceeded over the last 40 years. [EBC]

1095 Garritz, Amaya. Guía del Archivo Moctezuma-Miravalle. México: Univ. Nacional Autónoma de México, 1993. 169 p.: indexes.

Guide to the archive of two leading Mexican aristocratic families contains material from 1588–1905. Includes capsule biographies, thematic organization, detailed index, and a wealth of information about Mexico. Exceptionally informative guide to a valuable collection of documents that can be found in the archives of the City of Mexico. [EBC]

1096 Hernández Chávez, Alicia. Anenecuilco: memoria y vida de un pueblo. México: El Colegio de México, 1991. 261 p.: maps, plates.

Reconstruction of the history of Anenecuilco based on collection of the town's "primordial" or founding documents. Historian Hernández Chávez aptly uses this collection to make a case for the formation of a collective memory. [AL]

1097 Herrera Pérez, Octavio. Del señorío a la posrevolución: evolución histórica de una hacienda en el noreste de México; el caso de La Sauteña. (*Hist. Mex.,* 43:1, julio/sept. 1993, p. 5–49)

"Biography" of a rural estate in the former province of Nuevo Santander (now the northeastern state of Tamaulipas) illustrates conflicts created by desire for profit and modernization, the government's tax policies, and social revindications pursued by the Mexican revolution and the agrarian revolution. [AL]

Historical Text Archive: Latin America and Mexico. See item **37.**

1098 Historiografía española y norteamericana sobre México: coloquios de análisis historiográfico. Introducción, edición e índice por Alvaro Matute. México: Univ. Nacional Autónoma de México, Instituto de Investigaciones Históricas, 1992. 260 p.: bibl., index. (Serie Historia moderna y contemporánea; 24)

Interesting series of essays by Mexican historians about Spanish and US writers' and historians' visions of Mexican history. Organized largely around great writers and significant figures and events in Mexican history, work tends to neglect historical examinations of daily events. Nevertheless, provides a valuable entry point for interpreting Mexican history. Covers Gaos, Iglesias, Zamacois, Turner, visions of Zapata, 1847 war, etc. Variable quality. [EBC]

1099 Kollokvium istorikov SSSR i Meksiki, 1st, Moscow, 1988. I kollokvium istorikov SSSR i Meksiki [1st Colloquim of Soviet and Mexican Historians]. Redaktsionnaia kollegiia E.A. Larin *et al.* Moskva: Akademiia nauk SSSR, In-t vseobshchei istorii, 1990. 203 p.: bibl.

Published by the Institute of World History of the Soviet Academy of Sciences, these substantive scholarly papers were first presented at a gathering of historians in Moscow in Sept. 1988. They address questions of Soviet and Mexican historiography, focusing particularly on Latin American history and comparative approaches to Russian and Latin American historical developments. Thirteen papers are in Russian and six in Spanish. Topics include the problem of periodization in historical studies; Soviet study of Latin America, 1960s-80s; and especially Latin American revolutions and wars of independence, including Russia's role. The final paper, in Spanish, is an overview of bibliographies and documents in the Centro de Estudios de Historia de México Condumex. Designed to stimulate further research, the collection uses Russian and Western references. [B. Dash]

1100 Lenz, Hans. Historia del papel en México y cosas relacionadas, 1525–1950. México: M.A. Porrúa, 1990. 798 p.: bibl., ill. (some col.), index.

Surveys history of paper production in Mexico, a rarely discussed industry. Although technical, it furnishes data on labor and entrepreneurs and includes numerous illustrations. [AL]

1101 Limpiar y obedecer: la basura, el agua y la muerte en la Puebla de los Angeles, 1650–1925. Coordinación de Rosalva Loreto y Francisco J. Cervantes B. Puebla, Mexico: Claves Latinoamericanas, 1994. 288 p.: graphs, maps, tables.

Highly recommended, attractive collection of six essays on urban problems such as distribution of water, garbage collection and disposal, and public health policies. Carefully researched, this book opens new paths in the history of public health by noting changing cultural attitudes about sanitation and tracing the State's changing role regarding sanitary control. [EBC]

1102 MacLachlan, Colin M. and **William H. Beezley.** El Gran Pueblo: a history of greater Mexico. Englewood Cliffs, N.J.: Prentice Hall, 1994. 496 p.: bibl., ill., index, photos, maps.

Latest general history of Mexico in the 19th and 20th centuries up to the 1988 election. Although politics is emphasized, economic and social issues are not neglected. Special attention is given to problems in US border towns. Photographs in this book offer an important subtext message on Mexicans in Texas. Recommended for classroom use. [AL]

1103 Martínez Salazar, Angel and **Koldo San Sebastián.** Los vascos en México: estudio biográfico, histórico y bibliográfico. Vitoria, Spain: Gobierno Vasco, Lehendakaritza, 1992? 434 p., 16 p. of plates: bibl., ill., map.

Biographical dictionary of prominent Basque immigrants to Mexico from the 16th to 20th centuries. Useful reference. [AL]

Matos Moctezuma, Eduardo. Arqueología urbana en el centro de la Ciudad de México. See *HLAS 55:322.*

1104 McCaa, Robert. Women's position, family and fertility decline in Parral, Mexico, 1777–1930. (*in* Congreso de Historia Regional Comparada, *1st, México, 1989.* Actas. Ciudad Juárez, Mexico: Univ. Autónoma de Ciudad Juárez, 1990, p. 205–218, tables)

Author correlates family formation patterns and fertility in Parral for 160 years and concludes that beginning in the late 18th century the position of women underwent a significant deterioration accompanied by an increase in illegitimate birth. [AL]

1105 Muriá, José María *et al.* San Blas de Nayarit. Zapopan, Mexico: Colegio de Jalisco, 1993. 112 p.: bibl.

Papers from a 1992 conference on the history of San Blas examine Guadalajara's port from the perspective of the history of western Mexico and view its chronology in relation to events in the north and south. Good example of local history. [EBC]

1106 Nickel, Herbert J. Relaciones de trabajo en las haciendas de Puebla y Tlaxcala, 1740–1914: cuatro análisis sobre recluta-miento, peonaje, y remuneración. México: Univ. Iberoamericana, Depto. de Historia, 1987. 207 p.: bibl., ill.

This work contains four previously published essays, not easily available to Span-ish-speaking students. Nickel's well-docu-mented monographs are models of research on local labor conditions. [AL]

1107 Ortega y Medina, Juan Antonio. Re-flexiones históricas. Presentación de Eugenia Meyer. México: Consejo Nacional para la Cultura y las Artes, 1993. 357 p.: bibl. (Cien de México)

Posthumous collection of essays by historian Ortega y Medina (1913–92) is of his-toriographical interest. [AL]

1108 Pagaza García, Rafael; Teresa Rogerio Buendía and **Sofía Brito Ocampo.** Las obras de consulta mexicanas, siglos XVI al XX. México: Univ. Nacional Autónoma de México, 1990. 228 p., 190 p. of plates: bibl., ill. (Monografías/Centro Universitario de In-vestigaciones Bibliotecológicas; 12)

Catalog and history of reference works published in Mexico throughout its history. Of obvious interest to librarians, this work should be of use to cultural historians also. [AL]

Pérez-Rocha, Emma and **Gabriel Moedano.** Aportaciones a la investigación de archivos del México colonial y a la bibliohemerografía afromexicanista. See item **1209.**

1109 Prestar y pedir prestado: relaciones so-ciales y crédito en México del siglo XVI al XX. Coordinación de Marie-Nöelle Chamoux *et al.* México: Centro de Investiga-ciones y Estudios Superiores en Antropología Social; Centro de Estudios Mexicanos y Cen-troamericanos, 1993. 248 p.: bibl., ill., maps.

These 15 essays on credit policies and practices resulted from a conference in Paris in 1990. The work is divided into three sec-tions: the colonial period, the 19th century

and the 20th century. Gathers essays from well-established as well as younger histori-ans. Emphasizes case studies for the first two sections and general essays for the contempo-rary period. An anthropological emphasis gives this collection a special and important character. The essays indicate that since the 16th century, sophisticated and complex mechanisms of credit have been in place, sus-tained by key social networks still operative in contemporary Mexico. [AL]

1110 Rituals of rule, rituals of resistance: public celebrations and popular culture in Mexico. Edited by William H. Beezley, Cheryl English Martin, and William E. French. Wilmington, Del.: SR Books, 1994. 374 p.: bibl., ill. (Latin American silhouettes)

Valuable compilation of recent re-search on *mentalités* and popular culture be-tween the 18th-20th centuries considers im-pact of power and politics on festivals, ceremonies, confraternities, education, beau-tification of cities, and the rise of national celebrations. [EBC]

1111 Ruz, Mario Humberto. Savia india, floración ladina: apuntes para una his-toria de las fincas comitecas, siglos XVIII y XIX. México: Consejo Nacional para la Cul-tura y las Artes, 1992. 415 p.: bibl., ill. (Re-giones)

Study of controversial relations be-tween the Dominican Order as a property-owner and local indigenous landowners and laborers over resources in the region of Los Llanos, Chiapas. Although not a polished re-search work, it is based on archival data and helps to fill the historical void on small In-dian communities.

1112 Saucedo Zarco, Carmen. El Archivo Histórico Judicial de la Ciudad de Mé-xico. (*Anu. Estud. Am.*, 50:2, 1993, p. 413–420)

Brief but useful survey of holdings and present physical conditions of the judiciary archives in Mexico City. Only minimally catalogued and hardly used, this repository remains an important source of social history and judiciary procedures. [AL]

1113 Universidad Autónoma Benito Juárez de Oaxaca (Mexico). Biblioteca. La imagen y la palabra: libros del fondo biblio-gráfico de la Universidad Autónoma Benito Juárez de Oaxaca, octubre-diciembre de 1993.

Oaxaca, Mexico?: Museo de Arte Contemporáneo de Oaxaca, 1993? 64 p.: bibl., ill.

Useful guide to the rare book collection at the Univ. of Oaxaca. Although this is an incomplete guide that only suggests the wealth of the collection, it calls the attention of bibliophiles and scholars to a rich and relatively unknown source of colonial imprints. [AL]

1114 Vivir en Guadalajara: la ciudad y sus funciones. Coordinación de Carmen Castañeda García. Guadalajara, Mexico: Ayuntamiento de Guadalajara, 1992. 398 p.: bibl., ill. (Col. Guadalajara 450 años; 11)

Collection of 20 essays on the urban history of Guadalajara. Thematically grouped, they focus largely on 19th- and 20th-century history. These essays aspire to catch nuances of daily life, as well as larger issues of political and economic history. Of special interest are sections on women in the labor market and the politics of religion. [AL]

COLONIAL
General, Central, and South

1115 Abadie-Aicardi, Aníbal. La tradición institucional salmantina en los Libros de Claustros de la Universidad de México del Renacimiento a la Ilustración y la Independencia, 1551–1821. (*Jahrb. Gesch.*, 29, 1992, p. 1–46)

Uses minutes of university faculty meetings to study how traditional jurisprudence becomes institutionalized. [JM]

1116 Agila, Yves. Monnaie et société en Nouvelle Espagne. (*Bull. hisp./Bordeaux*, 95:1, jan./juin 1993, p. 5–27, tables)

Surveys differing opinions on the currency crisis in New Spain including the ill effects of adulterated coins, thus revealing political connotations in the perception of this issue. [AL]

1117 Alberro, Solange. Del gachupín al criollo: o de cómo los españoles de México dejaron de serlo. México: Colegio de México, Centro de Estudios Históricos, 1992. 234 p.: bibl. (Jornadas; 122)

Author investigates the many ways peninsular Spaniards began to adopt "native" habits and adapt to the cultural environment of the New World. Indigenous religious, culinary, and sexual practices affected the Spaniards, while the natives' world was also

changed under Spanish colonial rule. Alberro makes use of daily life incidents to explore acculturation in an amusing and clever work. [AL]

Alonso Gutiérrez, José Félix; Silvia Ávila Flores; and José Villalbazo Reyes. Guía del fondo Convento de Jesús María. See item **1081.**

1118 Aranda Romero, José Luis and **Agustín Grajales Porras.** Niños expósitos de la parroquia del Sarario de la ciudad de Puebla, México, a mediados del siglo XVIII. (*Anu. IEHS*, 6, 1991, p. 171–180, tables)

Good study of illegitimacy rates and child abandonment in the central dioceses of Puebla. Out-of-wedlock birth rates were high, but abandonment was unusual.

1119 Archivo General de la Nación (Mexico). Fundación de pueblos, t. 3542. Los cimarrones de Mazateopan. Edición de Fernando Winfield Capitaine. Xalapa, Mexico: Gobierno del Estado de Veracruz-Llave, 1992. 318 p.: bibl., ill., maps.

First complete printing of the archival documents related to the foundation of Guadalupe de Amapa, a town of run-away slaves. Documents are from 1767–70. Useful tool for interested researchers. [AL]

1120 Archivo Histórico de la Ciudad de Veracruz (Mexico). Catálogo de documentos coloniales, 1608–1810. Recopilación de Margarita de la Cruz del Angel et al. Veracruz, Mexico: H. Ayuntamiento de Veracruz, Archivo Histórico de la Ciudad de Veracruz; México: Secretaría de Gobernación, Archivo General de la Nación, 1993. 413 p.: ill., indexes.

Guide to the municipal archives of the first city of New Spain. Covers period between 1608–1810 in 114 volumes. Geographical, onomastic, and chronological indexes help researchers locate materials. [AL]

Bechtloff, Dagmar. La formación de una sociedad intercultural: las cofradías en el Michoacán colonial. See item **392.**

1121 Benítez, Fernando et al. El Galeón del Pacífico: Acapulco-Manila, 1565–1815. Guerrero, Mexico: Gobierno Constitucional del Estado de Guerrero, 1992. 253 p.: bibl., ill. (some col.), index, maps. (Biblioteca del sur)

Collection of essays by distinguished historians covers economic and cultural influences of the trans-Pacific trade. Pirates, coins, art, and maps are among themes reviewed. Beautifully illustrated. [AL]

1122 Berthe, Jean-Pierre. Estudios de historia de la Nueva España: de Sevilla a Manila. Mexico: Univ. de Guadalajara; Centre d'études mexicaines e centraméricaines, 1994. 318 p.: bibl., map. (Col. de documentos para la historia de Jalisco; 3)

A collection of 16 articles by well-known French historian previously published between 1956–92, mostly in French. Meticulous attention to detail and an interest in economic history has been his trademark. Useful for Spanish-speaking students of Mexican history. [AL]

1123 Boils Morales, Guillermo. Arquitectura y sociedad en Querétaro, siglo XVIII. México: Instituto de Investigaciones Sociales; Archivo Histórico del Estado, 1994. 225 p.: bibl., ill.

Containing large numbers of plans and photographs, and based on primary sources of art history, book chronicles the florescence of religious and civil architecture in relation to the spatial organization of the city. Includes information on both the builders and the planners. [EBC]

1124 Borah, Woodrow Wilson. Price trends of royal tribute commodities in Nueva Galicia, 1557–1598. Berkeley: Univ. of California Press, 1992. 265 p.: bibl., ill., index, map. (University of California publications. Ibero-Americana; 55)

Preceded by an erudite study of methodological problems, this useful work describes pricing of agricultural commodities in New Galicia in the second half of the 16th-century. Provides modern techniques for assessing prices and itemizes each product in separate sections. Buyers are profiled separately. Establishes differences between the Audiencias of Mexico and Guadalajara in market, production, and price patterns. [AL]

1125 Boyer, Richard E. Lives of the bigamists: marriage, family, and community in colonial Mexico. Albuquerque: Univ. of New Mexico Press, 1995. 340 p.: bibl., ill., index, map.

Intensive investigation into Inquisition records yields detailed life stories of a small number of plebian men and women and major life cycle events of about 200 others. Produces extensive insights into relationships between Inquisition and local communities, family histories, and religious beliefs. [EBC]

1126 Brading, David A. Church and State in Bourbon Mexico: the Diocese of Michoacán, 1749–1810. Cambridge; New York: Cambridge Univ. Press, 1994. 300 p.: bibl., index.

Collection of essays on the late 18th-century Church begins with the expulsion of the Jesuits and covers: 1) the secularization process; 2) special groups within the Church such as priests, nuns, confraternities; and 3) the cathedral canon and its relations with the Valladolid bishops. Especially interesting are chapters dedicated to devotional practice and popular religion. This well-crafted work ably renders a picture of the Church in a provincial setting. [AL]

1127 Bretos, Miguel A. La provincia de San Joseph de Yucatán: conversión y arquitectura religiosa en el país de los Mayas. (*Arch. Ibero-Am.*, 53:209/212, enero/dic. 1993, p. 67–104)

Study of Spanish church architecture and its architects in the Yucatán. [R. Haskett]

1128 Bustamante García, Jesús. Fray Bernardino de Sahagún: una revisión crítica de los manuscritos y de su proceso de composición. México: Univ. Nacional Autónoma de México, Instituto de Investigaciones Bibliográficas, Biblioteca Nacional [y] Hemeroteca Nacional, 1990. 516 p.: bibl.

Critical revision of Sahagún's writings. Follows the process of both writing and printing the works, and their idiosyncratic value in Sahagún's copious production. Excellent study with meticulous bibliographical work. [AL]

1129 Calvo, Thomas. Guadalajara y su región en el siglo XVII: población y economía. Guadalajara, Mexico: Centro de Estudios Mexicanos y Centroamericanos; H. Ayuntamiento de Guadalajara, 1992. 489 p.: bibl., graphs, ill., maps, tables. (Col. Guadalajara 450 años; 8)

This volume represents half of the author's doctoral thesis on Guadalajara and its region in the 17th century. A global history in the French tradition, it covers diverse themes: demography, migration and population patterns, family history, labor, agriculture, mining, commerce, title collection, and ecclesiastic credit. Numerous tables and graphs help envision the totality of the data. This monumental portrayal of a region and a period will stand unrivaled for many years. [AL]

1130 Calvo, Thomas et al. Xalisco, la voz de un pueblo en el siglo XVI. México: CIESAS; Centro de Estudios Mexicanos y Centroamericanos, 1993. 213 p.: bibl., map.

Edited translation of fragile, previously unknown Nahuatl documents of 16th-century Jalisco. Text in Nahuatl provided. Documents reflect economic and political struggles of indigenous communities against Spanish authorities, and their relationships with the religious authorities. These are excellent sources for the study of communal resistance and the inner structures of indigenous society. [AL]

1131 Canedo, Lino Gómez. Evangelización, cultura y promoción social: ensayos y estudios críticos sobre la contribución franciscana a los orígenes cristianos de México, siglos XVI-XVIII. Seleccionados y presentados con una extensa noticia bibliográfica de su autor por José Luis Soto Pérez. México: Editorial Porrúa, 1993. xliii, 845 p.: bibl., index, port. (Biblioteca Porrúa; 109)

Forty-three essays on Church history by the late Franciscan historian. Nearly one-fourth deal with general topics of Church history in Spanish America. The rest are divided chronologically and focus on the evangelization of New Spain. This selection enables historians to assess Father Lino's breadth of knowledge and his archival mastery. An appropriate tribute to a dedicated historian of his order and of the Church. [AL]

1132 Carvalho, Alma Margarita. La ilustración del despotismo en Chiapas, 1774–1821. México: Consejo Nacional para la Cultura y las Artes, 1994. 315 p.: bibl., maps. (Regiones)

Competent synthesis of Chiapas in the late 18th century stresses Central American orientation of this province (later to be annexed to Mexico) and the impact of Bourbon reforms on the three dominant socioeconomic groups in the region: the Church, the provincial elites, and the alcaldes mayores. [AL]

1133 Chávez Hayhoe, Arturo. Guadalajara en el siglo XVI. Guadalajara, Mexico: Ayuntamiento de Guadalajara, 1991. 2 v.: bibl., port. (Col. Guadalajara 450 años; 4–5)

Schematic history of Guadalajara in vignettes crafted by a well-known historian. Lack of overall organization makes this a difficult book to consult despite its wealth of information. For interested readers, topics such as slavery, health, hospitals, and the foundation of the city may merit investigation. [AL]

Ciudades mexicanas en la época colonial: exposición temporal, Museo Nacional de Historia, Castillo de Chapultepec. See item **83.**

Coloquio de Antropología e Historia Regionales, 12th, Zamora, Mexico, 1990. Herencia española en la cultura material de las regiones de México: casa, vestido y sustento. See item **1089.**

1134 Coloquio Internacional Sor Juana Inés de la Cruz y el Pensamiento Novohispano, Toluca, Mexico, 1995. Memoria. Toluca, Mexico: Univ. Autónoma del Estado de México; Instituto Mexiquense de Cultura, 1995. 532 p.: bibl., ill. (Biblioteca Sor Juana Inés de la Cruz)

Forty essays on Sor Juana written for a conference hosted by two leading cultural institutions in the state of Mexico. Although largely focusing on literary issues, works on music, archival sources, philosophy, and cinema make this an important interdisciplinary collection worth noting by colonialists. [AL]

1135 Congregaciones de pueblos en el Estado de México. Recopilación de María Teresa Jarquín. Zinacantepec, Mexico: Colegio Mexiquense, 1994. 310 p.: indexes. (Fuentes para la historia del Estado de México; 4)

Selection of documents related to the congregation of Indian towns between 1598–1606 in the present-day state of Mexico. Useful resource for historians. Thematic and onomastic indexes. [AL]

1136 Congreso de Americanistas, 1st, Badajoz, Spain, 1985. Hernán Cortés: hombre de empresa; actas. Valladolid, Spain: Casa-Museo de Colón y Seminario Americanista de la Univ., 1990. 351 p.: bibl., ill. (Bernal, serie americanista; 20)

Late publication of 1985 conference proceedings has a number of papers based on primary materials, but apparently does not reflect other new scholarship. Uneven collection of papers. [EBC]

1137 Cope, R. Douglas. The limits of racial domination: plebeian society in colonial Mexico City, 1660–1720. Madison: Univ. of Wisconsin Press, 1994. 220 p.: bibl., index.

Very good innovative study of life among the urban poor in 17th-century Mexico. Author deals with intricacies of race classification and race relations, material culture, labor recruitment, credit networks, and the 1692 riot in Mexico City. He interprets the latter as a temporary revolt of the non-elite against their "social betters" that produced a sentiment of camaraderie among the many ethnic groups making up plebian society. Strong archival research and easy reading commends this work. [AL]

1138 Cubillo Moreno, Gilda. Los dominios de la plata: el precio del auge, el peso del poder; empresarios y trabajadores en las minas de Pachuca y Zimapán, 1552–1620. México: Instituto Nacional de Antropología e Historia, 1991. 355 p.: bibl., ill., maps. (Col. Divulgación. Serie Historia)

Overview of early history of one of the least studied, but most important, mining *reales.* Concentrates on labor but also utilizes recently available Pachuca archives to inform us about other aspects of the region's economic history. [EBC]

Cummins, Victoria H. Blessed connections: sociological aspects of sainthood in colonial Mexico and Peru. See item **2392.**

1139 Daniel, Douglas A. Tactical factors in the Spanish conquest of the Aztecs. (*Anthropol. Q.,* 65:4, Oct, 1992, p. 187–194)

An examination of the conquest based heavily on Bernal Díaz and, somewhat secondarily, on Sahagún's *General History.* Argues that Spanish tactics, as reconstructed from the sources, were superior to the Aztecs', and that this, more than any technological or psychological factors, gave them victory. [R. Haskett]

1140 Documentalia del sur de Jalisco: siglo XVI. Recopilación de Thomas Hillerkuss. Zapopan, Mexico: Colegio de Jalisco; México: INAH, 1994. 537 p.: bibl., index, maps.

Carefully edited selection of archival materials illuminating social and economic issues of 16th-century Southern Jalisco (present-day Michoacán and Jalisco). Previously unpublished documents deal with boundary staking, official *visitas,* land grants, *encomenderos'* properties, evangelization, and Indian congregations. Good selection useful as training source for graduate students is also of interest to mature historians. [AL]

1141 Documentos para la historia urbana de Querétaro, siglos XVI y XVII: litigio entre los indios de la congregación y el convento de Santa Clara sobre derechos a las aguas con que regaban. Querétaro, Mexico: Archivo Histórico Municipal, 1994. 409 p.

Fifteen documents of important litigation over water rights among the Convent of Santa Clara, the Indians of Querétaro, and several Spanish land owners. A full introduction by José I. Urbiola Permisán contextualizes these sources as a prototype of colonial contestatory practices among typical representatives of colonial society. [AL]

1142 Echenique March, Felipe I. Indice del Ramo de Tierras de la Intendencia de Michoacán. México: Instituto Nacional de Antropología e Historia, 1993. 158 p.: index. (Col. Fuentes. Serie Historia)

Comprises all land titles and litigation for Michoacán based on the holdings of the National Archives of the Nation. There are four thematic indexes: 1) indigenous communities; 2) personal names; 3) town properties and geographical sites; and 4) jurisdictions. Useful to historians studying that area. [AL]

1143 Enciso Rojas, Dolores. La política regalista de Carlos III y el delito de bigamia. (*Estud. Hist. Novohisp.,* 11, 1991, p. 97–118)

Analyzes Charles III's secularization of crimes against the sacrament of marriage. Compares the impact of these changes in Spain and New Spain in the late 18th century. [JM]

1144 Escobar Olmedo, Armando Mauricio. Catálogo de documentos michoacanos en archivos españoles. v. 2. Morelia, Mexico: Univ. Michoacana de San Nicolás de Hidalgo, 1994? 1 v.

Covers documents between 1531–1812 in the Archivo General de Indias and Archivo Histórico Nacional. For vol. 1, see *HLAS 54: 1217.* [AL]

1145 Fernández, Rodolfo. Esclavos de ascendencia negra en Guadalajara en los siglos XVI y XVII. (*Estud. Hist. Novohisp.,* 11, 1991, p. 71–84, tables)

Investigates the role and demographic impact of African slaves in Guadalajara from the 16th-17th centuries. Based on archival sources. [JM]

1146 Fernández, Rodolfo. Latifundios y grupos dominantes en la historia de la provincia de Avalos. México: Instituto Nacional de Antropología e Historia; Editorial Agata, 1994. 192 p.: bibl., index. (Col. científica; 292)

Excellent detailed study of the process of land acquisition and perpetuation of interests in a wealthy agricultural and cattle-raising area. Strong on genealogical information on the dominant families. [AL]

1147 Florescano, Enrique. Memory, myth, and time in Mexico: from the Aztecs to Independence. Translated by Albert G. Bork and Kathryn R. Bork. Austin: Univ. of Texas Press, 1994. 282 p.: bibl., ill., index, map. (Translations from Latin America series)

Translation of *Memoria mexicana* (see *HLAS 52:964*), a well-crafted synthesis of precolumbian and colonial Mexico's historiography. Most useful to graduate students and teachers. [AL]

1148 El fuego de la inobediencia: autonomía y rebelión india en el Obispado de Oaxaca. Coordinación de Héctor Díaz-Polanco. México: CIESAS, 1992. 214 p.: bibl., maps. (Col. Miguel Othón de Mendizábal)

Five papers from a 1991 conference on the 1660–61 rebellion that began in Tehuantepec includes materials on social and economic conditions, ethnography of the Chontal, viewpoints of the two major ethnic protagonists, as well as reproductions of key documents. [EBC]

1149 Fuentes B., María Eugenia and **Virginia Guzmán M.** Guía documental del fondo jesuita. México: Biblioteca Nacional de Antropología e Historia, 1981. xxxv, 165 p.: bibl., indexes. (Cuadernos de la biblioteca. Serie Sección de manuscritos; 5)

Guide to the Jesuit section of the library of the National Museum of Anthropology and History, a rich source of manuscript materials. These papers belonged to the Jesuit Colleges of New Spain prior to the expulsion of the order in 1767. Materials include letters, legal contracts, sales, deeds, property titles, historical accounts, etc. Although poorly printed, this is a good guide to a very important collection. Name index. [AL]

1150 Garavaglia, Juan Carlos and **Juan Carlos Grosso.** Puebla desde una perspectiva microhistórica: la villa de Tepeaca y su entorno agrario; población, producción e intercambio, 1740–1870. México: Editorial Claves Latinoamericanas, 1994. 272 p.: bibl., ill., map.

Another valuable study by two historians who are specialists on this region. Addresses questions such as the rise and fall of population, the significance of increasing commercial ties to Veracruz, and the importance of indigenous production. A surprising result is that nearly half the families examined could be characterized as extended rather than nuclear. Agrarian history of the haciendas indicates that large turnover in land ownership occurred around the middle of the 19th century. [EBC]

1151 García Bernal, Manuela Cristina. Desarrollos indígena y ganadero en Yucatán. (*Hist. Mex.*, 43:3, enero/marzo 1994, p. 373–400, appendix, map, table)

Sustains thesis that since the late 17th century, the expansion of cattle estancias stimulated dispersal of the Indian population in Yucatán. Over time this encouraged changes to labor and property structure, since some estancias eventually changed to haciendas. Based on 1688 population census. For ethnohistorian's comment see item **444.** [AL]

García Moll, Roberto; Felipe R. Solís Olguín; and Jaime Bali. El tesoro de Moctezuma. See *HLAS 55:110.*

1152 Garritz, Amaya. Impresos novohispanos, 1808–1821. Coordinación de Virginia Guedea. Colaboración de Teresa Lozano Armendares. México: Univ. Nacional Autónoma de México, 1990. 2 v. (1347 p.): index. (Serie Bibliográfica/Instituto de Investigaciones Históricas; 9)

Alphabetical catalog of printed materials published in Mexico between 1808–21 and held in national and foreign repositories. Contains 2,911 diverse entries. War-related, administrative, and religious imprints form the bulk of the entries. [AL]

1153 Gerhard, Peter. Síntesis e índice de los mandamientos virreinales, 1548–1553. México: Univ. Nacional Autónoma de México, Instituto de Investigaciones Históricas, 1992. 774 p.: bibl., index, maps. (Serie documental; 21)

Index and annotations to viceregal orders issued under the first viceroy of New Spain, don Antonio de Mendoza, between 1548–53. Work is based on the only surviving records of the orders, two manuscript copies probably created a few years after the orders were issued. The copies, MS Kraus 140 and MS Ayer 1121, are held by the Library of Congress and the Newberry Library respectively. Provides annotations and introductory comments to each geographic section. Excellent guide to early viceregal administration. [AL]

1154 Gerhard, Peter. The southeast frontier of New Spain. Rev. ed. Norman: Univ. of Oklahoma Press, 1993. 219 p.: bibl., index, maps.

Updated bibliography of valuable 1979 work. For annotation of previous edition, see *HLAS 42:2038.*

1155 Gonzalbo Aizpuru, Pilar. Hacia una historia de la vida privada en la Nueva España. (*Hist. Mex.,* 42:2, oct./dic. 1992, p. 353–375, bibl.)

Studies daily activities of the people of New Spain, seeking to develop a profile of the private lives of the general populace. Defines and identifies differences between "public" and "private" lives. Along with secondary sources, cites chronicles of the conquest, diaries, histories, and private correspondence. [JM]

1156 González de la Vara, Martín. El estanco de la nieve. (*Estud. Hist. Novohisp.,* 11, 1991, p. 43–70)

Describes how cities were supplied with ice and evaluates costs to the public and benefits to the Crown of the monopoly. Excellent institutional study. [EBC]

1157 González Echegaray, María del Carmen. El Virrey Revillagigedo y sus orígenes. Santander, Spain: Diputación Regional de Cantabria, 1990. 103 p.: bibl., ill., maps (some col.).

Biography of notable 18th-century viceroy emphasizes Spanish genealogy rather than his professional accomplishments. [AL]

1158 González Muñoz, Victoria. Cabildos y grupos de poder en Yucatán, siglo XVII. Sevilla: Diputación Provincial de Sevilla, 1994. 372 p.: 1 map. (Publicaciones de la Excma. Diputación de Sevilla. Sección Historia. V centenario del descubrimiento de América; 19)

Excellent study of municipalities in Yucatán. Dissects the internal administrative structure and includes pithy biography of the men who ruled the cities. Notes a decline in local autonomy and a great dependence on encomienda and Indian labor. Backed by intensive research, this is a most commendable analytical work. [AL]

1159 González Rodríguez, Jaime. La difusión manuscrita de ideas en Nueva España, siglo XVI. (*Rev. Complut. Hist. Am.,* 18, 1992, p. 89–116, bibl., tables)

Intriguing study of the circulation of manuscripts and their role as venues of ideas in 16th-century New Spain. Focuses on Franciscan manuscripts and hypothesizes that Franciscans circulated manuscript sources among themselves to relieve the pressure of "official" ideas. [AL]

1160 Grajales Porras, Agustín and **José Luis Aranda Romero.** Hijos naturales del Sagrario Angelopolitano a mediados del siglo XVIII. (*in* Coloquio sobre Puebla, *2nd, Puebla, Mexico, 1991.* Memorias. Puebla, Mexico: Gobierno del Estado de Puebla, Comisión Puebla V Centenario, 1992, p. 21–32, tables)

Brief study of the rate of children born to unmarried parents in Puebla's main parish between 1750–59. Useful analytical tables. [AL]

1161 El Gran Michoacán: cuatro informes del obispado de Michoacán, 1759–1769. Preparación y estudio introductorio de Oscar Mazín. Zamora, Mexico: Colegio de Michoacán; Gobierno del Estado de Michoacán, 1986. 457 p.: bibl., maps.

Documentary collection of a series of reports on the dioceses of Michoacán prepared by the priests of 17 *alcaldías* and one *corregimiento.* Useful demographic and economic information for regional history. [AL]

1162 Greenleaf, Richard E. Persistence of native values: the Inquisition and the Indians of colonial Mexico. (*Americas/Francisc.,* 50:3, Jan. 1994, p. 351–376)

Accounts of first confrontations of "idolatrous" Indians and inquisitors of early New Spain confirms existence of non-Christian practices well after the conquest and the harsh methods used to uproot them. Posits that both were true and part of a broader process of acculturation in which Spanish violence was the expected reaction to indigenous resistance to Christianity. For an ethnohistorian's comments, see item **454.**[AL]

1163 Grosso, Juan Carlos. Mercados y región en el área central de México: San Juan de los Llanos y los pueblos de la Sierra Norte de Puebla, 1780–1840. (*Anu. IEHS,* 9, 1994, p. 169–212, bibl., graphs, tables)

Thorough study of merchants, merchandise, markets, and commercial activities in a key area of New Spain. A model of regional economic history. [AL]

1164 Grunberg, Bernard. The origins of the conquistadores of Mexico City. (*HAHR*, 74:2, May 1994, p. 259–283, graphs, maps, tables)

Prosopography of the conquistadors of Mexico City. Reviews the number of conquistadors and their geographical origins, in addition to other characteristics. [JM]

1165 Gutiérrez Gutiérrez, José Antonio. Los Altos de Jalisco: panorama histórico de una región y de su sociedad hasta 1821. México: Consejo Nacional para la Cultura y las Artes, 1991. 549 p.: bibl., maps. (Regiones)

Competent historical survey of a neo-Galician region with a strong sense of identity. [AL]

Hassig, Ross. Aztec and Spanish conquest in Mesoamerica. See *HLAS 54:491*.

1166 Hernández Rodríguez, Rosaura. Catálogo de documentos del siglo XVI del Archivo General del Estado de Tlaxcala. Tlaxcala, Mexico: Gobierno del Estado de Tlaxcala; México: Archivo General de la Nación, 1988. 3 v.

Guide to the notarial books of Tlaxcala in three volumes. Covers early 1570s-late 1590s. Several indexes help the reseacher utilize this valuable documentary collection. Also included are administrative and litigation documents from that period. [AL]

1167 Herrejón Peredo, Carlos. Hidalgo antes del Grito de Dolores. Morelia, Mexico: Centro de Estudios sobre la Cultura Nicolaita, Univ. Michoacana de San Nicolás de Hidalgo, 1992. 221 p.: bibl., ill. (some col.). (Biblioteca de nicolaitas notables; 46)

Collection of essays on Miguel Hidalgo. Includes Hidalgo's interesting translations into Spanish of a Latin text by Saint Jerome and of Moliere's *Tartuffe*. [AL]

1168 Herrejón Peredo, Carlos. Oratoria en Nueva España. (*Mem. Acad. Mex. Hist.*, 37, 1994, p. 153–174, bibl.)

Interesting essay on rhetoric of preaching and sermon-writing. Unusual exploration of cultural history. [AL]

1169 Hosotte, Paul. La noche triste, 1520: la dernière victoire du peuple du soleil. Paris: Economica, 1993. xvii, 142 p.: ill.,

maps. (Col. Campagnes & stratégies. Les grandes batailles; 10)

Reliably narrates this key moment in the Spanish conquest of Mexico for a broad audience. [A. Pérotin-Dumon]

Huerta, María Teresa. Empresarios del azúcar en el siglo XIX. See item **1337.**

1170 Ibarra, Antonio. La organización regional del mercado interno colonial novohispano: la economía de Guadalajara, 1770–1804. (*Anu. IEHS*, 9, 1994, p. 127–167, bibl., tables)

Excellent study of the regional economy of late 18th-century Guadalajara deals with production policies, revenues, internal markets, capital circulation, and overall economic development. [AL]

Indigenous revolts in Chiapas and the Andean highlands. See *HLAS 55:57.*

1171 Interpretaciones del siglo XVIII mexicano: el impacto de las reformas borbónicas. Coordinación de Josefina Zoraida Vázquez. México: Nueva Imagen, 1992. 215 p.: bibl., ill.

Revisionist history in six essays authored by well-known specialists. Intellectual crisis, fiscal bankruptcy, and ideological questioning of colonial policies are among topics under scrutiny. Highly recommended. [AL]

1172 Iriani, Ana V.; Aníbal A. Minnucci; and **Gustavo B. San Miguel.** Las crisis de mortalidad indígena en una parroquia novohispana: S. Francisco Tepeaca, 1738–1818. (*Anu. IEHS*, 6, 1991, p. 155–169, graphs, map, tables)

Investigates mortality crises in New Spain as part of larger demographic fluctuations in the region. Analysis is restricted to records of the indigenous population. [JM]

1173 Juárez Nieto, Carlos. La oligarquía y el poder político en Valladolid de Michoacán, 1785–1810. Morelia, Mexico: H. Congreso del Estado de Michoacán de Ocampo; CNCA-Instituto Nacional de Antropología e Historia; Instituto Michoacano de Cultura, 1994. 423 p.: bibl., ill. (some col.).

Study of an urban elite in the late colonial period. Based on printed and archival sources, work furnishes useful view of the group and the means it used to consolidate and perpetuate its power. [AL]

Kellogg, Susan. Hegemony out of conquest: the first two centuries of Spanish rule in central Mexico. See item **475.**

1174 **Kicza, John E.** Consumption and control: the Mexico City business community and commodity marketing in the eighteenth century. (*Estud. Hist. Novohisp.*, 12, 1992, p. 159–169)

Investigates commodity marketing in Mexico City in the Bourbon era. Highlights struggles between large estate owners and wholesalers for dominance and the fight of smaller dealers and processors to remain viable. [JM]

1175 **Klein, Herbert S.** Historia fiscal colonial: resultados y perspectivas. (*Hist. Mex.*, 42:2, oct./dic. 1992, p. 261–307, bibl.)

Historiographical overview of the state of the art in the history of colonial revenues. Pithy and useful. [AL]

Kuethe, Allan J. La desregulación comercial y la reforma imperial en la época de Carlos III: los casos de Nueva España y Cuba. See *HLAS 54:1913.*

1176 **Lameiras, José.** El encuentro de la piedra y el acero: la Mesoamérica militarista del siglo XVI que se opuso a la irrupción europea. Zamora, Mexico: El Colegio de Michoacán, 1994. 130 p.: bibl., ill., maps. (Col. Ensayos)

Describes military history of the Aztecs before the arrival of the Spaniards. Dwells on technical aspects of warfare and benefits of belonging to the miltary caste. [AL]

Landers, Jane. New research on the African experience in Spanish America and the Caribbean. See item **901.**

1177 **Langue, Frédérique.** El arbitrismo en el gremio minero novohispano o la representación de J. de la Borda y J. L. Lazaga, 1767: documentos. (*Anu. Estud. Am.*, 50:1, 1993, p. 269–302)

Relatively little-known document signed by two deputies representing the interests of New Spain's miners. They petitioned the Crown for reform and support of the mining enterprise in Mexico before the better known petition of 1774. Document reproduced in its entirety. [AL]

1178 **Lavrin, Asunción.** Espiritualidad en el claustro novohispano del siglo XVII. (*Colon. Lat. Am. Rev.*, 4:2, 1995, p. 155–179)

Article forms part of an issue dedicated to Sor Juana Inés de la Cruz. Examines various kinds of texts produced for and about nuns and analyzes how this literature informs us about spiritual exercises, devotions to Christ and Mary, visions and dreams, and mortifications of the body through fasting and flagellation. The ideal of the nun might be summarized as that of a strong woman able to withstand temptations. Places Sor Juana's writings within this tradition. [EBC]

1179 **Lenkersdorf, Gudrun.** Génesis histórica de Chiapas, 1522–1532: el conflicto entre Portocarrero y Mazariegos. México: Instituto de Investigaciones Filológicas, Univ. Nacional Autónoma de México, 1993. 294 p.: bibl., maps.

Revisionist study of the early years of the foundation of the province of Chiapa by its Spanish conqueror corrects misunderstandings by early chronicles about the feud between Diego de Mazariegos and Pedro Portocarrero and allocation of the territory to the Guatemala audiencia. Solid study based on archival sources. [AL]

1180 **León Cázares, María del Carmen.** Los mercedarios en Chiapas: ¿evangelizadores? (*Estud. Hist. Novohisp.*, 11, 1991, p. 11–43)

Analyzes reasons for the presence of members of the order Nuestra Señora de la Merced Redención de Cautivos (Mercedarios) in Chiapas. Argues that the main interest of this order was not missionary work, but rather collecting resources to "redeem" captives. [JM]

1181 **López Piñero, José María** and **José Pardo Tomás.** Nuevos materiales y noticias sobre la *Historia de las plantas de Nueva España* de Francisco Hernández. Valencia, Spain: Instituto de Estudios Documentales e Históricos sobre la Ciencia, Univ. de València-C.S.I.C., 1994. 387 p.: bibl., ill. (Cuadernos Valencianos de Historia de la Medicina y de la Ciencia; 44. Serie A, Monografías)

New essays by well-known historians of science on 16th-century Spanish scientist Francisco Hernández. Authors identify an unpublished text on the flora of New Spain and clarify a number of obscure points and factual mistakes on the publication, summaries, and outright plagiarism of Hernández's work. [AL]

1182 Luna Moreno, Carmen de. Alternativa en el siglo XVIII: franciscanos de la provincia del Santo Evangelio de México. (*Arch. Ibero-Am.*, 52:205/208, 1992, p. 343–371)

Surveys issue of *alternativa* in the Franciscan monasteries and growing lack of goodwill among members of this order. Spanish friars kept criollos outside the self-government rules. [AL]

1183 Maniau, Joaquín. Compendio de la historia de la real hacienda de Nueva España. Con notas y comentarios de Alberto María Carreño. Estudio preliminar de Marta Morineau Iduarte. México: Univ. Nacional Autónoma de México, Instituto de Investigaciones Jurídicas, 1995. xxviii, 149 p.: bibl. (Serie C—Estudios históricos; 49)

Reprint of a classic 1914 history of the exchequer in New Spain by a late colonial and early republican author. Contains extremely useful information on the administration of the royal exchequer in the last quarter of the 18th century as well as data on the origin of fiscal policies and taxation. [AL]

1184 Martin, Cheryl English. Modes of production in colonial Mexico: the case of Morelos. (*Estud. Hist. Novohisp.*, 12, 1992, p. 107–121)

Author seeks to show how labor and land ownership patterns deterred the development of a capitalistic economy, a process that only began in the mid-19th century. [AL]

1185 Martín Hernández, Francisco. Don Vasco de Quiroga: protector de los indios. Salamanca, Spain: Publicaciones Univ. Pontificia Salamanca; Caja Salamanca y Soria, 1993. 339 p.: bibl., col. ill., index. (Bibliotheca Salmanticensis. Estudios; 154)

The most recent biography of this attractive 16th-century humanist covers territory already discussed by preceeding studies. Mostly for general readers. [AL]

1186 Martíñez de Vega, María Elisa. Los mercaderes novohispanos: control virreinal y fraude fiscal en el primer tercio del siglo XVII. (*Rev. Complut. Hist. Am.*, 20, 1994, p. 87–128)

Broad picture of economic conditions of New Spain in the 17th century is preceeded by historiographic survey of older and more recent historical schools. Author sustains that Mexican merchant class held the key to reshaping the economy and making it less dependent on the mother country. [AL]

1187 Martínez López-Cano, María del Pilar. El crédito a largo plazo en el siglo XVI. México: Univ. Nacional Autónoma de México, 1995. 208 pages: bibl., tables.

Thorough study of credit in New Spain up to the middle of the 16th century. Based on archival sources, this work examines exhaustively the mechanisms of lending and borrowing, paying attention to financial as well as social factors. Surveys ecclesiastic, as well as lay, sources of credit and concludes that in this early period the Church had not yet become the preeminent lending institution. For specialists, but highly recommended. [AL]

1188 Mazín, Oscar and Marta Parada. Archivo Capitular de Administración Diocesana, Valladolid-Morelia: catálogo. v. 1. Michoacán, Mexico: Colegio de Michoacán; Gobierno del Estado de Michoacán, 1991. 1 v.: indexes.

Guide to the rich archival sources of the cathedral chapter of the bishopric of Michoacán contains records of the tithe collection, liens, chantries, and similar economic matters. Very useful. [AL]

1189 McCaa, Robert. Spanish and Nahuatl views on smallpox and demographic catastrophe in Mexico. (*J. Interdiscip. Hist.*, 25:3, Winter 1995, p. 397–431, table)

Rebuttal of Francis J. Brooks' "Revising the conquest of Mexico: smallpox, sources, and population." Argues that the demographic impact was significant. Extensive list of sources is included. For ethnohistorian's comment see item **497.** [JM]

1190 Mejías López, William. Hernán Cortés y su intolerancia hacia la religión azteca en el contexto de la situación de los conversos y moriscos. (*Bull. hisp./Bordeaux*, 95:2, juillet/déc. 1993, p. 623–646)

Well-written and argued study of Spanish law and attitudes towards those of other cultures and belief systems. Maintains that Cortes' intolerance of Mesoamericans and zealous pursuit of their conversion were manifestations of Spanish cultural attitudes. [R. Haskett]

1191 Melville, Elinor G.K. A plague of sheep: environmental consequences of the conquest of Mexico. Cambridge; New York: Cambridge Univ. Press, 1994. 203 p.: bibl., ill., index, map.

Studies environmental impact of the introduction of sheep in the valley of Mezquital. After a disastrous intensive experiment, the area changed to extensive pastoralism, although by then the region had become a mesquite desert dominated by private latifundia. [AL]

1192 Mexico in the age of democratic revolutions, 1750–1850. Edited by Jaime E. Rodríguez O. Boulder, Colo.: Lynne Rienner, 1994. 330 p.: bibl., ill., index.

Collection of essays examines key political issues before and after Mexican Independence in an attempt to identify continuities and changes. Discusses political personalities, constitutional reform, regional politics, the Church, and the nature of leadership in the mid-19th century. [AL]

1193 Miño Grijalva, Manuel. Estructura económica y crecimiento: la historiografía económica colonial mexicana. (*Hist. Mex.*, 42:2, oct./dic. 1992, p. 221–260)

Useful survey of recent trends in economic history. Assesses achievements and underlines the need to carry out research in several key areas. [AL]

1194 Morales, Francisco. Secularización de doctrinas: ¿fin de un modelo evangelizador en la Nueva España? (*Arch. Ibero-Am.*, 52:205/208, 1992, p. 465–495)

Traces history of secularization of Franciscan doctrines in New Spain (1574–1744). Details daily events and the weight of personalities (e.g., cowards, martyrs, and heroines). [AL]

1195 Morales Avendaño, Segundo Juan María. San Bartolomé de los Llanos en la historia de Chiapas. Tuxtla Gutiérrez, Mexico: Univ. Autónoma de Chiapas, 1986? 463 p.: bibl., ill. (Col. Chiapas; 4)

Exemplifies attempt to interpret local history. Local pride and genuine interest in the *patria chica* cannot compensate for the weak methodological training of the authors. Historiographical value of work lies in the

cultivation of this genre for general readers and the provision of abundant local data on a region that has lacked attention from historians and politicans. [AL]

1196 Moreno, Juan Joseph. Fragmentos de la vida y virtudes del V. Ilmo. y Rvmo. Sr. Dr. Don Vasco de Quiroga, primer obispo de la Sta. Iglesia Catedral de Michoacán y fundador del Real y Primitivo Colegio de San Nicolás Obispo de Valladolid. Morelia, Mexico: Balsal Editores, 1989. 230 p. (Col. Documentos y testimonios)

This second edition of an original 18th-century biography of Vasco de Quiroga includes rules for the organization of his pueblos and his testament.

Murillo Velarde, Pedro. Geographía de América. See item **940.**

1197 Museo Nacional del Virreinato (Mexico). Tepotzotlán y la Nueva España: memoria del coloquio. Coordinación de María del Consuelo Maquívar. Mexico: Museo Nacional del Virreinato, Instituto Nacional de Antropología e Historia, 1994. 341 p.: bibl., ill.

Papers presented at a conference on the role of Tepozotlán in New Spain. There is no unifying theme to this collection that contains papers on missionary activities, books and education, daily life, religion and religious practices, art, music, science, and the economy. The essays' quality is mixed, but those addressing cultural aspects of colonial life make this collection worthwhile. [AL]

1198 Myers, Kathleen A. A glimpse of family life in colonial Mexico: a nun's account. (*LARR*, 28:2, 1993, p. 63–87, bibl.)

Examines one nun's account of her family's life in rural colonial Mexico. Vol. 1 of work by Madre María de San José (1656–1719) highlights her secular life on an agricultural farm from 1656–87 and her 21-year struggle to become a nun. [JM]

1199 Nájera C., Martha Ilia. La formación de la oligarquía criolla en Ciudad Real de Chiapa: el caso Ortés de Velasco. México: Univ. Nacional Autónoma de México, Instituto de Investigaciones Filológicas, Centro de Estudios Mayas, 1993. 101 p.: bibl., ill., map. (Cuaderno; 22)

Traces formation of colonial elite in 16th-century Chiapa. Following the figure of

Francisco Ortés de Velasco, author illustrates the rise of a conquistador family through encomiendas, land ownership, marriages, and mayorazgo. Based on archival sources, this study is a good example of micro-family history and its potential to illustrate social economic networks and status. [AL]

1200 Nettel Ross, Margarita. Colonización y poblamiento del Obispado de Michoacán: período colonial. Morelia, Mexico: Gobierno del Estado, Instituto Michoacano de Cultura, 1990. 333 p.: bibl., ill., maps.

Survey synthesizes demographic settlement of the province of Michoacán. Useful visual aids. [AL]

1201 Newson, Linda A. The demographic collapse of native peoples of the Americas, 1492–1650. (*in* The meeting of two worlds: Europe and the Americas, 1492–1650. Edited by Warwick Bray. Oxford, England: Oxford Univ. Press; The British Academy, 1993, p. 247–288, bibl., ill., map, table)

Careful overview of recent revisionist work—including the author's own important contributions—on causes and dimensions of the demographic disaster. Newson also convincingly addresses why some peoples suffered more than others, and why some were able eventually to recover at least some demographic vigor. [R. Haskett]

1202 Noguez, Xavier. Documentos guadalupanos: un estudio sobre las fuentes de información tempranas en torno a las mariofanías en el Tepeyac. Toluca, Mexico: El Colegio Mexiquense; México: Fondo de Cultura Económica, 1993. 280 p.: bibl., ill. (Sección de obras de historia)

Model ethnohistorical study of the Virgin of Guadalupe concludes that the information considered to be the cult's earliest "history" has its origins in a group of traditions of collective creation (1521–1688) arising among Indians already acculturated to Christianity. Noguez's analysis has determined that while the medium of information was Hispanic, the source of the cult was indigenous. Concludes that a cult existed prior to 1563 when the first reported miracles were recorded. For ethnohistorian's comment see item 502. [EBC]

1203 Oliver Sánchez, Lilia Victoria. El Hospital Real de San Miguel de Belén, 1581–1802. Guadalajara: Univ. de Guadalajara, 1992. 326 p.: bibl., ill., index. (Libros de tiempo de ciencia; 6)

Examines history of medicine and development of colonial social welfare institutions within the context of the history of New Spain. [EBC]

1204 Ortega Noriega, Sergio *et al.* Amor y desamor: vivencias de parejas en la sociedad novohispana. México: Instituto Nacional de Antropología e Historia, 1992. 184 p.: bibl. (Col. Divulgación)

Eight studies on the subject of love—rejected, fulfilled, or unrequited—based on the analysis of archival materials. These entertaining vignettes further the reader's understanding of social history and gender relations. The topic remains in need of a general characterization. [AL]

Ortiz Lanz, José Enrique. Arquitectura militar de México. See item **118.**

1205 Ouweneel, Arij. Het verleden leefde voort in Antonio Pérez: Indiaanse "standennijd" in centraal Mexico, 1757–1761. = The past lived on in Antonio Pérez: Amerindian "class struggle" in central Mexico. (*Tijdschr. Geschied.*, 108, 1995, p. 24–49, maps)

Uses history of Amerindian shepherd, Antonio Pérez, to study Indian ethnicity in colonial times. Addresses some problems involved in this sort of research. Calls for dialogue between medievalists and colonial Latin Americanists. [R. Hoefte]

1206 Paredes Martínez, Carlos S, La región de Atlixco, Huaquechula y Tochimilco: la sociedad y su agricultura en el siglo XVI. México: Fondo de Cultura Económica, 1991. 182 p., 12 leaves of plates (some folded): bibl., ill. (some col.). (Col. Puebla)

Regional study traces socioeconomic organization before and after the conquest. Special attention is given to water control, land ownership, agricultural production, and labor. Useful review. [AL]

1207 Patch, Robert W. Maya and Spaniard in Yucatan, 1648–1812. Stanford, Calif.: Stanford Univ. Press, 1993. 329 p.: bibl., index, maps.

Excellent regional study ties together all previous studies by author while amplifying and incorporating a wealth of new details.

The social and economic structures of indigenous and Hispanic societies are shown to be intimately intertwined and difficult to fit into current economic ideas of historical development. By problematizing available information, author stimulates new avenues of inquiry into "peripheral" areas.

1208 Patronato Mexicano del V Centenario de Cortés. Cortés: navegante, político, arquitecto, economista y literato. Ed. conmemorativa, 1. ed. México: Editorial Diana, 1992. 467 p.: bibl., ill. (some col.), maps (some col.).

Prologue by Octavio Paz defines the purpose of this collection of essays: to exercise and liberate myth surrounding Hernán Cortés as a symbol of the conquest. The academic nature of these studies does not alter significantly the nature of the controversy over Cortés, but revisits well-known aspects of the history of the man and New Spain in the early colonial period in a bland effort to create objectivity about his figure and his actions. [AL]

1209 Pérez-Rocha, Emma and **Gabriel Moedano.** Aportaciones a la investigación de archivos del México colonial y a la bibliohemerografía afromexicanista. México: Instituto Nacional de Antropología e Historia, 1992. 64 p.: bibl. (Col. Fuentes. Serie Bibliografías)

Mostly a bibliography of works on the African population and culture in Mexico written between 1900–90. Despite its title, this publication does not cover archival resources. [AL]

1210 Pescador, Juan Javier and **Gustavo Garza.** La caja y general depósito del reino: la concentración comercial en la Ciudad de México a fines de la colonia, 1770–1790. (*Secuencia/México*, 23, mayo/agosto 1992, p. 5–46, bibl., graphs, ill., map, photos, tables)

Analyzes the commercial significance of Mexico City within the colonial economy during the last third of the 18th century. Looks specifically at networks of goods to and from the capital, as well as transportation access. [JM]

1211 Pescador, Juan Javier. De bautizados a fieles difuntos: familia y mentalidades en una parroquia urbana, Santa Catarina de

México, 1568–1820. México: Colegio de México, Centro de Estudios Demográficos y de Desarrollo Urbano, 1992. 400 p.: bibl., ill.

Thorough and imaginative monograph on the Mexico City parish of Santa Catarina de Sena contains a history of the episcopal organization, a demographic study comparing this parish with other regions of New Spain, an analysis of ethnic composition, a study of naming patterns as a reflection of popular devotions, as well as discussions of the *cofradías* and finances. The study also includes materials on the elite Fagoaga family and the architecture of the parish. The long time frame and the thorough exploration of the complete archive is especially commendable. [EBC]

1212 Pietschmann, Horst. Un testimonio del impacto del reformismo borbónico en Nueva España: la representación del intendente de Puebla de los Angeles de 27 junio de 1792. (*Jahrb. Gesch.*, 31, 1994, p. 1–38)

Analyzes a 1792 memorandum from the intendant of Puebla to the Spanish Crown. Contends that this document shows that independence was ultimately not the result of a struggle solely between peninsulares and criollos, but also between alliances and coalitians among diverse peoples. [JM]

1213 El poblamiento de México: una visión histórico-demográfica. t. 2, El México colonial. México: Secretaría de Gobernación, Consejo Nacional de Población, 1993. 1 v.

Survey of key features of colonial Mexico's demographic growth. Eight essays gathered by historians, demographers, and anthropologists synthesize state-of-the-art knowledge on the quantitative evolution of the population, its ethnic components, and colonial population policies. This glossy publication for general readers includes beautiful illustrations.

1214 Poole, Stafford. Our Lady of Guadalupe: the origins and sources of a Mexican national symbol, 1531–1797. Tuscon: Univ. of Arizona Press, 1995. 325 p.: bibl., facsim., index.

Rigorous historical analysis of many versions of the origins and development of the worship of the Virgin of Guadalupe. Destroys many long-held views and opinions about the Indian Juan Diego, the Nahuatl version of the apparition, and the image itself, supporting the thesis that Guadalupe must have been an Indian-painted image of The Immaculate Conception. Highly recommended. For ethnohistorian's comment, see item **510.** [AL]

1215 Poole, Stafford. Some observations on mission methods and native reactions in sixteenth-century New Spain. (*Americas/ Francisc.*, 50:3, Jan, 1994, p. 335–349)

Revisionist view of the evangelization methods used in 16th-century New Spain. Acknowledges syncretic practices and ponders nature of popular Catholicism in Spain. Explores how Spanish views on folklore, religion, and ritual influenced dogma taught to Indian neophytes. For ethnohistorian's comment see item **511.** [AL]

1216 Prontuario de documentos del Archivo de Indias sobre la Nueva Galicia. t. 1, Siglo XVI. Guadalajara, Mexico: Instituto Cultural Ignacio Dávila Garibi, 1986. 1 v.: index.

Guide to documents on New Galicia available at the Archivo de Indias in Seville. Thematically arranged, this brief guide provides scant help but could be very useful to a first-time researcher. [AL]

1217 Quezada, Sergio. Relación documental para la historia de la provincia de Yucatán, 1520–1844. Mérida, Mexico: Ediciones de la Univ. Autónoma de Yucatán, 1992. 398 p.: bibl., index. (Mérida, la de Yucatán y el quinto centenario)

Guide to documents for the history of colonial Yucatán in the Archivo General de la Nación (México), the Archivo General de Indias (Sevilla), and the Archivo Histórico Nacional (Madrid). Useful tool for reseach on judicial, economic, and administrative topics. [AL]

1218 Quiroga, Vasco de. *De debellandis Indis:* un tratado desconocido. Edición de René Acuña. México: Univ. Nacional Autónoma de México, Instituto de Investigaciones Filológicas, Centro de Estudios Clásicos, 1988. 351 p.: bibl., index. (Bibliotheca humanistica Mexicana; 1)

Translation from Latin of a study attributed to Vasco de Quiroga on the just rights of Spain to the Indies, which he upheld. Possibly part of *De debellandies Indies,* long considered lost. [AL]

1219 Ragon, Pierre. Les amours indiennes, ou, L'imaginaire du conquistador. Préface de Serge Gruzinski. Paris: A. Colin, 1992. 273 p.: bibl., index.

Following approach of Serge Gruzinski, Ragon identifies sexual archetypes and stereotypes that conquistadors applied to indigenous societies encountered in colonial Mexico. Shows origin of these concepts in Europeans' previous contacts with non-Christian Mediterranean cultures. Rich analysis, although lacking in gender perspective. [A. Pérotin-Dumon]

1220 Ramos Pérez, Demetrio. Hernán Cortés: mentalidad y propósitos. Madrid: Ediciones Rialp, 1992. 271 p.: bibl. (Forjadores de historia; 20)

Purports to show the real Cortés by analyzing his motivations, intentions, and tactics for dealing with his men, the indigenous peoples, and so forth. Cortés appears a clever schemer fundamentally in charge of his destiny. Based on works contemporary to Cortés as well as more recent interpretations. This work deifies Cortés in a new and different manner. [AL]

1221 Real Academia de la Historia (Spain). El tabaco en Nueva España: discurso leído el día 10 de mayo de 1992 en el acto de su recepción pública por el Excmo. Sr. D. Guillermo Céspedes del Castillo, y contestación por el Excmo. Sr. D. Gonzalo Anes y Álvarez de Castrillón. Madrid: Real Academia de la Historia, 1992. 219 p.: bibl., facsims., tables.

Comprehensive study of tobacco as an agricultural product and export commodity. Céspedes exhausts topic in a well-researched and documented study supplemented by numerous tables and illustrations. [AL]

1222 Reher, David Sven. Coyunturas económicas y fluctuaciones demográficas en México durante el siglo XVIII. (*in* Congresso sobre a História da População da América Latina, *1st, Ouro Preto, Brazil, 1989.* Actas. São Paulo: Fundação SEADE, 1990, p. 276–288, bibl., tables)

Sheds light on various aspects of the demographic and economic conditions in 18th-century Mexico. The relationship between the economy, population fecundity, mortality, and marriage are explored in this context. [JM]

1223 Reher, David Sven. Population pressure and living standards in late colonial Mexico. (*in* El poblamiento de las Américas, *Veracruz, 1992.* Actas. Liège, Belgium: International Union for the Scientific Study of Population, 1992, v. 1, p. 447–475, bibl., graphs, tables)

Notes that increased production did not translate to higher standards of living in late colonial Mexico. Investigates relationship between population trends and living standards during that period. [JM]

1224 Reyes G., Juan Carlos. El Santo Oficio de la Inquisición en Colima: tres documentos del siglo XVIII. Colima, Mexico: Univ. de Colima, Coordinación General de Extensión, 1993. 130 p.: bibl., ill., indexes. (Documentos colimenses; 2)

First document, from 1732, illuminates a fear of sorcery as well as ways in which Inquisitorial investigations crossed class lines. The second document, from 1772, illustrates a case of heresy—an alleged denial of the sainthood of Saint Ignatius of Loyola. The third, from 1775, reflects use of the Inquisition for personal ends. [L.R. Grahn]

1225 Robinson, David James and **Linda L. Greenow.** Catálogo del Archivo del Registro Público de la Propiedad de Guadalajara: Libros de hipotecas, 1566–1820. Guadalajara, Mexico: Gobierno de Jalisco, Secretaría General, Unidad Editorial, 1986. 256 p.: bibl., facsim., indexes, map. (Col. Historia. Documentos e investigaciones; 13)

Useful guide to books recording real estate liens in Guadalajara between 1721–1821. Brief introduction places documents in context. Will aid those interested in studying regional credit of the period. [AL]

1226 Rodríguez O., Jaime E. La transición de colonia a nación: Nueva España, 1820–1821. (*Hist. Mex.,* 43:2, oct./dic. 1993, p. 265–322, bibl.)

Reconstructs efforts of pro-autonomy forces in Mexico. Focuses on activity of secret organizations in furthering the cause of independence. [JM]

1227 Román Gutiérrez, José Francisco. Sociedad y evangelización en Nueva Galicia durante el siglo XVI. Zapopan, Mexico: El Colegio de Jalisco; México: Instituto Nacional de Antropología e Historia; Zacatecas,

Mexico: Univ. Autónoma de Zacatecas, 1993. 481 p.: bibl., maps.

Narrative history of the establishment of the bishopric of New Galicia. Written from the Spanish and the Roman Catholic Church viewpoint, it deals with the "how" of the spiritual conquest, the structural issues of evangelization, the establishment of jurisdictional boundaries, and the relation of church and State. Based on archival sources.

1228 Rubial García, Antonio. Tebaidas en el paraíso: los ermitaños de la Nueva España. (*Hist. Mex.,* 64:3, enero/marzo 1995, p. 355–383, bibl.)

Well-crafted survey of all the attempts to establish hermitages in New Spain, either by the regular orders or by individual friars. [AL]

1229 Ruiz Medrano, Ethelia. Los negocios de un arzobispo: el caso de Fray Alonso de Montúfar. (*Estud. Hist. Novohisp.,* 12, 1992, p. 63–83, appendices)

Detailed review of business affairs of an Archbishop of Mexico (1551–54) for whom the interests of this world seemed to have mattered more than those of the spirit. [AL]

1230 Ruz, Mario Humberto. Los linderos del agua: Francisco de Montejo y los orígenes del Tabasco colonial. Tabasco, Mexico: Gobierno del Estado de Tabasco, ICT Ediciones, 1991. 205 p.: bibl., ill.

Presentation of and commentary on a number of important documents linked to the early history of Spanish occupation of the Tabasco region. Focuses above all on Montejo. Important addition to the historical literature on the Spanish presence in the Americas; the title refers to the importance of the region's many rivers as boundaries for Spanish holdings of various kinds. [R. Haskett]

1231 Sánchez Fuertes, Cayetano. México, puente franciscano entre España y Filipinas. (*Arch. Ibero-Am.,* 52:205/208, 1992, p. 373–401)

Surveys linkages between New Spain and the Philippine Islands created by missionaries of St. Francis. [AL]

1232 Sánchez Maldonado, María Isabel. Diezmos y crédito eclesiástico: el diezmatorio de Acámbaro, 1724–1771. Zamora, Mexico: El Colegio de Michoacán, 1994. 146 p.: bibl., graphs, tables.

Provides wealth of information on the process of tithe collection, land ownership, and ecclesiastical credit in the region of Acámbaro, bishopric of Michoacán. Although several chapters are not well integrated, the work does provide an understanding of the interconnectedness of property ownership and credit availability that sustained agricultural production, social elites, and several key ecclesiastical institutions. [AL]

1233 **Scardaville, Michael C.** Hapsburg law and Bourbon order: State authority, popular unrest, and the criminal justice system in Bourbon Mexico City. (*Americas/Francisc.*, 50:4, April 1994, p. 501–525)

Study of colonial legal theory and jurisprudence. Concludes that punishment that was aimed to make the criminal pay a contribution to society also opened a door for rehabilitation. By tempering the practice of the law, magistrates sought to strengthen state allegiance, diffuse social tensions, and foster colonial dependency. Rebuts interpretation of the law as benefiting only the wealthy. [AL]

1234 **Scholes, France V.** and **Eleanor Burnham Adams.** Documents relating to the Mirones Expedition to the interior of Yucatán, 1621–1624. Spanish documents translated into English by Robert D. Wood. Additional notes by Frank E. Comparato. Culver City, Calif.: Labyrinthos, 1991. 50 p.: bibl., index, map.

One in a series of documents dealing with the pacification and evangelization of Yucatán. Translation and annotation place these unusual primary sources at the reach of students and general readers. [AL]

1235 **Sifvert, Anne Sofie.** Crónica de las monjas Brígidas de la Ciudad de México. Stockholm: Stockholms Univ., 1992. 221 p.: appendix, bibl.

Doctoral dissertation undertakes analysis of a newly-discovered chronicle of the foundation of the Brigitinne convent of Mexico City (1745). The chronicle was written by several different hands, possibly the nuns themselves. Analysis by the editor is meticulous and mostly linguistic; the text is of interest to social historians. Useful source. [AL]

Sor Juana Inés de la Cruz Project. See item 43.

1236 **Sor Juana y su mundo: una mirada actual.** Edición de Sara Poot Herrera. Investigación y textos de José Rogelio Alvarez *et al.* Colaboración de Pablo Brescia, Patricia Díaz Cayeros y Alejandro Rivas. Mexico: Univ. del Claustro de Sor Juana, Instituto de Investigaciones de la Cultura, 1995. 555 p.: bibl., ill. (some col.).

Eleven essays seek to recreate key aspects of the 17th-century world in which Sor Juana lived. Careful edition of the highest quality and pithy essays make this a banner publication on the poet. Collaborations from Silva Camarena, López Portillo, Poot Herrera, Lavrin, Bravo, Gallo, Alvarez, Checa, Pascual Buxó, Beuchot, Sabat de Rivers, Tenorio, and Glantz. [AL]

1237 **Soria, Víctor M.** La Casa de Moneda de México bajo la administración borbónica, 1733–1821. México: Univ. Autónoma Metropolitana, Unidad Iztapalapa, División de Ciencias Sociales y Humanidades, 1994. 279 p.: bibl. (Iztapalapa, texto y contexto; 18)

Well-researched monograph on a key financial institution offers detailed information on operations in the late colonial period. [AL]

1238 **Soria, Víctor M.** La incorporación del apartado del oro y la plata a la Casa de Moneda y sus resultados de operación, 1778–1805. (*Hist. Mex.*, 44:2, oct./dic. 1994, p. 269–298, bibl., tables)

Survey of the process of the Crown's appropriation of the key minting activities in New Spain and the appointment of its officials. [AL]

1239 **Stern, Peter.** *Gente de color quebrado:* Africans and Afromestizos in colonial Mexico. (*CLAHR/Albuquerque,* 3:2, Spring 1994, p. 185–205)

Surveys history of peoples of African descent in colonial Mexico, describing their occupational roles and the process of "mestizaje" that virtually erased all traces of this once clearly identifiable group. [JM]

1240 **Stern, Steve J.** The secret history of gender: women, men, and power in late colonial Mexico. Chapel Hill: Univ. of North Carolina Press, 1995. 478 p.: bibl., index, maps.

Wide-ranging exposition of primary

and secondary materials produced by and about the popular classes clarifies much in the visions and behavior of men and women in conflict and symbiosis with each other and with colonial authorities. Uses narrative, quantitative, and analytic tools to discuss difficult issues. [EBC]

1241 Tanck de Estrada, Dorothy. Escuelas y cajas de comunidad en Yucatán al final de la colonia. (*Hist. Mex.*, 43:3, enero/marzo 1994, p. 401–449, bibl., tables)

Asserts that toward the end of the 18th century the indigenous community's economic resources became a safety net for local governments. Argues that the use of these funds to establish schools and the government's takeover of these funds were related. [JM]

1242 Tenenbaum, Barbara A. The making of a fait accompli: Mexico and the Provincias Internas, 1776–1846. (*in* The origins of Mexican national politics, 1808–1847. Edited by Jaime E. Rodríguez O. Wilmington, Del.: Scholarly Resources, Inc., 1997, p. 85–109)

Lucid examination of the fiscal relationship between Central Mexico and the Northern Provinces discovers prosperity in the north reflected in the Treasury *cajas.* Concludes that far from being a drain on Mexico, the north paid its own expenses, as well as those that were the responsibility of the central government. [EBC]

1243 Thomas, Hugh. Conquest: Montezuma, Cortés, and the fall of Old Mexico. New York: Simon & Schuster, 1993. 832 p.: bibl., ill., index, maps.

Retelling of the Mexican conquest by masterful writer. Author has done his homework and gone beyond printed sources. Good reading. [AL]

1244 Tovar de Teresa, Guillermo. La Ciudad de México y la utopía en el siglo XVI. México: Seguros de México, 1987. 178 p.: bibl., ill. (some col.), maps (some col.)

Establishes the connection between Renaissance urban planning and Viceroy Antonio de Mendoza's conceptualization of the new city of Mexico. Good illustrations. [AL]

1245 Uchmany, Eva Alexandra. La vida entre el judaísmo y el cristianismo en la Nueva España, 1580–1606. México: Archivo General de la Nación; Fondo de Cultura Económica, 1992. 477 p.: bibl., ill., index. (Sección de obras de historia)

Traces history of a group of Portuguese Jews who migrated to New Spain and learned the outward forms of Christianity. A transcript of the Inquisitorial records has been compiled from the AGN, and from the Henry Charles Lea collection (Univ. of Pennsylvania) and G.R.G. Conway Collection (Thomas Gilchrease Institute of American History and Art, Tulsa, Okla.). Important contribution for understanding complexity of conversion process. [EBC]

Universidad Autónoma Benito Juárez de Oaxaca (Mexico). Biblioteca. La imagen y la palabra: libros del fondo bibliográfico de la Universidad Autónoma Benito Juárez de Oaxaca, octubre-diciembre de 1993. See item **1113.**

1246 Valero de García Lascuráin, Ana Rita. Solares y conquistadores: orígenes de la propiedad en la Ciudad de México. México: Instituto Nacional de Antropología e Historia, 1991. 302 p.: bibl., ill. (Col. Divulgación. Serie Historia)

Although based on published primary sources and secondary sources, this is a work of considerable originality as well as a careful summation of the early history of the city. [EBC]

1247 Los vascos en México y su Colegio de las Vizcaínas. Proyección y coordinación de Josefina Muriel. Coordinación editorial de Graciela Romandía de Cantú. Fotografía de Max Lobera *et al.* México: Instituto de Investigaciones Históricas, UNAM; Instituto de Investigaciones Estéticas, UNAM, 1987. 284 p.: bibl., ill. (some col.).

Richly illustrated, collective history of the Vizcaínas with special emphasis on architecture and the visual arts. Includes articles by Muriel, Pi-Suñer Llorens, Vargas Lugo, Porras Muñoz, among others. Indicates the riches to be found in the archive of the Colegio. [EBC]

1248 Viqueira, Pedro Juan. Tributo y sociedad en Chiapas, 1680–1721. (*Hist. Mex.*, 44:2, oct./dic. 1994, p. 237–267, bibl.)

Discusses role of fraud in the 1712 indigenous uprising in Chiapas. Analyzes the ongoing struggle for control of tribute in the region. [JM]

1249 Vollmer, Günter. Die Encomenderos, Encomiendas und Tributarios von Pánuco oder das verschwundene Land. (*Ibero-Am. Arch.*, 20:3/4, 1994, p. 279–336, appendices, bibl., graphs, tables)

By systematically analyzing all available colonial tax records and legal titles of the region for 1547–1663, author seeks to establish fate of earliest Mexican colonial territory and its indigenous population, the Huastec. [C.K. Converse]

1250 Vos, Jan de. Los enredos de Remesal: ensayo sobre la conquista de Chiapas. México: Consejo Nacional para la Cultura y las Artes, 1992. 239 p.: bibl., ill., maps. (Regiones)

Methodical study of the well-known history of Chiapas and Guatemala by Dominican Fr. Antonio de Remesal (1619). De Vos subjected the text to rigorous analysis substantiated by archival research and corrects numerous errors. Restricted to the period from 1524–29. Interesting and useful historiographical effort. [AL]

1251 Washington State University. The Regla papers: an indexed guide to the papers of the Romero de Terreros family and other colonial and early national Mexican families. Edited by John F. Guido and Lawrence R. Stark. Foreword by John E. Kicza. Pullman: Washington State Univ. Press, 1994. xx, 120 p.: ill., index.

Guide to the collection of colonial and 19th-century papers at Washington State Univ. Although no substitute for the valuable and detailed calendar produced by Jacquelyn Gaines in 1963, summarizes and adds a guide to the Jesuit Hacienda papers and miscellaneous materials, shedding light on Mexican 19th-century matters and on families who intermarried with the Regla family. [EBC]

1252 Wobeser, Gisela von. El agua como factor de conflicto en el agro novohispano, 1650–1821. (*Estud. Hist. Novohisp.*, 13, 1993, p. 135–146)

Contends that the struggle for water rights played an important role in agrarian conflicts of late 17th- and 18th-century New Spain. Argues that population increases and expansion of the haciendas resulted in an intense struggle for control of land and water resources. [JM]

1253 Wobeser, Gisela von. El crédito eclesiástico en la Nueva España, siglo XVIII. México: Univ. Nacional Autónoma de México, Instituto de Investigaciones Históricas, 1994. 275 p.: bibl.

Overview of credit mechanisms in the 18th century. Author studies sources, users, and institutions granting credit: nunneries, inquisitions, confraternities, chantries, etc. Numerous tables give readers the opportunity to sample information from primary credit sources. Useful survey of a topic that deserves greater historical attention. [AL]

1254 "Y por mí visto—" : mandamientos, ordenanzas, licencias y otras disposiciones virreinales del siglo XVI. Edición de Carlos S. Paredes Martínez. Recopilación de Víctor Cárdenas Morales, Iraís Piñón Flores y Trinidad Pulido Solís. México: CIESAS; Morelia, Mexico: Univ. Michoacana de San Nicolás de Hidalgo, 1994. 549 p.: bibl., indexes, maps.

Collection of 900 documents on 16th-century Michoacán includes primarily viceregal orders culled from three main documentary sources in Mexico and Spain. Useful for history of early colonial administration and indigenous affairs. [AL]

1255 Yáñez Díaz, Gonzalo. Espacios urbanos del siglo XVI en la región Puebla Tlaxcala. Puebla, Mexico: Gobierno del Estado de Puebla, Univ. Autónoma de Puebla; Comision Puebla V Centenario, 1991. 497 p.: bibl., ill., maps. (Col. V centenario)

Although based on published sources, the conceptualization of this study of 16th-century cities of the Puebla Tlaxcala region describes and analyzes the background of the Hispanic urban plan and compares and contrasts the plans of regional cities. [EBC]

1256 Zamudio Espinosa, Guadalupe Yolanda; María Elena Bribiesca Sumano; and J. Francisco Velázquez Mejía. Análisis diplomático, paleográfico e histórico-jurídico de la Carta Poder del siglo XVI. Toluca de Lerdo, Mexico: Centro de Investigación en Ciencias Sociales y Humanidades, U.A.E.M., 1989. vi, 93 leaves: bibl., ill.

Useful study of paleographic and morphological characters of 16th-century power-of-attorney documents, one of the most frequent legal documents of the period. Authors furnish 15 different models and provide researchers with the tools to follow others. Useful for all colonial historians. Printing is poor. [AL]

North and Borderlands

1257 Archivo Municipal de Saltillo (Mexico). El Señorío de San Esteban del Saltillo: voz y escritura nahuas, siglos XVII y XVIII. Recopilación de Eustaquio Celestino Solís. Saltillo, Mexico: Archivo Municipal de Saltillo, 1991. 193 p.: bibl.

Contains Spanish translations of 21 Nahua documents dating from 1613–1750. Collection includes routine matters such as wills as well as a 1658 petition to the Viceroy. [J. Britton]

1258 Archivo Municipal de Saltillo (Mexico). Temas del Virreinato: documentos del Archivo Municipal de Saltillo. Recopilación de Silvio Zavala con la colaboración de María del Carmen Velázquez. Saltillo, Mexico: Gobierno del Estado de Coahuila; México: Colegio de México, 1989. 293 p.

A collection of selected documents from Saltillo's archives, mostly from 17th and 18th centuries. Topics cover Indians, slaves, labor, civil administration, and others. Documents serve as examples of broader social and economic issues to be found in regional repositories. [AL]

1259 Brandes, Stanley. Las misiones de la Alta California como instrumentos de conquista. (*in* De palabra y obra en el Nuevo Mundo. v. 2, Encuentros interétnicos. Edición de Miguel León-Portilla *et al.* Madrid: Siglo Veintiuno Editores, 1992, p. 153–172)

Crushing critique of the Franciscan missions in California by a leading cultural anthropologist, based on an 1800 investigation and extensive secondary sources. [EBC]

1260 Chipman, Donald E. Spanish Texas, 1519–1821. Austin: Univ. of Texas Press, 1992. 343 p.: bibl., ill., index, maps.

While planned as text for Texas history classes, this one-volume study reflects considerable original research as well as a thorough review of the abundant secondary source materials. [EBC]

1261 Chipman, Donald E. Texas en la época colonial. Madrid: Editorial MAPFRE, 1992. 399 p.: bibl., ill., maps. (Col. España y Estados Unidos; 6. Col. MAPFRE 1492)

Historical survey focuses on people and institutions of Texas from native Americans of preconquest era to establishment of Spanish colonial empire and early stages of Anglo-American penetration. Organized chronologically with a good balance of social, political, and economic history. [J. Britton]

1262 Crosby, Harry. Antigua California: mission and colony on the peninsular frontier, 1697–1768. Albuquerque: Univ. of New Mexico Press, 1994. 556 p.: bibl., ill., index.

Important and thorough narrative of the history of Jesuit Baja California is a profusely detailed but exceptionally readable account of the Jesuit enterprise and a reclamation of its significance for the successful Spanish colonization of Upper California. [EBC]

1263 Cutter, Charles R. Community and the law in northern New Spain. (*Americas/Francisc.*, 50:4, April 1994, p. 467–480)

Revisionist interpretation of the meaning and usage of Hispanic law in New Spain and its northern provinces regards judiciary practice as "an interplay of royal will and popular sensibilities" accomodating community needs to jurisprudence theory. [AL]

1264 Engstrand, Iris Wilson. Arizona hispánica. Madrid: Editorial MAPFRE, 1992. 321 p.: bibl., index, maps. (Col. España y Estados Unidos; 10. Col. MAPFRE 1492)

Vol. 10 in a monographic series of works produced by MAPFRE on Spain and the US is an excellent cumulative history with useful bibliographies and an intelligent approach to the issues. Good collection of valuable maps. On the history of the Sonora-Arizona region, see also James E. Officer's *Hispanic Arizona, 1536–1856* (see *HLAS 52: 1120*). [EBC]

1265 Flagler, Edward K. Defensive policy and Indian relations in New Mexico during the tenure of governor Francisco Cuervo y Valdés, 1705–1707. (*Rev. Esp. Antropol. Am.*, 22, 1992, p. 89–104, bibl.)

Study of Indian policy in early 18th-century New Mexico argues that having learned from previous experience, the Spaniards permitted Pueblo peoples to maintain vestiges of their own religion in order to preserve them as allies against the Navajo, Apache, and possible European intruders. [EBC]

1266 Galán García, Agustín. Conflicto entre la autoridad militar y los religiosos de la Alta California, 1781–1792. (*Hisp. Sacra*, 40, julio/dic. 1988, p. 807–823)

Based on sources in Spain, traces conflict over the 1781 Reglamento de Presidios y Situados. Provides information about the 1780s in California. [EBC]

1267 Garate, Donald T. Basque names, nobility, and ethnicity on the Spanish frontier. (*CLAHR/Albuquerque*, 2 : 1, Winter 1993, p. 77–104, ill.)

Brings a wealth of documentation to the thesis that Basque ethnicity dominated the frontier. Notwithstanding the tone of ethnic advocacy often present in the investigation of this topic, Garate presents some little known and not well understood undercurrents to the history of New Mexico.

1268 González Rodríguez, Luis. El noroeste novohispano en la época colonial. México: Instituto de Investigaciones Antropológicas, UNAM; M.A. Porrúa Grupo Editor, 1993. 614 p.: bibl.

Thorough, almost encyclopedic description of the three ethnographic and geographic regions of northwestern New Spain, based on enormous amounts of documentation. Work remains close to its primary sources. Presents original materials as well as archival descriptions. [EBC]

1269 Jackson, Robert H. Indian population decline: the missions of northwestern New Spain, 1687–1840. Albuquerque: Univ. of New Mexico Press, 1994. 229 p.: bibl., ill., index, maps.

Based on parish registers and computer-assisted manipulations as well as comparative data for European communities. Concludes that the heavy population loss of Indian mission residents had the "unintentional but intended consequence" of freeing land and resources for non-Indian inhabitants. [EBC]

1270 Langue, Frédérique. Mines, terres et société à Zacatecas, Méxique: de la fin du XVIIe siècle à l'Independance. Préface de François Chevalier. Paris: Publications de la Sorbonne, 1992. 445 p.: bibl., ill., maps, tables.

Well-documented study based on archival sources in Mexico City, Zacatecas, Guadalajara, Seville, Madrid, Valladolid, and Paris. Presents *longue durée* panorama of famous silver-producing center in New Galicia. Along with cycles and conditions of mining economy, pursues social dynamics evolving in Zacatecas throughout the 18th century, thus pointing out the prototypical case of Basque immigrants who got rich, acquired great estates, and became noblemen. Such "seigneurial entrepreneurs" would endure in Mexico until the aftermath of independence. [T. Hampe-Martínez]

1271 Marchena Fernández, Juan. De franciscanos, apaches y ministros ilustrados en los pasos perdidos del norte de Nueva España. (*Arch. Ibero-Am.*, 52 : 205/208, 1992, p. 513–559, tables)

Based in part on a 1784 Real Orden and the investigation preceding its promulgation, this examination of royal policy after the expulsion of the Jesuits discerns less reliance on the military and a tendency to strengthen missions. [EBC]

1272 Mathes, Michael. Oasis culturales en la antigua California: las bibliotecas de las misiones de Baja California en 1773. (*Estud. Hist. Novohisp.*, 10, 1991, p. 369–442, bibl.)

Publication of a 1773 inventory of books owned by exiled Jesuits. Organized by mission, includes bibliographic identification of titles. [EBC]

1273 Mirafuentes Galván, José Luis. Agustín Ascuhul, el profeta de Moctezuma: milenarismo y aculturación en Sonora, Guaymas, 1737. (*in* Simposio de Historia y Antropología de Sonora, *16th, Hermosillo, México, 1993*. Memoria. Hermosillo, México: Instituto de Investigaciones Históricas, Univ. de Sonora, 1993, p. 157–171, bibl.)

Account and analysis of a millenarian movement of about 500 Indians who followed a prophet who called himself Moctezuma. Describes the despair of Indians, caught between demands of missions and settlers, who had been dismissed from work in the failing mining communities. [EBC]

1274 Norris, Jim. The Franciscans in New Mexico, 1692–1754: toward a new assessment. (*Americas/Francisc.*, 51:2, Oct. 1994, p. 151–171, tables)

Suggests periodization for quality of friars in New Mexico, finding quality level to be connected with increasingly solitary service on a frontier where Franciscans suffered constant transfers and tremendous difficulty learning native languages. [EBC]

1275 Phillips, George Harwood. Indians and intruders in central California, 1769–1849. Norman: Univ. of Oklahoma Press, 1993. 223 p.: bibl., ill., index. (The Civilization of the American Indian series; 207)

Important revisionist view of American conquest of California examines relations among Anglos, Californios, and Indians after the secularization of missions in the San Joaquin Valley. Concludes that strengthening Indian society in the interior—through addition of coastal Indians who had been released from missions and enriched by the sale of their commodities to New Mexico—debilitated Californio ranchers, and encouraged them to ally with Anglos in the 1840s, thus facilitating American conquest of California. [EBC]

1276 Picazo I Muntaner, Antoni. Presupuestos defensivos y económicos de la colonización de Texas. (*Arch. Ibero-Am.*, 53: 209/212, enero/dic. 1993, p. 315–323)

Argues that 17th-century French efforts to colonize Texas in order to find outlets for their contraband prompted the Spaniards to colonize Texas. [EBC]

1277 El Plan de Pitic de 1789 y las nuevas poblaciones proyectadas en las Provincias Internas de la Nueva España. Transcrito y editado por Joseph P. Sánchez. (*CLAHR/Albuquerque*, 2:4, Fall 1993, p. 449–467)

This transcription of an important letter describes the context in which modifications to the town-planning ordinances of the Laws of the Indies were suggested for the town of Hermosillo. See also item **1288.** [EBC]

1278 Porras Muñoz, Guillermo. El nuevo descubrimiento de San José del Parral. México: Univ. Nacional Autónoma de México, Instituto de Investigaciones Históricas,

1988. 245 p.: bibl. (Serie Historia novohispana; 39)

Annotated publication of a large collection of documents from the AGI concerning the foundation of Parral provides information to date unavailable about any other *real de minas.* Informative introduction. [EBC]

1279 Primer libro de actas de Cabildo de las Minas de los Zacatecas, 1557–1586. Paleografía, introducción e índices de Eugenio del Hoyo. Prólogo de Federico Sescosse. Zacatecas, Mexico: Edición del H. Ayuntamiento de Zacatecas, 1991. 190 p.: ill., indexes.

Recently discovered after being lost for many years, this first volume of the minutes of the municipality of the mines of Zacatecas is of great interest to historians. Covers 1557–86. [AL]

1280 Radding, Cynthia. Ciclos demográficos, trabajo y comunidad en los pueblos serranos de la Provincia de Sonora, siglo XVIII. (*in* Congresso sobre a História da População da América Latina, *1st, Ouro Preto, Brazil, 1989.* Actas. São Paulo: Fundação SEADE, 1990, p. 265–275, bibl., tables)

Suggests a new conceptualization of the organization of the indigenous population in relation to missions, the environment, secular economy, and household and family history. Through careful analysis of census materials and household composition, the author revises methods of analyzing and explaining Indian population decline in missions. [EBC]

1281 Radding, Cynthia. Work, labour and the market: the responses of farmers and semi-nomadic peoples to colonialism in North-West Mexico. (*Slavery Abolit.*, 15:2, Aug. 1994, p. 52–68)

Lucid theoretical overview explores gradual changes as a result of the establishment of missions and the proliferation of Hispanicized farmers among the Pima, Eudeve, and Opata peoples of Sonora. Nuanced views of productivity and the meaning of work in relation to the villages' cultural and economic organization. [EBC]

1282 Reff, Daniel T. Contextualizing missionary discourse: the Benavides *Memorials* of 1630 and 1634. (*J. Anthropol. Res.*, 50:1, Spring 1994, p. 51–67, bibl.)

Applies recent theory to the analysis of a 17th-century Franciscan text. Through a careful examination of the text, the author indicates how the worldview, as well as political and spiritual purposes, governed the writer's ethnographic vision. [EBC]

1283 Río, Ignacio del. Los grupos regionales de poder y el ejercicio de la autoridad política en la gobernación de Sonora y Sinaloa, 1732–1748. (*in* Simposio de Historia y Antropología de Sonora, *16th, Hermosillo, México, 1993.* Memoria. Hermosillo, México: Instituto de Investigaciones Históricas, Univ. de Sonora, 1993, p. 139–156)

Details shifting power relations between Jesuits and civil authorities during a time in which Jesuits won most of the battles. Also describes the results of the Visita of Pedro de Rivera to the presidios between 1724–28. [EBC]

1284 Ríos-Bustamante, Antonio José. Los Angeles, pueblo y región, 1781–1850: continuidad y adaptación en la periferia del norte mexicano. México: Instituto Nacional de Antropología e Historia, 1991. 384 p.: bibl., ill., maps. (Serie Historia. Col. Divulgación)

Analytic and narrative work places the history of Los Angeles within the context of the development of a region of northern Mexico. Various other questions and debates with earlier historians are considered. Based on secondary sources. [EBC]

1285 Ríos Zúñiga, Rosalina. La secularización de la enseñanza en Zacatecas: del Colegio de San Luis Gonzaga al Instituto Literario, 1784–1838. (*Hist. Mex.,* 44:2, oct./dic. 1994, p. 299–332, bibl.)

Based on new documentation, history of the principal advanced educational institution in Zacatecas emphasizes administration and finance. [EBC]

1286 Rock, Rosalind Z. *Mujeres de substancia:* case studies of women of property in Northern New Spain. (*CLAHR/Albuquerque,* 2:4, Fall 1993, p. 425–440)

Examines a small number of legal cases and testaments involving women. Lacks historiographic context, but contains descriptions of both social life and legal process. [EBC]

1287 Salinas Varona, Gregorio de. The 1693 expedition of Gregorio de Salinas Varona to sustain the missionaries among the

Tejas Indians. Edited by William C. Foster and Jack Jackson. Translated by Ned F. Brierly. (*Southwest. Hist. Q.,* 97:2, Oct. 1993, p. 265–311, map)

Translation, annotation, and extensive introduction to the record of geographic exploration. Valuable for its reconstruction of the 1693 route and its connections to modern landmarks. [EBC]

1288 Sanchez, Jane C. The Plan of Pitic: Galindo Navarro's letter to Teodoro de Croix, Comandante General de las Provincias Internas. (*CLAHR/Albuquerque,* 3:1, Winter 1994, p. 79–89, ill.)

Translation of correspondence related to the creation of the Plan of Pitic. This document, based on the Laws of the Indies, helped determine how subsequent frontier towns would be created and spatially organized. [EBC]

1289 Teja, Jesús F. de la. San Antonio de Béxar: a community on New Spain's northern frontier. Albuquerque: Univ. of New Mexico Press, 1995. 239 p.: bibl., ill., index.

Lucid and thoughtful review of the historical work on the northern frontier focuses on community formation instead of the customary emphasis on discrete elements such as presidio, mission, and ranches. Analyzes government policies, ethnic conflicts, floating populations, Canary Island migration, military settlers, and demographic materials. [EBC]

Tenenbaum, Barbara A. The making of a fait accompli: Mexico and the Provincias Internas, 1776–1846. See item **1242.**

1290 Vargas-Lobsinger, María. Formación y decadencia de una fortuna: los mayorazgos de San Miguel de Aguayo y de San Pedro del Alamo, 1583–1823. México: Univ. Nacional Autónoma de México, 1992. 237 p.: bibl., ill., index. (Serie historia novohispana; 48)

Detailed study of the economic history of one of the wealthiest families of New Spain. Despite its title, this study focuses mostly on the period 1700–1825. Rich in information, this is a tour de force for those interested in colonial elites and the administration of their properties. [AL]

Independence, Revolution, and Post-Revolution

BARBARA A. TENENBAUM, *Mexican Specialist, Hispanic Division, Library of Congress; Editor in Chief, Encyclopedia of Latin American History and Culture*
DON M. COERVER, *Professor of History, Texas Christian University*
SUZANNE B. PASZTOR, *Assistant Professor of History, University of the Pacific*

INDEPENDENCE TO REVOLUTION

SCHOLARLY WRITING ON MEXICAN HISTORY during the crucial years from 1810–1910 has reached a level of maturity unknown just a half decade ago. The steadily increasing professionalization of scholarship and the extraordinary improvement in Mexican archives are beginning to pay extravagant dividends in the excellence of recent research.

Mexican historians retain a fascination with politics—particularly with border studies—that has long been on the wane, with conspicuous and noteworthy exceptions, in the US. The meritorious trend whereby researchers examine regional responses to national policy and politics, noted in volume 54, continues to flourish. Although much remains to be done, these investigations show the limited impact of national dictates on regional behavior, in some cases provoking revolt rather than submission. However, if Serrano Alvarez is to be believed, such analyses will not necessarily lead to generalizations about the nation as a whole (item **1380**). Indeed, perhaps we are approaching a much greater appreciation for the difficulties of centralizing Mexico, even in terms of its scholarship, than previously thought. Can a revisionism about Porfirio Díaz on this score be far behind?

This biennium saw far fewer works on women's history and *microhistoria* and an enormous increase in economic studies, particularly for works examining the development of credit. Both the period of independence, 1808–21, and that between 1856–67 still remain significantly understudied, apart from the hagiography cherished in previous epochs. Nevertheless, this biennium saw major contributions from Guedea for the former period (items **1327** and **1328**) and Mallon for Puebla (item **1350**), which added to the works published previously by Cerutti on Monterey and the northeast (see *HLAS 54:1330* and *HLAS 54:1348*). Fortunately, thanks to new work by Sordo Cedeño (item **1383**), complementing the pioneering efforts of Noriega Elío (see *HLAS 50:1175*), the previously inscrutable centralist years seem more comprehensible. Art history, particularly in books of photography, has become very popular and can provide extraordinary insights into the Mexican soul. Particularly intriguing is the group of portraits of dead children from Ameca, Jalisco (item **1364**), providing evidence that in their depiction of the rush toward modernity, scholars are neglecting the other-worldly aspect of Mexican cosmology. Promising studies also appeared on the army, prisons, public health in both mining and urban environments, agrarian legislation, sugar and rubber plantations, wheat production, environment, and travelers' accounts.

Judging from the books and articles reviewed this biennium, reflecting publishing trends prior to 1995, we can expect to see a lively resurgence in sophisticated cultural analyses as more and more historians look into the creation of Mexican nationality. These will be a welcome complement to the excellent in-depth economic studies fostered by Marichal, Ludlow, Liehr, Cerutti, Carmagnani, and Grosso, as well as by the cadres of students they have trained. [BAT]

REVOLUTION AND POST-REVOLUTION

SUB-NATIONAL HISTORY PERSISTS as a major attraction for researchers. Wasserman examines the general issue of the regional approach to modern Mexican history (item **1622**) as well as providing an excellent example of it in his post-1910 study of the Chihuahuan elite (item **1623**). Regional studies range geographically from Baja California (items **1461** and **1436**) to Quintana Roo (item **1499**). Important state studies include Aguascalientes (item **1483**), Campeche (item **1394**), Guerrero (item **1584**), Michoacán (items **1590** and **1620**), Nuevo León (item **1473**), Sonora (item **1519**), Tlaxcala (item **1425**), Veracruz (item **1477**), and Yucatán (items **1507** and **1413**).

Agrarian studies continue as a major focus of research. Rivera Castro provides a collection of documents useful for understanding the general framework of agrarian reform (item **1580**). Although the emphasis continues to be on Cardenist policies, studies appeared that covered the pre-revolutionary period through the 1980s. Markiewicz provides a revisionist overview of the agrarian reform program from 1915–46, with an emphasis on the 1930s-40s (item **1529**). Cotter examines the technical side of 1920s-30s agriculture leading up to the Mexican Agricultural Project of 1943 (item **1450**), while Maldonado Aguirre connects the agrarian movement with the rise of the presidentialist State between 1920–34 (item **1526**). State-level studies of agrarian reform appeared for Chiapas (item **1579**), Sinaloa (item **1568**), Sonora (items **1522** and **1523**), and Zacatecas (item **1500**).

Interest in labor history declined moderately, with no multi-volume works issued during this biennium. The interaction between the government and labor is addressed in works by Ramírez Cuellar (item **1576**), Roxborough (item **1587**), and Tirado Villegas (item **1613**). The transnational aspect of labor is examined in Gonzáles (item **1482**) and Guerin-Gonzáles (item **1486**). Fuentes Díaz focuses on the tension between the worker activism encouraged by anarchist thought and the conservative social activism of the Catholic Church (item **1474**).

Historians continue to be concerned with economic development and the role of the government in the economy. Haber discusses both the historiography of Mexico's transition to an industrial economy as well as the process itself (item **1489**). Cerda reassesses the Porfirian economy and identifies important structural problems leading to the Revolution (item **1440**), while Cárdenas discusses the growing role of the national government in the economy from 1927–58 (item **1430**). The changing situation in the maquiladora industry is examined by Wilson (item **1625**) and Williams and Passe-Smith (item **1624**).

One notable trend is the production of more works focusing on women. Using oral history, prosopography, and biography, several authors have contributed to the knowledge of women's activities during the Revolution. Lau and Ramos review existing scholarship on this topic and provide an excellent summary of documents (item **1550**). *Las mujeres en la revolución mexicana* is a narrative and pictographic history with biographical sketches of the Porfirian and revolutionary eras (item **1549**). With a brief summary of the service records of 13 women contained in the Archivo de la Defensa Nacional, Monroy Pérez shows the varied roles of women during the Revolution (item **1545**). In *Vivencias femeninas de la revolución* (item **1415**), Basurto transcribes interviews with two sisters who were active in the Casa del Obrero Mundial. An extensive interview is the basis for *Carolina Escudero Luján*, a biography of Francisco J. Múgica's wife describing her experiences during the Revolution and detailing her political and social activities (item **1466**).

Four works that do not fit into the above categories also stand out: Britton provides an excellent survey and thought-provoking analysis of the images of the Revolution conveyed by US writers from 1910–60 (item **1420**); Brunk explores Zapata's relationship with urban intellectuals, and how that relationship influenced the gap between his regional rebellion and the national revolution (item **1422**); Camp furnishes a much needed examination of the development of the Mexican military (item **1427**); and Knight contributes to the ongoing debate over the significance of the Cárdenas Administration (item **1509**). [DC and SP]

INDEPENDENCE TO REVOLUTION

1291 Arnold, Linda. Vulgar and elegant: politics and procedure in early national Mexico. (*Americas/Francisc.*, 50:4, April 1994, p. 481–500)

Discussion of judicial procedures of *visita de cárcel* (prison interviews by judicial anthorities) and *amparo* (to protect Vicente García Torres, founder and publisher of *El Monitor Republicano*, from military persecution) tries to show how struggling with these issues helped define the nature of the state. Author's failure to place events in their proper political context, however, blunts her argument.

1292 Avila Palafox, Ricardo. Clientelismo y manipulación de los jefes políticos. (*in* Las formas y las políticas del dominio agrario: homenaje a François Chevalier. Coordinación de Ricardo Avila Palafox, Carlos Martínez Assad y Jean Meyer. Guadalajara, Mexico: Editorial Univ. de Guadalajara, 1992, p. 215–231)

Interesting look at the role of *jefes políticos*, arguing that they had little freedom vis-à-vis the governor of the state of Mexico, and used cooptation rather than repression.

1293 Banco de México. Recuerdos de México: gráfica del siglo XIX; colección del Banco de México, presentado en el Museo de San Carlos, mayo-julio de 1987. Investigación, selección de obras y de textos de Elena Horz de Vía. México: INBA; SEP; BM, 1987? 127 p.: bibl., ill. (some col.).

Beautiful compilation of views of 19th-century Mexico, mostly of the capital. Terrific illustrations, but let the scholar be aware that the images themselves often convey narratives of their own.

1294 Bastian, Jean Pierre. Metodismo y rebelión política en Tlaxcala, 1874–1920. (*in* Simposio Internacional de Investigaciones Socio-Históricas sobre Tlaxcala, *1st, Tlaxcala, México, 1985.* Memorias. Tlaxcala, Mexico: Gobierno del Estado de Tlaxcala, Instituto Tlaxcalteca de Cultura, Univ. Autónoma de Tlaxcala; México: Univ. Iberoamericana, 1986, p. 108–118, map)

Fascinating article concerning the relationships between Methodists and patriotic celebrations, resistance movements, rebellions, and the revolution in Tlaxcala. Recommended.

1295 Bazant de Saldaña, Mílada. Historia de la educación durante el Porfiriato. México: Colegio de México, Centro de Estudios Históricos, 1993. 297 p.: bibl. (Serie Historia de la educación)

Revealing look at how Porfirian ideology translated into educational planning and results. Essential for scholars of development.

1296 Bernecker, Walther L. Contrabando: ilegalidad y corrupción en el México decimonónico. (*Hist. Graf.*, 1:1, 1993, p. 127–155)

Offers theory of corruption as historical phenomenon and contends that Mexico became especially corrupt due to Spanish past. No statistics, but presents new German sources.

1297 Blázquez Domínguez, Carmen. Políticos y comerciantes en Veracruz y Xalapa: 1827–1829. Xalapa, Mexico: Comisión Estatal Conmemorativa del V Centenario del Encuentro de Dos Mundos, Gobierno del Estado de Veracruz, 1992. 147 p.: bibl. (Col. V centenario; 19)

Details the nature of the struggle between masonic lodges as well as that among Spanish and creole merchants, who thrived in Mexico's busiest and richest port. Heavily based on secondary sources.

1298 Bracamonte y Sosa, Pedro. Amos y sirvientes: las haciendas de Yucatán, 1789–1860. Mérida, Mexico: Univ. Autónoma de Yucatán, 1993. 274 p.: bibl., ill., maps. (Tratados)

Important work documents the transition from tribute payment to salaried labor on Yucatán haciendas, arguing that such transformation led to the Caste War. Also discusses the development of Yucatán ruling class. Recommended.

1299 Brown, Jonathan C. Trabajadores nativos y extranjeros en el México porfiriano. (*Siglo XIX*, 3:9, mayo/agosto 1994, p. 7–49)

Extensive survey of mostly US-born workers in Mexico, particularly in mining and railroads. Confirms view of significant anti-foreign worker prejudice and agitation especially after 1906, even as Mexicans began replacing foreign workers. Recommended.

1300 Carmagnani, Marcello. Estado y mercado: la economía pública del liberalismo mexicano, 1850–1911. México: El Colegio de México; Fideicomiso Historia de las Américas; Fondo de Cultura Económica, 1994. 439 p.: bibl., graphs, index, tables.

Major contribution to understanding the fiscal economy of Mexico during the crucial years of liberalism. Indispensable for any study of that period, although author tells only the official part of the story. Highly recommended.

1301 Carmagnani, Marcello *et al.* La fundación del Estado mexicano, 1821–1855. Coordinación de Josefina Zoraida Vázquez. México: Nueva Imagen, 1994. 187 p.: bibl. (Interpretaciones de la historia de México)

Five thought-provoking essays by Vázquez, Carmagnani, Hamnett, Di Tella, and Sordo Cedeño on the political history of Mexico, 1750–1854. See especially Carmagnani for an original survey of political organization bringing a wide range of sources to bear on the subject.

1302 Cerutti, Mario. Comerciantes y generalización del crédito laico en México, 1860–1910: experiencias regionales. (*Anu. IEHS*, 7, 1992, p. 211–236, bibl.)

Noteworthy examination of research on how merchants in various regions filled the credit gap after the Church left the business following the liberal reforms. Essential for those studying social history in various localities. As author notes, these results disprove allegations that merchants were parasitic, backward, or pre-bourgeois. Recommended.

1303 Chávez Chávez, Jorge. Justificación de la guerra contra los indios bárbaros: una acción del indigenismo mexicano. (*in* Congreso Internacional de Historia Regional Comparada 3rd, Ciudad Juárez, 1991. Actas. Edición de Ricardo León García. Ciudad Juárez, Mexico: Univ. Autónoma de Ciudad Juárez, 1992, p. 115–121)

Briefly looks at the official attitude toward Indians who resisted colonization. Goes a bit too far when stating that this also identifies those who resisted "order" and "progress." Perhaps true on the frontier, but not further inland.

1304 La Ciudad de México en la primera mitad del siglo XIX. v. 1, Economía y estructura urbana. v. 2, Gobierno y política; Sociedad y cultura. Recopilación de Regina Hernández. México: Instituto de Investigaciones Dr. José María Luis Mora, 1994. 2 v.: bibl., ill.

Fifteen essays detailing life in Mexico City from 1800–60 discuss everything from warehousing of foodstuffs to the nature of the workforce. Stronger on the economic and cultural than the political topics.

1305 Contreras Cruz, Carlos. Ciudad y salud en el Porfiriato: la política urbana y el saneamiento de Puebla, 1880–1906. (*Siglo XIX*, 1:3, junio 1992, p. 55–76, tables)

Ground-breaking article on public health concerns in Puebla. Indicates that there were scientists during the Porfiriato who advocated urban health policies. Promising research direction.

1306 El crecimiento de las ciudades noroccidentales. Coordinación de Jaime Olveda. Zapopan, Mexico: El Colegio de Jalisco; Colima, Mexico: Univ. de Colima; México: Instituto Nacional de Antropología e Historia, 1994. 325 p.: bibl., ill., maps.

Collection of essays on the cities of the northwest ranging from Tijuana south to Guadalajara and from Hermosillo to Zacatecas and Durango. Good introduction to urban development in a neglected region.

1307 Cruz Barrera, Nydia E. El despliegue del castigo: las penitenciarias porfirianas en México. (*in* Congreso Internacional de Historia Regional Comparada *3rd, Ciudad Juárez, 1991.* Actas. Edición de Ricardo León García. Ciudad Juárez, Mexico: Univ. Autónoma de Ciudad Juárez, 1992, p. 147–155)

Elementary article indicating many important research possibilities—prisons as instruments of reform as well as punishment, prisons as part of Porfirian order, prisons as mirror of Porfirian absorption of European and US thinking, etc.

1308 Cultura e identidad nacional. Recopilación de Roberto Blancarte. México: Consejo Nacional para la Cultura y las Artes; Fondo de Cultura Económica, 1994. 424 p.: bibl. (Sección de obras de historia)

Eleven essays on a panoply of little-studied subjects, mostly on pan-Americanism and indigenism, but also on Mexico's presence in Spain from 1886–1936 (Rosenzweig), and anti-Americanism in Mexico after 1847 (Suárez Aguello).

1309 Cunningham, Bob and **Harry P. Hewitt.** A "lovely land full of roses and thorns:" Emil Landberg and Mexico, 1835–1866. (*Southwest. Hist. Q.,* 98:3, Jan. 1995, p. 387–425, ill., maps, photos)

Uncritical examination of career of Danish emigré to Mexico who served in the army on the frontier during the 1850s and in the imperial army of the 1860s.

1310 Dachary, Alfredo César and **Stella Maris Arnaiz Burne.** La frontera Caribe de México en el XIX: una historia olvidada. (*Siglo XIX,* 3:7, oct. 1993, p. 33–62, map, tables)

Important look at a neglected subject discusses the decline, reemergence, and dismemberment of Yucatán in the context of its relations with Belize and Cozumel.

1311 Díaz, Porfirio. Memorias de Porfirio Díaz. v. 1–2. Prólogo de Moisés González Navarro. México: Consejo Nacional para la Cultura y las Artes, 1994. 2 v.: bibl. (Memorias mexicanas)

Díaz, that most mysterious of Mexican leaders, finished the first draft of this memoir in 1892. It concerns the time of his birth to the end of the war against the French and was printed in 100 numbered copies for close friends and associates. Apparently, the President never returned to the task.

The evolution of the Mexican political system. See *HLAS 55:2854.*

1312 Falcón, Romana. El Estado incapaz: lucha entre naciones; poder, territorio, "salvajes" y jefes de departamento. (*in* Las formas y las políticas del dominio agrario: homenaje a François Chevalier. Coordinación de Ricardo Avila Palafox, Carlos Martínez Assad, y Jean Meyer. Guadalajara, Mexico: Editorial Univ. de Guadalajara, 1992, p. 189–214)

Promising analysis of the relationship of the nation-state to its Texas-Coahuila frontier in the 1820s-30s. Contends that representatives of state and nation lacked authority, unlike experience during the viceregal period.

1313 Favre, Henri. Race et nation au Mexique de l'indépendance a la révolution. (*Annales/Paris,* 49:4, juillet/août 1994, p. 951–976)

Discussion of views on Indians including those of lesser-known figures like Francisco Pimentel, Vicente Riva Palacio, Francisco Cosmes, and José Limantour. Reveals the obvious contradiction in Mexican ideology between the idea of *mestizaje* and the negative attitude toward immigration.

Favret Tondato, Rita. Tenencia de la tierra en el estado de Coahuila, 1880–1987. See *HLAS 55:1378.*

1314 Los ferrocarriles y el General Manuel González: necesidad, negocios y política. Recopilación de Georgette Emilia José Valenzuela. México: Univ. Iberoamericana, 1994. 467 p.: bibl.

Introduction to González archive at the Biblioteca Iberoamericana details railroad projects undertaken during his administration. Crucial for understanding economic development from 1880 on.

1315 Figueroa Esquer, Raúl. El doctor Mora y la neutralidad británica durante la guerra entre México y Estado Unidos. (*Secuencia/México,* 16, enero/abril 1990, p. 5–28, ill.)

Details and perhaps exaggerates Mora's role in the negotiations of the Treaty of Guadalupe-Hidalgo. Brings new light to the story of Mora, but uses few English-language sources.

1316 Flores Clair, Eduardo. Trabajo, salud y muerte: Real del Monte, 1874. (*Siglo XIX*, 1:3, junio 1992, p. 9–28, graphs)

Important contribution to demographic and industrial history. Essay examines the ways of death in an infamous silver mine.

1317 Gálvez Medrano, Arturo. Regionalismo y gobierno general: el caso de Nuevo León y Coahuila, 1855–1864. Monterrey, Mexico: Gobierno del Estado de Nuevo León, Secretaría General, A.G.E.N.L., 1993. 208 p.: bibl., maps.

Fits in with current interest in regional vs. central authority theme (see items **1338** and **1326**). Author tends to give more credit to central government than other scholars.

Garavaglia, Juan Carlos and **Juan Carlos Grosso.** Puebla desde una perspectiva microhistórica: la villa de Tepeaca y su entorno agrario; población, producción e intercambio, 1740–1870. See item **1150.**

1318 García, Romualdo. Romualdo García. Monterrey, Mexico: MARCA, 1993. 59 p.: chiefly ill.

Affecting book of photographs by Guanajuato's premier turn-of-the-century photographer is considerably enhanced with a glorious commentary by Elena Poniatowska on images and their power.

1319 García Avila, Sergio and **Eduardo Miranda Arrieta.** Desorden social y criminalidad en Michoacán, 1825–1850. Prólogo de José Luis Soberanes Fernández. Morelia, Mexico: Supremo Tribunal de Justicia del Estado de Michoacán de Ocampo, 1994. 206 p.: bibl.

Lots of meat here for social historians interested in using local judicial archives to investigate general and sexual crimes ranging from vagrancy to sodomy. Recommended.

1320 García Quintanilla, Alejandra. Salud y progreso en Yucatán en el XIX: Mérida: el sarampión de 1882. (*Siglo XIX*, 1:3, junio 1992, p. 29–53, tables)

Clever article that uses the measles epidemic of 1882 and others to examine class distinctions in Mérida. Concludes that this epidemic played a part in quieting Maya resistance to henequen mechanization.

1321 Garrett, Jenkins. The Mexican-American War of 1846–1848: a bibliography of the holdings of the libraries, the University of Texas at Arlington. Prepared and edited by Katherine R. Goodwin. College Station: Texas A&M Univ. Press, 1995. 693 p.: bibl., ill., index. (Special collections publication; 2)

Useful bibliographic resource for scholars interested in the war and relations between northern Mexico and the US.

Garritz, Amaya. Impresos novohispanos, 1808–1821. See item **1152.**

1322 Giron, Nicole. Manuel Payno: un liberal en tono menor. (*Hist. Mex.*, 44:1, julio/sept. 1994, p. 5–35, bibl.)

Thoughtful discussion of what it meant to be a *moderado* in Mexican political life from 1855–67. Should help provide a new way to understand the political complexity of a difficult period.

1323 Gómez Tepexicuapan, Amparo. Veinte fotógrafos del siglo XIX. México: Instituto Nacional de Antropología e Historia, 1994. 59 p.: bibl., ill.

Misleading title for a small collection of relatively unknown photographers of the 1860s. Excellent for study of the period and for the development of photography in Mexico. Photo of historian Niceto de Zamacois by L. Veraza is a gem.

1324 González Martínez, Joaquín R. El movimiento regenerador de Sierra Gorda, 1847–1849. (*Estud. Latinoam./Poland*, 15, 1992, p. 167–186, map)

Argues that revolt had two layers—oligarchic and campesino—whose interests coincided for a time. When the peasants' interests ceased to be congruent with those of the oligarchy, the campesinos struggled onward to their defeat, leaving a legacy of revolt for years to come.

Grosso, Juan Carlos. Mercados y región en el área central de México: San Juan de los Llanos y los pueblos de la Sierra Norte de Puebla, 1780–1840. See item **1163.**

1325 Grosso, Juan Carlos. San Juan de los Llanos, 1780–1840: producción e intercambio en el centro de México. (*Siglo XIX*, 3:8, enero/abril 1994, p. 7–44, bibl., graph, maps, tables)

Well-researched article about agricultural production and marketing in Puebla shows that many peasants were wedded to the commercial economy and sold their produce either to Puebla City or to Veracruz, depending on the period. Recommended.

1326 Guardino, Peter. Barbarism or republican law?: Guerrero's peasants and national politics, 1820–1846. (*HAHR*, 75:2, May 1995, p. 185–213)

Important analysis of how villages in the present-day state of Guerrero reacted to centralist decrees and formed an important base of support for Mexican liberalism. Recommended.

1327 Guedea, Virginia. En busca de un gobierno alterno: los Guadalupes de México. México: Univ. Nacional Autónoma de México, Seminario de Rebeliones y Revoluciones en México, 1992. 412 p. (Serie Historia novohispana; 46)

Groundbreaking study of a creole movement to win the independence of New Spain. Tells us much about early politics of a supposedly hardly political time and includes biographical material on major actors. Recommended.

1328 Guedea, Virginia. Los procesos electorales insurgentes. (*Estud. Hist. Novohisp.*, 11, 1991, p. 201–249)

Examines process and formation of juntas among insurgent groups during Independence. Contends that these juntas can provide information on the motivations that different groups had in common to rise up in rebellion. [J. Maldonado]

1329 Güemez Pineda, Arturo. Liberalismo en tierras del caminante: Yucatán, 1812–1840. Zamora, Mexico: Colegio de Michoacán, 1994. 286 p.: ill. (Col. Investigaciones)

One of the few in-depth looks at the agrarian legislation of liberalism as it affected regional populations in Yucatán in general and Indian communities in particular. Recommended.

1330 Güemez Pineda, Arturo. La rebelión de Nohcacab: prefacio inédito de la guerra de castas. (*Relaciones/Zamora*, 13:52, otoño 1992, p. 167–202, map)

Impressive article that helps put Yucatán in better perspective with regard to its position in Mexico. In describing the revolt of isolated Nohcacab, draws attention to parallels with Texas on the one hand and other revolts at the same time on the other.

1331 Guillermo Kahlo, vida y obra: fotógrafo, 1872–1941; catálogo ilustrado. México: Consejo Nacional para la Cultura y las Artes, Instituto Nacional de Bellas Artes; Museo Estudio Diego Rivera; Museo Nacional de Arquitectura, 1993. 197 p.: bibl., ill.

Even in an exhibition devoted to *his* artistry, the Frida obsession dominates. His work, however, is gorgeous, reflecting a European sensibility let loose on Mexican vistas.

1332 Gutiérrez, Ludivina. Los estilos decimonónicos y porfirianos en Xalapa. Xalapa, Mexico: Univ. Veracruzana, 1986. 62 p.: bibl., ill.

Brief look at the stylistic changes wrought by economic growth and greater foreign influence in a key area of Mexico.

1333 Guzmán A., José Napoleón. Empresas y empresarios madereros en Michoacán, 1880–1915. (*Nuestra Hist./Caracas*, 4, enero/junio 1993, p. 73–88, photos)

Good beginning on the relations between excessive cutting, railroads, and mining in Michoacán. Nonetheless, article is somewhat poorly focused as author tries to say something about everything.

1334 Hamnett, Brian R. Juárez. London; New York: Longman, 1994. 301 p.: bibl., index, maps. (Profiles in power)

Based on primary as well as secondary materials, biography successfully strips away layers of mythology to present the most coherent and comprehensible Juárez yet seen. Good model for future authors when attempting the same for Santa Anna and Díaz. Recommended.

1335 Heath, Hilarie J. British merchant houses in Mexico, 1821–1860: conforming business practices and ethics. (*HAHR*, 73:2, May 1993, p. 261–290)

Opens new window on the issue of capital formation with an economist's look at the foreign commercial community. When read in tandem with Bernecker (item **1296**), depicts contraband in all its varied facets. Concludes with strange indictment of British merchants for not participating in infrastructural development.

1336 Henderson, Peter V.N. Modernization and change in Mexico: La Záculpa rubber plantation, 1890–1920. (*HAHR*, 73:2, May 1993, p. 235–260, tables)

Excellent analysis of the conditions in a Chiapan rubber plantation during tumultuous years. Provides good insights into what the revolution did and did not accomplish for plantation workers. Recommended.

1337 Huerta, María Teresa. Empresarios del azúcar en el siglo XIX. México: Instituto Nacional de Antropología e Historia, 1993. 192 p.: bibl. (Col. Divulgación)

Building on previous smaller studies of Isidoro de la Torre, author creates indispensible work on sugar plantation owners in what is now the state of Morelos from 1780–1870. A must read for those investigating capital formation in Mexico, the 1808 coup against Iturrigaray (Yermo was a member of this group), and the background to *Zapatismo*. Recommended.

1338 Ibarra Bellon, Araceli. ¿*Commercial jealousy* o reforma agraria?: origen y naturaleza del Motín de Tepic; 13 de diciembre de 1855. (*Bol. Am.*, 34:44, 1994, p. 111–135, bibl.)

Detailed analysis of the conflicts between locals, nationals, and foreigners in the port of Tepic. Provokes comparison with other similar revolts. Recommended.

Indigenous revolts in Chiapas and the Andean highlands. See *HLAS 55:57*.

1339 Indio, nación y comunidad en el México del siglo XIX. Coordinación de Antonio Escobar Ohmstede con la colaboración especial de Patricia Lagos Preisser. México: Centro de Estudios Mexicanos y Centroamericanos; Centro de Investigaciones y Estudios Superiores en Antropología Social, 1993. 399 p.: bibl., map.

Eighteen thoughtful essays on Indians in various parts of Mexico and their relationship to the State. Although all articles are worthwhile, see especially Thomson on Indians and military service and Meyer on the indigenismo of the Second Empire. Unfortunately, studies from the south and the west are not included.

1340 Jackson, Robert H. The impact of liberal policy on Mexico's northern frontier: mission secularization and the development of Alta California, 1812–1846. (*CLAHR/Albuquerque*, 2:2, Spring 1993, p. 195–225, tables)

Shows how liberal legislation in Mexico City mandating the secularization of missions in Alta California led to the development of large cattle ranches and a mobile work force, including former Indians.

1341 Juárez Flores, José Juan and **Francisco Téllez Guerrero.** Las finanzas municipales de la ciudad de Tlaxcala durante el segundo imperio. (*Siglo XIX*, 3:8, enero/abril 1994, p. 79–121, bibl., graphs)

Extremely important article on municipal finance proceeding from Téllez's previous work on Puebla (see *Historia Mexicana*, Vol. 39, No. 4, abril/junio 1990, p. 951–978). Constantly stresses how difficult it was to increase tax collections. Regrettably it does not indicate change, if any, during the Empire. Highly recommended.

1342 Juárez Nieto, Carlos. Formación de la conciencia nacional en una provincia mexicana: Valladolid de Michoacán, 1808–1830. (*in* Colección nuestra patria es América: nación, Estado y conciencia nacional. Edición de Jorge Núñez Sánchez, Quito: Editora Nacional, 1992, v. 2, p. 161–181)

Superficial article that pretends to discuss Michoacán's response to the imposition of national authority. Adds nothing new.

1343 Krauze, Enrique. Siglo de caudillos: biografía política de México, 1810–1910. Barcelona: Tusquets Editores, 1994. 349 p.: bibl., ill., index. (Col. Andanzas; 207)

Ironic, and ultimately misleading, general overview of 19th-century Mexican political history that manages to adopt the style of the "official story" while proposing to debunk it.

1344 Lempérière, Annick. La formación de las elites liberales en el México del siglo XIX: Instituto de Ciencias y Artes del estado de Oaxaca. (*Secuencia/México*, 30, sept./dic. 1994, p. 57–94, bibl., ill., tables)

Discussion of the impact of the Instituto de Ciencias y Artes on the formation of liberal society in Oaxaca. Discusses how the school prepared the State for the transition from a traditional to a progressive society. Unfortunately, author makes no attempt to integrate information with economic data to explain how so many students from such a poor state could attend. Recommended.

1345 Lerner, Victoria. Dos generaciones de viajeros mexicanos del siglo XIX frente a los Estados Unidos. (*Relaciones/Zamora*, 14:55, verano 1993, p. 41–72, bibl.)

Groundbreaking look at two generations of Mexican travelers to the US—the "critical" one (1860–77) and the "pessimistic" one (1880–1905). The first group had great hopes for a post-Civil War US, but the second saw its democracy corrupted. Contains bibliography for further research.

1346 Liehr, Reinhard. La función crediticia de los comerciantes en la ciudad de Puebla, México en la época anterior a los bancos, 1821–1864. (*Ibero-Am. Arch.*, 20:3/4, 1994, p. 381–398, bibl.)

Excellent, but somewhat mistitled, look at credit in all its various forms pre- and post-Independence includes examples up to 1840. Shows how secular creditors began to substitute for clerical ones following 1821. Recommended.

1347 Lira, Andrés. La recepción de la Revolución Francesa en México, 1821–1848: José María Luis Mora y Lucas Alamán. (*Cah. Am. lat.*, 10, 1991, p. 287–301)

Thought-provoking analysis of two of the principal thinkers of the first half of the 19th century. Curiously, Mora is revealed as leery of bloodshed, whereas Alamán thought it promoted a more lively society!

1348 Luna Zamora, Rogelio. A través del camino real: una primera aproximación a la historia del comercio entre regiones de Colima y Jalisco en el siglo XIX. (*Estud. Jalisc.*, 2, nov. 1990, p. 29–42, tables)

Interesting and hopefully model study of regional inter-relation between Jalisco and Colima and its port of Manzanillo.

1349 MacGrégor, Javier. Dos casos de persecución periodística durante el porfiriato. (*Estud. Hist. Mod. Contemp. Méx.*, 15, 1992, p. 65–84)

Although article does not probe its subject deeply enough, its ideas—the persecution of journalists and the use of selective prosecution to harass would-be opponents—are interesting in themselves and deserve further investigation, as do judicial sources used.

1350 Mallon, Florencia E. Peasant and nation: the making of postcolonial Mexico and Peru. Berkeley: Univ. of California Press, 1994. 472 p.: bibl., index, maps.

Intensely theoretical discussion of important issues, particularly concerning the period of the Reform and the Intervention as seen from the perspective of villagers from the Sierra del Puebla and Morelos. Recommended.

1351 Marichal, Carlos; Manuel Miño Grijalva; and Paolo Riguzzi. Historia de la hacienda pública del Estado de México, 1824–1990. v. 1–4. México: El Colegio Mexiquense; Gobierno del Estado de México, Secretaría de Finanzas y Planeación, 1994. 4 v.: bibl., ill.

Ambitious and extremely valuable set contains analysis (v. 1), governors' *memorias* from 1824–57 and 1870–90 (v. 2–3), and other sources (v. 4). Recommended for any student of Mexican finance.

1352 Marroni de Velázquez, María da Gloria. Los orígenes de la sociedad industrial en Coahuila, 1840–1940. Saltillo, Mexico: Archivo Municipal de Saltillo, 1992. 238 p.: bibl.

Good beginning to a study of industry in Coahuila, but it does not cover systemically the 100 years mentioned in its title; instead it contains isolated chapters with large gaps.

1353 Martínez Assad, Carlos R. Del fin del porfiriato a la Revolución en el sursureste de México. (*Hist. Mex.*, 43:3, enero/marzo 1994, p. 487–504)

Brisk overview of region including Yucatán, Campeche, Tabasco, and Veracruz during the period. Argues that, owing in part to continuing communication difficulties, the revolution took a vastly different form in first three than in the north and Morelos.

1354 McKellar, Margaret Maud. Life on a Mexican ranche. Edited by Dolores L. Latorre. Bethlehem, Pa.: Lehigh Univ. Press; London: Associated Univ. Presses, 1994. 238 p.: bibl., ill., index, maps.

Describes, from an American perspective, the daily happenings on a ranch in Coahuila once belonging to the Sánchez Navarro family. Another look at *Like Water for Chocolate* country.

Mexico in the age of democratic revolutions, 1750–1850. See item **1192**.

1355 Mexico in the age of democratic revolutions, 1750–1850. Edited by Jaime E. Rodríguez O. Boulder, Colo.: Lynne Rienner, 1994. 343 p.: bibl., ill., index.

Ten essays and two comments comprise one of the few collections devoted almost solely to political questions during an intensely political, though often overlooked, period. See especially Castro Gutiérrez on José de Gálvez, Patch on Yucatán, and Staples on the Church.

1356 Mexico through foreign eyes, 1850–1990 = visto por ojos extranjeros. Edited by Carole Naggar and Fred Ritchin. New York: W.W. Norton, 1993. 320 p.: ill. (some col.).

The work of 50 foreign photographers, most of which reflects the splendors of the country. Wonderful collection for documenting a universe of points of view.

1357 Meyers, William K. Forge of progress, crucible of revolt: origins of the Mexican Revolution in La Comarca Lagunera, 1880–1911. Albuquerque: Univ. of New Mexico Press, 1994. 293 p.: bibl., ill., index.

Investigates the heartland of Maderista support, showing how landowners often took the lead in radicalizing the region. Notes, however, that influence of the Magonistas and other anarchists will always be underrepresented due to paucity and disorganization of sources.

1358 Miller, Daniel R. The frustrations of a Mexican mine under U.S. ownership. (*Historian/Honor Society*, 55:3, Spring 1993, p. 483–500)

In-depth look at US investment in a Mexican mine, an experience that was filled with frustration and caused losses even with Guggenheim management.

1359 Miller, Simon. Wheat production in Europe and America: Mexican problems in comparative perspective, 1770–1910. (*Agric. Hist.*, 68:3, Summer 1994, p. 16–34)

Places Mexican wheat agriculture in context with examples drawn from England. Shows that Mexican labor productivity was indeed lower than in Europe. Growth of machinery accelerated productivity by the end of the Porfiriato. Recommended.

1360 Miranda Arrieta, Eduardo. Economía y comunicaciones en el estado de Guerrero, 1877–1910. Morelia, Mexico: Univ. Michoacana de San Nicolás de Hidalgo, Instituto de Investigaciones Históricas, Depto. de His-

toria de México, 1994. 198 p.: bibl., ill. (Estudios de historia mexicana; 1)

Shows that Porfirian modernity never really made it to Guerrero, with the exception of the northern zone connecting the Río Balsas to the center. The rest of the state, including Acapulco, remained separated from Mexico City even at the dawn of the revolution.

1361 Moctezuma Barragán, Javier. José María Iglesias y la justicia electoral. México: Univ. Nacional Autónoma de México, Instituto de Investigaciones Jurídicas, 1994. 447 p.: bibl., ill.; (Serie C—Estudios históricos; 42)

Caught between the nobility of Juárez and the political savvy of Díaz, Iglesias has too often been neglected. Author argues for the importance and sincerity of his legal beliefs. Should be read in tandem with *Juárez and Díaz: machine politics in Mexico* by Laurens Ballard Perry (see *HLAS 42:2229*).

1362 Montellano, Francisco. C.B. Waite, fotógrafo: una mirada diversa sobre el México de principios del siglo XX. Presentación de Aurelio de los Reyes. México: Consejo Nacional para la Cultura y las Artes; Grijalbo, 1994. 221 p.: bibl., ill. (some col.).

Fascinating collection of the work of a virtually unknown American photographer, C.B. Waite. Would have benefitted from an essay by a US art historian on US photography at the time. Particularly useful are photos of early-20th-century rubber industry in Chiapas.

1363 Morales Moreno, Luis Gerardo. Museo público e historia legítima en México. (*Hist. Graf.*, 1:1, 1993, p. 156–163)

Superficial stab at museum history; worthwhile as first step.

1364 Museo de San Carlos (Mexico). Tránsito de angelitos: iconografía funeraria infantil. México: Museo de San Carlos., 1988. 119 p.: bibl., ill.

Collection of 100 photos taken by Juan de Dios Machain, local photographer in Ameca, Jalisco. In this extraordinary book, art historian Gutierre Aceves Piña examines the relation between 19th-century photos of dead children and the paintings and iconography of the Virgin and saints in Spain and Mexico. A must for those wanting to understand modern Mexico's rural cosmology.

1365 Los negocios y las ganancias de la colonia al México moderno. Recopilación de Leonor Ludlow y Jorge Silva Riquer. México: Instituto de Investigaciones Dr. José María Luis Mora; Instituto de Investigaciones Históricas (UNAM), 1993. 506 p.: graphs, tables.

Twenty-three provocative essays on the history of all types of credit in Mexico, from clerical to mutual aid to agrarian to banks. See especially essays on transportation infrastructure by Grosso, Valle Pavón, Souto Mantecón, and Yuste.

1366 La noticia curiosa en el siglo XIX: antología. Recopilación de Roldán Peniche Barrera. Mérida, Mexico: Instituto de Seguridad Social de los Trabajadores del Estado de Yucatán, 1993. 138 p.: bibl., ill.

Fascinating source for the social history of Yucatán. Author includes brief introduction to this "human interest" story.

1367 Olveda, Jaime. Las viejas oligarquías y la reforma liberal: el caso de Guadalajara. (*Siglo XIX*, 2:4, oct. 1992, p. 9–30)

Largely theoretical article asserts that liberal reform did little to alter social relations in Guadalajara. Would have been more useful with the addition of full archival data of property sales, etc.

1368 Olvera Sandoval, José Antonio. Agricultura, riego y conflicto social en la región citrícola de Nuevo León, 1860–1910. (*Siglo XIX*, 2:5, feb. 1993, p. 59–78, table)

Analysis of citrus growing area of Montemorelos in Nuevo León, concentrating on the difficulties of procuring sufficient water.

1369 Orejel Salas, Hermelinda. Las mujeres que forjaron una nueva sociedad: trabajadoras y sindicalistas; del porfiriato a la etapa cardenista. (*in* Capítulos de historia de la ciudad de Guadalajara. Guadalajara, Mexico: Ayuntamiento de Guadalajara, 1992, p. 194–238, bibl., tables)

Thorough study of the female labor force and its unionization covers more than 75 years. Important contribution for labor historians. [A. Lavrin]

1370 Orozco, Víctor. Las guerras indias en la historia de Chihuahua: antología. Ciudad Juárez, Mexico: Univ. Autónoma de Ciudad Juárez; Instituto Chihuahuense de la Cultura, 1992. 458 p.: bibl., ill.

Collection of documents from 1771–1887 concerning the history of Indians in Chihuahua, told mostly by their enemies.

1371 Pérez Acevedo, Martín. Empresarios y empresas en Morelia, 1860–1910. Morelia, México: Univ. Michoacana de San Nicolás de Hidalgo, Instituto de Investigaciones Históricas, 1994. 259 p.: bibl., ill. (Col. Historia nuestra; 12)

In-depth studies of five major business figures in Morelia. Depiction of the economic climate of the area includes the reaction of other classes to their activities. Good beginning for a thorough study of capitalism in Michoacán.

1372 Pérez Toledo, Sonia. El pronunciamiento de julio de 1840 en la Ciudad de México. (*Estud. Hist. Mod. Contemp. Méx.*, 15, 1992, p. 31–45)

Attempts to explain popular classes' participation and non-participation in Gómez Farías-José Urrea abortive coup. Unfortunately, it sticks to predictable sources rather than going to judicial records, etc.

1373 El poblamiento de México: una visión histórico-demográfica. t. 3, México en el siglo XIX. México: Secretaría de Gobernación, Consejo Nacional de Población, 1993. 1 v.

Third volume in this excellent series. Includes nine thoughtful essays ranging from public policy on immigration (Illades Aguilar) to demographics (McCaa). Also includes brief summaries on European (González Navarro) and Asian (Ota Mishima) newcomers.

1374 El poder y el dinero: grupos y regiones mexicanos en el siglo XIX. Coordinación de Beatriz Rojas. México: Instituto Mora, 1994. 398 p.: bibl., ill.

Thirteen essays concerning economic and political power from independence to 1923. Those to be singled out among this uniformly excellent group are César Navarro Gallegos on a creole bishop during independence; Cecilia Noriega Elío on Congresses to 1857 (using statistical tools); and Rosa María Meyer Cosío on *empresarios españoles*.

1375 Reichstein, Andreas. ¿Era realmente inevitable?: ¿por qué México perdió Texas en 1836? (*Hist. Mex.*, 42:4, abril/junio 1993, p. 867–887, bibl.)

Puts the Texas rebellion more squarely into Mexican politics than ever before. In-

cludes valuable new insights on land speculation and political conflicts, and concludes
that Texas was lost because of avarice on both
sides.

1376 Rodríguez, Hipólito. Veracruz a fines
del siglo XIX: urbanización y acondi-
cionamiento portuario durante el Porfiriato.
(*in* Congreso Internacional de Historia Regional Comparada *3rd, Ciudad Juárez, 1991.*
Actas. Edición de Ricardo León García. Ciudad Juárez, Mexico: Univ. Autónoma de Ciudad Juárez, 1992, p. 135–146)
    Short evocative essay on the transfor-
mation of Mexico's most important port following the opening of its rail line to Mexico
City in 1873.

1377 Salvucci, Richard J. The origins and
progress of U.S.-Mexican Trade, 1825–
1884: "hoc opus, hic labor est." (*HAHR*, 71 : 4,
1991, p. 697–735, graphs, tables)
    Thought-provoking analysis of the cor-
relation among trade, tariffs, and politics as
they impact relations between the US and
Mexico. Indispensable for all who work in
this period. Those who have never studied
economics would have benefited had author
added a few short sentences introducing the
material.

1378 Sánchez Rodríguez, Martín. La herencia del pasado: la centralización de los
recursos acuíferos en México. (*Relaciones/
Zamora,* 14 : 54, primavera 1993, p. 21–41,
bibl., tables)
    Important contribution to both Mexi-
can legal and environmental history, article
discusses variety of decisions concerning
whether ownership of water rights in Mi-
chaocán went to the state or to the nation
prior to 1917 Constitution. Recommended.

1379 Schávelzon, Daniel. La arqueología del
imperialismo: la invasión francesa a
México, 1864–1867. (*Mesoamérica/Antigua,*
15 : 28, dic. 1994, p. 321–335, photo)
    Interesting account of how French in-
terest in Mexican antiquities led to the development of Mexican archaeology. Comments
on the blue-ribbon Commission Scientifique
au Mexique, established by Napoleon III at
the same time that a similar mission went to
Egypt. Nevertheless, gives short shrift to
homegrown interest in the past.

1380 Serrano Alvarez, Pablo. Clío y la historia regional mexicana: reflexiones metodológicas. (*Estud. Cult. Contemp.,* 6 : 18,
1994, p. 151–164, bibl.)
    One of the few attempts to look at re-
gional history methodologically. But if the
pattern of national chronology cannot be imposed on the study of regions, how do the latter contribute to the history of the whole?
Unwittingly elucidates the problem without
providing its solution.

1381 Serrano Ortega, José Antonio. El con-
tingente de sangre: los gobiernos estatales y departamentales y los métodos de reclutamiento del ejército permanente
mexicano, 1824–1844. México: Instituto Nacional de Antropología e Historia, 1993. 149
p.: bibl. (Col. Divulgación)
    Long-awaited work that is key for un-
derstanding the army and the all-important
relations between the various states and the
central government in 1842–44. Stresses the
importance of *compañías auxiliares* at the
state level and the reincarnation of the militias after the collapse of federalism.

1382 Skerritt Gardner, David. Rancheros sobre tierra fértil. Xalapa, Mexico: Univ.
Veracruzana, Dirección Editorial, 1993. 186
p.: ill. (Biblioteca/Universidad Veracruzana)
    Case study of Actopan, Veracruz and of
the nature of the *ranchero* there. Author
takes special pains to try to understand this
variant in the agricultural landscape, but
stops short of generalizing throughout the republic.

1383 Sordo Cedeño, Reynaldo. El congreso
en la primera república centralista. México: Colegio de México, Centro de Estudios
Históricos; Instituto Tecnológico Autónomo
de México, 1993. 472 p.: bibl.
    Supremely important study of the Con-
gress from 1834 to the reemergence of Santa
Anna in 1841. Finally sheds light on key players of the period who previously dwelt in the
shadows. Highly recommended.

1384 Staples, Anne. Bonanzas y borrascas
mineras: el Estado de México, 1821–
1876. Zinacantepec, Mexico: El Colegio Mexiquense, 1994. 375 p.: bibl., index, maps.
    Very important study of mining in the
state of Mexico. Includes attempt to connect
mining industry to political events. Hope-

fully there will be a second volume covering into the 20th century.

1385 **Tenenbaum, Barbara A.** Manuel Payno y los bandidos del erario mexicano, 1848–1873. (*Hist. Mex.*, 44 : 1, julio/sept. 1994, p. 73–106)

Details and clarifies Payno's role in the management of the Mexican national debt, expenditure of funds from the Treaty of Guadalupe-Hidalgo, and events surrounding intervention. Clarifies much that was previously obscure as well as enlightening the life of an important politician and leading writer of 19th-century Mexico. [E.B. Couturier]

1386 **Trujillo Bolio, Mario A.** Tres fuentes para la historia del crédito y las finanzas en la Ciudad de México durante el Segundo Imperio. (*Bol. Fuentes Hist. Econ. Méx.*, 5, sept./dic. 1991, p. 15–25)

Presents three important sources—Notarías, Archivo Judicial del Tribunal Superior, and *Directorio del Comercio del Imperio Mexicano* by Eugenio Maillefert—that help elucidate the financial transactions of the Empire in Mexico City.

1387 **Universidad Autónoma de Ciudad Juárez (Mexico).** Tomóchic: la revolución adelantada; resistencia y lucha de un pueblo de Chihuahua con el sistema porfirista, 1891–1892. Recopilación de Jesús Vargas Valdez. Ciudad Juárez, Mexico: Univ. Autónoma de Ciudad Juárez, 1994. 2 v.: bibl., ill., map. (Estudios regionales; 10)

Ten more articles on one of the most studied revolts in Mexican history, including two on Teresa Urrea and one on Cruz Chávez. Presents much new source material.

1388 **Vázquez, Josefina Zoraida.** Don Manuel Payno y la enseñanza de la historia. (*Hist. Mex.*, 44 : 1, julio/sept. 1994, p. 167–181)

Thoughtful and brief summary of Payno's history text for schools, emphasizing the national period and downplaying both the pre-colonial and conquest. Important source for future Payno biography.

1389 **Vázquez, Josefina Zoraida.** Un viejo tema: el federalismo y el centralismo. (*Hist. Mex.*, 42 : 3, enero/marzo 1993, p. 621–631, bibl.)

Presents perceptive historiographical review of recent publications on conflict between federalism and centralism in Mexico (1821–54) in an international context. [J. Britton]

1390 **Vázquez Mantecón, Carmen.** Espacio social y crisis política: La Sierra Gorda, 1850–1855. (*Mex. Stud.*, 9 : 1, June 1993, p. 47–70)

The Sierra Gorda became a haven for discontented and politically persecuted groups in the 19th century. Examines how local socioeconomic interest conflicted with Santa Anna's government in its attempt to convert the area into territory. [R.E. Looney]

1391 **Villalobos González, Martha H.** Las concesiones forestales en Quintana Roo a fines del porfiriato. (*Relaciones/Zamora*, 14 : 53, invierno 1993, p. 87–112, maps)

Somewhat misleading title since only a small fraction of article concerns this specific topic. Discusses how the Yucatecan elite, described so well by Wells, also participated, among others, in the exploitation of Quintana Roo. Tends to mitigate cries of dismemberment voiced by other yucatecos when Quintana Roo was separated juridically from the rest of the peninsula.

Washington State University. The Regla papers: an indexed guide to the papers of the Romero de Terreros family and other colonial and early national Mexican families. See item **1251.**

1392 **Zárate Toscano, Verónica.** Agustín de Iturbide: entre la memoria y el olvido. (*Secuencia/México*, 28, enero/abril 1994, p. 5–27, bibl., ill.)

Curious discussion of the development of some aspects of the Iturbide cult. Particularly enlightening on the disposition of his remains.

REVOLUTION AND POST-REVOLUTION

1393 **Abad de Santillán, Diego.** Historia de la Revolución Mexicana. Ensayos de Fredo Arias de la Canal y Fredo Arias King. México: Frente de Afirmación Hispanista, 1992. 618 p.: bibl., ill.

The author—anarchist, revolutionary, labor organizer, prolific translator—provides not a history of the Mexican Revolution, but rather a prehistory, with the narrative ending in 1910. Work contains lengthy essays by two other authors dealing with anarchism and liberalism.

1394 Abud Flores, José Alberto. Campeche: Revolución y movimiento social, 1911–1923. México: Instituto Nacional de Estudios Históricos de la Revolución Mexicana, Secretaría de Gobernación; Univ. Autónoma de Campeche, 1992. 133 p.: bibl., ill., maps. (Regiones)

Well-researched political history. Francisco Madero's revolt opened the door for privileged young *campechanos* who sought a role in the political life of the state but not structural change. Under the regime of Alvaro Obregón, Campeche experienced a greater opening of the political system, as attempts were made to accommodate various political factions and social groups.

1395 Aguilar Camín, Héctor and Lorenzo Meyer. In the shadow of the Mexican Revolution: contemporary Mexican history, 1910–1989. Translated by Luis Alberto Fierro. Austin: Univ. of Texas Press, 1993. 287 p.: bibl., index. (Translations from Latin America series)

Translation of work first published in 1989. Originally intended as part of an illustrated history of Mexico for a general audience, the current work is a revised and unillustrated overview for a more limited audience. The emphasis is on political and economic developments, especially the postwar failure of the political system to adapt to changing socioeconomic conditions. Good survey by two authors with contemporary political influence.

1396 Alanís Boyso, Rodolfo. Historia de la Revolución en el Estado de México: los zapatistas en el poder. Toluca: Gobierno del Estado de México, 1987. 252 p.: bibl., ill. (Textos históricos; 2)

Study of the major events in the state from Dec. 1914-Oct. 1915, when Gustavo Baz Prada served as Zapatista governor. Although the Zapatistas took steps to implement agrarian reform and improve conditions for workers, their programs were never fully realized.

1397 Alemán, Miguel. Remembranzas y testimonios. 2. ed. Miguel Hidalgo, México: Grijalbo, 1987. 437 p.: ill., index, ports. (Testimonios)

Memoir of the 58th Mexican president details his youth and his adult professional, political, and personal life.

1398 Alonso Alcocer, Primitivo. Cuando Quintana Roo fue desmembrado: 1931–1935. Chetumal, Mexico: Congreso del Estado, Quintana Roo, VI Legislatura; Municipio de Othón P. Blanco; Comité Directivo Estatal del PRI en Q. Roo, 1992. 299 p.: bibl., ill.

Over-wrought account of the ultimately-successful campaign to prevent the absorption of the territory of Quintana Roo by the neighboring states of Yucatán and Campeche.

1399 Altable Fernández, María Eugenia; Edith González Cruz; and Juan Preciado Llamas. Estudios de historia sudcaliforniana. La Paz, Mexico: Seminario de Investigación en Historia Regional, Univ. Autónoma de Baja California Sur, 1993. 191 p.: bibl., ill. (Serie científica)

Collection of three essays by individual authors dealing with the French Intervention, the Constitutionalist Revolution, and the Calles-Cárdenas transition in Baja California Sur. See also item **1436.**

1400 Alvarado, Salvador. Salvador Alvarado, estadista y pensador: antología. Recopilación y estudio introductorio de Francisco José Paoli Bolio. México: Fondo de Cultura Económica, 1994. 387 p.: bibl., ill. (Vida y pensamiento de México)

Collection of writings by the much-studied revolutionary general and controversial governor of Yucatán. Most of the work is devoted to selections from his most important publication, *La reconstrucción de México* (1919). Excellent introduction provides overview of Alvarado's career and political thought.

1401 Alvarez y Alvarez de la Cadena, José. Memorias de un constituyente. Recopilación de Alberto Enríquez Perea. México: El Nacional, 1992. 348 p.: bibl., ill.

Memoirs, writings, and speeches of a Michoacán deputy to the Constitutional Congress of 1916–17. Focuses on religious questions and Alvarez's role as an anti-clerical spokesman. Includes a section with biographical sketches and brief testimonials by congressional delegates.

1402 Amparán, Francisco José *et al.* Nueva historia de Torreón. Torreón, Mexico: R. Ayuntamiento de Torreón; Teatro Isauro Martínez; Consejo Nacional para la Cultura y las Artes, Programa Cultural de las Fronteras; Instituto Nacional de Bellas Artes, 1993. 325 p.: bibl., ill. (Cuesta de la fortuna. Serie Ayuntamiento 91–93)

Collection of essays by various authors tracing the history of Torreón and its surrounding area from colonial times to 1990. Most of the work deals with the Porfiriato and post-1910 period.

1403 Angeles Contreras, Jesús. El verdadero Felipe Angeles. Pachuca, Mexico: Univ. Autónoma de Hidalgo, 1992. 251 p.: bibl., ill.

Examination of the military career, political ideology, and revolutionary role played by the subject who is usually thought of as a *villista* general. Author sees Angeles as a martyr for *maderista* democratic ideals, a man who served "the other revolution" instead of the one that led to a "political dynasty usurping the popular will."

1404 Archivo General de la Nación (Mexico). Bailes y balas: Ciudad de México, 1921–1931. Curadora de la exposición, Mariana Yampolsky. México: Archivo General de la Nación, 1991. 95 p.: chiefly ill.

Eclectic collection of photographs, ranging from Obregón's funeral procession to topless dancers in a nightclub, depicting life in Mexico City during the 1920s. Photos are from the files of the *Fotografías de Actualidad* agency, currently housed in the AGN. Introductions to the different sections are brief, and the captions even briefer.

1405 Archivo Histórico del Estado de México. Ramo Revolución Mexicana: impresos y manuscritos, 1900–1932. v. 1. Toluca de Lerdo, Mexico?: Archivo Histórico del Estado de México, 1987. 1 v. (Serie Guías y catálogos; 1)

Annotated listing of over 1,000 documents covering a variety of topics and *municipios.*

1406 Arias González, Facundo. Historia de las relaciones del movimiento obrero con el campesino: el caso de la CROM y la Confederación Social Campesina Domingo Arenas, 1921–1929. (*in* Simposio Internacional de Investigaciones Socio-Históricas sobre Tlaxcala, *1st, Tlaxcala, Mexico, 1985.*

Memorias. Tlaxcala, México: Gobierno del Estado de Tlaxcala, Instituto Tlaxcalteca de Cultura, Univ. Autónoma de Tlaxcala; México: Univ. Iberoamericana, 1986, p. 149–157)

Brief exploration of conflicts between worker and campesino movements in Puebla. Although Puebla's working class responded in a variety of ways to agrarian issues, the Confederación Regional Obrera Mexicana opposed the division of land into *ejidos.* Ultimately both movements were subordinated to the revolutionary State and the conflict between them was institutionalized.

1407 Asamblea de ciudades: años 20s-50s, Ciudad de México; catálogo. Coordinación de textos Elsa Fujigaki Cruz y Ricardo de León Banuet. México: Museo del Palacio de Bellas Artes, 1992. 278 p.: ill. (some col.).

Catalog to accompany an exhibition at the Museo del Palacio de Bellas Artes. Work focuses on the many "cities" that made up Mexico City between 1920–60. The illustrations are excellent, but captions are often non-existent or uninformative.

1408 Aurrecoechea, Juan Manuel and **Armando Bartra.** Puros cuentos: la historia de la historieta en México. v. 2–3, 1934–50. México: Consejo Nacional para la Cultura y las Artes, Dirección General de Publicaciones; Dirección General de Culturas Populares, Museo Nacional de Culturas Populares; Grijalbo, 1994. 2 v.: ill. (some col.).

Invaluable work for the study of 20th-century popular culture. Needs better introduction, however, to place material in its international and national context.

1409 Auyón Gerardo, Eduardo. El dragón en el desierto: los pioneros chinos en Mexicali. Mexicali, Mexico?: Instituto de Cultura de Baja California, 1991. 199 p.: bibl., ill.

History of the influential Chinese community in Mexicali with considerable emphasis on its cultural impact. Extensively illustrated.

1410 Avila Espinosa, Felipe Arturo. La Ciudad de México ante la ocupación de las fuerzas villistas y zapatistas: diciembre de 1914-junio de 1915. (*Estud. Hist. Mod. Contemp. Méx.,* 14, 1991, p. 107–128)

Strong prejudices against the urban population prevented revolutionary forces from winning their allegiance. The revolutionaries were therefore regarded as foreign occupying forces. Clearly demonstrates the difficulties of trying to link an agrarian movement to urban dwellers.

1411 Avila Espinosa, Felipe Arturo. La Sociedad Mutualista y Moralizadora de Obreros del Distrito Federal, 1909–1911. (*Hist. Mex.*, 43:1, julio/sept. 1993, p. 117–154)

Well-organized discussion of the efforts by the governor of the Federal District, Guillermo de Landa y Escandón, to organize a mutualist society aimed at preempting the formation of more radical workers' organizations. This new organization preached the need for cooperation and harmony between workers and capitalists and sought to raise the civic consciousness and moral standards of members. After almost two years of organizational activity, the society was officially established in April 1911; within a matter of weeks, its patron—Porfirio Díaz—and its instigator, Governor Landa, would be in exile.

1412 Azuela, Mariano *et al.* Los fundadores de El Colegio Nacional vistos por sus colegas. Prefacio de Silvio Zavala. Edición e introducción de Miguel León-Portilla. México: El Colegio Nacional, 1983. 251 p., 14 leaves of plates: col. ports.

Collection of tributes to some of Mexico's leading intellectuals by some of Mexico's leading intellectuals on the 40th anniversary of the founding of El Colegio Nacional.

1413 Baños Ramírez, Othón. El cardenismo y la recomposición política de las regiones: el caso Yucatán. (*Relaciones/Zamora*, 14:53, invierno 1993, p. 167–196)

Author does a good job of sorting out the confused political situation existing in Yucatán in the 1920s-30s. The centralizing efforts under Calles and Cárdenas took place against a background of rural mobilization, the decline of the local Partido Socialista del Sureste, and competition between labor and agrarian groups. Cárdenas met the "proletarian demands of the workers" with an "authoritarian and centralist" agrarian reform program. See also item **1507.**

1414 Barradas, Celestino. Historia de la Iglesia en Veracruz. t. 2. Xalapa, Mexico: Ediciones San José, 1990? 1 v.: bibl., ill.

Uneven chronicle of the diocese of Veracruz, focusing on Bishop Joaquin Arcadio Pagaza. Most of the work is comprised of appendices giving detailed accounts of pastoral visits to various locations in the diocese. Vol. 2 covers the period from 1895–1918.

1415 Basurto, Jorge and **Guadalupe Viveros Pabello.** Vivencias femeninas de la Revolución [de] Jorge Basurto. Mi padre revolucionario [de] Guadalupe Viveros Pabello. México: Instituto Nacional de Estudios Históricos de la Revolución Mexicana, Secretaría de Gobernación, 1993. 140 p.: ill. (Col. Testimonio)

Two interesting recollections of the Mexican Revolution. The first is based on interviews with two sisters who were active in the Casa del Obrero Mundial. The second is an account of the activities of Felipe Gustavo Viveros Guiot, who fought against Huerta and Carranza.

1416 Binford, Leigh. Peasants and petty capitalists in southern Oaxacan sugar cane production and processing, 1930–1980. (*J. Lat. Am. Stud.*, 24:1, Feb. 1992, p. 33–55)

Shows that small producers have been able to operate profitably in competition with large mills and that this process has led to local accumulation of capital. Includes important comparative material. For ethnologist's comment see *HLAS 55:720.*

1417 Biografías de mujeres destacadas del Estado de Nuevo León. Nuevo León, Mexico: Gobierno del Estado de Nuevo León; Consejo Estatal de Población, 1992? 284 p.: ill., ports.

Uneven and unorganized collection of approximately 100 biographies, geared to more contemporary period.

1418 Blancarte, Roberto. Recent changes in Church-State relations in Mexico: an historical approach. (*J. Church State*, 35:4, Autumn 1993, p. 781–805)

Interesting study of recent changes in Mexico's constitution. Places reforms concerning the Catholic Church in a historical context. Argues that such reforms are part of an ongoing strategy by the Catholic hierarchy to recover its "social space" in Mexico.

1419 Blanco Velasco, Isabel. Tabasco: ¿rojo o creyente? Villahermosa, Mexico: Secretaría de Educación, Cultura y Recreación, Dirección de Educación Superior e Investigación Científica, 1992. 100 p.: appendix, bibl., ill. (Investigaciones. Historia)

Brief account of the Church-State conflict in Tabasco that eventually resulted in a violent confrontation between Church supporters and the authorities in May 1938. Appendix contains lengthy interview with Salvador Abascal, one of the principal organizers of the supporters of the Church.

1420 Britton, John A. Revolution and ideology: images of the Mexican Revolution in the United States. Lexington: Univ. Press of Kentucky, 1995. 271 p., 8 p. of plates: bibl., ill., index.

Survey of the images of the Revolution conveyed by US writers from 1910–60. Author establishes seven ideological categories into which these observers fall, ranging from "independent leftists" such as Frank Tannenbaum to "right wing racists" such as Jack London. The "liberal statist" ideology of writers such as Ernest Gruening has been the most influential.

1421 Brown, Jonathan C. Foreign and native-born workers in Porfirian Mexico. (*Am. Hist. Rev.*, 98:3, June 1993, p. 786–818, map, photos)

Study of rail and mining workers examines the complicated relationship between Mexicans and foreigners. Argues that although Mexican workers benefited from and welcomed the opportunities that came with the introduction of foreign capital, they also successfully resisted complete "proletarianization" and compelled the Mexican government to address the needs of workers.

1422 Brunk, Samuel. Zapata and the city boys: in search of a piece of the Revolution. (*HAHR*, 73:1, Feb. 1993, p. 33–65)

Important study of Zapatismo. Explores Zapata's relationship with the urban intellectuals that attempted to bridge the gap between his regional rebellion and the national Revolution. Suggests that such a bridge was never successfully built because intellectuals like Manuel Palafox refused to cooperate with Venustiano Carranza.

1423 Buchenau, Jürgen. Counter-intervention against Uncle Sam: Mexico's support for Nicaraguan nationalism. (*Americas/Francisc.*, 50:2, Oct. 1993, p. 207–232)

Examines Porfirio Díaz's policy toward Nicaragua using Mexican and European archives. Argues that Díaz pursued an assertive, nationalistic policy to prevent US intervention in Central America, while strengthening Mexico's influence in the region.

1424 Buffington, Robert. Revolutionary reform: the Mexican Revolution and the discourse on prison reform. (*Mex. Stud.*, 9:1, Winter 1993, p. 71–93)

Author traces the debate on prison reform from early Liberal period to the Constitutional Convention of 1916–17. The basic tenets of prison reform transcended the Revolution, and the post-revolutionary debate centered not on prison reform but on the issue of national government control. Constitution of 1917 retained the pre-1910 decentralized prison system.

1425 Buve, Raymond. La Revolución Mexicana: el caso de Tlaxcala a luz de las recientes tesis revisionistas. (*in* Simposio Internacional de Investigaciones Socio-Históricas sobre Tlaxcala, *1st, Tlaxcala, Mexico, 1985.* Memorias. Tlaxcala, México: Gobierno del Estado de Tlaxcala, Instituto Tlaxcalteca de Cultura, Univ. Autónoma de Tlaxcala; México: Univ. Iberoamericana, 1986, p. 119–134, map)

Revisionist survey argues that Tlaxcala's revolution was not simply a popular agrarian movement linked to Zapatismo, but rather, it reflected the demands of traditional agrarian elements and those of the state's more "modern," urban/worker sectors.

1426 Calles, Plutarco Elías. Correspondencia personal: 1919–1945. v. 2. Introducción, selección y notas de Carlos Macías. Hermosillo, Mexico: Gobierno del Estado de Sonora; Instituto Sonorense de Cultura; México: Fideicomiso Archivos Plutarco Elías Calles y Fernando Torreblanca; Fondo de Cultura Económica, 1991–1993. 1 v.: bibl., ill., indexes. (Vida y pensamiento de México)

Vol. 2 of a selection of documents from Calles' personal archive is divided into two sections: 1) on Mexico's diplomatic relations with the US, Europe, Spain, and Latin America; and 2) on internal political matters. Contains brief biographies of Calles' correspondents as well as an analytical index and detailed bibliography.

1427 Camp, Roderic Ai. Generals in the Palacio: the military in modern Mexico. New York: Oxford Univ. Press, 1992. 278 p.: bibl., index.

Excellent study of the evolution of the Mexican military, with attention to those factors that distinguish the Mexican military from other Latin American armed forces. Author examines the social and geographic background of the officer corps, the military education system, and the linkages between civilian and military groups.

1428 Camp, Roderic Ai. Mexican intellectuals and collective biography in the 20th century. (*in* Intellectuals in the twentieth-century Caribbean. London: Macmillan Caribbean, 1992, v. 2, p. 211–224)

Methodological discussion summarizing some of the author's findings from a larger study of Mexican intellectuals. Suggests that examination of autobiographies, biographies, and personal papers, as well as surveys and personal interviews can help contemporary scholars better understand the lives of Mexican intellectuals and the environment in which they work.

1429 Caraveo, Marcelo. Crónica de la Revolución, 1910–1929. Introducción y cronología de Guillermo Porras Muñoz. Presentación y notas de Jean Pierre Bastian. México: Editorial Trillas, 1992. 207 p.: bibl., ill., indexes, maps. (Linterna mágica; 19)

Chronicle of a Chihuahuan general who joined the Revolution with Pascual Orozco, fought against Madero and Carranza, and was forced into exile after rebelling against Calles. Includes several documents and letters, as well as the text of a 1954 interview with Caraveo.

1430 Cárdenas, Enrique. La hacienda pública y la política económica, 1927–1958. México: El Colegio de México; Fideicomiso Historia de las Américas; Fondo de Cultura Económica, 1994. 230 p.: bibl., graphs, tables.

Chronological examination of the increasingly significant role of the State in Mexico's economy, beginning with the Great Depression. Demonstrates the ways in which the Mexican government sought to promote development and counteract the effects of external events on the domestic economy.

1431 Cárdenas, Enrique. Población, mercado interno e inicios de la industrialización en México, 1880–1920. (*in* El poblamiento de las Américas, *Veracruz, 1992.* Actas. Liège, Belgium: International Union for the Scientific Study of Population, 1992, v. 1, p. 401–418, bibl.)

Brief, general survey of Mexico's economic development based on secondary sources. Shows that although the Mexican Revolution hurt Mexico's economy by causing the collapse of the financial market, other sectors, such as industry, mining, and oil suffered little from the fighting. By 1920, moreover, the financial market was recovering.

1432 Cárdenas Trueba, Olga and **Rubén Pliego Bernal.** Guía del Archivo de la Embajada de México en los Estados Unidos de América, 1910–1912. México: Secretaría de Relaciones Exteriores; Secretaría de Gobernación; Instituto Nacional de Estudios Históricos de la Revolución Mexicana, 1994. 313 p.: index. (Archivo histórico diplomático mexicano)

Helpful, comprehensive guide with an index that is thematic, onomastic, institutional, and geographic.

1433 Carr, Barry. Mexico: the perils of unity and the challenge of modernization. (*in* The Latin American left: from the fall of Allende to perestroika. Boulder, Colo.: Westview Press, 1993, p. 83–99)

An analysis of the fortunes of the Mexican left since the 1970s. Repression of the student movement and economic problems encouraged the left to transform itself through unification. Since 1988 however, the unity of the left has broken down, hampered by *caudillismo* and by an inability to create a viable program for economic growth and modernization.

1434 Casasola, Gustavo. Biografía ilustrada del General Emiliano Zapata. México: Editorial G. Casasola, 1994. 107 p.: chiefly ill., index. (Hechos y hombres de México)

Illustrated biography drawn from the Archivo Casasola-INAH contains very little in the way of narrative. Captions are informative but brief. See also item **1435** for illustrated biography of Francisco Villa in same series.

1435   Casasola, Gustavo. Biografía ilustrada del General Francisco Villa. México: Editorial G. Casasola, 1994. 148 p.: chiefly ill., index. (Hechos y hombres de México)

Another illustrated biography drawn from the Archivo Cassolo-INAH. Includes very little in the way of narrative, although brief captions are informative. See also item **1434** for illustrated biography of Emiliano Zapata in same series.

1436   Castro Burgoin, Domingo Valentín. El proceso histórico de la conversión de Baja California Sur en estado libre y soberano. La Paz, Mexico?: s.n., 1992. 102 p.: bibl.

Author, born and educated in Baja California Sur, chronicles the area's transition from district to territory to state in the face of a number of problems: geography, climate, isolation, invasion, internal struggles, and national political instability. See also item **1399.**

1437   Castro Castro, Juan. Economía de guerra durante la Revolución Mexicana: Sonora, 1913. (*in* Simposio de Historia y Antropología de Sonora, *16th, Hermosillo, México, 1993.* Memoria. Hermosillo, Mexico: Instituto de Investigaciones Históricas, Univ. de Sonora, 1993, p. 421–433, bibl.)

Study of revolutionary financing based on research in the State Archives of Sonora. Sonora's armed movement was supported with taxes on merchants and cattlemen, increases in export duties, the sale of cattle, the temporary confiscation of the lands of absent hacendados, and an extraordinary tax on the properties of enemies of the Revolution.

1438   Castro Martínez, Pedro Fernando. Adolfo de la Huerta y la Revolución Mexicana. México: Instituto Nacional de Estudios Históricos de la Revolución Mexicana; Secretaría de Gobernación; Univ. Autónoma Metropolitana, Unidad Iztapalapa, 1992. 170 p.: bibl., ill. (Biografías)

Basic biography of the Sonoran leader with little interpretation. Details De la Huerta's role in the Obregón government and the rebellion that forced him into exile.

1439   Ceballos Ramírez, Manuel and **José Miguel Romero de Solís.** Cien años de presencia y ausencia social cristiana, 1891–1991. México: IMDOSOC, 1992. 347 p.: ill.

Survey of Christian Social Doctrine and its impact on Mexico in commemoration of the centennial of the issuance of the papal encyclical on the condition of labor, *Rerum Novarum*. Extensively illustrated.

1440   Cerda, Luis. Causas económicas de la revolución mexicana. (*Rev. Mex. Sociol.,* 53:1, March 1991, pp. 307–347)

Suggestive article reanalyzes Mexican economic data for the period 1880–1910. Shows significant structural problems during the Porfiriato, which engendered economic difficulties leading to the Revolution.

1441   César Dachary, Alfredo A. and **Stella Maris Arnáiz Burne.** Bitácora de un viaje a la justicia: crónicas de una huelga olvidada. Caribe, Mexico: CIQRO, 1992. 117 p.: bibl.

Examination of the impact on international relations and union activities of the seizure of 16 Cuban fishing vessels by Mexican officials off the coast of Quintana Roo in March 1936. Includes brief appendices of official correspondence relating to the incident, but lacks notes or bibliography.

1442   La ciudadela de fuego: a ochenta años de la Decena Trágica. México: Consejo Nacional para la Cultura y las Artes; Biblioteca de México; Instituto Nacional de Antropología e Historia; Archivo General de la Nación; Instituto Nacional de Estudios Históricos de la Revolución Mexicana; Instituto de Investigaciones Dr. José Ma. Luis Mora, 1993. 151 p.: bibl., ill.

Commemorative issue marking the 80th anniversary of the overthrow of the Madero regime. Work includes a narrative of the events of the "ten tragic days" taken from the diaries of the famous journalist José Juan Tablada, a detailed chronology, and an essay on the photographs that make up the bulk of the work. See also item **1472.**

1443   Colegio Mexiquense. Diccionario biográfico e histórico de la Revolución Mexicana en el Estado de México. Coordinación de Roberto Blancarte. Zinacantepec, Mexico: Colegio Mexiquense; Instituto Mexiquense de Cultura, 1992. 298 p.: bibl., ill.

Useful reference work on a key state in the Revolution. Biographies constitute almost half of the work; other sections deal with military actions, political groups, workers' organizations, agrarian movements, popular culture, and state administrations.

1444 Collier, George A. The rebellion in Chiapas and the legacy of energy development. (*Mex. Stud.*, 10:2, Summer 1994, p. 371–384)

Examination of the complex background to current "zapatista" rebellion in an area where the PRI was institutionally weak. Author believes that energy policy since the 1970s and the economic restructuring begun in 1982 are at the root of the current unrest.

1445 La comunidad china del distrito norte de Baja California, 1910–1934. Mexicali: Instituto de Investigaciones Históricas del Estado de Baja California, 1990. 93 p.: bibl., ill.

Very interesting collection of essays, including an extensive overview by Evelyn Hu-DeHart, including information about both urban and rural Chinese.

1446 Concurso Estatal de Ensayo sobre la Historia de las Ligas de Comunidades Agrarias y Sindicatos Campesinos, 1st, Méxi-co?, 1987. Historia de las ligas de comunidades agrarias y sindicatos campesinos: Primer Concurso Estatal. v. 6, Golfo Centro. México: Confederación Nacional Campesina; Centro de Estudios Históricos del Agrarismo en México, 1988. 1 v.: bibl., ill., photos.

Brief but useful volume focused mainly on the 1920s and early 1930s, with information on the agrarian leader Ursulo Galván. Includes a number of interesting photographs.

1447 Congreso Internacional de Historia Regional Comparada, 3rd, Ciudad Juárez, Mexico, 1991. Actas. Edición de Ricardo León García. Ciudad Juárez, Mexico: Univ. Autónoma de Ciudad Juárez, 1992. 457 p.: bibl., ill., maps.

Forty-one papers on regional history of various parts of Mexico ranging in date from prehispanic to contemporary epochs. Major themes include "Society, Politics, and Elites;" "Regional Economic History;" "Religion, Education, and Culture;" "Art, Literature, and History;" and "Archaeology and Regional History." Notable scholars included are Katz, Altamirano, Calvo, Lau, Palomares, Meyer, and Pinet.

1448 Congreso Internacional sobre la Revolución Mexicana, San Luis Potosí, Mexico, 1990. Memoria. San Luis Potosí, Mexico: Gobierno del Estado de San Luis Potosí; México: Instituto Nacional de Estudios Históricos de la Revolución Mexicana, Secretaría de Gobernación, 1991. 2 v.: bibl., ill.

Series of papers pertaining to the Mexican Revolution. Subjects include women, journalism, economic and financial aspects of the Revolution, social classes and social groups, art, photography, and film.

1449 Contento y descontento en Jalisco, Michoacán y Morelos, 1906–1911. Recopilación de Shulamit Goldsmit, Alvaro Ochoa y Graciela de Garay Arellano. México: Univ. Iberoamericana, Depto. de Historia, 1991. 225 p.: bibl., maps.

An investigation of agrarian disputes and unrest in three Mexican states based on documents in the Colección Porfirio Díaz. Sections on Jalisco and Michoacán include a brief narrative and several supporting documents. A third section on Morelos includes only documents.

1450 Cotter, Joseph. The origins of the Green Revolution in Mexico: continuity and change? (*in* Latin America in the 1940s: war and postwar transitions. Edited by David Rock. Berkeley: Univ. of California Press, 1994, p. 224–247)

Explores Mexico's efforts in agricultural research and development during the 1920s-30s. Despite the government's emphasis on "scientific nationalism," such efforts underscored Mexico's reliance on foreign science and technology and paved the way for the Mexican Agricultural Project of 1943, established by the Rockefeller Foundation.

1451 Covo, Jacqueline. La prensa en la historiografía mexicana: problemas y perspectivas. (*Hist. Mex.*, 42:3, enero/marzo 1993, p. 689–710, bibl.)

General discussion of the possibilities and problems of using periodicals as historical sources, with suggestions for areas of further research.

1452 Cruz, Víctor de la. El general Charis y la pacificación del México postrevolucionario. México: Ediciones de la Casa Chata, CIESAS, 1993. 257 p.: bibl., ill.

An exploration of the activities of Heliodoro Charis Castro, who began as a leader of Zapotec rebels and was later incorporated into the revolutionary state under Alvaro Obregón. Places Charis' career in the context of the Zapotec struggle for autonomy.

1453 Debroise, Olivier and **Elizabeth Fuentes Rojas.** Fuga mexicana: un recorrido por la fotografía en México. México: Consejo Nacional para la Cultura y las Artes, 1994. 223 p.: bibl., ill., index. (Cultura contemporánea de México)

Brilliant compilation of photos that not only tell of the country, but also inform the reader of the lives of the photographers and the progress of the field. Recommended.

1454 Delgado de León, Bartolomé *et al.* Y dígalo que yo lo dije—: memorias de amor y vida en el Valle del Yaqui. Coordinación, análisis y testimonios sobre el periodista sonorense de Mayo Murrieta. Hermosillo, Mexico: Gobierno del Estado de Sonora, Secretaría de Fomento y Cultura, Instituto Sonorense de Cultura, 1994. 337 p.: ill. (Sonora; 11)

Reflections by and about Delgado de León, an educator, poet, prominent journalist, and political activist from the late 1940s to his death in 1974.

1455 Delgado Larios, Almudena. Un *nuevo 98* en una *Nueva España:* una lectura hispanoamericanista del conflicto yanqui-mexicano, 1910–1923. (*in* La formación de la imagen de América Latina en España, 1898–1989. Coordinación de Montserrat Huguet Santos, Antonio Niño y Pedro Pérez Herrero. Madrid: Organización de Estados Iberoamericanos para la Educación, la Ciencia y la Cultura (OEI), 1992, p. 279–311)

Interesting examination of Spain's view of US-Mexican relations during the Mexican Revolution. Based on an analysis of four Spanish periodicals. Spanish journalists tended to compare US intervention in Mexico's conflict with the earlier US involvement in Cuba. Mexico was depicted as the new defender of the "Hispanic race" against Yankee imperialism.

1456 Delgado Larios, Almudena. La Revolución Mexicana en la España de Alfonso XIII, 1910–1931. Madrid?: Junta de Castilla y León, Consejería de Cultura y Turismo, 1993. 359 p.: bibl. (Estudios de historia)

Interesting examination of the meaning of the Revolution as seen in Spain's newspapers of the same period. Spanish views of the Porfiriato, the agrarian and religious questions, education and labor reforms, and US-Mexican conflict during the Revolution re-flected Spain's struggles and encouraged debate on Spain's own problems.

1457 Diccionario histórico y biográfico de la Revolución Mexicana, t. 6, San Luis Potosí—Tabasco. t. 7, Tamaulipas—Zacatecas. t. 8, Sección internacional. México: Instituto Nacional de Estudios Históricos de la Revolución Mexicana, Secretaría de Gobernación, 1994. 3 v.: bibl., ill.

Major reference work organized by groupings of states published in honor of the 80th anniversary of the Revolution. Time period covered is 1890–1920. Work includes biographies, military actions, political groups, publications, conventions/congresses, plans and manifestos, popular songs and other cultural manifestations of the Revolution. Vol. 6 deals with San Luis Potosí, Sinaloa, Sonora, and Tabasco. Vol. 7 covers Tamaulipas, Tlaxcala, Veracruz, Yucatán, and Zacatecas. Vol. 8 treats the international aspects of the Revolution, describing foreign companies, espionage, armed intervention, mercenaries, arms dealers, the foreign press, and revolutionary activities by Mexicans living abroad. See *HLAS 54:1484* for review of vol. 2.

1458 Documentos del Archivo José F. Gómez. 2. ed., corr. México: Ediciones Toledo, 1988. 93 p., 8 leaves of plates: ill.

Documents from the archive of a local revolutionary in Oaxaca who rebelled and was killed in 1911. Efforts by the national government under the new Madero Administration to negotiate directly with the rebels led to conflict with state authorities.

1459 Domínguez Prats, Pilar. Refugiados canarios en México, 1939–1949. (*in* Coloquio de Historia Canario-Americana, *9th, Spain, 1990.* Actas. Las Palmas, Spain: Cabildo Insular de Gran Canaria, 1992, v. 1, p. 801–817, bibl.)

Examination of a small group of exiles that fled to Mexico during the Spanish Civil War. Provides a profile of the immigrants and discusses their experiences as new members of Mexico's economy and society. See also item **1543.**

1460 Domínguez Prats, Pilar. Voces del exilio: mujeres españolas en México, 1939–1950. Madrid?: Comunidad de Madrid, Dirección General de la Mujer, 1994. 294 p.: bibl., ill.

With much of the historiography of the Spanish exiles in Mexico centered on men and on those who were professionals and politically active, author seeks to complete the picture by focusing on experience of women in the exile process. Extensive use of interviews and archival sources.

1461 Duncan, Robert H. The Chinese and the economic development of northern Baja California, 1889–1929. (*HAHR*, 74:4, Nov. 1994, p. 615–647, map, tables)

Examines the history of Baja's Chinese population, a group that contributed to the region's early development. Unlike the Chinese in other areas of Mexico, those in Baja were easily accommodated in this isolated area, and ethnic tensions were rare.

1462 Eisenhower, John S.D. Intervention!: the United States and the Mexican Revolution, 1913–1917. New York: W.W. Norton, 1993. 393 p.: bibl., ill., index.

This study examining US efforts to shape the Revolution is geared toward a popular audience and uses secondary sources as well as some US military documents. Author argues that, in the broader scheme of things, US intervention was largely ineffectual.

1463 Ejército de ciegos: testimonios de la guerra chiapaneca entre carrancistas y rebeldes, 1914–1920. Selección y transcripción de Antonio García de León. México: Ediciones Toledo, 1991. 156 p.: bibl., ill., map.

Collection of ten personal accounts relating to the revolt in the central valleys of Chiapas against the *carrancista* "Mexican Army of Occupation." Eight accounts are by rebels of various affiliations while two are by *carrancistas.* Includes a good general introduction as well as introductions to the individual accounts.

1464 Enríquez Licón, Dora Elvia. Los estibadores de Manzanillo: conflictos por la hegemonía, 1934–1940. (*Estud. Hist. Mod. Contemp. Méx.*, 14, 1991, p. 177–193)

Study of conflict between CROM-affiliated union and CGT/CTM-affiliated union. The struggle was influenced by political developments at the local, state, and national levels. Although the CROM affiliate suffered a loss of power initially, by 1940 it had regained its dominant position.

1465 Escobar Toledo, Saúl *et al.* Pactos con el presente: las maneras de la historia contemporánea. Edición de Cuauhtémoc Velasco Avila. México: Instituto Nacional de Antropología e Historia, 1993. 96 p. (Col. científica; 266. Serie Historia)

Collection of five papers from a colloquium concerning the problems of dealing with Mexico's recent history and rescuing it from the hands of "more or less enlightened politicians and journalists."

1466 Escudero Luján, Carolina. Carolina Escudero Luján: una mujer en la historia de México; testimonio oral. Entrevistas de Guadalupe García Torres. Morelia, Mexico: Instituto Michoacano de Cultura, Centro de Estudios de la Revolución Mexicana Lázaro Cárdenas, Archivo de Historia Oral, 1992. 283 p.: bibl., ill.

Biography of a Chihuahuan woman based on an extensive interview conducted in 1985. Escudero Luján lived through the Revolution and was the wife of General Francisco J. Múgica. After her husband's death she remained politically and socially active.

1467 Esparza Santibáñez, Xavier I. La revolución en La Laguna. pt. 1, 1910–1913. Mexico: Univ. Autónoma de Coahuila, 1992. 1 v.: bibl., ill.

This study combines the author's narrative with extensive quotes from primary documents. Contains information on the Porfirian era, the Anti-Reelectionist movement and the Madero revolt, and the events of 1911–13.

1468 Estudios cuantitativos sobre la historia de México. Edición de Samuel Schmidt, James Wallace Wilkie y Manuel Esparza. México: Univ. Nacional Autónoma de México, 1988. 236 p.: bibl., ill.

Presentations from the third in a series of joint US-Mexico academic colloquia. Topics include economic policies of the 1976–82 *sexenio*, campesino movements, Mexico's population, and theories for quantitative history. Articles focus on Mexico City, Baja California, and the Mexican North.

The evolution of the Mexican political system. See *HLAS 55:2854.*

1469 Fábregas Puig, Andrés. Las fronteras y la formación de la nación: Chiapas. (*in* Coloquio de Antropología e Historia Regionales, *8th, Zamora, Mexico, 1986.* Edición de

Cecilia Noriega Elío. Zamora, Mexico: El Colegio de Michoacán, 1992, p. 615–627)

Somewhat confusing examination of the meaning of "frontier" and "nation" using the example of Chiapas. Argues that Chiapas, although politically linked to Mexico, is socially more akin to Central America. Contemporary Chiapas is characterized by political backwardness and economic overdevelopment.

Favret Tondato, Rita. Tenencia de la tierra en el estado de Coahuila, 1880–1987. See *HLAS 55:1378.*

1470 Fernlund, Kevin J. Senator Holm O. Bursum and the Mexican Ring, 1921–1924. (*N.M. Hist. Rev.*, 66:4, Oct. 1991, p. 433–453)

Shows New Mexico senator and businessman's important role in influencing US-Mexican relations in the 1910s and 1920s.

1471 Flores Hernández, Ivonne. Cusihuiríachi: minería e historia regional. Ciudad Juárez, Mexico: Univ. Autónoma de Ciudad Juárez, 1992. 160 p.: bibl., maps. (Estudios regionales; 5)

Analysis of the "social-historical process" of mining in the Cusihuiríachi region. Large foreign companies dominated mining in the area until the introduction of Cárdenas' "Mexicanization" policy, which not only encouraged greater participation by Mexican capital in mining but also provided federal support for small and medium mining operations.

1472 Flores Longoria, Samuel and **Rafael Soto Briones.** El difícil camino hacia la democracia: la lección de la Decena Trágica. Monterrey, Mexico: Gobierno del Estado de Nuevo León, 1993. 85 p.: bibl., ill. (La Sangre devota; 1)

Work issued to commemorate the 80th anniversary of the overthrow of the Madero regime. Includes a narrative of the "ten tragic days," a detailed chronology, and reflections by members of the Madero family. See also item **1442.**

1473 Flores Torres, Oscar. Burguesía, militares y movimiento obrero en Monterrey, 1909–1923: revolución y comuna empresarial. Monterrey, Mexico: Facultad de Filosofía y Letras, Univ. Autónoma de Nuevo León, 1991. 272 p.: bibl.

Useful study based on primary sources

in which the Mexican Revolution in Nuevo León is viewed within the context of local business interests and the labor movement. Good background starting in the 1880s. A section on the 1920–23 period gives an interesting view of President Alvaro Obregón's attitudes toward US business interests in Mexico and his relationship with business leaders in Monterrey as well as capital-labor relations in the region.

1474 Fuentes Díaz, Vicente. La clase obrera: entre el anarquismo y la religión. Presentación de José Francisco Ruiz Massieu. México: Univ. Nacional Autónoma de México, Coordinación de Humanidades, 1994. 313 p.: bibl.

Examination of two of the major influences on the working class by an active member of the Partido Revolucionario Institucional (PRI) focuses on the tension between worker activism encouraged by anarchist thought and the conservative social activism of the Catholic Church. Argues that the Church has historically been an obstacle to the development of worker solidarity.

1475 Gamboa Ojeda, Leticia. El financiamiento de la urbanización: la deuda interior del Ayuntamiento de Puebla en los mercados extranjeros, 1907–1914. (*Secuencia/México*, 23, mayo/agosto 1992, p. 99–124, bibl., ill., tables)

Study of Puebla's attempt to finance urban improvements through the issue of bonds backed by the Banco Central Mexicano and sold largely to foreign investors. Ultimate suspension of payments on the debt was due not to the Revolution but to the "persistent insolvency" of Puebla's Ayuntamiento.

1476 García Luna Ortega, Margarita. Huelgas de mineros en El Oro, Méx., 1911–1920. Toluca, Mexico?: Secretaría del Trabajo del Gobierno del Estado de México, 1993? 171 p.: bibl., ill.

Well-researched study of the working conditions of miners and their struggles against exploitation by mining companies. Provides a profile of El Oro during the Revolution, a survey of mining companies and their operations, and an exploration of several strikes.

1477 García Morales, Soledad. La rebelión delahuertista en Veracruz, 1923. Xalapa, Mexico: Univ. Veracruzana, 1986. 173 p.:

bibl., ill., index. (Biblioteca/Universidad Veracruzana)

Good description of the De la Huerta revolt at its center in Veracruz. The state was politically unsettled even before the revolt broke out due to the reforms implemented by Governor Adalberto Tejeda and the growing rift between Tejeda and President Obregón. Tejeda and his agrarian supporters helped put down the revolt, leading to a cabinet position for Tejeda in the new Calles Administration. See also item **1593.**

1478 Garza Toledo, Enrique de et al. Historia de la industria eléctrica en México. v. 1. México: Univ. Autónoma Metropolitana, Unidad Iztapalapa, División de Ciencias Sociales y Humanidades, 1994. 1 v.: bibl., ill. (Col. CSH)

Work traces evolution of electric industry from small, unregulated, private businesses to government-owned monopoly assigned a prominent role in national development plan. Examines economic, technological, and political factors; places considerable emphasis on the role of the labor movement.

1479 Gilly, Adolfo. La revolución interrumpida. Ed. corr. y aum. México: Ediciones Era, 1994. 367 p.: bibl. (Col. Problemas de México)

New edition of Gilly's 1971 work, a Marxist interpretation of the Revolution. Gilly sees Zapatismo as perhaps the truest expression of the Revolution and argues that the Revolution was "interrupted" after 1920 when Alvaro Obregón and others consolidated "bourgeois power."

1480 Gledhill, John. Casi nada: capitalismo, Estado y los campesinos de Guaracha. Zamora, Mexico: El Colegio de Michoacán, 1993. 732 p.: bibl., ill. (Col. Occidente)

Somewhat updated Spanish translation of work originally published in English in 1991 (see *HLAS 54:1500*).

1481 Gómez Alvarez, Cristina. Puebla, los obreros textiles en la Revolución, 1911–1918. Puebla, Mexico: Centro de Investigaciones Históricas y Sociales, 1989. 81 p.: bibl., ill. (Cuadernos de la Casa Presno; 9)

Examination of the evolution of the textile workers' movement in the traditional center of the Mexican textile industry from the triumph of Madero's revolution to the suppression of the strike of 1918. The workers suffered from weak organization and lack of ideology, focusing instead on immediate economic issues.

1482 Gonzales, Michael J. United States copper companies: the State and labour conflict in Mexico, 1900–1910. (*J. Lat. Am. Stud.*, 26:3, Oct. 1994, pp. 651–681)

Interpretation of the 1906 Cananea strike. Shows that the strike was primarily a response to economic issues, and that it helped encourage the development of a working class movement that would play an important role in the Mexican Revolution.

1483 González Esparza, Víctor Manuel. Jalones modernizadores: Aguascalientes en el siglo XX. Aguascalientes, Mexico: Instituto Cultural de Aguascalientes, 1992. 149 p.: bibl., ill. (Contemporáneos)

Careful examination of various aspects of the state's history from the Mexican Revolution to 1940, using demographic and economic statistics to explore the broader changes contributing to Aguascalientes' modernization. Includes a detailed discussion of agrarian reform in the aftermath of the revolution.

1484 González y González, Luis. La querencia. Guadalajara, Mexico: Editorial Hexágono, 1991. 160 p.: bibl.

Collection of five essays—most published previously—dealing with western Mexico (Nayarit, Aguascalientes, Colima, Jalisco, Guanajuato, and Michoacán).

1485 Gortari Rabiela, Rebeca de. Educación y la formación de la conciencia nacional. (*in* Coloquio de Antropología e Historia Regionales, *8th, Zamora, Mexico, 1986.* Edición de Cecilia Noriega Elío. Zamora, Mexico: El Colegio de Michoacán, 1992, p. 719–741)

Examines Mexico's attempt to use its educational system as a means of fostering nationalism. Focuses on the training and use of Mexican engineers from the Porfirian era through the Mexican Revolution. Technical and professional training was seen as a means of ending foreign dominance in areas that were crucial to Mexico's economic development.

1486 Guerin-Gonzales, Camille. Mexican workers and American dreams: immigration, repatriation, and California farm labor, 1900–1939. New Brunswick, N.J.: Rutgers Univ. Press, 1994. 197 p., 8 p. of plates: bibl., ill., index. (Class and culture)

Author examines the influx of more than 1,000,000 Mexican workers into California agriculture between 1900–30, the reversal of this movement in the 1930s, and the destabilizing effect that repatriation had on communities on both sides of the border. The workers were drawn by a shared vision of the "American Dream" but encountered problems due to competing ideas about freedom.

1487 Guillén, Fedro. Don Belisario: interpretación de un hombre y una época. Tuxtla Gutiérrez, Mexico: Gobierno del Estado de Chiapas, Instituto Chiapaneco de Cultura, 1994. 119 p.: bibl.

Biography of a physician and outspoken politican of the revolutionary era who openly denounced the regime of Victoriano Huerta and was later assassinated. Examines the influences on his life and political activities.

1488 Haber, Stephen H. Industrial concentration and the capital markets: a comparative study of Brazil, Mexico, and the United States, 1830–1930. (*J. Econ. Hist.*, 51: 3, Sept. 1991, p. 559–580, bibl., tables)

Excellent analysis of the features and development of the Mexican economy from the 19th century until 1930, focusing particularly on the cotton textile industry. Introduces a comparative perspective with the cases of Brazil and the US. For economist's comment see *HLAS 53:1495.*

1489 Haber, Stephen H. La industrialización de México: historiografía y análisis. (*Hist. Mex.*, 42:3, enero/marzo 1993, p. 649–688, bibl.)

Excellent discussion of both the historiography of Mexico's transition to an industrial economy as well as of the process itself. Until the 1980s, the historiography focused on the politics of development and saw industrialization as a relatively recent (World War II) phenomenon. More recent research has indicated that the industrialization process started in the early 19th century, with the transition to the mechanized factory underway by the 1890s.

1490 Las haciendas de Mazaquiahuac, el Rosario y el Moral: catálogo de la correspondencia de Antonio Castro Solórzano, su

administrador. no. 2, 1912–1913. no. 6, 1916–1917. Selección de María Eugenia Ponce Alcocer y Cecilia Güereña Gándara. México: Univ. Iberoamericana, Centro de Información Académica; Depto. de Historia, 1981, 1990. 2 v.: ill., index. (Catálogo de fondos documentales de la U.I.A. Serie Haciendas; 2, 6)

Catalog and selection of extremely interesting primary documents from the correspondence of the administrator of three haciendas in Tlaxala.

1491 Hale, Charles A. Frank Tannenbaum and the Mexican Revolution. (*HAHR*, 75:2, May 1995, p. 215–246)

Explores the major influences on Tannenbaum's development, including his participation in the International Workers of the World, and his education at Columbia Univ. and Brookings Graduate School. Suggests that such experiences influenced Tannenbaum's populist interpretation of the Mexican Revolution.

1492 Hernández Chávez, Alicia. Mexican presidentialism: a historical and institutional overview. (*Mex. Stud.*, 10:1, Winter 1994, p. 217–225)

Succinct overview of changes in presidentialism, from a relatively weak position in the 19th century, to the "imperial presidentialism" of the late Porfiriato and the birth of "contemporary presidentialism" in the 1929–36 period. The presidency was at its strongest from the 1940s-60s, but centralization had run its course by 1968. See also item **1495.**

1493 Hernández Chávez, Alicia. La tradición republicana del buen gobierno. México: El Colegio de México; Fondo de Cultura Económica, 1993. 224 p.

Author examines the evolution of Mexico's "republican political culture" from the independence movements to the Constitution of 1917. Approximately one-third of the work is devoted to the early years of the Revolution.

1494 Hernández Rodríguez, Rogelio. La formación del político mexicano: el caso de Carlos A. Madrazo. México: Colegio de México, Centro de Estudios Sociológicos, 1991. 207 p.: bibl., ill.

Study of the PRI official who made the first major—and unsuccessful—effort to promote internal reforms in the official party during the Díaz Ordaz Administration by emphasizing an appeal to youth. Madrazo continued to push for reform after leaving his PRI post, which led to his being considered a "dangerous politician." For political scientist's comment see *HLAS 55:2866.*

1495 Hernández Rodríguez, Rogelio. Inestabilidad política y presidencialismo en México. (*Mex. Stud.,* 10:1, Winter 1994, p. 187–216)

Examination of political actions by Salinas in three areas: elections, removal of state governors, and reform of the PRI. Author concludes that these actions have led to an even more personalistic and presidentialist system, thereby creating greater political instability. See also item **1492.**

1496 Hernández Romero, Amanda. General Miguel Saavedra Romero: quien en Celaya voló el brazo derecho al General Alvaro Obregón. Chihuahua, Mexico: Gobierno del Estado de Chihuahua, 1986. 88 p.: bibl., ill., photos, maps.

Brief biographical treatment, including photographs, newspaper clippings, and some primary documentation.

1497 Herrera, Celia. Pancho Villa facing history. New York: Vantage Press, 1993. 360 p.: ill.

First US edition of Herrera's 1939 book. A highly negative depiction of Villa intended to counter his heroic image. Based largely on accounts gathered from the families of Villa's victims and from the author's own recollections.

1498 Heyman, Josiah McConnell. Life and labor on the border: working people of northeastern Sonora, Mexico, 1886–1986. Tucson: Univ. of Arizona Press, 1991. 247 p.: bibl., ill., index, maps.

Micro- and macro-level study of working class families, especially those working on the US-owned copper mines in northeastern Sonora. Describes how working class experiences influenced socioeconomic conditions on both sides of the border. For ethnologist's comment see *HLAS 53:940.*

1499 Higuera, Antonio. Historia y hombres: el Comité Pro-Territorio de Quintana Roo. (*Relaciones/Zamora,* 12:46, primavera 1991, p. 7–36)

Study of the congressional process, begun in 1924 and culminating in 1931, to divide the territory of Quintana Roo and annex it to the states of Yucatán and Campeche, and of ensuing developments. After a massive out-migration and a general economic collapse, Cárdenas ordered the reintegration of the territory.

1500 Historia de la cuestión agraria mexicana: Estado de Zacatecas. v. 3, 1940–1985. Coordinación regional de José Sánchez Cortés. México: J. Pablos Editor; Gobierno del Estado de Zacatecas; Univ. Autónoma de Zacatecas, Centro de Estudios Históricos del Agrarismo en México, 1990–1992. 1 v.: bibl., ill., maps.

Careful and well-documented study with good economic and political data to back up its discussion of agrarian issues.

1501 Historia de las comunicaciones y los transportes en México. v. 10, El telégrafo. México: Secretaría de Comunicaciones y Transportes, 1988. 1 v.: bibl., ill.

Comprehensive, official history of the telegraph in Mexico. Includes an administrative history of the telegraph system and a discussion of the importance of the telegraph during the Mexican Revolution.

1502 Historia general de Tabasco. t. 1, Historia social. t. 2, Historia económica. Coordinación de Rosa María Romo López. Villahermosa, Mexico: Gobierno del Estado de Tabasco, Secretaría de Educación, Cultura y Recreación, 1994. 2 v.: bibl., ill., maps.

Extensive, well-researched history. Vol. 1 is dedicated to social history and contains sections on geography and population, the Catholic Church, education, and literature. Vol. 2 focuses on Tabasco's economic history from the colonial period to the contemporary era.

Indigenous revolts in Chiapas and the Andean highlands. See *HLAS 55:57.*

1503 Inéditos de La Cristiada. Recopilación de Luis Sandoval Godoy. Guadalajara, Mexico: Editorial Conexión Gráfica, 1990. 109 p. (Col. Letras jaliscienses de Editorial Conexión Gráfica)

Personal accounts of the *cristero* rebellion from participants on both sides of the struggle, all but one from the state of Jalisco.

1504 Una inmigración privilegiada: comerciantes, empresarios y profesionales españoles en México en los siglos XIX y XX. Recopiliación de Clara Eugenia Lida. Presentación de Nicolás Sánchez-Albornoz. Madrid: Alianza Editorial, 1994. 237 p.: bibl., ill. (Alianza América; 34)

Series of nine articles examining various aspects of the Spanish presence in Mexico from the early 19th century to the Spanish Civil War. Includes discussions of the growing importance of Spaniards in the Mexican economy and illustrates that Spanish immigrants came to occupy a respected position in Mexican society.

1505 Jablonska, Alejandra and **Juan Felipe Leal.** La Revolución Mexicana en el cine estadounidense, 1911–1916. (*Plural/México*, 21:241, oct. 1991, p. 24–31)

Shows that US films on the Mexican Revolution are related in form and style to the genre of the Western. Both have been used to display the moral and cultural superiority of the US over Mexico. The border is a favorite site, showing both political and cultural divisions.

1506 José C. Valadés, historiador y político. México: Univ. Nacional Autónoma de México, 1992. 112 p.: bibl., ill.

Collection of essays by various authors analyzing the controversial views of this journalist-politician-historian, best known for his writings on the Porfiriato and the Revolution.

1507 Joseph, Gilbert M. and **Allen Wells.** Un replanteamiento de la movilización revolucionaria mexicana: los tiempos de sublevación en Yucatán, 1909–1915. (*Hist. Mex.*, 43:3, enero/marzo 1994, p. 505–546, bibl., map)

Authors examine the mobilization and demobilization of popular forces during the "Madero opening." The popular movement in the peninsula was "fragmented and fragile," and a variety of factors—political, geographic, and economic—prevented it from evolving into a generalized rebellion. Part of a broader work soon to be published. See also item **1413.**

1508 Klesner, Joseph L. Modernization, economic crisis and electoral alignment in Mexico. (*Mex. Stud.*, 9:2, Summer 1993, p. 187–223)

Although coverage goes back to early 1960s, stress is on the elections of 1988 and 1991. Author concludes that a process of dealignment has taken place in which some groups have detached themselves from the

PRI but that realignment has not yet taken place. Although the PRI has lost its hegemony, it has still demonstrated an ability to dominate in this dealigned environment.

1509 Knight, Alan. *Cardenismo:* juggernaut or jalopy. (*J. Lat. Am. Stud.*, 26:1, Feb. 1994, p. 73–107)

Examines the historiographical debate on the era of Lázaro Cárdenas and argues that *cardenismo* was not as sucessful as is often assumed. Opposition to Cárdenas' radicalism often forced a retreat from that radicalism, and although decisive changes did occur, after 1940 *cardenismo* was merely an "institutional shell."

1510 Knight, Alan. Popular culture and the revolutionary State in Mexico, 1910–1940. (*HAHR*, 74:3, Aug. 1994, p. 395–444)

An analysis of Mexico's attempt to create a new State and a "new man" by forging a revolutionary culture. Emphasizes anticlericalism and the attempt to introduce socialist education. Argues that the revolutionary cultural program did not endure, and that socioeconomic changes were ultimately a more important outcome of the Revolution.

1511 Kowalenski, Stephen A. and **Jacqueline J. Saindon.** The spread of literacy in a Latin American peasant society: Oaxaca, Mexico, 1890–1980. (*Comp. Stud. Soc. Hist.*, 34:1, 1992, p. 110–140)

Essay uses extensive census data to examine the spatiotemporal variation in literacy. Concludes that spread of literacy may be enhanced on the one hand by labor markets, and on the other by social movements, such as the Mexican Revolution, which give impetus to education.

1512 Latapí de Kuhlmann, Paulina. La testamentaría de Alvaro Obregón en una época de crisis. (*Estud. Hist. Mod. Contemp. Méx.*, 14, 1991, p. 159–176, tables)

Based on documents of the Fondo Alvaro Obregón of the Fideicomiso Plutarco Elias Calles y Fernando Torreblanca, this article shows that Obregon's wealth, which for a time had been significant, was destroyed by his enormous debts to US commercial lenders and to the Mexican government, as well as by the crisis of 1926 and the Smoot-Hawley tariff. Shows clearly the vulnerabilities of private agricultural businesses to the vicissitudes of the US market.

1513 Leal, Juan Felipe and **Margarita Menegus Bornemann.** La quiebra de la Compañía Expendedora de Pulques, SCL, y la producción y comercialización del producto en las haciendas Mazaquiahuac y El Rosario, Tlaxcala, 1915–1920. (*in* Simposio Internacional de Investigaciones Socio-Históricas sobre Tlaxcala, *1st, Tlaxcala, Mexico, 1985.* Memorias. Tlaxcala, Mexico: Gobierno del Estado de Tlaxcala, Instituto Tlaxcalteca de Cultura, Univ. Autónoma de Tlaxcala; México: Univ. Iberoamericana, 1986, p. 135–148, ill., maps, tables)

Study traces the effects of the Mexican Revolution on Tlaxcala's pulque industry. Restrictions and taxes on the sale and production of pulque, as well as the temporary confiscation of property by the Constitutionalists, affected the industry but did not cause its demise.

1514 León Toral, Jesús de *et al.* El ejército y Fuerza Aérea mexicanos. México: Secretaría de la Defensa Nacional, 1992. 2 v. (693 p.): bibl., ill. (some col.).

Lavishly illustrated, highly detailed history of the Mexican army and air force. Vol. 1 carries the narrative to 1913. Vol. 2 covers the period from 1913–91, but there is little narrative after World War II.

1515 Lerner, Victoria. Espías mexicanos en tierras norteamericanas, 1914–1915. (*N.M. Hist. Rev.*, 69:3, July 1994, p. 230–247)

Author examines espionage activity in US territory by both Mexican nationals and US citizens. This activity took place in three main border areas: Sonora-Arizona-California; Chihuahua-Texas-New Mexico; and Tamaulipas-Coahuila-Nuevo Leon-Lower Rio Grande. Most of the attention is on *villista* activities. Additional emphasis on women's roles and on Mexican consulates.

1516 El liberalismo en México. Coordinación de Antonio Annino y Raymond Thomas Joseph Buve. Münster, Germany: Asociación de Historiadores Latinoamericanistas Europeos; Lit, 1993. 186 p.: bibl. (Cuadernos de historia latinoamericana; 1)

A series of six essays by European scholars. Takes 1812 as the starting point for the exploration of Mexican liberalism, which is seen as a key to understanding the formation of modern Mexico. Explores the meaning of liberalism and its impact on Mexicans and Mexico's governing structures.

1517 Lima Muñiz, Laura. Sierra de Agua: historia de una comunidad veracruzana. México: Univ. Autónoma Metropolitana, Unidad Iztapalapa, División de Ciencias Sociales y Humanidades, 1991. 108 p.: bibl., ill., maps. (Texto y contexto; 2)

Interesting study, based carefully on local and national primary sources and some oral history, on the conversion of two Veracruzan haciendas into an ejido community. Focuses on the period 1921–53.

1518 López González, Pedro. Nayarit, historia del periodismo. Tepic, Mexico: Asociación de Periodistas y Escritores del Estado de Nayarit; Gobierno del Estado de Nayarit, 1993. 79 p.: bibl., ill.

Examines major political and social issues in Mexico as reflected in Nayarit newspapers. Covers the period from 1833, when the first printing press arrived, through the 1950s. Includes a brief history of press censorship.

1519 López Ochoa, Marco Antonio. Sonora, tierra de caudillos: capitalismo y dominación en Sonora, 1880–1984. Prólogo de Raúl Olmedo Carranza. 2a ed. Hermosillo, Mexico?: s.n., 1989. 165 p.: bibl., maps.

Employing an eclectic methodology, the author traces the growth and growing contradictions of Sonoran capitalism. Maintains that an empresarial elite has historically controlled the state, culminating in the 1960s-70s in the over-exploitation of resources. The simultaneous failure of the national government's development plan led to the political and economic crisis of the 1980s.

1520 López Portillo, Felícitas. Las glorias del desarrollismo: el gobierno de Miguel Alemán. (*Secuencia/México*, 19, enero/abril 1991, p. 61–86, bibl., ill.)

Mostly traditional interpretation of Alemán's development policy, with particular emphasis on the background to the Alemán Administration.

1521 López Portillo, Felícitas. La revolución institucionalizada y sus censores. (*Cuad. Am.*, 6:31, enero/feb. 1992, p. 196–206)

Critical look at two articles published in the 1940s by Daniel Cosío Villegas and Jesús Silva Herzog that accused the administrations of Manuel Avila Camacho and Miguel Alemán of betraying the principles of the

1910 Revolution. The author finds their critiques equally applicable to the present period.

1522 Lorenzana Durán, Gustavo. Lázaro Cárdenas y el reparto agrario en los valles del Yaqui y Mayo, 1937–1938. (*in* Simposio de Historia y Antropología de Sonora, *16th, Hermosillo, Mexico, 1993. Memoria.* Hermosillo, Mexico: Instituto de Investigaciones Históricas, Univ. de Sonora, 1993, p. 471–488, bibl., tables)

Brief examination of land reform in Sonora. Details the extent of land redistribution in several pueblos, highlighting local conflicts over such changes. See also item **1523**.

1523 Lorenzana Durán, Gustavo. Política agraria y movimientos campesinos en los valles del Yaqui y Mayo, 1915–1934. Hermosillo, Mexico: Instituto de Investigaciones Históricas, Univ. de Sonora, 1991. 72 p.: bibl., ill. (Col. El Tejabán; 4)

Examination of the impact of agrarian legislation from Carranza's Law of Jan. 6, 1915 to the Agrarian Code of 1934 on the two key areas of agricultural production in Sonora. Author concludes that the "revolutionary compromise" between the peasants and the large landowners implemented by the government favored the large landowners and relegated the peasants to small, marginal properties. See also item **1522**.

1524 MacGregor, Josefina. Agentes confidenciales en México: España y su primer contacto oficial ante la revolución constitucionalista. (*Secuencia/México*, 24, sept./dic. 1992, p. 75–106, bibl., facsims., ill.)

This diplomatic history examines the activities of Spanish agent Manuel Walls y Merino who arrived in Mexico in 1914 to establish relations with the Constitutionalist movement. Walls successfully negotiated with Carranza and Villa for the protection of Mexico's Spanish residents, while paving the way for a smooth relationship with the Carranza regime.

1525 Madero vivo: a ochenta años de su sacrificio. Prólogo de Enrique Krauze. Coordinación de Fausto Zerón-Medina. 2a. ed. México: Clío, 1993. 123 p.: bibl., chiefly ill. (some col.), photos.

Collection of photographs dealing with the "Ten Tragic Days" in Feb. 1913. Photographs are accompanied by brief texts drawn from a variety of sources.

1526 Maldonado Aguirre, Serafín. De Tejeda a Cárdenas: el movimiento agrarista de la Revolución Mexicana, 1920–1934. Guadalajara, Mexico: Editorial Univ. de Guadalajara, 1992. 232 p.: bibl. (Col. Fin de milenio. Biblioteca Movimientos Sociales)

Well-researched and argued examination of the linkage between the agrarian movement and the rise of the presidentialist State, focusing on the two persons "most representative" of the movement. The agrarian movement is seen as ascending from regional power (Tejeda) to national power (Cárdenas). Although Tejeda contested for the presidency in 1934, he actually paved the way for the presidency for Cárdenas.

1527 Manifiestos, planes y documentos políticos del Oaxaca revolucionario, 1910–1920. Recopilación de Francisco José Ruiz Cervantes. Oaxaca, Mexico: Casa de la Cultura Oaxaqueña; CIDSTAO, 1987. 93 p.: bibl. (Col. Agua quemada. Fuentes para la historia de Oaxaca)

A collection of 27 documents from three archives and several printed sources.

1528 Manjarrez, Froylán C. La pluma y las palabras. Recopilación de Alberto Enríquez Perea. México: El Nacional, 1993. 442 p.: ill. (Col. Los Constituyentes de 1917)

Compilation of writings by politician who served at the Constitutional Convention of 1917 and later participated in the De La Huerta rebellion of 1923. The author returned to Mexico from exile in 1929 and embarked on a career as a prominent journalist. Selections are from the 1929–37 period and deal mainly with political themes.

1529 Markiewicz, Dana. The Mexican Revolution and the limits of agrarian reform, 1915–1946. Boulder, Colo.: Lynne Rienner Publishers, 1993. 215 p.: bibl., index.

Revisionist interpretation of land reform program, especially in the 1930s-40s. Author sees land distribution under Cárdenas as illusory and mostly reversible and believes that the Avila Camacho Administration was not a dramatic departure from the late Cárdenas years. Revolutionary governments developed a bureaucratic process of land grants aimed at retarding rather than facilitating land distribution. Based on a "revolutionary model of agrarian change" drawn from Marx, Engels, Lenin, and Trotsky.

1530 **Martin, JoAnn.** Contesting authenticity: battles over the representation of history in Morelos, Mexico. (*Ethnohistory/Society*, 40:3, Summer 1993, p. 438–465)

Interesting examination of the uses of history by peasants in Buena Vista, Morelos, and by the Mexican State. Demonstrates that the Partido Revolucionario Institucional has manipulated the history of the Mexican Revolution to help gain legitimacy, while Buena Vista villagers have challenged State authority by insisting on their own interpretation of that history.

1531 **Martínez Rescalvo, Mario O.** and **Jorge R. Obregón Téllez.** La Montaña de Guerrero: economía, historia y sociedad. México: Instituto Nacional Indigenista; Univ. Autónoma de Guerrero, Instituto de Investigación Científica, Area Humanístico-Social, 1991. 406 p.: bibl., maps. (Serie Economía y sociedad; 1)

Socioeconomic study of a region characterized by its large indigenous population and low standard of living. Highlights the region's history of indigenous unrest and agrarian struggles, which have continued in the post-Revolutionary era. Includes a statistical index.

1532 **Matute, Alvaro.** El fantasma de la intervención: los Estados Unidos y México en 1919. (*Estud. Hist. Mod. Contemp. Méx.*, 16, 1993, p. 79–100)

Examination of US-Mexican relations in 1919 with emphasis on pressure groups, the press, and the Jenkins case. Based primarily on the newspaper *El Universal*.

1533 **Matute, Alvaro.** La Revolución Mexicana: actores, escenarios y acciones; vida cultural y política, 1901–1929. México: Instituto Nacional de Estudios Históricos de la Revolución Mexicana, 1993. 268 p.: bibl., ill.

Collection of 19 articles by a well-known Mexican scholar. Most articles are from oral presentations and conference papers produced by Matute from 1976–91. They include studies of liberal thought in revolutionary Mexico, the Constitutionalist and National armies, the educational policies of José Vasconcelos, and Alvaro Obregón and the issue of *caudillismo* since the Revolution.

1534 **Meed, Douglas V.** Bloody border: riots, battles, and adventures along the turbulent U.S.-Mexican borderlands. Tucson,

Az.: Westernlore Press, 1992. 242 p.: bibl., ill., index. (Great West and Indian series; 58)

Episodic account of border events from the Cananea strike of 1906 to the Topete rebellion of 1929. Most of the emphasis is on the 1910–19 period. Numerous illustrations.

1535 **Menéndez, Carlos R.** La primera chispa de la Revolución Mexicana. Mérida, Mexico: Multicolor, 1988. 170 p., 8 leaves of plates: bibl., ill.

Account of the anti-Díaz uprising in Valladolid, Yucatán in June 1910, which was quickly suppressed. Author views revolt as precursor of the larger revolution that started in November. Work was written in 1916 and first published in 1919. Author was director of Mérida newspaper.

1536 **México en los años 20: procesos políticos y reconstrucción económica; siete estudios regionales.** Recopilación de Mario Cerutti. México: Claves Latinoamericanas; San Nicolás de los Garza: Facultad de Filosofía y Letras, Univ. Nacional Autónoma de Nuevo León, 1993. 338 p.: bibl.

Excellent collection of essays on a little-studied period of Mexico's history. Focuses on central and northern Mexico, specifically Chihuahua, Nuevo León, Veracruz, and Tlaxcala.

1537 **Meyer, Jean A.** Colima en la Cristiada. (*Estud. Hist. Mod. Contemp. Méx.*, 16, 1993, p. 101–173)

Preliminary examination of the Cristero Rebellion in the small, isolated state of Colima. The "profoundly Catholic society" of the state permitted the rebels to wage a classic guerrilla war against the forces of the central government. Author concludes that it is still too early for definitive statements about who the cristeros were and why they fought.

1538 **Meyer, Jean A.** Una historia política de la religión en el México contemporáneo. (*Hist. Mex.*, 42:3, enero/marzo 1993, p. 711–744, bibl., table)

After establishing the theoretical and historical background, author examines changes in politics and religion in the "contemporaneous" period (1960–90). The real point of departure is the 1930s, when the Catholic Church adopted a policy of "conditioned cooperation" with the State following the unsuccessful Cristero Rebellion. Author stresses the ability of the Church to adapt, even to the point of providing "postmodern opposition to modernity." Also covers Protestant activity during the period.

1539 Meyer Cosío, Francisco Javier. Tradición y progreso: la reforma agraria en Acámbaro, Guanajuato, 1915–1941. México: Instituto Nacional de Estudios Históricos de la Revolución Mexicana, 1993. 203 p.: bibl., ill., maps. (Investigación)

Well-researched study of the specific changes resulting from agrarian reform in one municipality. Provides a good survey of land tenancy patterns before the Revolution and a region-by-region examination of changes occurring after the Revolution.

1540 Miranda Correa, Eduardo. El Congreso Constituyente. Cerro de las Campanas, Mexico: Univ. Autónoma de Querétaro, Dirección Centros de Investigación, Centro de Investigaciones Sociales, 1988. 176 p.: bibl. (Temas de investigación; 13)

Good analysis of the forces that influenced the debates of the Constitutional Congress. Argues that the mobilization of campesinos and Mexican workers during the Revolution helped influence the Congress and ensure that the demands and aspirations of Mexico's popular classes were incorporated in the post-Revolutionary state.

1541 Moctezuma Barragán, Pablo. La vida y la lucha de Emiliano Zapata. México: Impresora Ideal, 1994. 179 p.: bibl.

General account, based on secondary sources, of Zapata and his movement by a modern activist and member of the Unión Popular Revolucionario Emiliano Zapata.

1542 Mohoff, George. The Russian colony of Guadalupe Molokans in Mexico. s.l.: s.n., s.d. 226 p.: ill., maps.

Well-illustrated and highly personal account of a group of Russian religious dissenters who settled in Baja California in the late Porfiriato. The colony began to decline in the 1930s and finally broke up in the 1960s under pressure from squatters.

1543 Molina Hurtado, María Mercedes. En tierra bien distante: refugiados españoles en Chiapas. Tuxtla Gutiérrez, Mexico: Gobierno del Estado de Chiapas, Consejo Estatal de Fomento a la Investigación y Difusión de la Cultura, DIF-Chiapas, Instituto Chiapaneco de Cultura, 1993. 229 p.: bibl., ill.

Description of the impact of republican refugees from Spain on the state of Chiapas.

While refugees began arriving in Mexico in 1937, they did not arrive in Chiapas in significant numbers until 1940. The formation of soccer teams was one of the most effective ways of integrating the exiles into local society. See also item **1459.**

1544 Monjarás-Ruiz, Jesús. Del estallido de la Revolución al asesinato de Madero: una versión periodística alemana. México: Fondo de Cultura Económica, 1988. 314 p.: bibl. (Col. popular; 369)

Series of articles reprinted from the German newspaper *Kolnische Zeitung.* Includes telegrams and letters written by Germans residing in Mexico during the Revolution, as well as articles of analysis by German journalists. Provides an interesting perspective on the fall of the Porfirian regime and the decline of Madero.

1545 Monroy Pérez, Adriana. Trece mujeres sonorenses en la Revolución. (*in* Simposio de Historia y Antropología de Sonora, *16th, Hermosillo, Mexico, 1993.* Memoria. Hermosillo, Mexico: Instituto de Investigaciones Históricas, Univ. de Sonora, 1993, p. 457–470, bibl.)

Brief presentation of the service records of 13 women contained in the Archivo de la Defensa Nacional. Details their various roles in the Revolution.

1546 Morales Martínez, Ignacio. Esteban B. Calderón: prócer revolucionario defensor de los derechos humanos. 2da. edición. Guadalajara, Mexico: Gobierno de Jalisco, Secretaría General, Unidad Editorial, 1987. 191 p.: appendix, bibl., ill. (Colección Historia. Serie Documentos e investigación; 32)

Second edition of a biography first published in 1967. Discusses Calderón's role as a leader of the 1906 Cananea strike, and details his activities during the Revolution. Appendix contains various documents, including speeches given by Calderón as a deputy to the Constitutional Congress.

1547 Morales Velarde, Francisco. Historia de las fábricas textiles en Jalisco. Zapopan, Mexico: H. Ayuntamiento Constitucional de Zapopan, 1992. 178 p.: ill.

Brief history, anecdotes, and personal recollections of Jalisco's textile factories by one who worked in them.

1548 Morelos: el estado. Coordinación de investigación de David Moctezuma Navarro y Medardo Tapia Uribe. Cuernavaca,

Mexico: Gobierno del Estado de Morelos; Letras Consultores en Comunicación Visual, 1993. 404 p.: bibl., ill. (some col.), maps.

Narrative and pictographic examination of Morelo's history, economy, society, and culture by a variety of authors. Includes an interesting discussion of the Revolution, including an evaluation of the image of Emiliano Zapata.

1549 Las mujeres en la Revolución Mexicana: 1884–1920. México: Cámara de Diputados, LV Legislatura; Instituto Nacional de Estudios Históricos de la Revolución Mexicana, 1992. 130 p.: bibl., ill.

Narrative and pictographic history that includes numerous biographical sketches. Topics include women activists of the Porfirian era, female militants during the Revolution, the feminist movement in the Yucatán, and the discussion of women's issues in the Constitutional Congress.

1550 Mujeres y revolución, 1900–1917. Estudio preliminar y recopilación de Ana Lau Jaiven y Carmen Ramos-Escandón. México: Instituto Nacional de Estudios Históricos de la Revolución Mexicana; Instituto Nacional de Antropología e Historia, 1993. 381 p.: bibl., ill.

Excellent study of women and the Mexican Revolution that combines information from existing scholarship with primary sources. Contains a brief examination of women's activities during the Revolution and a lengthy anthology of documents, including writings by both Mexican men and women that deal with women's issues.

1551 Muriá, José María. Bosquejo histórico de la Revolución en Jalisco. Zapopan, Mexico: Colegio de Jalisco; Guadalajara, Mexico: Gobierno de Jalisco, Secretaría de Educación, 1994. 36 p. (Ensayos jaliscienses)

Sketch of revolutionary activities in key state from 1908 to early 1930s. Emphasis is on the governorship of José Guadalupe Zuno (1923–26) and the political meddling of Calles in state affairs.

1552 Muriá, José María. Identidad e historia. Introducción de Guillermo de la Peña. Zapopan, Mexico: Colegio de Jalisco; México: INAH, 1994. 54 p.: bibl. (Ensayos jaliscienses)

Wide-ranging collection of essays relating to Jalisco region and regional history.

1553 Nieto, Rafael. Rafael Nieto: obras escogidas. Recopilación e introducción de Alberto Enríquez Perea. San Luis Potosí, Mexico: Comité Organizador San Luis 400, 1992. 2 v. (Col. Cuatro siglos. Serie Obras escogidas de autores potosinos; 6)

Collection of items by or relating to a prominent figure in the early years of the Revolution. Nieto served in the federal congress under Madero, as Subsecretary of Hacienda under Carranza, and as a delegate to the convention that drafted the Constitution of 1917. Vol. 2 deals with Nieto's controversial tenure as governor of San Luis Potosí (1919–23).

1554 Ochoa, Alvaro. La violencia en Michoacán: ahí viene Chávez García. Morelia, Mexico: Gobierno del Estado de Michoacán, Instituto Michoacano de Cultura, 1990. 315 p.: bibl., ill.

Study of a well-known bandit of the Revolutionary era, born in 1889 as José Inés García Chávez. Includes a biographical sketch of Chávez García, a lengthy section of documents dealing with his revolutionary activities, and a collection of stories and *corridos* about Chávez García.

1555 O'Dogherty, Laura. Restaurarlo todo en Cristo: Unión de Damas Católicas Mejicanas, 1920–1926. (*Estud. Hist. Mod. Contemp. Méx.*, 14, 1991, p. 129–158, tables)

Interesting discussion of an organization founded in Sept. 1920 with the support of the Bishop of Mexico City, one of several which the Mexican Catholic hierarchy hoped to use to oppose anti-clerical measures by the Obregón government. This group was linked closely to the most conservative wing of the Church.

1556 Orozco Zuarth, Marco A. Síntesis de Chiapas. Mexico: EDYSIS, 1994. 172 p.: bibl., ill., maps.

Basically a reference work on contemporary Chiapas. Devotes one chapter to the history of the state.

1557 Ortiz Garza, José Luis. México en guerra. México: Planeta, 1989. 230 p.: bibl., ill., index. (Col. Espejo de México; 2)

Well-researched study of foreign efforts to influence the Mexican mass media during World War II. Many of the propaganda techniques of World War II had been experimented with during World War I. Emphasis is on US activities due to availability of information, extent of US operations, and postwar effects of US involvement. Film was considered the most influential medium, and Walt Disney, the most effective film producer.

1558 Palacio Díaz, Alejandro del. Agonía y muerte de la Revolución Mexicana: el triunfo del sistema. 2. ed. corr. y aum. Azcapotzalco, Mexico: Esquemas; Univ. Autónoma Metropolitana, Unidad Azcapotzalco, 1991. 195 p.: bibl.

Author updates his gloomy assessment of the trajectory of the Mexican Revolution first published in 1986 with a chapter denouncing the Salinas Administration. Author retains his fundamental view that the rulers of the Revolution became the authors of the counterrevolution.

1559 Palacios Beltrán, Miguel R. and **Ana María León de Palacios.** Alvaro Obregón: caudillo e ideólogo de la reconstrucción nacional. Hermosillo, Mexico: Gobierno del Estado de Sonora, 1980. 177 p.: bibl., ill.

Brief, laudatory biography based on secondary sources examines Obregón's policies as president and defends his signing of the Bucareli Agreements as an act consistent with the 1917 Constitution and crucial in establishing a *modus vivendi* with the US.

1560 Palacios Santillán, Vicente *et al.* La Revolución Mexicana en Veracruz: los hombres y sus obras. Jalapa Enríquez, Mexico?: Cambio XXI Fundación Veracruz; Sección 32 del SNTE, 1992. 113 p.: bibl.

An alphabetized, annotated selection of people, items, and events dealing with the Revolution in Veracruz. Includes a chronology and a list of the state's governors.

1561 Partido Revolucionario Institucional (Mexico). Comité Ejecutivo Nacional, v. 1–3. Textos revolucionarios. Mexico: PRI, C.E.N., 1985. 3 v.: ill.

Mixed bag of revolutionary materials published by the National Executive Committee of the PRI to commemorate the 75th anniversary of the Revolution. Vol. 1 contains items ranging from precursor movements to revolutionary corridos. Work aimed at educating and motivating the party faithful.

1562 Peña, Guillermo de la. Poder agrario y ambigüedad revolucionaria: bandidos, caudillos y facciones. (*in* Las formas y las políticas del dominio agrario: homenaje a Fran-

çois Chevalier. Coordinación de Ricardo Avila Palafox, Carlos Martínez Assad, y Jean Meyer. Guadalajara, Mexico: Editorial Univ. de Guadalajara, 1992, p. 232–259, bibl.)

Interesting comparison of Mexican agrarian movements of the 1920s and social banditry in Brazil and Peru during the same period. Uses examples of Yucatán, Jalisco, and Veracruz to show the internal contradictions of such movements and their tendency to be easily co-opted.

1563 Pérez Bertruy, Ramona Isabel. Tomás Garrido Canabal y la conformación del poder revolucionario tabasqueño, 1914–1921. Villahermosa, Mexico: Gobierno del Estado de Tabasco, Secretaría de Educación, Cultura y Recreación, Dirección de Educación Superior e Investigación Científica, 1993. 111 p.: bibl. (Investigaciones. Historia)

Well-researched study on the emergence of a dominant caudillo in revolutionary Tabasco. As a political leader and provisional governor, Garrido Canabal successfully balanced the popular demands emanating from the Revolution with the demands of the national government and its project of "capitalist modernization."

1564 Pérez Mota, Luis Enrique. Chiapas: notas para una historia reciente. Tuxtla Gutiérrez, Mexico?: Univ. Autónoma de Chiapas; Instituto Chiapaneco de Cultura; Congreso del Estado, 1994. 445 p.: bibl.

Political history, based on secondary sources, with attention to the Mexican Revolution and the state's constitutional history. Other topics include economic development, social characteristics, local culture, and Chiapas' historical relationship with Central America.

1565 Pérez Olivares, Porfirio. Memorias: un dirigente agrario de Soledad de Doblado. Prólogo de Olivia Domínguez Pérez. Xalapa, Mexico: Univ. Veracruzana, 1992. 190 p.: bibl., ill. (Col. UV rescate; 35)

Memoirs of a person active in local politics and agrarian organization in the municipality of Soledad de Doblado, Veracruz, from the early 1930s to the early 1980s. Narrative ends in 1979.

1566 Poblett Miranda, Martha. José María Pino Suárez: semblanza. México: Instituto Nacional de Estudios Históricos de la Revolución Mexicana, 1986. 119 p.: bibl., ill.

Portrait of Madero's assassinated vice-president consists of a biography, 20 documents relating to his political activities from 1909–13, and six essays by his contemporaries.

1567 Polska-Meksyk, 1918–1988: zbiór dokumentów i materiałów [Poland-Mexico, 1918–1988: a collection of documents and materials]. Introduction by Jan Majewski. Warszawa, Poland: Ministerstwo Spraw Zagranicznych Polskiej Rzeczypospolitej Ludowej, 1989. 206 p.: bibl.

Brief history of Polish-Mexican relations, followed by a chronology of important dates in diplomatic relations between the two countries from the time Poland regained its independence in 1918 to April 13, 1989. Also includes, in chronological order, the texts of 74 documents relating to Polish-Mexican diplomatic relations. Concludes with a list of publications on Mexico published in Polish. [Z. Kantorosinski]

1568 Ponce, Francisco. Lo que el tiempo no se llevó: los conflictos agrarios en el sur de Sinaloa durante el periodo cardenista, 1935–1940. Culiacán, Mexico: Dirección de Investigación y Fomento de la Cultura Regional; Univ. Autónoma de Sinaloa, 1993. 112 p.: bibl.

Surveys part of Sinaloa's often-bloody struggle between agrarians and those opposed to land reform. Although the state's campesinos did succeed in partially destroying latifundia, land reform ultimately gave way to the needs of modernization.

1569 Portes Gil, Emilio. Emilio Portes Gil: un civil en la Revolución Mexicana. Entrevistas de Alicia Olivera de Bonfil. Ciudad Victoria, Mexico: Instituto Tamaulipeco de Cultura, Gobierno del Estado de Tamaulipas, 1989. 191 p.

Wide-ranging series of interviews conducted in Mexico City during June and July 1975. The former president provides his views on leading political events as well as political players from Porfirio Díaz to Lucio Cabañas.

1570 Portilla, Segundo. Los olvidados: Marcelo Craveo y el orozquismo serrano en Chihuahua. (*Relaciones/Zamora*, 12 : 47, verano 1991, p. 107–113)

Short discussion of a second-rank revolutionary leader who began his career within the *orozquista* movement. After its defeat, he was able to reintegrate himself into military and political life by joining forces with Alvaro Obregón.

1571 Pueblo en vilo: la fuerza de la costumbre; homenaje a Luis González y González. Edición de Alvaro Ochoa. Guadalajara, Mexico: El Colegio de Jalisco; México: El Colegio de México; Zamora, Mexico: El Colegio de Michoacán, 1994. 254 p.: bibl., ill.

Series of articles commemorating González's seminal work on San José de Gracia village and honoring his contributions to Mexican history.

1572 Puig, Juan. Entre el río Perla y el Nazas: la China decimonónica y sus braceros emigrantes, la colonia china de Torreón y la matanza de 1911. México: Consejo Nacional para la Cultura y las Artes, 1993. 321 p.: bibl., map. (Regiones)

Account of the massacre of Chinese at Torreón in May 1911 during the Madero revolt and the diplomatic negotations that ensued, lasting until 1934. Well researched, with extensive background provided (almost half of the work).

1573 Quintanilla, Susana. Los intelectuales y la política en la Revolución Mexicana: estudio de casos. (*Secuencia/México*, 24, sept./dic. 1992, p. 47–73, bibl., ill., maps)

Examines the relationship between intellectuals and the Mexican State from 1909–16, focusing on the activities of several members of the Ateneo de la Juventud. Argues that the Mexican Revolution created a new relationship between culture and power, a relationship in which intellectuals became dependent on military caudillos and true intellectual autonomy disappeared.

1574 Quintero Corral, Lucio. Pancho Villa derrotado en Tepehuanes, Dgo., al intentar tomar la Cd. de Durango, 1918. Ciudad Juárez, Mexico: L. Quintero Corral, 1990. 42 p.: bibl., ill.

Briefly recounts how federal troops commanded by Joaquín Amaro defeated Villa's forces in March 1918 as he was enroute to the city of Durango.

1575 Ramírez Carrillo, Luis Alfonso. De buhoneros a empresarios: la inmigración libanesa en el sureste de México. (*Hist. Mex.,* 43 : 3, enero/marzo 1994, p. 451–486, bibl., tables)

Examination of 20th-century Lebanese immigration in Yucatán, particularly Mérida. Most of the immigrants were Maronite Christians who settled originally in Mérida. The immigrants excelled at commerce and demonstrated considerable social mobility. By mid-century the descendants of the immigrants belonged mostly to the middle or upper classes.

1576 Ramírez Cuéllar, Héctor. Lombardo, un hombre de México. México: El Nacional, 1992. 379 p.: bibl.

Study of the life and thinking of one of Mexico's most influential labor leaders: Vicente Lombardo Toledano. Details his role in the development of the Confederación Regional Obrera Mexicana and the Confederación de Trabajadores de México. Also relates Lombardo's ideas on education, politics, and other issues.

1577 Ramírez Salazar, Carlos Arturo. Tanquián: el poder y su dinámica histórica en la huasteca potosina, 1870–1985. San Luis Potosí, Mexico: Archivo Histórico del Estado de San Luis Potosí, 1989. 178 p.: bibl., ill., maps.

History of a *municipio* in San Luis Potosí focuses on "the dominant class and its forms of domination." The most important components of the local elite are the cattle raisers who have adjusted to agrarian reform and blocked efforts at peasant organization. Coverage is evenly divided between pre- and post-revolutionary periods.

1578 Ramos, Marta E. Los militares revolucionarios: un mosaico de reivindicaciones y de oportunismo. (*Estud. Hist. Mod. Contemp. Méx.*, 16, 1993, p. 29–52)

In an effort to explain the gap between revolutionary rhetoric and revolutionary action, author examines a number of revolutionary leaders and their motives. While some sought agrarian reform, modernization, or democratization, others were driven by local and regional rivalries, a desire for power and wealth, or even an effort to preserve the status quo. Author emphasizes the heterogeneity of the Revolution, which was often a "mosaic of local movements."

1579 Reyes Ramos, María Eugenia. El reparto de tierras y la política agraria en Chiapas, 1914–1988. México: Univ. Nacional

Autónoma de México, Centro de Investigaciones Humanísticas de Mesoamérica y del Estado de Chiapas, 1992. 193 p.: bibl., ill., maps.

Timely examination of agrarian reform does much to explain current problems in southern Mexico. Author examines the interaction among political, social, and economic factors as well as among local, state, and federal officials. Current conflict is considerably more complicated than simplified notion of landless peasants versus big landowners. Numerous tables, maps, and charts.

1580 Rivera Castro, José and José Jesús Hernández Palomo. El agrarismo mexicano: textos y documentos, 1908–1984. Sevilla: Escuela de Estudios Hispano-Americanos, Consejo Superior de Investigaciones Científicas, 1991. 269 p., 7 p. of plates: bibl., ill. (Publicaciones de la Escuela de Estudios Hispano-Americanos; 359)

Collection of 30 basic readings and documents dealing with Mexico's agrarian problem from the eve of the Revolution to the contemporary era. Useful in understanding the main ideas and points of debate surrounding the agrarian issue. Includes texts of laws and decrees as well as good bibliography.

1581 Rivera Moreno, Donna *et al.* Xochiapulco: una gloria olvidada. Edición de Donna Rivera Moreno. Puebla, Mexico: Gobierno del Estado de Puebla; Dirección General de Culturas Populares, Unidad Regional Puebla; Comisión Puebla V Centenario, 1991. 303 p.: ill., maps. (Col. V centenario)

Collection of documents and articles dealing with the history of a municipality of Puebla. The indigenous population of Xochiapulco distinguished itself with its role in the May 5, 1862 battle against the French. Includes information on the Porfirian and Revolutionary eras as well as the 19th century.

1582 Rodicio García, Sara. La Cristiada: epopeya mejicana de los cristeros. (*Relig. Cult.*, 38:185, abril/junio 1993, p. 291–320, tables)

Exploration of the significance of the Cristero Rebellion, with frequent reference to Jean Meyer's work on this subject. Argues that the rebellion can be seen as part of a broader historical struggle for religious freedom that has manifested itself in various ways since the late colonial period.

1583 Rodríguez Centeno, Mabel M. La producción cafetalera mexicana: el caso de Córdoba, Veracruz. (*Hist. Mex.,* 43:1, julio/sept. 1993, p. 81–115, chart, graph)

Work is almost evenly divided between a general discussion of Mexican coffee production from the 1870s-1930s and a case study of Córdoba, Veracruz—a center for coffee production—during the same period. Author concludes that small and medium proprietors, rather than hacienda owners, dominated production in Córdoba and that the important role played by foreign-controlled producers in the late Porfiriato had yielded to dominance by Mexican propietors in the 1930s.

1584 Rodríguez Saldaña, Marcial. La desaparición de poderes en el Estado de Guerrero. Chilpancingo, Mexico: Univ. Autonóma de Guerrero, 1992. 201 p.: bibl.

Political and legal history explores the realities of federal-state relations, beginning in 1917. Four chapters examine the origins of the federal system and its role in the histories of Mexico and Guerrero. Seven chapters examine the several instances between 1911–75 in which Guerrero's state government was dissolved.

1585 Romero Gil, Juan Manuel. El Boleo, Santa Rosalía, Baja California Sur: un pueblo que se negó a morir, 1885–1954. Hermosillo, Mexico: Editorial Unísono, 1991. 434 p.: appendix, bibl., ill., maps.

History of an isolated copper mining town that emerged during the Porfiriato and was dominated by French investors. Examines worker organization in El Boleo and discusses the process by which the mining community was "Mexicanized" after 1954 when foreign investors left, threatening El Boleo with extinction. Well-researched study, including an appendix of documents.

1586 Rothstein, Frances. La crisis y los obreros en un municipio de Tlaxcala: San Cosme Mazatcochco, 1940–1984. (*in* Simposio Internacional de Investigaciones Socio-Históricas sobre Tlaxcala, *1st, Tlaxcala, Mexico, 1985*. Memorias. Tlaxcala, Mexico: Gobierno del Estado de Tlaxcala, Instituto Tlaxcalteca de Cultura, Univ. Autónoma de Tlaxcala; México: Univ. Iberoamericana, 1986, p. 166–170, bibl., tables)

Anthropologist's study of how a people have adapted themselves to economic change and crisis in Mexico. With the economic decline of the 1980s, residents of San Cosme have supplemented their incomes by using small plots of land for growing subsistence crops, and by marketing a variety of goods in the informal sector.

1587 Roxborough, Ian. Mexico. (*in* Latin America between the Second World War and the Cold War, 1944–1948. Edited by Leslie Bethell and Ian Roxborough. New York: Cambridge Univ. Press, 1992, p. 190–216)

Chapter on Mexico emphasizes the role of labor relations in providing the institutional foundations for the postwar "economic miracle." In "redefining the union scene," the Alemán Administration curbed the influence of more militant unions, insured the dominance of the CTM, and blocked the development of a union-linked political party challenging the PRI.

1588 Ruano, Leticia *et al.* José Guadalupe Zuno Hernández: vida, obra y pensamiento. Guadalajara, Mexico: Editorial Univ. de Guadalajara, 1992. 146 p.: bibl.

Four articles, with supporting documents, on the life and activities of a well-known intellectual and political figure from Jalisco. Focuses on Zuno's career as state governor during the 1920s, and includes discussions of his handling of the Church-State question, his quest for municipal autonomy, and his policies toward workers.

1589 Samaniego, Marco Antonio. El gremio de choferes y la línea internacional, 1920–1933. Tijuana, Mexico: Entrelíneas, 1991. 50 p.: bibl.

Brief history of a cab driver's union in Baja California and its struggle to protect its business along the border against the competition of North American companies.

1590 Sánchez, Martín. Grupos de poder y centralización política en México: el caso Michoacán, 1920–1924. México: Instituto Nacional de Estudios Históricos de la Revolución Mexicana, 1994. 263 p.: bibl., maps, ports. (Investigación)

Excellent discussion of the impact of Obregón's drive for centralization on Michoacán and the governorship of Gen. Francisco Múgica (1920–22). Author identifies three power groups (supporters of Múgica, followers of Pascual Ortiz Rubio, and the Catholics) and concludes that the fall of Múgica was the result of a clash between authority (Obregón) and revolutionary principles (Múgica). Ouster of Múgica meant the triumph of the center over all three power groups.

1591 Sánchez González, Agustín. Cuatro atentados presidenciales. México: Grupo Editorial Planeta, 1994. 188 p.: ill. (Espejo de México)

Interesting narrative of assassination attempts made on Porfirio Díaz, Alvaro Obregón, Pascual Ortiz Rubio, and Manuel Avila Camacho. Discusses the motives of assassins and would-be assassins, as well as the official investigations of each act.

1592 Sánchez González, Agustín. El general en La Bombilla: Alvaro Obregón, 1928, reelección y muerte. México: Editorial Planeta Mexicana, 1993. 219 p.: bibl., ill. (Espejo de México)

Examination of the assassination of Alvaro Obregón in 1928 and the various explanations offered about the event. Assembling an impressive cast of suspects in the killing, the author concludes that José de León Toral was solely responsible for the assassination.

1593 Sánchez Novelo, Faulo M. La rebelión delahuertista en Yucatán. Mérida, Mexico: Diario del Sureste, 1991. 95 p.: bibl., index.

Study of the impact of the *delahuertista* revolt on the state of Yucatán, whose controversial governor, Felipe Carrillo Puerto, supported Obregón and Calles. Carrillo Puerto was overthrown and executed, the execution being opposed by De la Huerta. Local rebels may have been opportunists using the revolt as a pretext to get rid of the governor and his policies. See also item **1477.**

1594 Schmidt, Samuel. The deterioration of the Mexican presidency: the years of Luis Echeverría. Translated and edited by Dan A. Cothran. Tucson: Univ. of Arizona Press, 1991. 250 p.: bibl., ill., index.

Generally unfavorable review of Echeverría's tenure as president, although author does indicate that Echeverría's problems were largely inherited and were not solved by later presidents either. Echeverría did not directly cause the decline in the Mexican presidency, which author sees as part of a more compli-cated process. Spanish edition was published in 1986.

1595 Schulze Schneider, Ingrid. La propaganda alemana en México durante la Primera Guerra Mundial. (*Anu. Dep. Hist./Madrid,* 5, 1993, p. 261–272, bibl.)

Brief survey of the efforts of Mexico's German colony to promote Germany's influence in Mexico during World War I. German propaganda took the form of newspapers, pamphlets, maps, and calendars depicting the campaigns of the Central Powers, as well as cultural propaganda through associations, schools, conferences, and the theater.

1596 Serrano Alvarez, Pablo. La batalla del espíritu: el movimiento sinarquista en El Bajío, 1932–1951. México: Consejo Nacional para la Cultura y las Artes, 1992. 2 v.: bibl., maps. (Regiones)

Extensively-researched study of this ultra-reactionary movement that was organized in the 1930s and remained a viable source of opposition to Mexico's post-revolutionary regime for over 15 years. The sinarquist movement represented a continuation of the Cristero Rebellion and included campaigns against caciquism, immorality, and socialism.

1597 Serrano Alvarez, Pablo. El proyecto sinarquista de la colonización de Baja California, 1941–1943. (*Rev. Indias,* 54:201, mayo/agosto 1994, p. 439–458)

Description of efforts by *sinarquista* leader Salvador Abascal to establish a *sinarquista* colony in Baja California with the support of the national and territorial governments. Abascal saw the project as a renewal of the missionary activity of the colonial period. Although the colony was established, it ultimately failed due to poor planning, inadequate financing, and leadership disagreements. See also item **1598.**

1598 Serrano Alvarez, Pablo. El sinarquismo en el Bajío mexicano, 1934–1951: historia de un movimiento social regional. (*Estud. Hist. Mod. Contemp. Méx.,* 14, 1991, p. 195–236, tables)

Well-organized examination of the evolution of *sinarquismo* in its regional base of the Bajío (Guanajuato, Michoacán, Jalisco, Querétaro), which author describes as "traditionalist, Hispanist, anti-communist, and ultra-Catholic." Even when the movement declined at the national level, it retained a strong presence in its regional base. See also item **1597**.

1599 Shadle, Stanley Frank. Andrés Molina Enríquez: Mexican land reformer of the revolutionary era. Tucson: Univ. of Arizona Press, 1994. 159 p., 1 p. of plates: bibl., index, ports. (PROFMEX series)

Examination of both the ideology and political involvement of one of the leading exponents of land reform in revolutionary Mexico. Author emphasizes the influence of Molina Enríquez on Article 27 of the Constitution of 1917 and his efforts to get successive administrations to implement his views on agrarian reform.

1600 Sifuentes Espinoza, Daniel. Itinerario político de Nuevo León, 1900–1929. Monterrey, Mexico?: Univ. Autónoma de Nuevo León, Centro de Información de Historia Regional, 1989. 1 v. (unpaged): bibl., ill. (Col. Folletos de historia del noreste; 9)

Brief political chronicle of early revolutionary period in key northern state. Most of the work is a collection of political programs put forward by various parties.

1601 Silva Herzog, Jesús. Obras escogidas. Presentación y selección de Alberto Enríquez Perea. San Luis Potosí, Mexico: Comité Organizador San Luis 400, 1992. 3 v. in 4 (2522 p.).: bibl. (Col. Cuatro siglos. Serie Obras escogidas de autores potosinos; 1)

"Selected" but still extensive collection of works drawn from a variety of sources by one of the most famous observers of and participants in 20th-century Mexican political and intellectual life. Topics range from autobiographical accounts to reflections on Don Quijote.

1602 Sotomayor Garza, Jesús G. Magnicidios. Torreón, Mexico: Editorial Nueva Aurora, 1994. 96 p.: bibl.

Collection of ten essays each devoted to an assassination or assassination attempt. Eight deal with 20th-century figures ranging from Francisco Madero to Luis Donaldo Colosio.

1603 Strauss Neuman, Martha. Wilson y Bryan ante Victoriano Huerta: ¿intervencionismo convencional o imperialismo moralista? La perspectiva norteamericana. (*Estud. Hist. Mod. Contemp. Méx.*, 11, 1988, p. 201–218)

Good—if not particularly original—analysis of the Wilson-Bryan policy toward Mexico during the Huerta regime. Author sees policy as simplistic and contradictory, with the two "archangels of democracy" unable to reconcile their moralistic foreign policy with its interventionist results.

1604 Tate, Michael L. Pershing's pets: Apache scouts in the Mexican punitive expedition. (*N.M. Hist. Rev.*, 66:1, Jan. 1991, p. 49–71)

Details the important role of Apache scouts in Pershing's forces and Carranza's successful request that they no longer be used.

1605 Taylor, Lawrence Douglas. La campaña magonista de 1911 en Baja California: el apogeo de la lucha revolucionaria del Partido Liberal Mexicano. Tijuana, Mexico: El Colegio de la Frontera Norte, 1992. 140 p.: bibl.

Argues against the view that this failed PLM rebellion was a filibustering expedition designed to establish a separate republic and to seek annexation by the US. Instead, it was part of a larger plan to transform Mexico's economy and society and, eventually, to destroy capitalist regimes worldwide.

1606 Taylor, Lawrence Douglas. La gran aventura en México: el papel de los voluntarios extranjeros en los ejércitos revolucionarios mexicanos, 1910–1915. México: Consejo Nacional para la Cultura y las Artes, 1993. 2 v.: bibl., maps. (Regiones)

Interesting study based on extensive archival research focuses on the role of foreign combatants in northern Mexico and discusses their backgrounds, motives for fighting, and relationship to Mexican revolutionaries. Although a numerical minority, foreigners had a significant impact on campaigns, particularly because of their technical expertise.

1607 Tello Díaz, Carlos. El exilio: un relato de familia. México: Cal y Arena, 1993. 479 p.: bibl., ill., index.

Parallel—and later converging—portraits of two of the most famous exile families of the Revolution: Díaz and Casasus. Story begins with Porfirio Díaz in exile in 1911 and ends with the families' return to Mexico in 1936. Extensive and excellent photographs.

1608 Tello Solís, Eduardo. Gral. Salvador Alvarado, soldado y estadista. Mérida, Mexico: s.n., 1994. 93 p.: bibl., ill.

Brief, basic biography of an important revolutionary figure based on secondary sources. Examines Alvarado's military activities and focuses on his social policies and thought.

1609 Testimonios de la revolución maderista en el estado de Oaxaca. Recopilación de Héctor Gerardo Martínez y Francie R. Chassen de López. Oaxaca, Mexico: Instituto de Investigaciones en Humanidades de la UABJO; Casa de la Cultura Oaxaqueña, 1987. 38 p. (Col. Agua quemada)

Collection of six essays previously published in newspapers or magazines by witnesses to or participants in the *maderista* revolt in Oaxaca.

1610 Testimonios de la Revolución Mexicana en Tamaulipas. Recopilación y notas de Jorge Trujillo Bautista. México: Instituto Nacional de Estudios Históricos de la Revolución Mexicana, Secretaría de Gobernación; Gobierno del Estado de Tamaulipas, Instituto Tamaulipeco de Cultura, 1992. 156 p.: bibl., ill. (Col. Testimonio)

Collection of 14 personal stories of the Mexican Revolution.

1611 Testimonios del proceso revolucionario de México. Entrevistas por Píndaro Urióstegui. México: Instituto Nacional de Estudios Históricos de la Revolución Mexicana, 1987. 694 p.: ill.

Series of nine interviews with participants in the Mexican Revolution, including Gen. Juan Barragán. Also includes a chapter of basic documents, such as the Plan de San Luis Potosí and the Plan de Ayala.

1612 Testimonios orales de la Revolución Mexicana en Oaxaca. México: Instituto Nacional de Antropología e Historia; S.E.P; Gobierno del Estado de Oaxaca, 1987. 247 p.: ill., maps.

Collection of interviews with 15 "ordinary" persons organized along ethnic categories. Compilers believe that interviews indicate a need to revise traditional view that such ethnic groups tended to be "on the margin" of the Revolution. Best small detail uncovered: one community had a contingent of "designated soldiers" that fought alongside

whichever revolutionary group controlled the area at the time, regardless of its ideology.

1613 Tirado Villegas, Gloria. Quiero morir como nací. Puebla, Mexico?: Instituto de Ciencias Sociales y Humanidades, Univ. Autónoma de Puebla, 1992. 106 p.: bibl., ill.

Biography of labor activist Guillermo Treviño Flores who helped to organize Mexico's first industrial union. Treviño was active in the Mexican Communist Party and opposed every administration from Calles to Carlos Salinas.

1614 Treviño Villarreal, Héctor Jaime. La revolución maderista en Nuevo León, 1910–1911. Monterrey, Mexico: Univ. Autónoma de Nuevo León, Centro de Información de Historia Regional, 1988. 42 p., 46 p. of plates (some folded): bibl., ill. (Col. Folletos de historia del noreste; 3)

Brief description of the leaders supporting the Madero revolt in Nuevo León, together with an explanation of why the revolt came late and in such a peaceful form. Based primarily on state archival sources. See also item **1615.**

1615 Treviño Villarreal, Mario. Los gobernantes villistas de Nuevo León, 1915. Monterrey, Mexico: Univ. Autónoma de Nuevo León, Centro de Información de Historia Regional, 1988? 48 p.: bibl., ill. (Col. Folletos de historia del noreste; 5)

Brief look (11 p. of narrative) at the short-lived governorships (Jan.-May 1915) of villista generals Felipe Angeles and Raúl Madero. See also item **1614.**

1616 Trueba Lara, José Luis. Los chinos en Sonora: una historia olvidada. Hermosillo, Mexico: Instituto de Investigaciones Históricas, Univ. de Sonora, 1990. 95 p.: bibl., ill. (Col. El tejabán; 2)

Useful collection of five articles dealing with a little-researched topic. Themes include Chinese immigration to Mexico, xenophobia, anti-Chinese campaigns in Sonora, and political conflict within Sonora's Chinese community. A concluding article discusses sources for the study of the Chinese in Mexico.

1617 Vaca, Agustín; Alma Dorantes; and Jaime Olveda. Fuentes hemerográficas jaliscienses para el estudio de la Revolución Mexicana. México: Instituto Nacional de Antropología e Historia, 1990. 486 p.: index. (Col. Fuentes)

Annotated list of items dealing with responses to the Revolution taken from 30 periodicals in the state of Jalisco during the period from 1910–20. Items are grouped according to topics ranging from military affairs to church activities. Most of the periodicals cited were published in Guadalajara.

1618 Valero Silva, José et al. Polvos de olvido: cultura y revolución. México: Univ. Autónoma Metropolitana, Unidad Azcapotzalco, División de Ciencias Sociales y Humanidades; Instituto Nacional de las Bellas Artes, 1993. 424 p.: bibl., ill.

Collection of lengthy essays by various authors dealing with the impact of the Revolution on the culture and daily life of those living in Mexico City and surrounding area. Topics include architecture, periodicals and pamphlets, women, musical groups, and poetry. Time period covered is 1910–17.

1619 Vargas González, Pablo E. Bernabé García: autobiografía del poder en un municipio michoacano. (*Relaciones/Zamora*, 46, Spring 1991, p. 129–151)

Study of the local cacique of San Pedro Caro in Michoacán who was active from the time of the Cárdenas Administration until 1982. García is shown as a positive example of a leader who negotiates material benefits for the campesino population, converting it into a base of support for the Mexican political system.

1620 Vargas González, Pablo E. Lealtades de la sumisión: caciquismo—poder local y regional en la Ciénega de Chapala, Michoacán. Zamora, Mexico: El Colegio de Michoacán, 1993. 286 p.: bibl. (Col. Occidente)

Author traces the evolution of local and regional political authority of Michoacán from 1910 to the mid-1980s. There were few major changes in the political and economic structures prior to 1930; the "democratic project" of Cárdenas in the 1930s gave way to a new caciquism which in turn was challenged by the growing influence of the "corporativist" state in the mid-1960s.

1621 Vázquez Gómez, Emilio et al. En torno a la democracia: el sufragio efectivo y la no reelección, 1890–1928. Ed. facsimilar. México: Instituto Nacional de Estudios Históricos de la Revolución Mexicana, Secretaría

de Gobernación, 1992. 613 p., 1 folded leaf: bibl., ports.

Commemorative publication of 15 pamphlets from 1890–1928 that represent Mexico's ongoing concern with effective suffrage during that period.

1622 Wasserman, Mark. The Mexican Revolution: region and theory, signifying nothing? (*LARR*, 25:1, 1990, p. 231–242)

Historiographical analysis of ten important books, including Alan Knight's *The Mexican Revolution* and John Tutino's *From insurrection to Revolution in Mexico.* Examines issues of periodization, theory and methodology, regional history, and popular culture as aspects of recent attempts by historians to interpret the Revolution. Champions the regional approach to modern Mexican history.

1623 Wasserman, Mark. Persistent oligarchs: elites and politics in Chihuahua, Mexico, 1910–1940. Durham, N.C.: Duke Univ. Press, 1993. 265 p.: bibl., index, map.

Excellent before-and-after study of the impact of the Revolution on the Chihuahuan elites. The author finds that a significant element of the old state elite survived through economic diversification, manipulation of the law, and intermarriage with the new revolutionary elite. The impact of the Revolution on local elites varied considerably, often due to location.

1624 Williams, Edward J. and **John T. Passé-Smith.** The unionization of the *maquiladora* industry: the Tamaulipan case in national context. San Diego, Calif.: Institute for Regional Studies of the Californias, San Diego State Univ., 1992. xv, 134 p.: bibl., index, map. (Border studies series; 4)

Study of the *maquiladora* industry in Tamaulipas, centering on Matamoros, Reynosa, and Nuevo Laredo. Authors demonstrate that the *maquiladora* experience in the area differs in important ways from the *maquiladora* pattern in other parts of Mexico, especially in the greater role played by unions in Tamaulipas.

1625 Wilson, Patricia Ann. Exports and local development: Mexico's new *maquiladoras*. Austin: Univ. of Texas Press, 1992. 161 p.: bibl., ill., index, map.

Examination of the capacity of the *maquiladoras* to generate domestic linkages that would further promote industrialization and economic diversification. Although some of the Mexican *maquiladoras* have gone beyond assembly to more capital-intensive activities, most foreign-owned *maquiladoras* make little use of domestic materials.

1626 Zebadúa, Emilio. Banqueros y revolucionarios: la soberanía financiera de México. México: Colegio de México; Fideicomiso Historia de las Américas; Fondo de Cultura Económica, 1994. 383 p.: bibl., index. (Sección de obras de historia. Serie Hacienda/ Fideicomiso Historia de las Américas)

Analysis of Mexico's financial recovery and growth from the "collapse" of the Mexican State in 1914–20s. Explores the relationship between national finances and national sovereignty. Based on correspondence between foreign bankers and the Secretaria de Hacienda, and on an analysis of budgets from the various revolutionary regimes.

CENTRAL AMERICA

STEPHEN WEBRE, *Professor of History, Louisiana Tech University*
DAVID MCCREERY, *Professor of History, Georgia State University*

SCHOLARLY OUTPUT IN CENTRAL AMERICAN history continues to grow and improve, in quantity and quality, with significant advances in selected areas. The impact of 1992's Columbus Quincentenary continues to be felt, most notably in the appearance of two monumental syntheses, the *Historia general de Centroamérica* (item **1633**) and the *Historia general de Guatemala* (item **1654**). Collaborative efforts by recognized specialists of various nationalities, these multi-volume works provide impressive evidence of the field's developing maturity and sophistication. There remains, of course, much to be done, and many important topics and even countries continue to be neglected.

For the colonial period, the critical bibliography compiled by W. George Lovell and Christopher H. Lutz (item **1662**) reveals the substantial progress made in demographic history in recent years. Significant new studies on colonial Guatemala include Lutz's own social and demographic study of Santiago de Guatemala (item **1664**) and Wendy Kramer's long-awaited analysis of the early encomienda (item **1658**). Our understanding of Guatemalan trade patterns and practices, both regional and imperial, is enhanced by Richmond F. Brown's study of powerful 18th-century merchant Juan Fermín de Aycinena (item **1646**) and José Antonio Fernández Molina's essay on the impact of the Salvadoran indigo boom on basic grain production and markets in the Maya highlands (item **1650**). There are works of comparable significance for Panama by Christopher Ward (item **1687**) and Alfredo Castillero Calvo (item **1647**). Colonial El Salvador, virtually ignored in the past, receives long-overdue attention in studies by Pedro Escalante Arce (item **1648**) and William R. Fowler (item **1651**).

Guatemala is the subject of a number of important new studies dealing with the national period. For the 19th century, these include major studies by Ralph Lee Woodward, Jr., on conservative caudillo Rafael Carrera (item **1800**) and David McCreery on rural life (item **1634**). The 1944–54 revolutionary period also continues to attract scholars. A major event is the publication of Francisco Villagrán Kramer's *Biografía política* (item **1795**), which prompted an immediate angry denial by Carlos Pellecer (item **1764**). Jim Handy has produced what may be the definitive study of the 1952–54 land reform (item **1729**).

Students of Nicaragua continue to focus on the 20th century and especially on Augusto C. Sandino and the Somoza dynasty. Knut Walter (item **1797**) shows Anastasio Somoza García's role in constructing the Nicaraguan State, while Jeffrey Gould (item **1724**) sets his regime in its Cold War context. The fall and subsequent assassination of Anastasio Somoza Debayle are the topics of new studies by former US ambassador to Nicaragua Lawrence Pezzullo (item **1766**) and by Claribel Alegría and D. J. Flakoll (item **1690**), respectively. Historians have yet to grapple seriously with the FSLN's unexpected electoral defeat and fall from power in 1990. Indeed, the excellent book on the Sandinista era by María Molero (item **1748**) evidences no premonition of the impending collapse, and Laura J. Enríquez (item **1715**) portrays the bourgeoisie as coming apart rather than coalescing into a coherent opposition. Harry E. Vanden and Gary Prevost (item **1792**), however, properly remind us of the implacable US determination to destroy the Nicaraguan economy while forcing an unaccustomed unity upon the opposition. Scholars of the Sandinista period will welcome two important collections of primary documents (items **1775** and **1755**).

Interest in women's experiences appears to be growing, especially in Costa Rica. Macarena Barahona (item **1695**) looks at the struggle for civil rights for women, while Juan José Marín (item **1746**) analyzes official discourse on prostitution in 1940s San José. Virginia Mora (item **1751**) surveys female labor in turn-of-the-century San José, a subject which Ana Lorena Carrillo also examines for Guatemala with a study of a 1925 strike by women coffee sorters (item **1702**). For Nicaragua, Anna Fernández (item **1718**) criticizes all sides for neglecting poor women's problems during the post-1979 Sandinista period.

Labor and agrarian studies continue to appear. For Honduras, works by Mario Argueta (item **1694**), Julio César Rivera (item **1770**), and Mario Posas (item **1767**) contribute to our knowledge of worker organization and especially the 1954 banana strike. Early stirrings of worker consciousness in Costa Rica are treated in new works by Víctor Hugo Acuña Ortega (item **1689**) and Carlos Hernández Rodríguez (item **1731**), while Deborah Levenson-Estrada (item **1742**) chronicles the courageous efforts of Guatemalan workers to organize and strike. Apart from studies by David McCreery on Guatemala (item **1634**) and Leticia Oyuela on Honduras (item **1636**), research on Costa Rica continues to dominate rural history, as evidenced by the recent contributions of Marc Edelman and Mitchell A. Seligson (item **1714**), Lowell Gudmundson (item **1726**), Ivan Molina Jiménez (item **1749**), and Mario Samper Kutschbach (item **1774**).

Finally, the activities of foreigners—adventurers, entrepreneurs, immigrants—are the subjects of several new works. In a lively narrative, Lester D. Langley and Thomas D. Schoonover tell tales of some of the more colorful individuals associated with the fruit companies (item **1740**). In his book on State-company relations in Guatemala (item **1711**), Paul J. Dosal treats the United Fruit Company critically, if somewhat sympathetically, while Diane K. Stanley offers a more positive appraisal of UFCO as a tropical pioneer (item **1786**). Only Ana Luisa Cerdas (item **1704**) reminds us of the company's less attractive side.

New works by Nancie L. González (item **1723**) and Darío Euraque (item **1716**) shed light on the little-studied question of Palestinian immigration to Honduras, while Mario Argueta (item **1693**) examines the German presence in that country. The German entrepreneurs who helped build the coffee industry in Guatemala's Alta Verapaz continue to inspire research as well. Stefan Karlen (item **1736**) discusses their economic and political interests, while Ricardo Terga (item **1789**) traces the impact on the local native population of the German immigrants' extramarital procreative urges.

GENERAL

1627 Bolland, O. Nigel. Colonization and slavery in Central America. (*Slavery Abolit.*, 15:2, Aug. 1994, p. 11–25)

General introduction emphasizes Indian slavery in Spanish provinces in 16th century and African slavery in British Honduras in the 18th and 19th centuries. Author has sounder grasp of the latter, but for both correctly notes persistence of forced labor in various guises following formal abolition.

1628 Cardenal, Rodolfo. The Church in Central America. (*in* The Church in Latin America, 1492–1992. Edited by Enrique Dussel. Kent, England: Burns & Oats; Maryknoll, N.Y.: Orbis Books, 1992, p. 243–270, bibl., map)

Good short survey from colonial period to 1980s, with a short bibliography.

1629 Documentos de la historia de Nicaragua 1523–1857. Recopilación de Antonio Esgueva Gómez. Managua: Univ. Centroamericana, Depto. de Filosofía e Historia, 1993. 252 p.: bibl., ill.

Collection designed for Nicaraguan university students features 97 primary documents in four thematic areas: conquest, independence, William Walker, and transit route question.

1630 Feldman, Lawrence H. Mountains of fire, lands that shake: earthquakes and volcanic eruptions in the historic past of Central America, 1505–1899. Culver City, CA: Labyrinthos, 1993. 295 p., 4 leaves of plates: bibl., ill. (some col.), index.

Annotated catalog of earthquakes and associated volcanic eruptions in Central America from 16th to late-19th century. Final chapter details 1835 eruption of volcano Cosigüín which affected entire isthmus. Many entries feature long descriptive quotations in original language.

1631 González, Nancie L. and **Charles D. Cheek.** Patrón de asentamiento de los caribes negros a principios del siglo XIX en Honduras: la búsqueda de un modo de vida. (*Yaxkin/Tegucigalpa*, 11:2, 1988, p. 89–108, bibl., maps, tables)

Citing archaeological and ethnographic evidence, authors argue that Carib settlement patterns on Central America's east coast were dictated more by possibilities of wage-earning employment, including serving as Spanish mercenaries, than by demands of fishing or horticulture. For anthropologists' review, see *HLAS 55:279.*

1632 Héroes al gusto y libros de moda: sociedad y cambio cultural en Costa Rica, 1750–1900. Edición de Iván Molina Jiménez y Steven Paul Palmer. San José: Editorial Porvenir; Plumsock Mesoamerican Studies, 1992. 211 p., 8 p. of plates: bibl., ill. (Col. Ensayos)

Six essays by various authors on topics such as material culture of late colonial Cartago, marriage in early-19th-century Central Valley, consumption patterns and popular entertainment in mid-19th-century San José, libraries and book trade, and conscious creation of national and nationalist culture in second half of 19th century. Theoretically-based and effectively researched in best Costa Rican scholarly tradition.

1633 Historia general de Centroamérica. v. 1, Historia antigua. v. 2, El régimen colonial, 1524–1750. v. 3, De la Ilustración al liberalismo, 1750–1870. v. 4, Las repúblicas agroexportadoras, 1870–1945. v. 5, De la posguerra a la crisis, 1945–1979. v. 6, Historia inmediata, 1979–1991. Coordinación general de Edelberto Torres-Rivas. Madrid: Comunidades Europeas; Sociedad Estatal Quinto Centenario; FLACSO, 1993. 6 v.: bibl., ill., index, maps.

Most ambitious modern synthesis yet of Central American history deliberately eschews traditional State-by-State treatment in favor of a more integrated chronological and topical approach. Uneven in places, but reasonably comprehensive and in general readable, informative, and representative of current scholarship.

1634 McCreery, David. Rural Guatemala, 1760–1940. Stanford, Calif.: Stanford Univ. Press, 1994. 450 p.: bibl., index, maps.

Comprehensive history of Guatemalan rural society in two centuries preceding the so-called Revolution of 1944. Detailed account of conditions in the countryside prior to rapid conversion to coffee production in the mid-19th century is followed by in-depth analysis of coffee's impact on the State and society, especially on indigenous communities, their land and labor. Thoroughly researched in archival sources and theoretically grounded in literature on transition to capitalism, in particular problem of "primitive accumulation."

1635 Molina Jiménez, Iván. Protocolos y mortuales: fuentes para la historia económica de Centroamérica, siglos XVI-XIX. (*Bol. Fuentes Hist. Econ. Méx.*, 6, enero/abril 1992, p. 15–23)

Explains value of notarial and probate records for research in economic history. Author describes most common types of instruments and explains their documentary importance. Extensive citations to exemplary studies emphasize recent work on Costa Rica to 1850.

1636 Oyuela, Irma Leticia de. Un siglo en la hacienda: estancias y haciendas ganaderas en la antigua Alcaldía Mayor de Tegucigalpa, 1670–1850. Tegucigalpa: Banco Central de Honduras, 1994. 191 p.: bibl., ill.

More than economic modes of production, haciendas in 18th- and 19th-century Honduras are better understood as terrains of cultural production, from regional mentalities to forms of gender relations. [D. Euraque]

500 años de lucha por la tierra: estudios sobre propiedad rural y refoma [i.e., reforma] agraria en Guatemala. See *HLAS 55:4656.*

1637 Torres-Rivas, Edelberto. History and society in Central America. Translated by Douglass Sullivan-González. Austin: Univ. of Texas Press, 1993. 193 p.: bibl., index, map. (Translations from Latin America series)

Translated, updated version of a 1969 *dependentista* classic that stresses the importance of alliances between local elites and international capital in determining national patterns of underdevelopment. An added chapter evaluates effects of negative growth rates in the 1980s and the results of the closing off of options for peaceful protest.

1638 Toussaint Ribot, Mónica. Belice: una historia olvidada. México: Instituto Mora; Centro de Estudios Mexicanos y Centroamericanos, 1993. 200 p.: appendix, bibl.

Summary of history of Belize from a Mexican perspective, including extensive chronological appendix, paralleling events in Belize with those in Mexico from the Conquest to present. No notes. Meant for general audience.

Vos, Jan de. La comunidad recreada: respuestas de los indios de Chiapas a la conquista. See item **546.**

1639 Weaver, Frederick Stirton. Inside the volcano: the history and political economy of Central America. Boulder, Colo.: Westview Press, 1994. 276 p.: bibl., ill., index. (Series in political economy and economic development in Latin America)

Meant as an undergraduate text, this overview of Central American history emphasizes 1930 to the present. Cautions against confusing smallness with lack of complexity and reminds the reader that each country has its own history resulting from interaction of internal circumstances with external forces. Complex, nuanced book requires and merits careful attention. For sociologist's comment see *HLAS 55:4689.*

1640 Williams, Robert Gregory. States and social evolution: coffee and the rise of national governments in Central America. Chapel Hill: Univ. of North Carolina Press, 1994. 395 p.: bibl., ill., index, maps.

Beginning with distinct recent histories of Central American republics, author argues that agrarian structures influence how the State treats non-elites and that regimes tend to reproduce earlier-established patterns, even when conditions change. Decisions made initially at the municipal level were key to development of coffee export production in each region, and, subsequently, in each State.

COLONIAL

1641 Alejos García, José. Los guatemaltecos de 1770 en la descripción de Pedro Cortés y Larraz. (*Estud. Cult. Maya,* 19, 1992, p. 215–268, bibl.)

Latest of many efforts to describe late-18th-century Guatemalan society relying solely on well-known published *visita* conducted 1768–70 by Archbishop Pedro Cortés y Larraz, distinguished in this case by good writing, clarity of analysis, and serious attempt to assess Cortés y Larraz's strengths and weaknesses as observer, interpreter, and reporter.

1642 Antonelli, Juan Bautista and **Diego López de Quintanilla.** Relación del Puerto de Caballos y su fortificación. Guatemala: Academia de Geografía e Historia de Guatemala, 1991. 36 p.: ill. (Publicación especial; 33)

Noted engineer Antonelli's 1590 report on colonial Honduras' Caribbean port describes local topography, population, and resources, as well as trade patterns and defense needs. Also, provides details on proposed overland route to the Pacific coast at the Gulf of Fonseca. Transcribed from original in AGI, Patronato, leg. 183.

1643 Araúz, Celestino Andrés and **Patricia Pizzurno Gelós.** El Panamá hispano, 1501–1821. Panamá: Comisión Nacional del Vo. Centenario—Encuentro de Dos Mundos—de España; Diario La Prensa de Panamá, 1991. 268 p.: bibl., ill.

For student and general readers. Professionally competent survey of colonial Panama exhibits good balance between traditional concerns (politics, war) and more contemporary ones (society, culture). Good bibliography of Spanish-language sources.

1644 Asenjo García, Frutos. Vasco Núñez de Balboa: el descubrimiento del Mar del Sur. Madrid: Silex, 1991. 224 p.: bibl. (Retratos de antaño)

Popular biography based on familiar printed sources portrays Balboa as a tragic hero whose promising career was treacherously cut short by villain Pedrarias Dávila.

1645 Bardales B., Rafael. Hernán Cortés en Honduras. Tegucigalpa: Editorial Universitaria, 1989. 139 p. (Col. Documentos; 3)

Brief retelling of familiar story of Cortés' expedition to Honduras (1525–26) accompanies text of conqueror's fifth letter to Charles V, dated Sept. 3, 1526.

1646 Brown, Richmond F. Profits, prestige, and persistence: Juan Fermín de Aycinena and the spirit of enterprise in the Kingdom of Guatemala. (*HAHR*, 75:3, Aug. 1995, p. 405–440, tables)

Long-needed substantial work on Aycinena (1729–96), a Navarrese immigrant who in his day became the wealthiest and most influential man in Central America. Richly detailed account of his career, family connections, and business activities made possible by the author's good fortune in gaining access to a trove of privately-held family papers.

1647 Castillero Calvo, Alfredo. El comercio regional del Caribe: el complejo portuario Cartagena-Portobelo, siglo XVI-XIX. (*in* Congreso Internacional de Historia Económ-

ica y Social de la Cuenca del Caribe, 1763–1898, 1st, San Juan, 1987. Actas San Juan: Centro de Estudios Avanzados de Puerto Rico y el Caribe, 1992, p. 293–373, graphs, maps, tables)

Overview from 1540s-1820s of Panama's changing role in the Caribbean regional trade system. Valuable on Portobelo's adjustment after the mid-17th century to decline of fleets and fairs. In the 18th century, slave trade franchise (*asiento*) and cash subsidy (*situado*) from Peru kept the isthmian service sector alive. Useful companion to Ward's *Imperial Panama* (see item **1687**).

1648 Escalante Arce, Pedro Antonio. Códice Sonsonate: crónicas hispánicas. San Salvador: Consejo Nacional para la Cultura y el Arte, Dirección General de Publicaciones e Impresos, 1992. 2 v.: bibl.

Collected essays on the *alcaldía mayor* of Sonsonate (modern Ahuachapán and Sonsonate departments, El Salvador), important in colonial period for cacao production and role in Pacific coastal trade. Traditional topics and approach, but thoroughly researched and well documented. Useful contribution on a neglected topic.

1649 Fe, riqueza y poder: antología crítica de documentos para la historia de Honduras. Recopilación de Irma Leticia de Oyuela. Tegucigalpa: Instituto Hondureño de Cultura Hispánica, 1992. 233 p.: bibl. (Publicaciones del Instituto Hondureño de Cultura Hispánica conmemorativas al V centenario del descubrimiento—encuentro de dos mundos; 1)

Collection of documents from colonial Honduras, chiefly wills. Organized topically by mining, *capellanías*, slavery, the family, and "The Image of the Eighteenth Century." Each section has a brief introduction but no notes or citations.

1650 Fernández Molina, José Antonio. Producción indígena y mercado urbano a finales del período colonial: la provisión de alimentos a la Ciudad de Guatemala. (*Rev. Hist./Heredia*, 26, julio/dic. 1992, p. 9–30, bibl. graphs, maps, table)

After the mid-18th century, the indigo boom created a market in El Salvador for wheat and maize produced in Guatemala's central valley. Resulting food shortages in Guatemala City led in turn to profitable new opportunities for pueblos of western Highlands, where cash crop production appears related to social differentiation and increasing ladinization.

1651 Fowler, William R., Jr. The living pay for the dead: trade, exploitation, and social change in early colonial Izalco, El Salvador. (*in* Ethnohistory and archaeology: approaches to postcontact change in the Americas. Edited by J. Daniel Rogers and Samuel M. Wilson. New York: Plenum Press, 1993, p. 181–199, bibl., map)

Impact in 16th century of Spanish conquest on Pipil communities in cacao-rich western El Salvador. Despite indigenous population decline, early integration into the world commodities market led to compensating in-migration, as well as unusually strong Spanish and ladino presence.

1652 García Añoveros, Jesús María. Discrepancias del Obispo y de los doctrineros con la Audiencia y los indígenas de Guatemala, 1687. (*Rev. Indias*, 52: 195/196, mayo/dic. 1992, p. 385–441)

Continuation of author's in-depth study (*HLAS 54: 1657*) of problems of ecclesiastical administration in late-17th-century Guatemala, based on report by Bishop Andrés de las Navas y Quevedo (1682–1701).

1653 Gosner, Kevin. Soldiers of the Virgin: the moral economy of a colonial Maya rebellion. Tucson: Univ. of Arizona Press, 1992. 227 p.: bibl., index, maps.

Fine study of Chiapas' Tzeltal revolt (1712–13) acknowledges tax and labor grievances but sees it mainly as spiritual revivalist movement. Author challenges traditional representations of colonial Maya society that stress model of "closed corporate community," cohesion, and solidarity.

1654 Historia general de Guatemala. v. 2, Dominación española, desde la Conquista hasta 1700 [edición de Ernesto Chinchilla Aguilar]. Edición general de Jorge Luján Muñoz. Guatemala: Asociación de Amigos del País, Fundación para la Cultura y el Desarrollo, 1993. 1 v: bibl., ill. (some col.), index, maps (some col.).

Colonial volume of projected multivolume work offers comprehensive coverage of Guatemalan history from conquest to the end of 17th century by principal authorities in the field. Particularly welcome are regional histories, unusually detailed maps, well-chosen illustrations (including many in color), and extensive up-to-date bibliography.

1655 Jones, Oakah L., Jr. Guatemala in the Spanish colonial period. Norman: Univ. of Oklahoma Press, 1994. 344 p.: bibl., ill., index, maps.

Disappointing attempt at long-needed synthesis of Guatemala's colonial history, weakened by factual errors and virtual omission of the 17th century.

1656 Jopling, Carol F. Indios y negros en Panamá en los siglos XVI y XVII: selecciones de los documentos del Archivo General de Indias. South Woodstock, Vt.: Plumsock Mesoamerican Studies; Antigua, Guatemala: Centro de Investigaciones Regionales de Mesoamérica, 1994. 612 p.: index.

More than 300 primary documents—some reproduced in their entirety, others excerpted—on indigenous and African experiences in 16th- and 17th-century Panama. Useful for historians, ethnohistorians, and archaeologists. Guide to reproduced AGI *legajos* and thorough subject indexing enhance value for researchers.

1657 Kramer, Wendy; William George Lovell; and Christopher H. Lutz. Encomienda and settlement: towards a historical geography of early colonial Guatemala. (*Yearbook/CLAG*, 16, 1990, p. 67–72, bibl., map, table)

In a report on continuing research, authors cite the value of records on individual *encomenderos* in reconstructing an early post-conquest history of Guatemala's indigenous communities.

1658 Kramer, Wendy. Encomienda politics in early colonial Guatemala, 1524–1544: dividing the spoils. Boulder, Colo.: Westview Press, 1994. 293 p.: bibl., ill., index, maps. (Dellplain Latin American studies; 31)

Major contribution to early history of *encomienda* and of Spanish Guatemala. Minute study of *probanzas de méritos* and other archival documentation reveals political divisions and rivalries among conquerors and early settlers. Argues encomienda in Guatemala dated from initial conquest in 1524, and not from time of implementation of New Laws in late 1540s as others have claimed.

1659 Kupperman, Karen Ordahl. A Puritan colony in the tropics: Providence Island, 1630–1641. (*in* Settlements in the Americas: cross-cultural perspectives. Edited by Ralph Bennett. Newark, Del.: Univ. of Delaware Press, 1993, p. 238–251)

Brief account of English Puritan settlement on Nicaragua's Santa Catalina island, earliest serious foreign challenge to Spanish security in Central America. Colony's rapid failure is explained in terms of events in England and Massachusetts Bay.

1660 León Viejo: Pompeya de América. Edición de Jorge Eduardo Arellano. Managua: Instituto Nicaragüense de Cultura; Comisión Nacional de la UNESCO, 1993. 160 p.: bibl., ill., maps.

Handy collection of essays and documents on Nicaragua's first capital city, founded in 1524 and abandoned in 1610.

1661 Libro viejo de la fundación de Guatemala. Edición crítica de Carmelo Sáenz de Santa María. Confrontación de la paleografía de María del Carmen Deola de Girón. Guatemala: Academia de Geografía e Historia de Guatemala; Comisión Interuniversitaria Guatemalteca de Conmemoración del Quinto Centenario del Descubrimiento de América, 1991. 228 p.: bibl., ill., index.

First volume of acts of cabildo of Santiago de Guatemala includes minutes of meetings from July 1524 through May 1530. Superseding an earlier edition (Guatemala City, 1934), new features include a critical introduction by Carmelo Sáenz de Santa María and records of early land distributions, 1528–38. Indispensable for any study of early Spanish activity in Guatemala.

López Medel, Tomás. Colonización de América: informes e testimonios, 1549–1572, por L. Pereña, C. Baciero, F. Maseda. See item **910.**

1662 Lovell, William George and **Christopher H. Lutz.** Demography and empire: a guide to the population history of Spanish Central America, 1500–1821. Boulder, Colo.: Westview Press, 1995. 190 p.: bibl., ill., index, maps. (Dellplain Latin American Studies; 33)

First-rate introduction to rapidly expanding field of demographic history of colonial Central America. Annotated bibliography of more than 200 recent studies, each commented critically and in depth, is prefaced by substantial introductory chapter in which editors, who are pioneers in the field, define current state of knowledge and trends in literature.

1663 Lovell, William George and **Christopher H. Lutz.** The historical demography of colonial Central America. (*Yearbook/ CLAG,* 17/18, 1990, p. 127–138, bibl., tables)

Based on exhaustive review of existing secondary literature, authors propose contact-era figure for native population of 5.1 million for all of Central America. They also suggest regional variations in population collapse and recovery, Spanish and African immigration, and race mixture, as well as questions still in need of research.

1664 Lutz, Christopher H. Santiago de Guatemala, 1541–1773: city, caste, and the colonial experience. Norman: Univ. of Oklahoma Press, 1994. 346 p.: bibl., ill., index, maps.

Major contribution to urban history traces development of population of colonial Santiago (modern Antigua Guatemala), emphasizing gradual failure of original Spanish model of segregated *repúblicas* as urbanization promoted mobility and miscegenation. Revised and updated version of Spanish-language original (see *HLAS 46:2349*).

1665 Markman, Sidney David. Extinct, fossilized, and transformed Pueblos de Indios in the Reino de Guatemala, 1540–ca. 1800. (*in* Settlements in the Americas: cross-cultural perspectives. Edited by Ralph Bennett. Newark, Del.: Univ. of Delaware Press, 1993, p. 53–77, bibl., facsims., maps, photos)

Brief history of urbanization in colonial Central America emphasizes Spanish practice of concentrating indigenous population into nucleated settlements, suggesting how some such settlements, especially in Highland Guatemala and Chiapas, retained essential spatial form and ethnic identity, while others either disappeared or evolved into Spanish-ladino communities.

1666 Megged, Amos. The rise of Creole identity in early colonial Guatemala: differential patterns in town and countryside. (*Soc. Hist./London,* 17:3, Oct. 1992, p. 421–440, maps, table)

Focusing on the late 16th and 17th centuries, author argues that racial and ethnic identities were socially constructed, not biologically determined. Among other conclusions, Guatemala's "Creole" population is seen as more rural and more racially mixed than is commonly supposed. Thought-provoking and useful, but loosely conceptualized.

1667 **Mejías, Sonia Alda.** Continuidad y resistencia: la comunidad indígena en Guatemala durante el período colonial. (*in* Memoria, creación e historia: luchar contra el olvido. Coordinación de Pilar García Jordán, Miguel Izard, y Javier Laviña. Barcelona: Universitat de Barcelona, 1993, p. 133–144, bibl.)

Summarizes recent scholarship on role in Maya cultural survival of synthesis at the community level of prehispanic traditions with imported institutions. This fresh insight is a reminder that weakness of state authority and primacy of local issues had parallels in contemporary Europe.

1668 **Mena García, María del Carmen.** Estructura demográfica de Veragua en el siglo XVIII. (*Anu. Estud. Am.*, 50:2, 1993, p. 345–412, graphs, tables)

Previously unpublished 1756 census of Veragua province (western Panama), found in AGI, Panamá, leg. 130. Analytical introduction facilitates interpretation of household-level data, revealing conditions in mestizo cattle-raising society on colonial frontier.

1669 **Molina Jiménez, Iván.** De lo devoto a lo profano: el comercio y la producción de libros en el Valle Central de Costa Rica, 1750–1850. (*Jahrb. Gesch.*, 31, 1994, p. 117–153, tables)

Sophisticated essay argues that books in late colonial Costa Rica were scarce at all social levels. Following independence, capitalization of agrarian sector and introduction of printing press brought rapid change. Availability and variety of books expanded in 1830s and 1840s, along with urbanization and growth of public education, occupational specialization, and more refined tastes in consumer goods and leisure activities.

1670 **Molina Montes de Oca, Carlos.** Garcimuñoz: la ciudad que nunca murió; los primeros cien días de Costa Rica. San José: Editorial Univ. Estatal a Distancia, 1993. 448 p.: bibl., ill., index, maps.

Detailed history of early settlement of Costa Rica focuses on frequently neglected western half of central valley, which did not achieve current dominance until 18th century. Locations of earliest unsuccessful Spanish settlements are identified with modern Desamparados (Garcimuñoz, 1561) and San José (Matarredondo site of Cartago, 1572).

1671 **Newson, Linda A.** Variaciones regionales en el impacto del dominio colonial español en las poblaciones indígenas de Honduras y Nicaragua. (*Mesoamérica/Antigua*, 13:24, dic. 1992, p. 297–312, maps, tables)

Brief synthesis stresses complexity of Spanish colonialism's impact on native population in Honduras and Nicaragua. Regional variations are due to different rates of decline and recovery, relative importance of disease, degree of violence and exploitation, character of native society, modes of control employed by conquerors, and nature and quantity of natural resources.

1672 **Palma Murga, Gustavo.** Fuentes para la historia económica de la América Central colonial en el Archivo General de Centroamérica. (*Bol. Fuentes Hist. Econ. Méx.*, 6, enero/abril 1992, p. 9–14)

Useful description enriched by reference to specific subject headings in AGCA's legendary *fichero*, which provides subject access to some 14,000 *legajos* personally processed by late archivist José Joaquín Pardo (1900–64).

1673 **Pastor F., Rodolfo.** De moros en la costa a negros de Castilla: respresentación y realidad en las crónicas del siglo XVII centroamericano. (*Hist. Mex.*, 44:2, oct./dic. 1994, p. 195–235, bibl.)

Thought-provoking essay weakened by unclear focus and careless proofreading. Objects of Creole paranoia at the beginning of the 17th century, African slaves and freedmen eventually became accepted as productive members of society and collaborators in domination over native population. *Mestizaje*, a key process in this transformation, is seen more as a factor of religious conversion than of actual biological mixture.

1674 **Patch, Robert W.** Imperial politics and local economy in colonial Central America, 1670–1770. (*Past Present*, 143, May 1994, p. 7–107, map, tables)

Corruption and coercion on part of local administrators enabled the Spanish Crown to govern Central America at minimal expense, while facilitating region's integration into commercial economy. Includes significant observations on sale of offices, origins of regional specialization, and varieties of native experience as consequence of integration.

1675 Pérez González, María Luisa. La organización socio-política del grupo Chol-Manché en Guatemala durante el siglo XVII: estudio preliminar. (*CLAHR/Albuquerque*, 2:1, Winter 1993, p. 57–75, appendix)

Contemporary Spanish sources shed light on the frontier Maya group which successfully resisted Spanish domination for almost two centuries. Price of success seen as dispersion and, ultimately, extinction.

1676 Recopilación de reales cédulas relativas a la provincia de Costa Rica, 1540–1802. Recopilación de Carlos Meléndez Chaverri. San José: Comisión Nacional de Conmemoraciones Históricas; Archivo Nacional de Costa Rica; Academia de Geografía e Historia de Costa Rica, 1992. 273 p.

Useful compendium identifies 99 royal decrees addressing Costa Rican issues or authorities. Texts of the great majority are reproduced, many for the first time.

1677 Robles Domínguez de Mazariegos, Mariano. Memoria histórica de la provincia de Chiapa, una de las de Guatemala. Tuxtla Gutiérrez, México: Rodrigo Nuñez Editores, 1992. 31 p.

Modern edition of important treatise presented to Cortes of Cádiz in 1813, when author served as deputy from Chiapas. Summarizes province's history and offers recommendations for promotion of economic development and improvement of lives of indigenous majority.

1678 Rodríguez González, Jamie. La universidad centroamericana durante el período colonial. (*Estud. Hist. Soc. Econ. Am.*, 11, 1994, p. 51–64)

Useful review of historiography of higher education in the colonial period emphasizes Guatemala's Univ. de San Carlos, the oldest and most studied of Central America's universities.

1679 Romero Vargas, Germán. La dominación europea de los indios de Nicaragua entre los siglos XVI y XIX. (*Am. Indíg.*, 53:1/2, enero/junio 1993, p. 9–21, map)

Brief essay based on forthcoming larger work. Spanish colonization of Pacific and central Nicaragua beginning in the 16th century is compared with English activities on Caribbean coast in 17th. Different conditions and modes of domination are seen as produc-

ing the east-west division that troubles present-day Nicaragua.

1680 Sanabria Martínez, Víctor. Datos cronológicos para la historia eclesiástica de Costa Rica, 1774–1821. Edición preparada por Vernor Manuel Rojas con la colaboración de Miguel Picado. San José?: Comisión Nacional de Evangelización de la Cultura, 1992. 232 p.: indexes.

During the 1920s and 1930s, San José Archbishop Sanabria continued work of scholarly predecessor Bernard Thiel, publishing abstracts of ecclesiastical records in two now-obscure Catholic periodicals. His material is gathered here in a single handy volume, enhanced in value by addition of name, place, and subject indexes.

1681 Sarabia Viejo, María Justina. La grana y el añil: técnicas tintóreas en México y América Central. Sevilla, Spain: Escuela de Estudios Hispano-Americanos de Sevilla, 1994. 222 p.: bibl., col. ill. (Publicaciones de la Escuela de Estudios Hispano-Americanos de Sevilla; 374)

Four colonial-era treatises on cochineal and indigo, including works by late-18th-century scientists José Antonio Alzate and José Mariano Moziño, describe techniques of cultivation and processing. Excellent illustrations, including several in color. Brief introduction to dye industry in Mexico and Guatemala places works in historical context.

1682 Solórzano, Flor de. La colonización inglesa en la costa del Caribe de Nicaragua: 1633–1787. (*Bol. Nicar. Bibliogr. Doc.*, 82, enero/marzo 1994, p. 107–122, bibl., tables)

Brief account of Nicaragua's so-called Mosquito region in the colonial period stresses the impact of British presence on native peoples and later development of Nicaragua. Based on familiar secondary sources. (Also appears in *América Indígena*, 53:1/2, enero/junio 1993, p. 41–60).

1683 Solórzano Fonseca, Juan Carlos. La búsqueda de oro y la resistencia indígena: campañas de exploración y conquista de Costa Rica, 1502–1610. (*Mesoamérica/Antigua*, 13:24, dic. 1992, p. 313–363)

Synthetic account based on published sources. Misplaced emphasis on the search for gold delayed effective colonization of

Costa Rica's central valley until the 1570s, when growth of the Panama market called attention to region's agricultural potential.

1684 Solórzano Fonseca, Juan Carlos. Conquista, colonización y resistencia indígena en Costa Rica. (*Rev. Hist./Heredia*, 25, enero/junio 1992, p. 191–205)

Based on published sources, this brief overview of Spanish efforts to extend control over what is today Costa Rica covers the entire colonial period and stresses regional differences in timing, approach, and indigenous response.

1685 Tous Mata, Meritxell and **Javier Martín Blanco.** El mundo precolombino en la memoria histórica de la Baja América Central. (*in* Memoria, creación e historia: luchar contra el olvido. Coordinación de Pilar García Jordán, Miguel Izard, y Javier Laviña. Barcelona: Universitat de Barcelona, 1993, p. 13–28, bibl.)

Dating possibly from mid-17th century, Nicaragua's popular dance drama "El güegüense" is seen here as survival of prehispanic traditions in emerging mestizo society, and as protest against colonial exploitation. Subtle word play in mixture of Spanish and Nahuatl spoken by the masses hid play's subversive intent from colonial authorities.

1686 Valdivieso, Antonio de. Cartas del Obispo Valdivieso. Selección de José Alvarez Lobo. Cusco, Perú: Centro de Estudios Regionales Andinos Bartolomé de las Casas, 1992. 230 p.: bibl. (Cuadernos para la historia de la evangelización en América Latina; 8)

Collected letters of Dominican friar Antonio de Valdivieso, bishop of León, Nicaragua, who was murdered by colonists in 1550. A contemporary of Las Casas and fellow critic of Spanish mistreatment of natives, Valdivieso is portrayed here as precursor of martyred priests of late-20th century.

1687 Ward, Christopher. Imperial Panama: commerce and conflict in isthmian America, 1550–1800. Albuquerque: Univ. of New Mexico Press, 1993. 272 p.: bibl., ill., index, maps.

In pathbreaking work on a neglected topic, the author's attempt to be comprehensive results in vagueness of focus and even factual errors, but the work is impressively researched and both scholars and general

readers will find it useful. Valuable features include meticulously reconstructed time series of fleet and fair data, history of fortifications, and bibliographic essay.

1688 Webre, Stephen. La crisis de autoridad en el siglo XVII tardío: Centroamérica bajo la presidencia de Don Jacinto de Barrios Leal, 1688–1695. (*Rev. Hist./Heredia*, 27, enero/junio 1993, p. 9–28)

Political crisis in a forgotten province in a forgotten century. Examination of the career of the late-17th-century president of the Audiencia of Guatemala illuminates problems plaguing the Hapsburg administration, including corruption, sale of office, Creole resistance to Crown initiatives, merchant tax evasion, contraband trade, and personalistic conflicts among administrators.

NATIONAL

1689 Acuña Ortega, Víctor Hugo. Artesanos, obreros y nación en Centroamérica en el período liberal, 1870–1930. (*Rev. Hist./Managua*, 2, 1992/93, p. 40–51, bibl., ill., photos)

Well-written essay based on secondary sources argues urban artisans and workers, not rural workers or Indians, were the first of "subaltern classes" to absorb "imagined community" of nationalism, proposed by late-19th-century liberal elites.

1690 Alegría, Claribel and **Darwin J. Flakoll.** Somoza: expediente cerrado; la historia de un ajusticiamiento. Managua: Latino Editores; Editorial El Gato Negro, 1993. 150 p.: ill.

Based largely on interviews, documents 1980 assassination of Anastasio Somoza Debayle in Paraguay by Argentine guerrillas. Publication delayed at request of the Argentine left to avoid appearance of terrorism during that country's redemocratization.

1691 Amaro, Nelson. Guatemala: historia despierta. Prólogo de Juan José Arévalo. Epílogo de Marco Vinicio Cerezo. Guatemala: IDESAC; Miami: Distribuidora Universal, 1992. 284 p.: bibl., ill.

Sweeping interpretation of Guatemala's history based on secondary sources argues social polarization has restricted changes that might encourage popular political participation. Both "violent left" and "exclusionary regime" are seen as obstacles to peace and democracy. For political scientist's comment see *HLAS 55:2974.*

1692 Araúz, Celestino Andrés and **Patricia Pizzurno Gelós.** El Panamá colombiano, 1821–1903. Panamá: Primer Banco de Ahorros y Diario La Prensa de Panamá, 1993. 303 p.: bibl., ill.

Focuses on Panama as a province of Colombia, 1821–1903. Meant as general overview chiefly of political events, with a single chapter on social and economic history. Based on archival and secondary sources, with chapter bibliographies but no notes.

1693 Argueta, Mario. Los alemanes en Honduras: datos para su estudio. Tegucigalpa: Centro de Documentación de Honduras, 1992. 80 p.: bibl., map.

Surveys activities of German immigrant merchants in Honduras from the late-19th century to WWII. US pressure and local elites anxious to take over properties finally undercut and destroyed immigrants' position. No German sources.

1694 Argueta, Mario. Historia de los sin historia, 1900–1948. Tegucigalpa: Editorial Guaymuras, 1992. 128 p.: bibl. (Col. Códices)

Excellent general introduction to 20th-century Honduran labor history emphasizes activities of miners and banana workers. This period is seen as a peak of *obrerismo nacional,* but the author argues internal divisions weakened laborers' efforts to organize and strike.

1695 Barahona Riera, Macarena. Las sufragistas de Costa Rica. San José: Editorial de la Univ. de Costa Rica, 1994. 195 p.: bibl., ill.

Details efforts of women from 1890s to gain civil rights, especially right to vote. These rights, which were not "given" but won by struggle of small number of women, were a necessary part of process of legitimizing representative democracy. Even today most Costa Ricans have trouble acknowledging the role of these women.

1696 Belice: sus fronteras y destino. Recopilación de Francesca Gargallo y Adalberto Santana. México: Univ. Nacional Autónoma de México, 1993. 233 p.: bibl., map. (Nuestra América; 32)

Proceedings of conference on Belize (Mexico City, 1989) with both Mexican and Belizean participants. Mostly brief with few notes or sources, papers treat variety of subjects, from Belize's racial make-up to Caribbean integration. Preface notes Guatemala's landmark 1991 recognition of Belizean independence.

1697 Bolaños Geyer, Alejandro. William Walker, el predestinado de los ojos grises: biografía. v. 2–4. St. Charles, Mo.: A. Bolaños Geyer, 1994? 3 v: bibl., ill., maps.

Spanish-language version of works annotated in *HLAS 54: 1699* (v. 3–4) and *HLAS 52:1421* (v. 2).

1698 Bolland, O. Nigel. "Indios bravos" or "gentle savages:" 19th-century views of the "Indians" of Belize and the Miskito Coast. (*Rev. Rev. Interam.,* 22:1/2, primavera 1992, p. 36–54, bibl.)

Compares changing views of Mosquito Indians over time as evidenced by English travelers and officials. Attitudes tended to reflect what the English wanted from Indians at the time. For example, after 1850, as commercial agriculture produced need for labor, racist views of "lazy natives" came to predominate.

Bourgois, Philippe. West Indian immigration to Central America and the origins of the banana industry. See *HLAS 55:4702.*

1699 Cabezas, Omar. Canción de amor para los hombres. Managua: Editorial Nueva Nicaragua, 1988. 579 p.: maps. (Biblioteca popular sandinista; 22)

Detailed personal account of struggle against Somoza, written between 1982–88 in popular language and in style of novel. Includes a glossary.

1700 Cáceres P., Jorge; Rafael Guidos Véjar; and Rafael Menjívar Larín. El Salvador: una historia sin lecciones. San José: FLACSO, 1988. 294 p.: bibl.

Three essays on El Salvador's history: 1) the 1948 Revolution, which is seen chiefly as a conflict between landowners and salaried workers; 2) the role of the State in promoting industry in late 1940s; and 3) social contradictions of "developmentalism" conceived solely in economic terms.

1701 Calloni, Stella. Panamá: pequeña Hiroshima. México: Publicaciones Mexicanas, 1991. 304 p.: bibl. (El Día en libros; 49. Sección Periodismo)

Journalistic account of events surrounding the 1989 US invasion of Panama. Accuses the US of continuing to "occupy" Panama and of covering up atrocities.

1702 Carrillo Padilla, Ana Lorena. Sufridas hijas del pueblo: la huelga de las escogedoras de café de 1925 in Guatemala. (*Mesoamérica/Antigua*, 15:27, junio 1994, p. 157–173)

Although first of its kind, 1925 strike of female coffee sorters for better hours and working conditions was part of wider range of protests that year. Supported by other workers and reported fairly in press, the strike was successful but some women may have been dismissed subsequently.

1703 Casanova F., Rafael. ¿Héroes o bandidos?: los problemas de interpretación de los conflictos políticos y sociales entre 1845 y 1849 en Nicaragua. (*Rev. Hist./Managua*, 2, 1992/93, p. 13–26, bibl., ill.)

Sees uprisings of the late 1840s as neither simple banditry nor class struggle, but as attempts of "prepolitical" groups, both poor and some elites, to resist other elites' efforts to build a stronger State based on increased tax collection and centralized control.

1704 Cerdas Albertazzi, Ana Luisa. El surgimiento del enclave bananero en el Pacífico Sur. (*Rev. Hist./Heredia*, 28, julio/dic. 1993, p. 117–159)

Shows tactics the United Fruit Company (UFCO) used after the 1930 contract to gain control of land and labor on west coast of Costa Rica. Unlike the Atlantic side, the Pacific area was already populated by small producers when the UFCO arrived, leading to conflict and violence. The company sought control by eliminating existing towns, restricting housing, and importing workers from Panama and Nicaragua.

1705 Cerdas Bockham, Dorita. Matrimonio y vida cotidiana en el graven central costarricense, 1851–1890. (*Rev. Hist./Heredia*, 26, julio/dic. 1992, p. 69–95)

In the 19th century, the Catholic Church reinforced ideology of the patriarchal family and inferiority of women. Author uses petitions for divorce to show problems women suffered in marriage and how they worked against them.

1706 Cerdas Cruz, Rodolfo. Costa Rica. (*in* Latin America between the Second World War and the Cold War, 1944–1948. Edited by Leslie Bethell and Ian Roxborough. New York: Cambridge Univ. Press, 1992, p. 280–299)

Good summary of events surrounding the 1948 Revolution. Initially the US supported Picado and tolerated activities of local communists, but by 1947 the embassy shifted to a more conservative position. "Visceral anticommunism" immobilized workers, contributing to the US's "first victory of the Cold War in Central America."

1707 Chomsky, Avi. West Indian workers in Costa Rican radical and nationalist ideology, 1900–1950. (*Americas/Francisc.*, 51:1, July 1994, p. 11–40)

Confronted with 1930s economic crisis, Costa Rican political leaders opted for racist nationalism, attacking West Indian immigrants as the cause of the country's problems. Communist Party efforts to sustain class analysis of the situation foundered on white hostility and West Indian conservatism.

1708 Clegern, Wayne M. Origins of liberal dictatorship in Central America: Guatemala, 1865–1873. Niwot: Univ. Press of Colorado, 1994. 166 p.: bibl., ill., index, map.

Presidencies of Vicente Cerna (1865–71) and Miguel García Granados (1871–73) form important transition period between Carrera's "Dictatorship of Thirty Years" and Liberal *Reforma*. Moderate reformers accomplished more than usually credited in terms of development, while congratulating themselves on avoiding Liberal "excesses."

1709 Cogley Quintero, J. Plinio. El dinámico e ingenioso Felipe Juan Bunau-Varilla y el canal por Panamá: la verdadera y dramática historia de nuestra separación de Colombia. Panamá?: s.n., 1990. 392 p.: bibl., port.

Attacks "official ideology" blaming Bunau-Varilla for an unfavorable canal treaty and dependent position of Panama. Bunau-Varilla did the best he possibly could under the circumstances, but oligarchy and subsequent politicians have repeatedly sold out to "imperialism."

1710 Dodd, Thomas J. Managing democracy in Central America: a case study; United States election supervision in Nicaragua, 1927–1933. Coral Gables, FL: North-South Center, Univ. of Miami; New Brunswick, N.J.: Transaction Publishers, 1992. 161 p.: bibl., ill.

Based on US and Nicaraguan archives and interviews from the 1960s, author documents US military and electoral involvement from 1927–1933. Sees electoral reform replacing military intervention and financial management as chief vehicle of US policy but finds the effort ultimately futile.

1711 Dosal, Paul Jaime. Doing business with the dictators: a political history of United Fruit in Guatemala, 1899–1944. Wilmington, Del.: SR Books, 1993. 256 p.: bibl., ill., index, maps. (Latin American silhouettes)

The United Fruit Company (UFCO) did not set the rules privileging corruption and influence peddling in early-20th-century Guatemala, but for half a century it played successfully by them at the expense of producers and consumers. Unlike in Honduras, fruit companies did not make and unmake Guatemalan governments.

1712 Dospital, Michelle. La construcción del Estado Nacional en Nicaragua: el proyecto sandinista, 1933–1934. (*Rev. Hist./Managua*, 2, 1992/93, p. 52–61, bibl., photos)

Evaluates Sandino's ideas on nationalism in years 1933–34, based on newspapers and letters. With the end of armed struggle, Sandino attempted to develop new vehicles to press popular concerns. Efforts threatened traditional parties and oligarchy, but Sandino's murder and the destruction of the Wiwilí settlement restored "business confidence."

1713 Dunkerley, James. Guatemala. (*in* Latin America between the Second World War and the Cold War, 1944–1948. Edited by Leslie Bethell and Ian Roxborough. New York: Cambridge Univ. Press, 1992, p. 300–326)

Guatemala was able to resist Cold War pressures for a decade because weakness of domestic opposition allowed the reform movement to consolidate unusual strength. Also, local events did not alarm the US until the Arana assassination and failed army coup removed "moderate" elements from politics. Ultimately, intervention resulted from fear that Guatemalan neutrality would threaten US hegemony in area.

1714 Edelman, Marc and **Mitchell A. Seligson.** Land inequality: a comparison of census data and property records in twentieth-century southern Costa Rica. (*HAHR*, 74: 3, Aug. 1994, p. 445–491, appendix, graphs, maps, tables)

Ingeniously combining census and cadastral records, authors show that in at least one area of Costa Rica land has become more democratically distributed since 1945, contradicting trends toward concentration that censuses alone appear to show and that theories of development predict.

1715 Enríquez, Laura J. Harvesting change: labor and agrarian reform in Nicaragua, 1979–1990. Chapel Hill: Univ. of North Carolina Press, 1991. 252 p.: bibl., ill., index.

Following a brief overview of Nicaraguan agriculture, Enríquez looks at Sandinista agrarian reform laws and at tensions they produced between subsistence and export sectors. Improving subsistence conditions lowered labor availability and raised labor costs to export sector, threatening needed export earnings. For economist's comment see *HLAS 53:1978*.

1716 Euraque, Darío. National formation, mestizaje and Arab Palestinian immigration to Honduras, 1880–1930s. (*Critique/St. Paul*, 6, Spring 1995, p. 25–37)

Palestinians arrived earlier and influenced Honduran society more profoundly than Nancie González (item **1723**) suggests, leading to racist immigration laws in 1929 and 1934 and conscious efforts to build mestizo national identity.

1717 Fernández González, Alvaro. "Todo empezó en el '53':" historia oral de un distrito liberacionista. (*Rev. Hist./Heredia*, 26, julio/dic. 1992, p. 97–142, bibl.)

Oral history of transformation of suburban section of San José from coffee district to residential area for urban wage earners. Repeated crises in the coffee economy and completion in 1953 of highway providing access to day work in the capital stimulated migration from the countryside. Support for the Partido Liberación Nacional is seen as linked to "material advances" sought and won from the State by community leaders.

1718 Fernández Poncela, Anna M. La participación económica y política de las mujeres nicaragüenses. (*Bol. Am.*, 33:42/43, 1992/93, p. 287–299, bibl., graphs, tables)

Discusses changing situation of "popular sector" women in Nicaragua, particularly since 1979. Criticizes both AMNLAE and FSLN for claiming to represent women but failing to address poor women's concerns adequately. Two or three jobs leave little time for mass organizations, while sexism bars those who do participate from power. Post-1990 changes have made things worse.

1719 Forster, Cindy. The time of "freedom:" San Marcos coffee workers and the radicalization of the Guatemalan National Revolution, 1944–1954. (*Radic. Hist. Rev.*, 58, Winter 1994, p. 35–79)

Indians of San Marcos remember reforms of 1944–54 as the product of their own struggle under home-grown leaders, not as a government gift or a result of Communist agitation. Tracing local leadership's development and relations with the State and Indian population, Forster shows Guatemalan Revolution before 1952 was not limited to urban middle class.

1720 García, Luis. El Jute. Redacción, prólogo y notas de Longino Becerra. Tegucigalpa: Univ. Nacional Autónoma de Honduras, Editorial Universitaria, 1991. 312 p. (Col. Realidad nacional; 33)

Edited recollections of campesino participant in failed guerrilla movement sponsored by Honduran Communist Party after the 1963 coup. Catalog of mistakes and handbook of what guerrillas ought not do, the text is a party exercise in self-criticism written in late 1960s-early 1970s but unpublished until 1991.

1721 Goldberg, Mark H. "Going bananas:" 100 years of American fruit ships in the Caribbean. Kings Point, N.Y.: American Merchant Marine Museum Foundation, 1993. 606 p.: bibl., ill. (American merchant marine history series; 3)

Intended for ship "buffs," compilation is also useful to economic and cultural historians. Provides photographs, design drawings, specifications, and other details for all US-owned ships engaged in Caribbean banana trade.

1722 González, María Victoria. La invasión a Panamá: un relato, un testimonio. Panamá: Ríos Editores, 1992. 168 p.: ill.

Journalistic account of 1989 US invasion of Panama. Faults brutality of invasion, incompetence of Panama's political and military leaders, and readiness of much of the population to loot. Clarifies the divisions existing among Panamanians themselves.

1723 González, Nancie L. Dollar, dove, and eagle: one hundred years of Palestinian migration to Honduras. Ann Arbor: Univ. of Michigan Press, 1992. 229 p.: bibl., ill., index.

Examines historical patterns of Palestinian migration from the West Bank to Honduras and immigrants' economic and social adaptations to a new environment. Some peddlers arrived early in 20th century but their numbers and importance grew in the 1950s following the partition of Palestine. Based on archival research and participant observation in Honduras and the West Bank.

1724 Gould, Jeffrey. Nicaragua. (*in* Latin America between the Second World War and the Cold War, 1944–1948. Edited by Leslie Bethell and Ian Roxborough. New York: Cambridge Univ. Press, 1992, p. 243–279)

Nicaragua in 1940s resembled the rest of Central America more than is usually imagined. During WWII Somoza appealed to urban workers with pro-labor "Populism," although he carefully excluded workers in agroindustry. As the Cold War grew, Somoza abandoned labor allies for 1947 "anti-communist" coup that won US favor.

1725 Gudmundson, Lowell and Héctor Lindo-Fuentes. Central America, 1821–1871: liberalism before liberal reform. Tuscaloosa: Univ. of Alabama Press, 1995. 156 p.: bibl., ill., index, maps.

In revisionist interpretation of half century after Central America's independence, authors argue that many economic changes (e.g., export agriculture promotion and port and road development) traditionally associated with late 19th-century Liberal reforms, were in fact already underway under preceding Conservative regimes. Original version appeared in vol. 3 of *Historia general de Centroamérica* (see item **1633**).

1726 Gudmundson, Lowell. Peasant, farmer, proletarian: class formation in a smallholder coffee economy, 1850–1950. (*in* Coffee, society, and power in Latin America. Edited by William Roseberry, Lowell Gudmundson, and Mario Samper Kutschback. Baltimore: Johns Hopkins Univ. Press, 1995, p. 112–150, map, tables)

Excellent overview of the development of the Costa Rican model of small-farmer coffee cultivation. Sees consolidation in the early-20th century of rural petty bourgeoisie, which adopted anti-labor and anti-Marxist reformism and benefitted from, more than prompted, post-1948 reforms.

1727 Guevara Mann, Carlos. Ilegitimidad y hegemonía: una interpretación histórica del militarismo panameño. Panamá: Editorial La Prensa, 1994. xxv, 176 p.: bibl.

Role of the military in Panama is tied to the illegitimacy of the State. From the 19th century, civilian politicians repeatedly violated the constitution and laws, keeping themselves in power with military backing. Since the 1960s, US policy has reinforced this pattern by supporting "institutionalized militarism" as best guarantee of hegemony.

1728 Hale, Charles R. Resistance and contradiction: Miskitu Indians and the Nicaraguan State, 1894–1987. Stanford, Calif.: Stanford Univ. Press, 1994. 296 p.: bibl., ill., index, maps.

In field research on Nicaragua's Atlantic Coast during 1985–88, author investigated confrontation between FSLN class analysis/assimilationist ideology and increasingly articulated ethnic identity of coastal Indians. This clash resulted in complex, nuanced alliances and contradictions within and between FSLN and Mosquitos that led toward mutual approximation.

1729 Handy, Jim. Revolution in the countryside: rural conflict and agrarian reform in Guatemala, 1944–1954. Chapel Hill: Univ. of North Carolina Press, 1994. 272 p.: bibl., index, maps.

Exemplary study of Guatemala's 1952–54 land reform, seen as opening a "Pandora's box" of class and ethnic conflict in the countryside, both within and between communities and local organizations. When the government failed to control conflict, rather than lose its monopoly on violence, the army turned against the revolution and toppled the elected president.

1730 Harpelle, Ronald N. Ethnicity, religion and repression: the denial of African heritage in Costa Rica. (*Can. J. Hist.*, 29:1, April 1994, p. 95–112)

Examines reaction of West Indian leaders and Costa Rican authorities to the spread of "African-influenced" religious sects in Puerto Limón during 1930s. When hysterical Spanish-language newspapers attacked "lunacy" of movements, black community leaders attempted to distance themselves and general population from them, fearing they would fuel discrimination.

1731 Hernández Rodríguez, Carlos. Trabajadores, empresarios y Estado: la dinámica de clases y los límites institucionales del conflicto, 1900–1943. (*Rev. Hist./Heredia*, 27, enero/junio 1993, p. 51–86, graph, tables)

Comparison of State reaction to labor agitation in 1903, 1920, and 1936 shows gradual redefinition of class relations setting the basis for social democracy in Costa Rica. Despite barriers, the working class has been active in politics since beginning of century.

1732 Herrera C., Miguel Angel. Nacionalismo e historiografía sobre la Guerra del 56: Nicaragua, 1850–1889. (*Rev. Hist./Managua*, 2, 1992/93, p. 27–39, bibl., ill., photos)

Histories written in the late-19th century reveal how elites sought to create an "imagined political community" as a basis for the nation, focusing on the filibuster episode to accentuate "us" vs. "them" and "local" vs. "national."

1733 Hilje Quirós, Brunilda. La colonización agrícola de Costa Rica, 1840–1940. San José: Univ. Nacional; Univ. Estatal a Distancia; Editorial Univ. Estatal a Distancia, 1991. 87 p.: bibl., ill., maps. (Nuestra historia; 10)

Meant for general readers, addition to *Nuestra Historia* series examines internal migrations provoked by coffee. Spontaneous migration was generally more successful than State-sponsored agricultural colonies because individual settlers had more resources.

1734 Hodges, Donald Clark. Sandino's communism: spiritual politics for the twenty-first century. Austin: Univ. of Texas Press, 1992. 246 p.: bibl., index.

More than simply a "nationalist with populist leanings," Sandino produced a distinctive synthesis of communism and anarchism rooted in the writings of pre-Marxist communists and spiritualism of "Magnetic-Spiritual School of the Universal Commune," a group headquartered in Buenos Aires during the early-20th century. For comment by philosophy specialist, see item bi94–13524.

1735 Holden, Robert H. The real diplomacy of violence: United States military power in Central America, 1950–1990. (*Int.*

Hist. Rev., 15:2, May 1993, p. 283–322, graphs)

During Cold War, US shifted from pre-WWII policy of direct, unilateral military intervention in Central America to cooperation with local armed forces, using military aid chiefly for political purposes. This new approach allowed "friendly" officers to repress internal opposition and "moderate" activities of "excessively nationalist" civilian politicians.

1736 Karlen, Stefan. Ausländische Wirtschaftsinteressen in Guatemala: Deutschland, 1871–1944. (*Jahrb. Gesch.*, 31, 1994, p. 267–303)

German economic presence in Guatemala reinforced export monoculture with efficiency and modern technology, causing conflict with local elites and US interests. During WWII, US cited Nazi influence as a pretext to force the Germans out. Relies heavily on US State Department and military intelligence records.

1737 Kit, Wade. The unionist experiment in Guatemala, 1920–1921: conciliation, disintegration, and the liberal *junta.* (*Americas/Francisc.*, 50:1, July 1993, p. 31–64)

Traces collapse of elite-popular coalition that brought down Guatemalan dictator Manuel Estrada Cabrera in 1920. Unionist rhetoric attracted artisans, students, and urban popular classes into national political life, but weaknesses of popular organizations prevented maintenance of involvement in face of attacks by military and oligarchy.

1738 Krenn, Michael L. Life with Somoza: the United States and dictatorship in Nicaragua, 1945–1954. (*SECOLAS Ann.*, 26, March 1995, p. 48–56)

Using US relations with Nicaragua as an example, author argues that post-war relations with Latin America were not determined entirely by anti-communism. Additional factor was growing sense that countries were not prepared politically or socially for democratic government. Dictators were better than possible instability.

1739 Laíno, Domingo. Somoza: el general comerciante. 3. ed. Asunción: Intercontinental Editora, 1989. 179 p.: bibl.

Details organization of Somoza family fortune before 1979, diagramming links with foreign, especially US-owned, companies.

1740 Langley, Lester D. and **Thomas David Schoonover.** The banana men: American mercenaries and entrepreneurs in Central America, 1880–1930. Lexington: Univ. Press of Kentucky, 1995. 219 p.: bibl., ill., index.

Follows activities of assorted North American entrepreneurs, mercenaries, and sociopaths in Central America around the turn of century, with particular attention to those employed by fruit companies, especially Lee Christmas.

1741 Leonard, Thomas M. A guide to Central American collections in the United States. Westport, Conn.: Greenwood Press, 1994. 186 p.: index. (Reference guides to archival and manuscript sources in world history, 1054–9110; 3)

Annotated list organized by state of manuscript holdings relating to Central America in US repositories. Includes name and country index.

1742 Levenson-Estrada, Deborah. Trade unionists against terror: Guatemala City, 1954–1985. Chapel Hill: Univ. of North Carolina Press, 1994. 288 p.: bibl., ill., index.

Using interviews and life stories and giving central importance to the 1984–85 strike against Guatemala City's Coca-Cola bottler, Levenson-Estrada examines unionization efforts in the face of constant violent repression. Organizing themselves on the basis of "decision" and "consciousness" without necessarily waiting for middle-class intellectual leadership, many workers linked union activities to Christian beliefs.

1743 Lizcano Fernández, Francisco. América Central en la segunda mitad del presente siglo: estructura social y niveles de vida. Toluca, Mexico: Univ. Autónoma del Estado de México, 1994. 106 p.: bibl. (Col. Historia; 15)

Brief treatment of economic and social conditions in Central America since WWII, approximately half of the volume is statistical tables. Countries reveal individual patterns, but generally incomes rose until 1970s, then stagnated or fell, while other social indicators, such as education and mortality rates, continued to improve.

1744 Longley, Kyle. Peaceful Costa Rica, the first battleground: the United States and the Costa Rican revolution of 1948. (*Americas/Francisc.*, 50:2, Oct. 1993, p. 149–175)

As a warm-up for 1954 and Guatemala, in 1948 US intervened indirectly in Costa Rica to help conservative opposition overthrow Teodoro Picado, a perceived Communist threat.

1745 Major, John. Prize possession: the United States and the Panama Canal, 1903–1979. Cambridge, England; New York: Cambridge Univ. Press, 1993. 432 p.: bibl., ill., index, map.

How the US built, operated, and defended the Panama Canal from the 19th century until 1979. Well-written, detailed, and relentlessly organized, book is flawed by lack of attention to Panamanian sources and, consequently, to Panamanian concerns.

1746 Marín Hernández, Juan José. Las causas de la prostitución josefina, 1939–1949: entre lo imaginario y el estigma. (*Rev. Hist./Heredia*, 27, enero/junio 1993, p. 87–108)

Analysis of official discourse on prostitution in Costa Rica's capital during the 1940s attributes the problem to poverty and lack of parental control, aggravated by those who actively corrupted girls for own uses and profit, by weak nature of the women, and by links of prostitution to other forms of crime.

1747 McNairn, Rosemarie M. British Honduras as Jamaica: a colonialist re-vision. (*SECOLAS Ann.*, 25, March 1994, p. 101–119)

Colonial discourse deconstructed to show how efforts of local whites to recreate a "civilized" Jamaica-style plantation colony in British Honduras clashed with the "other" in the form of uncontrolled Yucatan Maya, lawless local lower orders, and anarchic, priest-ridden republics of Central America.

1748 Molero, María. Nicaragua sandinista: del sueño a la realidad, 1979–1988. Managua: Coordinadora Regional de Investigaciones Económicas y Sociales; Madrid: Instituto de Estudios Políticos para América Latina y África; Barcelona: Fundación Bofil, 1988. 299 p.: bibl.

Solidly, but not embarrassingly, pro-Sandinista treatment of 1979–88, well-researched in local documents and Spanish-language secondary sources but ignoring extensive bibliography available in English. Admits FSLN mistakes with peasantry and Mosquitos but cites external aggression and unfavorable terms of trade as chief factors undercutting the economy and, hence, support for FSLN.

1749 Molina Jiménez, Iván. Los pequeños y medianos caficultores: la historia y la nación; Costa Rica 1890–1950. (*Caravelle/Toulouse*, 61, 1993, p. 61–73)

General overview of rise and relative decline of small coffee producers during late-19th and early-20th centuries argues that coffee produced stratification, destroying collective identity forged in colonial poverty. After 1880, elites invented national unity based on National War, followed after 1900 by gradual "redemocratization" of political life.

1750 Montgomery, Tommie Sue. Revolution in El Salvador: from civil strife to civil peace. Introduction by Ignacio Martín-Baró and Rodolfo Cardenal. 2nd ed. Boulder, Colo.: Westview Press, 1995. 344 p.: bibl., ill., index, maps.

Greatly expanded, updated version of 1982 edition by a political scientist with good contacts on both sides of Salvadoran conflict. Best single-volume treatment of the country's recent history argues that the FMLN must "broaden its base and form coalitions" to move successfully from guerrilla army to political party.

1751 Mora Carvajal, Virginia María. Los oficios femeninos urbanos en Costa Rica, 1864–1927. (*Mesoamérica/Antigua*, 15:27, junio 1994, p. 127–173, photo)

In turn-of-the-century Costa Rica *obreras* worked for low wages under exploitative conditions, performing chiefly manual labor associated with traditionally female tasks. Mora examines social context of various categories of female-dominated labor, including prostitution, and finds that modernization or mechanization of given job category tended to result in replacement of women by men.

1752 Morales, Gerardo. Cultura oligárquica y nueva intelectualidad en Costa Rica, 1880–1914. Heredia, Costa Rica: EUNA, 1993. 240 p.: bibl. (Col. Corubicí)

Hegemonic culture of Costa Rica's Oligarchic Republic at the end of the 19th century was elitist, exclusionary, and anti-democratic. After 1900, "la nueva intelectualidad," exemplified by the work of Omar Dengo, launched new journals seeking to include "social question" and "workers' question" in national debate.

1753 Nicaragua: a country study. Edited by Tim Merrill. 3rd ed. Washington: Federal Research Division, Library of Congress; Government Printing Office, 1994. 337 p.: bibl., ill., index, maps. (Area handbook series, 1057–5294. DA pam; 550–88)

Recent addition to the US Army country handbook series features chapters on history, society, economy, and government and politics prepared by authors such as Dennis Gilbert. Provides balanced description of events since 1979, including post-1990 elections. Good for identifying main parties, groups, etc.

1754 Nicaragua, a decade of revolution. Edited by Lou Dematteis with Chris Vail. Introduction by Eduardo Galeano. Text by Anthony Jenkins. New York: W.W. Norton, 1991. 168 p.: ill., map.

Powerful collection of black and white photographs from both sides of Nicaragua's civil war. Accompanying text tends to favor FSLN, but admits the revolution's errors.

1755 The Nirex collection: Nicaraguan revolution extracts; twelve years, 1978–1990. Recopilación de Porfirio R. Solórzano. Austin, TX: Litex, 1993. 10 v.: ill., indexes.

Ten volumes of photoreproduced articles, chapters, documents, papers, speeches, etc. related to Nicaragua since 1979. Roughly two-thirds are in English and rest mainly in Spanish. Organized topically and chronologically, with volumes on, for example, the economy (2), politics (2), culture, diplomacy, the church, and bibliographies. Good representation of various ideological orientations.

1756 Obregón, Clotilde María. Carrillo: una época y un hombre, 1835–1842. San José: Editorial Costa Rica, 1989. 245 p.: bibl., ill., index.

Labelled "architect of the State," early Costa Rican strongman Braulio Carrillo (1800–45) enhanced power of San José at the expense of other central valley cities, promoted national economy by paying off the country's share of federal debt and encouraging coffee production, prepared general law code, and expanded international commercial and diplomatic relations.

1757 Obregón, Clotilde María. El Río San Juan en la lucha de las potencias, 1821–1860. San José: Editorial Univ. Estatal a Distancia, 1993. 309 p.: bibl., ill., index, maps.

Great powers' interest in controlling possible canal route forced Costa Rica to accept an unjust and illogical border with Nicaragua. Although the country prevailed in the 1850 confrontation, US intervention gave disputed territory to Nicaragua.

1758 Obregón Loria, Rafael. Costa Rica y la guerra contra los filibusteros. Alajuela, Costa Rica: Museo Histórico Cultural Juan Santamaría; San José: Ministerio de Cultura, Juventud y Deportes, 1991. 409 p.: appendix, bibl., ill., index, col. map.

Difficult campaign in isolated area, Costa Rica's effort in 1850s to deny the San Juan River to filibusterers is an often-overlooked contribution to the National War. Account includes biographical encyclopedia of participants and appendix of ships trafficking on San Juan.

1759 Pakkasvirta, Jussi. Particularidad nacional en una revista continental: Costa Rica y *Repertorio Americano*, 1919–1930. (*Rev. Hist./Heredia*, 28, julio/dic. 1993, p. 89–115)

Analyzes image of Costa Rica given in *Repertorio Americano*. Generally following official line of white, democratic, prosperous, and civilized "exceptionality," after 1925 magazine became more radically anti-imperialist but remained within local elite discourse.

1760 Palacios A., Sergio. Reseña sobre la historia eclesiástica y civil de Honduras: el caso de la parroquia de San Francisco de Tatumbla. (*Yaxkin/Tegucigalpa*, 12:2, julio/dic. 1989, p. 5–43)

In 1888 the bishop of Comayagua ordered priests to collect local history to compensate for archives destroyed in civil wars. Responses are largely missing, but authors reproduce a historical summary and related documents for one parish.

1761 Palmer, Steven Paul. El consumo de heroína entre los artesanos de San José y el pánico moral de 1929. (*Rev. Hist./Heredia*, 25, enero/junio 1992, p. 29–63)

Apparent outbreak of drug addiction among local artisans in 1929 alarmed San José elites who saw a threat to morality and labor supply. In a resulting crackdown, police targeted small-scale sellers and "suspicious" characters, who were often convicted on little or no evidence.

1762 Peláez Almengor, Oscar Guillermo. La economía urbana de la Nueva Guatemala de la Asunción vista a través de los negocios de Francisco Cordón Batres: el abastecimiento de carne, 1871–1898. (*Mesoamérica/Antigua,* 15:27, junio 1994, p. 93–126, tables)

Citing notarial and other records, author details commerce in beef and cattle byproducts in late-19th-century Guatemala City. Shows how one individual used credit and government connections to monopolize trade but, in 1898 financial crisis, fell victim himself to debts owed to German export houses.

1763 Peláez Almengor, Oscar Guillermo. La Nueva Guatemala de la Asunción y los terremotos de 1917–18. Guatemala: Centro de Estudios Urbanos y Regionales, Univ. de San Carlos de Guatemala, 1994. 73 p.: bibl., ill.

Sees earthquake of 1917–18 and resulting conditions in the capital as a major cause of fall of Guatemalan dictator Manuel Estrada Cabrera (1898–1920). The government did little to alleviate suffering caused by the loss of working-class housing and employment or by subsequent epidemics.

1764 Pellecer, Carlos Manuel. Asalta-caminos en la historia de la revolución de octubre 1944. Guatemala: Artemis & Edinter, 1994. 79 p.

Blistering attack on Francisco Villagrán Kramer for his treatment of Pellecer in *Biografía política* (item **1795**), which, otherwise, author calls a useful book! Line-by-line refutation, but without sources or notes.

1765 Pérez Brignoli, Héctor. Indians, communists, and peasants: the 1932 rebellion in El Salvador. (*in* Coffee, society, and power in Latin America. Edited by William Roseberry, Lowell Gudmundson, and Mario Samper Kutschback. Baltimore: Johns Hopkins Univ. Press, 1995, p. 232–261, graph, maps, tables)

Surveys available sources and previous interpretations and concludes that the 1932 uprising was rooted in popular discontent provoked by coffee expansion but confined almost exclusively to heavily Indian areas. Added element of ethnic confrontation tipped population into revolt, and repression that followed virtually eliminated Indians from El Salvador's population.

1766 Pezzullo, Lawrence and **Ralph Pezzullo.** At the fall of Somoza. Pittsburgh, Penn.: Univ. of Pittsburgh Press, 1993. 303 p.: bibl., ill., index, maps. (Pitt Latin American series)

Fascinating insider account of the last days of Somoza's Nicaragua reinforces the picture given by Robert Pastor in *Condemned to repetition,* i.e., that the US embassy and Washington had little idea what was going on; that the US was "always behind the curve." Lawrence Pezzullo's own narrative is interspersed with Nicaraguan accounts of the fighting.

1767 Posas, Mario. Breve historia de las organizaciones sindicales de Honduras. Tegucigalpa: Friedrich Ebert Stiftung, 1986? 87 p.: bibl.

Traces worker organization from mutual aid associations in the late-19th century to unions of 1980s. Strikes of the 1920s and 1930s largely failed. In the 1940s dictator Tiburcio Carías Andino repressed organizing efforts, but the 1954 banana strike prompted a military populist to grant workers the right to organize and strike. Although largely failing to work together, unions have served as pressure groups within political parties.

1768 Ramírez Avendaño, Victoria. Jorge Volio y la revolución viviente. San Pedro de Montes de Oca, Costa Rica: Ediciones Guayacán, 1989. 222 p.: bibl., maps.

Foundation in 1921 of Costa Rica's Partido Reformista Nacional is seen as genuine expression of working class interests, challenging traditional, elite-driven parties and creating a new form of politics based on platforms, programs, and mass mobilizations, rather than on personalism.

1769 Ramos Guzmán, María Eugenia. Movimientos sociales: Estado-United Fruit Co.-trabajadores "el conflicto laboral de 1948–1949." (*Estudios/Guatemala,* 2, 1994, p. 59–75, bibl.)

Brief overview of the 1949 strike of banana workers against UFCO in Guatemala, based on newspapers and secondary sources.

Argues crisis developed from UFCO's refusal, supported by military and local elites, to deal with labor unions or accept binding arbitration called for by law.

1770 Rivera, Julio César et al. El silencio quedó atrás: testimonios de la huelga bananera de 1954. Recopilación de Marvin Barahona. Tegucigalpa: Editorial Guaymuras, 1994. 418 p.: bibl., ill. (Col. Talanquera)

Interviews with leaders of the great 1954 strike show range of ideological currents that motivated and sustained this national mobilization. [Darío Euraque]

1771 Robles, Arodys. Medición de la migración interna en Costa Rica, 1883–1950. (*in* Congresso sobre a História da População da América Latina, *1st, Ouro Preto, Brazil, 1989. Actas.* São Paulo: Fundação SEADE, 1990, p. 7–15, bibl., graph, map, tables)

Applying various statistical techniques to four censuses taken from 1883–1950, shows that population shifted in the late-19th century to area south of San José and toward the Atlantic coast. After 1900, streams continued to the Atlantic (until 1930), but movement also seen toward the Pacific coast and, subsequently, to the capital itself.

1772 Sagastume Fajardo, Alejandro S. El papel de la Iglesia de Centroamérica en la guerra contra William Walker, 1856–1860. (*Rev. Indias,* 53 : 198, mayo/agosto 1993, p. 529–544)

In 1840s, the Church in Nicaragua tried to intervene to end civil wars and in 1850s it supported opposition to William Walker as a "religious crusade." Walker's victory prompted clergy to work with him in name of peace, but outside Nicaragua Church continued to oppose filibusters, lending moral and financial support to the National War.

1773 Salinas, Marcos Rigoberto. Relaciones entre Iglesia y Estado en la República de El Salvador, 1821–1871. El Salvador: Arzobispado de San Salvador, 1992. 457 p.: facsims.

Extensively researched in Vatican archives, the book chronicles Salvadoran Church-State relations, culminating in the Concordat of 1862 and subsequent liberal separation of Church and State. Notes, but no bibliography or information on archives. Approximately one-third of the text reproduces original documents.

1774 Samper K., Mario. Policultivo, modernización y crisis: paradojas del cambio técnico-social en la caficultura centroamericana. (*Rev. Hist./Heredia,* 27, enero/junio 1993, p. 111–145)

Coffee cultivation takes variety of forms in Central America. Samper offers broad, comparative essay addressing questions regarding effects of introduction, expansion, and intensification of coffee production, how technical changes impact different forms of coffee production, and how such changes modify social relations of production.

1775 Sandinistas: key documents/documentos claves. Edited by Dennis L. Gilbert and David Block. Ithaca, N.Y.: Latin American Studies Program, Cornell Univ., 1990. 342 p.: bibl., ill.

Wide range of official FSLN materials, including internal party documents, public statements, and key speeches. Printed in facsimile and in original language. Where available, English translations are cited but not included.

1776 Seminario Estado, Clases Sociales y Cuestión Etnico-Nacional en Guatemala, *México, 1989–1990.* Guatemala, seminario estado, clases sociales y cuestión étnico-nacional. México: CEIDEC, 1992. 291 p.

These presentations made at a Mexico City seminar (1989–90), without sources or bibliographies, include several unrevised transcripts. Most reject "ethnopopulism" for Marxist approaches. Particularly useful are essays by Ibarra on 1920s, Porras Castejón on class and economic change between 1954–80, Hernández Ixcoy on peasant consciousness, and Bermúdez on "low intensity warfare."

1777 Serra, Yolanda Marco. Antecedentes históricos y actualidad de la participación política de la mujer panameña. (*in* Jornadas de Investigación interdisciplinaria sobre la Mujer, *9th, Madrid, 1992. La mujer latinoamericana ante el reto del siglo XXI.* Madrid: Ediciones de la Univ. Autónoma de Madrid, 1993, p. 95–112)

Surveys political activities of Panamanian women from 1903 to the present, based on a limited range of secondary sources. Early emphasis on education and work rights subsequently gave way to agitation for suffrage, whereas today hope is to bring women together around everyday problems such as abuse, access to health care, housing, etc.

1778 Sierra Fonseca, Rolando. Fuentes y bibliografía para el estudio de la historia de la Iglesia de Honduras. Tegucigalpa: Centro de Publicaciones, Obispado Choluteca, 1993. 106 p.: bibl. (Col. Padre Manuel Subirana; 9)

Unannotated bibliography of more than 1,600 items containing information on the Catholic Church in Honduras.

1779 Sierra Fonseca, Rolando. Iglesia y liberalismo en Honduras en el siglo XIX. Tegucigalpa: Centro de Publicaciones Obispado Choluteca, 1993. 98 p.: bibl. (Col. Padre Manuel Subirana; 6)

Conflicts between Catholic Church and State in Honduras were more complicated than recognized so far. Liberal clerics and Church authorities embodied complexities of issues at stake, particularly in 1820s and 1830s, and again in 1880s. [Darío Euraque]

1780 Silva, Margarita. Las fiestas cívico-electorales en San José y el reconocimiento de la autoridad de los elegidos, 1821–1870. (*Rev. Hist./Heredia,* 27, enero/junio 1993, p. 31–50)

Sees elections in mid-19th-century San José as collective public festivals in which men and women of all classes participated, a form of inclusionary regime legitimation modeled on *fiestas reales* of the colonial period.

1781 Soler, Giancarlo. La invasión a Panamá: estrategia y tácticas para el nuevo orden mundial. Panamá: CELA, 1993. 280 p.: bibl.

Failure of Panamanians to resolve internal conflicts opened divisions that the US could exploit for its own interests: destruction of the nation state and continued presence of US bases. The 1989 invasion returned oligarchy to power, but the regime is collapsing from incompetence and lack of popular support.

1782 Soler, Ricaurte. Panamá: historia de una crisis. México: Siglo Veintiuno Editores, 1989. 119 p.: bibl. (Historia inmediata)

Excellent short synthetic history of Panama says Omar Torrijos exposed, but was unable to resolve, contradictions of Panamanian society, while the post-1981 era witnessed partially successful counter-attack by oligarchy and "hongkongization" of Panama. Ac-

cording to author, the US destroyed Manuel Noriega for refusing to assist Contras in Nicaragua and as an excuse to abrogate 1977 canal treaties.

1783 Solís, Edwin and **Carlos González Pacheco.** El ejército en Costa Rica: poder político, poder militar, 1821–1890. San Pedro de Montes de Oca, Costa Rica: Guayacán, 1992. 204 p.: bibl., ill.

Expansion of coffee in 1870–90 required enhanced repressive capacity for the liberal State, prompting modernization of military, which developed corporate ideology demanding expanded political role for armed forces.

1784 Solórzano, Flor de. Reincorporación y saqueo de la Mosquitia. (*Am. Indíg.,* 53: 1/2, enero/junio 1993, p. 61–80, bibl.)

Between 1860–94, which saw "reincorporation" of Mosquitia, effective control of the region shifted from the UK to the US. Expansion of US-controlled banana, mining, and logging companies destroyed subsistence economy/society of Mosquitos.

1785 Spalding, Rose J. Capitalists and revolution in Nicaragua: opposition and accommodation, 1979–1993. Chapel Hill: Univ. of North Carolina Press, 1994. 314 p.: bibl., index, map.

Can capitalist bourgeoisie participate successfully in a revolution and, if so, on what terms? Structural analysis stresses class cohesion, but Spalding finds Nicaraguan capitalists remarkably uncohesive as a group. Many were ready to make individual deals with and within the Sandinista revolution.

1786 Stanley, Diane K. For the record: the United Fruit Company's sixty-six years in Guatemala. Guatemala: Centro Impresor Piedra Santa, 1994. 353 p.: bibl., ill., index.

UFCO's record in Guatemala, according to daughter of a company employee. Raised in the country, author challenges and effectively counters many criticisms of UFCO, but ultimately does not entirely dispel the "Black Legend," for which she blames historians. Good detail on plantation organization and lives of UFCO's foreign employees.

1787 Stoll, David. Between two armies in the Ixil towns of Guatemala. New York: Columbia Univ. Press, 1993. 383 p.: bibl., index, maps, photos, tables.

Most intimate account yet available of the impact of 1980s violence on Guatemala's rural indigenous population. Stoll finds inhabitants of the Ixil area largely sought neutrality between the army and guerrillas, while both groups regularly used violence to force the population to choose sides. Subtle treatment of complex reality. For ethnologist's comment see *HLAS 55:765.*

1788 Suter, Jan. Prosperität und Krise in einer Kaffeerepublik: Modernisierung, sozialer Wandel und politischer Umbruch in El Salvador, 1910–1945. Frankfurt: Vervuert, 1996. 711 p.: bibl., ill., maps, tables. (Editionen der Iberoamericana. Serie C, Geschichte und Gesellschaft; 2 = Ediciones de Iberoamericana. Serie C, Historia y sociedad; 2)

Impressive and empirically well-founded analysis of the political, social, and economic development of El Salvador. Focuses on origins and effects of various crises in the process of modernization. Author disagrees with idea of a mere "depression dictatorship" after world crisis of 1929, proposing instead his own concept of persistent elite conflicts over allocation of resources. Includes approximately 120 maps, lists, and tables. A bonanza for students of Central American social history. [H.M. Meding]

1789 Terga Cintrón, Ricardo. Almas gemelas: un estudio de la inserción alemana en las Verapaces y la consecuente relación entre los alemanes y los k'ekchíes. Cobán, Guatemala: Impr. y Tip. El Norte, 1991. 440 p.: bibl., ill.

Study of Kekchi-German relations in Guatemala's Alta Verapaz, based principally on interviews. Many German planters had multiple Indian mistresses and children before, during, and after their marriages to European wives. Much of the book is a genealogy tracing descendants of such relationships.

1790 Universidad Nacional (Costa Rica). Escuela de Historia. Tierra, café y sociedad: ensayos sobre la historia agraria centroamericana. Recopilación de Héctor Pérez Brignoli y Mario Samper K. San José: Programa Costa Rica, FLACSO, 1994. 589 p.: bibl., ill.

Papers presented at 1990 conference on agrarian societies organized by the Escuela de Historia, Univ. Nacional de Costa Rica (Heredia, Costa Rica). Provides useful introduction to comparative history of coffee in Central America. Different circumstances of crop's introduction and development seen as underlying distinctive social and political development of each isthmian republic. Sophisticated contributions by principal scholars in field. For sociologist's comment see *HLAS 55:4677.*

1791 Valladares de Ruiz, Mayra et al. La administración político-territorial en Guatemala: una aproximación histórica. Coordinación de Gustavo Palma Murga. Guatemala: Univ. de San Carlos de Guatemala, Escuela de Historia; Instituto de Investigaciones Históricas, Antropológicas y Arqueológicas, 1993. 187 p.: bibl., ill.

Essays by various authors examine political-administrative development of Guatemala from colony to present. Most simply summarize laws, but Dardón Flores' essay on 1871–1900 goes beyond to examine municipal revenues and services.

1792 Vanden, Harry E. and Gary Prevost. Democracy and socialism in Sandinista Nicaragua. Boulder, Colo.: L. Rienner, 1992. 172 p.: bibl., index.

The FSLN made genuine effort to construct socialist democracy in Nicaragua based on popular participation, as opposed to Soviet bureaucratization and US representative forms. Hampering and ultimately defeating the effort were party leadership's own verticalist tendencies, paucity of available theories or models, collapsing economy, and outside aggression.

1793 Vega Jiménez, Patricia. Los protagonistas de la prensa: los primeros escritores de periódicos costarricenses, 1833–1850. (*Rev. Hist./Heredia,* 28, julio/dic. 1993, p. 61–88, tables)

Who wrote for, published, and read newspapers in mid-19th-century Costa Rica? Analysis of newspapers and *mortuales* of better-known writers identifies 365 individuals who wrote at least once and 40 who wrote regularly. All came from middle and upper levels of society and had multiple occupations. With secularization of society after 1840, the number of priests who wrote declined.

1794 Vernooy, Ronnie. "Buscando trabajo": historia laboral del litoral atlántico. (*Wani/Managua*, 16, enero/marzo 1995, p. 23–35, photos)

History of work and labor relations on Nicaraguan coast as evidenced in life of 64-year-old forestry worker from Bluefields. Interspersing extended quotes with his own comments, author finds work opportunities depended heavily on information and assistance from the individual's social network.

1795 Villagrán Kramer, Francisco. Biografía política de Guatemala: los pactos políticos de 1944 a 1970. Guatemala: FLACSO-Guatemala-Costa Rica, 1993. 504 p.: bibl.

Examines "pacts" between elites and the military that, according to the author, underpinned Guatemalan politics from 1944 to 1970s and, by inference, still do. Based on archival research and interviews. Author, who himself participated in many events of the period, sets a new standard for political history written in Guatemala. For a dissent, see item **1764.**

1796 Walter, Knut and Philip J. Williams. The military and democratization in El Salvador. (*J. Interam. Stud. World Aff.*, 35:1, 1993, p. 39–88, bibl., tables)

The perception of many—especially the armed forces—in El Salvador that the military is the only institution capable of defending the State and guaranteeing stability hampers democratization. Little evidence exists of military willingness at present to cede autonomy or subject itself to civilian control.

1797 Walter, Knut. The regime of Anastasio Somoza, 1936–1956. Chapel Hill: Univ. of North Carolina Press, 1993. 303 p.: bibl., ill., index, map.

Somoza laid the groundwork for the modern State by neutralizing old regional *caudillos*, strengthening State apparatus, and using effective but not constant coercion of all groups. Stability resulted from political space the regime was unwilling or unable to close, shared interests of dominant elites, delivery of benefits to key groups, and repression. For political scientist's comment see *HLAS 55:3015.*

1798 Whitfield, Teresa. Paying the price: Ignacio Ellacuría and the murdered Jesuits of El Salvador. Philadelphia, Penn.: Temple Univ. Press, 1994. 505 p.: bibl., ill., index, maps.

"Neither straight biography, nor political or ecclesiastical history." Author interweaves the account of 1989 murder of six Jesuits at San Salvador's Univ. of Central America and subsequent investigation with the history of the Church's activities from the late 1940s. Research—chiefly interviews—is impressive, arguments convincing, and most historians could learn from the writing style of author, a filmmaker.

1799 Wilson, Richard. Maya resurgence in Guatemala: Q'eqchi' experiences. Norman: Univ. of Oklahoma Press, 1995. 373 p.: bibl., ill., index, maps.

The Kekchi of Guatemala's Alta Verapaz had their lives disrupted in 1970s by the base community movement, evangelicals, and impacts of cash-crop agriculture, in 1980s by civil war, and more recently by the ethnic revivalist movement. The cumulative effect has been to break up traditional community identification with local mountain spirits and replace it with pan-Kekchi identity based on language.

1800 Woodward, Ralph Lee. Rafael Carrera and the emergence of the Republic of Guatemala, 1821–1871. Athens: Univ. of Georgia Press, 1993. 630 p.: bibl., ill., index, maps.

Career of *caudillo* Carrera is used to examine thoroughly the political and economic life of Guatemala in the half century after independence. While the 1830s revolt was a popular reaction against ill-conceived liberal policies, once in office the conservatives did little for the Indians. Among Carrera's more important legacies were financial stabilization of the State and organization of the ladino-led national army.

1801 Wünderich, Volker. Sandino en la costa: de las Segovias al litoral Atlántico. Managua: Editorial Nueva Nicaragua, 1989. 167 p.: bibl.

Sandino's 1930 flight to the Atlantic coast gave him a view of national problems atypical of most Nicaraguan mestizos. He understood each people must develop its historical struggle based on its own experiences and with the tools available. Río Coco settlements were meant to "bridge" the country's ethnic and cultural differences.

THE CARIBBEAN, THE GUIANAS, AND THE SPANISH BORDERLANDS

EDWARD L. COX, *Associate Professor of History, Rice University, Houston*
ANNE PEROTIN-DUMON, *Professor of History, Pontificia Universidad Católica de Chile*
JOHN D. GARRIGUS, *Associate Professor of History, Jacksonville University*
JOSE M. HERNANDEZ, *Professor Emeritus of History, Georgetown University*
ROSEMARIJN HOEFTE, *Deputy Head, Department of Caribbean Studies, Royal Institute of Linguistics and Anthropology, The Netherlands*
TERESITA MARTINEZ-VERGNE, *Associate Professor of History, Macalester College*

BRITISH CARIBBEAN

A SURVEY OF RECENT PUBLICATIONS indicates that interest in the history of the British Caribbean remains healthy. Despite considerable variation in the areas and themes covered, some of the most important scholarly contributions center on immigration. Ordahl Kupperman, for example, offers a rich portrait of the early settlers on Providence Island who strove unsuccessfully to create a thriving colony that would have matched the mainland Puritan colonies (item **1890**). Equally significant are a number of fruitful studies on East Indians and Chinese in the late 19th and early 20th centuries, with the more useful publications covering the earlier period.

As in past volumes of the *Handbook*, slavery continues to provide serious and important discourse for a number of scholars. Stinchcombe invokes social theory to explain why sugar planters needed and sometimes created repressive governments to maintain repressive plantation labor systems (item **1964**). Placing Caribbean slavery and emancipation within the larger world context, he concludes that freedom was not necessarily a means of achieving the goals of the Enlightenment but rather another method of social control. This important work will undoubtedly stimulate considerable debate among slave studies scholars in the foreseeable future. Viotti da Costa's sophisticated work constitutes the most thorough examination to date of the factors surrounding the slave revolt and subsequent martyrdom of Reverend John Smith (item **2002**). Sheridan points to the harsh conditions that slaves in the British Windward Islands endured at a crucial period in the expansion of the plantation economy (item **1962**). Noting the important role white women played in slave societies of the US South, Beckles calls for serious inquiries into their contributions to Caribbean slave societies (item **1904**).

Nineteenth-century post-slavery adjustments and tensions are addressed in some excellent works. Heuman provides fresh insights into an important episode in Jamaica's social and political history, when growing disagreements between planters and workers led to the declaration of martial law, bloody suppression of the "insurrectionists," and ultimately the imposition of Crown Colony government (item **2028**). Butler discusses the impact of compensated emancipation on credit, landownership, finance, and trade (item **1989**). While her conclusions that the West India Interest's inflated claims about the disastrous impact that emancipation had on their holdings is hardly novel, Butler's study casts light on the increasing availability of credit, the involvement of women in plantation ownership, and the differences in the plight of Jamaican and Barbadian planters. Finally, Wilmot (item **2099**) and Craton (item **2128**) address the experiences and expressed priorities of ex-slaves amidst planter attempts to ensure that there was an adequate supply of laborers for the demands of plantation agriculture.

Importation of workers from overseas was a frequent device that planters in some islands employed to augment their labor supply. Look Lai's magisterial study deserves special mention for its sophisticated treatment of the importation of Asians into the region, and their working conditions there (item **2041**). Laurence's work, though somewhat more limited in scope, is equally useful and contains excellent tables of importation statistics and other information (item **2040**).

A number of fine studies address the contributions of these newer immigrants to the political economy of the host countries. Ramsaran provides a penetrating analysis of the remarkable growth in the mid- and late-20th century of the important East Indian business community in Trinidad (item **2193**), while Kartick discusses the unsuccessful attempts of Chinese immigrants to achieve self-sufficiency in British Guiana (item **2037**). Both Kelvin Singh (item **2200**) and H.P. Singh (item **2199**) concentrate on the political strivings of East Indians amidst the racial tensions of Trinidad's multi-ethnic society. Finally, Mudd (item **2061**) and Menezes (item **2055**) remind us of the important roles, especially in agriculture and mercantile activities, that East Indian and Portuguese immigrants played in the economic life of two colonies.

Bolland skillfully presents an excellent overview of the political disturbances that spread throughout the British Caribbean in the 1930s as a result of severe economic problems that adversely affected the disenfranchised workers (item **2112**). Walker-Kilkenny examines specific strike action in British Guiana (item **2096**), while Woolford deals artfully with the career of a Guyanese trade union leader and politician whose activism was spurred by labor discontent (item **2214**).

Finally, one of the most fascinating works reviewed this biennium on the modern period is authored by Fraser (item **2145**), who argues that US involvement in the British Caribbean did not begin in the 1960s-70s, but rather, much earlier, when the emergence of nationalist movements in the region led to British withdrawal and American assertion of hegemony. [ELC]

FRENCH AND DANISH CARIBBEAN

Three studies utilizing sophisticated methods of social analysis clarify our understanding of slave societies in the French Caribbean and French Guiana. Geggus furthers our knowledge of French slaves by looking systematically at the sex ratios, age, and ethnicity of those who left Africa and worked on plantations (item **1934**). Garrigus links the rise of a free-colored planter class in Saint-Domingue both to the dynamics of merchant economies on the periphery and to an official policy of race-recasting (item **1931**). Branson traces the history of 1,300 Saint-Domingue refugees—masters and slaves, men and women—in Philadelphia in the early 1800s (item **1909**). Mass labor migrations to the Caribbean are reassessed by three studies: Gemery and Horn (item **1881**) and Huetz de Lemps (item **1888**) examine 17th-century indentured servitude, while Renard covers the East Indian and African indentured servants in 19th-century Martinique and Guadeloupe (item **2076**).

In *HLAS 54* we signalled the growing attention to small islands in the interstices of imperial powers. This trend is confirmed by in-depth research on the 18th-century plantation economy, land use and technology, ethnic composition, and culture in Henri and Denise Parisis' "Le siècle du sucre à Saint-Martin français" (item **1954**) and Tyson's "On the Periphery of the Peripheries: the Cotton Plantations of St. Croix, Danish West Indies, 1735–1815" (item **1966**), beautifully matched by Hopkins' study of map-making (item **1938**). Pointing toward the same environmental history is Huyghues-Belrose's creative essay on the seaboard of French Guiana, drawing from archaeological, archival, and aerial records (item **1831**).

Of all the periods, the 19th century is best represented in the works annotated below, in particular for Guadeloupe. Meinier has documented how Guadeloupe's first qualified midwives confronted the male medical establishment (item **2056**). Dominique Taffin's reconstitution of a devastating cholera epidemic provides an unusual window on its post-emancipation society and is a good example of innovative cultural history (item **2089**). The centrality of sugar in the political economy of 19th-century French Lesser Antilles is best illuminated by Schnackenbourg's study of Ernest Souques, the first biography of Guadeloupe's most powerful *sucrier* and political "boss" (item **2086**), and Buffon's "L'affaire Zévallos," on the first self-management experience of socialist workers in a *centrale* (item **2115**). In addition, both Buffon and Schnackenbourg describe the colonial banks which presided over the sugar economy of Guadeloupe and Martinique for a century (items **1988** and **2085**). Corvington's last addition to his multi-volume work shows the Haitian capital in the 19th century asserting its political primacy and achieving its spatial boundaries and distinctive culture (item **2001**).

Contemporary history makes a breakthrough with three studies. Chathuant analyzes the intricacies of the island's domestic and international policies during World War II and its political culture under the spell of a collaborationist ideology (item **2120**). Donet-Vincent shows how France's infamous penal colonies in French Guiana ended (item **2133**). Mam-Lam-Fouck's *Histoire de la Guyane contemporaine, 1940–1982* covers *départementalisation* after the war, its modernization policy, new political deal, and quiet demographic revolution (item **2170**).

High standards in local history have been set by Lafleur's comprehensive monograph on Saint-Claude, one of Guadeloupe's oldest settlements (item **1834**). In "Histoire et identité des Antilles françaises," Pérotin-Dumon analyzes a century of historiography, from romanticism and positivism to the plantation society paradigm (item **1849**). An authoritative edition of Thomas Madiou, the founder of Haiti's national history, is a testimony to the scholarly capacity to overcome society's odds (item **1840**). [APD and JG]

DUTCH CARIBBEAN

Scholarly interest in plantations and slavery has continued unabated and has resulted in a number of important essays, most notably those by Oostindie (item **1953**) and Van Stipriaan (item **1965**), both published in English. Two important Dutch-language contributions on Suriname's slave and plantation systems by these same authors, Oostindie's *Roosenburg en Mon Bijou* (see *HLAS 52:1572*) and Van Stipriaan's *Surinaams contrast* (see *HLAS 54:2106*), have unfortunately not yet been translated into English. A.F. Paula's study of the exceptional case of slavery and abolition on the Dutch part of St. Maarten, *"Vrije" slaven*, should also be noted (see *HLAS 54: 2070*).

The recent political past of Suriname has also generated a number of publications, many of which were included in the most recent social sciences volume, *HLAS 55*. Dew's *The trouble in Suriname* chronicles events from its 1975 independence to 1993 (see *HLAS 55:3089*). More analytical are two essays by Gary Brana-Shute, one covering the same period ("Suriname: A Military and its Auxiliaries," see *HLAS 55:3087*) and the other the Amerindian insurgency in Suriname's interior ("An Inside-Out Insurgency," see *HLAS 55:782*), and one by Sedoc-Dahlberg on the transition to democracy ("Suriname: the Politics of Transition from Authoritarianism to Democracy, 1988–1992," see *HLAS 55:3093*). Meel's article goes back further in time and discusses the late 1950s and early 1960s, arguing that this was the period when Suriname could and should have become independent ("Verbroederingspolitiek en Nationalisme," see *HLAS 55:3092*). Two legal scholars, Munneke and Van Aller, look at the political history and constitutional and administrative future of The Netherlands Antilles and Aruba. In *Van kolonie tot Koninkrijksdeel* (item **1804**), Van Aller describes the political evolution of the islands, while in *Ambtsuitoefening en onafhankelijke controle in de Nederlandse Antillen en Aruba*, Munneke emphasizes the importance of administrative reforms to improve democratic control (see *HLAS 55:3077*).

The two most physically attractive books are by architects and discuss the buildings and lay-out of Saba and Willemstad, the capital of Curaçao. Buddingh' not only relates the architectural history of the area first settled by the Dutch and the synagoge Mikvé-Israël-Emanuel, but also provides an account of social life in early 18th-century Willemstad (item **1867**). Brugman uses Saba as a case study to call for more and better maintenance and preservation projects in the Caribbean (item **1814**). [RH]

PUERTO RICO

Although the now-familiar "new" historiography of the 1970s renewed its forces in the past two years to produce several works worthy of note, it is the continued output of writings on the island's political situation that is drawing more notice. These two trends are not unrelated—each is connected to the issues brought to the fore by the Quincentenary of the "discovery" of America: constant political domination by a foreign power; limited economic development in the context of global capitalism; ethnic and class conflict resulting from continuous migratory waves, etc. As a result, books and articles on the early colonial period and the 19th century deal with the impact on the colony of Spain's economic and political control of subordinate groups: women, populations of African descent, the working class, and so forth. Studies on the 20th century have continued to examine this history of subjection, describing, analyzing, denouncing, and reminiscing about the island's political trajectory under US rule. In both sets of writings, one can detect the influence of cultural studies and literary criticism, as discourse analysis, the review of literary texts, and the inclusion of popular understandings of historical processes march onto the field of history. Several reference works also resulted from the Quincentenary outflow.

Several factors affecting Puerto Rico's economy captured the attention of "new" historians in the last two years. Customary consideration was given to sugar and coffee, the export crops that sustained the landowning class for most of the 19th century. Novel in their use of sources and theoretical perspectives were works by Ayala (item **2105**), Camuñas Madera (item **1992**), and Pumarada O'Neill (item **1855**). The commercial establishment's links to the island's economy were revisited by Dávila Ruiz (item **2007**) and Cubano Iguina (item **2004**), both of whom expanded on traditional interpretations, in the former case, of the role of the US in Puerto Rico's commercial transactions and, in the latter, of that of Spanish-born merchants in the coffee economy. Studies of the oppressed included an outstanding contribution from González-Pérez (item **2024**), which argues that the near disappearance or absence of Africans in 19th-century Puerto Rican abolitionist and folkloric literature was due to the social and cultural integration of blacks and to the general desire for "whitening." In the field of women's studies, three excellent works, all three at the cutting edge of both theory and use of sources, must be mentioned: Baerga (item **2152**), Barceló Miller (item **2106**), and González García (item **2156**). Camuñas Madera (item **1991**), García (item **1821**), López Cantos (item **1894**), and Picó (item **1850**) offer interesting attempts at exploring historical questions of recent vintage. Díaz Quiñones (item **2009**) and Navarro García (item **2064**), along with the previously mentioned González Pérez, engaged quite successfully in discourse analysis of elite immigrant groups, of the religious-political hierarchy, and of the white bourgeoisie, respectively.

Political writings concentrated on the 20th century. Informative, descriptive, or "objective" accounts of the relationship between the US and Puerto Rico from the standpoint of the military, of the pro-statehood party, and of commonwealth supporters can be found, respectively, in Estades Font (item **2137**), Meléndez (item **2174**), and Zapata Oliveras (item **2216**). A more general work, with appended primary source material, is Perusse (item **2188**). Empowering in tone and denunciatory in content are Carrión *et al.* (item **2178**), Fernández (item **2140**), García Muñiz (item **2150**) and Rodríguez-Fatricelli (item **2194**).

Puerto Rico's two elder statesmen, Luis Muñoz Marín and Luis Ferré, both published memoirs in 1992. The second volume of Muñoz Marín's public autobiography, published posthumously, reflects on politics and government between 1940–52 (item **2177**). Ferré's memoir, narrated by his daughter Rosario, an established writer herself, is more personal in terms of style and content (item **2141**). Five works revolving around the construction of a national identity deserve a separate category: Acosta-Belén (item **1802**); Flores (item **2144**); González (item **2155**), Alvarez-Curbelo and Rodríguez Castro (item **2129**); and Delgado Cintrón (item **2130**).

A number of textbooks and general works deserve mention as well. Scarano (item **1859**) and Díaz Soler (item **1819**) wrote general histories, the latter covering exclusively the years of Spanish domination. Another installment of Adolfo de Hostos' *Tesauro de datos históricos* (item **1854**) covers entries up to the letter *R*. Scholars are also fortunate to have another volume of Eugenio María de Hostos' *Obras completas* available for consultation (item **2032**). [TMV]

CUBA, THE DOMINICAN REPUBLIC, AND THE SPANISH BORDERLANDS

The last biennium was somewhat disappointing, among other reasons because it failed to generate any major works related to the centennials of José Martí's death and the outbreak of the 1895–98 Cuban War of Independence. There continued to be almost a superabundance of materials, but the writing generally followed the pattern of previous years: no significant new trends developed, nor was there any appreciable improvement in the level of objectivity. Ideology and political preconceptions kept permeating historical output, particularly that of Cubans on both sides of the Florida Straits. As always, very little appeared that is truly memorable, but this merely serves to put in relief the noteworthy exceptions.

Among the works in the general category that deserve to be singled out is Moya Pons' concise history of the Dominican Republic (item **1844**), which certainly fills a gap in the literature in English. Equally deserving, although for different reasons, are Levine's study of the Jewish experience in Cuba (item **1838**) and Baud's analysis of the problems of the Haitian-Dominican frontier (item **2108**). Moreno Fraginals' slender volume is also an important addition to the history of Spanish immigration to Cuba (item **2058**).

None of the publications listed under the early colonial and late colonial headings needs to be specially mentioned, but the comparatively higher level of erudition of the works on the Spanish Borderlands ought to be highlighted. Notable among these works is the extremely useful *De Soto Chronicles,* an indispensable tool for researchers (item **1969**).

As in previous *HLAS* volumes, most of the entries annotated below refer to works on 19th-century topics. Thus it is not surprising that most of the above-average studies should appear in this subsection. Perhaps the most outstanding among them is the Herculean investigation of the Cuban slave market carried out by Bergad, Iglesias, and Barcia (item **1985**), a truly unparalleled work. Three Spanish scholars, Bahamonde, Cayuela, and Roldán de Montaud, also produced solid pieces of research on 19th-century Cuban politics, economics, and administration (items **1982, 1997, 1998, 2080, 2081,** and **2082**). These works, however, are only samples of the excellent materials generated by Spanish historians, who were also largely responsible for the publication of *Ramón La Sagra y Cuba* (item **2074**) and half a dozen serious studies on the Spanish-American War. In Cuba, the publication of extensive segments of the campaign diary of Carlos Manuel de Céspedes (the initiator of the 1868–78 War of Independence) made accessible to scholars material that had been presumed lost for over a century (item **1999**). This is a finding that is bound to amend, to some extent, the historical record of the war.

As to the studies on contemporary history, perhaps the most ambitious, though not necessarily the most successful, is Quirk's massive biography of Fidel Castro (item **2192**). Less ambitious, but more successful, is Paterson's inquiry into the reasons for Castro's triumph in Cuba, at least insofar as events in the US were concerned (item **2184**). But neither of these two works is as thorough as Bernardo Vega's probe into the relations between Trujillo and the US armed forces (item **2206**). The study, based on US and Dominican archival sources, should be required reading for all advocates of US military intervention in other countries. There are also two minor essays that, although less sweeping, are nevertheless interesting: O'Brien's discussion of General Electric's investments in Cuba (item **2181**) and Collazo's study of the Cuban banking crisis of 1920 (item **2122**). Had Collazo's approach to his subject been more balanced, his little book would have been far more thought-provoking. [JMH]

GENERAL

1802 Acosta-Belén, Edna. Ideología colonialista y cultura nacional puertorriqueña. (*in* De palabra y obra en el Nuevo Mundo. v. 1, Imágenes interétnicas. Edición de Miguel León-Portilla *et al.* Madrid: Siglo Veintiuno Editores, 1992, p. 463–498)

Proposes that colonialist ideology has shaped academic interpretations of Puerto Rican cultural identity. Traces images of Puerto Ricans across time—as constructed in textbooks, the press, films, government reports, anthropological studies. Describes early 20th-century depictions of "difference" and subsequent efforts to portray progress as due to US occupation. Offers detailed characterizations of docile Puerto Rican and immigrant types. [TMV]

1803 The African-Caribbean connection: historical and cultural perspectives. Edited by Alan Gregor Cobley and Alvin O. Thompson. Barbados: Dept. of History, Univ. of the West Indies; Natural Cultural Foundation, 1990. 171 p.: bibl., index, maps.

Important work examines African presence in Barbados and its implications for evolution of Barbadian society. Collection includes material on Africa-Caribbean linkages through migration and transference of ideas. Stresses African roots in Caribbean language and role of Caribbean peoples in anti-imperial movement in Africa and anti-apartheid campaigns in South Africa. [ELC]

1804 Aller, Hendrina Bernarda van. Van kolonie tot Koninkrijksdeel: de staatkundige geschiedenis van de Nederlandse Antillen en Aruba van 1634 to 1994 [From colony to part of the Kingdom: the constitutional history of the Netherlands Antilles and Aruba from 1634 to 1994]. Groningen, The Netherlands: Wolters-Noordhoff, 1994. 631 p.: bibl., index. (Dissertatie-serie / Vakgroep Staatsrecht Rijksuniversiteit Groningen; 1)

Detailed account of political and constitutional evolution of the Netherlands Antilles and Aruba is placed in economic, social, and cultural contexts. Emphasizes administration of the islands and political relations with The Netherlands in 20th century. Includes 19-page English summary and extensive bibliography and list of legal sources. [RH]

1805 Alofs, Luc. Slaven zonder plantage: slavernij en emancipatie op Aruba, 1750–1963 [Slaves without plantations: slavery and emancipation on Aruba, 1750–1963]. Oranjestad, Aruba: Charuba, 1996. 91 p.: appendix, bibl., ill., tables (Edición Educativo; 2)

First publication on slavery in Aruba is based on archival research in Aruba, The Netherlands, and Curaçao. Aruba did not have plantations and, compared to other Caribbean colonies, slavery was relatively unimportant. Appendix provides names of slave owners and emancipated slaves. [RH]

1806 Antonin, Arnold. Les idées haïtiennes et la révolution sud-américaine. Pétion-Ville, Haiti: Editions du Centre Pétion-Bolivar, 1990. 143 p., 5 leaves of plates: bibl., ill.

This wide-ranging publication includes an interesting 1980 report on Haitian immigrants in Caracas, mostly adults and 40 percent female. [APD]

1807 Arbell, Mordechai. La "nación" judía hispano-portuguesa del Caribe. (*Sefárdica/Buenos Aires*, 6:9, agosto 1992, p. 171–191, bibl., photos)

Overview of Jewish integration in the region is followed by a very useful summary of each community's history based on a thorough bibliography. [APD]

1808 Asuntos dominicanos en archivos ingleses. Edición de Bernardo Vega y Emilio Cordero Michel. Santo Domingo: Fundación Cultural Dominicana, 1993. 208 p.: bibl. (Publicaciones de la Fundación Cultural Dominicana)

Three of the documents reprinted in

this book may be categorized as travel literature. The other two refer to beginnings of the Trujillo era. [JMH]

1809 Baker, Patrick L. Centring the periphery: chaos, order, and the ethnohistory of Dominica. Jamaica: The Press, Univ. of the West Indies, 1994. 251 p.: bibl., ill., index, maps.

In this fairly successful attempt to understand society from the inside out, sociologist endeavors to explain changes that island experienced beginning in 17th century, and meaning of those changes for population and landscape. Despite somewhat unbalanced historical treatment, generally valuable for placing recent past within larger historical perspective. [ELC]

1810 Barbotin, Maurice. La péche à la nasse à Marie-Galante et la fabrication des nasses en bambou. (*Bull. Soc. hist. Guadeloupe*, 95/98, 1993, p. 3–40)

Rich piece of ethnohistory is written by foremost specialist of Marie-Galante, a dependency of Guadeloupe. Documents evolution of fishing ships, techniques, and tools. Shows that bow-nets were introduced by Europeans, replacing Carib use of bamboo. [APD]

1811 Bardin, Pierre. Un exemple de recherche: familles de nouveaux-libres. (*Généal. hist. Caraïbe*, 62, juillet/août 1994, p. 1092–1094)

Contributes to recent effort to systematize genealogical research on descendants of former slaves. [APD]

1812 Bernecker, Walther L. Kleine Geschichte Haitis. Frankfurt: Suhrkamp, 1996. 219 p.: bibl., tables.

A leading German expert on modern Latin American history provides well written, general overview of the history of Haiti. Describes political and social forces that shaped Haitian society, devoting considerable attention to social stratification as a legacy of colonialism. Also focuses on foreign rule and influences as constant factors in Haitian history. Views Haiti's prospects for the future with pessimism. [H.M. Meding]

1813 Bolland, O. Nigel. Current Caribbean research five centuries after Columbus. (*LARR*, 29:3, 1994, p. 202–219)

Review of eight books on Caribbean society includes sections entitled "The Indigenous Peoples and Colonization," "The Maroons of Jamaica and Suriname," and "Sugar, Slavery, and Freedom in Cuba, Puerto Rico, and Jamaica." Author mentions tendency in current scholarship to increasingly focus on smaller units of analysis, novel subjects, interdisciplinary research, and the continued legacy of colonialism. [B. Aguirre-López]

1814 Brugman, Frans H. The monuments of Saba: the island of Saba, a Caribbean example. Zutphen, The Netherlands: Walburg Instituut, 1995. 168 p.: bibl., ill. (some col.), maps (some col.), computer disk.

Alluring book focuses on traditional Saban architecture, including characteristic wooden cottages. Architect Brugman uses Saba as an example to present guidelines for maintenance and preservation projects in the Caribbean. Contains numerous drawings, some 30 b/w photograhs, and 21 color plates. Included diskette catalogs 10 percent of the photographic material and presents a complete bibliography. [RH]

1815 *Les Cahiers du patrimoine.* No. 11/12, jan./juin 1991, Dossier: Saint-Pierre, 1635–1902. Fort-de-France: Bureau du patrimoine du conseil régional de la Martinique.

Combines brief historical chronology of old Martinique port-town with description of its main public buildings, several testimonies on 1902 volcanic eruption that destroyed the city, and vignettes on literary and artistic activity (including that of women). Provides charming evocation of urban creole culture. [APD]

1816 Cash, Philip; Shirley C. Gordon; and Gail Saunders. Sources of Bahamian history. London; New York: Macmillan Caribbean, 1991. 374 p.: bibl., ill., index, map.

Valuable collection of documents consisting mostly of missionary reports, newspaper articles, letters, and official reports. Issues discussed include slavery, immigration, religious life, and economic conditions. Highly recommended for scholars of the region who wish to understand historical developments and the philosophy of the major figures from islands' past. [ELC]

1817 Coëta, René-Claude. Sinnamary: 1624–1848; une cité et des hommes. Préface de Elie Castor. Paris: L'Harmattan, 1992. 204 p.: bibl., ill.

Amateur genealogist hits upon rare documentation of 1840s slave cargo from Senegal. Fascinating details on descendants' families in western French Guiana. [APD]

Cultura cubana: una aproximación bibliográfica. See item **8.**

1818 Deen, Shamshu. Solving East Indian roots in Trinidad. Freeport Junction, Bahamas: H.E.M. Enterprises, 1994. 318 p.: bibl., ill., maps.

While reflecting author's attempt to reconstruct his own family history, book's greater significance rests in its highlighting of sources available for researching and understanding the history of East Indians in Trinidad. Of immense benefit to genealogists and others interested in reconstructing conditions faced by East Indian immigrants to Trinidad. [ELC]

1819 Díaz Soler, Luis M. Puerto Rico, desde sus orígenes hasta el cese de la dominación española. Río Piedras, P.R.: Editorial de la Univ. de Puerto Rico, 1994. 758 p.: bibl.

Organized as text for college-level course, book places island squarely in Spanish political context. As a consequence, author holds that island's struggle for cultural definition was interrupted by abrupt transfer to US domination. Because of author's long service in the classroom, volume acts as excellent reference source. [TMV]

1820 Espín Guillois, Vilma. La mujer en Cuba: historia; discursos, entrevistas, documentos. La Habana: Editorial de la Mujer, 1990. 117 p.

Far from a scholarly work, but still worthy of consideration in a largely neglected field. [JMH]

1821 García, Osvaldo. Fotografías para la historia de Puerto Rico, 1844–1952. 2. ed. Río Piedras, P. R.: Ediciones Huracán, 1993. 397 p.: bibl., index, photos.

Photographs alone make this book a treasure, although amount and quality of caption information vary. Notes advances in photographic techniques at several moments in history. [TMV]

1822 García Muñiz, Humberto and **Betsaida Vélez Natal.** Bibliografía militar del Caribe. Río Piedras, P.R.: Centro de Investigaciones Históricas, Facultad de Humanidades, Univ. de Puerto Rico-Recinto de Río Piedras,

1992. 177 p.: index. (Op. cit.—serie bibliográfica; 1)

Very useful research tool would have been even more helpful had authors included a brief comment about the value of at least the most important works. [JMH]

1823 Geggus, David P. Gabriel Debien, 1906–1990. (*HAHR*, 71 : 1, Feb. 1991, p. 140–142)

Obituary of French scholar who remains the single most important figure in historiography of pre-revolutionary Haiti. [JG]

1824 Geslin, Philippe. Archéologie de Saint-Pierre: novembre 1988. Dessins et relevés de Roger Mystille. Fort-de-France?: Collectif d'études et de recherches archéologiques de la Martinique; Assn. martiniquaise d'archéologie et d'ethnohistoire; Direction des antiquités préhistoriques et historiques de la Martinique, 1988. 94 p. : bibl., ill. (some col.). (Le Patrimoine archéologique de la Martinique; 3)

Report from the state agency responsible for archaeological excavation in historical quarter of Martinique's old port city provides: 1) maps showing spatial growth; 2) individual descriptions of buildings excavated; and 3) a note on building techniques and materials.

1825 Groot, Silvia W. de. Changing attitudes: politics of Maroons versus politics of the government in Surinam. (*in* International Conference of the Society of Caribbean Research, *1st, Berlin, 1988.* Proceedings. Frankfurt am Main: Vervuert, 1993, p. 7–20, bibl., tables)

Presents overview of relations between Maroons and Suriname government from 18th century to present. These relations are characterized by some constant factors as well as by changes and adjustments to existing situations. [RH]

1826 Guanche, Jesús. Significación canaria en el poblamiento hispánico de Cuba: los archivos parroquiales, 1690–1898. Prólogo de Sergio Valdés Bernal. La Laguna, Spain: Ayuntamiento de La Laguna, Centro de la Cultura Popular Canaria, 1992. 143 p.: bibl., ill. (Taller de historia; 12)

Based on research in 10 parochial archives, work confirms that of all migrations to Cuba, immigration from the Canary Islands during colonial period and early 20th

century was the most constant and contributed most to rapid growth of urban centers in central and western Cuba. A first-rate study. [JMH]

1827 Haïti à la une: une anthologie de la presse haïtienne de 1724 à 1934. v. 1, 1724–1864. Compilation de Jean Desquiron. Port-au-Prince: Imprimeur II, 1993. 1 v.: bibl.

Based on extensive research of Haitian newpapers and a comprehensive bibliography, combines historical survey of Haitian press, lists of periodicals and journalists, and excerpts from main titles throughout period covered. Particularly interesting data on provincial press and on that of the Haitian community in the Dominican Republic. [APD]

1828 Helg, Aline. Our rightful share: the Afro-Cuban struggle for equality, 1886–1912. Chapel Hill: Univ. of North Carolina Press, 1995. 361 p.: bibl., ill., index, map.

Well researched, but approaches subject from a "politically correct" US 1990s perspective. Too unbalanced to be a definitive study. Amounts to a monistic interpretation of Cuban history based on race and unsupported by the facts. [JMH]

1829 Hennessy, Alistair. The Hispanic and Francophone tradition. (*in* Intellectuals in the twentieth-century Caribbean. London: Macmillan Caribbean, 1992, v. 2, p. 1–35)

Thought-provoking piece on Hispanic and French intellectual traditions in the Caribbean, with reference to their English and Dutch counterparts, written by senior British scholar. Rich treatment of themes such as diaspora of literary authors, complexity of racial identity, political mobilization in universities, definition of intellectuals and their stances toward revolutions, and Caribbean-African connections. [APD]

1830 Hoogbergen, Wim S.M. Het kamp van Broos en Kaliko: de geschiedenis van een Afro-Surinaamse familie [The camp of Broos and Kaliko: the history of an Afro-Surinamese family]. Amsterdam: Prometheus, 1996. 212 p.: bibl., map, photos.

Well-written history focuses on the Suriname Maroon Landveld family, 1770–1994. Family members lived in the interior, on a deserted plantation, in Paramaribo, and in The Netherlands. Even though book is presented as oral history, most of pre-20th-century history is gleaned from archival sources and not supported by oral testimonies. [RH]

1831 Huyghues-Belrose, Vincent. Le littoral de la Guyane Française: perspectives historiques. (*Caribena/Martinique*, 2, 1992, p. 129–154, bibl., photos)

Creative essay focuses on environmental history of French Guyana coast, a "sphere of ephemeral achievements" in commercial agriculture from 1750 on. Drawing on physical and human geography, archival sources, field research, and aerial photography, analyzes initial obstacles, long-term handicaps, and development of water transportation. [APD]

1832 Jason, Mus-Cadynd Jean-Yves. Nature et état des fonds aux Archives Nationales d'Haïti. (*Chemins crit.*, 2:2, sept. 1991, p. 141–152, tables)

Important first report on status of long-neglected collections of the Archives Nationales d'Haïti clearly describes the different series and their state of physical preservation. [APD]

1833 Jourdain du Breuil, Yves. Histoire d l'habitation "Guischard" ou "Grand Parc" à la Basse-Terre de la Guadeloupe. (*Généal. hist. Caraïbe*, 67, jan. 1995, p. 1240–1243)

The remarkable stability enjoyed by a sugar estate and the richness of its documentation allows analysis of changing land use over almost three centuries. [APD]

Kulakova, N.N. Gaïtïĭsy: formirovanie ėtnosa (kolonial'naĭa ėpokha). See *HLAS 55: 811*.

1834 Lafleur, Gérard. Saint-Claude: histoire d'une commune de Guadeloupe. Préface de Simon Barlagne. Paris: Karthala, 1993. 362 p.: bibl., ill. (some col.), maps.

Fine example of local history successfully locates a microcosm within a broad framework. For a jurisdiction lying within old settlement of Basse-Terre, comprehensively reconstructs three centuries of plantation economy (first tobacco, ginger, and indigo; then sugar, coffee, and cattle; finally bananas and rum) as well as social changes brought about by French Revolution and abolition of slavery (new white local elites, a class of colored and black small planters, East Indian indentured workers). [APD]

1835 Lawaetz, Erik J. St. Croix: 500 years; pre-Columbus to 1990. Herning, Denmark: P. Kristensen, 1991. 494 p.: bibl., ill., index, maps.

Amateur historian from an old Dane-St. Croix family has compiled this wonderful social history of St. Croix with loving care. Rich iconography and data, particularly on 18th- and 19th-century free-coloreds (based on previous research by Eva Lawaetz); early 20th-century sugar plantations (based on 1891–1913 correspondence of his father, an overseer); and Hispanic immigrants from Puerto Rico, Vieques, and Culebra who came to work sugar in 1930s (based on interviews). [APD]

1836 Lebrón Saviñón, Mariano. Historia de la cultura dominicana. Santo Domingo: Comisión Oficial para la Celebración del Sesquicentenario de la Independencia Nacional, 1994. 3 v.: bibl., index. (Col. del sesquicentenario de la independencia nacional; 9)

Comprehensive study of Dominican intellectual life in its historical context is well written and documented. [JMH]

1837 Lenders, Maria. Strijders voor het Lam: leven en werk van Herrnhutter Broeders en -Zusters in Suriname, 1735–1900 [The Lamb's warriors: life and work of Moravian brothers and sisters in Suriname, 1735–1900]. Leiden, The Netherlands: KITLV Press, 1996. 451 p.: bibl., ill., map, photos. (KITLV Caribbean series; 16)

History of Moravian missionaries in Suriname provides detailed descriptions of daily lives of missionary families and their relations with each other and other population groups. Highlights interconnection between gender relations and class and race. Based on archival research in Germany, Suriname, and The Netherlands. [RH]

1838 Levine, Robert M. Tropical diaspora: the Jewish experience in Cuba. Gainesville: Univ. Press of Florida, 1993. 398 p.: bibl., ill., index, map.

Work is based, among other sources, on nearly 100 interviews with Cuban-Jewish immigrants, which lends it a lively quality. Also contains more than 75 rare photographs of Cuba and the Cuban Jewish community. Indeed a scholarly and well-written contribution. [JMH]

1839 López, José Ramón. Ensayos y artículos. Santo Domingo: Ediciones de la Fundación Corripio, 1991. 410 p.: ill. (Biblioteca de clásicos dominicanos; 10)

López, a journalist and fiction writer, stands out in the field of Dominican letters. Essays and articles included in this volume will certainly contribute to understanding politics and society in the Dominican Republic in late 19th and early 20th centuries. [JMH]

1840 Madiou, Thomas. Histoire d'Haïti. t. 1, 1492–1799. t. 2, 1799–1803. t. 3, 1804–1807. t. 4, 1807–1811. t. 5, 1811–1818. t. 6, 1819–1826. t. 7, 1827–1843. t. 8, 1843–1846. Port-au-Prince: H. Deschamps, 1985–1991. 8 v.: ill.

This authoritative and elegant edition by the first historian of the Haitian nation replaces that of 1922 and includes indexes and appendix of original documents.

1841 Marañón, Pedro Alonso. Los estudios superiores en Santo Domingo durante el período colonial: bibliografía crítica, metodogía y estado de la cuestión. (*Estud. Hist. Soc. Econ. Am.*, 11, 1994, p. 65–108, bibl.)

Extremely useful and enlightening bibliographical essay includes sober assessment of the current status of the study of higher education in the colonial period. [JMH]

1842 Mintz, Sidney W. Tasting food, tasting freedom. (*in* Slavery in the Americas. Edited by Wolfgang Binder. Würzburg, Germany: Königshausen and Neumann, 1993, p. 257–275, bibl.)

Highly original and significant essay concludes that food distribution and processing by slaves in Caribbean societies reflected enormous freedom of movement, "commercial maneuver, association and accumulation." Ultimately such activities may hold the key to understanding the totality of the slave experience, especially means of coping with slave life. [ELC]

1843 Moreno Fraginals, Manuel R. and **José J. Moreno Masó.** Guerra, migración y muerte: el ejército español en Cuba como vía migratoria. Gijón, Spain: Ediciones Júcar, 1993. 162 p.: bibl. (Cruzar el charco; 5)

Ground-breaking study focuses on Spanish armed forces as a vehicle for Spanish immigration into Cuba. [JMH]

1844 Moya Pons, Frank. The Dominican Republic: a national history. New Rochelle, N.Y.: Hispaniola Books Corporation, 1995. 544 p.: bibl., maps.

The only complete Dominican history available in English, this modern narrative of the economic, social, and political evolution of Dominican society from precolumbian times to present fills a gap in the literature. Includes a most useful bibliographic essay. [JMH]

1845 Obra historiográfica de Arturo Morales Carrión. Coordinación de María Dolores Luque de Sánchez y Juan E. Hernández-Cruz. San Germán, P.R.: Centro de Investigaciones Sociales del Caribe y América Latina, 1993. 80 p.: bibl.

Contains papers presented by leading historians at third conference organized to highlight Arturo Morales Carrión's contributions to Puerto Rican historiography. Authors collectively argue that Morales Carrión's work on 18th-century trade and 19th-century slavery, a product of the intellectual climate of the times, placed Puerto Rico's history in an international context. Also includes description of Morales Carrión's papers, available to the public as he himself organized them. [TMV]

1846 Olsen, Poul Erik. Toldvæsenet i Dansk Vestindien 1672–1917 [Customs administration in the Danish West Indies, 1672–1917]. Copenhagen: Toldhistorisk selskab, 1988. 261 p.: bibl., ill., index.

Work published by the Danish Customs Historical Society is illustrated with archival materials. Describes development of commercial policy and customs legislation for colonies in the Danish West Indies (St. Thomas, St. John, and St. Croix) acquired by Denmark in late 17th century and then sold to the US in 1917. First administered by the West Indian Guinea Co., the islands were placed under the Danish Crown in 1755. Laws, regulations, and uniforms of indigenous civil servants were created in Copenhagen for a different society, culture, and climate. Study acknowledges lack of supervision due to geographic distance and cultural differences, leading to problems such as inefficiency, bribery, and fraud. Notes significant role played by customs officials in the slave trade. Free trade area in current US

Virgin Islands is a heritage of Danish rule. [M.L. Bernal]

1847 Opatrný, Josef. Historical pre-conditions of the origin of the Cuban nation. Lewiston, N.Y.: E. Mellen Press, 1994. 248 p.: bibl., index.

Study of Cuba's origins by Eastern European scholar evidently well-versed in the literature on the subject. Some conclusions are worth pondering. [JMH]

1848 Paz Sánchez, Manuel de. Wangüemert y Cuba. v. 1. Prólogo de Consuelo Naranjo Orovio. Canary Islands: Centro de la Cultura Popular Canaria, 1991. 1 v.: bibl., ill. (Taller de Historia; 6)

Well-researched biography is nevertheless of doubtful relevancy in context of Canary Islanders' immigration to Cuba. Whether Wangüemert may be regarded as a prototype of these immigrants is highly debatable. [JMH]

1849 Pérotin-Dumon, Anne. Histoire et identité des Antilles françaises: les prémisses d'une historiographie moderne. (*Anu. Estud. Am.*, 51:2, 1994, p. 301–315)

First study of its kind, work analyzes dominant trends in French Caribbean historiography, 1840–1970. With 19th-century Romanticism, a historical tradition emerged that linked national independence and historical identity. Coinciding with the triumph of imperial history, positivism gave French Caribbean historiography the status of a discipline. In the 1940s an unprecedented social and intellectual mobilization in the Caribbean witnessed the decolonization of the French Empire. A new economic and social history of the French Antilles, breaking away from a markedly Eurocentric perspective, centered around the plantation society paradigm. [APD]

Pérotin-Dumon, Anne. Population, travail et urbanisme dans les villes de l'Amérique atlantique au XVIIIe siècle: Basse-Terre et Pointe-à-Pitre, Guadeloupe. See item **1955.**

1850 Picó, Fernando. El día menos pensado: historia de los presidiarios en Puerto Rico, 1793–1993. Río Piedras, P.R.: Ediciones Huracán, 1994. 198 p.: bibl., ill.

In an attempt to reach both a popular and scholarly readership, author presents

story of those convicted and serving jail sentences as history of marginalization, à la Annales school. Demonstrates familiarity with Foucault's work on social control and uniformity. Applies notion of "total institution" to show how prison infantilizes inmates and makes them dependent. Unfortunately, by purposefully identifying the "deviant" in socially conventional ways to indicate absurdity of the label, work never grapples with how "normality" is socially constructed. Creative use of sources—popular newspaper accounts, prisoners' idle comments, official handbooks on discipline, bureaucratic reports—illustrates value of imaginative research. [TMV]

1851 Porter, Whitworth and Mrs. Whitworth Porter. Views in the island of Dominica = Vues de la Dominique. Text by Lennox Honychurch and Geoffrey MacLean. Roseau, Dominica: Aquarela Galleries, 1988. 30 p.: ill. (some col.).

Collection of detailed photographs of buildings and other scenes from 18th-century Dominica also contains modern snaps of identical sites. Included are Government House, Roseau, and other aspects of local landscape. A brief commentary accompanies each. Includes foreword on present-day Dominica. Immensely valuable for individuals interested in island's history, landscape, and ecological changes. [ELC]

1852 Presencia judía en Santo Domingo. Edición de J. Alfonso Lockward. Santo Domingo: Taller, 1994. 231 p.: bibl.

Modest and unpretentious work helps fill a gap in Dominican historiography. [JMH]

1853 Los primeros turistas en Santo Domingo. Selección, prólogo y notas de Bernardo Vega. Santo Domingo: Fundación Cultural Dominicana, 1991. 315 p.: ill., indexes. (Publicaciones de la Fundación Cultural Dominicana)

Fascinating anthology relates impressions of some of the first foreigners who traveled to Dominican Republic between 1854 and 1929. As crucial for study of Dominican society as it is for exploring the prejudices of the island's visitors. [JMH]

1854 Puerto Rico. Oficina del Indice Histórico. Tesauro de datos históricos: índice compendioso de la literatura histórica de

Puerto Rico, incluyendo algunos datos inéditos, periodísticos y cartográficos. v. 2–4. Dirección de Aldofo de Hostos. Río Piedras, P.R.: Editorial de la Univ. de Puerto Rico, 1992–1994? 3 v.: bibl.

Carefully referenced compilation of popular and scholarly facts by noted historian serves as quick source for island's history up to mid-20th century. Conceptualized by the late Hostos as an alphabetical index, this work is at present 2/3 complete; four volumes are now in print. However, print format for such a publication may be considered somewhat impractical, considering the relative advantages of electronic bibliographic databases. For annotation of vol. 1, covering from A-E, see *HLAS 52:1599*. Vol. 2 covers F-H; vol. 3, I-M; and vol. 4, N-R. [TMV]

1855 Pumarada-O'Neill, Luis. La industria cafetalera de Puerto Rico, 1736–1969. San Juan: Oficina Estatal de Preservación Histórica, 1990. 195 p.: bibl., ill.

Relies on archaeological record, oral history, and architectural analysis to describe processes of production and marketing of coffee in 19th century. Maintains that coffee industry played an integral role in the development of Puerto Rican society. Offers valuable insights on connections between layout and function of the production units (*haciendas*) and the commercial establishments (*tahonas*). In addressing coffee industry's role in displacing peasants in the highlands and promoting foreign control of the economy, book must be placed among leading works on the subject by Baralt, Bergad, Buitrago Ortiz, and Picó. [TMV]

1856 Rossignol, Philippe and Bernadette Rossignol. Apports réciproques de la généalogie et de l'histoire antillaises. (*Généal. hist. Caraïbe*, 59, avril 1994, p. 1027–1031)

Experts in French Caribbean genealogy share their experience in promoting research with a historical bent. Stresses importance of migrations in the region, a factor that leads genealogical research beyond the borders of single islands. [APD]

1857 Rossignol, Philippe and Bernadette Rossignol. Familles parallèles à St. Domingue. (*Généal. hist. Caraïbe*, 62, juillet/août 1994, p. 1112–1114)

From careful reconstruction of both white and mulatto filial lines of 18th-century Saint Domingue planters, the best French Caribbean historical genealogists establish methodological guidelines for reconstructing genealogical filiation that has been partially obscured by racial prejudice. [APD]

1858 Sáez, José Luis. Breve resumen de historia de la Iglesia en Haití. (*Estud. Soc./Santo Domingo*, 27:98, oct./dic. 1994, p. 51–58)

Useful chronology of the Haitian Church from arrival of the first Franciscan missionaries (1493) to the 1993 assassination of Jean-Marie Vincent, a leading supporter of President Jean-Bertrand Aristide.

1859 Scarano, Francisco Antonio, Puerto Rico: cinco siglos de historia. San Juan: McGraw-Hill, 1993. 868 p.: bibl., ill. (some col.), index, maps.

High school textbook incorporates most recent historiographical currents in Puerto Rican history. Places island in Caribbean, Spanish-American, Spanish, and US context, as appropriate for time period. Rich in illustrations. [TMV]

1860 Sosa Rodríguez, Enrique. Importancia del contenido de los fondos del Archivo Nacional de Cuba para la historia de la República Dominicana. (*Ecos/Santo Domingo*, 1:2, 1993, p. 155–182, facsim.)

Lists and transcribes some of the Dominican papers extant in Cuba's National Archives. [JMH]

1861 Stranack, Ian. The Andrew and the Onions: the story of the Royal Navy in Bermuda, 1795–1975. 2nd ed. Bermuda: Bermuda Maritime Museum Press, 1990. 167 p.: bibl., ill., indexes, maps.

This second edition of the history of British Naval presence in Bermuda (first edition published in late 1970s) provides a lively account of British and Bermudan maritime history. Also includes discussion of US use of naval facilities in Bermuda as well as extremely valuable information on officers and daily activities at the base. [ELC]

1862 Tolentino Dipp, Hugo. Raza e historia en Santo Domingo: los orígenes del prejuicio racial en América. 2. ed. en castellano, versión ampliada. Santo Domingo: Fundación Cultural Dominicana, 1992. 296 p.: bibl., ill., index.

Author maintains that the servile work to which Africans and indigenous peoples were subjected was primarily responsible for the racial prejudices that arose in the New World. [JMH]

1863 Tolentino Rojas, Vicente. Historia de la division territorial [de la República Dominicana], 1492–1943. Santo Domingo: Sociedad Dominicana de Bibliófilos, 1993. 453 p.: bibl., ill., index, maps.

Although partially superseded by subsequent works, still a classic of Dominican history. [JMH]

1864 Venegas Delgado, Hernán. Regiones, provincias y localidades: historiografía regional cubana. Caracas: Fondo Editorial Tropykos, 1993. 118 p.: bibl.

Provides useful information about an important aspect of recent Cuban historiography. [JMH]

1865 Veuve, Serge. Saint-Pierre ville d'art et d'histoire. Martinique: Direction des antiquités historiques et préhistoriques de la Martinique; Collectif d'études et de recherches archéologiques de la Martinique, 1990. 103 p.: bibl., ill. (some col.), maps. (Col. Archéologie, patrimoine de la Martinique, 1145–2323; 5. Guides archéologiques de la Martinique; 1)

Guide to archaeological patrimony of Martinique's oldest port-town bears testimony to government's recent concern for historic preservation. [APD]

1866 Wonen in Suriname [Housing in Suriname]. (*OSO/Netherlands*, 11:1, 1992, p. 8–59, bibl., ill., photos)

Contains five articles on housing in Suriname. Discusses interior decoration in Paramaribo in 1920s, as well as Amerindian, Javanese, and East Indian architectural styles. [RH]

EARLY COLONIAL

Bernal Ponce, Juan. Ciudades del Caribe y Centroamérica: del siglo XV al siglo XIX. See item **148**.

1867 Buddingh', Bernard. Van Punt en Snoa: ontstaan en groei van Willemstad, Curaçao vanaf 1634; De Willemstad tussen 1700 en 1732 en de bouwgeschiedenis van de synagoge Mikvé Israël-Emanuel, 1730–1732 [Of

Punt and Snoa: the origin and development of Willemstad, Curaçao since 1634; Willemstad between 1700 and 1732; and the construction history of the Mikvé Israël-Emanuel Synagogue, 1730–1732]. 's-Hertogenbosch, The Netherlands: Aldus, 1994. 251 p.: bibl., ill. (some col.), maps (some col.).

Beautifully produced book is divided into sections describing development of De Punt, the area first settled by the Dutch; the reconstruction of a three-dimensional model of the town in the early 18th century; the various communities living in the town; and the Jewish presence in Curaçao. Includes 132 illustrations and a short summary in English. [RH]

1868 Burnard, Trevor. A failed settler society: marriage and demographic failure in early Jamaica. (*J. Soc. Hist.*, 28:1, Fall 1994, p. 63–82, bibl., tables)

Highly stimulating article examines reasons for Jamaica's failure to develop successfully as a settler society along the lines of other British North American colonies. Argues that demographic changes and high mortality rate among whites virtually doomed initial efforts. Island's development as plantation society accentuated earlier trends. [ELC]

1869 Camus, Michel Christian. Flibuste et pouvoir royal. (*Rev. Soc. haïti.*, 49:175, mars 1993, p. 5–15)

Specialist of early Haitian history traces efforts by the French crown in 1680s to curb activities of freebooters centered around Tortuga Island. Their employment as naval forces in rising imperial rivalries made this objective difficult to achieve. See also item **1870**. [APD]

1870 Camus, Michel Christian. L'île de la Tortue et la flibuste. (*Rev. Soc. haïti.*, 48:172, mars 1992, p. 1–7)

This comparison between Tortuga Island and the subsequent freebooting center of Jamaica shows latter's overwhelming preponderance. As a privateering base (and not just as a place of victualling), Jamaica issued most of the commissions after 1660 and inflicted major damage on Spanish shipping. The much-exaggerated fame of the freebooters of Tortuga stems from late additions to Oexquemelin's narrative, which attribute to the island actions that did not take place there. See also item **1869**. [APD]

1871 **Deagan, Kathleen A.** Europe's first foothold in the New World: La Isabela. (*Natl. Geogr. Mag.*, 181 : 1, Jan. 1992, p. 40–53, ill., map, photos)

Nicely illustrated, clearly written account combines recent findings in archaeology and history. See also item **1875**. [J. Britton]

1872 **Deagan, Kathleen A.** and **José María Cruxent.** From contact to *criollos*: the archaeology of Spanish colonization in Hispaniola. (*in* The meeting of two worlds: Europe and the Americas, 1492–1650. Edited by Warwick Bray. Oxford, England: Oxford Univ. Press; The British Academy, 1993, p. 67–103, bibl., ill., maps)

Examines archaeological projects in Hispaniola that provide data to explore the indigenous response to the arrival of Africans and Europeans, as well as the responses of the latter to the demands of colonial adjustment in the New World. For archaeologist's comment see *HLAS 55:493*. [JMH]

1873 **La découverte et la conquête de la Guadeloupe.** Direction de Alain Yacou et Jacques Adélaïde-Merlande. Pointe-à-Pitre, Guadeloupe: CERC, Univ. des Antilles et de la Guyane; Paris: Karthala, 1993. 303 p.: bibl., ill. (some col.), maps.

Guadeloupe historians explain to high school students the impact of Columbus' voyages on their island. Contributions by ethnologist Henri Petitjean-Roger stand out for their careful interpretation of the precolombian world and Carib linguistic heritage. [APD]

1874 **Deive, Carlos Esteban.** Las emigraciones canarias a Santo Domingo, siglos XVII y XVIII. Santo Domingo: Fundación Cultural Dominicana, 1991. 185 p.: bibl, map.

Solid piece of research based primarily on archival sources. [JMH]

1875 **Dobal, Carlos.** Como pudo ser La Isabela. Santiago, Dominican Republic: Depto. de Publicaciones, Pontificia Univ. Católica Madre y Maestra, 1988. 165 p.: bibl., ill., maps. (Col. Documentos; 128)

This history of the first city founded in the New World is the culmination of 20 years of research by the author. Work also led to construction of a maquette of the city. See also item **1871**. [JMH]

1876 **Flinkenflögel, Willem.** Nederlandse slavenhandel, 1621–1803. [Dutch slave trade, 1621–1803]. Utrecht, The Netherlands: Kosmos-Z&K Uitgevers, 1994. 136 p.: bibl., ill., index, maps. (Kosmos historisch)

Based on archival research, booklet on Dutch slave trade emphasizes its intercultural traits. First discusses economic, then ideological, aspects of the trade. The final chapter briefly surveys different forms of resistance, including vodun, rebellion, and marronage. Important recent studies on Suriname slavery and plantations are not listed in the bibliography. [RH]

1877 **Fuente, Alejandro de la.** Población y crecimiento en Cuba, siglos XVI y XVII: un estudio regional. (*Rev. Eur.*, 55, Dec. 1993, p. 59–93, bibl., graphs, tables)

Argues convincingly that demographic growth of Cuban villages in 17th century had to have been supported by parallel economic growth. Carefully written and researched. [JMH]

1878 **Games, Alison F.** Survival strategies in early Bermuda and Barbados. (*Rev. Rev. Interam.*, 22 : 1/2, primavera 1992, p. 55–71, bibl., tables)

By tracing experiences of some 5,000 17th-century immigrants from London, author examines islands' image in contemporary literature. Concludes that Barbadian immigrants fared much better than their Bermuda counterparts because of greater economic opportunities on Barbados, where land was available. [ELC]

1879 **García Rodríguez, Mercedes.** La Compañía del Mar del Sur y el asiento de esclavos en Cuba, 1715–1739. (*Santiago/Cuba*, 76, julio/dic. 1993, p. 121–170, bibl., tables)

Shows importance of slavery and slave trade in Cuba in first half of 18th century. [JMH]

1880 **Gautier, Arlette.** Les origines ethniques des esclaves déportés à Nippes, Saint-Domingue, de 1721 à 1770, d'après les archives notariales. (*Can. J. Afr. Stud.*, 23 : 1, 1989, p. 28–39, bibl., tables)

Uses notarial records to analyze ethnic composition of 1,812 African slaves in Saint Domingue's southern peninsula. Confirms that sex ratio and ethnic composition were closely linked in the colony, and casts doubt on importance of contraband slave trade to this region. [JG]

1881 Gemery, Henry A. and **James Horn.** British and French indentured servant migration to the Caribbean: a comparative study of 17th-century emigration and labor markets. (*in* El poblamiento de las Américas, *Veracruz, 1992*. Actas. Liège, Belgium: International Union for the Scientific Study of Population, 1992, v. 1, p. 283–299, bibl., tables)

Economic historians analyze major findings on unresolved issues about mass labor migrations during early Caribbean colonization. Indentured servants from both Britain and France were overwhelmingly male (women being shipped only when men were scarce), under 20, and from a broad social spectrum. However, British migration flow seems to have been four times larger than the French; the latter had other outlets within Europe, while for the many driven to English cities out of poverty, indentured immigration represented a unique option. [APD]

1882 Gravesande, Caesar N. Amerindian jurisdiction in the Guiana territory in the seventeenth and eighteenth centuries. (*Hist. Gaz.*, 44, May 1992, p. 2–14, map)

Supports view that Dutch jurisdiction over native peoples was more widespread than that of the Spanish. As officeholders in the realm of Dutch West India Company, some indigenous peoples fostered Dutch interests. Others served as slave catchers, acted to suppress slave revolts, and operated against enemies of the Dutch. [ELC]

1883 Gussinyer i Alfonso, Jordi. Congregación indígena y pueblos de indios en las Antillas, 1500–1525. (*Bol. Am.*, 34:44, 1994, p. 73–109, bibl.)

Examines failure of Spanish policy to establish towns of free indigenous peoples in the Antilles. Good piece of historical analysis. [JMH]

1884 Heijer, H.J. den. De geschiedenis van de WIC. Zutphen, The Netherlands: Walburg, 1994. 208 p.: bibl., ill., index, maps.

Richly illustrated, narrative history of the West-Indische Compagnie (WIC) from 1621–1791. First part discusses period of the "first WIC," including such themes as piracy, colonization, trade, and Dutch ventures in

Brazil. Second part concentrates on the "second WIC" and looks at internal organization, administration of the colonies, and the slave trade. Based on secondary literature and WIC archives in The Hague and Middelburg. [RH]

1885 Huerga, Alvaro. Los obispos de Puerto Rico en el siglo XVI. Ponce: Univ. Católica de Puerto Rico, 1988. 189 p.: bibl.

Three separate books (see also items **1886** and **1887**) trace ecclesiastical history of Puerto Rico through the tenure of bishops in 16th, 17th, and 18th centuries. Traditionally narrated and referenced, biographies contain rich data for social historians—witchcraft episodes, health and sanitary conditions, views on race, popular perceptions of government, etc. [TMV]

1886 Huerga, Alvaro. Los obispos de Puerto Rico en el siglo XVII. Ponce: Univ. Católica de Puerto Rico, 1989. 220 p.: bibl.

See item **1885.**

1887 Huerga, Alvaro. Los obispos de Puerto Rico en el siglo XVIII. Ponce: Univ. Católica de Puerto Rico, 1990. 228 p.: bibl.

See item **1885.**

1888 Huetz de Lemps, Christian. Indentured servants bound for the French Antilles. (*in* "To make America": European emigration in the early modern period. Berkeley: Univ. of California Press, 1991, p. 172–203)

French historian reviews the 17th-century practice, and draws from ongoing research to document changes after 1698: labor migrations became State-directed rather than spontaneous; migrations became centered in port of Bordeaux, replacing La Rochelle; and merchantmen were obliged to give free passage to from three to six servants, according to tonnage. In the 18th century an estimated 13,000 indentureds left the west and southwest inlands of France; they were all male and on average older than previous groups of indentured servants. [APD]

1889 Gli indios di Hispaniola e la prima colonizzazione europea in America. Edited by Brunetto Chiarelli. Firenze, Italy: Istituto geografico militare, 1991. 95 p.: bibl., ill. (some col.).

Contains proceedings of symposium on Hispaniola's indigenous peoples and first European settlers held in Florence, Italy, on

October 11, 1989. Included are reports of the scholars that made up the Commissione autonoma del progetto La Isabela. Extremely interesting and informative. [JMH]

Klooster, Wim and **Gert Oostindie.** El Caribe holandés en la época de la esclavitud. See item **1941.**

1890 Kupperman, Karen Ordahl. Providence Island, 1630–1641: the other Puritan colony. Cambridge; New York: Cambridge Univ. Press, 1993. 393 p.: bibl., index.

Sophisticated treatment of failed efforts by Providence Island Company to create prosperous colony. Rather than using local individuals familiar with environment, Company's backers initiated flawed design by promoting tenantry and sending from England officials and soldiers to protect their interests. Thus colony failed to follow path of other successful mainland Puritan colonies. Well documented. Excellent work. [ELC]

1891 Lafleur, Gérard. Les Caraïbes des Petites Antilles. Paris: Karthala, 1992. 270 p.: bibl.

Relying on archival records and French missionaries' chronicles, traces "Franco-British-Carib conflict" from 17th century to 1796. Expelled by European colonial powers from Lesser Antilles, Caribs sought refuge on the "neutral islands" of Saint Vincent and Dominica. Used as pawns by the European powers (but consistently siding with the French), they were finally deported to Honduras by the English after the English defeated the French at end of 18th century. Contains useful bibliography and list of archival sources. See also item **1892.** [APD]

1892 Lafleur, Gérard. The passing of a nation: the Carib Indians of the Lesser Antilles. (*in* Association of Caribbean Historians. Conference. *24th, Nassau, Bahamas, 1992.* Amerindians, Africans, Americans: three papers in Caribbean history presented at the 24th Annual Conference of the Association of Caribbean Historians, Nassau, The Bahamas. Mona, Jamaica: Univ. of the West Indies, 1993, p. 27–45)

Summarizes author's recent book on same topic (see item **1891.**) [APD]

1893 Langhorne, Elizabeth Coles. Worlds collide on Vieques: an intimate portrait from the time of Columbus. New York: Rivercross Pub., 1992. 88 p.: bibl., ill.

Short book written for a popular readership concentrates on native American perspective. [J. Britton]

1894 López Cantos, Angel. La religiosidad popular en Puerto Rico, siglo XVIII. s.l.: Centro de Estudios Avanzados de Puerto Rico y el Caribe, 1993. 65 p.: bibl.

Author cites rich materials and narrates enticing stories about popular beliefs and practices surrounding birth, life, and death within the Catholic tradition, topics virtually unexplored by historians. Unfortunately, rather than offering readers coherent explanations, this tiny book forces them to seek a satisfactory understanding elsewhere. [TMV]

Menezes, Mary Noel. The controversial question of protection and jurisdiction re: the Amerindians of Guyana. See item **1950.**

1895 Mira Caballos, Esteban. El pleito Diego Colón-Francisco de Solís: el primer proceso por malos tratos a los indios en La Española, 1509. (*Anu. Estud. Am.,* 50:2, 1993, p. 309–343)

Covers judicial proceedings crucial for understanding questions that have remained rather obscure, such as how Spanish and Indians really saw each other. [JMH]

1896 Moya Pons, Frank. Legitimación ideológica de la Conquista: el caso de La Española. (*in* De palabra y obra en el Nuevo Mundo. v. 2, Encuentros interétnicos. Edición de Miguel León-Portilla. Madrid: Siglo Veintiuno Editores, 1992, p. 63–78, tables)

This article actually examines the Conquest in Hispaniola. Author does not say a word about ideology or legitimation of the Spanish Conquest, which are far different subjects. [JMH]

1897 Ramos Gómez, Luis Javier. Cristóbal Colón y los indios taínos, de octubre de 1492 a diciembre de 1494. Valladolid, Spain: Casa-Museo de Colón; Seminario Americanista de la Univ. de Valladolid, 1993. 214 p.: bibl. (Cuadernos colombinos; 18)

Offers concise introduction to a well-studied subject. [JMH]

1898 Ramos Gómez, Luis Javier. Marzo y abril de 1494 en La Española: de la política de "conversación y familiaridad" a la de la "imposición y violencia." (*in* Memoria, creación e historia: luchar contra el olvido. Coordinación de Pilar García Jordán, Miguel

Izard y Javier Laviña. Barcelona: Univ. de Barcelona, 1993, p. 93–107, bibl.)

Offers dispassionate and informative analysis of change in Spanish policy vis-à-vis the indigenous peoples at beginning of the Conquest. [JMH]

1899   Sheridan, Richard B. Sugar and slavery: an economic history of the British West Indies, 1623–1775. Foreword by Hilary Beckles. Kingston: Canoe Press, 1994. 529 p.: bibl., index, maps.

Twenty-first anniversary reprint of book that has become standard reference for students of British Caribbean economic history (see *HLAS 38: 2833*). Shows transformation of islands' society and economy in response to demands of monocultural sugar cultivation. Contains new preface by Hilary Beckles, one of Sheridan's strongest supporters. Invaluable study. [ELC]

1900   Veloz Maggiolo, Marcio and **Elpidio Ortega.** La fundación de la villa de Santo Domingo: un estudio arqueo-histórico. Santo Domingo: Comisión Dominicana Permanente para la Celebración del Quinto Centenario del Descubrimiento y Evangelización de América, 1992. 277 p.: bibl., ill. (some col.), maps. (Col. Quinto centenario. Serie Historia de la ciudad; 1)

Informative, scholarly account of archaeological excavations carried out in late 1980s to determine location of the first village of Santo Domingo. [JMH]

LATE COLONIAL AND FRENCH REVOLUTIONARY PERIOD

1901   Adélaïde-Merlande, Jacques. La situation dans les colonies espagnoles d'Amérique en juillet 1808, vue par Victor Hugues. (*Espace caraïbe*, 1, 1993, p. 39–48)

Publishes original report forwarded to the French government by Victor Hugues, governor of French Guiana, following Napoleon's invasion of Spain. Hugues' appraisal of public opinion in Spanish-American colonies towards eventuality of French rule displays the political acumen of this well-known revolutionary figure. [APD]

1902   Amores Carredano, Juan Bosco. La Sociedad Económica de La Habana y los intentos de reforma universitaria en Cuba, 1793–1842. (*Estud. Hist. Soc. Econ. Am.*, 9, 1992, p. 369–394, graph)

Excellent contribution is based on serious research. Author knows the period well and certainly understands the problems that Cuba faced at the time. [JMH]

1903   La bataille de Vertières. (*Rev. Soc. haïti.*, 47:170, sept. 1991, p. 33–36)

Contemporary account by anonymous French author describes the Nov. 1803 capture of Cap Français by black armies. Includes several documents relating to surrender of the town. [JG]

1904   Beckles, Hilary. White women and slavery in the Caribbean. (*Hist. Workshop*, 36, Autumn 1993, p. 66–84, table)

Makes urgent plea for examination of role of white women in Caribbean slave societies. Were they the conscience of the system, as were their counterparts in US? Prior studies have relegated these women to an historical afterthought and contributed to the view of them as parasitic. This work points out that they were economic actors, managers of slave-based households, and conduits in the socio-ideological transmission. [ELC]

1905   Bénot, Yves. Comment la Convention a-t-elle voté l'abolition de l'esclavage en l'an II? (*Ann. hist. Revolut. fr.*, 293/294, juillet/sept. 1993, p. 349–361)

Argues, with evidence, that despite unanimity of the vote in the French Assemblée to abolish slavery in Feb. 1794, there still was considerable opposition to this measure in the revolutionary Convention. [JG]

1906   Bénot, Yves. La démence coloniale sous Napoléon: essai. Paris: Editions La Découverte, 1992. 407 p.: bibl., index. (Textes à l'appui. Série Histoire contemporaine)

In the vein of post-World War II anti-colonialist literature, journalist argues that colonial enterprises were an "integral part" of Napoleon's project of conquest. Although marred by a judgmental perspective on the period as a "return to colonial barbarism of the Ancien Régime," work is rich in original data. [APD]

Bernal Ponce, Juan. Ciudades del Caribe y Centroamérica: del siglo XV al siglo XIX. See item **148.**

1907   Bonneterre, Guy Gotreau Roussel. La dissidence de Marie-Galante. (*Généal. hist. Caraïbe*, 65, nov. 1994, p. 1188–1189)

Family papers throw light on originality of French revolutionary process in

Guadeloupe's dependency: white elites remained in power while taking measures to abolish slavery gradually. [APD]

1908 Bosman, L. Nieuw Amsterdam in Berbice, Guyana: de planning en bouw van een koloniale stad, 1764–1800 [Nieuw Amsterdam in Berbice, Guyana: planning and construction of a colonial town, 1764–1800]. Hilversum, The Netherlands: Verloren, 1994. 92 p.: bibl., ill., maps. (Zeven Provinciën reeks; 9)

Nice little monograph details the laborious decision-making process, or rather the lack thereof, for the planning and construction of Nieuw Amsterdam, in the context of Dutch colonial policy. Lack of knowledge, interest, and money in Holland—and shortage of capable personnel in Berbice—led to many delays and changes in the original plans. Within a few years after its construction the new town was conquered by the English, who renamed it New Amsterdam. [RH]

1909 Branson, Susan. Les réfugiés de Saint-Domingue à Philadelphie dans les années 1790 [St. Domingan refugees in the Philadelphia community in the 1790s]. (*in* Association of Caribbean Historians. Conference. *24th, Nassau, Bahamas, 1992.* Amerindians, Africans, Americans: three papers in Caribbean history presented at the 24th Annual Conference of the Association of Caribbean Historians, Nassau, The Bahamas. Mona, Jamaica: Univ. of the West Indies, 1993, p. 69–84)

Based on judicial records, offers a fascinating evocation of the 750 masters and 500 slaves who, following revolution in Saint Domingue, emigrated to the then largest US city. Documents unusual emancipation process: child slaves were contracted to work until reaching majority age in order to calm neighboring states anxious at the prospect of a massive emancipation had Pennsylvania law been enforced. Shows how *castes* were treated differently, and how their common Catholic culture set them apart from Philadelphians. Suggests possibility of tracing descendants of creole free-colored artisans. [APD]

1910 Brown, Wallace. The American Loyalists in Jamaica. (*J. Caribb. Hist.*, 26:2, 1992, p. 121–146, tables)

Argues that, with exception of the Na-tive Baptists who made a lasting contribution, the Loyalists' impact on Jamaica was minimal—especially when compared to their Bahamian counterparts—despite the considerable amount of money Jamaican authorities spent on assisting and relocating American Loyalists. [ELC]

1911 Brown, Wallace. The governorship of John Orde, 1783–1793: the Loyalist period in Dominica. (*J. Caribb. Hist.*, 24:2, 1990, p. 146–177, tables)

Claims that the major challenge facing Orde was settlement of American Loyalists. Author also discusses Orde's tumultuous relationship with his assembly, and difficulties he faced in dealing with maroon activity. The use of "favorable" petitions Orde received when he left the island as a measurement of the overall success of his administration demonstrates definite planter bias. [ELC]

1912 Butel, Paul. L'essor de l'économie de la plantation à Saint Domingue dans la deuxième moitié du XVIIIe siècle. (*Bull. Cent. hist. atl.*, 6, 1933, p. 61–75)

Assesses new findings on French colonial trade as well as on plantation management and profits. Stresses primacy of sugar among European demands for colonial goods, and Saint Domingue's unique asset of land diversity that allowed coffee as an alternative crop. [APD]

1913 El Caribe en la encrucijada de su historia, 1780–1840. Coordinación de Juan Manuel de la Serna. México: Univ. Nacional Autónoma de México, Coordinación de Humanidades, Centro Coordinador y Difusor de Estudios Latinoamericanos, 1993. 109 p.: bibl. (Panoramas de Nuestra América; 8)

Four of the scholarly papers included in this slender volume deal with aspects of Cuba's colonial history. [JMH]

1914 Carrington, Selwyn H. The American Revolution, British policy and the West Indian economy, 1775–1808. (*Rev. Rev. Interam.*, 22:1/2, primavera 1992, p. 72–108, bibl., tables)

Author asserts that because British Caribbean colonies experienced severe hardships during American Revolutionary War, most expected normalization of relationship with US in order to maintain their vitality. But their continued reliance on Ireland, England, or Canada forced them to "retain anti-capitalist methods of production in a fast developing finance capitalist society which had focused its development on industrialization." [ELC]

1915 Cauna de Ladevie, Jacques. La diaspora des colons de Saint-Domingue et le monde créole: le cas de la Jamaïque. (*Rev. fr. hist. Outre-mer*, 81:304, 1994, p. 333–359)

Following a good review of existing information about Saint Domingan colonists who fled to Jamaica during the French Revolution, work provides fresh data from private memoirs and genealogical records on: 1) the brief stay of most refugees, who were soon expelled by the English; 2) the streams of French prisoners of war, many of them colored and very different from royalist *émigres*; and 3) integration of coffee planters, French free-coloreds, and slaves who settled into Jamaican society and economy. [APD]

1916 Cauna de Ladevie, Jacques. Les difficultés de l'insertion pour un "petit-blanc" à Saint-Domingue: le cas type de Joinville-Gauban. (*Bull. Cent. hist. atl.*, 6, 1993, p. 99–115)

Based on printed autobiography, traces typical career of a young supervisor on a coffee (and then sugar) plantation. Provides fascinating details of French immigrants' life, social networks, race relations, and the extraordinarily hard work demanded by sugar-making. [APD]

1917 Cauna de Ladevie, Jacques. La famille et la descendance de Toussaint-Louverture. (*Rev. Soc. haïti.*, 46:164, sept./déc. 1989, p. 79–83)

Useful description of Haitian founding father's family. Traces his descendants in Haiti and France. [APD]

1918 Cauna de Ladevie, Jacques. Image et accueil de la Révolution française à Saint-Domingue. (*Conjonction/Port-au-Prince*, 181, 1989, p. 61–91)

Provides useful list of possibilities for future research in this field, including unexamined documents and personages, and new methodologies. [JG]

1919 Cauna de Ladevie, Jacques. M.J. Leremboure, premier maire de Port-au-Prince, 1791–1792. (*Rev. Soc. haïti.*, 46:164, sept./déc. 1989, p. 22–28)

Drawing on private papers held in south of France, gives biographical vignette of

colonial Haiti's first mayor during the Revolution, a wealthy planter and controversial figure assassinated in 1804. [APD]

1920 Cauna de Ladevie, Jacques. L'odyssée d'un esclave musulman du Sénégal à Versailles en passant par Tobago. (*Rev. Soc. haïti.*, 165, 1990, p. 59–61)

Publishes a 1787 document from the French National Archives describing a young Senegalese man who was sold into slavery by an English captain and who eventually came to the court at Versailles. [JG]

1921 Congreso Internacional de Historia Económica y Social de la Cuenca del Caribe, 1763–1898, 1st, San Juan, 1987. Primer Congreso Internacional de Historia Económica y Social de la Cuenca del Caribe, 1763–1898. San Juan, P.R.: Centro de Estudios Avanzados de Puerto Rico y el Caribe, 1992. 790 p.: bibl., ill., maps.

These papers presented at Interamerican University conference commemorating arrival of Europeans in Caribbean Basin cover a wide range of topics: slave trade and abolition, administrative and fiscal matters, trade and navigation, emigration, and social stratification. Contributors hail from almost all of the Spanish American republics, several European countries, and North America. Volume emphasizes interconnectedness of the Caribbean islands and treats them as a region. [TMV]

1922 Cuba ilustrada: la Real Comisión de Guantánamo, 1796–1802. Barcelona: Lunwerg Editores, 1991. 2 v.: col. ill., maps.

Vol. 1, an appealing book, beautifully printed and illustrated, includes a number of well-researched essays on the 18th-century expedition of the Conde del Mopox to explore and study Cuba's natural resources. Also includes catalogs of maps, blueprints, and other documents produced or used by Mopox expedition. Vol. 2 consists primarily of color reproductions of Guio's drawings of Cuban plants. [JMH]

1923 Debien, Gabriel. A propos du trésor de Toussaint-Louverture. (*Rev. Soc. haïti.*, 46:164, sept./déc. 1989, p. 84–93)

In one of his last publications, French pioneer in Caribbean history provides useful details on properties acquired by Toussaint-Louverture from the 1790s, when he rose to power. [APD]

1924 Deive, Carlos Esteban. Las emigraciones dominicanas a Cuba: 1795–1808. Santo Domingo: Fundación Cultural Dominicana, 1989. 159 p.: bibl.

Sheds light on the relatively unexplored subject of Saint Domingan emigration to Cuba. [JMH]

1925 Devezeau, Michel E.M.; Philippe Rossignol; and Bernadette Rossignol. La famille Devezeau aux Antilles. (*Généal. hist. Caraïbe*, 61, juillet/août 1994, p. 1064–1068)

Geneaology of a white planter family in late 18th-century Saint Domingue throws light on militia's role in colonial life and as a symbol of social status. [APD]

1926 Estrade, Paul and Anne Pérotin-Dumon. Les Antilles espagnoles, 1770–1855. (*in* Les révolutions dans le monde ibérique: soulèvement national et révolution libérale, état des questions. Talence, France: Presses universitaires de Bordeaux; Paris: Diffusion C.I.D., 1991, v. 2, p. 47–111)

Notwithstanding title, gives overview of independence era in Spanish and French Caribbean. French specialists analyze political and military evolution, and ideological, economic, and social forces impacting on it, in addition to reviewing the historiography and suggesting topics for further research. Pt. 1 assesses impact of the French Revolution and Pt. 2, the two liberal periods of Spanish colonial government (1810–12 and 1821–23). Covers wide range of topics including repeated invasions and occupations of Santo Domingo by Haitian armies of former slaves operating in the name of revolutionary France; "fidelity" to Spain by Cuban *hacendados* who also launched a successful sugar economy; and little-studied revolutionary movements on the Spanish islands in the 1830s-40s that demonstrated the growing differences among them. [APD]

1927 Fernández García, Angel Valentín. D. Felipe José de Trespalacios y Verdeja: obispo de Puerto Rico, erector del Obispado de La Habana y su primer obispo. Edición de Roberto Fernández Valledor. Ramey, P.R.: Editorial Datum, 1993. 284 p.: bibl., ill.

Extensively researched work is significant contribution to 18th-century history of Catholic Church in Cuba, Dominican Republic, and Puerto Rico. Archbishop Trespalacios is important because of his serious confrontations with secular authorities. [JMH]

1928 Fiehrer, Thomas M. Saint-Domingue/Haiti: Louisiana's Caribbean connection. (*La. Hist.*, 30, 1989, p. 431–435)

Offers rapid survey of colonial Haiti, the French Revolution, and resulting refugee tide, with an eye to illuminating Louisiana history. Based on secondary sources; some details are not entirely reliable. [JG]

Flinkenflögel, Willem. Nederlandse slavenhandel, 1621–1803. [Dutch slave trade, 1621–1803]. See item **1876.**

Fornet, Ambrosio. El libro en Cuba: siglos XVIII y XIX. See item **2017.**

1929 Forster, Robert. The French Revolution, people of color, and slavery. (*in* The global ramifications of the French Revolution. Washington: Woodrow Wilson Center Press; Cambridge, England; New York: Cambridge Univ. Press, 1994, p. 89–104)

A prominent historian of France examines impact of that country's refusal to consider how its revolution might be interpreted by colonial free people of color and by slaves. Essay, based on primary and secondary sources, focuses on Saint Domingue, paying greatest attention to the period 1789–91. [JG]

1930 Foubert, Bernard. Les habitations Laborde à Saint-Domingue dans la seconde moitié du XVIIIème siécle. (*Rev. Soc. haïti.*, 48:174, déc. 1992, p. 3–14)

Using an impressive array of public and private European sources, author reconstructs economy and society of three plantations in Les Cayes, southern Saint Domingue, from their beginnings in 1760s to their destruction from war, emigration, and desertion between 1793 and 1803. Findings include: 1) a good profit rate (7 percent) was achieved as a result of strong investment and management; 2) a predominance of Congolese-origin slaves (75 percent among 1,440); and 3) an absence of natural population growth, which correlated with reliance on slave trade. Valuable documentation of managers' repeated unsuccessful attempts during the revolutionary period to reestablish operations, and of struggles between coloreds and blacks for control. [APD]

1931 Garrigus, John D. Blue and brown: contraband indigo and the rise of a free colored planter class in French Saint-Domingue. (*Americas/Francisc.*, 50:2, Oct. 1993, p. 233–263, graphs, maps, tables)

Superbly researched article breaks new ground in history of patterns of race relations in context of 18th-century Atlantic merchant economies. Documents rise of colored indigo planters in peripheral region of southwest Saint Domingue and formation of their wealth, which was tied to contraband networks in Curaçao and Jamaica. Traces several generations of miscegenation on the part of French planters and prominent Jewish merchant families that, through marriages or consensual unions, blurred differences between whites and coloreds. An official recasting of race in 1760s-80s swelled free-colored category in the census and laid the ground for a social protest most forcefully articulated by Julien Raimond in the late Ancien Régime and in the French revolutionary assemblies. [APD]

1932 Garrigus, John D. Catalyst or catastrophe? Saint-Domingue's free men of color and the Battle of Savannah, 1779–1782. (*Rev. Rev. Interam.*, 22:1/2, primavera 1992, p. 109–125, bibl.)

Provides long-needed focus on colonial militias in French Caribbean and their significance in formation of a free-colored identity. Studies 545 freedmen veterans of the American Revolution, whom colonial authorities tried to transform into regular reserve troops upon their return to Saint Domingue. Freedmen proved reluctant to continue in a demanding service that brought them little. [APD]

1933 Geggus, David P. The demographic composition of the French Caribbean slave trade. (*in* French Colonial Historical Society. Meetings. *13th, Indiana Univ., South Bend, 1987* and *14th, Natchez, Miss., 1988.* Proceedings. Lanham, Md.: University Press of America, 1990, p. 14–30)

Drawing on the same primary sources used for his other articles on the slave trade (see item **1934**), Geggus again suggests that African suppliers exerted the most influence on the gender composition of this commerce. Explores effect of this composition on French Caribbean slave societies, noting that Saint Domingue, especially that area where the Haitian Revolution began in 1791, received an exceptional concentration of adult males as compared to Martinique and Guadeloupe. [JG]

1934 Geggus, David P. Sex ratio, age and ethnicity in the Atlantic slave trade: data from French shipping and plantation records. (*J. Afr. Hist.*, 30, 1989, p. 23–44)

Impressive research throws significant new light on French slave economy, particularly in offering human dimensions to hitherto undifferentiated African origins. Using Jean Mettas' compendium of French slave expeditions (see *HLAS 48:2449*) and author's own analysis of 13,000 individual cases registered in 400 plantation inventories (see *HLAS 48:2430* and *HLAS 52:1660*), work focuses on Saint Domingue rural slaves. Reveals much larger variations in demographic composition among slaves exported than previously known, such variations possibly result of organization of slave trade within Africa. Compellingly demonstrates importance of gender perspective in slavery studies, and opens path to further research on the more than 100 ethnic labels used to describe African origins—a challenge "to decipher rather than to dismiss." See also item **1933**. [APD]

1935 Geggus, David P. Sugar and coffee production in Saint Domingue and the shaping of the slave labor force. (*in* Cultivation and culture: labor and the shaping of slave life in the Americas. Charlottesville: Univ. of Virginia Press, 1993, p. 73–98)

Uses slave lists from 100 sugar plantations and 107 coffee estates to describe different social worlds created on each of these two plantatation types. Reveals that Saint Domingan plantations were generally smaller and more creolized than earlier scholars have suggested. Considers slaves' ethnic origins, gender ratio, and fertility for each plantation type, while noting that lives of coffee and sugar slaves also differed greatly depending on which of Saint Domingue's three provinces they inhabited. [JG]

1936 Gutiérrez Escudero, Antonio. Diferencias entre agricultores y ganaderos en Santo Domingo, siglo XVIII. (*Ecos/Santo Domingo*, 1:2, 1993, p. 45–76, tables)

Deals with conflict between regions controlled by cities of Santo Domingo and Santiago de los Caballeros, and shows how conflict was conditioned by presence of the French in the west of Hispaniola. Uses both primary and secondary sources. [JMH]

1937 Hernández González, Pablo J. La comarca de Vuelta Abajo, isla de Cuba, en 1755: recuento de un obispo ilustrado. (*Anu. Estud. Am.*, 50:1, 1993, p. 251–268)

Bishop Morel de Santa Cruz's report, transcribed in this article, is a key document for study of the Catholic Church in colonial Cuba. [JMH]

1938 Hopkins, Daniel. An extraordinary eighteenth-century map of the Danish sugar-plantation island St. Croix. (*Imago Mundi/London*, 41, 1989, p. 44–58, bibl., maps)

Analyzes cadastral and topographic map ca.1750 by Cronenberg and Jaegersberg that surpasses all others for its accuracy, beauty, and richness of information on St. Croix's economic development, land use, and settlements. [APD]

1939 Hurst, Ronald. The Golden Rock: an episode of the American War of Independence. London: Lee Cooper, 1996. 254 p.: map, photos.

Popular account relates capture of St. Eustatius in 1781. The British seized the island from the Dutch to put an end to its role as major supplier of arms and necessities to rebel Americans in the War of Independence. Based on contemporary records and secondary sources, but lacks bibliography and footnotes. [RH]

1940 Images de la révolution à St.-Domingue. Compilation de Michèle Oriol. Port-au-Prince: Fondation pour la recherche iconographique et documentaire: Editions Henri Deschamps, 1992. 197 p.: bibl., ill., maps (1 col.).

Combines handsome illustrations and official texts from the time of the Haitian Revolution with a brief chronology. [APD]

1941 Klooster, Wim and **Gert Oostindie.** El Caribe holandés en la época de la esclavitud. (*Anu. Estud. Am.*, 51:2, 1994, p. 233–259)

Provides elementary overview of historiography of Suriname and Dutch Leewards and Windwards from late 16th century to abolition of slavery in 1863. Also lists a number of documents on the Dutch (military) presence in the Caribbean held by the Archivo de Indias in Seville. [RH]

1942 König, Hans-Joachim. The *Código Negrero* of 1789: its background and its reverberations. (*in* Slavery in the Americas. Edited by Wolfgang Binder. Würzburg, Germany: Königshausen and Neumann, 1993, p. 141–150, bibl.)

Offers scholarly and enlightening discussion of the *Código*. [JMH]

1943 Lacerte, Robert K. The evolution of land and labour in the Haitian Revolution, 1791–1820. (*in* Caribbean freedom: society and economy from emancipation to the present. Kingston: Randle, 1993, p. 42–47, table)

Based largely on secondary sources, discusses landholding policy of Haiti's first political leaders. Concerned with reviving the economy, Toussaint Louverture tried to revive the plantations; but Pétion, by parcelling out lands, "decided the agrarian future of Haiti." [APD]

1944 Laurence, K.O. Tobago in wartime, 1793–1815. Barbados: The Press Univ. of the West Indies, 1995. 280 p.: bibl., ill., index, maps.

Examines impact of French revolutionary wars on Tobago's development. While his argument that wars impeded economic growth and hindered political stability is hardly earthshattering, he provides important data on slavery, economy, and population that places island more firmly in consciousness of historians of twin island nation of Trinidad and Tobago. [ELC]

1945 Le manuscrit de Mare-à-la-Roche. (*Rev. Soc. haïti.*, 47:170, sept. 1991, p. 22–32)

Publishes extracts from a planter's expense-and-copy book begun in 1774 and correspondence from 1783–1804. Author is identified only as "Agard au cap françois." [JG]

1946 Marichal, Carlos and **Matilde Souto Mantecón.** Silver and *situados:* New Spain and the financing of the Spanish Empire in the Caribbean in the eighteenth century. (*HAHR*, 74:4, Nov. 1994, p. 587–613, tables)

Although not a seminal article, work does break new ground as to importance of the *situados ultramarinos* and their role in complex finances of the Spanish Empire. [JMH]

1947 Marie-Sainte, Daniel. Les registres de catholicité et d'état civil de Goyave: balisage et parcours guidé. (*Généal. hist. Caraïbe*, 64, oct. 1994, p. 1168–1171)

Analysis of parish registers in Guadeloupe dating from 1759–1835 produces a microhistory of a slave society confronting institutional and political change. [APD]

Marrero, Leví. Cuba: economía y sociedad. v. 15, Azúcar, Ilustración y conciencia, 1763–1868: part III. See *HLAS 55:1696.*

1948 McDonald, Roderick A. The Duff House/Montcoffer Papers: a documentary source for the history of the British West Indies, with particular emphasis on Jamaica. (*J. Caribb. Hist.*, 26:2, 1992, p. 210–215)

Briefly describes plantation and other records of Scottish family. Records deal mostly with management and economic matters on Jamaican plantations for 18th century, although some address Caribbean-wide affairs especially relating to the American Revolution. Useful. [ELC]

1949 McGowan, Winston F. The French revolutionary period in Demerara-Essequibo, 1792–1802. (*Hist. Gaz.*, 55, April 1993, p. 2–18, ill., tables)

Argues that revolutionary period initially witnessed enormous economic uncertainty and political confusion in this Dutch colony. However, after 1796 takeover by British, political stability and economic growth ensued. Thus, revolutionary period constituted vital stage in transformation from Dutch to British influence and ultimately British possession. [ELC]

1950 Menezes, Mary Noel. The controversial question of protection and jurisdiction re: the Amerindians of Guyana. (*SWI Forum*, 9:1/2, Okt. 1992, p. 7–24, bibl., map, photo)

Author evaluates some stereotypical European attitudes towards indigenous peoples in British Guiana, and elucidates the ambivalent and difficult practical situation on which relations were based, especially regarding the administration of justice. [ELC]

1951 Noël, Eric. Le sucre des Iles, ou l'or blanc des Beauharnais à la fin de l'Ancien régime. (*Bull. Cent. hist. atl.*, 6, 1993, p. 77–98)

Thorough study focuses on well-man-aged sugar plantation in plain of Léogane, Saint Domingue, owned by French aristocratic family at end of 18th century. [APD]

1952 Oliver, Vere Langford. The monumental inscriptions in the churches and churchyards of the island of Barbados, British West Indies. 1st Borgo ed. San Bernardino, Calif.: Borgo Press; Glendale, Calif.: Sidewinder Press, 1989. 223 p.: bibl. (Stokvis studies in historical chronology and thought, 0270–5338; 13)

Originally published in 1915 in a limited edition of 200 copies, this compendium is a gold mine for genealogical research. Includes all churchyards as well as the Jewish burial-grounds in Bridgetown, with the latter indicating how many Sephardic Jews from Portugal had made their way there. [B. Tenenbaum]

1953 Oostindie, Gert. The Enlightenment, Christianity and the Suriname slave. (*J. Caribb. Hist.*, 26:2, 1992, p. 147–170)

Long overdue examination of development of Dutch abolitionist sentiment which, author argues, did not find expression until well after the 1790s. Importance of East Indies to Dutch economic and political interests partially explains this seeming disinterest in slavery issue in Suriname. Very useful. [ELC]

1954 Parisis, Denise and **Henri Parisis.** Le siècle du sucre à Saint-Martin français. (*Bull. Soc. hist. Guadeloupe*, 99/102, 1994, p. 5–208, bibl., ill., maps, photos, tables)

Superb study focuses on economy and society in French part of Saint Martin during sugar era (1780–1820). Combines archival and field research to give systematic documentation of buildings and machinery of Saint Martin's 35 sugar plantations. Especially novel is graphic reconstitution of previously unknown technology, such as toboggans for transporting sugarcane to the mill, and specific type of English furnaces. Also provides fascinating introduction to cosmopolitan society of French Caribbean diaspora on a small island outside orbit of the main colonial powers. [APD]

1955 Pérotin-Dumon, Anne. Population, travail et urbanisme dans les villes de l'Amérique atlantique au XVIIIe siècle: Basse-Terre et Pointe-à-Pitre, Guadeloupe. (*Bull. Cent. hist. atl.*, 6, 1993, p. 191–208)

Drawing from her work on Guadeloupe's colonial cities, author offers methodological comments on challenges to urban Caribbean history: 1) authorities, employing earlier administrative maps, are slow to grasp properly the urban character of these cities, making quantitative population assessments difficult; 2) reconstituting socioeconomic structure is made more complex by inclusion of data on female occupations; and 3) mutual dependence between port cities and plantations requires a fresh interpretive framework. [APD]

1956 Poitrineau, Abel. L'état et l'avenir des colonies françaises de plantation à la fin de l'Ancien Régime selon P.V. Malouet. (*Rev. Auvergne*, 104, 1990, p. 41–54)

Reviews late 18th-century and early 19th-century writings of this prominent colonial official who also owned valuable plantations in Saint-Domingue. Malouet supported French mercantilism but advocated a gradual loosening that would increase colonial productivity and profits. Though generally sympathetic to "Enlightened" opinion, Malouet nevertheless opposed slave emancipation on practical grounds. [JG]

1957 Porro Gutiérrez, Jesús María. Inquietudes en la parte española de la isla, sobre la sublevación de los esclavos en Saint-Domingue. (*Estud. Hist. Soc. Econ. Am.*, 10, 1993, p. 165–179)

Gathers reactions of Santo Domingo's colonial officials, particularly Governor García, toward revolution in French Saint-Domingue, 1790–95, and documents their support for rebellious slaves (who were, however, brought back to the French side by the 1794 abolition decree). Worthwhile primarily for use of Spanish colonial archives. [APD]

1958 Robinson, Carey. The iron thorn: the defeat of the British by the Jamaican Maroons. Kingston: Kingston Publishers Ltd., 1993. 273 p.: ill., maps.

Parts of this book were originally published as *The Fighting Maroons of Jamaica* (Kingston: W. Collins and Sangster, 1969). Popular, ideologically-driven work traces history of maroons from their initial emergence to outbreak of second maroon war of 1796. Pays scant attention to banishment of maroons to Nova Scotia. [ELC]

1959 Rossignol, Philippe and **Bernadette Rossignol.** Ascension sociale à Cayenne: descendance de soldats-habitants et d'artisans. (*Généal. hist. Caraïbe*, 56, jan. 1994, p. 962–967)

Genealogical research profiles two little-known classes in 18th-century French Guiana: the soldier-planter and the artisan. Shows male colonists' alliances with white and indigenous women and their integration into ranks of Cayenne notables. [APD]

1960 Rossignol, Philippe and **Bernadette Rossignol.** Gaspard Bayon, sénéchal de Guadeloupe. (*Généal. hist. Caraïbe*, 63, sept. 1994, p. 1122–1124)

Descriptive case study provides useful details about a little-known social group in 18th-century French Caribbean: the officers in royal courts. [APD]

1961 Sánchez Valverde, Antonio. Ensayos. Santo Domingo: Ediciones de la Fundación Corripio, 1988. 425 p.: bibl., ill. (some col.). (Biblioteca de clásicos dominicanos; 5)

Includes some of the most significant works from this Dominican classic, by one of the most colorful figures of 18th-century Dominican history. Also includes a solid study of Antonio Sánchez Valverde by Friar Cipriano de Utrera, and numerous annotations. [JMH]

1962 Sheridan, Richard B. The condition of the slaves in the settlement and economic development of the British Windward Islands, 1763–1775. (*J. Caribb. Hist.*, 24:2, 1990, p. 121–145, tables)

Concludes that because economic take-off of these islands occurred later than in other British Caribbean possessions, planters worked slaves hard and adopted policies that resulted in high mortality rates, low fertility rates, and an overall net annual decrease in the slave population, considerably greater than in other islands. [ELC]

1963 Stinchcombe, Arthur L. Freedom and oppression of slaves in the eighteenth-century Caribbean. (*Am. Sociol. Rev.*, 59:6, Dec. 1994, p. 911–929, bibl., map, tables)

Maintains that the nature of master-slave relationship depended on whether planter power was high or low, rather than on legal precepts and concepts. [JMH]

1964 **Stinchcombe, Arthur L.** Sugar island slavery in the age of Enlightenment: the political economy of the Caribbean world. Princeton, N.J.: Princeton Univ. Press, 1995. 361 p.: bibl., index, maps.

Work by sociologist applies social theory to explain why Caribbean planters required repressive regimes first to ensure prominence of slave labor in their enterprises and, after emancipation, to maintain equally repressive labor systems. Though based solely on secondary sources, very useful. [ELC]

1965 **Stipriaan, Alex van.** Debunking debts: image and reality of a colonial crisis; Suriname at the end of the 18th century. (*Itinerario/Leiden*, 19:1, 1995, p. 69–84, ill., photos, tables)

Discussion of 18th-century Dutch credit system shows that assumed relationship between 1773 Amsterdam Stock Exchange crisis and decay of Suriname plantation economy is one of the many myths permeating Suriname's historiography. Article is based on Chapter 7 of author's *Surinaams contrast* (see *HLAS 54:2106*). [RH]

1966 **Tyson, George F. Jr.** On the periphery of the peripheries: the cotton plantations of St. Croix, Danish West Indies, 1735–1815. (*J. Caribb. Hist.*, 26:1, 1992, p. 1–36, maps, tables)

Superbly researched study on cotton production era (1750–1800) is written by specialist on colonial Saint Croix. Representing one-third of island's plantations, cotton estates used drier, rocky soils unsuitable for sugar; were owned by modest planters (among them a sizable group of free-coloreds on marginal estates); and employed a quarter of Saint Croix's slaves, some of whom grew their own cotton on land allotted by their masters. [APD]

SPANISH BORDERLANDS

1967 **Cocker, William S.** The Columbian exchange in the Floridas: Scots, Spaniards, and Indians, 1783–1821. (*CLAHR/Albuquerque*, 3:3, Summer 1994, p. 305–325, maps, tables)

Scholarly account describes methods used by European merchants to squeeze land from the Indians. Relies basically on primary sources. [JMH]

1968 **Cross, crozier, and crucible: a volume celebrating the bicentennial of a Catholic Diocese in Louisiana.** Edited by Glenn R. Conrad. New Orleans, La.: Archdiocese of New Orleans; Center for Louisiana Studies, 1993. 683 p.: bibl., ill., index.

Rather than providing a new history of the Catholic Church in Lousiana, collection of essays covers various aspects of its growth and heritage. Diverse backgrounds and perspectives of the contributors make volume especially interesting. [JMH]

1969 **The De Soto chronicles: the expedition of Hernando de Soto to North America in 1539–1543.** Edited by Lawrence A. Clayton, Vernon James Knight, Jr., and Edward Carter Moore. Tuscaloosa: Univ. of Alabama Press, 1993. 2 v.: bibl., ill., index, maps.

Two volumes bring together English translations of the four primary accounts of the De Soto expedition and some relevant supplementary documents. The documents are newly annotated, preceded by literary and historical introductions, and followed by an extensive bibliography. [JMH]

Fiehrer, Thomas M. Saint-Domingue/Haiti: Louisiana's Caribbean connection. See item **1928.**

1970 **Goza, Wilián** and **Hugo Ludeña.** Gonzalo Silvestre: un soldado de Extremadura sobreviviente de la expedición de Hernando de Soto a La Florida, 1539–1543. (*in* Coloquios Históricos de Extremadura, *18th, Trujillo, Spain, 1989. Actas.* Cáceres, Spain: Institución Cultural El Brocense de la Excma. Diputación Provincial de Cáceres, 1991, p. 119–149, bibl., table)

Discusses Silvestre's career—including his role as an informant to Garcilaso de la Vega—and provides explication of several documents concerning Silvestre's part in Hernando de Soto's expedition. [J. Britton]

1971 **Grant, Ethan A.** The Natchez Revolt of 1781: a reconsideration. (*J. Miss. Hist.*, 57:4, Nov. 1994, p. 309–324, tables)

Interesting for its demonstration of an example of good and enlightened Spanish colonial government. [JMH]

1972 **Hudson, Joyce Rockwood.** Looking for De Soto: a search through the South for the Spaniard's trail. Athens: Univ. of Georgia Press, 1993. 230 p.: bibl., ill.

Travel story about a scholarly pursuit is informative and entertaining. [JMH]

1973 Inglis, G. Douglas. The character and some characters of Spanish Natchez. (*J. Miss. Hist.*, 56:1, Feb. 1994, p. 17–39, appendix.)

Drawing on repository of documents left behind by the Spaniards, author examines Natchez's peculiarities as a marriage of the Spanish and Anglo frontiers. [JMH]

1974 Kapitzke, Robert. The "Calamites of Florida": Father Solana, Governor Palacio y Valenzuela, and the desertions of 1758. (*Fla. Hist. Q.*, 72:1, July 1993, p. 1–18)

Scholarly work describes tensions that developed between religious and secular authorities in Florida during last ten years of First Spanish Period. [JMH]

1975 Kelley, James E., Jr. Juan Ponce de León's discovery of Florida: Herrera's narrative revisited. (*Rev. Hist. Am.*, 111, enero/junio 1991, p. 31–65, bibl.)

Provides new and modern translation of Herrera's narrative. Notes and commentaries are quite useful. [JMH]

1976 Landers, Jane. Black/Indian interaction in Spanish Florida. (*CLAHR/Albuquerque*, 2:2, Spring 1993, p. 141–162, ill.)

Based on records left by Spanish officials, work shows how blacks cooperated with native Americans and how both became allies of the Spaniards in their fight against land-hungry Georgians. [JMH]

Landers, Jane. New research on the African experience in Spanish America and the Caribbean. See item **901.**

1977 Schafer, Daniel L. "A class of the people neither freemen nor slaves": from Spanish to American race relations in Florida, 1821–1861. (*J. Soc. Hist.*, 26:3, Spring 1993, p. 587–609)

Argues that after Spain left Florida in 1821 the US replaced a mild and flexible system of race relations with a harsh two-caste system of slavery. Based on extensive research. [JMH]

19TH CENTURY

1978 Acosta de Arriba, Rafael. El fuego del señorío revolucionario. (*Santiago/Cuba*, 76, julio/dic. 1993, p. 171–190, bibl.)

Interesting and well-documented account focuses on fire that destroyed the city of Bayamo at beginning of first Cuban war of independence (1868–78). Article settles the question of who among Cuban insurgents was responsible for deciding to burn the city rather than surrender it to the Spaniards. [JMH]

1979 Acosta de Arriba, Rafael. La revolución de 1868–1878 y el desarrollo de las ideas en Cuba. (*Rev. Cuba. Cienc. Soc.*, 9:26, julio/dic. 1991, p. 100–114, bibl.)

Author's thesis is praiseworthy, but he has failed to develop it as fully as he should have done. [JMH]

1980 Alvarez Gutiérrez, Luis. La diplomacia alemana ante el conflicto Hispano-Norteamericano de 1897–1898: primeras tomas de posicion. (*Hispania/Madrid*, 54:186, enero/abril 1994, p. 201–256)

Based on extensive archival sources, work adds significant information to diplomatic history of US-Spanish conflict. [JMH]

Arxentina: destino da emigración española e galega, 1810–1910; documentos relacionados con ela. See item **2949.**

1981 Ayala, José Antonio. El contencioso masónico por el territorio en Puerto Rico a finales del siglo XIX, 1871–1899. (*Rev. Cent. Estud. Av.*, 8, enero/junio 1989, p. 98–117)

Institutional history of freemasonry in Puerto Rico in last three decades of 19th century is based on documents in Archivo Histórico Nacional in Salamanca and Gran Logia Soberana in Puerto Rico, as well as on printed sources. Deals with jurisdictional dispute over affiliation (*obediencia*). Vocabulary and treatment of issues make work suitable for the expert only. Analysis of masonic ideology within socioeconomic context is still lacking for Puerto Rico. [TMV]

1982 Bahamonde Magro, Angel and **José Gregorio Cayuela Fernández.** Hacer las Américas: las elites coloniales españolas en el siglo XIX. Madrid: Alianza Editorial, 1992. 390 p.: bibl., index. (Alianza América; 31)

First-rate study examines capital formation in 19th-century Cuba and its subsequent transfer to the metropolis. Study also dwells on political implications of these processes. Based on ample, meticulous research and on secondary sources. [JMH]

1983 Barón Fernández, José. La guerra hispano-norteamericana de 1898. Coruña, Spain: Ediciós do Castro, 1993. 273 p.: bibl., ill. (Historia)

Concise history based on primary and secondary sources is especially interesting because it reflects the Spanish point of view. [JMH]

1984 Baud, Michiel. Una frontera para cruzar: la sociedad rural a través de la frontera dominico-haitiana, 1870–1930. (*Estud. Soc./Santo Domingo*, 26:94, oct./dic. 1993, p. 5–28, bibl.)

A study of society in the frontier region between Haiti and the Dominican Republic in the 1870–1930 period. Includes sections on commerce and contraband, the introduction of sugar, and US presence, including military occupation. Points to the emergence of organized crime as a direct result of the American intervention in both countries, and to the greater control of the frontier region by the central states. [B. Aguirre-Lopez]

Baud, Michiel. Una frontera-refugio: dominicanos y haitianos contra el Estado, 1870–1930. See item **2108.**

Baud, Michiel. Historia de un sueño: los ferrocarriles públicos en la República Dominicana, 1880–1930. See item **2109.**

Beckles, Hilary. White women and slavery in the Caribbean. See item **1904.**

1985 Bergad, Laird W.; Fe Iglesias García; and María del Carmen Barcia Zequeira. The Cuban slave market, 1790–1880. Cambridge, England; New York: Cambridge Univ. Press, 1995. 245 p.: bibl., ill., index. (Cambridge Latin American series; 79)

Work is based on records of over 30,000 slave transactions from three separate locations in Cuba: La Habana, Santiago de Cuba, and Cienfuegos. No similar compilation of information exists on any other slave markets in Latin America or the Caribbean. [JMH]

1986 Boutin, Raymond. Notes sur les mariages à Pointe-Noire de 1850 a 1946. (*Etud. Guad.*, 5, fév. 1992, p. 127–133, graphs)

Work by best French Caribbean historical demographer is based on ongoing research on post-emancipation society of Guadeloupe. Analysis of population growth in two *communes* of Grande-Terre region shows that marriage had marginal role in formation of families in both, while immigration affected the two *communes* quite differently. A dry, healthy climate, four percent immigration rate, and balanced gender ratio gave Pointe-Noire a strong natural growth throughout 19th century, while malaria-plagued Petit-Canal experienced almost continuous negative growth, despite 16 percent immigration. [APD]

1987 Brasseur, Paul. Problèmes d'autorité en matière religieuse: l'érection des diocèses coloniaux, 1815–1851. (*MEFRIM*, 104: 2, 1992, p. 737–763)

Good study examines reorganization of the colonial Church following the French Revolution. Shows that abolitionists among newly-appointed clergy, in agreement with the government, contributed to launching the emancipation process. [APD]

1988 Buffon, Alain. La Banque de la Guadeloupe en 1895: le rapport Chaudié. (*Rev. Rev. Interam.*, 22:1/2, primavera 1992, p. 191–207, bibl.)

Specialist in monetary history documents banking system in French Lesser Antilles, 1851–1945. Formed with capital constituted by planters' abolition indemnities, colonial banks served primarily for local agricultural credit. Audit by French civil servant in the middle of sugar crisis shows growing circulation of paper money and other practices anticipating modern banking. [APD]

1989 Butler, Kathleen Mary. The economics of emancipation: Jamaica & Barbados, 1823–1843. Chapel Hill: Univ. of North Carolina Press, 1995. 198 p.: bibl., ill., index, maps.

Careful and sophisticated analysis examines impact of compensation on emancipation settlement and economy of two of Britain's Caribbean possessions. Argues that protectionism and credit had obscured inherent fragility of economies of both islands during final days of slavery. While grant relieved planter indebtedness, it failed to protect ailing and bankrupt sugar industry. [ELC]

1990 Cabrero, Leoncio. La integración de los libertos puertorriqueños en la comunidad ciudadana. (*in* Coloquio Internacional sobre Abolición de la Esclavitud, *Madrid, 1986.* Esclavitud y derechos humanos: la lucha por la libertad del negro en el siglo XIX; actas. Edición de Francisco de Solano y Agustín Guimerá. Madrid: Consejo Superior de Investigaciones Científicas, Centro de Estudios Históricos, Depto. de Historia de América, 1990, p. 293–317, appendices)

Based on documents from *El proceso abolicionista en Puerto Rico: documentos para su estudio* (San Juan: 1974), and from the Archivo Histórico Nacional, traces the problems of emancipation from the perspective of landowners (work contracts of *libertos* and indemnization), and of political conservatives who opposed liberal reforms on the part of the metropolitan government of Primo de Rivera. [TMV]

1991 Camuñas Madera, Ricardo R. Epidemias, plagas y marginación: la lucha contra la adversidad en Puerto Rico en los siglos XVIII y XIX. Puerto Rico: Editorial Universidad de América, 1992. 102 p.: bibl., port.

Argues that increased commercial activity and population growth facilitated spread of disease in 19th-century Puerto Rico. Landowners and merchants suffered impact of mid-century cholera epidemic as intensely as their slave populations, whose decrease raised slave prices. Slavery was weakened, and land changed hands to younger owners who favored modernization. Although a novel explanation for Puerto Rico's frustated attempts at economic progress, this thesis cannot be proved satisfactorily. [TMV]

1992 Camuñas Madera, Ricardo R. Hacendados y comerciantes en Puerto Rico en torno a la década revolucionaria de 1860. Mayagüez, P.R.: s.n., 1993. 194 p.: bibl., ill.

Reiterates conclusions of Olga Jiménez de Wagenheim (item **2094**) and Laird Bergad (*Coffee and the growth of agrarian capitalism in nineteenty-century Puerto Rico,* see *HLAS 46:2522*) regarding dislocations suffered by small-scale creole coffee producers due to economic domination by large landowners and foreign merchants at mid-century. Enriches understanding of political unrest by contextualizing it within both the western region of Puerto Rico where the Lares uprising of 1868 took root, and what Camuñas Madera calls the "revolutionary" decade of 1860. Lists numerous archives visited to obtain a sense of demographics and quality of town life. Concludes that a new generation imbued with capitalist ingenuity replaced the traditional elite of the early century. [TMV]

1993 Caribbean freedom: society and economy from emancipation to the present. Edited by Hilary Beckles and Verene Shep-

herd. Kingston: Randle; London: Currey, 1993. 581 p.: bibl.

Contains anthology of essays on modern Caribbean that previously appeared in scholarly journals. Some of the most original articles deal with emergence of peasantries and relationships between peasants and planters, social policy and class formation, and labor disturbances in early 20th century. This labor discontent heralded working class solidarity and emergence of political parties in British Caribbean as antecedents to decolonization movement. [ELC]

1994 Carretero García, Carmen. El fracaso de los proyectos universitarios en Puerto Rico a fines del siglo XIX. (*Estud. Hist. Soc. Econ. Am.,* 9, 1992, p. 143–154)

Provides chronological account of efforts to develop institutions of higher learning after 1868. After many obstacles—ideological, financial, personal—were overcome, foundation of Instituto de Estudios Superiores in 1888 by the Ateneo Puertorriqueño was result of liberal initiative from southern zone of the island, along with conservative support, limited financial contributions of donors, and defense of freedom of speech on the part of liberal governments in the metropolis. [TMV]

1995 Cartaya Cotta, Perla. La polémica de la esclavitud: José de la Luz y Caballero. La Habana: Editorial de Ciencias Sociales, 1988. 78 p. (Palabra de Cuba)

Actually a short biography of the noted 19th-century Cuban educator, work is noteworthy for its balanced assement of his ideas and personality. [JMH]

1996 Cassá, Roberto and **Genaro Rodríguez Morel.** Consideraciones alternativas acerca de las rebeliones de esclavos en Santo Domingo. (*Anu. Estud. Am.,* 50:1, 1993, p. 101–131)

Authors challenge traditional interpretations of slave rebellions in the Dominican Republic, maintaining that these rebellions were the result of class consciousness of the slaves.

1997 Cayuela Fernández, José Gregorio. Bahía de Ultramar: España y Cuba en el siglo XIX; el control de las relaciones coloniales. Madrid: Siglo Veintiuno Editores, 1993. 281 p.: bibl., index. (Historia)

Based largely on secondary sources, study focuses primarily on restructuring of the Cuba-Spain colonial relationship carried out by Capitán Gen. José Gutiérrez de la Concha in 1854–59. Work is important because of its emphasis on role played by pro-Spanish colonial elite. [JMH]

1998   Cayuela Fernández, José Gregorio. Los capitanes generales ante la cuestión de la abolición, 1854–1862. (*in* Coloquio Internacional sobre Abolición de la Esclavitud, *Madrid, 1986.* Esclavitud y derechos humanos: la lucha por la libertad del negro en el siglo XIX: actas. Edición de Francisco de Solano y Agustín Guimerá. Madrid: Consejo Superior de Investigaciones Científicas, Centro de Estudios Históricos, Depto. de Historia de América, 1990, p. 415–453, tables)

Important contribution focuses specifically on colonial administration of Capitán Gen. José Gutiérrez de la Concha. Also sheds light on administration of Capitán Gen. Francisco Serrano. [JMH]

1999   Céspedes, Carlos Manuel de. Carlos Manuel de Céspedes: el diario perdido. Edición de Eusebio Leal Spengler. La Habana: Editorial de Ciencias Sociales, 1992. 302 p.: bibl., ill., indexes. (Historia de Cuba)

Publication of these portions of the campaign diary of the man who began first Cuban war of independence (1868–78) is an epoch-making event in Cuban historiography. No essential changes will need to be introduced in the history of the war, but Céspedes' judgments of his fellow liberators and the behavior of the insurgent army will no doubt put to rest the more traditional and romantic narratives of the conflict. [JMH]

Congreso Internacional de Historia Económica y Social de la Cuenca del Caribe, 1763–1898, 1st, San Juan, 1987. Primer Congreso Internacional de Historia Económica y Social de la Cuenca del Caribe, 1763–1898. See item **1921.**

2000   Coradin, Jean. Histoire diplomatique d'Haïti. v. 1–2. Port-au-Prince: Edition des Antilles, 1988–93. 2 v: bibl., indexes.

Although based on secondary literature, useful for 19th-century diplomatic history. [APD]

2001   Corvington, Georges. Port-au-Prince au cours des ans. v. 4, La métropole haïtienne du XIXe siècle. 2. ed. Port-au-Prince: Impr. H. Deschamps, 1990? 1 v.

Volume is senior historian's latest addition to multifaceted history of Haiti's capital.

With help of press and cartographic sources, documents little-known modernization era—urban planning, introduction of electricity, water and sewer systems, public transportation, and markets. Shows that city's modern layout was set by 1880: merchant houses on the seaboard and residential neighborhoods on the periphery. Second part vividly evokes the making of a capital in spite of continuous political disturbances, as both a rising national bourgeoisie and popular neighborhoods gave the city a distinctive urban culture. Rich data on municipal, State, and police institutions, and on devastating epidemics related to its port function. [APD]

2002   Costa, Emília Viotti da. Crowns of glory, tears of blood: the Demerara slave rebellion of 1823. New York: Oxford Univ. Press, 1994. 378 p.: bibl., ill., index, maps.

Fascinating reconstruction of slavery and slave society in Demerara is gleaned mostly from complaints of slaves to missionaries and Protector of Slaves. Portrays society experiencing enormous tension during crucial transitional stage when amelioration of the slaves' living conditions and religious instruction challenged once and for all the fundamental bases on which slavery had long rested. Excellent. [ELC]

Craton, Michael J. Reshuffling the pack: the transition from slavery to other forms of labor in the British Caribbean. See item **2128.**

2003   The Cuba Commission report: a hidden history of the Chinese in Cuba; the original English-language text of 1876. Introduction by Denise Helly. Baltimore, Md.: Johns Hopkins Univ. Press, 1993. 156 p.: bibl., ill. (Johns Hopkins studies in Atlantic history and culture)

Reissue of a remarkable 19th-century document exposing abuses suffered by the more than 2,000 Chinese contract laborers brought to Cuba to work in the sugar industry. Introduction by Denise Helly provides historical context for this episode. [JMH]

2004   Cubano Iguina, Astrid. Un puente entre Mallorca y Puerto Rico: la emigración de Sóller, 1830–1930. Colombres, Spain: Archivo de Indianos, 1993. 184 p.: bibl., ill., maps. (Cruzar el charco; 7)

Well written and rich in analysis, this book stands out among the many case studies of immigration to Puerto Rico. Author argues that migration from Sóller, a municipality of Mallorca, resulted from a contraction of the citrus fruit industry and was directed to Puerto Rico through network arrangements. Singularity of Sóller case is more than offset by analysis of migrants' roles in Puerto Rican coffee economy. [TMV]

2005 Curnow, Ena. Manana, "detrás del Generalisimo": biografía de Bernarda Toro de Gómez. Miami, Fla.: Ediciones Universal, 1994. 1 v.

Offers unpretentious biographical portrait of wife of General Máximo Gómez, Commander-in-Chief of Cuban liberating army in 1895–98 war of independence. Book is nevertheless important because it contains liberal transcriptions of a large amount of previously unpublished correspondence between Gómez and his wife and children. Some of the letters are truly revealing. [JMH]

2006 Dain, Bruce. Haiti and Egypt in early black racial discourse in the United States. (*Slavery Abolit.*, 14:3, dec. 1993, p. 139–161)

Links rise of positive image of ancient Egypt and Ethiopia among free black activists in US in 1820s to failure of independent Haiti to disprove stereotypes about uncivilized blacks. [APD]

2007 Dávila Ruiz, Emma A. Apuntes sobre el comercio entre Puerto Rico y Gran Bretaña durante el siglo XIX. (*Bol. Cent. Invest. Hist.*, 7, 1992, p. 255–292)

In arguing that Puerto Rico and Great Britain enjoyed solid commercial relations during 19th century, author dispels commonly held view that US gradually came to control island's economy during this period. She concludes, then, that so-called Spanish-American War marked abrupt beginning of economic domination by US. Comparison with Cuba is most pertinent. [TMV]

2008 Delisle, Philippe. Les catéchismes à la Martinique dans la première moitié du XIX siècle révélateurs d'un réveil missionnaire. (*Rev. fr. hist. Outre-mer*, 82:307, 1995, p. 193–204)

Publication in 1839 of a first catechism for slaves in vernacular creole initiated a new missionary pedagogy of the Catholic Church, which was supported by the government. Showing that catechism's educational aspect was opposed by both white elites who feared

social subversion, and a rising elite of freedmen anxious about potential rivals, author throws light on colonial framework between the French Revolution and abolition of slavery, and new social forces emerging in 19th-century French Antilles. [APD]

2009 Díaz Quiñones, Arcadio. Salvador Brau i la ciutat lletrada porto-riquenya. (*in* Jornades d'Estudis Catalano-Americans, 2nd, Barcelona, 1986. Actes. Barcelona: Comissió Catalana del Cinquè Centenari del Descobiment d'Amèrica, 1987, p. 431–444)

Proposes that Catalan immigration at mid-19th century, rather than dividing Puerto Rican national identity, as José Luis González asserts, contributed to its shaping and even to autonomist inclinations. Focuses on figure of Salvador Brau, well-known historian and essayist of Catalan ascendancy, to highlight intellectual and ideological discourse that emanated from immigrant groups alongside their more visible and highly publicized commercial successes. [TMV]

2010 Documentos del primer gobierno dominicano: Junta Central Gubernativa, febrero-noviembre 1844. Recopilación de Julio G. Campillo Pérez. Santo Domingo: Comisión Oficial para la Celebración del Sesquicentenario de la Independencia Nacional, 1994. 160 p.: ill. (Col. Sesquicentenario de la independencia nacional; 5)

A very useful compilation of government documents from the Dominican Republic. [JMH]

2011 Domingo Acebroń, M. Dolores. Las expediciones a Cuba: apoyo a la insurrección cespedista, 1868–1878. (*Rev. Complut. Hist. Am.*, 18, 1992, p. 241–256, appendices)

To date this subject has been largely neglected by historians. In this context, an interesting contribution. [JMH]

2012 Doret, Michael R. Hannibal Price III, 1841–1893: auteur de *De la réhabilitation de la race noire par la République d'Haïti*. (*Rev. Soc. haïti.*, 49:175, mars 1993, p. 17–88, bibl.)

Notwithstanding its laudatory tone, work illuminates life and works of well-known author of *De la réhabilitation de la race noire par la République d'Haïti*, a cogent response to contemporary European theorists of white racial superiority. Stresses that Price combined nationalism with a commitment to democracy and a rejection of Haiti's militaristic state. [APD]

2013 Duharte Jiménez, Rafael. Rebeldía esclava en el Caribe. Xalapa, Mexico: Comisión Estatal Conmemorativa del V Centenario del Encuentro de Dos Mundos, Gobierno del Estado de Veracruz, 1992. 232 p.: bibl. (Col. V centenario; 10)

Interesting and well-researched essay focuses on comparative history of slave rebellions. [JMH]

Dye, Alan. Avoiding holdup: asset specificity and technical change in the Cuban sugar industry, 1889–1929. See item **2134.**

2014 Fernández, Aurea Matilde. España y Cuba, 1868–1898: revolución burguesa y relaciones coloniales. La Habana: Editorial de Ciencias Sociales, 1988. 243 p.: bibl. (Historia)

Author is a teacher of Spanish history at the Univ. de la Habana. In this study, based largely on printed sources, she emphasizes reciprocal influences between colony and metropolis in last third of 19th century. [JMH]

2015 Fernández Canales, Consuelo. Exposiciones de la opinión pública ante la abolición de la esclavitud en Puerto Rico, 1868–1873. (*in* Coloquio Internacional sobre Abolición de la Esclavitud, *Madrid, 1986.* Esclavitud y derechos humanos: la lucha por la libertad del negro en el siglo XIX; actas. Edición de Francisco de Solano y Agustín Guimerá. Madrid: Consejo Superior de Investigaciones Científicas, Centro de Estudios Históricos, Depto. de Historia de América, 1990, p. 279–291)

Presents novel analysis of efforts in favor of or against abolition by groups of citizens (*vecinos*), organizations, or individuals with a view to influencing legislation. Author concludes that public opinion had little influence in the deliberations of the Cortes. Successfully points to connection between economic and political reform from perspective of both the metropolis (Spain could hardly consider abolition in Puerto Rico when such action would likely pave the way for further political liberties in the face of Cuban war of independence) and the colony (after intense mobilization, reformers saw their program eradicated except for abolition after Pavía's rise to power in 1873). [TMV]

2016 Fletcher, Leonard P. The evolution of poor relief in Barbados, 1838–1900. (*J. Caribb. Hist.*, 26:2, 1992, p. 171–209, tables)

In a highly informative study, author claims that because State intervention in poor relief in 19th-century Barbados was present only minimally if at all, plight of poor and infirm was addressed mostly by benevolent bodies. Towards end of century, hesitant State involvement was noted. [ELC]

2017 Fornet, Ambrosio. El libro en Cuba: siglos XVIII y XIX. La Habana: Editorial Letras Cubanas, 1994. 239 p.: bibl., ill., index.

History of printing and publishing in Cuba covers 18th and 19th centuries. As a rule, publications by Spaniards are excluded. Well written and researched. Includes more than 300 valuable illustrations. [JMH]

2018 Frisch, Peter J. La chute du régime de Faustin Soulouque d'après un récit de Charles Haentjens [i.e., Haetjens]. (*Rev. Soc. haïti.*, 48:174, déc. 1992, p. 15–64)

Previously unpublished, privately-held manuscript by wealthy merchant close to political circles narrates 1858 army coup that overthrew emperor held responsible for Haiti's defeat by Santo Domingo. Conveys a sense of elite politicking and plotters' scant regard for Geffrard, chief of the army and their co-conspirator. [APD]

2019 García del Pino, César. Carlos García: comandante general de Vuelta Abajo. La Habana: Editorial de Ciencias Sociales, 1990. 164 p.: bibl., ill., index. (Historia de Cuba)

Author makes noteworthy attempt to show that during first Cuban war of independence, largely fought in eastern Cuba, there was also insurgent activity in western portion of the island. He also tries to vindicate memory of García, whom Spaniards regarded as a bandit. Author's perspective is narrow and some of his conclusions are not well founded. [JMH]

2020 García Mora, Luis Miguel. Un cubano en la restauración: la labor intelectual de Rafael Montoro, 1875–1878. (*Rev. Indias*, 52:195/196, mayo/dic. 1992, p. 443–475)

Written by a Spanish scholar, excellent in-depth study of Montoro's intellectual evolution fills a gap in writings on this Cuban politician. Balanced, objective, and well researched. [JMH]

2021 Gómez, Máximo. Máximo Gómez: una vida extraordinaria. Recopilación de Raúl Rodríguez La O. La Habana: Editora Política, 1986. 88 p.: bibl., ill.

Collection includes small number of previously unpublished letters of the General, some of which are truly important. [JMH]

2022 Gómez, Máximo. El pensamiento vivo de Máximo Gómez. v. 2. Recopilación de Bernardo García Domínguez. Santo Domingo: Ediciones CEDEE, 1992. 1 v: bibl.

Vol. 2 of anthology of the General's writings includes period from 1895 to his death. Although useful, work tends to leave out documents that might be detrimental to his name. For annotation of Vol. 1 see *HLAS* 54:2071. [JMH]

2023 Gómez Toro, Francisco. Papeles de Panchito. Selección, prólogo y notas de Bladimir Zamora. La Habana: Editora Abril, 1988. 195 p.: bibl., ill. (Col. Abril. Documentos)

Francisco Gómez Toro was the son of Gen. Máximo Gómez and worked closely with José Martí and Gen. Antonio Maceo, among other Cuban patriots, in 1890s. His papers, printed in this volume, are a significant source for study of 1895–98 Cuban war of independence. [JMH]

2024 González Pérez, Aníbal. Los amos también callan: apuntes sobre literatura y esclavitud en el Puerto Rico del siglo XIX. (*Rev. Inst. Cult. Puertorriq.*, 26:97, 1987, p. 19–23)

Focuses on dearth of abolitionist literature in Puerto Rico and absence of African characaters in folkloric production. Proposes as possible reasons for literary marginalization of black element the cultural and social integration of Africans and the desire for "whitening" of island. [TMV]

Hackshaw, John Milton. The Baptist denomination: a concise history commemorating one hundred and seventy five years, 1816–1991, of the establishment of the "company villages" and the Baptist faith in Trinidad and Tobago. See item **2158.**

2025 Haetjens, Charles. Quelques détails sur l'exécution d'Aimé Legros. (*Rev. Soc. haïti.*, 49:176, juin 1993, p. 77–84)

Reproduction of letter addressed to wealthy Haitian merchant close to political milieu captures atmosphere of a brief liberal interlude in grim 19th-century Haitian politics. [APD]

2026 Henríquez Ureña, Max and **José María Morillas.** El arzobispo Valera. Apéndices y selección de Rafael Bello Peguero. Santo Domingo: Arzobispado de Santo Domingo, Oficina de la Obra y Museos de la Catedral Metropolitana de Santo Domingo, Primada de Indias, 1991. 157 p.: appendices, bibl. (Serie Hombres de Iglesia; 6)

Reproduces significant documents about Valera and reprints two informative narratives of his life and times. Also includes fairly complete bibliography as well as a chronology prepared by Father José Luis Sáez, S.J. [JMH]

2027 Hernández Sandoica, Elena. Rafael María de Labra y Cadrana, 1841–1919: una biografía política. (*Rev. Indias*, 54:200, enero/abril 1994, p. 107–136)

Although the bibliography on Labra is rich in titles, this author purports to provide us with a new interpretation of Labra's so-called "American vocation." Interesting and provocative. [JMH]

2028 Heuman, Gad J. The killing time: the Morant Bay Rebellion in Jamaica. Knoxville: Univ. of Tennessee Press, 1994. 199 p.: bibl., index.

Relying heavily on massive amount of evidence collected by the Jamaican Royal Commission, as well as on colonial office correspondence and missionary reports, author provides modern, up-to-date analysis of social, political, and economic tensions in post-emancipation Jamaica that led to disturbances. Important work. [ELC]

2029 Hijano Pérez, María de los Angeles. El régimen municipal de la isla de Cuba en la segunda mitad del siglo XIX. (*Anu. Estud. Am.*, 50:2, 1993, p. 243–277)

Work is significant and well-documented contribution to literature on municipal government in Cuba. [JMH]

2030 Hilton, Sylvia L. The Spanish-American War of 1898: queries into the relationship between the press, public opinion and politics. (*Rev. Esp. Estud. Norteam.*, 5:7, 1994, p. 71–87, bibl.)

Sharp analysis examines relationship between the press, public opinion, and domestic politics, particularly on the Spanish side of the conflict. Shows clearly that there are still more questions than answers concerning the war, and that the matter is too complex to be settled in any facile way. [JMH]

2031 Hoefte, Rosemarijn. Free blacks and coloureds in plantation Suriname. (*Slavery Abolit.*, 17:1, April 1996, p. 102–129)

Based largely on 19th-century colonial records, contemporary sources, and recent studies, presents useful overview of group that, though numerically small, constituted important element in Suriname's free society. Topics covered include manumission, social organization and structure, family networks, education, and economic strivings. Suggests intertwining of race and class issues within the group and within larger society. Extremely useful vignettes on highly visible and successful individuals. [ELC]

2032 Hostos, Eugenio María de. Obras completas. v. 1, Literatura: t. 2, Cuento, teatro, poesía, ensayo. Introducción de Marcos F. Reyes Dávila. Ed. crítica, 1a ed. San Juan: Editorial del Instituto de Cultura Puertorriqueña; Río Piedras, P.R.: Editorial de la Univ. de Puerto Rico, 1988. 1 v.

Second volume of Hostos' literary writings continues effort of Univ. de Puerto Rico and Instituto de Cultura Puertorriqueña to publish all of Hostos' works. Includes short stories, plays, poems, essays, and book reviews by one of Puerto Rico's most influential social analysts and political thinkers. Introduction by Marcos Reyes Dávila emphasizes connections Hostos himself drew between his private life and the Caribbean island (*antillana*) trajectory. Indexes are extremely helpful. [TMV]

2033 Howard, Philip A. The Spanish colonial government's responses to the pan-nationalist agenda of the Afro-Cuban mutual aid societies, 1868–1895. (*Rev. Rev. Interam.*, 22:1/2, primavera 1992, p. 151–167, bibl.)

Well written and documented study, but the author should have taken into account that in 1895 there were still blacks who supported the Spanish colonial government against the Cuban insurgents. [JMH]

2034 Hu-DeHart, Evelyn. Chinese coolie labour in Cuba in the nineteenth century: free labour or neo-slavery? (*Slavery Abolit.*, 14:1, April 1993, p. 67–86)

Carefully written and researched work assesses condition of Chinese laborers in Cuba. Highly recommended. [JMH]

2035 Jennings, Lawrence. French anti-slavery under the Restoration: the Société de la morale chrétienne. (*Rev. fr. hist. Outre-mer*, 81:304, 1994, p. 321–331)

Authority on politics of France's 1848 abolition of slavery describes the first French abolitionist society. Founded in 1820s by Protestants as a charitable non-denominational organization, the society combined abolitionist goals with philanthropic work for slaves. It recruited among liberal opposition elites who would work for abolition after assuming power in 1830s. [APD]

2036 Jornadas sobre Cuba y su Historia, 1st, Madrid, 1991. Cuba, la perla de las Antillas: actas. Edición de Consuelo Naranjo Orovio y Tomás Mallo Gutiérrez. Madrid: Doce Calles; Consejo Superior de Investigaciones Científicas, 1994. 344 p.: bibl., ill., index.

Interesting anthology covers various aspects of 19th-century Cuba. While none of the essays is ground-breaking, most are worth reading. [JMH]

2037 Kartick, Reuben. O Tye Kim and the establishment of the Chinese settlement of Hopetown. (*Guyana Hist. J.*, 1, 1989, p. 37–50)

With land grant from the British Crown, Singapore-born missionary established settlement for disgruntled Chinese immigrants in 1865. Flooding and lack of subsistence crops compounded problems settlers encountered from hostile planter legislators. Natural population decrease and movement of youths to urban centers finally led to collapse of settlement after Kim's sudden departure following a major personal scandal. [ELC]

2038 Kirkpatrick, Margery. From the Middle Kingdom to the New World: aspects of the Chinese experience in migration to British Guiana. v. 1. Georgetown: M. Kirkpatrick, 1993. 1 v.: ill., maps, ports.

Author asserts that book is "about my family and others like them who came from 1853 to 1879 to work as indentured laborers in British Guiana." While drawing heavily on experiences of the Kirkpatricks, she includes useful data on, and incomplete family trees of, other members of Chinese community. [ELC]

2039 Lanaghan, Mrs. Antigua and the Antiguans. London: MacMillan Education, 1991. 2 v.: bibl.

Written by individual who lived on Antigua for some time, reprinted 19th-century classic deals with early history of British possession during its heyday. Despite claims that she was presenting "an impartial view of slavery and the free labour systems," author's anti-slavery sympathies are apparent. Includes important economic and demographic statistics on island, and genealogies of prominent families. [ELC]

2040 Laurence, K.O. A question of labour: indentured immigration into Trinidad and British Guiana, 1875–1917. New York: St. Martin's Press, 1994. 648 p.: bibl., index, maps.

Author's magnum opus, long overdue, fails to incorporate perspectives from recent studies that appeared since research was first conducted. Book's major importance rests in detailed information and useful statistics it provides on important subject. Discusses mortality, settlement, economic strivings, social organization, and termination of indentureship. [ELC]

2041 Look Lai, Walton. Indentured labor, Caribbean sugar: Chinese and Indian migrants to the British West Indies, 1838–1918. Introduction by Sidney W. Mintz. Baltimore, Md.: Johns Hopkins Univ. Press, 1993. 370 p.: bibl., index, maps. (Johns Hopkins studies in Atlantic history and culture)

Modern comprehensive examination of Chinese and Indian immigration into British Caribbean, especially major receiving colonies of Jamaica, Trinidad, and British Guiana. Addresses indentureship agreements that immigrants entered, non-indentured labor, and relationship between islands' agricultural and commercial growth. Argues for dialectical pluralist model for Caribbean, rather than traditional melting-pot syndrome. Pathbreaking study. [ELC]

2042 Luperón, Gregorio. Ideario de Luperón, 1839–1897. Recopilación de José Chez Checo. Santo Domingo: Ediciones de Taller, 1989. 354 p.: ill., indexes. (Biblioteca Taller; 274)

Useful anthology of writings by leader of Second Dominican Independence movement includes his thoughts on 11 different topics. Also contains very helpful chronology by Emilio Rodríguez Demorizi. [JMH]

2043 Mangar, Tota C. The rural and interior development policy of Henry Irving, 1882–1887. (*Hist. Gaz.*, 42, March 1992, p. 2–11, map)

Drawing heavily on material from Guyana's National Archives, author fruitfully examines tenure of colonial administrator whose "enlightened" policies spurred village development and improvement. By allocating funds for road construction, improving village governance, enhancing drainage and irrigation, and facilitating land purchase by East Indians, Irving helped undermine power of planter class. [ELC]

2044 Mangru, Simon. Anglican efforts to evangelize the East Indians in British Guiana, 1873–1898. (*Hist. Gaz.*, 61, Oct. 1993, p. 2–23, ill., tables)

Argues that, although evangelization started before 1850, it was systematized and extended during next two decades. Beginning in 1893, decreasing proselytization efforts by Britain and local Anglican church whose resources were diminishing led to overall decline in Anglican activities. Mostly institutional church history, with inadequate attention to actions, goals, and aspirations of East Indians. See also item **2045**. [ELC]

2045 Mangru, Simon. The role of the Anglicans in the evangelization of the East Indians in British Guiana, 1838–1919. (*Hist. Gaz.*, 57, June 1993, p. 2–19, ill.)

Presents overview of efforts by State Anglican church to work among East Indian laborers at height of migration. Concludes that differences between church leadership and planters militated against church achieving full potential in this field. See also item **2044**. [ELC]

2046 Marrero Zaldívar, Víctor Manuel. Cronología mínima del mayor general Vicente García González. Las Tunas, Cuba: Sección de Patrimonio Cultural, 1988. 58 p.: bibl., ill.

Noteworthy because of paucity of materials on this general. [JMH]

2047 Martí, José. El General Gómez. La Habana: Editora Política, 1986. 237 p.: bibl., port. (Col. Textos martianos)

Two-thirds of volume is made up of

letters from Martí to Gómez, most of them published previously. Remaining third is devoted to Gómez's writings, on Martí or addressed to Martí, some published for the first time. [JMH]

2048 Martínez-Fernández, Luis. El anexionismo dominicano y la lucha entre imperios durante la Primera República, 1844–1861. (*Rev. Rev. Interam.*, 22:1/2, primavera 1992, p. 168–190, bibl.)

Scholarly study emphasizes relevance of foreign factors in development of 19th-century annexationism in Dominican Republic. [JMH]

2049 Martínez-Fernández, Luis. The sweet and the bitter: Cuban and Puerto Rican responses to the mid-nineteenth-century sugar challenge. (*NWIG*, 67:1/2, 1993, p. 47–67, bibl.)

Provides succinct recapitulation of differences between sugar industries of Cuba and Puerto Rico in terms of timing, composition of planter class, access to capital resources, and reliance on slave labor force. Argues that in the face of crisis—what author calls the mid-19th-century sugar challenge—Cuba modernized and Puerto Rico diversified its agricultural production. [TMV]

2050 Mayer, Francine M. and **Carolyn E. Fick.** Slavery, slave emancipation and social reorganization in 19th-century Saint Barthélemy, French West Indies. (*in* El poblamiento de las Américas, *Veracruz, 1992.* Actas. Liège, Belgium: International Union for the Scientific Study of Population, 1992, v. 1, p. 233–259, bibl., graphs, tables)

Presents significant findings from research in progress on demographic changes experienced in this small island that faced economic decline following abolition of slavery. Although authors obscure their analysis somewhat by grouping free-coloreds with slaves, they convincingly link economic decline with trends toward feminization and creolization, and show that female-headed households persist as primary type of town residential unit. [APD]

2051 Mayo Santana, Raúl and **Mariano Negrón Portillo.** La familia esclava urbana en San Juan en el siglo XIX. (*Rev. Cienc. Soc./ Río Piedras*, 30:1/2, enero/junio 1993, p. 163–197, tables)

Part of a larger project, article reviews what is known about slavery in Puerto Rico in 19th century. Uses information from "Registro Central de Esclavos de 1872" to offer quantitative and historico-sociological analyses of slave families in San Juan. Tests hypothesis that slaves developed alternative forms of family life as adaptations to the oppression they suffered. [B. Aguirre-López]

2052 Maza Miquel, Manuel P. Desiderio Mesnier, 1852–1913: un sacerdote y patriota cubano para todos los tiempos. (*Estud. Soc./Santo Domingo*, 26:92, abril/junio 1993, p. 77–92, bibl.)

A significant contribution to the literature on Church-State relations during 1895–98 Cuban War of Independence. Based on extensive archival research. [JMH]

2053 Maza Miquel, Manuel P. León XIII, José Martí y el Padre McGlynn: un esforzado luchador social en Nueva York a fines del siglo XIX. (*Estud. Soc./Santo Domingo*, 24:84, abril/junio 1991, p. 43–63, bibl.)

Most commentators on Martí's assessment of the McGlynn affair know about either Martí or the Church; Father Maza is well versed about both. It will be hard to produce a more balanced and dispassionate study of the problem than this. [JMH]

2054 Mena Múgica, Mayra and **Severiano Hernández Vicente.** La administración autonómica española de Cuba en 1898: catálogo de la documentación de la Cámara de Representantes del Parlamento Insular y de la Presidencia del Consejo de Secretarios. Salamanca, Spain: Ediciones Univ. de Salamanca, 1994. 111 p.: bibl. (Obras de referencia; 6. Fuentes documentales de la administración española en el Archivo Nacional de Cuba.)

Research tool is useful for study of Cuban political institutions in late 19th century. [JMH]

2055 Menezes, Mary Noel. The winged impulse: the Madeiran Portuguese in Guyana; an economic, socio-cultural perspective. (*Guyana Hist. J.*, 1, 1989, p. 17–36)

Provides graphic analysis of reasons for Portuguese migration to British Guiana and Madeirans' economic contributions to the colony. Concludes that, apart from their role as financiers and business persons, the Madeiran influence was also notable in the socio-cultural realm, where they left their mark on religious festivals, cuisine, education, and fraternal and other self-help organizations. Excellent work. [ELC]

2056 Menier, Marie-Antoinette. Hommes sages contre sages-femmes à la Guadeloupe, 1829–1842. (*Bull. Soc. hist. Guadeloupe*, 87/90, 1991, p. 3–29, bibl.)

Welcome gender perspective is brought to burgeoning field of Caribbean medical history. Describes effort of two professional midwives sent by French government to Guadeloupe to teach obstetrics and professionalize midwifery, in the face of opposition from naval medical authorities. Their social origins and careers are illustrative of widows who characteristically entered teaching and medical professions in 19th century. [APD]

2057 Montejo Arrechea, Carmen Victoria. Sociedades de instrucción y recreo de pardos y morenos que existieron en Cuba colonial: período 1878–1898. Veracruz, Mexico: Gobierno del Estado de Veracruz, Instituto Veracruzano de Cultura, 1993. 138 p.: bibl.

Although not the first study published on the subject, this carefully written and researched work is probably the most orderly and systematic. [JMH]

2058 Moreno Fraginals, Manuel R. and José J. Moreno Masó. Análisis comparativo de las principales corrientes inmigratorias españolas hacia Cuba: 1846–1898. (*in* Coloquio de Historia Canario-Americana, *9th, Spain, 1990*. Actas. Las Palmas, Spain: Cabildo Insular de Gran Canaria, 1992, v. 1, p. 479–509, tables)

Study shows that from 1862–66, a period for which data appear to be more reliable, majority of Spanish immigrants into Cuba came from Asturias. Canary Islander immigrants were less numerous. [JMH]

2059 Moreno Masó, José J. La petjada dels catalans a Cuba: assaig sobre la presència catalana a Cuba durant la primera meitat del segle XIX. Barcelona: Generalitat de Catalunya, Comissió Amèrica i Catalunya, 1992, 1993. 108 p.: bibl., ill. (Col. Joan Orpí)

Although according to the title the book focuses primarily on first half of 19th century, it actually goes beyond that time limit. Sections devoted to analysis of sources and the bibliography are of special interest to historians. [JMH]

2060 Mörner, Magnus. Patterns of social stratification in the 18th- and 19th-century Caribbean: some comparative clarifications. (*Plant. Soc. Am.*, 3:2, 1993, p. 1–30, bibl., tables)

Sophisticated comparative study focuses on stratification in post-emancipation societies of Haiti, Martinique, Barbados, Jamaica, Cuba, and Puerto Rico. Also considers some of the general problems in comparative history. For ethnologist's comment see *HLAS 55:819*. [J. Britton]

2061 Mudd, Patricia Marirea. Portuguese Bermudians: early history and reference guide, 1849–1949. Louisville, Ky.: Historical Research Publishers, 1991. 704 p.: bibl., ill., index.

Aimed at demonstrating non-agricultural contributions of Portuguese migrants, book includes useful information on early Bermudan history and post-1850 Portuguese presence. Drawing heavily on local government gazettes, contains: surnames; ships' lists of migrants; marriage, birth, and death records; immigration applications and disposition of cases; and lists of unclaimed letters. Invaluable for genealogical research and local history. [ELC]

2062 La muerte de José Martí: versiones y discrepancias de Máximo Gómez. Antología, recopilación de documentos y notas de Florencio García-Cisneros. New York: Ediciones de Noticias de Arte, 1994. 1 v. (Col. Revisión histórica cubana)

To make Gen. Máximo Gómez responsible for the death of José Martí is a bit farfetched, but author makes other points that deserve close examination. [JMH]

Naranjo Orovio, Consuelo. Trabajo libre e inmigración española en Cuba: 1880–1930. See item **2180.**

2063 Navarro García, Jesús Raúl. Entre esclavos y constituciones: el colonialismo liberal de 1837 en Cuba. Sevilla, Spain: Escuela de Estudios Hispano-Americanos, 1991. 299 p.: bibl. (Publicaciones de la Escuela de Estudios Hispano-Americanos de Sevilla; 365. Col. Dos colores)

Author is certainly well versed in early 19th-century Caribbean history. A carefully written and researched study. [JMH]

2064 Navarro García, Jesús Raúl. Promotores religiosos de la educación superior en Puerto Rico a principios del siglo XIX. (*Estud. Hist. Soc. Econ. Am.*, 9, 1992, p. 355–368)

Explains actions of local religious hierarchy, especially of Nicolás Alonso de Andrade, by pointing to economic and ideological considerations of higher clergy. According to author, Church officials favored absolutist regimes not only because they provided financial security, but also because their political tenets fit well with conservative nature of Church doctrine. [TMV]

2065 Navarro García, Jesús Raúl. Los proyectos de universidad en Puerto Rico durante la primera mitad del siglo XIX: el marco socio-cultural. (*Estud. Hist. Soc. Econ. Am.*, 9, 1992, p. 131–141)

Analyzes establishment of Colegio de San Ildefonso in 1825 and Seminario Conciliar in 1832 as attempts to control ideological content of education. Likewise, foundation of the university met with obstacles from clergy and from metropolitan authorities who insisted on religious and political orthodoxy. [TMV]

2066 Núñez Florencio, Rafael. Los republicanos españoles ante el problema colonial: la cuestión cubana. (*Rev. Indias*, 53:198, mayo/agosto 1993, p. 545–561)

Provides clear, well-documented, and balanced assessment of the attitude of the Spanish Republicans. [JMH]

Obras completas de José Martí: iconografía, cronología. See item **19.**

2067 Offner, John L. The De Lôme letter: a Spanish and Cuban perspective. (*MACLAS: Lat. Am. Essays*, 4, 1991?, p. 79–87)

Focuses on new aspects of a much-studied subject. Whether President McKinley's policy toward Cuban insurgents would have been different had the Cuban junta been more cooperative is highly debatable. [JMH]

2068 Paquette, Robert L. and **Joseph C. Dorsey.** The Escoto Papers and Cuban slave resistance. (*Slavery Abolit.*, 15:3, Dec. 1994, p. 88–95, appendix, photo)

Article is crucial for study and understanding of slave resistance in colonial Cuba as Escoto Papers contain much significant information. [JMH]

2069 Paz Sánchez, Manuel de; José Fernández Fernández; and **Nelson López Novegil.** El bandolerismo en Cuba, 1800–1933: presencia canaria y protesta rural. Prólogo de María Poumier. Canary Islands: Centro de la Cultura Popular Canaria, 1993. 2 v.: bibl., ill., index. (Taller de Historia; 15, 16)

The most comprehensive survey to date of rural banditry in Cuba during the period, work makes ample use of primary sources but is oblivious to recent criticism of Hobsbawm's concept of "social banditry." Authors also embrace some very debatable interpretations of certain phases of Cuban history. Perhaps an excessively romantic view of some hero-villains. [JMH]

2070 Pérez Guzmán, Francisco. Bolívar y la independencia de Cuba. La Habana: Editorial Letras Cubanas, 1988. 195 p.: bibl.

Offers careful and impartial assessment of controversy about Bolívar's true intentions regarding independence of Cuba and Puerto Rico. [JMH]

2071 Persaud, Walter H. Benevolent rationality: a Foucauldian reading of the historiography of East Indians in 19th-century British Guiana. (*in* Forging identities and patterns of development in Latin America and the Caribbean. Edited by Harry P. Díaz, Joanna W.A. Rummens, and Patrick D.M. Taylor. Toronto: Canadian Scholars' Press, 1991, p. 289–311)

Uses Foucault's approach to dissect a number of modern histories of the East Indian experience in British Guiana. Contends that most writers read 19th-century texts as documents, without regard for fact that such "texts do not just tell us about East Indians in 19th century British Guiana but were active in producing East Indians of a century ago that we know today" (p. 292). Bemoans fact that today's dominant view stemmed from historians' highlighting only issues of interest to them. [ELC]

Peynado, Francisco José. Papeles y escritos de Francisco José Peynado, 1867–1933, prócer de la Tercera República. v. 1. See item **2189.**

2072 Poey Baró, Dionisio. La entrada de los aldamistas en la Guerra de los Diez Años. La Habana: Editorial de Ciencias Sociales, 1989. 114 p.: bibl. (Historia de Cuba)

Account is interesting but not entirely convincing. The preconceptions of the author are too obvious and his perspective is too narrow. [JMH]

2073 **Potter, Lesley M.** Indian and African-Guyanese village settlement patterns and inter-group relationships, 1871–1921. (*Hist. Gaz.*, 48, Sept. 1992, p. 2–15, ill.)

Through thorough examination of effects of official policy in influencing each group's location and in molding attitudes of members, author laments impact of partial separation of races on fostering of racial intolerance. Concludes that East Indians were more exclusive than Afro-Guyanese. [ELC]

2074 **Ramón de la Sagra y Cuba.** v. 1–2. Sada, Spain: Ediciós do Castro, 1992. 2 v.: bibl., ill. (Ensaio)

This solid, scholarly work perhaps will help put to rest the controversy about this important figure of colonial Cuba. Vol. 2, an anthology of La Sagra's writings on Cuba, includes an exhaustive bibliography. [JMH]

2075 **Recio Ferreras, Eloy.** Diario inédito escrito por un soldado español en la Guerra de Cuba, 1896–1899. (*Rev. Hist. Am.*, 112, julio/dic. 1991, p. 21–42, bibl.)

Diary tends to contradict veracity of most Cuban accounts of the 1895–98 War of Independence, which as a rule are too romantic and hagiographic. Also challenges view of the war offered by diaries of other Spanish soldiers. An important source that must be read in its entirety before passing judgment. [JMH]

2076 **Renard, Rosamunde.** Immigration and indentureship in the French West Indies, 1848–1870. (*in* Caribbean freedom: society and economy from emancipation to the present. Kingston: Randle, 1993, p. 161–167, tables)

Well-documented work looks at East Indian and African labor migrants chosen for their low costs to replace emancipated slaves in 1850s. Describes geographical origins, contractual conditions (including government subsidies to planters for migrants' passage and repatriation), poor diet and bad treatment, and their high level of strikes, desertion, and arson when their formal complaints failed to improve their lot. Underlines need for fresh study of labor-supplying regions and

of repatriation rates which were much higher in Martinique than in Guadeloupe. [APD]

2077 **Renard, Rosamunde.** Labour relations in Martinique and Guadeloupe, 1848–1870. (*J. Caribb. Hist.*, 26:1, 1992, p. 37–61, tables)

Author asserts that, following abolition of slavery, "a dependent and submissive labour force was transformed into one which was determined to take full advantage of its newly found independence from plantation labour." [APD]

2078 **Robles Muñoz, Cristóbal.** Negociar la paz en Cuba (1896–1897). (*Rev. Indias*, 53:198, mayo/agosto 1993, p. 493–527)

Author is one of the best exponents of the Spanish point of view regarding Spanish-American War. This article is highly recommended. [JMH]

2079 **Rodríguez Rodríguez, Aurea Verónica.** Bosquejo histórico de la enseñanza primaria en la isla de Cuba, 1790–1868. (*Arbor/Madrid*, 144:567, marzo 1993, p. 55–80, bibl., tables)

Sober assessment of primary education in Cuba at the time is based on primary and secondary sources. [JMH]

2080 **Roldán de Montaud, Inés.** Los partidos políticos y la polémica abolicionista tras la paz del Zanjón. (*in* Coloquio Internacional sobre Abolición de la Esclavitud, *Madrid, 1986*. Esclavitud y derechos humanos: la lucha por la libertad del negro en el siglo XIX; actas. Edición de Francisco de Solano y Agustín Guimerá. Madrid: Consejo Superior de Investigaciones Científicas, Centro de Estudios Históricos, Depto. de Historia de América, 1990, p. 499–513)

Brilliant study demolishes preconceptions and prejudices characteristic of previous works. Author knows the period quite well and has evidenced it once again. [JMH]

2081 **Roldán de Montaud, Inés.** La I República y Cuba. (*Rev. Complut. Hist. Am.*, 18, 1992, p. 257–279)

Required reading for all those interested in the period, about which author is most knowledgeable. [JMH]

2082 **Roldán de Montaud, Inés.** La Unión Constitucional y la política colonial de España en Cuba, 1868–1898. Madrid: Univ.

Complutense de Madrid, Facultad de Geografía y Historia, Depto. de Historia Contemporánea, 1991. 723 p.: bibl. (Col. Tesis doctorales; 296/91)

Well-researched doctoral dissertation is perhaps too long and detailed. Because of author's almost exclusive concentration on her topic, work also lacks perspective. However, makes undeniable contribution to our knowledge of a period largely neglected until very recently. [JMH]

2083 **Rose, James.** The repatriation controversy and the beginning of an East Indian village system. (*Guyana Hist. J.*, 1, 1989, p. 51–63)

Planters and local administrators promoted resident peasantry as method of keeping within the colony the labor and capital that might be unavailable if East Indians returned to their homeland. But plan failed because authorities never fully promoted a viable peasant class. Rather than furthering peasant interests, planter objectives remained paramount, eventually leading to renewed conflict. [ELC]

2084 **Sarracino, Rodolfo.** Cuba y Brazil: dos corrientes migratorias latinoamericanas de regreso a Africa en el siglo XIX. (*in* Colección nuestra patria es América: migraciones y vida urbana. Edición de Jorge Núñez Sánchez. Quito: Editora Nacional, 1992, v. 9, p. 13–41)

Based largely on secondary sources, work would not be noteworthy were it not for the lack of materials on the subject. [JMH]

2085 **Schnackenbourg, Christian.** La Banque de la Guadeloupe et la crise de change, 1895–1904. (*Bull. Soc. hist. Guadeloupe*, 87/90, 1991, p. 31–95, graph, table)

Drawing expertly from a recently opened archival collection, work examines management of a major financial crisis by State-controlled colonial bank and repercussions of crisis on local politics. Contrary to assertions of colored republican leaders, repeated by historians, white planters did not control bank's policy. The fact that the bank began distancing itself from the planters and maneuvered deftly between their lobby and that of the merchants signals planters' loss of influence in island's politics. A very worthy contribution to the literature on political economy of 19th-century sugar islands. [APD]

2086 **Schnackenbourg, Christian.** Un grand industriel guadeloupéen du XIXe siècle: Ernest Souques, 1831–1908. (*Bull. Soc. hist. Guadeloupe*, 95/98, 1993, p. 78–147)

Political biography of Guadeloupe's wealthiest and most powerful figure in second half of 19th century provides new vistas on modernization of sugar industry and rise of socialism. A Creole engineer who established the most advanced sugar factories in the Caribbean of the time, leader of white planter party, and owner of the main newspaper, Souques controlled island's politics. His turn-of-the-century confrontation with socialist leader Légitimus, an equally strong figure, ended in a famous *entente*. [APD]

2087 **Scott, Rebecca.** Former slaves: responses to emancipation in Cuba. (*in* Caribbean freedom: society and economy from emancipation to the present. Kingston: Randle, 1993, p. 21–27, table)

Shows that despite fears of slaveowners, abolition did not cause a disastrous flight of former slaves from plantation labor. [JMH]

2088 **Shepherd, Verene.** Indian females in Jamaica: an analysis of the population censuses, 1861–1943. (*Jam. Hist. Rev.*, 18, 1993, p. 18–29, tables)

Uses decennial censuses to discuss major characteristics of Jamaica's female East Indian population. Demonstrates their steady growth as percentage of population, although women never achieved numerical parity with men despite positive migration trends. Most women were engaged in agricultural activities, and tended to be at lower end of socioeconomic scale. Hard evidence supports long-held suspicions about main characteristics of this group. [ELC]

2089 **Taffin, Dominique.** Un passager clandestin?: le choléra à la Guadeloupe, 1865–1866. (*Bull. Soc. hist. Guadeloupe*, 83/86, 1990, p. 3–45, maps, tables)

Multi-layered cultural study based on original research examines 19th-century Guadeloupe's most devastating epidemic. Illuminating many changes in post-emancipation societies, work establishes that: 1) unlike previously well-known patterns of tropical disease, cholera spread to sugar-producing and mountainous regions far from ports, striking blacks and working women; 2) this spread was related to the unhealthy local living conditions of the poor; 3) because this pattern disproved traditional exogenous explanations, it provided elements for a social critique that authorities strove to smother; 4) the agricultural crisis caused by island's immobilization accelerated changes in the sugar industry; and 5) the eight percent population loss induced increased immigration of indentureds. [APD]

2090 Taverna Sánchez, Cristina. Hacia una concepción de la ciencia en el siglo XIX cubano: José de la Luz y Caballero. (*Santiago/ Cuba*, 75, junio 1993, p. 123–151, bibl.)

Work is basically a study of relationship between science and social progress in the thought of Luz y Caballero. [JMH]

2091 Thésée, Françoise. La révolte des esclaves du Carbet à la Martinique: octobre-novembre 1822. (*Rev. fr. hist. Outre-mer*, 80: 301, 4e trimestre 1993, p. 552–584)

Detailed reconstruction of Martinique's last great slave revolt relates the sequence of events and their geographic scope, socioeconomic characteristics of participants, master-slave relationships, and actions of main protagonists. Provides fascinating new data on militaristic style of the plot, the judicial inquiry conducted by authorities, and the publicly-staged executions meant to increase the impact of repression. [APD]

2092 Uría González, Jorge et al. Asturias y Cuba en torno al 98. Barcelona: Editorial Labor, 1994. 237 p.: bibl., maps. (Labor universitaria)

Topics covered in this volume have all been studied before, for Spain as a whole. However, by focusing specifically on the Asturias region and Asturian immigrants to Cuba, author has greatly enhanced our perspective of the subject. [JMH]

2093 Verteuil, Anthony de. Madrasi emigration to Trinidad, 1846–1916. (*Hist. Soc./Río Piedras*, 4, 1991, p. 75–94, ill., map, tables)

Drawing on sources in government archives as well as ships' registers, author examines origin, flow, and disposition of Madrasi laborers in Trinidad at high point of Indian migration. Also looks at religious and social background of immigrants, and ineffective efforts in Trinidad to Christianize them. [ELC]

2094 Wagenheim, Olga Jiménez de. Puerto Rico's revolt for independence: *El Grito de Lares*. Princeton, N.J.: M. Wiener Pub., 1993. 127 p.: bibl., ill., index, map.

When published for the first time in 1984, *El Grito de Lares* successfully demythified events surrounding Puerto Rico's failed attempt at independence in 1868. Available in English since 1985 (see *HLAS 50:1723*) and now reissued, title work complements Laird Bergad's excellent economic study of the period of coffee ascendancy, *Coffee and the growth of agrarian capitalism in nineteenth-century Puerto Rico* (see *HLAS 46:2522*). Wagenheim's contribution lies in her detailed accounts of participant motivations obtained through a careful examination of court proceedings against those arrested after the event—landowners, slaves, merchants, shopkeepers, and others. [TMV]

2095 Walker, George P.J. The life of Daniel Gateward Davis: first bishop of Antigua. St. Kitts, West Indies: Creole Pub. Co., 1992. 156 p.: bibl., ill.

In brief study, author provides sketch of a priest and later bishop who presided over diocese of the Leeward Islands at the crucial transitional period after abolition of slavery. Mostly biographical, work fails to weave Davis' tenure into societal and political changes. [ELC]

2096 Walker-Kilkenny, Roberta. The Leonora strike of 1939. (*Hist. Gaz.*, 46, July 1992, p. 2–9, map, tables)

Argues that consolidation of estates between 1838–1938 afforded little scope for workers to bargain for improved working conditions or enhanced wages. Examines course of strike that necessitated setting up of commission of inquiry. Trade unionism was result of enhanced working-class consciousness. [ELC]

2097 Walvin, James. The life and times of Henry Clarke of Jamaica, 1828–1907. Ilford, England; Portland, Oregon: F. Cass, 1994. 155 p., 2 p. of plates: bibl., ill.

Making ample use of extensive diaries and other writings remaining on island, author has meticulously recreated life of this cleric, teacher, businessman, and politician. Book provides excellent portrait of Clarke and of late 19th-century Jamaica. Demonstrates loneliness of this important social and moral critic who was appreciated in death though virtually scorned while alive. [ELC]

The War of 1898 and U.S. interventions, 1898–1934: an encyclopedia. See item **2211.**

2098 Willock, Roger. Bulwark of empire: Bermuda's fortified naval base, 1860–1920. 2nd ed. Old Royal Navy Dockyard, Bermuda: Bermuda Maritime Museum Press, 1988. 189 p.: bibl., ill., index.

Provides historical background and relates methods of employing most of Bermuda's 19th-century forts. Offers spirited defense of argument that fortifications were constructed for defense of Naval Base rather than of the island. Provides insights on experiences of individuals who served in forts, fruitful discussion of North America and West Indian Squadron, and examination of Bermuda's role in international history. Highly important tome. [ELC]

2099 Wilmot, Swithin R. Politics and labour conflicts in Jamaica, 1838–1865. (*Hist. Soc./Río Piedras,* 4, 1991, p. 95–106, tables)

Examines meaning of freedom for ex-slaves. Discusses their involvement in politics and efforts to build new systems of labor on estates. Whereas they asked for full participation in the political realm, on the estates they limited their demands to autonomy. [ELC]

2100 Woolford, Hazel M. The reaction of the press to the Compulsory Denominational Education Bill of 1876. (*Hist. Gaz.,* 39, Dec. 1991, p. 2–12, ill., tables)

Author contends that cynicism over this bill, introduced in British Guiana so soon after passage of controversial act of 1870, effectively doomed it from the start. East Indians were generally opposed to it and preferred to send their children to nonsectarian schools. Resulted in high absentee rate among children. [ELC]

2101 Yacou, Alain. La insurgencia negra en la isla de Cuba en la primera mitad del siglo XIX. (*Rev. Indias,* 53:197, enero/abril 1993, p. 23–51)

Work is interesting contribution to a field in which scarcity of reliable documentation makes possible a great variety of generalizations. [JMH]

20TH CENTURY

Acosta-Belén, Edna. Ideología colonialista y cultura nacional puertorriqueña. See item **1802.**

2102 Alvarez-Tabío Albo, Emma. Vida, mansión y muerte de la burgesía cubana. Prólogo de Roberto Segre. La Habana: Editorial Letras Cubanas, 1989. 196 p.: bibl., ill. (Ensayo. Giraldilla)

Basically an architectural study of residences that wealthy Cubans built for themselves from 1900–1944. Useful given the dearth of materials on the subject. [JMH]

2103 Aparicio Laurencio, Angel. Blas Hernández y la revolución de 1933: la campaña en los campos de Cuba. Edición y prólogo a cargo de Jorge Hernández Martín. Miami, Fla.: Ediciones Universal, 1994. 183 p.: bibl., ill. (Col. Cuba y sus jueces)

This little book's purpose is to correct the historical record about Juan Blas Hernández, a Cuban guerrilla leader of the 1930s, and to expose alleged falsifications of the history of the 1933 revolution. Author's critique of Hugh Thomas' well-known work on Cuba (see *HLAS 34:2069a*) is unmitigated and rather severe. Recommended reading for all those interested in the period. [JMH]

2104 Auguste, Claude B. L'Union nationale des étudiants haïtiens, U.N.E.H. (*Rev. Soc. haïti.,* 48:174, déc. 1992, p. 65–90)

Haitian historian who helped found country's first student federation in 1960 recalls opposition to Duvalier, which was strong in the education sector of an otherwise weak union movement. Describes federation's Marxist, internationalist line and its total repression by dictatorship. [APD]

2105 Ayala, César J. La nueva plantación antillana, 1898–1934. (*Op. Cit./Río Piedras,* 8, 1994, p. 121–165)

Author explores Susan Archer Mann's theory regarding adoption of pre-capitalist relations of agricultural production when there are large discrepancies between time of work and time of production such as occurs in the sugar industry. Comparison between Puerto Rico and Cuba suggests that solutions ranged from flexible production to on-time deliveries on the part of *colonos* (providers of raw cane to the central mill), but hardly included an expansion of pre-capitalist structures. [TMV]

2106 Barceló Miller, María de Fátima. La mujer en la literatura histórica puertorriqueña de Brau a la Generación del 40. (*Rev. Inst. Cult. Puertorriq.*, 26:97, 1987, p. 12–18, bibl.)

Traces trajectory of historians' writing about women, beginning with Salvador Brau's progressive stance regarding potential of women at turn of the century, through nostalgic construction of passive role of women of 1930s generation, to reaffirmation of women's insignificance in discourse of 1940s. The "new historiography" of late 1960s, author argues, liberated island's history from bourgeois domination and paved way for incorporation of women on an equal footing in the writing of history. [TMV]

2107 Barcia Zequeira, María del Carmen. Los primeros partidos políticos burgueses de Cuba. (*Arbor/Madrid,* 144:567, marzo 1993, p. 101–116)

Although interesting because of dearth of materials on the subject, work is politically motivated and permeated by ideology. [JMH]

Baud, Michiel. Una frontera para cruzar: la sociedad rural a través de la frontera dominico-haitiana, 1870–1930. See item **1984.**

2108 Baud, Michiel. Una frontera-refugio: dominicanos y haitianos contra el Estado, 1870–1930. (*Estud. Soc. /Santo Domingo,* 26:92, abril/junio 1993, p. 39–64, bibl.)

Author's thesis is that Haitian-Dominican frontier should be regarded as a socioeconomic universe rather than an area of Haitian penetration. Based largely on primary sources. [JMH]

2109 Baud, Michiel. Historia de un sueño: los ferrocarriles públicos en la República Dominicana, 1880–1930. Santo Domingo: Fundación Cultural Dominicana, 1993. 145 p., 7 p. of plates: bibl., ill.

Scholarly study examines rise and fall of the Cibao railroads. Although profusely annotated, work suffers from lack of a bibliographical essay. [JMH]

2110 Betances, Emelio. The formation of the Dominican capitalist State and the United States military occupation of 1916–1924. (*MACLAS: Lat. Am. Essays,* 4, 1991?, p. 231–253, bibl.)

Shows how US policy vis-à-vis local political elites changed in the effort to organize a strong national government. Well documented and carefully written. [JMH]

2111 Bojórquez Urzaiz, Carlos. Cubanos patriotas en Yucatán. Mérida, Mexico: Fomento Editorial, Univ. Autónoma de Yucatán, Facultad de Antropología, 1988. 132 p.: bibl.

Curious account of Cuban conspiratorial activities in Yucatán during anti-Batista struggle, written by a Mexican anthropologist who is unquestionably a fervent admirer of Fidel Castro. [JMH]

2112 Bolland, O. Nigel. On the march: labour rebellions in the British Caribbean, 1934–39. Kingston: Ian Randle Publishers; London: James Currey Publishers, 1995. 216 p.: bibl., index, map.

Important study examines wave of labor unrest that rocked Anglophone Caribbean in 1930s. Author evaluates background causes of unrest; details occurrences on each colony; and offers interpretation of long-term consequences. Growth of trade unionism and emergence of political parties are major results of these disturbances, with considerable political change coming later. Good work. [ELC]

Boutin, Raymond. Notes sur les mariages à Pointe-Noire de 1850 a 1946. See item **1986.**

2113 Brache Batista, Anselmo. Constanza, Maimón y Estero Hondo: testimonios e investigación sobre los acontecimientos. 2. ed. ampliada y corr. Santo Domingo: Taller, 1993. 344 p.: bibl., ill.

Unpretentious but informative, and occasionally even suggestive, account focuses on Cuba-sponsored invasion of the Dominican Republic in 1959. Author probably exaggerates invasion's impact on subsequent events. [JMH]

2114 Browne, Whitman T. From commoner to king: Robert L. Bradshaw, crusader for dignity and justice in the Caribbean. Lanham, Md.: Univ. Press of America, 1992. 425 p.: bibl., ill., index.

First biography of St. Kitts trade unionist and politician who was active in working-class politics on island from 1944–78 is based on extensive interviews with, among others, Bradshaw's family members, and is generally sympathetic to him. As book contains many inaccuracies, especially when venturing beyond St. Kitts, it should be read with caution. [ELC]

2115 Buffon, Alain. L'affaire Zévallos: une expérience d'autogestion en Guadeloupe au début du siècle. (*Bull. Soc. hist. Guadeloupe*, 95/98, 1993, p. 41–77)

Offers new approach to new topic. In 1905 one of the island's most important sugar factories, or *centrales*, declared bankruptcy. In an attempt to reorganize production on a new basis, socialist leaders united small planters and tried to diversify crops. Their innovative policy failed, however, when dumping by white planters drove down sugar prices. Buffon locates this first experiment in self-management in context of rising socialism that followed sugar crisis of 1884–95, as republican France began to reduce its unconditional support of the white Creole oligarchy. [APD]

Buffon, Alain. La Banque de la Guadeloupe en 1895: le rapport Chaudié. See item **1988.**

2116 C.L.R. James's Caribbean. Edited by Paget Henry and Paul Buhle. Durham, N.C.: Duke Univ. Press, 1992. 287 p.: bibl., ill., index.

Extremely useful collection of essays deals with work, life, and influence on regional politics and culture of preeminent Caribbean man of letters and political critic. Authors contend that James advocated efforts towards mass organizations, regional unity, and participatory politics by workers to address the problem of underdevelopment in Caribbean countries. [ELC]

2117 *Les Cahiers du patrimoine.* No. 9, juillet/août/sept. 1990 [et] No. 10, oct./nov./déc. 1990, Dossier: Fort-de-France dans les années 30, v. 1–2. Fort-de-France: Bureau du Patrimoine du Conseil Régional de la Martinique.

Vol. 1 of this fascinating two-part monograph on Martinique's capital draws judiciously from professional historians as well as literary authors. Vol. 1 focuses on a wide range of topics—water and canal system, public buildings, epidemics, etc. Vol. 2 covers Martinique's collective housing, games and social gatherings in popular neighborhoods, its memory of hurricanes and other cataclysms, and voluntary social services organized by women in early 20th century. Volumes bear testimony to growing recent interest in urban cultural history in the Caribbean. [APD]

Caribbean freedom: society and economy from emancipation to the present. See item **1993.**

2118 Castro Pereda, Rafael. Idioma, historia y nación: ensayos de Rafael Castro Pereda y documentos históricos sobre la *Ley del Idioma.* Puerto Rico: Editorial Talleres, 1993. 237 p.: ill.

A collection that includes important government documents regarding historical changes in the official language status of Puerto Rico from the US takeover to the present, as well as several of Castro Pereda's essays on the most recent struggles of the Puerto Rican people to assert themselves as a Spanish-speaking nation and combat internal and external assimilationist language policies. [E. Acosta-Belén]

2119 Chamberlain, Mary. Renters and farmers: the Barbadian plantation tenantry system, 1917–1937. (*J. Caribb. Hist.*, 24:2, 1990, p. 195–225)

Studies six neighboring villages around three plantations in St. Phillip's parish. Based largely on oral testimonies, author concludes that though divisions tended to make negotiation for improved conditions difficult, workers were never defeated, though they may have been outwardly despondent. [ELC]

2120 Chathuant, Dominique. La Guadeloupe dans l'obédience de Vichy, 1940/1943. (*Bull. Soc. hist. Guadeloupe*, 91/94, 1992, p. 3–40, graph, maps, table)

Study on French Lesser Antilles during World War II enlarges scope of Caribbean political history through careful assessment of policies of colonial authorities in response to a complex international scene. French Antilles were surrounded by English islands supporting *France Libre*, and were increasingly entering the orbit of latter's ally, the US. Study deftly weaves ideological, economic, cultural, and social strands to depict internal dynamics of a *vichyste* regime in a tropical colony. Provides myriad fresh data on local politics, women, agricultural policy, etc. Departing from previous superficial studies, shows that exaggerated reputations of Vichy authorities cut off from France did not, in fact, give them effective local leverage. [APD]

2121 Cincuenta años de exilio español en Puerto Rico y el Caribe, 1939–1989: memorias del congreso conmemorativo celebrado en San Juan de Puerto Rico. Sada, Spain: Ediciós do Castro, 1991. 364 p.: bibl., ill. (Serie Documentos/Ediciós do Castro; 87)

Contains collection of papers, of uneven quality, presented at the "Congreso sobre el Impacto de la Guerra Civil Española y el Exilio Español en Puerto Rico y el Caribe" in 1989. Leading academic figures from Europe, US, and Latin America describe activities of Spanish exiles during 1930s and 1940s, when islands of Hispanic Caribbean were reconstituting themselves culturally as well as politically and economically. Essays cover Spanish presence in politics and society, literature, and the arts. One section is dedicated to women's contributions. [TMV]

2122 Collazo Pérez, Enrique. Una pelea cubana contra los monopolios: un estudio sobre el crac bancario de 1920. Oviedo, Spain: Vicerrectorado de Relaciones Institucionales, 1994. 93 p.: bibl., ill. (Resultados de la cooperación de la Univ. de Oviedo con Iberoamérica; 1)

Work is well researched but written from excessively nationalistic Cuban perspective. The same material may be interpreted in an entirely different way, even accepting basic opposition between Cuban and US interests. [JMH]

Colón, Jesús. The way it was, and other writings. See item **3554.**

2123 Conflict and change in Cuba. Edited by Enrique A. Baloyra and James A. Morris. Albuquerque: Univ. of New Mexico Press, 1993. 347 p.: bibl., index, map.

Praiseworthy attempt to determine why Cuba has not yet gone the way of its erstwhile Communist allies in Eastern Europe and the Soviet Union is highly recommended for readers interested in the subject. For political scientist's comment see *HLAS 55:3116.* [JMH]

2124 Constable, Pamela. Haiti: a nation in despair, a policy adrift. (*Curr. Hist.*, 93: 581, March 1994, p. 108–115)

Reviews efforts to restore Jean-Bertrand Aristide to Haitian presidency. Focuses on events leading to Oct. 1993 withdrawal of the USS Harlan County and impact of that event. [JG]

2125 Contrera, Nelio. Julio Antonio Mella: el joven precursor. La Habana: Editora Política, 1987. 112 p.: bibl., ill.

Interesting portrait of Mella is based on reminiscences of men and women who knew him. [JMH]

2126 Cordero Michel, Emilio. Las expediciones de junio de 1959. (*Estud. Soc./ Santo Domingo*, 25:88, abril/junio 1992, p. 35–66, bibl., tables)

Author contends that although expeditions in question failed, they had an impact on the events that culminated in the downfall of Trujillo. [JMH]

2127 Córdova, Gonzalo F. Resident Commissioner Santiago Iglesias and his times. Río Piedras: Editorial de la Univ. de Puerto Rico, 1993. 513 p.: bibl., ill.

Traditional political biography profiles Santiago Iglesias Pantín, a Spanish-born, early 20th-century labor activist, leader of the Partido Socialista, which allied with the Unión Republicana to win elections on the island in 1932 and 1936. Based on US Congressional Record and on papers of Iglesias himself, book concentrates on his role as Resident Commissioner in 1930s. Work is strong on context, providing a rich description of Puerto Rico in the three periods covered: 1896–1917, when Iglesias allied his cause to that of Samuel Gompers and the American Federation of Labor; 1917–32, when the Partido Socialista was created to channel labor demands; and 1932–39, when Iglesias became active in Washington politics. It is unfortunate that the wealth of information the author uncovered, and detailed chronology he offers, are used only to vindicate the figure of Iglesias as a "realistic and pragmatic" advocate of the working class who achieved reform by working the system. By not addressing Iglesias' pro-US, anti-independence, non-socialist stand, Córdova leaves unexplored the interconnections between labor politics, party affiliations, and nationalist discourse. [TMV]

2128 Craton, Michael J. Reshuffling the pack: the transition from slavery to other forms of labor in the British Caribbean. (*NWIG*, 68:1/2, 1994, p. 23–75, bibl.)

Argues that change for exploited working class in British Caribbean did not come with emancipation, but, rather haltingly, in the wake of labor uprisings from 1930s onward. The introduction of East Indian immigrants into the region stifled working class solidarity in 19th century while augmenting labor supply. [ELC]

2129 Del nacionalismo al populismo: cultura y política en Puerto Rico. Edición de Silvia Alvarez-Curbelo y María Elena Rodríguez Castro. Río Piedras, P.R.: Decanato de Estudios Graduados e Investigación, Recinto de Río Piedras, Univ. de Puerto Rico; Ediciones Huracán, 1993. 205 p.: bibl.

Selected from papers presented at the Primer Encuentro de Historiadores sponsored by the Dept. of History at the Univ. of Puerto Rico in 1990, these essays examine a number of important formulations in both the political and the intellectual arenas of the 1930s and 1940s. The most provocative articles are those by the two editors: Alvarez-Curbelo on the mythical foundations of Muñoz Marín's populist discourse and Rodríguez-Castro on the "Foro de 1940" as the meeting ground for social reform and Creole tradition. Other articles, of uneven quality, revolve around issues of nationalism and Hispanicism, the role of the social sciences, US foreign policy, and underdevelopment. The entire volume is exemplary of the exciting possibilities that grow out of cooperation between researchers of literature and history. [TMV]

2130 Delgado Cintrón, Carmelo. Del verbo se trata: idioma nacional y periodismo en Rafael Castro Pereda. (*Rev. Juríd. Univ. P.R.*, 62:1, 1993, p. 1–50)

Presents retrospective on literary journalistic production promoting Spanish language and, by extension, Puerto Rican culture. Highlights originators of this tradition (among many others, José de Diego, Rosendo Matienzo Cintrón, Vicente Balbás Capó, Nemesio Canales, César Andreu Iglesias) as well as more recent examples (Nilita Vientós Gastón, Juan Antonio Corretjer, Manuel Maldonado Denis, Salvador Tió, and—the figure around whom the rest of the article revolves—Rafael Castro Pereda). Traces struggle to re-establish Spanish as the language of instruction in island's public schools; to make Spanish the official language of the court system; and to declare Spanish the official language of the commonwealth (as a consequence, making English a foreign language). Triumphant tone of article is tempered by fact that, immediately after publication, leg-

islation approved by pro-statehood party in power declared both English and Spanish official languages of Puerto Rico. [TMV]

2131 Derby, Robin L.H. and Richard Turits. Historias de terror y los terrores de la historia: la masacre haitiana de 1937 en la República Dominicana. (*Estud. Soc./Santo Domingo*, 26:92, abril/junio 1993, p. 65–76)

Perceptive reassessment of 1937 massacre of Haitians carried out by dictator Trujillo shows how the concept of a hostile Haiti was developed by the Dominican ruler in order to justify the killing. [JMH]

Dew, Edward M. The trouble in Suriname, 1975–1993. See *HLAS 55:3089.*

Dijk, Frank Jan van. Sociological means: colonial reactions to the radicalization of Rastafari in Jamaica. See *HLAS 55:4719.*

2132 Domínguez, Jaime de Jesús. La sociedad dominicana a principios del siglo XX. Santo Domingo: Comisión Oficial para la Celebración del Sesquicentenario de la Independencia Nacional, 1994. 535 p.: bibl. (Col. del sesquicentenario de la independencia nacional; 7)

Balanced, well-written, and fairly well researched account by Dominican scholar. Those interested in events that led US to occupy the country should take this work into account. [JMH]

2133 Donet-Vincent, Danielle. La fin du bagne, 1923–1953. Rennes, France: Editions Ouest-France, 1992. 190 p.: bibl., ill., map. (De mémoire d'homme: l'histoire. Université/Editions Ouest-France)

Excellent account focuses on end of French penal colonies in French Guiana, the oldest and most important of such settlements, during implementation of pre-war legislation in 1923–53. Analyzes interplay of various factors in 1920–40s that led to reform: 1) reports in French popular press, above all by Albert Londres, on atrocious living conditions; 2) humanitarian mission by Salvation Army and social critique by Charles Péan; 3) mounting opposition in French Guiana and political campaigns under the Popular Front, resumed by French Guianese politicians after the war. [APD]

2134 Dye, Alan. Avoiding holdup: asset specificity and technical change in the Cuban sugar industry, 1889–1929. (*J. Econ.*

Hist., 54:3, Sept. 1994, p. 628–653, maps, tables)

Offers novel explanation of reasons for the shift of the center of gravity of Cuban sugar production from west to east after independence. Well-documented and carefully written. [JMH]

2135 Emancipation IV: a series of lectures to commemorate the 150th anniversary of emancipation. Edited by Woodville Marshall. Kingston: Canoe Press, 1993. 136 p.: bibl., index.

Essays concentrate on 20th-century Barbados. Topics covered include women in the work force, socioeconomic transformation of Barbados from 1865–1937, emergence of small business, housing policy since 1936, education for development, and Barbados within the larger Caribbean and international dimension. Though aimed at popular audience, very useful for specialists. [ELC]

2136 Encinosa, Enrique G. Cuba en guerra: historia de la oposición anti-castrista 1959–1993. Miami, Fla.: Endowment for Cuban American Studies, 1994. 389 p.: bibl., ill., index, map, ports.

This early attempt to write history of anti-Castro movement, a subject highly controversial and still insufficiently documented, is uncritical and hagiographic in tone. [JMH]

2137 Estades Font, María E. Poder militar y política en Puerto Rico, 1898–1918. (*Cuad. Am.*, 8:46, julio/agosto 1994, p. 187–204)

Places early 20th-century military buildup, including recruitment of Puerto Ricans for US army, within larger strategic interests of US in Caribbean and Central America. Argues that naval supremacy in region necessitated direct political control of island. External considerations, then, affected Puerto Rico's own historical development in its early years as US colony. [TMV]

2138 Evans, Walker. Walker Evans: Havana 1933. Essay by Gilles Mora. Sequence by John T. Hill. Translated by Christie McDonald. New York: Pantheon Books, 1989. 111 p.: bibl., chiefly photos.

Evans' photographs record only one narrow aspect of a very complex reality at the time: besides Evans' Havana, several other Havanas existed that he did not cover. [JMH]

2139 Fabre, F. and G. Stehle. Le cyclone de 1928 à la Pointe-à-Pitre. (*Bull. Soc. hist. Guadeloupe*, 91/94, 1992, p. 41–72, ill., map, photos)

Vivid, hour-by-hour account of 1928 hurricane that caused 600 deaths in Pointe-à-Pitre, Guadeloupe's main port city, written by priest who witnessed the event. Accompanied by historical photos, work is worthwhile contribution to history of cataclysms. [APD]

2140 Fernandez, Ronald. The disenchanted island: Puerto Rico and the United States in the twentieth century. Foreword by William M. Kunstler and Ronald L. Kuby. New York: Praeger, 1992. 264 p.: bibl., index.

Denounces US ignorance and self-serving objectives in century-long formal relationship with Puerto Rico. Dismisses enhanced commonwealth status as permanent political option for island. Condemns dependence on mainland as possible component of both statehood and independence alternatives. Exhorts Puerto Ricans to achieve change based on national pride through peaceful means. Valuable because of use of materials from presidential libraries and congressional records. For international relations specialist's comment see *HLAS 53:4663*. [TMV]

2141 Ferré, Luis Alberto. Memorias de Ponce: autobiografía de Luis A. Ferré. Narración de Rosario Ferré. Barcelona: Grupo Editorial Norma, 1992. 135 p.: ill. (some col.).

As daughter Rosario explains in foreword, the memoir combines the private and public, the subjective and objective, reinforcing and challenging characteristics of feminine and masculine Latin American autobiographical narratives. Elder statesman Ferré combines Ponce street scenes and his political "struggles" to advance the cause of statehood, business ventures, and philanthropic activities with moving stories of friends, family, and love. Newspaper articles, poems, speeches, and photographs are appended. [TMV]

2142 Ferrera Herrera, Alberto. El Granma: la aventura del siglo. La Habana: Editorial Capitán San Luis, 1990. 183 p.: bibl., ill.

Studies in detail the steps presumably taken by US to prevent and defeat Castro's landing in Cuba in 1956. Author draws most of his conclusions from Batista's military records. [JMH]

2143 Fifty years later: antislavery, capital-ism and modernity in the Dutch orbit.
Edited by Gert Oostindie. Leiden, The Netherlands: KITLV Press, 1995. 272 p.: bibl., index, map. (Caribbean series; 15)

First work extensively examining antislavery in the Dutch world, this collection of 12 essays by Dutch and US scholars focuses on antislavery, capitalism, and modernization in The Netherlands and its colonies in the Americas, Asia, and Africa. Anchor article is by Seymour Drescher. [RH]

2144 Flores, Juan. Divided borders: essays on Puerto Rican identity. Houston, Tex.: Arte Público Press, 1993. 252 p.: bibl., ill.

Essays collectively challenge notion that culture is static and self-preserving. In the US, author argues, Puerto Ricans' identity is forged out of interactions between workers, ethnic groups, immigrants, and others as they resist hegemonic demands to assimilate. Examines vast literary production of Puerto Rican and other Latino writers to show how language and culture serve to affirm a self-fashioned identity that is neither mainstream nor schizophrenic. Author's command of history and language make this a remarkable comment on Puerto Rican culture. For literary perspective, see item **3601**. [TMV]

2145 Fraser, Cary. Ambivalent anti-colonialism: the United States and the genesis of West Indian independence, 1940–1964. Westport, Conn.: Greenwood Press, 1994. 233 p.: bibl., index. (Contributions in Latin American studies, 1054–6790; 3)

Pathbreaking study examines interaction of Caribbean nationalists with British and US policymakers, British cooperation with US to remain premier political power in region, and US efforts to promote "order" through limiting new powers' international activities. Argues that 1964 political defeat of Cheddi Jagan in British Guiana demonstrated that the reality of political independence was actually a transition to American sphere of influence. [ELC]

2146 Gaillard, Gusti-Klara. Haiti d'un impérialisme a un autre, 1918–1941. (*Rev. Soc. haïti.*, 48:172, Mars 1992, p. 48–58)

This examination of the decline of French diplomatic and financial interests in Haiti from 1918–41 is to be commended for its analysis of the process by which French property was liquidated. [APD]

2147 Gaillard, Roger. La république exterminatrice. v. 4, La guerre civile, une option dramatique, 15 juillet-31 décembre 1902. Port-au-Prince: R. Gaillard, 1993. 1 v: appendices, bibl., photos.

Foremost specialist pursues his study of Haitian politics in the age of US imperialism. This volume focuses on struggle between democratic civilian forces and the military at beginning of the 20th century. Argues that expulsion of important liberal leader Anténor Firmin had lasting effects in turning Haiti away from a modern constitutional regime. [APD]

2148 Gálvez Rodríguez, William. Frank: entre el sol y la montaña. v. 1–2. La Habana: Unión de Escritores y Artistas de Cuba, 1991. 2 v.: bibl., ill.

This panegyric rather than scholarly work not only mixes fiction with reality, but also deals very superficially with crucial aspects of Frank País' revolutionary career and his relations with Castro. [JMH]

2149 García-Carranza, Araceli. Bibliografía del Asalto al Cuartel Moncada: suplemento 1973–1987. La Habana: Editorial Política, 1989. 125 p.: index.

Updates bibliography compiled by Mirian Hernández (see item **2160**). [JMH]

2150 García Muñiz, Humberto. Los últimos treinta años, 1898–1930: un manuscrito inédito de Frank Tannenbaum sobre Puerto Rico. (*Op. Cit./Río Piedras*, 7, 1992, p. 145–208)

Frank Tannenbaum's unpublished manuscript on Puerto Rico's first 30 years under US rule serves as springboard for author's comments regarding both Tannenbaum and the product of his work on the island. Tannenbaum's contribution to Brookings Institution's *Porto Rico and its problems* (Washington: 1930), the most "objective of three books published in the 1930s about island's society and economy, is presented in context of a brief biography of him (one of Latin American history's giants). Precisely because of Tannenbaum's political trajectory, García Muñiz laments fact that, even though Tannenbaum was quick to denounce effects of monoculture on Puerto Rico's population (and his piece was therefore excluded from the full report, García Muñiz speculates), he failed to take issue with political consequences of colonial domination. [TMV]

2151 Gautier de Alvarez, Josefina. Escondido: mi 30 de mayo. Santo Domingo: Editora Taller, 1993. 202 p.: ill.

Author reminisces about her participation in assassination of Trujillo. She became involved in the event by hiding one of the most prominent of the dictator's executioners. [JMH]

2152 Género y trabajo: la industria de la aguja en Puerto Rico y el Caribe hispánico. Edición de María del Carmen Baerga. San Juan: Editorial de la Univ. de Puerto Rico, 1993. 321 p.: bibl., ill.

Collection of essays examines female-dominated textile manufacturing industry. Solid theoretical underpinnings and thorough analysis of data make entire volume an outstanding contribution to field of gender studies. Various essays explore key notions such as connection between what appear to be archaic and traditional methods in the periphery (e.g., outwork) and factory production in the metropolis; labeling of women's work as marginal to industrial production, therefore its devaluation and concomitant low wages; the supposedly innate dexterity of women; and impact of wage work on women's position in the household. The Dominican Republic and Cuba are included in some pieces by way of comparison. [TMV]

2153 Gentles, Janet. Percival Jamaica: his life and work. Kingston: Paschal Press, 1993. 106 p.: bibl., ill.

Biography of Percival William Gibson—presbyter, educator, and crusader for social justice. The first Jamaican to become Anglican bishop of the island, Gibson had a profound impact on the lives of countless Jamaicans in both the secular and non-secular spheres. [ELC]

Giacalone, Rita. Cambios políticos y sociales en Curazao, 1969–1989. See *HLAS 55:4730.*

2154 Girvan, D.T.M. Working together for development: D.T.M. Girvan on cooperatives and community development, 1939–1968. Compiled and edited by Norman Girvan. Foreword by Philip Sherlock. Kingston: Institute of Jamaica Publications, 1993. 424 p.: ill., index, photos.

Highly informative collection of Girvan's papers, compiled and edited by his son, deals mostly with community programs, cooperatives, and Jamaican welfare system

between 1930–60. In wake of riots and labor discontent, all recognized the need for a fresh approach to problem-solving and for promoting development and social awakening. Includes Girvan's keen insights on Ecuador and Chile, where he also worked. [ELC]

2155 González, José Luis. Puerto Rico: the four-storeyed country and other essays. Translated by Gerald Guinness. Princeton, N.J.: M. Wiener Pub., 1993. 135 p.: bibl.

Originally published in Spanish (Río Piedras: 1980), work is once again a timely contribution to ongoing debate about what constitutes a national culture. Publication in English adds to both literature on cultural studies and the definition process Puerto Ricans are currently undergoing as a result of political circumstances. Author argues in main essay that Afro-Antilleans, white landowners, urban professionals, and managerial class contributed successively to defining Puerto Rican identity. Excellent introduction by Gerald Guiness gives coherence to González's separate pieces on several aspects of culture "from below," and provides context for more controversial issues raised by author. [TMV]

2156 González García, Lydia Milagros. Una puntada en el tiempo: la industria de la aguja en Puerto Rico, 1900–1929. Puerto Rico: CEREP, CIPAF, 1990. 139 p.: bibl., ill., maps. (Col. Teoría)

Pioneer effort in field of women's studies, book describes early 20th-century clothing industry and, within it, women's home work. Successfully argues that incorporation of women into textile labor force is linked to larger process of proletarianization of peasants as laborers for sugar industry. Focuses on social and economic impact of textile manufacturing on the island: role of US companies and local intermediaries, interactions between members of working families, class relations, etc. Interviews with elderly needlework artisans provide rich descriptions that dovetail with statistical analysis of the period. [TMV]

2157 Guerrero, Miguel. El golpe de estado. Santo Domingo: Editora Corripio, 1993. 381 p.: bibl., ill., index.

Journalistic account of events that led to overthrow of Dominican President Juan Bosch in 1963 is informative and readable. [JMH]

2158 Hackshaw, John Milton. The Baptist denomination: a concise history commemorating one hundred and seventy five years, 1816–1991, of the establishment of the "company villages" and the Baptist faith in Trinidad and Tobago. Foreward by Allan J. Parkes. Trinidad and Tobago: Amphy and Bashana Jackson Memorial Society, 1992. 152 p.

Fruitful treatment focuses on Baptists in Trinidad from early 19th century to present. Author details obstacles imposed by colonial authorities to hinder ability of Baptists to worship as they pleased. Includes discussion of persecution of Shouters, and of final efforts by Baptists to obtain "respectability" as a prelude to removal of discriminatory laws. [ELC]

2159 Hector, Michel. Solidarité et luttes politiques en Haïti: l'action internationale de Joseph Jolibois Fils, 1927–1936. (*Rev. Soc. haïti.*, 49:176, juin 1993, p. 7–53)

Article is welcome addition to Hector's solid research on Haiti's role in anti-imperialist mobilization in the Americas during first half of 20th century. Documents international tour made by Jolibois, known for his commitment to democracy, to capitalize on sympathy Haiti (and Nicaragua) attracted in 1920s because of US occupation. [APD]

2160 Hernández, Mirian. Bibliografía del Asalto al Cuartel Moncada. La Habana: Editorial Orbe, Instituto Cubano del Libro, 1975. 361 p.: index.

A useful research tool. For update, see item **2149.** [JMH]

2161 Historia de la banca en la República Dominicana. Santo Domingo: Banco Antillano; Museo Nacional de Historia y Geografía, 1986? 80 p.: ill.

Proceedings of a symposium focus on a largely neglected, albeit crucial, aspect of Dominican history. [JMH]

2162 Hylton Edwards, Stewart. Lengthening shadows: birth and revolt of the Trinidad army. Trinidad: Inprint Caribbean, 1982. 154 p., 11 p. of plates: ill. (some col.), index.

Provides stimulating insider's account of the Trinidad Regiment, especially of crucial 1960s military disturbances and subsequent court-martial of coup leaders. Includes lengthy correspondence with some of the principal players in failed revolt. Also sheds light on political maneuvering in the newly independent island when Black Power ideology threatened political stability. [ELC]

2163 Inoa, Orlando. Estado y campesinos al inicio de la era de Trujillo. Santo Domingo: Librería La Trinitaria, 1994. 262 p.: bibl.

Analyzes hardships to which Trujillo subjected Dominican peasants when he rose to power. Includes a commendable bibliographical essay. [JMH]

2164 Jiménez, Félix. Cómo fue el gobierno de Juan Bosch?. Santo Domingo: Editora Alfa y Omega, 1988. 445 p.: ill.

Collects and reprints documents which, according to author, show that Bosch's ephemeral 1963 presidency actually mapped out the road that Dominican rulers have followed ever since. [JMH]

2165 Kennedy y Bosch: aporte al estudio de las relaciones internacionales del gobierno constitucional de 1963. Edición de Bernardo Vega. Santo Domingo: Fundación Cultural Dominicana, 1993. 545 p.: bibl., index.

Author himself admits that he could examine only part of available documentation and that consequently no definitive conclusions may be drawn from his research. He has nevertheless provided us with a very solid point of departure. [JMH]

2166 Lancaster, Alan. The unconquered wilderness: a historical analysis of the failure to open the hinterland of British Guiana, 1901–1919. (*Hist. Gaz.*, 58, July 1993, p. 2–22, ill.)

Presents succinct analysis of problems authorities encountered in establishing interior settlements that they hoped would promote agricultural diversification. Unfortunately, availability of land stimulated, rather than lessened, sugar cultivation and had a negative effect on the embryonic railroad scheme, which was unable to attract capital from sugar ventures. Difficulties also stemmed from an inadequate population for settlement and railroad construction. [ELC]

2167 Liss, Sheldon B. Fidel!: Castro's political and social thought. Boulder, Colo.: Westview Press, 1994. 246 p.: bibl., index. (Latin American perspectives series; 13)

Work is a useful yet premature anthology of Castro's thought. Given Castro's volatile personality, no one can be sure that his intellectual profile is complete as yet. [JMH]

2168 López, José Ramón. Diario: enero-agosto de 1921. Santo Domingo: Ediciones de la Fundación Corripio, 1991. 398 p.: ill. (Biblioteca de clásicos dominicanos; 11)

Covering period immediately preceding author's death, work records his views and political opinions rather than his intimate thoughts. [JMH]

2169 Lutchman, Harold A. Constitutional developments in British Guiana during the Second World War. (*Hist. Gaz.*, 50, Nov. 1992, p. 2–15, ill.)

Author discusses limited constitutional advances country experienced as a result of 1930s disturbances. Demonstrates that changes failed to address fundamental socioeconomic problems. Introduction of universal adult suffrage in 1950s empowered masses who voted into office a government committed to changing the status quo. Herein lies backdrop to suspension of constitution in 1953. [ELC]

2170 Mam-Lam-Fouck, Serge. Histoire de la Guyane contemporaine, 1940–1982: les mutations économiques, sociales et politiques. Paris: Editions caribéennes, 1992. 446 p.: bibl., index.

Continuation of Mam-Lam-Fouck's previous work (see *HLAS 50:1675*) provides comprehensive treatment of economic, demographic, and political transformations in French Guiana from 1946–82 brought about by *départementalisation*. Shows that Guianese politicians actively sought a closer integration with the metropolis. Disappointment followed excessive earlier expectations when agricultural development produced limited results, while genuine achievements such as eradication of tropical diseases were underestimated. Fueled by Guianese studying in France, public discontent grew after 1958, leading to autonomist movements in the 1970s; however, *régionalisation* in 1982 was greeted with indifference. Author stresses demographic explosion resulting from sanitary improvements and Caribbean immigration in 1980s, which led to tensions between newcomers and Creole and Amerindian communities. This contribution to the history of French decolonization and of the uncertain Caribbean identity is a must for libraries. [APD]

2171 Manville, Marcel. Les Antilles sans fard. Paris: L'Harmattan, 1992. 271 p.: bibl.

Author, a Martinique lawyer born into a colored family of artisans and a veteran of World War II, organized later Caribbean immigrants in France. Work is latest addition to growing list of memoirs by French Antillan political figures. [APD]

2172 Maríñez, Pablo A. Agroindustria, Estado y clases sociales en la era de Trujillo, 1935–1960. Santo Domingo: Fundación Cultural Dominicana, 1993. 142 p.: bibl.

Author maintains that economic development of the Dominican Republic in 1935–60 was the work of the Trujillo group and did not result in emergence of a bourgeois class. The political instability that has characterized recent Dominican history is the consequence of this process. [JMH]

2173 Massari, Roberto. Che Guevara: grandeza y riesgo de la utopía. Tafalla, Spain: Txalaparta, 1992. 402 p.: bibl., ill. (Gebara; 14)

Biography is worth reading despite author's excessive admiration for Guevara and work's consequent hagiographic tone. To state that an acknowledged utopian such as the Argentine guerrilla was the number two man of the Cuban Revolution is a bit farfetched. [JMH]

2174 Meléndez, Edgardo. Movimiento anexionista en Puerto Rico. Río Piedras: Editorial de la Univ. de Puerto Rico, 1993. 292 p.: bibl.

Sophisticated analysis considers ideological shifts within pro-statehood position as reflecting social and economic transformations on the island. Particularly revealing are author's explanations for cross-class support for the Partido Nuevo Progresista, the party's "reformist" stance, and changes in its leadership style. Work offers new perspectives on island's inability to transform itself into a national state. For political scientist's comment on English-language edition, see *HLAS 53: 3558*. [TMV]

2175 Mora, Juan Miguel de. Misión de prensa en Santo Domingo. México?: s.n, 1990. 95 p., 16 p. of plates: ill.

Highly critical journalistic account of beginnings of US military occupation of the

Dominican Republic in 1965, written by a Mexican newspaperman. [JMH]

2176 Morell-Romero, José. Revolution in Cuba: memoirs of a combatant. Tallahassee, Fla.: Suncoast Professional Pub. Corp., 1993. 125 p.: ill.

Author played only a secondary role in events covered by his reminiscences, which for the most part tend to be rather succinct. They do have a corroborative value however, and cannot be ignored. [JMH]

Mudd, Patricia Marirea. Portuguese Bermudians: early history and reference guide, 1849–1949. See item **2061.**

2177 Muñoz Marín, Luis. Memorias: autobiografía pública. v. 2, 1940–1952. San Germán, P.R.: Univ. Interamericana de Puerto Rico, 1992. 1 v.

Vol. 2 of Luis Muñoz Marín's memoirs begins with electoral victory of the Partido Popular Democrático in 1940 and ends with approval of 1952 Constitution that established commonwealth status. Work is a candid defense of the Estado Libre Asociado, of which Muñoz was the architect, and is also a more general reflection of politics and government in this period. Perhaps because of the nature of related events, or because Muñoz did not have enough time to edit his own writing before his death, this volume does not read as coherently as did vol. 1. (San Juan: Univ. Interamericana de Puerto Rico, 1982). Nevertheless, this volume is indispensable for understanding a crucial time in Puerto Rican history, and is revealing as a self-portrait of a key figure. [TMV]

2178 La nación puertorriqueña: ensayos en torno a Pedro Albizu Campos. Edición de Juan Manuel Carrión, Teresa C. Gracia Ruiz, y Carlos Rodríguez-Fraticelli. San Juan: Editorial de la Univ. de Puerto Rico, 1993. 280 p.: bibl., ill.

Contains excellent collection of essays by well-known academics of various disciplines. Themes covered include evolution of nationalist leader's political thought, his juridical experiences, and his postmortem imaging by independence supporters. Postmodern conceptualizations of nationalism and a thorough understanding of Caribbean politics at mid-century make several contributions truly outstanding. [TMV]

2179 Naranjo Orovio, Consuelo. Del campo a la bodega: recuerdos de gallegos en Cuba, siglo XX. Sada, Spain: Ediciós do Castro, 1988. 269 p.: bibl., ill. (Documentos para a historia contemporánea de Galicia; 50)

Relies on oral history to supplement archival information. However, data provided on important subjects such as economic activities of the immigrants are based largely on secondary sources. Discussion of immigrants' politics reflects author's own political proclivities. [JMH]

2180 Naranjo Orovio, Consuelo. Trabajo libre e inmigración española en Cuba: 1880–1930. (*Rev. Indias,* 52: 195/196, mayo/dic. 1992, p. 749–794)

Informative statistical study is based on Cuban and Spanish sources. [JMH]

2181 O'Brien, Thomas F. The revolutionary mission: American enterprise in Cuba. (*Am. Hist. Rev.,* 98: 3, June 1993, p. 765–785, photo)

Fascinating study of turbulent history of General Electric's investments in Cuba includes Cuban response to corporation's activities, which were typical of multinational corporate culture. [JMH]

2182 Olsen, Scott H. Reverend L. Ton Evans and the United States occupation of Haiti. (*Caribb. Stud.,* 26: 1/2, 1993, p. 23–47)

Evans was a Welsh Baptist missionary who worked in Haiti from 1917–19. Despite his hope that US occupation would end the country's extreme poverty and political corruption as well as the exhorbitant European demands, Evans bore witness to the racism and excesses committed by occupation forces, which fueled rural banditry as a form of peasant nationalist struggle. Demonstrates that "missionaries can be a fruitful locus for studying foreign policy implementation through non-State means." [APD]

2183 Panton, David. Jamaica's Michael Manley: the great transformation, 1972–92. Foreword by Rex Nettleford. Kingston: Kingston Publishers Limited, 1993. 225 p.: bibl., ill., index.

Author examines reasons for Jamaican Prime Minister's sudden switch from State-driven socialism to market-driven economy in early 1980s. Concludes that island's dependence on international markets and changes in international political and economic scene limited policy options. Hence pragmatic re-evaluation of past policies spurred adoption of strategies most appropriate for Jamaica's future. [ELC]

2184 Paterson, Thomas G. Contesting Castro: the United States and the triumph of the Cuban Revolution. New York: Oxford Univ. Press, 1994. 352 p.: bibl., ill., index.

Thoroughly documented explanation of US failure to block Castro's rise to power is especially recommendable for presentation of US side of the story, obviously the author's forte. Some of his conclusions are nevertheless open to refinement. [JMH]

2185 Payne, Hugh W.L. The expulsion of the People's Progressive Party from the government of British Guiana in 1953. (*Hist. Gaz.*, 51, Dec. 1992, p. 2–17, ill.)

While adding little to previous knowledge of reasons for British Government's suspension of British Guiana's constitution, essay contributes to knowledge of documentation on the subject. Draws on newspaper reports and speeches by parliamentarians and local officials to conclude that threat of communist takeover was actually overreaction by British ministers opposed to political advances in colony. [ELC]

2186 Peña Batlle, Manuel Arturo. Previo a la dictadura: la etapa liberal. Compilación, presentación y comentarios de Bernardo Vega. Santo Domingo: Fundación Peña Batlle, 1991. 277 p.: bibl., ill., index. (Obras; 2)

Contains compilation of political articles published by this Dominican intellectual prior to Trujillo's dictatorship. Explanatory notes and commentaries by Bernardo Vega greatly enhance the value of the volume. [JMH]

2187 Pérez, Louis A. Essays on Cuban history: historiography and research. Gainesville: Univ. Press of Florida, 1995. 306 p.: bibl., index.

Most of the chapters in this monograph present aspects of Cuban history at the turn of the century. Work includes extended treatment of the US military intervention, the Cuban communities in Tampa and Ybor City, and attempts at cultural domination through education and religion. A second emphasis, on the more recent period, includes

analysis of the post-1959 army, US-Cuban relations, and a review of the literature on Cuba. Also includes valuable descriptions of archival information available for research in Cuba and Spain. [B. Aguirre-López]

Pérez-Stable, Marifeli. The Cuban Revolution: origins, course, and legacy. See *HLAS 55:4769.*

2188 Perusse, Roland I. The United States and Puerto Rico: the struggle for equality. Malabar, Fla.: R.E. Krieger Pub. Co., 1990. 181 p.: bibl., index.

Concise introduction places in chronological order the issues relevant to controversy over political status of Puerto Rico. Author contends that equality can be achieved only through statehood or independence. Lengthy list of primary readings promotes use of book as text. [TMV]

2189 Peynado, Francisco José. Papeles y escritos de Francisco José Peynado, 1867–1933, prócer de la Tercera República. v. 1. Recopilación de Juan Daniel Balcácer. Santo Domingo: Fundación Peynado Alvarez, 1994. 1 v: indexes.

Despite generally hagiographic tone of the volume (which also includes writings on Peynado), work might be useful for those interested in the evacuation of the Dominican Republic by US troops in 1924. [JMH]

2190 Potter, Lesley M. The Amerindians of Guyana and their environment. (*Hist. Gaz.*, 52, Jan. 1992, p. 2–19, ill.)

Argues that traditional success of Amerindians in effectively exploiting their environment for survival is now being challenged by social changes and economic activities engendered by cultural contacts and "modernization." [ELC]

2191 Potter, Lesley M. The paddy proletariat and the dependent peasantry: East Indian rice-growers in British Guiana, 1895–1920. (*Hist. Gaz.*, 47, Aug. 1992, p. 2–14, map)

Sophisticated analysis examines role of East Indian rice growers in fostering emergence of vibrant industry. Occasionally labor demands of expanding sugar industry and wishes of Indian proletariat for self sufficiency conflicted. But employment on plantations was still necessary to supplement meagre earnings from expanded rice industry.

Hence terms "paddy proletariat" and "dependent peasantry." [ELC]

2192 Quirk, Robert E. Fidel Castro. New York: Norton, 1993. 898 p.: bibl., ill., index, maps.

Nearly 900-page exertion by a newcomer to Cubanology is based largely on US secondary sources. Work is too long for an introduction to Castro and too concise for a full treatment of the subject. Last half of volume is an account of the revolution rather than a biography of its prime mover. [JMH]

2193 Ramsaran, Dave. Breaking the bonds of indentureship: Indo-Trinidadians in business. St. Augustine, Trinidad: I.S.E.R., The Univ. of the West Indies, 1993. 162 p.: bibl., col. ill.

Drawing on information contained in eight case studies, author provides succinct treatment of increasing participation of Indo-Trinidadians in the private sector. Argues that East Indians, who came to Trinidad later and under circumstances different from Africans, made pragmatic and rational efforts to enter business as means of accumulating wealth and enhancing social advancement. [ELC]

2194 Rodríguez-Fraticelli, Carlos. U.S. solidarity with Puerto Rico: Rockwell Kent, 1937. (in Colonial dilemma: critical perspectives on contemporary Puerto Rico. Edited by Edwin Meléndez and Edgardo Meléndez. Boston: South End Press, 1993, p. 189–198)

Recounts fascinating episode surrounding artist Rockwell Kent's commission to paint a mural for the US Post Office in 1937. His project stirred controversy among both US officials (who rejected its anti-colonial message) and island politicians (who objected to Kent's depiction of Puerto Ricans). Unfortunately, author does not do much more than narrate. [TMV]

2195 Ros, Enrique. Playa Girón: la verdadera historia. Miami, Fla.: Ediciones Universal, 1994. 314 p.: bibl., ill., port. (Col. Cuba y sus jueces)

Although far from a definitive account, work is certainly the best documented Cuban exile version of the Bay of Pigs fiasco published thus far. Book is based partly on research and partly on personal reminiscences

of author and other participants in the event. [JMH]

2196 Sainton, Jean-Pierre. Rosan Girard: chronique d'une vie politique en Guadeloupe. Pointe-à-Pitre: Jasor; Paris: Karthala, 1993. 455 p.: bibl., ill.

Historian interviews well-known political figure on his socialist roots and trajectory from communism to advocacy of independence. Evokes political culture of French Antilles after 1945 and situation of communist militants persecuted by local authorities, even though their party supported the socialists in power during the Cold War. [APD]

2197 Sandiford, Keith A.P. Combermere School under G.B.R. Burton, 1897–1925. (J. Caribb. Stud., 7:1, Spring 1989, p. 99–113)

Penetrating study focuses on a Barbadian secondary school during an important phase of its evolution. Author claims that important legacies of the Burton era are still present at the school today. School still serves as premier source of black educational pride in the island. [ELC]

Shepherd, Verene. Indian females in Jamaica: an analysis of the population censuses, 1861–1943. See item **2088**.

2198 Sims, Harold. Cuba. (in Latin America between the Second World War and the Cold War, 1944–1948. Edited by Leslie Bethell and Ian Roxborough. New York: Cambridge Univ. Press, 1992, p. 217–242)

Essentially a concise history of Cuba's labor movement between World War II and early 1950s, work relies entirely on secondary sources. However, author has managed to produce a fairly balanced, if somewhat superficial, account. [JMH]

2199 Singh, Hari Prasad. The Indian struggle for justice and equality against black racism in Trinidad and Tobago: 1956–1962. Compiled and introduced by Indian Review Press. Foreword by John La Guerre. Couva, Trinidad: Indian Review Press, 1993. 128 p.

Contains speeches and writings of Singh, regarded as "Father of Indian Nationalism in Trinidad." Demonstrates how heated the debates on race relations were in the 1960s. Singh's position is that at the time when Eric Williams championed an anti-colonial agenda, East Indians in Trinidad were being relegated to second-class citizenship by many who promoted black nationalism. [ELC]

2200 Singh, Kelvin. Race and class struggles in a colonial state: Trinidad 1917–1945. Calgary, Canada: Univ. of Calgary Press; Kingston: The Press, Univ. of the West Indies, 1994. 284 p.: bibl., index.

While island's internal struggles occurred along racial lines, class divisions revealed themselves through actions of educated leaders of major racial groups. By 1930s, transethnic collaboration was forged against power of ruling class. The limited successes of Afro-Caribbean and Indo-Caribbean political leaders, however, would seem to call into question author's roseate picture of racial cooperation. Passionate arguments. [ELC]

Subervi-Velez, Federico A.; Nitza M. Hernández López; and **Aline Frambes-Buxeda.** Los medios de comunicación masiva en Puerto Rico. See *HLAS 55:4791.*

2201 Suriname en de Tweede Wereldoorlog [Suriname and the Second World War]. (*OSO/Netherlands,* 14:2, 1995, p. 133–203, bibl., photos, tables)

Article focuses on political, economic, and social consequences of World War II on Suriname. Topics discussed include increasing economic dependence on bauxite, growing political consciousness and nationalism, volunteers from Suriname who served in Dutch East Indies, and internment in Suriname of "politically dangerous" individuals from Suriname, South Africa, and Dutch East Indies. [RH]

2202 Taylor, Frank. To hell with paradise: history of the Jamaica tourist industry. Pittsburgh: Univ. of Pittsburgh Press, 1993. 239 p.: bibl., ill., index, photos. (Pitt Latin American series)

Attributes Jamaica's modern-day tourist attractiveness to local authorities' conscious effort to recast the island's traditional image as graveyard for whites. Demonstrates industry's exponential growth in 1990s, and concludes that it now serves as virtual lifeblood of nation's economy. [ELC]

La tercera raíz: presencia africana en Puerto Rico. See *HLAS 55:4794.*

2203 Tribute to a scholar: appreciating C.L.R. James. Edited by Bishnu Ragoonath. Kingston: Consortium Graduate School of Social Sciences, 1990. 114 p.: bibl.

Essays by students of the Consortium Graduate School of Social Sciences (Univ. of the West Indies and Univ. of Guyana) review some of the more important writings of James and measure their applicability to today's Caribbean and world developments. Includes excellent introduction on James' life and thought. [ELC]

2204 Valdés Vivó, Raúl. El gran secreto: cubanos en el Camino Ho Chi Minh. La Habana: Editora Política, 1990. 247 p.

When the Vietnamese government divulged the foreign contribution to the maintenance of the celebrated Ho Chi Minh Trail, the former Cuban ambassador to Vietnam decided to go public about the Cuban share of that effort. Fascinating reading. [JMH]

2205 Vassell, Linnette. The movement for the vote for women, 1918–1919. (*Jam. Hist. Rev.,* 18, 1993, p. 40–54)

Traces struggle for franchise for Jamaican women through pages of the *Daily Gleaner,* a Jamaican newspaper. Points out that men were prominent in the campaign, acting out of enlightened self-interest and out of fear that women might mount more militant campaign for themselves. Very useful article. [ELC]

2206 Vega, Bernardo. Trujillo y las fuerzas armadas norteamericanas. Santo Domingo: Fundación Cultural Dominicana, 1992. 520 p.: bibl., ill., index.

Shows conclusively how US Marine Corps officers helped Trujillo consolidate his dictatorship in 1930s. Based on extensive archival research in the Dominican Republic and US. [JMH]

2207 Vega Suñol, José. Presencia norteamericana en el área nororiental de Cuba: etnicidad y cultura. Holguín, Cuba: Ediciones Holguín, 1991. 211 p.: bibl. (Ensayo)

The author had to leave out more than half of his manuscript, but readers must not overlook what he was able to publish because it covers a subject on which very little has been written. [JMH]

2208 El 23 de febrero de 1930, o, La más anunciada revolución de América. Recopilación de Bernardo Vega. Santo Domingo: Fundación Cultural Dominicana, 1989. 83 p.

Shows conclusively that Trujillo's rise

to power was clearly anticipated by most Dominican writers and journalists. [JMH]

2209   Vinat de la Mata, Raquel. Las obreras de la aguja: un sector olvidado. (*Nuestra Hist./Caracas,* 3, julio/dic. 1992, p. 53–74, tables)

Had author supported her findings with appropiate references to her sources, this article would be an important contribution to the field of women's studies in Cuba. [JMH]

Walker-Kilkenny, Roberta. The Leonora strike of 1939. See item **2096.**

2210   Walker-Kilkenny, Roberta. Women in social and political stuggle in British Guiana, 1946–1953. (*Hist. Gaz.,* 49, Oct. 1992, p. 2–18, ill.)

Author contends that expansion of franchise increased possibilities for women already involved in welfare organizations and cottage industries. Politically organized, they addressed housing situation, working conditions for domestic laborers, and ultimately franchise. Despite disintegration of nascent political organizations, women's consciousness was enhanced considerably. [ELC]

2211   The War of 1898 and U.S. interventions, 1898–1934: an encyclopedia. Edited by Benjamin R. Beede. New York: Garland, 1994. 751 p.: bibl., index, maps. (Garland reference library of the humanities; 933. Military history of the United States; 2)

Although format of the book is not necessarily conducive to great scholarship, work could have benefitted from collaboration of Spanish, Cuban, and other Spanish-American historians. As it is, some of the entries are weak, and others are marred by obvious mistakes. One of book's most indicative shortcomings is the lack of an entry on Carlos Finlay, one of the most important figures of the period. [JMH]

2212   Williams, Eric Eustace. Eric E. Williams speaks: essays on colonialism and independence. Edited by Selwyn Reginald Cudjoe. Wellesley, Mass.: Calaloux Publications; Amherst: Univ. of Massachusetts Press, 1993. 436 p.: bibl., ill., index.

Collection of important speeches of Trinidad politician and Caribbean historian covers wide range of issues relating to Caribbean's status and destiny. Includes essays by editor on Williams as public speaker, by George Lamming on political change in Trinidad, by C.L.R. James on the 1960 Party Convention, and by Erica Williams-Connell on women's issues. [ELC]

Willock, Roger. Bulwark of empire: Bermuda's fortified naval base, 1860–1920. See item **2098.**

2213   Winocur, Marcos. La burguesía azucarera cubana: estructura capitalista y definición política en la coyuntura insurreccional de 1952–1959. (*in* Colección nuestra patria es América: historia económica de América Latina. Edición de Jorge Núñez Sánchez. Quito: Editora Nacional, 1992, v. 7, p. 181–204)

Author has merely scratched the surface of a subject that deserves further investigation. [JMH]

2214   Woolford, Hazel M. Hubert Nathaniel Crichlow: the crusader. (*Hist. Gaz.,* 43, April 1992, p. 2–11, ill.)

Interesting biography of British Guiana labor union organizer of early 20th century, who laid the foundation for a strong trade union movement in Guyana and whose activities spanned the interests of Caribbean workers as a whole. Crichlow was a "politician, social worker, trade unionist, and fearless leader." [ELC]

2215   Zanetti Lecuona, Oscar. Las clases de la sociedad cubana en vísperas de la revolución. (*Arbor/Madrid,* 144:567, marzo 1993, p. 135–164, tables)

The unemployed have been largely left out of author's analysis of Cuban society, which is far more acceptable as far as the higher classes are concerned. [JMH]

2216   Zapata Oliveras, Carlos R. Nuevos caminos hacia viejos objetivos: Estados Unidos y el establecimiento del Estado Libre Asociado de Puerto Rico, 1945–1953. Río Piedras?: Comisión Puertorriqueña para la Celebración del Quinto Centenario del Descubrimiento de América y Puerto Rico, 1991. 471 p.: bibl., ill.

Chronological and descriptive account examines practical and conceptual obstacles encountered by those who shaped the idea of commonwealth (*estado libre asociado*) as a status option for Puerto Rico in 1940s-50s. Focuses on Luis Muñoz Marín, the ideologue of the Partido Popular Democrático, and on Antonio Fernós Isern, Puerto Rico's Resident Commissioner in Washington. Although author intends the book to be an impartial narrative of key events, work's value lies in its detailed examination of documentation highlighting the changing relations between Puerto Rico and US and their respective representatives. [TMV]

SPANISH SOUTH AMERICA
General

MICHAEL T. HAMERLY, *Independent Consultant, Seattle, Washington*

2217 Alzate Angel, Beatriz. Historia documental en la frontera de los tres límites. (*in* Simposio Desarrollos Recientes en la Historia de los Llanos del Orinoco: Colombia y Venezuela, *New Orleans, 1991.* Café, caballo y hamaca: visión histórica del Llano. Quito: Ediciones Abya-Yala; Bogotá: Orinoquia Siglo XXI, 1992, p. 195–214, maps, tables)

Working paper relates ongoing historical research on area where Colombia, Brazil, and Venezuela meet. Apparently based entirely on travel accounts, ranging in time from 1744 through 1989. [MTH]

2218 Archivo Nacional del Ecuador. Guía de los fondos documentales del Archivo Nacional del Ecuador. v. 1–2. Dirección y supervisión de Grecia Vasco de Escudero. Quito: Consejo Nacional de Archivos, 1994. 2 v.

This most complete and up-to-date checklist of holdings of the main branch of the Archivo Nacional del Ecuador supplements, but does not replace, previous, more specific guides to the Archivo. [MTH]

Asociacionismo, trabajo e identidad étnica: los italianos en América Latina en una perspectiva comparada. See item **2950.**

2219 Congreso Ecuatoriano de Historia, *1st*, *Quito, 1993.* La producción historiográfica sobre el Ecuador en los últimos 25 años: memoria. (*Procesos/Quito,* 5, segundo semestre 1993, p. 1–123, bibl., table)

Publishes five *ponencias* on the historiography of Ecuador as presented at the first Congreso Ecuatoriano de Historia, held in Quito 16–19 Nov. 1993. Conjointly the most detailed analysis and evaluation of the state of history, including prehistory and ethnohistory, in and on Ecuador to date. All five authors are not only nationals, but trained and practicing professionals. The most noteworthy contributions are Rosemarie Terán Najas' "La historia económica y social sobre la época colonial ecuatoriana: un balance de la producción historiográfica en los últimos 25 años" and Juan J. Paz y Miño Cepeda's "La historiografía económica del Ecuador sobre el s. XIX y XX en los últimos 25 años." See also Jorge Núñez Sánchez's *La historiografía ecuatoriana contemporánea, 1970–1994* (Quito: Univ. Central del Ecuador, 1994). [MTH]

2220 Estados y naciones en los Andes: hacia una historia comparativa; Bolivia, Colombia, Ecuador, Perú. Compilación de Jean Paul Deler y Yves Saint-Geours. Lima: Instituto de Estudios Peruanos; Instituto Francés de Estudios Andinos, 1986. 2 v.: bibl., ill. (Historia andina; 11. Col. Travaux de l'IFEA; 33)

Publishes proceedings of the Coloquio de Historia Andina sponsored by the Institut français d'études andines in Lima in Aug., 1984. The majority of participants are leading historians of 19th- and 20th-century history of Colombia, Ecuador, Peru, and Bolivia. Volumes are exceptionally important for treatment of sources, oral as well as archival; continuity and change; regional societies; external influences, especially commercial, and Andean responses thereto; the nation-state; ideology and political representation; violence and conflict. Should be read as a whole because participants are comparative in approach, not just in discussions following each round of papers, but in the presentations themselves. [MTH]

2221 López-Ocón, Leoncio. Las actividades americanistas del naturalista español Marcos Jiménez de la Espada. (*in* Jornadas sobre "España y las expediciones científicas en América y Filipinas," *1st, Madrid, 1991*. La ciencia española en ultramar: actas. Madrid: Doce Calles, 1991, p. 362–380, photos)

Provides useful summary of a new, apparently yet-to-be published book-length study of life and oeuvre of the scholar who introduced Hispanists to the *relaciones geográficas* of the Perus. If this article is any indication, López-Ocón's forthcoming *De viajero naturalista a historiador* will be well worth reading. [MTH]

2222 Nueva historia del Ecuador. v. 12, Ensayos generales I; v. 13, Ensayos generales II; v. 14, Cronología comparada de la historia ecuatoriana. Edición de Enrique Ayala Mora. Quito: Corporación Editora Nacional; Grijalbo, 1994–1995? 3 v.

Vols. 12–13 of this 15-volume, truly new history of Ecuador (only the last volume of which remained to be published as of Dec. 1995) consist of 14 eminently readable and quite insightful overviews of the historical geography and the demographic, economic, ethno-, political, regional, and social history of Ecuador during the colonial and national periods. Vol. 13 includes useful, but far from complete, name and place indexes for vols. 1–13. Vol. 14 consists of side-by-side timetables of developments and events in Ecuador, the Americas, and the world. For a description of other volumes in this series, see *HLAS 52: 2114, HLAS 54:745*, and *HLAS 54:2679–2683*. [MTH]

2223 Oleas G., Angel F. Catálogo modelo: Biblioteca del Convento de Santo Domingo, Quito. Dirección Técnica de María Eugenia Mieles V. Quito: Instituto Nacional de Patrimonio Cultural; Consejo Nacional de Ciencia y Tecnología; Brussels: Reino de Bélgica; Quito: Comunidad Dominicana de Quito, 1992. 347 p.: ill. (Patrimonio documental ecuatoriano. Catálogos; 1)

Samples published holdings of the Biblioteca del Convento de Santo Domingo in Quito to exemplify level-three description of library materials according to internationally agreed upon standards. Too limited to be of any use to subject specialists, this catalog describes only 250 titles out of an inventory of 30,972 volumes. But the ongoing processing of the manuscript and print collections of the Dominicans in Quito should make their important holdings more accessible and better known. [MTH]

Colonial Period

MICHAEL T. HAMERLY, *Independent Consultant, Seattle, Washington*
SUSAN M. SOCOLOW, *Professor of History, Emory University*
LANCE R. GRAHN, *Associate Professor and Assistant Chairperson of the Department of History, Marquette University*

WE HAVE HAD TO LIMIT our introductory remarks even more in this *Handbook* than in *HLAS 54* inasmuch as historians continue to produce an exceptionally abundant and succulent harvest. Even applying more stringent criteria for inclusion, an unprecedented number of new and recent articles, books, and published sources, altogether 504 items, proved to be worthy of our table.

Insofar as general works are concerned, the most appealing is *Estados y naciones en los Andes* (item **2220**), in which historians of Colombia, Ecuador, Peru, and Bolivia adopt a truly comparative approach to the century and a half following the independence of their countries. Turning to the colonial period proper, it should be noted that the proceedings of the 1986 Symposium on the Earth-Measuring Expedition of 1736 were finally forthcoming (item **2238**). In addition, the compiler and other particulars of the early 17th-century *relaciones geográficas* have now been established (see vol. 1 of the new critical edition, item **2240**). [MTH]

VENEZUELA

Historiographical trends for colonial Venezuela remain much as they have been in recent years. The topics of slavery, independence, cacao production, and regionalism again dominate this biennium. In part, this continuity of research agendas reflects the productivity of the Academia Nacional de Historia, but it also demonstrates the investigative energy that these subjects still generate. Historians of colonial Venezuela are putting together these well-worn themes in new combinations that give them fresh life and interest.

Tronconis de Veracoechea (item **2271**) and Rojas (item **2270**), for example, illustrate that the 1795 Coro slave revolt is still accorded national significance for its representation of nascent and multicultural sentiment for independence. Nonetheless, the several articles on civil unrest in the late 18th century (items **2275, 2246, 2270, 2271,** and **2253**) delineate the unique combination of slave rebelliousness, class conflict, French revolutionary ideology, and international commercial relationships that fostered Venezuelan nationhood.

The generally localized nature of these historical events and modern studies points to the continuing sway of regional and local perspectives. Economic and mission history have been defined as much as aspects of geographical identity, as activities situated in a particular place. Thus, whether it be studies of cacao production (items **2248, 2265,** and **2264**) or examinations of Capuchin and Jesuit missions (items **2272, 2254,** and **2261**), a sense of place dominates the work. The titles of three recent books, *Tierra, gobierno local y actividad misionera en la comunidad indígena del oriente venezolano* (item **2254**), *The town of San Felipe and colonial cacao economies* (item **2265**), and *La Nueva Segovia de Bariquiçimeto* (item **2245**) exemplify the analytical prominence of locality. At the same time, these three studies typify how microanalysis illustrates larger patterns of colonial life, such as ethnic tensions, international trade, and material culture, respectively.

The aforementioned book on Bariquiçimeto by Avellán de Tamayo also represents the strength of recent reference works (item **2245**). In the long run, this study will likely prove valuable both as a handbook on material and popular culture and as an exemplary municipal history. Similarly, Vaccari de Venturini's survey of Venezuelan governors (item **2273**) and Grases' historiographical essay (item **2251**) are welcome research tools that invite continuing investigation.

NUEVA GRANADA

As with colonial Venezuela, the trends of recent colonial Colombian historiography are familiar. For example, biographical studies of well-known figures, such as José Celestino Mutis and Antonio de la Torre y Miranda, continue to multiply. Duque Gómez's tribute to Mutis illustrates the positive tone that characterizes these works, as well as the national historical pride vested in this famous teacher and investigator (item **2286**). Historians gave similarly high praise to Torre (items **2294** and **2301**) and Antonio Caballero y Góngora (item **2304**). Gratifyingly, modern biographers increasingly place their protagonists in a fuller scientific or political context. The splendid two-volume set, *Mutis y la Real Expedición Botánica* (item **2302**), and the articles by Restrepo Forero (item **2305**) and Ruiz Martínez (item **2306**) clarify the intellectual dynamics and modernity of late Bourbon culture in the viceroyalty.

The thematic significance of Indian *resguardos* is equally evident this biennium in the work of Velásquez (item **2312**), Sosa Abella (item **2309**), González (item

2289), and Luna (item **2296**). The institutional core, reiterated by the reissue of González's 1970 text, remains sound. The analyses by Sosa Abella and Tovar (item **2311**) exhibit the development and continuing potential of *resguardo* social history.

Regional history represents a third major historiographical focus in recent years. Here, the work and influence of Germán Colmenares is particularly evident (item **2283**). His own emphasis on the dynamic interplay between social and economic development is used by others, such as Suárez de Alvarez (item **2310**), Mejía Prado (item **2300**), and Díaz López (item **2284**), to elucidate regional distinctiveness, structures, and identities.

Finally, Anthony McFarlane's *Colombia before independence* (item **2299**) and the Archivo General de la Nación's *Censo-guía y estadística de los archivos de Antioquia* (item **2282**) deserve special mention. McFarlane's study of 18th-century New Granada puts customary themes such as regionalism and viceregal accomplishment into a long-needed synthesis of the Bourbon century. With its wealth of information, the archival guide for Antioquia should facilitate and foster not only regional and local history, but also analyses of the breadth of colonial society. [LG]

QUITO

Historical and related output on the former Presidency of Quito has been much more substantial and of a higher quality in recent years than reported in *HLAS 54*. Furthermore, so much good work has been done of late and continues to be done that reporting upon everything of significance will be the work of at least the two forthcoming *Handbooks* (Vols. 58 and 60). The recent robustness of Ecuadorian historiography is not without its down side, however; for instance, the Banco Central del Ecuador's *Cultura* ceased publication about ten years ago. Fortunately, the Banco's *Revista Ecuatoriana de Historia Económica* is still going strong, and a major new journal, *Procesos: Revista Ecuatoriana de Historia*, appeared in 1991.

Other major developments include the passing of the Old Guard. The aging Jorge Salvador Lara (b. 1926), whose recent credits include a new general history of Ecuador (item **2373**) and the most comprehensive history of the city of Quito to date (item **2374**), will probably turn out to be the last of the great traditional historians. The demise of the aficionados and of the autodidacts is more than compensated for by the appearance of a substantial group of recently trained nationals, including women, mostly from the Pontificia Universidad Católica del Ecuador and the Facultad Latinoamericana de Ciencias Sociales, both in Quito. The caliber of productivity of the new historians and of their mentors is impressive as evidenced in this *Handbook*, for example, in the original theses on the protectorate of Indians (item **2317**), on the Chota River Valley (item **2327**), and on the cinchona trade (item **2353**).

Several more North American and European scholars have joined the ranks of colonial-period Ecuadorianists. See, for example, Newson's long-anticipated *Life and death in early colonial Ecuador* (item **2354**) or Volland's also long-awaited study of the postconquest history of the Indians of the coast, (item **2381**). Other researchers have added to their impressive earlier works with major new monographs, most notably Minchom, *The people of Quito* (item **2351**); Ortiz de la Tabla Ducasse, *Los encomenderos de Quito* (item **2355**); and Powers, *Andean journeys* (item **2363**). Neither should one ignore the lesser gems by the Spaniard Paniagua Pérez (items **2357** and **2358**) or the Frenchman Poloni (items **2359** and **2360**), or, for other recent developments, *La producción historiográfica sobre el Ecuador en los últimos 25 años* (item **2219**).

PERU

The harvest of works on Lower Peru continues to be extraordinarily bountiful. Alarco has produced yet another volume in his monumental history of Peru (item **2225**). Much more important are the mostly new *Compendio histórico del Perú*—of which vols. 2–4 are devoted to the colonial period (item **2389**)—and Lazo García's extraordinarily rich and exceptionally important history of money in Upper as well as Lower Peru (item **2429**). Just as impressive is Macera's *Precios del Perú* (item **2432**). Both Lazo García's and Macera's works are major benchmarks in Peruvian historiography. Not only do they add enormously to our knowledge of the colonial period, but they will force considerable reworking thereof.

Indeed almost all of the recent and new work on the colonial period of Peru proper is impressive in one way or another. To single out one or more articles or other books for additional commendation would be to slight far too many authors and their works. But I would be remiss in not calling attention to Barriga Calle's not-at-all morbid "La experiencia de la muerte en Lima" (item **2382**), Hampe Martínez's thoughtful and thought-provoking "Hacia una nueva periodización de la historia del Perú colonial" (item **2413**), Henige's deliciously truculent "Counting the encounter" (item **2417**), or Iwasaki Cauti's fascinating "Mujeres al borde de la perfección" (item **2424**). To be invidious, the most readable new book in English struck this contributor to be Mills' *An evil lost to view?* (item **2438**), and the most readable in Spanish to be Alfonso W. Quiroz's *Deudas olvidadas* (item **2450**). Both works, moreover, are original and important contributions.

ALTO PERU

There continue to be at least as many, if not more, North Americans and Europeans at work on the history of Upper Peru as there are Bolivians. Insofar as the production of the last few years is concerned, the large number of major monographs in general and of books in English in particular is especially significant. A substantial and quite comprehensive body of literature on the colonial period now exists in English, bolstered by the appearance of at least six new books during the last biennium. Furthermore, Bolivian historiography has become so healthy that scholars no longer hesitate to reexamine previously-studied regions or materials. To wit, Jackson takes on Larson in his reexamination of the agrarian history of Cochabamba (item **2478**) and Klein reassesses his own data in his ongoing studies of the demography and economy of La Paz province (item **2480**). At the same time, less well-known areas have come under close scrutiny. Both Cornblit and Zulawski, for example, considerably enhance and elucidate the history of the mining town and district of Oruro (items **2475** and **2487**).

CHILE

Output on the former Captaincy General of Chile remains much the same: substantial, sophisticated, and almost exclusively in the hands of national scholars. Flusche appears to be the only North American publishing regularly on the colonial period (items **2494** and **2495**). Why this should be so when there are so many North Americans and Europeans working on Quito and Lower and Upper Peru eludes this contributor. Although the majority of studies annotated here rework known ground, some innovative work, such as Vargas Cariola's pioneering essay on daily military life in the 17th century (item **2510**) or Sánchez's wholly original "Régimen Económico de una Parroquia Rural" (item **2504**), did appear. As usual, appreciably more articles—almost all of which were of a high caliber—than books were published.

Clearly the least interesting as well as longest book was Retamal Favereau, Celis Atria, and Muñoz Correa's minute but lackluster *Familias fundadoras de Chile* (item **2503**). The most exciting and the best monograph—in this contributor's opinion—was Bravo Lira's *El absolutismo ilustrado en Hispanoamérica: Chile, 1760–1860, de Carlos III a Portales y Montt* (item **2491**). [MTH]

RIO DE LA PLATA

The major debate in colonial Argentine historiography continues to be the great "gaucho-peasant" controversy. It now seems clear that the peasants have, at least temporarily, been victorious, but the discussion continues as to the condition of the newly discovered and ubiquitous peasantry. Among the most productive and best scholars, Gelman (items **2564, 2562,** and **2563**), Garavaglia (items **2557, 2556, 2560,** and **2606**), and Mayo (item **2593**) are the dominant figures, but important contributions to a further understanding of the economy of the frontier are also being made by Canedo (items **2534** and **2535**). While these scholars present a picture of a relatively prosperous peasantry, Gresores sees that same peasantry as a landless, exploited proletariat (items **2569** and **2570**). A related interest in the history of Indian-Spanish relations along the *bonarense* frontier continues (items **2526, 2582,** and **2583**).

There has also been a strong interest in the history of bureaucrats and bureaucracy, focusing primarily, but not exclusively, on the Viceregal period (items **2469, 2515, 2544, 2545, 2613, 2618, 2625, 2634,** and **2635**) and on educational reforms under the Bourbons (items **2522** and **2523**).

Important demographic studies have emerged, ranging from whole populations to subgroups, among them the meticulous work of Celton (items **2541** and **2542**), Ferreyra (item **2554**), Arcondo (item **2513**), Boleda (item **2529**), García Belsunce (item **2561**), Lorandi and Ferreiro (item **2577**), and Ruedi and Somoza (item **2620**). The first three of these historians also reflect the growth of strong work on the history of Córdoba (see also Punta, item **2609** and Romero Cabrera, items **2615** and **2616**) and a general interest in regions of the Interior. The history of colonial women is also becoming a consistent and interesting topic for *rioplatense* historiography (items **2580, 2581, 2584,** and **914**), and work is beginning to appear on criminality (items **2524** and **2608**).

Very few studies of the colonial history of the Banda Oriental (present-day Uruguay) have appeared. On the other hand, a respectable amount of work centers on colonial Paraguay and northern Argentina, including several studies on the Jesuit missions (items **2528, 2547, 2555, 2575, 2579,** and **2578**) and *reducciones* (items **2538, 2537, 2550,** and **2571**). One notes in much of this new work an attempt to understand conquest and the mission experience from the standpoint of the native peoples (items **2619** and **2630**).

We note an increasing number of journal articles dealing with colonial Río de la Plata at the same time as there has been an abrupt decline in the number of published monographs dealing with the region. [SMS]

GENERAL

2224 Acarete, *du Biscay.* La route de l'argent. Présentation de Jean-Paul Duviols. Paris: Editions Utz; Distique, 1992. 140 p.: bibl., ill.

New edition of the important, but long out-of-print, 17th-century travel account *Relation des voyages du sieur Accarette dans la riuiere de la Plate* (Paris, 1672). Acarete (Accarette in French, Ascarate in Spanish) was a Basque merchant who made two voyages to the Río de la Plata in 1657–59 and 1660. During his first excursion he also traveled overland to Potosí via Córdoba, Santiago del Estero, Salta, and Jujuy. Acarete reports on contraband trade between Upper Peru and Buenos Aires and on the state of Spanish defenses. [MTH]

2225 Alarco, Eugenio. El hombre peruano en su historia. v. 7, La historia dorada de la colonia. Lima: s.n., 1992. 1 v.

Vol. 7 in a monumental history of Peru from prehistoric times through the present, this tome covers viceroyalty at large from late 1500s through first third of 1700s in considerable yet curious detail. This traditional or Old Guard history, albeit one organized more or less thematically, is apparently compiled mostly from *relaciones* of viceroys and *actas* of *cabildos*. However, this is supposition since sources and studies on which work is based are scheduled to be included in next volume, *La historia negra de la colonia*. Recommended reading for retired colonialists and insatiable Peruvianists. [MTH]

2226 Cahill, David. Colour by numbers: racial and ethnic categories in the Viceroyalty of Peru, 1532–1824. (*J. Lat. Am. Stud.*, 26:2, May 1994, p. 324–346)

Well-articulated essay examines ethnic distinctions in the Perus before and after the Spanish conquest. An important contribution to ongoing debate as to meaning and significance of racial terminology employed by conquerors and conquered. [MTH]

2227 Coloquio Internacional Sociedad y Expansión, *Lima, 1994.* Actas. v. 1, Antecedentes y aspectos de la expansión europea en su primera etapa, siglo XVI. Lima: Univ. de Lima, 1994. 1 v.: bibl.

This volume includes essays on various aspects of relationships between the Old and New Worlds, especially between Spain and Peru, from 16th through 18th centuries. Few of the papers, presented mostly by Peruvian scholars, contribute new data or interpretations. Nonetheless, this set is important because it exemplifies not just the maturation of historiography in Peru, but a refreshing expansion of interests on the part of Peruvian scholars. [MTH]

2228 Descubrimientos españoles en el Mar del Sur. v. 1–3. Madrid: Editorial Naval, 1992. 3 v.: bibl., ill. (some col.), index, maps (some col.).

Multiauthored, multivolume history of Spanish voyages of discovery and exploration in the Pacific from Magellan's and Elcano's circumnavigation through voyages of Mourelle de la Rúa is based on archival, as well as published, sources and studies. A superior reference work on Spain in the Pacific. Well illustrated, mostly with reproductions of coeval drawings and maps. [MTH]

2229 Economía y comercio en América Hispana. Edición de Guillermo Bravo Acevedo. Santiago: Departamento de Ciencias Históricas, Facultad de Filosofía y Humanidades, Univ. de Chile, 1990. 174 p.: bibl., maps. (Serie Nuevo mundo, 0176-7571; 5)

Six essays by José Luis Martínez C., María Angélica Apey Rivera, Osvaldo Silva Galdames, Rodolfo Urbina Burgos, Guillermo Bravo Acevedo, and Hernán Asdrúbal Silva, respectively, on settlements and access to resources in the Atacama in 1600s, on Arica as a waystop in trade between Lower and Upper Peru, on war and barter between colonists, soldiers, and the Mapuche, on commerce of Chilote in late 1700s, on private-sector trade between Chile and Peru in mid 1700s, and on maritime traffic between the Spanish Mediterranean and Río de la Plata from 1778–96. Original contributions to economic and regional history of 17th- and 18th-century Peru, Upper Peru, Chile, and Río de la Plata. [MTH]

2230 Marzal, Manuel María. La utopía posible: indios y jesuitas en la América colonial, 1549–1767. v. 1., Brasil, Perú, Paraguay y Nuevo Reino. Lima: Pontificia Univ. Católica del Perú, 1992. 1 v.: bibl.

Anthology contains excerpts from accounts of Jesuit missionaries in their provinces of Brazil, Peru, Paraguay, and Nuevo Reino de Granada. Editor has selected passages that exemplify ethnographic value of the chronicles as well as the activities of the missionaries. Ably woven together with commentary. [MTH]

2231 Mazzeo de Vivó, Cristina Ana. Esclavitud y acumulación mercantil: el tráfico negrero en el contexto de las reformas borbónicas. (*Histórica/Lima*, 17:2, dic. 1993, p. 149–178, bibl., map, tables)

Contributes some original data on slave trade between Buenos Aires and Lima in late 18th and early 19th centuries. Especially concerned with the traffic engaged in by the *limeño* José Antonio de Lavalle y Cortés, the

Conde de Premio Real. Based on author's master's thesis. [MTH]

2232 Miño Grijalva, Manuel. La manufacturera colonial: aspectos comparativos entre el obraje andino y el novohispano. (*Rev. Ecuat. Hist. Econ.*, 2:4, 1988, p. 13–61)

Comparative study focuses on textile manufacturing in the Presidency of Quito, Lower Peru, and New Spain. An abridged version of this work was published in 1989 (see *HLAS 52:816*). [MTH]

2233 Minta, Stephen. Aguirre: the re-creation of a sixteenth-century journey across South America. New York: H. Holt, 1994. 244 p.: bibl., ill., index.

Minta's well-written and entertaining account of his reenactment of Aguirre's search for El Dorado is as close as most readers can or probably would want to come to what the intrepid Basque suffered in the 1550s, or for that matter, what Minta himself endured 430 years later in retracing Aguirre's peregrination. [MTH]

2234 Nouvelles certaines des isles du Peru: fac-similé de l'édition originale. Texte rapproché du français moderne par Hélène Cazes. Suivi de Nouvelles du Pérou, de Miguel de Estete. Texte présenté par Isabel Soto-Alliot. Traduit de l'espagnol par Angeles Muñoz et Rosine Gars. Édition publiée sous la direction d'Isabel Soto-Alliot. Préface de Pierre Chaunu. Thaon, France: Amiot-Lenganey, 1992. 80 p.: bibl. (Essais)

First work, an exceptionally important primary source on the discovery and conquest of what are now Ecuador and Peru (Paris: 1534), is reprinted in photofacsimile and in modern typeface. Volume also publishes coeval French version of Estete's *Noticia del Perú* (1535). Authorities disagree as to authorship of letters on which *Nouvelles certaines* was based, but they agree that authors of the letters were eyewitnesses. [MTH]

2235 O'Phelan Godoy, Scarlett. Rebeliones andinas anticoloniales: Nueva Granada, Perú y Charcas entre el siglo XVIII y el XIX. (*Anu. Estud. Am.*, 49, 1992, p. 395–440)

Comparative study examines 1765 rebellion of *barrios* of Quito, 1780–81 rebellion of Túpac Amaru in Lower and Upper Peru, and 1781 rebellion of *comuneros* in Socorro. Also considers relationships between those rebellions and 1809–14 movements for independence in Quito and Lower and Upper Peru.

Important essay replete with fresh insights and new interpretations is written by leading student of unrest among the Andean peoples during late colonial and independence periods. [MTH]

2236 Peire, Jaime. La manipulación de los capítulos provinciales, las élites, y el imaginario socio-político colonial tardío. (*Anu. Estud. Am.*, 50:1, 1993, p. 13–54, tables, graphs)

Exceptionally interesting study of the ways and means used by local elites to co-opt the office of provincial in the Mercedarian order throughout Spanish America in late 1700s. Also looks at discourse between provincials, archbishops, viceroys, *audiencias,* and other authorities of the period regarding political and social developments as well as ecclesiastical matters. [MTH]

2237 Sáiz, Blanca. Bibliografía sobre Alejandro Malaspina: y acerca de la Expedición Malaspina y de los marinos y científicos que en ella participaron. Madrid: Ediciones El Museo Universal, 1992. 469 p.: index.

Extensive, but not altogether satisfactory, bibliography of materials on the Malaspina Expedition and its component members. Lists 1,064 published articles and books and an additional 70 unpublished items, including theses. Many of the descriptions are incomplete or secondhand in origin (i.e., compiler unverified). Also the subject index is so general as to be almost useless. [MTH]

2238 Simposio por los 250 Años de la Misión Científica Franco-Española a la América Ecuatorial, *Quito, 1986.* Ponencias. (*Bol. Acad. Nac. Hist./Quito*, 72:153/154, 1989 [i.e., 1993], p. 4–405; 73:155/156, 1990 [i.e., 1994], p. 9–211, graphs, ill., tables)

Publishes proceedings of symposium held in Quito in July 1986 on earth measuring expedition of 1736. Only those papers having something original to say have been annotated individually in this chapter. [MTH]

2239 Tardieu, Jean-Pierre. Los jesuitas y la "Lengua de Angola" en Perú, siglo XVII. (*Rev. Indias*, 53:198, mayo/agosto 1993, p. 627–637)

Reviews what is known regarding efforts of Jesuit priests in Upper Peru and the Río de la Plata to master Bantu in order to work more effectively with slaves, at least those brought from Angola region. Whether or not Fathers Torres Bello's and López de

Castilla's grammar and dictionary, apparently compiled in early 1600s, were ever published remains to be ascertained. [MTH]

2240 Valencia, Pedro de. Relaciones de Indias. v. 1, Nueva Granada y Virreinato de Perú. Estudios introductorios y notas históricas de Jesús Paniagua Pérez. Edición crítica de Francisco Javier Fuente Fernández. León, Spain: Secretariado de Publicaciones de la Univ. de León, 1993. 519 p.

Recent research has revealed that the well-known *Relaciones geográficas* of early 17th century were drafted by Pedro de Valencia in 1607 and 1608, utilizing responses received to the questionnaire he prepared in 1604. This volume consists of new transcriptions, replete with explanatory notes based on manuscript originals in the Biblioteca Nacional de Madrid, of: "Los Quijos," "Panamá," "Portobelo," "Tunja," "Nuestra Señora de Leiva," "Villar Don Pardo," "Los Pueblos de la Villa de el Villar Don Pardo" (i.e., Riobamba and its indigenous towns), "Guayaquil y Portoviejo," "Jaén de Bracamoros," "Relación de San Leandro de Jaén, Baeza y Guayaquil," "Santiago de la Frontera y su Distrito." In brief, a critical edition of a major group of primary sources. [MTH]

Walter, Rolf. Der Traum vom Eldorado: die deutsche Conquista in Venezuela im 16. Jahrhundert. See item **2274.**

2241 Zeuske, Michael. Francisco de Miranda und die Entdeckung Europas: eine Biographie. Münster, Germany: Lit, 1995 298 p.: bibl. (Hamburger Ibero-Amerika Studien; Bd. 5)

Narrative biography of Francisco de Miranda, the "proto-leader" of Spanish American independence, presented in a lively and literary manner. Author has employed a fictionalized reconstruction of certain dialogues and situations to lend a sense of intimacy to his narrative. Most of the book is devoted to Miranda's own "discovery" of Europe and to the circumstances surrounding the creation of his innovative political model for the Americas. Zeuske, however, does not regard Miranda as a social revolutionary because of his consistent aristocratic aspirations. [T. Hampe-Martínez]

2242 Zuidema, R. Tom. Guamán Pomo between the arts of Europe and the Andes. (*Colon. Lat. Am. Rev.,* 3:1/2, 1994, p. 37–85, bibl., ill.)

Guamán Poma must be read and viewed not simply as a compound—far from homogeneous—mixture of European and Andean, but through a multiplicity of ideological and iconographic filters in order to determine what he was trying to say and depict. In this case, Zuidema discusses "the drawings-cum-text of Mama Huaco and Huayna Capac," and the why and the how thereof. [MTH]

VENEZUELA

2243 Andreo García, Juan. La intendencia en Venezuela: Don Esteban Fernández de León, intendente de Caracas, 1791–1803. Murcia, Spain: Univ. de Murcia, 1991. 281 p.: bibl. (Cuadernos; 25)

Well-researched economic history focuses on Venezuela's fourth *intendente.* Examines the institution and the man during a period marked by trade liberalization, a war with England, and creation of the Consulado. Concludes that intendente correctly concentrated on tobacco revenues and cost cutting to raise royal income. Excellent analysis of difficult Real Hacienda data. [K. Waldron]

2244 Arcila Farías, Eduardo. Comercio en el área del Caribe y hacienda pública de Venezuela en la segunda mitad del XVIII. (*in* Congreso Internacional de Historia Económica y Social de la Cuenca del Caribe, 1763–1898, *1st, San Juan, 1987.* Actas. San Juan: Centro de Estudios Avanzados de Puerto Rico y el Caribe, 1992, p. 279–292, tables)

Worthwhile compilation includes statistics on Venezuelan flour exports (1601–50), cacao exports (1651–1824), and ship traffic for Caracas-La Guaira (1601–1738). [LRG]

2245 Avellán de Tamayo, Nieves. La Nueva Segovia de Bariquiçimeto. v. 1–2. Caracas: Academia Nacional de la Historia, 1992. 2 v.: bibl., ill., indexes, maps. (Biblioteca de la Academia Nacional de la Historia: Fuentes para la historia colonial de Venezuela; 213–214)

Impressive encyclopedic history of an important colonial city is packed with carefully documented detail. Distinguished by its architectural and paleographical emphases, work is valuable resource for local history in general. [LRG]

2246 Brito Figueroa, Federico. Venezuela colonial: las rebeliones de esclavos y la Revolución Francesa. (*Caravelle/Toulouse*, 54, 1990, p. 263–289, bibl., tables)

Seeking to delineate formation of Venezuelan national identity, Brito reiterates that late 18th-century rebellions of slaves and other oppressed social groups represented conscious efforts to attain the sociopolitical goals of the French Revolution. See also items **2270, 2271, 2277,** and **2253.** [LRG]

2247 Chacón Rodríguez, David R. La defensa de las costas venezolanas de la Guaira, Punta Brava y Puerto Cabello, frente al ataque inglés de 1743 según la documentación existente en el Archivo General de Indias. Caracas?: República de Venezuela, Armada; Cádiz, Spain: Bazán, 1991? 252 p.: appendices, bibl., ill. (some col.), maps.

Provides useful, if at times mundane, military history of British Navy's unsuccessful attacks against Venezuelan coastal defenses in spring of 1743. Narrative is nicely illustrated with contemporary maps and enriched by substantial documentary appendices. [LRG]

2248 Chacón S., Résmil E. El desarollo de la propiedad cacaotera en Caucagua durante el siglo XVIII. (*Estud. Hist. Soc. Econ. Am.*, 11, 1994, p. 321–326)

Brief survey examines cacao production in Caucagua region (modern Venezuelan state of Miranda). Exploitation of this high-quality cacao spurred rapid local development and solidified Venezuelan cacao production. Primacy of cacao crystallized in 18th century in response to European demands. [LRG]

2249 Francisco de Miranda en Francia. Presentación de André-Jean Libourel. Compilación y prólogo de Edgardo Mondolfi. Caracas: Embajada de Francia en Venezuela; Monte Avila Editores, 1992. 370 p. (Documentos)

Bilingual work reprints documents relating Miranda's actions at Valmy and during Belgian campaign, and his treason trial before the French Tribunal Criminel Révolutionnaire. [K. Waldron]

2250 González Oropeza, Hermann. La evangelización fundante en la Venezuela Oriental. (*in* La evangelización fundante en América Latina: estudio histórico del siglo

XVI. Bogotá: Consejo Episcopal Latinoamericano, 1990, p. 83–231, appendix)

Lengthy article summarizes ecclesiastical activity in eastern Venezuela, including Margarita and Trinidad. Major dispute of 16th century was between dioceses of Puerto Rico and Santo Domingo over domination of territories. [K. Waldron]

2251 Grases, Pedro. Estudio crítico sobre la bibliografía de la Real Compañía Guipuzcoana de Caracas, 1728–1785. (*Bol. Inst. Riva-Agüero*, 16, 1989, p. 303–316, bibl.)

Valuable historiographical work surveys monographs written in 18th, 19th, and 20th centuries. Organized chronologically by date of publication, titles tend to represent general studies of Venezuela; few works specifically treat the Real Compañía. Hussey's *The Caracas Company, 1728–1784* (see *HLAS 40:2295*) remains unmatched. The works of Vicente de Amézaga Aresti are also highlighted. [LRG]

2252 Hutten, Philipp von. Das Gold der Neuen Welt: die Papiere des Welser-Konquistadors und Generalkapitäns von Venezuela, Philipp von Hutten 1534–1541. Herausgegeben von Eberhard Schmitt und Friedrich Karl von Hutten. Hildburghausen, Germany: Verlag Frankenschwelle, 1996. 209 p.: bibl., ill. (some col.), index, maps.

Well-presented collection of unpublished materials concerning von Hutten is drawn from his family archives as well as additional previously published material. Includes short biographies of persons mentioned in von Hutten's letters. Von Hutten's unpublished letters retain morphology, but not original acronyms and punctuation, of 16th-century German. Authors add clarifying notations. [C.K. Converse]

2253 Langue, Frédérique. Desterrar el vicio y serenar las conciencias: mendicidad y pobreza en la Caracas del siglo XVIII. (*Rev. Indias*, 54:201, mayo/agosto 1994, p. 355–381, table)

Slave and *pardo* rebellions in 1749, 1795, and 1797 indicate that class conflict characterized late colonial society in Venezuela. Elites' oppression of indigent in Caracas demonstrated urban upper class fear of the poor. Contrasts with other studies of popular unrest (items **2246, 2277,** and **2271**) that instead focus on external sources of the development of sentiment for independence. [LRG]

Langue, Frédérique. Las élites en América española: actitudes y mentalidades. See item **902.**

2254 Laserna Gaitán, Antonio Ignacio.
Tierra, gobierno local y actividad misionera en la comunidad indígena del oriente venezolano: la visita a la provincia de Cumaná de Don Luis de Chávez y Mendoza, 1783–1784. Caracas: Academia Nacional de la Historia, 1993. 427 p.: ill., maps. (Biblioteca de la Academia Nacional de la Historia. Fuentes para la historia colonial de Venezuela; 219)

Despite its subtitle, this book is an almost encyclopedic collection of short essays on the geography and ethnography of Cumaná, Capuchin evangelization of the area, Chávez's visit itself, agriculture and land tenure, and the *corregimiento*. The work provides a solid foundation for ethnohistorical research on Nueva Andalucía. [LRG]

2255 López Bohórquez, Alí Enrique. El archivo de la Real Audiencia de Caracas: estado actual de las fuentes documentales para su estudio. (*Bol. Acad. Nac. Hist./Caracas*, 74:294, abril/junio 1991, p. 55–61)

Archive of the Real Audiencia never existed as a separate depository; many documents were lost during independence wars. Sections exist in Spanish archives, Archivo General de la Nación, and other Caracas archives. Expert on the Real Audiencia describes what remains and where; enough materials remain to reconstruct colonial history. [K. Waldron]

Martínez de Salinas, María Luisa. Castilla ante el Nuevo Mundo: la trayectoria indiana del gobernador Bernardo de Vargas Machuca. See item **2297.**

2256 Meza, Robinzon. La élite caraqueña frente a la reorganización político-administrativa de Venezuela en el último cuarto del siglo XVIII. (*Islas/Santa Clara*, 100, sept./dic. 1991, p. 7–19)

Concise analysis focuses on conflict between Cabildo, Capitán General, Real Audiencia, and Consulado. *Criollos* opposed royal policy limiting commerce, creating a tobacco monopoly, interfering in cabildo affairs, and promoting the *pardo* group. No new material, but still a useful summary. [K. Waldron]

2257 Michelena y Rojas, Francisco. Exploración oficial. Edición crítica, introducción e índices de Nelly Arvelo de Jiménez y Horacio Biord Castillo. Iquitos, Peru: CETA; IIAP, 1989. 693 p., 4 plates of leaves (some folded): bibl., ill., maps, indexes. (Monumenta amazónica. C, Agentes gubernamentales; 1)

Part of Proyecto Monumenta Amazónica, this sixth volume is devoted to historic documents. Francisco Michelena y Rojas, born in Venezuela in 1801, was a diplomat and later governor of Amazonas. He wrote of his explorations by river, showing sensitivity to indigenous cultures. Valuable to anthropologists and historians. [K. Waldron]

2258 Miguel López, Isabel. Relaciones comerciales entre Santander y La Guayra, 1786–1795. (*Bol. Acad. Nac. Hist./Caracas*, 73:291, julio/sept. 1990, p. 115–149, appendices, graphs, tables)

La Guaira was the destination of 12 percent of all ships leaving Santander, Spain. Sailing to Venezuela loaded with textiles, flour, iron, and steel, the ships returned to Spain with gold, silver, cacao, cotton, and coffee. Trade grew rapidly after 1789 with Venezuela's inclusion in the free trade policy until European hostilities of mid-1790s interrupted shipping. Miguel relies on customs records and ship registries of both ports to demonstrate activity. [K. Waldron]

2259 Miranda, Francisco de. Colombeia. v. 9–11, Revolución Francesa. Prefacio de J. L. Salcedo-Bastardo. Introdución bibliografía, prólogo y notas de Josefina Rodríguez de Alonso. Caracas: Ediciones de la Presidencia de la República, 1991–1992? 3 v.

These three volumes of Miranda's archive cover period 1790–93 when he was active in the French Revolution. Vol. 9 documents correspondence with William Pitt. Vol. 10 covers two months in 1792 when Miranda fought alongside French troops. Vol. 11 details his Belgian campaign. Most entries are translated from the original English or French publications. [K. Waldron]

2260 Misión secreta en Puerto Cabello y viaje a Caracas en 1783. Prólogo, investigación, traducción y notas de Carlos F. Duarte. Caracas: Fundación Pampero, 1991. 442 p.: bibl., ill. (some col.), indexes, maps.

Little-known primary sources were written by members of a French naval squadron that stopped in Puerto Cabello in 1783. Led by Marqués de Vaudreuil, squadron sailed from Boston to Venezuela. Brief extracts of diaries contain amusing observations about food, women, dances, and social customs. [K. Waldron]

2261 Misiones jesuíticas en la Orinoquía, 1625–1767. v. 1–2. Edición de José del Rey Fajardo *et al.* San Cristóbal, Venezuela: Univ. Católica del Táchira, 1992. 2 v.: bibl., maps.

Valuable collection of essays in historical missiology goes beyond book's title. Most of the contributions examine Jesuit evangelization in several regions of southern Venezuela, but anthology also includes useful overviews of Spanish American mission history and studies of Jesuit education. [LRG]

2262 Montoya, Miguel. La evolución político-territorial de Mérida, 1558–1914. Mérida, Venezuela: Univ. de Los Andes, Consejo de Publicaciones, 1993. 177 p.: bibl., ill., maps. (Textos de la Univ. de los Andes. Col. 500 años de qué?)

Brief history of Venezuelan Mérida seeks to clarify province's political identity and to establish region's colonial uniqueness. Devoted largely to colonial period. [LRG]

2263 Ortega, Miguel Angel. La esclavitud en el contexto agropecuario colonial: siglo XVIII. Caracas: Editorial APICUM, 1992. 110 p.: bibl., ill. (Col. "El Otro discurso"; 2)

Comparative regional analysis of slavery in province of Caracas, c. 1730–80, examines role of Afrovenezuelans in production of cacao, sugarcane, and livestock. Useful example of an Afrocentric perspective. See also item **2265**. [LRG]

2264 Piñero, Eugenio. Accounting practices in a colonial economy: a case study of cacao haciendas in Venezuela, 1700–1770. (*CLAHR/Albuquerque*, 1:1, Fall 1992, p. 37–66, tables)

Utilizing administrative records of Hacienda Cumanibare, Piñero provides useful survey of the business side of cacao production. Covers not only bookkeeping but also labor management, business expenses, and internal investment strategies. [LRG]

2265 Piñero, Eugenio. The town of San Felipe and colonial cacao economies. Philadelphia: American Philosophical Society, 1994. 189 p.: bibl., index. (Transactions of the American Philosophical Society, 0065–9746: 84, pt. 3)

Local study of cacao economy argues for staple thesis of economic growth. Cacao production in Caracas province, for example, fostered rationalization of cattle-ranching in the southern Llanos as haciendas' need for hides and beef increased. Worthwhile exmination of Amerindian roles in cacao production as well. This study parallels Miguel Angel Ortega's work (see item **2263**). [LRG]

2266 Ponce de Behrens, Marianela. Para la memoria venezolana. Caracas: Academia Nacional de la Historia, 1990. 321 p.: bibl., index (Biblioteca de la Academia Nacional de la Historia. Estudios, monografías y ensayos; 125)

Anthology inventories career of an influential historian. Work includes seven essays on gubernatorial *residencias* from 16th-18th centuries, two on slavery, 24 biographical profiles, and nine brief pieces on 19th-century constitutions. [LRG]

2267 Rey Fajardo, José del. La expulsión de los jesuitas de Venezuela, 1767–1768. San Cristóbal, Venezuela: Univ. Católica del Táchira, 1990. 398 p.: bibl., index.

Despite title, work is not a history of the subject. Compendium of documents includes inventory of Jesuit libraries and archives at the Colegio of Mérida and Caracas and at eight missions. Compilation done as part of inventory of confiscated Jesuit properties. Material presented in publications by same author. [K. Waldron]

2268 Rodríguez Campos, Manuel. La economía venezolana en los primeros años de la emancipación: influencias de autores españoles de los siglos XVIII y XIX en las críticas de José Rafael Revenga y Antonio Leocadio Guzmán. (*Rev. Indias*, 50:189, mayo/agosto 1990, p. 473–507)

Provides rare economic overview of post-independent Venezuela in transition from Spanish to English trading system. Indebted, needing new export markets, its agriculture destroyed, Venezuela turned to England for loans, imports, and ideas. English laissez-faire and traditional Spanish economists influenced Ministro de Hacienda José Rafael Revenga and Ministro del Interior Antonio Leocadio Guzmán, both of whom preferred State intervention, protectionism, and less dependence upon foreign wealth. [K. Waldron]

2269 Rodríguez Mirabal, Adelina. El régimen de tenencia de la tierra en los Llanos venezolanos: figuras jurídicas, económicas y sociales. (*in* Simposio Desarrollos Recientes en la Historia de los Llanos del Orinoco: Colombia y Venezuela, *New Orleans, 1991.* Café, caballo y hamaca: visión histórica del Llano. Quito: Ediciones Abya-Yala; Bogotá: Orinoquia Siglo XXI, 1992, p. 105–119, maps)

Examines in brief the southward colonizing push into the Llanos of Apure in late 18th century. Beginning with sporadic incursions by missionaries and herders c. 1750 and intensifying with organized expansion in 1780s, cattle ranching became focus of social conflict in the region. Livestock raising developed at the expense of indigenous communities and missionary effectiveness. [LRG]

2270 Rojas, Reinaldo. Rebeliones de esclavos negros en Venezuela antes y después de 1789. (*Estud. Hist. Soc. Econ. Am.*, 10, 1993, p. 151–164)

Survey of 18th-century slave rebellions defends periodization of 1500–1750, 1750–1804, and 1804–1830, even though author describes periods 1500–1789 and 1789–1847. Prior to 1790, slaves concretized idea of freedom in formation of cimarron communities, demonstrating rejection of their role in the cacao economy. Inspiration from Jacobin ideology of the French and Haitian Revolutions marked the second period. See also items **2271** and **2298.** [LRG]

Testigos norteamericanos de la expedición de Miranda: John Sherman, Moses Smith, Henry Ingersoll. See item **2677.**

2271 Tronconis de Veracoechea, Ermila. Aspectos de la esclavitud negra en Venezuela y el Caribe, 1750–1854. (*in* Congreso Internacional de Historia Económica y Social de la Cuenca del Caribe, 1763–1898, *1st, San Juan, 1987.* Actas. San Juan: Centro de Estudios Avanzados de Puerto Rico y el Caribe, 1992, p. 41–59, bibl.)

Placing history of slavery in context of Venezuelan-Caribbean commercial relations,

author finds parallel ideological intercourse that fostered both slave rebelliousness and national independence. Growing influence of liberalism culminated in Venezuelan abolition of slavery in 1854. See also item **2270.** [LRG]

2272 Ugalde, Luis. Mentalidad económica y proyectos de colonización en Guayana en los siglos XVIII y XIX: el caso de la Compañia Manoa en el delta del Orinoco. v. 1–2. Caracas: Academia Nacional de Ciencias Económicas, 1994. 2 v.: bibl., ill. (Serie Tesis; 8)

Broadly contextualizing his study in the familiar civilization-barbarism dichotomy of Latin American socioeconomic analysis, and utilizing the Orinoco delta as a focal point, Ugalde critiques Venezuelan economic planning from c. 1700 to c. 1930. Development strategies for the Guayana Region, ranging from Capuchin evangelization in 1720s to concessions granted to Manoa and Orinoco Companies 200 years later, failed and left Orinoco delta underdeveloped. [LRG]

2273 Vaccari de Venturini, Letizia. Sobre gobernadores y residencias en la Provincia de Venezuela, siglos XVI, XVII, XVIII. Caracas: Academia Nacional de la Historia, 1992. 266 p.: bibl. (Biblioteca de la Academia Nacional de la Historia. Fuentes para la historia colonial de Venezuela; 217)

Valuable political history handbook and research tool. In addition to the narrative discussion of governors and their political contexts, which includes a nice summary of corruption, the book includes a list of governors and a glossary. [LRG]

2274 Walter, Rolf. Der Traum vom Eldorado: die deutsche Conquista in Venezuela im 16. Jahrhundert. München: Eberhard, 1992. 152 p.: bibl., ill. (Schriften zu Lateinamerika; 3)

Well-researched, concise history focuses on Germans as merchants, investors, and public officials rather than as "soldiers of fortune" in 16th-century South America, especially in Venezuela where they had been granted considerable user rights by Spain. [C.K. Converse]

2275 Zubiri Marín, M. Teresa. Mandato de los pueblos indios de América: los comuneros de Mérida; una reacción contra la política colonial española del siglo XVII en

Venezuela. (*Bol. Am.*, 32:41, 1991, p. 7–19, bibl.)

Overly brief, but nonetheless useful, survey examines civil unrest in Maracaibo province in 1781. Less well known than contemporary uprisings in Nueva Granada and Peru, this *comunero* rebellion also illustrates popular displeasure with invigorated tax collection and the tobacco monopoly, as well as gestation of sentiment for independence. [LRG]

NUEVA GRANADA

2276 Alonso, Carlos. Agustín de Coruña: segundo obispo de Popayán, +1589. Valladolid, Spain: Ed. Estudio Agustiniano, 1993. 236 p.: bibl., col. ill. (Monografías de misiones y misioneros agustinos; 9)

Presents solid survey of life of Agustín de Coruña, one of the most important of the early Augustinians in the New World. Coruña played a major role in religious life of New Spain and New Castile, having been one of the first members of his order in Mexico as well as the second bishop of Popayán (1566–89). [MTH]

2277 Borja, Jaime. Barbarización y redes de indoctrinamiento en los negros: cosmovisiones en Cartagena, siglo XVII y XVIII. (*in* Coloquio Contribución Africana a la Cultura de las Américas, *1st, Bogotá, 1992.* Actas. Bogotá: Instituto Colombiano de Antropología, Colcultura, 1993, p. 241–254)

Relying on writings of Fr. Alonso de Sandoval, work examines ideological processes by which Spaniards in Cartagena de Indias came to demonize African slaves. Despite paternalism of Spanish thought, Iberian imagination created a new social reality based on the fear of things unfamiliar, the idea of the savage, and the prevailing negative attitude towards Muslims. See also item **2298.** [LRG]

2278 Böttcher, Nikolaus. Aufstieg und Fall eines atlantischen Handelsimperiums: Portugiesische Kaufleute und Sklavenhändler in Cartagena de Indias von 1580 bis zur Mitte des 17. Jahrhunderts. Frankfurt am Main, Germany: Vervuert, 1995. 265 p.: bibl. (Berliner Lateinamerika-Forschungen; 4)

Well-documented study based on PhD dissertation (Freie Univ. Berlin) focuses on community of Portuguese merchants of Sephardic descent who migrated to Cartagena de Indias during the late 16th and early 17th centuries. Uses social and economic approach based on primary sources in Spain and Colombia to depict Jewish traditional practices and their subsequent inquisitorial repression. Also analyzes the Atlantic slave trade, which was ruled by *negrero* traders established in Cartagena. A most valuable contribution to the history of commercial entrepreneurship, religious intolerance, and social minorities in colonial Spanish America. [T. Hampe-Martínez]

2279 Caldas, Francisco José de. Francisco José de Caldas, un peregrino de las ciencias. Edición de Jeanne Chenu. Madrid: Historia 16, 1992. 357 p.: bibl., map. (Crónicas de América; 72)

Contains Caldas' letters to José Celestino Mutis, Santiago Arroyo, and María Manuela Barahonda. Caldas led the famous Real Expedición Botánica del Nuevo Reyno de Granada, a well-studied topic. Chenu's excellent introduction places Caldas within European intellectual climate of the period while noting his unique scientific contributions. Letters to his fiancée reveal human side of the scientist. Excellent one-volume study. [K. Waldron]

2280 Casado Arboniés, Manuel. La producción de esmeraldas en el Nuevo Reino de Granada: la Caja Real de Muzo, 1595–1709. (*Estud. Hist. Soc. Econ. Am.*, 10, 1993, p. 37–59, graphs, map, tables)

Parallels author's earlier studies of treasury of Antioquia and estimates of gold production in that mining region. Utilizing deposits of the royal *quintos* (amounts equal to 20 percent) in the treasury of Muzo, author calculates that legal production of emeralds in 17th century approached levels of 1595–1607 only during period 1620–24; that from 1664–66 production slowly fell; and that production recovered in second half of the century, peaking in 1687. [LRG]

2281 Castillo Mathieu, Nicolás del. Descubrimiento y conquista de Colombia, 1500–1550. 2a ed., rev. y complementada. Bogotá: Ediciones Gamma, 1990. 204 p.: bibl., ill., maps.

Written for a general audience, this work by a well-known historian scans familiar historical territory of early 16th-century Colombia. A clear and efficient survey of the conquest era in both the Caribbean and Pacific regions. [LRG]

2282 Censo-guía y estadística de los archivos de Antioquia. Dirección editorial de Gladys M. de de la Cuadra. Bogotá: Archivo General de la Nación, Ministerio de Gobierno, 1992. 303 p.: bibl., index.

Excellent and comprehensive guide to large and small archives ranges from provincial, diocesan, and university holdings to dozens of municipal, notarial, and parochial collections. Includes brief indications of holdings and details archives' administration, including addresses, hours of operation, personnel, and conditions. [LRG]

2283 Colmenares, Germán. El tránsito a sociedades campesinas de dos sociedades esclavistas en la Nueva Granada, Cartagena-Popayán, 1780–1850. (*in* Congreso Internacional de Historia Económica y Social de la Cuenca del Caribe, 1763–1898, *1st, San Juan, 1987.* Actas. San Juan: Centro de Estudios Avanzados de Puerto Rico y el Caribe, 1992, p. 77–103, tables)

Offers insightful critique of work of Hermes Tovar, Adolfo Meisel, and Orlando Fals Borda on 18th-century economy of Cartagena province, as well as useful comparisons of slavery and agribusiness in the Cauca Valley and Cartagena province. Colmenares argues that dissolution of slave society between 1780–1850 contributed to lack of economic development in early 19th century along Caribbean coast. See also item **2300.** [LRG]

2284 Díaz López, Zamira. Oro, sociedad y economía: el sistema colonial en la Gobernación de Popayán, 1533–1733. Bogotá: Banco de la República, 1994. 318 p.: bibl., ill., index, maps. (Col. bibliográfica Banco de la República. Historia colombiana)

Important work examines fiscal and social aspects of gold mining in Popayán, connecting gold cycles to societal and regional development of the area. Supports a standard interpretation of conquest-era abuse of indigenous laborers, late 17th-century provincial economic decline, and Chocó-led economic recovery in early Bourbon period. [LRG]

2285 Documentos inéditos para la historia de Boyacá y Colombia. v. 1. Recopilación de Ulises Rojas. Tunja, Colombia: Academia Boyacense de Historia, 1991. 1 v. (Biblioteca de la Academia Boyacense de Historia. Serie Obras fundamentales; 10)

Eclectic collection from Archivo General de Indias and Tunja archives includes interesting selections on Tuatés, Muzos, and Muiscas. Letter of *cacique* Diego de Torres, 1584, to the King, citing 22 grievances against Spanish colonists, is noteworthy. [K. Waldron]

2286 Duque Gómez, Luis. La influencia de Mutis en el Nuevo Reino de Granada y su ejercicio de la medicina. (*Senderos/Bogotá,* 5:25/26, agosto 1993, p. 494–511, ill.)

Another tribute to José Celestino Mutis credits 18th-century scientist with a legacy of Colombian faith in liberty and democracy as well as with wide-ranging scientific advancements. Overview of Mutis' career relies on quotations from Guillermo Hernández de Alba's edition of his diary. [LRG]

2287 Earle, Rebecca. The Spanish political crisis of 1820 and the loss of New Granada. (*CLAHR/Albuquerque,* 3:3, Summer 1994, p. 253–279)

As in Mexico, the Spanish political crisis of 1820 had repercussions in Nueva Granada. Despite Viceroy Juan Sámano's efforts to insulate Cartagena from news of the liberal revolt, growing liberal pressure there overwhelmed royalist cause and hastened independence. [LRG]

2288 Garrido, Margarita. Reclamos y representaciones: variaciones sobre la política en el Nuevo Reino de Granada, 1770–1815. Bogotá: Banco de la República, 1993. 414 p.: bibl., index, map. (Col. bibliográfica Banco de la República. Historia colombiana)

Divided into parts for 1770–1810 and 1810–15, study of political culture compares ideology, experience, and identity among three social groups: Creole political elites, white and mestizo town citizenries, and Hispanicized indigenous peoples. Conclusions about group identities are familiar, but the analysis provides a useful context for the *comunero* revolt and independence.

2289 González, Margarita. El resguardo en el Nuevo Reino de Granada. 3. ed. Bogotá: El Ancora Editores, 1992. 175 p.: bibl., ill.

Latest edition of this work, first published in 1970 (see *HLAS 40:3135a*), remains a valuable overview of indigenous policy and administration in Nueva Granada. Offers straightforward explication of fundamental institutions such as *resguardo, corregimiento,* and *mita* within context of evolving politics, demographics, land tenure patterns, and labor dynamics. [LRG]

2290 Grahn, Lance R. An irresoluble dilemma: smuggling in New Granada, 1713–1763. (*in* International Congress of Americanists, *45th, Bogotá, 1985*. Historia. Bogotá: Ediciones Uniandes, 1988, p. 21–44, tables)

Focusing on Riohacha, Santa Marta, and Cartagena, relates dependence upon contraband for basic food supplies. Coast guard, designed to intercept illegal trade, acquiesced out of necessity. Treasuries benefitted from seizures but costs of defense were high. Uses records from the Treasuries of the three provinces. [K. Waldron]

2291 Gutiérrez, José. Enigmas y arcano del delirio de la conquista: rudimentos de legalidad y anarquía de la mentalidad colombiana, de Bastidas a Quesada. Bogotá: Spiridón, 1993? 301 p.: bibl., ill., maps.

Author brings together history and Freudian psychoanalysis to explore mentality of the conquistadores located mainly in and near Nueva Granada. Although he examines several individuals such as Pedrarias and Pedro Fernández de Lugo, main focus is on Gonzalo Jiménez de Quesada. [J. Britton]

2292 Kuethe, Allan J. The early reforms of Charles III in New Granada. (*in* International Congress of Americanists, *45th, Bogotá, 1985*. Historia. Bogotá: Ediciones Uniandes, 1988, p. 69–80)

Cogent overview of dynamics of court politics includes examination of rise and fall of Marqués of Esquilache, which affected Caroline imperial reform in 1760s-70s. Useful study for placing singularity of Bourbon reform in Nueva Granada in a larger imperial context. [LRG]

2293 León Linares, Guillermo. Las instituciones y la legalidad en los Llanos Orientales de Colombia: la colonia y la república. (*in* Simposio Desarrollos Recientes en la Historia de los Llanos del Orinoco: Colombia y Venezuela, *New Orleans, 1991*. Café, ca-

ballo y hamaca: visión histórica del Llano. Quito: Ediciones Abya-Yala; Bogotá: Orinoquia Siglo XXI, 1992, p. 123–166)

Disjointed essay uses early colonization of Colombian Llanos and late 18th-century development of *latifundio* to demonstrate that metropolitan vision for crown-centered imperial unity failed to take hold in the face of American realities and private initiative. [LRG]

López Medel, Tomás. Colonización de América: informes e testimonios, 1549–1572, por L. Pereña, C. Baciero, F. Maseda. See item **910.**

2294 Lucena Giraldo, Manuel. Las nuevas poblaciones de Cartagena de Indias, 1774–1794. (*Rev. Indias,* 53:199, sept./dic. 1993, p. 761–781, tables)

Places effort to establish new settlements in province of Cartagena in context of late 18th-century Bourbon reform. Antonio de la Torre y Miranda's 1776 description of internal colonization indicates a pattern of failure despite population figures that suggest otherwise. Nonetheless, his diary, which was published in 1794, remains an important polemical defense of this project. See also item **2301.** [LRG]

2295 Luna, Lola G. La Nación Chimila: un caso de resistencia indígena en la gobernación de Santa Marta. (*in* Encuentros Debate América Latina Ayer y Hoy, *3rd, Barcelona, 1991*. Conquista y resistencia en la historia de América = Conquista i resistència en la història d'Amèrica. Coordinación de Pilar García Jordán y Miquel Izard. Barcelona: Publicacions Univ. de Barcelona, 1992, p. 123–137, bibl.)

Useful discussion focuses on important feature of indigenous-Spanish relations in northern Nueva Granada. Steadfastly occupying agriculturally rich areas of Santa Marta province, the Chimilas resisted subjugation to colonial institutions until end of 18th century when Spanish soldiers finally defeated them. See also item **2296.** [LRG]

2296 Luna, Lola G. Resguardos coloniales de Santa Marta y Cartagena y resistencia indígena. Bogotá: Fondo de Promoción de la Cultura del Banco Popular, 1993. 318 p.: bibl., index, maps. (Biblioteca Banco Popular; 141)

Textually concise revised doctoral thesis evidences vitality of regional history and continued historiographical importance of Chimila resistance to Spanish colonialism. Examines persistence of *resguardo* system in northern Nueva Granada in spite of its not being strictly enforced there. A documentary index by year enhances book's usefulness. See also item **2295**. [LRG]

2297 Martínez de Salinas, María Luisa. Castilla ante el Nuevo Mundo: la trayectoria indiana del gobernador Bernardo de Vargas Machuca. Valladolid, Spain: Diputación Provincial de Valladolid, 1991. 247 p.: bibl., ill.

Interesting biography of Vargas Machuca (1555–1622) examines his colonial career, which ranged from municipal and military leadership in Portobelo to governorship of island of Margarita. Nicely illustrates early 17th-century political affairs along Caribbean littoral of South America. [LRG]

2298 Maya Restrepo, Adriana. Las brujas de Zaragoza: resistencia y cimarronaje en las minas de Antioquia, Colombia, 1619–1622. (*Am. Negra*, 4, dic. 1992, p. 85–99, bibl.)

Relying on a single case of witchcraft from Antioquia province, which Inquisition investigated in 1618–22, author argues that colonial authorities and slave owners demonized religious practices of African slaves. Alleged gatherings of witches were actually meetings at which slaves maintained community and jointly resisted their bondage. See also item **2277**. [LRG]

2299 McFarlane, Anthony. Colombia before independence: economy, society, and politics under Bourbon rule. New York: Cambridge Univ. Press, 1993. 399 p.: bibl., ill., index, maps. (Cambridge Latin American studies; 75)

This long-needed and impressive history of 18th-century Nueva Granada is a now essential text for the viceregal period. Especially strong for its late 18th-century economic analyses, work is also a valuable examination of limitations of Bourbon reform, relative strength of Nueva Granada's political and cultural forces, and influence of regionalism. [LRG]

2300 Mejía Prado, Eduardo. Orígen del campesino Vallecaucano. Cali, Colombia: Editorial Facultad de Humanidades, 1993. 149 p.: bibl.

Reflecting historiographical importance of Germán Colmenares' work (see item **2283**), this regional study posits that 19th-century peasant communities in the Cauca Valley developed in 18th-century context of changing demographics, dissolution of slavery, and evolving peasant land tenure. [LRG]

Michelena y Rojas, Francisco. Exploración oficial. See item **2257**.

2301 Moreno de Angel, Pilar. Antonio de la Torre y Miranda, viajero y poblador, siglo XVIII. Bogotá: Planeta, 1993. 266 p.: bibl., ill., maps.

Useful, though standard, biography of Torre y Miranda (1734–1805), one of Nueva Granada's most notable public servants. A singular individual who served as a military officer, government official, explorer, and amateur botanist, Torre y Miranda personified much of late 18th-century Colombian history. See also item **2294**. [LRG]

2302 Mutis y la Real Expedición Botánica del Nuevo Reyno de Granada. v. 1–2. Coordinación científica de María Pilar de San Pío Aladrén. Bogotá: Villegas Editores; Barcelona: Lunwerg Editores, 1992. 2 v.: bibl., col. ill.

Exquisite boxed-set combines first-rate essays on work and legacy of José Celestino Mutis with wonderful color plates. The illustrations alone make this a superior resource for studies of 18th-century culture, the history of science (especially botany), and Nueva Granada biography. See also item **2305**. [LRG]

2303 Pumar Martínez, Carmen. Los cabildos revolucionarios en el Nuevo Reino de Granada. (*Estud. Hist. Soc. Econ. Am.*, 10, 1993, p. 181–206)

Effective examination of role of cabildos, particularly cabildo of Cartagena, in the development of Nueva Granadan independence. Following failed attempts to create a national monarchy and to effect a military coup, revolutionary leaders turned to the cabildo as preferred agent of political change, thus making municipal councils a locus of metropolitan-colonial rivalry. [LRG]

2304 Ramos, Demetrio. Caballero y Góngora, mandatario de Nueva Granada, Virrey del Caribe: notas de historia social y desarrollo económico, tras la paz de 1783. (*in* Congreso Internacional de Historia Económica y Social de la Cuenca del Caribe, 1763–

1898, 1st, San Juan, 1987. Actas. San Juan: Centro de Estudios Avanzados de Puerto Rico y el Caribe, 1992, p. 123–166)

Positive review of Antonio de Caballero y Góngora's viceregal career (1782–89) notes archbishop's social conscience, political skill, scientific interest, and patriotic intent. Because the archbishop-viceroy wanted Nueva Granada to rival Peru, he sought especially to develop the Caribbean regions of the viceroyalty. [LRG]

2305 Restrepo Forero, Olga. José Celestino Mutis: el papel del saber en el Nuevo Reino. (*Anu. Colomb. Hist. Soc. Cult.*, 18/19, 1990/91, p. 47–99)

Blends historiography and biography in an evaluation of Mutis' career. Accomplishments of the well-known botanical expedition of 1783–1792 notwithstanding, the multi-faceted scholar's greatest contribution to Nueva Granadan society was his teaching, through which he diffused scientific knowledge. See also item **2302.** [LRG]

2306 Ruiz Martínez, Eduardo. Bibliotecas neogranadinas durante la Ilustración. (*Senderos/Bogotá*, 5:25/26, agosto 1993, p. 587–612, ill.)

Brief biographical sketches of José Celestino Mutis, Manuel Benito de Castro, Francisco de Paula Santander, and Miguel Antonio Caro demonstrate the presence, albeit limited, of both the books and ideas of the Enlightenment in late 18th- and early 19th-century Bogotá. [LRG]

2307 Ruiz Rivera, Julián B. Prestaciones mitayas en el Nuevo Reino de Granada. (*in* Jornadas de Historiadores Americanistas, 2nd, Santafé, Spain, 1988. América: encuentro y asimilación; Actas. Edición de Joaquín A. Muñoz Mendoza. Granada, Spain: Diputación Provincial de Granada, 1989, p. 159–175)

Uses a few examples to note perpetual conflict between Spanish and indigenous peoples regarding forced labor. Legal records reveal native attempts to reduce numbers of participants, at times successful. Concludes that legal restraints did prevent worst abuses. [K. Waldron]

2308 Silva, Renán. Las epidemias de viruela de 1782 y 1802 en la Nueva Granada: contribución a un análisis histórico de los procesos de apropiación de modelos cultura-

les. Cali, Colombia: Univ. del Valle, 1992. 173 p.: bibl. (Col. de edición previa. Serie Investigaciones)

Casting public health concerns and Bourbon-era epidemiology in analytical framework of cultural modernization, author argues that responses to late 18th-century epidemics, including introduction of vaccines in 1804, represent revalorization of human life and establishment of "planes de emergency"—social spaces in which new sociocultural models would crystallize. [LRG]

2309 Sosa Abella, Guillermo. Labradores, tejedores y ladrones: hurtos y homicidios en la provincia de Tunja, 1745–1810. Bogotá: Instituto Colombiano de Cultura Hispánica, 1993. 152 p.: bibl. (Col. Cuadernos de historia colonial; 1)

Utilizes criminal activity to analyze social behavior within highland *resguardo* communities. This study of popular culture as reflected in acts of flight, theft, homicide, and drunkenness is an important step forward for studies of Nueva Granada *resguardos.* [LRG]

2310 Suárez de Alvarez, Ivonne. El papel del oro en la formación regional de Antioquia. (*in* International Congress of Americanists, 45th, Bogotá, 1985. Historia. Bogotá: Ediciones Uniandes, 1988, p. 141–154, bibl.)

Presents solid, albeit unexceptional, argument that Antioquia regional uniqueness derived principally from gold mining, which in turn determined societal relationships among Spaniards, indigenous peoples, blacks, and mestizos in the province; commercial networks; frontier expansion; and, most importantly, human interaction with the physical environment. [LRG]

2311 Tovar Pinzón, Hermes. Colombia: lo diverso, lo multiple y la magnitud dispersa. (*Maguaré/Bogotá*, 7:8, 1992, p. 45–79, graphs, tables)

Provocative essay argues that 16th-century Spaniards attempted to impose a spatial unity of sorts on socioeconomic regions of Nueva Granada. Tovar draws on textual criticism of 16th-century chronicles, especially those of Jorge Robledo's expeditions (1539–42); ethnographical references to conquest-era indigenous cultures; demographic estimates; and reflections on the institutions of conquest and early colonialism. [LRG]

2312 **Velázquez, Nelly.** Los resguardos de indios en la provincia de Mérida del Nuevo Reino de Granada, siglo XVII, y la integración sociocultural. (*in* Encuentros Debate América Latina Ayer y Hoy, *3rd, Barcelona, 1991.* Conquista y resistencia en la historia de América = Conquesta i resistència en la història d'Amèrica. Coordinación de Pilar García Jordán y Miquel Izard. Barcelona: Publicacions Univ. de Barcelona, 1992, p. 111–121, bibl.)

Makes suggestive argument that 17th-century colonial government intended *resguardos* to normalize indigenous-Spanish relations, to further integration of indigenous communities into colonial society, and to facilitate indigenous accommodation to demands of the Atlantic economy. Useful article for comparison of regional successes and failures in implementation of indigenous relocation. [LRG]

QUITO

2313 **Actas del Cabildo Colonial de San Francisco de Quito de 1658 a 1663.** Transcripción de Judith Paredes Zamara. Revisión de Diego Chiriboga Murgueitio. Quito: Archivo Municipal de Quito, 1993. 512 p. (Publicaciones del Archivo Municipal de Quito; 36)

Continues publication—suspended since 1969—of minutes of the Cabildo of Quito. See also item **2314.** [MTH]

2314 **Actas del Cabildo Colonial de San Francisco de Quito de 1664 a 1669.** Prólogo de Jorge Salvador Lara. Transcripción de Judith Paredes Zamara. Revisión de Diego Chiriboga Murgueitio. Quito: Archivo Municipal de Quito, 1995. 514 p. (Publicaciones del Archivo Municipal de Quito; 37)

This volume and earlier work (see item **2313**) are basic sources for reconstruction of history of the city and the Corregimiento de Quito during mid-colonial period. [MTH]

2315 **Andrien, Kenneth J.** The State and dependency in late colonial and early republican Ecuador. (*in* The political economy of Spanish America in the age of revolution, 1750–1850. Albuquerque: Univ. of New Mexico Press, 1994, p. 169–195, tables)

Utilizes dependency literature as qualitative framework, and treasury records of Quito, Guayaquil, and Cuenca as quantitative basis to reassess role of the State in economic development of Ecuador during late colonial, independence, and early national periods. Concludes that the State "promoted economic policies that created a discriminatory, arbitrary, and irrational economic environment for promoting sustained, autonomous development." [MTH]

2316 **Arosemena, Guillermo.** El comercio exterior del Ecuador. v. 1–3. Guayaquil, Ecuador: G. Arosemena, 1992. 3 v.: bibl., ill.

Presents first attempt to quantify and analyze the import-export sector of the economy of Ecuador from late 16th through late 20th centuries. Based entirely on published sources and secondary studies, vol. 1 covers colonial period; vol. 2, 1821–1920; and vol. 3, 1921–1990. Although poorly formatted and not as methodologically sophisticated nor as comprehensively researched as one would like (author is clearly an amateur historian; there are glaring gaps in the bibliographies), on the whole a worthwhile work that pulls together considerable information. Especially interesting are detailed discussions of planters, traders, and bankers. Here author has an insider's advantage, being himself a member of Guayaquil elite and an entrepreneur. [MTH]

2317 **Bonnett Vélez, Diana.** Los protectores de naturales en la Audiencia de Quito: siglos XVII y XVIII. Quito: Facultad Latinoamericana de Ciencias Sociales, Sede Ecuador, 1992. 153 p.: bibl., ill., maps. (Col. Tesis. Historia)

Well-researched master's thesis focuses on the Protectorado de Naturales, whose area of responsibility covered what are now Ecuador and southern Colombia. Examines the office and analyzes a number of cases relating to land and labor disputes and tribute impositions. An historiographic first for Ecuador. [MTH]

2318 **Borchart de Moreno, Christiana Renate** and **Segundo E. Moreno Yáñez.** Balance y tendencias de la historia socio-económica ecuatoriana, siglo XVIII. Quito: FLACSO, 1990. 50 p.: bibl. (Documentos de Trabajo; 5)

Work covers virtually the same material presented in authors' previous study, "La Historia Socioeconómica Ecuatoriana del Siglo XVIII: Análisis y Tendencias" (see *HLAS 52:2085*). [MTH]

2319 Borchart de Moreno, Christiana Renate. Mujeres quiteñas y crisis colonial: las actividades económicas femeninas entre 1780–1830. (*in* Jornadas de Investigación Interdisciplinaria sobre la Mujer, *9th, Madrid, 1992.* La mujer latinoamericana ante el reto del siglo XXI. Madrid: Ediciones de la Univ. Autónoma de Madrid, 1993, p. 319–332)

Work covers virtually the same material presented in her previous study, "La Imbelicidad y el Coraje: la Participación Feminina en la Economía Colonial, Quito, 1780–1830" (see *HLAS 54:2323*). [MTH]

2320 Büschges, Christian. Familie, Ehre und Macht: Konzept und soziale Wirklichkeit des Adels in der Stadt Quito, Ecuador während der späten Kolonialzeit, 1765–1822. Stuttgart: F. Steiner, 1996. 318 p.: bibl (Beiträge zur Kolonial- und Überseegeschichte; 66)

Significant contribution to the history of upper-class formation and domination in colonial Spanish America, this monograph focuses on the *nobleza* of Quito in the late 18th century. This aristocratic group (which included about 500 individuals) consisted not only of entitled nobility and *caballeros,* but also of high-ranking officers from the bureaucracy, the Church, and the militia. Their social and economic activities are described in detail. By intentionally refusing to use the term *elite,* Büschges emphasizes that the *nobleza quiteña* was more of a traditional society, based on large landed estates. [T. Hampe-Martínez]

2321 Carmona Moreno, Félix. Fray Luis López de Solís, O.S.A.: figura estelar de la evangelización de América. Madrid: Editorial Revista Agustiniana, 1993. 223 p.: bibl., index. (Historia viva; 6)

Presents solid biography of third bishop of Quito (1594–1605). Solís stabilized ecclesiastical organization and promoted Christianization of the diocese. He convoked and presided over the second and third synods, and founded the Seminario de San Luis (the forerunner of the Univ. Central del Ecuador) as well as several other important institutions. [MTH]

2322 Carrión, Alejandro. En el reino de los golillas. Quito: Banco Central del Ecuador, Centro de Investigación y Cultura, 1991.

177 p.: bibl. (Obras completas de Alejandro Carrión; 13)

History at its best and at its worst. Contains series of well-told, but undocumented and not altogether accurate, vignettes. Valuable nonetheless because author understands and uncovers the mentality of his ancestors better than some of his academic counterparts. [MTH]

2323 Ceinos Manzano, María Jesús. El origen de los colegios jesuitas de la Provincia Quitense y su incidencia en la educación. (*Estud. Hist. Soc. Econ. Am.,* 11, 1994, p. 231–237, bibl.)

Brief essay focuses on economic bases of Jesuit schools in the Audiencia of Quito and the educational labors of the Society. Includes some new archival data. [MTH]

2324 Chacón Zhapán, Juan; Pedro Soto; and **Diego Mora.** Historia de la Gobernación de Cuenca, 1777–1820: estudio económico-social. Cuenca, Ecuador: Consejo Nacional de Universidades y Escuelas Politécnicas (CONUEP); Univ. de Cuenca, Instituto de Investigaciones Sociales (IDIS); Municipalidad de Cuenca, Dirección de Cultura; Casa de la Cultura Ecuatoriana, Núcleo del Azuay; Gobernación del Azuay, 1993. 545 p.

Notwithstanding subtitle, work is a comprehensive history of what are now the provinces of Cañar and Azuay, from establishment of the Gobierno Político y Militar de Cuenca in 1777 through establishment of the Provincia Libre e Independiente de Cuenca in 1820. Like principal author's previous work (see item **2325**), volume is based almost entirely on archival materials. Includes 319 p. of demographic and economic time-series data. Chapter on population and corresponding time series, however, is methodologically flawed and therefore unreliable. [MTH]

2325 Chacón Zhapán, Juan. Historia del Corregimiento de Cuenca, 1557–1777. Quito: Banco Central del Ecuador, 1990. 675 p.: tables

Author's dissertation is a solid, comprehensive history of what are now the provinces of Cañar and Azuay, from the Spanish Conquest through establishment of the Gobierno Político y Militar de Cuenca. Based almost entirely on original research, work includes 185 pages of previously unpublished sources. [MTH]

2326 Colmenares, Germán. La hacienda en la sierra norte del Ecuador: fundamentos económicos y sociales de una diferenciación nacional, 1800–1870. (*Procesos/Quito,* 2, 1992, p. 3–50, tables)

Economic and social analysis examines haciendas in northern and central highlands during first two-thirds of 19th century. Especially concerned with differences between agrarian regimes of neocolonial Ecuador and Colombia, and impact of sluggish and, in some local districts, negative population growth on labor arrangements. A pioneering study based on a substantial quantitative matrix compiled from notarial records. [MTH]

2327 Coronel Feijoo, Rosario. El valle sangriento: de los indígenas de la coca y el algodón a la hacienda cañera jesuita, 1580–1700. Quito: Facultad Latinoamericana de Ciencias Sociales, Sede Ecuador; Abya-Yala, 1991. 172 p.: bibl., ill., maps. (Col. Tesis. Historia; 4)

Original master's thesis relates what happened to indigenous peoples of the Chota River Valley in 1600s and how they came to be replaced for the most part by black slaves in 1700s. Adds appreciably to demographic and economic history, and indirectly to ethnohistory, of the northern highlands. Yet another historiographic first for Ecuador. [MTH]

2328 Descalzi, Ricardo. Historias de la Real Audiencia de Quito. v. 1–4. Quito: Escuela Politécnica del Ejército, 1990. 4 v.: bibl., ill.

In this curious yet interesting set of pocket books, author sheds some light on various aspects of history of the city and the Audiencia of Quito that have not received adequate attention. Vol. 1 is entitled *Historia colonial de la plaza mayor;* Vol. 2, *Historia de las misiones amazónicas;* Vol. 3, *Agua, higiene y medicina de la Quito colonial;* and Vol. 4, *Alzamientos y revoluciones en la colonia.* Although these *historias* lack tables of contents, indexes, and proper documentation, clearly the late Descalzi knew the colonial period well. [MTH]

2329 Fernández Rueda, Sonia. Historiografía de la arquitectura en la época colonial: algunas consideraciones. (*Procesos/Quito,* 2, 1992, p. 105–117)

Traditionally almost the only, and in-

disputably the most prolific, student of architecture of the colonial period in Ecuador was José Gabriel Navarro (1883–1965). Recently, however, there has been a renaissance of interest and several new studies by other scholars, resultant in part from recent restoration projects. Parenthetically, Navarro was also an outstanding student of sculpture and painting (see, for example, item **200**). [MTH]

2330 Fuentealba, Gerardo. Forasteros, comunidades indígenas, Estado y grupos de poder en la Audiencia de Quito, siglo XVIII. (*Rev. Ecuat. Hist. Econ.,* 4:8, 1990, p. 59–98)

Reexamines increase in *forasteros* in 18th century. Maintains that indigenous peoples employed migration as tactic to reduce amount of tribute they were charged; to avoid mita; and to obtain and retain land and its usage. Karen Power (see item **2363**) substantiates Fuentealba's first two conclusions for 16th and 17th centuries. Fuentealba also reexamines largely successful efforts of the State under the Bourbons to rationalize tribute schedules and exact more tribute, as well as the socioeconomic consequences thereof. [MTH]

González Pujana, Laura. Minería y trabajo indígena en los Andes, Guamanga y Zaruma. See item **2404.**

2331 Guevara Gil, Jorge Armando and **Frank Salomon.** A "personal visit:" colonial political ritual and the making of Indians in the Andes. (*Colon. Lat. Am. Rev.,* 3:1/2, 1994, p. 3–36, bibl.)

The *visita* in question is that of 1623 to the Collaguazos. Authors appear to advocate that researchers should steep themelves in the totality, not just the mentality, of the time and place and then somehow recreate and explicate that decidedly other time and place in postmodern qualitative terminology.

2332 Hamerly, Michael T. Demografía y morfología de Guayaquil, 1756–1814. (*Bol. Acad. Nac. Hist./Quito,* 73:155/156, 1990, p. 157–172, graph, tables)

New study examines growth of population of Guayaquil, and of the port city as an entity, during late colonial period. Utilizes parish registers—for the first time in the case of the historical demography of Guayaquil—as well as *padrones* and other coeval enumerations, specifically of houses and *pulperías.* [MTH]

2333 Herzog, Tamar. Sobre justicia, honor y grado militar en Quito, s. XVIII. (*Procesos/Quito*, 6, 1994, p. 49–57)

Examines claims of civilian presidents of the Audiencia of Quito in 1700s to title of Capitán-General in addition to those of Presidente and Gobernador-General. Illuminates overlapping concepts of "justice, honor, and military rank" and therefore illustrates social mentalities of period. [MTH]

2334 Hirschkind, Lynn. History of the Indian population of Cañar. (*CLAHR/Albuquerque*, 4:3, Summer 1995, p. 311–342, map)

Reviews postconquest history of ethnic group known as the Cañari. Maintains that for a variety of reasons, including displacement and decimation by the Incas and as well as by Spanish conquistadores and colonists, the indigenous population of modern provinces of Cañar and Azuay long since ceased to be distinctive and, in fact, eventually came to consist simply of what may be described as highland Quechua speakers. [MTH]

2335 Jornadas de Historia Social, *14th, Zaruma, Ecuador, 1992.* Zaruma: cuatro siglos de peregrinaje histórico; memorias. Quito: Corporación Ecuatoriana de Amigos de la Genealogía, 1992. 297 p.: bibl., ill. (Col. Medio milenio; 7)

Contains proceedings of social and genealogical conference held in and on Zaruma. Majority of *ponencias* are genealogical in focus, yet volume as a whole examines and delineates for the first time many aspects of history of this all but forgotten town in the southern sierra, a major gold mining center during the early colonial period. [MTH]

2336 Jurado Noboa, Fernando. Algunas reflexiones sobre la tenencia de los esclavos en la colonia, 1536–1826. (*Bol. Arch. Nac. Hist.*, 22, agosto 1992, p. 93–101)

Research notes on slaves in colonial Ecuador, drawn mostly from notarial records. [MTH]

2337 Jurado Noboa, Fernando. La migración internacional a Quito entre 1534 y 1934. v. 1–3. Quito: Sociedad Amigos de la Genealogía, 1989–1993. 3 v.: bibl., ill., index. (Col. SAG; segunda serie, 51–53)

Biographical and genealogical dictionary lists Europeans and Latin Americans who settled or resided in Quito at one time or another. Vol. 1 covers entries A-CL; vol. 2, CO-GAZ; and vol. 3, G-L. An important set, but like the majority of Sociedad Amigos de la Genealogía (a.k.a. Corporación Ecuatoriana de Amigos de la Genealogía) publications, work is poorly edited and badly reproduced. [MTH]

2338 Langue, Frédérique. Minas ecuatorianas de principios del siglo XIX: "sanguijuelas" y "holgazanes." (*Rev. Arch. Nac. Hist. Azuay*, 6, 1986, p. 101–124, table)

Provides novel reexamination of state of mining in early 1800s. Based on reports in Archivo General de Indias on the yet to be worked silver veins in the central highlands (Condorasto) and the still being worked but virtually depleted gold mines in the southern highlands (Zaruma). Significant contribution to economic history of late colonial period. [MTH]

2339 Lavallé, Bernard. El cuestionamiento de la esclavitud en Quito a finales de la época colonial. (*Procesos/Quito*, 6, 1994, p. 23–48)

Original study focuses on the scrutiny of slavery as a morally acceptable institution during late colonial period, interestingly enough carried out by slaves as well as masters. Also examines ways in which slaves could obtain or were granted freedom. A significant contribution to social history of the time and place. See also item **2340.** [MTH]

2340 Lavallé, Bernard. Lógica esclavista y resistencia negra en los Andes ecuatorianos a finales del siglo XVIII. (*Rev. Indias*, 53: 199, sept./dic. 1993, p. 699–722)

Delineates and documents three instances of slave resistance (through flight) to abusive treatment by lay administrators and new owners of former Jesuit estates in northern highlands. A study of a neglected aspect of late colonial social history. See also item **1912.** [MTH]

2341 Laviana Cuetos, María Luisa. Problemas metodológicos en el estudio de la Real Hacienda: ingreso bruto e ingreso neto en las cajas de Guayaquil, 1757–1804. (*in* Colección nuestra patria es América: historia económica de América Latina. Edición de Jorge Núñez Sánchez. Quito: Editora Nacional, 1992, v. 7, p. 3–20, graph, tables)

Reconsideration of methodological issues relating to study of fiscal records is part of author's apparently long since completed but yet to be published *La Real Hacienda de Guayaquil, 1757–1804.* [MTH]

2342 Lenz-Volland, Birgit and **Martin Volland.** Indianische Meersalzproduktion im kolonialzeitlichen Ecuador. (*in* Beiträge zur Kulturgeschichte des westlichen Südamerika. Opladen, Germany: Westdeutschler Verlag, 1990, p. 86–112, bibl., maps)

Gives history of production of and trade in sea salt during colonial period. Primary salt pans were located at or near Bahía de Caráquez, Charapotó, Santa Elena, Morro, and Puná, and were subject to European encroachment. [MTH]

2343 Libro cuarto de Cabildos de Cuenca, 1575–1578. Versión paleográfica de Juan Chacón Zhapán. Cuenca, Ecuador: Archivo Histórico Municipal; Xerox del Ecuador, 1982. 774 p.: index.

Includes original text in photofacsimile. Indexed. Continues publication of Chacón Zhapán's transcription of minutes of Cabildo de Cuenca, beginning with *Libro segundo*, corresponding to the years 1563–69 (Guayaquil, Ecuador: 1977), as initiated by Archivo Histórico Guayas. *Libro primero*, corresponding to 1557–63, transcribed by Jorge A. Garcés, appeared in 1938. *Libro tercero*, corresponding to 1569–75, has been missing from Archivo Histórico Municipal de Cuenca for some years. See also items **2344, 2345,** and **2346.** [MTH]

2344 Libro de Cabildos de Cuenca, 1800–1810. Versión paleográfica de Juan Chacón Zhapán. Cuenca, Ecuador: Banco Central del Ecuador, Centro de Investigación y Cultura, 1991. 2 v.

Publishes recently recovered volumes corresponding to 1800–10. Transcribed by Chacón Zhapán and some of his students. Not indexed. This work, like its predecessors (see items **2343, 2345,** and **2346**), is a basic source for reconstruction of history of the city and of the Corregimiento/Gobierno Político y Militar de Cuenca. [MTH]

2345 Libro quinto de Cabildos de Cuenca, 1579–1587. Versión paleográfica de Juan Chacón Zhapán. Cuenca, Ecuador: Archivo Histórico Municipal; Xerox del Ecuador, 1988. 645 p.: index.

Covers years 1579–87. Indexed. See also items **2343, 2344,** and **2346.** [MTH]

2346 Libro sexto de Cabildos de Cuenca, 1587–1591. Versión paleográfica de Juan Chacón Zhapán. Cuenca, Ecuador: Archivo Histórico Municipal; Xerox del Ecuador, 1990. 262 p.

Covers years 1587–91. No index. See also items **2343, 2344,** and **2345.** [MTH]

2347 Lucena Salmoral, Manuel. La ciudad de Quito hacia mil ochocientos. (*Anu. Estud. Am.*, 51:1, 1994, p. 143–164)

Working paper on city of Quito c. 1800 examines morphology, infrastructure, economy, and pastimes of the city and its inhabitants. Based on archival research in Ecuador and Spain. [MTH]

2348 Lucena Salmoral, Manuel. La ciudad perdida de Logroño y la última fundación misional en el Reino de Quito, 1818: oro, jíbaros y misioneros. (*Estud. Hist. Soc. Econ. Am.*, 10, 1993, p. 217–232)

Documents 1816 "rediscovery" of ghost town of Logroño, previously a center of placer mining, and 1818 foundation of a new mission—possibly the last in colonial Spanish South America—that of San José de Bomboiza (now Gualaquiza) in Shuar (Jivaro) territory. [MTH]

2349 Lucena Salmoral, Manuel. La delimitación hispano-portuguesa y la frontera regional quiteña. (*Procesos/Quito*, 4, 1993, p. 21–39)

Gives brief overview of labors of Marañón Commission (1778–1804), especially of work of Francisco Requena, and a preliminary analysis of Requena's 1785 "Descripción del Gobierno de Maynas." Requena's work was recently published by María del Carmen Martín Rubio in *Historia de Maynas: un paraíso perdido en el Amazonas* (see *HLAS 54:722*), and independently by Pilar Ponce Leiva in *Relaciones histórico-geográficas de la Audiencia de Quito*, vol. 2 (see *HLAS 54:2345*). [MTH]

2350 Lucena Salmoral, Manuel. La población del Reino de Quito en la época de reformismo borbónico: circa 1784. (*Rev. Indias*, 54:200, enero/abril 1994, p. 33–81, tables)

New attempt to establish size and characteristics of population of Audiencia de

Quito during late colonial period utilizes *padrones* of 1770s-80s, especially those of or c. 1784. Among author's more curious conclusions is that Cuenca was more populous than Quito. Although this is correct for census units that included rural as well as urban parishes, the opposite held true for the actual cities. [MTH]

2351 Minchom, Martin. The people of Quito, 1690–1810: change and unrest in the underclass. Boulder, Colo.: Westview Press, 1994. 297 p.: bibl., ill., index. (Dellplain Latin American studies; 32)

Although not analyzed or interpreted as well as one would like, work is a major contribution to study of Quito during second half of colonial period. Provides a much-needed demographic base for ongoing reexamination of economic and social history of the capital. Breaks new ground with focus on "non-elite" and illumination of many themes such as socio-racial status and mobility, religious riots, and civil disturbances, especially that of 1765. [MTH]

2352 Moreno Egas, Jorge. Observancia religiosa del pueblo de Quito en 1797. (*in* Colección nuestra patria es America: la cultura en la historia. Edición de Jorge Núñez Sánchez. Quito: Editora Nacional, 1992, v. 8, p. 33–51, tables)

Quantifies religious observance of people of Quito in 1797, utilizing parish returns for that year. Tabulates by sex and ethnic group numbers of parishioners who complied with canonical precept to confess and to receive communion at least once a year. [MTH]

2353 Moya Torres, Alba. Auge y crisis de la cascarilla en la Audiencia de Quito, siglo XVIII. Quito: Facultad Latinoamericana de Ciencias Sociales, Sede Ecuador, 1994. 251 p.: bibl. (Serie Tesis. Historia)

Yet another original master's thesis from FLACSO in Quito, work outlines, to some extent fleshes out, and analyzes a far from exhausted chapter in the economic history of Ecuador: the trade in cinchona bark— the source of quinine. A solid study based on archival research in Cuenca and Quito. [MTH]

2354 Newson, Linda A. Life and death in early colonial Ecuador. Norman: Univ. of Oklahoma Press, 1995. 517 p.: bibl., index,

maps, tables (The civilization of the American Indian series; 214)

A substantial, sophisticated study on the yet to be wholly resolved questions of how large the native populations of the coast, the highlands, and the Oriente were on the eve of the Inca and Spanish conquests and by how much they declined as a direct or indirect consequence thereof. Includes a detailed, sound, scholarly discussion of the lands and peoples of prehispanic Ecuador. Employs qualitative as well as quantitative analysis. [MTH]

2355 Ortiz de la Tabla Ducasse, Javier. Los encomenderos de Quito, 1534–1660: origen y evolución de una elite colonial. Sevilla, Spain: Escuela de Estudios Hispano-Americanos, 1993. 377 p.: bibl., index. (Publicaciones de la Escuela de Estudios Hispano-Americanos de Sevilla; 368)

First major study of encomienda holders in the highlands is a social history pieced together from a wide variety of sources, mostly original. Remarkable tour-de-force inasmuch as encomienda records per se for Audiencia de Quito do not appear to have survived. Elucidates emergence of local elite in early colonial period. Well written, analyzed, and interpreted; however, more time lines, especially with the genealogical tables, and discussion thereof, would have been helpful [MTH]

2356 Ospina, Pablo. La región de los Quijos: una tierra despojada de poderes, 1578–1608. (*Procesos/Quito*, 3, segundo semestre 1992, p. 3–31, bibl. graphs, map)

Methodologically sophisticated, yet eminently readable, study examines role of religion in pacification and settlement of the Oriente, indigenous uprising of 1578, reaction of the highlands to and aftermath of the rebellion, and formation of indigenous and white frontiers. Altogether an exceptionally important contribution to early history of Ecuador's future eastern provinces. [MTH]

2357 Paniagua Pérez, Jesús. El Cristo de Girón en el siglo XVIII. (*Rev. Arch. Nac. Hist. Azuay*, 6, 1986, p. 71–100)

Multifaceted analysis examines economic, ideological, and social aspects of the "cult" of Christ of Girón (prov. of Azuay) in 1700s. Includes data on activities of the corresponding brotherhood (*cofradía*). Based on original research in Archivo Nacional de Historia, Sección del Azuay. [MTH]

2358 Paniagua Pérez, Jesús. Los oratorios en la Audiencia de Quito. (*Bol. Arch. Nac. Hist.*, 22, agosto 1992, p. 103–123)

Well-documented study examines economic and social aspects of cult of Nuestra Señora de Guadalupe, especially of the affiliate brotherhood (*cofradía*), as well as the sanctuary in Guápulo and the financing of the shrine's construction and ornamentation. [MTH]

2359 Poloni, Jacques. Achats et ventes de terres par les indiens de Cuenca au XVIIe siècle: éléments de conjoncture économique et de stratification sociale. (*Bull. Inst. fr. étud. andin.*, 21:1, 1992, p. 279–310, bibl., graphs, maps, tables)

Analyzes 1,118 notarial records from 1592–1699 of land sales by indigenous peoples in *corregimiento* of Cuenca in order to construct a quantitative matrix for study of various aspects of economic and social history of the region and of its indigenous inhabitants during mid-colonial period. A wholly original (for Ecuador), methodologically sophisticated, and extraordinarily important piece of work. See also item **2360.** [MTH]

2360 Poloni, Jacques. Mesure du métissage à Cuenca d'après le recensement de 1778. (*Mélanges/Paris*, 28:2, 1992, p. 101–122, maps, tables)

Analyzes ethnic composition of city and district of Cuenca, utilizing detailed returns of 1778 census. Argues that mestizos were "classified" as whites, at least for purposes of enumeration. Advances historical demography of southern highlands, and constitutes major step towards providing quantitative base for reconstruction of region's social history. See also item **2359.** [MTH]

2361 Ponce, Pilar. La educación disputada: repaso bibliográfico sobre la enseñanza universitaria en la Audiencia de Quito. (*Estud. Hist. Soc. Econ. Am.*, 11, 1994, p. 137–150, bibl.)

Useful but incomplete review of limited literature on universities in Quito during colonial period is an interesting attempt to establish benchmarks in the history of the future Univ. Central del Ecuador (the only university in the country until 1868). [MTH]

2362 Ponce, Pilar. Un espacio para la controversia: la Audiencia de Quito en el siglo XVIII. (*Rev. Indias*, 52:195/196, mayo/dic. 1992, p. 839–865)

Critical review examines traditional view, dating from coeval cries of decadence and despair, of economy of the highlands in 1700s as being in a state of crisis, and recent literature on the more or less concurrent economic boom on the coast. Ponce maintains that, at worst, the textile-dependent economy of northern and central highlands was in trouble, but that economy of more diversified southern lowlands was modestly prosperous, perhaps even growing. [MTH]

2363 Powers, Karen Vieira. Andean journeys: migration, ethnogenesis, and the State in colonial Quito. Albuquerque: Univ. of New Mexico Press, 1995. 236 p.: bibl., ill., index, maps.

Employs qualitative as well as quantitative analysis to determine why native population of Audiencia de Quito, especially of northern and central highlands, increased during first half of colonial period. Powers finds principal cause to have been migration, endogenous as well as exogenous, and secondary cause to have been falsification of data by *caciques* and census takers. Author also examines cultural dynamics and socioeconomic implications of migration. Clearly written and well reasoned, work is exceptionally important contribution to demographic, economic, and social history of the highlands. See also Powers' separately published dissertation (item **2365,**), of which this book is much more than a mere revision. See also item **2330.** [MTH]

2364 Powers, Karen Vieira. The battle for bodies and souls in the colonial North Andes: intraecclesiastical struggles and the politics of migration. (*HAHR*, 75:1, Feb. 1995, p. 31–56)

Fascinating essay relates attempts by secular clergy and regular orders, especially Franciscans, to manipulate "lower caste agency, in the form of Indian population movements and resultant *mestizaje*," for institutional or personal purposes, including struggle between seculars and regulars for parishes and supremacy, in *corregimiento* of Latacunga (Audiencia de Quito) in 1600s. Enriches and enlivens multiple aspects of the historiography of the central highlands. [MTH]

2365 Powers, Karen Vieira. Prendas con pies: migraciones indígenas y supervivencia cultural en la Audiencia de Quito. Quito: Abya-Yala, 1994. 429 p.: bibl., maps, tables.

Spanish version of author's 1990 PhD dissertation, *Indian migration and sociopolitical change in the Audiencia of Quito* (New York Univ.), is more detailed than her 1995 book (see item **2363**), but not as well articulated. [MTH]

2366 Ramón Valarezo, Galo. Loja y Zaruma: entre las minas y las mulas, 1557–1700. (*Rev. Ecuat. Hist. Econ.*, 4:7, 1990, p. 111–143)

Novel study focuses on rise (1580s and 1590s) and decline (1620s and 1630s) of gold mining in Zaruma, and on impact of initial prosperity and subsequent pauperization and quasi-depopulation of Zaruma on the *hacendados* and economy of Loja. Based on considerable original research. [MTH]

2367 Ramos Gómez, Luis José. La acusación contra el Presidente Electo Dn. José de Araujo y Río, sobre la introducción de mercancías ilícitas a su llegada a Quito en diciembre de 1736. (*Bol. Acad. Nac. Hist./ Quito*, 72:153/154, p. 249–272)

Analyzes undoubtedly true charges that President-Elect Araujo introduced merchandise illicitly prior to and upon taking office. Perhaps only novelty in the charges is amount and "blatancy" of traffic. Inasmuch as Araujo "donated" 26,000 pesos—probably borrowed—to obtain office, he needed to recover his investment. A comparative study by author on ways and means in which presidents of Audiencia de Quito financed and/or enriched themselves would now be useful. See also items **2368, 2369,** and *HLAS 54: 2343.* [MTH]

2368 Ramos Gómez, Luis José. El "bien común" como pretexto del presidente José de Araujo para crear una compañía de soldados y prohibir el aguardiente de caña en Quito en 1737. (*Rev. Andin.*, 11:2, dic. 1993, p. 381–402, bibl.)

Apparently President Araujo established a company of soldiers not only for his protection and that of his spouse but to enforce the prohibition of the distillation and sale of sugarcane aguardiente. It seems Araujo

was less concerned with the public good than he was with lining Victorino Montero's and indirectly his own pocket. Brother-in-law Montero was the local distributer of grape aguardiente. See also items **2367, 2369,** and *HLAS 54:2343.* [MTH]

2369 Ramos Gómez, Luis José. La pugna por el poder local en Quito entre 1737 y 1745 según el proceso contra el Presidente de la Audiencia, José de Araujo y Río. (*Rev. Complut. Hist. Am.*, 18, 1992, p. 180–196)

In yet another chapter in his ongoing study of the *residencia* of Araujo, Ramos Gómez once again takes up theme of the power struggle between the "outsider" president and the local elite, some of whose members were allied with Araujo. One of the more interesting outcomes of the clash was appointment of a locally-born successor to the president. See also items **2367, 2368,** and *HLAS 54: 2343.* [MTH]

2370 Reig Satorres, José. Guayaquil, su relevancia histórica. Guayaquil, Ecuador: Ediciones del Centro Universitario Los Esteros, 1991. 154 p.: appendices

Cogent reexamination replete with documentary appendices relates continuing controversy surrounding temporary transfer/annexation of the Gobierno Político y Militar de Guayaquil to the Viceroyalty of Peru in early 1800s. Controversy is continuing because historians still debate particulars and significance of the transfer, and because Peruvians still claim Guayaquil and the central and southern coast of Ecuador as theirs by right according to the doctrine of *uti possidetis* of 1810. [MTH]

2371 Rueda Novoa, Rocío. La ruta a la Mar del Sur: un proyecto de las elites serranas en Esmeraldas, s. XVIII. (*Procesos/ Quito*, 3, segundo semestre 1992, p. 33–54, maps)

Adds some new data to well-known attempts of Quito to open an alternative route to the coast via northern province of Esmeraldas. Focuses particularly on Barón de Carondelet's Malbucho project. [MTH]

2372 Sala Catalá, José and **Antonio Lafuente.** Ciencia colonial y roles profesionales en la América española del siglo XVIII: el caso de la Audiencia de Quito. (*in* Colección nuestra patria es América: la cultura en la historia. Edición de Jorge Núñez

Sánchez. Quito: Editora Nacional, 1992, v. 8, p. 53–71, bibl.)

Brief study concentrates on cartography, cosmology, and local scientific interests in navigation. Reflects some primary research. [J. Britton]

2373 **Salvador Lara, Jorge.** Breve historia contemporánea del Ecuador. México: Fondo de Cultura Económica, 1994. 638 p.: bibl., index.

New, somewhat anachronistic, yet worthwhile, general history of Ecuador from 30,000 BCE through 1992, written by current director of Academia Nacional de Historia and Museo Histórico (Quito). Emphasizes political and cultural developments, but does not entirely neglect economic and social aspects. Includes brief bibliographic essay and onomastic index. [MTH]

2374 **Salvador Lara, Jorge.** Quito. Madrid: Editorial MAPFRE, 1992. 404 p.: bibl., ill., index, maps. (Col. Ciudades de Iberoamérica; 5. Col. MAPFRE 1492)

History of city of Quito covers prehispanic times through present. Amenably written, but author sacrifices coverage to style. Strong on prehistory of Ecuador (notwithstanding Salvador Lara's belief in the Reino de Quito) and independence years, the two periods in which author has specialized. Weaker on middle colonial and early national periods, and on daily life and other aspects of social history. [MTH]

2375 **Soasti, Guadalupe.** Obrajeros y comerciantes en Riobamba, s. XVII. (Procesos/Quito, 1, 1994, p. 5–22, bibl., tables)

An almost wholly original, data-rich study examines production of textiles in the corregimiento of Riobamba in 17th century and of traffic in textiles with Lima. Delineates role of key families such as the Cepeda and of their obrajes (in this case, Chambo). [MTH]

2376 **Tapia Tamayo, Amílcar.** Pueblos y doctrinas de la antigua Provincia de los Pastos. Quito?: Sociedad Ecuatoriana de Investigaciones Históricas y Geográficas; Tulcán, Ecuador: Diócesis de Tulcán, 1992. 124 p.: bibl.

Well-researched history by one of Ecuador's new professionally-trained scholars focuses on indigenous parishes of Tulcán, Huaca, Tusa, and Puntal, all of which were

entrusted to the Mercedarians and located in what would become the province of Carchi. Tapia Tamayo is rapidly emerging as an authority on his native province, the history of which had been neglected. See also his *Los puntales: pueblo importante de los Pastos* (Quito: Ministerio de Educación Pública, 1989). [MTH]

2377 **Terán Najas, Rosemarie.** Censos, capellanías y elites: aspectos sociales del crédito en Quito colonial, primera mitad del s. XVIII. (Procesos/Quito, 1, 1991, p, 23–48)

Studies utilization of loans from ecclesiastical entities and endowments of chaplaincies as vehicles of credit by elite of the city of Quito during the first half of 1700s. Also examines social aspects thereof. A well-researched and novel contribution. [MTH]

2378 **Valencia Llano, Alonso.** Elites, burocracia, clero y sectores populares en la Independencia Quiteña, 1809–1812. (Procesos/Quito, 3, segundo semestre 1992, p. 55–101, tables)

Prosopographic study examines titled nobility, military officers, and clergy—royalist/loyalist as well as patriot/insurgent—of late colonial/early independent Quito. Sheds considerable light on motivations and actions of the "men of August." One of the most original and significant contributions in some time to the study of the rise of Ecuadorian independence movements. [MTH]

2379 **Viforcos Marinas, María Isabel.** Los recogimientos: de centros de integración social a cárceles privadas; Santa Marta de Quito. (Anu. Estud. Am., 50:2, 1993, p. 59–92, map)

Founded in 1595 by the bishop of Quito as a reformatory for dissolute women, a refuge for abused wives, and an orphanage, Santa Marta became a private prison for mestizas and indias during 1600s. An original contribution to little-known history of penal and welfare institutions. [MTH]

2380 **Villegas, Juan.** Negros y mulatos esclavos: Audiencia de Quito. Montevideo: Centro de Estudios de Historia Americana, 1992. 25 leaves: bibl. (Investigaciones de historia nacional y americana; 1. Esclavos negros, Quito; 1. V centenario del descubrimiento de América)

Working paper on 13 cases heard by Audiencia of Quito involving black slaves, between 1656–1746, is of interest only to specialists. [MTH]

2381 **Volland, Martin.** Indianische Bevölkerungsgeschichte im Corregimiento Guayaquil, 1548–1765. Bonn: Holos, 1994. 315 p.: bibl., ill., maps. . (Mundus Reihe Alt-Amerikanistik; 10)

Author's PhD dissertation. A history of the postconquest decline and resurgence—apparently beginning sometime during the early 18th century—of the autochthonous population of the former Corregimiento of Guayaqil. The decimation of the district's ethnic groups began c. 1531 and continued at least through 1605, and probably later. The data thus far recovered for the 17th century, however, are too fragmentary to determine approximately when the decline ceased. Also advances knowledge of encomiendas and repartimientos of the region. Expands upon the historical demographic work of Julio Estrada Ycaza, Michael T. Hamerly, and María Luisa Laviana Cuetos. Based on several years of original research in Spanish, Ecuadorian, and Colombian repositories. [MTH]

PERU

Assadourian, Carlos Sempat. La economía colonial: la transferencia del sistema productivo europeo en Nueva España y el Perú. See item 801.

2382 **Barriga Calle, Irma.** La experiencia de la muerte en Lima: siglo XVII. (*Apuntes/Lima*, 31, 1992, p. 81–102)

Fascinating essay examines a subject often unexplored today, but which was a familiar part of everyday life in previous centuries: the experience of death and its ramifications. Focusing on 17th-century Lima, this study makes an important contribution to the history of private life and contemporary thought. [MTH]

2383 **Behar Astudillo, Rosa.** Santa Rosa de Lima: un análisis psicosocial de la anorexia. (*Rev. Cienc. Soc./Valparaíso*, 32/33, 1989, p. 257–263, bibl.)

Interesting work by a psychiatrist attempts to determine extent to and ways in which anorexia might have influenced the behavior and personality of Saint Rose of Lima. See also item 2424. [MTH]

2384 **Bradley, Peter T.** The defence of Peru, 1648–1700. (*Jahrb. Gesch.*, 29, 1992, p. 91–120)

Continues author's earlier work *The defence of Peru: 1600–1648* (see *HLAS 40: 3192*). Bradley finds that Crown and viceroys made little more than token efforts to maintain and enhance defenses of the Viceroyalty during second half of 17th century, and that the private sector increasingly had to fill the breach. See also Bradley's contribution to *Compendio histórico del Perú* (item 2389). [MTH]

2385 **Bronner, Fred.** Church, Crown, and commerce in seventeenth-century Lima: a synoptic interpretation. (*Jahrb. Gesch.*, 29, 1992, p. 75–89)

Maintains that "private enterprise founded the Spanish-American empire and a near-capitalist spirit pervaded it and held it together." A thought-provoking reexamination of the socioeconomic structure and ethos of the City of the Kings in the 1600s. [MTH]

2386 **Burga, Manuel.** Rasgos fundamentales de la historia agraria peruana, s. XVI-XVIII. (*Procesos/Quito*, 1, 1991, p. 49–67, bibl.)

Insightful reexamination of economic cycles and crises utilizes tithe records of Archdiocese of Lima to establish cycles in agrarian history of central Peru during second half of colonial period: 1) marked depression during first half, if not first two-thirds, of 1700s; 2) stagnation between 1768–82; and 3) recovery between 1783–1818. See also item 2413. [MTH]

2387 **Burns, Kathryn.** Amor y rebelión en 1782: el caso de Mariano Túpac Amaru y María Mejía. (*Histórica/Lima*, 16:2, dic. 1992, p. 131–176, bibl.)

Publishes and analyzes a curious but inconclusive manuscript in the Biblioteca Nacional del Perú regarding the apparently frustrated love affair between Mariano Túpac Amaru, a son of the rebel José Gabriel, with the "chola" María Mejía. Provides tantalizing glimpse of private life in *cacique* class and of the not infrequent interference of Church and State in affairs of the heart and flesh. María was found to be pregnant, presumably by Mariano, when she was "deposited" in a convent in Cusco. [MTH]

2388 Celestino, Olinda. Les confréries religieuses a Lima. (*Arch. sci. soc. relig.*, 37:80, oct./déc. 1992, p. 167–191, bibl., tables)

Provides general overview of confraternities in Lima: membership, activities, internal organization, etc. Suggests that political activities of confraternities deserve better treatment in historical literature. [A. Lavrin]

2389 Compendio histórico del Perú. t. 2–4. Edición, producción, ilustración, diagramación y epígrafes de Carlos Milla Batres. Lima: Editorial Milla Batres, 1993. 3 v.: bibl., ill. (some col.).

Vols. 2–4 of this deluxe, mostly new, lavishly illustrated general history of Peru cover colonial period. Vol. 2 includes a solid synthesis of traditional and recent scholarship, including ethnohistorical, on European discovery, Spanish conquest, and the early colonial period by Teodoro Hampe-Martínez, and a long essay on naval defenses of the Viceroyalty in 1500s-1600s by Peter T. Bradley (see also item **2384**). Vol. 3, on 17th century, is a reprise of corresponding chapters in Rubén Vargas Ugarte's *Historia general del Perú* as originally issued by the same publisher in 1966 . Vol. 4, on 18th and early 19th centuries, is a series of original essays on viceroys and their administrations, Bourbon reforms, art, literature, and the economy. [MTH]

2390 Congreso Peruano de Historia Eclesiástica, 1st, Arequipa, 1990. La evangelización del Perú: siglos XVI y XVII; actas. Arequipa, Peru: s.n., 1990. 595 p.: bibl., ill.

Congress proceedings focus on colonial period and Peru proper. Except for two papers on Maynas, the Congress took up four themes: 1) evangelization; 2) role of the Church in formation of nationality; 3) social thought and action of the Church; and 4) the Church in Arequipa. Presentations vary in originality and sophistication. Several cover new or lesser-known ground, most notably those on the Church in Arequipa; however, the majority, especially those dealing with missionary activities, rework well-known fields. Many of the papers are detailed and well documented. Altogether a significant contribution to history of the Catholic Church and faith in the Viceroyalty, notwithstanding the built-in biases of the majority of participants. [MTH]

2391 Cruz Rodríguez , María Agueda. Las universidades del Perú: fuentes y bibliografía crítica, metodología y estado de la cuestión. (*Estud. Hist. Soc. Econ. Am.*, 11, 1994, p. 151–180, bibl.)

Well-structured, highly informative essay focuses on the historiography and state of the archives of colonial Peruvian universities: San Marcos in Lima, San Ignacio and San Antonio in Cusco, and San Cristóbal in Huamanga. [MTH]

2392 Cummins, Victoria H. Blessed connections: sociological aspects of sainthood in colonial Mexico and Peru. (*CLAHR/Albuquerque*, 3:1, Winter 1994, p. 1–18)

Comparative study examines careers of the virtually forgotten Pedro Moya de Contreras, third archbishop of Mexico, and the renowned St. Toribio Alfonso Mogrovejo, second archbishop of Lima. Although Cummins finds that both men were deserving of "sainthood," only Mogrovejo was beatified and canonized, apparently because he enjoyed better personal and family connections and because of Peru's need to have a saint of its own. See also items **2424, 2436, 2426,** and **2423.** [MTH]

2393 Damian, Carol. Artist and patron in colonial Cuzco: workshops, contracts, and a petition for independence. (*CLAHR/Albuquerque*, 4:1, Winter 1995, p. 25–53)

Refreshingly different article focuses on the Escuela de Bellas Artes de Cusco. Utilizing notarial records, Damian examines social and economic aspects of the production of religious art by Spanish, mestizo, and indigenous artisans and artists during second half of 17th and first half of 18th centuries. Her discussion of Spanish production for indigenous persons and of indigenous production for Spaniards is enlightening. [MTH]

2394 Diez Hurtado, Alejandro. El poder de las varas: los cabildos en Piura a fines de la colonia. (*Apuntes/Lima*, 30, 1992, p. 81–90, chart)

Stresses that not only did some indigenous communities use Spanish institutions (in this case, the cabildo) for their own purposes, including survival, but also that Andean history is far more complex than some scholars seem to realize. Therefore the region's history should not be subject to the facile generalizations that continue to be made. [MTH]

2395 Domínguez Faura, Nicanor. Aguas y legislación en los valles de Lima: el repartimiento de 1617. (*Bol. Inst. Riva-Agüero*, 15, 1988, p. 117–154, bibl., maps)

Study of water supply and demand, and regulating legislation, in the Rimac Valley from late 1500s-early 1600s offers an original contribution to history and historical geography of the central coast. [MTH]

2396 Domínguez I., Manuel F. El Colegio franciscano de Propaganda Fide de Moquegua, 1775–1825 (*Arch. Ibero-Am.*, 52: 205/208, 1992, p. 221–254)

Well-documented study chronicles final 50 years of the Franciscan institution in the Diocese of Arequipa and its missionary activities among "pagans" of the Altiplano and of the Upper Amazon Basin. Useful but anachronistic in approach and coverage. [MTH]

2397 Durán Montero, María Antonia. Lima en 1613: aspectos urbanos. (*Anu. Estud. Am.*, 49, 1992, p. 171–188, plan)

Examination of housing and occupations in urban Lima in 1613 is based on Contreras' *Padrón de indios de Lima en 1613* (see *HLAS 34:1149*). Includes a reconstructed plan of the city. Disagrees with Bromley and Barbagelata's *Evolución urbana de la ciudad de Lima* (see *HLAS 11:2542*) regarding assignation of coeval numbering of streets. [MTH]

2398 Durand Flórez, Luis. El proceso de independencia en el Sur Andino: Cuzco y La Paz, 1805. Lima: Univ. de Lima, 1993. 529 p.: bibl., maps. (Publicaciones de la Universidad de Lima)

Durand's thesis is that between 1782 and 1800 the "Sur Andino" (the Peruvian/Bolivian Altiplano, considered an integral, distinct region by author) moved from *reformismo autonomista* (criollos and mestizos united) to *separatismo* (criollos and mestizos divided politically). Provocative, important work reflects considerable research; however, Durand rambles in time and space, and quotes excessively from every conceivable author and then some. [MTH]

2399 Fernández Alonso, Serena. Un noble canario en el gobierno local indiano: el Marqués de Casa Hermosa en la Intendencia de Puno. (*in* Coloquio de Historia Canario-Americana, *9th, Spain, 1990.* Actas. Las Pal-mas, Spain: Cabildo Insular de Gran Canaria, 1992, v. 1, p. 717–736)

Attempts to vindicate the maligned Marqués de Casa Hermosa, a late 18th-century *intendente* of Puno. Well-researched, although somewhat lacking in objectivity. [MTH]

2400 Fernández Alonso, Serena. Perfil biográfico y acción de gobierno de Don Jorge Escobedo y Alarcón. (*Rev. Indias*, 52: 195/196, mayo/dic. 1992, p. 365–383)

Well-researched sketch of life and career of last Visitador-General of Peru. [MTH]

2401 Fernández Martín, Luis. Hernando Pizarro en el Castillo de la Mota. Valladolid, Spain: Junta de Castilla y León, Consejería de Cultura y Bienestar Social, 1991. 78 p.: bibl., ill. (some col.).

Detailed, objective, insightful, well-researched account relates what happened to the Pizarros and their fortune during years Hernando was imprisoned in Mota de Medina (1543–61). Replete with appropriate, magnificently reproduced illustrations. [MTH]

2402 Fraser, Valerie. Architecture and ambition: the case of the Jesuits in the Viceroyalty of Perú. (*Hist. Workshop*, 34, Autumn 1992, p. 17–32, ill. maps)

Interesting, albeit somewhat rambling and not altogether coherent, essay examines the "theocratic empire," which, the author maintains, the Jesuits endeavored to establish for themselves in the Viceroyalty of Peru. Focuses to some extent on Order's acquisition of the Amarucancha or former palace of Huayna Capac in Cuzco, the Jesuits' conversion of the palace into a church and college, and their utilization of the symbolic site as a power base. [MTH]

2403 Gareis, Iris. "República de Indios"—"República de Españoles:" reinterpretación actual de conceptos andinos coloniales. (*Jahrb. Gesch.*, 30, 1993, p. 259–277)

Thought-provoking essay focuses on persistence of the two republics, or continuing cleavage between indigenous and *mistis* in modern Peru; on utilizaton of the myth of *inkarrí*, or belief in the return of a salvific Inca by Túpac Amaru II and other indigenous leaders of late colonial period; and on interaction between separatism, insurgency, and millenarianism. [MTH]

2404 González Pujana, Laura. Minería y trabajo indígena en los Andes, Guamanga y Zaruma. (*Rev. Complut. Hist. Am.*, 18, 1992, p. 117–131)

Comparative study looks at 14th-century assignment of indigenous labor to the mines of Guamanga and Zaruma in what are now Peru and Ecuador. Doubly interesting for its examination of the Mita de Zaruma, a virtually unknown chapter in the history of the Audencia of Quito. [MTH]

2405 Gremios coloniales peruanos. Presentación de Francisco Quiroz Chueca. Lima: Univ. Nacional Mayor de San Marcos, Seminario de Historia Rural Andina, 1991. 98 p.: bibl.

Compendium of 16 sources from 1558–1826 for reconstruction of the history of guilds in Lima is useful only for its examples of surviving primary materials on guilds—the functions, membership, organization, and significance of which have barely begun to be adumbrated in the literature. [MTH]

2406 Griffiths, Nicholas. "Inquisition of the Indians?:" the inquisitorial model and the repression of Andean religion in seventeenth-century Peru. (*CLAHR/Albuquerque*, 3:1, Winter 1994, p. 19–38)

Reexamines underlying beliefs and misperceptions of the Extirpation and reasons for its failure. Maintains that the conquerors failed to impose their own faith on the conquered because the former misunderstood and misinterpreted the latter. Hence, for example, persecution of *hechiceros* probably enhanced the reputation of native priests and shamans among the peoples of the Andes. [MTH]

2407 Guevara Gil, Jorge Armando. Propiedad agraria y derecho colonial: los documentos de la Hacienda Santotis, Cuzco, 1543–1822. Lima: Pontificia Univ. Católica del Perú, Fondo Editorial, 1993. 572 p.: bibl., maps.

Extraordinary work relates history of Hacienda Santotis, a sizable property in the outskirts of Cuzco, from its mid-16th century beginnings through end of colonial period. Even more extraordinary is the principal source on which this work is based: *Expediente de los títulos de propiedad de la Hacienda Santotis, Cuzco, 1543–1822* (reproduced

on pp. 309–539). The fact that the hacienda once belonged to the author's family, and author's background in law and ethnohistory, enhance the value of this outstanding contribution to the agrarian, legal, and social history of the Altiplano. [MTH]

2408 Guibovich Pérez, Pedro. La cultura libresca de un converso procesado por la Inquisición de Lima. (*Hist. Cult./Lima*, 20, 1990, p. 133–160)

Analyzes the personal library of Manuel Baptista Peres, who was sentenced to death and executed by the Inquisition in 1638. *Converso* Peres was extraordinarily well read in history and religion regardless of his status as a possible lapsed Catholic. [MTH]

2409 Guibovich Pérez, Pedro. Fray Juan de Almaraz: calificador de la Inquisición de Lima, siglo XVI. (*CHELA*, 4, 1989, p. 31–45, appendix)

Essay relates life, activities, and mentality of 16th-century advisor to the Inquisition—a criollo, son of a royal official, an Augustinian, and a member of the faculty of Univ. de San Marcos. While a minor chapter in the history of the Inquisition, work opens a promising new avenue of research. [MTH]

2410 Guibovich Pérez, Pedro. El testamento e inventario de bienes de Espinosa Medrano. (*Histórica/Lima*, 16:1, junio 1992, p. 1–31, bibl.)

Publishes with brief commentary the last will and testament (1681) of Dr. Juan de Espinosa Medrano, a wealthy member of the clergy of Cuzco. Exemplifies importance of wills and testaments as significant sources of social and economic data. [MTH]

2411 Hampe Martínez, Teodoro. Bibliotecas privadas en el mundo colonial: la difusión de libros e ideas en el Virreinato del Perú, siglos XVI-XVII. Frankfurt: Vervuert; Madrid: Iberoamericana, 1996. 307 p.: bibl., index. (Textos de estudios coloniales y de la Independencia; 1)

Anthology of 25 previously published essays focus on private libraries, the world of ideas, and the book trade in the Viceroyalty of Peru. Major contribution to the intellectual history of the colonial period. For the particulars of some of these studies see *HLAS 48: 2747; HLAS 52:1032, 2012, and 2152–2155; and HLAS 54:2380.* [MTH]

2412 Hampe Martínez, Teodoro. Control
moral y represión ideológica: la Inquisición en el Perú, 1570–1820. (*Bol. Inst. Riva-
Agüero*, 16, 1989, p. 253–263, bibl.)
   Provides overview of what is known
about history and, in passing, historiography
of the Inquisition in Peru. Also reevaluates
the Inquisition in light of the canons of modern historiographic concerns by relating what
the study thereof offers for those endeavoring
to reconstruct and understand the social
structures and mentalities of the time and
place. [MTH]

2413 Hampe Martínez, Teodoro. Hacia una
nueva periodificación de la historia del
Perú colonial: factores económicos, políticos
y sociales. (*Jahrb. Gesch.*, 29, 1992, p. 47–74)
   Exceptionally important essay focuses
on periodization of the colonial period, taking
into account economic, social, and political
factors as they have become better known.
Hampe Martínez suggests the following chronology: 1) "formación de las estructuras de
dominación colonial" (1530–80); 2) "apogeo
de plata y consolidación de la economía interna" (1580–1650); 3) "florecimiento del sistema de hacienda y mercados regionales"
(1650–1720); 4) "presión fiscal y retos en la
dominación colonial" (1720–80); and 5) "rom-
pimiento de las estructuras de dominación española" (1780–1820). See also item **2386.**
[MTH]

2414 Hampe Martínez, Teodoro. Notas sobre población y tributo indígena en Cajamarca, primera mitad del siglo XVII. (*Bol.
Inst. Riva-Agüero*, 14, 1986/87, p. 65–81,
tables)
   Contains research notes on state and
movement of indigenous population in district of Cajamarca during first half of 1600s,
on organization of indigenous peoples in encomiendas, on amount and nature of tribute
required of them, and on the labor quota or
mita to which they were subjected. [MTH].

2415 Hampe Martínez, Teodoro. La Revolu-
cion Francesa vista por el *Mercurio
Peruano*: cambio político vs. reformismo
criollo. (*Bol. Inst. Riva-Agüero*, 15, 1988,
p. 163–178)
   Hampe Martínez finds that the Sociedad de Amantes del País, as revealed in their
publication *Mercurio Peruano*, rejected the
excesses of the French Revolution inasmuch

as the Creole aristocrats who comprised the
society aspired at most to administrative reforms that would result in "good government" and equal treatment for Spaniards of
European birth and those born in the colonies. [MTH]

2416 Hampe Martínez, Teodoro. Sumaria
bibliografía sobre los cronistas del
Perú. (*Bol. Bibl. Nac.*, 40:93/94, 1985,
p. 5–57)
   Useful bibliography of modern editions
and studies of the chroniclers of 16th and
17th centuries lists 525 articles and books. Includes an author index. [MTH]

2417 Henige, David. Counting the encounter: the pernicious appeal of verisimili-
tude. (*CLAHR/Albuquerque*, 2:3, Summer
1993, p. 325–361, tables)
   Takes to task advocates of the "disease
model," especially Noble David Cook.
Whether Peru had as many indigenous
peoples before contact or circa 1520 as Cook
advocates (see *HLAS 46:2695*) or, as Henige
advocates, substantially fewer circa 1525 sans
"virtually impossible" preceding epidemics,
is beyond the ken of the *Handbook*, but the
wary and the weary of the "numbers game"
will enjoy and perhaps profit from Henige's
critique. [MTH]

2418 Heras, Julián. Significado y extensión
de la obra misionera de Ocopa en el
siglo XVIII. (*Arch. Ibero-Am.*, 52:205/208,
1992, p. 209–219)
   Gives favorable review of expansion of
Franciscan missionary activities in 1700s, especially those radiating from Ocopa. [MTH]

2419 Herzog, Tamar. La Gaceta de Lima,
1756–1761: la reestructuración de la
realidad y sus funciones. (*Histórica/Lima*, 16:
1, junio 1992, p. 33–61, bibl. tables)
   In a revealing analysis of contents of
recently reprinted *Gaceta de Lima*, Herzog
argues that it should be read not as a newspaper, but as a chronicle of "una ciudad señorial
que pasa su tiempo y gasta su energía en actividades ceremoniales, en donde la paz y la
armonía prevalecen." But as such the *Gaceta*
was and remains a key source for studying the
mentality of the late colonial elite of the City
of the Kings. [MTH]

2420 Hinojosa C., Iván. El nudo colonial: la
violencia en el movimiento tupama-
rista. (*in* Congreso Nacional de Investiga-

ciónes en Historia, *1st, Lima, 1984.* Actas. Lima: CONCYTEC, v. 1, 1991, p. 61–75, bibl.)

Maintains that only a violent revolution could have overthrown the existing order, but that the exploited failed to find a way to break the yoke of colonial society. Also claims that violence of the *tupamaristas* was met by an even greater violence of repression. [MTH]

2421 Holguín Callo, Oswaldo. El doctor Diego de Salinas, 1558–1595: primeros lances de un limeño ambicioso. (*Bol. Inst. Riva-Agüero,* 14, 1986/1987, p. 9–63)

Detailed, apparently exhaustively researched biography of an early colonial period first-generation *limeño* and academician. Author does not address degree to which Salinas' ambitions and aspirations were representative of members of his caste and class. [MTH]

2422 Huertas Vallejos, Lorenzo. Introducción al estudio de la producción de vinos y aguardientes en Ica: siglos XVI al XVIII. (*Hist. Cult./Lima,* 21, 1991/92, p. 161–216, appendix, bibl., photos, tables)

Working paper examines production of wines and aguardientes in the Ica Valley. The history of *pisco* has been neglected by historians despite its importance to the economy of the Peruvian central coast. [MTH]

Indigenous revolts in Chiapas and the Andean highlands. See *HLAS 55:57.*

2423 Iwasaki Cauti, Fernando. Fray Martín de Porras: santo, ensalmador y sacamuelas. (*Colon. Lat. Am. Rev.,* 3:1/2, 1994, p. 159–184, bibl.)

Work is not a standard biography of the Peruvian who became a saint despite his "illegitimacy," his "mixed blood," or his lack of social standing; rather, it is a fascinating essay depicting the mentality of the times, witchcraft and medicine in early colonial Lima and the thin line between the two, Porres' practice of faith healing and dental extractions, and the reasons for his reputation as a miracle worker. See also items **2424, 2392,** and **2426.** [MTH]

2424 Iwasaki Cauti, Fernando. Mujeres al borde de la perfección: Rosa de Santa María y las alumbradas de Lima. (*HAHR,* 73: 4, Nov. 1993, p. 581–613, appendix)

Attempts to place Rosa de Santa María

within religious and ideological context by examining lives and practices of other "holy women" of the time and place. In the process sheds considerable light on subculture of *beatas* and on the fine line between those seen as devout and pious and those viewed with suspicion and hostility. One of the few modern studies of sainthood in Peru. See also items **2383, 2392, 2426,** and **2423.** [MTH]

2425 Iwasaki Cauti, Fernando. Toros y sociedad en Lima colonial. (*Anu. Estud. Am.,* 49, 1992, p. 311–333, appendix)

Insightful essay focuses on bullfighting in Lima from foundation of the city in 1532 to construction of the Plaza de Acho in 1766. Especially concerned with social aspects of the "sport" (e.g., its "takeover by plebians"). [MTH]

2426 Iwasaki Cauti, Fernando. Vidas de santos y santas vidas: hagiografías reales e imaginarias en Lima colonial. (*Anu. Estud. Am.,* 51:1, 1994, p. 47–64)

Provides scintillating albeit brief glimpse of popular culture and mentality in colonial Lima as gleaned from discourse analysis of 17th- and 18th-century hagiographies. A promising venue of research. See also items **2392, 2424,** and **2423.** [MTH]

2427 Jaramillo, Miguel. Migraciones y formación de mercados laborales: la fuerza de trabajo indígena de Lima a comienzos del siglo XVII. (*Economía/Lima,* 15:29/ 30, junio/dic. 1992, p. 265–320, bibl., tables)

Quantitative study of indigenous labor in early 17th-century Lima is based on well-known 1613 *padrón* and on notary records of the period. Jaramillo examines origins, length of residence, occupations, salaries, and motivations of migrants to the city. Enhances our knowledge of demographic, economic, and social history of the capital of the conquerors. [MTH]

2428 Juan, Jorge and **Antonio de Ulloa.** Noticias secretas de América. Edición de Luis Javier Ramos Gómez. Madrid: Historia 16, 1991. 778 p.: bibl. (Crónicas de América; 63)

New edition of standard 18th-century document. Lengthy introductory essay and textual footnotes by Ramos Gómez reflect his thorough investigations of the various manuscripts used to produce this volume. [J. Britton]

2429 Lazo García, Carlos. Economía colonial y régimen monetario: Perú, siglos XVI-XIX. v. 1–3. Lima: Banco Central de Reserva del Perú, Fondo Editorial, 1992. 3 v.: bibl., ill. (some col.), maps.

Monumental work focuses on history of money in Lower and Upper Peru. Vols. 1–2 thoroughly examine production and periodic debasement of gold and silver coins in the Perus, and vol. 3 consists of detailed time series of the production of the mints of Lima and Potosí. An exceptionally important contribution to economic history of the Viceroyalty and one that, like Macera's *Precios del Perú* (see item **2432**), will alter elemental interpretations and prove to be a rich source for the profession for many years to come. [MTH]

2430 Lockhart, James. Spanish Peru, 1532–1560: a social history. 2nd ed. Madison: Univ. of Wisconsin Press, 1994. 320 p.: bibl., ill., index.

Lockhart's 1968 work (see *HLAS 32: 2240*) has been changed only marginally. [MTH]

2431 Lohmann Villena, Guillermo. Los corsos: una hornada monopolista en el Perú en el siglo XVI. (*Anu. Estud. Am.*, 51:1, 1994, p. 15–45)

Details and documents extent to which Corsicans played a prominent role in intra-imperial and intercolonial trade. Focuses on their activities in Lima in 1500s. Supplements studies of Enriqueta Vila Vilar, especially *Los Corzo y los Mañara: tipos y arquetipos del mercader con América* (see item **990**. [MTH]

2432 Macera, Pablo et al. Precios del Perú: siglos XVI-XIX; fuentes. v. 1–3. Computación de Walter Carnero et al. Lima: Fondo Editorial, Banco Central de Reserva, 1992? 3 v.: ill., tables.

Consists of time series of mean annual prices (in reales) of 347 products for which some diachronic data have been found for Lima, Trujillo, Pisco, Ica, Huamanga, Huancavelica, Moquegua, Arequipa, and Cuzco, and for 39 haciendas on the coast and in the highlands, from 1569–1824. Data are presented in tables and bar charts. Although Macera insists that this work is "exclusivamente documentario," it includes indices for 35 products for Lima with mean prices as of 1801–10 as base. Methodology employed is

delineated in the introduction. Sources from which this monumental database was compiled are almost entirely institutional in origin. The 39 haciendas, for example, were or had been Jesuit properties. An impressive piece of work that will revolutionize the analysis and interpretation of economic history of the colonial period. See also item **2429**. [MTH]

2433 Málaga Medina, Alejandro. Amanecer hispano de Arequipa. (*Bol. Inst. Riva-Agüero*, 16, 1989, p. 105–114, bibl.)

Ably recapitulates early years of Spanish Arequipa and its role in civil wars of the 1500s. Author is a prominent historian as well as a native son. [MTH]

2434 Mannarelli, María Emma. Pecados públicos: la ilegitimidad en Lima, siglo XVII. Lima: Ediciones Flora Tristán, 1993. 324 p.: bibl.

Fascinating, pioneering study examines sexual relationships, social inequalities, concubinage, adultery, illegitimacy, dishonored women, and fate of abandoned infants in 17th-century Lima. A revision of author's PhD thesis (Columbia Univ., 1992), work is based largely on research in Archivo de la Beneficencia Pública de Lima and Archivo Arzobispal de Lima. [MTH]

2435 Marzal, Manuel María. Del paternalismo colonial al moderno indigenismo en el Perú. (*in* De palabra y obra en el Nuevo Mundo. v. 2, Encuentros interétnicos. Edición de Miguel León-Portilla et al. Madrid: Siglo Veintiuno Editores, 1992, p. 127–152)

Interesting essay is written by a Peruvian historian of ideas whose work is not nearly as well known as it should be. In this piece Marzal examines *indigenismo* of Toledo, Solórzano y Pereyra, Acosta, and Calancha on the one hand, and of Castro Pozo, Valcárcel, Mariátegui, and Belaúnde on the other. Unfortunately, Marzal stops short of comparing the thinking of 20th-century intellectuals with that of their colonial-period predecessors. [MTH]

2436 McGlone, Mary M. The King's surprise: the mission methodology of Toribio de Mogrovejo. (*Americas/Francisc.*, 50: 1, July 1993, p. 65–83)

Author relates that Philip II expected Mogrovejo to be an organization man and to organize the Church in Peru, but that the future saint turned out to be a maverick and a missionary imbued with the same spirit as Las Casas and his followers. See also item **2392.** [MTH]

2437 Mejías Alvarez, María Jesús. Muerte regia en cuatro ciudades peruanas del barroco. (*Anu. Estud. Am.*, 49, 1992, p. 189–205)

Outlines funeral honors accorded to Philip III by Castrovirreina and by Lima in 1621, to Prince Baltasar Carlos by Arequipa in 1647, and to Carlos II by Trujillo in 1701. Potentially interesting piece is handicapped by limited understanding of time and place. [MTH]

Memoria del Nuevo Mundo: Castilla-La Mancha y América en el Quinto Centenario. See item **928.**

2438 Mills, Kenneth. An evil lost to view?: an investigation of post-evangelisation Andean religion in mid-colonial Peru. Liverpool, England: Institute of Latin American Studies, Univ. of Liverpool, 1994. 147 p.: bibl. (Monograph series; 18)

Relates a "microhistory," not a "case study," of religious life in a single parish (San Pedro de Acas, Cajatambo) in Archdiocese of Lima in mid-17th century. Examines multiplicity of ways in which Andean religious beliefs and practices and Catholicism interacted at institutional and individual levels. Excellent example of qualitative research as it should be: multidisciplinarian in analysis and sophisticated in interpretation, yet written clearly enough for both generalists and specialists. [MTH]

2439 Morlon, Pierre. De las relaciones entre clima de altura y agricultura de la sierra del Perú en los textos de los siglos XVI y XVII. (*Bull. Inst. fr. étud. andin.*, 21:3, 1992, p. 929–959, bibl., maps)

Working paper on inadequately known history of climate in Peru is based on coeval chronicles. Author agrees with students of contemporary climate that two seasons prevail in the Andes, at least in the Central Andes: the wet and the dry. Argues that sources studied demonstrate that precipitation was greater in the 1500s and 1600s than in the 1900s, and therefore that agriculture was more productive at higher altitudes at that time than at present. [MTH]

2440 Navarro Azcue, Concepción and Carmen Ruigómez Gómez. La ordenanza de intendentes y las comunidades indígenas del Virreinato peruano: una reforma insuficiente. (*Rev. Complut. Hist. Am.*, 19, 1993, p. 209–231)

Authors maintain that impact of *intendencia* system on indigenous population of Peru has been inadequately studied; yet work provides little new information. [MTH]

2441 Nieto Vélez, Armando. Francisco del Castillo: el Apostol de Lima. Lima: Pontificia Univ. Católica del Perú; Fondo Editorial, 1992. 335 p.: bibl., ill., ports.

Provides detailed and heavily documented, but nonetheless official and therefore not altogether objective, biography of the Jesuit Francisco del Castillo (1615–73), noted for his concern and care for the poor and slaves, and currently a candidate for beatification. [MTH]

2442 Noack, Karoline. Die Visitation des Gregorio González de Cuenca—1566–67—in der Nordregion des Vizekönigreiches Peru: gesellschaftliche Relevanz von Rechtsordnung und Rechtsanwendung. Frankfurt am Main; New York: Lang, 1996. 310 p.: bibl. (Europäische Hochschulschriften. Reihe III, Geschichte und ihre Hilfswissenschaften, 0531–7320; 717.)

Work based on PhD dissertation (Freie Univ. Berlin) carefully analyzes proceedings of the *visita* by Gregorio González de Cuenca to the province of Trujillo, northern Peru. Author rightly presents González de Cuenca as a precursor to a series of administrative reforms imposed by Viceroy Toledo during the 1570s. Noack also challenges notion of the presumptive continuity of prehispanic institutions within the colonial system, noting that native Andean communities disintegrated regardless of the reintroduction of their traditions. [T. Hampe-Martínez]

2443 O'Phelan Godoy, Scarlett. Tiempo inmemorial, tiempo colonial: un estudio de casos. (*Procesos/Quito*, 4, 1993, p. 3–20, bibl.)

Fascinating study recalls various instances in which *caciques*, ecclesiastics, and private citizens of the Perus appealed to "time immemorial" or "traditional usage" during late 1700s-early 1800s to oppose alterations or changes provoked by Bourbon Reforms concerning possession of land, contributions or taxes, right of succession, and ritual practices. [MTH]

2444 O'Phelan Godoy, Scarlett. L'Utopie andine: discours parallèle à la fin de l'époque coloniale. (*Annales/Paris*, 49:2, mars/avril 1994, p. 471–495)

Examines ideological basis of 18th-century indigenous rebellions, from that of Juan Santos Atahualpa in 1742 through that of Túpac Amaru 38 years later, mostly among *caciques* of Cuzco region. Central to the "parallel discourse" was belief not only in the return of the Inca but in restoration of the Tawantinsuyu without the *mistis.* [MTH]

2445 O'Phelan Godoy, Scarlett. Vivir y morir en el mineral de Hualgayoc a fines de la colonia. (*Jahrb. Gesch.*, 30, 1993, p. 75–127)

"To live in and to die . . ." reconstructs rapid rise and equally rapid fall of Hualgayoc (discovered in 1771), the second most important center of silver mining in Peru proper in late-18th century. Depletion, wars for independence, and epidemics of typhus and smallpox were responsible for demise of the mines. Yet another of O'Phelan's significant contributions to regional as well as socioeconomic history of late colonial period. [MTH]

2446 Oré, Luis Jerónimo de. *Symbolo Catholico Indiano.* Lima: Australis, 1992. 462 p.: bibl., facsims., ill. (Col. Ars historiae)

Photofacsimile edition of a work originally published in Lima by Antonio Ricardo in 1598. Initially important as a treatise for proselytizing native peoples of the Andes, the *Symbolo Catholico Indiano* is now a major linguistic as well as ethnohistorical source inasmuch as Oré has appended and translated into Quechua and Aymara the *Symbolum Sancti Athanasii* (p. 211–458). This edition includes a prologue by Julián Heras and an introductory study by Noble David Cook. [MTH]

2447 Pacheco Sandoval, Marino et al. Pasco en la colonia: estudios de historia económica y social. Lima?: Labor, 1992. 160 p.: bibl., ill., maps.

Anthology of original essays on mining district of Cerro de Pasco. Marino Pacheco Sandoval discourses in some detail on history

of the *villa* and its hinterland from prehispanic times through 1700s; Alejandro Reyes Flores examines demography, economy, and society of the region in 1700s; and César Espinoza Claudio and José Boza Monteverde study uprising of 1780. Major contribution to regional history. [MTH]

2448 Pardo Sandoval, Teresa. Un impreso peruano desconocido. (*Bol. Inst. Riva-Agüero*, 15, 1988, p. 155–162, bibl.)

Exhaustive description of a heretofore unregistered imprint, a 1641 sermon authored by Pedro de Reyna Maldonado and printed in Lima by Jorge López de Herrera, is of interest primarily to bibliographers and specialists in minutiae. [MTH]

2449 Porro, Nelly R. El Señor Santiago en tierras del antiguo Incario. (*in* Estudios en homenaje a Don Claudio Sánchez-Albornoz en sus 90 años: anexos de *Cuadernos de Historia de España.* Buenos Aires: Instituto de Historia de España, 1990, v. 6, p. 177–215)

Reexamines texts of 16th and 17th centuries to demonstrate that the patron saint of Spain was not only invoked by Spaniards in battle and in danger but that the Hispanic Santiago was merged with the Apo Illapa (one of the general *huacas* of Andean ethnic groups, the material manifestation of whom was thunder and lighting) at least in some places, during early colonial period. [MTH]

2450 Quiroz, Alfonso W. Deudas olvidadas: instrumentos de crédito en la economía colonial peruana, 1750–1820. Lima: Pontificia Univ. Católica del Perú, Fondo Editorial, 1993. 233 p., 1 folded leaf of plates: bibl., ill., index.

Exceptionally readable monograph on a virtually forgotten topic, the role of credit, by a specialist in financial history. Quiroz examines importance of credit in the economy of the Viceroyalty, credit mechanisms c. 1750, dismantling of the traditional system of credit under the Bourbons and its partial replacement by an alliance between the Treasury and the commercial elite, and what went wrong during first years of the Republic. For a précis of this pioneering work see author's "Reassessing the Role of Credit in Late Colonial Peru: *Censos, Escrituras*, and *Imposiciones*" (HAHR, 74:2, May 1994, p. 193–230). [MTH]

2451 Ramírez, Susan E. Instability at the top: a social history of the landed elite in colonial Peru. (*CLAHR/Albuquerque*, 3:3, Summer 1994, p. 327–346, map, tables)

Prosopographic study of landed elite of Lambayeque area of the north coast defines, quantifies, and documents questions of "exclusivity, wealth, and durability of elite families." Ramírez finds that, for the most part, "the landed elite was unstable, open, and in constant flux." An important contribution to regional and social history. [MTH]

2452 Ramírez, Susan E. The world upside down: cross-cultural contact and conflict in sixteenth-century Peru. Stanford, Calif.: Stanford Univ. Press, 1996. 234 p.: bibl., ill., index, maps.

Refreshingly well-written, reasoned, and articulated study of continuity and change on the north coast of Peru during the early colonial period. Reconstructs and illuminates multiple aspects of indigenous society on the eve of and during the first 50 years following the Spanish conquest. Offsets the somewhat static image of Tawantinsuyu and the early Spanish colony as usually seen from Cuzco and Lima. Exceptionally important contribution to the historiography of the Andean region. [MTH]

2453 Ramos, Gabriela. La fortuna del inquisidor: Inquisición y poder en el Perú, 1594–1611. (*CHELA*, 4, 1989, p. 89–122, appendix, bibl.)

Detailed, well-researched study relates ways and means by which the Inquisitor Pedro Ordóñez Florez enriched himself through his office. However, as author reminds us, Ordóñez Florez and society at large viewed the Holy Office as a family business as well as a guardian of the faith. [MTH]

2454 Regalado de Hurtado, Liliana. Religión y evangelización en Vilcabamba, 1572–1602. Lima: Pontificia Univ. Católica del Perú, Fondo Editorial, 1992. 232 p.: bibl.

Study of Spanish colonization of Vilcabamba following first defeat of Túpac Amaru (1572), and of initial Augustinian and Jesuit efforts to evangelize rainforest peoples of the Antisuyu. Well researched, but methodologically unsophisticated and limited in scope. [MTH]

2455 Rivera-Rodas, Oscar. El encuentro de dos mundos: la escritura de Dios a la voz mutilada. (*CLAHR/Albuquerque*, 3:4, Fall 1994, p. 423–455)

Employs discourse analysis to determine what may be recovered of the lost, as well as altered and, therefore, "mutilated voice of the Andes." Focuses on 1533 encounter between conquerors and indigenous authority as represented in Titu Cussi Yupangui's 1570 *Ynstruçion*, Felipe Guamán Poma de Ayala's 1615 *Nueva corónica y buen gobierno* (see *HLAS 2:228*), and Inca Garcilaso de la Vega's 1609 and 1617 *Comentarios reales* (see *HLAS 9:3774*). [MTH]

2456 Rizo-Patrón, Paul. La familia noble en la Lima borbónica: patrones matrimoniales y dotales. (*Bol. Inst. Riva-Agüero*, 16, 1989, p. 265–302, bibl., tables)

Second chapter of noteworthy senior thesis on titled members of the elite in 18th-century Lima. For annotation of first chapter see *HLAS 54:2407*.

2457 Romero, Fernando. Safari africano y compraventa de esclavos para el Perú: 1412–1818. Lima: Instituto de Estudios Peruanos; Univ. Nacional San Cristóbal de Huamanga, 1994. 275 p.: bibl. (Serie Estudios históricos; 14)

Work marks first attempt by any scholar to write a general history of the slave trade, direct as well as indirect, between Africa and Peru. A solid, albeit somewhat prosaic, study. [MTH]

2458 Sala i Vila, Núria. La constitución de Cádiz y su impacto en el gobierno de las comunidades indígenas en el Virreinato del Perú. (*Bol. Am.*, 33:42/43, 1992/93, p. 51–70)

Examines impact of temporary abolition (1812–14) of legal distinction between the *República de españoles* and the *República de indios*. Absolutists like Virrey Abascal and various *subdelegados* and *intendentes* opposed the constitutional changes, especially those relating to election of municipal officers. The majority of Creoles were none too happy about indigenous peoples being granted electoral equality either, and also did what they could to frustrate reforms. [MTH]

2459 Sánchez Moreno Bayarri, Víctor N.
Arequipa colonial y las fuentes de
su historia: estudio crítico. Lima: Aserprensa,
1987. 409 p.: bibl.
Basic guide to and analysis of published materials (studies and primary sources)
on Arequipa during colonial period. Includes
North American and European contributions
but only if available in Spanish. A welcome
vademecum; however, does not include information on city's archives, libraries, museums, or private collections. [MTH]

2460 Seiner L., Lizardo. Producción agrícola
y comercio inter-zonal: el Partido de
Arica en el período colonial tardío, 1790–
1814. (*Bol. Inst. Riva-Agüero,* 16, 1989,
p. 135–148, bibl., graph, table)
Working paper focuses on agricultural
base of economy of the Partido de Arica during late colonial period, and on the traffic, especially in aguardiente, via mule trains between Arica and the Altiplano. [MTH]

2461 Serrano Mangas, Fernando. Vascos y
extremeños en el Nuevo Mundo dur-
ante el siglo XVII: un conflicto por el poder.
Mérida, Spain: Asamblea de Extremadura,
1993. 116 p.: bibl.
Detailed study examines tumultuous
political and social ramifications of arrival of
Basques in Peru in 1630s, particularly their
conflict with resident Spanish (mainly Extre-
maduran) population. Based largely on archival research. [J. Britton]

2462 Stern, Steve J. Peru's Indian peoples
and the challenge of Spanish conquest:
Huamanga to 1640. 2nd ed. Madison: Univ.
of Wisconsin Press, 1993. 295 p.: bibl., ill., index, map.
Textually the same as the original edition (see *HLAS 46:2728*), but includes a new
prologue, "Paradigms of Conquest: History,
Historiography, and Politics" (annotated in
HLAS 54:1067). An essay placing Stern's
book more specifically within context of Peruvian historiography would have been welcome. [MTH]

2463 Tardieu, Jean-Pierre. Le soldat noir au
Pérou: XVIe-XVIIe siècles. (*Mélanges/
Paris,* 28:2, 1992, p. 87–100)
Outlines history of blacks in armed
forces of Peru from their initial appearance as
slaves of conquistadors through formation of

companies of free blacks in late-17th century.
[MTH]

2464 Travada, Ventura. Suelo de Arequipa
convertido en cielo. Peru: Ignacio Prado
Pastor, 1993. 859 p.: bibl.
Facsimile edition of a holographic mid-
18th-century chronicle of city of Arequipa.
Although relatively easy to decipher, a transcription of this account (heretofore never
published in its entirety) would have been
more useful. Includes a "Nota Introductoria"
by Eusebio Quiroz Paz Soldán as well as a
"Nota del Editor." [MTH]

2465 Unzueta Echevarría, Antonio. Juan Domingo de Zamácola y Jáuregui y su
obra social, cultural y literaria en el Perú,
siglo XVIII. Vitoria, Spain: Servicio Central
de Publicaciones del Gobierno Vasco, 1992.
154 p.: bibl., ill., index. (Amerika eta euskaldunak = América y los vascos; 3)
Original biography of little-known
Basque who spent almost all of his adult life
(45 years) as curate of Cayma (or Caima), in
outskirts of Arequipa. Zamácola not only
tried to improve material and spiritual life
of his parishioners, but also was a prolific
writer. His most important work was an unpublished, apparently lost *Historia general
de Arequipa.* [MTH]

2466 Vega, Juan José. Pizarro en Piura.
Lima?: Instituto Cambio y Desarrollo,
1993. 371 p.: appendices, bibl., ill., index. (Colección S.E.C.)
Detailed history of early years of Piura
consists of five parts: 1) discovery of Piura in
1528 and its incorporation into Spanish Empire; 2) Francisco Pizarro in the Valle de la
Chira; 3) the Spanish foundation and first
weeks of San Miguel de Piura; 4) Francisco Pizarro in the Valle del Piura; and 5) appendices
relating what happened in and to Piura during
next several years. [MTH]

2467 Viforcos Marinas, María Isabel and **Jesús Paniagua Pérez.** El leonés don Cristóbal Vaca de Castro, gobernador y organizador del Perú. Madrid?: s.n., 1991. 151 p.: bibl.,
col. ill., maps.
Biography of first royally appointed
gobernador of Peru. Vaca de Castro defeated
the Almagristas and was responsible for
much of the initial organization of the Vice-

royalty. Well researched and written, handsomely printed and illustrated. [MTH]

Vila Vilar, Luisa. El viaje de Amédée Frézier por la América meridional. See item **2511.**

2468 Zamalloa Armejo, Raúl. La polémica entre el *Mercurio Peruano* y el *Semanario Crítico,* 1791. (*Histórica/Lima,* 17:1, julio 1993, p. 109–118)

Revisionist study focuses on shortlived *Semanario Crítico* (Lima, 1791; 16 nos.), and its editor, Juan Antonio de Olavarrieta, a Franciscan friar. Zamalloa maintains that Olavarrieta was a true liberal, a man of the masses as well as a man of the Enlightenment. [MTH]

ALTO PERU

2469 Acevedo, Edberto Oscar. Las intendencias altoperuanas en el Virreinato del Río de la Plata. Buenos Aires: Academia Nacional de la Historia, 1992. 592 p.: bibl., index. (Col. del quinto centenario del descubrimiento de América; 4)

Detailed study of late 18th-century *intendencias* of Alto Peru (Cochabamba, La Paz, Charcas, Potosí and Puno) includes discussions of political, religious, economic, and social ramifications of institutional reform. This important book is rich in data and based on wide-ranging primary sources. [SMS]

2470 Acevedo, Edberto Oscar. Policía y buen gobierno en Charcas. (*An. Univ. Chile,* 20, agosto 1989, p. 211–231)

Preliminary study of gubernatorial dispositions relating to "good government" and other civic matters is of some interest to specialists. [MTH]

2471 Barragán, Rossana and **Sinclair Thomson.** Los lobos hambrientos y el tributo a Dios: conflictos sociales en torno a los diezmos en Charcas colonial. (*Rev. Andin.,* 11:2, dic. 1993, p. 305–348, appendix, bibl.)

Informative, original working study focuses on inadequately explored aspect of history of Alto Perú: the role of tithes as a source of income for colonial elites and as a source of conflict, not just tension, between conquered and colonizers. Examines several tithe-related rebellions and riots of second half of 1700s. [MTH]

2472 Bidondo, Emilio A. El pronunciamiento del 25 de Mayo de 1809 en la docta Chuquisaca. (*Invest. Ens.,* 40, enero/dic. 1990, p. 191–205, bibl.)

Contains some new data on Sucre's initial "cry for independence." Of interest primarily to specialists and native sons and daughters. [MTH]

2473 Block, David. Mission culture on the upper Amazon: native tradition, Jesuit enterprise & secular policy in Moxos, 1660–1880. Lincoln: Univ. of Nebraska Press, 1994. 240 p.: bibl., ill., index, maps.

Solid history of Moxos (departamento of El Beni since 1842) covers its earliest days as a Jesuit mission province through the rubber boom of 1870s. Examines European settlement and exploitation of the region, as well as what happened to its native peoples under the Jesuits and Spanish/Bolivian rule and exploitation. Exceptionally important contribution to ethnohistory, historical demography, and mission and economic history of northeastern Bolivia during second half of colonial period and early national period. [MTH]

2474 Cañedo-Argüelles Fabrega, Teresa. Potosí: la versión aymara de un mito europeo; la minería y sus efectos en las sociedades andinas del siglo XVII, la provincia de Pacajes. Madrid: Editorial Catriel, 1993. 127 p.: bibl., ill. (Col. Ensayo)

Minor work of limited importance contains some archival data on impact of Potosí and the mita on demography, economy, and society of the *yungas* in 1600s. Originally presented as a licentiate thesis in 1976. [MTH]

2475 Cornblit, Oscar. Power and violence in the colonial city: Oruro from the mining renaissance to the rebellion of Túpac Amaru, 1740–1782. Translated by Elizabeth Ladd Glick. Cambridge; New York: Cambridge Univ. Press, 1995. 230 p.: bibl., ill., index, maps. (Cambridge Latin American studies; 76)

Well-researched and written political history of Oruro covers 40 years prior to and during the great rebellion of 1780–81. Examines and elucidates relationships between public and private life, and the achievement, consolidation, use, and sometimes loss of power. Also adds appreciably to knowledge and understanding of Túpac Amaru rebellion. Many years in the making, a superior and sophisticated study. Chronologically complements Zulawski's work (see item **2487**). [MTH]

Durand Flórez, Luis. El proceso de independencia en el Sur Andino: Cuzco y La Paz, 1805. See item **2398**.

2476 González Rodríguez, María de la Paz. La Universidad de San Francisco Xavier de Chuquisaca, Alto Perú: bibliografía crítica y estado de la cuestión. (*Estud. Hist. Soc. Econ. Am.*, 11, 1994, p. 181–188)

Useful review of limited historiography on the university includes published and unpublished source suggestions that would enable production of a thematically and chronologically more complete history of this multisecular, exceptionally important institution of higher learning. [MTH]

Indigenous revolts in Chiapas and the Andean highlands. See *HLAS 55:57*.

2477 Jackson, Robert H. and José Gordillo Claure. Formación, crisis y transformación de la estructura agraria de Cochabamba: el caso de la hacienda de Paucarpata y de la comunidad del Passo, 1538–1645 y 1872–1929. (*Rev. Indias*, 53:199, sept./dic. 1993, p. 723–760, tables)

Case study of hacienda of Paucarpata and community of Passo in the Valle Bajo of Cochabamba covers two critical junctures: the early history or formation of the hacienda, and impact of changes in government policies and the market on the estate and community in late 19th and early 20th centuries. Also examines relationships between the hacienda and the community, especially conflicts over land and water. Exemplifies many of the points Jackson makes in his book (see item **2478**). [MTH]

2478 Jackson, Robert H. Regional markets and agrarian transformation in Bolivia: Cochabamba, 1539–1960. Albuquerque: Univ. of New Mexico Press, 1994. 283 p.: bibl., ill., index, maps.

Like Brooke Larson's 1988 work, *Colonialism and agrarian transformation in Bolivia: Cochabamba, 1550–1900* (see *HLAS 52:2196*), Jackson's book promises somewhat more than it delivers. Although Jackson really stops in 1929, except for a brief postscript on 1953 agrarian reform, he does provide a major revisionist study of the agrarian history of Cochabamba from Spanish Conquest

through early 20th century. Jackson takes issue with Larson and with Gustavo Rodríguez Ostria who claim that Cochabamba hacienda owners were rentiers. [MTH]

2479 Klein, Herbert S. Demographic structure of peasant populations in colonial Spanish America: the case of Alto Perú in the late 18th century. (*in* El poblamiento de las Américas, *Veracruz, 1992*. Actas. Liège, Belgium: International Union for the Scientific Study of Population, 1992, v. 1, p. 67–104, tables)

Revised study examines hacienda and free community populations of Pacajes and Chulmani, circa 1786. Primarily concerned with "the impact of wealth and land access on the demographic characteristics of the peasant populations . . ." [MTH]

2480 Klein, Herbert S. Haciendas and ayllus: rural society in the Bolivian Andes in the eighteenth and nineteenth centuries. Stanford, Calif.: Stanford Univ. Press, 1993. 230 p.: bibl., ill., index.

Work is not altogether old wine in a new bottle inasmuch as Klein has reworked the demographic and economic data on the province of La Paz, which has been the focus of his work for many years (see *HLAS 44: 2715, HLAS 50:1976, HLAS 54:2439–2440,* and item **2479**). Also, here Klein has added an introduction, conclusion, bibliography, and index. A major contribution to the study of population and rural history, not just of Bolivia, but of Latin America as a whole in the 1700s and 1800s. [MTH]

Lazo García, Carlos. Economía colonial y régimen monetario: Perú, siglos XVI-XIX. v. 1–3. See item **2429**.

2481 Maldini, Gerardo. La celébre polémica dieciochesca entre Francisco de Viedma y el P. Antonio Cumajuncosa. (*Am. Merid.,* 9, oct. 1989, p. 51–57)

Offers tantalizing tidbits from the 35 *legajos* in the Archivo del Convento Francisco de Tarija regarding the "Asunto Viedma," or the prolonged 18th-century dispute between the Gobernador Intendente de Cochabamba and the prefect of the local Franciscans regarding Viedma's proposed plan of government for the missions. One hopes that this piece will encourage a full-scale study of this fascinating polemic. [MTH]

O'Phelan Godoy, Scarlett. Tiempo inmemorial, tiempo colonial: un estudio de casos. See item **2443.**

Porro, Nelly R. El Señor Santiago en tierras del antiguo Incario. See item **2449.**

2482 Romero Romero, Catalina. Tres bibliotecas jesuitas en pueblos de misión: Buenavista, Paila y Santa Rosa, en la región de Moxos. (*Rev. Indias*, 52 : 195/196, mayo/dic. 1992, p. 889–921)

Discusses and inventories monographic holdings of three 18th-century Jesuit missions in the Moxos. Somewhat superficial. [MTH]

Saguier, Eduardo R. La corrupción de la burocracia colonial borbónica y los orígenes del federalismo: el caso del Virreinato del Río de la Plata. See item **2625.**

2483 Sánchez-Concha Barrios, Rafael. Las expediciones descubridoras: la entrada desde Larecaja hasta Tarija, 1539–1540. (*Bol. Inst. Riva-Agüero*, 16, 1989, p. 75–104, bibl., tables, map)

Working paper focuses on a virtually forgotten and apparently not particularly lucrative exploratory expedition of 1539–1540, captained by Pedro de Candia. Reconstructs route taken between the Altiplano and Chiriguano country, and, for 71 members of the expedition, establishes names, origins, and previous experience as conquistadors. [MTH]

2484 Schramm, Raimund. Fronteras y territorialidad: repartición étnica y política colonizadora en Los Charcas, valles de Ayopaya y Mizque. (*Jahrb. Gesch.*, 30, 1993, p. 1–26)

Case study relates efforts by ethnic groups (the Soras and Chuys in the Ayopaya and Mizque valleys, respectively), to preserve some of their preconquest rights and privileges, especially ownership and use of land vis-à-vis dispossession and encroachments by Europeans during and immediately following the Spanish Conquest. [MTH]

2485 Solano, Francisco de. Elites y calidad de vida en Chucuito a mediados del siglo XVII, segun la correspondencia privada de un noble gaditano. (*Histórica/Lima*, 16:2, dic. 1992, p. 221–270, bibl.)

Publishes and analyzes 1652–73 letters of Rafael de Sopranis Boquin de Bocanegra, Barrizzio y Gentil Estopiñán in which Rafael describes his life and activities in Chucuito to his elder brother Simón de Sopranis, Regidor Perpetuo de Cádiz. Given apparent scarcity of private correspondence still in existence, work provides a rare glimpse into daily life of a Spanish merchant and of the social sphere in which he and other privileged members of society functioned in the Altiplano during mid-colonial period. [MTH]

2486 Tandeter, Enrique. Coercion and market: silver mining in colonial Potosí, 1692–1826. Albuquerque: Univ. of New Mexico Press, 1993. 332 p.: bibl., ill., index, map.

Prize-winning English version of *Coacción y mercado* (see *HLAS 54:2451*) complements Peter Bakewell's *Miners of the Red Mountain* and *Silver and entrepreneurship in seventeenth-century Potosí* (see *HLAS 48 : 2766* and *HLAS 52:2188*) and Jeffrey A. Cole's *The Potosí Mita, 1573–1700* (see *HLAS 48:2767*) diachronically and, for the most part, thematically. [MTH]

2487 Zulawski, Ann. They eat from their labor: work and social change in colonial Bolivia. Pittsburgh: Univ. of Pittsburgh Press, 1994. 238 p.: bibl., ill., index, maps. (Pitt Latin American series)

Incorporates and elaborates on author's continuing work on indigenous population, migration, and labor in 1600s and on the related issues of gender and class (see also *HLAS 50:1983, HLAS 52:2202,* and *HLAS 54:2454–2455*). Particularly concerned with major mining center of Oruro, the history of which is now better known thanks to both Zulawski and Cornblit (see item **2475**). Work also examines frontier zone of Pilaya y Paspaya. Important contribution to the economic, ethno-, and social history of the Altiplano. [MTH]

CHILE

2488 Barrientos Grandón, Javier. Los oidores honorarios: notas para su estudio. (*An. Univ. Chile*, 20, agosto 1989, p. 233–247)

Archival research supports this institutional study of the Audiencia of Chile. [J. Britton]

2489 Bascuñán, Pilar. A 400 años de la llegada de los jesuitas a Chile, 1593–1993. Investigación de María Angélica Echenique. Santiago: Editorial Los Andes, 1993. 111 p.: bibl., ill. (some col.).

Unabashedly pro-Jesuit study recapitulates order's activities in Chile from 1593 through their expulsion in 1767 and from their return in 1815 through present. Redeemed to some extent by interesting illustrations. [MTH]

2490 Bengoa, José. Conquista y barbarie: ensayo crítico acerca de la conquista de Chile. Santiago: Ediciones SUR, 1992. 131 p.: bibl. (Col. Estudios históricos)

Provocative essay relates the many ways in which current and past misconceptions of indigenous peoples as barbarians at worst or noble savages at best have affected the history and historiography of Chile, more often than not with tragic consequences for native Americans. Hardly a novel approach, but Bengoa's systematic reexamination of Spanish Conquest and subsequent wars with the Mapuches is insightful. [MTH]

2491 Bravo Lira, Bernardino. El absolutismo ilustrado en Hispanoamérica: Chile, 1760–1860, de Carlos III a Portales y Montt. Santiago: Editorial Universitaria, 1994. 487 p.: bibl., ill., indexes. (Col. Imagen de Chile)

Novel study relates extent to which enlightened despotism prevailed in Chile after as well as before independence: during late colonial period under tutelage of Carlos III from afar, and during early national period under quasi-monarchs Diego Portales and Manuel Montt at home. Engaging and coherent in exposition; insightful and provocative in interpretation; interestingly and tellingly illustrated. Political history at its best. [MTH]

2492 Casanueva, Fernando. Una peste de viruelas en la región de la frontera de guerra hispanoamericana en el Reino de Chile, 1791. (*Rev. Hist./Heredia,* 26, julio/dic. 1992, p. 31–65, maps, table)

Analyzes 1791 outbreak of smallpox among indigenous peoples of southern frontier. Especially concerned with political, military, financial, and missionary facets, and implications of the epidemic for the State, the army, and the Church. Based on coeval sources. [MTH]

2493 Cerda Pincheira, Patricia. La función del Ejército en la frontera del Bío-Bío durante el siglo XVII. (*Rev. Hist./Concepción,* 2:2, 1992, p. 103–113)

Somewhat different essay on functions of the army in the south in 1600s stresses colonizing role of recruits and importance of their mostly indigenous consorts in shaping local society. [MTH]

2494 Flusche, Della M. Church and State in the diocese of Santiago, Chile, 1620–1677: a study of rural parishes. (*CLAHR/Albuquerque,* 4:3, Summer 1995, p. 241–259)

Case study focuses on issue of financial support for rural parishes. Exemplifies ways and means in which royal, regional, and ecclesiastical bureauracies interacted and attempted to reach compromise solutions to problems of jurisdictionally overlapping colonial rule. [MTH]

2495 Flusche, Della M. Doña Isabel Osorio de Cáceres: Chilean matriarch. (*CLAHR/Albuquerque,* 3:1, Winter 1994, p. 39–71)

Detailed reconstruction of life of an early colonial-period *criolla* relates how she and her husband, a high-ranking member of the local *audiencia,* consolidated and expanded their estates and fortunes; how Doña Isabel managed finances independently of her spouse; and how she tempered ownership of black slaves and exploitation of indigenous charges with Christian charity "as she understood it." Significant contribution to history of women in Chile. [MTH]

2496 González Abuter, Tulio and **Ricardo Acuña Casas.** Los Angeles durante la colonia. Concepción, Chile: Editora Aníbal Pinto, 1990. 168 p.: bibl., ill. (some col.), maps.

Detailed, well-researched history of Santa María de los Angeles (prov. of Bío Bío) covers early 18th-century origins through end of colonial period. [MTH]

2497 Grubessich S., Arturo. Esclavitud en Chile durante el siglo XVIII: el matrimonio como una forma de integración social. (*Rev. Hist./Concepción,* 2:2, 1992, p. 115–128, tables)

Examines late-colonial-period efforts of Church and State to humanize slavery by recognizing right of slaves not just to marry but to select their own partners, including free persons, and right of married slaves not to be separated from their spouses. Also quantifies choices of married slaves throughout Chile in 1700s. Finds that a significant number of slaves wedded free persons. [MTH]

2498 Miranda Becerra, Diego. Policía en el Reyno de Chile. Chile: Depto. de Estudios Históricos, Instituto Superior de Ciencias Policiales, Carabineros de Chile, 1992. 286 p.: bibl.

Somewhat prosaic work focuses on history of the police in colonial Chile. However, author, a retired military officer, has done some original research and organized his material thematically as well as chronologically. In the process he sheds light on a topic largely ignored in Chilean historiography. [MTH]

2499 Mora Cañada, Adela. Bibliografía crítica, metodología y estado de la cuestión en la historiografía sobre la universidad colonial en Chile. (*Estud. Hist. Soc. Econ. Am.*, 11, 1994, p. 189–205)

Critically evaluates literature on higher education during colonial period. Concludes that the facts and sources have been established, but argues that it is time to move beyond scientific and institutional history. [MTH]

2500 Muñoz Correa, Juan Guillermo. Documentos relativos a indígenas: Chile Central, siglo XVII. Santiago: Univ. de Santiago de Chile, 1992. 99 p.

Curious compilation reprints miscellaneous documents dating from 1603–1708, having to do in one way or another with indigenous peoples in central Chile. The most interesting is abstract of "Partidas de Enterramientos de Indios en la Doctrina de Chimbarongo" (1665–82). [MTH]

2501 Pacheco Silva, Arnoldo. Una economía de conquista: Concepción, siglo XVI. (*Rev. Hist./Concepción*, 1:1, 1991, p. 25–44, maps)

Highly schematic, thoughtful essay examines economy of Concepción during the Conquest and early colonial period. Focuses on the "peculiar aspects" of what author identifies as an "economy of conquest" (namely, transitory nature of the economy and fragility of emerging new society as well as the precariousness of life). [MTH]

2502 Pinedo, Javier. Reflexiones en torno al Abate Juan Ignacio Molina, la Ilustración, y el *Ensayo sobre la historia natural de Chile.* (*Universum/Talca*, 7, 1992, p. 21–40, bibl. ill. map)

These "reflections" on the thought of Molina (1740–1829) focus especially on ex-

tent to which Molina was abreast of intellectual developments in Europe, particularly as manifested in his 1810 work on natural history of Chile. Prelude to author's larger study (in progress) on history of ideas in the colony during 1700s. [MTH]

2503 Retamal Favereau, Julio; Carlos Celis Atria; and Juan Guillermo Muñoz Correa. Familias fundadoras de Chile, 1540–1600. Santiago: Dirección de Bibliotecas, Archivos y Museos; Zig-Zag; V Centenario Llegada de Cristóbal Colón a América, Comisión Nacional Preparatoria-Chile, 1992. 827 p.: bibl., index.

Study of 71 of Chile's oldest families in Chile summarizes early history and traces descendents of each "founding father" through 1990. Rich in information but skewed by bias, resultant to some extent from subjects studied and sources consulted. According to authors, eight of the founders were *caballeros* (mostly *notorios*) and an additional 36 were *hidalgos*, but only five were clearly *pecheros* or commoners. [MTH]

2504 Sánchez, Raúl. Régimen económico de una parroquia rural: Rauquén, 1664–1794. (*Universum/Talca*, 4:1, primer semestre 1989, p. 37–51, facsims., map, tables)

Detailed analysis of financial history of a *doctrina de indios* or rural parish in southern Chile is wholly original contribution to ecclesiastical and economic history of the colony. [MTH]

2505 Tezanos Pinto Schomburgk, Sergio de. Medicina colonial chilena: siglo XVI. (*Rev. Chil. Hist. Geogr.*, 159, 1991, p. 95–128)

Eminently readable work attempts "to make sense" of history of medicine during early colonial period. Author analyzes and interprets facts and figures all too frequently paraded on their own in the literature. [MTH]

2506 Triviños, Gilberto. La polilla de la guerra en el Reino de Chile. Santiago?: Editorial La Noria, 1994. 208 p.: bibl. (Col. Aguas firmes; 5)

Employs discourse analysis to examine historical literature, some of which Triviños reinterprets as fictionalized history if not historical fiction, on European perception of the Mapuche, especially accounts by missionaries, soldiers, captives, and "squawmen" who knew the people firsthand. Author makes the point that whenever we read histories of "others," we should take into account how culture affects what was/is written, as well as our contemporary interpretation of the written word. [MTH]

2507 Urbina Burgos, Rodolfo. Apuntes sobre encomiendas y encomenderos en Chiloé. (*An. Univ. Chile*, 20, agosto 1989, p. 595–620, tables)

Consists of research notes on grants to indigenous peoples and their beneficiaries in Chiloé during 1600s and first half of 1700s. See also item **2508.** [MTH]

2508 Urbina Burgos, Rodolfo. Notas sobre las tierras de indios de Chile en la segunda mitad del siglo XVIII. (*Notas Hist. Geogr.*, 3, 1992, p. 83–113, tables)

Additional research notes focusing this time on indigenous lands and related issues throughout the colony during second half of 1700s. See also item **2507.** [MTH]

2509 Valenzuela Márquez, Jaime. Aspectos de la devoción barroca en Chile colonial. (*CLAHR/Albuquerque*, 4:3, Summer 1995, p. 261–286)

Interesting essay focuses on popular religious practices in 17th-century Santiago. [MTH]

2510 Vargas Cariola, Juan Eduardo. Estilo de vida en el Ejército de Chile durante el siglo XVII. (*Rev. Indias*, 53:198, mayo/agosto 1993, p. 425–457)

Pioneering essay on heretofore neglected aspect of military history of Chile describes how soldiers lived in 1600s, giving specific information on their housing, dress, diet, leisure activities, camaraderie, and religious practices. Reconstruction of daily military life in colonial period is restricted by unavailability of service and related records. [MTH]

2511 Vila Vilar, Luisa. El viaje de Amedée Frézier por la América meridional. Sevilla, Spain: Diputación Provincial de Sevilla; Consejería de Cultura de la Junta de Andalucía, 1991. 385 p.: bibl., ill., maps. (Publicaciones de la Excm. Diputación Provincial de Sevilla. Sección Historia. V centenario del descubrimiento de América; 12)

Detailed analysis of Frézier's *Relation du voyage de la Mer du Sud aux côtes du Chily et du Perou, fait pendant les années 1712, 1713 & 1714* (Paris, 1716) is liberally interspersed with passages from the work. The most interesting feature of this study is the chapter entitled "Frézier y la Literatura de Viajes." [MTH]

Villalobos R., Sergio. Chile y su historia. See item **2935.**

RIO DE LA PLATA

Acarete, *du Biscay.* La route de l'argent. See item **2224.**

2512 Acevedo, Alba M. Primeros apóstoles indios en la evangelización: algunos casos extraídos de las *Cartas Anuas* de la Compañía de Jesús, 1609–1637. (*Rev. Hist. Am. Argent.*, 16:31/32, 1991/92, p. 87–98)

Stresses role of lay people, including indigenous, in the evangelization process. Author concentrates on Mendoza, using published Jesuit reports (*Cartas Anuas*) as her primary source. [SMS]

2513 Arcondo, Aníbal B. Mortalidad general, mortalidad epidémica y comportamiento de la población de Córdoba durante el siglo XVIII. (*Desarro. Econ.*, 33:129, abril/junio 1993, p. 67–85, graphs, table)

Concentrating on mortality, author discusses three important epidemics in first half of 18th century (1717–20, 1729, 1742). Second half of century was marked by a general improvement in economic and health conditions, the disappearance of mortality crises, and an increasing number of births (baptisms). An interesting article. [SMS]

2514 Arcondo, Aníbal B. El ocaso de una sociedad estamental: Córdoba entre 1700 y 1760. Córdoba, Argentina?: Univ. Nacional de Córdoba, Dirección General de Publicaciones, 1992. 309 p.: bibl., ill.

Important study of Córdoba during first half of 18th century examines both economic situation and social ramifications of the local economy. Arcondo's original dissertation, a study of prices of local and imported goods, while still at the center of this study, has been much amplified. [SMS]

2515 Arias Divito, Juan Carlos. Consumo de tabaco y real hacienda. (*in* Estudios en homenaje a Don Claudio Sánchez-Albornoz en sus 90 años: anexos de *Cuadernos de Historia de España.* Buenos Aires: Instituto de Historia de España, 1990, v. 6, p. 3–16, bibl., tables)

Author continues his work on the Dirección General de Tabacos y Naipes, concentrating here on tobacco tastes in different regions of the Viceroyalty. See also items **2516** and **2544**. [SMS]

2516 Arias Divito, Juan Carlos. Notas sobre el consumo de tabaco en la Intendencia de Salta, 1779–1809. (*Res Gesta*, 30, julio/dic. 1991, p. 5–39, table)

Arias Divito reviews the report of Francisco de Paula Sanz, first Director General of the tobacco monopoly (Real Renta de Tabacos y Naipes del Virreinato del Río de la Plata), and follows with a region-by-region discussion of consumption patterns. In general, Sanz was quite accurate in his observations and predictions; tobacco was widely consumed by both sexes, although there were regional variations in the preferred product. See also items **2515** and **2544**. [SMS]

2517 Armando, Adriana Beatriz. Un acercamiento al Chaco Austral a mediados del siglo XVIII: el relato de Dobrizhoffer y los conflictos fronterizos. (*Anu. IEHS*, 9, 1994, p. 215–226)

In this reading of Martin Dobrizhoffer's *Historia de los abipones* as a frontier narrative, author pays special attention to the 18th-century Jesuit's presentation of space, war, and chiefship among the Chaco peoples. For English version of Dobrizhoffer's work, see *HLAS 34:2322*. [SMS]

2518 Asenjo Sedano, Carlos. El ánima del maestre: la fundación de Buenos Ayres por los andaluces. Sevilla, Spain: Muñoz Moya y Montraveta, 1993. 251 p. (Serie Narrativa)

This "biography" of the *adelantado* Pedro de Mendoza, founder of the first ill-fated city of Buenos Aires, is really a historical novel, lacking any mention of sources; as such it raises interesting questions as to where history ends and literary invention begins. [SMS]

2519 Avellá Cháfer, Francisco. La biblioteca del primer obispo de Buenos Aires, Fray Pedro de Carranza. (*Invest. Ens.*, 40, enero/dic. 1990, p. 235–238)

Brief article reviews personal library of Carranza, a Carmelite monk and first bishop of Buenos Aires. Not surprisingly, the 253 volumes owned by the bishop in 1628 were overwhelmingly biblical commentaries and books of sermons. [SMS]

2520 Avonto, Luigi. "La Sierra de la Plata" y otros ensayos: historias de italianos en el Nuevo Mundo, 1492–1550. Montevideo: Ediciones El Galeón, 1993. 235 p.: bibl., ill., maps. (Col. Historia ; 6)

Series of articles on the "discovery" of America and the Río de la Plata region stresses contribution of Italian statesmen, captains, pilots, and seamen. Avonto credits the Italians with fomenting myth of 16th-century America as a land of limitless riches. [SMS]

2521 Avonto, Luigi. Sulla scia di Vespucci: il viaggio al Río de la Plata della *Newen Zeytung Auss Presill Landt*. (*Quaderni/São Paulo*, 4, giugno 1993, p. 79–122)

Discusses "probable" 1501 voyage of the Florentine Amérigo Vespucci to Río de la Plata coast, based on an analysis of the *Newen Zeytung auss Presillg Landt* (1514). [SMS]

2522 Baldó i Lacomba, Marc. La enseñanza de los *saberes útiles* en el Río de la Plata, 1790–1810. (*Estud. Hist. Soc. Econ. Am.*, 9, 1992, p. 423–445)

Article on educational aspects of the Bourbon Reforms in the Río de la Plata concentrates on creation of new institutions of learning. Author focuses on schools of the Consulado de Comercio de Buenos Aires, specifically those intended to teach technical subjects to the middle sectors of society: the Escuela de Náutica, La Academia de Geometría y Dibujo, and the projected Escuela de Química. Author finds that the reforms were marked by excellent projects but sparse results due to feeble funding by the Crown and weak local planning. [SMS]

2523 Baldó i Lacomba, Marc. La universidad colonial hispanoamericana, 1538–1810: bibliografía crítica, metodología y estado de la cuestión; el Río de la Plata. (*Estud. Hist. Soc. Econ. Am.*, 11, 1994, p. 207–229, bibl.)

Interesting overview is followed by a lengthy bibliography of historical work on Univ. de Córdoba and the Colegio de San Carlos. Author also summarizes results of his research on history of these institutions after expulsion of the Jesuits, stressing increased tension between the university and the *cabildo* as well as weakened financial state of the major institutions of higher education in the Viceroyalty. [SMS]

2524 Barreneche, Osvaldo. "Esos torpes dezeos:" delitos y desviaciones sexuales en Buenos Aires, 1760–1810. (*in* Estudios de historia colonial. La Plata, Argentina: Univ. Nacional de La Plata, 1993, p. 29–45)

Presents analysis, much influenced by Foucault, of discourse involving sexual crimes, primarily rape. Author looks at social groups involved, the judicial process, major lines of defense, and punishment. [SMS]

2525 Barros Franco, José Miguel. Rey don Felipe: plano de una fundación hispana en el Estrecho de Magallanes. (*Rev. Hist. Naval*, 11:40, 1993, p. 27–40, ill., photos)

Discusses map drawn up in 1584 that, according to author, shows location of ill-fated Patagonian settlement of Nombre de Jesús. The settlement, undertaken by Sarmiento de Gamboa, was supported by the Crown as a deterrent to English incursion in the Straits of Magellan. [SMS]

2526 Battista, Susana and Claudia Ríos. Las relaciones hispano-indígenas en la frontera bonaerense, 1580–1630. (*in* Estudios de historia colonial. La Plata, Argentina: Univ. Nacional de La Plata, 1993, p. 47–87, bibl.)

In keeping with general revision of history of Spanish-indigenous relationships along the Buenos Aires frontier, authors examine period following successful re-founding of the city. They find that periods of warfare alternated with those of peace, determined by Spanish need for labor; that while the indigenous peoples resisted subjugation, they did not resort to raiding Spanish settlements; and that the missions failed because they did not adjust to indigenous values and culture. [SMS]

2527 Bazán, Armando Raúl. El mestizaje americano y la formación de la sociedad criolla: el caso especial del Tucumán. (*Invest. Ens.*, 42, enero/dic. 1992, p. 217–238)

In reaction to what author sees as a rebirth of the Black Legend, he underscores importance of social, cultural, and racial *mestizaje* in America and, more specifically, in Tucumán. [SMS]

2528 Blumers, Teresa. La contabilidad en las reducciones guaraníes. Asunción: Centro de Estudios Antropológicos, Univ. Católica, 1992. 345 p.: appendices, bibl. (Biblioteca paraguaya de antropología; 15)

Interesting study based on 150 years of Jesuit fiscal accounts from their Guaraní missions provides important data on tribute, population, production, consumption, circulation of currencies, and profit. Author reproduces several accounts in her appendices. [SMS]

2529 Boleda, Mario. Demografía histórica del noroeste argentino: dinámica demográfica hacia fines del siglo XVIII. Salta, Argentina: Grupo de Estudios Socio-Demográficos, 1992. 42 p.: bibl., graphs, tables. (Cuadernos del Gredos; 15)

Demographic study based on three nominative lists of population uses stable models to generate birth, death, and fertility estimates. [SMS]

2530 Bruno, Cayetano. Gobernantes beneméritos de la evangelización en el Río de la Plata y el Tucumán: época española. Rosario, Argentina: Ediciones Didascalia, 1993. 196 p.: bibl. (Col. 500 años; 11)

Brief chapters on 28 governors from 16th to 18th centuries who are deemed to have been particularly active in furthering evangelization of indigenous peoples. [SMS]

2531 Bruno, Cayetano. Las reducciones jesuíticas de indios guaraníes, 1609–1818. Rosario, Argentina: Ediciones Didascalia, 1991. 170 p.: bibl., col. ill., maps.

Overview of the Jesuit Guaraní missions is written by the pre-eminent Argentine church historian. Bruno sees Jesuits in a most positive light, commending both their spiritual accomplishments as well as their work in fending off Portuguese expansion. Expulsion of the Order is seen as nothing less than the work of Satan. [SMS]

2532 Campagna Caballero, Ernesto. La población esclava en ciudades puertos del Río de la Plata: Montevideo y Buenos Aires. (*in* Congresso sobre a História da População da América Latina, *1st, Ouro Preto, Brazil, 1989*. Actas. São Paulo: Fundação SEADE, 1990, p. 218–225, bibl., graphs, tables)

Demographic analysis of slave population of Buenos Aires and Montevideo is unfortunately marred by a dense and pretentious literary style replete with dependency jargon. [SMS]

2533 Campos, Presentació; Vicente Genovès; and Emili Gómez Nadal. El valencià Jaume Rasquí, governador del Plata, 1557–1559. Introducció i edició de Manuel Ardit. Pròleg d'Alfons Cucó. Valencia, Spain: Generalitat Valenciana, 1987. 150 p.: bibl.

Reprints Gómez Nadal's 1931 article concerning a mid-16th-century attempt by the Valencian Jaime Rasquin, a member of the Irala expedition, to buy the governorship of the region. Volume also contains Santoya *relación* detailing the case and other related documents. [SMS]

2534 Canedo, Mariana. La ganadería de mulas en la campaña bonaerense: una aproximación a las estrategias de producción y comercialización en la segunda mitad del siglo XVIII. (*in* Huellas en la tierra: indios, agricultores y hacendados en la pampa bonaerense. Recopilación de Raúl Mandrini y Andrea Reguera. Tandil, Argentina: Univ. Nacional del Centro, IEHS, 1993, p. 147–160, appendix, graph, table)

Study based on analysis of 18 estate inventories from Partido de los Arroyos finds that both large and small landowners were engaged in diversified ranching in which sheep, mules, and horses accounted for up to 40 percent of their animal capital. An interesting article. [SMS]

2535 Canedo, Mariana. Propiedades, propietarios y ocupantes: la tierra y la familia en la campaña de Buenos Aires; "el Pago de Los Arroyos," 1600–1750. (*Bol. Inst. Hist. Ravignani*, 7, primer semestre 1993, p. 7–29, graphs)

Studies land circulation in one zone of rural Buenos Aires. Author finds that up to 1,720 large tracts of land passed intact from generation to generation. After 1750, increased colonization and creation of a market for land was reflected in sale of land to non-family members. [SMS]

2536 Cañedo-Argüelles Fabrega, Teresa. Principios de ecología cultural en la configuración de un territorio de frontera: la Mesopotamia Argentina en el siglo XVII. (*Estud. Ibero-Am./Porto Alegre*, 17:2, dez. 1991, p. 73–91, map)

Looks at ecological, demographic, and geographical factors that affected Spanish colonization patterns in the Corrientes-Missiones-Entre Rios area. [SMS]

2537 Cañedo-Argüelles Fabrega, Teresa. La provincia de Corrientes en los siglos XVI y XVII: un modelo de colonización en el Alto Paraná. Madrid: Consejo Superior de Investigaciones Científicas, Centro de Estudios Históricos, Depto. de Historia de América, 1988. 257 p.: bibl., col. ill., maps. (Col. Tierra nueva e cielo nuevo; 23. V centenario del descubrimiento de América)

Interesting study of isolated region of the Río de la Plata concentrates on 16th and 17th centuries. Author looks at the major precolumbian indigenous cultures of the region, role of Church and State in the European colonization process, and formation of both urban and rural mission societies. [SMS]

2538 Cañedo-Argüelles Fabrega, Teresa. Las reducciones en el Alto Paraná. (*in* De palabra y obra en el Nuevo Mundo. v. 2, Encuentros interétnicos. Edición de Miguel León-Portilla *et al.* Madrid: Siglo Veintiuno Editores, 1992, p. 195–216, table)

Work examines inter-ethnic relationships during first 100 years of Spanish colonization in region of Alto Paraná. Author compares acculturation process in Asunción with that of Corrientes, pointing out that in latter region the *reducciones* imposed a strict separation of the indigenous from the Spanish population, thus limiting process of racial and cultural mestizaje. [SMS]

2539 Carrazzoni, José Andrés. Félix de Azara: peripecias de un sabio. (*Todo es Hist.*, 329, dic. 1994, p. 8–42, bibl., ill., map, photos)

Rather lengthy article in a popular history magazine focuses on Enlightenment scientist and social observer who spent 20 years studying the flora, fauna, and inhabitants of Río de la Plata. [SMS]

2540 Cartas anuas de la Provincia Jesuítica del Paraguay, 1632 a 1634. Introducción de Ernesto J.A. Maeder. Buenos Aires: Academia Nacional de la Historia, 1990. 229 p.: ill., indexes.

Contains transcription of report sent from Jesuit province of Paraguay (including Tucumán, Buenos Aires and Paraguay) to Rome covering activities in their *colegios, reducciones,* and missions. [SMS]

2541 Celton, Dora Estela. Fecundidad de las esclavas en la Córdoba colonial. (*Rev. Junta Prov. Hist. Córdoba*, 15, 1993, p. 29–48, graphs, tables)

Overview of growth of slave population in late 18th-century Córdoba is followed by analysis of slave women's fertility using "own-children estimates."

2542 Celton, Dora Estela. La mortalidad y fecundidad en los siglos XVIII y XIX en ciertas regiones de la Argentina. (*in* El poblamiento de las Américas, *Veracruz, 1992.* Actas. Liège, Belgium: International Union for the Scientific Study of Population, 1992, v. 2, p. 177–194, bibl., tables)

Demographic study relates mortality and fertility in city of Córdoba and other regions from 1778 to mid-19th century. Author uses various techniques of indirect estimate ("retrospective projection," "growth equations," and "own-children estimates") to calculate average life span and fertility rates. [SMS]

2543 Colombres, Carlos Luque. Los protectores de naturales en Córdoba. (*Rev. Junta Prov. Hist. Córdoba*, 15, 1993, p. 91–111)

One of the last articles by the late Cordoban historian finds origin of 16th-century idea of protecting indigenous peoples in a biblical injunction against oppression. Injunction led to creation of a cabildo officer charged specifically with preventing abuse of indigenous peoples. [SMS]

2544 Cooney, Jerry W. La Dirección General de la Real Renta de Tabacos and the decline of the royal tobacco monopoly in Paraguay, 1779–1800. (*CLAHR/Albuquerque*, 1: 1, Fall 1992, p. 101–115)

Author traces decline of the royal tobacco monopoly in Paraguay to 1789, when a heavy inventory of Paraguayan product caused a far-reaching and ultimately disastrous change in policy. See also items **2516** and **2515.** [SMS]

2545 Cooney, Jerry W. Fraude y burócratas: tabaco y Paraguay, 1789–1790. (*Parag. Sociol.*, 29:85, sept./dic. 1992, p. 29–40)

In another strong article by the dean of American scholars of colonial Paraguay, Cooney argues that Bourbon Reforms degenerated into bureaucratic routine and corruption by

1790s, and uses example of the tobacco monopoly in Paraguay to prove his point. [SMS]

2546 Cruz, Josefina. La gesta heróica de los fundadores de Córdoba. Buenos Aires: R.J. Pellegrini Impressiones, 1993. 176 p.: bibl., ill.

A romanticized biography recounts life of doña Luisa Martel de los Ríos, widow of Sebastián Garcilaso de la Vega and wife of Jerónimo Luis de Cabrera. Doña Luisa accompanied her husband, named governor and *adelantado* of Tucumán by Viceroy Toledo, as Cabrera conquered new territory and founded Spanish cities, Córdoba among them. Uses much literary invention, but at least provides some bibliography. [SMS]

2547 Dalcin, Ignacio. Em busca de uma "terra sem males": as reduções jesuíticas guaranis, evangelização e catequese nos Sete Povos das Missões. Porto Alegre, Brazil: Edições EST; Palmarinca, 1993. 159 p.: bibl., ill., maps.

Study of Jesuit missions with special attention to the Sete Povos area is preceeded by a brief but interesting historiographical essay. Author attempts to look at the missions through Guarani eyes, underlining experience, religious life, and doctrinal understanding of the indigenous people. [SMS]

2548 Damianovich, Alejandro A. Las anotaciones del diario de Juan Francisco Aguirre sobre el curato y pueblo del Rosario, 1796. (*Res Gesta*, 30, julio/dic. 1991, p. 135–157)

Discusses information on town of Rosario contained in unpublished portion of the journal of Juan Francisco Aguirre. According to author, Aguirre, who visited, lived in, and traveled through the region between 1781–1801, provides fairly accurate information about the region. [SMS]

2549 Del Guayra a las Falkland: memoriales olvidados del siglo XVIII. Recopilación de Edith Vidal Rossi. Canelones, Uruguay: Tall. Gráf. Vanguardia, 1988. 96 p.: bibl., ill., maps.

Four relatively little-known texts report on state of Río de la Plata region at end of 18th century. Included are two bishops' reports on entire region (1772 and 1776), and two reports written by the Count of Liniers to Floridablanca on the Maldonado region (draft and finished product). The compiler concludes with discussion taken from 19th-century historian Francisco Javier Brabo on Spanish-Portuguese territorial settlements. [SMS]

2550 Durán Estragó, Margarita. The Reductions. (*in* The Church in Latin America, 1492–1992. Edited by Enrique Dussel. Kent, England: Burns & Oats; Maryknoll, N.Y.: Orbis Books, 1992, p. 351–362, bibl., facsim.)

Overview of the *reducciones* in America concentrates on those of Paraguay. Author stresses development of the idea of "reducing" the indigenous peoples so as to evangelize them, as well as changes in missionizing philosophy. [SMS]

2551 Fernández, Ariosto. La orden Franciscana en Montevideo y su labor docente, 1767–1814. (*Hoy Hist.*, 11:62, marzo/abril 1994, p. 30–40, photos)

Author discusses attempts by Franciscans to provide primary and secondary education in Montevideo after expulsion of the Jesuits. [SMS]

2552 Fernández, Juan Patricio. Relación historial de las misiones de indios chiquitos que en el Paraguay tienen los padres de la Compañía de Jesús, 1726. Presentación y notas de Daniel J. Santamaría. Jujuy, Argentina: Univ. Nacional de Jujuy, Centro de Estudios Indígenas y Coloniales, 1994. 229 p. (Biblioteca de Historia y Antropología; 2)

Little known 18th-century work relates history of Jesuit missions among the Chiquitos. Useful introduction and notes by Santamaría. An important ethnohistorical as well as mission history source and the only currently available edition of this work. [MTH]

2553 Fernández Alexander de Schorr, Adela. Ibatín y la Thoma: orígenes de San Miguel de Tucumán; vicisitudes de una ciudad. San Miguel de Tucumán, Argentina: Ediciones Estrella Federal, Secretaría de Post-Grado de la U.N.T., 1993. 64 p.: bibl., ill.

Brief study outlines multiple problems confronting 16th-century founders of the city of San Miguel de Tucumán. Because of hostility of the indigenous population, the city was repeatedly attacked and had to be moved. Author seems more intent on detailing the moving of religious images than on relating details to any larger picture of conquest and expansion. [SMS]

2554 Ferreyra, María del Carmen. El matrimonio en Córdoba durante el siglo XVII: algunas referencias demográficas. (*Cuad. Hist./Córdoba*, 1, 1994, p. 5–21, bibl., tables)

Important article examines marriage patterns in 17th-century Córdoba. Author combines parish register information with material culled from dowry papers and wills to study rates of marriage, nativity, location (urban vs. rural), and race. Ferreyra's work not only suggests degree to which parish records underestimated marriages; it also points to importance of male in-migration and its possible link to economic conditions. [SMS]

2555 Ganson, Barbara. "Like children under wise parental sway:" passive portrayals of the Guaraní Indians in European literature and *The Mission.* (*CLAHR/Albuquerque*, 3:4, Fall 1994, p. 399–422, appendix)

A discussion of the image of the Guarani and the Jesuit misions in Paraguay constructed by European authors from Voltaire to the film writers of *The Mission.* The author argues that these images responded more to European political agendas than to Guarani realities. [SMS]

2556 Garavaglia, Juan Carlos. La agricultura del trigo en las estancias de la campaña bonaerense: tecnología y empresas productivas. (*in* Huellas en la tierra: indios, agricultores y hacendados en la pampa bonaerense. Recopilación de Raúl Mandrini y Andrea Reguera. Tandil, Argentina: Univ. Nacional del Centro, IEHS, 1993, p. 91–120, graphs, tables)

In this additional piece in the author's revisionist view of the *porteño* countryside, Garavaglia argues that wheat was not produced solely by small farmers, but that the crop played an important part in the production cycle of *estancias*. Furthermore, according to author, wheat cultivation complemented cattle raising. Using estate inventories, Garavaglia concludes that many *estancias* were in fact dedicated to mixed farming. [SMS]

2557 Garavaglia, Juan Carlos. Las chacras y quintas de Buenos Aires: ejido y campaña, 1750–1815. (*in* Huellas en la tierra: indios, agricultores y hacendados en la pampa bonaerense. Recopilación de Raúl Mandrini y Andrés Reguera. Tandil, Argentina: Univ. Nacional del Centro, IEHS, 1993, p. 121–146, graphs, tables)

Using estate inventories as well as tithe records, Garavaglia discusses a range of smaller agricultural properties in the Buenos Aires countryside. He argues that there was a yeomanry class in the rural regions with considerable investments in slaves, oxen, carts and agricultural produce. [SMS]

2558 Garavaglia, Juan Carlos. De la carne al cuero: los mercados para los productos pecuarios; Buenos Aires y su campaña, 1700–1825. (*Anu. IEHS*, 9, 1994, p. 61–96, bibl., graphs, tables)

Supplementing his earlier study of commercialization of wheat, flour, and bread (*Bol. Inst. Hist. Ravignani*, 3:4, 1991, p. 7–29), Garavaglia now concentrates on meat (and to a lesser degree, hides). This important article looks at questions of market structure, supply and demand, per capita consumption, and prices, underlining how creation of meat-salting plants (*saladeros*) fundamentally changed the market. [SMS]

2559 Garavaglia, Juan Carlos and **Raúl Fradkin.** Hombres y mujeres de la colonia. Buenos Aires: Editorial Sudamericana, 1992. 279 p.: bibl., ill., maps. (Sudamericana joven. Ensayo; 4)

Series of dramatic vignettes, written in semi-novelistic form, illustrate colonial life throughout Río de la Plata area. Authors include brief chapters on issues as wide ranging as the reception of the Viceroy, a rural female weaver, an urban slave, and migrant workers. Book represents interesting attempt to use history of everyday life and at least some everyday people to relate colonial history to college and secondary students. [SMS]

2560 Garavaglia, Juan Carlos. Los labradores de San Isidro, siglos XVIII-XIX. (*Desarro. Econ.*, 32:128, enero/marzo 1993, p. 513–542, graphs, tables)

Examines agrarian landowning systems in San Isidro during late colonial and early national periods. Garavaglia repeats that region had large number of small farmers who were more than simple peasants; that agriculture, especially wheat farming, continued to be important in the region; and that slave labor was a considerable factor in production of wheat. [SMS]

2561 García Belsunce, César A. Natalidad y bautismos en el pago de Magdalena, 1738–1765. (*Invest. Ens.*, 42, enero/dic. 1992, p. 269–289, graphs, tables)

As part of a larger study of population of the *pago* of La Magdalena in 18th century, author studies births with special attention to race and legitimacy. Study is important since it is the first to examine certain aspects of rural population patterns in the Buenos Aires region. [SMS]

2562 Gelman, Jorge. Los caminos del mercado: campesinos, estancieros y pulperos en una región del Río de la Plata colonial. (*LARR*, 28:2, 1993, p. 89–118, bibl., tables)

One of the foremost historians of the late colonial countryside in the Río de la Plata examines relationships of both large and small producers in the Colonia-Soriano region. He finds that both types of producers were closely tied to the market; and that the high degree of dependency on commercializing production put small producers in a weak position vis-à-vis market forces and local middlemen. [SMS]

2563 Gelman, Jorge. Formas de explotación agraria y estructura de la población en un medio rural colonial: el Río de la Plata a fines del siglo XVIII. (*in* El poblamiento de las Américas, *Veracruz, 1992.* Actas. Liège, Belgium: International Union for the Scientific Study of Population, 1992, v. 1, p. 105–122, bibl., tables)

Demographic study of several rural zones of the Banda Oriental (Soriano, Colonia and Paysandú) at end of 18th century suggests that transformation from a zone of small farms to larger cattle ranches affected the sexual composition of the population. [SMS]

2564 Gelman, Jorge. La historia agraria del Río de la Plata colonial: balance y perspectivas de las investigaciones recientes. (*in* Colección nuestra patria es América: historia económica de América Latina. Edición de Jorge Núñez Sánchez. Quito: Editora Nacional, 1992, v. 7, p. 61–80)

Gives brief, interesting overview of revisionist approach to *porteño* rural history, which has stressed regional variation, mixed agriculture and ranching, small farmers, and *estancieros*. Reviews those topics to which a new literature has made important contributions, and suggests topics that remain to be studied. [SMS]

2565 Gelman, Jorge. Mundo rural y mercados: una estancia y las formas de circulación mercantil en la campaña rioplatense tardíocolonial. (*Rev. Indias*, 52:195/196, mayo/dic. 1992, p. 477–514, tables)

Continuation of Gelman's work is based on records from the Estancia de las Vacas. Here author analyzes how the *estancia* attempted to maximize its profits, looking at both the commercial relationship between the *estancia* and the urban market, and its attempts to pay its workers in goods rather than cash. An interesting and detailed study. [SMS]

2566 González Rodríguez, Adolfo Luis. Encomienda y propiedad de la tierra en Córdoba durante los siglos XVI y XVII. (*Rev. Complut. Hist. Am.*, 18, 1992, p. 143–153, appendix)

Article is another contribution to the great *encomienda-hacienda* debate. Author agrees with Chevalier, arguing that in Córdoba the granting of *encomiendas* of indigenous peoples to Spanish settlers in effect also gave the Spaniards rights to the land on which the indigenous population lived. [SMS]

2567 Gotta, Claudia. Una aproximación histórica al problema del ganado como *moneda* en Norpatagonia, siglos XVIII-XIX. (*Anu. IEHS*, 8, 1993, p. 13–26, bibl.)

Over-theorized discussion, chock-full of quotes from anthropological, economic, and historical literature, repeats thesis that cattle and captives were used as mediums of exchange among the indigenous societies of the *pampas*. [SMS]

2568 Gould, Eduardo Sergio. La ilusión de los metales: experiencias mineras en Córdoba hacia mediados del siglo XVIII. (*in* Historia de los argentinos. Argentina: Asociación de Fabricantes Argentinos de Coca-Cola, 1990, p. 99–149, tables)

Examines an ill-fated attempt to mine gold in Córdoba sierras in 1748–49. Author attributes the failure to insufficient capital investment and low levels of technology. [SBS]

2569 Gresores, Gabriela and **Carlos M. Birocco.** Arrendamientos desalojos y subordinación campesina: elementos para el análisis de la campaña bonaerense en el siglo XVIII. Buenos Aires: F.G. Cambeiro, 1992. 109 p.: bibl. (Col. Estudios coloniales y de la independencia americana)

Slim volume consists of two articles. The first, by Gresores, is based on two 1799 legal cases involving squatters in San Vicente; the second, by Birocco, analyzes land rental contracts between 1700–55. Gresores, using Marxist terminology, sees colonial large landowners oppressing the landless peasants, thus creating a landless proletariat and class antagonism in colonial rural society. Birocco, less ideological, stresses the mechanisms that landowners used to preserve control of their land. Details of 22 rental contracts are included. [SMS]

2570 Gresores, Gabriela and **Gabriela Martínez Dougnac.** En torno a la economía y la sociedad rioplatenses en el siglo XVIII: debates historiográficos actuales. (*Rev. Ciclos*, 2:3, 1992, p. 173–195)

Critique of articles by Garavaglia, Gelman, and Marquiegui is written by their most vocal Marxist opponents. In this on-going debate about nature of *porteño* rural society in 18th century, authors emphasize oppression and class antagonism, stressing that laborers were coerced into indenture while small farmers were subject to onerous sharecropping arrangements. [SMS]

Guanes de Laíno, Rafaela. Familias sin tierra en Paraguay. See *HLAS 55:4989*.

2571 Gullón Abao, Alberto José. Las reducciones del este de la provincia del Tucumán en la segunda mitad del siglo XVIII, bajo la administración franciscana. (*Arch. Ibero-Am.*, 52:205/208, 1992, p. 255–276, graphs, map, table)

Study looks at Jesuit *reducciones* after they passed into Franciscan hands, this time in Tucumán. Concludes that although the Franciscans were confronted with grave problems including hostile indigenous populations and a seriously damaged mission infrastructure, they were generally successful in defending the frontier. [SMS]

2572 Las Indias españolas: crónicas del descubrimiento y el Uruguay primitivo. Montevideo: Ediciones de la Banda Oriental; Instituto de Cooperación Iberoamericana, 1992. 139 p.: bibl.

Contains series of postmodern literary essays on early chronicles of discovery of America, with a few "texts" thrown in for good measure. Among other topics discussed is *otredad*.

2573 Jornadas sobre Historia Rioplatense en el Período Hispánico, *Buenos Aires and Colonia, Argentina, 1992.* Ponencias. v. 1–2. Buenos Aires: Univ. del Museo Social Argentino, 1993. 2 v.: bibl.

Two volumes contain short papers that draw on traditional *rioplatense* bibliography, adding some details to history of local institutions or individuals. Vol. 2 improves slightly on Vol. 1 in that it includes pagination as well as text of a 1757 Montevideo census. [SMS]

Kleinpenning, Jan M.G. Peopling the Purple Land: a historical geography of rural Uruguay, 1500–1915. See *HLAS 55:2619.*

2574 Kurchan, Mario D. Historia postal del Río de la Plata hacia la época de las invasiones inglesas = River Plate postal history: period, 1800/1810. Argentina: M.D.K., 1992. 72 p.: bibl., facsims., maps.

English-Spanish edition, which, under the guise of studying the English invasions, presents bits and pieces on mail service before and after the invasions. Illustrated with facsimile copies of various documents. [SMS]

2575 Lacombe, Robert. Guaranis et jésuites: un combat pour la liberté, 1610–1707. Préface de Jean Lacouture; Diffusion Karthala, 1993. 301 p.: bibl., ill., index, maps.

Interesting general study of Jesuit missions draws heavily on 16th-, 17th-, and 18th-century published sources. Lacombe sees seeds of political independence in mission autonomy. [SMS]

2576 Laguarda Trías, Rolando A. La carta más antigua escrita en territorio uruguayo. Montevideo: Impr. Militar, 1992. 116 p.: bibl., ill.

Facsimile edition and transcription of a lengthy letter written by Luis Ramírez, crew member in the Sebastian Cabot expedition, describing his experiences from the departure from Spain in 1526 to 1528. [SMS]

2577 Lorandi, Ana María and **Juan Pablo Ferreiro.** De la crisis a la estabilidad: la sociedad nativa en Tucumán a fines del siglo XVII y comienzos del XVIII. (*Mem. Am.,* 1, 1991, p. 57–101, bibl., map, table)

Analyzes several demographic sources with the goal of understanding the patterns of control over, dispersion of, and tribute exacted from indigenous population after its de-

feat in the lengthy Calchaquí wars. Article contains a wealth of information on various ethnic groups and *encomiendas* in the region. [SMS]

2578 Maeder, Ernesto J.A. Un debate tardío sobre la libertad de los guaraníes de misiones. (*Hisp. Sacra,* 46:93, enero/junio 1994, p. 191–205)

Arguing that Guarani missions were not demographically stable, but rather constantly affected by internal and external factors, Maeder summarizes much of his recent work by dividing missions' demographic history into five distinct stages. An interesting article. [SMS]

2579 Maeder, Ernesto J.A. Las misiones de Guaraníes: historia demográfica y conflictos con la sociedad colonial, 1641–1807. (*in* Congresso sobre a História da População da América Latina, *1st, Ouro Preto, Brazil, 1989.* Actas. São Paulo: Fundação SEADE, 1990, p. 41–50, bibl., graph, tables)

Considers the various debates about treatment of the Guarani following expulsion of the Jesuits, including the discussion in Spain during the first decade of 19th century. Maeder believes that it was Belgrano who, paradoxically, finally implemented the liberal solutions of Spanish Enlightenment thinkers. [SMS]

2580 Mallo, Silvia. Hombres, mujeres y honor: injurias, calumnias y difamación en Buenos Aires, 1770–1840; un aspecto de la mentalidad vigente. (*in* Estudios de historia colonial. La Plata, Argentina: Univ. Nacional de La Plata, 1993, p. 9–26)

Examines ways in which gender, social class, and race shaped and defined insults to an individual's honor and defamation of character. Also discusses which actions and insults were considered offensive, and the punishments exacted. [SMS]

Mallo, Silvia. Justicia, divorcio, alimentos y malos tratos en El Río de la Plata, 1766–1857. See item **3063.**

2581 Mallo, Silvia. La libertad en el discurso del Estado, de amos y esclavos, 1780–1830. (*Rev. Hist. Am.,* 112, julio/dic. 1991, p. 121–146, bibl.)

Interesting article, based primarily on judicial cases, reviews ideas and attitudes towards freeing of slaves during late colonial and early independence periods in Argentina. Mallo suggests that during independence period, slaveowners attempted to limit freedom or at least redefine it within servitude, while slaves demonstrated an increased willingness to fight for freedom. [SMS]

2582 Mandrini, Raúl J. Guerra y paz en la frontera bonaerense durante el siglo XVIII. (*Cienc. Hoy*, 4:23, marzo/abril 1993, p. 27–35, bibl., ill., maps, photos)

Overview of indigenous-Spanish relations along 18th-century Buenos Aires frontier stresses that periods of war alternated with those of peace, and that both war and peace were economic strategies, as a commercial interdependence between both sides of the border developed. [SMS]

2583 Mandrini, Raúl J. Indios y fronteras en la área pampeana, siglos XVI-XIX: balance y perspectivas. (*Anu. IEHS*, 7, 1992, p. 59–73, appendix)

Reviews recent historical, ethnohistorical, and archeological work on indigenous peoples of Pampas region up to 19th century. Mandrini stresses revisions of the more traditional historiography that tended to see the Pampas as an empty space and its indigenous inhabitants as savage nomads. [SMS]

2584 Mariluz Urquijo, José María. Francisco Bruno de Rivarola, feminista virreinal. (*in* Estudios en homenaje a Don Claudio Sánchez-Albornoz en sus 90 años: anexos de *Cuadernos de Historia de España*. Buenos Aires: Instituto de Historia de España, 1990, v. 6, p. 113–125)

Stressing that 18th century was a time of re-evaluation of role of women in Buenos Aires as well as in Spain, author reviews vision of women presented in Buenos Aires' first newspapers. He then concentrates on Francisco Bruno de Rivarola, author of *Religión y fidelidad argentinas* (1809), arguing that Rivarola was the first *porteño* feminist. [SMS]

2585 Martín de Codoni, Elvira. El Alferez Real: símbolo de una fidelidad a través de tres siglos. (*Rev. Hist. Am. Argent.*, 16:31/32, 1991/92, p. 55–85)

Examines cabildo office of *alferez real* (royal standard bearer) from its inception to 1812. Author concentrates on holder's role in festivities of each city's patron saint, and includes detailed information on those who held this office in Mendoza. [SMS]

2586 Martínez de Sánchez, Ana María. Infraestructura del abasto de carne a la ciudad de Córdoba: Los Corrales, 1738–1810. (*Anu. Estud. Am.*, 50:2, 1993, p. 129–161, ill., photo, table)

Discusses municipal corrals and slaughterhouse as well as tax collected on cattle entering corrals in Córdoba. Author provides much information but little analysis, concluding simply that improvement of the meat supply was another of Intendente Sobremonte's progressive reforms. [SMS]

2587 Martínez de Sánchez, Ana María. Oficios concejiles y funcionarios encargados del control del abasto en la ciudad de Córdoba. (*Invest. Ens.*, 43, enero/dic. 1993, p. 435–449)

Reviews duties of the three officials of Córdoba cabildo involved in matters of food supply for the city: the *fiel ejecutor*, the *mayordomo de corrales*, and the *fiel de medidas*. [SMS]

2588 Martínez Martín, Carmen and **Rafael Carbonell de Masy.** Análisis comparativo de las "Cartas Anuas" de la provincia jesuítica del Paraguay, 1618–1619, con dos documentos previos. (*Rev. Complut. Hist. Am.*, 18, 1992, p. 159–178)

Briefly discusses periodical reports, prepared by the Jesuit Provincial, on Jesuits' activities in missions of Paraguay and Uruguay. Authors append some unpublished letters sent by missionaries in the field to the Provincial that provide further information about the missions. [SMS]

2589 Martínez Martín, Carmen. Apuntes biográficos del marino D. Joaquín de Olivares y Centeno y su viaje a la Patagonia. (*Rev. Hist. Naval*, 11:43, 1993, p. 105–113)

Brief biography of leader of 1745–46 naval expedition to explore the Patagonian coast includes some information about the expedition itself. [SMS]

2590 Martínez Martín, Carmen. La colaboración de la Iglesia en la organización territorial de la Governación del Tucumán, ss. XVI-XVIII. (*Invest. Ens.*, 40, enero/dic. 1990, p. 297–334)

Article stresses importance of the Church and evangelization in determining the spatial organization of the colonial Governación de Tucumán. Author also reviews principal problems produced by religious organization of the territory. [SMS]

2591 Mayo, Carlos A.; María A. Diez; and Carmen S. Cantera. Amor, ausencia y destitución: el drama de Victoria Antonia de Pesoa; una historia del mundo colonial. (*Invest. Ens.*, 43, enero/dic. 1993, p. 321–335)

Brief biography of Victoria Antonio de Pesoa based on her letters to her husband and other primary sources provides interesting insights into life of women in late colonial Río de la Plata. [SMS]

2592 Mayo, Carlos A. and Jaime Peire. Iglesia y crédito colonial: la política de los conventos de Buenos Aires, 1767–1810. (*Rev. Hist. Am.*, 112, julio/dic. 1991, p. 147–157, bibl.)

Discusses role of the convents of Buenos Aires in providing capital in the form of loans to merchants, landowners, artisans, and others. Authors find the friars acting as rational bankers, interested in the viability of their loans rather than in any charitable actions. [SMS]

2593 Mayo, Carlos A. and Amalia Labrubesse de Díaz. Terratenientes, soldados y cautivos: la frontera, 1737–1815. Mar del Plata, Argentina: Univ. Nacional de Mar del Plata, Colegio Nacional Dr. Arturo U. Illia, Grupo Sociedad y Estado, 1993. 137 p.: bibl. (Pesquizas e investigaciones, 0327–6538)

Consists of three essays originally completed in 1986: the first presents a general overview of problem of the frontier in late colonial Buenos Aires; second and longest piece investigates life along the frontier; concluding essay concentrates on land distribution in San Vicente region. Another solid contribution to rural history of the Río de la Plata, a continuing "fertile field." [SMS]

Maza, Juan Isidro. Historia de Malargüe. See item **3070.**

Maza, Juan Isidro. Mujeres en la historia de Mendoza. See item **3071.**

2594 McGeagh, Robert. Thomas Fields and the precursors of the Guaraní *reducciones*. (*CLAHR/Albuquerque*, 2:1, Winter 1993, p. 35–55)

Interesting discussion focuses on work of Thomas Fields, an Irish Jesuit, whose labors in Paraguay at end of 16th century laid the foundation for creation of the Jesuit mission system a few years later. [SMS]

2595 Missões jesuítico-guaranis: fontes bibliográficas. Porto Alegre, Brazil?: Missões 300 Anos; Governo do Estado do Rio Grande do Sul, 1991? 65 p.

Three bibliographies of books and articles on the Jesuit missions and the Guaraní. [SMS]

2596 Molina de Muñoz Moraleda, Stella Maris and Ernesto Muñoz Moraleda. Temas del Tucumán. San Miguel de Tucumán, Argentina: Secretaría de Post-Grado, Univ. Nacional de Tucumán, 1994. 480 p.: bibl., maps.

Contains group of widely divergent articles written over past 20 years by husband and wife historians from Tucumán. Pieces range from studies of Marian cult in evangelization of 16th-century Tucumán to discussion of late 19th-century sugar industry. Most of the articles on the colonial era are concerned with Church or institutional history, adding some detail but little interpretation to the historical record. [SMS]

2597 Monsalvo de Bonduel, Beatríz Susana. Las comunicaciones en la provincia de San Juan durante la época colonial y el siglo XIX. (*Actas Am.*, 1:1, 1994, p. 65–84, bibl., ill., maps)

Gives overview of transportation and communication (primarily mail) systems from precolumbian era to 19th century. According to Monsalvo, the Spanish Crown was little interested in problems of communications in America and simply copied the Peninsular mail system for the New World. [SMS]

2598 Montoya, Ramón A. El paso del virrey Cevallos por las tierras del Plata. Buenos Aires: Junta de Estudios Históricos del Puerto Nuestra Señora Santa María de Buen Ayre, 1991. 35 p.

Brief biography of Pedro de Cevallos, based entirely on secondary sources, concentrates on his nine months in the newly created office of Viceroy of Río de la Plata. Favorably compares his vision of the Indian frontier to that of Gen. Roca. [SMS]

2599 Narancio, Edmundo M. Mercedes otorgadas a los pobladores de la ciudad de Montevideo al tiempo de su fundación. (*An. Univ. Chile*, 20, agosto 1989, p. 373–399, appendix)

Review of Spanish efforts to found the city of Montevideo is followed by discussion of legal privileges granted to first settlers. Appendix includes transcription of Bruno de Zabala's decree outlining rights and responsibilities of the settlers. [SMS]

2600 Navarro Floria, Pedro and **Andrea Nicoletti.** Formación y apertura de una oligarquía criolla en el Buenos Aires virreinal. (*in* Historia de los argentinos. Buenos Aires?: Asociación de Fabricantes Argentinos de Coca-Cola, 1990, p. 175–214, graphs, tables)

Discusses membership and attitudes of two organizations, the Cabildo and the Consulado, through which the "mercantile oligarchy" of Buenos Aires exercised their power. Stresses role of family networks and clans in both institutions. [SMS]

Orsi, René. Dorrego y la unidad rioplatense. See item **3084.**

2601 Padula Perkins, Jorge Eduardo. Un periodismo sin periódico. (*Todo es Hist.*, 313, agosto 1993, p. 88–91, bibl., facsim.)

Provides brief overview of chronicle of Ulrich Schmidel, author of first book about the Mendoza expedition, *Viaje al Río de la Plata* (Buenos Aires: Cabaut y Cía., 1903).

2602 Pérez, Osvaldo. El Montevideo colonial a la luz de un nuevo censo. (*Hoy Hist.*, 11:63, mayo/junio 1994, p. 25–32, ill., tables)

Description of Montevideo is based on a newly discovered census taken in 1757. Includes letter from the *gobernador*, José Joaquín de Viana, to Pedro de Cavallos providing additional descriptive data on the population of the region. [SMS]

Petit Muñoz, Eugenio. Artigas: federalismo y soberanía. See item **3204.**

2603 Piana de Cuestas, Josefina. Visita a los indios de servicio de la ciudad de Córdoba del Tucumán en 1598. (*Historiogr. Bibliogr. Am.*, 31:1, 1987, p. 27–61, bibl.)

Transcribes a 1598 unpublished *visita* undertaken by Antonio de Aguilar Vellicia. The *visitador* provided information on indigenous people, in this case those held by 17 *encomenderos* of Córdoba. [SMS]

2604 Plá, Josefina. Historia cultural. v. 1–4. Edición de Miguel Angel Fernández. Asunción: RP Ediciones; Instituto de Cooperación Iberoamericana, 1991–1993. 4 v.: bibl., ill. (Obras completas)

The collected works Josefina Plá, Paraguayan artist, essayist, and *pensadora*, cover a range of topics, from the Jesuit missions, Spanish influence on Paraguayan culture, and Paraguayan crafts, to thoughts on the Paraguayan *imaginería*. Unfortunately this edition fails to provide the original publication dates and places for the works included. [SMS]

2605 Platero, Tomás. Nuestra gran abuela María Clara: una historia de la esclavitud hacia la libertad. (*Afro-Hisp. Rev.*, 13:1, Spring 1994, p. 52–54)

Beginning with María Clara, a Río de la Plata black slave who first appears in the notary records in 1771, author traces his family through 18th- and 19th-century documents. [SMS]

2606 Población, sociedad, familia y migraciones en el espacio rioplatense: siglos XVIII y XIX. Recopilación de Juan Carlos Garavaglia y José Luis Moreno. Buenos Aires?: Cántaro, 1993. 187 p.: bibl., ill. (Col. de estudios socio-políticos; 6)

This edited volume, consisting of six essays by three distinguished historians (Garavaglia, Moreno, Gelman) and two fine younger scholars (Mariana Canedo and José Mateo), continues a revision of Argentine rural history. All authors stress regional ecologies, economies, and societies within the Buenos Aires hinterland. A strong collection of articles. [SMS]

2607 Prieto, Justo. Paraguay: la provincia gigante de las Indias; análisis espectral de una pequeña nación mediterránea. Asunción: Archivo del Liberalismo, 1988. 243 p.: bibl., ill.

Liberal nationalistic overview of Paraguayan history from precolumbian times to 1935 stresses uniqueness of Paraguayan landscape and experience. Subtext of book is a warning against Paraguayan involvement in the Cono Sur. [SMS]

2608 Pugliese, María Rosa. La prisión por deudas en el Río de la Plata a finales del período hispánico. (*An. Univ. Chile*, 20, agosto 1989, p. 425–472)

Examines forms of legal recourse available for punishing debtors, including debtors' prison. Discusses conditions that prevented imprisonment (including noble status and gender), as well as strategies used to avoid jail or to reduce sentences. This solid article concentrates on the period 1750–1810. [SMS]

2609 Punta, Ana Inés. Los intercambios comerciales de Córdoba con el puerto de Buenos Aires en la segunda mitad del siglo XVIII: el sector de los comerciantes. (*Anu. IEHS*, 9, 1994, p. 35–60, bibl., tables)

Studies economic activities of Córdoba merchants in last decades of 18th century. Finds that the region increased exports, especially of textiles and hides, to Buenos Aires, as the city, in spite of its distance from the port, gained greater participation in international markets. [SMS]

2610 Pusineri Scala, Carlos Alberto. Historia de la moneda paraguaya, siglos XVI al XIX. Asunción: Comisión Nacional Quinto Centenario Paraguay; Editorial Don Bosco, 1992. 192 p.: bibl., ill.

Study of coinage gives much attention to economic and social conditions under which money circulated. Far broader than a simple numismatic study, book also discusses mechanisms used in a specie-poor region instead of money, legislation that attempted to staunch the flow of silver out of the region, and background to the issuing of a few commemorative coins. [SMS]

2611 V centenario en el Río de la Plata: pioneros, adelantados, caminantes, fundadores. Selección, ordenamiento y notas de Alvaro Barros-Lémez. Prólogo de Antonio Mercader. Montevideo?: Comisión Nacional Preparatoria de la Conmemoración del V Centenario del Descubrimiento de América, 1992. 144 p.: bibl., ill., maps.

Contains selection of excerpts from explorers, travelers, adventurers, and government officials in Río de la Plata region, with emphasis on the Banda Oriental. Included are Vespucci, Hernandarias, Paucke, Azara, and Artigas.

2612 Quiroga Micheo, Ernesto. El hermano Bernardo, el gran pecador. (*Todo es Hist.*, 312, julio 1993, p. 48–59, facsims., ill., map)

Popular article focuses on Bernardo Sánchez, an early 17th-century lay figure who, after amassing a fortune in Ecuador, traveled to Chile and then to Río de la Plata in the guise of a religious pilgrim. "El Pecador Bernardo" not only advanced charitable causes (he founded a primary school in Buenos Aires), he also carried out official inspections, reporting directly back to King Philip III. [SMS]

2613 Rees Jones, Ricardo. El superintendente Manuel Ignacio Fernández, 1778–1783: las reformas borbónicas en el Virreinato de Buenos Aires. Buenos Aires: Instituto de Investigaciones de Historia del Derecho, 1992. 371 p.: bibl.

Solid biography of Manuel Ignacio Fernández, Bourbon bureaucrat and first *intendente* of the Río de la Plata, is based on extensive documentary evidence and concentrates on weighing Fernández's successes and failures. [SMS]

2614 Rela, Walter. Viajeros, marinos y naturalistas en la Banda Oriental del siglo XVIII. Montevideo: Ediciones de la Plaza, 1992. 139 p.: bibl., ill., maps (some col.).

Brief overview of social, political, military, and economic history of 18th-century Montevideo and surrounding region is followed by selections from travelers (Paucke, Millau, Pernetty, Bougainville, Aguirre, Azara, Concolorcovo and members of the Malaspina Expedition, among others). Each selection is preceded by biographical notes on the respective author. [SMS]

2615 Romero Cabrera, Liliáns Betty. Aproximación a la Córdoba del siglo XVIII. (*Invest. Ens.*, 40, enero/dic. 1990, p. 383–404, bibl.)

Discussion of late 18th-century Córdoba underlines role of the Cabildo, commerce, the slave trade, and the mule trade in the social, political, and economic development of the city. [SMS]

2616 Romero Cabrera, Liliáns Betty. La "Casa de Allende" y la clase dirigente: 1750–1810. Córdoba, Argentina: Junta Provincial de Historia de Córdoba, 1993. 210 p.: bibl., maps. (Serie Libros de la Junta Provincial de Historia de Córdoba, 0327-0554; 13)

After a general introduction to the commerce of late 18th-century Córdoba, author concentrates on the Allende clan, an important family in commerce and local politics. Author sees the American-born Allendes as representing a Creole bourgeoisie, arguing that in their struggle for power they were precursors of Independence Movement. [SMS]

2617 Romero Carranza, Ambrosio; Alberto Rodríguez Varela; and Eduardo Ventura. Historia política y constitucional de la Argentina. v. 1, Desde el período hispánico hasta 1824. Buenos Aires: A-Z Editora, 1993. 1 v.

Interesting discussion of provincial constitutions in effect during the period studied. [J.T. Criscenti]

2618 Romero de Viola, Blanca R. Paraguay siglo dieciocho: período de transición. Asunción?: Ediciones Comuneros, 1987. 278 p.: bibl., ill., maps.

Concentrates on political and military accomplishments of Agustín Fernando de Pinedo (*gobernador, 1772–78*), who is portrayed as principal figure in bringing Bourbon Reforms to Paraguay. According to author, Pinedo founded the *reducciones* along the Río Paraguay in order to end *encomienda* system and benefit the Royal Treasury.

2619 Roulet, Florencia. La resistencia de los guaraní del Paraguay a la conquista española, 1537–1556. Posadas, Argentina: Editorial Universitaria, Univ. Nacional de Misiones, 1993. 302 p.: bibl., map. (Los Tesistas)

Discusses first 20 years of Spanish-Guaraní contact (1537–56), examining both Spanish actions and Guaraní reactions. Guaraní insistence on retaining their warrior culture led to a general rebellion in 1545–46, and to eventual defeat of the originally planned "friendship and alliance." [SMS]

2620 Ruedi, Nora and **Jorge L. Somoza.** Estimación de la mortalidad de jesuitas, nacidos entre 1550 y 1749, que vivieron en las misiones del Paraguay: Cuenca del Plata. (*in* Congresso sobre a História da População da América Latina, *1st, Ouro Preto, Brazil, 1989.* Actas. São Paulo: Fundação SEADE, 1990, p. 88–97, bibl., graphs, tables)

Using published data on Jesuits in Paraguay, authors undertake a sophisticated demographic study of mortality among the group. They find that Jesuits between ages 20–29 had an average life expectancy of 38.6 to 40.7. [SMS]

2621 Saban, Mario Javier. Judíos conversos. v. 2, Los hebreos, nuestros hermanos mayores. Buenos Aires: Editorial Distal, 1991. 1 v.: bibl.

Second volume of Saban's three-part study of *conversos* in Río de la Plata region includes brief overview of Jewish Portuguese diaspora, and two pieces claiming that founders of both Salta and Córdoba were descendants of Spanish Jewish families. Includes reproductions of documents referring to Portuguese, Portuguese Jews, and heresy in

the region. Partial genealogies of *converso* families also are included. For Vol. 1, see *HLAS 54:2567*; for Vol. 3, see item **2622**. [SMS]

2622 Saban, Mario Javier. Judíos conversos. v. 3, Los marranos y la economía en el Río de la Plata. Buenos Aires: Editorial Galerna, 1993. 1 v.: bibl.

Third volume of this work on the *conversos* stresses commercial activities of the Portuguese Jews, dividing history of the group into three periods: 1580–1619, a period of growth and consolidation; 1619–1654, a period of incorporation into local society and loss of identity fueled by increasing strength of the Inquisition; and 1654–1680, a period of disappearance of Portuguese Jews from the region. Again, documents are scattered throughout the text and there is a lengthy section of partial genealogies of distinguished Argentine families of *converso* origin. For Vol. 1, see *HLAS 54:2567*; for Vol. 2, see item **2621**. [SMS]

2623 Saguier, Eduardo R. El combate contra la "limpieza de sangre" en los orígenes de la emancipación argentina: el uso del estigma de la bastardía y del origen racial como mecanismos de defensa de las elites coloniales. (*Rev. Hist. Am.*, 110, julio/dic. 1990, p. 155–198, bibl.)

Relates various cases in which either racial origins or illegitimacy were used to challenge an individual's position or marital plans. Saguier believes that these cases from interior regions of the Viceroyalty must have contributed to the independence movement, but never explains exactly how or why. [SMS]

2624 Saguier, Eduardo R. Las contradicciones entre el fuero militar y el poder político en el Virreinato del Río de la Plata. (*Rev. Eur.*, 56, June 1994, p. 55–73, bibl.)

Examines role of the *fuero militar* in interior regions of the Viceroyalty. As in many of his articles, Saguier provides a wide-ranging discussion of theoretical literature and details from archival cases, but is somewhat vague in his conclusions. Here, for example, he finds that in some cases the *milicia* created social mobility, while in other cases it did not. [SMS]

2625 Saguier, Eduardo R. La corrupción de la burocracia colonial borbónica y los orígenes del federalismo: el caso del Virreinato del Río de la Plata. (*Jahrb. Gesch.*, 29, 1992, p. 149–177)

Positing an intimate connection between colonial corruption in 18th century and emergence of federalism, Saguier discusses several cases of abuse of office in Alto Perú and the interior regions of Río de la Plata. He concludes that these cases produced a deepening resentment against Spanish and *porteño* bureaucrats. [SMS]

2626 Saguier, Eduardo R. Las crisis de circulación y la lucha contra el monopolio comercial español en los orígenes de la revolución de independencia: el caso de Buenos Aires en el siglo XVIII. (*Rev. Complut. Hist. Am.*, 19, 1993, p. 149–194, bibl., tables)

Using various numerical series culled from notary papers and other documents, author identifies what he considers to be seven periods of commercial expansion followed by seven crises. These crises somehow explain why region failed to develop an autonomous commercial bourgeoisie or to effectively fight against the Ancient Regime. As in many of his articles, Saguier draws from a wide range of theoretical and other readings, but fails to present a sharp, coherent argument. [SMS]

2627 Saguier, Eduardo R. La crisis de un estado colonial: balance de la cuestión rioplatense. (*Anu. Estud. Am.*, 49:2, 1992, p. 65–91)

Using a review of historians' arguments about the nature of the commercial class of Buenos Aires (was it an aristocratic group or a bourgeoisie) as a pretext, author attacks work of José Carlos Chiaramonte. He also finds fault with unnamed others who fail to understand that colonial institutions were "simply spaces where the relations of power were inscribed." [SMS]

2628 Saguier, Eduardo R. El parentesco como mecanismo de consolidación política de un patriciado colonial: el caso de las provincias rioplatenses del virreinato peruano, 1700–1776. (*Estud. Hist. Soc. Econ. Am.*, 10, 1993, p. 61–116, bibl., tables)

Again working on the cities of the interior, Saguier follows selected genealogies to show how certain elite families maintained political power through the 18th century. He interprets their actions as resistance to the power of the Spanish Crown. [SMS]

2629 Saguier, Eduardo R. Las pautas hereditarias del regimen capellánico rioplatense. (*Americas/Francisc.*, 51:3, Jan. 1995, p. 369–392)

Examines use of endowed chaplaincies in the Río de la Plata, a practice which author believes demonstrates the instability of the local elite and aids in understanding construction of the collective imagination leading to independence. [SMS]

2630 Santamaría, Daniel J. Del tabaco al incienso: reducción y conversión en las misiones Jesuitas de las selvas sudamericanas, siglos XVII y XVIII. San Salvador de Jujuy, Argentina: Centro de Estudios Indígenas y Coloniales, Univ. Nacional de Jujuy, 1994. 176 p.: bibl.

Important study concentrates on process of attracting indigenous peoples to Jesuit *reducciones* and converting them to Christianity. Author compares four different regions of Jesuit missionary activity (the Orinoco, the Maynas district of present-day Ecuador, the Moxos, and the Chiquitos missions of Alto Perú), carefully comparing Jesuit expectations and indigenous responses as well as discussing social and economic impact of the mission experience on indigenous peoples. Maps would have been extremely helpful. [SMS]

2631 Seoane, María Isabel. Las órdenes religiosas y el derecho de sepultura en el Buenos Aires del siglo XVII. (*An. Univ. Chile*, 20, agosto 1989, p. 551–583)

Analysis of funeral customs in 17th-century Buenos Aires is based on notary records. Looks at place of burial and dress of the deceased as well as ceremonies at the funeral and afterward. [SMS]

2632 Silva, Hernán Asdrúbal. Reformas, guerras y tráfico canario-rioplatense. (*in* Coloquio de Historia Canario-Americana, *9th, Spain, 1990.* Actas. Las Palmas, Spain: Cabildo Insular de Gran Canaria, 1992, v. 2, p. 717–730, bibl., graphs, tables)

Reviews commercial connections between Río de la Plata and the Canary Islands that resulted from the 1796 war between Spain and Great Britain and continued up to 1810. [SMS]

2633 Soules, María Inés. El poblamiento de La Rioja durante el período hispánico. (*in* Estudios en homenaje a Don Claudio Sánchez-Albornoz en sus 90 años: anexos de *Cuadernos de Historia de España*. Buenos Aires: Instituto de Historia de España, 1990, v. 6, p. 355–377, map)

Provides descriptive overview of development of the city of La Rioja from its founding in 1591 to end of the colonial period. In spite of title, article is weak on information about the population of the city. [SMS]

2634 Urquiza, Fernando Carlos. Etiquetas y conflictos: el obispo, el virrey y el cabildo en el Río de la Plata en la segunda mitad del siglo XVIII. (*Anu. Estud. Am.*, 50:1, 1993, p. 55–100)

Interesting article reviews conflicts over questions of etiquette between religious and secular authorities. Author divides conflicts into two periods (1750–76 and 1776–

1810), arguing that continual conflicts between the Viceroy and the Bishop and increased friction in the second period were the result of a changed equilibrium in the local power structure. [SMS]

2635 Zapico, Hilda Raquel. El cabildo porteño: su injerencia y actividad en el campo eclesiástico, 1589–1640. (*Rev. Hist. Am. Argent.*, 16:31/32, 1991/92, p. 21–54, bibl.)

Author traces role of *porteño* cabildo as the local representative of royal power, and the royal right of Church patronage. She finds that while Buenos Aires was a religious society, its display of religiousity was never as marked as it was in other colonial cities. [SMS]

19th and 20th Centuries
Venezuela

PETER S. LINDER, *Assistant Professor of History, New Mexico Highlands University*
INES QUINTERO, *Instituto de Estudios Hispanoamericanos, Universidad de Venezuela*

ADVANCES IN VENEZUELAN HISTORIOGRAPHY noted in vols. 52 and 54 of the *Handbook* have continued this biennium. Twentieth-century politics remains the focus of most works reviewed; however, a substantial number of useful studies have emerged in other areas, in particular in economic, social, and intellectual history.

Recent economic and social histories often stress the role played by the State and public policy. Salazar-Carrillo takes a critical look at government petroleum and investment policy since 1958 to explain current economic woes (item **2676**). Yarrington examines expanding State power and intrusiveness in land privatization and rural proletarianization in a particular region of western Venezuela (item **2682**). Encontrela and Saneugenios focus on the role of public funding priorities in determining access to higher education (and the quality of that education) in the 20th century (item **2656**). Also notable is González Deluca's study of Caracas merchants, which provides insights into Venezuelan society, based on research on the activities of one of its more significant social groups (item **2657**).

A number of economic histories also challenge prevailing views of foreign capital's role in Venezuela's economy. Harwich Vallenilla provides a new perspective on the role of foreign concerns in a case study of the New York & Bermúdez Company (item **2659**). The same author has also edited a two-volume collection of case studies that demonstrate the limits of foreign capital's influence before the oil boom of the 1920s (item **2662**).

In labor history, institutional studies remain the rule, although the quality of those works has improved greatly. In his study of the labor movement since 1958,

Ellner concludes that the State's ability to control the demands of organized labor has frequently been exaggerated, and will be lessened in the future (item **2654**).

A number of significant works in 19th-century intellectual history have appeared. Arratia (item **2642**) and Pino Iturrieta (item **2672**) have studied the role of elite intellectuals in the political and social conflicts of the early republic. Pino Iturrieta has also produced a study of prevalent ideas and concepts about women's roles in 19th-century society (item **2673**). In the introduction to an edited volume of the writings of Rómulo Betancourt, Sosa Abascal critically analyzes the economic and political ideas of one of the founders of modern Venezuela (item **2645**).

Some striking changes in political history also deserve mention. One is a growing interest in the politics of the 19th century. For example, Urdaneta Quintero examines the impact of conflicts with the central government in shaping a distinct regional consciousness among the political and economic elite of Maracaibo after independence (item **2679**).

A number of works reflect recent political crises and scandals. Historians are beginning to reevaluate the advent of democracy and, in particular, the roles of Venezuela's leading political parties. Valero investigates the role of foreign governments in the rise and fall of the first Acción Democrática government (item **2680**). Recent studies also demonstrate a new concern with regional political differences. For example, Angulo Rivas investigates the origins of COPEI as a Catholic political organization profoundly shaped by the Andean region in which it first appeared (item **2639**).

2636 Acosta, Cecilio *et al.* Pensamiento conservador del siglo XIX: antología. Selección y estudio preliminar de Elías Pino Iturrieta. Caracas: Monte Avila Editores, 1992. 579 p.: bibl. (Biblioteca del Pensamiento Venezolano José Antonio Páez; 5)

Selección, comentario y análisis de los textos políticos y económicos de los autores más representativos del pensamiento conservador venezolano. Se exponen las diferencias y especificidades del discurso conservador en relación con aspectos como las reformas económicas, la participación popular y la libertad de imprenta. Está organizado temáticamente.

2637 Acuña, Guido. Pérez Jiménez, un gendarme innecesario: libro testimonial de la resistencia, 1948–1958. Caracas: Pomaire, 1989. 385 p.: ill., index. (Col. Testimonios)

Acción Democrática activist and labor leader's memoirs of 44 months' imprisonment in a concentration camp of the Pérez Jiménez regime. Reflects elderly activist's recent disillusionment with political scandals of the 1980s and 1990s. Useful for political and labor history of the Pérez Jiménez era.

2638 Angulo Rivas, Alfredo. Adiós a la utopía. Caracas: Univ. de los Andes; Alfadil Ediciones, 1993. 169 p.: bibl. (Col. Trópicos; 50)

Positive interpretation of rise of Acción Democrática and its most important early leader, Rómulo Betancourt. Asserts that Acción Democrática and Betancourt came to power and became a leading political force in Venezuela because of intimate understanding of social structure and divisions. Also argues that early successes led to recent authoritarianism and corruption.

2639 Angulo Rivas, Alfredo. Los Andes de Venezuela: un estudio de historia política. Mérida, Venezuela: Univ. de Los Andes, Ediciones del Rectorado, 1993. 140 p.: bibl., ill.

Regional political study analyzes origins and initial development of COPEI from a conservative Catholic regional organization in Táchira and Mérida to a national political power. Attributes Acción Democrática's failure to develop a strong following in Andean states to the local perception of it as anti-Catholic and anti-Andean.

2640 Archivo de Rómulo Betancourt. t. 3, 1931. Caracas: Editorial Fundación Rómulo Betancourt, 1992. 1 v.: ill., indexes.

Selections from Betancourt's papers from 1931, including Plan of Barranquilla. Seeks to demonstrate that, despite an apparent reduction in militancy and radicalism, Betancourt remained ideologically consistent.

2641 Arráiz, Antonio. Los días de la ira: las guerras civiles en Venezuela, 1830–1903. Recopilación y hemerografía por Néstor Tablante y Garrido. Prólogo de Pedro Beroes. Valencia, Venezuela: Vadell Hnos., 1991. 214 p.: bibl.

Crónica y análisis de las revueltas ocurridas en Venezuela desde la disolución de la Gran Colombia hasta la última revolución caudillista de 1903. El autor ofrece una guía de gran utilidad para conocer las motivaciones y protagonistas de los distintos episodios bélicos que alteraron la vida política venezolana durante el siglo XIX.

2642 Arratia, Alejandro. Etica y democracia en Fermín Toro. Caracas: Monte Avila Editores Latinoamericana, 1993. 178 p.: bibl. (Estudios)

Brief, but interesting investigation of ideology and political thought of a leading 19th-century conservative leader, as reflected in writings on politics, economy, and society. Asserts that at least some of Venezuela's post-independence elite sought to create a workable and just republic, in part by adapting European ideologies to conditions then existing in Venezuela.

2643 Banko, Catalina. Los comerciantes extranjeros de La Guaira frente a las reformas económicas de José Tadeo Monagas, 1848–1850. (*Tierra Firme*, 12:45, abril/junio 1994, p. 175–186)

Investigation of mercantile reactions to changes in government credit and financial policies of the Monagas Administration. Asserts that foreign merchants used economic power and influence of their home governments to blunt or derail policies that threatened their interests, in particular attempts to limit the rights of creditors.

2644 Barnola Q., Isaías. Matías Salazar: un caudillo del siglo XIX venezolano. Caracas: Fundarte, Alcaldía de Caracas, 1993. 148 p.: bibl. (Col. Rescate; 9)

Biography of a military leader of the Federal War era. Matías Salazar, one of the most successful generals of the liberal cause, helped ensure its triumph in the west, only to be displaced and eventually executed by order of Guzmán Blanco. Illustrative of political climate after the Federal War, and means and conditions by which Antonio Guzmán Blanco came to power in 1870.

2645 Betancourt, Rómulo. La segunda independencia de Venezuela: compilación de la columna "Economía y Finanzas" del diario *Ahora*, 1937–1939. v. 1–3. Estudio introductorio de Arturo Sosa Abascal. Caracas: Fundación Rómulo Betancourt, 1992. 3 v.: bibl. (Col. Tiempo Vigente; 3–5)

Análisis exhaustivo del pensamiento económico de Betancourt, su diagnóstico de Venezuela, sus ideas en torno al petróleo, la agricultura, el papel del Estado, el capital extranjero, la situación social y educativa. Se ofrece un balance crítico del proyecto de modernización de Betancourt para Venezuela. Ver *HLAS 55:3252* para el comentario del cientista político.

2646 Bracho, Jorge. El positivismo y la enseñanza de la historia en Venezuela. Caracas: Fondo Editorial Tropykos, 1995. 142 p.: bibl. (Col. Historia Alzada; 2)

Revisión de los preceptos teóricos del positivismo presentes en Venezuela y su incidencia en la elaboración historiográfica de los siglos XIX y XX, así como su impacto sobre el proceso educativo a partir de la imposición de un modelo interpretativo guiado por las pautas de positivismo como escuela historiográfica.

2647 Bruzual, Blas *et al*. Pensamiento liberal del siglo XIX: antología. Selección y estudio preliminar de Inés Mercedes Quintero Montiel. Caracas: Monte Avila Editores, 1992. 329 p.: bibl. (Biblioteca del Pensamiento Venezolano José Antonio Páez; 4)

Selección, comentario y análisis de los textos políticos y económicos fundamentales del pensamiento liberal venezolano a partir de la edificación de la República en 1830. Se exponen las características del discurso liberal en relación con temas como la alternabilidad, los partidos políticos, la libertad de imprenta, los excesos del liberalismo económico, la cuestión agraria y el Estado interventor. Ver item **4986** para el comentario del filósofo.

2648 Cardozo Galué, Germán. La elite intelectual maracaibera a fines del siglo XIX. (*Tierra Firme*, 12:45, abril/junio 1994, p. 127–146, bibl., graphs, table)

A quantitative analysis of "intellectual production" in Maracaibo at the end of the last century, coinciding with peak of regional agroexport boom. Argues for a regional intellectual golden age, measured by increases in publication of books and newspapers from the 1870s to the 1920s and emergence of a number of regional—and even national—literary and intellectual figures. Useful indicator of direction for future research.

2649 Carvallo, Gastón. Próceres, caudillos y rebeldes: crisis del sistema de dominación, 1830–1908. Caracas: Grijalbo, 1994. 263 p.

Estudio sociopolítico del siglo XIX venezolano en el cual se analizan las bases económicas y sociales de los sectores dominantes, la estructuración del sistema de dominación, sus contradicciones y el agotamiento del modelo así como las características y respuestas de los sectores dominados frente a la hegemonía de las oligarquías.

2650 Castro Leiva, Luis. The dictatorship of virtue or opulence of commerce. (*Jahrb. Gesch.*, 29, 1992, p. 195–240)

A complex study of how the concepts of liberty and virtue shaped political discourse in 19th-century Latin America and Venezuela, and influenced the adoption of neoliberal political and economic systems currently in place in Latin America.

2651 Consalvi, Simón Alberto. Grover Cleveland y la controversia Venezuela-Gran Bretaña. Washington?: Tierra de Gracia Editores, 1992. 223 p.: ill. (Historia de papel)

Análisis de los documentos de la intervención norteamericana en el episodio de las reclamaciones venezolanas contra Gran Bretaña por el Esequibo. Se destaca la posición norteamericana frente a las aspiraciones británicas como una forma de reafirmar la Doctrina Monroe en un momento en que a EE.UU. le interesaba consolidar su presencia en América Latina. El volumen incluye los textos fundamentales de la controversia.

2652 Cunill Grau, Pedro et al. Venezuela contemporánea, 1974–1989. Prólogo de Ramón J. Velásquez. Caracas: Fundación Eugenio Mendoza, 1989. 823 p.: bibl.

Volumen colectivo que recoge la dinámica política, económica, institucional, cultural, geográfica y social de Venezuela. Se trata de una útil guía para el estudio de los principales aspectos de la sociedad venezolana de los últimos veinticinco años.

2653 Dávila, Luis Ricardo. Rómulo Betancourt and the development of Venezuelan nationalism, 1930–1945. (*Bull. Lat. Am. Res.*, 12:1, Jan. 1993, p. 49–63)

Detailed study and content analysis of Betancourt's writings during a crucial 15-year period. Author concludes that Acción Democrática leader's conceptualization of nationalism evolved away from anti-imperialism toward a more moderate economic nationalism, stressing political democracy and cooperation with foreign capital.

2654 Ellner, Steve. Organized labor in Venezuela, 1958–1991: behavior and concerns in a democratic setting. Wilmington, Del.: SR Books, 1993. 247 p.: bibl., index. (Latin American Silhouettes)

Based on extensive interviews with members of the labor movement, this sophisticated institutional study of organized labor challenges the assumptions of Venezuelan exceptionalism. Demonstrates internal political and economic divisions of the labor movement, and concludes that labor's traditional role as a source of political and social stability cannot necessarily be expected to continue in the future.

2655 Ellner, Steve. Venezuela. (*in* Latin America between the Second World War and the Cold War, 1944–1948. Edited by Leslie Bethell and Ian Roxborough. New York: Cambridge Univ. Press, 1992, p. 147–169)

Discussion of controversies surrounding the 1945 coup and the Acción Democrática government of 1945–48. Asserts that the Acción Democrática government that came to power through the 1945 coup was not revolutionary and had a stormy relationship with the parties of the far left, and that the US grew increasingly hostile because of a changing world-view and the onset of the Cold War.

2656 Escontrela N., Ramón and Amadeo Saneugenio S. El proceso histórico de incorporación de los diversos grupos sociales a la educación superior venezolana. (*Bol. Acad. Nac. Hist./Caracas*, 76:303, julio/sept. 1993, p. 75–93, bibl.)

A provocative analysis of differential access to higher education. Documents "democratization" of access to higher education in Venezuela since 1958. Author observes that, despite dramatic expansion in higher education in the 1960s-70s, economic crises beginning in the early 1980s and increasing emphasis on "technocratic" education have led to most resources going to institutions patronized by scions of upper and middle classes at the expense of those serving members of the lower classes.

2657 González Deluca, María Elena. Los comerciantes de Caracas: cien años de acción y testimonio de la Cámara de Comercio de Caracas. Caracas: La Cámara, 1994. 848 p.: bibl., index.

Estudio de la evolución de la Cámara de Comercio de Caracas y el gremio mercantil desde su fundación en 1893. Se aborda el tema de las prácticas del sector mercantil, sus relaciones con otros sectores económicos así como la capacidad de poder del gremio y su influencia económica durante un siglo de intensa actividad.

2658 Guaithero Díaz, Genaro. Yo, el bandolero. Caracas: Centauro, 1993. 525 p.

Memoir of a guerrilla of the leftist insurgency of 1960s. A demythologizing look at guerrilla war, and a trenchant critique of its young leadership. Of peasant origins, author argues that leadership failed because of distance from and ignorance of people they purported to represent.

2659 Harwich Vallenilla, Nikita. Asfalto y revolución: la New York & Bermúdez Company. Presentación de Ramón J. Velásquez. Prólogo de David Ruiz Chataing. Caracas: Fundación para el Rescate del Acervo Documental Venezolano; Monte Avila Editores, 1992. 543 p.: bibl., ill. (Documentos)

Comprehensively documented study of difficulties faced by the first foreign firm attempting to develop Venezuelan hydrocarbon resources. Challenging the prevailing arguments that stress dominance of foreign capital in the 19th century, argues that, before the oil boom, most foreign concerns made limited profits, faced severe difficulties in dealing with national authorities, and concentrated in areas deficient in national investment.

2660 Harwich Vallenilla, Nikita. Imaginario colectivo e identidad nacional: tres etapas en la enseñanza de la historia de Venezuela. (*in* Jornadas de Investigación Histórica, *1st, Univ. Central de Venezuela, 1990. Actas.*

Caracas: Univ. Central de Venezuela, 1991, p. 273–295, tables)

A study of how teaching of Venezuelan history in schools gradually developed to reflect nation-building concerns of a national elite. Concludes that intellectual elite used teaching of history to promote their version of a national vision.

2661 Historia de las finanzas públicas en Venezuela. Siglo XX. v. 79, pt. 1, 4. Planificación y ordenación por Tomás Enrique Carrillo Batalla. Caracas: Academia Nacional de la Historia, 1988–1994. 2 v.: bibl. (Biblioteca de la Academia Nacional de la Historia. Serie Economía y Finanzas de Venezuela; 142, 147)

Useful collection of documents detail congressional debates regarding budgetary matters following the return of Acción Democrática to power. For comments on earlier volumes see *HLAS 53:2108.*

2662 Inversiones extranjeras en Venezuela, siglo XIX. v. 1–2. Coordinación de Nikita Harwich Vallenilla. Caracas: Academia Nacional de Ciencias Económicas, 1992–1994. 2 v.: bibl.

Highly useful collection of case studies examines actions of specific foreign enterprises in Venezuela prior to the advent of the oil industry. Illustrates that direct foreign investment in Venezuela during 19th century was limited in scope, did not dominate the economy, and concentrated primarily in areas not controlled by established Venezuelan interests. Quality of essays is uneven.

2663 Lárez, Fermín. El movimiento sindical y la lucha política en Venezuela, 1936–1959. Caracas: Monte Avila Editores Latinoamericana: Instituto Nacional de Altos Estudios Sindicales, 1992. 212 p. (Documentos)

Useful study seeking to investigate difficulties experienced by union movement to organize and bargain while divided internally by ideology and politics. An introductory essay is followed by interviews of key labor leaders.

2664 Lucena Salmoral, Manuel. Incidencia del comercio exterior en la caída de la primera república de Venezuela. (*in* Congreso Internacional de Historia Económica y Social de la Cuenca del Caribe, *1763–1898, 1st, San Juan, 1987. Actas.* San Juan: Centro de Estudios Avanzados de Puerto Rico y el Caribe, 1992, p. 411–453, graphs, tables)

Concise summary of forthcoming book. Based on a careful analysis of import-export statistics between 1807–12, author concludes that the principal cause of the fall of the First Republic was not the earthquake of 1812 or the royalist's advance or Miranda's dictatorship, but the economic crisis produced by the collapse of trade. [J. Rausch]

2665 Lucena Salmoral, Manuel. Los mercados exteriores de Caracas a comienzos de la independencia. Caracas: Academia Nacional de la Historia, 1992. 396 p.: bibl., ill. (Biblioteca de la Academia Nacional de la Historia. Fuentes para la Historia Republicana de Venezuela; 51)

Based on a detailed analysis of trade records, author attributes collapse of the First Republic to a crisis in international trade.

2666 Moleiro, Rodolfo. De la dictadura a la democracia: Eleazar López Contreras, lindero y puente entre dos épocas. 3. ed. Caracas: Editorial Pomaire Venezuela, 1993. 503 p.: bibl., ill.

Study stresses democratic and libertarian aspects of the presidential administrations following the death of Juan Vicente Gómez, and a critique of the coup that brought Acción Democrática to power.

Muñoz L., Carlos A. El Estado venezolano y su política regional. See *HLAS 55:4846.*

2667 Núñez de Cáceres, Pedro. Memorias. Caracas: Instituto Autónomo Biblioteca Nacional; Fundación para el Rescate del Acervo Documental Venezolano, 1993. 767 p.

Excerpts from memoirs of a lawyer and educator active in politics in mid-19th century Venezuela offer acerbic commentary on factional divisions and society of Caracas and Venezuela in the years leading up to the outbreak of the Federal War.

2668 Oduber, Fernando. San Antonio de Los Altos: desestructuración de la propiedad territorial de la junta comunera, 1914–1970. Caracas: Ediciones Los Heraldos Negros, 1994. 421 p.: bibl., ill.

Useful long-term study of rural land tenure in a region near Caracas. Making extensive use of registry archives, documents dissolution of a traditional communal land-holding through State intervention, acquisition of communal land by outsiders, and finally rapid expansion of Caracas since 1930s.

2669 Parra, Teresa de la. Influencia de las mujeres en la formación del alma americana. Introducción de R.J. Lovera De-Sola. Caracas: Fundarte; Alcaldía del Municipio Libertador, 1991. 126 p. (Col. Delta; 28)

Originally published in 1961, this essay had been delivered as a lecture by this Venezuelan writer in Bogotá in 1930. Title is misleading, for Teresa de la Parra says far less about the "influencia de la mujer en la formación del alma americana" than about independence history in general. Nevertheless, this is a bibliographical jewel for a variety of reasons, and certainly merits publication. R.J. Lovera De-Sola offers an excellent introduction (47 p.), well documented with 98 footnotes. [R.L. Williams]

2670 Pérez Jiménez, Marcos. Pérez Jiménez: tres décadas después. Entrevista de Alfredo Angulo Rivas. Mérida, Venezuela: Univ. de Los Andes, 1994. 93 p.

El entrevistado expone su concepción del poder, la justificación de su mandato, su crítica al régimen democrático, así como información diversa sobre los alcances de su régimen. Constituye un testimonio político para el estudio de ese polémico período de la historia venezolana estudiado escasamente y con una gran carga de partidarismo.

2671 Pino Iturrieta, Elías *et al.* Antonio Guzmán Blanco y su época. Coordinación de Inés Mercedes Quintero Montiel. Caracas: Monte Avila Editores Latinoamericana, 1994. 211 p.: bibl. (Documentos)

Libro colectivo sobre el período de gobierno de Antonio Guzmán Blanco (1870–88) en el cual se analizan los aspectos más relevantes de la dinámica política, económica, cultural y social de la Venezuela de entonces, acompañado de un estudio exhaustivo de las fuentes del período. El libro ofrece una útil síntesis del proceso de cambios que constituyó el regimen guzmancista.

2672 Pino Iturrieta, Elías. Las ideas de los primeros venezolanos. Caracas: Monte Avila Editores Latinoamericana, 1993. 157 p.: bibl. (Estudios)

Intellectual history of the early republic focuses on political and social ideas of a number of *caraqueño* elite intellectuals that were selected by José Antonio Páez after the collapse of Gran Colombia to develop a republican system of government. Argues that these intellectuals failed to establish a long-lasting, stable political and social order because of their attempts to prevent social change and limit access to wealth and political power.

2673 Pino Iturrieta, Elías. Ventaneras y castas, diabólicas y honestas. Caracas: Planeta, 1993. 143 p.: bibl. (Col. Voces de la Historia)

Examines how the Church viewed women after independence in early- and mid-19th century and its attempts to regulate their lives. Argues that independence brought no change to traditional views of roles and status of women; there was only a change in tactics from institutional punishment to publicity for women who violated traditional norms.

2674 Rodríguez, José Angel. El paisaje del riel en Trujillo, 1880–1945. Caracas: Academia Nacional de la Historia, 1994. 224 p.: bibl., ill., map. (Biblioteca de la Academia Nacional de la Historia. Estudios, Monografías y Ensayos; 162)

Investigation of economic, environmental, and social impacts of the Ferrocarril de La Ceiba, the railroad built in the late-19th century to connect Lake Maracaibo with the Andean piedmont. Drawing upon archival materials, oral histories, newspapers, and published documents, concludes that rail development brought only limited agricultural and commercial benefits while resulting in substantial environmental destruction, social and economic disruption, and rapid expansion of some urban centers.

2675 Rojas, Clara Marina. El inicio del juego democrático en Venezuela: un análisis de las elecciones 1946–1947. Caracas: Academia Nacional de la Historia, 1992. 108 p.: bibl. (Biblioteca de la Academia Nacional de la Historia. Fuentes para la Historia Republicana de Venezuela; 50)

Studies the regional and social sources of support for the four most important political parties of 1945–48 in order to understand electoral victory of Acción Democrática. Asserts that Acción Democrática owed its triumph to a peasantry mobilized by promises of agrarian reform.

2676 Salazar-Carrillo, Jorge and **Roberto D. Cruz.** Oil and development in Venezuela during the twentieth century. Westport, Conn.: Praeger, 1994. 280 p.: bibl., index, tables.

Dry, but useful study based primarily on published government statistics investigates petroleum's role in Venezuela's economy from 1910–90. Argues that State investment and taxation policies, rather than the oil industry itself, are to blame for recent economic problems and general failure to develop. For economist's comment see *HLAS 55:1744.*

2677 Testigos norteamericanos de la expedición de Miranda: John Sherman, Moses Smith, Henry Ingersoll. Selección, traducción y prólogo de Edgardo Mondolfi. Presentación de Margot Boulton de Bottome. Caracas: Centro Venezolano Americano; Monte Avila Editores, 1992. 191 p. (Documentos)

Testimonios fundamentales de John Sherman, Moses Smith y Henry Ingersoll, quienes acompañaron a Francisco de Miranda en su aventura política en 1806. Se recrean los juicios políticos acerca del episodio, los detalles de la empresa, los conflictos y contradicciones del proyecto y las vicisitudes que padecieron en el intento.

2678 Texera Arnal, Yolanda. La exploración botánica en Venezuela, 1754–1950. Caracas: Fondo Editorial Acta Científica Venezolana, 1991. 186 p.: bibl., index, map. (Col. de Estudios Sociales de la Ciencia del Fondo Editorial Acta Científica Venezolana)

Estudio de la exploración botánica desde las primeras expediciones europeas hasta su consolidación como una disciplina científica en la universidad. Se ofrece un inventario pormenorizado de los botánicos que visitaron el país, así como de las iniciativas, proyectos y realizaciones que permitieron el establecimiento de la botánica como una actividad científica. Está acompañado de índices y cuadros.

2679 Urdaneta Quintero, Arlene. El Zulia en el septenio de Guzmán Blanco. Zulia, Venezuela: Consejo de Desarrollo Científico y Humanístico, Centro de Estudios Históricos, Facultad de Humanidades y Educación, Univ. de Zulia; Caracas: Fondo Editorial Tropykos, 1992. 185 p.: bibl., maps.

Well-argued and well-documented study of 19th-century conflicts between regional elites and the liberal central government. Chronicles efforts by Antonio Guzmán Blanco and *caraqueño* elite to centralize and modernize the nation, efforts that were manifested in Zulia by the closing of the Maracaibo customs house. Concludes that pressures from the central government led financial and commercial elites of Maracaibo to develop political maturity and a strong sense of regional identity that informed later conflicts between the central government and region.

2680 Valero, Jorge. ¿Cómo llegó Acción Democrática al poder en 1945? Caracas: Fondo Editorial Tropykos, 1993. 166 p.: bibl., ill.

A study of circumstances under which Acción Democrática came to power in 1945, relying on US and British foreign relations documents. Author argues that Acción Democrática did not bring down the Medina Angarita government, asserting that divisions within the military and Medina's own indecisiveness created circumstances that brought the social democratic party to power. Also maintains that foreign powers—in particular the US and Great Britain—had no role in the 1945 coup, although they quickly established amicable working relations with Gallegos and Betancourt.

2681 Velásquez, Ramón J. La caída del liberalismo amarillo: tiempo y drama de Antonio Paredes. Caracas: Editorial Planeta, 1993. 553 p.

Ultima reedición de ésta crónica exhaustiva acerca del desmantelamiento del sistema caudillista en las últimas décadas del siglo XIX y primeros años del siglo XX. A través del estudio de las actuaciones políticas de Antonio Paredes, caudillo liberal, se reconstruye el proceso que pone fin a la hegemonía del Partido Liberal Amarillo en Venezuela.

2682 Yarrington, Doug. Public land settlement, privatization, and peasant protest in Duaca, Venezuela, 1870–1936. (*HAHR*, 74:1, Feb. 1994, p. 33–61, map, table)

Important regional study focusing on district of Duaca in the state of Lara uses a variety of archival and published sources. Examines how growing power of central government accelerated coffee cultivation, land privatization, and peasant proletarianization. Argues that political centralization under Gómez made it possible for local and national elites to appropriate public lands and convert the occupants into tenants, giving elites access to peasant labor.

Colombia and Ecuador

JANE M. RAUSCH, *Professor of History, University of Massachusetts-Amherst*

DURING THE PAST 30 YEARS, the study of history as a serious academic discipline in Colombia has steadily matured. Although Velandia's valuable book on the Academia Colombiana de Historia (item **2734**) reminds us not to negate the contributions of traditional historians, there is a new generation of scholars, trained by history faculties at Colombian universities and also abroad, who are posing new questions, experimenting with methodologies, and exploring untapped archives. This transformation is reflected in the articles edited since 1963 by members of the History Dept. of the Univ. Nacional in Bogotá and published in the *Anuario Colombiano de Historia Social y de la Cultura,* several of which are annotated below, and by the high quality and varied themes of papers presented at the Congreso Nacional de Historia de Colombia held at the Univ. Industrial de Santander (8th, Bucaramanga, 1992, item **2703**). Perhaps the best indication, however, is the groundbreaking *La historia al final del milenio* (item **2691**), in which Colombian and foreign historians critically evaluate the status of research on a variety of colonial and national topics. Their essays attest to the enormous strides made in historiography in recent years and to the vigor of Colombian intellectual life in spite of the country's political travails.

With regard to the publication of documents, a trend noted in previous years, this report includes descriptions of four collections (items **2704, 2683, 2684,** and **2685.**) that complete the 80-volume project begun in 1986 by the Fundación Francisco Paula de Santander with the goal of making available modern, critical editions of Santander's correspondence, diaries, and other documents related to his life and times. Enhanced by introductory essays and notations on methodology, these volumes supersede older existing editions. Especially valuable is *Santander y los libros* (item **2683**), which includes, in addition to a catalog of Santander's library at the time of his death, a list of all the volumes in the Fundación project, indexed by title and author.

Another collaborative project worthy of mention is *Historia de las fuerzas militares de Colombia,* sponsored by the Ministry of Defense and edited by Gen. Alvaro Valencia Tovar (item **2711**). Modeled after the *Nueva historia de Colombia* (see *HLAS 52:2367–2372*), the set includes three volumes on the army and one each on the air force, navy, and national police. The texts consist of essays written by 14 active or retired officers. Containing up-to-date bibliographies, maps, and photographs, the books promise to be valuable reference works for many decades. *Conflicto amazónico 1932/1934,* also edited by Valencia Tovar, is an anthology of essays by military historians focusing on Colombia's war with Peru over Leticia (item **2702**).

Turning now to monographs and articles, biography, regional history, and La Violencia remain popular topics, although methodologies vary considerably. Restrepo Restrepo combines the first two subjects in his impressive study of Antioqueñan lawyer, Pedro Antonio Restrepo Escovar (item **2720**). Utilizing Restrepo Escovar's diaries written between 1859–99, the author shows how one man's career can illustrate major regional developments of the late-19th century. More classic in approach are Antei's study of the early years of Agustín Codazzi (item **2690**) and a new edition of Grillo's life of Santander, *El hombre de las leyes* (item **2710**), while the volumes dealing with Manuela Sáenz (item **2749**) and Vicente Lizcano (item **2735**) combine selections from their writings with biographical essays by contemporary scholars. Two contrasting monographs, one a *tesis de grado* (item **2732**) and the other a more personal memoir (item **2709**), offer insights into the career of Jorge Eliécer Gaitán.

Among the regional studies, Clavijo Ocampo (item **2701**) and Valencia Llano (item **2731**) use local notarial records. In his analysis of 19th-century Antioqueñan colonization, Eduardo Santa adds oral testimony and personal experience to these materials to demonstrate that the pioneer movement was spontaneous (item **2724**). In *Nación y etnias,* a geographer and a historian provide an excellent introduction to the understudied Amazon region (item **2707**), while *Historia económica y social del Caribe colombiano* offers a survey of the Caribbean coast from 1498–1994 (item **2699**).

Continuing unabated is the interest in La Violencia, which, as Ricardo Peñaranda noted in 1992, "has produced the most voluminous set of studies on a single subject ever seen in Colombian historiography" (see p. 294 of *Violence in Colombia,* reviewed in *HLAS 52:2394*). Sáenz Rovner's revised dissertation shows that although powerful Colombian industrialists did not cause La Violencia, they took advantage of it between 1945–50 to increase their political and economic influence (item **2722**). Barbosa Estepa uses oral testimony and printed sources to analyze the origin and characteristics of La Violencia within the unique history of the Llanos (item **2695**). Alape has completed the second volume of his biography of FARC leader Pedro Antonio Marín (item **2718**), and recent guerrilla movements of the 1980s are the subject of articles by Ortiz (item **2718**) and Chernick and Jiménez (item **2700**). Most importantly, in his stimulating sociocultural history of the development of Colombian identity in the 20th century (item **2729**), Uribe Celis places La Violencia in a broader context, suggesting that the ideological nature of politics, rapid modernization, and failure to develop true democracy have perpetuated the phenomenon.

Historical research in Ecuador still lags behind that of Colombia, but the papers presented at international seminars on the "Significance of Liberalism in Ecuador" (item **2743**) and on Ecuador's African roots (item **2736**) reveal that new as well as traditional topics are attracting scholarly attention. Among noteworthy monographs dealing with the 19th century are Darío Lara's well-researched biography of LaFond de Lurcy (item **2742**), whose account of his experiences in Ecuador is an important source for the independence era, and Tobar Donoso's examination of the evolution of the legal status of Indians with regard to tithing, debt peonage, and agrarian reform (item **2750**).

For the 20th century, Vol. 12 of the *Nueva historia del Ecuador,* edited by Ayala Mora, offers essays by knowledgeable historians on urban development, provincial organization, demography, and regionalism (item **2746**). There are two fine studies of five-time president José María Velasco Ibarra: Maiguashca's article examining the socioeconomic conditions that led to the emergence of *velasquismo* (item **2745**) and De la Torre's dissertation focusing on the caudillo's early career (item **2751**). Ycaza Cortez extends his history of labor to cover the post-WWII era (item **2752**), and finally, Goffin's survey of the growth of fundamentalist Protestant groups is a sobering indictment of their impact on native cultures and the environment (item **2741**).

SANTANDEREANA

2683   Fundación para la Conmemoración del Bicentenario del Natalicio y el Sesquicentenario de la Muerte del General Francisco de Paula Santander. Santander y los libros. Bogotá: Fundación para la Conmemoración del Bicentenario del Natalicio y el Sesquicentenario de la Muerte del General Francisco de Paula Santander, 1993. 3 v. (Biblioteca de la Presidencia de la República)

Concluding three-volume set in the 80-volume series published between 1988–93 by the Fundación Francisco de Paula Santander. Vol. 1 describes the editorial project, reviews earlier editions of the Archivo Santander, and lists errors located in the 24-volume Archivo Santander (1913–32) uncovered by Gustavo Otero Muñoz. Vol. 2 has brief biography of Santander and a catalogue of his library at the time of his death. Vol. 3 lists all volumes in the Fundación Francisco de Paula Santander series, indexed by title and author. It also includes listings of all places, statues, monuments, etc. named after Santander in Colombia.

2684   Fundación para la Conmemoración del Bicentenario del Natalicio y el Sesquicentenario de la Muerte del General Francisco de Paula Santander. Santander y los ingleses, 1832–1840. v. 1–2. Recopilación de Malcolm D. Deas y Efraín Sánchez. Bogotá: Fundación para la Conmemoración del Bicentenario del Natalicio y el Sesquicentenario de la Muerte del General Francisco de Paula Santander, 1991. 2 v.: indexes. (Biblioteca de la Presidencia de la República) (Col. Documentos; 70–71. Biblioteca de la Presidencia de la República)

Compilation of British Foreign Office consular reports from 1832–40 chosen to give insight to the British appraisal of Santander's Administration. Vol. 1 features correspondence between William Turner and Lord Palmerston. Vol. 2 includes documents related to the trial and imprisonment of consul Joseph Russell in Panama, 1836–37. Original documents followed by Spanish translations. Fine introduction by Malcolm Deas provides historical context.

2685 Hall, Francis and **William Duane.** Santander y la opinión angloamericana: visión de viajeros y periódicos, 1821–1840. Repertorio noticioso de *Niles' Weekly Register, The Albion, New York Daily Advertiser.* Recopilación de David Sowell. Bogotá: Fundación para la Conmemoración del Bicentenario del Natalicio y el Sesquicentenario de la Muerte del General Francisco de Paula Santander, 1991. 523 p.: ill., indexes. (Biblioteca de la Presidencia de la República)

Anthology of writings about Colombia and New Granada by North American and British travelers and journalists. Includes accounts by Benthamist Col. Francis Hall (1824) and Col. William Duane (1823–24) and articles reporting political events published from 1821–40 in the *Niles' Weekly Register* (Baltimore), *The Albion* (New York) and the *New York Daily Advertiser.* This is the first new edition of the Hall work in either English or Spanish since 1824. As Sowell's excellent introduction suggests, the periodicals reveal North American concerns with regard to Colombia and a grudging admiration for Santander.

COLOMBIA

2686 Acevedo Carmona, Darío. Consideraciones críticas sobre la historiografía de los artesanos del siglo XIX. (*Anu. Colomb. Hist. Soc. Cult.,* 18/19, 1990/91, p. 125–144, bibl.)

Valuable review of 15 studies on 19th-century artisans suggesting a need for a more critical examination of primary sources. Does not cite recent work by David Sowell.

2687 Aguilera Peña, Mario and **Renán Vega Cantor.** Ideal democrático y revuelta popular: bosquejo histórico de la mentalidad política popular en Colombia, 1781–1948. Bogotá: Instituto María Cano, 1991. 251 p.: bibl., ill.

Prize-winning analysis studies impact of the ideology of the French Revolution (1789) on Colombian popular consciousness and political history. Emphasis on Independence era, events of 1848, Regeneration, 1920s socialism and Gaitanismo. Helpful charts. Extensive bibliography.

2688 Alape, Arturo. Tirofijo: los sueños y las montañas, 1964–1984. Bogotá: Planeta, 1994. 295 p.: bibl. (Col. Documento)

Vol. 2 of Alape's biography of guerrilla leader Pedro Antonio Marín covers the 20 years from his founding of the Fuerzas Armadas Revolucionarias de Colombia (FARC) to signing of peace treaty with the Betancur government in 1984. Well-written, objective, and draws on extensive interviews and documentation. For Vol. 1, see *HLAS 52:2340.*

Alvarez Gutiérrez, Jaime. Carta a su Alteza, el Micer de Aragón, Señor de Castilla y Don de Parte del Mundo, Juan Carlos Alfonso Víctor María de Todos los Santos, Rey de España . . . See item **791.**

2689 Alvarez Restrepo, Antonio. Testimonio de un hijo del siglo. Bogotá: Fondo Cultural Cafetero, 1992. 373 p.: ill. (Ediciones Fondo Cultural Cafetero; 29)

Memoirs of the Banco Cafetero's founder, a prominent conservative who held a variety of government posts under Laureano Gómez and the National Front. Alvarez discusses 20th-century events and public figures as well as themes of national interest such as the La Violencia and the fall of Rojas Pinilla.

2690 Antei, Giorgio. Los héroes errantes: historia de Agustín Codazzi, 1793–1822. Bogotá: Planeta Colombiana Editorial, 1993. 540 p.: bibl., ill., index.

Examines childhood in Lugo, education in Pavia, and early military career of Italian-born colonel and engineer who headed the Chorographic Commission, 1849–59. Forthcoming second volume will cover his mature years from 1822–59. Draws on Italian, Colombian and US archives. Meticulous footnotes, extensive bibliography.

2691 Archila Neira, Mauricio *et al.* La historia al final del milenio: ensayos de historiografía colombiana y latinoamericana. v. 1–2. Recopilación de Bernardo Tovar Zambrano. Bogotá: Editorial Univ. Nacional, Facultad de Ciencias Humanas, Depto. de Historia, 1994. 2 v. (792 p.): bibl., ill.

Ground-breaking collaborative undertaking assesses the state of Colombian historiography at the end of the 20th century. Eight history professors from the Univ. Nacional review colonial-era research; 19th-century economic and social movements; 20th-century politics, social movements, and La

Violencia; and history of science. Other essays by leading US, French, English, and German historians examine writings of their countrymen on Colombia. Essential volumes for research libraries and serious scholars.

2692 Atehortúa, Adolfo León and **Humberto Vélez R.** Estado y fuerzas armadas en Colombia: 1886–1953. Cali, Colombia: Pontificia Univ. Javeriana, Seccional Cali; Bogotá: T.M. Editores, 1994. 235 p.: bibl. (Sociología y política. Académica)

Historical survey of military institutions from their origins to mid-20th century. Emphasizes formation, corporative values, perceptions of democracy, and civil-military relations. Pioneering work, intended to raise questions for further research. Includes extensive bibliography.

2693 Ayala Diago, César Augusto. El discurso de la conciliación: análisis cuantitativo de las intervenciones de Gustavo Rojas Pinilla entre 1952 y 1959. (*Anu. Colomb. Hist. Soc. Cult.*, 18/19, 1990/91, p. 205–243, tables)

Uses "content analysis" of key speeches made by Rojas Pinilla in 1953–54 and 1957 to show how the general adapted his public pronouncements to a new political age. Provides insight into the appeal of Alianza Nacional Popular (ANAPO) in the 1970s.

2694 Ayala Diago, César Augusto. El Movimiento de Acción Nacional (MAN): movilización y confluencia de idearios políticos durante el gobierno de Gustavo Rojas Pinilla. (*Anu. Colomb. Hist. Soc. Cult.*, 20, 1992, p. 44–70)

Examines aborted attempt by Rojas Pinilla supporters to create a third party in 1955. Argues that their failure was a victory for the Conservative bloc and marked the beginning of confrontations between the government and the press and the Church, resulting in the overthrow of the government.

2695 Barbosa Estepa, Reinaldo. Guadalupe y sus centauros: memorias de la insurrección llanera. Bogotá: Instituto de Estudios Políticos y Relaciones Internacionales de la Univ. Nacional; CEREC, 1992. 285 p.: bibl., maps. (Serie Historia contemporánea y realidad nacional; 31)

Uses oral testimony and printed sources to analyze origins and characteristics

of La Violencia from 1930–57 within the context of the unique history of the Llanos. Regards the movement as a revolution that revealed "inherent contradictions in a society that had developed at the margin of the national economic, social and cultural processes." Well-written and researched.

2696 Bejarano Avila, Jesús Antonio. Historia económica y desarrollo: la historiografía económica sobre los siglos XIX y XX en Colombia. Bogotá: CEREC, 1994. 291 p.: bibl. (Serie Textos; 22)

Comprehensive review of 1,300 books, articles, and theses published from 1950–80 dealing with Colombian economic history. Identifies predominant themes and discusses strengths and weaknesses of past and current research. Excellent bibliography. Fundamental source for reviewing historiography by foreign and national scholars.

2697 Bermúdez, Alberto. Historias de un pueblo rebelde: el Quindío, de la conquista al Departamento. Armenia, Colombia: Univ. del Quindío, 1992. 131 p.: bibl.

History of Quindío from 1541 to 1980s stresses that its creation as a department in 1966 was not the result of La Violencia, but rather, the consequence of a genuine sense of popular autonomy felt by the people. Good introduction to regional history.

Bermúdez Q., Suzy. Hijas, esposas y amantes: género, clase, etnia y edad en la historia de América Latina. See item **687.**

2698 Braun, Herbert, Our guerrillas, our sidewalks : a journey into the violence of Colombia / Herbert Braun. Niwot, Colo. : University Press of Colorado, c1994. ix, 239 p. : ill. ;

Spell-binding account of the 1988 kidnapping and subsequent rescue of American oilman Jake Gambini by ELN guerrillas. The author, leftist historian and brother-in-law of the victim, provides broad historical context and a narrative from three points of view: those of the guerrillas, Gambini, and his own. An intensely personal assessment of the impact of decades-long violence on contemporary Colombia.

2699 Castillo Mathieu, Nicolás del *et al.* Historia económica y social del Caribe colombiano. Bogotá: Ediciones Uninorte, Centro de Estudios Regionales; ECOE Ediciones, 1994. 370 p.: bibl., ill., maps. (Col. Textos universitarios de ECOE Ediciones. Col. Documentos; 72)

Eight scholars trace history of the Colombian Caribbean coast from 1498–1994. Arranged chronologically, essays emphasize economic and social developments. Two-thirds of book deals with national period. A chapter on San Andrés and Providencia Islands is especially helpful. Overall, the best history of this region to date.

2700 Chernick, Marc W. and **Michael F. Jiménez.** Popular liberalism, radical democracy, and Marxism: leftist politics in contemporary Colombia, 1974–1991. (*in* The Latin American left: from the fall of Allende to perestroika. Boulder, Colo.: Westview Press, 1993, p. 61–81)

Balanced review of recent guerrilla movements. Argues that "leftist politics after 1974 are best understood as the working out of long-standing forms of opposition to elite rule within a major redesign of Colombian capitalism and the State." Authors predict that opposition to oligarchical rule will continue to find "its customary expression" despite steps toward a more inclusive political system under Gaviria.

2701 Clavijo Ocampo, Hernán. Formación histórica de las elites locales en el Tolima. pt. 1–2. Bogotá: Fondo de Promoción de la Cultura del Banco Popular, 1993. 2 v.: bibl., map. (Biblioteca Banco Popular; 139–140)

Ground-breaking study on economic role of elites in Tolima based on local notarial records and other sources in regional and national archives. Vol. 1 covers 1600–1813; Vol. 2 considers development of mining, ranching, aguardiente monopoly, tobacco, and rice between 1814–1930. Prologue by Malcolm Deas describes the study as a "great mine" of information.

2702 Conflicto amazónico: 1932–1934. Dirección de Alvaro Valencia Tovar. Colombia: Villegas Editores, 1994. 303 p.: bibl., ill., maps.

Essays by military officers discuss various aspects of the Colombian-Peruvian conflict in the Amazon town of Leticia. Sponsored by the Ministry of Defense, the volume is lavishly illustrated with rare photographs from the period and includes some first-hand accounts. Excellent introduction to events

that triggered a unique outpouring of Colombian nationalism.

2703 Congreso Nacional de Historia de Colombia, 8th, Bucaramanga, 1992. Memorias. v. 1–3. Recopilación de Amado Guerrero Rincón. Bucaramanga, Colombia: Univ. Industrial de Santander, Facultad de Ciencias Humanas, Depto. de Historia; s.l.: Comisión V Centenario Colombia, 1993. 3 v.: bibl.

Papers in Vol. 1 deal with frontier, regional, urban and business history. Those in Vol. 2 mostly relate to the colonial period and treat the Columbus sesquicentennial. Vol. 3 covers political history from colony to present, social movements, and La Violencia. The breadth and high quality of these papers attest to the increasing professionalization of the study of history at Colombian universities.

2704 La Convención de Ocaña, 1828. v. 1–3. Bogotá: Fundación para la Conmemoración del Bicentenario del Natalicio y el Sesquicentenario de la Muerte del General Francisco de Paula Santander, 1993. 3 v.: bibl., ill., indexes. (Biblioteca de la Presidencia de la República)

Compilation of documents relating to the congress that met from March 2 to June 11, 1828 to revise the Constitution of 1821. Vol. 1 contains the acts of the sessions as well as ancillary materials such as declarations by municipalities, pronouncements by military officers, and government decrees dated from Aug. 21, 1826 to April 4, 1828. Vol. 2 includes ancillary documents dated from April 5 to June 16, 1828. Vol. 3 has ancillary documents dated from June 16 to Sept. 12, 1828 and a collection of official and private correspondence related to the congress. All volumes indexed by place, name and subject.

2705 Deas, Malcolm D. Del poder y la gramática: y otros ensayos sobre historia, política y literatura colombianas. Bogotá: Tercer Mundo Editores, 1993. 346 p.: bibl. (Historia)

Deas is a British historian renowned in Colombia for his studies of Colombian history and politics. Since arriving there in 1963, he has become part of the intellectual and political scene in Colombia as few foreign scholars have. This fine volume contains a prologue written by his longtime friend, former President Alfonso López Michelsen, followed by 13 essays on 19th-century Colombia. His essays on history are well informed and incisive, and his two essays on literature (one on Vargas Vila and another on Conrad's *Nostromo*) are equally impressive. [R.L. Williams]

2706 Deas, Malcolm D. Miguel Antonio Caro and friends: grammar and power in Colombia. (*Hist. Workshop,* 34, Autumn 1992, p. 47–71)

Sprightly, well-written, intriguing analysis of prominent role played by grammarian presidents Miguel Antonio Caro and Rufino Ciervo in Conservative Party hegemony from 1885–1930. Concludes that Conservative concern for pure language reflected their desire for connections with the past—a search for "things old, uncontaminated and essentially Spanish."

2707 Domínguez, Camilo and **Augusto Gómez.** Nación y etnias: conflictos territoriales en la Amazonia colombiana, 1750–1933. Bogotá: Disloque Editores, 1994. 245 p.: bibl., graphs, maps.

Geographical-historical analysis of integration of Amazon region into effective Colombian control during 19th and 20th centuries. Well-written text draws on archival sources and is divided into three sections: 1) the construction of nationalism in the Colombian Amazon; 2) Indian and white population movements; and 3) economic activities, especially quinine and rubber extraction. Excellent maps, graphs, and bibliography. Essential introduction to topic.

2708 Gómez, Augusto; Ana Cristina Lesmes; and Claudia Rocha. Caucherías y conflicto colombo-peruano: testimonios 1904–1934. Bogotá: Disloque Editores, 1995. 318 p.: bibl., ill., map.

First-hand accounts by Indians and soldiers involved in the Putumayo rubber scandal or in some phase of Colombian-Peruvian relations from 1903–33. Editors use these testimonies—most previously unpublished—to show how private interests and extractive economic activities turned the Amazon into a "Green Hell."

2709 Gómez Aristizábal, Horacio. Jorge Eliécer Gaitán y las conquistas sociales en Colombia. Bogotá: Publicaciones Univ. Central: Instituto Colombiano de Estudios Latinoamericanos y del Caribe, 1991. 223 p.: bibl.

Thoughtful biography of Gaitán focusing on his personality, goals, ideology, and struggle for social justice. Argues that he helped forge social consciousness in Colombia and was the first to involve the masses in his political strategy. Includes bibliography but no footnotes.

2710 Grillo, Max. Santander y los ignorados. v. 1–2. Estudio crítico-biográfico, selección y notas preliminares de Hernando Salazar Patiño. Manizales, Colombia?: Publicación Gobernación de Caldas, 1991. 2 v. (Biblioteca de autores caldenses. Col. clásica; 1)

Grillo (1868–1949) was a Liberal journalist, historian, poet, and important member of the modernismo movement. Vol. 1 includes informative introductory essay on Grillo's life and significance of his works, followed by his memoir of the War of The Thousand Days, *Emociones de la Guerra* (1903). Vol. 2 reprints his classic biography of Santander, *El Hombre de las leyes* (1940), and 17 short essays originally published in journals.

Guerrero Barón, Javier. Los años del olvido: Boyacá y los orígenes de la violencia. See *HLAS 55:4816.*

2711 Historia de las fuerzas militares de Colombia. v. 1–6. Dirección de Alvaro Valencia Tovar. Bogotá: Planeta, 1993. 6 v.: bibl., ill., indexes.

Multi-volume survey of the history of Colombia's armed forces and police from conquest to 1991, compiled by a team of 14 military historians under the direction of Gen. Alvaro Valencia Tovar. Vols. 1–3 trace the evolution of the army from colonial times to present; Vol. 4 deals with the navy; Vol. 5, the air force; and Vol. 6, the police. Contributors are active or retired military personnel who maintain objectivity and achieve high intellectual standards. Fills an enormous void in historical literature and promises to be a useful reference tool for many years.

2712 Iriarte, Alfredo. Toros de Altamira y Lascaux a las arenas colombianas: mitos, leyendas, historias. Bogotá: Amazonas Editores, 1992. 157 p.: ill. (some col.).

Lavishly illustrated coffee-table book offers well-written survey of bullfighting in Colombia from colonial times to the present. Compares the sport's development in various cities and examines its role as a theme in art and literature. No bibliography or footnotes.

2713 Koonings, Kees and **Menno Vellinga.** Origen y consolidación de la burguesía industrial en Antioquia. (*in* Burguesías e industria en América Latina y Europa meridional. Recopilación de Mario Cerutti y Menno Vellinga. Madrid: Alianza Editorial, 1989, p. 55–104, appendix, bibl., tables)

Two Dutch scholars review previous theories explaining Antioqueñan entrepreneurship and offer their own interpretation that considers both internal and external factors in a concrete historical context.

Maiguashca, Juan. Las clases subalternas en los años treinta. See *HLAS 55:1813.*

2714 Martínez Carreño, Aída. Sastres y modistas: notas alrededor de la historia del traje en Colombia. (*Bol. Cult. Bibliogr.,* 28:28, 1991, p. 61–75, ill.)

Brief survey of dressmaking in New Granada from the 16th to the late 19th centuries notes the gradual transformation of a male-dominated craft to one practiced primarily by women. Well-documented and illustrated but directed to a popular audience.

2715 Medina, Medófilo. Obispos, curas y elecciones, 1929–1930. (*Anu. Colomb. Hist. Soc. Cult.,* 18/19, 1990/91, p. 185–204)

Intriguing analysis of clerical participation in the 1929–30 electoral campaign. Uses contemporary periodical sources to underscore ideological schism between Archbishop Perdomo and other bishops. Demonstrates that the election marked the end of the traditional role played by the Catholic hierarchy in Colombian politics, with serious repercussions in the decades to come.

2716 Obregón Torres, Diana. La sociedad de naturalistas neogranadinos a la invención de una tradición. (*Interciencia/Caracas,* 17:3, May/June 1992, p. 135–140, bibl.)

Analysis of the ephemeral existence of the Sociedad de Naturalistas Neogranadinos (1859–61). Argues that despite efforts of members to keep alive the scientific tradition begun by the Botanical Expedition in New Granada, their society failed because Colombian elites were too preoccupied with business and politics to support scientific endeavors.

2717 Ocampo Trujillo, José Fernando. Ensayos sobre historia de Colombia. Manizales, Colombia: Impr. Departamental,

1988. 172 p.: bibl. (Biblioteca de escritores caldenses)

Four polemical but well-researched essays focus on Manizales' role in the wars of 1860 and 1876; the antecedents of Regeneration, 1875–85; López Pumarejo's *revolución en marcha* as an impediment to radical social and economic change; and events between 1946–53 that paved the way for the National Front.

2718 Ortiz S., Carlos Miguel. Violencia política de los ochenta: elementos para una reflexión histórica. (*Anu. Colomb. Hist. Soc. Cult.,* 18/19, 1990/91, p. 245–280)

Analysis of guerrilla movements of the 1980s stresses their continuity with the guerrilla groups of the 1940s and 1950s. Concludes that such forms of anti-social behavior will continue as long as the make-up of the Colombian State remains unchanged.

2719 Pinzón de Lewin, Patricia. El ejército y las elecciones: ensayo histórico. Bogotá: CEREC, 1994. 205 p.: bibl. (Serie Historia contemporánea y realidad nacional; 33)

Draws on *Memorias de Guerra* and Ministerio de Gobierno documents in the Archivo Nacional (Bogotá) to trace role of military as voters and as an instrument for ensuring orderly elections from 1810 to National Front period. Concludes that since the 1907 reform, with the exception of the Rojas Pinilla regime, the military has eschewed partisanship and facilitated peaceful elections.

2720 Restrepo Restrepo, Jorge Alberto. Retrato de un patriarca antioqueño: Pedro Antonio Restrepo Escovar, 1815–1899; abogado, político, educador y fundador de Andes. Bogotá: Banco de la República, 1992. 469 p.: bibl., ill., index. (Col. bibliográfica Banco de la República. Historia colombiano)

Innovative study of the founder of Andes, an Antioquian town, based on diaries written between 1858–99. Presents Restrepo Escovar as "paradigmatic" of a way of living and of an epoch in Antioquia. Demonstrates that biography, largely neglected by economic and social historians, complements and challenges interpretations drawn from a more generalized approach to history.

2721 Romero Moreno, María Eugenia. Ensayos orinoquenses. Bogotá: Orinoquia Siglo XXI, 1988. 113 p.: bibl., ill., maps.

Ten essays survey demography, history,

society and culture of the Colombian llanos. Author is anthropologist with broad experience on the region. Includes examples of folksongs and poems and a bibliography of 18th- and 19th-century travel accounts. Excellent, up-to-date introduction.

2722 Sáenz Rovner, Eduardo. La ofensiva empresarial: industriales, políticos y violencia en los años 40 en Colombia. Bogotá: Ediciones Uniandes; Tercer Mundo Editores, 1992. 279 p., 16 p. of plates: bibl., ill. (Historia económica)

Revised dissertation (Brandeis Univ., 1988) uses previously unexplored archival material, including the papers of ANDI (Asociación Nacional de Industriales), to trace influence of powerful industrialists in Colombian politics and society between 1945–50. Argues that although industrialists were not the cause of La Violencia, they took advantage of it to increase their power. Major contribution to an under-studied era.

2723 Salazar Santos, Santiago. Alfonso López Pumarejo: mis recuerdos sobre su vida y su obra. Bogotá: Bolivar; Univ. Externado de Colombia, 1993? 229 p., 8 p. of plates: ill.

Personal recollections about López Pumarejo, by a colleague and former Colombian ambassador to Canada. Provides insight into the personality, character and political life of the man described as "the most original and influential liberal leader in Colombian political history of this century and the most civilized gentleman (*hombre civil*) that I have known."

2724 Santa, Eduardo. La colonización antioqueña: una empresa de caminos. Bogotá: TM Editores, 1993. 312 p.: bibl. (Historia)

Uses archival materials, traveler accounts, and oral testimony to argue convincingly that the movement was spontaneous, as pioneers cut roads through the wilderness and built resting places (*fondas camineras*) around which towns soon emerged. Later congress passed laws to stimulate the foundation of towns and roads, which became the source of economic and industrial development.

2725 Sourdis de De la Vega, Adelaida. Cartagena de Indias durante la Primera República, 1810–1815. Bogotá: Banco de la República, 1988. 160 p.: bibl., map. (Col. bibliográfica Banco de la República. Historia colombiana)

Narrative history based on careful review of archival documents on Bogotá, Cartagena, and Segovia. Argues that the destructive Spanish seige of 1815 capped a process of deterioration begun by the violent struggle between autonomists and *independentistas*, and that Cartagena's defeat doomed the Caribbean coast, with the exception of Barranquilla, to stagnation during the 19th century.

2726 Sowell, David. La Caja de Ahorros de Bogotá, 1846–1865: artisans, credit, development, and savings in early national Colombia. (*HAHR*, 73:4, Nov. 1993, p. 615–638, tables)

Examines the Caja de Ahorros as a "neo-Bourbon initiative." Concludes that the Caja filled a banking vacancy as "perhaps only a government-sponsored agency could," but that it nevertheless failed to stimulate development or growth of small industries around Bogotá.

2727 Torres Carrillo, Alfonso. Estudios sobre pobladores urbanos en Colombia: balance y perspectivas. (*Maguaré/Bogotá*, 9, 1993, p. 131–146, photo)

Lamenting the lack of attention paid to the role of urban masses in contemporary Colombian history, author critiques studies done to date and outlines a methodology for recovering the history of the urban barrio.

2728 Tovar Pinzón, Hermes. Que nos tengan en cuenta: colonos, empresarios y aldeas; Colombia, 1800–1900. Bogotá: Tercer Mundo Editores, 1995. 256 p.

Prize-winning study uses regional archival sources to compare colonization movements on the frontiers of Antioquia, Santander, and Tolima. Argues that frontier society reflected attributes of distinctive regions rather than a common national identity. Challenges previous theories by showing that "*convivencia* between State, *colonos* and *empresarios* made possible an economy of sufficiency for thousands of poor people."

2729 Uribe Celis, Carlos. La mentalidad del colombiano: cultura y sociedad en el siglo XX. Bogotá: Ediciones Alborada; Editorial Nueva América, 1992. 209 p.: bibl.

Stimulating exploration of Colombian identity by a sociologist thoroughly grounded in cultural history. Pt. 1 surveys developments by decade from the turn of the century to the 1960s. Pt. 2 examines the continuum of violence and cites as causes the ideological nature of Colombian politics and the disruption caused by rapid modernization after WWI. Pt. 3 speculates on what it means to be Colombian.

2730 Uribe Uribe, Julián. Memorias de Julián Uribe Uribe. Prólogo y notas de Edgar Toro Sánchez. Bogotá: Banco de la República, 1994. 623 p.: bibl., ill., indexes, maps. (Col. bibliográfica Banco de la República. Historia colombiana)

Uribe Uribe (1857–1930) was an Antioqueñan engineer who directed construction of the Pacific railroad linking Cali with Buenaventura. His memoirs, published for the first time, provide insight into political and economic events as well as the careers of his brothers Rafael and Tomás. Prologue by Toro Sánchez contains a brief biography. His notes and index enhance volume's utility.

2731 Valencia Llano, Alonso. Empresarios y políticos en el Estado Soberano del Cauca: 1860–1895. Cali, Colombia: Editorial Facultad de Humanidades, Especialización en la Enseñanza de las Ciencias Sociales, Historia de Colombia, 1993. 327 p.: bibl.

Meticulous economic history draws on regional archival sources to answer the question, "Why did successful economic enterprises exist in Cauca during an age in which little capital could be risked because of the unstable political climate?" Includes chapters on educational reform, colonization, and communication as well as on production and commerce.

2732 Vásquez Higuera, Julio César. Gaitán: mito y realidad de un caudillo. Prólogo de Horacio Serpa Uribe. 2. ed. Tunja, Colombia: Talleres de Servicios Gráficos, 1992. 348 p.: bibl., ill.

Well-researched *tesis de grado* covers four topics: 1) Gaitán as theorist, lawyer, and politician; 2) origin and collapse of his political movement, UNIR; 3) causes and consequences of the April 9 assassination; and 4) enduring impact of Gaitán's ideology. Author is lawyer, administrator, and former mayor of Paipa (Boyacá). Assessment of Gaitán's legacy for contemporary Colombia is especially interesting.

2733 Vázquez Carrizosa, Alfredo. Historia diplomática de Colombia. v. 1. Bogotá: Pontificia Univ. Javeriana, Maestría en Relaciones Internacionales, 1993. 1 v.: bibl.

Comprehensive survey of Gran Colombian diplomacy during rule of Bolívar and Santander, 1819–30. Covers relations with other Spanish American states and the Holy See; the Panama Conference of 1826; border disputes; and efforts to establish a monarchy.

Vázquez Cobo, Alfredo. Pro patria: la expedición militar al Amazonas en el Conflicto de Leticia. See *HLAS 55:4280.*

2734 Velandia, Roberto. La Academia Colombiana de Historia. Bogotá: Editorial Kelly, 1988. 114 p.: bibl., ports.

Straightforward history of the Academia from its founding in 1902 to 1988. Includes lists of all former and present members, archives, publications, and activities. Useful reference tool.

2735 Villanueva Martínez, Orlando *et al.* Biófilo Panclasta, el eterno prisionero: aventuras y desventuras de un anarquista colombiano. Bogotá: Ediciones Proyecto Cultural Alas de Xué, 1992. 357 p.: bibl., ill.

Vicente Lizcano (1879–1942), whose pseudonym was Biófilo Panclasta, was a Colombian-born anarchist active in Russia, Turkey, Spain, Italy, US, and Venezuela. Believing him to be unfairly ignored by Colombian academics, five collaborators present his biography and a selection of his newspaper articles and letters, and suggest his importance to 20th-century history.

ECUADOR

Andrien, Kenneth J. The State and dependency in late colonial and early republican Ecuador. See item **2315.**

Arosemena, Guillermo. El comercio exterior del Ecuador. v. 1–3. See item **2316.**

2736 Congreso El Negro en la Historia, *3rd, Esmeraldas, Ecuador, 1992* El Negro en la historia: raíces africanas en la nacionalidad ecuatoriana. Coordinación de Rafael Savoia. Quito: Centro Cultural Afroecuatoriano, 1992. 239 p.: bibl., ill., maps. (Col. Medio milenio; 9. Col. CCA; 3)

Seventeen papers reveal growing scholarly interest in African contribution to Ecuadorian history. Topics cover colonial and national eras and include demography, African roots, slavery, and genealogies. Ten papers concern Esmeraldas. Others deal with Valle del Chota, Cuenca del Río Mira, Guayaquil and Zamura. For papers from the second conference, see *HLAS 54:2670.*

2737 Corral Burbano de Lara, Fabián *et al.* El Chagra. Quito: Impr. Mariscal, 1993. 180 p.: bibl., ill. (chiefly col.).

Multifaceted portrait of the Ecuadorian "chagra" or cowboy as an essential national type. Coffee-table book with lavishly illustrated chapters on cowboys, horses, riding equipment, rodeos, fiestas, and houses. Includes glossary and bibliography.

2738 Davis, Roger P. The local dynamics of national dissent: the Ecuadorian *pronunciamientos* of 1826. (*Historian/Honor Society,* 55:2, Winter 1993, p. 289–302, maps)

Comparative analysis of the Guayaquil, Quito, and Cuenca *pronunciamientos* issued between July and Sept. 1826 in opposition to Santander in Bogotá and in support of Bolívar and the new Bolivian Constitution. Argues that "the outlines of early Ecuador" can be discerned in these local dynamics of national dissent.

Demélas-Bohy, Marie-Danielle. L'invention politique: Bolivie, Equateur, Pérou au XIXe siècle. See item **2773.**

2739 Destruge Illingworth, Camilo. Urvina, el presidente: biografía del General José María Urvina. Quito: Banco Central del Ecuador, 1992. 309 p.: ill., index. (Col. histórica; 23)

First printed edition of a biography written between 1911–13 about Liberal Gen. José María Urvina (1808–91), who dominated Ecuadorian history between 1845–60. Author was a Liberal, journalist, historian, and director of the Biblioteca Municipal of Guayaquil. Well-documented manuscript presents positive image of Urvina and remains the most detailed study of his career to date.

2740 Eguiguren Valdivieso, Genaro. El gobierno federal de Loja: la crisis de 1858. Quito: Corporación Editora Nacional, 1992. 131 p.: bibl., ill., map. (Biblioteca de ciencias sociales; 41)

Study of federal government established in Loja Province 1859–61. Explores difficulties confronting Ecuadorians in creating a unified state in the early national era. Relies primarily on published sources. Useful monograph on a little known subject.

2741 Goffin, Alvin Matthew. The rise of Protestant evangelism in Ecuador, 1895–1990. Gainesville: Univ. Press of Florida, 1994. 189 p.: bibl., ill., index, maps.

Traces growth of fundamentalist Protestant groups in context of nationalism, imperialism, religious tolerance, and cultural hegemony. Describes response of Catholic Church and indigenous peoples. Acknowledges some positive influences but emphasizes that these movements have disrupted native cultures, exploited the natural environment, and failed to promote social justice. Sobering indictment, carefully researched and written.

Jurado Noboa, Fernando. La migración internacional a Quito entre 1534 y 1934. v. 1–3. See item **2337.**

2742 Lara, A. Darío. Gabriel Lafond de Lurcy: viajero y testigo de la historia ecuatoriana. Quito: Banco Central del Ecuador, 1988. 317 p.: bibl., ill. (Col. histórica; 16)

Scholarly biography of Lafond de Lurcy (1801–76) who lived in Ecuador from 1820–28 and whose book, *Voyagers dans les Amériques* (Paris, 1847), is a key source for the independence era. Lara supports authenticity of the controversial Lafond letter concerning the Guayaquil interview. Informative and well-written. Lacks index, but includes extensive bibliography.

2743 El liberalismo en el Ecuador: de la gesta al porvenir. Edición de Blasco Peñaherrera Padilla. Quito: Corporación Editora Nacional; Fundación Eloy Alfaro; Fundación Friedrich Naumann, 1991. 258 p.: bibl. (Col. Temas; 3)

Collection of papers and comments presented at a 1990 international seminar on "The Significance of Liberalism in Ecuador" held to commemorate the Revolution of June 5, 1895. Authors include academics, politicians, and journalists who discuss the past and future of Liberalism, still regarded as the most popular political movement in Ecuador.

2744 López R., Fernando. Nacimiento de una región: propuesta de historia económica y social de Santo Domingo de los Colorados entre 1860 y 1960. Quito: Municipalidad de Santo Domingo, 1992. 265 p.: bibl., ill.

Located between Quito and the coast, Santo Domingo de los Colorados grew from fewer than 4,000 inhabitants at the beginning of the 20th century to more than 30,000 by 1960. This study analyzes various factors promoting development. Includes many documents related to land grants and colonization. Excellent bibliography.

2745 Maiguashca, Juan. Los sectores subalternos en los años 30 y el aparecimiento del velasquismo. (*in* Las crisis en el Ecuador: los treinta y ochenta. Quito: Corporación Editora Nacional, 1991, p. 79–93, table)

Well-researched essay argues that economic diversification in Ecuador between 1920–50 led to a dislocation in traditional relations between the dominant and subdominant social classes. This change enabled the masses to take advantage of new opportunities to play an active role in the political movement created by José Velasco Ibarra.

2746 Nueva historia del Ecuador. v. 12, Ensayos generales I. Espacio, población, región. Edición de Enrique Ayala Mora. Quito: Corporación Editora Nacional: Grijalbo, 1992? 1 v.: bibl., ill., maps, tables.

Part of 15-volume series edited by Enrique Ayala Mora, Vol. 12 contains essays by Ecuadorian scholars on urban and provincial organization, demography, and regionalism during the 20th century. Others trace history of Amazonas, Galápagos Islands, and efforts to establish international borders. Includes excerpts from key documents, helpful summaries, maps and bibliography, but no index. Excellent introduction to these topics. For review of earlier volumes, see *HLAS 54:2679.*

2747 Pensamiento de Pedro Moncayo. Edición de Enrique Ayala Mora. Quito: Corporación Editora Nacional, 1993. 213 p.: bibl., indexes. (Biblioteca de ciencias sociales; 20)

Moncayo (1807–88), a journalist, diplomat, historian, lawyer, and member of Liberal party, was a major public figure in Ecuador from 1830 until his death. This volume combines a selection of his speeches in parliament (1845–58) with six essays examining his life by Ecuadorian scholars.

2748 Rodríguez, Linda Alexander. Las finanzas públicas en el Ecuador liberal, 1895–1925. (*Secuencia/México,* 23, mayo/agosto 1992, p. 125–172, bibl., ill., tables)

Wide-ranging survey of all aspects of public finance during Liberal era. Topics include regionalization, commerce, taxation, foreign debt, budgets, banking policies, and the coup of 1925. Numerous statistical tables provide fundamental data for economic historians.

2749 Sáenz, Manuela. Patriota y amante de usted: Manuela Sáenz y el Libertador; diarios inéditos. Textos de Elena Poniatowska *et al.* México: Editorial Diana, 1993. 297 p.: ill.

Correspondence between Bolívar and Manuela Sáenz, arranged with excerpts from the latter's diaries of Quito (1822) and Paita (1840–46), document their evolving relationship. Includes brief biography of Sáenz by Carlos Alvarez Saa and commentaries by Elena Poniatowska, Miguel Bonasso, and Hans Dieterich Steffan. Good introduction to a still-understudied topic.

Salvador Lara, Jorge. Breve historia contemporánea del Ecuador. See item **2373.**

2750 Tobar Donoso, Julio. El indio en el Ecuador independiente. Quito: Pontificia Univ. Católica del Ecuador, 1992. 554 p.: index.

Careful examination of legal status of Indians in Ecuador from 1830–1970. Focus is on tithing, debt peonage, and agrarian reform. Author was a lawyer who helped to develop some 20th-century reforms. Footnotes but no bibliography.

2751 Torre, Carlos de la. La seducción velasquista. Quito: Ediciones Libri Mundi, Enrique Grosse-Luemern; Facultad Latinoamericana de Ciencias Sociales FLACSO-Sede Ecuador, 1993. 261 p.: bibl., ill.

PhD dissertation draws on archival and periodical materials to examine the early career of José María Velasco Ibarra, five-time president of Ecuador, and the social and political movements of the 1930s and 1940s that brought him to power for the second time in 1944. Important contribution to the study of 20th-century populism.

Valencia Llano, Alonso. Elites, burocracia, clero y sectores populares en la Independencia Quiteña, 1809–1812. See item **2378.**

2752 Ycaza Cortez, Patricio. Lucha sindical
y popular en un período de transición
(*in* El Ecuador de la Postguerra. Quito: Banco
Central de Ecuador, 1992, v. 2, p. 543–568,
bibl.)
    Surveys strikes, struggles, and adjust-

ments of working class labor organizations
during the transition period between 1948–70
when the economy changed from being predominantly *agroexportadora* to *agrominera-
exportadora*, with considerable, although
late-developing, industrial growth.

Peru

NILS P. JACOBSEN, *Associate Professor, University of Illinois, Urbana-Champaign*

IN THE PREVIOUS VOLUME, *HLAS 54*, the sense predominated that historiography on republican Peru was in a phase of open-ended transition, with a balance
between old and new themes and approaches. Now the shape of the new predominant approaches is beginning to come into focus. The new methods examine linkages between culture, economy, society, and politics, including the hidden meanings
of doctrines, institutions, and practices, while admitting a plurality of voices and
twisted paths, all of which makes it more difficult for the historian to proclaim the
inevitability of outcomes.

Perhaps the field where these shifting sensitivities and approaches to Peruvian
history have produced the most interesting work reviewed for this volume is in what
could be called the "new political history." Two distinct conceptual approaches,
often at odds with each other, characterize recent studies in this field: 1) the Gramscian notion of hegemony; and 2) discourse analysis and the concept of political culture pioneered by French historians, such as Roger Chartier and Maurice Agulhon.
Mallon's study of the role of peasants in the formation of the Mexican and Peruvian nation-states is clearly the most important recent work using the first line of
approach (item **2791**). She demonstrates innovative ways of exploring the impact
of peasants on local and national power structures, but leaves the reader with the
depressingly pessimistic notion that Peruvian governments, for decades after the
mid-1880s, relied entirely on repression in their attempts to extend the writ of Lima
across the national territory. Thurner (item **2811**) and Méndez (item **2795**) are pursu-
ing similar issues as they explore the lack of connection between highland peasant
notions of republican citizenship and the exclusivist national identity espoused by
Creole elites. In his essay on the social bases of politics in a northern highland province, Taylor suggests that changing social structures in fact reinforced clientelism
and caudillo politics rather than weakening them (item **2810**).

During the current reporting period, the most important example of the second line of new political history—concerned primarily with discourse analysis and
the construction of a national political culture—is Demélas' work (item **2773**). Her
comparative study examines the Andean countries' "seduction" by democratic politics arising out of the French and American Revolutions. According to her model,
which follows that of François Xavier Guerra, politics adapted in strange and unexpected ways, while society remained "traditional." Less methodologically ambitious, but similarly revisionist in its conclusions, is the work by Mc Evoy about Manuel Pardo and the early Civilista Party, which rejects the conventional dismissal of
Pardo and his group as nouveau-riche guano contractors who seized the State merely

because of class interests (item **2794**). Instead, she credits Pardo for a far-reaching modernization project for the State and economy, with broad popular participation. Gootenberg also suggests that Pardo and other writers on economic affairs during the guano age presented sound proposals for national development, even though they never were applied (item **2784**).

As Irurozqui points out, this potential for revisionism arises primarily because liberal and Marxist teleological notions about Peruvian history are no longer tenable (item **2787**). Certainly this rejection of much of the historical writing produced between the 1960s-80s provides the impetus for Planas' somewhat simplistic, revisionist studies on the Generation of 1900 (item **2800**) and the Leguía regime (item **2801**). He suggests that during the aristocratic republic there existed fragile but significant developments towards pluralism and a more inclusive polity, which were destroyed through the "autocracy" of the Leguía regime.

Beyond the studies already mentioned by Gootenberg and Méndez, a number of historians published articles concerning political and social ideas. The excellent study by Dawe and Taylor on Enrique López Albújar's notions of banditry clearly demonstrates the complex amalgam of local knowledge and imported fashionable ideas present in an influential reformist author's representation of Peruvian social reality (item **2772**). De la Cadena enriches our understanding of indigenismo in Cusco, and, more generally, the construction of ethnicity, by relating both to the crucial social norm of "decencia" (item **2763**). Martínez Riaza (item **2793**) and González Calleja (item **2783**) underscore the drifting of conservative and authoritarian intellectuals and politicians in Peru between the 1920s and early 1940s towards the regimes of Primo de Rivera, Franco, and Mussolini, while the structural and institutional bases for emulating southern European corporatists and fascists remained weak in Peru.

A cultural approach to major themes in the history of republican Peru is just beginning to receive more attention. Majluf's suggestive essay on the growing use of monuments to shape popular memories demonstrates the important implications of this kind of research (item **2789**). Tamayo Herrera's preliminary study on the changing rituals of death in Lima (item **2809**) whets our appetite for more studies on rituals, both public and private, concerning life cycle events, and civil and religious celebrations.

One topic that continues to receive less attention than it deserves in the historiography of republican Peru is the history of women and, more broadly, of gender relations. Villavicencio's study has brought to light the surprising extent of women's participation in literary circles during the 1870s-80s and in various labor and reform organizations during the early-20th century (item **2815**). In addition, Cecilia Blondet has given us a cogent analysis of the surge in women's organizations since the early 1970s (item **2760**). Yet we still do not have any significant studies on the impact of gender relations on major issues in republican history.

Work on aspects of Peru's multi-ethnic character, on the position of its subalterns, and on immigration continued vigorously during this reporting period. Beyond the publications on highland Andean peasantries already mentioned, the most important achievements reviewed here were two major studies by Hünefeldt (item **2786**) and Aguirre (item **2754**) on the final phase of slavery and its abolition. More than earlier works, these publications stress the Afro-Peruvians' agency and their surprising space for negotiation with slave owners and various intermediary groups. Aguirre's depiction of early post-independence Lima society as atomistic and non-corporatist poses a major challenge to conventional conceptions.

New immigrant groups in 19th- and 20th-century Peru continue to receive considerable attention. Bonfiglio has written a well-documented, innovative monograph on Italian immigrants that offers new insights on the peculiar politics of this relatively small, but highly influential group (item **2761**). Trazegnies Granda's monumental epic on the fate of one Chinese coolie constitutes a successful exploration of a new way to write the history of those who are neither famous nor mighty (item **2812**). Furthermore, Rodríguez Pastor (item **2804**) and Lausent-Herrera (item **2788**) have published valuable accounts of the social and religious behavior of Chinese Peruvians.

Much of the best historiography on post-independence Peru continues to have a regional focus. One previously neglected region, Amazonia and the eastern piedmont of the Andes, is finally receiving the attention it deserves. A project at the Univ. de Barcelona has resulted in a string of publications by García Jordán (items **2780, 2781,** and **2782**) and Sala i Vila (item **2806**) that contribute much to our understanding of the contests and negotiations from the 1880s-1910s between the Catholic Church, the Peruvian State, and rubber entrepreneurs over control of the native population. The works present a plausible model for the distinct character of colonization in different southern Andean piedmont regions. Coomes and Barham (item **2769**) use neoclassical economic axioms to propose a thorough reinterpretation of the rubber boom throughout Amazonia, beyond the borders of Peru. Finally, the late Jesús Víctor San Román has given us an uneven, but serious and useful overview of the economic and social development of the Peruvian Amazon region since conquest (item **2807**).

Most contributions to economic history during this reporting period also have a regional focus. Burga's long essay on the agrarian conjunctures in central Peru, both coastal and highland, between the late colonial period and the 1850s demonstrates the tremendously diverse economic conditions from valley to valley and between production controlled by hacendados and that carried out by peasants (item **2762**). Two solid articles by Deustua underscore the important role of peasants and muleteers in the functioning of central Peru's regional markets, still articulated around the silver mines by the mid-19th century (items **2774** and **2775**). Contreras' close reading of land transactions among peasants in the Mantaro valley during the late 19th and early 20th centuries is a powerful reminder of how localized ethnic practices could shape economic behavior, even during periods of advanced market penetration (item **2768**). In the north, Bazán Alfaro and Gómez Cumpa suggest that it was not commodities but labor migration that defined regions by the time of the sugar estates' boom after 1890 (item **2759**). Overall, it appears that scholarly work on Peru's economic history is still declining, however. Martínez Alier's call for utilizing ecological models as a crucial method for understanding changing material conditions has so far found little echo, either (item **2792**).

Visual images are gaining in importance for our understanding of history. Three beautiful volumes in this reporting period fit this pattern. Mould de Pease and Longhi have assembled extraordinary photos and paintings in an up-beat nationalist volume showing how Peru became the diverse nation it is today (item **2798**). The editors of the volume on *pisco* bring to life every phase of its production, from the vineyards to the distilleries and bottling (item **2771**). But pride of place here belongs to the Smithsonian Institution's edition of selected photos by Martín Chambi (item **2765**), whose fame as one of the great photographers of the 20th century continues to grow. Better than any text, these photographs make clear how complicated Cusco regional society was during the mid-20th century: embracing the modern world, yet holding fast to its proud indigenous and colonial Spanish past. Chambi's work shows his mastery of profound, multifaceted visions.

2753 **Aguirre, Carlos.** Agentes de su propia emancipación: manumisión de esclavos en Lima, Perú, 1821–1854. (*Am. Negra*, 4, dic. 1992, p. 101–136, bibl., tables)

Closely related to chapter of author's book *Agentes de su propia libertad: los esclavos de Lima y la desintegración de la esclavitud, 1821–1854* (item **2754**). Article traces structures of slave emancipation in Lima and complex strategies employed by the slaves themselves to achieve that end.

2754 **Aguirre, Carlos.** Agentes de su propia libertad: los esclavos de Lima y la desintegración de la esclavitud, 1821–1854. Lima: Pontificia Univ. Católica del Perú, Fondo Editorial, 1993. 335 p.: bibl.

Major study of final period of slavery in Lima and its surrounding valleys. Contains chapters on the composition of the slave population (and its entrenchment in rural and urban society); the slave market; slaves' legal strategies to gain freedom; and extra-legal strategies such as marronage, banditry, and rebellions, although there is scant evidence for the last of these strategies. To widen their space for negotiation for better treatment and freedom, individual slaves skillfully exploited the new republican legal and political environment, as well as existing market pressures. Based on thorough archival research.

2755 **Alayza Escardó, Francisco.** Historia de la cirugía en el Perú. Lima: Editorial Monterrico, 1992. 413 p.: bibl., ill.

Impressive encyclopedic overview of surgical practices and leading surgeons, as well as hospitals, medical training, medical associations, and surgical publications from the prehispanic period to mid-2oth century. Written by distinguished surgeon and public health official, based on thorough bibliography of published works.

2756 **Alvarez-Calderón Gerbolini, Annalyda** *et al.* La historia del Perú en la *Revista de la Universidad Católica.* Lima: Pontificia Univ. Católica del Perú, Fondo Editorial, 1993. 218 p.

Selection of important essays on various themes of Peruvian history—from the fall of the Inca Empire to early opera performances in Lima from 1814–40s—published in the Catholic Univ.'s *Revista* (1935–60) by leading historians, including Raúl Porras Barrenechea, Rubén Vargas Ugarte, and José de la Riva Agüero. There is also an index of all articles published in this important journal (1932–60), including numerous entries on philosophy and the history and modern doctrine of Catholicism in Peru.

2757 **Antología del Cuzco.** Recopilación de Raúl Porras Barrenechea. Fotografías de Martín Chambi. Lima: Fundación M.J. Bustamante de la Fuente, 1992. 426 p.: ill.

Careful reedition of Porras' valuable selection of testimonies about Cusco, from 16th-century chroniclers to 2oth-century travelers, scholars, and poets. The addition of some of Martín Chambi's photographs further enriches the volume.

2758 **Basadre, Jorge.** Perú, problema y posibilidad; y otros ensayos. Selección, prólogo y cronología de David Sobrevilla. Bibliografía de Miguel Angel Rodríguez. Caracas: Biblioteca Ayacucho, 1992. 426 p.: bibl. (Biblioteca Ayacucho; 177)

In addition to being the most analytical work on Peruvian history by the foremost historian of the republican era, the volume contains Basadre's illuminating essays on the poet José María Eguren, the great issues of Peruvian civilization, and the overall meaning of history. Sobrevilla's carefully drawn biographic and intellectual portrait is important. Rodríguez's bibliography of works by and about Basadre is helpful, although probably incomplete.

2759 **Bazán Alfaro, Inés** and **José Gómez Cumpa.** Enganche y formación de espacios regionales en el Perú: Lambayeque, 1860–1930. (*in* Congreso Nacional de Investigaciones en Historia, *1st, Lima, 1984.* Actas. Lima, CONCYTEC, 1991, v. 1, p. 249–267)

The rise of modern capitalist sugar plantations on the north coast led to the integration of three distinct regional spaces, linking coastal valleys with a highland hinterland. The major cause for the rise of these spaces was the labor shortage on the coast and the development of labor recruitment (i.e., *enganche*) in the highlands. Authors stress regional differences between spaces created around the valleys of Jequetepeque, Chicama and Santa Catalina, and the Lambayeque and Zaña valleys.

2760 **Blondet, Cecilia.** Out of the kitchens and onto the streets: women's activism in Peru. (*in* The challenge of local feminisms:

women's movements in global perspective. Boulder, Colo.: Westview Press, 1995, p. 251–275, photos, table)

Overview of the spectacular growth of women's organizations since the early 1970s. Author sees a conjunction of structural (economic, educational) and ideological reasons for this growth, and stresses that the heterogeneity of women's organizations reflects the disaggregated process of fundamental change underway in the country.

2761 Bonfiglio, Giovanni. Los italianos en la sociedad peruana: una visión histórica. Lima: Asociación Italianos del Perú, 1993. 334 p.: bibl., index, map.

Major study of Italian immigrants, focusing on the 1840–1930 period, shows continuities since the arrival of Genoese mariners in the 1530s. Author highlights the peculiar patterns of Italian immigration to Peru compared with major streams to the Southern Cone and the US, and contributes much information on the economic, social, and political integration of Italians in the host country. Based on exhaustive research with printed sources and some archival materials, this is an important work.

2762 Burga, Manuel. El Perú central, 1770–1860: disparidades regionales y la primera crisis agrícola republicana. (*in* América Latina en la época de Simón Bolívar: la formación de las economías nacionales y los intereses europeos, 1800–1850. Edición de Reinhard Liehr. Berlin: Colloquium Verlag, 1989, p. 227–310, graphs, maps, tables)

Ambitious and highly complex quantitative study of agricultural production and conjunctures in central Peru during late colonial and early republican periods, based on tithe records. Draws a complex contrastive image of crises and booms, differentiating coastal and highland regions, and Spanish and indigenous economic activities. Suggests that crises in Peru's links with the world economy benefit interior production zones.

Bushnell, David and **Neill Macaulay.** The emergence of Latin America in the nineteenth century. See item **1004.**

2763 Cadena, Marisol de la. Decencia y cultura política: los indigenistas del Cuzco en los años veinte. (*Rev. Andin.*, 12:1, julio 1994, p. 79–133, bibl.)

Important essay about the construction of ethnicity in early 20th-century Cusco. Author suggests that "decencia" (honor) is the normative criterion through which ideologies and practices of ethnic hierarchies are created. The elite indigenistas never could escape this framework and thus remained paternalistic and hierarchical in their approach to Indians.

2764 Castro Vásquez, Aquilino. Hanan Huanca: historia de Huanca Alta y de los pueblos del Valle del Mantaro; desde sus orígenes hasta la República. Lima: Asociación Editorial Stella, 1992. 414 p., 16 p. of plates: bibl., ill. (some col.), map.

Local history of western Huancayo province in the central sierra. Provides encyclopedic detail through wars of independence, but sketchy thereafter. Rejecting everything Spanish, author insists on calling even the modern inhabitants of the region by prehispanic ethnic categories.

2765 Chambi, Martín. Martín Chambi: photographs, 1920–1950. Foreword by Mario Vargas Llosa. Introductions by Edward Ranney and Publio López Mondéjar. Translation from the Spanish by Margaret Sayers Peden. Washington: Smithsonian Institution Press, 1993. 120 p.: chiefly ill.

Beautiful edition of some key photographs by one of the greatest photographers of the 20th century. A native of a village in Puno dept., Chambi established a photo studio in Cusco where his work ranged from portraits of weddings and celebrations to ethnographic images of Indians and street scenes. His work is always on knife's edge between artistry and keen social observation, between exoticizing the specimens of Cusco society and demonstrating their modernity. Invaluable for understanding southern Andean society and culture in the mid-20th century.

2766 Clayton, Lawrence A. Las relaciones peruano-estadounidenses desde la Independencia hasta el siglo XX. Lima: Univ. de Lima, Facultad de Ciencias Humanas, 1993. 160 p. (Cuadernos de Historia/Santiago; 16)

Seven lectures on themes of US-Peruvian relations since the 1820s delivered at the Univ. de Lima in 1988. Also includes a preliminary effort to synthesize work on this topic. Author stresses domestic forces shaping the policies of each country towards the other, and the multifaceted nature of these forces.

2767 Compendio histórico del Perú. t. 5, La Independencia, 1780–1824; La República, 1826–1899 [de] Luis Durand Flórez. t. 6, La República, 1900–1993 [de] Luis Durand Flórez; El arte republicano, s. XIX-XX [de] Luis E. Wuffarden; Historia económica del Perú, s. XIX-XX [de] Luis Ponce Vega. Edición, producción, ilustración, diagramación y epígrafes de Carlos Milla Batres. Lima: Editorial Milla Batres, 1993. 2 v.: ill. (some col.).

Conventional synthesis of Peru's republican history by Luis Durand Florez: Vol. 5 covers period from the Túpac Amaru's rebellion to the end of the Piérola Administration, and Vol. 6 covers 20th century. Emphasis is political, and the interpretation often follows that of Jorge Basadre. Vol. 6 also contains sections on the economic history and the arts of republican Peru. Volumes are richly illustrated with many, often rarely seen, photographs and prints.

2768 Contreras, Carlos. Mercado de tierras y sociedad campesina: el Valle del Mantaro en el siglo XIX. (*Hist. Cult./Lima*, 20, 1990, p. 243–265, bibl.)

Important study of land transactions and notions of land property among peasants of central Peruvian highlands between late-19th and early-20th century, based on research in notarial archives. Author establishes that even when the land market became more active in the communities, familial and communal customary rights limiting individual property notions did not disappear.

2769 Coomes, Oliver T. and Bradford L. Barham. The Amazon rubber boom: labor control, resistance, and failed plantation development revisited. (*HAHR*, 74:2, May 1994, p. 231–257)

Authors present a fundamental critique of conventional dependency, Marxist, and ecological analyses of the rubber boom. They reject the notions that labor relations were primarily based on force and that no capital was accumulated within the region. Based on neo-classical economic theory, they stress the rational, competitive nature of the rubber enterprises and explain that the failure to develop a viable plantation complex was due to the scarcity of labor, high opportunity cost of capital, and the long maturation of

planted rubber trees. Based largely on application of economic theory to printed sources and secondary literature. See also item **3276.**

2770 Cornejo Polar, Jorge. Intelectuales, artistas y Estado en el Perú del siglo XX. Lima: Univ. de Lima, Facultad de Ciencias Humanas, 1993. 161 p.: bibl. (Cuadernos de Historia/Santiago; 17)

Statistical analysis of the impact of 80 intellectuals and 80 artists on the politics and the public sphere in 20th-century Peru, resulting in the conclusion that some of those intellectuals and artists who had least access to official power had the greatest public impact.

2771 Crónicas y relaciones que se refieren al origen y virtudes del pisco, bebida tradicional y patrimonio del Perú. Lima: Banco Latino, 1990. xx, 129 p.: ill. (some col.).

Richly illustrated description of the history, development, and social significance of Peruvian brandy, and the coastal valleys where it is produced (e.g., Chincha, Pisco, Ica, Moquegua).

2772 Dawe, John and **Lewis Taylor.** Enrique López Albújar and the study of Peruvian brigandage. (*Bull. Lat. Am. Res.*, 13:3, Sept. 1994, p. 247–280, maps)

Excellent critical appraisal of the complex and thoughtful depiction of banditry by the jurist, journalist, and indigenista author López Albújar (1872–1966). His regionally differentiated analysis of banditry reveals influences of the European positivist school of criminology and some racism, along with a social-reformist and ethnographic bent. López Albújar anticipated many of the findings of Eric Hobsbawm's studies of banditry in the late 1950s.

Delgado Díaz del Olmo, César *et al.* Otras pieles: género, historia y cultura. See item **3627.**

2773 Demélas-Bohy, Marie-Danielle. L'invention politique: Bolivie, Equateur, Pérou au XIXe siècle. Paris: Editions Recherche sur les civilisations, 1992. 620 p.: bibl., ill., index, maps.

Major study of Andean political cultures from the late colonial period to the 1920s is based on varying levels of research for each of the three countries, with the most thorough for Bolivia and the least for Peru.

Pt. 1 deals with the 1780–1825 period, juxtaposing a traditional society steeped in pre-Tridentine Christianity and suddenly "seduced" by modern, democratic politics; Pt. 2 deals with compromises "invented" to bridge this chasm between social traditionalism and political modernity during the century after independence. Author places much emphasis on discourse, symbolism, and political ideas, and relatively little on social and economic processes influencing political struggles.

2774 Deustua, José. Mining markets, peasants, and power in 19th-century Peru. (*LARR,* 29:1, 1994, p. 29–54, bibl.)

Provides evidence for peasants' important role in supplying Andean markets with foodstuffs and transportation services, a role which began to decline notably towards the end of the 19th century. Mine owners used debt mechanisms to control the peasant labor force, presumably in order to create a free wage-labor market, while the peasant mineworkers sought to resist their proletarianization. Author highlights the paradox between the participation of Andean peasants in markets construed as free and impersonal, and their extreme powerlessness and status as second-class citizens.

2775 Deustua, José. Routes, roads, and silver trade in Cerro de Pasco, 1820–1860: the internal market in nineteenth-century Peru. (*HAHR,* 74:1, Feb. 1994, p. 1–31, map, tables)

Through an archival study of routes of supply for Central Andean silver mines during the first half century after independence, the author concludes that mining created a complex internal market. Lima merchants advancing credit to the miners and purchasing the silver were the primary beneficiaries of this economic activity. Study contains detailed information on routes used in the silver economy and commodities carried over them.

Drake, Paul W. International crises and popular movements in Latin America: Chile and Peru from the Great Depression to the Cold War. See item **2888.**

2776 Estenssoro, Juan Carlos *et al.* La historiografía peruana en debate. (*Apuntes/Lima,* 33, segundo semestre 1993, p. 113–120)

Five brief essays about recent work on major issues of Peruvian history from the colonial period to the 20th century.

2777 Fernández Alonso, Serena. Las montoneras como expresión política armada en el camino hacia la constitucionalidad del Perú republicano: siglo XIX. (*Anu. Estud. Am.,* 50:1, 1993, p. 163–180)

Author first analyzes the political activities of Nicolás de Piérola frome the 1870s on, and then focuses on actions of the *montoneras*—irregular local troops—in the civil war of 1894–95. Piérola is portrayed as a decisive modernizer of Peru's political culture who returned constitutional rule to the nation. The *montoneras* are portrayed as spontaneous popular forces.

2778 Flores Galindo, Alberto *et al.* Encuentros: historia y movimientos sociales en el Perú. Entrevistas por Carlos Arroyo. Lima?: MemoriAngosta, 1989. 172 p.: bibl. (Serie Historia)

Interviews with 14 mostly Marxist Peruvian historians and anthropologists about their work and their vision of Peruvian history, from the Incaic period to present. Several reveal the internal debates within Peruvian historiography and show the fascinating point of transition when Marxism began to lose its dominance among Peruvian intellectuals. Especially interesting is a long, unusually polemical "prologue" by Alberto Flores Galindo.

2779 Galdo Gutiérrez, Virgilio. Ayacucho, conflictos y pobreza: historia regional, siglos XVI-XIX. Ayacucho: Univ. Nacional San Cristóbal de Huamanga, 1992. 220 p.: bibl., ill., maps.

Highly informative synthesis of regional history, from prehispanic ethnic kingdoms to end of the 19th century. Stresses economic patterns, social and political movements, and education. Based on thorough knowledge of published material and some archival sources.

2780 García Jordán, Pilar. El indio es la caña, los patrones son el trapiche y el jugo de la caña son los aviadores: reflexiones sobre la explotación chauchera en el Ucayali en los inicios del siglo XX. (*Bol. Am.,* 35:45, 1995, p. 61–85, appendix, bibl., maps)

In order to incorporate the native peoples into the "civilized" national polity, during the rubber boom era (1880s-1910) the Peruvian State and the Catholic Church worked hand-in-glove to extend the administrative infrastructure to the Peruvian Amazon. Using the example of the apostolic prefecture of the Ucayali, author demonstrates frequent conflicts between missionaries and rubber entrepreneurs whose draconian labor recruitment ended up depopulating many mission towns.

2781 García Jordán, Pilar. La misión del Putumayo, 1912–1921: religión, política y diplomacia ante la explotación indígena. (*in* Memoria, creación e historia: luchar contra el olvido. Coordinación de Pilar García Jordán, Miguel Izard, y Javier Laviña. Barcelona: Univ. de Barcelona, 1993, p. 255–272)

In response to the public outcry against the genocidal exploitation of the natives of the Putumayo by Julio Arana's rubber company, the Vatican and the Peruvian and British governments negotiated the establishment of missions in the region. These failed to stop the exploitation of the Indians, however. Well-documented study highlights how the ruthless rubber business, conflicts between Peruvian and Colombian sovereignty, and fears over Anglo-Saxon Protestant intrusions all contributed to the failure to protect the native population.

2782 García Jordán, Pilar. Reflexiones sobre el darwinismo social, inmigración y colonización: mitos de los grupos modernizadores peruanos, 1821–1919. (*Bull. Inst. fr. étud. andin.*, 21:3, 1992, p. 961–975, bibl.)

Survey of essays, pamphlets, and legislative projects appearing in Peru between the 1840s and early 20th century exalting the need for European immigration. Extremes of Social Darwinism and racism were reached during the 1890s and the first decade of the 20th century.

Gareis, Iris. "República de Indios"—"República de Españoles:" reinterpretación actual de conceptos andinos coloniales. See item **2403.**

2783 González Calleja, Eduardo. La derecha latinoamericana en busca de un modelo fascista: la limitada influencia del falangismo en el Perú, 1936–1945. (*Rev. Complut. Hist. Am.*, 20, 1994, p. 229–255)

Discusses distinct reactionary movements in Peru between Sánchez Cerro's Unión Revolucionaria and the regional organizations of the Falange. Concludes that the rhetorical support by Peru's conservative and aristocratic intellectuals for a "mimetic fascism" during the late 1930s was far stronger than the actual government alignment with or mass support for Franco's Spain or fascist Italy.

2784 Gootenberg, Paul. Imagining development: economic ideas in Peru's "fictitious prosperity" of guano, 1840–1880. Berkeley: Univ. of California Press, 1993. 243 p.: bibl., index, map.

Presents thorough analysis and novel interpretation of the economic thought of leading politicians and intellectuals of the guano age. Argues that these writers on economic issues proposed creative new paths out of the disequilibrium between consumption and production created by the guano boom, but that these policies were never implemented due to the resistance of vested interests.

Gootenberg, Paul. Niveles de precios en Lima del siglo diecinueve: algunos datos e interpretaciones. See *HLAS 55:1945.*

2785 Haworth, Nigel. Peru. (*in* Latin America between the Second World War and the Cold War, 1944–1948. Edited by Leslie Bethell and Ian Roxborough. New York: Cambridge Univ. Press, 1992, p. 170–189)

Based on US diplomatic correspondence, author presents detailed account of the politics of the Bustamante Administration (1945–48) and its ultimate overthrow by Gen. Odría's military coup. Stresses favorable view of APRA in US State Dept. circles, and declining US support for the Bustamante Administration.

Holland, Charles. Noticias de Buenos Aires, el Paraguay, Chile y el Perú: cartas del ciudadano inglés Charles Holland, 1820–1826. See item **3045.**

2786 Hünefeldt, Christine. Paying the price of freedom: family and labor among Lima's slaves, 1800–1854. Berkeley: Univ. of California Press, 1994. 269 p.: bibl., index.

Important study of slavery in Lima and its surrounding valleys in the half century preceding abolition in 1854, with similar overall interpretation as that of Carlos Aguirre's 1993 study (see item **2754**). Author stresses multiple strategies of slave families to gain freedom as primary cause for the terminal crisis of slavery in Peru. Study connects family structures and strategies with slaves' migratory patterns from countryside to Lima, their networks of friends and patrons in the city, and their search for the most advantageous working conditions. Author uncovers a surprising level of negotiation by slaves, even in public spaces such as the courts, and highlights the central role of women in the emancipation process.

Indigenous revolts in Chiapas and the Andean highlands. See *HLAS* 55:57.

2787 Irurozqui, Marta. El Perú de Leguía: derroteros y extravíos historiográficos. (*Apuntes/Lima*, 34, primer semestre 1994, p. 85–101)

Criticizes most Marxist and liberal historians writing on early-20th century Peru during the 1970s-80s for imposing ideological categories onto their historical subjects, based on their own disappointment with modern Peru. Author's alternative is an analysis of internal conflicts among various elite sectors so as to determine means and discourse through which elites sought to establish hegemony.

2788 Lausent-Herrera, Isabelle. La cristianización de los chinos en el Perú: integración, sumisón y resistencia. (*Bull. Inst. fr. étud. andin.*, 21:3, 1992, p. 977-1007, bibl., photos)

The missionary activities of Jesuits and Franciscans among Chinese Peruvians created some of the powerful institutions that allowed the Chinese community to maintain its own cultural identity. Important study of baptisms, marriages, last rites, syncretism, and Chinese secret societies from the 1860s to the mid-20th century.

López-Ocón, Leoncio. Las actividades americanistas del naturalista español Marcos Jiménez de la Espada. See item **2221.**

2789 Majluf, Natalia. Escultura y espacio público: Lima, 1850–1879. Lima: IEP, 1994. 1 v. (Documento de trabajo; 67)

In the mid-19th century the government began to place monuments in Lima's plazas and create new monumental plazas. Author interprets this as the expression of a new notion of public space and the government's attempt to shape the people's collec-

tive memory towards a certain version of the nation, an attempt which the author considers a failure.

2790 Mallon, Florencia E. De ciudadano a "otro:" resistencia nacional, formación del Estado y visiones campesinas sobre la nación en Junín. (*Rev. Andin.*, 12:1, julio 1994, p. 7–78, bibl., map)

Spanish translation of one of the chapters of author's book, *Peasant and nation: The making of postcolonial Mexico and Peru* (items **1350** and **2791**).

2791 Mallon, Florencia E. Peasant and nation: the making of postcolonial Mexico and Peru. Berkeley: Univ. of California Press, 1994. 472 p.: bibl., index, map.

The Peruvian section of this comparative work deals with peasants' role in Junín and Cajamarca depts. in the formation of the Peruvian nation during the profound crisis provoked by the War of the Pacific and its aftermath (1882–95). Using Gramscian notions, author argues that A.A. Cáceres abandoned his coalition with Junín's peasants soon after the departure of the Chileans and began to pursue a policy of exclusion that only deepened under Nicolás de Piérola after 1895. Counter-hegemonic projects of the peasantry were repressed by force. In Cajamarca neither peasants nor the departmental elites ever sought to construct a hegemonic regime, mobilizing instead for purely anti-statist and anti-fiscal motives. Important, if controversial, study based on thorough reconstruction of local politics and society. For Mexican specialist's review, see item **1350.**

2792 Martínez-Alier, Juan. La interpretación ecologista de la historia socioeconómica: algunos ejemplos andinos. (*Rev. Andin.*, 8:1, julio 1990, p. 9–46, bibl.)

Brief discussion of several major postconquest economic activities in the Andes—Bolivian mining, the Peruvian guano boom and coastal fishmeal production, and agricultural production for regional and international markets—aims to demonstrate a persistent drain of energy or caloric units to the detriment of future generations. Author considers Andean peasants and miners to be frequent practitioners of an "egalitarian ecology of the poor," and discusses various theoretical debates about the implications of such movements.

2793 **Martínez Riaza, Ascensión.** El Perú y
España durante el oncenio: el hispanismo en el discurso oficial y en las manifestaciones simbólicas, 1919–1930. (*Histórica/
Lima*, 18:2, dic. 1994, p. 335–363, bibl.)
During the 1920s various currents of
political and cultural "hispanism" flourished
in Peru and contributed to binding closely the
ties between the authoritarian Leguía and
Primo de Rivera regimes. Suggestive, if unsystematic, exploration of important topic.

Marzal, Manuel María. Del paternalismo colonial al moderno indigenismo en el Perú. See
item **2435.**

2794 **Mc Evoy, Carmen.** Un proyecto nacional en el siglo XIX: Manuel Pardo y
su visión del Perú. Lima: Pontificia Univ. Católica del Perú, Fondo Editorial, 1994. 354 p.:
bibl.
Challenging the long-dominant dependency interpretation of guano-age politics, author portrays Pardo and the early Partido Civil
as putting forth a serious and progressive "national project" aimed at raising production in
all sectors of the Peruvian economy and integrating the nation through railroads. Focuses
on Pardo's political ideas and on his popular
mobilization in the presidential campaign of
1871–72. While based on thorough research,
work accepts Pardo's pronouncements
uncritically.

2795 **Méndez G., Cecilia and Luis Torrejón.**
Arrestados y encarcelados de Lima:
aproximaciones a una caracterización social para la segunda mitad del siglo XIX.
(*in* Congreso Nacional de Investigaciones
en Historia, *1st, Lima, 1984.* Actas. Lima,
CONCYTEC, 1991, v. 1, p. 149–164, tables)
Brief analysis of arrests and convic-
tions in Lima for twenty-two years (1877–99),
according to type of crime as well as trade,
nationality, and race of the individual arrested. Authors find significant decrease in
arrested artisans, increase of day laborers and
unemployed. Indians and mestizos are over-
represented among the arrested.

2796 **Méndez G., Cecilia.** *Incas sí, indios no:*
note on Peruvian Creole nationalism
and its contemporary crisis. (*J. Lat. Am.
Stud.*, 28:1, Feb. 1996, p. 197–225)
During the Peruvian-Bolivian Confederation (1836–39), Creole individuals in Lima
ridiculed Andrés Santa Cruz as Indian and
considered that the *patria* had been invaded
by barbarians. Author contrasts idealization
of Incas with denigration of contemporary Indians by elite Creoles around Felipe Pardo,
and suggests that this attitude has continued
to be typical of Creole nationalism to the
present day.

2797 **Mendoza Meléndez, Eduardo.** La campaña de la Breña. v. 1–2. 3. ed., rev.,
corr. y aum. Lima: F. Aliaga, 1993. 2 v.: ill.
(some col.), maps.
The most thoroughly researched military history of the resistance campaign
(1882–83) against the Chilean troops by irregular troops under Andrés Avelino Cáceres
and peasant *montoneras* from the central
highlands. Book contains novel information
about the material conditions and the precise
composition of these troops.

Peña, Guillermo de la. Poder agrario y ambigüedad revolucionaria: bandidos, caudillos y
facciones. See item **1562.**

2798 **El Perú emergente: la nación de la mil
interpretaciones.** Lima?: Nuevas Ideas,
1993. 131 p.: ill. (some col.).
Compilation of extraordinary paintings, drawings, and photos accompanied
by brief texts all designed to illustrate the
gradual emergence—between the 16th and
late 20th centuries—of a multifaceted, multi-
ethnic Peruvian nation.

2799 **Perú, hombre e historia.** v. 3, La República [de] Franklin Pease G.Y. Lima:
EDUBANCO, 1993. 1 v.: bibl., ill. (some col.),
maps.
Thoughtful, although uneven, overview of central themes of Peru's republican
history by noted colonial historian. Especially
useful as an introduction to some of the recent historiographical debates, the volume is
strongest for the period up to 1930.

2800 **Planas Silva, Pedro.** El 900: balance y
recuperación. Lima: CITDEC, 1994. v.
1: bibl., index.
Author wishes to rescue the Generation of 1900—led by Francisco García Calderón, José de la Riva Agüero and Victor Andrés
Belaúnde—from the neglect or contempt
their ideas and politics have elicited from the
majority of Marxist-influenced Peruvian intellectuals since the 1920s. Focuses on the
student demonstrations of 1911, the organiza-

tion and program of the futurist Partido Nacional Democrático of 1915, and the ideas of the young V.A. Belaúnde. Author distances this generation from the *civilistas*, highlights their reformism and proximity to indigenismo, and discusses the evolution of their democratic ideas. Although unsystematic and driven by a preconceived agenda, this is an important study based on considerable original research.

2801 Planas Silva, Pedro. La República Autocrática. Lima: Fundación Friedrich Ebert, 1994. 263 p.: bibl.

Single-minded, ferocious critique of Augusto Leguía's 1919–30 presidency, portrayed as historical analogue to the Fujimori regime after the *autogolpe* of April 5, 1992. Author is concerned with democratic, pluralist institution-building and political practices of compromise. He views the *República Aristocrática* (1895–1919) as having established fragile, limited pluralist traditions, which were rudely destroyed by Leguía. Although the book contains many important insights and is based on considerable research, this is not a balanced appraisal of Leguía's *oncenio*, as it contains little attempt to deal with his substantive policies.

Quiroz, Alfonso W. Deudas olvidadas: instrumentos de crédito en la economía colonial peruana, 1750–1820. See item **2450**.

2802 Quiroz Paz Soldán, Eusebio. Visión histórica de Arequipa: 1540–1990. Arequipa, Peru: UNSA, 1991. 364 p.: bibl., ill., maps.

Collection of articles by one of the authorities on republican Arequipa deals with social, economic, and political aspects of the history of the city and its region.

2803 Revesz, Bruno *et al.* Piura: región y sociedad; derrotero bibliográfico para el desarrollo. Piura, Peru: Centro de Investigación y Promoción del Campesinado; Cusco, Peru: Centro de Estudios Regionales Andinos Bartolomé de Las Casas, 1996. 766 p.: indexes. (Archivos de historia andina, 1022–0879; 22)

Singular, exhaustive regional bibliography (2,166 items) of the important northern Peruvian dept. of Piura. Includes brief annotations of the more important works and covers everything from archaeology and linguistics to fisheries and modern finance. Easily accessible volume is clearly organized and includes four systematic indices.

2804 Rodríguez Pastor, Humberto. Asiáticos en la costa: cimarronaje, rebeliones y suicidio, siglo XIX. (*in* Congreso Nacional de Investigaciones en Historia, 1st, Lima, 1984. Actas. Lima, CONCYTEC, 1991, v. 1, p. 101–147, graphs, tables)

After an overview of the situation of coolies on coastal estates and their forms of resistance, author focuses on incidence of marronage among coolies, finding it to be surprisingly frequent, especially during the 1870s to early 1880s.

2805 Saiz, Odorico. Restauración de la Orden Franciscana en el Perú en el siglo XIX. Lima: Provincia Misionera de San Francisco Solano, Convento de los Descalzos, RIMAC, 1993. 253 p.: bibl., ill., maps. (Serie V centenario, franciscanos evangelizadores del Perú; 6)

Well-researched, informative study of the reestablishment of the Franciscan Order in Peru, following its dissolution during the independence period. To be more precise, a monograph on the restoration of the Colegio de Santa Rosa de Ocopa (1826–51) under the good offices of Father Andrés Herrero, and of the foundation of the Colegio Apostólico de Santa María de los Angeles de Lima in 1852. Important contribution to the missionary history of the early national period. [MTH]

2806 Sala i Vila, Núria. La conquista de la selva en el sur andino, 1824–1929: el desarrollo de una frontera interna. (*in* Memoria, creación e historia: luchar contra el olvido. Coordinación de Pilar García Jordán, Miguel Izard y Javier Laviña. Barcelona: Univ. de Barcelona, 1993, p. 241–254)

Presents innovative, complex scheme to explain the incorporation of various Amazonian regions in southern Peru, each shaped by different local and national projects as well as international boundary conflicts. Stresses differences among the social, economic, and political processes and structures in regions from Ayacucho to Madre de Dios.

2807 San Román, Jesús Víctor. Perfiles históricos de la amazonía peruana. 2. ed. Corregida y aumentada por Martha Rodríguez. Iquitos, Peru: Centro de Estudios Teológicos de la Amazonía; Centro Amazónico de Antropología y Aplicación Práctica; Instituto de Investigaciones de la Amazonía Peruana, 1994. 274 p.: bibl., ill.

New updated edition of 1975 publication by Augustinian priest and Amazon researcher broadly outlines the economic and social development of the Peruvian Amazon since the conquest, with much sympathy for the position of the region's native ethnic groups. Based on published sources and administrative records from a provincial archive in Moyobamba.

2808 Super, John C. History, Indians, and university reform in Cuzco. (*Historian/Honor Society*, 56:2, Winter 1994, p. 325–338)

Demonstrates that the study of Incaic and Andean history became a central concern of the university reform movement in Cusco from 1909–20s. History, viewed as essential for exalting the greatness of Andean civilization, thus became linked to the efforts of Cusco's indigenistas.

2809 Tamayo Herrera, José. La muerte en Lima, 1780–1990. Lima: Univ. de Lima, Facultad de Ciencias Humanas, 1992. 102 p.: bibl. (Cuadernos de Historia/Santiago; 15)

Preliminary results of study of wills, architecture and iconography of cemeteries, and ritual aspects of funerals from the late colonial period to present. Author stresses the secularization and laicization of funeral practices, including class differences. Detects a "necrolatry" among Lima's elites, the uncritical eulogization of deceased public figures who were completely shunned before their deaths.

2810 Taylor, Lewis. Society and politics in late nineteenth century Peru: Contumazá, 1876–1900. Liverpool, England: Institute of Latin American Studies, Univ. of Liverpool, 1990. 75 p.: bibl., maps. (Working paper/Institute of Latin American Studies, Univ. of Liverpool; 11)

Politics in the northern highlands during the late-19th century showed no change from a longer-standing, personalistic caudillo pattern. The State was ineffective in imposing law and order, as long-standing clientelistic factions waged recurrent fighting for control of local power. These political structures were reinforced by an increasingly mobile "proletarianized" or "semi-proletarianized" rural and urban population. Closely argued

essay based on thorough research in local archives.

2811 Thurner, Mark. *Republicanos* and *la comunidad de Peruanos:* unimagined political communities in postcolonial Andean Peru. (*J. Lat. Am. Stud.*, 27:2, May 1995, p. 291–318)

Based on archival research in Ancash dept. and the Gramscian concept of hegemony and subaltern studies, author presents novel ideas on the politics of Andean community peasants and nation-state formation between independence and the 1880s. The Indians developed their own form of republicanism, derived from colonial communal roots. Elite politicians rejected this republicanism and excluded the Indians from active political participation.

2812 Trazegnies Granda, Fernando de. En el país de las colinas de arena: reflexiones sobre la inmigración china en el Perú del s. XIX desde la perspectiva del derecho. Lima: Pontificia Univ. Católica del Perú, Fondo Editorial, 1994. 2 v.: bibl., ill.

Vol. 1 of two long volumes is a fictionalized account of the trials and tribulations of one poor Cantonese petty trader who is taken as a coolie to Peru and sold to work on the guano islands and a cotton hacienda. Finally freed, he establishes his own small trading company. Based on exhaustive research, through its vivid style this fictionalized history brings to life well-known facts about the conditions of coolies. Vol. 2 is an erudite treatise on legal issues surrounding the coolie trade and rights and obligations of coolies in Peru.

2813 Valdizán Gamio, José. Historia naval del Perú. t. 5. Prólogo de Luis E. Valcárcel. Lima: Ministerio de Marina, Dirección General de Intereses Marítimos, 1993. 1 v.: bibl., ill., indexes.

Another volume in the narrative history of the ships and men of the Peruvian navy, covering the naval campaigns of the War of the Pacific until the virtual elimination of the Peruvian navy at the battle of Angamos (Oct. 8, 1879).

2814 Vida y obra de Víctor Raúl Haya de la Torre. v. 1. Lima: Instituto Cambio y Desarrollo, 1990. 1 v.: bibl., ill. (Col. Historia política; 1)

Of the three essays in this volume, only the one by Planas and Vallenas on the growth of Haya's ideology from 1926 to the mid-1940s merits some attention, because— from a pro-Aprista perspective—it concedes the complete shift of nearly all key positions, despite Haya's own affirmation to the contrary. Authors see the 1926–28 period as the creative period in Haya's political thought, when he attempted to apply Lenin's notions about semi-colonial countries to Latin American realities. They see a gradual and accelerating "retraction" of all early radical positions setting in as early as the electoral campaign of 1931, but interpret it as the full acceptance of democratic, pluralist politics. For philosopher's comment, see item **5032.**

2815 Villavicencio F., Maritza. Del silencio a la palabra: mujeres peruanas en los siglos XIX y XX. Edición de Margarita Zegarra. Lima: Centro de la Mujer Peruana Flora Tristán, 1992. 220 p.: bibl.

Ambitious, although uneven, analysis of the changing social, cultural, and political role of women, especially between 1870–1930. Chapters focus on the surprising generation of female authors publishing during the 1870s-80s and on the social transformations of Lima's women, including their early activities in politics, labor struggles, and feminist organizations between 1890s-1930.

Bolivia

ERICK D. LANGER, *Associate Professor of History, Carnegie Mellon University*

BOLIVIAN HISTORY HAS ACHIEVED a greater level of maturity with the appearance on the scene of a number of well-trained younger scholars. Local and regional history has benefited from this trend (items **2866, 2864,** and **2855**), and more-established scholars have also continued to contribute (items **2843** and **2846**). Cochabamba has always merited special attention (items **2837, 2858, 2861,** and **2859**). There is a new research emphasis on the long-neglected eastern lowlands (items **2829** and **2861**), including a compendium of articles on the Chiriguanos, an important indigenous group (item **2824**). The new generation of scholars, often with close ties to the countryside around La Paz, also has focused on the highland indigenous peoples in a series of valuable studies (items **2819, 2825, 2835,** and **2848**). The elite view of the highland indigenous peoples also has received some attention from intellectual historians (items **2836** and **2863**).

Less attention has been paid to the independence wars. Just's exhaustive study on the early independence movement in Chuquisaca (item **2839**) and Arnade's retrospective essay provide new views (item **2820**). Fortunately, the first 50 years after independence is finally receiving its due. Major studies of debt in the early republican period (item **2851**), of the frontier policies of President José Ballivián (item **2833**), and of the conception of liberal discourse in southern mining towns (item **2856**) are providing new insights to this understudied period. Publication of Melchor María Mercado's naive paintings (item **2849**) and that of an 1830s essay on the economic state of the country at that time, with a series of recent scholarly analyses on the essay (item **2821**), also advance our knowledge for this period.

Bolivia's economy during most of its history has depended upon mining, and a number of new studies fill important gaps in the literature on this topic (e.g., item **2860**). Silver mining has been largely neglected, except for one polemical work on the entrepreneurs in the Atacama desert (item **2855**). Tin mining, however, including its technological aspects (items **2827** and **2853**), is finally receiving the proper attention from a host of scholars (items **2817, 2826,** and **2852**). Another study examines mining from the perspective of labor from the 19th century onward (item **2862**).

A relatively new field in the historiography of Bolivia is that of the Catholic Church and its missions in the republican period. While general histories remain sketchy (item **2838**), the study of the Franciscan missions in the southeastern section of the country has received considerable attention in analytic studies (items **4083** and **2844**) as well as in a reprint of a classic 19th-century treatise by Corrado (item **2828**). In addition, one author examines the role of the Catholic Church as a political force in the late-20th century (item **2840**).

As always, 20th-century political history is alive and well. For the era prior to the Chaco War, both the Republican Party (item **2817**) and the Socialists (item **2847**) receive their due. Gallego Margaleff covers extensively the "military socialism" of the post-Chaco-War military regimes of the 1930s (items **2832, 2830,** and **2831**), while the leftist leader José Arze is the subject of another important biography (item **2816**). The Che Guevara guerrilla episode in the late 1960s continues to fascinate (items **2834** and **2823**), but more recent events, such as the Popular Assembly period in 1970 (item **2865**) and the formation of the leftist Movimiento de Izquierda Revolucionaria (MIR) are finally deemed worthy of attention (item **2854**).

Herbert Klein has provided us with two excellent overviews of Bolivian history; one, a revised edition of his general history (item **2841**), and the other, a review of recent works (item **2842**). In addition, the *Anuario*, a new periodical published out of Sucre by the Archivo y Biblioteca Nacionales de Bolivia, provides reviews and historiographic essays, further indicating the vitality of historical research in Bolivia.

2816 **Abecia López, Valentín.** José Antonio Arze y Arze: inventario. La Paz: Librería Editorial Juventud, 1992. 150 p.: bibl.

Favorable biography of important leftist politician, with almost exclusive focus on Arze's political activities.

2817 **Albarracín Millán, Juan.** Bolivia: el desentrañamiento del estaño; los republicanos en la historia de Bolivia. La Paz: Ediciones AKAPANA, 1993. 271 p.: bibl., ill., index.

In this first volume in a promised series on the 1920–50 period, author lays out the foundation for his argument that the increasing predominance of tin-mining baron Simón I. Patiño brought about the political degeneration of the Republican Party administrations that held power. Sketches the tin mining industry from WWI to the formation of Patiño Mines in 1923. Lacks footnotes.

2818 *Anuario.* 1994/95. Sucre, Bolivia: Talleres Gráficos Tupac Katari; Archivo y Biblioteca Nacionales de Bolivia.

Important new publication to appear annually. First issue, a commemorative volume for the long-time and recently deceased director of the National Archives, contains valuable articles by virtually all important historians working on Bolivia. Consists of three parts: 1) "General Topics;" 2) "Bibliographic and Archival Essays;" and 3) "Reviews." Extremely useful for recent work on women, independence, and mining, as well as on archival research possibilities in Bolivia. See also items **2860** and **2820.**

2819 **Arias, Juan Félix.** Historia de una esperanza: los apoderados espiritualistas de Chuquisaca, 1936–1964. La Paz: Aruwiyiri, 1994. 185 p. (Agresión Colonial y Resistencia Indígena; 3)

Intriguing case study of an indigenous movement in southern Bolivia that moved from revindication of Indian lands in the 1930s to a millenarian religious organization.

2820 **Arnade, Charles W.** Una nueva mirada a la creación de Bolivia. (*Anuario/ Sucre*, 1994/95, p. 73–88)

Author compares his classic work on independence published in the 1950s to later works about the nature of the Bolivian independence movement. Results in a polemical but useful introduction to historiography on Bolivian independence in the second half of this century.

2821 Barragán, Rossana *et al.* Bosquejo del estado en que se halla la riqueza nacional de Bolivia, presentado al examen de la Nación por un aldeano, hijo de ella, año de 1830. Coordinación de Ana María Lema. La Paz: Plural Editores; Facultad de Humanidades y Ciencias de la Educación, Univ. Mayor de San Andrés, 1994. 282 p.: bibl. (Col. Academia; 2)

Pt. 1 is a critical annotated edition of important 19th-century essay against free trade, revealing much about economic and social conditions in early republican Bolivia. Pt. 2 includes pieces by seven scholars evaluating and contextualizing the essay and its anonymous author.

2822 Bieber, León E. La política militar alemana en Bolivia, 1900–1935. (*LARR*, 29:1, 1994, p. 85–106, bibl., tables)

Unlike earlier interpretations, Bieber shows that Germany did not foster military training in Bolivia, but that many of the ties with German officers came in a private capacity. German arms sales were important to Bolivia, but not to Germany.

Block, David. Mission culture on the upper Amazon: native tradition, Jesuit enterprise & secular policy in Moxos, 1660–1880. See item **2473.**

2823 El Che en Bolivia: documentos y testimonios. Recopilación y notas de Carlos Soria Galvarro. v. 1, El PCB antes, durante y después. v. 2, Su último combate. La Paz: CEDOIN, 1992–1993. 2 v.: ill. (Col. Historia y documento)

Useful collection of published accounts and photos on the last hours of Che Guevara's life in Bolivia. Purpose is to show that Che was captured alive and later assassinated by the military.

2824 Chiriguano. Edición de Jürgen Riester. Santa Cruz de la Sierra, Bolivia: Apoyo para el Campesino Indígena del Oriente Boliviano, 1994. 674 p.: bibl., ill. (Pueblos indígenas de las tierra bajas de Bolivia; 3)

Collection of articles by major scholars, most previously published in different languages, on the Chiriguano peoples of southwestern Bolivia. Includes chapters on historical aspects by Sanabria, Saignes, Combés, Langer, Schuchard, and Meliá. Anthropological section, with heavy emphasis on Izozog region and religion, includes contributions by Albó, Riester, Hirsch, Zarzycki, Zolezzi, López, and Simon de Souza.

2825 Condori Chura, Leandro and **Esteban Ticona Alejo.** El escribano de los caciques apoderados = Kasikinakan puriraru-nakan qillqiripa. La Paz: Hisbol; THOA, 1992. 284 p.: ill. (Serie Testimonios; 7)

Important autobiography of Aymara indigenous leader who was active in the first half of the 20th century. Firsthand description of Indian resistance to the process of hacienda expansion on the Bolivian altiplano.

2826 Contreras C., Manuel E. and **Mario Napoleón Pacheco T.** Medio siglo de minería mediana en Bolivia, 1939–1989. La Paz: Biblioteca Minera Boliviana, 1989. 164 p.: bibl., ill. (Biblioteca Minera Boliviana; 4)

Important contribution to mining historiography describes development of the National Association of Medium-Sized Miners, discusses changes in levels of production, and analyzes medium-sized mining companies and their impact on the Bolivian economy.

2827 Contreras C., Manuel E. Tecnología moderna en los Andes: minería e ingeniería en Bolivia en el siglo XX. La Paz: Biblioteca Minera Boliviana, 1994. 137 p.: bibl., ill., maps. (Biblioteca minera boliviana; 8)

Excellent introduction to the history of tin mining; Pt. 1 provides a general history, whereas Pt. 2 details the development of mining engineers in Bolivia and their competition with foreign counterparts. Pt. 3 is a valuable bibliographic essay on tin mining in Bolivia.

2828 Corrado, Alejandro María and **Antonio Comajuncosa.** El colegio franciscano de Tarija y sus misiones. v. 1–2. 2. ed., con introducción y nuevos apéndices. Tarija, Bolivia: Editorial Offset Franciscana, 1990. 2 v. 641 p.: appendices, ill., map.

Important reprint (with some additions by the editor) of the 1884 classic, narrating the history of the Franciscan missions among the indigenous peoples of southeastern Bolivia in the colonial and the republican periods, by Comajuncosa and Corrado, respectively. Great source on history of the Bolivian Chaco region and of the city of Tarija from the Franciscan perspective.

Demélas-Bohy, Marie-Danielle. L'invention politique: Bolivie, Equateur, Pérou au XIXe siècle. See item **2773.**

2829 **Durán Ribera, Emilio** and **Guillermo Pinckert Justiniano.** La revolución igualitaria de Andrés Ibáñez. Santa Cruz de la Sierra, Bolivia: Editorial Universitaria, 1988. 279 p.: bibl., port., facsims.

Detailed account of the federalist rebellion of 1876–77 in the Santa Cruz region under the leadership of the Socialist-inspired Ibáñez. Although it failed and its leader was executed, the Ibáñez rebellion served as a cry for regional autonomy in the prosperous Santa Cruz department.

2830 **Gallego Margaleff, Ferran.** Ejército, nacionalismo y reformismo en América Latina: la gestión de Germán Busch en Bolivia. Barcelona: PPU, 1992. 300 p.: bibl. (LHU; 13)

Detailed narrative account of politics under the nationalist-reformist military dictator in the 1930s is Pt. 2 of author's doctoral thesis. Larger view is obscured by emphasis on political maneuverings. For Pt. 1, see item **2831.**

2831 **Gallego Margaleff, Ferran.** Los orígenes del reformismo militar en América Latina: la gestión de David Toro en Bolivia. Barcelona: PPU, 1991. 225 p.: bibl. (LHU; 11)

A dense and detailed narrative account of the period leading up to and through the regime of the "military socialist" president in the aftermath of the Chaco War. Author does not make clear the larger implications for the study of military reformism. Pt. 1 of author's doctoral thesis; for Pt. 2, see item **2830.**

2832 **Gallego Margaleff, Ferran.** La política económica del "socialismo militar" boliviano. (*Anu. Estud. Am.*, 50:1, 1993, p. 213–234)

Demonstrates structural constraints of reformist economic policies of military socialists of the Toro and Busch regimes in the 1930s. Moreover, the reformist conceptualization of the new economic programs and sheer fiscal needs impeded a coherent modernization of the economy.

2833 **Greever, Janet Groff.** José Ballivián y el oriente boliviano. Traducción, prólogo, y notas de José Luis Roca. La Paz: Empresa Editora Siglo, 1987. 253 p.: bibl., indexes, maps.

Pioneering and well-documented study of largely neglected period and region examines mid-19th-century efforts of President Ballivián to colonize Bolivia's eastern lowlands in the Amazon and Chaco regions, as well as find fluvial routes to the Atlantic.

2834 **Guevara, Ernesto.** The Bolivian diary of Ernesto Che Guevara. Edited by Mary-Alice Waters. New York: Pathfinder, 1994. 467 p.: bibl., ill., index, maps.

An excellent edition of the guerrilla leader's diary, with maps and photos to explain Guevara's failed Bolivian campaign.

2835 **Huanca, Tomás.** Los procesos de desestructuración en las comunidades andinas a fines del siglo XIX: altiplano lacustre. (*in* Coloquio Estado y Región en los Andes, Cusco, Peru, 1984. Actas. Cusco, Peru: Centro de Estudios Rurales Andinos Bartolomé de las Casas, 1987, p. 45–86, bibl., tables)

Important local study of alienation of Indians from their community land in northern highlands. Especially valuable for detailed analysis of the effects of Melgarejo laws in the 1860s.

2836 **Irurozqui, Marta.** ¿Qué hacer con el indio?: un análisis de las obras de Franz Tamayo y Alcides Arguedas. (*Rev. Indias*, 52: 195/196, mayo/dic. 1992, p. 559–587)

Analysis of the two most important early 20th-century Bolivian intellectuals, showing how the definition of the "Indian problem" was profoundly conservative because both tried to find solutions for continued Creole hegemony and essentially blamed the backwardness of Bolivia on the Indians.

Jackson, Robert H. and **José Gordillo Claure.** Formación, crisis y transformación de la estructura agraria de Cochabamba: el caso de la hacienda de Paucarpata y de la comunidad del Passo, 1538–1645 y 1872–1929. See item **2477.**

2837 **Jackson, Robert H.** Regional markets and agrarian transformation in Bolivia: Cochabamba, 1539–1960. Albuquerque: Univ. of New Mexico Press, 1994. 283 p.: bibl., ill., index, maps.

Argues that the division of haciendas into peasant smallholdings in Cochabamba occurred during the 19th century as a result of liberal policies, including the decline of regional markets, the increase in free trade, and the construction of railroads.

2838 **Just, Estanislao.** Aproximación a la historia de la Iglesia en Bolivia. La Paz: Editorial Don Bosco, 1987. 87 p.: bibl. (Yachay. Temas monográficos; 1)

Brief outline of Catholic Church history in Bolivia from the conquest to the present day, written by an important Jesuit historian. Schematic emphasis on administrative matters, broken down regionally by bishoprics.

2839 Just, Estanislao. Comienzo de la independencia en el Alto Perú: los sucesos de Chuquisaca, 1809. Sucre, Bolivia: Editorial Judicial, 1994. 858 p.: appendix, bibl., ill.

This massive tome, with an extensive documentary appendix, is the definitive account of one of the first patriotic revolts in South America. Shows that the Creole revolutionaries were for true independence, based on Enlightenment doctrines learned at the Univ. of Charcas.

2840 Klaiber, Jeffrey. The Catholic Church's role as mediator: Bolivia, 1968–1989. (*J. Church State*, 35:2, Spring 1993, p. 351–365)

The Catholic Church has proved instrumental in the mediation between various political forces in Bolivia, as this analysis shows. The need for Church interference in Bolivian politics shows the fragility of democratic processes in the country.

2841 Klein, Herbert S. Bolivia: the evolution of a multi-ethnic society. 2nd ed. New York: Oxford Univ. Press, 1992. 343 p.: bibl., index, maps. (Latin American histories)

Second edition of best history of Bolivia written in any language. Includes social and economic history as well as political developments. Updated only by adding events since 1980s to the last chapter; also offers revised and very useful bibliographic essay.

2842 Klein, Herbert S. Recent trends in Bolivian studies. (*LARR*, 31:1, 1996, p. 162–170)

Useful synopsis of some recent publications on Bolivia. Notes include comprehensive recent bibliographies on mining, elites, recent politics, and peasantry in Bolivia.

2843 Langer, Erick D. and Gina L. Hames. Commerce and credit on the periphery: Tarija merchants, 1830–1914. (*HAHR*, 74:2, May 1994, p. 285–316, maps, tables)

Investigates the predominant role that merchants in Tarija played in the commercial development of southern Bolivia. Employs new methodology, through use of probate and merchant records, to reconstruct retail and wholesale commercial networks. Shows how different groups participated in trade.

2844 Langer, Erick D. Mission land tenure on the southeastern Bolivian frontier, 1845–1949. (*Americas/Francisc.*, 50:3, Jan. 1994, p. 399–418, table)

Using the Franciscan missions among the Chiriguanos as an example, shows how land distribution within missions reveals economic and power structures. In this case, control over land indicates that mission Indians wielded relatively great command over their own lives.

2845 Langer, Erick D. Missions and the frontier economy: the case of the Franciscan missions among the Chiriguanos, 1845–1930. (*in* The new Latin American mission history. Lincoln: Univ. of Nebraska Press, 1995, p. 49–76)

Analyzes missions in southeastern Bolivia according to their economic impact as labor sources, producers of agricultural and artisanal goods, and markets. Provides a new means of assessing the vital importance of missions in frontier economy.

2846 Lofstrom, William Lee. Cobija y el litoral boliviano, vistos por ojos extranjeros: 1825–1880. La Paz: Editorial Quipus; Verónica, Mauro Bertero, 1991. 138 p.: bibl., ill., maps.

A useful compendium of traveler's accounts, translated into Spanish, describes Bolivia's most important Pacific port of the 19th century. Also includes lengthy introductions to accounts, placing accounts and authors in their appropriate contexts.

López-Ocón, Leoncio. Las actividades americanistas del naturalista español Marcos Jiménez de la Espada. See item **2221.**

2847 Lorini, Irma. El movimiento socialista "embrionario" en Bolivia, 1920–1939: entre nuevas ideas y residuos de la sociedad tradicional. La Paz: Editorial Los Amigos del Libro, 1994. 303 p.: bibl. (Col. Historia; NA 491)

Exhaustive, but overly academic, book tracing the intellectual history of socialism in Bolivia finds that foreign influence was small and late, in part due to lack of European immigration. Highlights career of Tristán Marof, founder of modern socialism in Bolivia.

2848 Mamani Condori, Carlos B. Taraqu,
1866–1935: masacre, guerra y "renovación" en la biografía de Eduardo L. Nina
Qhispi. La Paz: Ediciones Aruwiyiri, 1991.
172 p.: bibl., ill. (Serie Agresión colonial y resistencia indígena)
    Well-conceived local case study of the
northern altiplano region and an Aymara indigenous leader details the struggle between
Creoles and Indians over land and indigenous
rights during the period of greatest hacienda
expansion.

Méndez G., Cecilia. *Incas sí, indios no:* note
on Peruvian Creole nationalism and its contemporary crisis. See item **2796.**

Mendoza Meléndez, Eduardo. La campaña de
la Breña. v. 1–2. See item **2797.**

2849 Mercado, Melchor María. Album de
paisajes, tipos humanos y costumbres
de Bolivia, 1841–1869. Sucre: Banco Central
de Bolivia; Archivo Nacional de Bolivia; Biblioteca Nacional de Bolivia, 1991. 239 p.:
bibl., ill. (some col.), index.
    Beautiful reproductions of watercolor
paintings in naive style are a significant
source of information for mid-19th century
life in Bolivia. Includes Mercado's short diary
of voyage to eastern lowlands, as well as exhaustive biography of the painter and description of his paintings by Gunnar Mendoza.

2850 Meyer Aragón, Carlos. En ambos frentes: memorias de un ex combatiente
mutilado en la Guerra del Chaco. Asunción:
Impr. Zamphirópolos, 1987. 75 p.
    Reprint of a Chaco War participant's
personal account, first published in Asunción
in 1935. The author, a Bolivian who was
taken prisoner, was so critical of his own side
that his account was published in Paraguay
and he was sentenced to death by a Bolivian
tribunal. The sentence was never carried out.
[J. Horowitz]

2851 Millington, Thomas. Debt politics after independence: the funding conflict
in Bolivia. Gainesville: Univ. Press of Florida,
1992. 172 p.: bibl., index. (Univ. of Florida social sciences monograph; 79)
    Argues that Bolivia lost much of its fi-
nancial autonomy during the Sucre Administration in the 1820s by emphasizing "floating
debt" rather than more rational "funded
debt" schemes. Sees the hacienda owners'

rentier mentality in rural Bolivia to be the
result of these policies.

2852 Mitre, Antonio. Bajo un cielo de estaño: fulgor y ocaso del metal en Bolivia. La Paz: Asociación Nacional de Mineros
Medianos; ILDIS, 1993. 307 p.: bibl. (Biblioteca Minera Boliviana; 6)
    Excellent treatment of the Bolivian tin
mining industry before 1952, including its
turn-of-the-century inception, mine ownership, and labor conditions, is strongest on
the first three decades of the 20th century.
Curiously, includes little treatment of Simón
Patiño, the most important mine owner.

2853 Mitre, Antonio. El enigma de los hor-
nos: la economía política de la fundi-
ción de estaña; el proceso boliviano a la luz de
otras experiencias. La Paz: Asociación Nacional de Mineros Medianos: ILDIS, 1993. 143
p.: bibl. (Biblioteca Minera Boliviana; 7)
    Examines reasons that tin smelters
were not built until after WWII in Bolivia. Rejects both nationalist and liberal theses; instead points to the structure of the tin mining
industry, lack of protectionism, and tin miners' lack of autonomy from the Bolivian State.

Morales, Waltraud Q. Bolivia: land of struggle. See *HLAS 55:3336.*

Pastore, Carlos. El Gran Chaco en la formación territorial del Paraguay: etapas de su incorporación. See item **3158.**

2854 Peñaranda de del Granado, Susana and
Omar Chávez Zamorano. El MIR entre
el pasado y el presente. La Paz: Artes Gráficas
Latina, 1992. 535 p.: bibl., ill.
    Sympathetic biography of leftist party
traces its origins as revolutionary party in the
early 1970s, to its accession to power as a
centrist party in the 1989 election. Extremely
detailed and well-documented.

2855 Pérez Torrico, Alexis. El estado oligár-
quico y los empresarios de Atacama,
1871–1878. La Paz: Ediciones Gráficas E.G.,
1994. 211 p.: bibl., map.
    Polemical but well-documented study
of elites in the little-studied Atacama region
just before the War of the Pacific (1879–84).
Finds that a weak Bolivian government (with
its laissez-faire ideology) and the Bolivian oligarchy, allied with Chilean capitalists, sold
out national interests in silver mining, ni-
trates, and railroad deals.

2856 Platt, Tristan. Divine protection and liberal damnation: exchanging metaphors in nineteenth-century Potosí. (*in* Contesting markets: analyses of ideology, discourse and practice. Edinburgh, Scotland: Edinburgh Univ. Press, 1992, p. 131–158)

Provocative essay attacks economic liberal interpretation of Bolivian history by showing that liberalism is an ideological construction. Argues for a different conception of history by examining protectionism, tribute, and the meaning of money and profit through the lens of economic relations between Indians and Creoles in mid-19th century Potosí. For Spanish translation, see item **2857.**

2857 Platt, Tristan. Protección divina y perdición liberal: poéticas del intercambio en el Potosí del siglo XIX. (*Rev. Andin.*, 11:2, dic. 1993, p. 349–380, bibl.)

For review of the English-language original, see item **2856.**

2858 Rivera Pizarro, Alberto. Los terratenientes de Cochabamba. Cochabamba, Bolivia: CERES; FACES, 1992. 136 p.

Shows how the Cochabamba landlord class kept its identity, despite widespread peasant smallholdings. Detailed analysis of land tenure patterns in first half of 20th century also suggests that widespread peasant upheavals from the 1940s onward brought about the complete decline of the hacienda system.

2859 Rodríguez Ostria, Gustavo. La construcción de una región: Cochabamba y su historia, siglos XIX-XX. Cochabamba, Bolivia: Univ. Mayor de San Simón, Facultad de Ciencias Económicas y Sociología, 1995. 196 p.: bibl., map.

Collection of essays, most previously published, discusses the modernization of Cochabamba, fiestas, Indian communities, famines, worker-student alliances, and elite efforts to revitalize mining in Oruro.

2860 Rodríguez Ostria, Gustavo. El peso del mineral: un balance de la historiografía minera boliviana colonial y republicana. (*Anuario/Sucre*, 1994/95, p. 91–107)

The most complete bibliographical essay on mining in Bolivia covers aspects of production, mine labor, technology, and working-class "mining culture." Shows that many regions and some aspects, such as small mining enterprises, have not yet been studied adequately. See also item **2818.**

2861 Rodríguez Ostria, Gustavo. Poder central y proyecto regional, Cochabamba y Santa Cruz en los siglos XIX y XX. Bolivia: ILDIS; IDAES, 1993. 168 p.: bibl.

Important series of essays shows how centrally-located Cochabamba and frontier Santa Cruz developed in the late-19th and 20th centuries through changes in internal markets. Last section examines regionalist impulses between the Great Depression and 1965, with Bolivian national feelings emerging victorious.

2862 Rodríguez Ostria, Gustavo. El socavón y el sindicato: ensayos históricos sobre los trabajadores mineros, siglos XIX-XX. La Paz: ILDIS, 1991. 166 p.: bibl., ill.

Collection of brilliant essays, many published earlier, applying framework pioneered by E.P. Thompson for mine labor in Bolivia. Finds mining economy and labor discipline were determined by agricultural cycle, festivals, and theft of minerals in the 19th century. In the 20th century, labor affected mining through unions and political involvement.

Ruiz-Tagle Orrego, Emilio. Bolivia y Chile: el conflicto del Pacífico. See item **2926.**

2863 Sarkisyanz, Manuel. Kollasuyo: indianische Geschichte der Republik Bolivien; Propheten des indianischen Aufbruchs. Idstein, Deutschland: Schulz-Kirchner, 1993. 683 p.: bibl., index.

The title is a bit deceptive, for rather than being an Indian history, it is an exhaustive intellectual history of what non-Indians (mainly elite figures) have said about the Indians. Sarkisyanz covers from Belzu in the mid-19th century to the CONDEPA (Conciencia de Patria) party of today. Despite problems, sees Indianist consciousness rising and becoming part of the mainstream.

2864 Soux, María Luisa. La coca liberal: producción y circulación a principios del siglo XX. La Paz: Misión de Cooperación Técnica Holandesa; Centro de Información para el Desarrollo, 1993. 212 p.: bibl., ill., maps. (Col. Historia agraria)

Valuable study of coca in Yungas province (La Paz), the traditional region of coca cultivation. Ranges from discussion of tenure system and coca production in Yungas, to the commercialization of coca in La Paz, Bolivia, and the world.

2865 **Strengers, Jeroen.** La Asamblea Popular: Bolivia, 1971. La Paz: Sistema de Documentación e Información Sindical; Ediciones Gráficas EG, 1991. 272 p.: bibl., ill., index. (Col. Tiempo de historia)

A journalistic account of the 1970 Torres regime, recounted in detail from the perspective of leftist labor unions.

2866 **Torres Sejas, Angel.** Oruro en su historia. La Paz: Librería Editorial Juventud, 1994. 720 p.: bibl., ill.

Exhaustive narrative history of the department of Oruro, from its pre-Tiwanaku population to 1994.

2867 **Whitehead, Laurence.** Bolivia. (*in* Latin America between the Second World War and the Cold War, 1944–1948. Edited by Leslie Bethell and Ian Roxborough. New York: Cambridge Univ. Press, 1992, p. 120–146, table)

A provocative political account, in which the effects of international affairs in the 1940s (and subsequent labeling of Bolivian political forces according to international formulas) are shown to have distorted national politics. Argues that the 1952 Revolution might have occurred earlier and been more reformist had this labeling not occurred.

Chile

WILLIAM F. SATER, *Professor of History, California State University, Long Beach*

THE WORKS REVIEWED THIS BIENNIUM reflect Chilean historiography's increased interest in a more detailed study of the role of ethnic minorities in the formation of the *raza chilena*. New material has appeared focusing on different aspects of the lives and contributions of immigrants from Italy, England, Spain, and Germany as well as of Sephardic Jews who settled in Chile. Agosín's lyrical memories of her sometimes traumatic childhood as a Jew surrounded by Nazis in Osorno is a welcome combination of literary and historical insights (item **2868**). Similarly, Blancpain's work on the French is a pleasure to read, but, like a good mystery story, it simply ends too soon; with luck he will provide us additional insights by expanding on this slim volume (item **2874**).

On a more general level, Collier and Sater (item **2882**) have written a treatment of Chile, which, while less specialized than Gonzalo Vial's ongoing project, covers a longer period, 1804–1994.

Economic topics remain a favorite area for research. Spearheaded by a younger generation of historians, such as Luis Ortega (items **2917** and **2918**), Julio Pinto Vallejos (items **2919** and **2920**), René Millar, Juan Eduardo Vargas (item **2934**), and Ricardo Couyoumdjian *et al.*, new works dealing with various aspects of industrialization, commerce, mining—particularly the coal industry—and the labor movement, have appeared. Couyoumdjian *et al.'s Historia de la Bolsa de Comercio de Santiago, 1893–1993* is a tour de force which, while hard reading, is clearly worth the effort (item **2885**). Millars' general economic history for the 1820–1925 period (item **2912**) is an extremely well researched and very welcome addition to Chilean historiography, supplanting Fetter's seminal study, *Monetary inflation in Chile*, (Princeton, N.J.: Princeton Univ. Press, 1931). Let us hope Millar will continue along this vein of research and produce a second volume dealing with the post-1925 period.

Political historians are finally turning their eyes to the post-1930 epoch. Barnard (item **2872**) and Etchepare (item **2890**) concentrated to great effect on the events leading up to the passage of the infamous *ley maldita*, while Grugel (item **2897**) studied the forces that enabled the less-than-brilliant Carlos Ibáñez (his nickname while a cadet at the *Escuela Militar* was "the Mule") to get elected to a second presidential term. Fermandois' chronicle of the tedious negotiations between US creditors and Chile over Santiago's international debts demonstrates the ability of so-called dependent countries to protect their pocketbook, much to the woe of their creditors (item **2891**).

Two particularly worthwhile bibliographical works appeared this year. The volume by Retamal and Villalobos (item **2923**) is a marvelous source for anyone seeking information published in Chilean journals on a wide variety of topics. Another essential research tool is Sagredo's updated bibliography included in the second edition of Cariola Sutler and Sunkel's *Un siglo de historia económica de Chile, 1830–1930* (item **2880**). The breadth of both bibliographical works is extremely comprehensive. All historians should consult these publications as a prelude to serious research.

Local history, which has often been an important area for study, seems to have lost favor among scholars of Chilean history. Still, Martinic's two-volume work on Magallanes is particularly noteworthy, providing a detailed analysis of this southernmost province (item **2907**).

The emergence of Chile's educational institutions increasingly has attracted the attention of various scholars. For instance, Sol Serrano's excellent study of the Univ. de Chile traces the development of the nation's preeminent, and for years the sole, provider of college degrees (item **2929**). Some historians are investigating institutions or customs that, for better or worse, reveal the darker side of Chilean society. Camus' article on Santiago's 19th-century mental asylum is particularly interesting (item **2878**), while León's fascination with cemeteries enlightens, though it does not always elate (item **2903**).

It would benefit scholars if more research aids, such as those produced by Retamal, Villalobos, and Sagredo, were published. Nonetheless, the recent publication of books and articles on the post-1925 period, particularly on the 1930s and the 1940s, is opening up new and most welcome vistas. Clearly, the high quality of recent research and the new areas under investigation indicate how singularly vital is Chilean historiography. The founding of new journals, moreover, affords younger scholars additional outlets for their historical discoveries.

2868 Agosin, Marjorie. A cross and a star: memoirs of a Jewish girl in Chile. Translated by Celeste Kostopulos-Cooperman. Albuquerque: Univ. of New Mexico Press, 1995. 179 p.: ill.

As a Jewish girl raised in Osorno during the heyday of the Nazis, Agosin discovered that Chile's south proved a fertile ground for National Socialism, as it still does today. A combination of flashbacks and more traditional memoir style, this charming study, in lovely prose, reveals the message of immigrant alienation. For translation specialist's comment, see item **4605.**

2869 Agulhon, Maurice et al. Formas de sociabilidad en Chile, 1840–1940. Santiago: Fundación Mario Góngora; Vivaria, 1992. 393 p.: bibl.

Eighteen essays describe various forums—including fire companies, mutual aid societies, the ubiquitous *tertulias,* and cafes—that created opportunities for Chileans to meet. Some authors provide excellent insights into the character of 19th- and 20th-century Chilean society. Extremely useful for social and intellectual historians.

2870 Antezana-Pernet, Corinne. Peace in the world and democracy at home: the Chilean women's movement in the 1940s. (*in* Latin America in the 1940s: war and postwar transitions. Edited by David Rock. Berkeley: Univ. of California Press, 1994, p. 166–186)

As women participated more in the economy, and their status improved, they demanded political representation. World War II, rather than domestic political elements, helped them to achieve this goal. The women's movement later faltered like other political movements, a victim of the restrictive domestic environment.

2871 Aránguiz Donoso, Horacio. Notas para el estudio de los bancos extranjeros en Chile, 1889–1971. (*Historia/Santiago*, 27, 1993, p. 19–68, tables)

The government regulated foreign-owned banks to ensure that they retained enough capital to pay both their taxes and their depositors, and to guarantee that they did not enjoy advantages. Based largely on congressional debates, work traces hostility toward foreign banks, which culminated in their nationalization under Allende. Useful for economic historians, although more detail would have been helpful.

2872 Barnard, Andrew. Chile. (*in* Latin America between the Second World War and the Cold War, 1944–1948. Edited by Leslie Bethell and Ian Roxborough. New York: Cambridge Univ. Press, 1992, p. 66–91)

Domestic issues, particularly the struggle between Socialists and Communists, led González Videla to pass the *ley maldita*. Although the US clearly favored such legislation, US capacity to influence the Moneda (Chile's presidential palace) seems to have been limited. Although somewhat complicated, this well-researched study is one of the few to explain this critical period.

2873 Barros Van Buren, Mario. Historia diplomática de Chile, 1541–1938. Prólogo y una introducción a la segunda edición de Jaime Eyzaguirre. 2. ed. (actualizada a 1958). Santiago: Editorial A. Bello, 1990. 891 p., 120 p. of plates: bibl., ill., index, maps.

Presumably revised and updated, work unsuccessfully attempts to cover 1938–58 in less than 60 pages. While the core of the old work remains useful, no new research has been added. Important only for those who do not have the first edition.

Bascuñán, Pilar. A 400 años de la llegada de los jesuitas a Chile, 1593–1993. See item **2489.**

2874 Blancpain, Jean-Pierre. Francia y los franceses en Chile, 1700–1980. Santiago: Hachette, 1987. 355 p.: bibl., ill., maps. (Col. Histo-Hachette)

Charming work based on a variety of materials integrates entertaining and educational anecdotes. Although raising more questions than it answers, study provides an entertaining, albeit brief, examination of the French and their impact, not only on Chile, but on Chileans as well.

2875 Brahm García, Enrique. Del soldado romántico al soldado profesional: revolución en el pensamiento militar chileno, 1885–1940. (*Historia/Santiago*, 25, 1990, p. 5–37, bibl.)

Under German tutelage, Chileans envisioned war as a scientific enterprise that would benefit society and that, to be successful, required introduction of conscription and integration of foreign examples. Interesting work, despite its tendency to give more importance to theory than to the reality of the Chilean army.

2876 Bravo Elizondo, Pedro. Santa María de Iquique, 1907: documentos para su historia. Santiago: Ediciones del Litoral; Editorial Cuarto Propio, 1993. 218 p.: bibl.

Provides reader with material drawn from the local press, official archives, and eyewitnesses—including foreign diplomats—about the 1907 massacre. Explains the background to the strike, and the demonstrations that led to the bloodshed. Useful for those involved in labor history.

Bravo Lira, Bernardino. El absolutismo ilustrado en Hispanoamérica: Chile, 1760–1860, de Carlos III a Portales y Montt. See item **2491.**

2877 Bravo Valdivieso, Fernando; Francisco Bulnes Serrano; and **Gonzalo Vial Correa.** Balmaceda y la guerra civil. Santiago: Editorial Fundación, 1991. 445 p.: bibl., ill., index.

Conventional study of the Balmaceda period, the Civil War, and Balmaceda's ultimate suicide. Lacks scholarly appeal.

2878 Camus Gayán, Pablo. Filantropía, medicina y locura: la Casa de Orates de Santiago, 1852–1894. (*Historia/Santiago,* 27, 1993, p. 89–140)

Focusing on mental health, author shows change in societal values and increasing ability of physicians to treat and cure the mentally ill rather than institutionalize them. Novel study, using original sources, of a frequently ignored institution.

2879 Cárdenas G., Mario. Grupos marginados en los inicios de la era republicana: vagabundos, mendigos e indigentes. (*Cuad. Hist./Santiago,* 1, dic. 1991, p. 47–62, bibl.)

Both Church and State made numerous efforts to provide some support for the sick, abandoned, and destitute, while controlling criminal classes and beggars. Uses primary sources to describe these efforts. Although lacking focus, article is nonetheless interesting for social historians.

2880 Cariola Sutter, Carmen and **Osvaldo Sunkel.** Un siglo de historia económica de Chile, 1830–1930. Bibliografía revisada y actualizada por Rafael Sagredo B. Santiago: Editorial Universitaria, 1990. 397 p.: bibl., index. (Col. Imagen de Chile)

The core of this work, an essay on the impact of the nitrate industry augmented by numerous charts, is enriched mightily by Sagredo's bibliography, which has brought the original entries up to date. Excellent work and an essential tool for all who seek to investigate Chilean economic history.

2881 Chile since independence. Edited by Leslie Bethell. Cambridge, England; New York: Cambridge Univ. Press, 1993. 240 p.: bibl., index, maps.

Contains articles on Chile from vols. 3, 5, and 8 of *The Cambridge history of Latin America.* For annotations of those volumes, see *HLAS 48:1808, HLAS 50:955,* and *HLAS 54:1110.*

2882 Collier, Simon and **William F. Sater.** A history of Chile, 1808–1994. New York: Cambridge Univ. Press, 1996. 427 p.: bibl., ill., maps. (Cambridge Latin American studies; 82)

This remarkable and most readable synthesis of Chilean history from 1808–1994, including some colonial background, does justice to the significance of the 19th century for subsequent periods. Includes a welcome emphasis on culture, both high and low, as well as a focus on politics and economics. Authors' treatment is not devoid of drama, which they present with sensitivity, especially the Unidad Popular years, the period of military dictatorship, and the more recent transition to civilian rule. Highly recommended work serves as a substantive reference for scholars and valuable introduction for undergraduates. [Iván Jaksić]

2883 Converse, Christel K. Culture and nationalism among the German-Chileans in the 1930s. (*MACLAS: Lat. Am. Essays,* 4, 1991?, p. 117–124)

Perceptive article drawn from author's dissertation, *The rise and fall of Nazi influence among the German-Chileans,* the only work available so far on the topic. Traces historical, socioeconomic, and cultural trajectory of an influential ethnic group. Thoroughly documented work based on US, Chilean, and German primary sources. [Ed.]

2884 Cordero, Fernando. Chile, siglo XIX: de la milicia a la guardia cívica. (*Ibero-Am./Stockholm,* 22:1, 1992, p. 83–97, tables)

Utilizing mainly secondary sources, article concludes that the Chilean National Guard constituted an integral and effective back-up to the regular military, an assertion certainly not confirmed by historical events nor demonstrated by the author.

2885 Couyoumdjian, Juan Ricardo; René Millar; and **Josefina Tocornal.** Historia de la Bolsa de Comercio de Santiago, 1893–1993: un siglo de mercado de valores en Chile. Santiago: Bolsa de Comercio de Santiago, 1993. 768 p.: index, tables.

Using an impressive number of primary sources, authors provide a magisterial study of the Santiago Bolsa, explaining its workings while simultaneously discussing other aspects of Chilean economic history. Includes valuable biographical information as well as tables tracing the rise and fall of the stock market and various companies. Relying almost exclusively on primary materials, this is an essential work for economic historians.

2886 Crispi, Paula de Dios. Inmigrar en Chile: estudio de una cadena migratoria hispana. Santiago: Dirección de Bibliotecas, Archivos y Museos, Centro de Investigaciones Diego Barros Arana, 1993.

172 p.: bibl., ill. (Col. Sociedad y cultura; 5)

Essay on immigration to Chile melded with the experiences of the Franco brothers and their relatives who settled in Curicó after 1907. Includes useful charts on Spanish immigration to Chile. Narrowly focused, yet an excellent source for immigration experts.

2887 Crozier, Ronald D. La industria del yodo, 1815–1915. (*Historia/Santiago*, 27, 1993, p. 141–212, bibl., graphs, tables)

Emphasizing technical aspects of the iodine industry, work provides overview of this often neglected aspect of Chile's mining sector. Although extremely specialized, contains useful data on mining production.

2888 Drake, Paul W. International crises and popular movements in Latin America: Chile and Peru from the Great Depression to the Cold War. (*in* Latin America in the 1940s: war and postwar transitions. Edited by David Rock. Berkeley: Univ. of California Press, 1994, p. 109–140)

While domestic forces were significant beginning with the Depression and particularly after the onset of the Cold War, the US did influence movements for change in Peru and Chile. As a result, the impact of reform elements in both nations was limited. Valuable article employs wide range of sources for diplomatic historians.

2889 Estrada, Baldomero. La colectividad italiana de Santiago de Chile a través de la Sociedad de Socorros Mutuos "Italia," 1880–1920. (*in* Asociacionismo, trabajo e identidad étnica: los italianos en América Latina en una perspectiva comparada. Recopilación de Fernando J. Devoto y Eduardo J. Miguez. Buenos Aires: Centro de Estudios Migratorios Latinoamericanos (CEMLA); Instituto de Estudios Históricos y Sociales (IEHS), 1992, p. 59–76, appendix, tables)

Generalizations about the Italian community, particularly in Santiago and Valparaíso. Tries to demonstrate that Italian immigrants appeared better educated and more skilled than the Chilean population and that they generally prospered while holding down jobs in urban commerce. Although sparse sources limit its impact, work is still useful for ethnic historians.

2890 Etchepare Jensen, Jaime. El advenimiento de Gabriel González Videla al gobierno y el fracaso de la Unión Nacional, 1946–1948. (*Rev. Hist./Concepción*, 2:2, 1992, p. 73–101)

Using mainly secondary sources, studies the events leading up to the election of González Videla, his break with the Communists, and the passage of the Law for the Defense of Democracy. More narrative than analytical, work nonetheless provides a good overview of post-WWII Chile.

2891 Fermandois, Joaquín. Del unilateralismo a la negociación: Chile, Estados Unidos y la deuda de largo plazo, 1934–1938. (*Historia/Santiago*, 26, 1991/92, p. 71–115)

Relying heavily on US archival materials as well as on Chilean sources, demonstrates how Chile managed to wring concessions from the Yankee bond holders during the Great Depression. Despite its lengthy narrative, diplomatic historians will profit from this valuable work on a painful subject in US-Chilean relations.

2892 Frei Montalva, Eduardo. Memorias—1911–1934—y correspondencias con Gabriela Mistral y Jacques Maritain. Santiago: Planeta, 1989. 221 p.: bibl., ill. (Espejo de Chile; 5)

Disappointing volume by Chile's first Christian Democratic president. Because work tends to emphasize his early years, it is not essential for historians, although it is useful for Frei's view on his earliest activities.

2893 Garay Vera, Cristián. Bibliografía y fuentes para la relación chileno-española entre 1936–1939. (*Rev. Chil. Humanid.*, 13, 1992, p. 117–131, appendix)

Detailed analysis of primary and secondary materials describing Spanish-Chilean relations. Highly specialized but nonetheless essential work for diplomatic historians.

2894 Gazmuri Riveros, Cristián. El "48" chileno: igualitarios, reformistas, radicales, masones y bomberos. Santiago: Editorial Universitaria, 1992. 276 p.: bibl., ill., maps. (Col. Imagen de Chile)

The 1848 European Revolution produced a generation of Chileans who supported reform and staffed the new voluntary groups such as fire companies and Masons. These organizations became the basis for a new political wave, the Partido Radical, whose members subsequently became leaders in the Republic. Well-researched, insightful book.

González Abuter, Tulio. Negociaciones chileno-argentinas de límites, 1871–1881: historia de una década. See *HLAS 55:4250.*

2895 González Pizarro, José Antonio. Claudio Gay y la historiografía chilena: el contexto histórico-cultural en la formulación de una concepción historiográfica. (*Rev. Chil. Hist. Geogr.,* 158, 1990, p. 103–125)

The French naturalist first taught science and then history at various Chilean educational institutions. Using primary sources plus Gay's works, author shows how Gay incorporated Chilean examples into his lectures. While not a groundbreaking work, useful for intellectual historians.

2896 Gross, Patricio. Santiago de Chile: ideología y modelos urbanos. (*EURE/Santiago,* 16:48, junio 1990, p. 67–85, bibl.)

Isolating the poor from the affluent constituted the goal of Santiago's urban planners. Elites refused to modernize the city or its transportation system, or to improve living conditions, thus keeping the poor on the periphery while the comfortable classes lived around the city center. Essential work for social historians.

2897 Grugel, Jean. Populism and the political system in Chile: Ibañismo, 1952–1958. (*Bull. Lat. Am. Res.,* 11:2, May 1992, p. 169–186, bibl.)

Ibáñez's election introduced new forces into Chile, and populism remained part of the nation's political culture even after the end of his second term. Brief but otherwise excellent introduction to a study of the forces that brought the General of Hope to power in 1952, forces which survived thereafter.

2898 Heller, Friedrich Paul. Colonia Dignidad: von der Psychosekte zum Folterlager. Stuttgart, Germany: Schmetterling, 1993. 308 p.: bibl., ill., index, map.

Publicist's attempt to connect controversial community of post-World War II German immigrants with activities of Chile's intelligence services (DINA). Relies on variety of sources, some questionable or undocumented. Nevertheless, book merits attention because it raises questions and provides data on topics in need of further research. [C.K. Converse]

Holland, Charles. Noticias de Buenos Aires, el Paraguay, Chile y el Perú: cartas del ciudadano inglés Charles Holland, 1820–1826. See item **3045.**

2899 Izquierdo Fernández, Gonzalo. Las sociedades ilustrados en el mundo agrario español y la Sociedad de Agricultura en Chile. (*Bol. Acad. Chil. Hist.,* 55:99, p. 229–256)

The Sociedad Nacional de Agricultura, a development of Enlightenment thought, sought to introduce technical change and to improve the lot of Chile's peasants. After 1870, the members, increasingly tied to business, emphasized new techniques and implements rather than social change. Based on primary materials, this work benefits economic historians.

2900 Jaksic, Ivan. Sarmiento y la prensa chilena del siglo XIX. (*Historia/Santiago,* 26, 1991/92, p. 117–144, tables)

Despite limitations of restrictive laws, the press, sometimes with government subsidies, flourished. Among its luminaries was Sarmiento, who saw the press as an instrument of progress and who put his services at the disposal of the Montt Administration. While stressing Sarmiento, article provides brief intellectual history of Chile.

2901 Jocelyn-Holt Letelier, Alfredo. Institucionalidad liberal y universidad en el Chile decimonónico. (*Universum/Talca,* 6, 1991, p. 65–84, photos)

Portales and his cohorts were not Conservatives but Liberals, and the Republic they established, while perhaps authoritarian, did not signal a restoration of Spanish conservatism. Similarly, the newly created Univ. de Chile was a Liberal institution, founded to create a cultured society. This densely written study is not particularly convincing.

2902 Kiernan, Victor. Chile from war to revolution, 1879–1891. (*Hist. Workshop,* 34, Autumn 1992, p. 72–91)

Using a limited number of sources—many of them biased—author paints traditional picture of Balmaceda as martyr. Old wine in a new bottle.

2903 León León, Marco Antonio. De la capilla a la fosa común: el Cementerio Católico Parroquial de Santiago, 1878–1932. (*Historia/Santiago,* 27, 1993, p. 331–375, graph, map, photos, table)

Santiago's Cementerio Católico, founded to ensure that the presence of heretics, or worse, would not jeopardize the eternal rest of the devout, became the focus of a Church-State conflict in the 1880s that took years to resolve. Interesting, albeit morbid, study of an oft-neglected institution, using mainly secondary works.

2904 Lobos Araya, Marina. La legislación carbonífera chilena: un ejemplo de casuismo y pragmatismo en el siglo XIX. (*Hist. Nuestra*, 2, 1990, p. 48–74, bibl., tables)

The coal-mining domestic elite pressured the government to pass new Mining Codes plus ancillary protectionist laws, encouraging the mining of coal and its local consumption. The need for higher grade British coal, however, forced the government to strike a balance between protectionism and more open trade policies. Although author's research is somewhat lacking, study is nonetheless useful.

2905 Loveman, Brian. The political left in Chile, 1973–1990. (*in* The Latin American left: from the fall of Allende to Perestroika. Boulder, Colo.: Westview Press, 1993, p. 23–39)

Fearing a counterrevolution, the Left has tempered its rhetoric and restrained its activities since Pinochet's fall. While certain elements still advocate class struggle, most favor consensus over confrontation, isolating the more militant faction but restoring a degree of political involvement. Good overview of the various political groups and their goals.

2906 Lowden, Pamela. The Ecumenical Committee for Peace in Chile, 1973–1975: the foundation of moral opposition to authoritarian rule in Chile. (*Bull. Lat. Am. Res.*, 12:2, May 1993, p. 189–203, bibl.)

By providing legal aid to detainees and testimony about human rights violations, the Comité de Cooperación para la Paz en Chile (and its successor, the Vicaría de la Solidaridad) saved the detained, sought to discover the whereabouts of the disappeared, and proved crucial in marshaling anti-government sentiment during the Pinochet years. Uses limited sources to describe an important organization.

2907 Martinic Beros, Mateo. Historia de la región magallánica. v. 1–2. Punta Arenas, Chile: Univ. de Magallanes, 1992. 2 v. (1423 p.): bibl., indexes, maps.

Study on Magallanes by the area's lead-ing historian traces evolution of Chile's south from its settlement to the present. Based on extensive research and the result of years of effort, it is a splendid local history.

2908 Matus González, Mario. Vivencia de los sefardíes. Santiago: Univ. de Chile, 1993. 1 v.

Using written and oral sources, describes history of Sephardic Jewish immigration to Chile and profiles the members of the immigrant community. An insightful look at how a frequently ignored group settled and prospered. Essential for those interested in history of ethnic communities and immigration.

2909 Mayo, John. British merchants in Chile and on Mexico's west coast in the mid-nineteenth century: the age of isolation. (*Historia/Santiago*, 26, 1991/92, p. 145–171)

Attracted by domestic stability and the rule of law, British merchants eschewed Mexico for Chile, where they prospered. In neither country, however, did the English seek to impose their will or to alter local conditions. Relying on British sources, which may have skewed his conclusions, author traces growth of what became an important ethnic group in Chile.

2910 Medina Aravena, Juan Andrés. La Central Unica de Trabajadores y el gobierno de la Unidad Popular: auge y desaparición. (*Rev. Hist./Concepción*, 1:1, 1991, p. 63–86)

The CUT became almost symbiotically entwined with the Allende government, virtually controlling the labor movement and even participating in the government's decision-making. Pinochet used CUT's involvement as a rationalization for suspending the union. Not especially well-researched or insightful, but may be helpful for labor specialists.

Mendoza Meléndez, Eduardo. La campaña de la Breña. v. 1–2. See item **2797.**

Meneses Ciuffardi, Emilio. El factor naval en las relaciones entre Chile y los Estados Unidos, 1881–1951. See *HLAS 55:4255.*

2911 Michel Slasar, José A. El presbítero Guillermo Viviani Contreras y el sindicalismo cristiano. (*Anu. Hist. Iglesia Chile*, 10, 1992, p. 103–115)

Viviani organized Catholic unions and

founded a newspaper to advance workers' interests, stop the spread of Marxist and anarchist ideas, and prevent a destructive class war. Author uses the priest's words to prove his thesis. May be useful to labor historians.

2912 Millar Carvacho, René. Políticas y teorías monetarias en Chile, 1810–1925. Santiago: Univ. Gabriela Mistral, 1994. 1 v.

Richly detailed and meticulously researched study describing Chile's monetary history employs an enormous range of primary and secondary works. Millar describes the evolution of Chile's monetary and banking system, along with the various, generally unsuccessful, attempts to return to the gold standard. All economic historians will need this splendid work.

2913 Miller, Rory. Transferencia de técnicas: la construcción y administración de ferrocarriles en la costa occidental de Sudamérica. (*Siglo XIX*, 3:7, oct. 1993, p. 65–102, maps)

The building of railroads permitted a transfer of technology that enabled Chile to develop a cadre of local specialists to run these rail lines, but local industry rarely provided rolling stock. Interesting study based on a good mix of primary and secondary sources. Includes examples other than Chile.

2914 Muñoz Gomá, María Angélica. El Partido Conservador y su postura ante la educación secundaria: Ministerio de Abdón Cifuentes, 1871–1873. (*Historia/Santiago*, 27, 1993, p. 377–423)

More narrative than analytical, uses mainly clerical journals and congressional sessions to study debate on the State's role as university gatekeeper. Conservatives, who saw education as buttressing status quo, clashed with Liberals, who did not agree. This conflict ultimately led to Cifuentes' resignation. Narrowly focused piece is not without merit.

2915 Mybes, Fritz. Die Geschichte der aus der deutschen Einwanderung entstandenen lutherischen Kirchen in Chile: von den Anfängen bis zum Jahre 1975. Düsseldorf, Germany: Archiv der Evangelischen Kirche im Rheinland, 1993. 225 p.: bibl., ill., indexes. (Schriften des Archivs der Evangelischen Kirche im Rheinland; 5)

Meticulously detailed chronology of development of Chile's Lutheran church and its transformation from an ethnic institution to an ecumenical one, which resulted in its division in 1975. However, author treads very lightly on church's role during its Nazi-oriented ethnic period. Book's value lies in its numerous German and German-Chilean documentary sources. [C.K. Converse]

2916 Norambuena Carrasco, Carmen. Inmigración, agricultura y ciudades intermedias, 1880–1930. (*Cuad. Hist./Santiago*, 1, dic. 1991, p. 105–126, tables)

As the south began to produce wheat, cities, which were tied to the local economy, emerged and grew, becoming centers of commerce as well as outposts of culture and education. When the wheat boom ended, most of these cities—with the exception of Temuco—stagnated. Good introduction to the fluctuating fortunes of urban centers.

2917 Ortega, Luis. La frontera carbonífera, 1840–1900. (*Mapocho/Santiago*, 31, primer semestre 1992, p. 131–148, table)

The south became the arena for sometimes violent struggles as coal miners sought higher salaries and better treatment. Clearly demonstrates, through a rich combination of sources, that the *salitreras* were not the only incubator for the formation of a working class. Essential for labor and economic historians.

2918 Ortega, Luis. El proceso de industrialización en Chile, 1850–1930. (*Historia/Santiago*, 26, 1991/92, p. 213–246)

Due to the post-1850 infusion of capital and the introduction of new technology and transport, an industrial base was created, particularly along the Santiago-Valparaíso and Tome and Lota axes. Increasingly able to satisfy domestic needs, new industries also provided the basis for subsequent expansion. Essential study for economic historians.

2919 Pinto Vallejos, Julio. Cortar raíces, criar fama: el peonaje chileno en la fase inicial del ciclo salitrero, 1850–1879. (*Historia/Santiago*, 27, 1993, p. 425–447)

Many Chileans arrived in the north before 1897, made the transition to salaried worker, possessed a sense of identity, and had acquired experience in redressing their grievances. Offers tentative explanations for the delay before workers launched a general strike. Appealing to economic and social historians.

2920 Pinto Vallejos, Julio. La transición laboral en el norte salitrero: la provincia de Tarapacá y los orígenes del proletariado en Chile, 1870–1890. (*Historia/Santiago*, 25, 1990, p. 207–228, bibl.)

Isolated in the north, sorely exploited, and without access to the traditional means of protection, miners turned to violence in 1890 and launched a general strike. Using a good mix of sources, author sees the *salitreros* as the crucible for the creation of the Chilean working class. Certainly worthy of study.

2921 Pozo, José del. Rebeldes, reformistas y revolucionarios: una historia oral de la izquierda chilena en la época de la Unidad Popular. Santiago: Ediciones Documentas, 1992. 375 p.: bibl., maps.

Using 120 interviews with Chileans from different socioeconomic classes, geographical areas, and political affiliations, author provides overview of the left's attitudes and motivations during the Allende Period. Excellent study provides an understanding of how things looked "from below."

2922 Ramírez Morales, Fenando. Apuntes para una historia ecológica de Chile. (*Cuad. Hist./Santiago*, 1, dic. 1991, p. 148–198, tables)

Breaking new ground, author traces evolution of legislation to protect wildlife, sea animals, and forests from abuse. Strongly rooted in congressional debates and laws, this important study addresses environmental history in Chile.

2923 Retamal Avila, Julio and **Sergio Villalobos R.** Bibliografía histórica chilena: revistas chilenas, 1843–1978. Santiago: Dirección de Bibliotecas, Archivos y Museos, Centro de Investigaciones Diego Barros Arana, 1993. 363 p.: index.

Superb bibliographical tool covers more than 50 publications that appeared between 1843–1978. In addition to a detailed breakdown by topic, includes bibliographical essay. Essential for all researchers.

2924 Retamal Avila, Julio. Características físicas del chileno del siglo XVII. (*Historia/Santiago*, 27, 1993, p. 449–504, graphs, table)

Apparently Chileans' physical stature has changed, although author is unclear as to whether this is due to mestization or simply to changes in descriptive terminology. Not

surprisingly, concludes that in the 17th century, members of the upper class were taller, whiter, and in better physical condition than others. Hardly scientific work is of limited value.

2925 Rodríguez Villegas, Hernán. Santiago en 1900. Fotografías del Centro de Documentación Iconográfica del Museo Histórico Nacional, de la donación ESSO Chile Petrolera Ltda. Santiago: Museo Histórico Nacional; Esso, 1986. 1 v. (unpaged): ill.

A lovely walk down memory lane, with photographs of Santiago from first quarter of this century. Not essential, but a worthwhile book showing Santiago when it was smaller, more tranquil, and less polluted.

2926 Ruiz-Tagle Orrego, Emilio. Bolivia y Chile: el conflicto del Pacífico. Santiago: Editorial Andrés Bello, 1992. 173 p.: bibl.

Career diplomat provides standard treatment of the conflict, with fewer sources and less insight than normal. Not for serious scholars.

2927 Salinas Meza, René. Una comunidad inmigrante: los alemanes en Valparaíso, 1860–1960: estudio demográfico. (*Jahrb. Gesch.*, 29, 1992, p. 309–342, graphs, tables)

Generalizations on the German-Chilean population, based on a very small sample of Valparaíso Evangelicals. Indicates that Germans married later than most Chileans, selected their spouses from within their community, and produced fewer children.

2928 Serrano, Sol. La Revolución Francesa y la formación del sistema nacional de educación en Chile. (*Cah. Am. lat.*, 10, 1990, p. 237–262)

Although lacking economic resources, Chile tried to copy the French educational system. The result was a system of *liceos* and the Univ. de Chile, which complemented but did not displace existing clerical institutions. Establishment of normal schools also enhanced the State's presence. A fine study of Chile's seminal educational institutions.

2929 Serrano, Sol. Universidad y nación: Chile en el siglo XIX. Santiago: Editorial Universitaria, 1994. 276 p.: bibl. (Col. Imagen de Chile)

Under the aegis of the secular State, the university disseminated knowledge and, through entrance examinations for higher education, ensured the quality of the professional faculties. The university became an instrument of modernization, integration, and secularization. All intellectual historians should consult this amply researched, superb institutional study.

2930 Stuven, Ana María. Polémica y cultura política chilena, 1840–1850. (*Historia/Santiago*, 25, 1990, p. 229–253, bibl.)

Polemical political debates were allowed to occur, providing they remained within certain genteel boundaries and only the *gente decente* participated. By questioning the role of the Church, and thus fundamental institutions, Santiago Arcos, a critic of Chilean society, threatened the old order and precipitated a crisis, setting limits for debate. Intellectual historians will find the focus of this work interesting.

2931 Valdivia Ortiz de Zárate, Verónica. Las Milicias Socialistas, 1934–1941. (*Mapocho/Santiago*, 33, primer semestre 1993, p. 157–180)

Created to defend the socialists from the Milicia Republicana, the Milicias Socialistas evolved into a tool to bring socialism to Chile by militarizing the Partido Socialista. The army's support of the Frente Popular, as well as divisions within the Left, led to the dissolution of the militias. Excellent use of primary materials.

2932 Valenzuela, Luis. The Chilean copper-smelting industry in the mid-nineteenth century: phases of expansion and stagnation, 1834–58. (*J. Lat. Am. Stud.*, 24:3, Oct. 1992, p. 507–550, tables)

Copper exports increased due to lower costs for transportation and imported coal as well as the introduction of new technology. Rising export levels stimulated other areas of Chile's economy, providing both the State and the private sector with substantial income. Excellent study employing both British and Chilean sources.

2933 Valenzuela Márquez, Jaime. Bandidaje rural en Chile central: Curicó, 1850–1900. Santiago: Dirección de Bibliotecas, Archivos y Museos, Centro de Investigaciones Diego Barros Arana, 1991. 159 p.: bibl., ill., maps. (Col. Sociedad y cultura; 1)

Contrary to Hobsbawm, argues that those who turned to banditry after being displaced by the labor system preyed not on the rich and certainly refused to share their booty with the poor. View of Curicó's dark side based on archival sources shows agrarian life to be less than idyllic.

2934 Vargas Cariola, Juan Eduardo. José Tomás Ramos Font: una fortuna chilena del siglo XIX. Santiago: Fundación Mario Góngora; Ediciones Univ. Católica de Chile, 1988. 271 p.: bibl., ill., facsims., ports. (Investigaciones)

Focuses on Ramos Font to explain how commerce and finance were conducted in mid- to late-19th century Valparaíso. Ramos Font succeeded because he needed relatively little capital and faced limited foreign competition. After 1900, however, Chilean capitalists could no longer compete. Well-researched, biographically based business history.

2935 Villalobos R., Sergio. Chile y su historia. Santiago: Editorial Universitaria, 1993. 391 p.: ill., maps. (Col. Imagen de Chile)

Textbook designed for general study of Chilean history. Written for a popular audience by one of Chile's leading historians, work accents the colonial period and the early Republic.

2936 Villalobos R., Sergio et al. La época de Balmaceda. Santiago: Dirección de Bibliotecas, Archivos y Museos, Centro de Investigaciones Diego Barros Arana, 1992. 123 p.: bibl., ill. (some col.).

Splendid essays on Balmaceda and the 1891 Revolution. Especially useful are those by Martínez and Subercaseaux, describing the economy and cultural life. Grez's demonstration of how the Democratic Party split over supporting Balmaceda and Couyoumdjian's treatment of the reaction of various foreign powers to the Civil War round out this excellent study.

2937 Volk, Steven S. Mine owners, money-lenders, and the State in mid-nineteenth-century Chile: transitions and conflicts. (*HAHR*, 73:1, Feb. 1993, p. 67–98, table)

Chile only belatedly developed a banking system, in part because elites did not consider it essential. They subsequently did so, although it is not clear when this conversion occurred. Work relies on limited sources, many of them secondary, and is somewhat unfocused, but historians will find it nonetheless useful.

Argentina, Paraguay, and Uruguay

JOSEPH T. CRISCENTI, *Professor Emeritus of History, Boston College*
JOEL HOROWITZ, *Associate Professor of History, Saint Bonaventure University*

AS IN PAST REPORTING PERIODS, the historical writings annotated for this volume of the *Handbook* focus more on the post-1880 years than on the earlier decades. Furthermore, unlike in previous years, this biennium includes a considerable amount of writing on the period after 1930, much of it designed for popular audiences. Women historians, primarily from Argentina, have been very active, but foreign scholars are less evident than before. Argentine economic historians and demographers studying the pre-1880 years, often working with incomplete data, are revealing previously ignored or overlooked facets of the economic and social reality of the region.

The historical writings reviewed here on 19th-century Argentina, Paraguay and Uruguay have several characteristics in common. They challenge the so-called official history of each country; they study the slow process whereby one colonial institution and then another was replaced by modern institutions; and they examine the various adjustments that were made as the region was integrated into the world economy. There is an awareness that the political and military leaders of the independence movement were products of a society in which two outlooks, colonial and modern, coexisted. The existence of a colonial outlook helps to explain the continuing debate over whether the Viceroyalty of Río de la Plata became the Argentine nation in 1810, and whether Artigas assumed that Uruguay eventually would become a part of that nation. For Uruguayans, the issues have always been whether the republic was created by the natives or Great Britain, and whether a small State can financially survive. The colonial frame of reference also accounts for the ease with which contemporaries served Hispanic American countries other than their own, for national distinctions appeared only gradually. Gandia has described the unhitching of Spanish politics from Río de la Plata politics, and the converting of a civil war into a war for independence (item **3113**). While colonial customs and outlooks lingered into the 20th century in the interior, in the port cities the transition to a modern outlook was encouraged by elites under the influence of French culture ca. 1840 and by the rising influx of European immigrants.

Nevertheless, the tension between colonial and modern outlooks persisted throughout most of the 19th century, for the modernization of political institutions and the economy proceeded slowly. The literary figures who labored for modernization—Bartolomé Mitre, Vicente Fidel López, Domingo F. Sarmiento, for example—justified their political conduct and criticized their Argentine, Paraguayan, and Uruguayan enemies when they wrote the first historical accounts of the period. A later generation of scholars, as some of the works annotated below indicate, has worked assiduously in the national and provincial archives, rehabilitating many of the people who were misrepresented in earlier histories. Bosch has also called attention to the important contributions made by the graduates of the Escuela Normal de Paraná (item **2973**).

Currently, scholars tend to see the military caudillo as a popular leader, rather than as the authoritarian or despotic figure portrayed by earlier historians. In the province of Facundo Quiroga, they note, the *cabildo abierto* of elected representatives and the military caudillo appeared alongside a functioning government during the war for independence, and the military caudillo observed the law and the rights of the people (item **3032**). The *cabildo abierto* eventually gave way to a legislative body, and the military caudillo disappeared by 1880. In the province of Córdoba, the fate of the military caudillo was determined when the regional commercial class entered politics. Although historians presently doubt that the military caudillo obstructed nation-building, they do believe that President Bartolomé Mitre employed foreign military officers to impose on the country the political organization that he favored. After the Paraguayan War, there began in Argentina, Paraguay, and Uruguay a gradual transition from military to civilian government.

The aims of Brazilian foreign policy in the Río de la Plata after the overthrow of Rosas are also receiving renewed attention. Paraguayan appreciation of Brazil has increased with the realization that the Baron de Caxias and Brazilian troops opposed having Bartolomé Mitre, an enemy, as their general during the Paraguayan War. Some Argentines, believing that Brazil wanted to dominate the Argentine provinces after the fall of Rosas, are trying to establish whether Brazil played a role in the Entre Ríos revolutions of the 1870s. Other scholars are assessing the importance of the competition between Peninsular and Creole merchants in the Interior Provinces, and their inter- and intra-provincial activities, in an attempt to determine the level of prosperity that existed in the Interior Provinces after 1810.

With the steady influx of immigrants and economic growth, both society and the economy gradually modernized. Construction industries in Buenos Aires and Montevideo were kept busy by the arrival of immigrants in need of housing and by the demand of the new urban elite for modern structures. In works on the pre-1880 period, immigrants who settled in the city of Buenos Aires have received more attention than those who spread out into the province of Buenos Aires and Patagonia and blended with the existing populations to form new societies. As immigrants entering Argentina tended to avoid the northwestern provinces, criollo society managed to survive there into the 20th century. Buenos Aires and Montevideo were not, however, the final destinations of all immigrants.

Since the 1960s, Argentine scholars have devoted increased attention to immigrant groups and settlements south of Buenos Aires, with impressive results. A number of microhistories of estancias and pueblos are annotated below. Noteworthy in these histories are the descriptions of collaboration between the Creoles, immigrants, and Christian and non-Christian Indians as they adapted to changes in the export cycle, the reactions of different estancia owners to new market demands, and the appearance of a distinct labor market in each region. The failure of immigrants to lose their ethnic identities and become citizens led to the writing of textbooks, primarily used in Buenos Aires, that sought to defend criollo culture, create national feelings, and build sympathy for the military. The overall aim of this education was the creation of "good citizens;" it was not until about 1879 that an exaggerated nationalism appeared. Nevertheless, gaps in the literature of immigration do remain. The history of ethnic groups and the mixing of races in Uruguay, for example, remains largely unwritten. Other less studied topics include early rural labor conflicts, especially in the littoral. Also lightly touched upon is the hispanization of indigenous peoples that took place throughout the country, and the survival into the 20th century of indigenous pueblos with "rights." The rights of some colonies in the province of Santa Fe are likewise poorly understood.

Economic progress was not uniform throughout the region. The province of Santa Fe presumably lost its economic independence and became dependent on Buenos Aires during the Rosas period. The degree of industrialization that took place in Paraguay prior to 1864 is still contested; the available quantitative data does not permit a definitive answer. Everywhere rural inhabitants were reluctant to abandon their agricultural pursuits or to accept a national currency: in some areas, the barter system continued to exist late into the 19th century. Research has confirmed the existence of small farmers, using family labor, for most of the century. On the southern frontier of the province of Buenos Aires small farmers were seemingly not anxious to acquire more lands than they could cultivate nor to secure titles to their lands. They coexisted with large landowners, a minority group consisting mostly of Frenchmen and Spaniards, and often supported the same policies.

Demographers working with 19th-century sources that are unreliable or not entirely satisfying have been able to reach interesting, though often tentative, conclusions for particular geographical regions and towns. Until recently, demographic studies based on census data emphasized the size of a community, and the composition, occupations, and ages of its people, with little attention paid to marriages, perhaps because priests were not always available to perform and record religious marriages, and civil marriages were not instituted until after 1860. Some censuses do reveal how men outside the city of Buenos Aires viewed themselves: in the poor province of Corrientes they said they were aristocrats, members of a *familia decente,* or members of a *pueblo;* in Tandil, men characterized themselves as artisans. The censuses are evidently silent on the means of support available to women in regions where they outnumbered the men. In Uruguay, according to one scholar, there are different interpretations of the roles of the women who found themselves in these circumstances. Although many immigrants were unwilling until 1906 to identify their nationality, demographers have been able to establish the movement of immigrants beyond the city of Buenos Aires, the rapidity with which they adopted local marriage customs, and their rise to dominance in various communities. Numerous records also indicate when the debt laws and the *papeleta* requirement were not enforced. [JTC]

Publishing on post-1880 Argentina has followed many of the same patterns as those established in earlier periods. The more than ten years since the restoration of democracy have permitted a flourishing of the historical profession in Argentina. An avalanche of good, solid, and occasionally excellent work has been written. However, the decline of the publishing industry, among other factors, has meant that much of the best work is in article or short book form, with a scarcity of longer monographs. Many longer works are intended for the popular market and deal with events of the most recent decades, which, while useful, are frequently not what a professional historian would desire. The preponderance of articles places a serious burden on the researcher, due to the sporadic publication and limited circulation of many of these journals. When journals can be located, however, readers are exposed to a multiplicity of fine studies, demonstrating the tremendous progress of Argentine historiography in the last decade.

Compared to work produced during the past several bienniums, there has been an increasing concentration on the years after 1930. This reflects, in part, the reaction to changes inside Argentine society. For example, the shedding of the economic legacies of the post-1943 governments has led to an attempt to rehabilitate the neo-conservative governments of the 1930s. Intended for large audiences, these works paint sympathetic portraits. Fraga's biography of Gen. Agustín P. Justo is paradigmatic of this trend (see *HLAS 54:2962*). Similarly, the authors' attitudes can be summed up by the title of the book by Aguinaga and Azaretto, *Ni década, ni infame: del '30 al '43* (item **2941**). We can expect to see much more work on the

1930s now that Fraga has had the Uriburu and Justo papers at the National Archive organized and cataloged, making these papers undoubtedly the most accessible segment of that archive's vast holdings (item **3030**). Privitellio's excellent discussion of political mobilization for Justo in the city of Buenos Aires in 1931 gives us an indication of the type of research that is now possible (item **3102**).

Several other trends have surfaced. While the provinces and rural areas have received more attention in the literature, several extremely interesting studies of Buenos Aires have increased our knowledge of its physical nature, as well as its politics. Gutman and Hardoy have written an excellent study of the physical evolution of Buenos Aires, with an emphasis on the period after 1880 (item **3037**). Walter has written what, in a sense, is a continuation of James Scobie's classical study of the city, but with much more emphasis on the political sphere (item **3145**). Our knowledge of porteño material culture during the 18th and 19th centuries has been greatly improved by Schávelzon's report on a five-year archaeological project to excavate 17 sites in the city (item **3122**). Still, the number of studies on the rural economy, immigration, and even labor unrest outside of the capital marks a decided decentralization of historiographical work. In part this reflects the improving quality of the universities outside Buenos Aires, but also a growing realization of the importance of the rest of the nation.

The burgeoning studies of immigration continue to widen and deepen. Much recent work has turned its gaze beyond Buenos Aires, with some attention paid to the regions beyond the pampas. Many are microstudies, a primary component of which has been the examination of mutual aid associations. These studies reveal a great deal about the nature of immigrant communities, but as Devoto argues in the book that he edited with Míguez, if these studies are going to continue to be useful, they will have to ask new types of questions (item **2950**). New sources are also important. The opening of the Foreign Ministry archives has permitted Klich to present an important vision of the place of Syrio-Lebanese in Argentina through the largely aborted attempts of the Ottoman Empire to defend them (item **3052**). There has been, as well, a series of popular or commemorative volumes that present interesting information, especially photographs (items **2999** and **3100**). One study particularly worth noting is that of Jarach and Smolensky on some two thousand Italian Jews who fled to Argentina between 1938–42 (item **3050**). The authors, who participated in this migration, have included fascinating transcripts of the interviews upon which much of the book is based.

Labor and working class history also constitutes a significant area of research. It is the one area in which English language works dominate. Here too the emphasis is on the post-1930 period, with much more attention being paid to regions away from Buenos Aires. These works should begin to force generalizations based on Buenos Aires-centered research to be refined or placed in a wider context. For example, Pastoriza has presented a study of the labor movement in Mar del Plata during the 1930s-40s (item **3087**). Furthermore, Brennan has written a pathbreaking book on Córdoba during the 1950s-1970s that focuses on automobile and light and power workers, in which he argues that the work process helped dictate the path taken by labor (item **2979**). This study, which also gives us an excellent picture of the *cordobazo*, should prevent future works on labor in this period from using the earlier Buenos Aires-centered approach. James produced an excellent study examining the cementing of ties between peronism and the working class from 1955–73 (item **3049**). Raising the discussion of populism to a new level, this work will be at the center of all discussions on the period for years to come. Previous studies of strife on the pampas focused on tenant farmers, but Ansaldi has now edited a series of investigations of unrest among rural workers that rocked the pampas in the first four decades of this century (item **3000**). Official histories of the left written from the perspective of dissenting leftist groups give readers a different perspective on events (items **3083** and **3140**).

While our vision of rural social structures on the pampas during the late-colonial period has undergone a complete revolution, less change has occurred in our understanding of this area in the 20th century. Still, a number of studies of specific localities and estancias continue to show that land-use and tenancy patterns were extremely complex, and that the stereotypes developed several decades ago of the rootless and constantly moving tenant farmers are far too simple. While much of the writing is at the micro level, Adelman has produced a study comparing credit availability among grain producers in the provinces of Saskatchewan and Buenos Aires (item **2940**), and Moreyra has written a large-scale, thorough monograph on rural production in Córdoba (item **3077**).

Remarkably little writing has focused on political history between 1880–1930, even when one accepts a very wide definition of "political." There are exceptions, some noted above, and here, too, attention has turned to areas beyond the capital (item **3003**). The majority of the political work is on the period after 1945. There are two especially noteworthy studies of the peronist era. Bitrán has written a detailed study of the Congress on Productivity, called by the first peronist government, in which he argues that the congress was an important step in creating a multi-class coalition as the balance tipped against the workers (item **2966**). Plotkin published a pathbreaking book that explores how the peronist State attempted to create a new culture for Argentina (item **3092**). This same work provides the fullest picture yet of the Eva Perón Foundation.

The desire to explore the long agony of Argentina's decline that began under Perón has produced considerable writing, not primarily monographs, but explorations of fragments of reality written with a large audience in mind. There is a predominance of biography, autobiography, and collections of documents. Most examine the attempts of Argentine society to adjust to the conditions created after the fall of Perón in 1955 and the turmoil this produced. There are also official histories of two presidents of the 1960s. Of particular interest is Graham-Yooll's compilation of information on that period (item **3034**), including a detailed chronology from 1955 to March 1976 and a list of political deaths for 1975, and Anzorena's collection of personal accounts of the formation of the Juventud Peronista (item **2946**). The only real attempts to tie this era together are Halperín Donghi's short but intriguing essay (item **3039**), and Romero's interesting and worthwhile overview of the years between Yrigoyen and Menem (item **3115**).

The level of writing on modern Argentine history is extremely high. Many studies have focused on small, defined topics, and have been much more oriented to the provinces than in previous reporting periods. Both are welcome trends. Political history of all types has become less important. As in the historiography of many regions of the world, there is a need to unite some of the emerging trends and produce new paradigms, if only to start questioning once again the value of received wisdom.

The writing on post-1880 Paraguay is still very sparse and frequently traditional, concentrating on the Chaco War and institutions, or defending party politics. There are several important exceptions. Rivarola has produced an excellent examination, based on a French dissertation, of the formation of the Paraguayan working class and the creation of a labor movement between 1870 and 1931 (item **3163**), taking us a crucial step further in labor studies. Caballero Aquino has aided the study of recent history by putting together a moving collection of oral histories of women opposed to the Stroessner regime (item **3161**). Writing in English, Lewis has produced an important revisionist political history for the years between 1869 and 1940 based on the personal data of 950 individuals (item **3156**).

The historical writing on Uruguay for the period after 1880 is extremely professional and, unlike the writing on Argentina, it is found in books rather than articles. Three major themes appear to have dominated during the past two years. First, there has been an interest in Uruguayan historiography. Ribeiro (item **3207**), Soler (item **3214**), and Torres Wilson (item **3215**) all produced balanced, but very different, examinations of the trends and tendencies in the recent writing of Uruguayan history. Also emerging is a sophisticated picture of the interconnectiveness between the economy and the political system. Caetano examines how economic pressure groups came to be a crucial force within political parties between 1916–30 (item **3179**). Rilla looks at Batlle's tax reform policies and the opposition that they produced (item **3208**). Jacob (item **3191**) and Labraga (item **3193**) studied different aspects of the economy and their relationship with the State. Third, there has been considerable interest in the working class, especially anarchism and in the parties of the left. Uruguayan historians have been very conscious of historical work on the other bank of the Río de la Plata, while their counterparts across the river have not, with the principal exception being the collection edited by Devoto and Ferrari (item **3003**). [JH]

ARGENTINA

2938 Acosta, María Elena. Gobierno y oposición en el Congreso durante la Presidencia de Illia, 1963–1966. Buenos Aires: Instituto Torcuato di Tella, 1993. 36 p. (Documento de Trabajo; 120)

Examines make-up and comportment of the two Congresses with which Illia's government had to deal. Argues that while the Radicals never had a majority in the Cámara de Diputados, the Congress was reasonably successful in passing laws. After the 1965 election, the increasingly determined opposition made the administration's position more difficult. [JH]

2939 Adelman, Jeremy. Una cosecha esquiva: los socialistas y el campo antes de la primera guerra mundial. (*Anu. IEHS*, 4, 1989, p. 293–333)

Demonstrates that rural tenants and wage earners did not want to change the agricultural system established between 1870 and 1880 and did not think of themselves as members of a class, whereas the socialists wanted to change the socioeconomic structure and create a new class of landowners. [JTC]

2940 Adelman, Jeremy. Financiamiento y expansión agrícola en la Argentina y el Canadá, 1890–1914. (*Rev. Ciclos*, 2:3, 1992, p. 3–21, tables)

Compares credit available to grain producers in Buenos Aires and Saskatchewan provinces. Shows that nature of landholding influenced availability of credit. In Argentina predominance of tenant farming made obtaining credit more difficult for grain producers as banks focused their attention on large landholders. The more even distribution of land in Canada helped produce a wider availability of credit. [JH]

2941 Aguinaga, Carlos E. and **Roberto A. Azaretto.** Ni década, ni infame, del '30 al '43. Prólogo de Rosendo Fraga. Buenos Aires: J. Baudino, 1991. 303 p.: bibl.

An open attempt to create a positive conservative portrait of the 1930s, authors stress what they see as the accomplishments of the era, especially of Agustín P. Justo. [JH]

2942 Alarcón, Roque. Cordobazo. Córdoba, Argentina?: Editorial Enmarque, 1989. 157 p.: ill.

Written to celebrate 20th anniversary of the Cordobazo and intended for a popular audience, work is based on newspaper accounts and interviews and has no scholarly apparatus. Provides detailed account of the event but little in the way of context. [JH]

2943 Alberdi, Juan Bautista and José Cayetano Borbón. Correspondencia Alberdi-Borbón, 1858–1861. Edición de Carolina Barros. Buenos Aires: Editorial Centro de Estudios Unión para la Nueva Mayoría, 1991. 110 p.: bibl. (Col. Estudios; 7)

Introduction describes relationship between José Cayetano Borbón and Alberdi. The heart of the book is 35 letters exchanged from 1858–61 while Alberdi was in Europe and the merchant Borbón remained in Buenos Aires. Work presents interesting view of Argentine politics, but is just a small segment of a 30-year correspondence. [JH]

2944 Aliata, Fernando. Edilicia privada y crecimiento urbano en el Buenos Aires posrevolucionario, 1824–1827. (*Bol. Inst. Hist. Ravignani,* 7, primer semestre 1993, p. 59–92)

Explains influence of road building and foreigners on direction of urban expansion, and transition of the traditional home with three patios to a "modern" house. Corrects theory that no building took place between 1810–51, and that colonial styles and forms persisted. [JTC]

2945 Ansaldi, Waldo. Cosecha roja, la conflictividad obrera rural en la región pampeana, 1900–1937. (*Rev. Parag. Sociol.,* 27:79, sept./dic. 1990, p. 47–72)

Excellent introduction to problems encountered in any study of rural conflicts centers on rural labor conflicts of 1917–22 in provinces of Buenos Aires, Entre Ríos, Córdoba, and Santa Fe. [JTC]

2946 Anzorena, Oscar R. JP: historia de la Juventud Peronista, 1955–1988. Buenos Aires: Ediciones del Cordón, 1989. 224 p., 6 p. of plates: ill.

Not really a history of the Juventud Peronista, but rather a series of extremely interesting accounts by some of its leaders of their own experiences. Author does little more than join them together. Accounts are all from the left-wing of the movement. [JH]

2947 Arrosagaray, Enrique. Los Villaflor de Avellaneda. Buenos Aires: Ediciones de la Flor, 1993. 254 p.

A local union leader and his wife reminisce about living conditions, work experiences, politics, and their relations with the military governments. Claim that October 17, 1945, demonstration was organized in Avellaneda without any outside interference. Based on conversations with Villaflors in 1990. [JTC]

2948 Arturo Frondizi, historia y problemática de un estadista. v. 5, El gobernante. Dirección de Roberto Gustavo Pisarello Virasoro y Emilia Edda Menotti. Prólogo de Enrique de Gandía. Buenos Aires: Ediciones Depalma, 1983- . 1 v.

Interesting collection of information on Frondizi's presidency includes some overarching examinations of aspects of his term in office, such as industrialization policies, rationalization of the administration, mining and electrical policies, and culture and education. Also discussed are resignation of the vice president and one of the many military crises. Part of a larger examination of his presidency written by his supporters. [JH]

2949 Arxentina: destino da emigración española e galega, 1810–1910; documentos relacionados con ela. Recopilación de Xosé Antón López Taboada. Vigo, Spain: Unipro Editorial, 1993. 417 p.

Analysis of origins, employment skills, income, and distribution of Spanish and Galician immigrants who arrived primarily in last quarter of 19th century is supported by collection of documents (pp. 61–399). Immigration to Cuba is also discussed. [JTC]

2950 Asociacionismo, trabajo e identidad étnica: los italianos en América Latina en una perspectiva comparada. Recopilación de Fernando J. Devoto y Eduardo José Míguez. Buenos Aires: CEMLA-CSER-IEHS, 1992. 358 p.: bibl.

Series of 17 papers from a conference held in Luján in 1988 which is divided into two sections. The first looks at communal associations and group identity; the second examines role of ethnicity in the workplace. Latter section is particularly important because of previous dearth of studies. While there are articles on Chile, Uruguay, Brazil, and Italy, the overwhelming concentration is on Argentina. Some essays look at other immigrants, thereby placing study of Italians in perspective. [JH]

2951 Les aveyronnais dans La Pampa: fondation, développement et vie de la colonie aveyronnaise de Pigüé, Argentine, 1884–1974. Coordination de Jean Andreu, Bartolomé Bennassar et Romain Gaignard. 2nd edition. Toulouse, France: Editions Privat; Presses Universitaires du Mirail, 1993. 287 p.: bibl., ill., index, maps, tables.

A group of researchers—geographers, historians, philologists—from the Institut pluridisciplinaire d'études sur l'Amérique latine de Toulouse (IPEALT) have produced this comprehensive study of a small French colony established for a century in Pigüé, a village 600 km southwest of Buenos Aires. The 200 immigrants, originally from Aveyron, were able to reshape in the *pampas* their traditions, language, music, and technology, as well as to develop a prosperous economy based on wheat and cattle. Completely revises and updates first edition (Toulouse, France: Privat, 1977). [T. Hampe-Martinez]

2952 La aviación naval en la guerra del Atlántico Sud. Buenos Aires: Instituto Aeronaval, 1991- . 5 v.

Series of five pamphlets gives accounts of activities of different units of the Argentine naval air force during Malvinas/Falkland War. Accounts are detailed and straightforward, although these are official histories. [JH]

2953 Azcona Pastor, José Manuel. Los paraísos posibles: historia de la emigración vasca a Argentina y Uruguay en el siglo XIX. Bilbao, Spain: Univ. de Deusto, 1992. 333 p.: bibl., ill.

Presents a broad overview of Basque immigration to the Río de la Plata in 19th century, stressing ability of the Basques to adapt to their new environment without losing their ethnic identity. Noteworthy description of reasons for immigrating and the conditions under which immigration took place. [JTC]

2954 Baer, James A. Street, block, and neighborhood: residency patterns, community networks, and the 1895 Argentine manuscript census. (*Americas/Francisc.*, 51:1, July 1994, p. 89–101, maps, tables)

Maintains that tenants banded together in tenant leagues because they were all affected by rising housing costs and poor housing conditions. [JTC]

2955 Barba, Fernando Enrique. Federales y Liberales, 1861–1880. (*Bol. Acad. Nac. Hist./Buenos Aires*, 62/63, 1989/90, p. 373–393, bibl.)

In a thought-provoking essay, writer describes breakup and reorganization of Argentine political parties after Battle of Pavón. [JTC]

2956 Barbería, Elsa Mabel. Los dueños de la tierra en la Patagonia austral. (*Todo es Hist.*, 318, enero 1994, p. 16–40, bibl., photos, tables)

Detailed account of settlement of province of Santa Cruz is enriched with short biographies of major landowners stressing their family connections and the methods they used to acquire their lands. Concludes that the English were not the dominant landowners; that *latifundistas* were not in the majority; and that absentee landowners were a minority. [JTC]

2957 Barrancos, Dora. Cultura y educación en el temprano sindicalismo revolucionario. (*Anuario/Rosario*, 14, 1989/90, p. 183–205)

Describes origins of revolutionary syndicalism, its rejection of intellectuals, the ideas of its leaders, and its educational efforts to create class consciousness among Argentine workers. [JTC]

2958 Basile, Clemente. Una guerra poco conocida. v. 1–2. San Salvador de Jujuy, Argentina: Univ. Nacional de Jujuy, 1993. 2 v.: bibl. (Col. Arte-ciencia. Serie Jujuy en el pasado)

Collection of documents relates military history of Argentine war against the Confederación Perú-Boliviana and international mediation of the dispute. [JTC]

2959 Batalla, Pablo Eugenio and **Fernando Rizzi.** Arturo Illia. Buenos Aires: Fundación Arturo Illia para la Democracia y la Paz, 1990. 160 p.: bibl.

Contains two prize-winning essays from a contest to commemorate Illia, held soon after his death. Essay by Batalla is a thoughtful examination of Illia's political economy. Rizzi has written a short sketch of Illia's presidency. [JH]

2960 Bazán, Armando Raúl. El noroeste y la Argentina contemporánea, 1853–1992. Buenos Aires: Plus Ultra, 1992. 477 p.: bibl.

Successful attempt to view history of six provinces—Santiago del Estero, Catamarca, La Rioja, Jujuy, Tucumán, and Salta—as an entity without losing sight of their role in the nation is well written and incorporates latest scholarship. [JTC]

2961 Bellucci, Mabel and Adriana Rofman. Mujeres: entre el movimiento social y el Estado; historia y balance de la Subsecretaría de la Mujer de la Nación, 1984–1989 (*Todo es Hist.*, 285, marzo 1991, p. 65–70)

Members of a short-lived agency discuss origins of the feminist movement and the shortcomings of an agency established to promote issues of concern to women. The failure of the agency is attributed to lack of political and public support. [JTC]

2962 Bergmann, Günther J. Auslandsdeutsche in Paraguay, Brasilien, Argentinien. Bad Münstereifel, Germany: Westkreuz, 1994. 256 p.: bibl., ill.

Study concentrates on 19th- and 20th-century German-speaking immigrants in the Río Paraná region, including Austrians, Swiss, Jews, and Eastern European ethnic Germans. Author also frequently refers to immigrant communities elsewhere in South America. Extensive bibliography consists almost entirely of German-language archival and published sources. [C.K. Converse]

2963 Bianchi, Susana. "El Ejemplo Peronista": valores morales y proyecto social, 1951–1954. (*Anu. IEHS*, 4, 1989, p. 371–402)

A textual analysis of "El Ejemplo Peronista," a regular feature of the periodical *Mundo Peronista*, reveals a Peronist society in which men prepare for the working world and women for the domestic world, and in which man moves up the social ladder by his own efforts. The popular classes are not to threaten the existing class structure, the capitalists, or the patriarchs. [JTC]

2964 Bidondo, Emilio A. and Susana Margarita Ramírez. Juan Ignacio de Gorriti: sacerdote y patricio. Buenos Aires: Ediciones Univ. del Salvador, 1987. 283 p.: bibl., ill.

In a brief biography of Gorriti, authors call attention to unverifiable statements appearing in older biographies. Includes over 100 pages of documents that show evolution in Gorriti's political ideas from federalism to unitarianism. [JTC]

2965 Bignone, Reynaldo B.A. El último de facto: la liquidación del Proceso; memoria y testimonio. Buenos Aires: PLANETA, 1992. 299 p., 8 p. of plates: ill. (Espejo de la Argentina)

Political and service memoir of military president who assumed power after Argentina's defeat in the Falklands/Malvinas War. Primarily covers the period from coup of 1976 until turning over of power to the civilian government in 1983. Focus is on internal workings of the military and author's attempts to justify the military's actions. [JH]

2966 Bitrán, Rafael. El Congreso de la Productividad. Buenos Aires: El Bloque, 1994. 381 p.: bibl., ill. (Col. Perspectiva histórica)

Balanced and detailed work examines the Congreso Nacional de Productividad y Bienestar called by first Peronist government to help counter the increasingly bad economic situation. Author looks at events that led up to the congress as well as its impact. He sees the attempt to increase production as important in establishing a multi-class political movement by helping to tilt the political-economic process against the workers.[JH]

2967 Blacha, Noemí M. Girbal de. Azúcar, poder político y propuestas de concentración para el Noroeste Argentino en los años '20: las conferencias de gobernadores de 1926–1927. (*Desarro. Econ.*, 34:133, abril/junio 1994, p. 107–122)

Blends economic and political analysis. Studies attempt by northwestern governors of 1920s to face problems created by the crisis in the sugar industry. [JH]

2968 Blacha, Noemí M. Girbal de. Tradición y modernización en la agricultura cerealera argentina, 1910–1930: comportamiento y propuestas de los ingenieros agrónomos. (*Jahrb. Gesch.*, 29, 1992, p. 369–395)

Discusses formation of a professional class of agronomists, and their proposals for educating the small farmer, increasing crop and animal production, agrarian legislation, and agricultural research.[JTC]

2969 Bohdziewicz, Jorge C. La tentativa de mediación chilena durante el bloqueo francés a la Confederación Argentina. (*Am. Merid.*, 8, julio 1988, p. 7–19)

Describes a little-known incident in which the Chilean government, at the urging of the local French agent, offered in 1839 to mediate the dispute between France and Buenos Aires government. Rosas rejected the offer. [JTC]

2970 Bolsi, Alfredo S.C. La fuerza de trabajo en la ciudad de Corrientes, 1820–1868. Buenos Aires: Academia Nacional de Geografía, 1989. 72 p.: bibl. (Publicación especial; 3)

Analysis of census data highlights concentration of land in a few hands and a population in which there were always more women than men and native-born professionals and artisans were gradually replacing foreign-born workers. [JTC]

2971 Bonura, Elena. Aproximaciones al estudio del problema monetario de las Provincias Unidas del Río de la Plata, 1810–1820. (*Historiogr. Rioplat.*, 4, 1992, p. 39–84)

Impressive analysis examines difficulties a new State encountered when it sought to create a national currency while fighting for its independence and maintaining free trade. [JTC]

2972 Bordi de Ragucci, Olga N. Cólera e inmigración, 1880–1900. Buenos Aires: Editorial Leviatán, 1992. 189 p.: bibl. (Col. Otra historia)

Examines origins and effectiveness of administrative policies to guard against immigrants introducing infectious diseases, and the opposition of foreign diplomats and shipping companies to them. Based on Argentine and Italian archives. [JTC]

2973 Bosch, Beatriz. Cordobeses en la Escuela Normal del Paraná. (*Invest. Ens.*, 42, enero/dic. 1992, p. 209–216)

Lists students from Córdoba who received a liberal education at the school between 1871–1919, and briefly describes their careers after graduation. Calls attention to importance of the school. [JTC]

2974 Bosch, Beatriz. La revolución del 1st de Mayo de 1851, según uno de sus protagonistas. (*Invest. Ens.*, 40, enero/dic. 1990, p. 145–157)

Demonstrates that Juan Francisco Seguí in his *Memorias* misrepresented achievements of Justo José de Urquiza, as well as his own relations with Urquiza. [JTC]

2975 Bouvard, Marguerite Guzman. Revolutionizing motherhood: the mothers of the Plaza de Mayo. Wilmington, Del.: Schol-

arly Resources, Inc., 1994. 278 p.: bibl., ill., index. (Latin American silhouettes)

Relates history of the Mothers of the Plaza de Mayo from founding in 1977 through first years of Menem presidency. The mothers formed the organization to protest disappearance of their children during the military regime of 1970s. Much of the material is based on interviews with the members. For political scientist's comment see item *HLAS 55:3508.* [JH]

2976 Braslavsky, Cecilia. Los usos de la historia en la educación argentina: con especial referencia a los libros de texto para las escuelas primarias, 1853–1916. Buenos Aires: Facultad Latinoamericana de Ciencias Sociales, 1992. 54 p. (Serie documentos e informes de investigación; 133)

Analysis of elementary school texts reveals that their authors used history in a variety of ways to build a model moral conscience and not a national conscience. Two of the prevalent themes were militarism and anti-indigenism. How influential the textbooks were is debatable because teachers did not all receive the same training and school attendance was low. Schools evidently failed to build a national identity, but they did teach all their students to read and write in the same language. See also item **2977**. [JTC]

2977 Braslavsky, Cecilia. Los usos de la historia en los libros de texto para las escuelas primarias argentinas: 1916–1930. Buenos Aires: Facultad Latinoamericana de Ciencias Sociales, 1993. 45 p. (Serie de documentos e informes de investigación; 144)

Author analyzes historical content of primary school books during first era of the Unión Cívica Radical. She examines the creation of myths and the depiction of values and the past. See also item **2976**. [JH]

2978 Bravo, María Celia. Cuestión regional: azúcar y crisis cañera en Tucumán durante la primera presidencia de Yrigoyen. (*Ruralia/Buenos Aires*, 4, oct. 1993, p. 45–60, bibl., tables)

Focuses on interconnectedness between the crisis in the sugar industry and constant political crises in Tucumán during first presidency of Yrigoyen. Argues that crucial elements were the problems in the sugar industry combined with national government's unwillingness to deal with them. The newly democratic government was more interested in urban areas with large numbers of voters, such as Buenos Aires, and therefore favored consumers over producers. [JH]

2979 Brennan, James P. The labor wars in Córdoba, 1955–1976: ideology, work, and labor politics in an Argentine industrial city. Cambridge, Mass.: Harvard Univ. Press, 1994. 440 p.: bibl., ill., index, map. (Harvard historical studies; 116)

Examines creation of a working class and of a unique labor movement in Córdoba, factors which should transform the vision of labor politics in the entire country. Looks specifically at situation of the light and power workers, but devotes greatest attention to the automobile workers. Author focuses on the work process and how it shaped workers' vision of their world. Contains excellent discussion of the *cordobazo*. Book is well documented. [JH]

2980 Bruno, Cayetano. Terrorismo y antiterrorismo en los albores de la emancipación. (*Invest. Ens.*, 40, enero/dic. 1990, p. 69–113, bibl.)

Documented study examines destructive and anti-*porteño* results of the Moreno policy of terrorism, and efforts of Belgrano and San Martín to re-create enthusiasm for independence movement in the provinces. [JTC]

2981 Buchrucker, Cristián. Nacionalismo y peronismo: la Argentina en la crisis ideológica mundial, 1927–1955. Buenos Aires: Editorial Sudamericana, 1987. 410 p.: bibl. (Col. Historia y cultura)

Monographic study compares Peronism with fascism and nationalism of 1930s, and assesses impact of Peronism and nationalism on Argentine political ideas. Concludes that Peronism was not fascism. [JTC]

2982 Busto, Jorge A. Indios y blancos, sal y ganado mas allá de la frontera: Patagones, 1820–1830. (*Anu. IEHS*, 8, 1993, p. 27–45, bibl.)

Excellent discussion focuses on economic transformation and on common interests developed with indigenous peoples that allowed El Carmen, an obscure outpost, to survive. [JTC]

2983 Calviño, Adolfo Rubens. La crisis de 1890 a través del Congreso. v. 2, pts. 1–2, El estallido, 1890–1891. Buenos Aires:

Centro Editor de América Latina, 1989-. 2 v.: bibl. (Biblioteca Política argentina; 397–398)

Detailed description of response to the crisis is based primarily on congressional debates and correspondence between Ricardo Pillado and Victorino de la Plaza. [JTC]

2984 Camarero, Hernán and **Alejandro Schneider.** La polémica Penelón-Marotta: marxismo y sindicalismo soreliano, 1912–1918. Prólogo de Emilio J. Corbière. Buenos Aires: Centro Editor de América Latina, 1991. 97 p.: bibl. (Biblioteca Política argentina; 326)

Analyzes ideological debate between two minority factions within the Partido Socialista—Marxist socialists and the "revolutionary syndicalists" of Georges Sorel, a debate which contributed to formation of the International Socialist Party and the Partido Comunista de la Argentina. [JTC]

2985 Campi, Daniel. Captación y retención de la mano de obra por endeudamiento: el caso de Tucumán en la segunda mitad del siglo XIX. (*Rev. Ciclos*, 1:1, 1991, p. 149–167, tables.)

Documented study tentatively suggests why debt peonage system failed to assure landowners and industrialists control of a stable labor force. [JTC]

2986 Caponnetto, Antonio. Contribución bibliográfica para el estudio del revisionismo histórico argentino. (*Historiogr. Rioplat.*, 4, 1992, p. 137–179)

Annotated bibliography lists works discussing historical revisionism. Includes works both for and against. Each work is described in relatively neutral terms. [JH]

2987 Cárdenas de Monner Sans, María Inés. Alvaro Barros: un militar digno. Buenos Aires: Editorial Leviatán; Ediciones Siglo Veinte, 1992. 127 p.: bibl. (Col. Otra historia)

Discusses frontier experiences of first governor of territory of Patagonia, as well as his publications on frontier conditions and proposed solutions for frontier problems. [JTC]

2988 Carpena, Ricardo and **Claudio A. Jacquelin.** El intocable: la historia secreta de Lorenzo Miguel, el último mandamás de la Argentina. Buenos Aires: Editorial Sudamericana, 1994. 351 p.: bibl.

Popular biography of longtime head of

the metalworkers union and for decades the most powerful union leader in Argentina is written by two journalists. Based on 157 oral interviews but with no footnotes; thus it is impossible to trace sources of the stories. [JH]

2989 Carrera, Nicolás Iñigo. La huelga general de masas de enero de 1936: un hecho borrado de la historia de la clase obrera Argentina. (*Anu. IEHS*, 9, 1994, p. 289–315, map, tables)

Creates a typology for general strikes and then discusses the large general strike of Jan. 1936 which grew out of a construction workers' strike. [JH]

2990 Castro, Donald S. "Entre bueyes no hay cornadas" = Among equals there are no disagreements; the Argentine popular theater as a source for the historian. (*in* Seminar on the Acquisition of Latin American Library Materials, 35th, Rio de Janeiro, 1990. Continuity and change in Brazil and the Southern Cone: research trends and library collections for the year 2000. Albuquerque: SALALM Secretariat, General Library, Univ. of New Mexico, 1992, p. 41–59, bibl.)

Calls attention to the *sainete porteño* (or *sainete criollo*), a "short jocular play," as a source for insights into experiences and attitudes of the *porteño* lower classes from 1890–1930. [JTC]

2991 Cava Mesa, María Begoña; Luis Fernando Contreras; and Francisco Javier Pérez. Sociedad "Laurak Bat" de Buenos Aires. Vitoria, Spain: Servicio Central de Publicaciones del Gobierno Vasco, 1992. 292 p.: bibl., ill., maps. (Amerika eta euskaldunak = América y los vascos; 17)

Study of Laurak Bat, the communal organization of Basques from Spain covers period 1877 (date of its founding)-1990. While the authors attempt to place the work within the framework of larger forces in the society, the most interesting parts are drawn from organization's own financial and membership records. Also important is the description of the shifts in Basques' image of themselves. [JH]

2992 Centro Educativo Sefaradí para Latinoamérica (Argentina) Presencia sefaradí en la Argentina. Buenos Aires: Centro Educativo Sefaradí para Latinoamérica, 1992. 203 p.: bibl., ill. (some col.).

Official and well-done history of the Sephardic community of Argentina, especially Buenos Aires, concentrates mostly on establishment of the official institutions of the various segments of the community. The numerous photographs add to work's usefulness. [JH]

2993 Chiaramonte, José Carlos; Guillermo Ernesto Cussianovich; and Sonia Tedeschi de Brunet. Finanzas públicas y política interprovincial: Santa Fe y su dependencia de Buenos Aires en tiempos de Estanislao López. (*Bol. Inst. Hist. Ravignani*, 8, 1993, p. 77–116, map, tables)

Financial data found in provincial and national archives for 1824–39 suggest that as the provincial economy declined, Estanislao López became more supportive of Rosas to assure continuance of subsidies from Buenos Aires. [JTC]

2994 Chiaramonte, José Carlos. Mercaderes del litoral: economía y sociedad en la provincia de Corrientes, primera mitad del siglo XIX. México: Fondo de Cultura Económica, 1991. 275 p.: bibl., ill., map. (Sección de obras de historia)

A prominent scholar assembles articles he wrote from 1974–85 on the role of the province of Corrientes in the 1821–38 national organization dispute and on the dynamics of the economy, society, and internal administration of the province itself. [JTC]

2995 Chiaramonte, José Carlos and Pablo Buchbinder. Provincias, caudillos, nación y la historiografía constitucionalista argentina, 1853–1930. (*Anu. IEHS*, 7, 1992, p. 93–120)

Authors review perspectives of historians and constitutionalists from mid-19th century to the 1920s on origins of the Argentine nation, the issue of federalism, and role of the caudillos. [JTC]

2996 Ciafardo, Eduardo O. Los niños en la ciudad de Buenos Aires, 1890–1910. Buenos Aires: Centro Editor de América Latina, 1992. 95 p.: bibl. (Biblioteca Política argentina; 361)

Briefly describes lives of children in the three social classes into which he divides Buenos Aires: the poor, the middle sector, and the elite. While presenting a good impressionistic description, author is unable to go further because of his lack of additional sources. [JH]

2997 Ciafardo, Eduardo O. La práctica bené-
fica y el control de los sectores populares de la ciudad de Buenos Aires, 1890–1910.
(*Rev. Indias*, 54:201, mayo/agosto 1994,
p. 383–408)

Attributes rise of charitable institutions directed and staffed by women of the
traditional middle and popular classes to a desire to reduce crime, immorality, and poverty
among the urban poor without resorting to
violence and repressive measures. Role of
positivist philosophy in development of social control strategy is noted. [JTC]

2998 Cichero, Marta. Cartas peligrosas
de Perón. Buenos Aires: Planeta, 1992.
342 p., 8 p. of plates: bibl., ill. (Espejo de la
Argentina)

This depiction of the Peronist resistance, 1955–58, based on fragments of oral interviews and documents—especially letters,
is intended for a popular audience. The principal source is Father Hernán Benítez, and book
contains full transcripts of letters between
him and Perón. Benítez disagreed with the
use of violence. Documents and interviews
were also obtained from Armando Carbo,
Raúl Lagomarsino, and Guillermo Patricio
Kelly, among others. [JH]

2999 Colonia Mauricio: 100 años. Carlos
Casares, Argentina: Comisión Centenario Colonización Judía en Colonia Mauricio, 1991. 152 p.: bibl., ill., photos.

This well-done volume commemorat-
ing the 100th anniversary of the founding of
Colonia Mauricio in Carlos Casares (Buenos
Aires prov.) by the Jewish Colonization Society of Baron Hirsch is a well-assembled combination of short historical pieces, memoirs,
and photographs. [JH]

3000 Conflictos obrero-rurales pampeanos,
1900–1937. v. 1–3. Recopilación de
Waldo Ansaldi. Buenos Aires: Centro Editor
de América Latina, 1993. 3 v.: bibl. (Biblioteca
Política argentina; 402–404)

A series of important studies focuses
on a much neglected topic: rural labor unrest
in the Pampas region. While covering period
1900–37, emphasis is on massive unrest of
1916–22, with articles discussing the situation in provinces of Buenos Aires, Córdoba,
Entre Ríos, and Santa Fe. Ansaldi begins the
work with an insightful essay providing a unifying theme. [JH]

3001 Congreso del Centenario de la Revolu-
ción del '90, *Córdoba, Argentina,*
1990. Actas. v. 1–2. Córdoba, Argentina:
Junta Provincial de Historia de Córdoba,
1993. 2 v.: bibl.

These 30 papers present new data on
1890s political, economic, and educational
conditions in Santa Fe prov. and interior provinces. The rise of the Unión Cívica Radical is
also examined. [JTC]

3002 Congreso Internacional Conmemora-
tivo del Bicentenario del Nacimiento
del General Don Martín Miguel de Güemes,
Salta, Argentina, 1985. Ponencias. Buenos
Aires: Secretaría Parlamentaria, Dirección
Publicaciones, 1989. 490 p.: bibl.

Collection of essays includes a significant reevaluation of Güemes and of conditions in Salta prov. at the time. Also describes
reception of the 1819 Constitution in the interior provinces. [JTC]

3003 La construcción de las democracias rio-
platenses: proyectos institucionales y
prácticas políticas, 1900–1930. Recopilación
de Fernando J. Devoto y Marcela P. Ferrari.
Buenos Aires: Editorial Biblos, Univ. Nacional de Mar del Plata, 1994. 268 p.: bibl., ill.

Series of well-done articles is result of
a 1993 conference held in Mar del Plata on
politics and emergence of the first democratic
electoral systems in Argentina and Uruguay.
Two articles look at voting in Uruguay in first
part of this century; the remainder focus on
Argentina. One article looks at connection
between social and electoral reform; three examine politics in Buenos Aires prov.; another
looks at Córdoba. Two studies of Mar del
Plata and one on the city of Santa Fe are also
included. [JH]

3004 Control social en Córdoba: la papeleta
de conchabo, 1772–1892; documentos
para su estudio. Introducción y selección de
Marcela González de Martínez. Córdoba, Argentina: Centro de Estudios Históricos, 1994.
86 p.: bibl. (Serie Documental)

Describes existence of the *papeleta*
(pass) from colonial times to 1902, noting
that the laws prescribing it were not consistently enforced and that its purpose was to
keep the *nobles* separate from the *plebyos*.
[JTC]

3005 Converso, Félix E. ¿Los créditos com-
pulsivos deterioraron económicamente
a los mercaderes españoles?: nueva informa-

ción para el caso Córdoba, 1806–1830. (*Anu. Estud. Am.*, 50:2, 1993, p. 163–186, appendix, tables)

The forced loans made by Spanish merchants to national and provincial governments from 1810–30 followed traditional procedures; did not prevent the lenders from continuing and profiting from their mercantile activities; and were eventually repaid. [JTC]

3006 Converso, Félix E. La lenta formación de capitales: familias, comercio y poder en Córdoba, 1850–1880. Córdoba, Argentina: Junta Provincial de Historia de Córdoba, 1993. 225 p.: bibl., ill. (Junta Provincial de Historia de Córdoba: 0327–0554; 12)

Important study examines origins and growth of a regional commercial class that acted as an intermediary between the ports of Buenos Aires and Rosario and the interior provinces, and that displaced the military caudillo in provincial politics. [JTC]

3007 Cordone, Hector G. Apuntes sobre la evolución de la historia sindical en la Argentina: una aproximación bibliográfica. Buenos Aires: Centro de Estudios e Investigaciones Laborales (CEIL), Consejo Nacional de Investigaciones Científicas y Técnicas; 1992. 57 p.: appendix, bibl. (Documentos de trabajo; 32)

Intelligent overview of writings on Argentine labor until 1986 emphasizes work done in Spanish. A listing of more recent books and articles is appended. [JH]

3008 Costa Méndez, Nicanor, Malvinas: ésta es la historia. Buenos Aires: Editorial Sudamericana, 1993. 335 p., 8 p. of plates: bibl., ill.

Narrowly construed memoir deals primarily with period Dec. 1981-June 1982, when author was Foreign Minister and the Falkland/Malvinas War occurred. Author, who died before he could make revisions, attempts to justify his actions. [JH]

3009 Cresto, Juan José. Los libres del sur: cronología y reflexiones sobre la revolución de 1839. Buenos Aires: Alfar Editora, 1993. 143 p.: ill.

An interesting, but unfocused inquiry into an 1839 rebellion against the Rosas dictatorship led by hacendados from the southern communities of Dolores, Vidal, and Chas-

comús. Includes facsimiles of key archival documents.

3010 Crisafulli, Gustavo. Por nacer entre océano y pampa: Bahía Blanca y su hinterland, 1880–1914. (*in* Huellas en la tierra: indios, agricultores y hacendados en la pampa bonaerense. Recopilación de Raúl Mandrini y Andrea Reguera. Tandil, Argentina: Univ. Nacional del Centro, IEHS, 1993, p. 275–287, tables)

Excellent work discusses transition of Bahía Blanca from a small fortress to the third Argentine port as it experienced expansion and decline of woolen exports, rise of agricultural exports, appearance of small industrial shops, and increase in the number of tenant farmers. [JTC]

3011 Cuccorese, Horacio Juan. Proteccionismo y liberalismo en tiempo histórico de la Confederación Argentina: contribución al estudio de la historia del pensamiento económico argentino. (*Nuestra Hist./Buenos Aires*, 18:35/36, dic. 1990, p. 267–286)

Analyzes arguments advanced by Pedro de Angelis and José María Roxas y Patrón of Buenos Aires in favor of free trade, and of Pedro Ferré of Corrientes for protectionism. [JTC]

3012 Curia de Villecco, María Elena and **Víctor Hugo Bolognini.** Inmigración en Tucumán. San Miguel de Tucumán, Argentina: Instituto de Historia y Pensamiento Argentinos, Facultad de Filosofía y Letras, Programa No. 64—CIUNT, Univ. Nacional de Tucumán, 1992. 168 p.: bibl., ill.

Series of well-documented studies of immigrants in Tucumán prov. includes a study of marriage patterns of various groups and a more tightly focused examination of marriage patterns and related issues among Spaniards and Italians. Work also looks at two immigration chains from Italy, one from the south and the other from the north, and includes a study of an Italian mutual aid society. [JH]

3013 Devoto, Fernando J. ¿Inventando a los Italianos?: imágenes de los primeros inmigrantes en Buenos Aires, 1810–1880. (*Anu. IEHS*, 7, 1992, p. 121–135)

Excellent study looks at trend among ethnic historians to "invent" images of Italian immigrants without analyzing their sources and without noting that immigrants' perceptions of their origins would differ from the beliefs about such origins held by the people around them. [JTC]

3014 Di Tella, Torcuato S. Torcuato Di Tella: industria y política. Buenos Aires: Tesis, Grupo Editorial Norma, 1993. 165 p.: bibl., ill.

Short biography of the Italian industrialist who founded the manufacturing firm Sociedad Industrial Americana de Maquinarias (SIAM) is written by his son, a well-known sociologist. By the time of Di Tella's death, SIAM was the largest such firm in Argentina. Using both family and company papers, author presents a picture of the man, the immigrant milieu, and the running of an industrial company. [JH]

3015 Duarte, María Amalia. Repercusiones de la revolución de 1874: la misión de José Hernández a Buenos Aires. (*Invest. Ens.*, 40, enero/dic. 1990, p. 159–189)

Well-documented study focuses on divisions within political party of Gen. Ricardo López Jordán (hijo) and on his decision not to support the *mitrista* revolution of 1874. See also item **3016.** [JTC]

3016 Duarte, María Amalia. Tiempos de rebelión, 1870–1873. Buenos Aires: Academia Nacional de la Historia, 1988. 408 p.: bibl. (Biblioteca de historia argentina y americana; 20)

Provides exhaustive analysis of revolutionary movement led by Gen. Ricardo López Jordán (hijo) in Entre Ríos prov. and of President Sarmiento's response. See also item **3015.** [JTC]

3017 Escudé, Carlos. Cultura política y contenidos educativos: el caso de Argentina. (*in* Le ombre del passato: dimensioni culturali e psicosociali di un processo di democratizzazione; Argentina e i suoi fantasmi. Torino, Italy: G. Giappichelli, 1992, p. 111–154)

Maintains that plan for "patriotic education" adopted by conservative positivists in 1908 to protect *criollo* culture from the massive influx of immigrants furthered authoritarianism, militarism, and an exaggerated nationalism. Based on a review of elementary and secondary school textbooks used from 1879–1986. [JTC]

3018 Esteban, Edgardo and **Gustavo Romero Borri.** Iluminados por el fuego: confesiones de un soldado que combatió en Malvinas. Buenos Aires: Editorial Sudamericana, c1993. 212 p.

Intriguing first-person account of Falkland/Malvinas conflict is written by a private who fought in the war. Work details author's own experiences; shows hardships and absurdities of the war; and describes homecoming offered to returning veterans. [JH]

3019 Estrada, Marcos de. Manuel de Sarratea: prócer de la Revolución y de la Independencia. Buenos Aires: Ediciones Barreda,1985. 425 p., 31 p. of plates: bibl., ill.

Documented study focuses on an able diplomat who served his country during the first half of 19th century. Corrects accounts offered by previous historians. [JTC]

3020 *Estudios de Historia Rural.* Vol. 2, 1992, Tierras y sociedad rural en la provincia de Buenos Aires. La Plata, Argentina: Univ. Nacional de La Plata, Centro de Estudios Histórico-Rurales.

Volume contains three interesting and important articles on rural history. The first examines the early history of the Sociedad Rural Argentina from its founding in 1866 to 1878. Looks at nature of membership and leadership, and argues that membership was not limited to wool producers but was more varied. The second examines occupation of land in the *partido* of Chascomús from 1779–1821. Final essay examines usefulness of court records for study of rural history in Buenos Aires prov. [JH]

3021 Feierstein, Ricardo. Historia de los judíos argentinos. Buenos Aires: Planeta, 1993. 418 p.: bibl., ill., maps, photos. (Espejo de la Argentina)

Popular but extensive history of the Jews in Argentina which is well illustrated with photographs. [JH]

3022 Ferreira Soaje, José Vicente. Historia de Córdoba en la primera mitad del siglo XIX: las luchas civiles y el rol protagónico cumplido por los Reynafé. v. 1–2. Córdoba, Argentina: Municipalidad de Córdoba, 1991. 2 v.: bibl.

Biographies of Reynafé brothers based primarily on provincial archives of Córdoba emphasize contest between external and internal provincial forces for control of a pivotal province. Volumes analyze administration of Gen. José María Paz and assassination of Juan Facundo Quiroga. [JTC]

3023 Fraga, Rosendo. Argentina en las urnas: 1931–1991. Buenos Aires: Editorial Centro de Estudios Unión para la Nueva Mayoría, 1992. 225 p. (Col. Análisis político; 8)

Presents electoral statistics emphasizing period after 1983. No information is given on congressional elections before 1983, and election results are not broken down below provincial level. [JH]

3024 Fraga, Rosendo. Carlos Saavedra Lamas: estudio preliminar. Con la colaboracíon de Raúl Alberto Gatica. Buenos Aires: Editorial Centro de Estudios Unión para la Nueva Mayoría, 1991. 116 p. (Col. Estudios; 8)

Contains a brief biographical sketch and reprints 14 documents on foreign policy from the Archivo del General Agustín P. Justo. Also lists and briefly describes all documents pertaining to foreign policy included in the Justo papers and those of Julio A. Roca that are preserved in the Archivo General de la Nación. Briefly describes Saavedra Lamas' papers that are still privately held. [JH]

3025 Fraga, Rosendo. El ejército y el derrocamiento de Frondizi. (*Todo es Hist.*, 300, junio/julio 1992, p. 38–71, photos)

Describes in detail the maneuvering within the military that led to overthrow of Frondizi with the approval of the Navy and the political parties. Based on the notes of the Ministro de Defensa and a memorandum prepared by his secretary. [JTC]

3026 Frydenberg, Julio and Miguel Ruffo. La semana roja de 1909. v. 1–2. Buenos Aires: Centro Editor de América Latina, 1992. 2 v.: bibl. (Biblioteca Política argentina; 358–359)

Authors maintain that the May 1909 general strike in Buenos Aires was a political strike of the proletariat against repressive police tactics, and that the strike was settled by negotiations between the strikers and the government. [JTC]

Gandía, Enrique de. El General Enrique Martínez en la historia de la Argentina y del Uruguay. See item **3189.**

3027 Gandía, Enrique de. Historia política argentina. v. 7, El caudillismo. Buenos Aires: Editorial Claridad, 1988- . 1 v.

Reviews and critiques past and present interpretations of Argentine political history from 1805–22, and sees independence movement as a by-product of the political struggles in Spain itself. [JTC]

3028 García-Godoy, Christián. Tomás Godoy Cruz: su tiempo, su vida, su drama; ensayo crítico. Washington: Full Life/Vida Plena; Impressions In Ink, 1991. 811 p.: bibl., ill., indexes.

A descendant presents first documented biography of an important provincial leader who collaborated with San Martín. [JTC]

3029 García Heras, Raúl. State intervention in urban passenger transportation: the Transport Corporation of Buenos Aires, 1939–1962. (*HAHR*, 74:1, Feb. 1994, p. 83–110, tables)

Examines government attempt to coordinate and control public transport in Buenos Aires and gives reasons for the government's failure. Article concentrates on administrative and economic problems created by government policies and ideologies. Written from primary sources located in Argentina, Great Britain, and the US. [JH]

3030 Giraldes, María Teresa. Fondo documental del presidente Agustín P. Justo. Buenos Aires: Editorial Centro de Estudios Unión para la Nueva Mayoría, 1991. 100 p. (Col. Estudios; 2. Col. Referencia. Serie Descriptores)

Guide and catalog to Justo papers held in the Archivo General de la Nación. Most of the papers are from his presidency, 1932–38. This excellent guide should allow researchers easy access to his extensive papers. [JH]

3031 Gironés de Sánchez, Isabel. La inmigración europea en la Provincia de San Juan, 1852–1910. San Juan, Argentina: Univ. Nacional de San Juan, Facultad de Filosofía, Humanidades y Artes, Instituto de Historia Regional y Argentina, 1989. 81 p.: bibl.

Based on records in the provincial archives and reports in the local press, reconstructs immigrant flow, settlement patterns of the different ethnic groups, and economic improvements produced by the immigrants. [JTC]

3032 Goldman, Noemí. Legalidad y legitimidad en el caudillismo: Juan Facundo Quiroga y La Rioja en el interior rioplatense, 1810–1835. (*Bol. Inst. Hist. Ravignani*, 7, 1993, p. 31–58)

The available documents reveal that a legislative body manifesting provincial sovereignty appeared while the government was performing its traditional functions and caudillismo was on the rise. [JTC]

3033 González Bernaldo, Pilar. El levantamiento de 1829: el imaginario social y sus implicaciones políticas en un conflicto rural. (*Anu. IEHS*, 2, 1987, p. 137–176, graphs, map)

Re-examines in depth the rural revolt in southern Buenos Aires province that occurred prior to rise of Rosas. Concludes that revolt was not a social protest movement, but simply a protest against the changes in traditional society brought about by the advance of the large *estancia*. [JTC]

3034 Graham-Yooll, Andrew. De Perón a Videla. Buenos Aires: Editorial Legasa, 1989. 557 p.: appendices, bibl.

Originally intended to be published in mid-1976 by the then *Buenos Aires Herald* reporter, work is principally a detailed political chronology of the period September 1955-March 1976. Appendices include complete lists of cabinet ministers, author's famous list of political deaths in 1975, a chronology of evolution of the press from 1973–76, and a list of political periodicals published during the same period. [JH]

3035 Granados, Osvaldo. Jorge Antonio, el testigo. Buenos Aires: Peña Lillo Editor, 1988. 216 p., 16 p. of plates: ill.

Woven together with author's own commentaries are his long and interesting interviews with Jorge Antonio—financier, political figure, and friend of Juan Perón. While work moves around chronologically, Antonio does have interesting things to say, especially about the first Perón era. [JH]

3036 Gravil, Roger. Foreign interference in Argentina in the mid-1940s. (*Estud. Latinoam./Poland*, 14:pt. 2, 1992, p. 43–63)

Attempts to revise the standard academic view of British hostility to the rise of Perón. Basing his argument primarily on British government documents, claims that British's new Labor Party government favored Perón. [JH]

3037 Gutman, Margarita and Jorge Enrique Hardoy. Buenos Aires: historia urbana del área metropolitana. Madrid: Editorial MAPFRE, 1992. 374 p.: bibl., ill., index, maps. (Col. Ciudades de Iberoamérica; 13. Col. MAPFRE 1492)

Gives history of physical development of greater Buenos Aires since city's founding. Emphasis is on period following 1880. While growth is placed within the context of population, economic, and transportation changes, work concentrates on physical environment, architecture, and urban planning. [JH]

3038 Guzmán, Carlos Alberto. San Martín, 1824–1850. Buenos Aires: Círculo Militar, 1993. 192 p.: bibl., ill. (Biblioteca del oficial; 750)

Chronicles an obscure period in life of San Martín; corrects misinformation circulated by his enemies in Buenos Aires; and emphasizes his determination to remain aloof from all political struggles. Documented study. [JTC]

3039 Halperín Donghi, Tulio. La larga agonía de la Argentina peronista. Buenos Aires: Ariel, 1994. 142 p.

Short, insightful essay examines in a historical context the slow, painful collapse of the society that was created by the first Peronist experience. Halperín Donghi sees the hyperinflation that occurred at the end of the Alfonsín administration as marking the final collapse of the system. [JH]

3040 Halperín Donghi, Tulio et al. Sarmiento, author of a nation. Berkeley: Univ. of California Press, 1994. 398 p.: bibl., index.

Nineteen scholars, primarily specialists in Spanish literature, call attention to various aspects of Sarmiento's career, writings, and ideas. [JTC]

3041 Herrero, Antonio Miguel. Monte Chingolo: la ultima batalla del E.R.P. (*Todo es Hist.*, 284, feb. 1991, p. 6–41)

Chronological history relates origins and actions of the Ejército Revolucionario del Pueblo (ERP) and its denouement at the battle of Monte Chingolo. Among the nine documents published are statements by army officers, an ex-leader of the ERP, and Julio Santucho. [JTC]

3042 Herz, Enrique Germán. La Revolución del 90. Buenos Aires: Emecé Editores, 1991. 270 p.: bibl., ill.

Essayist maintains that objectives of the revolution were to end a cycle of provincial presidents and to restore control of the national government to the *porteño* elite. [JTC]

3043 Historia de Neuquén. Buenos Aires: Plus Ultra, 1993. 426 p.: bibl., ill., map. (Col. Historia de nuestras provincias; 16)

Collection of well-written and documented essays discusses developments in the area prior to and after its military conquest and settlement. [JTC]

3044 Historia y género. Recopilación de Dora Barrancos. Buenos Aires: Centro Editor de América Latina, 1993. 126 p.: bibl. (Biblioteca Política argentina; 439)

Five articles by various authors deal with gender as a key element of analysis. Three examine women in Argentina. Donna Guy writes on women's rights in 19th century; Mirta Lobato on women workers in Berisso; and Sandra McGee Deutsch on women and the political right in Argentina, Brazil, and Chile. [JH]

3045 Holland, Charles. Noticias de Buenos Aires, el Paraguay, Chile y el Perú: cartas del ciudadano inglés Charles Holland, 1820–1826. Presentación e introducción de León Tenenbaum. Traducción de Mabel Susana Godfrid de Tenenbaum y León Tenenbaum. Buenos Aires: Fundación Banco de Boston, 1990. 90 p.: ill.

Only one of the 18 interesting letters published here was written in Buenos Aires; the others originated in Chile and Peru. In the letters, Holland comments on the mining craze in the two countries and its effects, and on the new governments' need for new loans to pay the interest on existing loans. [JTC]

3046 Hopkins, A.G. Informal empire in Argentina: an alternative view. (*J. Lat. Am. Stud.*, 26:2, May 1994, p. 469–484)

Argues that informal imperialism existed because of Argentina's dependence on British finance and credit. [JTC]

3047 Informes españoles sobre Argentina. v. 1, Urquiza-Derqui-Mitre, 1852–1868. Recopilación de Isidoro J. Ruiz Moreno. Buenos Aires: Univ. del Museo Social Argentino, 1993- . 1 v.

The Spanish minister informs his government on relations between Buenos Aires prov. and the Argentine Confederation, the onset and progress of the Paraguayan War, the revolutionary movements in the interior provinces, and the presidential elections of 1868. [JTC]

3048 La inmigración española en Mendoza: cuatro estudios monográficos. Dirección de Marta López de Pederzoli. Mendoza, Argentina: Consulado General de España, 1989. 253 p.: bibl., ill., maps (some col.).

Work contains four studies on Spanish immigration to Mendoza prov. One examines lives of two Spanish doctors; another the impact of the Spanish Civil War on the province; the third, the connection between Spanish immigration and the development of viniculture; and the fourth, views of Spanish immigrants held by the press between 1880–1930. [JH]

3049 James, Daniel. Resistance and integration: Peronism and the Argentine working class, 1946–1976. Cambridge, England; New York: Cambridge Univ. Press, 1988. 303 p.: bibl., index. (Cambridge Latin American studies; 64)

Brilliant analysis examines relationship between Peronism, the working class, and the unions from 1955–73. Demonstrates how and why Peronism became more firmly entrenched in the working class after 1955. Also examines way in which unions shifted their nature under impact of the larger political scene. Finally, looks at sources of the power of unions and their leaders. [JH]

3050 Jarach, Vera and **Eleonora M. Smolensky.** Colectividad judía italiana emigrada a la Argentina, 1937–1943. Prólogo de Ernesto Sábato. Buenos Aires: Centro Editor de América Latina, 1993. 140 p.: appendices, bibl. (Biblioteca Política argentina; 394)

The authors, who were among some 2,000 Italian Jews who fled to Argentina between 1938–1942, have created an interesting study. Based largely on interviews, work concentrates on the problems faced by Italian Jews in adjusting to the new society. Fascinating transcripts of interviews are included as appendices. [JH]

3051 Jordán, Alberto R. El proceso: 1976/1983. Buenos Aires: Emecé Editores, 1993. 454 p.: bibl., ill., index, maps.

In this useful analysis, author's chief goal is to offer a detailed and systematic evaluation of the activities of the most recent Argentine military government. While not unsympathetic to some of the military's goals, he finds that the regime was a massive failure. [JH]

3052 Klich, Ignacio. Argentine-Ottoman relations and their impact on immigrants from the Middle East: a history of unfulfilled expectations, 1910–1915. (*Americas/Francisc.*, 50:2, Oct. 1993, p. 177–205, table)

Based principally on material found in the archive of the Argentine Foreign Ministry, work examines short-lived diplomatic representation of the Ottoman Empire in Argentina and diplomats' attempt to protect and shape the local Syro-Lebanese community. The diplomats had little success, but article helps illuminate the position of the community in the larger society. See also item **3053.** [JH]

3053 Klich, Ignacio. *Criollos* and Arabic speakers in Argentina: an uneasy *pas de deux*, 1888–1914. (*in* The Lebanese in the world: a century of emigration. London: Centre for Lebanese Studies, 1992, p. 243–284, tables, photos)

Thoughtful discussion focuses on immigration of Arabic-speakers (defined as Syro-Lebanese, Syrian, and/or Ottoman subjects) to Argentina, their hostile reception, and their eventual assimilation. See also item **3052.** [JTC]

3054 Klich, Ignacio. Perón, Braden y el antisemitismo: opinión pública e imagen internacional. (*Rev. Ciclos*, 2:2, 1992, p. 5–38)

Essayist presents a detailed and documented analysis demonstrating that Perón was not antisemitic or fascist, and wanted to draw closer to the US. Perón's maneuvers were obstructed by Argentine nationalists, by the press and Jews of North America, and by Spruille Braden. To win North American aproval, Perón favored the creation of a Jewish state. See also item **3055.** [JTC]

3055 Klich, Ignacio. Peronistas y Radicales ante las aspiraciones sionistas en Palestina. (*Desarro. Econ.*, 34:133, abril/junio 1994, p. 75–94)

Worthwhile article is based on archival research in UK, US, Canada, and Israel. Klich

shows that Argentines' attitude towards creation of Israel was much more complex than is usually thought, and that both Peronists and Radicals shared similar beliefs. Article sheds light on general attitudes of Argentines towards Jews. See also item **3054.** [JH]

3056 Korzeniewicz, Roberto P. Labor unrest in Argentina, 1930–1943. (*LARR*, 28:1, 1993, p. 7–40, bibl., tables)

Re-evaluates nature of labor unrest, based on creation of the first nationwide set of strike statistics. Data is culled from *La Prensa.* Author shows existence of widespread unrest in the interior, especially in agriculture. Emphasizes role of the Communists in late 1930s. Also available in Spanish as *Malestar laboral en la Argentina, 1930–1943* (Buenos Aires: Centro de Estudios e Investigaciones Laborales, Consejo Nacional de Investigaciones Científicas y Técnicas, 1992, 50 p.). [JH]

3057 Larra, Raúl. Savio, el argentino que forjó el acero. Prólogo de Adolfo Dorfman. Buenos Aires: Centro Editor de America Latina, 1992. 139 p.: (Biblioteca Política argentina; 381)

Reprint of sympathetic 10-year old biography (Buenos Aires: Ediciones Anfora, 1980) of the Argentine general who pushed for military-led industrialization, especially in steel. Solid, but little in the way of scholarly apparatus. Interesting prologue by Adolfo Dorfman outlines state of Argentine manufacturing at the time of publication. [JH]

3058 Lázzaro, Silvia B. Estado, capital extranjero y sistema portuario argentino, 1880–1914. v. 1–2. Buenos Aires: Centro Editor de América Latina, 1992. 2 v.: bibl. (Biblioteca Política argentina; 365–366)

Writing in the framework of dependency theory, Lázzaro has produced a detailed analysis of the building of modern ports, linking such construction to the development of trade. Argues that the role of foreign capital and its monopoly power hindered long-term development. [JH]

3059 Lewis, Daniel. Internal and external convergence: the collapse of Argentine grain farming. (*in* Latin America in the 1940s: war and postwar transitions. Edited by David Rock. Berkeley: Univ. of California Press, 1994, p. 209–223, tables)

Argues that collapse of grain farming

in postwar Argentina is not due to traditional explanations—Peronist economics or structural problems. According to author, three conditions dealt final blow after a long period of weakness: 1) no new land available; 2) end of labor flexibility; and 3) inability to obtain new technology. [JH]

3060 López, Jeannette. La mujer y la historia argentina. Buenos Aires: Editorial Plus Ultra, 1991. 150 p.: bibl., facsims.
Provides brief biographies of 24 Argentine women. [JTC]

3061 López, Mario Justo. Historia de los ferrocarriles de la Provincia de Buenos Aires, 1857–1886. Buenos Aires?: Lumiere, 1991. 281 p.: bibl., ill., maps.
Examines policies governing provincial and national railroads in Buenos Aires prov., 1857–88. [JTC]

3062 Malamud, Carlos. Lisandro de la Torre y el debate de las carnes. (*Anu. IEHS*, 7, 1992, p. 137–165)
Re-examines the famous senate debate of 1935, which followed the signing of the Roca-Runciman Pact, on the results of an investigation of the market for meat. Focuses on Lisandro de la Torre, and argues that the debate was not about imperialism but was an attack on the government, and that there was no winner. Based on a rereading of the senate records. [JH]

3063 Mallo, Silvia. Justicia, divorcio, alimentos y malos tratos en El Río de la Plata, 1766–1857. (*Invest. Ens.*, 42, enero/dic. 1992, p. 373–400, tables)
Analysis of 117 divorces reveals that the attitude towards marriage and the role of each partner in the marriage underwent a change during the period; that women initiated most divorce proceedings for poor treatment; and that some men defended the rights of women. Most of the divorces studied took place in Buenos Aires and Montevideo. [JTC]

3064 Maluendres, Sergio. De condiciones y posibilidades: los agricultores del sureste productivo del Territorio Nacional de La Pampa. (*in* Huellas en la tierra: indios, agricultores y hacendados en la pampa bonaerense. Recopilación de Raúl Mandrini y Andrea Reguera. Tandil, Argentina: Univ. Nacional del Centro, IEHS, 1993, p. 289–323, graph, tables)

Evaluates development of agriculture in southeast La Pampa with special emphasis on the *departamento* of Guatraché. Author looks at relationship of farming and herding, availability of credit, the nature of yields, and reasons for some farmers having higher yields than others. Author's conclusion for the latter is that having capital was key. [JH]

3065 Marco, Miguel Angel de. Carlos Casado del Alisal y el progreso argentino. Rosario, Argentina: Instituto Argentino de Cultura Hispánica, 1993. 277 p.: bibl., ill.
Biography of a Spanish immigrant who arrived in Rosario in 1857 and became a successful banker, railroad promoter, and wheat and maté merchant. See also item **3068**. [JTC]

3066 Marco, Miguel Angel de et al. Historia de Santa Fe. Rosario, Argentina: Librería APIS, 1992. 238 p.: bibl., ill., maps.
Intended for use by students, work is a straightfoward, up-to-date history of the province. Concentrates mostly on political history, but other aspects of the society are also considered. While there are no footnotes, it is obvious that authors have consulted a wide range of printed and archival sources. [JH]

3067 Marco, Miguel Angel de. Juan B. Arengo y los innovadores rosarinos ante la necesidad de reformar la ley electoral de la nación y de la provincia de Santa Fe en la última década del siglo XIX. (*Invest. Ens.*, 43, enero/dic. 1993, p. 385–408)
Excellent work discusses efforts of Spanish republicans, especially Arengo, to promote laws that would assure honest provincial elections and do away with political revolutions. See also item **3066**. [JTC]

3068 Marco, Miguel Angel de et al. Rosario. v. 2., Política, cultura, economía, sociedad—desde 1916 hasta nuestros días. 2a ed. Buenos Aires: Fundación Banco de Boston, 1988- . 1 v.
The four essays on the political, economic, and social history of the port city from 1916–89 rely on municipal records, census data, and the local press. See also item **3065**. [JTC]

3069 Marquiegui, Dedier Norberto. Asociacionismo, liderazgo étnico e identidad: un enfoque comparado, Luján, 1876–1920. (*Stud. Emigr.*, 31:115, set. 1994, p. 427–460, tables)

After examining historians' uses of mutual aid associations in discussing immigration, author looks at five such organizations based in Luján. Three are Italian, one French, and the other Spanish. Compares regional origins and occupational status for members and leaders of each organization. Based on detailed, if uneven, records of mutual aid societies. [JH]

3070 **Maza, Juan Isidro.** Historia de Malargüe. Mendoza, Argentina: Univ. Nacional de Cuyo, Facultad de Filosofía y Letras, 1991. 351 p.: ill. . (Col. Historia de los departamentos: Mendoza; 1)

Series of essays discusses relations with indigenous peoples in Mendoza and Neuquén in pre- and post-independence years, creation of the *departamento* of Marlagüe, and developments in the *departamento* to 1900. [JTC]

3071 **Maza, Juan Isidro.** Mujeres en la historia de Mendoza. Buenos Aires: Fundación Banco de Boston, 1989. 118 p., 15 p. of plates: ill.

Presents brief biographies of women who were prominent in the province from colonial to modern times. Indigenous women are included. [JTC]

3072 **Meding, Holger M.** Flucht vor Nürnberg?: deutsche und österreichische Einwanderung in Argentinien, 1945–1955. Köln, Germany: Böhlau Verlag, 1992. 311 p.: bibl., index, photos.

Well-written, concise history and analysis of German immigration to Argentina is based on extensive research in Argentine and German archives, almost 100 interviews, and international secondary literature. Meding's examination of Argentine immigration policy, international assistance to legal and illegal emigration, and the political motivation and sociological and demographic origins of the immigrants results in a valuable contribution to Argentine and immigration history. See also item **3073.** [C.K. Converse]

3073 **Meding, Holger M.** German emigration to Argentina and the illegal brain drain to the Plate, 1945–1955. (*Jahrb. Gesch.,* 29, 1992, p. 397–419, tables)

Overview of German postwar emigration to Argentina is written from a German perspective. While recognizing the shady past of some of the emigrants, author views their arrival as good for both Argentina and Germany. Author used archives in both Germany and Argentina, and conducted interviews. See also item **3372.** [JH]

3074 **Mercado, María Cecilia.** Algunas cifras atinentes a la evolución poblacional de la region NOA, siglo XIX. Salta, Argentina: Grupo de Estudios Socio-Demográficos, 1988. 42 p.: bibl., graphs, maps, tables. (Cuadernos del Gredos; 6)

Examination of available population figures for 19th-century northwest Argentina, giving special emphasis to Salta. [JH]

3075 **Michelini, Pedro E.** Perón, develando incógnitas: algunos hechos poco claros de su vida política. Buenos Aires: Corregidor, 1993. 159 p.: ill.

Michelini, who became Juan Perón's legal representative in Argentina in 1965, has put together a series of documents and letters written by Perón. There is almost no editing, and little indication of context is given. The majority of the documents, and the most interesting, are letters written to Michelini in late 1960s. [JH]

3076 **Míguez, Eduardo José.** La frontera de Buenos Aires en el siglo XIX: población y mercado de trabajo. (*in* Huellas en la tierra: indios, agricultores y hacendados en la pampa bonaerense. Recopilación de Raúl Mandrini y Andrea Reguera. Tandil, Argentina: Univ. Nacional del Centro, IEHS, 1993, p. 191–208, table)

Instructive discussion relates problems presented by the sources available for a study of the frontier, and by the terms used in describing the structure of the labor market in Tandil from 1869–95. [JTC]

Monsalvo de Bonduel, Beatríz Susana. Las comunicaciones en la provincia de San Juan durante la época colonial y el siglo XIX. See item **2597.**

3077 **Moreyra de Alba, Beatriz Ines.** La producción agropecuaria cordobesa, 1880–1930: cambios, transformaciones y permanencias. Córdoba, Argentina: Centro de Estudios Históricos, 1992. 585 p.: bibl., ill., maps.

Extremely detailed and thorough work examines changing agricultural production and grazing patterns in the province. Careful attention is given to regional differentiation and to change over time. Also emphasizes types and sizes of landholdings, availability of credit, and comparisons with the rest of the nation. [JH]

3078 Muscará, Juan Carlos. La frontera sur de Córdoba a mediados del siglo XIX. Córdoba, Argentina: Atenea Editorial, 1994? 27 p.: bibl. (Col. Cuadernos de historia; 1)

Valuable discussion based on provincial archives relates methods used to maintain peace on the provincial borders and to negotiate with indigenous *caciques.* [JTC]

3079 Musri, Dora Davire de. Plan revolucionario de operaciones de Mariano Moreno. San Juan, Argentina: Univ. Nacional de San Juan, Facultad de Filosofía, Humanidades y Artes, 1988. 46 p.: bibl.

Reviews available evidence on authorship of the plan, and concludes that the revolutionary leaders in Buenos Aires, contrary to liberal historians, did not intend to avoid the use of terror. [JTC]

3080 Newton, Ronald C. Ducini, prominenti, antifascisti: Italian fascism and the Italo-Argentine collectivity. (*Americas/Francisc.*, 51:1, July 1994, p. 41–66)

Well-done study relates attempt, directed from Italy, to implant Fascism among the Italian community in Argentina. Examines Fascists' rather limited successes and creation of Italian anti-Fascist organizations in Argentina. Author draws most of his information from Italian archives and the Argentine Italian-language press. [JH]

3081 Ochoa de Eguileor, Jorge and **Eduardo Valdés.** Dónde durmieron nuestros abuelos?: los hoteles de inmigrantes en la Capital Federal. Buenos Aires: Fundación URBE, 1991. 203 p., 29 p. of plates: ill., maps.

Description of hotels where immigrants stayed between 1857 and 1920, and of the laws that applied to these lodgings, is based on archival research. [JTC]

3082 Olivera, Graciela. El campo comunero de la Isla Verde: transición desde el régimen comunal al privado de la tierra, La Rioja, siglos XIX y XX. (*Ruralia/Buenos Aires*, 4, oct. 1993, p. 61–80, graphs, photos, tables)

Examination of a cattle-raising region relates its progression from a traditional communal mode of property holding to a more "modern" form. The dominant economic activity evolved from raising cattle intended for export to Chile, to production of charcoal, to modern cattle establishments. [JH]

3083 Oriolo, Jordán. Antiesbozo de la historia del Partido Comunista: 1918–1928. v. 1–2. Buenos Aires: Centro Editor de América Latina, 1994. 2 v. (Biblioteca Política argentina; 476–477)

Critique of official histories of the Partido Comunista de la Argentina was written with the intention of discrediting the Party's longtime leaders: Vittorio Codovilla and Orestes and Rodolfo Ghioldi. While the author has sympathy for the goals of the Party, he has analyzed small details carefully. Author is the son of Cayetano Oriolo, an early Communist leader who was purged from the Party in the 1920s. [JH]

3084 Orsi, René. Dorrego y la unidad rioplatense. La Plata, Argentina: Subsecretaría de Cultura, 1991. 711 p.: bibl. (Col. Pensamiento nacional)

Long overdue monographic study focuses on a federalist politician whose efforts to unite the political parties and to create one nation en el Río de la Plata were thwarted by *Unitarios* in his cabinet. [JTC]

3085 Páez de la Torre, Carlos. Vida de don Alfredo Guzmán, 1855–1951. Tucumán, Argentina: Estación Experimental Agro-Industrial Obispo Colombres, 1989. 187 p.: bibl., ill. .

Alfredo Guzmán was an agro-industrialist (principally sugar), philanthropist, and conservative politician who for 70 years played a leading role in Tucumán prov. This very traditional biography focuses on his business and philanthropic activities. [JH]

3086 Palacios, Héctor A. Historia del movimiento obrero argentino. v. 2–3. Buenos Aires?: H.A. Palacios, 1992- . 2 v.: bibl.

Vols. 2–3 give overview of the labor movement from 1930–71, from perspective of left-wing nationalism, specifically Trotskyism. Work is comprehensive but is based on secondary sources and lacks scholarly apparatus. [JH]

3087 Pastoriza, Elisa. Los trabajadores de Mar del Plata en vísperas del peronismo. Buenos Aires: Centro Editor de América Latina, 1993. 140 p.: appendix, bibl. (Biblioteca Política argentina; 427)

This well-crafted study of labor movement in Mar del Plata in 1930s and 1940s places events in the context of the theoretical arguments about rise of Peronism, but also in the social and economic context of the resort. Work also contains an appendix discussing a key workers' library. Based on extensive use of archival sources and periodicals. [JH]

3088 Pavoni, Norma Leonor. Córdoba y el gobierno nacional: una etapa en el proceso fundacional del estado argentino, 1852–1862. v. 1–2. Córdoba, Argentina: Banco de la Provincia de Córdoba, 1993. 2 v.: bibl., maps.

Analysis of contemporary sources concludes that economic growth of the province was prevented partly by financial difficulties of the State and the absence of credit institutions. Vol. 2 reprints a valuable collection of unedited documents found in provincial and private archives. [JTC]

3089 Perón, Juan Domingo. Cartas del exilio. Selección, introducción y apéndices de Samuel Amaral y William E. Ratliff. Buenos Aires: Editorial Legasa, 1991. 237 p.: ill. (Ensayo crítico)

Contains 41 previously unpublished letters written by Perón between December 1, 1955 and April 8, 1969. All but three date from 1955–57, and most are to Hipólito Jesús Paz, a former foreign minister, and to María de la Cruz who was Perón's contact in Chile. Excellent introduction. [JH]

3090 Piccagli, Américo E. and Zulma Taurizano. Historia documental de San Pedro, provincia de Buenos Aires. v. 2, De la villa al pueblo, 1809–1854. Buenos Aires: Editores R. de Armas & Asoc., 1990. 1 v.: bibl., ill.

Fascinating study relates political and economic activities in a river port. [JTC]

3091 Pignatelli, Adrián. Ricardo Balbín, el presidente postergado. v. 1–2. Buenos Aires: Centro Editor de América Latina, 1992. 2 v.: bibl. (Biblioteca Política argentina; 363–364)

Well-researched biography of a political leader, four times a candidate for president, stresses his relations with Juan Perón and intra- and inter-party struggles from 1943–76. Based on press accounts, party documents, and interviews with people who knew Balbín. [JTC]

3092 Plotkin, Mariano Ben. Mañana es San Perón: propaganda, rituales políticos y educación en el régimen peronista, 1946–1955. Buenos Aires: Ariel Historia Argentina, 1994. 348 p.: bibl.

Excellent, pathbreaking work explores Perón regime's attempt to create a new culture for Argentina in order to establish regime's legitimacy and expand its base of support. Author examines alteration of October 17 and May 1 celebrations. He also looks at politicalization of the educational system and gives best description yet of the Fundación Eva Perón. Pays particular attention to attempts to appeal to women and children. [JH]

3093 Poenitz, Erich Luis W.E. Misiones y los guaraní-misioneros en Entre Ríos. (Bol. Acad. Nac. Hist./Buenos Aires, 62/63, 1989/1990, p. 459–477)

Brief account relates settling in Entre Ríos prov. of Guarani from the Jesuit missions, their Hispanicization, and their efforts to defend the independence of Misiones prov. [JTC]

3094 Popescu, Oreste. La doctrina industrial de Carlos Pellegrini. (An. Acad. Nac. Cienc. Econ., 35, 1990, p. 187–203)

Outlines national and foreign origins of the economic philosophy of Pellegrini and of Vicente Fidel López, founder of the first Argentine school of economics. These economists held that the government should protect nascent industries from imports and promote regional development. [JTC]

3095 Populismo en San Juan y Mendoza. Recopilación de Pablo Lacoste. Buenos Aires: Centro Editor de América Latina, 1994. 126 p.: bibl. (Biblioteca Política argentina; 454)

Three chapters address unique populism of the two Andean provinces. The first examines this variety of populism within context of the wider literature on that subject; the second looks at *bloquismo* in San Juan from 1930–41; and final essay discusses a local caudillo in Mendoza. [JH]

3096 Posada, Marcelo Germán. La conformación del perfil del empresariado pecuario: el caso del partido de Mercedes (Buenos Aires, Argentina), 1850–1890. (Rev. Hist. Am., 112, julio/dic. 1991, p. 159–177, bibl., graphs, map, tables)

Examination of census figures for 1881, 1885, and 1895 suggests that large landowners responded quickly to changes in market demand for wool and hides, and that immigrants were the main source of a paid labor force. [JTC]

3097 Pozzi, Pablo A. Argentina 1976–1982: resistencia obrera y apertura democrática. (*Estud. Latinoam./Poland*, 15, 1992, p. 187–219, tables)

Argues that labor unrest during military dictatorship of 1976–82 furthered opening toward democracy. Claims that strikes and other activities prevented the military from fully carrying out its plans, especially in the economic sphere. [JH]

3098 Pozzi, Pablo A. and **Alejandro Schneider.** "Combatiendo al capital": crisis y recomposición de la clase obrera argentina, 1983–1993. Buenos Aires?: El Bloque Editorial, 1993. 221 p.: bibl.

Arguing from a Marxist perspective, authors claim that despite apparent weakening of the labor movement, a renewed sense of combativeness, manifesting itself in new forms, is discernible among the working class. Based on periodical literature and interviews with individual workers. [JH]

3099 Pozzi, Pablo A. Oposición obrera a la dictadura, 1976–1982. Buenos Aires: Editorial Contrapunto, 1988. 203 p.: bibl. (Col. Memoria y presente)

Stresses worker resistance to the military rulers of the Proceso was greater than is usually thought. Also examines union leadership's complex relationships with the military. Largely based on the publications of Argentines living abroad during the military dictatorship. [JH]

3100 Presencia alemana en la Argentina = Deutsche Präsenz in Argentinien. Proyecto y dirección de Manrique Zago. Investigación histórica e iconográfica de Peter Alemann. Buenos Aires: M. Zago Ediciones, 1992. 252 p.: bibl., maps, photos.

Popular history of Germans in Argentina is made interesting by numerous photographs. [JH]

3101 Prieto, Agustina. Ciudad y barrio obrero: un análisis comparado de la vida cotidiana de los trabajadores de Rosario, 1890–1914. (*in* Colección nuestra patria es América: migraciones y vida urbana. Edición de Jorge Nuñez Sánchez. Quito: Editora Nacional, 1992, v. 9, p. 149–174)

Examination of working class living conditions in Rosario with focus on two neighborhoods removed from the center of the city. Unlike more central *barrios*, these neighborhoods were distinctly working class. [JH]

3102 Privitellio, Luciano de. Sociedad urbana y actores políticos en Buenos Aires: el "partido" independiente en 1931. (*Bol. Inst. Hist. Ravignani*, 9, 1994, p. 75–96)

Making excellent use of the recently opened Justo Archives, author has given us the best discussion to date of the creation of a political organization. He examines the creation of political backing for Justo in the capital in 1931. [JH]

3103 Quesada, Juan Isidro. Félix Frías en Chile, 1843–1848: capítulo de la biografía de este prócer. (*Invest. Ens.*, 43, enero/dic. 1993, p. 471–514)

Excellent introduction to a *porteño* intellectual who served as a Bolivian diplomat; represented *El Mercurio* of Chile in Paris; opposed Rosas for family and political reasons; and defended the Catholic religion. Quotes extensively from private correspondence. [JTC]

3104 Quijada Mauriño, Mónica. De Perón a Alberdi: selectividad étnica y construcción nacional en la política inmigratoria argentina. (*Rev. Indias*, 52:195/196, mayo/dic. 1992, p. 867–888)

Exceptional analysis focuses on ideas of nation-building that consistently guided Argentine immigration policy from 1810–1952. [JTC]

3105 Quijada Mauriño, Mónica. Política inmigratoria del primer Peronismo: las negociaciones con España. (*Rev. Eur.*, 47, Dec. 1989, p. 43–64)

Documented analysis examines negotiations leading to the Convention of 1948 in which Argentina sought Catholic technicians and farming and pastoral specialists from Spain for its infant industries and colonization projects. Bureaucracies of both countries prevented implementation of the agreement. [JTC]

3106 Quijada Mauriño, Mónica. *Zollverein* e integración sudamericana en la política exterior peronista, 1946–1955: análisis de un caso de nacionalismo hispanoamericanista. (*Jahrb. Gesch.*, 30, 1993, p. 371–408)

Argues that Peronist foreign policy was neither disorganized nor expanisionist. The regime attempted to create a Latin American common market but was responding to ideas that had been present in Argentina for decades. Much of the information is from Spanish archives. [JH]

3107 Rapoport, Mario. Argentina. (*in* Latin America between the Second World War and the Cold War, 1944–1948. Edited by Leslie Bethell and Ian Roxborough. New York: Cambridge Univ. Press, 1992, p. 92–119)

Basing his work almost entirely on secondary sources, author analyzes how and why the left was displaced in Argentina in the direct aftermath of World War II. Argues that unlike the situation in the rest of Latin America what occurred in Argentina was not a product of the Cold War, but of World War II and the rise of Juan Perón. [JH]

3108 Reguera, Andrea. Arrendamientos y formas de acceso a la producción en el sur bonaerense: el caso de una estancia del partido de Necochea, primera mited el siglo XX. (*in* Huellas en la tierra: indios, agricultores y hacendados en la pampa bonaerense. Recopilación de Raúl Mandrini y Andrea Reguera. Tandil, Argentina: Univ. Nacional del Centro, IEHS, 1993, p. 241–274, graphs, maps, tables)

Well-done study details land use and land holding in southeast Buenos Aires prov. After a general discussion of the nature of tenant farming and the passage in 1921 of a law to regulate the activity, author looks at practices on the Martínez family *estancia*. Study is based largely on family's detailed archive. Land use patterns were extremely complex and 1921 legislation had little impact. See also item **3109**. [JH]

3109 Reguera, Andrea. Trabajo humano, trabajo mecánico: cadena de oficios entre ciudad y campo en el sur bonaerense, siglos XIX y XX. (*Anu. IEHS*, 6, 1991, p. 113–136, bibl., tables)

Detailed account describes an *estancia* in Necochea (Buenos Aires prov.), examining organization, recruitment, and payment of a labor force, adjustments to mechanization, and relations with neighboring towns. See also item **3108**. [JTC]

3110 La Revolución de 1890: libro-homenaje en su centenario. Buenos Aires: Camara de Diputados de la Nación, 1992. 148 p.: ill.

Collection of news reports, documents, and statements by participants in the revolution and by other contemporaries serves to record a crucial moment in Argentine history. [JTC]

3111 Riekenberg, Michael. Nationbildung, sozialer Wandel und Geschichtsbewusstein am Río de la Plata, 1810–1916. Frankfurt: Vervuert, 1995. 333 p.: bibl., index. (Americana Eystettensia. Serie B, Monographien, Studien, Essays; 6)

Historical essay on sense of nationhood in River Plate region (1810–1916) uses an extensive bibliography, including school texts, to trace historical-political symbolism. Also portrays process of nation building and conceptual development of nationhood against background of sociopolitical interrelationships. Notes that anti-imperialist sentiments and uniquely American notions of the World War I era combined with *Hispanidad* and gaucho culture, a mixture that stabilized society in a symbolic sense and created an optimistic and future-oriented sense of history in the region. [C.K. Converse]

3112 Rock, David. Authoritarian Argentina: the Nationalist movement, its history, and its impact. Berkeley: Univ. of California Press, 1993. 320 p.: bibl., index.

Examines ideological roots of 1970s military regime to help explain the horrors the regime produced. To do this, Rock has thoroughly explored political ideas and ideology of the nationalist right in Argentina throughout this century. While a work of intellectual history, it is tied to the changing political currents. [JH]

3113 Rodríguez, Adolfo Enrique. La policía de Buenos Aires después de la Batalla de Caseros y durante la época de la separación de la provincia de la Confederación. (*Publ. Inst. Estud. Iberoam.*, 8:6, 1989, p. 147–176, photos, map)

Valuable study examines security

forces from their collapse following the battle to their reorganization and recomposition by end of the 1850s. [JTC]

3114 Rojas, Isaac Francisco. Memorias del almirante Isaac F. Rojas: conversaciones con Jorge L. González-Crespo. Buenos Aires: Planeta, 1993. 601 p.: ill.

González-Crespo has edited a series of oral remembrances by Admiral Rojas in which Rojas recounts his political and naval activities from his entrance in the service until 1958. Pays particular attention to the Revolución Libertadora of 1955 and its immediate aftermath when Rojas was vice president. González-Crespo has included detailed explanatory footnotes, many with information from naval archives. Also includes an appendix with some interesting facsimiles of documents. [JH]

3115 Romero, Luis Alberto. Breve historia contemporánea de la Argentina. Buenos Aires: Fondo de Cultura Económica, 1994. 414 p.: bibl., index. (Col. popular; 505)

Balanced, insightful overview of Argentine history from election of Yrigoyen in 1916 to 1993 is based on latest historiography. Although unfootnoted, contains a good bibliography and index. Combines political, economic, and social history, with emphasis on the first two. [JH]

3116 Romero, Luis Alberto. Buenos Aires: la sociedad criolla, 1810–1850. (*Hoy Hist.*, 11:61, enero/feb. 1994, p. 48–61)

Excellent study describes disruptions and accommodations that took place as the colonial elite gave way to a new elite and as rural criollo society survived beside another with partially or totally Europeanized elements. [JTC]

3117 Ruiz Moreno, Isidoro J. España, Rosas y Urquiza: las relaciones oficiales. (*in* Estudios en homenaje a Don Claudio Sánchez-Albornoz en sus 90 años: anexos de *Cuadernos de Historia de España.* Buenos Aires: Instituto de Historia de España, 1990, v. 6, p. 293–331)

Presents documented description of the long negotiations (1845–60) that led to Spain's recognition of Argentine independence. [JTC]

Sagastizábal, Leandro de *et al.* Argentina 1880–1943: Estado, economía y sociedad,

aproximaciones a su estudio. See *HLAS 55: 3575.*

3118 Sánchez de Bustamante, Teófilo. Del pasado jujeño: investigaciones históricas. Jujuy, Argentina: Univ. Nacional de Jujuy, 1988. 187 p.: bibl., ill. (Col. Arte-ciencia. Serie Jujuy en el pasado)

Describes land holdings, elementary education, and the Pueyrredón family tree in first decades of the 19th century. [JTC]

3119 Santamaría, Daniel J. and **Marcelo Lagos.** Historia y etnografía de las tierras bajas del norte argentino: trabajo realizado y perspectivas. (*Anu. IEHS*, 7, 1992, p. 75–92)

Chronologically based examination of writings on the Argentine Chaco and its peoples begins with first written accounts. Examines nature of the works, their purposes, and their limitations. Authors make several interesting suggestions about the need to combine history and anthropology. [JH]

3120 Santomauro, Héctor N. La generación argentina de 1880: vicisitudes del proceso social, político y económico, 1862–1916. Tandil, Argentina: Unicornio Centro Editor, 1992. 189 p.: bibl. (Col. Biblioteca de hoy)

Traces influence of positivism in Argentina from 1862–80, and denies that any plan to establish a model country existed. [JTC]

3121 Santos Martínez, Pedro. La coalición internacional que derrocó a Rosas. (*Nuestra Hist./Buenos Aires*, 18:35/36, dic. 1990, p. 237–266)

Well-researched essay describes in detail the methods used by Brazil to accomplish what author regards as the country's objectives: the overthrow of Rosas and establishment of its dominance in the Río de la Plata. [JTC]

3122 Schávelzon, Daniel. Arqueología histórica de Buenos Aires. v. 1, La cultura material porteña de los siglos XVIII y XIX. Buenos Aires: Corregidor, 1991- . 1 v.: bibl., ill., map.

During a five-year period, author led the excavation of 17 sites in the city of Buenos Aires. These systematic archeological investigations uncovered a great deal of information about material culture of the 18th and 19th centuries. This work helps fill important lacunae in our knowledge of living conditions in the capital. [JH]

3123 Segreti, Carlos S.A. El unitarismo argentino: notas para su estudio en la etapa 1810–1819. Buenos Aires: A-Z Editora, 1991. 185 p.: bibl.

Essayist distinguishes between centralism and a unitarian state; maintains that formation of the Argentine State was implicitly agreed upon in 1810; and describes gradual break-up of the *intendencia* system inherited from the colonial period. [JTC]

3124 Segreti, Carlos S.A. Las vías de hecho en el conflicto con Francia e Inglaterra en 1845. (*Invest. Ens.*, 43, enero/dic. 1993, p. 65–125)

Detailed analysis of diplomatic correspondence exchanged between Rosas and the English and French ministers confirms author's view that Rosas ably defended the Argentine position. [JTC]

3125 Senén González, Santiago and **Fabián Bosoer.** El hombre de hierro: Vandor, Rucci, Miguel, Brunelli. Buenos Aires: Corregidor, 1993. 157 p.: bibl., ill.

Four short biographies of the leaders of the Unión Obrera Metalúrgica (UOM) from late 1950s to 1993. UOM dominated union politics during that time, and authors have presented a balanced picture of the leadership. [JH]

3126 Serulnikov, Sergio. When looting becomes a right: urban poverty and food riots in Argentina. (*Lat. Am. Perspect.*, 21:3, Summer 1994, p. 69–89, bibl.)

Analyzes food riots that broke out in May and June 1989 in the wake of Carlos Menem's election and a wave of hyperinflation. Author looks at the riots in the context of social protest. While based on newspaper accounts, analysis is well done and thoughtful. [JH]

3127 Sheinin, David. Defying infection: Argentine foot-and-mouth disease policy, 1900–1930. (*Can. J. Hist.*, 29:3, Dec. 1994, p. 501–523)

Well-done work reexamines controversy between Argentina and US over closing of the US market to Argentine beef because of prevalence of hoof-and-mouth disease in Argentina. Sheinin sees the controversy and misunderstandings as based primarily on the differing views of the nature of the problem. Research was done in British, US, and Argentine archives. [JH]

3128 Sidicaro, Ricardo. La política mirada desde arriba: las ideas del diario *La Nación*, 1909–1989. Buenos Aires: Editorial Sudamericana, 1993. 545 p.: bibl. (Col. Historia y cultura)

Analyzes editorial positions of this important paper which saw itself as representing the interests of the elites and the nation. Covers views on politics, social questions, and economics. Author does a good job of placing the editorial positions in context. Coverage is of necessity uneven. [JH]

3129 Siegrist de Gentile, Nora. Inmigración vasca en la ciudad de Buenos Aires, 1830–1850. Vitoria, Spain: Servicio Central de Publicaciones, Gobierno Vasco, 1992. 168 p.: bibl., ill., maps. (Amerika eta euskaldunak = América y los vascos; 14)

Analysis of the Spanish census of 1857 and of Buenos Aires census of 1855 shows that most Basques came from provinces of Guipúzcoa and Navarro, and that they settled in the *juzgado* of Catedral al Sur in the city of Buenos Aires. [JTC]

3130 Siepe, Raimundo. Yrigoyen, la Primera Guerra Mundial y las relaciones económicas. Buenos Aires: Centro Editor de América Latina, 1992. 129 p.: bibl. (Biblioteca Política argentina; 388)

Looks at Yrigoyen's policy of aggressive neutrality during World War I. Basing his work on secondary sources and archival sources in Spanish, author defends and praises Yrigoyen. Also includes a discussion of Argentina's trade with US and Great Britain from 1916–21. [JH]

3131 Silva, Hernán Asdrúbal. La actividad de los agentes de inmigración argentinos y la competencia por canalizar el flujo inmigratorio español. (*Rev. Indias*, 53:199, sept./dic. 1993, p. 799–805)

Brief study examines efforts and impacts of Argentine immigration agents in Spain prior to 1880. [JH]

3132 Silva, Hernán Asdrúbal; Adriana Beatriz Gerpe; and **Adriana Beatriz Martino.** Bibliografía sobre el impacto inmigratorio masivo en la Argentina, 1850–1930. (*in* Bibliografía sobre el impacto del proceso inmigratorio masivo en el Cono Sur de América: Argentina, Brasil, Chile, Uruguay. México: Instituto Panamericano de Geografía e Historia, 1984, v. 1, p. 9–109)

Important bibliography attempts to cover all aspects of immigration to Argentina and the role of immigrants once there. While a crucial source, work's usefulness is hindered by its style of organization and lack of annotation. Somewhat dated, but remains a good place to begin looking for older sources. [JH]

3133 Simposio de Historia Regional, 1st, San Juan, Argentina, 1987. Actas. San Juan, Argentina: Univ. Nacional de San Juan, Instituto de Historia Regional y Argentina Héctor Domingo Arias, 1994. 103 p.: bibl. (Estudios y monografías; 4)

Papers presented at the symposium discuss organization of provincial archives of Mendoza and San Juan, and works of historians interested in the Argentine northwest. [JTC]

3134 Sindicatos como los de antes—. Recopilación de Torcuato S. Di Tella. Buenos Aires: Editorial Biblos; Fundación Simón Rodríguez, 1993. 214 p.: bibl. (Col. Cuadernos Simón Rodríguez; 24)

Interesting collection of articles on unions includes short introduction by the editor. Includes two reprints: 1) Luis Lotito, "El Proletariado Tucumano a Comienzos del Siglo" (which originally appeared in a syndicalist journal in 1907 and 1908), and 2) Celia Durruty, "La Federación Obrera Nacional de la Construcción" (a selection from the author's *Clase obrera y peronismo*—see *HLAS 32: 2533a*). The four original articles are: 1) Graciela Climent and Ana María Mendes Diz, "La Industria Azucarera y los Comienzos del Movimiento Obrero en Tucumán;" 2) María del Carmen Arnaiz, "Un Oasis en el Desierto: la Unión Obrera Departamental de Concepción del Uruguay, 1920–1946;" 3) Laura Kalmanowiecki, "La Unión Sindical Argentina: de la Revolución Prometida a la Incorporación en el Sistema Político;" and 4) Torcuato S. Di Tella, "La Unión Obrera Textil, 1930–1945." [JH]

3135 Suriano, Juan. El Estado argentino frente a los trabajadores urbanos: política social y represion, 1880–1916. (*Anuario/Rosario*, 14, 1989/90, p. 109–136)

Describes slow reaction of national government to social problems created by rapid influx of immigrants; the creation of a municipal police force and national labor department; and the reliance on European and US models for resolving similar problems. [JTC]

3136 Szusterman, Celia. Frondizi and the politics of developmentalism in Argentina, 1955–62. Pittsburgh: Univ. of Pittsburgh Press, 1993. 318 p.: bibl., index. (Pitt Latin American series)

Believing that Argentina's problems are rooted in politics, author presents an extremely detailed analysis of Frondizi's rise to the presidency and his time in power. Also looks at growth of the ideology of development. Based on extensive interviews, the periodical press, and diplomatic archives in both US and Great Britain. [JH]

3137 Tolcachier, Fabiana Sabina. Asociaciones israelitas en el partido de Villarino. (*Stud. Emigr.*, 31:115, set. 1994, p. 461–493, graphs, tables)

Well-done work looks at five Jewish organizations in a *partido* near Bahía Blanca. Argues that, unlike other ethnic groups in different regions, these organizations did not separate the members from the larger community. Author believes the reason might be the newness of the region when Jews began to settle there. [JH]

3138 Tozzioli, Aldo. Teodelina, 1875–1982. (*Universidad/Santa Fe*, 101, mayo 1991, p. 77–118, tables)

Excellent discussion of origins and development of an important colony in Santa Fe prov. [JTC]

3139 Trifone, Víctor and Gustavo Svarzman. La repercusión de la Guerra Civil Española en la Argentina, 1936–1939. Buenos Aires: Centro Editor de América Latina, 1993. 105 p.: bibl. (Biblioteca Política argentina; 409)

Brief study examines impact of the Spanish Civil War on Argentine society. Shows which groups supported which side, and why. Also looks at tensions that the war created inside Argentina. [JH]

3140 El trotskismo obrero e internacionalista en la Argentina. v. 1, Del GOM a la Federación Bonaerense del PSRN, 1943–1955. Coordinación de Ernesto González. Buenos Aires: Editorial Antídoto, 1995. 251 p.

Provides official history of a faction of the Trotskyist movement (Grupo Obrero

Marxista—the faction led by Nahuel Moreno and currently known as Movimiento al Socialismo—MAS). Presents a different and interesting picture of the left and the union movement during the Perón regime. Based mostly on party archives and interviews with party leaders. [JH]

3141 Urquiza Almandoz, Oscar F. La revolución radical de 1893 y la provincia de Entre Ríos. (*Invest. Ens.*, 43, enero/dic. 1993, p. 353–383)

Provides detailed account of participation of the Guardia Nacional de Entre Ríos in suppressing a revolution in Santa Fe prov. [JTC]

Vázquez-Presedo, Vicente. Auge y decadencia de la economía argentina desde 1776. See *HLAS 55:2091.*

3142 Villarino, Emilio. Batallón 5: el Batallón de Infantería de Marina No. 5 en la Guerra de las Malvinas. Prólogo de Carlos Büsser. Buenos Aires: Aller Atucha, 1992. 201 p.: ill., maps.

Relates activities of Batallón de Infantería de Marina No. 5 in the Falkland/Malvinas War. Author is a journalist currently employed by the Navy. Clearly based on interviews with unit members, but lacks footnotes. [JH]

3143 La vuelta de Don Juan Manuel: ciento diez autores y protagonistas hablan de Rosas. Recopilación de Fermín Chávez. Buenos Aires: Distribuidora y Editora Theoria, 1991. 302 p.

Contains reproductions of letters, poems, and dramatic pieces that speak favorably of Rosas and are not well known. Each author is identified by a brief biographical sketch. [JTC]

3144 Waispek, Carlos Alberto. Balsa 44: relato de un sobreviviente del crucero A.R.A. General Belgrano. Buenos Aires: Editorial Vinciguerra, 1994. 158 p.: port.

Memoir of a survivor of the Argentine cruiser, *General Belgrano*, sunk by the British during the Falkland/Malvinas War. [JH]

3145 Walter, Richard J. Politics and urban growth in Buenos Aires, 1910–1942. Cambridge; New York: Cambridge Univ. Press, 1993. 278 p.: bibl., ill., index, maps. (Cambridge Latin American studies; 73)

Intended in some senses as a continua-

tion of James Scobie's masterful *Buenos Aires: plaza to suburb, 1870–1910* (see *HLAS 38:3850*), this is a worthy successor. The focus is different, as title suggests. While discussing the life of the city and its growth and urban development, primary emphasis is the impact of politics on Buenos Aires. Based on diverse sources, book extends greatly our understanding of the development of the city. [JH]

3146 Wedovoy, Enrique. La estancia, ¿explotación capitalista o feudal? (*Todo es Hist.*, 318, enero 1994 p. 60–78, ill., photos)

Maintains that the *estancia* became part of the commercial economic system, but the native owner resisted change and the English were responsible for the progress made. [JTC]

3147 Zavala, Juan Tulio. Años vividos: política y revolución. San Luis, Argentina: Editorial Univ. San Luis, 1987. 335 p.: ill.

An educator and journalist of San Luis (1857–1923) recalls living conditions and educational climate when province was undergoing modernization. Also describes in detail his leadership of local members of the Unión Cívica Radical during the political struggles of 1885–1922. [JTC]

3148 Zeberio, Blanca. En torno a los orígenes sociales y las estrategias de emigración: el caso de los leoneses en la campaña sur de Buenos Aires, 1900–1930. (*Rev. Indias*, 54:201, mayo/agosto 1994, p. 409–437, graphs, table)

Studies large migration of Spaniards from León to southern Buenos Aires prov. Article looks at reasons for migration, pattern of family migrations, and migrants' success rate. Based on research in both Spain and Argentina. [JH]

3149 Zeberio, Blanca. La situación de los chacareros arrendatarios en la pampa húmeda: una discusión inacabada. (*in* Huellas en la tierra: indios, agricultores y hacendados en la pampa bonaerense. Recopilación de Raúl Mandrini y Andrea Reguera. Tandil, Argentina: Univ. Nacional del Centro, IEHS, 1993, p. 209–239, tables)

Combines overview of existing literature on tenant farming in Buenos Aires prov. in first decades of 20th century with discussion of specific situation in grain areas of southeast Buenos Aires. Conditions were more complex than is usually thought. Ownership increased over time; however, renters often remained on the same land for years, owned farm machinery, and controlled sizeable pieces of land. [JH]

PARAGUAY

Bergmann, Günther J. Auslandsdeutsche in Paraguay, Brasilien, Argentinien. See item **2962.**

3150 Estigarribia, José Félix. Memorias del mariscal José Félix Estigarribia. [Edición de Graciela Estigarribia de Fernández.] Prólogo de Rafael Eladio Velázquez. Asunción: Intercontinental Editora, 1989. 235 p.: maps.

The commander of the Paraguayan forces during the Chaco War recalls his military strategy and tactics, and impact of inadequate logistical. [JTC]

3151 Ferreira Pérez, Saturnino. Antecedentes del Centro Democrático: el golpe del 18 de octubre de 1891, su fusión con el Partido Liberal Histórico y dos páginas de sangre. Asunción: Ediciones Comuneros, 1988. 337 p.

Presents history of the political parties as seen through newspaper editorials published from 1890–95 and 1918–23. [JTC]

Franco, Rafael. Memorias militares. v. 2. See *HLAS 55:3597.*

3152 Frutos Pane, Juan Manuel. Ensayos republicanos: historia y doctrina colorada. Asunción: Editorial Clásicos Colorados, 1988. 198 p.: bibl., ill.

Short pieces and essays dealing with the Partido Colorado are written by a longtime activist. The most interesting sections are those describing author's own party activities. [JH]

3153 Galeano, Alfredo. Recuerdos y reflexiones de un soldado. Asunción: Criterio Ediciones; RP Ediciones, 1990. 202 p.: bibl., ill.

A combination of history, memoir, and thoughts about the proper role of the armed forces in Paraguayan society is written by a retired military officer. The most interesting segments discuss author's participation in the Chaco War as a young officer and his crucial role in the revolt of 1947. [JH]

Ganson, Barbara. "Like children under wise parental sway:" passive portrayals of the Guaraní Indians in European literature and *The Mission.* See item **2555.**

Guanes de Laíno, Rafaela. Familias sin tierra en Paraguay. See *HLAS 55:4989.*

3154 Heyn Schupp, Carlos Antonio. Iglesia y estado en el proceso de emancipación política del Paraguay, 1811–1853: con un centenar de documentos sobre el tema. Asunción: Editorial Don Bosco, 1991. 289 p.: appendix, bibl.

General introduction to Church-State relations includes an appendix of valuable documents drawn from Paraguayan, Spanish, and Vatican archives. [JTC]

Holland, Charles. Noticias de Buenos Aires, el Paraguay, Chile y el Perú: cartas del ciudadano inglés Charles Holland, 1820–1826. See item **3045.**

3155 Klassen, Peter P. Die Mennoniten in Paraguay: Reich Gottes und Reich dieser Welt. Bolanden-Weierhof, Germany: Mennonitischer Geschichtsverein, 1988. 383 p.: bibl., ill. index.

Paraguayan Mennonite writes about his community. Describes historical, religious, and cultural development of Russian Mennonites in Paraguay, their settlement, and their daily life in the Chaco region. [C.K. Converse]

3156 Lewis, Paul H. Political parties and generations in Paraguay's Liberal era, 1869–1940. Chapel Hill: Univ. of North Carolina Press, 1993. 227 p.: bibl., index, maps.

Detailed study looks at politics from the fall of Francisco Solano López to final defeat of the Liberals. Argues that for much of the period no critical difference in ideology existed between the two key political parties, and emphasizes role of generations in political shifts. Based on collection of personal data for 950 individuals. Demonstrates that majority of the founders of both the Partido Colorado and the Partido Liberal had opposed López. [JH]

Meyer Aragón, Carlos. En ambos frentes: memorias de un ex combatiente mutilado en la Guerra del Chaco. See item **2850.**

3157 Olmedo Alvarenga, Agustín. Historia del Colegio Militar Mariscal Francisco Solano López, 1915–1985. v. 1–2. Asunción:

Impr. Militar de la Dirección de Publicaciones Militares, 1990. 2 v.: bibl., ill. (some col.).

Official history of the Paraguayan officers' school is based on school's own documentation, some of which is reprinted. Contains biographical information on commanders and lists activites, but has little on what was taught or on daily lives of the students. [JH]

3158 Pastore, Carlos. El Gran Chaco en la formación territorial del Paraguay: etapas de su incorporación. Asunción: Criterio-Ediciones, 1989. 284 p.: bibl., maps.

A Liberal historian examines measures taken by Paraguay to defend Chaco region from Bolivia. Concentrates on period beween 1852–1928, emphasizing defense of the actions of Eligio Ayala. Includes large number of documents. [JH]

3159 Pastore, Mario. State-led industrialisation: the evidence on Paraguay, 1852–1870. (*J. Lat. Am. Stud.*, 26:2, May 1994, p. 295–324, tables)

Maintains that little evidence exists to support revisionist school's theoretical assumptions that Paraguay experienced industrial growth prior to 1864. Suggests that the State pursued mercantilist policies. [JTC]

Plá, Josefina. Historia cultural. v. 1–4. See item **2604.**

3160 La polémica francesa sobre la Guerra Grande. Selección, traducción, notas y comentarios de Milda Rivarola. Asunción: Editorial Histórica, 1988. 279 p.: bibl., ill., maps.

Pt. 1 of two-part work consists of translations of four articles written by a French anarquist. Pt. 2 contains extracts of French consular reports written between 1864–1870. Two views of Paraguay: one positive, one negative. [JTC]

3161 Por orden superior. Entrevistas organizadas por Olga Caballero Aquino. Prólogo de Esther Prieto. Asunción: Ediciones Ñandutí Vive; Intercontinental Editora, 1989. 181 p.

Collection of oral histories of women who opposed Stroessner regime. The women are from a wide spectrum of political groups: Liberals, Colorados, Febreristas, Communists, and Christian Democrats. Contains

wrenching accounts of torture, exile, and isolation. The oral histories make clear the difficulties involved in political activity and the interconnectedness between Paraguay and Argentina. [JH]

3162 La Revolución de 1904. Recopilación de Leandro Prieto Yegros. Asunción: Editorial Cuadernos Republicanos, 1990. 341 p.: bibl.

Publishes extracts from the works of participants, Liberal journalists, and a Socialist, all seeking to explain the Revolution of 1904. [JTC]

Riart, Gustavo Adolfo. El Partido Liberal y el ejército. See *HLAS 55.*

Riekenberg, Michael. Nationbildung, sozialer Wandel und Geschichtsbewusstsein am Río de la Plata, 1810–1916. See item **3111.**

3163 Rivarola, Milda. Obreros, utopías & revoluciones: formación de las clases trabajadoras en el Paraguay liberal, 1870–1931. Asunción: CDE, 1993. 317 p.: bibl., ill.

Excellent, dense, fact-filled work examines creation and condition of a Paraguayan working class, and development and evolution of a labor movement. Ties these developments to the larger political system. Based largely on French diplomatic archives and documentary material collected by Francisco Gaona, work contains copious footnotes. [JH]

3164 Rodríguez Alcalá de González Oddone, Beatriz. El íntimo universo de Eugenio Alejandrino Garay. Asunción: Intercontinental Editora, 1991. 167 p.: ill.

Brief biography of Eugenio is based on his letters to his wife.[JTC]

3165 Saguier, Miguel Abdón and **Manuel Pesoa.** 18 de octubre. Asunción: Criterio Ediciones, 1991. 268 p.

Examines period between 1887–91 as the lead-up to the nearly successful Liberal revolt of Oct. 1891. Using extensive quotations from newspapers, especially *El Independiente,* authors give detailed account that is partisanly Liberal. [JH]

3166 Salum-Flecha, Antonio. Historia diplomática del Paraguay de 1869 a 1990. 4. ed., corr. y aum. Asunción: Ediciones Comuneros, 1990. 269 p.: bibl., ill., maps.

The author, a lawyer, journalist, and

Partido Colorado politician, wrote this diplomatic history to be a university textbook. Based entirely on secondary works, focuses primarily on boundary disputes with Paraguay's neighbors. [JH]

3167 Schmitt, Peter Adolf. Paraguay y Europa, 1811–1870. Traducción de Frank M. Samson. Asunción: s.n., 1990. 402 p.: bibl., ill.

Presents close examination of diplomatic relations between Paraguay and European countries. Includes laudatory appraisal of accomplishments of Carlos Antonio López. Bibliography is a valuable guide to the literature. [JTC]

3168 Silvera Alvarez, Cecilia. Telémaco Silvera: un demócrata republicano; vida y escritos. Asunción: Imprenta Salesiana, 1992. 314 p.: bibl., ill.

Brief biography of Silvera and a collection of his journal articles reflect on his interest in agrarian and labor problems and government reform. [JTC]

3169 Tajima, Hisatoshi. Historia del Paraguay del siglo XIX, 1811–1870. Asunción: Centro Paraguayo de Estudios Sociológicos, 1988. 125 p.: bibl. (Serie Historia social)

Maintains that the dependency theory does not apply to Paraguay, as country obtained political and economic independence early in 19th century. [JTC]

3170 Whigham, Thomas. La transformación económica del Paraguay: una perspectiva oficial de 1863. (*Rev. Parag. Sociol.*, 30: 86, enero/abril 1993, p. 67–70)

Article in the official press optimistically discusses potential for industrialization. [JTC]

URUGUAY

3171 Abadie-Aicardi, Aníbal. El Dr. Otto Woysch y el Uruguay de 1857–1863: mentalidad pastoral, ideas y crítica cultural. (*Am. Merid.*, 9, oct. 1989, p. 7–38, photo)

Discusses reflections by a German minister of the Lutheran Reformed Church during his assignment in Montevideo, as recorded in his book *Comunicaciones sobre la vida social y eclesiástica en la República del Uruguay*, originally published in German, in 1864. [JTC]

3172 Acosta y Lara, Eduardo F. La guerra de los charrúas en la Banda Oriental. v. 1–2. Montevideo: Librería Linardi y Risso, 1989. 2 v.: bibl., ill.

Collection of documents touches on relations of the Charrúas, Guaraní, Minúan, Abipón, and Guaycurú tribes—Christian and non-Christian alike—with the Spanish in 18th century and first decades of the independence era. Very revealing on the degree of cooperation between the Spaniards and the indigenous peoples. [JTC]

3173 Aguirre Ramírez, Gonzalo. La Revolución del Quebracho y la conciliación: de Ellauri a Tajes, 1873–1886. Montevideo: Barreiro y Ramos-Editores, 1989. 205 p.: bibl.

Detailed study examines origins of the revolution against General Máximo Santos that resulted in re-establishment of civilian government. Documents on pages 140 to 201. [JTC]

3174 Alfaro, Milita. Carnaval: una historia social de Montevideo desde la perspectiva de la fiesta. v. 1., El carnaval heroico, 1800–1872. Montevideo: Ediciones Trilce, 1991- . 1 v: bibl.

Interesting look at carnival in Montevideo from 1800–72 relates how the celebration changed from the wild disorder of the early years to a more formal event. Author argues that this process reflects the changes in the larger society and gives the historian a window for examining those changes. [JH]

3175 Arteaga, Juan José *et al.* Estudio bibliográfico sobre el impacto del proceso inmigratorio en el Uruguay en el período 1830–1930. (*in* Bibliografía sobre el impacto del proceso inmigratorio masivo en el Cono Sur de América: Argentina, Brasil, Chile, Uruguay. México: Instituto Panamericano de Geografía e Historia, 1984, v. 1, p. 189–207)

Unannotated guide to 367 works found in Montevideo libraries that refer to impact of immigration on the country. Does not include publications found in libraries organized by different immigrant groups. [JTC]

Azcona Pastor, José Manuel. Los paraísos posibles: historia de la emigración vasca a Argentina y Uruguay en el siglo XIX. See item **2953.**

3176 Barrios Pintos, Aníbal. La Villa de Nuestra Señora del Rosario: proceso fundacional, sus primeros años. Montevideo:

Intendencia Municipal de Colonia, 1992. 84 p.: bibl., ill., maps.

History of the town of Rosario, *departamento* of Colonia, from its founding in 1772 to 1834. Based on archives on both sides of the Río de la Plata, provides detailed analysis of both institutional and economic development. Overwhelming emphasis is on period before 1810. [JH]

3177 Batlle y Ordóñez, José. ¿Reforma o revolución?: la polémica Batlle-Mibelli, 1917. Edición de Milton I. Vanger. Montevideo: Ediciones de la Banda Oriental, 1989. 260 p.: bibl. (Temas del siglo XX; 40)

Examines polemic between José Batlle y Ordóñez and the Socialist Celestino Mibelli that appeared in *El Día* in 1917. A key theme was the role of the military in Uruguay. The exchange helped Batlle define the difference between the Colorados and the Socialistas. Contains a good introduction by Milton I. Vanger. [JH]

3178 Bértola, Luis. La industria manufacturera uruguaya, 1913–1961: un enfoque sectorial de su crecimiento, fluctuaciones y crisis. Montevideo: Facultad de Ciencias Sociales; CIEDUR, 1991. 328 p.: bibl., ill.

Sophisticated analysis of industrial growth in Uruguay. Author presents theoretical analysis, elaborate sets of data, and explanations for growth or lack thereof, and ties his examination to wider problems in the economy. Data for manufacturing is broken down by sector. [JH]

3179 Caetano, Gerardo. La república conservadora, 1916–1929. v. 1–2. Montevideo?: Editorial Fin de Siglo, 1992- . 2 v.: bibl. (Col. Raíces)

Sophisticated analysis of the political system of Uruguay covers period from true opening of the political system and first defeat of Batlle to 1929. Emphasis is on the creation of economic pressure groups and their role in the creation of an archipelago of political movements which dominated the conservative State albeit from within the traditional parties. [JH]

3180 Cassina de Nogara, Alba G. Hacia una democracia integral: apuntes para una historia del feminismo en Uruguay. Montevideo?: Consejo Nacional de Mujeres de Uruguay, 1990. 156 p.: bibl., ill.

A rapid review of the feminist movement in Uruguay. [JTC]

La construcción de las democracias rioplatenses: proyectos institucionales y prácticas políticas, 1900–1930. See item **3003.**

3181 Corredera Rossi, Ketty. Inmigración italiana en el Uruguay: 1860–1920. Montevideo?: Proyección, 1989. 139 p.: bibl., ill. (Serie Migraciones; 1)

Studies descendants of Waldenses and Italians from Basilicata, Italy, who settled in Colonia. Presents case studies of three Genovese brothers who succeeded as entrepreneurs and became members of the middle class. [JTC]

3182 La diplomacia de la Patria Vieja: 1811–1820. Recopilación y advertencia de Juan E. Pivel Devoto y Rodolfo Fonseca Muñoz. Montevideo: Ministerio de Relaciones Exteriores, Instituto Artigas del Servicio Exterior, 1990. 407 p.: indexes. (Ediciones del Instituto Artigas del Servicio Exterior.)

Contains the diplomatic correspondence between Artigas and Asunción, Buenos Aires, Cádiz, Montevideo, and Río Grande del Sur. [JTC]

3183 Dutrénit Bielous, Silvia. El maremoto militar y el archipiélago partidario: testimonios para la historia reciente de los partidos políticos uruguayos. Prólogo de Gerardo Caetano. Montevideo: Instituto Mora; Ediciones de Ciencias Sociales, 1994. 326 p.

Author believes that political parties are the center of Uruguayan politics and that the existence of a military dictatorship does not totally alter this. After a relatively short introduction detailing party activity under military rule, 1973–84, author presents 16 interviews about this period with key leaders from all the major political parties. Among the interviewees are Jorge Batlle, Julio Sanguinetti, Líber Seregni, and Luis Alberto Lacalle. [JH]

3184 Echenique, Carlos A. Prudencio Vázquez y Vega: aspectos destacables de su ascendencia y de su acción intelectual. Montevideo: Impr. Cooperativa, 1989. 208 p.: bibl.

Biography of a distant relative of Artigas who belonged to the Partido Constitucional and the "Radicales de 1871," and who edited the regional newspaper, *La Revista de Melo.* Vázquez y Vega defended the radical ideas of the university generation of 1868. [JTC]

3185 Fernández Cabrelli, Alfonso. Artigas: el hombre frente al mito. v. 1. Montevideo?: s.n., 1991- . 1 v.: bibl., ill., maps.

Emphasizes that Artigas belonged to a society composed of colonial and modern elements and that his values were drawn from both groups. Documented and well written. [JTC]

3186 Fernández Cabrelli, Alfonso. Iglesia ultramontana y masonería en la transformación de la sociedad oriental. Montevideo: Ediciones América Una, 1990. 388 p.: bibl., ill.

Studies unsuccessful efforts of the national clergy, influenced by the struggle between the Masons and the Church in Europe, to reform the Uruguayan Church and to prevent the separation of Church and State and the secularization of education. [JTC]

3187 Ferreiro, Felipe. Estudios históricos e internacionales. Montevideo: Ministerio de Relaciones Exteriores, Instituto Artigas del Servicio Exterior, 1989. 339 p., 6 leaves of plates: ill.

Most of the 28 essays in this collection focus on the first decades of the independence era. Essays appeared originally in various periodicals or as prologues to books published between 1925–54. Many of the essays reflect the ongoing reevaluation of Artigas. [JTC]

3188 Frega, Ana and Yvette Trochon. Los fundamentos del Estado empresario, 1903–1933. (*Cuad. CLAEH*, 58/59, 1991, p. 115–137, table)

Essayists argue that Batlle y Ordóñez was not embracing socialism when he advanced State intervention in the economy; rather, his goal was for public agencies to create jobs. [JTC]

3189 Gandía, Enrique de. El General Enrique Martínez en la historia de la Argentina y del Uruguay. (*Bol. Acad. Nac. Hist./Buenos Aires*, 62/63, 1989/90, p. 293–320)

Biography of an Uruguayan general (1789–1870) emphasizes his contributions to the independence movement, his revelations on the activities of the Masons, and his involvement in Argentine and Uruguayan politics. Martínez himself was a Mason. [JTC]

3190 Jacob, Raúl. Los bancos extranjeros, 1911–1938. (*Rev. Nac./Montevideo*, 239, sept. 1993, p. 111–125)

Gives brief overview of foreign banking in Uruguay, its scope, and its role. [JH]

3191 Jacob, Raúl. Modelo batllista: ¿variación sobre un viejo tema?. Montevideo: Proyección, 1988. 175 p.: bibl., ill. (Col. Historia; 5)

Work is composed principally of two well-documented studies of development of the service economy between 1900–30. The first concentrates on the problems and opportunities presented by transportation (ports, railroads, and shipping), and also looks at the meat trade with Río Grande (Brazil). The second examines the development, first in Montevideo and later in other localities, of tourism connected to the sea. [JH]

3192 José Batlle y Ordóñez: documentos para el estudio de su vida y de su obra. ser 8, pt. 1, vols. 1–7. Montevideo: Poder Legislativo, Cámara de Representantes, 1989- . 7 v.

Volumes record actions taken at the Convención Nacional del Partido Colorado (1920–29). [JTC]

Kleinpenning, Jan M.G. Peopling the Purple Land: a historical geography of rural Uruguay, 1500–1915. See *HLAS 55:2619.*

3193 Labraga, Alfonso *et al.* Energía y política en el Uruguay del siglo XX. v. 1. Montevideo: Ediciones de la Banda Oriental, 1991- . 1 v: bibl. (Temas del siglo XX; 45)

Briefly analyzes fuel needs and government policies that accompanied them, from traditional firewood and charcoal to coal and then petroleum. Also includes discussion of related transportation policies. [JH]

3194 López d'Alesandro, Fernando. Historia de la izquierda uruguaya. v. 1–3 (in 4). Montevideo?: Ediciones del Nuevo Mundo, 1988- . 4 v.: bibl.

Detailed examination of the Uruguayan left from the utopian socialists to creation of the Partido Comunista del Uruguay and the division of the anarchists in the wake of the Bolshevik Revolution. Focus is on the political with some attention to the ideological. Work becomes more detailed as it moves closer to the present. Author has consulted a wide range of sources, especially periodicals. [JH]

3195 Mañé Garzón, Fernando and **Angel Ayestarán.** El gringo de confianza: memorias de un médico alemán en Montevideo, entre el fin de la Guerra del Paraguay y el Civilismo, 1867–1892; su actuación obstétrica y quirúrgica [por] Ricardo Pou Ferrari. Montevideo: s.n., 1992. 310 p.: bibl., ill., indexes.

Reprints interesting memoirs of Carl Brendel, a German doctor who lived in Montevideo between 1867–92. Throws light not only on the development of the medical profession, but also on life in the German community and on politics. Detailed footnotes make clear references. Includes two introductions: the first is general and the second, by Ricardo Pou Ferrari, details Brendel's role in the development of medicine in Uruguay. [JH]

3196 Marenales Rossi, Martha. La aventura vasca: destino—Montevideo. Traducción, procesamiento y corrección de Ana Guarnerio. Montevideo: Editorial Gamacor Producciones, 1991. 335 p.: appendices, bibl., ill. (some col.), maps.

Impressive study relates migration of French and Spanish Basques to Uruguay and their successful adaptation to their adopted country. Based on statistics collected in France, Spain, and Uruguay. Annexes contain names of many immigrants, their point of origin, and their occupations for the years 1840–72. [JTC]

3197 Mariluz Urquijo, José María. Notas sobre la imprenta oriental de los Ayllones. (*Invest. Ens.*, 42, enero/dic. 1992, p. 49–56)

Short biographies of two Bolivian typographers who established a short-lived press in Montevideo, 1821–27. [JTC]

3198 Méndez Vives, Enrique. La tiza y el sable: vida cotidiana en el Uruguay de Varela y Latorre. Montevideo: Editorial Fin de Siglo, 1993. 165 p.: bibl., ill. (Col. Raíces)

Presents a picture of daily life in Montevideo based on news items that appeared in the press between 1876–80. [JTC]

3199 Nahum, Benjamín *et al.* Crisis política y recuperación económica, 1930–1958. Montevideo: Ediciones de la Banda Oriental, 1987. 164 p.: bibl. (Historia uruguaya; 7)

Written as a text for advanced high school students, presents a straightforward and well-done examination of the period 1930–58. Concentrates on politics and the economy, providing much detail. [JH]

3200 Nahum, Benjamín *et al.* El fin del Uruguay liberal: 1959–1973. Montevideo: Ediciones de la Banda Oriental, 1990. 184 p.: bibl., ill. (Historia uruguaya; 8)

Relates appearance of urban guerrillas and authoritarian State with military support, results of the economic crisis of the 1950s. [JTC]

3201 Narancio, Edmundo M. La independencia de Uruguay. Madrid: Editorial MAPFRE, 1992. 415 p.: bibl., ill., index, maps. (Col. Independencia de Iberoamérica; 4. Col. MAPFRE 1492)

Well-written work summarizes current scholarship pertaining to early struggle to create an independent Uruguay. A collection of documents (p. 341–378), brief biographies of important personages of the period, and a bibliography filled with useful notes add to value of the volume. [JTC]

3202 O'Neill Cuesta, Fernando. Anarquistas de acción en Montevideo, 1927–1937. Montevideo: Editorial Recortes, 1993. 403 p.: bibl., col. ill.

Work combines memoir with historical research. Looks at anarchists who took direct action in Montevideo between 1927–37. Author became an anarchist in prison where he met many of those who appear in his book. Author is sympathetic to, but at times critical of, these activists. [JH]

3203 Padrón Favre, Oscar. Historia de Durazno. Montevideo?: Intendencia Municipal de Durazno, 1992. 464 p.: bibl., ill. (some col.), maps.

Initial institutional, military, and social history of a politically important town and *departamento* is well documented. [JTC]

3204 Petit Muñoz, Eugenio. Artigas: federalismo y soberanía. Montevideo: Univ. de la República, Facultad de Humanidades y Ciencias, Depto. de Publicaciones, 1988. 117 p.: bibl.

In this collection of previously published articles (many of them shortened for this volume), author maintains that Artigas believed that a confederation of the provinces in the Río de la Plata would precede formation of a federal state. [JTC]

3205 Pivel Devoto, Juan E.; Guillermo Stewart Vargas; and Felipe Ferreiro. Oribe: las raíces de lo blanco. Montevideo?: Secretaría de Asuntos Sociales, Partido Nacional; Ediciones de la Banda Oriental, 1987. 90 p.

Three historians describe the personality of Oribe. [JTC]

3206 Puiggrós, Ernesto; María del Carmen Medina Pintado; and Uruguay R. Vega Castillos. La inmigración española en el Uruguay: catalanes, gallegos y vascos. México: Organización de los Estados Americanos, Instituto Panamericano de Geografía e Historia, 1991. 129 p.: bibl. (Pub.; 455. Serie Inmigración; 7)

Five essays discuss Spanish immigration to Uruguay from independence to 1940. The first examines general flow of immigrants to Uruguay; second provides introductory material on Spanish immigration; and last three look at Catalans, Galicians, and Basques with most emphasis on important figures from these communities and the founding of institutions. [JH]

3207 Ribeiro, Ana. Historia e historiadores nacionales, 1940–1990: del ensayo sociológico a la historia de las mentalidades. Montevideo: Ediciones de la Plaza, 1991. 83 p.: bibl.

In a prize-winning essay from a contest held by the Academia Nacional de Letras, author presents a dispassionate examination of the tendencies and trends in the writing of Uruguayan history over last half century. [JH]

Riekenberg, Michael. Nationbildung, sozialer Wandel und Geschichtsbewusstsein am Río de la Plata, 1810–1916. See item **3111.**

3208 Rilla, José Pedro. La mala cara del reformismo: impucstos, estado y política en el Uruguay, 1903–1916. Montevideo: Arca, 1992. 279 p.: bibl., ill.

In a study of the tax reform policies of José Batlle y Ordóñez, author carefully examines existing tax policies and the goals and motives of the reformers. Also looks at the economic and philosophical underpinnings of resistance to change. An intriguing combination of economic, political, and intellectual history. [JH]

3209 Rodríguez, Ana María. América Latina entre dos imperialismos: la prensa británica de Montevideo frente a la penetración

norteamericana, 1889–1899. Montevideo: Univ. de la República, Facultad de Humanidades y Ciencias, Depto. de Publicaciones, 1988. 175 p.: bibl.

A review of the British press in Montevideo suggests that the British did not fear economic competition with the US but rather wanted the US to intervene in the Río de la Plata in the interest of stability and peace. [JTC]

3210 Rodríguez Díaz, Universindo. Los sectores populares en el Uruguay del novecientos. v. 1, 1907–1911. Montevideo: Editorial Compañero, 1989- . 1 v.: bibl., ill.

Examination of the popular classes in 1910–11 is based on a detailed use of the press, both working class and national. 1911 saw Uruguay's first general strike. Study examines efforts to organize against the high cost of living, especially housing, and conditions within a number of industries. Surveys conditions of unions and the strikes which took place. Also looks at the organization of women. [JH]

3211 Rodríguez Villamil, Silvia. Mujeres uruguayas a fines del siglo XIX: ¿cómo hacer su historia? (*Bol. Am.*, 33:42/43, 1992/93, p. 71–85, bibl.)

Presents excellent introduction to history of women as a specialty. Includes brief commentaries on current Uruguayan works and research on women, and calls attention to areas deserving investigation. [JTC]

3212 Sapriza, Graciela. Los caminos de una ilusión: 1913, huelga de mujeres en Juan Lacaze. Montevideo: Editorial Fin de Siglo, 1993. 131 p.: bibl., ill. (Col. Raíces)

Presents portrait of a predominantly female textile workers' strike in Puerto Sauce. Gives much emphasis to a picture of the town. Draws on periodicals, archives, and memories of descendents. Helps move labor history's focus away from Montevideo. [JH]

3213 Seminario Mujeres e Historia en el Uruguay, *Montevideo, 1991*. Actas. Coordinación de Silvia Rodríguez Villamil. Montevideo: Grecmu; LOGOS; FESUR, 1992. 264 p.: bibl.

Contains nine papers delivered at a 1991 conference, with accompanying comments. The most valuable deal with Uruguay, and include a study of the historiography of women and an analysis of primary and secondary school texts and their visions of women. [JH]

3214 **Soler, Leticia.** La historiografía uruguaya contemporánea: aproximación a su estudio. Montevideo: Ediciones de la Banda Oriental, 1993. 98 p.: bibl. (Temas universitarios; 11)

Attempts to present a balanced examination of recent developments in the writing of Uruguayan history, with particular attention to the Marxist and "Nueva Historia" schools. [JH]

3215 **Torres Wilson, José de.** ¿Quiénes escribieron nuestra historia?: 1940–1990. Montevideo?: Ediciones de la Planta, 1992. 158 p.: bibl.

Author, who is both a Nacionalista activist and a professional historian, examines trends in Uruguayan historiography over a 50-year period, especially the movement away from classical styles and themes to the so-called new history. Carefully ties authors to their politics. Discussion of works he believes important is arranged by publication date. [JH]

3216 **Trías, Vivián.** Imperialismo en el Uruguay. Prólogo de Guillermo Chifflet. Montevideo: Cámara de Representantes, República Oriental del Uruguay, 1991. 197 p.: bibl., ill. (Selección de obrás de Vivián Trías. Serie Patria chica; 10)

Collection of essays by a leading Uruguayan educator and congressman who applies the dependency theory in his discussion of the past and future of his country. [JTC]

Vázquez Franco, Guillermo and **Juan Manuel Casal.** Historia política y social de Iberoamérica: investigaciones y ensayos. See item **1044.**

3217 **Vázquez Franco, Guillermo.** La historia y sus mitos: a propósito de un libro de Real de Azúa, comentarios, digresiones, reflexiones. Montevideo: Cal y Canto; Distribuye Gussi, 1994. 193 p.: bibl.

In thoughtful essays, author questions the "official" history and idealization of Artigas, the existence of Uruguay as an independent state, and the concept of federation. He is follower of Real de Azúa. [JTC]

BRAZIL

DAIN BORGES, *Associate Professor of History, University of California, San Diego*
JOAN E. MEZNAR, *Associate Professor of History, Westmont College*

BRAZILIAN GRADUATE PROGRAMS IN HISTORY have boomed since their expansion in the late 1970s. As of 1989, they were granting about one hundred master's and twenty doctoral degrees per year. During the 1980s, though many master's theses were published in book form, book publishing did not increase apace with thesis research (for discussion of these trends, see Fico and Polito, item **3301**). In the last three or four years, Brazilian historians have complained of a frustrating backlog of unpublished dissertation research and a decrease in book publication in Brazil, a trend that is not limited to the discipline of history (see the "Editor's Note" to *HLAS 54*, p. xxi, regarding this reduction in Brazil's monographic publishing).

Almost certainly, therefore, the explosion of historical research will be more apparent in the form of published journal articles, rather than monographs. Unfortunately, Brazilian scholarly journals have been historically short-lived and poorly indexed. Furthermore, few libraries in the US have collected them consistently. A selective guide such as the *Handbook*, which reviews not only journal articles, but also monographs, conference papers, and book chapters, is necessarily limited by space and editorial considerations and therefore can identify only a portion of contemporary research. Until indexing of Brazilian periodicals improves, it will be increasingly difficult to canvass all new contributions on a given topic. To help ensure a more complete review of recent literature, scholars planning advanced research (particularly on São Paulo, Rio de Janeiro, or Minas Gerais) should consult indexes to theses, such as those published periodically by the Univ. de São Paulo. These indexes are increasingly available on-line through Brazilian library catalogs. (UT-LANIC maintains a list of web links to various Latin American libraries at http://info.lanic.utexas.edu/la/region/library/).

New bibliographical tools include Camargo on the first 19th-century press (item **3235**), a catalog of the Casa de Cultura Josué Montello library on Maranhão (item **3220**), Massi and Pontes on Brazilianists (item **3331**), guides to the archives of Prudente de Moraes and Rodrigues Alves at the Instituto Histórico e Geográfico Brasileiro (item **3313**), and Lewin on the archives of Epitácio Pessoa (item **3323**).

For the early colonial period, Miceli has written an excellent social history of the world of European sailors and the voyages of discovery (item **3251**). Ribeiro's useful edited volume of primary materials documenting the expansion of the Portuguese in Brazil is available in Spanish as well as Portuguese (items **3243** and **3259**). The works of Weckmann, Giucci, Bosi, and Araújo address the emergence of Brazilian culture in the 16th century (items **3269, 3244, 3233,** and **3227**).

Interest in the role of indigenous peoples continues to grow. Justo Guedes and Monteiro discuss the importance of indigenous labor in southern Brazil (items **3245** and **3252**), while Barickman examines the indigenous presence in coastal Bahia (item **3232**), and Cambraia and Mendes focus on Minas Gerais (item **3236**). Maybury-Lewis (item **3222**) analyzes policy toward indigenous peoples in broad regional and historical contexts. Hoornaert's edited volume deals with relations between Christian missionaries and indigenous peoples in the Amazon region (item **3221**).

Work on African slavery also continues apace. Volpato's excellent work on Mato Grosso (item **3268**), Salles' on Goiás (item **3261**), and Cabral's on Maranhão (item **3234**) provide evidence as to the continued importance of regional studies. Barickman's article on slave provision grounds in 19th-century Bahia is an important contribution, situating Brazilian rural slavery in a comparative context (item **3231**).

In the field of Afro-Brazilian history, Silva's biography of Dom Obá II d'Africa and Verger's compilation of life stories offer fascinating insights into slavery and urban life in the 19th century (items **3360** and **3368**). Hanchard and Nascimento provide important views of race and politics in the 20th century (items **3310** and **3223**).

Much interesting research continues to be done on women and families. Comparisons between slaves and free families (items **3250, 3317, 3315,** and **3346**), the role of godparenthood (items **3342** and **3317**), analyses of prostitution (items **3362** and **3365**), and explorations into the meanings of marriage in patriarchal society (items **3241, 3247, 3357, 3262,** and **3230**) provide some of the important themes in the ongoing debates. Most of the work concentrates on the southeast region of the country during the colonial period and the 19th century. One hopes that new research will bring the discussion into the 20th century and broaden the geographical perspective.

For the national period, the largest category of titles published is that of local municipal histories. The fission of municipalities in southern states (101 new municipalities were created in Rio Grande do Sul between 1980–90), as well as the centenaries of the foundation of many immigrant *colônias*, provides occasion for a bumper crop of local histories. Most of these are sponsored by small-town mayors, written by amateur antiquarians, and equipped with a minimal scholarly apparatus.

While they have not been annotated here, such local histories have potential as sources in future research.

Historiography of the 19th century shows no strong focus outside of the studies of slavery discussed above. Treatments of politics and elite ideology include Cavaliero's popular narrative of independence in English (item **3239**), Besouchet on Pedro II (item **3278**), and Ridings on commercial associations (item **1026**). Dissertation research in progress in Brazil and the US should soon yield much-needed studies of county-level politics under the Empire; in this vein, Souza provides an idiosyncratic, creative comparison of identity in Serro and Diamantina (item **3366**). A thematic issue of the *Luso-Brazilian Review* illuminates the regional context of the Canudos rebellion of 1897 (item **3374**).

Historiography of the Republic continues to follow familiar themes in social history. There are many studies of immigration: Lesser on Jews and Lebanese (item **3318**), Grun on Armenians (item **3308**), Monteiro on policies in Minas (item **3337**), and Brito (item **3287**) and Richter (item **3353**) on Germans. The works by Lindsay on return migration to Lagos (item **3325**), Dreher on immigration and the Church (item **3312**), and Dawsey on Confederates (item **3291**) bridge the 19th and 20th centuries. Furthermore, the studies of immigrants cited here are only a fraction of a literature composed primarily of amateur genealogical and local studies. There is a new interest in the culture of cities in the 20th century: Araújo discusses family and the rise of the pursuit of "pleasure" in Rio de Janeiro (item **3275**); Pesavento studies social issues in Porto Alegre (item **3349**); and Pimentel examines urban housing and the failure of the modernist urban utopia (item **3350**). The bold interpretation of social modernity and literary modernism in São Paulo in the 1920s by Sevcenko is an indispensable analysis of urban mentalities (item **3359**).

Works on the literary modernism of the 1920s, as exemplified by Gomes (item **3306**), the volume on Buarque de Holanda (item **3358**), and essays in the special issue of *Luso-Brazilian Review* dedicated to Richard Morse (item **3293**), demonstrate the flourishing of intellectual and cultural history. New biographies and interpretations of Gilberto Freyre by Chacon (item **3289**), Needell (item **3341**), and Morse (item **3293**) add to debates discussed in the review essay by Borges (item **3284**). The *Luso-Brazilian Review's* special issue on images of women discusses film and radio (item **3290**). Diverse topics on intellectual relations between France and Brazil are also explored (item **3311**). Needell (item **3340**), Skidmore (item **3364**), and Borges (item **3285**) discuss dimensions of racial ideology.

Political and labor history dominate the post-1920 historiography. Political histories of *coronelismo* have dwindled, but the debate over "who ruled" during the Republic continues, with contributions by Topik (item **3367**) and Perissinotto (item **3347**). Interpretations of *tenentismo* and the 1920s abound; see Pacheco Borges (item **3286**), Keith (item **3314**), Pesavento (item **3348**), Diacon (item **3296**) and Prestes (item **3352**), as well as Lira on the bandit Lampião (item **3327**). Whether government in the 1930s was totalitarian preoccupies Cancelli in his work on the police (item **3288**), as well as the authors of the historiographical essays in Silva (item **3300**). Lesser's excellent case study of Jewish immigration provides a more nuanced view of the words and deeds of the Estado Novo government (item **3320**). The Communist movement continues to magnetize attention and polemics. Malta creates a heroic fiction from documents of the Communist rebellion of 1935 (item **3330**), while Waack demolishes its icons (item **3371**); Bethell discusses 1947 (item **3279**), and Mir examines the 1960s guerrillas (item **3333**). Post-1945 studies emphasize the political and labor legacy of Getúlio Vargas, demonstrated by a special issue of the *Luso-Brazilian Review* (item **3304**), Bodea on parties in Rio Grande do Sul populism (item

3282), Wolfe on labor (item **3373**), and, notably, Lobo's important compilation of research and statistics on Rio's union politics (item **3355**). Brazilian historians are debating the utility of oral history, as evidenced in Levine and Meihy's biography of Carolina Maria de Jesus (item **3322**) and interviews compiled by Ferreira (item **3298**) and Araújo, Soares, and Castro (item **3370**) for the Fundação Getúlio Vargas/CPDOC oral history project.

Aside from the topical treatment of a variety of issues in Ridings' book on 19th-century commercial associations (item **3354**), business and economic history appears primarily in articles. Barham and Coomes provide polemical reevaluations of the developmental impact of the Amazon rubber boom (items **3276** and **3292**). Blasenheim discusses 19th-century railroads in Minas (item **3281**), and Boone studies streetcar contracts in Rio (item **3283**). Versiani compares the labor supply in various cities and regions during the period of early industrialization (item **3369**). Haber analyzes the textile sector during the Depression in an article with broad implications (item **3309**), offering an interesting counterpoint to Topik (item **3367**) and Ridings on lobbying the State (item **3354**).

GENERAL

3218   Arquivo Público do Estado da Bahia (Brazil). Guia de fontes para a história da escravidão negra na Bahia. Salvador, Brazil: Arquivo Público do Estado da Bahia, 1988. 218 p.: bibl. (Publicações APEB. Série Ordens régias; 1)

Contains index of *ordens régias* dating from 1648–1822 related to African slavery. Also includes extensive bibliography of sources on slavery found in public libraries and private archives in Salvador.

3219   Arquivo Público Estadual (Vitória, Brazil). Fontes para a história da escravidão negra no Espírito Santo. Vitória, Brazil: APE, 1988. 130 p. (Col. Memória capixaba. Série Instrumentos de pesquisa; 2)

Guide to materials related to slavery was published as part of centennial commemoration of abolition in 1988. Includes manuscript and published resources housed in the Arquivo Público Estadual of Espírito Santo and its library, as well as materials from notarial and church archives in 18 municipalities.

Carelli, Mario. Cultures croisées: histoire des échanges culturels entre la France et le Brésil, de la découverte aux temps modernes. See *HLAS 55:5153.*

3220   Casa de Cultura Josué Montello (São Luís, Brazil). Fontes de pesquisa para a história do Maranhão. São Luís, Brazil: Casa de Cultura Josué Montello, 1992. 282 p.: indexes. (Catálogos / Casa de Cultura Josué Montello; 3)

Annotated catalog to the Casa de Cultura's holdings on history of Maranhão includes 730 entries.

3221   História da Igreja na Amazônia. Coordenação de Eduardo Hoornaert. Petrópolis, Brazil: Vozes, 1992. 416 p.: bibl., ill., maps. (Publicações CID. História; 12)

Covering period from early European contact to 20th century, volume includes chapters by a variety of scholars who are largely critical of Catholic and Protestant missionary work in the Amazon, and sensitive to the perspective of indigenous peoples.

3222   Maybury-Lewis, David. Una crónica amarga: el Brasil y los indios. (*in* De palabra y obra en el Nuevo Mundo. v. 2, Encuentros interétnicos. Edición de Miguel León-Portilla *et al.* Madrid: Siglo Veintiuno Editores, 1992, p. 97–120)

Broad historical overview of political and social policy toward indigenous peoples argues that a consistent indigenous policy was never formulated primarily because Brazilian officials believed that indigenous peoples would disappear as "civilization" spread and miscegenation increased.

3223   Nascimento, Abdias do and **Elisa Larkin Nascimento.** Africans in Brazil: a Pan-African perspective. Trenton, N.J.: Africa World Press, 1992. 218 p.: bibl., index.

Includes autobiographical essay as well as text of several presentations at African world events from 1987–91. Abdias do Nascimento, an Afro-Brazilian playwright and artist, was elected to the Brazilian Congress in

1983 and to the Senate in 1990. Good bibliographic essay.

3224 Porto, Carlos Eugênio. Roteiro do Piauí. 2a. ed., atualizada. Teresina, Brazil: Companhia Editora do Piauí, 1994? 188 p.: bibl., ill., maps.

History of Piauí written by a medical doctor covers settlement of the region, its place in the independence movement, and its economic base of livestock and agricultural production. Also discusses impact of disease on the region in 19th and 20th centuries.

3225 Stubbe, Hannes. Über die Kindheit der afrobrasilianischen Sklavem. (in Amerikaner wider Willen: Beiträge zur Sklaverei in Lateinamerika und ihren Folgen. Frankfurt: Vervuert Verlag, 1994, p. 203–230, tables)

Study is based almost exclusively on Brazilian sources. Includes medical and missionary reports and psychological studies, and raises issue of early brutalization of Brazilian-born slaves. While slave mothers were rented out or sold as wetnurses, their infants were separated and de-socialized. Stubbe calls for further studies of the psychological and social development of slaves. [C.K. Converse]

COLONIAL

3226 Alexandre, Valentim. Os sentidos do Império: questão nacional e questão colonial na crise do Antigo Regime português. Porto, Portugal: Edições Afrontamento, 1993. 837 p.: bibl. (Biblioteca das ciências do homem; 5)

Political and diplomatic history of collapse of Luso-Brazilian system covers period from 1796–1831. Argues that opposition to colonial rule was tied to politics and ideology, as well as to economics.

3227 Araújo, Emanuel O. O teatro dos vícios: transgressão e transigência na sociedade urbana colonial. Rio de Janeiro: J. Olympio Editora, 1993. 362 p.: bibl.

History of public life in Brazilian cities concludes that distance from the Portuguese king and the royal court contributed to widespread corruption in Brazilian society.

3228 Ávila, Cristina and **Maria do Carmo Andrade Gomes.** O negro no barroco mineiro: o caso da Igreja do Rosário de Ouro Preto. (Rev. Dep. Hist./Belo Horizonte, 6, junho 1988, p. 69–76, bibl.)

Addresses paradoxes of Catholicism of slave population, arguing that, on the one hand, slaves used the religion to continue African practices and that syncretism was more pronounced than conversion. On the other hand, work demonstrates that slaves also were rooted in a colonial society and produced artwork that was overwhelmingly European in style and form.

3229 Azeredo Coutinho, José Joaquim da Cunha de. Ensaio econômico sobre o comércio de Portugal e suas colônias. Introdução e direção de edição de Jorge Miguel Pedreira. Lisboa: Banco de Portugal, 1992. 141 p.: bibl., indexes. (Col. de obras clássicas do pensamento econômico português; 3)

Reprint of four works published between 1791 and 1804.

3230 Bacellar, Carlos de Almeida Prado. Família, herança e poder em São Paulo, 1765–1855. São Paulo: Centro de Estudos de Demografia Histórica da América Latina, Univ. de São Paulo, Faculdade de Filosofia, Letras e Ciências Humanas, 1991. 99 p.: bibl. (Estudos CEDHAL; 7)

Revised M.A. thesis examines transition from subsistence agriculture to sugar mills and then to coffee plantations in Itú, Jundiaí, and Moji Mirim. Argues that family wealth provided means for economic expansion; thus, capital generated by sugar production funded the successful transition to coffee.

3231 Barickman, B.J. "A bit of land, which they call *roça*:" slave provision grounds in the Bahian Recôncavo, 1780–1860. (HAHR, 74:4, Nov. 1994, p. 649–687, table)

Excellent article demonstrates that although Bahian slaves had access to provision grounds, they did not become important suppliers of food in the Recôncavo. Free farmers, often using slave labor themselves, controlled those markets. *Roças* nonetheless were important: by allowing slaves a certain amount of autonomy, they changed the meaning of slavery.

3232 Barickman, B.J. "Tame Indians," "wild heathens," and settlers in southern Bahia in the late eighteenth and early nineteenth centuries. (Americas/Francisc., 51:3, Jan. 1995, p. 325–368)

Arguing that the presence of indigenous peoples, and Portuguese attempts to deal with them, shaped development of Porto Seguro in early-19th century, author marshalls surprising evidence that indigenous peoples continued to influence settlement along the Brazilian coast as late as the early Empire.

3233 Bosi, Alfredo. Dialética da colonização. São Paulo: Companhia das Letras, 1992. 404 p.: bibl., ill.

Collection of essays on creation of a Brazilian colonial culture includes chapters on ethnic relations, slavery, religion, and trade.

3234 Cabral, Maria do Socorro Coelho. Caminhos do gado: conquista e ocupação do sul do Maranhão. São Luís, Brazil: Edições SECMA, 1992. 265 p.: bibl., maps.

Pioneering political, social, and economic study focuses on the *sertão* of Bom Pastos in southern Maranhão. Describes how, in distinct contrast to plantations around São Luís, the preponderance of cattle ranches in the south created a patriarchal society in which local power fell to large landowners.

3235 Camargo, Ana Maria de Almeida and **Rubens Borba de Moraes.** Bibliografia da Impressão Régia do Rio de Janeiro, 1808–1822. São Paulo: Edusp; Livraria Kosmos Editora, 1993. 2 v.: ill., index.

Well-done update of Valle Cabral bibliography of works from first printing press in Brazil includes descriptions and annotations.

3236 Cambraia, Ricardo de Bastos and **Fábio Faria Mendes.** A colonização dos sertões do leste mineiro: políticas de ocupação territorial num regime escravista, 1780–1836. (*Rev. Dep. Hist./Belo Horizonte*, 6, junho 1988, p. 129–136)

Authors examine attempts to colonize *sertões* of eastern Minas Gerais. The region became particularly attractive after the Portuguese court arrived in Rio de Janeiro in 1808; but as the frontier penetrated the interior of Minas, conflicts between indigenous peoples and new settlers increased.

3237 Campos, Adalgisa Arantes. Notas sobre os rituais de morte na sociedade escravista. (*Rev. Dep. Hist./Belo Horizonte*, 6, junho 1988, p. 109–122, ill.)

Examines survival of African practices in burial rites of colonial Brazil.

3238 Carvalho, Flávio Mendes. Raízes judaicas no Brasil: o arquivo secreto da Inquisição. São Paulo: Editora Nova Arcadia, 1992. 416 p.: bibl., ill.

List of names of condemned Portuguese and Brazilian Jews, compiled alphabetically by surname, is transcribed from Lisbon Inquisition lists across centuries. Includes data such as age and profession, but lack of cross-indexing makes it more a memorial than a useful scholarly tool.

3239 Cavaliero, Roderick. The independence of Brazil. London: I.B. Tauris for British Academic Press; New York: St. Martin's Press, 1993. 231 p.: bibl., ill., index, map.

Lively narrative of politics, 1807–31, explains Brazilian independence largely in terms of British and Portuguese interests, policies, and strategies. Rich in anecdotal lore, but slights social issues and ignores pre-1807 history. Based on travelers' accounts and secondary literature as of 1975. For a more current synthesis see *HLAS 52:2974.*

3240 Costa, Iraci del Nero da. Arraia-miúda: um estudo sobre os não-proprietários de escravos no Brasil. São Paulo: Univ. de São Paulo, Faculdade de Economia e Administração, Depto. de Economia, 1990. 172 leaves: bibl., maps.

Examines role of free poor (defined as those who did not own slaves) in 18th- and 19th-century Brazil, concluding that existing historiography does not adequately acknowledge significance of this group. Uses statistical evidence to demonstrate that non-slaveholders participated in all areas of the Brazilian economy.

3241 Del Priore, Mary. Ao sul do corpo: condição feminina, maternidades e mentalidades no Brasil Colônia. Brasília: Edunb; Rio de Janeiro: J. Olympio Editora, 1993. 358 p.: bibl., ill.

Study of women in colonial Brazil illustrates how women gained power from marriage and motherhood, thus subverting attempts to domesticate them.

3242 Ferlini, Vera Lucia Amaral. Estrutura agrária e relações de poder em sociedades escravistas: perspectivas de pesquisas de critérios de organização empresarial e de mentalidade econômicas na período colonial. (*Rev. Bras. Hist.*, 11:22, março/agôsto 1991, p. 35–47)

Argues that economic data must be addressed with as much care as any other source, since the way individuals record their economic information is as ideologically laden as the way they describe any other aspect of their lives.

3243 La fundación de Brasil: testimonios 1500–1700. Prólogo de Darcy Ribeiro. Selección de textos de Darcy Ribeiro y Carlos de Araújo Moreira Neto. Notas introductorias a los textos-testimonio de Carlos de Araújo Moreira Neto. Cuadro sinóptico de Gisele Jacon de A. Moreira. Caracas: Biblioteca Ayacucho, 1992. 603 p.: index. (Biblioteca Ayacucho; 185)

A collection of primary material (including Inquisition documents, papal bulls, travelers' observations, and letters) is brought together to illustrate creation of colonial Brazil. Emphasizes internal contradictions of emerging Brazilian society.

3244 Giucci, Guillermo. Sem fé, lei ou rei: Brasil, 1500–1532. Tradução de Carlos Nougué. Rio de Janeiro: Rocco, 1993. 239 p.: bibl., index.

Discusses influence of European Renaissance culture on Portuguese attempts to understand what they found in Brazil.

3245 Guedes, Max Justo. As bandeiras ignoram o Tratado de Tordesilhas e ampliam o espaço geográfico brasileiro. (*Nação Def.*, 19:70, abril/junho 1994, p. 63–86, maps, tables)

Argues that demand for Indian slaves to work in expanding sugar industry spurred *bandeirante* attacks against Jesuit mission Indians in Spanish territory, thus pushing Brazilian territorial limits well beyond the Tordesillas line.

3246 Høiris, Ole. Sandfærdig beretning om og beskrivelse af et vildt, nøgent, grusomt, kannibalistisk folks land, beliggende i den nye verden, Amerika, 1557 [A true report and description of a wild, barren, gruesome, cannibalistic peoples' country located in the New World, America, 1557.] Højbjerg, Denmark: Forlaget Intervention Press, 1992. 127 p.: bibl.

Hans Stadens' 1557 account concerning his stay in Brazil and the consequences of colonization for the indigenous peoples is translated from German into Danish. Useful introduction provides excellent historical

background on European interests in 16th-century Brazil. [I. Schjellerup]

3247 Lewkowicz, Ida. As mulheres mineiras e o casamento: estratégias individuais e familiares nos séculos XVIII e XIX. (*História/ São Paulo*, 12, 1993, p. 13–28, bibl.)

Interesting analysis of marriages, especially those of 18th century, finds that formal unions were important even among the poor. Concludes that personal interest converged with State and religious concerns to promote an orderly, yet ultimately misogynistic, society.

3248 Lipiner, Elias. Izaque de Castro: o mancebo que veio preso do Brasil. Recife, Brazil: Fundação Joaquim Nabuco, Editora Massangana, 1992. 321 p.: bibl., ill., index. (Série Descobrimentos; 1)

Based on Inquisition records, this story of a young Jewish man weaves together connections between Portugal, Holland, and Brazil in 17th century.

3249 Medeiros, Maria do Céu. Igreja e dominação no Brasil escravista: o caso dos oratorianos de Pernambuco, 1659–1830. João Pessoa, Brazil: CCHLA; Idéia, 1993. 193 p.: bibl., ill., map.

A revised M.A. thesis, this study of Oratorian missionaries in Pernambuco analyzes cooperation between Church and State and its tragic consequences for indigenous peoples and African slaves. Links to the State ultimately undermined the order itself: by siding with the Portuguese in the Guerra dos Mascates, Oratorians made themselves unwelcome in Brazil after independence.

3250 Metcalf, Alida C. A família escrava no Brasil colonial: um estudo de caso em São Paulo. (*in* Congresso sobre a História da População da América Latina, *1st, Ouro Preto, Brazil, 1989*. Actas. São Paulo: Fundação SEADE, 1990, p. 205–212, bibl., graph, tables)

Focusing on Santana de Parnaíba, author finds much common ground between slave and free families. For example, slaves often did marry formally; slave women had fertility rates comparable to those of free women; and nuclear families (of both slave and free) were far more common than matrifocal families or single living. Nonetheless, Metcalf concludes that the lot of slave families was precarious, especially if the owner died and the family was broken up in the estate settlement.

3251 Miceli, Paulo Celso. O ponto onde estamos: viagens e viajantes na história da expansão e da conquista; Portugal, séculos XV e XVI. São Paulo: Scritta, 1994. 237 p.: bibl.

Presents absorbing social history of sailors and life aboard ship in 15th and 16th centuries. Beginning with description of Lisbon (the port, the poor, epidemics, religion), story proceeds to the ship itself, the hierarchy aboard ship, and day-to-day life of the sailors. Provides a good sense of uncertainties and anxieties sailors faced during their time at sea.

3252 Monteiro, John Manuel. São Paulo en la economía colonial: nuevas perspectivas sobre viejas cuestiones. (*in* Colección nuestra patria es América: historia económica de América Latina. Edición de Jorge Nuñez Sánchez. Quito: Editora Nacional, 1992, v. 7, p. 81–110, tables)

As he has done in other work, Monteiro demonstrates that indigenous slave labor was an essential component of commercial agriculture in colonial São Paulo. Indigenous peoples produced foodstuffs for the internal market, and inexpensively transported products to the coast. The decline in indigenous slavery, therefore, undermined commercial agriculture in São Paulo.

3253 Nova história da expansão portuguesa. v. 6, O império luso-brasileiro, 1500–1620. Coordenção de Harold Johnson e Maria Beatriz Nizza da Silva. Direção de Joel Serrão e Antônio Henrique R. de Oliveira Marques. Lisboa: Editorial Estampa, 1986 -. 1 v.

Political, social, and economic history of the Portuguese Empire covers period from discovery of Brazil through the union with Spain.

3254 Novinsky, Anita. La Inquisición y la burguesía brasileña, siglo XVIII. (*CHELA,* 4, 1989, p. 65–75, tables)

Author claims that 18th-century gold rush increased the Catholic Church's fear of New Christians, considered potential threats to the power of the Church in the colony. Yet Inquisition attacks against New Christians in early-18th century, the author concludes, destroyed an emerging bourgeoisie and relegated Brazil to backwardness.

3255 Ramos, Donald. From Minho to Minas: the Portuguese roots of the *mineiro* family. (*HAHR,* 73:4, Nov. 1993, p. 639–662, tables)

Author finds significant continuities of experience among men from northern Portugal who emigrated to Brazil.

3256 Ramos, Donald. A mulher e a família em Vila Rica do Ouro Preto: 1754–1838. (*in* Congresso sobre a História da População da América Latina, 1st, Ouro Preto, Brazil, 1989. Actas. São Paulo: Fundação SEADE, 1990, p. 154–163, bibl., tables)

Argues that economic conditions contributed to large number of single women heads of household in Vila Rica.

3257 Raposo, Luciano. O avêsso da memória: cotidiano e trabalho da mulher em Minas Gerais no século XVIII. Prefácio de Laura de Mello e Souza. Brasília: Edunb; Rio de Janeiro: J. Olympio Editora, 1993. 249 p.: bibl., ill., maps.

Important work on women in colonial Minas Gerais. The wealth from the mines, bringing as it did riches for a few and poverty and misery for many, provides context for examining varied roles of women. Focuses on poor women and their place in the family, in religion, and in commerce.

3258 Reis, Liana Maria. Mulheres de ouro: as negras de tabuleiro nas Minas Gerais do século XVIII. (*Rev. Dep. Hist./Belo Horizonte,* 8, jan. 1989, p. 72–85, bibl.)

Female slaves working as vendors illuminate urban slavery in 18th-century Minas Gerais. Concludes that practice of allowing slaves in urban settings to work for earnings did not undermine, but rather reinforced, the existing slave system.

3259 Ribeiro, Darcy and Carlos de Araújo Moreira Neto. A fundação do Brasil: testemunhos, 1500–1700. Petrópolis, Brazil: Vozes, 1992. 447 p.: bibl., ill., index, map.

Collection of primary documents addresses first 200 years of Portuguese expansion in Brazil. Selection includes papal documents, travelers' descriptions, reports from government officials, and Jesuit accounts.

3260 Saldanha, Antônio Vasconcelos de. As capitanias e o regime senhorial na expansão ultramarina portuguesa. Prefácio de Frédéric Mauro. Funchal, Portugal: Secretaria

Regional do Turismo, Cultura e Emigração; Centro de Estudos de História do Atlântico, 1992. 343 p.: bibl. (Col. Memórias; 7)

Originally a thesis completed at the Faculdade de Direito of the Univ. de Lisboa, this history of Portuguese law discusses the common legal basis for land ownership in Brazil, the Atlantic islands, and West Africa.

3261 Salles, Gilka Vasconcelos Ferreira de. Economia e escravidão na Capitania de Goiás. Goiânia, Brazil: CEGRAF, UFG, 1992. 369 p.: bibl., ill., maps. (Col. Documentos goianos; 24. Publicação; 187)

Economic history of colonial Goiás gives particular attention to role of slaves in gold and diamond mining, cattle ranching, manufacturing, and commerce.

3262 Samara, Eni de Mesquita. Patriarcalismo, família e poder na sociedade brasileira, séculos XVI-XIX. (*Rev. Bras. Hist.*, 11:22, março/agôsto 1991, p. 7–33, bibl.)

Using evidence from São Paulo province, author examines changes and continuities in role of the family in colonial and imperial Brazil, arguing that regional and class variations must be taken into account in order to understand family structure in Brazil.

3263 Santos, Corcino Medeiros dos. O Rio de Janeiro e a conjuntura atlântica. Rio de Janeiro: Expressão e Cultura, 1993. 290 p.: bibl., ill.

Highlights importance of Atlantic Ocean in the circulation of goods between Europe, America, Africa, India, and the South Sea Islands; and the place of the port of Rio de Janeiro in this trade system. Concludes that 1808 arrival of the Portuguese court in Rio allowed for Brazil's full participation in the international economy.

3264 Serrão, Joaquim Veríssimo. O tempo dos Filipes em Portugal e no Brasil, 1580–1668: estudos históricos. Lisboa: Edições Colibri, 1994. 343 p.: bibl., maps. (Colibri história; 5)

Collection of 11 essays focuses on politics in Portugal and Brazil under Spanish Hapsburgs. While Spanish rule damaged Portuguese interests in the East (opening the way for British involvement in that region), it did serve to integrate Brazil into the Atlantic world, solidifying Portuguese control in that colony.

3265 Silva, Maria Beatriz Nizza da. O sagrado e o profano nas festas do Brasil colonial. (*Rev. Ciênc. Hist.*, 8, 1993, p. 105–110)

Author claims that festivals in colonial Brazil, while reinforcing hierarchy, also provided space for participation of those at the bottom of the social pyramid, including slaves, women, and gypsies. The meshing of the secular and the religious, she concludes, indicates that colonial Brazil was becoming increasingly European.

3266 Vergolino-Henry, Anaiza and **Arthur Napoleão Figueiredo.** A presença africana na Amazônia colonial: uma notícia histórica. Belém, Brazil: Governo do Estado do Pará, Secretaria de Estado de Cultura, Arquivo Público do Pará; Falangola Editora, 1990. 280 p.: bibl., ill., index, maps. (Documentos históricos; 1)

Examines previously unpublished documents related to Africans, housed in the Arquivo Público do Pará. Covers period 1733–1815, but is especially rich for the Pombaline years (1751–59).

3267 Viotti, Hélio Abranches. O anel e a pedra: dissertações históricas. Belo Horizonte, Brazil: Editora Itatiaia, 1993. 412 p.: bibl. (Col. Reconquista do Brasil; 2a. ser., v. 175)

Collection of previously published essays focuses on role of the Jesuits, especially Father José de Anchieta, in colonial Brazil.

3268 Volpato, Luiza Rios Ricci. Cativos do sertão: vida cotidiana e escravidão em Cuiabá em 1850–1888. São Paulo: Editora Marco Zero; Cuiabá, Brazil?: Editora da Univ. Federal de Mato Grosso, 1993. 251 p.: bibl., ill.

Explores daily life of slaves in 19th-century Mato Grosso. Includes excellent description of town of Cuiabá and of repercussions of the Paraguayan War on everyday life in that remote province.

3269 Weckmann, Luis. La herencia medieval del Brasil. México: Fondo de Cultura Económica, 1993. 400 p.: bibl., ill., index. (Sección de obras de historia)

Explains Portugal's colonial expansion in Brazil as a product of the medieval character, and concludes that this type of colonial experience accounts for survival of Portuguese feudalism at all levels of Brazilian culture.

NATIONAL

3270 Almeida, Antônio de. Movimentos sociais e história popular: Santo André nos anos 70 e 80. São Paulo: Editora Marco Zero: Programa Nacional do Centenário da República e Bicentenário da Inconfidência Mineira, MCT/CNPq, 1992. 117 p.: bibl. (Col. Onde está a República. Biblioteca da República)

Short but detailed study focuses on interaction between social movements and public authorities during opening to more competitive politics in an industrial city that is part of São Paulo metropolis. Outlines process of intermittent protests around perennial issues (inflation, day care, floods, buses). Charts fluctuations of institutionalized neighborhood associations between independent protest and passive co-optation. Based on newspaper accounts, fieldwork, and some association documents.

3271 Almeida, Maria Amélia. O ideário feminista na Bahia nos anos 30. (*História/São Paulo*, 12, 1993, p. 63–83, bibl.)

Finds that feminism, as it emerged in Bahia in 1930s, was anchored in values of an educated middle-class. Feminists favored progress, democracy, and peace, with a special emphasis on equal political rights for women. Feminism attracted both support and opposition primarily from the middle class. Concludes that most Bahian women were excluded from the feminist movement.

Amazon: Nihonjin ni yoru 6onen no Ijūshi [Amazon: 60 years of Japanese immigration]. See *HLAS 55:2625.*

3272 Um americano intranqüilo. Praia de Botafogo, Brazil: Editora da Fundação Getulio Vargas, CPDOC, 1992. 77 p.: bibl.

Short collection of essays in honor of Richard Morse includes reminiscences and critiques of Morse's arguments presented in *O espelho de Próspero* (São Paulo: Companhia das Letras, 1988). Essays by Antônio Cândido, Carlos Guilherme Mota, Francisco Falcon, Haroldo de Campos, José Murilo de Carvalho, and Roberto da Matta. See also item **3293.**

3273 Andrews, George Reid. Desigualidad racial en Brasil y en Estados Unidos: un estudio estadístico comparado. (*Desarro. Econ.*, 33:130, julio/sept. 1993, p. 185–216, graphs, tables)

Using evidence from census and demographic records, claims that from 1950–80 racial inequality lessened in the US and increased in Brazil. In US, African-Americans migrated to areas with better economic opportunities and benefited from implementation of affirmative action policies. In Brazil, on the other hand, the economic growth favored the top 20 percent of the population, mainly the white elite.

3274 Anuário do Museu da Inconfidência. No. 9, 1993. Ouro Preto, Brazil: Museu da Inconfidência.

Papers from 1992 conference on Tiradentes and 1789 independence conspiracy are of uneven quality but contain some significant contributions. Diverse topics, but give notable emphasis to cultural history of the movement. Contributions by Kenneth Maxwell, Antônio Cândido, Francisco Iglesias, and others.

3275 Araújo, Rosa Maria Barboza de. A vocação do prazer: a cidade e a família no Rio de Janeiro republicano. Prefácio de Richard Morse. Rio de Janeiro: Rocco, 1993. 406 p.: bibl., ill.

Wide-ranging over myriad topics, work concerns families and urban daily life, from 1890–1920. Founded on contrast between realms of "house" and "street" that has become central in urban sociology of Brazil. Demonstrates that after urban reforms of 1903–06, families of all classes found the "vocation" for public play and leisure that characterizes modern Rio. Based on secondary literature, the press, and a notable collection of private papers from the Lacombe family.

3276 Barham, Bradford L. and Oliver T. Coomes. Reinterpreting the Amazon rubber boom: investment, the State, and Dutch disease. (*LARR*, 29:2, 1994, p. 73–109, bibl., table)

Reanalyzing secondary literature on the rubber boom, argues that the very profitability of rubber boom prevented development in the Amazon by discouraging investment in production of other tradable goods and by effecting a monopoly on State policy support. This created an economy extraordinarily vulnerable to the rubber bust. See also item **3292.**

Barickman, B.J. "A bit of land, which they call *roça*:" slave provision grounds in the Bahian Recôncavo, 1780–1860. See item **3231.**

3277 Belluz, Carlos Alberto Del Bel. Santa Rita do Passa Quatro: imagens da época do café. São Paulo: Azevedo de Paula e Barbuio Empreendimentos S/C; Incorporadora Azevedo de Paula, 1991. 174 p.: bibl., ill., map, photos.

Local history album of a São Paulo municipality during region's coffee boom, 1886–1920s, is distinguished by abundant photographs documenting town and plantations.

Beozzo, José Oscar. Brasil: 500 anos de migrações: povos indígenas, escravos africanos e brasileiros, imigrantes europeus e asiáticos. See *HLAS 55:5147.*

Bergmann, Günther J. Auslandsdeutsche in Paraguay, Brasilien, Argentinien. See item **2962.**

3278 Besouchet, Lídia. Pedro II e o século XIX. 2a. ed. rev. e ampliada. Rio de Janeiro: Editora Nova Fronteira, 1993. 683 p.: bibl., index.

Substantial biography of Pedro II is highly skewed toward his relations with French society and French intellectuals. Draws on secondary and primary sources, especially French archives. For annotation of first edition of this work (entitled *Exílio e morte do Imperador*) see *HLAS 40:4069.*

3279 Bethell, Leslie. Brazil. (*in* Latin America between the Second World War and the Cold War, 1944–1948. Edited by Leslie Bethell and Ian Roxborough. New York: Cambridge Univ. Press, 1992, p. 33–65)

A chapter in a volume of studies analyzing the dialectic of domestic and international factors in postwar openings, work chronicles political opening following 1945, emphasizing growth of the Partido Comunista do Brasil and its proscription in 1947.

3280 Bideau, Alain and Sérgio Odilon Nadalin. Histórias de vida e análise demográfica da fecundidade: abordagens complementares para uma história de comportamento social. (*in* Congresso sobre a História da População da América Latina, 1st, Ouro Preto, Brazil, 1989. Actas. São Paulo: Fundação SEADE, 1990, p. 131–141, bibl., graphs, tables)

Examines birthrates as a way of tracing acculturation of German/Swiss Lutheran immigrants from peasant foreigners to bourgeois Brazilians.

3281 Blasenheim, Peter L. Railroads in nineteenth-century Minas Gerais. (*J. Lat. Am. Stud.*, 26:2, May 1994, p. 347–374, maps, tables)

Traces interests of companies, planters, and elites of other regions in construction of railroads throughout the Mata coffee zone, and analyzes outcomes of railroad overbuilding. Based on government reports and newspapers.

3282 Bodea, Miguel. Trabalhismo e populismo no Rio Grande do Sul. Porto Alegre, Brazil: Editora da Univ. Federal do Rio Grande do Sul, 1992. 212 p.: bibl.

Thoughtful interpretation analyzes relations between national politics and Partido Trabalhista Brasileiro in Rio Grande do Sul, 1945–54, focusing on complementary aims of Getúlio Vargas (modernization, inclusion of workers, nationalism) and Alberto Pasqualini (building a coherent labor party). Argues that, contrary to many theories of Latin American populism, Vargas' populism emerged from parties rather than from a charismatic connection to the masses. Provides detailed analysis of candidacies and parties in state elections, based on newspapers, interviews, and election returns. Portions of political narrative are transparently partisan in support of Leonel Brizola, who was a presidential aspirant in late 1980s when work was written.

3283 Boone, Christopher. Streetcars and politics in Rio de Janeiro: private enterprise versus municipal government in the provision of mass transit, 1903–1920. (*J. Lat. Am. Stud.*, 27:2, May 1995, p. 343–366)

Relates how the Rio de Janeiro Tramway, Light and Power Company (the "Light") negotiated a monopoly contract in 1907, the favorable terms of which were ultimately reversed by inflation. Interesting case study of bargaining between foreign capital and governments. Based on Brazilian and Canadian archives, newspapers, and government documents.

3284 Borges, Dain. Brazilian social thought of the 1930s. (*Luso-Braz. Rev.*, 31:2, Winter 1994, p. 137–150)

Surveys recent debates on significance of pioneering historical essays by Sérgio Buarque de Holanda, Caio Prado Júnior, and Gilberto Freyre in highly ideologized 1930s.

3285 Borges, Dain. "Puffy, ugly, slothful and inert": degeneration in Brazilian social thought, 1880–1940. (*J. Lat. Am. Stud.*, 25:2, May 1993, p. 235–256)

Degeneration as psychiatric concept and as loose metaphor shaped three themes in nation's social criticism: laziness destroyed character; diverse mentalities threatened national integrity; and exploitative social relations were parasitic. Even criticism of racism was shaped by themes of degeneration. Many social reforms were proposed as therapies for degeneration.

3286 Borges, Vavy Pacheco. Tenentismo e revolução brasiliana. São Paulo: Editora Brasiliense, 1992. 259 p.: bibl., ill.

Studies invention of the label *tenentes* in military-civilian politics in São Paulo, 1930–32, to argue that *tenentismo* is a dubious construct deriving from partisan polemics. Based on secondary literature and the newspaper of the Legião Revolucionária of São Paulo.

3287 Brito, Maria Helena de Oliveira. A colônia alemã do Uvá: 1924–1954. Goiânia, Brazil: CEGRAF-UGF, 1992. 149 p.: bibl., ill., maps. (Col. Documentos goianos; 20)

Studies a relatively unsuccessful German farm colony, notable because it was founded by the state government of Goiás well after the heyday of sponsored colonies. Goal of developing internal markets in an isolated region was frustrated by condition of the soil and lack of infrastructure. Reworked master's thesis, based on government documents and interviews with surviving members, most of whom obtained title to land around 1954.

3288 Cancelli, Elizabeth. O mundo da violência: a polícia da era Vargas. Brasília: Editora Univ. de Brasília, 1993. 227 p.: bibl.

Denunciation of vicious police repression and intimidation, 1930–45, is well-documented, using Brazilian and US government archives. Valuable for specialists, but fabricates tenuous thesis that expanded police violence, which ranged from harassing travelers to closing foreign-language schools to maintaining ghastly prisons, proves formation of a totalitarian state in 1930. Disregards counter-

evidence of police repression before 1930 (see *HLAS 54:3320* and *3396*).

3289 Chacon, Vamireh. Gilberto Freyre: uma biografia intelectual. Recife, Brazil: Fundação Joaquim Nabuco, Editora Massangana; São Paulo: Companhia Editora Nacional, 1993. 312 p.: bibl., ill. (Série Documentos; 40. Brasiliana; 387)

Useful chronology up to publication of *Casa-grande & senzala* in 1933 emphasizes Freyre's education in US. Includes new archival information, but interpretations follow Freyre's memoirs rather uncritically. See also item **3341.**

3290 Changing images of the Brazilian woman: studies of female sexuality in literature, mass media, and criminal trials, 1884–1992. (*Luso-Braz. Rev.*, 30:1, Summer 1993, p. 1–139)

Thematic issue focuses on 20th-century representations of women. Contributions include Margaret Rago summarizing her findings on prostitution (see *HLAS 54:3407*); Marta de Abreu Esteves and Sueann Caulfield discussing shifts in conceptions of female virginity, 1890–1940; Amelia Simpson on Xuxa; Alcir Lenharo and Marta Avancini on radio singers in 1940s and 1950s; and Luís Filipe Ribeiro and Maria Fernanda Baptista Bicalho on women in novels and silent film.

3291 The Confederados: Old South immigrants in Brazil. Edited by Cyrus Bassett Dawsey and James M. Dawsey. Tuscaloosa: Univ. of Alabama Press, 1995. 273 p.: bibl., ill., index, maps.

Diverse, uneven collection of essays emphasizes cultural themes: relations to Masonry, Brazilian modernizers, and early Protestant missions; role of family networks in recruiting colonists, and of marriages in perpetuating the communities; ethnic identity as expressed in Southern English and self-identification as *americanos* or *confederados*. Includes new version of memoir of settler Sarah Bellona Smith Ferguson.

3292 Coomes, Oliver T. and **Bradford L. Barham.** The Amazon rubber boom: labor control, resistance, and failed plantation development revisited. (*HAHR*, 74:2, May 1994, p. 231–257)

Reinterpretation of literature on rubber boom argues that plantations did not develop because rubber tapping was relatively efficient and profitable, enough so to preempt plantation ventures. See also items **3276** and **2769.**

3293 Culture and ideology in the Americas: essays in honor of Richard M. Morse. (*Luso-Braz. Rev.*, 32:2, Winter 1995, p. 1–107)
Thematic issue reflects Morse's recent work on the ideologies underlying social relations and intellectual history of modernism. Dain Borges, Florestan Fernandes, and Enrique Krauze provide evaluations of Morse's career, as well as a complete bibliography of Morse's work. Essays by Morse, Gilda de Mello e Souza, Dain Borges, and Harry Hoetink discuss the place of literary modernism and Gilberto Freyre in the development of a Brazilian social thought engaged with popular culture, especially rural and Afro-Brazilian cultures. Antônio Cândido and Helena Bousquet Bomeny discuss modernism and long-term trends in literature. See also item **3272.**

3294 De homens e máquinas. v. 1, Roberto Mange e a formação profissional. v. 2, Acervo Roberto Mange—inventário analítico. São Paulo: SENAI, 1991. 2 v.: bibl., ill. (some col.), index.
Biography of Roberto Mange, a pioneer of Brazilian industrial psychology, testing, and training who headed the Serviço Nacional de Aprendizagem Industrial (SENAI) vocational training institute from 1942–55. Places his life in context of rationalization of industrial work in Brazil, educational policy in 1930s and 1940s, and founding of SENAI. Based on secondary sources, archival papers, and interviews; richly illustrated with photographs. Vol. 2 catalogs holdings of Mange's papers at the Arquivo de História Social Edgard Leuenroth of UNICAMP.

3295 Della Cava, Ralph. Thinking about current Vatican policy in Central and East Europe and the utility of the "Brazilian paradigm." (*J. Lat. Am. Stud.*, 25:2, May 1993, p. 257–281)
Essay argues that successes and problems of "missionary" policy of the Catholic Church in Brazil since 1950 provide a useful model for predicting course of Church's future policy in Central and Eastern Europe. Subtly traces comparisons that illuminate both Brazilian and European issues.

3296 Diacon, Todd. Bringing the countryside back in: a case study of military intervention as State-building in the Brazilian Old

Republic. (*J. Lat. Am. Stud.*, 27:3, Oct. 1995, p. 569–592)
Argues that some military officers who fought against the 1912–16 Contestado Rebellion were transformed ideologically and became more reformist and nationalist.

3297 Dutra, Eliana Regina de Freitas; Douglas Cole Libby; and Sheila Brandão Baggio. Das sombras do tráfico às luzes do século: notas sobre uma discussão parlamentar. (*Rev. Dep. Hist./Belo Horizonte*, 6, junho 1988, p. 77–108)
Authors explore changes in Brazilian lawmakers' views of importance of free labor and of "progress" through mechanization. Their analysis of debates in parliament between 1837 and 1850 demonstrates that far more than British coercion was involved in ending African slave trade to Brazil.

3298 Entre-vistas: abordagens e usos da história oral. Coordenação de Marieta de Moraes Ferreira. Rio de Janeiro: Editora da Fundação Getúlio Vargas, 1994. 172 p.: bibl. (Ciências sociais)
Collection of essays on the Programa de História Oral of the Fundação Getúlio Vargas reflects current controversies among Brazilian historians regarding project's aims and methods. Several essays analyze interviews with post-1964 government and opposition elites: officers, economists, students.

3299 Exil in Brasilien: die deutschsprachige Emigration, 1933–1945; eine Ausstellung des Deutschen Exilarchivs 1933–1945, die Deutsche Bibliothek, Frankfurt am Main. Edited by Christine Hohnschopp and Frank Wende. Leipzig: Deutsche Bibliothek, 1994. 173 p.: bibl., ill. (Sonderveröffentlichungen / Deutsche Bibliothek; 21)
Small volume introduced by Patrik von zur Mühlen accompanies exhibit on German-speaking and Jewish exiles in Brazil (1933–45) organized by the Deutsche Bibliothek in Frankfurt. Book consists of over 50 biographies, letters, memoirs, interviews, and excerpts from publications provided by the Bibliothek's Deutsche Exilarchiv and other European archives. [C.K. Converse]

3300 O feixe e o prisma: uma revisão do Estado Novo. v. 1, O feixe: o autoritarismo como questão teórica e historiográfica. Organização de José Luiz Werneck da Silva. Rio de Janeiro: J. Zahar Editor, 1991 -. 1 v. (Col. Jubileu)

Useful collection of brief historiographical and interpretive essays drawn from a symposium on Getúlio Vargas' Estado Novo regime. Includes recollections of Vargas by Luiz Carlos Prestes and Décio Freitas. Several contributors compare the Estado Novo with European authoritarian regimes.

3301 Fico, Carlos and **Ronald Polito.** A história no Brasil, 1980–1989: elementos para uma avaliação historiográfica. v. 1. Prefácio de Carlos Guilherme Mota. Ouro Preto, Brazil: UFOP, 1992 -. 1 v.: bibl., ill., index.

Survey of outcomes of expansion of the history profession in late 1970s covers university programs, journals, associations, congresses and symposia, and publishers. Primarily statistical rather than evaluative approach, based on higher education and publishing statistics.

Franco, Gustavo Henrique Barroso. A década republicana: o Brasil e a economia internacional, 1888–1900. See *HLAS 55:2144.*

3302 Freitas Filho, Almir Pita. Tecnologia e escravidão no Brasil: aspectos da modernização agrícola nas exposições nacionais da segunda metade do século XIX, 1861–1881. (*Rev. Bras. Hist.,* 11:22, março/agôsto 1991, p. 71–92, bibl.)

Using catalogs and reports from five national expositions from 1861–81, author concludes that Brazilians saw no basic incompatibility between mechanization and slavery.

3303 Galliza, Diana Soares de. O processo emancipatório na Paraíba: as manumissões. (*Rev. Inst. Hist. Geogr. Para.,* 82:25, dez. 1991, p. 67–86,tables)

Excellent study of manumissions in northeastern province of Paraíba demonstrates variety of means slaves found with which to buy freedom (ranging from production of cotton to cattle ranching, real estate, and even winning lottery tickets). Also argues that women were manumitted in greater numbers than men, in part because interprovincial slave trade after 1850 skewed the slave population in Paraíba, leaving a greater proportion of enslaved women in the province.

3304 Getúlio Vargas and his legacy. (*Luso-Braz. Rev.,* 31:2, Winter 1994, p. 1–150)

Thematic issue emphasizes legacy of Vargas in culture and labor relations. Contributions include Joel Wolfe arguing that, since most labor reforms did not extend beyond Rio de Janeiro, workers' politics cannot be understood as a reaction to those reforms; Ângela de Castro Gomes evaluating the Partido Trabalhista Brasileiro after Vargas' suicide; Jeffrey Lesser on definitions of national identity in relation to Jewish and Arab immigrants; Daryle Williams on propaganda and historical preservation policy; Mary Lou Daniels on factory novels; and Dain Borges reviewing historiography on social thought of 1930s. Of special interest is Randal Johnson's dense description of "dynamics of the literary field" in Brazil, 1930–45, mapping changes in publishing, criticism, roles of intellectuals, and the canon of Brazilian literature.

3305 Gobineau, Arthur, *comte de.* Arthur de Gobineau et le Brésil: correspondance diplomatique du ministre de France à Rio de Janeiro, 1869–1870. Texte établie, présenté et annoté par Jean François de Raymond. Grenoble, France: Presses Universitaires de Grenoble, 1990. 190 p.: bibl., ill., index.

Official dispatches concentrating on reports of Paraguayan War are less colorful than Gobineau's published private correspondence. Combines careful annotations and an introductory essay with an overview of Brazil, ca. 1870.

3306 Gomes, Angela de Castro. Essa gente do Rio . . . os intelectuais cariocas e o modernismo. (*Estud. Hist./Rio de Janeiro,* 11, jan./junho 1993, p. 62–77)

Preliminary report on literary *modernismo* outside São Paulo emphasizes Manuel Bandeira, Graça Aranha, Sérgio Buarque de Holanda and the journal *Estética* (1924). Places Rio modernists in a milieu dominated by the official Academia de Letras, "traditional" bohemia, and Catholic circles.

3307 Groot, C.F.G. de Brazilian Catholicism and the ultramontane reform, 1850–1930. Amsterdam: CEDLA, 1996. 209 p.: bibl. (Latin American studies; 75)

Study of ultramontanism in Minas Gerais, Rio de Janeiro, and São Paulo focuses on whether ultramontane reform succeeded in transforming Brazilian Catholics into a homogeneous religious community. Also discusses reform of the Church and clergy, and the peculiarly Brazilian character of these reforms. [R. Hoefte]

3308 Grün, Roberto. Negócios & famílias: armênios em São Paulo. São Paulo: IDESP, Editora Sumaré, 1992. 100 p.: bibl., ill. (Série Imigração, 0103–7730)

Short essay on São Paulo's Armenian community, based on 24 interviews, is preliminary to a longer study. Speculates on sociological determinants of ethnic self-definition (as being above all different from "Turks"), specialization in the shoe business, and reactions to pressure for assimilation from institutions such as the university.

3309 Haber, Stephen H. Business enterprise and the Great Depression in Brazil: a study of profits and losses in textile manufacturing. (*Bus. Hist. Rev.*, 66:2, Summer 1992, p. 335–363, tables)

Important investigation examines cotton textile industry's reaction to the Great Depression. Argues that the crisis was deeper for many firms than aggregate output statistics indicate. Unprofitable Brazilian manufacturers reacted by lobbying the State to limit competition, rather than by reinvesting. Based on firm accounts and government documents.

3310 Hanchard, Michael George. Orpheus and power: the Movimento Negro of Rio de Janeiro and São Paulo, Brazil, 1945–1988. Princeton, N.J.: Princeton Univ. Press, 1994. 203 p.: bibl., index.

Using the *Movimento Negro* to illustrate how racial hegemony constrains effective political action in Brazil, author urges Afro-Brazilians to take a more self-critical and international position in order to work effectively for political change.

3311 Images réciproques du Brésil et de la France: actes du colloque organisé dans le cadre du projet France-Brésil. Coordination de Solange Parvaux et Jean Revel-Mouroz. Paris: IHEAL, 1991. 2 v.: bibl., ill. (Col. Travaux et mémoires de l'IHEAL; 46. Série Thèses et colloques; 2)

Voluminous bilingual collection from 1987 conference on images in television and mass media, schools, and scholarly circles, emphasizes stereotyping of Brazil's image in France and constructive reception of French ideas and sciences in Brazil.

3312 Imigrações e história da Igreja no Brasil. Organização de Martin Noberto Dreher. Aparecida, Brazil: Editora Santuário; São Paulo: Comissão de Estudos de História da Igreja na América Latina, 1993. 192 p.: bibl.

Papers from a symposium of major Church historians addresses topics such as State policy regarding religion and immigration, transformations of Protestantism among immigrants, European priests and the Romanization of Catholic practices, the *capelas* of Italian immigrants, and syncretism among Japanese immigrants. Generally good essays, surprisingly rich in suggesting dialectical connections among these topics.

3313 Instituto Histórico e Geográfico Brasileiro. Arquivos presidenciais. v. 1–2. Comentários e notas de Herculano Gomes Mathias. Rio de Janeiro: Instituto Histórico e Geográfico Brasileiro, 1990 -. 2 v.: bibl.

Vol. 1, *Prudente de Morais,* is a guide to 2,241 documents, mostly presidential correspondence from 1894–98. Transcribes selected personal documents and correspondence on matters such as the Federalista rebellion and the Canudos rebellion. Vol. 2, *Rodrigues Alves,* is a guide to 1,000 documents including Rodrigues Alves' personal notebooks, political and presidential correspondence, documents on coffee finance question, and notes of his biographer Afonso Arinos de Melo Franco. Transcribes selected papers.

3314 Keith, Henry H. Soldados salvadores: as revoltas militares brasileiras de 1922 e 1924, em perspectiva histórica. Tradução de Antonio Patriota. Rio de Janeiro: Biblioteca do Exército Editora, 1989. 293 p.: bibl. (Publicação / Biblioteca do Exército Editora; 581. Col. General Benício; 270)

Unrevised translation of 1969 dissertation traces rise of the military's "savior" role in politics through 1924. Narrative history is based largely on secondary literature, with some use of US consular dispatches.

3315 Knox, Miridan Britto. Demografia escrava no Piauí. (*in* Congresso sobre a História da População da América Latina, 1st, Ouro Preto, Brazil, 1989. Actas. São Paulo: Fundação SEADE, 1990, p. 244–250, bibl., tables)

Uses slave lists compiled at time of the Free Birth Law along with material from 1872 census to give a picture of slavery (and slave families) in Piauí. Finds that few slaves married and that families were primarily matrifocal.

3316 Komissarov, Boris Nikolaevich. Da Sibéria à Amazônia: a vida de Langsdorff. Prefácio de Marcos Pinto Braga. Brasília: Edições Langsdorff, 1992. 135 p.: bibl.

Sketch biography of German-born naturalist who visited Brazil ca. 1803–30, and was Russian consul in Rio 1813–19, is based partly on documents and collections in Russian archives. See also *HLAS 54:3240.* For collections of watercolors and drawings from his voyages see *HLAS 50:2701* and *HLAS 54: 3284.*

3317 Kuznesof, Elizabeth Anne. Ilegitimidade, raça e laços de família no Brasil do século XIX: uma análise da informação de censos e de batismos para São Paulo e Rio de Janeiro. (*in* Congresso sobre a História da População da América Latina, *1st, Ouro Preto, Brazil, 1989.* Actas. São Paulo: Fundação SEADE, 1990, p. 164–174, tables)

Examines illegitimacy and its connections to race and family. Author is particularly interested in how social practices concerning godparenthood varied depending on race and/or legitimacy of the child. Finds few hard and fast rules: while members of social extremes (slave/unmarried and free white/ married) were more prone to uniformity in practice, there was much diversity in the large middle segment.

3318 Lesser, Jeffrey H. From pedlars to proprietors: Lebanese, Syrian and Jewish immigrants in Brazil. (*in* The Lebanese in the world: a century of emigration. London: Centre for Lebanese Studies, 1992, p. 393–410, table)

Survey of 1880–1950 experience focuses on factors that led Brazilians to confuse the ethnic groups: urban residence and occupational specialization in peddling, commerce, and small industry. Emphasizes analysis of negative characterizations by Brazilian sociologists and nativists in 1920s and 1930s.

3319 Lesser, Jeffrey H. The immigration and integration of Polish Jews in Brazil, 1924–1934. (*Americas/Francisc.*, 51:2, Oct. 1994, p. 173–191, tables)

Succinct overview of migration discussed at greater length in item **3320.**

3320 Lesser, Jeffrey H. Welcoming the undesirables: Brazil and the Jewish question. Berkeley: Univ. of California Press, 1994. 208 p.: bibl., ill., index.

Fascinating portraits of vacillations and deceptions in Estado Novo policymaking, and of anti-semitic dimension to Brazilian nationalism, emerge from a case study of Jewish migration and refugee policies from 1920s through 1940s. Meticulously documented with extensive research in Brazilian, British, and US archives. See also item **3319.**

3321 Levine, Robert M. The cautionary tale of Carolina Maria de Jesús. (*LARR*, 29: 1, 1994, p. 55–83, bibl.)

Presents excellent brief biography of Carolina Maria de Jesus, the São Paulo *favelada* who catapulted into international prominence with the publication of her diary *Quarto de despejo* (see *HLAS 25:4741*). (Work was also published in English under the title *Child of the dark*—see *HLAS 25: 4740.*) Examines Carolina's failure to prosper despite success of her work. Author claims that she did not fit into the accepted mold of champion of the poor and was, therefore, never accepted by the Brazilian middle class, elite, or even by Brazilian scholars. See also item **3322.**

3322 Levine, Robert M. and **José Carlos Sebe Bom Meihy.** The life and death of Carolina Maria de Jesus. Albuquerque: Univ. of New Mexico Press, 1995. 162 p.: bibl., ill., index, map. (Diálogos)

Biography of author of *Quarto de despejo* (see item **3321**) discusses what led her to publish her denunciation of shantytown conditions and how she reacted to the fame and money that followed its publication. Reflects on race and social mobility in Brazil. Transcribes interviews with family members.

3323 Lewin, Linda. The papers of Epitácio Pessoa: an archival note and personal comment. pt. 1. (*Luso-Braz. Rev.*, 32:1, Summer 1995, p. 69–82)

Pt. 1 of 2, work describes the Arquivo de Epitácio Pessoa, deposited in the Instituto Histórico e Geográfico Brasileiro along with other family papers. Pt. 2 was published in 1996.

3324 Lima, Roberto Kant de and **Magali Alonso de Lima.** Capoeira e cidadania: negritude e identidade no Brasil republicano. (*Rev. Antropol./São Paulo,* 34, 1991, p. 143–182, bibl.)

Examines responses to practice of *capoeira* as a way to address race and labor constructs in the transition from slavery to industrial society and in the definition of citizenship in 20th-century Brazil.

3325 Lindsay, Lisa A. "To return to the bosom of their fatherland": Brazilian immigrants in nineteenth-century Lagos. (*Slavery Abolit.*, 15:1, April 1994, p. 22–50)

Argues that Brazilian freedmen "returning" to Lagos often inserted themselves as middlemen of ambivalent identity between Europeans and Africans. By the end of the century, hardening colonial racial divisions and the end of return migration diminished their role. Extensively based on Nigerian notarial and probate documents, government documents, and secondary literature.

3326 Lins, Cristovão. Jari: 70 anos de história. Almeirim, Brazil?: Prefeitura Municipal de Almeirim, 1991. 236 p.: bibl., ill.

Chronicles four phases of administration of Amazonian *latifúndio* that became controversial in its third phase as Daniel Ludwig's monumental Projeto Jari, 1967–81. Author was an employee both under Ludwig and during following nationalization phase. Narrative is mostly undocumented, but parts are memoirs of an eyewitness.

3327 Lira, João Gomes de. Lampião: memórias de um soldado de volante. Recife, Brazil: Governo do Estado de Pernambuco, Secretaria de Educação, Cultura e Esportes/FUNDARPE; Companhia Editora de Pernambuco, 1990. 665 p.: ill. (Biblioteca comunitária de Pernambuco. Memória; 03)

Entertaining, rich compilation contains mostly undocumented stories and anecdotes about the career of the bandit, 1919–38, and the military campaigns against him. Focus on Lampião's connections with the conflicts of his home town of Nazaré illuminates dimensions of enmity in the backlands.

3328 Lustosa, Isabel. Histórias de presidentes: a República no Catete. Petrópolis, Brazil: Editora Vozes; Rio de Janeiro: Fundação Casa de Rui Barbosa, 1989. 182 p.: bibl., ill.

Album contains profiles of each president who occupied the Catete Palace in Rio de Janeiro, 1897–1960, as portrayed in caricature, popular songs, and anecdotes. Well-selected, fresh anthology of caricatures may interest scholars. Disappointingly slim coverage of Getúlio Vargas' presidencies.

3329 Malczewski, Zdzisław. Obecność Polaków i Polonii w Rio de Janeiro. Lublin, Poland: Oddz. Lubelski Stowarzyszenia Wspólnota Polska, 1995. 350 p.: bibl., ill. (some col.), index. (Biblioteka Polonii. Seria A; Studia, 1233–0272; 8)

Well-documented work on history of Polish emigration to Brazil, particularly to Rio de Janeiro, focuses mainly on question of urban emigration. Covers 1840–1955 period, and includes topics such as activities of "Polonia" (Polish colony) in Brazil on behalf of Poland, Polish contributions to the development of Rio and the Brazilian nation, Polish diplomatic activity, and "Polonia" in Rio. [Z. Kantorosinski]

3330 Malta, Maria Helena. A intentona de vovó Mariana. Rio de Janeiro: Editora Rosa dos Tempos, 1991. 240 p.: bibl., index.

Didactic historical novel contrasts banal anxiety of contemporary middle-class concerns in Rio and the utopian optimism of the 1935 Communist coup attempt. Frames documentary chapters (drawn from interviews, memoirs, and documents of the revolt) as dreamy recollections of "granny Mariana," a stubborn survivor of the period. Footnotes, bibliography, and an index of names permit the reader to reconstruct sources.

3331 Massi, Fernanda Peixoto and Heloísa André Pontes. Guia biobibliográfico dos brasilianistas: obras e autores editados no Brasil entre 1930 e 1988. São Paulo: Editora Sumaré, 1992. 125 p.: indexes.

Annotated bibliography lists books published in Brazil by 99 foreign-born historians and social scientists (mostly from France and US). Includes capsule biographies derived from standard reference works.

3332 Mindlin, José E. Uma vida entre livros: reencontros com o tempo. São Paulo: EDUSP; Companhia das Letras, 1997. 231 p.: ill., indexes, maps.

In 19 chapters, Mindlin recounts his adventures in assembling a 30,000-volume collection. This bibliophile's memoirs encompass his teenage years and his decades as an entrepreneur, as well as his more recent years as a political, economic, and cultural advisor. Indexes, captivating illustrations, and excellent graphic design add to the volume's appeal. Tying the book together is Mindlin's plain and seductive language, which entrances while enlightening the reader about Mindlin's favorite authors (. . . "in Brazil, Machado"), as well as friends (such as Drummond). An ingenious introduction to shelves brimming with books, each one of them with a unique history, this work attests to Mindlin's conviction that "I talk with my books as with friends. . . . Yet the books are *not* my property. A library makes no sense without readers." [I. Siqueira Wiarda]

3333 Mir, Luís. A revolução impossível. São Paulo: Editora Best Seller, 1994. 755 p.: bibl., ill.

Chronicles the Partido Comunista Brasileiro and its offshoots such as Ação Libertadora Nacional under military dictatorship from 1964 to roughly 1971. Based primarily on newspapers and periodicals, work is a critical but sympathetic narrative that emphasizes disillusionment with armed resistance.

3334 Mitre, Antonio and **Tania Quintaneiro.** Viagem conturbada por um rio tranqüilo: conflitos diplomáticos em torno da navegação do Amazonas no século XIX. (*Rev. Dep. Hist./Belo Horizonte*, 4, junho 1987, p. 44–84)

Broadens perspectives on disputes over river navigation between Brazil and US, 1820–67, by showing how neighboring countries of Bolivia, Peru, Ecuador, and Nueva Granada were each pulled into the conflict at different times. Based on Brazilian and US government documents.

3335 Momentos do livro no Brasil. Projecto e coordenação geral de Fernando Paixão. Coordenação de pesquisa e texto de Maria Celeste Mira. São Paulo: Editora Ática, 1996. 215 p.: bibl., ill. (some col.), index.

Excellent and unique review of broadly-defined Brazilian publishing history, from the precursors Laemmert and Garnier at the turn of the century to today's books on tape and CD-ROM. As with L. Hallewell's *O livro no Brasil*, (1985), this is an essential source for scholars and bibliophiles. Well organized and visually appealing, with a detailed index and an interesting chronology. Enlivened throughout with examples of cover pages, caricatures of authors, and woodblock illustrations, the focus is on the eclectic vision of those who were among the most dynamic leaders in the publishing industry in 20th-century Brazil. [I. Siqueira Wiarda]

3336 Monteiro, Mário Ypiranga. Negritude e modernidade: a trajetória de Eduardo Gonçalves Ribeiro. Manaus, Brazil: Governo do Estado do Amazonas, 1990. 161 p.: bibl., ill. (some col.), map.

Potpourri of chapters pays homage to black military officer who was governor of Amazonas in 1890s. Defends his record, especially his modernizing public works. Attractive photographs of turn-of-the-century Manaus.

3337 Monteiro, Norma de Góes. Imigração e colonização em Minas, 1889–1930. Belo Horizonte, Brazil: Editora Itatiaia, 1994. 213 p.: bibl. (Col. Reconquista do Brasil; 2a. sér.,188)

Chronicles state policy, noting ritualistic reiteration of decrees. Distinguishes period of emphasis on subsidized immigration of foreign laborers for coffee plantations (1892–98) from later policies establishing native and foreign settler colonies (1907–30). Apparently unrevised 1973 doctoral thesis is based on official documents, especially legislation.

Moraes, João Quartim de. A esquerda militar no Brasil. v. 1, Da conspiração republicana à guerrilha dos tenentes. See *HLAS 55:3739.*

3338 Moraes Neto, Geneton and **Joel Silveira.** Nitroglicerina pura. Rio de Janeiro: Editora Record, 1992. 235 p.: bibl., ill., index.

Overblown "exposé" drawn from British Foreign Office confidential dossier, unflattering profiles of Brazilian 1930s politicians are followed by reminiscences by Silveira about journalism and censorship under Vargas' Estado Novo.

Na contracorrente da história: documentos da Liga Comunista Internacionalista, 1930–1933. See *HLAS 55:3741.*

3339 Naro, Nancy Priscilla Smith. At the heart of the transition: land and labor in Rio de Janeiro, Brazil, 1870–90. (*Hist. Soc./Río Piedras*, 4, 1991, p. 9–41, tables, ill.)

Case study of *municípios* of Vassouras and Rio Bonito, state of Rio de Janeiro, argues that the much-studied abolition of slavery coincided with a less-documented conflict between planters and squatters. Eviction and tenantry lawsuits over improvements to land suggest that planters' transition to free labor also entailed renegotiating relations with landless farmers. Interesting for comparisons with São Paulo state.

3340 Needell, Jeffrey D. History, race, and the State in the thought of Oliveira Viana. (*HAHR*, 75 : 1, Feb. 1995, p. 1–30)

Stresses that a belief in the Brazilian people's racial incapacity for liberal citizenship lay at the root of Oliveira Viana's still-influential model of authoritarian corporatism.

3341 Needell, Jeffrey D. Identity, race, gender, and modernity in the origins of Gilberto Freyre's *oeuvre*. (*Am. Hist. Rev.*, 100 : 1, Feb. 1995, p. 51–77)

Carefully documented psycho-bio-graphical work analyzes how a personal identity crisis and reaction against modernity led Freyre to construct an influential historical legend of Brazil in *Casa-grande & senzala* (1933): that miscegenation and racial domination had created a society that was at once patriarchal and democratic. See also item **3289.**

3342 Neves, Maria de Fátima Rodrigues das. Ampliando a família escrava: compadrio de escravos em São Paulo do século XIX. (*in* Congresso sobre a História da População da América Latina, *1st, Ouro Preto, Brazil, 1989*. Actas. São Paulo: Fundação SEADE, 1990, p. 237–243, bibl., graphs, tables)

Argues that godparenthood allowed slaves to choose ways to extend family ties. Finds that in São Paulo they did so by selecting men (there were more godfathers than godmothers) and by creating links to the free community, although not to the master.

3343 Niedersächsische Staats- und Universitätsbibliothek Göttingen (Germany). Neues Heimatland Brasilien: Texte und Bilder zur kulturellen Entwicklung der deutschbrasilianischen Bevölkerung in Südbrasilien; Begleitband zur Ausstellung, 10.01.-19.02.1994. Compiled by Sandra Messele-Wieser and Lothar Wieser. Göttingen, Germany: Niedersächsische Staats- und Universitätsbibliothek, 1993. 84 p.: bibl., facsims. (Göttinger Bibliotheksschriften: 0943–951X; 4)

Focuses on German settlement in southern Brazil (1808–1945). Includes facsimiles of documents, excerpts of laws, letters, and accounts of immigrants' experiences drawn from 19th- and 20th-century newspapers and calendars. Bibliography is based on collections of the Niedersächsische Staats-

und Universitätsbibliothek Göttingen. [C.K. Converse]

3344 Nunes, Sebastião G. História do Brasil. Sabará, Brazil: Edições Dubolso; Mazza, 1992. 221 p.: bibl., ill., index.

Literary parody frames satirical vignettes as alphabetical entries in an historical dictionary. Commentary on official legend, civic heroes, and pretentious intellectuals is relentlessly debasing and scatalogical.

3345 Paiva, Clotilde Andrade and **Douglas Cole Libby.** The middle path: alternative patterns of slave demographics in 19th century Minas Gerais. (*in* El poblamiento de las Américas, *Veracruz, 1992*. Actas. Liège, Belgium: International Union for the Scientific Study of Population, 1992, v. 1, p. 185–232, graphs, tables)

Demographic study focuses on slave population in Minas Gerais, two generations after bust of the gold rush. Among other points, argues that natural increase of the Brazilian slave population occurred even during period of the African slave trade.

3346 Paiva, Clotilde Andrade and **Herbert S. Klein.** Slave and free in nineteenth-century Minas Gerais: Campanha in 1831. (*Slavery Abolit.*, 15 : 1, April 1994, p. 1–21, graphs, tables)

Study of Minas Gerais, a region that in 19th century was only secondarily attached to the export economy, highlights importance of slaves, and particularly women, in production of foodstuffs and in textile and weaving industries geared toward the São Paulo and Rio de Janeiro markets. Authors argue that evidence from Minas Gerais suggests that the slave population could have been self-sustaining despite the significant numbers of African-born in the slave population.

Peña, Guillermo de la. Poder agrario y ambigüedad revolucionaria: bandidos, caudillos y facciones. See item **1562.**

3347 Perissinotto, Renato Monseff. Classes dominantes e hegemonia na República Velha. Campinas, Brazil: Editora da Unicamp, 1994. 251 p.: bibl. (Série Pesquisas)

Revised master's thesis in sociology, based entirely on secondary literature, distinguishes divisions within São Paulo's ruling class. Argues that inter-state political "regionalism" expressed reactions of other class segments to São Paulo's coffee-commercial interests which exercised hegemony in conjunction with foreign capital.

3348 Pesavento, Sandra Jatahy. Borges de Medeiros. Porto Alegre, Brazil: IEL, 1990. 128 p.: bibl. (Rio Grande político)

Biographical essay on governor and boss of Rio Grande do Sul during the First Republic is based on secondary sources. Includes anthology of his writings and speeches. Succinct statement of conventional interpretation that Borges de Medeiros and his generation, through their influence on Getúlio Vargas, translated positivist republican ideology into administrative practices for Brazil's post-1930 authoritarian, interventionist State.

3349 Pesavento, Sandra Jatahy. O cotidiano da república: elites e povo na virada do século. Porto Alegre, Brazil: Editora da Univ. Federal do Rio Grande do Sul, 1990. 87 p.: bibl., ill. (Síntese rio-grandense; 3)

Light essay on Porto Alegre social issues in 1890s juxtaposes points of view of establishment newspapers with proletarian newspapers. Many quotations.

3350 Pimentel, Thaïs Velloso Cougo. A torre Kubitschek: trajetória de um projeto em 30 anos de Brasil. Belo Horizonte, Brazil: Governo do Estado de Minas Gerais, Secretaria de Estado da Cultura, 1993. 181 p.: bibl., ill.

Modest but thoughtful study focuses on a massive apartment complex in Belo Horizonte, designed by Oscar Niemeyer in 1951 and plagued by construction delays and social problems, that became a symbol of the failure of Brazil's modernist utopia. Interesting supplement to James Holston's *Modernist city* (Univ. of Chicago Press, 1989) and Gilberto Velho's *A utopia urbana* (Rio de Janeiro: Zahar Editores, 1973). Based on interviews, press reports, government documents.

3351 Portinho, José Gomes. Achegas à Araripe: guerra civil no RGS. Organização e notas de Mário Pacheco Dornelles. Porto Alegre, Brazil: M.P. Dornelles, 1990. 101 p.: bibl., index.

Contains transcription of notes by a former officer of the Farrapos Revolution, written in the margins of his copy of Tristão de Alencar Araripe's *Guerra civil no Rio Grande do Sul* (Rio de Janeiro: 1881), disput-

ing facts and interpretations. Interesting to specialists, but intelligible only in conjunction with Araripe's volume.

3352 Prestes, Anita Leocádia. Os militares e a reação republicana: as origens do tenentismo. Petrópolis, Brazil: Vozes, 1994. 96 p.: bibl., ill.

Brief, mostly narrative essay based on secondary literature and preliminary research in papers of Nilo Peçanha. Argues that revolutionary *tenentista* movement of junior officers did not derive from military political culture. Instead, the movement mobilized during campaign of fortuitous 1921–22 *reação republicana* coalition of disgruntled, pro-Hermes de Fonseca officers and dissident politicians, against the official candidate Bernardes.

Resende, Maria Efigênia Lage de. Às vésperas de 37: o novo/velho discurso da ordem conservadora. See *HLAS 55:3759.*

3353 Richter, Klaus. A Sociedade Colonizadora Hanseática de 1897 e a colonização do interior de Joinville e Blumenau. Florianópolis, Brazil: Editora da UFSC; Blumenau, Brazil: Editora da FURB, 1992. 106 p.: bibl., ill., map.

Thorough, illustrated study of a commercial immigrant colonization company that failed financially but introduced ca. 4,700 German colonists to Santa Catarina. Considers German-imperialist aims of directors, conflicts of interest between directors and colonists. Based extensively on primary documents from local and German archives.

3354 Ridings, Eugene. Business interest groups in nineteenth-century Brazil. Cambridge, England; New York: Cambridge Univ. Press, 1994. 377 p.: bibl., ill., index. (Cambridge Latin American studies; 78)

Rich, pioneering study of the *associações comerciais* of major cities documents their lobbying and influence. Illuminates many topics, including credit, taxation and infrastructure, foreign capitalists' positions on labor, and balance between agricultural and industrial interests. Extensively researched, mainly in Brazilian and British archives.

3355 Rio de Janeiro operário: natureza do Estado e conjuntura econômica, condições de vida e consciência de classe, 1930–

1970. Coordenação de Eulália Maria Lahmeyer Lobo. Rio de Janeiro: Access Editora, 1992. 461 p.: bibl., ill.

Important compilation of research team's coordinated studies of labor politics, wages and prices, strikes, and workplace health emphasizes militancy and responses to the State. Extensive tables are based on government documents; charts of strikes are compiled from press and other sources. Aims to demonstrate that Rio de Janeiro militancy was equivalent to São Paulo's.

3356 Ruuth, Anders. Igreja Universal do Reino de Deus: Gudsrikets universella kyrka; en brasiliansk kyrkobildning. Stockholm: Almqvist & Wiksell International, 1995. 351 p.: appendix, bibl., ill., map. (Bibliotheca theologiae practicae; 54)

Carefully documented study by Swedish scholar (and Lutheran theologian) examines Brazil's Igreja Universal do Reino de Deus, or Pentecostal Church of the Kingdom of God. Established in 1977, the church has become one of the fastest growing Pentecostal churches in Latin America. Through use of modern marketing methods, radio, and television, the church had expanded into more than 1,000 congregations throughout Brazil by the 1990s. Impressive appendix (50 p.) includes bibliography (30 p.), tables, charts, acronyms, etc. [M.L. Bernal]

3357 Samara, Eni de Mesquita. Mulheres brasileiras: direitos e alternativas em sociedades patriarcais, seculos XVIII e XIX. (*in* Jornadas de Investigación Interdisciplinaria sobre la Mujer, *9th, Madrid, 1992. La mujer latinoamericana ante el reto del siglo XXI.* Madrid: Ediciones de la Univ. Autónoma de Madrid, 1993, p. 39–52, bibl.)

Focusing on legal status of women before republican government curbed the control of the Church, author offers a particularly interesting discussion of women's options when they separated from their husbands.

Sarracino, Rodolfo. Cuba y Brazil: dos corrientes migratorias latinoamericanas de regreso a Africa en el siglo XIX. See item **2084.**

3358 Sérgio Buarque de Holanda: vida e obra. São Paulo: Secretaria de Estado da Cultura; Univ. de São Paulo, 1988. 158 p.: bibl., ill.

Good collection of biographical and critical essays on major Brazilian historian and essayist includes extensive bibliography of his publications.

Series retrospectivas do Paraná. See item **20.**

3359 Sevcenko, Nicolau. Orfeu extático na metrópole: São Paulo, sociedade e cultura nos frementes anos 20. São Paulo: Companhia das Letras, 1992. 390 p.: bibl., ill., index.

Outstanding if sometimes tendentious work interprets transformation of São Paulo into a frenetic, mechanized metropolis, where experience of daily life was theatrical. Connects crisis of European metropolitan culture and European modernist art to crisis of São Paulo's intellectuals. Discusses responses to a sense of loss of identity in São Paulo by Blaise Cendrars (expressed in his work *Etc. . . ., etc. . . .:um livro 100% brasileiro,* annotated in *HLAS 42: 6398*); the 1922 Semana de Arte Moderna; Sérgio Buarque de Holanda; and others. Based largely on a critical reading of newspapers as documents and interpretations of urban phenomena such as soccer, automobile traffic, floods, tenements, aviation, and Carnival.

3360 Silva, Eduardo da. Prince of the people: the life and times of a Brazilian free man of colour. London; New York: Verso, 1993. 219 p.: bibl., ill., index, map.

Life story of Cândido da Fonseca Galvão, who called himself Dom Obá II d'Africa, provides fascinating portrait of daily life in Rio de Janeiro—with special emphasis on the role of slaves, ex-slaves, and free men of color—from the Paraguayan War to the beginning of the Republic.

Silva, José Luiz Foresti Werneck da. As duas faces da moeda: a política externa do Brasil monárquico, 1831–1876. See *HLAS 55:4385.*

3361 Silva, Maria Beatriz Nizza da. Vida privada e quotidiano no Brasil: na época de D. Maria I e D. João VI. Lisboa: Editorial Estampa, 1993. 359 p.: bibl., ill. (some col.). (Referência / Editorial Estampa; 4)

Collection of essays oriented toward specialists centers on marriage, illegitimacy, inheritance, and clergy more than on "daily life." Rich in archival documentation, especially ecclesiastical records. Includes contributions by David Higgs and Guilherme Pereira das Neves.

3362 Silva, Marinete dos Santos. Escravidão e prostituição: das várias utilidades de uma negra escrava. (*Rev. Dep. Hist./Belo Horizonte*, 6, junho 1988, p. 123–127)

Pioneering study focuses on slave prostitutes in Rio de Janeiro during 1860s and 1870s. Author finds that it was poor women slaveholders who most often subjected their female slaves to prostitution. See also item **3365.**

3363 Silva, Vera Alice Cardoso e. Da bateia à enxada: aspectos do sistema servil e da economia mineira em perspectiva, 1800–1870. (*Rev. Dep. Hist./Belo Horizonte*, 6, junho 1988, p. 47–68, bibl., tables)

Demonstrates that slaves in Minas Gerais remained heavily concentrated in mining areas despite decline of mining and rising importance of agriculture in 19th century.

3364 Skidmore, Thomas E. Bi-racial U.S.A. vs. multi-racial Brazil: is the contrast still valid? (*J. Lat. Am. Stud.*, 25:2, May 1993, p. 373–386)

Exploratory essay examines change in realities and perceptions of race relations. There is more evidence of polarization in Brazil, just when racial categories may be becoming less polarized in US. Suggests avenues for further research. For sociologist's comment see *HLAS 55:5202.*

3365 Soares, Luís Carlos. Rameiras, ilhoas, polacas—: a prostituição no Rio de Janeiro do século XIX. São Paulo: Editora Atica, 1992. 118 p.: bibl. (Ensaios; 132)

Work is particularly concerned with role of slavery in the practice of and debate around prostitution in Rio de Janeiro during 19th century. Examines social and racial divisions among prostitutes, as well as expectations that the State might regulate public prostitution (involving free women) and eliminate clandestine prostitution (involving slave women). See also item **3362.**

3366 Souza, José Moreira de. Cidade: momentos e processos; Serro e Diamantina na formação do norte mineiro no século XIX. São Paulo: ANPOCS; Marco Zero, 1993. 265 p.: bibl.

Interesting comparison of two small neighboring cities as loci of relations among "strangers." Organized around schematic sociological categories, but led by its docu-

ments into detailed analyses of liberal ideals and citizenship, the establishment of municipal cemeteries, attitudes toward railroads and progress, small-town ethos, outcomes of economic decline. Creative thesis, based on local archives and press.

3367 Topik, Steven. The oligarchy and the State: Brazil, 1889–1930. (*in* International Congress of Americanists, 45th, Bogotá, 1985. Historia. Bogotá: Ediciones Uniandes, 1988, p. 87–104)

Surveys relations between classes and the State. Concentrated oligarchies easily controlled the State and wanted little from it except favorable finance and trade policy. Both foreign and domestic capitalists negotiated favors and concessions from the State in equivalently personalist fashion until ca. 1914–30, when interest groups grew more important.

3368 Verger, Pierre. Os libertos: sete caminhos na liberdade de escravos da Bahia no século XIX. Salvador, Brazil: Corrupio; Fundação Cultural, Estado da Bahia, 1992. 140 p.: bibl., ill., map. (Baianada; 10)

Compilation of life stories links 19th-century Brazil and Africa. Gives examples of seven different paths pursued by freed Africans, centering around religious choices (adherence to Christianity, Islam, or African faiths, or some combination of these three) and economic possibilities.

3369 Versiani, Flávio R. Labor supply in early Brazilian industrialization. (*in* El poblamiento de las Américas, Veracruz, 1992. Actas. Liège, Belgium: International Union for the Scientific Study of Population, 1992, v. 1, p. 419–446)

Examines differences in wage and skill levels across regions, 1872–1920, concluding that access of São Paulo industry to skilled workers was a more significant factor in industrialization than access to an "unlimited" supply of labor from rural areas.

3370 Visões do golpe: a memória militar sobre 1964. Introdução e organização de Maria Celina d'Araújo, Gláucio Ary Dillon Soares, e Celso Castro. Rio de Janeiro: Relume Dumará, 1994. 256 p.: bibl., index.

Contains segments from 12 interviews collected by the Programa de História Oral of the Centro de Pesquisa e Documentação de História Contemporânea do Brasil. Not surprisingly, direct questions on motivations for the 1964 coup and on aims of early military governments elicit mostly formulaic, clichéd recollections. Cohort interviewed were colonels, not generals, in 1964; several later held intelligence posts.

3371 Waack, William. Camaradas: nos arquivos de Moscou, a história secreta da revolução brasileira de 1935. São Paulo: Companhia das Letras, 1993. 381 p.: bibl., ill., index.

Important revisionist account of relations among Luis Carlos Prestes, Moscow, and Partido Comunista do Brasil, 1929–38, emphasizes practical and seamy aspects of Party's financing and coordination by COMINTERN. Debunks romantic legend of Olga Benario. Paints 1935 Communist rebellion as absurd outcome of generic COMINTERN directives. Some details of the conspiracy emerge from previously secret documents in Russian archives.

3372 Wagner, Reinhardt W. Deutsche als Ersatz für Sklaven: Arbeitsmigranten aus Deutschland in der brasilianischen Provinz São Paulo, 1847–1914. Frankfurt am Main: Vervuert Verlag, 1995. 202 p.: bibl., graphs, maps, tables.

Provides critical examination of São Paulo coffee growers' unique replacement of slave labor with the *parceria* system consisting of lease/share-cropping and contract labor. Also examines system's effect on German and Swiss immigrants who comprised two-thirds of such labor. Based on extensive research in Brazilian and German archives. [C.K. Converse]

3373 Wolfe, Joel. "Father of the Poor" or "Mother of the Rich?": Getúlio Vargas, industrial workers, and construction of class, gender, and populism in São Paulo, 1930–1954. (*Radic. Hist. Rev.*, 58, Winter 1994, p. 80–111, ill.)

Analyzes workers' letters to Vargas. Letters indicate that populism was actually workers' wary exchange of political support in return for Vargas' support of their grievances against bosses and elites. Women's letters show that they disagreed with paternalistic Estado Novo ideology opposing women's work.

3374 The world out of which Canudos came. (*Luso-Braz. Rev.*, 30:2, Winter 1993, p. 1–116)

Thematic issue emphasizes Bahian context and origins of Canudos religious community, 1893–96, rather than the war against Canudos. Gives a measure of the state of debates concerning Canudos. Contributions include Gerald Greenfield and Dain Borges on urban perceptions of country people and reactions to their insubordination; Robert Levine and Consuelo Novais Sampaio on social structure of Salvador and political powers in state of Bahia; and Lori Madden and José Calazans discussing interpretations of Canudos. Of special interest is Alexandre Otten's essay reinterpreting the sermons of Antônio Conselheiro as reflections of relatively orthodox Catholic doctrine rather than apocalyptic messianism.

JOURNAL ABBREVIATIONS

Actas Am. Actas Americanas. Univ. de La Serena, Facultad de Humanidades. La Serena, Chile.

Afro-Hisp. Rev. Afro-Hispanic Review. Univ. of Missouri-Columbia. Columbia, Missouri.

Agric. Hist. Agricultural History. Agricultural History Society. Univ. of Calif. Press. Berkeley.

Allpanchis/Cusco. Allpanchis. Instituto de Pastoral Andina. Cusco, Peru.

Am. Anthropol. American Anthropologist. American Anthropological Assn., Washington.

Am. Econ. Rev. The American Economic Review. American Economic Assn., Evanston, Ill.

Am. Hist. Rev. The American Historical Review. American Historical Assn., Washington.

Am. Indíg. América Indígena. Instituto Indigenista Interamericano. México.

Am. Merid. América Meridional. Sociedad Regional de Ciencias Humanas. Montevideo.

Am. Negra. América Negra. Pontificia Univ. Javeriana. Bogotá.

Am. Sociol. Rev. American Sociological Review. American Sociological Assn., Washington.

Americas/Francisc. The Americas. Academy of American Franciscan History. Washington.

An. Acad. Nac. Cienc. Econ. Anales de la Academia Nacional de Ciencias Económicas. Buenos Aires.

An. Arqueol. Etnol. Anales de Arqueología y Etnología. Univ. Nacional de Cuyo, Facultad de Filosofía y Letras. Mendoza, Argentina.

An. Hist. Contemp. Anales de Historia Contemporánea. Cátedra de Historia Contemporánea, Univ. de Murcia. Murcia, Spain.

An. Mus. Am. Anales del Museo de América. Museo de América. Madrid.

An. Univ. Chile. Anales de la Universidad de Chile. Santiago.

An. Valent. Anales Valentinos: Revista de Filosofía y Teología. Facultad de Teología San Vicente Ferrer. Valencia, Spain.

Anc. Mesoam. Ancient Mesoamerica. Cambridge Univ. Press. Cambridge, England.

Ann. hist. Révolut. fr. Annales historiques de la Révolution française. Société des Études Robespierristes; Firmin-Didot. Reims, Paris.

Annales/Paris. Annales. Centre national de la recherche scientifique de la VIe Section de l'Ecole pratique des hautes études. Paris.

Anthropol. Q. Anthropological Quarterly. Catholic Univ. of America, Catholic Anthropological Conference. Washington.

Anu. Colomb. Hist. Soc. Cult. Anuario Colombiano de Historia Social y de la Cultura. Univ. Nacional de Colombia, Facultad de Ciencias Humanas, Depto. de Historia. Bogotá.

Anu. Dep. Hist./Madrid. Anuario del Departmento de Historia. Depto. de Historia, Univ. Complutense de Madrid.

Anu. Estud. Am. Anuario de Estudios Americanos. Consejo Superior de Investigaciones Científicas; Univ. de Sevilla, Escuela de Estudios Hispano-Americanos. Sevilla, Spain.

Anu. Hist. Iglesia Chile. Anuario de Historia de la Iglesia en Chile. Seminario Pontificio Mayor. Santiago.

Anu. IEHS. Anuario IEHS. Univ. Nacional del Centro de la Provincia de Buenos Aires, Instituto de Estudios Histórico-Sociales. Tandil, Argentina.

Anu. Mus. Inconfidência. Anuario do Museu da Inconfidência. Museo Inconfidência. Ouro Preto, Brazil.

Anuario/Rosario. Anuario. Univ. Nacional de Rosario, Escuela de Historia. Argentina.

Anuario/Sucre. Anuario. Talleres Gráficos Túpac Katari. Archivo y Biblioteca Nacionales de Bolivia. Sucre.

Apuntes/Lima. Apuntes. Univ. del Pacífico, Centro de Investigación. Lima.

Arbor/Madrid. Arbor. Consejo Superior de Investigaciones Científicas. Madrid.

Arch. Francisc. Hist. Archivum Franciscanum Historicum. Collegio S. Bonaventura. Rome.

Arch. Ibero-Am. Archivo Ibero-Americano. Revista de Estudios Históricos. Los Padres Franciscanos. Madrid.

Arch. sci. soc. relig. Archives de sciences sociales des religions. Centre nationale de la recherche scientifique. Paris.

Archaeology/New York. Archaeology. Archaeology Institute of America. New York.

Art J. Art Journal. The College Art Assn., New York.

Bol. Acad. Chil. Hist. Boletín de la Academia Chilena de la Historia. Santiago.

Bol. Acad. Nac. Hist./Buenos Aires. Boletín de la Academia Nacional de la Historia. Buenos Aires.

Bol. Acad. Nac. Hist./Caracas. Boletín de la Academia Nacional de la Historia. Caracas.

Bol. Acad. Nac. Hist./Quito. Boletín de la Academia Nacional de Historia. Quito.

Bol. Am. Boletín Americanista. Univ. de Barcelona, Facultad de Geografía e Historia, Depto. de Historia de América. Barcelona.

Bol. Arch. Nac. Hist. Boletín del Archivo Nacional de Historia. Quito.

Bol. Bibl. Nac. Boletín de la Biblioteca Nacional. Biblioteca Nacional. Lima.

Bol. Cent. Invest. Hist. Boletín del Centro de Investigaciones Históricas. Facultad de Humanidades, Univ. de Puerto Rico. Río Piedras.

Bol. Cult. Bibliogr. Boletín Cultural y Bibliográfico. Banco de la República; Biblioteca Luis-Angel Arango. Bogotá.

Bol. Fuentes Hist. Econ. Méx. Boletín de Fuentes para la Historia Económica de México. Centro de Estudios Históricos, El Colegio de México. México.

Bol. Inst. Hist. Ravignani. Boletín del Instituto de Historia Argentina y Americana Dr. Emilio Ravignani. Facultad de Filosofía y Letras, Univ. de Buenos Aires.

Bol. Inst. Riva-Agüero. Boletín del Instituto Riva-Agüero. Pontificia Univ. Católica del Perú. Lima.

Bol. Nicar. Bibliogr. Doc. Boletín Nicaragüense de Bibliografía y Documentación. Biblioteca, Banco Central de Nicaragua. Managua.

Bull. Cent. hist. atl. Bulletin du Centre d'histoire des espaces atlantiques. Talence-Cedex, France.

Bull. hisp./Bordeaux. Bulletin hispanique. Univ. de Bordeaux; Centre national de la recherche scientifique. Bordeaux, France.

Bull. Inst. fr. étud. andin. Bulletin de l'Institut français d'études andines. Lima.

Bull. Lat. Am. Res. Bulletin of Latin American Research. Society for Latin American Studies. Oxford, England.

Bull. Soc. hist. Guadeloupe. Bulletin de la Société d'histoire de la Guadeloupe. Archives départamentales avec le concours du Conseil général de la Guadeloupe. Basse-Terre, Guadeloupe.

Bus. Hist. Rev. Business History Review. Harvard Univ. Graduate School of Business Administration. Boston, Mass.

Cah. Am. lat. Cahiers des Amériques latines. Paris.

Cah. patrim. Les cahiers du patrimoine. Bureau du patrimoine du Conseil régional de la Martinique. Fort-de-France.

Can. J. Afr. Stud. Canadian Journal of African Studies. Assn. of African Studies. Ottawa, Canada.

Can. J. Hist. Canadian Journal of History. Univ. of Saskatchewan. Saskatoon, Canada.

Caravelle/Toulouse. Caravelle. Cahiers du monde hispanique et luso-brésilien. Univ. de Toulouse, Institute d'études hispaniques, hispano-americaines et luso-brésiliennes. Toulouse, France.

Caribb. Stud. Caribbean Studies. Univ. of Puerto Rico, Institute of Caribbean Studies. Río Piedras.

Caribena/Martinique. Caribena: cahiers d'études américanistes de la Caraïbe. Centre d'études et de recherches archéologiques (CERA). Martinique.

CHELA. Cuadernos para la Historia de la Evangelización en América Latina: CHELA. Centro Bartolomé de las Casas. Cusco, Peru.

Chemins crit. Chemins critiques: revue haïtiano-caraïbéenne. Société sciences-arts-littérature. Port-au-Prince, Haiti.

Cienc. Hoy. Ciencia Hoy. Asociación Ciencia Hoy; Morgan Antártica. Buenos Aires.

CLAHR/Albuquerque. Colonial Latin American Historical Review. Spanish Colonial Research Center, Univ. of New Mexico. Albuquerque.

Colon. Lat. Am. Rev. Colonial Latin American Review. Simon H. Rifkind Center for the Humanities, Dept. of Romance Languages, City College of New York. New York.

Comp. Stud. Soc. Hist. Comparative Studies in Society and History. Society for the Comparative Study of Society and History; Cambridge Univ. Press. London.

Conjonction/Port-au-Prince. Conjonction. Bulletin de l'Institut français d'Haïti. Port-au-Prince.

Critique/St. Paul. Critique: Journal of Critical Studies of the Middle East. Center for Critical Studies of the Middle East. St. Paul, Minn.

Cuad. Am. Cuadernos Americanos. Editorial Cultura. México.

Cuad. CLAEH. Cuadernos del CLAEH. Centro Latinoamericano de Economía Humana. Montevideo.

Cuad. Hist./Córdoba. Cuadernos de Historia. Instituto de Historia del Derecho y de las Ideas Políticas. Córdoba, Argentina.

Cuad. Hist./Santiago. Cuadernos de Historia. Univ. de Chile, Facultad de Humanidades y Educación, Depto. de Ciencias Históricas. Santiago.

Curr. Hist. Current History. Philadelphia, Penn.

Desarro. Econ. Desarrollo Económico. Instituto de Desarrollo Económico y Social. Buenos Aires.

Diogenes/Philosophy. Diogenes. International Council for Philosophy and Humanistic Studies (Paris); Berg Publishers. Oxford, England.

Econ. Soc. Hist. Neth. Economic and Social History in the Netherlands. Nederlandsch Economisch-Historisch Archief. Amsterdam.

Economía/Lima. Economía. Depto. de Economía, Pontificia Univ. Católica del Perú. Lima.

Ecos/Santo Domingo. Ecos. Instituto de Historia, Univ. Autónoma de Santo Domingo.

Espace Caraïbe. Espace Caraïbe. Maison des Pays Ibériques, Univ. M. de Montaigne, Bordeaux, France; Centre d'Études et de Recherches Caraïbéennes, Univ. des Antilles et de la Guyane, Pointe-à-Pitre, Guadeloupe.

Estud. Cult. Contemp. Estudios sobre las Culturas Contemporáneas. Centro Universitario de Investigaciones Sociales, Univ. de Colima. México.

Estud. Cult. Maya. Estudios de Cultura Maya. Centro de Estudios Mayas, Univ. Nacional Autónoma de México. México.

Estud. Cult. Náhuatl. Estudios de Cultura Náhuatl. Instituto de Investigaciones Históricas, Univ. Nacional Autónoma de México. México.

Estud. Hist. Mod. Contemp. Méx. Estudios de Historia Moderna y Contemporánea de México. Univ. Nacional Autónoma de México. México.

Estud. Hist. Novohisp. Estudios de Historia Novohispana. Univ. Nacional Autónoma de México. México.

Estud. Hist./Rio de Janeiro. Estudos Históricos. Associação de Pesquisa e Documentação Histórica. Rio de Janeiro.

Estud. Hist. Rural. Estudios de Historia Rural. Univ. Nacional de La Plata, Centro de Estudios Histórico-Rurales. La Plata, Argentina.

Estud. Hist. Soc. Econ. Am. Estudios de Historia Social y Económica de América. Univ. de Alcalá de Henares. Madrid.

Estud. Ibero-Am./Porto Alegre. Estudos Ibero-Americanos. Pontifícia Univ. Católica do Rio Grande do Sul, Depto. de História. Porto Alegre, Brazil.

Estud. Jalisc. Estudios Jaliscienses. Univ. de Guadalajara. Guadalajara, Mexico.

Estud. Latinoam./Poland. Estudios Latinoamericanos. Academia de Ciencias de Polonia, Instituto de Historia. Wrocław.

Estud. Soc./Santo Domingo. Estudios Sociales. Centro de Estudios Sociales Juan Montalvo, SJ. Santo Domingo.

Estudios/Guatemala. Estudios. Instituto de Investigaciones Históricas, Antropológicas, y Arqueológicas, Univ. de San Carlos de Guatemala. Guatemala.

Ethnohistory/Columbus. Ethnohistory: the Bulletin of the Ohio Valley Historic Indian Conference. Columbus, Ohio.

Ethnohistory/Society. Ethnohistory. American Society for Ethnohistory. Duke Univ., Durham, N.C.

Etud. Guad. Etudes Guadeloupéennes. Association guadeloupéenne de recherches et d'études. Abymes, Guadeloupe.

EURE/Santiago. EURE: Revista Latinoamericana de Estudios Urbanos Regionales. Centro de Desarrollo Urbano y Regional, Univ. Católica de Chile. Santiago.

Fla. Hist. Q. The Florida Historical Quarterly. The Florida Historical Society. Jacksonville, Fla.

Généal. hist. Caraïbe. Généalogie et histoire de la Caraïbe. Assn. de la généalogie et histoire de la Caraïbe. Le Pecq, France.

Guyana Hist. J. Guyana Historical Journal. History Society, Dept. of History, Univ. of Guyana. Georgetown.

HAHR. Hispanic American Historical Review. Conference on Latin American History of the American Historical Assn.; Duke Univ. Press. Durham, N.C.

Hisp. Sacra. Hispania Sacra: Revista de Historia Eclesiástica de España. Centro de Estudios Históricos, Instituto Enrique Flórez. Madrid.

Hispania/Madrid. Hispania. Instituto Jerónimo Zurita, Consejo Superior de Investigaciones Científicas. Madrid.

Hist. Cult./Lima. Historia y Cultura. Museo Nacional de Historia. Lima.

Hist. Gaz. History Gazcttc. Univ. of Guyana, History Society. Turkeyen, Guyana.

Hist. Graf. Historia y Grafía. Depto. de Historia, Univ. Iberoamericana. México.

Hist. Mex. Historia Mexicana. Colegio de México. México.

Hist. Nuestra. Historia Nuestra. Concepción, Chile.

Hist. Relig. History of Religions. Univ. of Chicago. Chicago, Ill.

Hist. Res./Oxford. Historical Research. Institute of Historical Research. Oxford, England.

Hist. Soc./Río Piedras. Historia y Sociedad. Depto. de Historia, Univ. de Puerto Rico. Río Piedras.

Hist. Workshop. History Workshop. Ruskin College, Oxford Univ., Oxford, England.

Historia/Santiago. Historia. Univ. Católica de Chile. Instituto de Historia. Santiago.

História/São Paulo. História. Fundação para o Desenvolvimento da Univ. Estadual Paulista, Instituto de Letras, História e Psicologia. São Paulo.

Historian/Honor Society. The Historian. Phi Alpha Theta, National Honor Society in History; Univ. of Pennsylvania. Univ. Park, Penn.

Histórica/Lima. Histórica. Pontificia Univ. Católica del Perú, Depto. de Humanidades. Lima.

Historiogr. Bibliogr. Am. Historiografía y Bibliografía Americanista. Escuela de Estudios Hispano-Americanos de Sevilla. Sevilla, Spain.

Historiogr. Rioplat. Historiografía Rioplatense. Instituto Bibliográfico Antonio Zinny. Buenos Aires.

Homme/Paris. L'Homme. Laboratoire d'anthropologie, Collège de France. Paris.

Hoy Hist. Hoy es Historia: Revista Bimestral de Historia Nacional e Iberoamericana. Editorial Raíces. Montevideo.

Ibero-Am. Arch. Ibero-Amerikanisches Archiv. Ibero-Amerikanisches Institut. Berlin.

Ibero-Am./Stockholm. Ibero-Americana: Nordic Journal of Latin American Studies. Institute of Latin American Studies, Univ. of Stockholm.

Imago Mundi/London. Imago Mundi: the Journal of the International Society for the History of Cartography. King's College. London.

Int. Hist. Rev. The International History Review. Univ. of Toronto Press. Downsview, Ontario, Canada.

Int. Soc. Sci. J. International Social Science Journal. Blackwell Publishers. Oxford, England.

Interciencia/Caracas. Interciencia. Asociación Interciencia. Caracas.

Invest. Ens. Investigaciones y Ensayos. Academia Nacional de la Historia. Buenos Aires.

Islas/Santa Clara. Islas. Univ. Central de Las Villas. Santa Clara, Cuba.

Itinerario/Leiden. Itinerario. Leiden Centre for the History of European Expansion. Leiden, The Netherlands.

J. Afr. Hist. Journal of African History. Cambridge Univ. Press. London.

J. Anthropol. Res. Journal of Anthropological Research. Univ. of New Mexico. Albuquerque, N.M.

J. Caribb. Hist. The Journal of Caribbean History. Caribbean Univ. Press. St. Lawrence, Barbados.

J. Caribb. Stud. Journal of Caribbean Studies. Assn. of Caribbean Studies. Coral Gables, Fla.

J. Church State. Journal of Church and State. J.M. Dawson Studies in Church and State, Baylor Univ., Waco, Tex.

J. Econ. Hist. The Journal of Economic History. Economic History Assn.; Univ. of Kansas. Lawrence.

J. Interam. Stud. World Aff. Journal of Interamerican Studies and World Affairs. Institute of Interamerican Studies, Univ. of Miami. Coral Gables, Fla.

J. Interdiscip. Hist. The Journal of Interdisciplinary History. The MIT Press. Cambridge, Mass.

J. Lat. Am. Stud. Journal of Latin American Studies. Centers or Institutes of Latin American Studies at the Universities of Cambridge, Glasgow, Liverpool, London, and Oxford. Cambridge Univ. Press. London.

J. Miss. Hist. The Journal of Mississippi History. Mississippi Historical Society; Mississippi Dept. of Archives and History. Jackson, Miss.

J. Soc. Hist. Journal of Social History. Carnegie Mellon Univ., Pittsburgh, Penn.

Jahrb. Gesch. Jahrbuch für Geschichte von Staat, Wirtschaft und Gesellschaft Lateinamerikas. Köln, Germany.

Jam. Hist. Rev. The Jamaican Historical Review. The Jamaican Historical Society. Kingston.

La. Hist. Louisiana History. Louisiana Historical Assn., Lafayette, La.

La Mei Shi Yan Jiu Tong Xun. La Mei Shi Yan Jiu Tong Xun [Latin American History Newsletter]. s.n., Beijing?.

LARR. Latin American Research Review. Latin American Research Review Board. Univ. of New Mexico, Albuquerque, N.M.

Lat. Am. Perspect. Latin American Perspectives. Univ. of California. Newbury Park, Calif.

Li Shi Yan Jiu. Li Shi Yan Jiu [Chinese History Research]. Renmin Zhubanshe [People's Publishing House]. Beijing.

Luso-Braz. Rev. Luso-Brazilian Review. Univ. of Wisconsin Press. Madison, Wis.

MACLAS Lat. Am. Essays. MACLAS Latin American Essays. Middle Atlantic Council of Latin American Studies. New Brunswick, N.J.

Maguaré/Bogotá. Maguaré. Depto. de Antropología, Univ. Nacional de Colombia. Bogotá.

Mapocho/Santiago. Mapocho. Biblioteca Nacional. Santiago.

MEFRIM. Mélanges de l'Ecole française de Rome: Italie et Méditerranée. L'Ecole française de Rome. Rome.

Mélanges/Paris. Mélanges de la Casa de Velázquez. Ecole des hautes études hispaniques. Paris.

Mem. Acad. Mex. Hist. Memorias de la Academia Mexicana de la Historia. México.

Mem. Am. Memoria Americana. Instituto de Ciencias Antropológicas, Facultad de Filosofía y Letras, Univ. de Buenos Aires.

Mesoamérica/Antigua. Mesoamérica. Centro de Investigaciones Regionales de Mesoamérica. Antigua, Guatemala.

Mex. Stud. Mexican Studies/Estudios Mexicanos. Univ. of California, Berkeley.

N.M. Hist. Rev. New Mexico Historical Review. Historical Society of New Mexico; Univ. of New Mexico. Albuquerque, N.M.

N.Y. Rev. Books. The New York Review of Books. New York.

Nação Def. Nação e Defesa. Estudos Políticos do Gabinete de Estudos e Planeamento do Estado-Maior do Exército. Lisboa.

Nariz Diablo. Nariz del Diablo. Centro de Investigaciones y Estudios Socio-Económicos. Quito.

Natl. Geogr. Mag. National Geographic Magazine. National Geographic Society. Washington.

New Sch. New Scholar. Univ. of California, Committee on Hispanic Civilization and Center for Chicano Studies. Santa Barbara.

Notas Hist. Geogr. Notas Históricas y Geográficas. Univ. de Playa Ancha. Valparaiso, Chile.

Nuestra Hist./Buenos Aires. Nuestra Historia. Fundación Nuestra Historia. Buenos Aires.

Nuestra Hist./Caracas. Nuestra Historia. Litografía Litota. Caracas.

NWIG. New West Indian Guide/Nieuwe West Indische Gids. KITLV Press. Leiden, The Netherlands.

Op. Cit./Río Piedras. Op. Cit.: Boletín del Centro de Investigaciones Históricas. Depto.

de Historia, Facultad de Humanidades, Univ. de Puerto Rico. Río Piedras.

OSO/Netherlands. OSO. Stichring Instituut ter Bevordering van de Surinamistick (IBS) te Nijmegen. Nijmegen, The Netherlands.

Past Present. Past and Present. London.

Plant. Soc. Am. Plantation Society in the Americas. Univ. of New Orleans.

Plural/México. Plural. Excelsior Compañía Editorial. México.

Procesos/Quito. Procesos. Corporación Editora Nacional. Quito.

Publ. Inst. Estud. Iberoam. Publicaciones del Instituto de Estudios Iberoamericanos. Instituto de Estudios Iberamericanos. Buenos Aires.

Quaderni/São Paulo. Quaderni. Istituto Italiano di Cultura; Istituto Cultural Italo-Brasileiro. São Paulo.

Radic. Hist. Rev. Radical History Review. Mid-Atlantic Radical Historians' Organization. New York.

Razón Fe. Razón y Fe. La Compañía de Jesús. Madrid.

Relaciones/Zamora. Relaciones. El Colegio de Michoacán. Zamora, Mexico.

Relig. Cult. Religión y Cultura. Madrid.

Res Gesta. Res Gesta. Instituto de Historia, Facultad de Derecho y Ciencias Sociales, Univ. Católica Argentina. Rosario, Argentina.

Res/Harvard. Res. Peabody Museum of Archaeology and Ethnology, Harvard Univ., Cambridge, Mass.

Rev. Andin. Revista Andina. Centro Bartolomé de las Casas. Cusco, Peru.

Rev. Antropol./São Paulo. Revista de Antropologia. Univ. de São Paulo, Faculdade de Filosofia, Letras e Ciências Humanas; Associação Brasileira de Antropologia. São Paulo.

Rev. Arch. Nac. Hist. Azuay. Revista del Archivo Nacional de Historia, Sección del Azuay. Casa de la Cultura Ecuatoriana, Núcleo del Azuay. Cuenca, Ecuador.

Rev. Auvergne. Revue d'Auvergne. Société des Amis de l'Université de Clermont. Clermont-Ferrand, France.

Rev. Bras. Hist. Revista Brasileira de História. Associação Nacional dos Professores Universitários de História (ANPUH). São Paulo.

Rev. Cent. Estud. Av. La Revista del Centro de Estudios Avanzados de Puerto Rico y el Caribe. San Juan.

Rev. Chil. Hist. Geogr. Revista Chilena de Historia y Geografía. Sociedad Chilena de Historia y Geografía. Santiago.

Rev. Chil. Humanid. Revista Chilena de Humanidades. Facultad de Filosofía, Humanidades y Educación, Univ. de Chile. Santiago.

Rev. Ciclos. Revista Ciclos en la Historia, Economía y la Sociedad. Fundación de Investigaciones Históricas, Económicas y Sociales, Facultad de Ciencias Económicas, Univ. de Buenos Aires. Buenos Aires.

Rev. Ciênc. Hist. Revista de Ciências Históricas. Univ. Portucalense. Porto, Portugal.

Rev. Cienc. Soc./Río Piedras. Revista de Ciencias Sociales. Univ. de Puerto Rico, Colegio de Ciencias Sociales. Río Piedras.

Rev. Cienc. Soc./Valparaíso. Revista de Ciencias Sociales. Facultad de Derecho y Ciencias Sociales, Univ. de Valparaíso. Chile.

Rev. Colomb. Antropol. Revista Colombiana de Antropología. Ministerio de Educación Nacional, Instituto Colombiano de Antropología. Bogotá.

Rev. Complut. Hist. Am. Revista Complutense de Historia de América. Facultad de Geografía e Historia, Univ. Complutense de Madrid.

Rev. Cuba. Cienc. Soc. Revista Cubana de Ciencias Sociales. Centro de Estudios Filosóficos, Academia de Ciencias de Cuba. La Habana.

Rev. Dep. Hist./Belo Horizonte. Revista do Departamento de História. Univ. Federal de Minas Gerais. Belo Horizonte, Brazil.

Rev. Ecuat. Hist. Econ. Revista Ecuatoriana de Historia Económica. Banco Central del Ecuador, Centro de Investigación y Cultura. Quito.

Rev. Esp. Antropol. Am. Revista Española de Antropología Americana. Facultad de Geografía e Historia. Univ. Complutense de Madrid.

Rev. Esp. Estud. Norteam. Revista Española de Estudios Norteamericanos. Centro de Estudios Norteamericanos, Univ. de Alcalá de Henares. Spain.

Rev. Eur. Revista Europea de Estudios Latinoamericanos y del Caribe = European Review of Latin American and Caribbean Studies. Center for Latin American Research and Documentation; Royal Institute of Linguistics and Anthropology. Amsterdam.

Rev. fr. hist. Outre-mer. Revue française d'histoire d'Outre-mer. Société de l'histoire des colonies françaises. Paris.

Rev. Hist. Am. Revista de Historia de América. Instituto Panamericano de Geografía e Historia, Comisión de Historia. México.

Rev. Hist. Am. Argent. Revista de Historia Americana y Argentina. Univ. Nacional de Cuyo, Instituto de Historia. Mendoza, Argentina.

Rev. Hist./Concepción. Revista de Historia. Depto. de Ciencias Históricas y Sociales, Univ. de Concepción, Chile.

Rev. Hist./Heredia. Revista de Historia. Univ. Nacional de Costa Rica, Escuela de Historia. Heredia, Costa Rica.

Rev. Hist./Managua. Revista de Historia. Instituto de Historia de Nicaragua. Managua.

Rev. Hist. Naval. Revista de Historia Naval. Instituto de Historia y Cultura Naval Armada Española. Madrid.

Rev. hist./Paris. Revue historique. Presses Univ. de France. Paris.

Rev. Indias. Revista de Indias. Consejo Superior de Investigaciones Científicas, Instituto Gonzalo Fernández de Oviedo. Madrid.

Rev. Inst. Cult. Puertorriq. Revista del Instituto de Cultura Puertorriqueña. San Juan.

Rev. Inst. Hist. Geogr. Para. Revista do Instituto Histórico e Geográfico Paraibano. Univ. Federal da Paraíba. João Pessoa, Brazil.

Rev. Junta Prov. Hist. Córdoba. Revista de la Junta Provincial de Historia de Córdoba. Córdoba, Argentina.

Rev. Juríd. Univ. P.R. Revista Jurídica de la Universidad de Puerto Rico. Escuela de Derecho, Univ. de Puerto Rico. Río Piedras.

Rev. Mex. Sociol. Revista Mexicana de Sociología. Instituto de Investigaciones Sociales, Univ. Nacional Autónoma de México. México.

Rev. Nac./Montevideo. Revista Nacional. Ministerio de Instrucción Pública. Montevideo.

Rev. Occident. Revista de Occidente. Madrid.

Rev. Parag. Sociol. Revista Paraguaya de Sociología. Centro Paraguayo de Estudios Sociológicos. Asunción.

Rev. Rev. Interam. Revista/Review Interamericana. Inter-American Univ. Press. Hato Rey, Puerto Rico.

Rev. Soc. haïti. Revue de la Société haïtienne d'histoire et de géographie. Port-au-Prince.

Ruralia/Buenos Aires. Ruralia: Revista Argentina de Estudios Agrarios. FLACSO; Ediciones Imago Mundi. Buenos Aires.

Santiago/Cuba. Santiago. Univ. de Oriente. Santiago, Cuba.

Sarance/Otavalo. Sarance. Instituto Otavaleño de Antropología. Otavalo, Ecuador.

SECOLAS Ann. SECOLAS Annals. Southeastern Conference on Latin American Studies; West Georgia College. Carrollton, Ga.

Secuencia/México. Secuencia. Instituto Mora. México.

Sefárdica/Buenos Aires. Sefárdica. Centro de Investigación y Difusión de la Cultura Sefardí. Buenos Aires.

Senderos/Bogotá. Senderos. Biblioteca Nacional de Colombia. Bogotá.

Siglo XIX. Siglo XIX. Facultad de Filosofía y Letras, Univ. Autónoma de Nuevo León. Monterrey, Mexico.

Slavery Abolit. Slavery & Abolition. Frank Cass & Co., Ltd., London.

Soc. Compass. Social Compass. The International Catholic Institute for Social-Ecclesiastical Research. The Hague.

Soc. Hist./London. Social History. Methuen. London.

Southwest. Hist. Q. Southwestern Historical Quarterly. The Texas State Historical Assn., Austin, Tex.

Stud. Emigr. Studi Emigrazione. Centro Studi Emigrazione. Rome.

Stud. Hist. Hist. Mod. Studia Historica: Historia Moderna. Univ. de Salamanca. Salamanca, Spain.

SWI Forum. SWI Forum voor Kunst, Kultuur en Wetenschop. De Stichting. Paramaribo, Suriname.

Tierra Firme. Tierra Firme. Caracas.

Tijdschr. Geschied. Tijdschrift voor Geschiedenis. P. Noordhoff. Groningen, Netherlands.

Todo es Hist. Todo es Historia. Buenos Aires.

UCLA Hist. J. UCLA Historical Journal. Univ. of California, Dept. of History. Los Angeles.

Universidad/Santa Fe. La Universidad. Univ. Nacional del Litoral. Santa Fe, Argentina.

Universum/Talca. Universum. Univ. de Talca. Talca, Chile.

Wampum/Leiden. Wampum. Archeologisch Centrum. Leiden, The Netherlands.

Wani/Managua. Wani: Una Revista sobre la Costa Atlántica. Centro Investigaciones y Documentación de la Costa Atlántica. Managua.

Yaxkin/Tegucigalpa. Yaxkin. Instituto Hondureño de Antropología e Historia. Tegucigalpa.

Yearbook/CLAG. Yearbook. Conference of Latin Americanist Geographers; Ball State Univ., Muncie, Ind.

Yumtzilob/Leiden. Yumtzilob: Tijdschrift over de Americas. Archeologisch Centrum. Leiden, The Netherlands.

LITERATURE

SPANISH AMERICA
General

SARA CASTRO-KLAREN, *Professor of Hispanic and Italian Studies, The Johns Hopkins University*

THIS BIENNIUM HAS BROUGHT A MIXTURE of anthologies, histories, monographs, and, of course, collections of essays; there are considerably fewer interviews and conference proceedings. Books inspired by the commemoration of the Quincentenary continue to appear and, to judge by the announcements of American university presses, there are still a few more to come. On the anthology front, David William Foster has made a major contribution (item **3388**). We also welcome John Keller and Rafael Aguirre's revised edition of *Hispanoamérica en su literatura* (item **3389**). Both should serve as points of departure for future anthological projects. It is unfortunate that Darío Villanueva and José María Viña Liste (item **3403**) and Ricardo Gullón (item **3381**), the Spanish editors of an anthology and a dictionary, respectively, did not avail themselves of the model provided by these solidly researched works and their intelligent and informed organization. Graduate and undergraduate students will also benefit from Naomi Lindstrom's original and well-grounded history of 20th-century literature (item **3393**).

The emergence of a new interest in history is reflected in three monographs. Raymond Souza's study of the weight of history in the modern novel (item **3401**) provides an interesting companion for Seymour Menton's study of the new historical novel (item **3395**). Aníbal González's history of journalism and the development of fiction in Latin America diverges from the much propounded thesis that locates the genre's origin and character in the early Spanish chroniclers (item **3386**). However, the most important studies reviewed in this section are those influenced by post-structuralist theory that use history and historiography to pose radical questions about the conceptual underpinnings of our understanding of cultural history. Following the lead of *Imagined communities* by Benedict Anderson, Ileana Rodríguez examines the role of gender and ethnicity in relation to the ideology of the nation-state as written in the fiction of women writers (item **3399**). Iris Zavala studies the relations of colonialism and *modernismo,* and in so doing transforms our understanding of not only the "literary" movement, but also of the period when Latin American intellectuals set out to create "their own" project of emancipatory modernity (item **3404**). Though very difficult to read because of their complex entwining with post-structural theory, the two books mentioned above, along with the collection of essays edited by Stephen Bell (item **5026**), present a series of complex, urgent, and vexing issues concerning Latin American cultural production.

The problems that these authors identify, conceptualize and attempt to analyze—colonialism, subject formation, nation formation, gender/ethnicity, "hispanism," historiography—will continue to be major topics for the next decade. As the field continues to evolve from literary criticism into cultural criticism, the importance of historical research will bring forth new knowledge.

3375 Arrom, José Juan. Imaginación del Nuevo Mundo: diez estudios sobre los inicios de la narrativa hispanoamericana. México: Siglo Veintiuno Editores, 1991. 196 p.: bibl. (Lingüística y teoría literaria)

Holds to thesis that texts written by Columbus, Las Casas, Gonzalo Fernández de Oviedo and José de Acosta lay the foundation for Spanish American narrative. Author claims that the partially autobiographical accounts of the conquest of Mexico create a space between history and fiction that remains unchallenged until modern times. Arrom's method includes short biographical notes on each "cronista," assessment of the current value of their work as a reliable source, and analysis of selected passages from the chronicles. Points out the voyage to America of medieval narrative forms such as catastrophe, humorous medieval stories and fictional biography. Based on ample and sound scholarship, these essays are useful to those interested in colonial letters, and in particular, their relationship to both Spanish narrative forms and Amerindian narrative arts.

Bibliografía en CD-ROM de la *Nueva Revista de Filología Hispánica*. See item **2.**

Brotherston, Gordon. Book of the fourth world: reading the Native Americas through their literature. See item **401.**

3376 Catelli, Nora *et al.* La crítica literaria española frente a la literatura latinoamericana. Coordinación de Leonor Fleming y María Teresa Bosque La[s]tra. México: Univ. Nacional Autónoma de México, Coordinación de Humanidades, Centro Coordinador y Difusor de Estudios Latinoamericanos, 1993. 220 p.: bibl. (Panoramas de nuestra América; 2)

Several young Spanish academics write on the reception of Latin American literature in Spain. Book's preface states that past literary relations between Latin America and Spain have been marked by mutual and willful ignorance of each other. Nora Castelli writes that "para comprender el tipo de relaciones literarias existentes entre América Latina y España hay que abandonar toda consideración acerca de la hermandad de las lenguas y desarrollo paralelo de la vida literaria de ambos continentes." She notes that the reception of Latin American literature in Spain does not differ from the reception accorded any other foreign literature. Same is true in Latin America of Spanish literature. Interesting sample of critical work by young Spaniards who want to join the international field of Latin American studies and abandon the neo-colonial pretensions of a homogenizing "Hispanism."

3377 Colonial discourse and post-colonial theory: a reader. Edited and introduced by Patrick Williams and Laura Chrisman. New York: Columbia Univ. Press, 1994. 570 p.: bibl., index.

Edward Said's *Orientalism* (1978) inaugurated a new mode of inquiry into texts written about areas absorbed by Europe's colonial expansion. Said's inquiry led to the "new" field of colonial discourse-analysis. Bill Ashcroft, Gareth Griffiths and Helen Tiffin's *The Empire writes back* (1989) inaugurates a new theoretical field, beyond Said's orientalism, to investigate the emergence of texts authored by colonial subjects or "post-colonial theory." Approaches developed by former subjects of the British Empire share many theoretical and cultural concerns with Latin American intellectual history. Includes selections from Frantz Fanon, Edward Said, Gayatri Spivak, Denis Porter, Jenny Sharp, Stuart Hall, etc. Highly recommended for those investigating new paradigms in cultural criticism and intellectual history.

3378 Contextos: literatura y sociedad latinoamericanas del siglo XIX. Edición de Evelyn Picón Garfield e Iván A. Schulman. Urbana: Univ. of Illinois Press, 1991. 115 p.:

Worthwhile collection of selected papers on modernismo and modernity and national identities from a US-USSR symposium (Urbana, Ill., 1987). Diverse group of scholars use differing approaches and methodologies.

Of special interest are: Kuteischikova and Kemskov on formation of national consciousness; Zubritski on Juan Wallparimachi Mayta and the formation of Quechua national consciousness; and Picón Gardfield on Guatimotzin, a new in-depth reading of this neglected novel. Schulman shows how Gertrudis Gómez de Avellaneda used "historical" data from chronicles in combination with fictional representations, in order to "intuir civilizaciones y utilizar las crónicas para comentar no solo sobre procesos históricos sino sobre la sociedad de la epoca." In his essay on literature and slavery in Puerto Rico, Aníbal González sets out to correct the apparent and shocking inexistence of abolitionist literature in Puerto Rico. Finds that it is the various forms of "popular" literature "folklore, adivinanzas, cuentos, canciones" where the image of the Puerto Rican African American can be recovered. This legacy is later captured in *La noche oscura del Niño Avilés* (1984) by Edgardo Rodriguez Juliá and the short stories by Ana Lydia Vega in *Encancaramblado* (1983).

3379 Critical theory, cultural politics, and Latin American narrative. Edited by Steven M. Bell, Albert H. Le May, and Leonard Orr. Notre Dame: Univ. of Notre Dame Press, 1993. 227 p.: bibl.

Essays such as Fredric Jameson's "Exogamy and Letters in Late Capitalism," Mary Louise Pratt's "Criticism in the Contact Zone," and Fernando Coronil's "Challenging Colonial Histories" provide good examples of the challenges posed by post-structuralism to the notion of "nation" and by implication to the standing category of "national literatures." "Hispanism," that ill-defined umbrella term, under which the study of Latin American letters has been institutionalized, is indicated as a problem. Neil Larson points out that the indisputable cultural triumph of Latin American fiction has not been matched by a corresponding social and political emancipation from imperial bonds. Excellent volume posing urgent questions in the field of cultural criticism and its possible definitions in the North American academy. Highly recommended for all graduate programs as well as for those engaged in curriculum discussions.

Cueva, Agustín. Literatura y conciencia histórica en América Latina. See item **3618.**

3380 De la ironía a lo grotesco: en algunos textos literarios hispanoamericanos. Iztapalapa: Univ. Autónoma Metropolitana, 1992. 221 p.: bibl., ill.

Seven essays on irony in a variety of Spanish American texts, plus two translations of articles originally published in French. Although irony is the theme that links the essays, authors have found the need to draw on other related tropes: satire, parody, the grotesque, humor, etc. Authors cover assortment of works from different periods: colonial poetry to Modernismo to Rosario Castellanos. Of interest to anyone working with irony, two theoretical pieces from the French magazine *Poétique.*

3381 Diccionario de literatura española e hispanoamericana. v. 1–2. Dirigido por Ricardo Gullón. Prólogo de Fernando Lázaro Carreter. Asesores Pedro Cátedra *et al.* Secretario, Javier Blasco. Edición de Carmen Criado. Madrid: Alianza Editorial, 1993. 2 v. (2024 p.).: bibl., index. (Alianza diccionarios)

Two-volume dictionary composed mainly of entries of authors and critics from Spain and Spanish America. There are also definitions for broad terms, such as: "Literatura Infantil Española," "Teatro Medieval," "La Novela Histórica," "Modernismo," etc. Interesting and useful list of past winners of literary awards is under "Premios Literarios." End of vol. 2 includes index of works cited in the "Diccionario" to facilitate searches. Extremely useful reference for broad public and most useful for fact-finding. Emphasizes Peninsular over Spanish American literature.

3382 A dream of light & shadow: portraits of Latin American women writers. Edited by Marjorie Agosin. Albuquerque: Univ. of New Mexico Press, 1995. 342 p.: bibl.

Sixteen portraits of Latin American writers sensitively introduced by poet and writer Agosin. Women selected for this anthology are creative and preoccupied by issues concerning women and marginalized groups, education, and political injustice. Essays on each writer written by distinguished literary critics. Useful for classroom purposes and general reading. [A. Lavrin]

3383 Echavarren Welker, Roberto. Margen de ficción: poéticas de la narrativa hispanoamericana. México: Editorial J. Mortiz,

1992. 141 p.: bibl. (Cuadernos de Joaquín Mortiz)

Book is divided into two sections: "Disciplinas" and "Lecturas." Pt. 1 is a theoretical study of what the author calls the literary margin (margen literario). Combines pschoanalysis, anthropology, and philosophy to offer an understanding of the virtue of writing/reading. Writing and reading imply a singular, liberating experience for the "hablante" from the institutions that regulate him (or her). Pt. 2 comprises seven readings on transgression from the margin (e.g., Unamuno, Macedonio Fernández, and Borges; context and mise-en-scène in Rulfo; reality and imagination in Onetti; fetish and fading of the subject in Puig; writing and voice in Sylvia Molloy and Ricardo Piglia; and writing and dictatorship in Severo Sarduy and Reinaldo Arenas). Complicated theoretical base makes for difficult reading but author offers innovative interpretations of works produced by important writers "on the margin."

3384 Escritores de América: 31 entrevistas publicadas en *Revista de Libros* de *El Mercurio.* Santiago?: Editorial Los Andes, 1993. 306 p.: ill. (Serie Diálogos)

Interviews of 31 Latin American authors, including five female writers, that first appeared in the *Revista de Libros* in Chile. Some interesting personal anecdotes and revealing commentaries by some of Latin America's best known writers: from Adolfo Bioy Casares to Mario Vargas Llosa. Fun and light reading. Each is accompanied by an excellent sketch of the interviewee by Jimmy Scott.

Fuentes, Carlos. Geografía de la novela. See item **3489.**

3385 Glickman, Nora. Jewish women writers in Latin America. (*in* Women of the word: Jewish women and Jewish writing. Edited by Judith R. Baskin. Detroit: Wayne State University Press, 1994, p. 299–322)

Provides short descriptions of the work of several Argentine and Mexican Jewish women. For some, writing becomes a unique way of understanding and finding identity. For others, it is an exploration of their hybrid condition as both challenge and asset. Some, like Teresa Porzekanski and Margo Glantz, recover voices of the past in albums, records, and folktales. Others, like Gloria Gervitz

and Sabina Berman, commemorate bonds between mother and daughter. The novels of Alicia Steinberg reflect generational conflicts and refer to contemporary politics with sarcasm and disdain. Steinberg is particularly interested in the changing role of Yiddish for each new generation of Latin American Jewish writers. A good guide to a subject of growing in importance in the field of Latin American intellectual history.

Gomes, Angela de Castro. Essa gente do Rio . . . os intelectuais cariocas e o modernismo. See item **3306.**

3386 González, Aníbal. Journalism and the development of Spanish American narrative. Cambridge, England; New York: Cambridge Univ. Press, 1993. 165 p.: bibl., index. (Cambridge studies in Latin American and Iberian literature; 8)

Intelligent, well-researched, and innovative investigation of the interaction between modernity, journalism and literature in Spanish America. Clear and readable, work that defines all broad terms (e.g., modernity, journalism, discourse, etc.). Asks why so many Spanish American authors are/were journalists and why fiction writers use journalistic discourse and devices (e.g., Fernández de Lizardi, Sarmiento, Ricardo Palma, the Modernists, Borges, García Márquez, Vargas Llosa, Elena Poniatowska). Author suggests that Spanish America's first self-proclaimed novel, *El Periquillo Sarniento,* was a covert form of journalism, a pamphlet masquerading as a work of narrative fiction to escape censorship. *Facundo* was a pamphlet that became a novel. Finally, with contemporary writers, journalism seems to help focus ethical or moral reflections which articulate Spanish American narratives. Highly recommended.

3387 Graham-Yooll, Andrew. After the despots: Latin American views and interviews. Edited by Norman Thomas di Giovanni. London: Bloomsbury, 1991. 218 p.: index.

Highly readable collection of essays and interviews with well-known authors. Concerns political uncertainty of the 1980s. Interviews and discussions reveal anger, impotence, and disgust felt by writers confronting military dictatorships, as well as cautious optimism that has accompanied the transition to democracy. Authentic voices well worth hearing.

3388 Handbook of Latin American literature. Compiled by David William Foster. 2nd ed. New York: Garland Pub., 1992. 799 p.: bibl., index. (Garland reference library of the humanities; 1459)

Revised edition of the 1987 *Handbook.* New chapters are: "Latino Writing in the United States," "Paraliterature," and "Film." Each is a comprehensive essay concerning the national literature of a particular Latin American country. Each chapter includes annotated bibliography and useful listing of general references on Latin American literature.

3389 Hispanoamérica en su literatura. Edited by Nicholson B. Adams *et al.* Revised by John E. Keller and Rafael A. Aguirre. 2nd ed. New York: W.W. Norton, 1993. 538 p.: ill., 2 maps.

Revised 2nd ed. of an anthology of Spanish-American letters aimed at intermediate university courses. Includes selections of 47 authors representing poetry, short story, essay, novel, letter, and personal memoir (no theater). This edition adds sections on the "boom" and on contemporary writers, and includes more female writers (e.g., Gertrudis Gómez de Avellaneda, Isabel Allende, Hilda Perera). Divided into four main sections: 1) Colonial Literature, 2) 19th Century, 3) 20th Century: 1900–1960; and 4) 20th Century: After 1960. Useful anthology although it already needs to be updated (e.g., Manuel Puig, d. 1990). See also Foster's anthology (item **3394**).

3390 Imagination, emblems, and expressions: essays on Latin American, Caribbean, and continental culture and identity. Edited by Helen Ryan-Ranson. Bowling Green, OH: Bowling Green State Univ. Popular Press, 1993. 382 p.: bibl.

Volume of 24 essays dedicated to the theme of culture and identity in Latin America and the Caribbean. Book concerns quest for identity that has become of paramount importance to the people of the Western Hemisphere. *HLAS* readers will find the five essays on Latin American culture and identity most interesting and pertinent to their research. Recommended for its insightful essays and particularly useful to those interested in cultural studies.

3391 Kadir, Djelal. The other writing: postcolonial essays in Latin America's writing culture. West Lafayette, Ind.: Purdue Univ. Press, 1993. 220 p.: bibl., index.

Collection of essays on Borges, Paz, Fuentes, García Márquez, Vargas Llosa, Donoso, and Diamela Eltit. Each essay is a dazzling reading of the text in question. A comparatist by training and a voracious reader by habit, Kadir places each text in a rich web of Western culture. Kadir writes amply on theory which he believes to be a form of fiction. Collection offers original readings on the sublime in *Cristóbal Nonato* and *Terra Nostra,* places *Cien años de soledad* in the context of Milton's *Paradise lost.* On the whole this critic attempts to read other-wise, the work of writers who, aware of a tradition that circumscribes them, write in self-conscious ways in order to produce alternate modes of knowing.

3392 Kaminsky, Amy K. Reading the body politic: feminist criticism and Latin American women writers. Minneapolis: Univ. of Minnesota Press, 1993. 176 p.: bibl., index.

Clearly reasoned and well-integrated book explores questions of exile, torture, the body, testimony, and lesbian cartographies in women's writing. Kaminsky sees the limits of genre theory as an appropriate tool for reading Elena Garro's *Los recuerdos del porvenir,* for example. Aware of the silence that has surrounded the lesbian writer in Latin America, Kaminsky offers a readical and sensitive discussion of the issue by focusing on the fiction of Cristina Peri-Rossi, and Sylvia Molloy. Acknowledges the feminist postulates, leadership and struggle for ordinary Latin American women who daily organize in search of democracy across institutional spaces, from the domestic to the public arena of party politics and theorizing. Highlights theoretical work of Chilean sociologist Julieta Kirkwood. Informed, intelligent, clearly written, this book is highly recommended for those interested in metropolitan feminist theories and their problematic connection with Latin American women's writing and other social practices.

La escritura del cuento. See item **3522.**

Latbook: libros y revistas argentinas en Internet. See item **40.**

Latino 3. See *HLAS 55:36.*

Latino literature web page. See item **41.**

3393 **Lindstrom, Naomi.** Twentieth-century Spanish American fiction. Austin: Univ. of Texas Press, 1994. 246 p.: bibl., index. (Texas Pan American series)

Readable, well-organized, soundly researched introduction to Latin American fiction. Relies on the best of current research on individual authors, periods, and literary movements. Combines empirical information on biography and period with insightful and careful readings of canonical works. Solid treatments of modernismo, realism and naturalism, avant-guard, fantastic modes, the boom and its antecedents, the postboom and new voices. Particularly noteworthy is the consistent treatment of writing by women. Fills important vacuum created by the production of anthologies which lack a critical and bibliographic structure. Highly recommended for college courses and Master's level instruction.

3394 **Literatura hispanoamericana: una antología.** Edited by David William Foster. Con la colaboración de Roberto Forns Broggi *et al.* New York: Garland Pub., 1994. 1215 p. (Garland reference library of the humanities; 1693)

Starting with Bartolomé de las Casas, this anthology moves on through the centuries right up to Rigoberta Menchú. Includes introductory notes and brief bio-bibliographic notes on each author. Includes precolumbian texts. Selection criteria reflects current debates on the canon. Unlike several other recent anthologies Foster's selects full chapters and even a full play. Includes many women writers left out of previous collections (e.g., Rosario Castellanos and Gertrudis Avellaneda). Texts are representative of the best of many writers, periods, and movements (e.g., Martí, Sarmiento, Mistral, Vallejo, Borges, and Cortázar). Selections are not easy. Anthology is for senior or graduate students. Excellent and recommended for use in conjunction with companion critical volume.

3395 **Menton, Seymour.** Latin America's new historical novel. Austin: Univ. of Texas Press, 1993. 228 p.: bibl., index. (The Texas Pan American series)

Interesting, clear reliable account of the new historical novel (1949–92). Particu-

larly useful chronology for establishing limits of this sub-genre. Explores differences between the old and new historical novel, a difference which is not based on date of publication but rather on aesthetic criteria which divides the enormous fictional production since 1949. The "New" is decidedly postmodern. Subsequent chapters provide in-depth readings of individual novels (e.g., *La guerra del fin del mundo,* 1981; *Los perros del paraíso,* 1987; *Noticias del Imperio,* 1987). Most interesting chapter treats several novels about Simón Bolívar. Also worthwhile is the last grouping on "Jewish Latin American Novels." Lays down solid basis for future work on a fascinating corpus.

MLA International Bibliography [CD-ROM]. See item **17.**

3396 **Molloy, Sylvia.** Too Wilde for comfort: desire and ideology in fin-de-siècle Latin America. (*in* Negotiating lesbian and gay subjects. Edited by Monica Dorenkamp and Richard Henke. New York: Routledge, 1995, p. 35–52)

Examines reactions of José Martí in New York to the person (body and dress) of Oscar Wilde together with Rubén Darío's obituary on Wilde's death. Makes the case that in the appreciations of both modernista writers there is an "anxious machismo" that asserts a panicked normative we. Following Octavio Paz's claim that the modernista appropriation of European decadence at the turn of the century is a sign of regeneration in Latin America, Molloy points out that this entrance into modernity is rather patchy. Decadent pleasures of the body are viewed as part of what Dario calls the "red flower of sexual aberrations" and homosexual panic marks the suppression of the male body not only in Darío and Martí but especially in Rodó.

3397 **Morales T., Leónidas.** Figuras literarias, rupturas culturales: modernidad e identidades culturales tradicionales. Santiago: Pehuén, 1993. 164 p.: bibl. (Ensayo)

Seven essays on four Latin American authors (Horacio Quiroga, José E. Rivera, José M. Arguedas, and Violeta Parra), written over 27 years. The essays on the first three authors look at systems of connotations and the construction of determined narrative figures. Quiroga's characters in Misiones create a community figure: the "global village" of

Misiones. Rivera's *La vorágine* allows the construction of two other figures: the myth of the voyage to hell or "el país de los muertos." In Arguedas, the structure of the narrative language, becomes the stylistic figure of a seductive social utopia. It is the process of modernity in Spanish America and the ruptures that it creates that explain the creation of these literary figures.

Mundo latino: rincón literario. See item **42.**

3398 Payne, Johnny. Conquest of the new word: experimental fiction and translation in the Americas. Austin: Univ. of Texas Press, 1993. 292 p.: bibl., index. (The Texas Pan American series)

Readings of "boom and postboom" authors from Argentina and Uruguay. Payne includes Borges in the "boom" because he first appeared in translation with the younger generation of "boom" writers. Focusing on Buenos Aires and Montevideo, there are comparisons with US writers in order to allow the similarities and disparities in their own cultural grounding to become more salient. The "boom" as a phenomenon seems to have reinforced many long-standing stereotypes of Latin America. Translation of these works failed to provide US readers with a more complex view of history and politics. Excellent study emphasizes careful, close readings of modern South American fiction against its political and cultural grounding. Recommended reading.

Payne, Judith A. and **Earl E. Fitz.** Ambiguity and gender in the new novel of Brazil and Spanish America: a comparative assessment. See item **4335.**

3399 Rodríguez, Ileana. House/garden/nation: space, gender, and ethnicity in post-colonial Latin American literatures by women. Translated by Robert Carr and Ileana Rodríguez. Durham, NC: Duke Univ. Press, 1994. 223 p.: bibl., index. (Post-contemporary interventions)

Studies the intersection of gender, nation, and ethnicity in times of transition. Author draws from her own experience as a member of the Sandinista government and from current theoretical discussion on nation and narration. She dwells on the fact that the Sandinista defeat in Nicaragua is followed by the government of Doña Violeta Chamorro and compares her to authors and heroines examined in the book. Ranging widely over Latin American history, this well-researched and intelligently conceived interpretation of the fiction of nation formation is an important book.

Schwartz, Jorge. Vanguardas latino-americanas: polêmicas, manifestos e textos críticos. See item **4340.**

3400 Sklodowska, Elzbieta. Testimonio hispanoamericano: historia, teoría, poética. New York: Peter Lang, 1992. 219 p.: bibl.

Departs from Miguel Barnet's thesis on testimonial narrative as the answer to the so-called crisis of the bourgeois novel. Examines major claims made by the critics for the testimonial narrative as a distinct genre. Attempts a typology of her own in order to clarify the meaning of the term "testimonio." Clearly written, well-researched, comprehensive, and reliable summary and analysis of the critical debate on "testimonio." Includes good bibliography.

3401 Souza, Raymond D. La historia en la novela hispanoamericana moderna. Bogotá: Tercer Mundo Editores, 1988. 199 p.: bibl. (Crítica literaria)

Study of the reciprocal action between history and literature in contemporary Spanish American novels (since 1960). Concentrates on the topological and epistemological strategies used by authors, focusing on the similarities as opposed to the differences between history and fiction. Investigates how contemporary Latin American writers use historic events as inspiration in the writing of their novels, and the literary aspects of this process. Authors discussed are: Rosario Aguilar (Nicaragua), Gustavo Alvarez Gardeazábal (Colombia), Reinaldo Arenas (Cuba), Alejo Carpentier (Cuba), Carlos Fuentes (Mexico), Mario Vargas Llosa (Peru), and Ernesto Sábato (Argentina). They have been unable to dominate or even assimilate their history into the present. The intensification of history in contemporary Spanish American novels is healthy; problems cannot be resolved if they are not recognized and articulated.

Teorías de los cuentistas. See item **3526.**

3402 Varela, Félix. Jicoténcal. Edición de Luis Leal y Rodolfo J. Cortina. Houston, Tex.: Arte Público Press, 1995. xlvii, 164 p.: bibl., index.

Para Leal y Cortina se trata de la primera novela histórica escrita en el Nuevo Mundo y quizás la primera en castellano. La aservación es debatible, pero este relato del siglo XIX de la alianza entre Hernán Cortés y Tlaxcala y de la traición al joven general Jicoténcal, es de enorme interés histórico, a lo cual contribuye las notas, la bibliografía, los dos índices y la aguda introducción histórica-crítica.

3403   Villanueva, Darío and **José María Viña Liste.** Trayectoria de la novela hispano-americana actual: del "realismo mágico" a los años ochenta. Madrid: Espasa Calpe, 1991. 453 p.: bibl. (Col. Austral; 222. Filología)

Study of the last 50 years of Hispanic American novels. The year 1940 is taken as point of departure from traditional themes and forms. Consists of four parts: 1) a long introduction; 2) authors born 1900–20; 3) authors born 1921–40; and 4) a short section on latest novelists. Most women writers, however, are not included. Book seems to have been prepared with Spanish students in mind.

3404   Zavala, Iris M. Colonialism and culture: Hispanic modernisms and the social imaginary. Bloomington: Indiana Univ. Press, 1992. 240 p.: bibl., index.

Brilliant, taxing but worthwhile revision of modernismo in Spanish America and its Spanish counterpart. Ranges widely on poststructuralism and post-Marxist theory. Challenging and comprehensive book is an ambitious rethinking of the cultural history of a key period in Latin America. Particularly innovative is the chapter on heterology and popular culture. Highly recommended for cultural criticism and intellectual history.

Zavala, Lauro. Humor, ironía y lectura: las fronteras de la escritura literaria. See item **3527.**

Colonial Period

ALVARO FELIX BOLAÑOS, *Associate Professor of Spanish, University of Florida*

LOS ESTUDIOS DE LAS LETRAS del período colonial hispanoamericano se han estado ocupando últimamente no sólo de la exploración de nuevos textos y la reconsideración de otros previamente estudiados sino también de la reflexión sobre la metodología de su estudio. "Discurso colonial" es el concepto que más se ha utilizado en la última década para designar tales textos que un número, cada vez más creciente, de latinoamericanistas tiende a estudiar, cuestionando la experiencia colonizadora europea en el Nuevo Mundo. Sin embargo, la gran popularidad y la innegable versatilidad de este concepto no revelan su claridad sino más bien su carácter controversial y, con alguna frecuencia, su problemática aplicabilidad a todos los textos de cuatro siglos de dominación española en América (ver item **3405**).

La historiadora Patricia Seed ha realizado una de las más claras y pertinentes reflexiones sobre el desarrollo de lo que ella llama "movimiento interdisciplinario" en el que la crítica literaria, la antropología y la historia han hecho sus aportes para el estudio de textos sobre situaciones coloniales que no pueden ser ya satisfactoriamente estudiados por una sola disciplina. En su muy importante ensayo-reseña titulado "Colonial and Post-Colonial Discourse" (item **3419**), Seed intenta definir este nuevo movimiento que para el caso latinoamericano, según ella, responde a los estímulos intelectuales de estudiosos no europeos de la experiencia colonialista inglesa. Este necesario y saludable esfuerzo de sistematización de una prominente tendencia de lectura de los textos coloniales supuso cierta institucionalización de una disciplina cuyo principal objetivo ha sido la crítica al colonialismo de ayer y de hoy. También planteó la aplicabilidad del término a la muy amplia y compleja totalidad de textos coloniales desde 1492 hasta fines del siglo XVIII. Tal intento de institucionalización y generalización de términos y metodologías propició una de las más importantes controversias—entre Seed, Walter Mignolo (item **3413**), Hernán Vidal (item **3422**) y Rolena Adorno (item **3405**)—hasta la fecha realizadas sobre la metodología en los estudios de las letras del período colonial hispanoamericano. Este debate es de obligada lectura para todos aquellos interesados en el desarrollo de los estudios coloniales.

Pero el término "discurso colonial," utilizado en la gran mayoría de los trabajos aquí reseñados, ha sido, a pesar de su carácter controversial, el resultado de un intento de encontrar una lengua franca en un campo de estudio transitado en la última década no solamente por críticos literarios (dedicados principalmente al estudio de las derivaciones americanas de la estética renacentista) sino por estudiosos de la historia, la antropología y la etnografía. El término "discurso colonial" está, entonces, unido a un consenso entre historiadores, antropólogos y críticos literarios sobre varios aspectos: 1) la necesidad de estudiar las letras del período colonial hispanoamericano en el contexto de una crítica al colonialismo; 2) partir de la idea de la opacidad del lenguaje y la multiplicidad de sus significados, lo cual obliga a considerar múltiples posibilidades de interpretación de los discursos en cualquier época y circunstancia; 3) considerar el colonialismo y la tiranía de las interpretaciones unívocas que propicia de las palabras, las frases y los textos como presupuesto necesario unido a las implicaciones políticas de tal univocidad ayer y hoy. En tal perspectiva, como será notorio en la mayoría de los estudios aquí reseñados, se tiende a explorar las cartas, crónicas, relaciones, la poesía épica, lírica y el teatro, atendiendo a las relaciones entre el manejo del lenguaje y el dominio colonialista en el Nuevo Mundo. Se tiende también a revelar en tales estructuras verbales las voces suprimidas, marginadas o desvirtuadas por su condición racial, étnica, social o de sexo en los textos historiográficos o literarios y, finalmente, se intenta reivindicar la validez de textos compuestos en sistemas de transmisión de conocimiento distintos al alfabeto europeo, como los textos orales y pictoideográficos de culturas precolombinas antes y después de la llegada de los españoles.

Quizás el estudio más importante publicado en los últimos años sobre el problema de la relación entre el legado del Renacimiento en las letras del período colonial latinoamericano y el complejo proceso del ejercicio del poder (político, cultural, económico) colonialista en la América hispana es *The darker side of the Renaissance* de Walter Mignolo (item **3414**). Este estupendo trabajo no solamente ofrece una propuesta de estudio de las letras coloniales como expresión del dominio colonialista europeo sobre la lengua, la memoria y el territorio americanos sino también, y principalmente, una alternativa crítica ante el reto intelectual lanzado por estudiosos de la experiencia colonialista inglesa a partir del siglo XVIII y quienes han podido incorporar su estudio de tales experiencias en las discusiones sobre el postmodernismo. Mignolo, un latinoamericano escribiendo desde los Estados Unidos, replantea la posición de enunciación de una crítica al colonialismo e intenta una descolonización de la disciplina interdisciplinaria ejercida.

El cuestionamiento de la universalidad del alfabeto como único medio de transmisión de conocimientos y de la estética y tradición cultural renacentistas como única forma de validar expresiones artísticas y culturales en cualquier parte del mundo ha sido también el punto partida de dos trabajos fundamentales para el estudio de las letras mesoamericanas y andinas desde la llegada de los españoles: en *Escribir en el aire: ensayo sobre la heterogeneidad sociocultural en las literaturas andinas*, Antonio Cornejo Polar demuestra la inoperancia de intentos homogeneizadores (nacionalistas y lingüísticos) en los estudios de las expresiones culturales de los Andes desde 1532 hasta hoy (item **3409**); en *Nahuas and Spaniards: postconquest central Mexican history and philology,* James Lockhart le devuelve la voz al indígena nahua durante dos siglos de documentación forense española para sugerir la complejidad de los procesos de dominación, transculturación y resistencia al poder colonial (item **3412**).

En esta línea de la lectura de la voz oculta de los nativos americanos existen estudios de "relaciones" de exploración que se han construido en torno a su silenciación. En este sentido son fundamentales los aportes de Maureen Ahern (items **3425** y **3426**) y José Rabasa (item **3449**) sobre la historiografía española del suroeste norteamericano en el siglo XVI. Este interés en las voces de los americanos en estos tempranos testimonios ha llamado también la atención de estudios de perspectivas antropológicas como los formidables trabajos de Daniel Reff (item **3451**) y Hanne Veber (item **3458**) sobre las relaciones de Fray Marcos de Niza y Cabeza de Vaca, respectivamente. Igualmente la voz de la mujer y su condición como escritora en la sociedad colonial han sido objeto de importantes aportes como la edición y estudio de la autobiografía de la monja mexicana María de San José, realizada por Kathleen Myers (item **3442**), y el estudio sobre la vida de la traductora española María Antonio del Río y Arnedo radicada en América en el siglo XVIII, por Daisy Rípodas (item **3452**). Una importante reflexión sobre el espacio literario de la mujer en la colonia ha sido realizada también por Adriana Valdés (item **3420**). Por su parte, Antonio Alatorre nos ofrece una primera edición moderna de la poesía profana de Sor Juana Inés de la Cruz, titulada *Enigmas ofrecidos a la casa del placer,* de obligada lectura para los interesados en la poesía de la monja (item **3463**).

Llama la atención (además del ya mencionado estudio de Cornejo Polar) la cantidad y buena calidad de estudios sobre el área andina en los últimos años. Verónica Salles-Reese persiste en sus sugestivas relecturas de las "relaciones" de nativos americanos en el Perú (item **3455**). Miguel Nieto nos ofrece una edición de un poema épico de 1537 sobre la conquista del Perú que viene a enriquecer el panorama épico anterior al poema de Ercilla (item **3460**). Juan Espinosa Medrano ha sido objeto de mucha atención, en especial, su prosa (items **3464, 3438** y **3453**). Pero el mayor aporte al mejor conocimiento de un autor peruano del siglo XVIII realizado últimamente es el estudio de la vida y obra de Pedro Peralta Barnuevo y la edición, y traducción al inglés, de su hasta ahora perdida sátira (*Diálogo de los muertos: la causa académica* por Jerry Williams, item **3465**). Merece también mención el formidable trabajo de Guillermo Lohman Villena sobre la identidad de la llamada Amarilis peruana (item **3441**). El panorama de los estudios sobre las letras coloniales se ha comenzado a enriquecer últimamente también con sólidos e importantes aportes sobre el Cono Sur, entre los que merecen mención las sugestivas reflexiones sobre la construcción colonial de una idea de patria chilena de Castillo Sandoval (item **3430**), la reconsideración del canon de la literatura colonial del Uruguay de Gustavo Verdesio (item **3421**), y la nueva edición de *La araucana* de Isaías Lerner (item **3461**).

GENERAL

3405 Adorno, Rolena. Reconsidering colonial discourse for sixteenth- and seventeenth-century Spanish America. (*LARR,* 28: 3, 1993, p. 135–145)

Importantísima contribución al debate sobre el concepto de "discurso colonial" prociado por Patricia Seed y ante el que Adorno reconsidera su posición. Cuestiona aplicabilidad de este concepto a textos coloniales latinoamericanos de los siglos XVI y XVII. Para ella tal concepto es aplicable solo a partir del siglo XVIII por varias razones: 1) "discurso colonial" ubicado históricamente corresponde solo a estudios literarios y crítica culturales preocupados por la experiencia colonialista y postcolonialista anglo-europea; 2) España y sus posesiones en siglos XVI y XVII, por diferencias temporales, geográficas y culturales, se resisten a este paradigma intelectual; y 3) concepto de "discursos de dominación" unido a conflictos de diferencias raciales y culturales posible de articular a partir del siglo XVIII en Latinoamérica no tiene cabida en el mundo de valores realistas, cortesanos y caballerescos de cronistas o autores como Sor Juana. Saludable cuestionamiento de atrayente noción de homogeneidad (histórica, ideológica, cultural) que tiende a rezumar de concepto generalizante de "discurso colonial."

3406 América Latina: palavra, literatura e cultura. v. 1, A situação colonial. Organização de Ana Pizarro. São Paulo: Memorial; Campinas, Brazil: Editora da UNICAMP, 1993. v. 1: ill.

Historia cultural, sociología de la cultura, historia literaria, y de las ideas, semiología, crítica literaria, antropología cultural y simbólica son algunas disciplinas a que recurren los 23 excelentes y heterogéneos trabajos (incluyendo la introducción de Pizarro) reunidos sobre las diversas formas discursivas del período colonial de Hispanoamérica y el Brasil. Exploran temas de la formación de una imagen de América y los americanos, el Barroco, la Ilustración, el espacio de la mujer en la colonia, teorías de la lengua y la literatura en América colonial y la idea de la ciudad. Tienen en común la búsqueda de lecturas creadoras, apertura de perspectivas críticas y la noción de Latinoamérica como una estructura global integrada históricamente y culturalmente. Colaboradores: Angel Rama, Martin Lienhard, Gordon Brotherston, Walter Mignolo, John Beverly, Iris Zavala, Edith Pimentel Pinto, Rolena Adorno, etc. Una de las mejores colecciones de ensayos sobre las letras del período colonial en los últimos años.

3407 Coded encounters: writing, gender, and ethnicity in colonial Latin America. Edited by Francisco Javier Cevallos-Candau *et al.* Amherst: Univ. of Massachussetts Press, 1994. 298 p.: bibl., ill., index.

Selección de 15 trabajos del simposio "Reflections of Social Reality: Writing in Colonial Latin America" (Amherst, Mass., 1990). Dividido en cinco secciones: 1) representaciones textuales y gráficas del Nuevo Mundo; 2) institucionalización de la colonia; 3) resistencia cultural en textos andinos; 4) mujeres en la colonia; y 5) sátira y literatura de viajes en siglos XVIII y XIX. La mayoría de los trabajos, de distintas aproximaciones disciplinarias, tienen en común saludable actitud de no estar lidiando con un pasado muerto sino con problemas de la historia y la cultura latinoamericanas todavía vigentes hoy.

3408 Cornejo Polar, Antonio. Los comienzos de la heterogeneidad en las literaturas andinas: voz y letra en el "diálogo" de Cajamarca. (*Rev. Crít. Lit. Latinoam.*, 17:33, 1990, p. 155–207)

Comprender la literatura andina supone aceptar la insoluble y recíprocamente agresiva repulsión de la oralidad y la escritura como dos conciencias en choque desde su encuentro. Cornejo examina el "grado cero" de tal interacción en el "diálogo" entre Atahualpa y el Padre Valverde en Cajamarca en 1532 a través de las crónicas y su huella en posteriores danzas, canciones rituales y obras teatrales. Sólida alternativa al bilingüismo, multilingüismo o el dialogismo en el estudio de la literatura latinoamericana.

3409 Cornejo Polar, Antonio. Escribir en el aire: ensayo sobre la heterogeneidad socio-cultural en las literaturas andinas. Lima: Editorial Horizonte, 1994. 245 p. (Crítica literaria; 11)

Propone estudiar literatura latinoamericana incluyendo expresiones orales y escritas producidas por diversos sujetos sociales y culturales heterogéneos y conflictivos en el multiculturalismo de los Andes. Analizando unidades discursivas emblemáticas del área cultural andina (desde "diálogo" del cura Valverde y Atahualpa en 1532 hasta el testimonio de hoy) Cornejo plantea, en este importante aporte, falacia de los discursos homogeneizantes y propone heterogeneidad como único elemento globalizante de un corpus literario irreductible a las "bellas letras" o a un canon unido a idea de nación.

3410 Giucci, Guillermo. La conquista de lo maravilloso: el Nuevo Mundo. Montevideo: Ediciones de Juan Darién, 1992. 271 p.: bibl., ill., maps.

Examen de evolución del discurso de lo maravilloso que liga lo remoto a lo portentoso y al enriquecimiento rápido en Asia, primero, en América, después. Especial atención a textos sobre expediciones originadas en España y cobijadas por estricto sentido de legitimidad jurídica y religiosa (de Colón al Caribe, de Pánfilo de Narváez a la Florida y de Diego de Sanabria al Río de la Plata) y cuyos fracasos ejemplifican quiebra de este discurso y su transformación en aviso, para el lector del siglo XVI, y el de hoy—según Giucci—, sobre la pobreza de la ilusión americana.

3411 Historia y ficción: crónicas de América. Coordinación de Ysla Campbell. Ciudad Juárez, México: Univ. Autónoma de Ciudad Juárez, 1992. 277 p.: bibl. (Col. Conmemorativa quinto centenario del encuentro de dos mundos; 2)

Colección de 10 ensayos (sin prólogo introductorio) de críticos de variadas nacionalidades sobre textos del siglo XVI y XVII: 1) historiográficos e históricos de Pérez de Oliva, Fernández de Oviedo, Las Casas, franciscanos de Nueva España, Gaspar de Carvajal, Inca Garcilaso, Bernal Díaz, Malaspina; 2) y literarios de Sor Juana Inés de la Cruz y varios autores de poemas épicos. Variedad de aproximaciones (crítica cultural, glorificación de tradición hispánica en América, binomio historia/literatura en las crónicas, etc.) y de temas. Volumen conmemorativo del "Quinto Centenario del Encuentro de Dos Mundos" sin criterios claros de selección.

3412 Lockhart, James. Nahuas and Spaniards: postconquest central Mexican history and philology. Stanford, Calif.: Stanford Univ. Press; Los Angeles: UCLA Latin American Center Publications, Univ. of California, Los Angeles, 1991. 304 p.: bibl., 1 map. (Nahuatl studies series; 3. UCLA Latin American studies; 76)

Examen de dos siglos de testimonio en lengua nahuatl (anales, contratos de compraventa, actas de cabildo, testamentos, litigios, etc.) para dilucidar naturaleza del sujeto colonial nahua con base en lo que dice de sí mismo en su propia lengua. De los mejores aportes al esclarecimiento de interacciones y transformaciones de la lengua y cultura nahuas bajo la dominación española. Concluye que estructuras culturales indígenas sobrevivieron en México por más tiempo del tradicionalmente pensado.

3413 Mignolo, Walter. Colonial and postcolonial discourse: cultural critique or academic colonialism? (*LARR*, 28:3, 1993, p. 120–134, bibl.)

Respuesta y confrontación a concepto de "discurso colonial" de Patricia Seed (item **3419**). Aclara que crítica al discurso colonial no es fenómeno de los años 80 y 90 (señala aportes de O'Gorman en 1958 y Angel Rama en 1982); cuestiona rigidez de posición del intelectual que escribe sobre situaciones coloniales sugerida por Seed (la del intelectual no occidental escribiendo sobre Latinoamérica desde Europa o EEUU) resultante en un monólogo académico de estudiosos del discurso colonial sin escuchar voces políticamente comprometidas del período y territorio coloniales y postcoloniales. Rechaza limitación del concepto de "colonial discourse" pues deja de lado textos no transmitidos por medio del alfabeto y propone el de "colonial semiosis." Gran aporte a propuesta de mayor compromiso de intelectuales con implicaciones políticas de la producción cultural en situaciones coloniales.

3414 Mignolo, Walter. The darker side of the Renaissance: literacy, territoriality, and colonization. Ann Arbor: Univ. of Michigan Press, 1995. 426 p.: bibl., ill., index, maps.

El predominio de idea europea del alfabeto como único medio de reunir y transmitir conocimientos está problematizado aquí en su relación directa con la colonización del Nuevo Mundo. Recurriendo a diversas disciplinas—literatura, historia, semiótica, historiografía, cartografía, teoría cultural, geografía, lingüística—este estupendo estudio examina procesos de colonización de lenguas, memorias y espacio que tuvieron lugar a partir de la irrupción de América en la conciencia europea. Enfasis en conexiones entre escritura alfabética, organizaciones sociales y control político en América. De lectura obligada para interesados en historia, literatura y cultura del Nuevo Mundo y el Renacimiento, y en los debates contemporáneos sobre la relatividad de los discursos históricos, etnográficos y antropológicos.

3415 Murray, James C. Spanish chronicles of the Indies: sixteenth century. New York: Twayne Publishers, 1994. 188 p.: bibl., index. (Twayne's world authors series; TWAS 847. Spanish literature)

Manual de consulta general para lectores no especializados de habla inglesa sobre cartas, crónicas, relaciones e historias relativas a presencia hispana en América en el siglo XVI. Limitado a autores españoles, y gobernado por dualidad historia/ficción, equiparará tales textos con obras literarias del Siglo de Oro español. Los descubrimientos, conquista, exploración, evangelización y colonización son para Murray movimientos históricos que estructuran su trabajo. Util para estudiantes si se tienen en cuenta estas limitaciones.

3416 Prieto Inzunza, Angélica. La pasión en las crónicas. México: Plaza y Valdés, 1992. 123 p.: bibl., ill.

Implantando un modelo semiótico a textos disímiles ("requerimiento," crónicas de Cortés, Bernal Díaz, Las Casas, un relato de ficción contemporáneo), autora celebra coraje del conquistador y dramatiza ferocidad del conquistado examinando sus diversas "pasiones:" indiferencia de Palacios Rubios, indignación de Bernal, agudeza de Cortés, venganza de los indios caribes, etc. Interesante a veces, poco aporta a comprensión de implicaciones políticas y culturales del contacto entre europeos y americanos en el siglo XVI.

3417 Relaciones literarias entre España y América en los siglos XVI y XVII. Coordinación de Ysla Campbell. Ciudad Juárez, Mexico: Univ. Autónoma de Ciudad Juárez, 1992. 281 p.: bibl. (Col. Conmemorativa quinto centenario del encuentro de dos mundos; 1)

Colección de 12 ensayos que examinan la ingerencia del Nuevo Mundo como tema en desarrollo de grupo selecto de obras literarias españolas de los siglos XVI y XVII. Siete ensayos están dedicados a la comedia; los demás al romancero, la picaresca, la escritura conventual femenina y a la suerte americana del motivo del ruiseñor cantor desde el *Diario* de Colón hasta el Modernismo. Centro de reflexión es más literatura del Siglo de Oro español que cultura americana de esa época.

3418 Revista Iberoamericana. Número especial, Vol. 61, No. 170/171, 1995, Literatura colonial: identidad y conquista en América. Edición de Mabel Moraña. Pittsburgh: Univ. of Pittsburgh.

Heterogéneo conjunto de 17 estudios (incluyendo dos notas y sección de reseñas), muchos de orientación interdisciplinaria, sobre canonización, colonización, construcción del sujeto colonial, identidad, análisis de obras particulares, estudios comparativos, ordenamiento historiográfico y adopción, adaptación o subversión de modelos culturales europeos en los diversos discursos americanos y euroamericanos. Saludable énfasis, en muchos de los trabajos, en las implicaciones de estos problemas en la compleja diversidad (alteridad, diferencia) social y cultural americana desde el período colonial hasta hoy. Primer volumen de dos dedicados a las letras coloniales.

3419 Seed, Patricia. Colonial and postcolonial discourse. (*LARR*, 26:3, 1991, p. 181–200)

Ensayo-reseña de cinco importantes trabajos interdisciplinarios sobre problemas de la historia y la literatura en el contexto de la colonización europea en el Caribe, la América hispana y las Filipinas que, según Seed, inauguran un movimiento interdisciplinario (recurriendo a historia, crítica literaria y antropología cultural) denominado "Colonial and Postcolonial Discourse." En él, la problematización del lenguaje político y el contexto político de la lengua literaria permite abandonar simple preocupación con la literatura canónica y se enfoca en la crítica de las relaciones de poder en las sociedades en situaciones coloniales. La implícita institucionalización de esta disciplina en el mundo académico de Occidente que hace Seed, la problemática amplitud (sobre cinco siglos de colonialismo) del término "discurso colonial" y la rigidez del lugar de enunciación utilizado por los intelectuales anticoloniastas que escriben produjo saludable debate con latinoamericanistas como Rolena Adorno (item **3405**), Hernán Vidal (item **3422**) y Walter Mignolo (item **3413**) en esta misma revista (Vol. 28, No. 3, 1993). De obligada lectura para interesados en localización de los discursos coloniales en contexto de los debates intelectuales contemporáneos sobre postestructuralismo, estudios subalternos, nuevo historicismo y teoría feminista.

3420 Valdés, Adriana. El espacio literario de la mujer en la colonia. (*in* Ver desde la mujer. Santiago: Ediciones La Morada; Editorial Cuarto Propio, 1992, p. 83–105, bibl.)

Considerando escritura conventual de mujeres como un "macro-discurso" que concentró mayoría de escritos de mujeres latinoamericanas de la colonia, Valdés cuestiona tradicionales criterios de canonización literaria que marginaron estos innumerables escritos. Examina casos de la Madre Castillo (Colombia), María de San Joseph y Sor Juana Inés de la Cruz (México), Ursula Suárez (Chile), como propuesta de estudio de textos cuestionablemente desvalorizados hasta hoy. Aporte simultáneo al de Electa Arenal y Stacey Schlau en *Untold Sisters.*

3421 Verdesio, Gustavo. Una ausencia en el canon: los discursos coloniales sobre el Uruguay en el marco de la historiografía uruguaya y los estudios coloniales latinoamericanos. (*Rev. Iberoam.*, 61:170–71, enero/junio 1995, p. 249–268)

El estrecho criterio "belleletrístico" de historias de literatura tanto uruguaya como hispanoamericana ha excluído textos coloniales sobre Uruguay. Basado en propuesta teórica de W. Mignolo, Verdesio propone ampliar límites selectivos para incluir formas discursivas de carácter estético y diversos tipos de formaciones verbales (actas, capitulaciones, cédulas reales, etc.) cuyo referente es el universo colonial del Uruguay. Interesante propuesta de redefinición del corpus discursivo colonial tanto uruguayo como latinoamericano.

3422 Vidal, Hernán. The concept of colonial and postcolonial discourse: a perspective from literary criticism. (*LARR*, 28:3, 1993, p. 113–119)

Aporte al debate generado por el ensayo-reseña de Patricia Seed (item **3419**). Señalando condición de literatura como institución y crítica literaria como profesión, y necesidad de intelectuales latinoamericanistas de enfrentar violencia del neoliberalismo capitalista ante el vacío político que dejó la caída del bloque soviético, Vidal llama la atención sobre peligro de institucionalización del nuevo movimiento intelectual en que cae Seed al crear la categoría de "Colonial and Postcolonial Discourse." Propone, como alternativa, abandono del estudio de técnica e identidad de textos privilegiados por el canon y ocuparse—desde una posición política definida—de identidad de productores de cultura. Esto, según él, permitirá construcción de un espacio público en el que dialoguen las culturas popular y oficial y se articulen voces de marginados.

3423 Zavala, Iris M. La ética de la violencia: identidad y silencio en 1492. (*Rev. Iberoam.*, 61:170/171, enero/junio 1995, p. 13–26)

Recurriendo a noción nietzscheana del pensamiento ético (medio ideológico para legitimar opresión) y las bajtininas de la ética y el silencio, Zavala realiza sugestiva interpretación de hechos históricos de 1492–93 contados por Colón para sugerir que el primer texto cultural sobre América (el *Diario*) es una interpretación "racional" típica de Occidente que configura una sociedad basada en el dominio y la colonización de europeos sobre americanos. Amplias digresiones teóricas vuelven pesada su lectura.

INDIVIDUAL STUDIES

3424 Adorno, Rolena. The politics of publication: Bartolomé de Las Casas's *The devastation of the Indies.* (*NWIG*, 67:3/4, 1993, p. 285–292)

Artículo-reseña sobre traducción al inglés de la *Brevísima* de Las Casas por Herma Briffault e introducción de Bill Donovan (ver *HLAS 38:2173a* and *HLAS 54:949*) que llama la atención sobre frecuente fracaso intelectual de publicaciones en circunstancias de aniversario. Corrige numerosos errores de traducción al igual que erróneos datos de la introducción sobre la biografía de Las Casas y el contexto histórico y político que traicionan el contenido y el significado de la inmensa obra del dominico.

3425 Ahern, Maureen. *La relación de la jornada de Cíbola:* los espacios orales y culturales. (*in* Congreso del Instituto Internacional de Literatura Iberoamericana, *28th*, Providence, R.I., *1990*. Conquista y contraconquista: la escritura del Nuevo Mundo. México: Colegio de México; Providence, R.I.: Brown Univ., 1994, p. 187–199)

Estudio de *Relación* de Pedro de Castañeda y Nájcera (1563?) sobre la destructiva (para nativos) y frustrada (para españoles) expedición de Francisco Vázquez de Coronado en busca de ciudades de Cíbola (1540–42). Recurriendo a de Certeau, Ahern destaca cuatro "espacios de interacción" (de oralidad, de los capitanes, de transgresión y violencia, culturales) producidos entre la producción del "texto" y el "otro" para lograr "credibilidad." Atención a implicaciones etnográficas, geográficas y diferencias culturales permiten articular una de las mas sugestivas lecturas de la presencia indígena en textos españoles de exploración.

3426 Ahern, Maureen. La relación como glosa, guía y memoria: Nuevo México, 1581–1582. (*Rev. Iberoam.*, 61:170/171, enero/junio 1995, p. 41–55)

Estudio de inédita *Relación y concudio del viaje y suceso que Francisco Sánchez Chamuscado con ocho soldados sus compañeros hizo en el descubrimiento del nuevo México y tierra nueba* (1582) de Hernán Gallegos destacando su uso de estrategias discursivas de Cabeza de Vaca sobre contacto entre españoles y americanos para construir nuevo espacio cultural de conversión, explotación y colonización. Examen de fisuras del discurso de Gallegos que revelan férrea resistencia indígena ante violencia de invasores precursora de gran rebelión de Los Pueblos de fines del siglo XVII. Otro sólido aporte de Ahern a la exposición de silenciadas voces indígenas.

3427 Beckjord, Sarah J. 'Con sal y ají y tomates:' las redes textuales de Bernal Díaz en el caso de Cholula. (*Rev. Iberoam.*, 61:170/171, enero/junio 1995, p. 147–160)

Inspirada en ensayo de Rolena Adorno (ver *HLAS 52:3292*) sobre impugnación anti-encomendera de Las Casas como real estímulo de la escritura de Bernal Díaz, Beckjord compara las versiones de Cortés, Oviedo, Gómara, Las Casas y el mismo Bernal sobre la masacre de Cholula como construcciones intertextuales gobernadas por intereses políticos y personales concretos. Aunque poco agrega a la tesis central de Adorno, ejemplifica muy bien ambiguos esfuerzos de composición histórica ante cambiantes circunstancias legales y políticas de la colonización del Nuevo Mundo.

3428 Bolaños, Alvaro Félix. Barbarie y canibalismo en la retórica colonial: los indios Pijaos de Fray Pedro Simón. Bogotá: CEREC, 1994. 243 p.: bibl., ill., maps.

Enfocado en textos históricos, en particular *Noticias historiales de las conquistas de Tierra Firme en las Indias Occidentales* (1627), sobre guerra entre colonizadores españoles e indios pijaos del Nuevo Reino de Granada, intenta explicar cómo y por qué se construyen clisés racistas sobre nativos americanos y sugiere razones de su persistencia

hoy. Enfasis en construcción retórica de imagen monstruosa y destructible del pijao y su legado en la escritura de la historia colombiana que aspira a justificar brutal campaña de exterminio de estos indios en el siglo XVII.

3429 Bolaños, Alvaro Félix. Sobre "relaciones" e identidades en crisis: el "otro" lado del ex-cautivo Alonso Ramírez. (*Rev. Crít. Lit. Latinoam.*, 21:42, 1995, p. 131–160)

Partiendo de considerar *Infortunios de Alonso Ramírez* como "relación" cuyo intento es decir "la verdad," artículo reflexiona sobre razones de la necesidad del texto de construir espacios "bárbaros" en los que el nativo americano es menos amenazante que el pirata inglés. Atiende a implicaciones de esta redistribución de espacios culturales denigrantes en cuestión de doble autoría de *Infortunios:* testimonio oral de Ramírez y transcripción de Sigüenza.

3430 Castillo Sandoval, Roberto. ¿Una misma cosa con la vuestra?: Ercilla, Pedro de Oña y la apropiación post-colonial de la patria araucana. (*Rev. Iberoam.*, 61:170/171, enero/junio 1995, p. 232–247)

Excelente desmantelamiento de nociones del americanismo de Ercilla y pro-colonialismo de Oña en torno al intento criollo por construir una idea de territorialidad nacional desde el siglo XVI hasta hoy. El cisma entre Arauco (barbarie indígena) y Chile (civilización hispana) es un mito erciliano que ha desvirtuado la idea de "patria" en Chile. Para Castillo es el Oña identificado culturalmente con lo indígena, y no el Ercilla fluctuante entre la idealización y salvajización del indio, quien mejor articula una noción de la nacionalidad como espacio reclamado por indígenas y euroamericanos.

3431 Codding, Mitchell A. Perfecting the geography of New Spain: Alzate and the cartographic legacy of Sigüenza y Góngora. (*Colon. Lat. Am. Rev.*, 3:1/2, 1994, p. 185–219)

Bien documentada exposición de contribuciones cartográficas de Sigüenza y Góngora sobre Nueva España y su posterior desarrollo a manos de José Antonio Alzate (1737–99), entusiasta de avances científicos y enciclopedistas quien las transmitió a la posteridad publicando en México los mapas resultantes (1768–95). Util ubicación de este legado en México y Europa de la época, pero no problematiza implicaciones políticas y culturales de una cartografía utilizada por militares, marinos, jueces, viajeros y monarcas pro-imperialistas para mejor control colonialista.

3432 Cortijo Ocaña, Antonio. Creación de una voz de autoridad en Bartolomé de Las Casas: estudio del "Prólogo" de la *Historia de las Indias*. (*Rev. Iberoam.*, 61:170/171, enero/junio 1995, p. 220–229)

En este "Prólogo"—manifiesto teórico sobre como concebir escritura de historia— Las Casas anticipa problemas de recepción de su *Historia de las Indias* enunciando distintos discursos (humanista, jurista, teológico, de asunto maravilloso) para los distintos receptores que tiene en mente. Espera así, según Cortijo, reconciliar la controversial defensa de los indios con las expectativas tradicionales de los lectores. Buena contextualización del Las Casas teórico de la historia en la tradición historiográfica clásica, medieval y renacentista.

3433 Galster, Ingrid. Aguirre, oder, Die Willkür der Nachwelt: die Rebellion des baskischen Konquistadors Lope de Aguirre in Historiographie und Geschichtsfiktion, 1561–1992. Frankfurt a. Main: Vervuert, 1996. 938 p.: bibl., ill.

How does one explain the numerous historical recreations devoted to Lope de Aguirre's rebellion since the 16th century? Galster, a German specialist in Romance languages and civilizations, undertakes an ambitious review of works—chronicles, biographies, novels, poems, films, and even comic-strips—which exalt or denigrate Aguirre's personality and deeds. After exploring the arbitrary and other deviations from historical "truth" inherent to these reconstructions, Galster argues that all such "histories" depend on personal and ideological motives and contain some fictional elements. [T. Hampe-Martínez]

3434 Gerassi-Navarro, Nina. Huarochirí: recordando las voces del pasado en los mitos de creación. (*Rev. Iberoam.*, 61:170/171, enero/junio 1995, p. 95–105)

Sólido análisis comparativo y de perspectiva literaria sobre transformación y resistencia de mitos prehispánicos de creación en recopilaciones de mitos andinos de un texto del siglo XVII y otro del XX: *Tratado sobre los dioses falsos* (1608) del cura Francisco de Avila y *Huarochirí 400 años después* (1977) de Alejandro Ortiz. Ejemplifica manera en que las culturas andinas entendieron el encuentro con la española y retuvieron o transformaron su propia voz y tradición.

3435 Giorgi, Diógenes de. Martín del Barco Centenera: cronista fundamental del Río de la Plata. Montevideo: Ediciones del Nuevo Mundo, 1989. 236 p.: bibl., facsims. (Biblioteca Hernandarias de historia colonial rioplatense)

Examen del poema épico "Argentina y Conquista del Río de la Plata" (Lisboa, 1602) que se propone reivindicar su valor como fuente histórica y probar que Uruguay tiene en Barco Centenera a su primer cronista. Tales objetivos limitan estudio a los primeros 14 cantos referentes al hoy territorio uruguayo. Breve epílogo sobre la crítica historiográfica y literaria del poema. Estudio de escaso valor fuera de los propósitos nacionalistas del autor.

3436 Gonzalez Martínez, José Luis. Garcilaso Inca de la Vega: un hombre entre dos razas. (*Rev. Hist. Am.*, 110, julio/dic. 1990, p. 19–35, bibl.)

Breve pero excelente reflexión sobre tensión entre abstracto concepto de mestizaje y concreta y trágica condición de mestizo del Inca en su justificación y defensa de la cultura del pasado incaico ante el público lector europeo. Para González, Garcilaso, como autor que intenta sintetizar la herencia del colonizador español y el indio colonizado, no es producto de un conflicto resuelto sino testigo de un conflicto pendiente relacionado con la tragedia de los pueblos indígenas del presente.

Harris, Max. The dialogical theatre: dramatizations of the conquest of Mexico and the question of the other. See item **459.**

3437 Herman, Susan. Conquest and discovery: subversion of the fall in *El carnero*. (*MLN/Baltimore*, 108, 1993, p. 283–301)

Intenta leer *El carnero*, no como colección de *historielas*, sino como un todo en cuya organicidad Freyle presenta en su acerba y sistemática crítica al sistema colonial. Rechaza nociones cristianas de "pecado original" y "redención" de otros críticos y propone que Freyle, en su búsqueda del origen del mal en el Nuevo Reino de Granada, revisa/subvierte noción bíblica de 'Caída' (pérdida del paraíso) para lograr tal organicidad. Muchas conjeturas poco convincentes. Idea expresada desde hace 17 años (tesis doctoral de 1978).

3438 Hopkins Rodríguez, Eduardo. El humor en el *Apologético* de Juan de Espinosa Medrano. (*Bol. Inst. Riva-Agüero*, 15, 1988, p. 31–40)

Interesante examen del *Apologético* como obra que a la vez alaba (a Luis de Góngora) y vitupera (a Manuel de Faria, detractor del poeta cordobés) mediante mordaz manejo del humor. Degradación al opositor, elogio al defendido, diversión del lector y logro de su complicidad usando sutilmente asociaciones, adjetivaciones, con estilo culto y vulgar, cumplen función de autoenaltecimiento del genio del autor cuzqueño, según Rodríguez.

3439 Inca Garcilaso de la Vega: primer mestizo de América; estudios. Lima?: Instituto Cambio y Desarrollo, 1993. 395 p.: bibl., ill.

Reedición de 19 trabajos entre artículos, conferencias, un poema encomiástico, prólogos a ediciones de obras del Inca, etc. publicados previamente en libros, revistas y periódicos (1916–93) sobre obra y persona del autor con motivo del vigésimo noveno aniversario de la creación de la Univ. Inca Garcilaso de la Vega. Selección intenta unirse en torno al tema del mestizaje como alternativa del Inca ante el trauma, aún sin resolver hoy, causado por la conquista. Animo conmemorativo admite otros temas y aproximaciones de autores tan diversos como José de la Riva Agüero, Ricardo Rojas, Alfredo Yepes Miranda, Raúl Porras Barrenechea, José Durand, Max Hernández, etc.

3440 Lerner, Isaías. La visión humanística de América: Gonzalo Fernández de Oviedo. (*in* La indias (América) en la literatura del siglo de oro. Edited by Ignacio Arellano. Kassel, Germany: Edition Reichenberger, 1992, p. 3–22)

Aunque se propone hablar del impacto de América en la visión humanística de Oviedo, destaca tres aspectos con que *Silva de varia lección* (1540) de Pedro Mexía contribuye en composición de *Historia general y natural de las Indias* de Oviedo: 1) idea de historia general como miscelánea de material curioso; 2) defensa de uso de castellano en vez de latín; y 3) actitud crítica frente a modelos

clásicos como Plinio. Deja en claro conexión entre Mexía y Oviedo. Sugerencia de que estos tres aspectos existen en la *Historia* debido a influencia de la *Silva* no convence.

3441 Lohmann Villena, Guillermo. "Amarilis indiana:" identificación y semblanza. Lima: Pontificia Univ. Católica del Perú, Fondo Editorial, 1993. 381 p.: bibl., ill.

Lohmann se une a larga lista de críticos que desde principios del siglo XIX han intentado identificar a la autora del poema "Epístola de Amarilis a Belardo," compuesto entre 1615–16 y dedicado a Lope de Vega. Retomando propuesta de Francisco Rubén Berroa y Bernedo de 1939 y mediante lectura detenida de claves del poema (con amplia documentación de archivos), concluye que la poeta peruana no pudo ser otra que María de Rojas y Garay, descendiente de colonizadores españoles. Impresionante pesquisa que mucho ilumina el contexto histórico y literario español y peruano del siglo XVII a pesar de depender de una conjetura.

3442 María de San José, Madre. Word from New Spain: the spiritual autobiography of Madre María de San José, 1656–1719. Critical edition and introduction by Kathleen A. Myers. Liverpool, England: Liverpool Univ. Press, 1993. 234 p. (Hispanic studies TRAC (Textual research and criticism); 4)

Cuidadosa primera edición completa del vol. 1 (de 12 que constituyen la obra total) de la "vida" espiritual de la monja mexicana (orden Agustinas Recoletas) escrita en 1703. Narra historia de su conversión e ingreso al convento en contra de férrea e insidiosa oposición familiar. Excelente estudio introductorio contextualizando histórica y literariamente el texto y caracterizándolo como crónica de gran esfuerzo de expresión de voz femenina, de sutiles estrategias subvertoras, contra manipulador control del confesor que ordenó su escritura.

3443 Mejías López, William. Las ideas de la guerra justa en Ercilla y en *La Araucana*. Santiago: Editorial Universitaria, 1992. 199 p.: bibl. (Col. Imagen de Chile)

Intento de lectura "política" de *La araucana* en la que la clemencia de una guerra justa contra los indios propuesta por Ercilla equivale a una defensa de éstos comparable y conectada con la de Victoria y Las Casas. Bien documentado estudio aunque reducido a celebración del "pro-indigenismo" de Ercilla y su lealtad al expansionismo imperial y legal español. Confunde la común protesta libresca contra excesos en la guerra contra los indios (de un Victoria) con radical cuestionamiento de presencia hispana en América (del dominico).

3444 Mejías López, William. Principios indigenistas de Pedro de Oña presentes en "Arauco Domado." (*Quad. Ibero-Am.*, 73, giugno 1993, p. 77–94)

La existencia de una tradición lascasista en el Virreinato del Perú y la influencia, también indigenista—según él—de Ercilla, explican la condena del maltrato de los indios y de la encomienda como institución hecha por Oña en "Arauco Domado." Abundante y útil información histórico-literaria en torno a los poemas épicos de tema americano del siglo XVI.

3445 Merrim, Stephanie. Catalina de Erauso: from anomaly to icon. (*in* Coded encounters: writing, gender and ethnicity in colonial Latin America. Amherst: Univ. of Massachusetts Press, 1994, p. 177–205)

Examina razones por las que esta aventura, delincuente, conquistadora y exitosa trasvestida monja alferez, en el contexto de la conflictiva y contradictoria época barroca, logra manipular los medios contemporáneos de comunicación para promocionar su imagen pública como anomalía digna de celebración y premio; señala sorprendentes similitudes con el caso de Sor Juana Inés de la Cruz en sus transacciones con la cultura cortesana del barroco mexicano. De aproximación cultural y es uno de los mejores estudios sobre la subjetividad femenina en situaciones coloniales hasta la fecha.

3446 Miró Quesada S., Aurelio and **Roberto Quevedo.** Lucas de Mendoza y su "Canción Lyrica:" dos estudios. Asunción: Editorial El Gráfico, 1986. 58 p., 2 folded leaves: bibl., ill.

Estudio biográfico y genealógico (con facsímiles de documentos) de Fray Lucas de Mendoza (1584–1636), primer poeta paraguayo radicado después en Lima. Reproducción de "Canción Lyrica," su único poema conocido, compuesto a propósito de las exequias de la Reina Margarita, esposa de Felipe III, en 1612. Importante divulgación de la obra de un poeta alabado por Lope de Vega en su *Laurel de Apolo.*

3447 Myers, Kathleen A. Imitación, revisión y amazonas en la *Historia general y natural* de Fernández de Oviedo. (*Rev. Iberoam.*, 61: 170/171, enero/junio 1995, p. 161–173)

Mediante riguroso examen comparativo de frecuentes enmiendas, adiciones y revisiones en manuscritos y ediciones de la *Historia general,* se ilustra fluctuación entre imitación de modelos europeos (ej., Plinio) y el empiricismo historiográfico autorizado por experiencias del autor en el Nuevo Mundo. El caso de las amazonas demuestra, según Myers, que a veces la tradición cultural europea se impone como medio para entender a América y se convierte en ocasión para reescribir viejos mitos europeos rompiendo, así, saludable cuestionamiento de Oviedo de sus modelos en otras ocasiones.

3448 Pailler, Claire and **Jean-Marie Pailler.** Una América verdaderamente latina: los historiadores romanos y el Inca Garcilaso en la perspectiva de G. Dumezil. (*Histórica/ Lima,* 17:2, dic. 1993, p. 179–222, bibl.)

La herencia cultural greco-latina que domina sobre la España desde la que escribe el Inca explica, según los Pailler, tanto similitudes de estructura y propósito da la historia de los reyes de Roma de historiadores romanos como la de los reyes Incas de Garcilaso y el "latinismo" de la obra del mestizo. Estudio comparativo, rico en detalles interesantes, escaso en originalidades, que busca explicar intento de legitimación de obra del Inca ante auditorio eurocentrista del siglo XVII.

3449 Rabasa, Jose. De la *allegoresis* etnográfica en *Los Naufragios* de Alvar Núñez Cabeza de Vaca. (*Rev. Iberoam.,* 61:170/171, 1995, p. 175–185)

Rechazando la reducción de lo "extraño" a expresiones de lo "literario" en *Naufragios,* propone una lectura que resalte la empatía del autor con lo diferente y los problemas historiográficos en el registro de costumbres contrarias a los valores de Occidente. Usando la *allegoresis* (decir una cosa y significar otra) Cabeza de Vaca conscientemente presenta la otredad de un pueblo y al mismo tiempo cuestiona sus propias cultura y escritura logrando uno de los testimonios etnográficos mas auténticos del "encuentro" de americanos y europeos.

3450 Ramírez Ribes, María. Un amor por el diálogo: el Inca Garcilaso de la Vega. Prólogo de Arturo Uslar Pietri. Caracas: Monte Avila Editores, 1992. 196 p.: bibl. (Estudios)

El feliz encuentro del Occidente altivo y el Incario menoscabado por su falta de alfabeto, son dos mundos, en apariencia contrapuestos que el Inca Garcilaso logra armonizar. En ese armonioso diálogo cultural, en el que mestizaje, tolerancia, comprensión y amor son la base, encuentra la literatura hispanoamericana su origen y la razón "de su gloria." Ingenuo y celebratorio estudio sobre identidad latinoamericana que visualiza mestizaje como espacio carente de conflictos sociales, raciales, culturales y económicos.

3451 Reff, Daniel T. Anthropological analysis of exploration texts: cultural discourse and the ethnographical import of Fray Marcos de Niza's journey to Cibola. (*Am. Anthropol.*, 93:3, 1991, p. 636–655)

Demuestra que prejuicios teóricos y culturales (tanto contra el fraile explorador como contra las culturas americanas) de antropólogos e historiadores que descartaban a Fray Marcos por mentiroso o equivocado les impidió a éstos aprovechar riqueza de información arqueológica de su "relación" sobre la vida y destino final de las culturas Hohokam y Trincheras del suroeste norteamericano. Deja en claro que análisis del discurso de textos de exploración es útil para la antropología y la etnografía.

3452 Rípodas Ardanaz, Daisy. Una ignorada escritora en la Charcas finicolonial: María Antonia de Río y Aenedo. (*Invest. Ens.*, 43, enero/dic. 1993, p. 167–207, appendix)

Historía de la vida de María Antonio de Río y Arnedo (n. Arévalo, España 1775), una de las muchas traductoras españolas del francés al castellano, quien viajó a América con su esposo y participó a su laso activa y a veces turbulentamente en la vida literaria, social y política americana. Interesante caso representativo (en Argentina y Bolivia) de tribulaciones de una mujer que intenta integrar su condición femenina con la de escritora a fines del siglo XVIII. Variada y útil documentación histórica y de archivo.

3453 Rodríguez Garrido, José A. Aproximación a la oratoria sagrada de Espinosa Medrano. (*Bol. Inst. Riva-Agüero*, 15, 1988, p. 11–32)

La prosa de "El Lunarejo" no es narrativa sino expositiva y, con la excepción del *Apologético*, todos sus textos en prosa están destinados a la recitación más que la lectura. Con tal presupuesto Rodríguez ubica la prosa de Espinosa Medrano—en especial la colección de sermones titulada *Novena maravilla*—en la tradición y técnicas medievales y renacentistas de la oratoria sagrada. Importante artículo a pesar del énfasis, en tono panegerista, en la voz autoexaltadora de "El Lunarejo" en los textos analizados.

3454 Ross, Kathleen. The baroque narrative of Carlos de Sigüenza y Góngora: a new world paradise. Cambridge, England; New York: Cambridge Univ. Press, 1993. 220 p.: bibl., index. (Cambridge studies in Latin American and Iberian literature; 9)

Estudio de la heterogeneidad y complejidad de la narrativa barroca hispanoamericana y su contexto cultural a través de Sigüenza y Góngora. Recurriendo a teoría de la narrativa, historiografía y crítica feminista, Ross examina esfuerzos de Sigüenza por colocar al Nuevo Mundo en el contexto de cultura europea. Enfasis en el *Paraíso occidental* (1684)—historia de fundación de conventos mexicanos—a partir del cual reflexiona sobre problemas del sexo, raza y la subjetividad criolla a través del examen de estrategias retóricas del varón Sigüenza apropiándose de la escritura de las monjas. Intenta así señalar la diferencia entre el barroco de Indias y el español.

3455 Salles-Reese, Verónica. Yo don Joan de Santacruz Pachacuti Yamqui Salcamaygua . . . digo. (*Rev. Iberoam.*, 61:170/171, enero/junio 1995, p. 107–118)

Estimulante y convincente lectura de *Relación de las antigüedades deste reyno del Pirú* (1613) de Joan de Santacruz como texto contestatario y de defensa ante la violenta ofensiva antiidolátrica lanzada por el cura Francisco de Avila desde 1610. Como alternativa a anteriores lecturas—que descartan texto como discurso histórico o lo idealizan como verídico o subversivo—Salles-Reese dilucida sutiles estrategias de resistencia de Santacruz y niega su supuesto colaboracionismo con Avila y su total sumisión a él.

Sor Juana Inés de la Cruz Project. See item
43.

3456 Stolley, Karen. *El lazarillo de ciegos
caminantes:* un itinerario crítico. Hanover, NH: Ediciones del Norte, 1992. 224 p.:
bibl. (Puertas 88)

Rigurosa y sugestiva lectura atendiendo a complejo y violento enfrentamiento
de dos esfuerzos de composición discursiva de
disímiles entes literarios creados por Carrió
de la Vandera: el blanco visitador español y el
oscuro indio Concolorcorvo. Destacando carácter eminentemente dialógico y confronta-
cional y la sutil y polivalente construcción
verbal de esta obra—por encima de su valor
testimonial y documental—Stolley intenta
revisar y confrontar casi dos siglos de lectura
de *El lazarillo.* Excelente y de obligada lectura para interesados en la obra de Carrió.

3457 Tavard, George Henry. Juana Inés de la
Cruz and the theology of beauty: the
first Mexican theology. Notre Dame, Ind.:
Univ. of Notre Dame Press, 1991. 239 p.:
bibl., index.

Distinto enfoque de la obra poética
de Sor Juana de un profesional de la teología.
Explica las referencias bíblicas, mitológicas
greco-romanas, egipcias, así como sus conceptos de la naturaleza de Cristo, la Virgen, la
bondad divina, etc. en el contexto de la ideología contrarreformista. Considera el silencio
final de Sor Juana como un acto voluntario y
triunfalista. Escasa habilidad con textos originales y rasgos de la cultura hispana menos-
caban un tanto su aporte.

3458 Veber, Hanne. Dialectics of discovery:
Cabeza de Vaca in Texas and Florida,
1528–36. (*Folk/Copenhagen,* 34, 1992,
p. 119–143, map)

Sugestiva lectura antropológica de
Naufragios de Cabeza de Vaca como la historia de la confrontación de dos sistemas de
valores y tipos de praxis incongruentes. Los
papeles de shamanes e hijos del sol adquiridos
por los náufragos en su lucha por la supervivencia entre las sociedades indígenas representan un caso de mutua influencia en que
categorías culturales indígenas estructuran
prácticas de los españoles, y en que éstos, lle-
vando a cabo tales categorías culturales, son
capaces de remodelarlas.

TEXTS, EDITIONS, ANTHOLOGIES

3459 Bolaños, Joaquín. La portentosa vida de
la Muerte, emperatriz de los sepulcros,
vengadora de los agravios del Altísimo y muy
señora de la humana naturaleza. Edición crítica, introducción y notas de Blanca López de
Mariscal. México: Colegio de México, Centro
de Estudios Lingüísticos y Literarios, 1992.
407 p.: bibl., ill. (Biblioteca novohispana; 2)

Narración episódica, buscando entre-
tenimiento y reflexión moral, unificada por la
Muerte como personaje central. Ligada a tradición de relatos medievales y renacentistas
españoles en que la Muerte le recuerda a la
humanidad la brevedad de la vida y la ilusión
de las jerarquías terrenas. La sátira y los cuadros de costumbres anuncian *El periquillo
sarniento.* Excelente y útil introducción y
buen trabajo editorial.

**3460 "La Conquista del Perú:" poema he-
roico de 1537.** Anónimo. Edición, introducción y notas de Miguel Nieto Nuño.
Cáceres: Institución Cultural El Brocense de
la Excma. Diputación Provincial de Cáceres,
1992. xxviii, 80 p.: bibl.

Nueva edición del único poema conocido sobre la conquista del Perú. Su composición en 1537, según conjetura Nieto, lo convierte en primer poema heroico extenso de la
conquista de America (32 años antes que *La
araucana*). Tiene a Francisco Pizarro como
héroe y está dividido en dos partes (sobre primeros viajes de exploración y sobre jornada de
Cajamarca). Atribuído antes a Miguel de Estete, Francisco de Xerez, etc. por otros críticos, es para Nieto un poema heroico de valor
histórico escrito por autor anónimo cercano
a los hechos narrados en 273 coplas de arte
mayor.

Damrosch, David. The aesthetics of conquest: Aztec poetry before and after Cortés.
See item **428.**

3461 Ercilla y Zúñiga, Alonso de. La Araucana. Edición de Isaías Lerner. Madrid:
Cátedra, 1993. 1026 p.: bibl., ill., indexes. (Letras hispánicas; 359)

Edición basada en la póstuma de Madrid de 1597, la más completa por contener
114 cantos extras ausentes de la edición generalmente considerada definitiva (Madrid,
1589–90) por José Toribio Medina y José Durand. El nuevo fragmento, sobre conquista del

Sur de Chile, corresponde a tema de la cuarta parte prometida por Ercilla y halló espacio en edición póstuma gracias a idóneos editores conocedores de proyectos literarios del autor, según conjetura Lerner. Amplitud, rigurosidad y utilidad de introducción y notas al texto la convierten en nueva excelente edición.

3462 Ferrero, Carlos S. Versificadores y poetas en la Nueva Granada. v. 1. Colombia?: s.n., 1989? v. 1: bibl., ill. (Martes Culturales de la Asociación Ferrero Ramírez de Arellano. Col. Asociación Ferrero Ramírez de Arellano; 5)

Interesante antología de poesía del siglo XVI del Nuevo Reino de Granada escrita por conquistadores y primeros pobladores españoles del área de Santa Fe de Bogotá y Tunja principalmente (de las primeras ciudades fundadas a partir de 1538). Malograda por fárrago de biografías y exaltadas lecciones histórico-literarias glorificadoras del "fervor" conquistador y fundacional de los españoles. Aunque incluye bibliografía, no está clara fuente de poemas antologizados.

3463 Juana Inés de la Cruz, Sor. Enigmas: ofrecidos a la Casa del Placer por Juana Inés de la Cruz. Edición y estudio de Antonio Alatorre. México: Colegio de México, Centro de Estudios Lingüísticos y Literarios, 1994. 173 p.: ill.

Edición moderna de los *Enigmas*, intrincadas adivinanzas en verso (del tipo de las propuestas por la Esfinge clásica) escritos por Sor Juana entre 1692–93 por encargo de un grupo de monjas portuguesas admiradoras suyas y quienes estaban organizadas en una asociación literaria llamada "la Casa del Plazer." Basada en primera edición de Lisboa de 1695. Excelente estudio del editor de estas últimas composiciones "mundanas" de la monja y sobre sus problemas textuales. De obligada referencia para interesados en la poesía de Sor Juana.

Teatro dieciochesco de Nueva España. See item **4267.**

3464 Toro Montalvo, César. *La novena maravilla:* joya de la prosa colonial hispanoamericana. (*Fénix/Lima,* 34/35, 1989, p. 119–168, ill.)

Edición parcial de selección de sermones que "El Lunarejo" dio entre 1656–85 en Perú y publicada en Madrid en 1695 por sus discípulos. Obra en prosa menos conocida y reeditada que el *Apologético* con el que comparte exuberante despliegue de artificios culteranos y conceptistas. Prólogo ofrece buen resumen de la atención crítica recibida por la obra durante dos siglos. Exceso de ponderación de su valor y del significado de esta edición para "el curso de la historia de las letras coloniales del siglo XVII" limita su mérito.

Toro Montalvo, César. Literatura peruana: de los incas a la época contemporánea. See item **3644.**

3465 Williams, Jerry M. Censorship and art in pre-Enlightenment Lima: Pedro de Peralta Barnuevo's *Diálogo de los muertos; la causa académica.* Potomac, Md.: Scripta Humanistica, 1994. 1 v.: bibl. (Scripta Humanistica; 110)

Este importante trabajo confronta reputación de Peralta como autor conforme con el status quo por medio de: 1) excelente y bien documentado estudio de la vida y obra del autor y, 2) publicación y traducción al inglés de recientemente descubierta sátira alegórica de Peralta que ridiculiza las actividades de las academias literarias limeñas frecuentadas por él: *Diálogo de los muertos: la causa académica,* escrito entre 1725–31. Propone así reevaluación del valor literario de la obra de Peralta.

3466 Zatrilla y Vico, Joseph, *Conde de Villasalto.* Poema heroico al merecido aplauso del único oráculo de las musas, glorioso asombro de los ingenios y célebre fénix de la poesía, la esclarecida y venerable señora Sor Juana Inés de la Cruz, religiosa profesa en el Convento de San Jerónimo de la Imperial Ciudad de México. Escribióle José Zatrilla y Vico. Ed. facsímile. Monterrey, Mexico: Producciones Al Voleo el Troquel, 1993. xi, 38 p.: ill.

Primera edición moderna y facsimilar de 100 rebuscadas octavas reales escritas en 1696, a pocos meses de la muerte de Sor Juana, en exorbitante alabanza de ella. El sardo Zatrilla, quien debió conocer las ediciones españolas de la poesía de la monja de 1689–92, es más conocido como autor de novelas sobre ardientes enredos amorosos con tono moralizante. Importante para evaluar reacción del lector europeo de Sor Juana en su época.

20th Century Prose Fiction
Mexico

JOSE MANUEL GARCIA-GARCIA, *Assistant Professor of Spanish, New Mexico State University*

CONTINUAMOS BAJO EL SIGNO de dos generaciones dominantes: la Generación del 68 y la generación que he bautizado con el nombre de Generación Postista. La Generación del 68 ya ha sido ampliamente estudiada por Enrique Krauze en su importante ensayo "Cuatro Estaciones de la Cultura Mexicana" (*Vuelta*, Vol. 60, nov. 1981, p. 27–42). Los representantes de la G-68, caracterizadas por su actitud de crítica social y su postura política *anti-establishment*, están en contra de todo lo viejo y lo solemne; por eso exaltan el lenguaje carnavalesco de la Onda. Son, en primera instancia, los traviesos de la literatura. Aspiran a ser contemporáneos del mundo en rebelión: son los protagonistas de las jornadas del 68 y los que ensayan con los géneros marginales del periodismo cultural, con Carlos Monsiváis siendo el caso más señalado. La Generación del 68 vivió en carne propia la terrible masacre del 2 de octubre del 1968 y respondió con una literatura del desengaño, literatura que hasta la fecha sigue produciéndose. Ver, por ejemplo, la obra de José Agustín (item **3467**) o la novela deprimente de René Avilés Fabila (item **3469**) o la biografía novelada de Gustavo Hilares (item **3495**). Los jóvenes del 68 se encontraban ante la disyuntiva de vivir en la extrema izquierda o sobrevivir en la inercia.

La generación posterior a la del 68 es la nacida entre 1951 y 1965. Ellos heredaron las ideas de Octavio Paz y Carlos Monsiváis. Sin embargo, más que seguir la "tradición de la ruptura" han buscado el sincretismo cultural. Esta es la generación que comienza ahora a dominar el panorama de la literatura contemporánea mexicana. Según Paz en "El Romanticismo y la Poesía Contemporánea," hoy asistimos "al crepúsculo de la estética del cambio" (*Vuelta*, Vol. 127, junio 1987, p. 26). El arte y la literatura en México han perdido sus poderes de rebelión: hoy estamos ante el "arte de la convergencia." Para Monsiváis, hoy nos encontramos en la era de la crisis a todos niveles: los jóvenes de la actual generación han respondido con un abigarrado sincretismo, una especie de neobarroco o literatura híbrida *conscientemente* paródica. Sin Marx y sin Rousseau, han guiado sus búsquedas hacia las nacientes teorías postestructuralistas de la posmodernidad. En esta "nueva estética" participan algunos de la Generación del 68, como Monsiváis (*Por mi madre, bohemios*, item **3509**), Jorge Ayala Blanco (n. 1942), Paco Ignacio Taibo II (n. 1949), Laura Esquivel (n. 1950) y Angeles Mastretta (n. 1949). Hoy vivimos bajo el signo de los tiempos ya estudiado por Monsiváis en "Muerte y Resurrección del Nacionalismo Mexicano" (*Nexos*, Vol. 109, enero 1987, p. 13–22). Vivimos la época de los post: estamos en un "posnacionalismo" que consiste en una democratización violenta de la vida social, el rechazo de los panoramas unificadores, el gusto por la fragmentación y el neolocalismo, tipo Armando Ramírez (item **3510**) o Luis Humberto Crosthwaite (items **3480** y **3481**). También, como señala Monsiváis, la actual literatura está consolidándose en los temas homosexuales y feministas con propuestas diferentes y sofisticadas. Los escritores actuales de la Generación Postista son ajenos al marxismo de viejo cuño: su contracultura se opone aun a los valores morales de la generación anterior. Ver, por ejemplo las novelas de Carmen Boullosa (n. Distrito Federal, 1951, items **3474** y **3473**) y Martha Cerda (n. Guadalajara, 1952, item **3477**). La Generación Postista tiene también excelentes representantes en la literatura gay; Luis Zapata (n. Guerrero, 1951) José Joaquín Blanco (n. 1951) y Luis Montaño (n. Sonora, 1955–85) son tres de los más destacados escritores de este género. También otras voces han enriquecido la cultura postista: Enrique Serna (n. 1959), autor de *Uno soñaba que era rey* (item **3514**), el periodista cultural Pablo Espinosa (n. Veracruz, 1956) y el cronista de lo fantástico, Oscar de la Borbolla (n. 1951). Otros escritores de la Generación Postista que comienzan a desarrollarse dentro de este espíritu de época son: Guillermo J. Fadanelli, Ricardo Chávez Castañeda, Alfredo Espinosa y los críticos Lauro Zavala y Christopher Domínguez.

Pero al mismo tiempo, siguen publicando sus nostalgias los reconocidos Carlos Fuentes y Elena Garro. En el México actual, coexisten los gustos de la modernidad y la postmodernidad y se relacionan a regañadientes las generaciones culturales mexicanas. Hay ahora un después, "después del 68" y como dijera en una ocasión Octavio Paz, quien ha visto el rostro de la esperanza, nunca podrá olvidarla. Con ese espíritu, concluimos que la literatura mexicana de fin de siglo está reencontrando los fructíferos caminos de la contracultura que estábamos esperando.

PROSE FICTION

3467 Agustín, José. Camas de campo/campos de batalla. Puebla, Mexico: Benemérita Univ. Autónoma de Puebla, 1993. 160 p. (Col. Meridiano)

Son 16 ensayos de temas diversos y tono coloquial ameno que nos informan acerca de los pleitos de familia entre Jung y Freud ("Dos Gruesos Frente a Frente"), y entre los grupos culturales mexicanos dirigidos por Octavio Paz ("derechista") y Carlos Monsiváis ("izquierdista"). También nos enteramos de los aciertos y errores de los amigos, enemigos y aliados del escritor José Agustín. Es un libro polémico, hecho desde el campo mismo de batalla.

3468 Anteo, Mario. Las trampas del jardín. Monterrey, Mexico: Ediciones Castillo, 1994. 163 p. (Col. Más allá; 2)

Consiste de 22 cuentos con personajes descritos en forma realista. Nos adentramos a las rutinas de seres frustrados incapaces de cambiar sus destinos. En el cuento "Las Trampas del Jardín," el personaje central no vacila en abandonar la posibilidad de un adulterio. En "Crux de Histrión," el payasito barrachín cumple su rutina a pesar de la desesperanza y de una formidable cruda que lo quema. Y en "Amor Omar," un saxofonista debe olvidarse de la mujer de sus sueños al descubrir que ella es, literalmente, el diablo.

3469 Avilés Fabila, René. Réquiem por un suicida. Madrid: Libertarias/Prodhufi, 1993. 210 p. (Narrativa; 49)

Novela de tesis. Apasionada defensa del suicida Gustavo Treviño, narrador-personaje que ha vivido muy bien, ha sido guerrillero, escritor, mujeriego, posmarxista, tanatólogo, y suicida retro-romántico. Al final de su biografía, una de sus amantes: "camina lentamente hacia la salida del cementerio. Oprime la urna [de sus cenizas] con amor." Este libro es un irónico réquiem de la Razón Marxista de los años 70.

3470 Betancourt, Ignacio. Ajuste de cuentos. México: Editorial Océano, 1995. 170 p.

El título es justo; es una edición de relatos escritos entre 1976–91. Dominan el humor quevedesco y el amor por la jerga desparpajada. "De cómo Guadalupe Bajó a La Montaña y Todo lo Demás" es el mejor de los relatos seleccionados. Una pandilla secuestra a la Virgen de Guadalupe, la oculta en una cantina y exige rescate. México se indigna y los ladrones, desesperados, se atrincheran en el centro de la capital. Allí mueren aplastados, mientras la Virgen asciende, para caer luego, reventada por un municionazo. Sin duda, Betancourt es el provocador más moralizante del cuento mexicano.

3471 Borbolla, Oscar de la. Asalto al infierno. México: Joaquín Mortiz, 1993. 147 p.

Ocho relatos donde los personajes buscan la aventura gratuita y acaban de buscaroba-muertos ("Aventura en la Tumba") o participan en un ataque directo al Diablo ("Asalto al Infierno") o confunden el amor, la realidad y la fantasía ("El Club de las Amazonas"). De la Borbolla utiliza el humor para describir los fracasos de sus personajes. Y no pocas veces, se incluye él mismo como protagonista.

3472 Borbolla, Oscar de la. Todo está permitido. México: Grupo Editorial Planeta, 1994. 133 p. (Col. Narrativa 21)

Novela donde la sensual Gabriela aprende a vivir de los vividores-machistas mexicanos. El narrador nos lleva por los momentos más intensos y plenos de gozo sexual de la heroína. La chica es de una hermosura renacentista, una Doña Bárbara mexicana que vive su picaresca vida hasta lograr su objetivo: ser rica e independiente. Sin duda, Borbolla escribe como feminista, pero sin salirse del estereotipo literario de la pícara rebelde.

3473 Boullosa, Carmen. Duerme. Madrid: Santillana; Buenos Aires: Aguilar, Altea, Taurus, Alfaguara, 1994. 146 p. (Alfaguara hispánica; 128)

Son los albores del Nuevo Mundo y la francesa Claire, aventurera travesti, quien vuelve a la vida gracias a la magia de la india Inés, ha perdido su disfraz-identidad masculina y ahora es una mujer que los hombres violan y maltratan. Sin embargo, logra sobrevivir en ese mundo de horror. Boullosa nos ha dado un personaje que reúne las características del héroe épico y del ser marginal, profundamente subversivo.

3474 Boullosa, Carmen. La milagrosa: novela. México: Ediciones Era, 1993. 113 p. (Biblioteca Era)

Novela policiaca, política y fantástica. La protagonista es una bella joven que sueña milagros que se cumplen en la vida real y es acosada por la corrupción, representada por el malvado Felipe Morales. Afortunadamente, el investigador privado (alcóholico, rompehuelgas) Aureliano Jiménez ayuda a la joven Milagrosa a escapar de los mil y un peligros que la acechan. La estructura de la novela envuelve al lector y lo lleva a un viaje por los sueños de la protagonista y las voces de los beneficiados de la magia de la curandera. También es una

novela de amor rosa y de persecuciones de película de acción.

3475 Carballido, Emilio. Flor de abismo. 143 p. (Grandes narradores)

Integra tres novelas cortas (o tres relatos largos). "Flor de Abismo" se trata del ascenso y caída de un poeta nacional. Un héroe trágico, el sentimiento de culpa lo destruye después de que en su finca ocurren desgracias fatales. "Sobre Virtudes Teologales" se trata de una beata ciega y desheredada que se casa con un viejo-rico y vive un final feliz. Esta noveleta atrae por su tono de remembranza nostálgica. "El Sol" que trata de tres hombres enloquecidos por la bella, inocente y campirana Hortensia. Ocurre un crimen pasional que le da un tono de intriga y suspenso a la historia. Puede decirse que "Flor de Abismo" es un ramillete de nostalgias.

3476 Carballo, Marco Aurelio. La novela de Betoven y otros relatos. México: Katún, 1986. 130 p. (Prosa contemporánea; 19)

Contiene 16 cuentos bien hechos, de tono realista, de temacotidianos y humor textual. En "Primaballerina" un joven travesti no entiende por qué el público masculino prefiere a las mujeres bailarinas. En "La Noche Aciaga en que el Sargento Apodaca se le Puso al Brinco al Capitán Necoechea" un policía enano, macho y prepotente, acaba medio rostizado por un pobre mesero asustado. "Posdata de la Posdata" un atropellado lleva como única identificación una carta de amor melodramático. Y en "Mi Amigo el Tigre" una mesera casi mata a un pobre diablo, todo por una miserable propina.

3477 Cerda, Martha. La señora Rodríguez y otros mundos. México: J. Mortiz, 1990. 181 p. (Serie del volador)

No sabemos si es una colección de cuentos con novela o novela con cuentos intercalados (entre capítulo y capítulo). Si es una colección de cuentos, diremos que son un *patchwork* de narraciones cortas, sin tema dominante y unidas por el azar. Si es novela, diremos que se trata de un personaje femenino y su bolsa mágica. La narración es una mezcla perfecta entre la farsa y la parodia de algunos modelos literarios (por ejemplo, de *Un tal Lucas* de Julio Cortázar y *Niebla* de Miguel de Unamuno). El estilo de la autora es sencillo y a la vez cáustico. De los personajes vemos sólo rasgos exagerados, grotescos, fugaces.

3478 Cerda, Martha. Y apenas era miércoles. México: J. Mortiz, 1993. 84 p. (Cuarto creciente)

Ficción y testimonio se unen para tejer la historia de 11 personajes que viven los momentos previos a la explosión ocurrida el 22 de abril de 1992 en Guadalajara. Es también una denuncia de la negligencia oficial e informativa de México. Cerda utiliza la narración simultánea y la descripción intimista o intrahistórica para ir creando la tensión previa al terrible desenlace.

3479 Chávez Castañeda, Ricardo. La guerra enana del jardín. Benito Juárez, Mexico: J. Mortiz, 1993. 145 p. (Premios bellas artes de literatura)

Son 12 cuentos escritos en un lenguaje de fácil lectura. Destacan las narraciones siguientes: "Bien Podría Llamarse Vida Tomada," donde un joven destruye su matrimonio al dedicarse a escribir narraciones mediocres; "La Guerra Enana del Jardín," en el que un narrador se dedica a buscar un tema y un punto de vista de una historia que no termina de hacer; "El Diario del Perro Muerto," la historia de unos jóvenes que se dedican a escribir un *scrap-book* y que acabarán enterrándolo simbólicamente. Los cuentos de Chávez tienen tres constantes: son un homenaje a Julio Cortázar, tienen intenciones metaficcionales y son una abigarrada referencia a los comics mexicanos y norteamericanos.

3480 Crosthwaite, Luis Humberto. El gran preténder. México: Consejo Nacional para la Cultura y las Artes, 1992. 97 p. (Fondo editorial tierra adentro; 46)

Esta novela de nostalgia es la evocación del cholo-macho "Saico" y sus amigos marginados. Es la sucesión de viñetas donde se retrata la violencia chola o pandillera. Las mujeres se pelean por el "Saico;" éste se pelea por ellas y todos acaban víctimas de sí mismos y de la gran pandilla oficial de Tijuana, la policía fronteriza. A pesar de la moraleja neo-naturalista de la historia, Crosthwaite logra un ritmo poético encantador.

3481 Crosthwaite, Luis Humberto. La luna siempre será un amor difícil. México: ECO, 1994. 180 p.: ill. (OsaMayor; 11)

Novela que podría calificarse de *post-modern* porque es un híbrido de subgéneros (epistolar y documental). También es un juego paródico de Bernal Díaz del Castillo y Laura Esquivel. El conquistador Balboa y su mujer escapan del desempleo capitalino y van a Tijuana donde viven una serie de aventuras de corte picaresco. En esta novela también hay juegos visuales y caligramas.

Diccionario bio-bibliográfico de escritores de México, 1920–1970. See item **9.**

3482 Espinosa Becerra, Pablo. No por mucho madrugar se redacta más temprano. México: Consejo Nacional para la Cultura y las Artes, 1994. 379 p.

Espinosa quiere ser el Monsiváis de la generación de escritores mexicanos de fin de siglo. Su estilo es en ocasiones poético, en otras, francamente relajiento. Y uno se emociona hasta las lágrimas con textos como "Oye Lennon: ¿el sueño ha terminado?." Se divierte con la nostalgia de la lucha libre en "Del Arte del Pancracio" y se deja manipular sentimentalmente con textos que evocan a grupos de rock (U2) y de otros amos de la industria del espectáculo. Espinosa es el neocronista de la frase exacta y memorable.

3483 Espinosa Becerra, Pablo. Si me han de matar mañana, lo redacto de una vez. México: Leega; INBA, 1988. 132 p.

Ganador del Premio Bellas Artes de Literatura y de Periodismo Cultural, esta colección de crónicas es de gran calidad. Uno disfruta la descripción de la cantante de ranchero en Bellas Artes ("Lola la Grande"), del caos generado por una película pésima ("Lola la Trailera") y de las multitudes atolondradas ante las cámaras de televisión ("12 de Diciembre, la Basílica"). Con Espinosa, el género del neocronismo mexicano logra una gran calidad literaria.

3484 Esquivel, Laura. La ley del amor. Barcelona: Plaza & Janés, 1995. 276 p.: col. ill., 1 digital sound disc. (Ave fénix. Serie mayor; 38)

Novela llena de sorpresas, incluye un disco compacto para acompañar los viajes por el tiempo de los personajes y dibujos de monitos que interrumpen la narración para mostrarnos momentos epifánicos. Historia mezcla de *new age*, novelarrosa, ciencia-ficción y de un humor literario involuntario. Los personajes reencarnan para deshacer sus entuertos pretéritos o para consumar un amor que en alguna de sus vidas les fue negado. Esquivel es una escritora que tiene demasiada imaginación.

3485 Estañol, Bruno. Ni el reino de otro mundo. México: J. Mortiz, 1991. 125 p. (Premios bellas artes de literatura)

Son 13 cuentos donde los perdedores del mundo relatan sus desventuras: el pícaro Benjamín, mujeriego y tomador ("¡Vas a Acabar como el Tío Benjamín!"); el impulsivo Frank que abandona a su familia, seis hijos y esposa, por 34.000 dólares y un nuevo amor ("Ni el Reino de Otro Mundo"); los alcohólicos y mariguanos, frustrados amantes de la loca Vilma ("Ménage a Trois"); y los despistados ladrones de bancos ("El Gran Asalto"). Estañol utiliza una prosa sin adornos y con multiplicidad de puntos de vista.

3486 Fadanelli, Guillermo J. El día que la vea la voy a matar. México: Grijalbo, 1992. 160 p. (Narrativa)

Son 32 cuentos con personajes nacidos del teatro del absurdo, la nota roja y del existencialismo camusiano. Fadanelli sabe contar, con toda la calma del mundo, los intentos de un loco por atravesar de un golpe las paredes ("Rogelio contra el Muro") o los juegos violentos de un joven contra una anciana ("Mi Mamá me Mima"). Se burla de García Márquez ("Cuento de Realismo Mágico") y nos narra una fiesta de locos, donde hay mutilaciones y risas sin par ("Mi Tía Clarita"). Esta nueva voz narrativa intenta ser el Roland Topor mexicano.

3487 Fernández Perera, Manuel. La especie desconocida. Fotografías de Lola Alvarez Bravo. México: Editorial Quinqué, 1988. 82 p.: ill.

Libro de fábulas divertidas, sobrias y poéticas. En "La Mona de Seda," una mona se viste de seda y se queda. En "G.S.," una cucaracha kafkiana intenta hablar en el momento de ser aplastada. Y en "La Segunda Tentación," Adán es víctima de las paradojas intelectuales de la sofista y tentadora serpiente bíblica. Fernández continúa las técnicas seductoras del maestro Augusto Monterroso.

3488 Fuentes, Carlos. Diana, o, La cazadora solitaria. Madrid: Santillana, 1994. 224 p. (Alfaguara hispánica; 130)

Biografía-ensayo de un supuesto escritor cuarentón, agobiado por los sucesos políticos ocurridos entre 1965–75. Se vale de los temas del erotismo y el amor imposible para meditar acerca de los horrores de la época. Por esta novela desfilan personajes reales y ficticios que entrecruzan sus destinos con Diana Soren, especie de María Félix y Tania, la guerrillera. También es una vuelta a algunos de los temas del autor: Don Juan, los políticos norteamericanos y los símbolos aztecas.

3489 Fuentes, Carlos. Geografía de la novela. México: Fondo de Cultura Económica, 1993. 178 p. (Col. Tierra firme)

En esta Reunión de ensayos de diferentes épocas (1974, 1991, 1993) hay una diversidad de argumentos y temas, incluyendo: la defensa de la novela como género literario y el brillante elogio a escritores reconocidos como Jorge Luis Borges, Milán Kundera e Italo Calvino. Fuentes también ingresa a la discusión posmoderna: ha muerto el eurocentrismo (y/o el chovinismo literario); ahora estamos ante el nacimiento del policentrismo. Y para documentar esta nueva experiencia humana, la palabra escrita es más necesaria que nunca. En este compendio ensayístico, Fuentes nos ofrece una visión optimista del futuro.

3490 Fuentes, Carlos. El mal del tiempo. Madrid: Alfaguara, c1994. 2 v.

Bajo este título Fuentes reúne cinco novelas cortas. En *Constancia*, domina los temas del dolor y exilio. En *La desdichada*, Toño y Bernardo evocan con nostalgia al México que vivieron. En *El prisionero de Las Lomas*, se desarrolla la sátira de un neopícaro mexicano, sarnoso por la corrupción oficial. En *Viva mi fama*, los símbolos de la tauromaquia y el arte pictórico encarnan en el torero Rubén Oliva (antípoda de Pedro Romero) y en el pintor Don Francisco Goya. El tema dominante de *Gente de razón* es el de la arquitectura y sus diversos estratos simbólicos y culturales. Es una visión post-apocalíptica, continuación de la novela *Cristóbal Nonato*.

3491 Fuentes, Carlos. Tres discursos para dos aldeas. Buenos Aires: Fondo de Cultura Económica, 1993. 107 p. (Col. popular; 489)

Incluye tres de los discursos más destacados de Fuentes. El primero, pronunciado con motivo del Premio Miguel de Cervantes en 1987, es una meditación en torno al idioma español y a la simbología moderna de *El Quijote*. El segundo discurso fue pronunciado en la UNESCO en 1991 y se trata de los efectos culturales del descubrimiento de América. El último discurso abarca la situación mundial después de la Guerra Fría.

3492 Gardea, Jesús. Difícil de atrapar: cuentos. México: Joaquín Mortiz, 1995. 127 p. (Serie del volador)

El estilo de Gardea es poético y telegráfico. Una frase condensa varias oraciones y el lector debe ir "llenando" las insinuaciones y los huecos o elipsis. Hay un fraseo minimalista que se duplica en el lenguaje de los personajes, quienes hablan como Gardea narra. En este mundo saturado de silencios y de frases corta, nos llenamos del erotismo de "Livia y los Sueños" y de la soledad de "La Loca Maravilla," cuentos que atrapan con facilidad, porque están hechos con oficio y a fuego lento.

3493 Garro, Elena. Busca mi esquela y primer amor. Monterrey, Mexico: Ediciones Castillo, 1996. 110 p.

En "Busca mi Esquela," Miguel encuentra a la joven Irene-Paulina huyendo por las calles oscuras de la ciudad. Se enamoran. La joven lo visita cuando quiere, pero Miguel no sabe nada de ella. Al final, descubre que Paulina se ha casado con otro. Garro logra mantener la tensión mediante el misterio que envuelve la conducta de la joven. En "Primer Amor," una niña recuerda su aventura en un pueblito francés. Allí conoce a Siegfried, un adolescente prisionero de guerra. Este se enamora de la madre de la niña. Pero al final él muere tratando de rescatar a la chica. Esta comprende entonces, que Siegfried fue su primer amor.

3494 González de Alba, Luis. Agapi mu. México: Aguilar, León y Cal Editores, 1993. 204 p. (Cal y arena)

Novela de tema homosexual. Enrique está muriendo de SIDA, mientras su compañero David filosofa, se enamora de José, viaja y tiene relaciones sexuales con un gran número de personajes anónimos en cines de tercera. No hay dramatismo en la narración. Todo ocurre sin aspavientos: Enrique muere, David conoce nuevos amores y la vida sigue igual. El narrador busca (y logra) la mitificación del erotismo porno-sensual de sus personajes.

3495 Hilares, Gustavo. Memorias de la guerra de los justos. México: Cal y Arena, 1996. 1 v.

Buen ejemplo de que la novela realista en México goza de buena salud y tiene magníficos narradores. Hilares nos coloca en el centro de la vida de la guerrilla urbana mexicana de los años 70. Los poderosos fantasmas de Oseas, Genaro Vázquez Rojas y Lucio Cabañas vuelven para desmitificar sus luchas y para mostrarnos sus contradicciones, a veces ridículas. Este libro sí es un saldo de cuentas; es el apasionado desencanto de un sobreviviente del naufragio posmarxista.

Inventario de voces: visión retrospectiva de la literatura sonorense. See item **3903.**

3496 Isunza, Fabián. Reveses. Edición de Alfredo Espinosa. Chihuahua, Mexico: Ediciones Azar, 1994. 136 p.

No sabemos si Fabián es Alfredo Espinosa (el que firma como recolector de los escritos de Isunza). Lo cierto es que es una colección de aforismos y meditaciones en torno al amor que "embellece el rostro de sus víctimas;" a la escritura ("el arte de escupir hacia arriba") y del año ("Flor del jardín prohibido"), un tema espinoso, tocado con el sútil encanto de un poeta maldito de fin de siglo XX. Es un texto que habla de placeres "marginales," sin recurrir al chiste fácil.

3497 Jodorowsky, Alexandro. Sombras al mediodía. Santiago: Dolmen Ediciones, 1995. 200 p. (Escritores de Chile)

Colección de fábulas y haikús. Jodorowsky juega con la lógica visual ("El Conocimiento" y "Dentrofuera"), el psicoanálisis ("La Mujer que se Esfuma" y "Amor Filial") y las reflexiones filosóficas ("El Primer y el Ultimo Hombre. ¿Qué Podrán Decirse?"). Este autor chileno-mexicano es un Fernando Arrabal mezcla de René Magritte, es teatro del absurdo e imagen filosofal, minimalista y desconcertante. Es la continuidad de "los grandes" que están escribiendo sus últimas obras.

3498 Lavín, Guillermo. Final de cuento. México: Consejo Nacional para la Cultura y las Artes, 1993. 113 p. (Fondo editorial tierra adentro; 83)

Libro de 17 cuentos de ambiente cortazariano. "La Máscara" es el relato de un demonio carnavalesco que tiene el don de cambiar de rostros. "Fin de Cuento" se trata de un narrador que se imagina intocable y es asesinado por uno de sus personajes. En "Cuerpo Tomado," Julio Cortázar vuelve a escribir sus cuentos a través de un escritor joven. A pesar de la brevedad de sus relatos Lavín sabe cómo crear atmósferas cargadas de suspenso.

3499 López Páez, Jorge. Doña Herlinda y su hijo y otros hijos. México: Fondo de Cultura Económica, 1993. 323 p. (Col. popular; 483)

Contiene 13 cuentos de corte realista en que el lector debe ir descubriendo las pistas que llevan al mundo secreto de los personajes. Por ejemplo, en "Doña Herlinda y su Hijo" y "Herlinda Primera o Primero Herlinda," la historia se trata de una familia de provincia que oculta bajo un pesado manto de convenciones sociales la relación homosexual y el adulterio de los "hijos," perfectamente controlados por la matriarcal Doña Herlinda. Es un excelente juego de máscaras, tradiciones, apariencias y realidades.

3500 Márquez Vázquez, Luis. Rubor de betabel. México: Grupo Editorial Planeta, 1994. 177 p. (Col. Narrativa 21)

Esta novela ganadora del Premio "Agustín Yáñez" es una obra excéntrica por su exagerado convencionalismo literario. Se trata de la vida melodramática del arquitecto Fernando y su hermosa, pero descocada esposa, la buena Ariadna. Cuando la mujercita se mete a estudiar arte dramático, la vida se le hace una telenovela, con hombres malos que la seducen y esposos que se autodestruyen por amor. Al final, parece que Fernando y Ariadna se reconcilian, pero vuelven a las incompatibilidades y Ariadna huye a Guadalajara. Es una novela para soportar la terrible condición de ser cornudo, clasemediero, mexicano y aburrido.

3501 Martínez, Herminio. Diario maldito de Nuño de Guzmán. Mexico: Editorial Diana, 1990. 237 p.

Estamos a principios del siglo 16 y el narrador es el mismísimo Presidente de la primera Real Audiencia de México, Nuño de Guzmán. Martínez echa mano de las crónicas de la época, las leyendas y los datos dispersos para darle un tono coherente a su novela histórica. Otro elemento atractivo: el lenguaje es una mezcla lúdica de arcaismos y neologismos. Es un magnífico logro.

3502 Martínez Castro, Leticia et al. El vértigo del erotismo. México: EDAMEX, Univ. Autónoma Metropolitana, 1996. 176 p.

Antología de cuentos eróticos, casi todos hechos por escritoras jóvenes. Los mejores relatos son: "Erotismo Frutal" de Norma Macías, donde un hombre palpa, saborea y desecha un virginal durazno; "Paloma" de Julieta Cortés Martínez, acerca de la animalidad literal y poética de una mujer; "Amor Prohibido" de Mariana Gumá, donde un pez en su pecera sueña con ser presa erótica de un gato blanco; "Basilio y Judith" de Claudia Segura Medina, en el que descubrimos a la mitad del relato que estamos ante la relación sexual entre un perro y su dueña; y "37.2 C" de Edith Villanueva Silés, donde la imagen de un espejo nos cuenta los juegos íntimos de su figura-dueña.

3503 Mastretta, Angeles. Puerto libre. México: Cal y Arena, 1993. 176 p.

Muestrario de relatos que son aforismos ("¿Quién Insulta, el Alma o la Lengua?" Porque es la lengua, la que guarda "el vivo recuerdo del cobijo que otra le dio entre juegos"). Mastretta ha logrado una preciosa colección de viñetas llenas de nostalgias. La escritora sostiene en los 29 relatos un tono intimista, juguetón y reflexivo; un poco Poniatowska, un poco Loaeza, pero siempre es la Mastretta de *Arráncame la vida.*

3504 Molina, Silvia. Un hombre cerca. 2. ed. México: Cal y Arena, 1993. 112 p.

Son siete cuentos de corte realista e intimista. Destacan "Domingo" la historia de una mujer que recuerda sus domingos de la infancia y gusta de imaginar la vida cotidiana de su amante; y "Hospital," la relación de amor-odio entre un hombre mediocre y su hija menospreciada. La narrativa de Molina es un viaje nostálgico, lleno de música y ambientes de clase media.

3505 Monsiváis, Carlos. El género epistolar: un homenaje a manera de carta abierta. México: Miguel Angel Porrua, 1991. 99 p.

Esta colección de cartas personales, públicas y políticas del siglo 18 al 20 es una larga, lujosa y bien documentada crónica del sub-género epistolar. Monsiváis señala la importancia de estos documentos: representan un hecho democrático en un ambiente social antidemocrático; son ejercicios literarios y muestrarios del "espíritu de una época." El cronista acierta al dar a la luz pública esa parte de la historia mexicana, que parece no ser de nuestra incumbencia.

3506 La palabra en juego: el nuevo cuento mexicano. Selección, introducción y notas de Lauro Zavala. Toluca, Mexico: Univ. Autónoma del Estado de México, 1993. 167 p.: bibl. (Col. 500 años de América)

Estos 21 cuentos fueron originalmente publicados entre 1986–92. Zavala señala que son relatos breves, bien hechos y con el tono lúdico del cuento actual mexicano. Relatos memorables son: "Madonna de Guadalupe" de Juan Villoro, en el que los jóvenes se desviven literalmente por la distraída Rocío La Bella; "Los Locos Somos otro Cosmos" de Oscar de la Borbolla, donde sólo se usa la vocal "o" pero sin embargo los diálogos son coherentes y las descripciones perfectas; y "La Ultima Visita" de Enrique Serna, una excelente micro-farsa en prosa que se trata de una familia pleitera que simula, a duras penas, ser refinada y discreta.

3507 Pitol, Sergio. Domar a la divina garza. Barcelona: Anagrama, 1988. 203 p. (Narrativas hispánicas; 68)

El licenciado Dante de la Estrella es presumido y se cree modesto, es ridículo y se cree refinado. Pierde siempre en todo: ante sus amigos, sus sirvientes y el lector. Acaba siempre llorando y batido en su propio excremento. Domar a la divina garza significa perder escandalosamente el juego de las envidias y los ataques personales. Esta novela retrata el mundo mediocre de una clase media en decadencia.

3508 Poniatowska, Elena. Luz y luna, las lunitas. Fotografías de Graciela Iturbide. México: Ediciones Era, 1994. 208 p.: ill. (some col.).

La cronista-novelista Poniatowska nos ofrece una antología de sus ensayos acerca de la mujer mexicana. Las descripciones son ingenuas, emotivas, juguetonas y nostálgicas. Así, leemos con cariño, el ambiente de un mercado en el Distrito Federal de principios de siglo (en "El Ultimo Guajolote"), y del destino de la gran Jesusa Palancares, y de las fotografías de Graciela Iturbide, y del matriarcado en Juchitán, y, de las hierberas de Huamantla. Este libro es una crónica-ficcionalizada en honor a las mujeres que los antropólogos machos no quisieron documentar.

3509 Por mi madre, bohemios. v. 1. Comentarios y alabanzas de Carlos Monsiváis. Selección de textos de Alejandro Brito. Ilus-

traciones y cuidado ornamental de Rafael Barajas ("El Fisgón"). Mexico: LaJornada Ediciones, 1993. 1 v.: ill. (Serie Atrás de la raya)

Es la muy esperada antología de declaraciones oficiales que son autogoles, autodevaluaciones, contradicciones, manifestaciones claras de cinismo y de humor involuntario de "secretarios de estado, gobernadores, senadores, diputados, empresarios, obispos, hombres de pro y columnas de la sociedad." Esta selección de declaraciones de los Pro-Hombres Mexicanos abarca del 29 de nov. 1989 al 30 de oct. 1990. Fueron originalmente recopiladas por Monsiváis y publicadas en *La Jornada.*

3510 Ramírez, Armando. Tepito. México: Grijalbo, 1989. 121 p.

Es una excursión por los laberintos del barrio de Tepito, ofrecido por el sabroso narrador de historias de ese mítico lugar, cuna del albur y del omnipresente naco. Los de Tepito son seres que han sido maltratados por la vida: la prostituta, el boxeador, el fayuquero, el raterillo y las guapas adolescentes que abandonan el barrio por desprecio a la pobreza. Esta novela es también una parodia de la crónica, tan de moda en el México contemporáneo.

3511 Rulfo, Juan. Los cuadernos de Juan Rulfo. Presentación de Clara Aparicio de Rulfo. Transcripción y nota de Yvette Jiménez de Báez. México: Ediciones Era, 1994. 183 p.: ill.

Colección de textos inacabados, fragmentos de Pedro Páramo, borradores y apuntes varios demuestran la desesperación de Rulfo, que no logró superar su propio estilo. Aunque la idea original fue la de mostrar la "cocina" literaria de ese autor y de recuperar el "hilo de su pensamiento creador," el resultado es un libro polémico que Rulfo, perfeccionista, no hubiera publicado. Puede servir, sin embargo, como ejemplo para los nuevos escritores.

3512 Ruvalcaba, Eusebio. Jueves Santo. México: Editorial Joaquín Mortiz, 1994. 122 p. (Premios bellas artes de literatura)

Estos 13 cuentos fueron reunidos para jugar con nuestra actitud políticamente correcta. Hay personajes que matan para pertenecer a un grupo de borrachos ("Lo Ultimo que Recuerdo es que Estaba Bailando con la Quinceañera") o que enloquecen en un arrebato místico ("Paréntesis Citadino") o que se visten de vaquero enano y fornican con sus caballos para sentirse "Búfalo Kid" ("El Revólver más Rápido del Oeste") o que se disfraza de "Santa Clos" para descubrir su verdadera vocación pedofílica ("Cascabel"). A pesar de los temas, no hay moraleja, ni estilo escandaloso. Estamos ante una literatura freudiana, narrada por un escritor realista.

3513 Sefchovich, Sara. La señora de los sueños. México: Grupo Editorial Paneta, 1993. 295 p. (Col. Fábula)

Una señora descubre su condición de esclava del hogar y comienza a modificar su conducta. Primero, debe soñarse ser una mujer árabe tradicionista, luego, una rusa poderosa, después, una revolucionaria cubana y una prostituta de New York. Al final de la novela, ella descubre que su fuerza radica en el poder de la imaginación y de los sueños. Su familia, mientras tanto, no entiende qué ha pasado con la señora. Esta novela es muy esquemática en su estructura, pero se lee con gusto solidario, gracias a su tono coloquial y a su mensaje feminista de última moda.

3514 Serna, Enrique. Uno soñaba que era rey. México: Plaza y Valdés, 1989. 312 p.

Novela donde los personajes de la Onda de Agustín y Sainz han envejecido. Ahora son los pilares del cinismo y la corrupción oficiales; tienen hijos mata-nacos y hacen concursos donde los pobres se juegan la vida y mueren. Es la entretejida historia de clasemedieros, mediospobres, pobres-pobres y desesperados sin remedio. El México grotesco de la crisis anterior a la Crisis. Esta novela es una amarga y humorística sátira social contra los que pueblan el infierno de la capital.

3515 Taibo, Paco Ignacio. Máscara azteca y el doctor Niebla (después del golpe). México: Aguilar, Altea, Taurus, Alfaguara, 1996. 91 p. (Alfaguara)

En el México del año 2002 el Doctor Niebla, alter ego de todos los que luchan contra el mal gobierno, se une al Máscara Azteca para crear un equipo de locos contra el orden establecido. Sus tácticas incluyen la multiplicación de personalidades, el asalto sorpresivo y no planeado, y la mitificación de los rebeldes. Taibo nos entretiene con una narración llena de elipsis y des-ordenamientos fríamente calculados. Esta novela nos recuerda a *El Libro de Manuel* de Julio Cortázar.

3516 Taibo, Paco Ignacio. Nomás los muertos están bien contentos. México: Joaquín Mortiz, 1994. 202 p. (Serie del volador)

Consta de nueve cuentos y un guión de cine, escritos entre 1989–93. Destacan por su calidad: "Los Maravillosos Olores de la Vida," donde Marcial, matón de la policía judicial, se suicida desesperado de olerse a muerto; "Mariachis Muertos Sonriendo," donde un novelista escribe del Chato, fotógrafo de Nota Roja, y la narración se detiene y vuelve a continuar cuando el Chato llama por teléfono al narrador. Humor sangriento y crímenes sin solución son otros de los elementos dominantes de este libro.

3517 Zapata, Alfredo. Esquina bajan. Monterrey, Mexico: Ediciones Castillo, 1994. 171 p. (Col. Más allá; 3)

Es una colección de crónicas periodísticas que son viñetas de personajes provincianos. A tres páginas por personaje, nos enteramos de la vida inútil de un enano presumido ("Un Enano Místico"); de la Lupe, nacida para mentar-madres ("Lupe Rayos"); y del papelero excéntrico, sobreviviente de un incendio ("El Drácula de la Treviño"). Zapata sabe darnos una sensación de extrañamiento, aún cuando aplica técnicas periodísticas del siglo pasado.

3518 Zapata, Luis. La hermana secreta de Angélica María. México: Cal y Arena, 1989. 159 p.

Tragicomedia de un hermafrodita que de joven introvertido (Alvaro), pasó a ser la segunda Novia de México (Alba María) y luego la voluptuosa Alexina (*freak* de la cirugía mágica del Doctor Morán). Es la historia de un personaje sin identidad ni cordura; escaparate de la psiquiatría, muestrario de angustias. Al final de la novela, sabremos que su mundo fue construido en el caldo del infierno de un manicomio. A pesar del tema, Zapata nos ofrece un narrador juguetón y una serie de situaciones de comedia de enredos.

LITERARY CRITICISM AND HISTORY

3519 Carballo, Emmanuel. Bibliografía de la novela mexicana del siglo XX. México: Univ. Nacional Autónoma de México, Coordinación de Difusión Cultural, 1988. 233 p.: ill. (Serie Textos; 2)

Un trabajo de gran valor académico,

sobre todo en México, donde no hay acceso a la información bibliográfica de la producción literaria. Se divide en tres partes: 1) un prólogo corto de Carballo; 2) una bibliografía que va de 1900–87; y, 3) una recomposición por orden alfabético de la misma bibliografía. Aunque basada en investigaciones de algunos mexicanistas informados, sin embargo la bibliografía no está actualizada suficientemente. Es una lástima que Carballo ignore a investigadores de la talla de John S. Brushwood.

3520 García-García, José Manuel. La inmaculada concepción del humor: teoría, antología y crítica del humor literario mexicano. Chihuahua, Mexico: Ediciones del Azar, 1995. 191 p.: bibl., ill.

El libro se divide en tres partes: 1) un glosario teórico en torno a las nociones del humor literario; 2) una antología de 584 citas y fragmentos tomados de la literatura mexicana contemporánea (1950–95); y 3) tres estudios acerca del humor literario mexicano. El primer estudio es cronológico; el segundo es una serie de anotaciones en torno a los 64 escritores citados y, el último es un estudio del sarcasmo en la poesía de Minerva Margarita Villarreal. Este libro puede leerse a la manera de *Rayuela* de Cortázar o de los *Fragmentos de un discurso amoroso* de Roland Barthes.

3521 García Núñez, Fernando. Fabulación de la fe: Carlos Fuentes. Xalapa, Mexico: Univ. Veracruzana, 1989. 127 p.: bibl. (Biblioteca)

García Nuñez utiliza el concepto teológico de Presciencia Divina ("el modo de conocer simultáneo, total y eterno de Dios") para analizar los sujetos, las voces y los métodos narrativos en *Aura, Cumpleaños* y *Una familia lejana*, la trilogía clásica de Fuentes. También estudia el tema de la herejía en *Terra Nostra* y el concepto del libre albedrío en *La cabeza de la hidra*. En la última parte de este estudio tenemos una biografía selecta y parcialmente anotada. Un libro para estudiosos de la obra de Carlos Fuentes.

3522 La escritura del cuento. Selección, introducción y notas de Lauro Zavala. México: Univ. Nacional Autónoma de México, Coordinación de Difusión Cultural, Dirección de Literatura; Univ. Autónoma Metropolitana-Xochimilco, 1993–1995. 1 v. (Teorías del cuento; 2. Textos de difusión cultural: Serie El Estudio)

En otra experiencia enriquecedora, Zavala nos ofrece 38 testimonios literarios acerca de la creación del relato. Autores como Jorge Luis Borges, Sergio Pitol y Vicente Leñero nos hablan de ese viaje que une inspiración y oficio para crear en la redondez de un cuento. Zavala ha incluido también a maestros del relato policiaco moderno. Este libro anecdotario es fuente de información para los que comienzan el oficio de la escritura.

3523 Medina, Dante. Zona de la escritura. México: Univ. de Guadalajara, 1994. 72 p.

En esta colección de ensayos breves en torno a la escritura, Medina reflexiona en torno a la creación literaria, utilizando el párrafo aforístico. Por ejemplo, nos dice que "el azar en literatura, siempre tiene razón" y que "la literatura es el lugar privilegiado de los desacuerdos." Para escritores que no han meditado mucho acerca de la cocina literaria.

3524 Pfeiffer, Erna. Entrevistas: diez escritoras mexicanas desde bastidores. Frankfurt am Main: Vervuert Verlag, 1992. 170 p.: bibl., ports.

Diez entrevistadas responden con ingenuidad y crudeza a las preguntas de Pfeiffer. Carmen Boullosa habla de sus actividades culturales en el Distrito Federal y Margo Glantz de su visión de la literatura escrita por mujeres. Angela Mastretta habla de su éxito comercial y María Luisa Puga de su experiencia como creadora literaria. Pfeiffer incluye también a Julieta Campos, Elsa Cross e Inés Arredondo. Es un libro para documentar el tema de la literatura femenina-feminista.

3525 Ramos Díaz, Martín. La novela mexicana en Estados Unidos, 1940–1990. México: Univ. Autónoma del Estado de México, 1994. 254 p.: bibl. (Col. La abeja en la colmena; 33)

Panorama general de una academia norteamericana que estudia la novelística de México. Ramos nos informa de las opiniones de Joseph Sommers, John S. Brushwood, Ann Ducan y otros. A través de ellos, vemos la evolución de la novela (1940–90), ahora analizada por investigadores como Fernando García Núñez y Danny Anderson. Para Ramos, la figura académica dominante es el investigador John S. Brushwood. Un manual muy útil para estudiantes de literatura.

3526 **Teorías de los cuentistas.** Recopilación de Lauro Zavala. México: Univ. Nacional Autónoma de México, Coordinación de Difusión Cultural, Dirección de Literatura; Univ. Autónoma Metropolitana-Xochimilco, 1993. 396 p.: bibl. (Teorías del cuento; 1. Textos de difusión cultural. Serie El Estudio)

Zavala será el enciclopedista de la academia mexicana; aquí reúne las voces de 31 cuentistas que hablan, con brevedad y elocuencia, del cuento. Unos proponen decálogos (Horacio Quiroga), otros antidecálogos (Jorge Luis Borges y Julio Cortázar) y otros más, proponen reinterpretaciones lúdicas en relación al oficio literario (Oscar de la Borbolla). Libro para cuentistas y para los estudiosos del cuento.

3527 **Zavala, Lauro.** Humor, ironía y lectura: las fronteras de la escritura literaria. Col. Villa Quietud, Mexico: Univ. Autónoma Metropolitana, Unidad Xochimilco, 1993. 216 p.: bibl., ill. (Col. Ensayos)

Es un libro que estudia el humor del indígena mexicana y de metodología aplicada al humor étnico y a la ironía textual moderna. Zavala incluye su excelente estudio "Humor e Ironía en el Cuento Mexicano Contemporáneo." Entre los cuentistas estudiados, con disciplina académica y conocimiento de causa, están: Hugo Hiriart, Lazlo Moussong y Emiliano Pérez Cruz.

Central America

RENE PRIETO, *Professor of Spanish, Southern Methodist University*

WORKING BEYOND THE NARROW CONFINES OF POLITICAL boundaries, providing new role models for Latin American women, and reshaping the world according to their ideals, Central American women authors continue to surpass themselves in their writing. Curiously—although, not surprisingly—a handful have come up with plots in which upper- and middle-class women themselves fall in love with leftist militants and revolutionaries. In Claribel Alegría's *Despierta mi bien despierta* (item **3528**), and Gioconda Belli's *La mujer habitada* (item **3529**) the authors fantasize about women who discover the need to revolt against a sick society. Depiction of social revolution in these stories comes hand in hand with the portrayal of sexual liberation; emancipated female protagonists suggest new roles for Latin American women, exhorting them to engage in reshaping their lives.

As Central American women authors currently portray her, the new Latin American heroine is not merely equal to man; morally and spiritually, she is his superior. The estranged heroine in Belli's *Sofía de los presagios* (item **3530**) is gifted with qualities of intuition and tenderness that empower her as a role model, making her better able to shape her country than the many men under whose direction it has been foundering since independence. These books suggest that when a civilization persists in destroying itself, it becomes essential to shift the focus of power towards such revolutionary women. Is this desire for a shift simply wishful thinking or is it a sense of foreboding? Are women ready to claim the superiority that so many Central American authors attribute to their gender?

Ready or not, the voice of Central American women is stronger than ever. In Costa Rica, where it seems nearly half the regional novels are being published, there is even a new literary monographic series entitled "Narrativa Ellas Cuentan." Edited by Linda Berrón, this series publishes books by and about women such as *Relatos de mujeres: antología de narradoras de Costa Rica* (item **3537**). Other important works written by Costa Rican women include *Tierra de espejismos* (item **3541**), by Julieta Pinto, founder and first director of the Dept. of Literature of the National University, and *Responso por el niño Juan Manuel,* by the equally prolific Carmen Naranjo (item **3538**). Naranjo has long been concerned with the portrayal of identity, but this interest is by no means exclusive to Central America's female authors.

In *Los molinos de Dios* (item **3531**), Alberto Cañas explores the story of a family who made its fortune in the coffee plantations of Costa Rica, and in *La otra cara* (item **3536**), originally written in the Kanjobal language, Gaspar Pedro González questions from within the Mayan identity and its relationship to ladino culture. Last but not least, in the story "Sos una Bicha" from *Elvira y el arcángel: historias sin cuento 1990* (item **3534**), David Escobar Galindo sketches a dialogue with a young prostitute in an attempt to define who she really is, and where she comes from. Identity—whether in matters of gender, ethnicity or age—is the leading preoccupation of most authors writing in Central America today.

PROSE FICTION

3528 Alegría, Claribel. Despierta mi bien despierta. San Salvador: UCA Editores, 1986. 75 p. (Col. Gavidia; 22)

Conflictive love between a socialite aspiring to become a writer and a leftist militant. With hope and lucidity, Alegría exposes the cancer rotting at the core of Salvadoran society.

3529 Belli, Gioconda. La mujer habitada. México: Editorial Diana, 1988. 342 p. (Diana literaria)

Nicaragua's indigenous past is fused together with the revolutionary present in poet Belli's first novel. Told in two interwoven voices, and portrayed in two different historical settings, this sensual and poetic work shows how similar women's struggles have always been, and reveals the path oppressed groups need to follow in order to become free.

3530 Belli, Gioconda. Sofía de los presagios. Managua: Editorial Vanguardia, 1990. 374 p. (El Hilo azul)

Rite-of-passage novel in which the estranged heroine searches for her long-lost mother and discovers, against her expectations, that she was not abandoned as a child. Infused with necromancy and eroticism, this fascinating study of female marginality portrays strong bonds that tie women together, even after death.

3531 Cañas, Alberto F. Los molinos de Dios. San José: Red Editorial Iberoamericana Centroamérica, 1992. 416 p.

These happy and unhappy tales of a family that made its fortune in the coffee plantations of Costa Rica paint a vast frieze of Central American life over the last 130 years.

3532 Chávez Alfaro, Lizandro. Vino de carne y hierro. Managua: Anama, 1993. 166 p.

Black humor and a defiant but pained optimism permeate the 13 stories in this collection. "Primera Vez/Ultima Vez" combines sensuality with revolutionary fatalism, while "Ojos Bajo la Mar" depicts the tenacity needed to overcome terrible odds.

3533 Ducoudray, Louis A. Los ojos del arrecife. San José: Editorial Fernández-Arce, 1992. 231 p.: ill. (Creación literaria; 1)

Award-winning stories portray life in the Caribbean archipelago. The language in "La Niña de las Flores Eternas" and "Los Ojos del Arrecife" is particularly suggestive and reminiscent of Alejo Carpentier's sultry baroque style.

3534 Escobar Galindo, David. Elvira y el arcángel: historias sin cuento 1990. San Salvador: UCA Editores, 1993. 238 p. (Col. Gavidia. Serie menor; 47)

Like those included in two companion volumes published earlier, these stories focus on current events in El Salvador. The blend of sensuality and social concerns in stories like "Sos una Bicha" are typical of contemporary Central American literature.

3535 Escobar Galindo, David. Los fuegos del azar. San Salvador: Impr. Ricaldone, 1993. 101 p.

Imbued with nostalgia and pessimism, these short stories make evident, once again, this author's love of language. As in most recent collections of stories published in Central America, this one includes at least one tale ("Ruleta Rusa") that portrays political unrest and the rigors of martial law.

3536 González, Gaspar Pedro. La otra cara. Guatemala: Editorial Cultura, Ministerio de Cultura y Deportes, 1992. 249 p.: ill. (Col. Narrativa guatemalteca siglo XX; 16. Serie Miguel Angel Asturias)

Originally written in Kanjobal (one of 20 Mayan languages spoken in Guatemala), this finely wrought tale describes strained relationships between Indians and ladinos from the seldom written perspective of the former.

3537 Naranjo, Carmen et al. Relatos de mujeres: antología de narradoras de Costa Rica. Prólogo de Sonia Marta Mora. Recopilación y presentación de Linda Berrón. San José: Editorial Mujeres, 1993. 201 p.: ill. (Colección Narrativa. Ellas cuentan)

Short stories written by 24 women, some of whom are famous (Julieta Pinto, Irma Prego, Rima de Vallbona). Methods and approaches are extraordinarily varied and include accounts based on 19th-century judiciary files ("Andrea Perdió la Honra el Día de San Lorenzo," by Tatiana Lobo), and lists of things to do today and tomorrow ("Infinitas Partes de un Temperamento," by Carmen Naranjo). Biographical index is appended.

3538 Naranjo, Carmen. Responso por el niño Juan Manuel. San José: Editorial Universitaria Centroamericana, 1991. 192 p. (Col. Séptimo día)

Carmen Naranjo is not just a good writer; she is a great one. This poetic story of an acutely lonely boy who invents a playmate for himself demonstrates her ability beyond a shadow of a doubt.

3539 Núñez Soto, Orlando. El vuelo de las abejas. Managua: CIPRES, 1993. 215 p.

A woman's fantasies are turned inside out in this fascinating drama of a psychoanalyst who succumbs to his patient's fear of cannibalism.

3540 Pinto, Julieta. Cuentos de la tierra. Ilustrado por Fco. Amighetti. San José: Editorial Costa Rica, 1993. 109 p.: ill.

Sensitive portrayals of rivers, blind horses, and filial love give ample proof of Pinto's talent and susceptibility.

3541 Pinto, Julieta. Tierra de espejismos: novela. San José: Editorial Univ. Estatal a Distancia, 1991. 191 p. (Col. Vieja y nueva narrativa costarricense; 7)

The struggle of peasants to forge ahead and hold on to their property illustrates the problem of land ownership and the need to create a more equitable society.

3542 Ramírez, Sergio. Clave de sol: cuentos. Managua: Editorial Nueva Nicaragua, 1992. 206 p.

Love and revolution come to the fore in "La Múcura que está en el Suelo," one of the typically ironic stories in this collection. "Kalimán el Magnífico y la Pérfida Mesalina," and "Ilusión Perdida" strongly suggest that all love is ultimately fraught with lies.

Hispanic Caribbean

EDNA ACOSTA-BELEN, *Distinguished Service Professor of Latin American and Caribbean Studies, State University of New York-Albany*
UVA DE ARAGON, *Assistant Director, Cuban Research Center, Florida International University*

PUERTO RICO

THE 1990s PUERTO RICAN literary scene continues to be characterized by the increasing visibility of women writers and by the work of Puerto Rican writers who were born or reside in the US. Regarding the latter group, these authors write in English, Spanish, or bilingually and some, after many years, are beginning to receive increased critical attention from scholars in Puerto Rico. As a result, more of the works originally published in English are being translated into Spanish. The most notable example is Esmeralda Santiago's *Cuando era puertorriqueña* (item **3585**), a novel about the new Puerto Rican identity of those who straddle the cultures of the island and the US. Similarly, there is an increasing number of literary works by island writers being translated into English. Also worthy of mentioning are crossover writing attempts such as Rosario Ferré's *House in the lagoon* (item **3563**), the first novel by this renowned island author originally written in English.

The anthology *Del silencio al estallido: narrativa femenina puertorriqueña* (item **3556**), edited by Ramón Luis Acevedo, reasserts the existence of a women's poetic tradition in Puerto Rican literature since the 1930s. Nonetheless, it has been only in recent decades that women writers have made significant inroads into the traditional canon of Puerto Rican prose fiction.

Writing outside the mainstream of Puerto Rican letters, a younger generation of relatively unknown short fiction writers from the 1980s and 1990s was introduced in José Angel Rosado's anthology *El rostro y la máscara: antología alterna de cuentistas puertorriqueños contemporáneos* (item **3582**). According to the editor, these authors share a condition of marginality and represent a kind of literary theorization and experimentation that differs from those of more established writers. Along with the work of the younger generation, writers from the generations of the 1950s and 1940s continue to publish, as exemplified by the recent prose fiction works of Emilio Díaz Valcárcel (item **3558**), Pedro Juan Soto (item **3587**), and Enrique Laguerre (item **3565**).

One of the most relevant critical works of the last few years is Juan Gelpí's *Literatura y paternalismo en Puerto Rico* (item **3603**). In this insightful collection of essays, the well-known critic denounces the culturally nationalistic and patriarchal character of Puerto Rico's literary canon, which began to form in the late-19th century. He also illustrates how contemporary Puerto Rican writers, several women authors among them, are transgressing the traditional canon and bringing innovative trends and styles into Puerto Rican letters. In *Reapropiaciones: cultura y nueva escritura en Puerto Rico* (see *HLAS 54:3869*), another renowned critic, Peruvian Julio Ortega, reaffirms the flourishing of a new Puerto Rican writing style represented by authors who combine carnavalesque and Baroque elements with the popular discourse of mass urban culture. This new way of writing is illustrated by the narratives of Luis Rafael Sánchez (item **3611**), Edgardo Rodríguez Juliá, and Rosario Ferré (item **3562**), and the poetry of Angela María Dávila, Joserramón Melendes (items **3570** and **4121**), and José Luis Vega, among others. Another important critical contribution is found in Ana Lydia Vega's *Esperando a Loló y otros delirios generacionales* (item **3612**), in which, with her characteristic irreverence and sense of humor, the acclaimed prose fiction writer confronts some of the myths and conventions of Puerto Rican literary traditions, describing what feminist and women's literature, including her own, represent to different audiences.

There are two collections of critical essays that also deserve mention since they follow the intellectual tradition established by Puerto Rican writers and literary critics of previous generations who analyzed the links between the island's colonial status and the role of culture and language in the anticolonial struggle. With his collection of essays, *La memoria rota* (item **3600**), Arcadio Díaz Quiñones makes a significant contribution to the discussion of how the island's colonial status impinges upon historical memory and the construction of Puerto Rico's national identity. The notion that Puerto Rican culture should be extended beyond island borders to include the US experience is becoming quite central to the analysis of

Puerto Rican reality and several critics are recognizing that these connections are necessary to fully understand the myths and distortions that permeate the island's national discourse. A clearer vision of these linkages is advanced in Juan Flores' *Divided borders: essays on Puerto Rican identity* (item **3601**), a compilation of some of Flores' best known essays, including his Casa de Las Américas award-winning critical essay on Antonio S. Pedreira's insular vision, and those dealing with the development of Puerto Rican literature and the structuring of Puerto Rican identity in the US.

New inroads in establishing the transnational sociocultural connections between US Latino populations and their corresponding Latin American and Caribbean countries of origin are being made in *The Latino Review of Books,* a journal for critical thought and dialogue. In addition to reviewing books and materials, this new journal publishes provocative articles on the cultural merging of borders taking place in the Americas. [EA-B]

CUBA AND THE DOMINICAN REPUBLIC

Desde sus inicios más remotos, cuando Colón plasmara en su diario la impresión que le produjo "la tierra más fermosa," la literatura cubana ha estado marcada por la distancia. Es decir, por su condición de extramuros, o, más exactamente, extramares. Actualmente, dada la situación económica y política del país, esta característica se agudiza. Nos encontramos, pues, ante una narrativa peregrina en cuanto a su lugar de publicación (inclusive los escritores que viven en la isla han comenzado a publicar fuera), aunque no necesariamente universal en su temática y aliento.

Conviene anotar que las casas editoriales de España están publicando a un gran número de autores cubanos, independientemente de su lugar de residencia o su filiación ideológica. No sólo en este territorio editorial se observa el reencuentro de una literatura escindida a partir de 1959, sino que dentro de Cuba desde hace pocos años han comenzado a incluirse textos de exiliados en revistas y antologías como en el caso de *Estatuas de sal* (item **3560**). Muestra del auge de la literatura cubana en España es el Premio Sonrisa Vertical (1996) otorgado a José Carlos Somoza y el éxito de librería de *Te di la vida entera* (item **3590**) de Zoé Valdés, finalista del Premio Planeta (1996).

La autora que más atención ha recibido, tanto en ventas como en crítica, ha sido precisamente Valdés con sus dos novelas, *La nada cotidiana* (item **3589**) y *Te di la vida entera.* Valdés, nacida en 1959, el mismo año del triunfo de la Revolución, ahora exiliada en París, expone en sus textos el derrumbe material y psíquico de Cuba después de la caída del comunismo soviético. También Jesús Díaz, quien se fue de la isla en fecha relativamente reciente, trata en *La piel y la máscara* (item **3557**) la dualidad que necesitan asumir los individuos para sobrevivir en la isla. Contraria a la literatura de los primeros años de exilio, nostálgica y mitificadora, estas obras, aunque escritas en el exterior, denuncian desde dentro, deconstruyen, demitifican. Sin embargo, en ocasiones, especialmente en el caso de Valdés, el absurdo de la realidad que intentan reflejar invade excesivamente la forma literaria.

Una de las tendencias más claras de estos años es el impulso que ha tomado el género del cuento, como lo evidencia la publicación de varias antologías, tanto en Miami (item **3574**) como en Cuba (item **3560**) y en España (items **3555** y **3577**), y el saldo mayor de colecciones de narraciones cortas publicadas que de novelas.

En Cuba las nuevas promociones se han ido apartando un tanto de los tonos sentenciosos y grandilocuentes y de los temas sociales, para explorar con una mirada mucho más intimista y cotidiana el mundo del individuo de a pie o de personajes marginales. También el humor—muchas veces negro—es una característica común en los escritores más jóvenes. Otro aspecto de interés, en ambas orillas, es la creciente presencia del tema de la mujer (items **3560** y **3578**), lo cual puede observarse por igual en la crítica (items **3609** y **3608**).

Entre las reediciones, las más sobresalientes son *Jicoténcal* de Félix Varela (item **3402**), un texto injustamente olvidado, y *El reino de este mundo* de Alejo Carpentier (item **3552**). Es también de interés la recopilación de textos, algunos inéditos, otros publicados anteriormente, de autores como José Lezama Lima (items **3567** y **293**) y Guillermo Cabrera Infante (items **3551** y **3550**). En cuanto a la crítica, puede observarse que sus intereses son muy variados, pues los estudios van desde lo más inmediato, como los autores de la década del 80 (item **3606**), hasta importantes períodos (item **3598**) y autores (item **3594**) de la era republicana. A 100 años de su independencia de España, y a pesar de los cataclismos políticos (o tal vez, estimulados por los mismos) la narrativa cubana sorprende por su ecléctica riqueza.

En la República Dominicana puede observarse que continúa favoreciéndose el género del cuento corto y que la temática se mantiene íntimamente ligada a los problemas sociopolíticos. [UA]

PROSE FICTION

3543 Abreu Adorno, Manuel. No todas las suecas son rubias. San Juan: Instituto de Cultura Puertorriqueña, 1991. 176 p. (Serie Letras contemporáneas)

A posthumous autobiographical novel by a writer who began to receive literary recognition for his collection of short stories *Llegaron los hippies* (1978), published before his death at a young age. This engaging novel focuses on the failed amorous relationship between a Swedish woman and a Puerto Rican bohemian living in Paris and the clashes produced by their different cultures and sensibilities.

3544 Antología del cuento psicológico de la República Dominicana. Prólogo de Antonio Zaglul y Josefina Zaiter de Zaglul. Recopilación, introducción y notas de Domingo Hernández Contreras. Santo Domingo: Univ. Iberoamericana, 1995. 272 p.: bibl., index. (Col. Textos universitarios; 9)

Dividida en tres etapas—la de los precursores, la de transición (1930–60) y la contemporánea—esta muestra de cuentos psicológicos confirma la riqueza del género en el país. La segunda etapa es la más prolífera, pero la tercera profundiza con mayor destreza en el mundo interior del individuo.

3545 Aponte Alsina, Marta. Angélica furiosa. Cayey, P.R.: Sopa de Letras Editores, 1994. 162 p.: ill.

This first novel by this recognized literary critic demonstrates once again her talents as a skillful narrator. The story moves around the powerful character of Angélica, a sorcerer who is unable to speak until a shocking secret is revealed to her by her granddaughter.

3546 Arenas, Reinaldo. Adiós a mamá: de La Habana a Nueva York. Prólogo de Mario Vargas Llosa. Barcelona: Ediciones Altera, 1995. 177 p.

Ocho cuentos póstumos de Arenas que basculan entre un mundo aniquilado por el comunismo y otro, sin ángeles, incapaz de saciar la furia de este indómito rebelde. Narraciones que aunan lo mágico al crudo realismo, la profanación a la ternura, el humor al desamparo, el desenfreno sexual al derrumbe humano. Arenas muestra aquí su pleno dominio del género y del lenguaje.

3547 Arrillaga, María. Mañana valentina. San Juan: Instituto de Cultura Puertorriqueña; Santiago: Editorial Cuarto Propio, 1995. 228 p. (Serie Narrativa)

The protagonist of this experimental narrative is a woman oscillating between the two different cultural and linguistic worlds of New York and Puerto Rico, trying to reassert her identity and personal freedom as a woman.

3548 Arroyo, Anita. Cuentos del caribe. Miami: Ediciones Universal, 1992. 64 p. (Col. Caniquí)

Con Curaçao, Martinica, Nassau,

Haití, Saint Thomas y Puerto Rico como escenarios, estos cuentos muestran retazos de las muchas culturas que se entrecruzan bajo la magia del trópico. Fiel a la sensibilidad social presente desde sus primeras obras, la autora no olvida que el embrujo de estas islas muchas veces disimula la pobreza en que se debaten sus clases más necesitadas.

3549 Bragado Bretaña, Reinaldo. En torno al cero. Miami: Editorial Outsider, 1994. 97 p.

Alejados de los derroteros del realismo, la denuncia social o el testimonio, estos cuentos se instalan en esa otra cara de la cuentística cubana: lo fantástico. Con el uso de la técnica del cuento cerrado a lo Poe y lo Quiroga, y lecturas bien asimiladas de Julio Verne, George Wells, Ray Bradbury, Rod Sterling y Jorge Luis Borges, Bragado se adentra en las zonas del horror, el misterio y la ciencia ficción.

3550 Cabrera Infante, Guillermo. Ella cantaba boleros. Madrid: Santillana, 1996. 309 p. (Alfaguara)

Ella cantaba boleros estaba destinado a ser el capítulo final de *Tres tristes tigres*. El autor lo publica ahora como una historia independiente, siguiendo el consejo que hace más de treinta años le diera Mario Vargas Llosa. Para complacer a otro amigo escritor, Javier Marías, también incluye el último capítulo de *La Habana para un infante difunto*. Estos finales que ahora se publican juntos pero no revueltos van unidos por los mismos demonios: el Dante de Infante y las noches habaneras de Cabrera.

3551 Cabrera Infante, Guillermo. Mi música extremada. Edición de Rosa María Pereda. Madrid: Espasa Calpe, 1996. 399 p.

Esta colección de textos sobre el amor y la música del autor cubano, extraídos de sus libros, cobra ritmo de habanera o de bolero, de acuerdo con el grado de nostalgia que aporte el lector.

3552 Carpentier, Alejo. El reino de este mundo. Introducción de Federico Acevedo. Río Piedras, P.R.: Editorial de la Univ. de Puerto Rico, 1994. xlix, 136 p.: bibl. (Col. caribeña)

Reedición de la novela de Carpentier publicada originalmente en 1949 sobre la epopeya del pueblo haitiano contra la esclavitud que desembocó en la independencia política

así como sobre el desarrollo de la sociedad postcolonial. La introducción de Acevedo facilita el acercamiento al texto.

3553 Collazo, Miguel. Estación central. La Habana: Editorial Letras Cubanas, Instituto Cubano del Libro; Cali, Colombia: Prensa Moderna Impresores; 1993. 261 p.

Dos personajes protagónicos y dos recorridos de La Habana con el telón de fondo de la Cuba de 1947 durante el gobierno de Ramón Grau San Martín.

3554 Colón, Jesús. The way it was, and other writings. Edited with an introductory essay by Edna Acosta-Belén and Virginia Sánchez Korrol. Houston, Tex.: Arte Público Press, 1993. 127 p.: bibl., ill.

Selection of anecdotal writings by Jesús Colón, a Puerto Rican journalist and community activist who lived in New York City between 1917–74, including selections of his unfinished testimonial account of the evolution of the New York Puerto Rican community.

3555 Cuentos desde La Habana: últimos narradores cubanos. Selección e introducción de Omar Felipe Mauri Sierra. Alicante, Spain: Aguaclara, 1996. 190 p. (Anaquel narrativa; 35)

Dos docenas de jóvenes autores, en su mayoría desconocidos, contribuyen a esta antología, con una amplia variedad de temas, técnicas y personajes. Junto a los obreros y soldados, tan presentes en la literatura cubana contemporánea, encontramos *hippies*, *punkys*, ancianos, solitarios, suicidas, homosexuales y dementes. El mundo de los jóvenes, la familia, la pareja, el sexo, la cultura y la sociedad se abordan con humor, intimismo y autenticidad. Una bocanada de aire fresco, muestra de las novísimas tendencias de la narrativa en la isla.

3556 Del silencio al estallido: narrativa femenina puertorriqueña. Estudio, selección y notas de Ramón L. Acevedo. Río Piedras, P.R.: Editorial Cultural, 1991. 259 p.: bibl., ill.

This anthology of short stories by contemporary Puerto Rican women writers includes an extensive introductory essay in which Acevedo highlights the presence of women writers during different historical periods and characterizes the prose fiction of some of the best known contemporary women authors. He also emphasizes the feminist character of some of the most recent women's literary production.

3557 Díaz, Jesús. La piel y la máscara. Barcelona: Editorial Anagrama, 1996. 227 p. (Narrativas hispánicas; 193)

A través de la narración del proceso de filmación de una película, se crea un juego de espejos, de pieles y de máscaras, en cuyo fondo late una metáfora sobre la relación entre el arte y la vida, entre la realidad y su apariencia en la Cuba de hoy.

3558 Díaz Valcárcel, Emilio. Taller de invenciones. Río Piedras, P.R.: Editorial Cultural, 1993. 155 p.

In this novel, a group of aspiring writers attending a writing workshop discovers the many different texts, narrative tones, and perspectives that result from an author's imagination and inventiveness. The renowned Puerto Rican writer, Emilio Díaz Valcárcel, conducted the workshop.

3559 Dos siglos de literatura dominicana: s. XIX–XX. t. 3–4, Prosa. Selección, prólogo y notas de José Alcántara Almánzar. Santo Domingo: Comisión Oficial para la Celebración del Sesquicentenario de la Independencia Nacional; Editorial Corripio, 1996. 425, 406 p.: bibl., ill. (Col. Sesquicentenario de la independencia nacional; 10)

Amplia muestra de cuentos, fragmentos de novelas y ensayos con énfasis en el presente siglo. Se evidencia la fuerte tendencia a la narración breve, la renovación del género en las últimas décadas y la mayor riqueza de técnicas narrativas. Se ha desplazado el foco de interés de la vida rural a los complejos problemas urbanos contemporáneos. La praxis política—violencia, represión, muerte—es también tema recurrente.

3560 Estatuas de sal: cuentistas cubanas contemporáneas; panorama crítico, 1959–1995. Recopilación de Mirta Yáñez y Marilyn Bobes. La Habana: Ediciones Unión, 1996. 384 p.

Antología de narraciones cortas escritas por mujeres. Aunque recoge muestras anterior al 1959, el grueso se dedica a cuentos de autoras nacidas entre 1931–72, que empezaron a publicar después de la Revolución. Incluye narradoras del exilio, aunque en una proporción ínfima. El ensayo introductorio y los dos del apéndice señalan el creciente interés que ha tomado a partir de 1980 la investigación del discurso femenino en Cuba.

3561 Fernández Gordián, Osvaldo. La guerra de Vietnam: tragedia puertorriqueña. San Juan: s.n., 1994. 197 p.

Written by a Vietnam veteran, the value of this collection of stories lies in its attempt to capture the tragedy of the war as much as to recognize the forgotten lives of Puerto Rican soldiers who died or participated in the conflict.

3562 Ferré, Rosario. La batalla de las vírgenes. San Juan: Editorial de la Univ. de Puerto Rico, 1993. 121 p.

Pages of diaries, letters, and newspaper articles are juxtaposed with various narrative voices to relate the experiences of a Spanish priest and an adulterous woman caught in the absurdity and turmoil of daily life in modern Puerto Rico.

3563 Ferré, Rosario. The house on the lagoon. New York: Farrar, Straus and Giroux, 1995. 407 p.: ill.

The first novel written in English by one of Puerto Rico's most gifted authors. Through this absorbing family epic, the author captures the complexity of Puerto Rican society including class, racial, and political conflicts.

3564 Imbert-Brugal, Carmen. Distinguida señora. Santo Domingo: Amigo del Hogar, 1995. 230 p.

Novela que se desarrolla en el contexto caribeño marcado por la voluptuosidad y la represión. El texto es desigual, a ratos necesitado de mayor revisión, a ratos con pasajes o frases sorprendentes, como rayazos luminosos.

3565 Laguerre, Enrique A. Los gemelos. Río Piedras, P.R.: Editorial Cultural, 1992. 144 p.

Through the conflictive lives of twin brothers, the master of the Puerto Rican telluric novel creates another story of remembrances and nostalgia for a bygone rural world.

3566 Leante, César. Desnudo femenino y otros cuentos. Madrid: Pliegos, 1995. 143 p. (Pliegos de narrativa)

Del realismo a la fantasía, de la búsqueda de la tierra prometida a la exploración de la enigmática psicología humana, del cuento cerrado a lo Poe, a las técnicas narrativas afines al *boom*, este pequeño volumen muestra una variedad de registros que hacen también desigual la calidad y originalidad de los cuentos.

3567 Lezama Lima, José. Fascinación de la memoria: textos inéditos; con un estudio sobre *Orígenes* de Cintio Vitier. Selección y prólogo de Iván González Cruz. La Habana: Editorial Letras Cubanas, 1993. 337 p.: bibl.

Compilación de textos inéditos, hallados todavía sin transcribir en los archivos del autor. Los siete capítulos agrupan poesías, cuentos, conferencias, epistolario, ensayos, pensamientos y materiales de ficción. Este volumen contribuye a ofrecer una visión humana e inclusive sencilla, aunque no por eso menos rica y compleja, del autor de *Paradiso.*

3568 Llano Rodríguez, Eduardo del. Los doce apóstatas. La Habana: Editorial Letras Cubanas, 1994. 91 p. (Pinos nuevos)

Novela breve, fantástica, humorística y adolorida, que se enfrenta a problemas contemporáneos y eternos con frustración y esperanza.

3569 Márquez-Sterling, Manuel. La cúpula. Miami: Ediciones Universal, 1995. 233 p. (Col. Caniquí; 784–9)

Novela histórica-alegórica que se desenvuelve de 1926–33, durante el Machadato. La cúpula del Capitolio y la ciénaga sobre la cual se construye el edificio sirven de símbolos de los más altos ideales patrióticos así como de los males políticos, económicos, sociales y morales de la joven república.

3570 Melendes, Joserramón. Secretum. Río Piedras, P.R.: QueAse, 1993. 159 p.: ill.

This group of encoded essays reflects the complex philosophical and intellectual frameworks embedded in this poet's writing and his affinity for linguistic experimentation.

3571 Meshad, Adrián. Llévense a esos que cantan en la Esmeralda. San José: Editorial Universitaria Centroamericana, 1994. 135 p. (Col. Séptimo día)

Reaparecen temas tradicionales de la literatura latinoamericana y la estructura clásica del cuento a lo Poe, Quiroga o Hernández-Catá.

3572 Montero, Mayra. Tú, la oscuridad. Barcelona: Tusquets Editores, 1995. 241 p. (Col. Andanzas; 243)

Esta historia de un herpetólogo en busca de una rana roja en extinción en los montes de Haití entremezcla supersticiones, leyendas, locura, sangre, muerte y violencia. El lenguaje es directo y la trama llena del suspenso de una novela policiaca, pero el fondo de esta novela guarda los misterios de una raza, una selva y una isla.

3573 Muller, Alberto. Monólogo con Yolanda: novela sobre las sombras de una isla. Miami: Ediciones Universal, 1995. 126 p. (Col. Caniquí)

Esta crónica de una isla y de sus habitantes es una alegoría de la historia de Cuba y una visión del futuro de paz y armonía que sueña el autor para el país. Cierta tendencia a las frases aforísticas hace que la novela roce la peligrosa línea hacia el didactismo. Los elementos de realismo mágico y un lirismo—quizás excesivo, pero auténtico—son sus mayores logros.

3574 Narrativa y libertad: cuentos cubanos de la diáspora. Selección, introducción y notas de Julio E. Hernández-Miyares. Miami: Ediciones Universal, 1996. 1 v. (Col. antologias)

Cuentos de más de doscientos autores del exilio a través de cuatro generaciones y casi cuatro décadas. La nostalgia, la denuncia, las ansias de regreso y la sed de libertad son los cuatro puntos cardinales sobre los que se asienta esta narrativa comprometida. La compilación se resiente de una gran irregularidad en la calidad de los textos. La demora que sufrió la publicación de tan monumental empeño ha hecho que las notas biobibliográficas no estén al día, lo cual es también lamentable.

3575 Nos-y-Otros (Cuba). Basura y otros desperdicios. La Habana: Editorial Letras Cubanas, 1994. 93 p. (Pinos nuevos)

Colección de cuentos cortos llenos de un humor, a veces negro, y de irreverencias. El propio mundo de la creación literaria es objeto de las adoloridas burlas de los autores, Eduardo del Llano Rodríguez y Luis Felipe Calvo Bolaños, miembros de la agrupación teatral-literaria Nos-y-Otros creada en La Habana en 1982.

3576 Ortega, Gregorio. Los dinosaurios y otros relatos. Edición de Luis Alonso Girgado. A Coruña, Spain: Editorial Tambre, 1993. 146 p.: bibl. (Tambre-narrativa)

Una docena de cuentos cortos de filiación fantástica aunque algunos como "El framboyán" se inscriben en una línea netamente realista. El influjo de los relatos de aventura y de la novela negra norteamericana es evidente.

3577 Paz, Senel et al. La isla contada: el cuento contemporáneo en Cuba. Recopilación de Francisco López Sacha. Prólogo de Manuel Vázquez Montalbán. 2a. edición. Donostia, Spain: Tercera Prensa-Hirugarren-Prentsa, 1996. 241 p. (Literatura; 5)

Esta veintena de cuentos da una muestra de la narrativa corta dentro de la isla a partir de 1980. En estos autores, la revolución y los problemas sociales pasan a un segundo plano y se ve un mayor énfasis en la vivencia individual que en períodos anteriores. La mirada del niño y el adolescente, los temas amorosos, sexuales y éticos predominan. Algunos temas tabúes en los 70, tales como el homosexualismo, la prostitución, el exilio, y la angustia existencial del ser humano, se tratan con mayor—aunque no total—libertad.

3578 Perera, Hilda. La noche de Ina. Madrid: Ediciones Libertarias, 1993. 94 p. (Los Libros del avefénix; 29)

La autora mezcla dos géneros (la novela y el teatro) y dos técnicas literarias (el monólogo interior y el diálogo) para contrastar la forma en que piensan y sienten una mujer posmenopáusica y las nuevas generaciones que la rodean. El resultado es un cuadro patético de desencuentros, ya no sólo generacionales, sino existenciales.

3579 Ramos, Juan Antonio. En casa de Guillermo Tell. Río Piedras, P.R.: Editorial Plaza Mayor, 1991. 101 p. (Biblioteca de autores de Puerto Rico)

A new collection of short stories by one of the leading writers of the 1980s. In this particular collection, the author captures, with his characteristic humor and irony, the nightmarish and alienating aspects of daily life on the island.

3580 Rodríguez, Rolando. Cuba, 1930: república angelical. Madrid: Ediciones Endymión, 1995. 780 p. (Narrativa)

Ambiciosa novela histórica, basada en fuentes documentales directas, sobre la revolución de 1930 contra la tiranía de Gerardo Machado. Los personajes son los protagonistas de aquella historia: grupos de estudiantes, oficiales y sargentos del ejército. Se recrea la atmósfera de un momento apasionado en los anales de un país.

3581 Rosales, Guillermo. El juego de la viola. Miami: Ediciones Universal, 1994. 95 p. (Col. Caniquí)

Esta breve novela póstuma fue publicada con más de un cuarto de siglo de retraso, pues fue escrita en La Habana en 1968. Dieciséis breves capítulos narrados desde el punto de mira de un niño revelan un mundo de personajes infantiles, miedo a crecer y una escondida y fiera ternura.

3582 El rostro y la máscara: antología alterna de cuentistas puertorriqueños contemporáneos. Selección y prólogo de José Angel Rosado. San Juan: Editorial Isla Negra; Editorial de la Univ. de Puerto Rico, 1995. 203 p.: ill.

This anthology of Puerto Rican short fiction introduces a little known younger generation of writers of the 1990s who remain marginal to the mainstream of Puerto Rican letters. Rather than focusing on the more common sociocultural and political concerns of prior generations, the works of these writers emphasize the psychological and existential complexities of daily life, often challenging or transgressing the borders between fantasy and reality.

3583 Saínz Blanco, Alfredo. Mi más querido fantasma. Holguín, Cuba: Ediciones Holguín, 1993. 100 p. (Col. de la ciudad)

Delicioso conjunto de crónicas literarias desde una columna de cultura en la prensa de provincia. Saínz Blanco establece un puente hacia el lector amparado por el equilibrio entre las imprescindibles referencias librescas y su sensibilidad poética. El punto de mira personal provoca la observación aguda o tierna, sencilla o profunda, pero siempre inédita y sorprendente.

3584 Sánchez, Luis Rafael. La guagua aérea. 2. ed. Río Piedras, P.R.: Editorial Cultural, 1994. 214 p.

The most internationally acclaimed author of his generation puts together a selection of some of his best known newspaper articles, including the famous text that bears the title of this collection, and several interviews with him published in Spanish-language newspapers. The thematic unity of the volume is created by the metaphor of the

airbus, the back and forth migratory movement of Puerto Ricans between the island and
the US.

3585 Santiago, Esmeralda. Cuando era puertorriqueña. New York: Vintage Books,
1994. 1 v. (Vintage español)
Autobiographical novel about the new
Puerto Rican identity of those who straddle
the cultures of the island and US. This is the
author's own translation of her acclaimed
novel *When I Was Puerto Rican* (Reading,
Mass.: Addison-Wesley, 1993).

3586 Somoza, José Carlos. Silencio de
Blanca. Barcelona: Tusquets Ediciones,
1996. 199 p.
En este texto el autor concibe el erotismo como una ceremonia, un ritual en que
el acercamiento sutil y las distancias reme-
dan el ritmo preciso y triste de un Nocturno
de Chopin.

3587 Soto, Pedro Juan. Memoria de mi am-
nesia. Río Piedras, P.R.: Editorial Cultural, 1991. 134 p.: ill.
Narrative centers around the investigation and absurd realities surrounding the suspicious death of a female psychiatric patient.
The story is told through the juxtaposition of
the narrative voices of the woman, her husband, the psychiatrist, and the investigator.

3588 Stanley Rondón, Avelino. La máscara
del tiempo. Santo Domingo: Editora
Búho, 1996. 105 p.
Un prólogo y diez relatos, muestra de
la nueva narrativa dominicana y de que los
viejos problemas del país y del continente,
especialmente el caudillismo y el abuso del
poder, continúan vigentes.

3589 Valdés, Zoé. La nada cotidiana. Buenos
Aires: Emecé Editores, 1996. 171 p.
Patria, la protagonista de esta novela,
nace, como la autora, en La Habana en 1959,
el mismo año del triunfo de la Revolución en
Cuba, y es miembro de esa generación que
creció bajo el signo de la ilusión y el sacrificio
por un futuro mejor, y de adulta se encuentra
de bruces frente a la frustración, las penurias,
la apatía: la nada cotidiana. Para sobrevivir,
se escuda tras la coraza del oportunismo a medida que pasa de un amo/amante a otro. Con
lenguaje desenfadado, se combina lo erótico
con lo político, lo cotidiano con lo metafísico
en un texto que aspira al más crudo realismo

pero que en cuyo tejido el lector experimen-
tado puede descubrir algunas trampas.

3590 Valdés, Zoé. Te di la vida entera. Barcelona: Planeta, 1996. 362 p. (Col. Autores españoles e hispanoamericanos)
A través de la historia de sesenta años
de la vida de una mujer cubana, la autora nos
lleva de La Habana nocturna, sensual y única
de la década de los 50 a la miseria y la degradación de los tiempos presentes. El lenguaje
desenfadado de novelas anteriores se convierte aquí en franco desparpajo. Un intento
de homenaje a Guillermo Cabrera Infante que
se queda en un pastiche con algunos ingeniosos juegos de palabras.

3591 Vázquez Díaz, René. La Isla del Cundeamor. Madrid: Santillana, 1995.
311 p. (Alfaguara)
La novela bascula de Miami Beach a
Cuba (la real y la inventada), de la Biblia al
bolero, de la intuición poética a lo vulgar, de
Fidel Castro a Betty Boop, del Arca de Noé a
la isla de cundeamor, o la utopía de los trópicos. Es la historia de una obsesión cubana.

3592 Victoria, Carlos. La travesía secreta.
Miami: Ediciones Universal, 1994.
477 p. (Col. Caniquí)
Desde los patios de la escuela secundaria, hasta el sueño de un mensaje en una
botella a la deriva, la travesía secreta del adolescente Marcos Manuel Velazco recorre laberintos artísticos, religiosos, políticos y sociales en busca de la verdad. Esta novela es el
canto de un cisne, el bello-trágico lamento de
una generación que se enfrenta a su muerte
espiritual.

3593 Vidal Ortiz, Guillermo. Matarile. La
Habana: Editorial Letras Cubanas,
1993. 165 p. (Letras cubanas)
Sueños, realidades e invenciones tran-
sitan por la menta del protagonista y de este
texto-letanía que extiende una aguda mirada
sobre los problemas sociales de la vida contemporánea y la eterna miseria del ser
humano.

LITERARY CRITICISM
AND HISTORY

3594 Aragón, Uva de. Alfonso Hernández-
Catá, un escritor cubano, salmantino y
universal. Salamanca, Spain: Cátedra de Poé-

tica Fray Luis de León, Univ. Pontificia de Salamanca, 1996. 179 p.: bibl., ill.

Compuesto de siete capítulos (con bibliografía, acta de nacimiento y fotografías de la familia del escritor), abarca desde un perfil biográfico hasta análisis temático, estructural y estilístico de la obra de Hernández Catá, que lleva huellas no sólo del modernismo hispanoamericano sino también de la literatura española y universal. Escritor de cuentos, fábulas, novelas, teatro, poesía y ensayos, Hernández Catá es considerado un excelente prosista modernista. Un aspecto esencial en su obra, según la autora, es su sensibilidad social respeto a los personajes marginados, la burguesía, la mujer, el homosexualidad, el racismo y la protesta política y social. Este estudio biográfico y comentario general de su narrativa muestra que, además de ser diplomático, Hernández Catá figuró en los círculos literarios más importantes de su época. Su obra revela una angustia existencial y un presentimiento constante de la muerte. [D. Gerdes]

3595 El arte narrativo de Hilda Perera: de *Cuentos de Apolo* **a** *La noche de Ina.* Edición de Luis A. Jiménez y Ellen Lismore Leeder. Miami: Ediciones Universal, 1996. 180 p.: bibl. (Col. Caniquí)

La continua búsqueda de identidad de los personajes, el registro de voces maternas que aparecen muchas veces silenciadas, las experiencias del exilio en el individuo, las mujeres y la familia, y la subversión de oposiciones binarias del discurso dominante de la cultura masculina se revelan como algunas de las coordenadas de la narrativa de Hilda Perera.

3596 Barquet, Jesús J. Consagración de La Habana: las peculiaridades del grupo Orígenes en el proceso cultural cubano. Miami: Iberian Studies Institute, North-South Center, Univ. of Miami, 1992. 103 p.: bibl. (Letras de oro)

Análisis de aspectos generacionales estéticos y culturales, poco estudiados con anterioridad, del influyente grupo cultural Orígenes. Se defiende la tesis de que la actitud aparentemente elitista de estos escritores fue en realidad una forma de regeneración, no sólo cultural, sino también social. Es de especial interés el estudio de las revistas literarias de la época.

3597 Bertot, Lillian. The literary imagination of the Mariel generation. Miami: Endowment for Cuban American Studies, Cuban American National Foundation, 1995. 105 p.: bibl.

En un lenguaje preciso y claro, la autora analiza las obras de Reinaldo Arenas, Roberto Valero, Miguel Correa y otros de la generación del Mariel con especial énfasis en sus aspectos de denuncia sociopolítica de la Revolución y de etapas anteriores.

3598 Cairo Ballester, Ana. La revolución del 30 en la narrativa y el testimonio cubanos. La Habana: Editorial Letras Cubanas, 1993. 431 p.: bibl. (Giraldilla)

Un libro que viene a llenar un vacío en el estudio de la narrativa testimonial contra la dictadura de Machado. Excelente trabajo de investigación que se resiente, como mucha de la crítica cubana, del uso y abuso de clichés, tanto en el lenguaje como en los juicios sociopolíticos.

3599 Chaple, Sergio. Estudios de narrativa cubana. La Habana: Ediciones Unión, 1996. 313 p.

Una aproximación a la obra de cuatro importantes narradores cubanos—Alfonso Hernández-Catá, Félix Pita Rodríguez, Onelio Jorge Cardoso y Alejo Carpentier—a partir de los principios conceptuales y metodológicos del estructuralismo sueco. Incluye también un ensayo sobre *Tilín García* (1939), la única novela del pintor Carlos Enríquez.

Del silencio al estallido: narrativa femenina puertorriqueña. See item **3556.**

3600 Díaz Quiñones, Arcadio. La memoria rota. Río Piedras, P.R.: Huracán, 1993. 180 p.: index. (Col. La nave y el puerto)

Following the Puerto Rican intellectual tradition established by Puerto Rican writers and literary critics of prior generations, the author makes a significant contribution to the analysis of how Puerto Rico's colonial status impinges upon the development of its national culture. Some of these essays were previously published in scattered sources and are unified by the author's attempt to ponder the continuities, disruptions, and omissions in Puerto Rico's historical memory.

3601 Flores, Juan. Divided borders: essays on Puerto Rican identity. Houston, Tex.: Arte Público Press, 1993. 252 p.: bibl., ill.

This volume includes some of the best known essays on Puerto Rican identity by one of the leading critics of US Puerto Rican literature. In addition to discussing stages in the development of Puerto Rican letters in the US, the author analyzes the processes that led to a transformation of Puerto Rican culture, rejecting the traditional assimilationist arguments in favor of a new cultural consciousness. For historian's comment see item **2144**.

3602 **Fuentes, José Lorenzo** and **Manuel Díaz Martínez.** The Cuban writer. (*Cuba. Stud.*, 24, 1994, p. 143–153)

Transcripción de las intervenciones de los dos autores cubanos en una mesa redonda en Amherst Univ., con preguntas de panelistas y del público. Se discute principalmente la relación entre la escritura y el poder en Cuba desde el punto de vista de dos intelectuales perseguidos por el Estado.

3603 **Gelpí, Juan.** Literatura y paternalismo en Puerto Rico. San Juan: Editorial de la Univ. de Puerto Rico, 1993. 201 p.: bibl. (Col. caribeña)

One of the most relevant critical works of the last few years. This well-known critic provides an insightful analysis of the culturally nationalistic and patriarchal character of Puerto Rico's literary canon and illustrates how several contemporary Puerto Rican prose fiction writers such as Luis Rafael Sánchez, Edgardo Rodríguez Juliá, Ana Lydia Vega, Rosario Ferré, Manuel Ramos Otero are transgressing it.

3604 **Gerón, Cándido.** Juan Bosch: vida y obra narrativa. Santo Domingo: Editora Alfa y Omega, 1993. 300 p.: bibl.

Minucioso estudio sobre la metodología y los arquetipos de la cuentística de Bosch. *Cuento de Navidad* se toma de ejemplo para el análisis de la simbología social y humana. Se analizan por igual otros textos. El exceso de adjetivos elogiosos restan seriedad al trabajo.

3605 **González-Pérez, Armando.** Acercamiento a la literatura afrocubana: ensayos de interpretación. Miami: Ediciones Universal, 1994. 212 p.: bibl., ill. (Col. Ebano y canela)

Util colección de estudios para un primer acercamiento a la literatura la literatura afrocubana. Se estudian todos los géneros y se incluyen autores de dentro y fuera de la isla.

A pesar de la variedad de aproximaciones críticas, los estudios carecen de profundidad y la selección de los autores incluidos podría ser más cuidadosa.

3606 **Huertas, Begoña.** Ensayo de un cambio: la narrativa cubana de los '80. 130 p.: bibl.

Dentro del marco del "período de rectificación" de la década de los 80 que aporta un ánimo renovador en el ámbito cultural cubano, surge, según la autora, una nueva corriente literaria que reacciona contra ciertas pautas estéticas del pasado. Se abandona la retórica épica y los barroquismos verbales para dar paso a una visión intimista, subjetiva. La perspectiva cotidiana incorpora a los textos un tono desenfadado, un talante demitificador y una saludable dosis de humor. Aún así, este estudio, como la gran mayoría de la crítica escrita en Cuba, no logra desprenderse de un enfoque influido por la realidad sociopolítica.

3607 *The Latino Review of Books: a Publication for Critical Thought and Dialogue.* Vol. 1, 1995. Albany, NY: Univ. at Albany, SUNY, CELAC, Center for Latino, Latin American, and Caribbean Studies.

A forum for stimulating critical thought and dialogue about the linkages and intersections between the Americas, North and South. This journal also attempts to transcend or redefine the conventional boundaries that have constrained the study and understanding of the people of Latin America and the Caribbean and their counterpart populations in the US. Published three times a year.

Lezama Lima, José. La visualidad infinita. See item **293**.

3608 **Loynaz, Dulce María.** Canto a la mujer: compilación de textos. Pinar del Río, Cuba: Ediciones Hnos. Loynaz, 1993. 2 v.

Conferencias, ensayos y poemas que ofrecen la visión de la autora de varias figuras femeninas, desde Isabel la Católica y Sor Juana Inés de la Cruz, hasta las poetas del continente e incluyendo a sus compatriotas, algunas más lejanas en el tiempo, como Gertrudis Gómez de Avellaneda, y otras más recientes. Visión penetrante, sensible e iluminadora de la Dulce María Loynaz.

3609 **Montero, Susana.** La narrativa femenina cubana, 1923–1958. (*Cuad. Hispanoam.*, 544, oct. 1995, p. 19–42)

Un recuento básico de la narrativa femenina cubana a partir del Primer Congreso Nacional de Mujeres en La Habana hasta el advenimiento de la Revolución. Montero establece bien la relación entre esta narrativa y la vida sociopolítica del país. Excelente punto de partida para cualquier estudio de la narrativa femenina cubana de esos años.

3610 Soto, Francisco. Reinaldo Arenas: the pentagonía. Gainesville: Univ. Press of Florida, 1994. 193 p.: bibl., index.

Este estudio enfoca la pentagonía *Celestino antes del alba, El palacio de las blanquísimas mofetas, Otra vez el mar, El color del verano* y *El asalto* como novelas de testimonio, dentro del contexto del entusiasmo que cobró la narrativa testimonial a partir del triunfo de la Revolución Cubana.

3611 Vázquez Arce, Carmen. Por la vereda tropical: notas sobre la cuentística de Luis Rafael Sánchez. Buenos Aires: Ediciones de la Flor, 1994. 244 p.: bibl.

Making use of Barthes' critical theory, the author provides an insightful analysis of Sánchez's short stories and their relationship to his subsequent novels, which gained him international recognition. She sees Sánchez's short stories as a major step in forging a new path for Puerto Rican prose fiction.

3612 Vega, Ana Lydia. Esperando a Loló y otros delirios generacionales. San Juan: Editorial de la Univ. de Puerto Rico, 1994. 111 p.: ill.

This volume includes lectures and newspaper articles by the renowned prose fiction writer. With her characteristic irreverence and sense of humor, the author sharply confronts some of the myths, conventions, and obsessions of Puerto Rican literary tradition, including what feminist and women's literature, including her own, represent to different audiences.

3613 22 conferencias de literatura puertorriqueña. Edición de Edgar Martínez Masdeu. San Juan: Librería Editorial Ateneo, 1994. 606 p.: bibl., port.

An uneven collection of 22 lectures on Puerto Rican literature given by well-known scholars at the Ateneo Puertorriqueño. Of particular interest are those dealing with women's literature, contemporary theater, US Puerto Rican writers, and Black poetry.

Andean Countries

RAYMOND L. WILLIAMS, *Professor of Spanish, University of California, Riverside*
CESAR FERREIRA, *Assistant Professor of Spanish, University of Oklahoma*

COLOMBIA AND VENEZUELA

MUCH OF THE LITERARY CRITICISM published in Colombia during this biennium has dealt with Gabriel García Márquez. Several new volumes have been written on his work, including an analytical study by Edward Hood (item **3615**). Although in Venezuela scholars and critics have dedicated themselves to a larger variety of writers, one notable trend is the rebirth of interest in the fiction writer Guillermo Meneses (items **3646** and **3645**). Critics of Venezuela continue to dedicate studies to traditional figures: for instance, Colombian historian and literary critic Otto Morales Benítez published a biographical study of Rómulo Gallegos (item **3651**). Meanwhile, the Venezuelan critic Javier Lasarte Valcárcel and the Colombian critic Luz Mery Giraldo each published broad studies on a variety of contemporary topics (items **3647** and **3616**).

The late 1980s and early 1990s Colombian publishing boom—led by Tercer Mundo Editores and Planet Editorial—abated somewhat, but Gabriel García Márquez, R.H. Moreno-Durán, and Alvaro Mutis remained prominent on the literary scene. Among the younger established novelists, Fernando Vallejo, Eduardo García Aguilar, Andrés Hoyos, Evelio Rosero Diago, and Pedro Sorela were visible in Colombia. Promising new figures to appear on the Colombian literary scene were Boris Salazar, Roberto Rubiano Vargas, and Hugo Chaparro Valderrama; each openly exhibits the influence of television, film, or the media.

In Venezuela, Salvador Garmendia (item **3755**) remained one of the major figures of the contemporary novel, along with writers of the later generation, such as José Balza (items **3750** and **3751**). The historical novel continued to be a predominant form in Venezuela, and one of the most accomplished creators of this type of fiction was Denzil Romero (items **3765** and **3766**). Two younger fiction writers who continued to make inroads in Venezuelan letters were Ednodio Quintero (item **3764**) and Gustavo Luis Carrera (item **3752**).

A comprehensive vision of literature in the Andean region was made available in several excellent anthologies that bear witness to the heterogeneity and vitality of modern fiction in the region: Harold Kremer (item **3664**), Gustavo Luis Carrera (item **3752**), and Antonio Bastardo (item **3754**) compiled fine anthologies that well represent Colombia and Venezuela. [RLW]

PERU, ECUADOR, BOLIVIA

La más reciente producción literaria en el Perú se caracterizó por la aparición de nuevos títulos de sus tres escritores contemporáneos más consagrados: Alfredo Bryce Echenique, Julio Ramón Ribeyro y Mario Vargas Llosa. Bryce Echenique publicó una de sus novelas más ambiciosas, *No me esperen en abril* (item **3718**), junto con una valiosa antología de toda su obra titulada *Para que duela menos* (item **3719**). Ribeyro reunió todos sus relatos en un grueso volumen bajo el título *Cuentos completos* (item **3736**) y reeditó su novela *Cambio de guardia* (item **3735**). Fallecido en 1994, Ribeyro también publicó una *Antología personal* (item **3734**), un libro que da cuenta de los muchos géneros que cultivó el autor a lo largo de su carrera. Vargas Llosa entregó una novela situada en la sierra peruana, *Lituma en los Andes* (item **3743**), y un interesante volumen de ensayos, *Desafíos a la libertad* (item **3742**).

Entre los escritores más jóvenes, cabe destacar la aparición de una serie de novelas escritas por mujeres, entre las que destacan *Ximena de dos caminos* de Laura Riesco (item **3737**), *El copista* de Teresa Ruiz Rosas (item **3739**), y *Las dos caras del deseo* de Carmen Ollé (item **3732**). La novela negra, un género escasamente tratado en la literatura peruana, tuvo en Alonso Cueto con *Deseo de noche* (item **3724**) y Fernando Ampuero con *Caramelo verde* (item **3712**) a dos de sus mejores cultivadores, mientras que la novela indigenista mostró su vigencia con la publicación de *País de Jauja* de Edgardo Rivera Martínez (item **3738**) y de una importante edición anotada de *Los ríos profundos* de José María Arguedas a cargo de Ricardo González Vigil (item **3716**).

En el campo de la crítica, cabe destacar la aparición de trabajos críticos sobre la obra de Bryce Echenique a cargo de José Luis de la Fuente y Julio Ortega, así como tres nuevos estudios sobre la obra de Vargas Llosa publicados por Nélida Flórez, Rita Gnutzmann y José Rodríguez Elizondo, respectivamente. A la vasta bibliografía existente sobre la narrativa indigenista peruana, con particular interés en la obra de José María Arguedas, se sumaron nuevos estudios de Antonio Cornejo Polar, Tomás Escajadillo y Elena Aibar-Ray. Ismael P. Márquez llevó a cabo un importante trabajo sobre el fenómeno de La Violencia y su representación ficcional en *La retórica de la violencia en tres novelas peruanas* (item **3635**).

En el Ecuador, gran parte de su literatura se instaló dentro de una amplia reflexión sobre la tradición y la modernidad en la sociedad. Además de la práctica de una escritura más experimental a cargo de escritores jóvenes como Huilo Ruales

Hualca (item **3700**), llama la atención el amplio cultivo del cuento entre sus escritores. Entre ellos destacan los libros de Jorge Dávila Vázquez, Iván Egüez, Raúl Pérez Torres, Marco Antonio Rodríguez, Abdón Ubidia y Jorge Velasco Mackenzie. En la novela, cabe subrayar la reedición de obras de figuras canónicas de la narrativa ecuatoriana como Nelson Estupiñán Bass, Alfredo Pareja Diezcanseco, Humberto Salvador y Alicia Yánez Cossío, así como los nuevos aportes de Francisco Proaño Arandi, Néstor Taboada Terán y Luis Zúñiga. Las novelas de éstos dos últimos se instalan en el género de la novela histórica.

En el campo de la crítica, una importante contribución fue el *Indice de la narrativa ecuatoriana* (item **3619**), de gran utilidad para estudiosos de la literatura ecuatoriana contemporánea. Un abarcador estudio de Alberto Rengifo sobre la obra de Alfredo Pareja Diezcanseco (item **3621**) y otro de Patricia Varas sobre la narrativa ecuatoriana a partir de la década del 70 (item **3622**) son volúmenes de consulta indispensable sobre el tema.

En Bolivia, su nueva literatura tuvo como telón de fondo la problemática del mundo indígena y la inestabilidad histórica de su sociedad. Tal es el caso de la novela *El viaje* de René Poppe, autor de reconocida trayectoria en la literatura de ese país (item **3657**). El cuento encontró importantes cultivadores en autores como Paz Padilla Osinaga (item **3655**), Carlos Saavedra Weise (item **3658**) y Manuel Vargas (item **3662**). De especial interés en el género del minicuento es el volumen de Edmundo Paz Soldán, *Desapariciones* (item **3656**), finalista en el concurso "Letras de Oro" para escritores de habla hispana en los Estados Unidos. [CF]

LITERARY CRITICISM AND HISTORY
Bolivia

Cornejo Polar, Antonio. Escribir en el aire: ensayo sobre la heterogeneidad socio-cultural en las literaturas andinas. See item **3625**.

Colombia

3614 Escobar, Eduardo. Nadaísmo crónico y demás epidemias. Bogotá: Arango Editores, 1991. 198 p. (Testimonio)

Escobar, best known in Colombia as an irreverent poet, painter, and essayist associated with the iconoclastic writers of the 1960s *nadaísta* movement in Colombia, has published 13 books. This volume consists of 20 personal testimonies published in newspapers over the past 20 years, mostly in *El Tiempo*. Most deal with the 1960s and the cultural scene in Colombia during that period. Escobar's narcissism is flagrant, but that was an important part of *nadaísmo*. Very worthwhile documentation.

3615 Hood, Edward Waters. La ficción de Gabriel García Márquez: repetición e intertextualidad. New York: P. Lang, 1993. 229 p.: bibl., ill., indexes. (American university studies. Series II, Romance languages and literature, 0740–9257; 195)

Revised doctoral dissertation analyzes repetition and intertextuality in García Márquez's early fiction to his writing of the 1970s. Includes *La hojarasca, El coronel no tiene quien le escriba, Cien años de soledad,* and *La increíble y triste historia de la cándida Eréndira y su abuela desalmada*. Reviews theoretical ideas about repetition and intertextuality, covering theorists and authors such as Derrida, Deleuze, Miller, Kundera, Durrenmatt, Calvino, Freud, Camus, and Genette. Examines the repetition of plots, characters, and episodes in García Márquez's work. Very careful and thorough study; of interest to García Márquez scholars.

3616 La novela colombiana ante la crítica, 1975–1990. Coordinación y recopilación de Luz Mery Giraldo B. Cali, Colombia: Editorial Facultad de Humanidades; Bogotá: Centro Editorial Javeriano, 1994. 372 p.: bibl. (Crítica)

Colombian professor and critic compiled 19 articles for this volume in which she offers a prologue explaining that Isaacs, Rivera, García Márquez, and Mutis have defined the Colombian novel. She also clarifies why

Cien años de soledad (1967) was a turning point for the Colombian novel. Work is divided into three parts: 1) "La Nueva Narrativa Colombiana;" 2) "Una Tradición Renovadora;" and 3) "¿Quién mata al padre?" Novelists discussed are major writers, including Manuel Zapata Olivella, Héctor Rojas Herazo, Alvaro Mutis, Albalucía Angel, Fanny Buitrago, R.H. Moreno-Durán, Luis Fayad, Rodrigo Parra Sandoval, Oscar Collazos, Alvaro Pineda Botero, José Luis Garcés, Antonio Caballero, Marvel Moreno, Fernando Vallejo, and Marco Tulio Aguilera Garramuño. Very useful and worthwhile volume of critical studies.

3617 —para que mis amigos me quieran más—: homenaje a Gabriel García Márquez. Selección y prólogo de J.G. Cobo Borda. Bogotá: Siglo del Hombre Editores, 1992. 424 p.: bibl., ill.

Colombian critic and poet Cobo Borda explains that this book is a celebration of two important landmarks: the 25th anniversary of *Cien Años de Soledad* and García Márquez's 65th birthday, both celebrated in 1992. Includes uneven pieces by writers, journalists, translators, scholars, and friends organized in three parts: 1) "Imágenes" provides 18 general essays on the author and his work; 2) "Temas" contains 13 pieces on his work in general; and 3) "Variaciones" consists of essays on specific works. An excellent witness to García Márquez's talent and international following.

Ecuador

Cornejo Polar, Antonio. Escribir en el aire: ensayo sobre la heterogeneidad socio-cultural en las literaturas andinas. See item **3625.**

3618 Cueva, Agustín. Literatura y conciencia histórica en América Latina. Quito: Planeta, 1993. 167 p.: bibl. (Obras de Agustín Cueva; 7. Col. País de la amistad)

Media docena de ensayos sobre diversos autores latinoamericanos y una interesante reflexión sobre el Ecuador y su literatura entre 1920–60.

3619 Indice de la narrativa ecuatoriana. Edición de Gladys Jaramillo Buendía, Raúl Pérez Torres y Simón Zavala Guzmán. Quito: Editora Nacional, 1992. 752 p.: bibl.

Excelente libro de referencia que contiene información bibliográfica detallada de la producción narrativa ecuatoriana entre 1960–91. Incluye breve información biográfica y referencias críticas de 190 autores ecuatorianos.

3620 Ojeda, Enrique. Ensayos sobre las obras de Jorge Icaza: con una entrevista a este escritor. Quito: Edit. Casa de la Cultura Ecuatoriana, 1991. 138 p.: bibl.

Redición de cuatro estudios sobre la obra del indigenista ecuatoriano. Su novedad radica en la inclusión de una carta y una entrevista con el autor, hasta ahora inéditas. Este último documento es de interés para cualquier estudioso sobre la obra de Icaza.

3621 Rengifo A., Alberto B. La narrativa de Alfredo Pareja Diezcanseco. Quito: Banco Central del Ecuador, 1990. 411 p.: bibl. (Biblioteca de la revista Cultura; 5)

Ambicioso estudio sobre la obra de uno de los más importantes novelistas de la Generación del 30 en el Ecuador. Rengifo se concentra en los libros más importantes de Pareja (*El muelle, La manticora*, etc.), basando su análisis en las teorías de Luckacs, Goldmann y Barthes.

3622 Varas, Patricia. Narrativa y cultura nacional. Quito?: Abrapalabra Editores, 1993. 221 p.: bibl.

La relación literatura-cultura es abordada en este ensayo, con especial énfasis en el realismo social y el indigenismo, hasta llegar a la actual narrativa ecuatoriana. Su autora ilustra el tema socio-cultural con la literatura urbana producida a partir de 1970 por autores como Iván Egüez, Raúl Pérez Torres y Jorge Velasco Mackenzie.

Peru

3623 Aibar Ray, Elena. Identidad y resistencia cultural en las obras de José María Arguedas. Lima: Pontificia Univ. Católica del Perú, Fondo Editorial, 1992. 292 p.: bibl.

Estudio sobre las novelas *Los ríos profundos, Todas las sangres* y *El zorro de arriba y el zorro de abajo*. Más allá de la clásica problemática de la identidad de los protagonistas y la supervivencia de la cultura quechua, este estudio busca esclarecer nociones de transculturación y mestizaje en la literatura indigenista con una base antropológica, al tiempo que analiza las bases ideológicas de la obra del autor.

3624 Arguedas, José María and **Manuel Moreno Jimeno.** José María Arguedas: la letra inmortal; correspondencia con Manuel Moreno Jimeno. Edición de Roland Forgues. Lima: Ediciones de los Ríos Profundos, 1993. 163 p.: ill.

Interesante libro que ilustra la amistad personal y literaria entre ambos escritores peruanos. Dividido en dos partes, la primera reúne las cartas de Moreno Jimeno a Arguedas y la segunda, sin duda la más interesante, las de Arguedas escritas a Moreno Jimeno. El editor añade una serie de notas críticas a los textos que ayudan a aclarar dudas sobre la información expresada en las cartas. Util volumen para conocer una serie de opiniones literarias y datos íntimos de ambos escritores.

3625 Cornejo Polar, Antonio. Escribir en el aire: ensayo sobre la heterogeneidad socio-cultural en las literaturas andinas. Lima: Editorial Horizonte, 1994. 245 p. (Critica literaria; 11)

Importante ensayo que repasa la heterogeneidad de las voces de la literatura andina del Ecuador, Perú y Bolivia, sus formas orales y escritas, y sus relaciones con la historia. El libro combina reflexiones sobre diversos autores, entre ellos, el Inca Garcilaso, Juan León Mera, Clorinda Matto de Turner, César Vallejo, Ciro Alegría, Alcides Arguedas, etc.

3626 El cuento peruano hasta 1919. Selección, prólogo y notas de Ricardo González Vigil. Lima: Petroperú, Ediciones COPE, 1992. 2 v. (800 p.): bibl. (El cuento peruano; 6)

Vol. 6 (en dos tomos) de una antología que reúne los cuentos más representativos de la etnoliteratura y la tradición oral (el Inca Garcilaso, Bartolomé de las Casas, etc.), así textos más recientes sobre el costumbrismo, y la Ilustración en la literatura (Palma, Ascencio y Segura, Olavide, García Calderón, Valdelomar, etc.).

3627 Delgado Díaz del Olmo, César et al. Otras pieles: género, historia y cultura. Recopilación de Maruja Barrig y Narda Henríquez Ayin. Lima: Pontificia Univ. Católica del Perú, 1995. 156 p.: bibl.

Recopilación de nueve ensayos de diversos historiadores y literatos que debaten la historia y la narrativa peruana del siglo XX haciendo énfasis en las relaciones de género y la construcción de identidades. Libro de consulta indispensable para estudiar el fenómeno de la literatura femenina en el Perú.

3628 Elmore, Peter. Los muros invisibles: Lima y la modernidad en la novela del siglo XX. Lima: Mosca Azul Editores; El Caballo Rojo Ediciones, 1993. 230 p.: bibl.

Estudio crítico que examina la experiencia urbana de la modernidad en la novelística peruana del siglo XX. Los textos comentados son *La casa de cartón* de Adán; *Duque* de Diez-Canseco; *Yawar fiesta* de María Arguedas; *El mundo es ancho y ajeno* de Alegría; *Los geniecillos dominicales* de Ribeyro; *Conversación en La Catedral* de Vargas Llosa; y *Un mundo para Julius* de Bryce Echenique.

3629 Escajadillo, Tomás G. Narradores peruanos del siglo XX. 2. ed. Lima: Editorial Lumen, 1994. 249 p.: bibl. (Col. Prisma; 6)

Libro que reúne siete ensayos críticos sobre autores canónicos de la literatura peruana del siglo XX. Estos incluyen a López Albújar, García Calderón, Diez-Canseco, Alegría, Arguedas, Salazar Bondy, Scorza y Bryce Echenique. Aunque tradicional en su aporte crítico, la lectura de cada uno de estos textos siempre puede ser un buen punto de partida para conocer la obra de cada uno de los escritores mencionados.

3630 Escajadillo, Tomás G. La narrativa indigenista peruana. Lima: Amaru Editores, 1994. 333 p.: bibl.

Libro que revisa a los autores canónicos del indigenismo peruano (López Albújar, Alegría, Arguedas, Scorza, etc.) y su impacto a largo plazo en la historia literaria peruana de este siglo. El autor discute también nuevas corrientes neo-indigenistas a partir de 1971. Contiene una exhaustiva bibliografía sobre el tema.

3631 Flórez, Nélida. La mujer en la novela de Mario Vargas Llosa. Lima: s.n., 1993. 111 p.: bibl.

Novedoso y necesario estudio sobre el tema de la mujer en la obra de Vargas Llosa. Aunque algo esquemático y simplista en sus comentarios sobre los personajes femeninos del autor, tiene valiosas reflexiones sobre el realismo de estos personajes, su extracción social y su lugar en la sociedad que Vargas Llosa evoca en su narrativa.

3632 Fuente, José Luis de la. Cómo leer a Alfredo Bryce Echenique. Madrid: Ediciones Júcar, 1994. 218 p.

Libro que proporciona una visión panorámica de toda la obra de uno de los autores peruanos contemporáneos más importantes. Además de una breve biografía de Bryce, se incluye un análisis de los temas y estilos en sus cuentos y sus novelas desde *Un mundo para Julius* (1970) hasta *La última mudanza de Felipe Carrillo* (1988). La bibliografía al final del ensayo es una de las más exhaustivas publicadas hasta el momento sobre el autor.

3633 Gnutzmann, Rita. Cómo leer a Mario Vargas Llosa. Gijón, Spain: Ediciones Júcar, 1992. 202 p.: bibl. (Guías de lectura Júcar; 13)

Esta es una buena guía introductoria para el lector interesado en conocer toda la obra de Vargas Llosa. Se revisa la vida del autor, sus opiniones sobre la literatura y las diversas etapas de su prolífica carrera como escritor desde *Los jefes* hasta *Elogio de la madrastra*. También se incluye una útil bibliografía.

3634 Loayza, Luis. El sol de Lima. 2. ed., corr. y aum. México: Fondo de Cultura Económica, 1993. 190 p. (Col. Tierra firme)

Nueva edición de un importante libro de ensayos publicado por primera vez en 1974. Además de conocidos textos sobre el Inca Garcilaso, El Lunarejo, Ricardo Palma, Abraham Valdelomar, Martín Adán y Sebastián Salazar Bondy, entre otros, esta edición incluye nuevos textos sobre personajes peruanos en la literatura europea, el costumbrismo y Julio Ramón Ribeyro.

3635 Márquez, Ismael P. La retórica de la violencia en tres novelas peruanas. New York: P. Lang, 1994. 124 p.: bibl. (University of Texas studies in contemporary Spanish-American fiction, 0888–8787; 7)

Valioso ensayo crítico que examina el tema de la violencia, sus causas históricas en la sociedad peruana y sus matices ideológicos. Para ello, el autor ha escogido tres textos canónicos de la narrativa peruana contemporánea: *Los ríos profundos* de Arguedas, *Cambio de guardia* de Ribeyro e *Historia de Mayta* de Vargas Llosa. Incluye una excelente bibliografía sobre el tema.

3636 Los mundos de Alfredo Bryce Echenique: textos críticos. Edición de César Ferreira y Ismael P. Márquez. Lima: Pontificia Univ. Católica del Perú, Fondo Editorial, 1994. 320 p.: bibl.

Colección de ensayos críticos sobre

toda la obra de uno de los novelistas peruanos contemporáneos más importantes. El libro incluye textos en los que el propio autor comenta su quehacer literario y sus ideas sobre la literatura, así como una variedad de apreciaciones críticas que revisan el desarrollo de su obra desde su primer libro de cuentos *Huerto cerrado* (1968), pasando por toda su obra novelística y su libro de memorias *Permiso para vivir* (1993).

3637 Ortega, Julio. El hilo del habla: la narrativa de Alfredo Bryce Echenique. Guadalajara, Mexico: Univ. de Guadalajara, 1994. 147 p.: bibl. (Col. del Centro de Estudios Literarios)

Estudio crítico sobre la obra de Bryce Echenique. Incluye cuatro breves ensayos sobre las novelas más importantes del autor y una larga entrevista con el mismo. Asimismo, incluye una larga sección de opiniones del propio Bryce sobre su vida y obra y una bibliografía general.

3638 Porras Barrenechea, Raúl. La marca del escritor. Edición de Luis Loayza. México: Fondo de Cultura Económica, 1994. 138 p.

Loayza reúne en este libro una selección antológica de los ensayos literarios de uno de los pensadores peruanos más influyentes de este siglo. Entre estos destacan los comentarios de Porras sobre los mitos incaicos, Rodrigo Orgóñez, el Inca Garcilaso, Sánchez Carrión y Luis Benjamín Cisneros. El prólogo de Loayza destaca la influencia del pensamiento de Porras y su vigencia en la cultura peruana del siglo XX.

3639 Ribeyro, Julio Ramón. Ribeyro, la palabra inmortal. Entrevistas con Jorge Coaguila. Lima: J. Campodónico/Editor, 1995. 132 p.: bibl. (Col. del sol blanco)

Junto con un breve comentario crítico sobre la obra de Ribeyro, este libro recoge seis entrevistas al autor realizadas entre 1991–93. Además de diversos comentarios de boca del autor sobre sus libros más recientes—los aforismos de *Dichos de Lúder* (1989), el cuarto volumen de cuentos de *La palabra del mudo* (1992) y su diario íntimo *La tentación del fracaso* (1992),—se incluyen seis relatos inéditos de Ribeyro. Una amplia bibliografía sobre las muchas entrevistas que concedió en vida el escritor complementan un útil volumen.

3640 Rodríguez Elizondo, José. Vargas Llosa: historia de un doble parricidio. Santiago?: Editorial La Noria, 1993. 71 p.

Ensayo que analiza *El pez en el agua*, las memorias políticas del novelista peruano publicadas en 1993. Rodríguez Elizondo centra su atención en los vínculos afectivos del escritor con su padre biológico, con quien siempre mantuvo una relación conflictiva, y con su padre intelectual, el pensador francés Jean Paul Sartre, de quien Vargas Llosa se alejó en la década de los 80. Interesante análisis sobre las relaciones entre vida y literatura, hecho que pone en evidencia las muchas lecturas que admite el polémico libro de Vargas Llosa.

3641 Rodríguez Rea, Miguel Angel. El Perú y su literatura: guía bibliográfica. Lima: Pontificia Univ. Católica del Perú, Fondo Editorial, 1992. 251 p.: indexes. (Textos universitarios)

Una útil guía bibliográfica para estudiar la literatura peruana. El recopilador divide los diversos acápites de su libro en historias generales, antologías, diccionarios, bibliografías y hemerografías, ensayos y estudios críticos, índices onomásticos e índices temáticos. Un libro valioso para consultar algún tema o autor de la literatura peruana.

Sánchez León, Abelardo. La balada del gol perdido. See item **3740.**

3642 Thorne, Carlos. Páginas de extramuros. Lima: Editorial Irene, 1993. 124 p.

Variada colección de artículos de este prolífico novelista contemporáneo. En ellos reflexiona sobre el oficio del escritor, el cuento en el Perú, la generación del 50, la novela de la dictadura, la novela de la ciudad en el Perú, y la literatura latinoamericana. También le dedica artículos a autores de su preferencia como César Vallejo, James Joyce, Ortega y Gasset, Alejo Carpentier y Marta Lynch, entre otros. Interesante antología para conocer las preferencias literarias del escritor.

3643 Toro Montalvo, César. Historia de la literatura peruana. v. 3, Emancipación. v. 4, Costumbrismo y literatura negra del Perú. v. 5, Romanticismo. Lima: Editorial San Marcos, 1991–94. 3 v.: bibl.

Tres nuevos volúmenes de historia de la literatura peruana que se unen a un proyecto total de 10 tomos. Además del análisis de cada período histórico anunciado en el tí-

tulo de cada libro, el autor opta siempre por incluir una serie de apéndices en los que presente útil información sobre autores y textos de particular relevancia para el período literario en cuestión. Para una reseña de vol. 1, ver *HLAS 54:3925.*

3644 Toro Montalvo, César. Literatura peruana: de los incas a la época contemporánea. Lima: A.F.A. Editores, 1994. 824 p.: bibl., ill.

Grueso volumen que es en realidad un compendio del proyecto en 10 tomos de este historiador de la literatura peruana (ver item **3643**). El libro está dividido por períodos históricos y los autores más destacados de esa época. También se incluye una bibliografía para cada período histórico en cuestión. Tanto este volumen como la historia en 10 tomos de este autor vienen a llenar el vacío dejado por las historias de Augusto Tamayo Vargas y Luis Alberto Sánchez.

Venezuela

3645 Araujo, Orlando *et al.* Guillermo Meneses ante la crítica. Prólogo de Hugo Achugar. Selección y recopilación de Javier Valcárcel Lasarte y Hugo Achugar. Caracas: Monte Avila Editores, 1992. 279 p.: bibl. (Ante la crítica)

Venezuelan writers and critics have paid particular attention recently to the superb Venezuelan fiction writer Guillermo Meneses, who published during the 1930–60s. Consists of articles and brief notes on Meneses, as well as interviews with him organized in two parts: 1) 16 fine essays and notes; and 2) 26 reviews and four previously published interviews on Meneses' work. A useful volume.

3646 Azócar de Campos, Elba. Innovaciones en la cuentística de Guillermo Meneses. Presentación de Miguel Angel Burelli Rivas. Prólogo de Pedro Díaz Seijas. Caracas: Univ. Simón Bolívar, Instituto de Altos Estudios de América Latina; Fundación Bicentenario de Simón Bolívar, 1992. 117 p.: bibl.

Study of Meneses' short fiction contains a presentation by Miguel Angel Burelli Rivas, prologue by Pedro Díaz Seijas, introduction by the author, and a study of 10 stories by Meneses: "La Balandra *Isabel* Llegó esta Tarde," "Adolescencia," "Borrachera," "Luna," "El Duque," "Un Destino Cumplido," "Alias El Rey," "Tardío Regreso a Través de un Espejo," "La Mano Junto al Muro," and "El Destino de un Dios Olvidado." Author follows with concluding chapter about innovations in the writer's work and a bio-bibliographical note about him.

3647 Lasarte Valcárcel, Javier. Sobre literatura venezolana. Caracas: Ediciones La Casa de Bello, 1992. 172 p.: bibl. (Col. Zona tórrida; 41. Letras universitarias)

Lasarte's nine lengthy studies of 20th-century Venezuelan literature consist of independent essays, all of them informed and intelligent, rather than one coherent book. Authors discussed are: Teresa de la Parra, Arturo Uslar Pietri, Julio Garmendia, Guillermo Meneses, Salvador Garmendia, Rómulo Gallegos, and several poets.

3648 López Alvarez, Luis. Literatura e identidad en Venezuela. Barcelona: PPU, 1991. 199 p.: appendix, bibl., ill. (Universitas; 14. Serie Ediciones y estudios. Estudios)

Latin America's cultural debate on identity remains alive after over a century. This book-length essay explores the subject in the Venezuelan context. López Alvarez, a Spaniard who has researched the debate in great scholarly detail, defines Venezuela as a nation in search of identity. The work is arranged in two parts: 1) the search since independence; and 2) 20th-century literary manifestations of the debate. Appendix includes an overview of publishing houses in Venezuela. Unfortunately, the intelligent presentation of ideas dissipates towards the end.

3649 Márquez Rodríguez, Alexis. Historia y ficción en la novela venezolana. Caracas: Monte Avila Editores, 1991. 257 p.: bibl. (Estudios)

Having written essays on the historical novel for some time, Márquez Rodríguez has become an authority on the subject. Introduction examines the historical novel in Venezuela from the colonial period through the 19th century. An overview of all historical novels published in Venezuela is then provided, followed by individual studies of historical novels by Arturo Uslar Pietri, Enrique Bernardo Núñez, Miguel Otero Silva, and Francisco Herrera. Informative volume is impressive in its breadth and scholarship, but Márquez Rodríguez appears unaware of Lukacs' theory on issues of history and fiction.

3650 Medina, José Ramón. Noventa años de literatura venezolana, 1900–1990. Cronología y bibliografía de Horacio Jorge Becco. Caracas: Monte Avila Editores, 1993. 634 p.: bibl., indexes. (Estudios)

Critical and chronological history of Venezuelan literature (1900–90s) discusses major trends, by generation. Emphasizes major writers and major works and includes appendices with excellent chronologies on the Venezuelan essay, poetry, novel, and short story. Well informed and useful guide to the nation's literature.

3651 Morales Benítez, Otto. Rómulo Gallegos: identidad del escritor y del político. Caracas: Ediciones del Congreso de la República, 1993. 190 p.: bibl., ill., index.

Morales Benítez, author of 34 books on cultural, political, and historical topics since the 1970s, is one of Colombia's most prolific historians. Many of these books are written from a sense of civic duty and involve Venezuela, a nation he has always admired far more than his compatriots. This volume provides an excellent overview of the public and political life of the prominent Venezuelan writer Rómulo Gallegos and an in-depth look at his political ideas. A very positive portrait of Gallegos emerges, especially of his notions about Latin American identity. Informative and useful book by one of Colombia's most respected public figures.

Parra, Teresa de la. Influencia de las mujeres en la formación del alma americana. See item **2669.**

PROSE FICTION
Bolivia

3652 Avila Echazú, Edgar. El Códice de tunupa. Cochabamba, Bolivia: Editorial Serrano, 1993. 151 p.

Volumen de nueve cuentos cuyos relatos incluyen temas que examinan acontecimientos históricos en Bolivia, el mundo indígena y diversas vivencias infantiles y juveniles. El narrador utiliza una serie de voces narrativas con destreza y habilidad.

3653 Bruzonic, Erika D. Cegados por la luz: relatos. La Paz: Editorial Don Bosco, 1992. 85 p.

Heterogéneo libro de cuentos que contiene ocho relatos de esta periodista y narradora. La cotidianidad del mundo femenino, la libertad política, el surrealismo expresionista, las contradicciones del mundo tecnológico y la deshumanización de la explosión demográfica son algunos de los temas tratados.

3654 Morales Durán, Agustín. Fiestas de Tarija: cuentos testimoniales de medio siglo. Tarija, Bolivia: Editorial Universitaria Juan Misael Saracho, 1991. 125 p.: ill.

Colección de cuentos sobre la zona sur de Tarija. Su protagonista principal es el hombre de esta tierra, el chapaco. En torno a este personaje, el autor retrata la identidad social y colectiva de ese pueblo, con frecuentes incursiones en su folklore y sus diversas expresiones sociales colectivas.

3655 Padilla Osinaga, Paz. La covacha del loco: el deleite morboso de lo profano. Santa Cruz de la Sierra, Bolivia: Editora El País, 1993. 89 p.

Nueva colección de cuentos de este joven escritor que incluye tres relatos en los que se mezclan con sutil habilidad la experimentación verbal, lo real, lo fantástico y lo grotesco. Por ello, a menudo establece una relación lúdica entre autor y lector. La creación literaria en sí emerge como el gran tema de estos textos.

3656 Paz Soldán, Edmundo. Desapariciones. La Paz?: Edición Centro I. Patiño, 1994. 150 p.

Excelente colección de minicuentos. Muchos de ellos giran en torno a existencias cotidianas que examinan temas como el amor, la soledad o la duda existencial. Al mismo tiempo, se incluyen textos que dialogan con la literatura fantástica y el absurdo. Destaca el estilo equilibrado y sobrio de narrar.

3657 Poppe, René. El viaje. La Paz: Ediciones Casa de la Cultura, Alcaldía Municipal, 1993. 109 p.

Novela corta de uno de los más importantes narradores bolivianos contemporáneos. Se combina con habilidad el tratamiento de temas amorosos y la vida literaria. El mundo de la mina y la inestabilidad política de Bolivia sirven de trasfondo para narrar una amena historia donde el viaje sirve de *leitmotif.* Destaca en este relato el uso de una prosa concisa y trabajada, así como un ágil diálogo que sugiere más de lo que se narra a primera vista.

3658 Saavedra Weise, Carlos. El ojo del general y otros relatos. Santa Cruz, Bolivia: Editora El País, 1993. 156 p.

Libro de 12 cuentos cuyo trasfondo es con frecuencia el de la dictadura militar. Por ello, muchos de los personajes y situaciones narradas son alegorías del terror, la muerte y el abuso de poder. Todos estos temas resultan parte de una memoria colectiva que el libro desea evocar y rescatar a través de narraciones de corte clásico pero efectivas.

3659 Sáenz, Jaime. Los papeles de Narciso Lima-Achá. La Paz: Instituto Boliviano de Cultura, 1991. 511 p.

Novela de uno de los poetas latinoamericanos más originales del siglo XX. Varios de los recursos poéticos propios de la obra de este poeta boliviano son llevados con eficacia al género narrativo. A través del juego de autores apócrifos y de sus relaciones intertextuales, la novela organiza su estructura, que atenta contra su mismo orden, así como contra las concepciones de autoridad y autoría textual. [O. Rivera Rodas]

3660 Soria Gamarra, Oscar. Sepan de este andar: antología de cuentos. La Paz: Univ. Mayor de San Andrés, 1991. 280 p.

Cuentos que giran en torno a la identidad social del trabajador boliviano (el campesino, el minero, etc.). Atrapados en su frugalidad material y su marginalidad psicológica y cultural, las frustradas luchas sociales de estos personajes revelan aspectos de una sociedad convulsionada. Guionista de cine, su autor demuestra agilidad y destreza para recrear situaciones a menudo muy dramáticas a través de la palabra.

3661 Teixidó, Raúl. Jardín umbrío. Cochabamba, Bolivia: Editorial Los Amigos del Libro, 1994. 163 p.: ill. (Col. Literatura de hoy; 659)

Ganador del Premio Nacional de Cuento, Teixidó es un importante escritor boliviano de la década del 60. Este volumen reúne cuatro trabajos en prosa donde el autor revela algunas claves de su quehacer artístico. Destaca entre ellos "Memoria de la Luz," un interesante texto autobiográfico que ayuda a conocer mejor su vida y su obra.

3662 Vargas, Manuel. Montes Claros. La Paz: Ediciones Casa de la Cultura, H. Alcaldía Municipal, 1992. 107 p.: ill.

Colección de 14 cuentos de este conocido escritor. Como en gran parte de su obra, su escenario es el mundo rural y campesino de Bolivia. La geografía física por la que deambulan sus personajes es también el espejo de una geografía humana, pues sus protagonistas son producto y consecuencia de ese mundo, desde sus momentos más elevados hasta los más dolorosos. Contiene un interesante prólogo de Jesús Urzagasti.

Colombia

3663 Abad Faciolince, Héctor Joaquín.
Asuntos de un hidalgo disoluto. Bogotá: T-M Editores, 1994. 232 p. (Narrativa contemporánea. Col. Prisma)
Narrated by a character who is a 71-year-old Colombian millionaire, this work is a modern Colombian version of the Spanish picaresque novel. Contains chapter subtitles from many of those 17th-century novels, as well as picaresque adventures. Protagonist tells of his education, religious upbringing, seduction, lovers, adultery, family, and trip to Italy, among other adventures. For this narrator, and perhaps for the young Abad Faciolince (b. 1958), writing is life. This first novel is one of the better works of fiction to appear recently in Colombia.

3664 Antología del cuento vallecaucano. Recopilación y prólogo de Harold Kremer. Cali, Colombia: Ediciones Univ. del Valle, 1992. 258 p. (Col. Literatura. Autores vallecaucanos)
Accomplished short-story writer Harold Kremer has anthologized 21 stories from the Valle del Cauca region of Colombia. He has selected some of Colombia's best writers, including Enrique Buenaventura, Rodrigo Parra Sandoval, Oscar Collazos, Fernando Cruz Kronfly, Armando Romero, Gustavo Alvarez Gardeazábal, Umberto Valverde, Marco Tulio Aguilera Garramuño, Andrés Caicedo, Gustavo González Zafra, and Boris Salazar. Kremer also offers a prologue.

3665 Badrán Padauí, Pedro. Lecciones de vértigo. Bogotá: Planeta, 1994. 144 p.
Badrán Padauí (b. 1960) published a volume of short stories prior to this first novel. Narrator's first paragraph explains the basic premise of the entire book: his neighborhood in Bogotá has risen far into the sky and is floating above the city. He, his family, and his neighborhood friends spend the the

following pages dealing with life as it presents itself under these bizarre conditions. Difficult situations and circumstances arise, most of which elicit humor because of their parallels with daily life in Bogotá under normal conditions. Light, allegorical novel suggests that Badrán Padauí is among the more talented of Colombia's youngest novelists.

3666 Chaparro Valderrama, Hugo. El capítulo de Ferneli. Bogotá: Arango Editores, 1992. 285 p.: ill. (Opera prima)
Known as a young journalist and short-story writer in Colombia, Chaparro Valderrama obviously has a passion for detective fiction and American film. His characters conceive of reality as chance, but this metafictional work has origins in detective fiction, horror movies, newspapers, and the very act of creation. An outgrowth of Cortázar's *Hopscotch*, this novel also resonates with Sue Grafton, Alfred Kubin, Raymond Chandler, Rubem Fonseca, Luis Rafael Sánchez, and the Carlos Fuentes of *Hydra head.* The protagonist is a writer who writes to understand, and the result is a highly innovative and entertaining novel.

3667 Escobar Velásquez, Mario. Canto rodado. Bogotá: Planeta, 1991. 284 p. (Autores colombianos)
Colombia's Antioquia region has produced a venerable tradition of rural storytellers, a tradition that has included Tomás Carrasquilla and Manuel Mejía Vallejo. Escobar Velásquez has written several novels that participate in this tradition of stories with strong plots, energetic characters, and violent actions. This rural novel of solitude and love follows the same tradition. His characters are once again afflicted souls surrounded by crisis and conflict. This well-written novel confirms author's place as one of the most powerful among Colombia's conventional writers.

3668 García Aguilar, Eduardo. Urbes luminosas: relatos. Bogotá: Instituto Colombiano de Cultura, 1993. 152 p. (Escritores colombianos en la diáspora; 6)
Author of several volumes of fiction, García Aguilar has broken from conventional modes with this book, offering a series of entertaining travel chronicles with an apparent touch of fiction. His travels and stays in Europe, the US, and Latin America usually find him working in menial jobs and observing the subcultures of the world. Typical settings for

his experiences are kitchens, train stations, and cheap hotels. In Stockholm he finds a Polish lover in a warehouse and gets to know a novelist. In a brothel of Panama, he observes the spectacle of a sex show, seeing all types of female and male bodies for sale to foreigners. In a hospital, he reads Rousseau and Faulkner. He befriends the marginal artists of San Francisco and the trash collectors in Mexico City. His experiences are inevitably bizarre, and his writing superb.

3669 García Márquez, Gabriel. Del amor y otros demonios. Barcelona: Mondadori, 1994. 190 p. (Literatura Mondadori; 12)

The Nobel Laureate has set this novel during the colonial period in a region of South America, which, although unnamed, bears remarkable similarity to the Caribbean coast of Colombia. The plot begins immediately when Sierva María, the daughter of the Marquis de Casalduero, is bitten by a rabid dog in the marketplace as she prepares to celebrate her 12th birthday. The rest of the story flows from this event, but often moves back in time. The lethargic Marquis finds his purpose in attempting to save his daughter's life. There's a touch of Caribbean magic (in the form of *santería*), plenty of the expected imagination, and more complexity than in most of García Márquez's recent writing.

3670 García Márquez, Gabriel. Diatriba de amor contra un hombre sentado: monólogo en un acto. Bogotá: Arango Editores, 1994. 69 p. (Teatro colombiano)

In this short play, a woman delivers a monologue for the entire work. Graciela's husband remains seated for her entire monologue, as she reviews their 25-year marriage, rethinking the justice of everything that has been said and done. For this silver wedding anniversary, she reaches the early conclusion that "nothing is so much like hell as a happy marriage." This and other lines remind us that the author is García Márquez, and that he has lost nothing of his ability to formulate just the right phrase. Towards the end of his career, García Márquez the feminist has surfaced.

3671 Hoyos, Andrés. Conviene a los felices permanecer en casa. Bogotá: Altamir Ediciones, 1992. 301 p. (Novela)

Andrés Hoyos (b. 1953), who has published a novel and short fiction, has been gaining a fine reputation recently in Colombia. This historical novel dealing with conflicts among the leaders who created Colombia is set during the early-19th century and the wars of independence. The language and structure are traditional, and the plot develops chronologically. Effective satire of Colombian society during the wars of independence. This novel confirms once again Hoyos' well-earned reputation.

3672 Hoyos, Andrés. "Los viudos" y otros cuentos. Bogotá: T-M Editores, 1994. 306 p. (Narrativa. Col. Prisma)

The title story is set in the period of the Spanish Inquisition and tells of a dying sinner asked to confess the details of his heretic books or be denied absolution. The narrator suggests that today we are all "widows of heresy," for heresy is still alive today. After establishing his primary interests, this self-consciously heretic writer relates urban stories about writing, victims, and exiles. Author of two novels prior to the publication of these 12 stories, Hoyos (b. 1953) is establishing himself as one of Colombia's very best young urban writers.

3673 Illán Bacca, Ramón. Crónicas casi históricas. Prólogo de Germán Vargas. Barranquilla, Colombia: Ediciones Uninorte, 1990. 140 p.: ill.

Illán Bacca is a well-known writer of Colombia's Caribbean coast, particularly Barranquilla, where he teaches and publishes in local newspapers. His previous works of fiction are *Marihuana para Goering* (short stories) and *Déborah Kruel* (novel). This work consists of 40 published journalistic pieces dealing with a broad range of subjects, preceded by a prologue by Colombian journalist and critic. Illán Bacca's interests encompass literature, film, music, history, television, art, and politics. His tone is light; his commentaries are often informative and always entertaining.

3674 Louis Lakah, Soad. La Lío y otras mujeres. Bogotá: Plaza & Janés Editores, 1994. 123 p.

Soad Louis Lakah became a recognized short fiction writer in Colombia in the 1980s when she and a well-respected group of young writers in Montería, Colombia were associated with the literary magazine *El Túnel*. This first novel begins with the literary convention of the discovered manuscripts published by the narrator, supposedly with no revisions. The female protagonist lives a rural 20th-century Colombian version of a picaresque novel, operating as a witch in a magical world. This a light and easy-to-read first novel.

3675 Restrepo, Laura. La isla de la pasión. México: Planeta, 1992. 321 p.: bibl. (Col. Narrativa 21)

Investigative account about a group of Mexican soldiers who were sent to a distant island in the Pacific Ocean during the Mexican Revolution, and abandoned for several years. Restrepo, known in Colombia as a journalist and writer of popular fiction, combines both types of writing in this work, relating both the story and her own story of searching for information about this bizarre episode in Mexican history. She interviews elderly survivors, reprints documents related to the events, and interviews those familiar with the events on the island. All of this research is combined with a considerable amount of fiction writing, making for good reading.

3676 Rosero Diago, Evelio. Señor que no conoce la luna. Bogotá: Planeta, 1992. 101 p.: ill.

One of Colombia's most interesting young writers, Evelio Rosero Diago (b. 1958) has already published two novels and several volumes of short fiction. His fictional world is populated by desperate, tortured, and unstable characters who are presented without names, ages, or clear individual identities; some are identified as "los desnudos" (the naked ones) and others as "los vestidos" (the dressed ones). Rosero Diago challenges his readers to find logic in a perverse and tortuous world.

3677 Rubiano Vargas, Roberto. El informe de Galves y otros *thrillers*. Bogotá: Tercer Mundo Editores, 1993. 160 p. (Narrativa contemporánea. Col. Prisma)

Author of two books of fiction, this writer from Bogotá communicates well the experience of life in Colombia's capital in these detective stories set in an ambience of generalized crime, violence, and intrigue. The urban setting is ugly, but Rubiano Vargas' fiction is a pleasure to read because of his masterful appropriation of the narrative strategies and even the style of Jorge Luis Borges. Con-

sequently, these are stories with labyrinths, partial manuscripts, and the like. Rubiano Vargas is an atypical writer for Colombia, and quite accomplished.

3678 Salazar T., Boris. Caravana. Cali, Colombia: Ediciones Univ. del Valle, 1992. 111 p. (Col. Literatura)

Characters in these short fictions do not belong to any particular place. Instead, they seem to flee from a Colombia in ruins, finding distraction in constant movement, and survival only in telling stories. Salazar is fascinated with a variety of urban settings, as well as with the encounter between these settings and his characters. Another intriguing book by this uniquely talented young writer (b. 1955) who has lived in Cali, Colombia, and New York.

3679 Salazar T., Boris. La otra selva. Bogotá: Tercer Mundo Editores, 1991. 199 p. (Narrativa contemporánea. Col. Prisma)

This is the first novel of one of Colombia's most interesting young writers (b. 1955). Written in New York while Salazar was in graduate school, *La otra selva* is a fictional account of the last days in the life of Colombia's classic writer José Eustasio Rivera and takes place over a few months in 1928. Narrated in multiple voices, this novel contains numerous self-referential comments. Very well written and intriguing fictional account of Rivera and the status of writing in Colombia today.

3680 Silva, Juan Manuel. El Conde de Cuchicute. Bogotá: Altamir, 1991. 329 p.

The Count of Cuchicute, an historical figure in early-20th-century Colombia, was a quite novelesque character known as a fighter and woman chaser. After detailed historical research, Silva has written his first novel on this unorthodox and bizarre character. Silva writes well in the traditional style, but shows no interest in innovation.

3681 Sorela, Pedro. Aire de mar en Gádor. 1. ed. en Colombia. Bogotá: Tercer Mundo Editores, 1993. 272 p. (Narrativa contemporánea. Col. Prisma)

Known as a journalist in Spain, this Spanish-Colombian binational author has begun writing fiction and literary criticism in recent years. With this novel, which deals with human relations and involves multiple encounters and separations, Sorela exhibits a mature use of language and a good sense of humor in the form of satire. Sorela has a great sense for plot and intrigue. Certainly an interesting talent to appear in the Colombian context.

3682 Sorela, Pedro. Fin del viento. Madrid: Santillana, 1994. 287 p. (Alfaguara hispánica; 111)

Sorela's third novel, a futuristic work that deals with the birth of a war at the end of this century, is also a satire of European society. Author constructs a novel of epic proportions, divided into three parts, with ample action. This Colombian-Spanish writer is a master at developing plot and keeping the reader both intrigued and entertained.

3683 Sorela, Pedro. Ladrón de árboles. México: Ediciones Corunda, 1993. 121 p.: ill. (OsaMayor; 9)

This Colombian-Spanish author writes in Spain, but mostly about Latin American subjects. His style is generally traditional, as it is in these 16 stories. Sorela uses a variety of European and Latin American settings to develop the stories' urban protagonists. Very good sense for story-telling and style.

3684 Valencia Jaramillo, Jorge. El corazón derrotado. Bogotá: Planeta, 1992. 271 p.: ill.

Valencia Jaramillo has been a prominent figure in Colombia's cultural and political scene over the past two decades, occupying several political positions and serving as a great promoter of literature and the arts. Although he is not known as a writer, he has published this curious volume, which contains thoughts, memories, and poems on three subjects: love, forgetting, and death. Three short essays are followed by numerous poems. A pleasant souvenir of an important presence in Colombia.

3685 Vallejo, Fernando. Entre fantasmas. Bogotá: Planeta, 1993. 178 p. (El río del tiempo; 6)

Vallejo's novels in recent years have given him the well-earned reputation as one of Colombia's most irreverent writers. Most are devastating critiques of social mores in Medellín and among Colombia's upper class. He also deals with heretofore unspoken topics for most serious Colombian fiction writers, such as homosexuality. In this work, the first-person narrator, a vague and self-conscious entity, is a film director in Mexico, and the novel moves between Columbia and Mexico (where Vallejo himself has lived and written over the past few years). Author's new thematic interest is aging, but he remains interested in the flow of time (a theme in his previous novels). His tone is still irreverent and satiric. Another very well-written novel by Vallejo.

3686 Zapata Olivella, Manuel. Hemingway, el cazador de la muerte. Bogotá: Arango Editores, 1993. 347 p. (Narrativa colombiana)

Zapata Olivella's narrative maps have often been broad, and he continues this tradition by placing Ernest Hemingway in contact with himself in Africa. In this first-person narration, Hemingway is in Kenya in 1961 with a young lover, searching for a myth to photograph and narrate. Zapata Olivella finds the Africa of Latin America in this region, an Africa as rich in flora and fauna as the first Europeans found in Colombia. Author proves once again that he is one of the most imaginative novelists in Colombia and the entire Caribbean region.

Ecuador

3687 Benites Vinueza, Leopoldo. Argonautas de la selva: los descubridores del Amazonas. Estudio introductorio y notas de Oswaldo Encalada Vásquez. Quito: Libresa, 1992. 382 p. (Col. Antares; 78)

Nueva edición en la prestigiosa colección "Antares" de esta clásica novela histórica sobre Francisco de Orellana y el descubrimiento del Amazonas, publicada por primera vez en 1945. Incluye un amplio estudio crítico que repasa la vida y obra del autor y la importancia de esta novela en el contexto de la historia literaria de su país.

3688 Casares, Olivia. Zoonidos: cuentos de la naturaleza. 2. ed. Ecuador: Abrapalabra Editores, 1993. 103 p.

Conjunto de relatos que pertenece al mundo de la la zoología y, por extensión, a la literatura infantil. Sin embargo, este libro admite también una lectura adulta, pues una y otra vez alude simbólicamente a la organización social de los animales como espejo de la sociedad humana. Su prosa es de una falsa inocencia pues encierra una reflexión de valores básicos sobre la existencia.

3689 Chiriboga, Luz Argentina. Bajo la piel de los tambores: novela. Quito: Editorial Casa de la Cultura Ecuatoriana, 1991. 155 p.

Primera novela de esta conocida escritora. Su tema es la educación sentimental de una mujer en la costa del Ecuador. El progresivo descubrimiento del mundo urbano y social al que se enfrenta la protagonista a medida que se afianza su identidad adulta sirve de comentario sobre los falsos valores de una sociedad pacata y rígida.

3690 Cuento contigo: antología del cuento ecuatoriano. Recopilación de Cecilia Ansaldo Briones. Guayaquil, Ecuador: Univ. Católica de Santiago de Guayaquil; Quito: Univ. Andina Simón Bolívar, Subsede Quito, 1993. 334 p.

Excelente antología del cuento ecuatoriano que reúne textos de 40 autores. De gran valor para cualquier estudioso del género pues proporciona un amplio panorama del cuento ecuatoriano en los siglos XIX y XX. Además de un interesante estudio que discute la evolución del género en el Ecuador, se incluye una nota introductoria sobre la vida y obra de cada autor.

3691 Dávila Vázquez, Jorge. El dominio escondido. Estudio introductorio y notas de Felipe Aguilar. Quito: Libresa, 1992. 250 p.: bibl. (Col. Antares; 74)

Antología de cuentos de este importante narrador ecuatoriano. Su escenario general es la ciudad de Cuenca. En la aparente vida apacible de esa ciudad provinciana se retrata la existencia de una serie de personajes, muchos de ellos femeninos, cuyas vidas rutinarias y solitarias a menudo encarnan los conflictos entre una vieja moral y el arribo de la modernidad. El autor desarrolla una variedad de técnicas narrativas que ilustran su gran talento en el género. Incluye un valioso estudio introductorio.

3692 Egüez, Iván. Historias leves. Quito: Abrapalabra Editores, 1994. 142 p.

Colección de cuentos donde este importante escritor incursiona en el mundo de la parodia y el humor. En estos relatos las historias se suceden en varios sitios del planeta, a menudo desafiando la realidad virtual. La solemnidad del hecho literario es puesta en entredicho ante el tono burlón y lúdico de los textos.

3693 Estupiñán Bass, Nelson. El crepúsculo. Edición de Alejandro Sigüenza G. Quito: Editora Nacional, 1992. 156 p.

Nueva novela con matices de realismo social como muchas de las obras de este escritor. La industria del caucho en la zona de Esmeraldas y la explotación de la población negra de esa región ecuatoriana resaltan como los temas más salientes. La novela está escrita con un formato epistolar, hechoque se presta para una interesante experimentación narrativa.

3694 Páez, Santiago. Profundo en la galaxia. Quito: Abrapalabra Editores, 1994. 140 p.

Novedosa colección de siete cuentos de ciencia ficción. Una de sus mayores virtudes es la creación de mundos futuristas con motivos y símbolos provenientes de la cultura indígena ecuatoriana.

3695 Pareja y Díez Canseco, Alfredo. Baldomera. Las pequeñas estaturas. Selección, prólogo, cronología y bibliografía de Edmundo Ribadeneira. Caracas: Biblioteca Ayacucho, 1991. 388 p.: bibl. (Biblioteca Ayacucho; 169)

Nueva edición anotada de dos novelas de este importante miembro de la llamada Generación del 30 en el Ecuador en la prestigiosa colección Ayacucho. Estas llamadas novelas-río reflejan la herencia naturalista de Zola y son amplios frescos de la sociedad ecuatoriana de la primera parte del siglo XX, con una multiplicidad de personajes.

3696 Pérez Torres, Raúl. Cuentos escogidos. Estudio introductorio y notas de Luz Marina de la Torre. Quito: Libresa, 1991. 258 p.: bibl. (Col. Antares; 64)

Antología de relatos de este importante escritor, uno de los cultivadores más asiduos del cuento en Ecuador. La pobreza de la vida citadina, la alienación y el fracaso son algunos de sus temas. Un amplio estudio introductorio da cuenta del lugar de este autor en la narrativa ecuatoriana reciente.

3697 Proaño Arandi, Francisco. Del otro lado de las cosas. Quito: Editorial El Conejo, 1993. 182 p. (Col. Ecuador/letras)

La ciudad de Quito, su centro histórico y una vieja casona que se derrumba, simbolizando el fin de una anacrónica burguesía de principios de siglo, son los elementos básicos de esta novela. A ellos se une un narrador-protagonista, otrora revolucionario de la década de los 70, que se debate en una crisis de identidad entre lo nuevo y lo viejo. El arribo de la modernidad y sus difíciles consecuencias hacen de esta novela una lectura necesaria en la narrativa ecuatoriana actual.

3698 Proaño Arandi, Francisco. Oposición a la magia. Estudio introductorio, cronología y notas de Julio Pazos Barrera. Quito: Libresa, 1994. 151 p. (Col. Antares; 102)

Redición de una colección de nueve relatos de este prolífico escritor ecuatoriano. Aunque el libro permite una lectura independiente de cada cuento, a estos relatos los caracteriza un experimentalismo verbal que se ilustra en la autoconciencia de la escritura, atmósferas oscuras y asfixiantes, personajes de rostros vagos y desfigurados y un sistema de alusiones de personajes mitológicos.

3699 Rodríguez, Marco Antonio. Cuentos del rincón. Estudio introductorio y notas por Manuel Zabala Ruiz. Quito: Libresa, 1991. 155 p.: bibl., ill. (Col. Antares; 68)

Primer libro de relatos de este importante narrador ecuatoriano. A través de diferentes experiencias que lo llevan a ingresar finalmente al mundo adulto, el joven protagonista de estos cuentos va descubriendo el mundo con temor e incertidumbre. El prólogo revisa toda la trayectoria literaria del autor.

3700 Ruales Hualca, Huilo. Loca para loca la loca: cuentos para despeinarse la cara. Quito: Eskeletra Editorial, 1989. 157 p.: ill. (Col. La Lulupa)

Heterodoxa colección de más de una veintena de cuentos y minicuentos de este importante narrador que apareció en la literatura ecuatoriana en la década de los 80. La locura, la violencia, la muerte y los muchos fantasmas que atormentan a sus personajes se expresan a través de una escritura que destaca por su carácter iconoclasta, irreverente y experimental.

3701 Salvador, Humberto. En la ciudad he perdido una novela. Estudio introductorio y notas de María del Carmen Fernández. Quito: Libresa, 1993. 244 p.: bibl., ill. (Col. Antares; 94)

Edición crítica de la novela del escritor guayaquileño, publicada por primera vez en 1930. Escrita durante el auge del indigenismo, esta novela tiene entre sus temas el cuestio-namiento de la creación literaria, el realismo socialista, las teorías freudianas y la aparición del arte cinematográfico.

3702 Samaniego Salazar, Filoteo. Sobre sismos y otros miedos. Madrid: Editorial Verbum, 1991. 169 p. (Narrativa)

Interesante reflexión novelada sobre el hombre contemporáneo en el Ecuador. Aunque de corte existencialista, el autor recurre en su narración a ciertos tópicos que dialogan con la tradición de la novela de la tierra (los terremotos y otras fuerzas naturales) que se postulan como determinantes en las vidas de sus personajes y a menudo son un espejo de sus quimeras personales.

3703 Taboada Terán, Néstor. Angelina Yupanki, marquesa de la Conquista. Barcelona: Apóstrofe, 1992. 255 p. (Novela histórica)

Novela que narra los enfrentamientos de españoles e incas en la captura de Atahualpa, así como la posterior guerra civil entre Diego de Almagro y Francisco Pizarro durante la conquista del Perú. Su protagonista es una mujer indígena, esposa de Pizarro y amante del cronista Juan de Betanzos. Este libro es una importante contribución al género de la novela histórica.

3704 Terán, Enrique. Camino de llanto = Huacay-ñán. Quito: Editorial El Conejo, 1994. 193 p. (Grandes autores ecuatorianos)

Novela inédita de este conocido autor ecuatoriano de la década de los 30. Es un relato de viaje que tiene como tema la historia amorosa de dos jóvenes. A través de esta relación se insertan una serie de comentarios filosóficos, estéticos y políticos con elementos de un romanticismo tardío y un acercamiento al realismo socialista.

3705 Torre Flor, Carlos de la. Voces en torno al abuelo: novela. Quito: Editorial Casa de la Cultura Ecuatoriana, 1992. 162 p.

Novela que gira en torno a la figura patriarcal de un abuelo. El personaje sirve para retratar los legados de una clase criolla terrateniente, y una forma de vida que se desdobla entre una sociedad rural y urbana. Esa división acaba por poner en conflicto los viejos valores tradicionales de una sociedad que también debe modernizarse. La humanidad del protagonista y de las figuras que giran en torno a él es uno de los rasgos más salientes de esta novela.

3706 Ubidia, Abdón. Cuentos escogidos. Estudio introductorio de Jorge Dávila Vázquez y Alexandra Astudillo Figueroa. Quito: Libresa, 1993. 214 p. (Col. Antares; 95)

Antología que reúne 15 cuentos de este importante narrador ecuatoriano. Su temática gira en torno al fracaso del cambio social en una sociedad conservadora, encerrada en la tradición. Su prosa es pulcra, buscando siempre un balance entre lo coloquial y lo experimental. Contiene un excelente estudio introductorio.

3707 Ubidia, Abdón. Divertinventos: libro de fantasías y utopías. 1. ed en esta colección. Quito: Editorial Grijalbo Ecuatoriana, 1989. 111 p. (El Espejo de tinta)

Heterogénea colección de cuentos y minicuentos de este importante narrador ecuatoriano. Escritos con un estilo ligero y ameno, estos relatos trascienden muchas veces los límites formales de la realidad, al tiempo que plantean inquietudes sobre temas como el amor, el tiempo, la muerte, etc.

3708 Vallejo Corral, Raúl. Fiesta de solitarios. Quito: Editorial El Conejo, 1992. 178 p.: ill. (Col. Ecuador/premios)

Excelente colección de 11 cuentos donde se destacan figuras solitarias, sumidas en una profunda tristeza y la marginalidad psicológica. Por ello, los amores perdidos, los encuentros con la muerte, el exilio físico e interior resaltan como rasgos claves de estos personajes, retratados con un estilo narrativo siempre efectivo y elegante.

3709 Velasco Mackenzie, Jorge. Desde una oscura vigilia: cuentos. Quito?: Abrapalabra Editores, 1992. 120 p.

Colección de 10 cuentos cuya temática gira en torno a la ciudad de Guayaquil. En ese escenario urbano, sus protagonistas dramatizan el final simbólico de una ciudad y una vida. Como los personajes de Onetti, son figuras solitarias que viven existencias mediocres y tediosas.

3710 Yánez Cossío, Alicia. Bruna, soroche y los tíos. Estudio introductorio y notas de Sara Beatriz Vanégas Cobeña. 4. ed. Quito: Libresa, 1991. 319 p.: bibl. (Col. Antares; 67)

Nueva edición de la novela de una de las escritoras más importantes de este siglo en el Ecuadora. Su trama describe las peripecias interiores de una adolescente que busca reafirmar su identidad individual en un contexto social lleno de falsas convicciones religiosas y morales, propias de una sociedad provinciana y falsa. Contiene un interesante estudio crítico sobre la obra de la novelista.

3711 Zúñiga Paredes, Luis. Manuela: novela. Ecuador: Abrapalabra Editores, 1991. 197 p.: ill.

Novela histórica donde el autor incursiona en la humanidad de Manuela Sáenz, la compañera y amante de Simón Bolívar. El autor recrea con acierto el oscurantismo de la sociedad colonial, el tratamiento de las mujeres y la psicología de la protagonista en ese contexto. Una interesante contribución sobre dos figuras históricas cuyo tratamiento literario no deja de tener interés para los escritores contemporáneos.

Peru

3712 Ampuero, Fernando. Caramelo verde. Lima: J. Campodónico, 1992. 134 p. (Col. del sol blanco)

Tercera novela de este narrador y periodista que incursiona en la novela negra. El mundo de las drogas, el dinero y la corrupción le sirven al escritor para hacer un comentario sobre la violencia y el poder en el Perú contemporáneo.

3713 Ampuero, Fernando. Malos modales. Lima: J. Campodónico, 1994. 172 p. (Col. del sol blanco)

Colección de cuentos cuyos personajes son miembros de la clase media peruana. Muchos de ellos son individuos jóvenes que con frecuencia entran en conflicto con una vieja moral tradicional. Aunque por momentos de factura irregular, muchos de estos textos son un retrato sociológico irónico y penetrante del grupo social en cuestión.

3714 Arévalo, Javier. Nocturno de ron y gatos. Lima: PEISA, 1994. 219 p. (Serie del río hablador)

Novela que tiene como protagonistas a un grupo de jóvenes intelectuales en la Lima contemporánea. Marcados por el hastío y la frustración que el medio les ofrece para desarrollar su vocación, estos artistas malditos se refugian en el mundo nocturno de la bohemia, el sexo y las drogas. Un vasto comentario sobre la nueva generación de escritores e intelectuales peruanos (más jóvenes), y su desencantada relación con la ciudad y la sociedad a la que pertenecen.

3715 Arguedas, José María. Un mundo de monstruos y de fuego. Selección e introducción de Abelardo Oquendo. México: Fondo de Cultura Económica, 1993. 222 p.: bibl. (Col. Tierra firme)

Antología de Arguedas con selecciones de sus cuentos, *Los ríos profundos* y *El zorro de arriba y el zorro de abajo.* También se incluyen testimonios biográficos y reflexiones del autor sobre la novela. El excelente prólogo del recopilador complementa un volumen de importante consulta para estudiosos del indigenismo y del novelista.

3716 Arguedas, José María. Los ríos profundos. Edición de Ricardo González Vigil. Madrid: Cátedra, 1995. 462 p.: bibl., ill. (Letras hispánicas; 392)

Edición anotada de la novela más importante de Arguedas. Incluye un largo prólogo sobre la vida y obra del autor, así como valiosas consideraciones sobre el significado de esta novela en la historia literaria del indigenismo peruano. El texto de la novela está rigurosamente comentado y se incluye una valiosa bibliografía. Un aporte importante para el estudio de la obra arguediana.

3717 Bellatin, Mario. Salón de belleza. Lima: J. Campodónico, 1994. 78 p. (Col. del sol blanco)

Fino cultivador de la novela corta, este joven escritor es una de las voces más novedosas aparecidas en el Perú en los últimos años. Bellatin es dueño de una prosa experimental que siempre busca sugerir un mundo que trasciende los límites convencionales de la realidad. El libro narra la vida de un homosexual trasvesti, dueño de una peluquería en la que van a morir las víctimas de un mal incurable. La enfermedad como tema literario es tratado con eficacia y madurez narrativa.

3718 Bryce Echenique, Alfredo. No me esperen en abril. Barcelona: Anagrama, 1995. 611 p. (Narrativas hispánicas; 178)

En esta nueva novela, Bryce retorna al mundo de la alta burguesía limeña a través de su protagonista adolescente, Manongo Sterne, personaje reminiscente del protagonista infantil de su primera novela *Un mundo para Julius.* Además de ser una novela de inicia-

ción sentimental, este libro es un vasto retrato de la clase alta peruana desde la década del 50 hasta nuestros días. Como siempre, la oralidad, el humor y la ironía son elementos importantes en la elaboración del relato.

3719 Bryce Echenique, Alfredo. Para que duela menos. Edición de Juan Angel Juristo. Madrid: Espasa Calpe, 1995. 315 p.: bibl., ill.

Antología de toda la obra de este importante escritor contemporáneo que incluye fragmentos de sus novelas, cuentos, artículos periodísticos y sus memorias. Contiene un largo estudio introductorio a cargo del editor del volumen y una selecta bibliografía crítica. Excelente visión panorámica de la obra de Bryce Echenique.

3720 Carrasco, Fátima. El europeo. Lima: El Santo Oficio, 1995. 163 p.

Primera novela de esta escritora. Novela de adolescencia que aunque algo convencional en sus temas (el inicio en la vida amorosa, los parámetros sociales que impiden la libertad de acción a sus personajes), está narrada con ironía y amable ternura. Plantea la problemática de la aparición de una nueva generación en la sociedad peruana contemporánea y sus desencuentros con una vieja moral.

3721 Cisneros, Antonio. El libro del buen salvaje: crónicas de viaje, crónicas de viejo. Lima: Peisa, 1994. 210 p. (Serie Crónicas contemporáneas)

Segundo libro que reúne crónicas periodísticas de este importante poeta peruano. Con una prosa ágil, Cisneros se muestra como un agudo conocedor de la vida peruana, así como un hombre viajero y cosmopolita. Sus crónicas combinan con gracia e ironía la experiencia personal y generacional, lo sublime y lo ridículo.

3722 Cuento peruano contemporáneo. Selección, nota introductoria y edición de Rafael Dávila Franco. Lima?: Ediciones San Gabriel, 1991. 188 p.

Antología que incluye 19 cuentos de importantes cultivadores del relato en el Perú en el siglo XX, entre ellos, López Albújar, Valdelomar, Diez Canseco, Alegría, Arguedas, Vargas Vicuña, Ribeyro, Reinoso, Martínez, Gálvez Ronceros, Rivera Martínez, Gutiérrez, Pérez Huarancca y Jara. Llama la atención la ausencia de Vargas Llosa y Bryce Echenique.

3723 Cueto, Alonso. Amores de invierno. Lima: Editorial Apoyo, 1994. 98 p.

Tercer libro de cuentos de este joven escritor, aparecido en la década de los 80. Muchos de estos relatos se caracterizan por su brevedad. Como en muchas de sus obras anteriores, sus personajes buscan en el dinero, el amor y la muerte un paraíso que los redima de la monotonía e insignificancia de su vida diaria.

3724 Cueto, Alonso. Deseo de noche. Lima: Editorial Apoyo, 1993. 94 p.

Relato que se instala dentro del género de la novela negra. A pesar de su brevedad, la narración combina con eficacia el juego entre la realidad y la fantasía, el erotismo y cierto comentario social sobre la clase media peruana. Novedosa contribución al género detectivesco en el Perú.

3725 Higa Oshiro, Augusto. Final del porvenir. Lima: Milla Batres, 1992. 186 p.: ill.

Situada en un barrio popular de la ciudad de Lima, esta novela tiene como tema la problemática urbana y los conflictivos procesos étnicos y culturales por los que atraviesa la sociedad peruana contemporánea. Su prosa es ágil y privilegia un lenguaje musical, lleno de humor y cierto lirismo para narrar. Pero, sobre todo, es un testimonio social de la vida desesperada de gentes andinas en la barriada limeña.

3726 Hinostroza, Rodolfo. Fata Morgana: novela. Lima: ASA Ediciones, 1994. 319 p.: ill.

Novela que tiene como protagonista la vida de un escritor latinoamericano expatriado en Europa. El texto está narrado a dos tiempos, con planos de la narración que continuamente se cruzan. Entre sus muchos elementos destacan el tema erótico y el acto creador de la escritura. Interesante contrapunto entre la fantasía erótica y la fantasía intelectual, lo racional e irracional, remitiéndonos al concepto de la escritura automática surrealista y el psicoanálisis freudiano.

3727 Jara, Cronwell. Patíbulo para un caballo. Lima: Mosca Azul Editores, 1989. 377 p.

Primera novela de este reconocido cuentista que narra la fundación y resistencia de una barriada. El realismo y la violencia institucional ejercida por el mundo del poder,

así como la marginalidad de sus protagonistas se combinan con eficacia para poner en evidencia la tensión existente entre el mundo andino y la modernidad urbana.

3728 Malca, Oscar. Al final de la calle. Illustraciones de Piero Quijano. 3a ed. Lima: Ediciones El Santo Oficio, 1994. 193 p.: ill.

Lima es el escenario de un protagonista de la clase media que resume su existencia entre el fútbol, el sexo, la droga y la música rock. Como otros miembros de la generación de escritores a la que pertenece el autor, la vida diaria de la ciudad y sus espacios sórdidos, bohemios y violentos retratan una cotidianidad marcada por la frustración juvenil y el tedio existencial.

3729 Mellet, Viviana. La mujer alada. Lima: Peisa, 1994. 91 p. (Serie del río hablador)

Doce relatos de esta joven cuentista peruana que basa su imaginario en un contrapunto entre lo cotidiano y lo absurdo. Sus personajes habitan un mundo urbano plagado de soledad e incomunicación. No obstante, también están presentes hechos que irrumpen en ese mundo con sorpresa e ironía.

3730 Nieto Degregori, Luis. Señores destos reynos: cuentos. Lima: PEISA, 1994. 154 p. (Serie del río hablador)

Novela histórica situada en el Cusco de los siglos XVI, XVIII y XX. Este libro se instala dentro de la tendencia revisionista de la novela histórica en América Latina que concibe la fuente historiográfica como un posible producto de la ficción. El autor recrea momentos claves de la historia incaica peruana (las rebeliones de Manco Inca y Túpac Amaru, por ejemplo), extendiendo el impacto de esos acontecimientos hasta el presente.

3731 Niño de Guzmán, Guillermo. Una mujer no hace un verano. 2. ed. Lima: J. Campodónico Editor, 1996. 1 v. (Col. Del sol blanco)

Segundo libro de cuentos de este escritor perteneciente a la generación de los 80. Los personajes de estos relatos se debaten entre la duda existencial, la soledad, el desamor y el peligro. A menudo el trasfondo de sus aventuras es el mundo urbano nocturno y el mar, que aparece representado como un elemento de simbología múltiple.

3732 Ollé, Carmen. Las dos caras del deseo. Lima: PEISA, 1994. 277 p. (Serie del río hablador)

Primera novela de esta conocida poeta. La protagonista es profesora de una universidad y observa con asombro su propia crisis existencial que es, a la vez, espejo de la crisis social peruana desde una perspectiva femenina. Dividido en dos partes, el relato transcurre en Lima y luego en un pequeño pueblo de los EE.UU., donde su protagonista trabaja como obrera.

3733 Palma, Ricardo. Tradiciones peruanas. Coordinación de Julio Ortega. Ed. crítica, 1. ed. Nanterre, France: Allca XXe, Univ. Paris X, Centre de recherches latino-américaines, 1993. 658 p.: bibl. (Col. Archivos; 23)

Extensa edición anotada de 100 tradiciones de Ricardo Palma. Auspiciada por la UNESCO, este volumen está coordinado por Julio Ortega. Incluye interesantes comentarios de dos escritores peruanos, Luis Loayza y Alfredo Bryce Echenique, y una serie de estudios críticos de especialistas sobre la obra de Palma como Merlin Compton, Alberto Escobar, Aníbal González, Roy Tanner, Bernard Lavallé, Henry Bonneville, Alexandru Georgescu, Fernando Unzueta y José Miguel Oviedo. También se incluye una extensa bibliografía sobre el autor.

3734 Ribeyro, Julio Ramón. Antología personal. México: Fondo de Cultura Económica, 1994. 238 p.: bibl. (Col. Tierra firme)

Este libro reúne un muestrario interesante de toda la obra de Ribeyro preparado por el propio autor. A lo largo de su carrera literaria, Ribeyro cultivó todos los géneros: la novela, el cuento, el teatro, la prosa corta, el ensayo y el diario íntimo. El libro incluye también un fragmento de su autobiografía, que el autor comenzó a escribir poco antes de su muerte en 1994.

3735 Ribeyro, Julio Ramón. Cambio de guardia. Barcelona: Tusquets Editores, 1994. 307 p. (Col. Andanzas; 215)

Primera edición española de esta importante novela de Ribeyro, publicada por primera vez en 1973. Su trasfondo es la dictadura del General Manuel Odría en la década de los años 50 en el Perú. En medio de una escritura experimental para un narrador más bien clásico, la novela es un comentario sobre la clase oligárquica y el poder que ella ostenta a través de un militar inepto y corrupto.

3736 Ribeyro, Julio Ramón. Cuentos completos. Prólogo de Alfredo Bryce Echenique. Madrid: Santillana, 1994. 749 p. (Alfaguara)

Volumen que reúne toda la obra cuentística (con algunos textos inéditos) de uno de los narradores más importantes de este siglo en el Perú. El libro incluye un importante prólogo que revisa los grandes temas del autor: la frustración de la clase media peruana; la marginalidad física y psicológica; el conflicto social y urbano en la sociedad peruana contemporánea. La variada experimentación estilística de Ribeyro y su gran talento con el género corto quedan de manifiesto.

3737 Riesco, Laura. Ximena de dos caminos. 236 p. (Serie del río hablador)

Riesco ofrece una versión femenina de los conflictos irreconciliables entre la costa y la sierra peruana al narrar la infancia de Ximena en la ciudad andina de La Oroya. Reaparece aquí la clásica problemática de la narrativa indigenista, pero la sensibilidad femenina de la narración le añade un novedoso matiz al tema.

3738 Rivera Martínez, J. Edgardo. Páis de Jauja: novela. Lima: La Voz Ediciones, 1993. 515 p.

Una de las novelas más importantes de la narrativa indigenista peruana reciente. Situado en la ciudad de Jauja, este libro narra la infancia de Claudio y su paulatino descubrimiento del mundo andino. El protagonista vive en carne propia las contradicciones internas de la sociedad peruana cuando entra en contacto con el espacio dominante de la costa peruana. La novela dialoga de cerca con obras clásicas del género indigenista como *El mundo es ancho y ajeno* de Ciro Alegría y *Los ríos profundos* de José María Arguedas.

3739 Ruiz Rosas, Teresa. El copista. Barcelona: Editorial Anagrama, 1994. 123 p. (Narrativas hispánicas; 171)

Novela corta, finalista del premio de Herralde de Novela en España. Utilizando el género epistolar, narra la relación amorosa entre un "copista" de música y una mujer. La música ocupa un papel protagánico en el relato, pero su mayor novedad radica en el contrapunto entre una voz masculina y otra femenina para narrar la misma historia.

3740 Sánchez León, Abelardo. La balada del gol perdido. Lima: Ediciones Noviembre Trece, 1993. 214 p.

Recopilación de crónicas periodísticas de este conocido poeta y novelista. Muchos de estos textos versan sobre el deporte y el fútbol, asuntos que utiliza el escritor, sociólogo de profesión, para hacer una serie de comentarios sobre la idiosincrasia peruana. En su último acápite, el libro reúne una serie de artículos sobre poetas y escritores peruanos (Salazar Bondy, Bryce Echenique, Cisneros, entre otros).

3741 Silva-Santisteban, Rocío. Me perturbas. Lima: Ediciones El Santo Oficio, 1995. 107 p.

Primer libro de cuentos de esta conocida poeta peruana de la generación del 80. El universo de estos relatos está marcado por la autodestrucción, la violencia psicológica, la soledad y el desencanto. Aunque los cuentos son algo desiguales en su factura, su autora logra configurar un imaginario propio.

3742 Vargas Llosa, Mario. Desafíos a la libertad. 1. ed. española. Madrid: El País; Aguilar, 1994. 319 p.: indexes. (El nuevo siglo)

Selección de artículos publicados entre 1990–94 en los que el novelista reflexiona sobre lo que él denomina la "cultura de la libertad:" la política europea tras la caída del muro de Berlín; el ultranacionalismo; la tradición autoritaria en América Latina y la defensa de la economía neoliberal, entre otros temas.

3743 Vargas Llosa, Mario. Lituma en los Andes. Barcelona, España: Planeta, 1993. 312 p. (Col. Autores españoles e hispano-americanos)

Libro que marca el retorno a la novela del escritor peruano de más renombre internacional. Vargas Llosa utiliza su conocido personaje, el sargento Lituma, para explorar los mitos del mundo andino, y los temas de la violencia y el terrorismo en el Perú contemporáneo. A pesar de ser una de sus novelas menos logradas, es siempre un texto de prosa bien trabajada y una contribución a la polémica entre el mundo indígena y el mundo costeño en la sociedad peruana.

3744 Verástegui, Enrique. Taki onqoy. Lima: Lluvia Editores, 1993. 200 p.

Libro que combina el verso, el drama, la prosa creativa y el ensayo para contar una huelga armada de campesinos en un valle cerca de Lima. Tal variedad de voces narrativas culmina en una enorme utopía: la instauración de una nueva República del Tahuantinsuyo. Sin duda uno de los libros más experimentales del conocido poeta peruano.

3745 Verástegui, Enrique. Terceto de Lima. Lima: Milla Batres Editorial, 1992. 218 p.

Libro que reúne tres novelas cortas de este importante poeta de la generación del 70. Los tres textos, "Teorema del Anarquista Ilustrado," "Retrato de Pareja con Pandilla de Primavera" y "Ensayo sobre la Pasión Andina" tienen como protagonistas a una generación de jóvenes intelectuales, probablemente las del mismo Verástegui, que se entregan a la vida bohemia. Lima y su cambiante identidad es el escenario de las aventuras de estos personajes que expresan una existencia marcada por la frustración y el desencanto.

3746 Zavaleta, Carlos Eduardo. Niebla cerrada. Lima: Lluvia Editores, 1995. 1 v.

Nueva edición de un volumen de cuentos publicado por primera vez en 1970. Este libro forma parte de los cuentos completos de este prolífico narrador, perteneciente a la generación del 50. Además de los tres relatos que aquí se incluyen, esta edición lleva un amplio prólogo del autor, titulado "Autobiografía fugaz," que le permite al lector situarse en el contexto histórico en el que se inscribe el trabajo ensayístico y narrativo del escritor.

3747 Zavaleta, Carlos Eduardo. El padre del tigre: cuentos completos. Lima: Lluvia Editores, 1993. 196 p.

Noveno libro de cuentos de este prolífico narrador, perteneciente a la generación del 50. Este volumen incluye 11 cuentos, escritos en su mayoría entre 1988–90. Muchos de ellos están situados en ciudades extranjeras (La Paz, Londres, Madrid) para destacar el tema de la incomunicación en un espacio cultural ajeno. Otros temas son el terrorismo, la educación sentimental, la inquietud política y la evocación juvenil en la Lima de los años 50.

Venezuela

3748 Agudo Freytes, Raúl. Miguel de Buría. Caracas: Alfadil Ediciones, 1991. 101 p. (Col. Orinoco; 40)

Agudo Freytes (b. 1914) is not well

known in the Venezuelan literary world because his publications have been primarily in the social sciences. *Miguel de Buría*, a historical novel using all conventions of 19th-century fiction, is set in 16th-century Nueva Andalucía during the reign of Charles V; it includes historical characters from the colonial oligarchy. Discovery of gold on the shores of the Buría River attracts conquerors to the region and an African character named Miguel organizes a rebellion, causing the arrival of troops from Spain. Good plot and dramatic ending.

3749 Arribas, Carlos. No pidamos la luna: fotogramas imposibles. Caracas: Monte Avila Editores Latinoamericana, 1993. 142 p. (Col. Las Formas del fuego. Narrativa)

This volume of 10 stories is the first by this young Venezuelan writer (b. 1958). His fictions rewrite motifs from films and his characters are movie figures such as Tarzan, Rita Hayworth, Rock Hudson, and James Dean. Result is a postmodern and entertaining playing with movie clichés.

3750 Balza, José. Ejercicios narrativos. México: Coordinación de Difusión Cultural, Dirección de Literatura, UNAM, 1992. 167 p. (Textos de difusión cultural. Serie Rayuela internacional)

In the vein of several postmodern writers affected by poststructuralist theories of intertextuality, Balza's "narrative exercises" consist of writing and rewriting his own previously published texts and those of others. Balza, who is always experimental, pushing the limits of the written word, is clearly aware of the canon and the experiments that precede him, for his writing echoes both. Interesting book includes 24 short and innovative fictional pieces.

3751 Balza, José. Tres ejercicios narrativos: *Marzo anterior; Largo; Setecientas palmeras plantadas en el mismo lugar.* Prólogo de Víctor Bravo. Caracas: Monte Avila Editores, 1992. 335 p. (Continentes)

In the less experimental period of his early career, Balza published his first novels under the titles of *Marzo anterior* (1965), *Largo* (1968), and *Setecientas palmeras plantadas en el mismo lugar* (1974). These three texts can now be read as innovative fiction. They refer back to Balza's home region of the Venezuelan Delta and offer a reflection on the city, eroticism, death, and history. Balza's fragmented subjects and fluid language reveal a postmodern aesthetic. Important volume for the development of modern and postmodern fiction in Venezuela.

3752 Carrera, Gustavo Luis. Cuentos. Selección y prólogo de Luis Barrera Linares. Caracas: Monte Avila Editores Latinoamericana, 1992. 176 p. (Continentes)

Selection of Carrera's best stories. Carrera began as a writer of social protest literature in the 1960s, and his short stories have evolved over the years. He identifies with Poe, Chekhov, Quiroga, and Cortázar. These 14 stories, well written in the traditional molds of Poe and Quiroga, are set in the Venezuelan llanos or his hometown of Cumaná. Anthology confirms artistry of Carrera as Venezuela's modern-day Horacio Quiroga.

3753 Casanova, Eduardo. La noche de Abel. Caracas: Monte Avila Editores, 1991. 118 p. (Continentes)

Author of five novels, short stories, essays, and theater, Casanova is one of numerous contemporary Venezuelan writers interested primarily in rewriting history. The novel's historical setting is the early-19th-century struggle for independence with all accompanying violence and chaos. José Antonio de Sucre, Simón Bolivar, and other independence fighters are all central to the novel, and speak in lengthy dialogues. Most dialogue concerns nationhood; most action centers on military movements of characters facing death. Casanova is a very conventional writer of historical novels.

3754 Díaz Sánchez, Ramón *et al.* Narradores de *El Nacional*, 1946–1992. Prólogo de Domingo Miliani. Edición de Antonio Bastardo. Caracas: Monte Avila Editores Latinoamericana, 1992. 551 p. (Continentes)

Since 1946, the Venezuelan newspaper *El Nacional* has held a national short story contest and awarded prizes to some of the most accomplished contemporary fiction writers in Venezuela. Here Bastardo has compiled 48 of the winning stories. Authors include Laura Antillano, Igor Delgado Senior, Ramón Díaz Sánchez, Angel Gustavo Infante, Humberto Mata, Guillermo Meneses, Carlos Noguera, Ednodio Quintero, Ana Teresa Torres, and Arturo Uslar Pietri.

3755 Garmendia, Salvador. El Capitán Kid: novela. 1. ed. venezolana. Caracas: Grijalbo, 1988. 273 p. (Cantaclaro)

Garmendia has published much serious and sober fiction, usually dealing with characters suffering anguish in the town of Altagracia. Here he ventures into the fantasy world of childhood memories and children's literature, although this work is addressed to adults. Characters move in and out of this fantasy world and Altagracia. This is one of Garmendia's better novels and, like some of his later writing, it is written in a light and colloquial style.

3756 Herrera Luque, Francisco J. 1998. Prólogo de Alexis Márquez Rodríguez. 1ra. ed. venezolana. Caracas: Grijalbo, 1992. 181 p. (Col. La tuna de oro)

Herrera Luque (1927–91) was a Venezuelan psychiatrist who published three volumes of essays and six novels, most analyzing and reconsidering national history and national identity. Found after his death and written towards the end of his life, *1998* is a political novel that critic Alexis Márquez Rodríguez identifies as *novela de política ficción.* Indeed, the plot revolves around political intrigues, with virtually no characterization or concern over style. Nevertheless, this entertaining book correctly predicts much of the region's politics in the 1990s.

3757 Infante, Angel Gustavo. Yo soy la rumba. 1ra. ed. venezolana. Caracas: Grijalbo; Mondadori, 1992. 141 p. (Col. La Tuna de oro)

Infante's first novel is in line with Francisco Massiani's fiction and the Mexican *Onda* in its emphasis on youth and the young subculture of American rock and Caribbean music. Divided into two parts, the novel consists of brief anecdotes which hang together loosely and could be read as short stories emphasizing the 1960–70s. Nostalgic and entertaining book which uses very conventional language for this type of fiction. One of Venezuela's promising young writers.

3758 Massiani, Francisco. Relatos. Prólogo Carlos Noguera. Caracas: Monte Avila Editores, 1991. 214 p.: bibl., ill. (Continentes)

Massiani has dedicated an entire career to writing about adolescent themes, both in his novels and short stories. This volume contains stories originally published under titles

Las primeras hojas de la noche (1970) and *El llanero solitario tiene la cabeza pelada como un cepillo de dientes* (1975) (see *HLAS 40: 6795*). Almost all deal with themes of rites of passage and are written in a simple, direct, and often colloquial style that characterizes Massiani's fiction. Many also have a touch of humor arising from either the situations or the language. Fine prologue offers analysis of both theme and technique.

3759 Mata Gil, Milagros. Mata el caracol. Caracas: Monte Avila Editores, 1992. 157 p. (Continentes)

Author of several volumes of fiction and essays on literature, Mata Gil is one of Venezuela's most prominent contemporary women writers. She generally follows the innovative path of her mentor José Balza. In this novel, one of the author's most experimental texts, Eloísa finds some notebooks at home and uses them to reconstruct family history and her father's struggle to escape death and time. Innovative basic structure alternates between monologues, letters, fragments of poems, and other texts. As in her previous texts, Mata Gil's main thematic interests are sexuality and power.

3760 Memoria y cuento: 30 años de narrativa venezolana, 1960–1990. Selección, presentación y notas de Luis Barrera Linares. Caracas: Contexto Audiovisual 3; Pomaire, 1992. 314 p.

Fine short story writer Barrera Linares has compiled a short fiction anthology of young Venezuelan writers. Brief introduction is followed by 31 stories by: Laura Antillano (b. 1950), José Balza (b. 1939), Luis Britto García (b. 1940), Igor Senior Delgado (b. 1942), Angel Gustavo Infante (b. 1959), Eduardo Liendo (b. 1941), Francisco Massiani (b. 1944), Milagros Mata Gil (b. 1950), Humberto Mata (b. 1949), Carlos Noguera (b. 1943), Ednodio Quintero (b. 1947), and Denzil Romero (b. 1939). Highly recommended.

3761 Meneses, Guillermo. Obras completas. v. 1, *Canción de negros; Campeones; El mestizo José Vargas.* Caracas: Ediciones La Casa de Bello, 1992. 1 v. (Col. Zona tórrida; 32. Obras completas)

The upsurge of recent critical studies on the Venezuelan writer Guillermo Meneses (1911–78; see items **3645** and **3646**) is just one indicator of his importance among contemporary Venezuelan writers. The republication of Meneses' complete works is another demonstration of his seminal importance. Vol. 1 of seven projected volumes includes three early novels that are revealing in the context of the author's total work, for in them we see Meneses the traditionalist and regionalist before his more innovative writings of the 1950s–60s. Vol. 1 indicates that future volumes will contain two more novels, short stories, theater, and numerous essays.

3762 Oropeza, José Napoleón. La guerra de los caracoles. Caracas: Monte Avila Editores, 1991. 108 p. (Continentes)

Fictional worlds of these eight stories are inhabited by the ghosts of Kafka, Faulkner, and Rulfo, who haunt characters whose human relationships are framed in intense inner worlds. Oropeza is an impressive stylist, using short sentences and effective language. He cites Marc Chagall's statement that "all our interior world is reality," and then proceeds to convince the reader of this truth. Born in 1950, Oropeza is a young but mature writer.

3763 Policastro, Cristina. La casa de las virtudes. 1ra. ed. venezolana. Caracas: Grijalbo Mondadori, 1992. 181 p. (Col. La tuna de oro)

Known in Venezuela as a journalist and critic since the mid-1980s, Policastro had several careers before discovering fiction writing. This first novel reveals all the technical sophistication one could expect from a veteran writer. Characters move in a literary world, but are not protected from confronting the difficulties of daily life and death. Policastro communicates a palpable excitement with the act of creation in this self-conscious and playful book. Perhaps slightly overwritten.

3764 Quintero, Ednodio. "Cabeza de Cabra" y otros relatos. Prólogo de Julio Miranda. Caracas: Monte Avila Editores Latinoamericana, 1993. 203 p. (Continentes)

Quintero teaches at the university level in Mérida, Venezuela, and began publishing fiction in the 1970s. Volume's 44 stories have been reorganized and rewritten since their original publication over a 15-year period. To these 44, the author adds the title story, "Cabeza de Cabra." These stories present tortured characters, erotic dream worlds, perverse actions, and black humor. Stories attest to Quintero's broad range of abilities with the short story form. Stories vary in length from just a few lines to short novelettes rich in intertextuality.

3765 Romero, Denzil. Grand tour: epístasis. Caracas: Alfadil; Barcelona: Laia, 1987. 354 p. (Col. Orinoco; 8)

Continuation of his novel La tragedia del Generalísimo, this work relates the Generalísimo's travels around Europe in the late-18th century. In 55 brief chapters (or segments), a modern voice directs the narrative in a second person tú to the general as he visits London and various parts of England, Rotterdam, several German cities, Vienna, and Prague. He engages the political and intellectual leaders of the period, including Alexander von Humboldt, in conversation. Fine, dense, erudite, and consistently well-written novel. Essayistic digressions are somewhat heavy handed at times.

3766 Romero, Denzil. Tonatio Castilán o un tal dios Sol. Caracas: Monte Avila Editores Latinoamericana, 1993. 198 p. (Continentes)

The historical novel has been very important in Latin America in recent years, and Romero is one of Venezuela's better historical novelists. Most of his novels are set in Venezuela, but this one takes place in Mexico. Romero recreates from his childhood the entire life of Don Pedro de Alvarado, called "Tonatio" (Son of the Sun) by the Mayas. A captain for Hernán Cortés, Alvarado later became the governor of Guatemala. Romero's explorations of Latin American identity demonstrate his fine knowledge of historical fact and his impressive use of language.

3767 Uslar Pietri, Arturo. Cuentos de la realidad mágica. Madrid: Narrativa Mondadori, 1992. 244 p.

A giant among Venezuelan writers, Uslar Pietri is often remembered outside of his homeland as the author of Las lanzas coloradas and other novels, rather than as a superb short story writer. This volume contains 21 of his best stories that originally appeared in Barrabás y otros relatos (1928), Red (1936), Treinta hombres y sus sombras (1949), and Pasos y pasajeros (1966). Valuable and timely publication.

Chile

JOSE PROMIS, *Professor of Latin American Literature and Literary Criticism, University of Arizona*

DURANTE LOS ULTIMOS AÑOS la producción narrativa se ha favorecido con la actividad de editoriales internacionales que han abierto oficinas en el país. La mayor difusión que por este medio pueden alcanzar los narradores chilenos principiantes y el reconocimiento que siguen obteniendo en el extranjero autores como José Donoso, Isabel Allende, Marcela Serrano, Ariel Dorfman y Antonio Skármeta son alicientes que influyen de manera positiva en los escritores jóvenes. A este ambiente propicio se agrega también la creación de una serie de estimulantes concursos literarios. Varios autores citados aquí han recibido galardones de este tipo: Ramón Díaz Eterovic (item **3775**), Antonio Gil (item **3779**), Jorge Guzmán (item **3783**) entre otros.

El exilio político sufrido por numerosos narradores chilenos ha iniciado un proceso de sedimentación literaria. La narrativa testimonial—manifestación dominante de dicho asunto hace unos años atrás—ha dejado paso a relatos en que el exilio es focalizado desde una perspectiva eminentemente artística que sin ignorar sus notas dramáticas de desarraigo, fracaso y desesperación, trata de iluminar aquellos aspectos no considerados en el discurso testimonial de fuerte perspectiva ideológica. *Cobro revertido*, de Leandro Urbina (item **3799**), constituye un excelente ejemplo de esta nueva manera de tratar el tema. Pero además, la experiencia del exilio ha producido también un mayor cosmopolitismo de la novela, tanto en lo que se refiere a sus temas y espacios (ver *La hija del mercader de Venecia* de Rodrigo Atria, item **3769**), como a la voluntad de ensayar formas génericas que hasta ahora eran poco usuales en Chile (ver *Nombre de torero* de Luis Sepúlveda (item **3796**).

El interés por formas narrativas novedosas debe ser justificado no sólo como una consecuencia del exilio, sino también como efecto de las circunstancias históricas vividas en Chile bajo el régimen militar. Es significativa, por ejemplo, la aparición de relatos policiales, como *Angeles y solitarios* de Ramón Díaz Eterovic (item **3775**), o de la llamada "narrativa negra," a que se adscriben los cuentos de Tomás Harris (item **3784**). Con estos relatos se pretende representar una atmósfera de opresión y oscuridad que muchos autores consideran que no ha desaparecido aún del espacio nacional.

La riqueza genérica que exhibe la prosa de ficción en los últimos tres años se comprueba también en la definitiva presencia de una narrativa femenina que propone una mirada alternativa a la literatura escrita por varones. Un relato de Lucía Guerra (item **3781**) representa bien esta visión descanonificadora y los cuentos de Andrea Maturana (item **3791**) ejemplifican la manera como las narradoras pertenecientes a promociones más jóvenes ejercen tal mirada. Con la publicación de *Antigua vida mía*, Marcela Serrano se sitúa como una de las más destacadas novelistas de esta tendencia (item **3797**). En *Paula*, Isabel Allende ofrece, por otra parte, un testimonio interesantísimo sobre la formación literaria de la narradora chilena más conocida nacional e internacionalmente (item **3768**).

La producción de los tres últimos años revela también un marcado interés por la llamada "nueva novela histórica," con la cual se pretende un doble objetivo: desacreditar la visión tradicional de la historia y proponer nuevas alternativas de interpretación llenando imaginariamente los espacios que el discurso histórico tradicional ha dejado vacíos. Las novelas de Gustavo Gil (item **3779**) y Eduardo Labarca (item **3785**) constituyen dos interesantes ejemplos de esta tendencia, pero su expresión artística más lograda es el relato *Ay mama Inés,* de Jorge Guzmán (item **3783**), que ofrece una interesantísima reinterpretación de los orígenes y el sentido de la nacionalidad chilena.

En la actividad llevada a cabo por autores de generaciones anteriores sobresalen la nueva edición de *Eloy,* de Carlos Droguett, una de las mejores novelas chilenas contemporáneas, cuyo texto ha de considerarse ahora definitivo ya que fue revisado y corregido por el propio autor (item **3777**); el Premio Nacional de Literatura 1994 otorgado al novelista, cuentista y ensayista Jorge Edwards (item **3805**); y la nueva novela de José Donoso, *Donde van a morir los elefantes* (item **3776**), que renueva algunas imágenes características de su mundo narrativo a la vez que continúa la reflexión sobre el género que ha iniciado en relatos anteriores. Vale anotar que esta misma preocupación hacia la teoría a través de la ficción está presente también en autores más jóvenes, como Darío Oses en *Machos tristes* (item **3792**) y Marco Antonio de la Parra en *La pérdida del tiempo* (item **3794**).

PROSE FICTION

3768 Allende, Isabel. Paula. Barcelona: Plaza & Janés, 1994. 365 p. (Ave fénix. Serie mayor; 23)

Relato de memorias que la autora escribió dirigiéndolo a su hija, quien permanecía en estado comatoso en un hospital español. Posee valor de testimonio y documento debido a las interesantes informaciones que entrega sobre aspectos biográficos, sobre la génesis y sobre determinados elementos del contenido de sus principales novelas.

3769 Atria, Rodrigo. La hija del mercader de Venecia. Santiago: Planeta, 1995. 228 p. (Biblioteca del sur)

Historia de las aventuras de dos mujeres italianas que viajan desde Venecia a Chile en el momento en que este país se independiza definitivamente del dominio español. Narrada con un lenguaje de inusual riqueza. Las peripecias de sus personajes permiten que el autor destruya el mito sarmientino que identificaba a la civilización con Europa y a la barbarie con América.

3770 Cerda, Carlos. Morir en Berlín. Santiago: Planeta, 1993. 250 p. (Biblioteca del sur)

Historia sobre las vicisitudes, angustias y esperanzas de los exiliados chilenos en Berlín. El narrador descubre la presencia de una segunda frontera, esta vez invisible, que los sigue separando aun lejos de su patria. Un lenguaje excelentemente trabajado colabora a crear la atmósfera de opresión que los persigue.

3771 Cerda, Carlos. Primer tiempo. Santiago: Editorial Andrés Bello, 1995. 203 p.

Se reúnen cuentos del autor que habían aparecido en diversas revistas y antologías publicadas fuera de Chile. Relatos de excelente factura narrativa que lo demuestran como uno de los más interesantes narradores chilenos actuales.

Ciencia y cultura en Chile. See item **5.**

3772 Cosas del mar y otros relatos. Santiago?: Narradores Novísimos; Municipalidad de El Bosque, 1993. 86 p.

Selección de los mejores cuentos presentados al concurso nacional Eusebio Lillo, de la Municipalidad de El Bosque en Santiago. Permite conocer a algunos de los novísimos cuentistas chilenos.

3773 Couve, Adolfo. La comedia del arte. Santiago: Planeta, 1995. 154 p. (Biblioteca del sur)

Novela de sobresalientes valores estilísticos que gira en torno a una temática que siempre ha obsesionado al autor: la definición y la función del arte, así como la condición y la responsabilidad que compete desempeñar al artista en su tiempo.

3774 Cuentos con *walkman*. Edición de Alberto Fuguet y Sergio Gómez. Santiago: Planeta, 1993. 287 p. (Biblioteca del sur)

Excelente selección de cuentos de autores cuyas edades fluctúan entre 17–25 años. Los relatos configuran la visión de mundo característica de la más reciente generación de escritores chilenos. Trae un prólogo con interesantes informaciones sobre esta misma promoción.

3775 Díaz Eterović, Ramón. Angeles y solitarios. Santiago: Planeta, 1995. 277 p. (Biblioteca del sur)

En 1995 recibió el primer premio del concurso de novela inédita del Consejo Nacional del Libro y la Cultura con el título *Morir de madrugada*. Relato en que la estructura de la novela policial se utiliza con fines testimoniales: mostrar las fisuras y lacras que caracterizan a la sociedad donde el delito se comete.

3776 Donoso, José. Dónde van a morir los elefantes. Madrid: Santillana, 1995. 409 p. (Alfaguara)

Novela supuestamente escrita por Gustavo Zuleta, profesor chileno contratado en una universidad del medioeste norteamericano. Jugar con la credulidad del lector permite que Donoso proyecte su visión paródica del mundo académico estadounidense. Sin duda, una de las mejores novelas del período que además ratifica nuevamente a su autor como el mejor narrador chileno contemporáneo.

3777 Droguett, Carlos. Eloy. Prólogo de Alain Sicard. Santiago: Editorial Universitaria, 1993. 196 p. (Col. Los contemporáneos)

Edición importantísima para los estudiosos de Droguett debido a que el propio autor corrigió el texto de la novela publicada en 1967 por la misma Editorial Universitaria. Debe ser considerada por lo tanto la edición definitiva de una de las más importantes novelas chilenas contemporáneas.

3778 Fuguet, Alberto. Por favor, rebobinar. Santiago: Planeta, 1994. 308 p. (Biblioteca del sur)

Novela que representa muy bien la temática de la mirada hacia el pasado y la de la búsqueda de las raíces que se reitera significativamente en las generaciones de narradores chilenos más jóvenes, y que utilizan como recurso para explicar las condiciones del presente.

3779 Gil, Antonio. Hijo de mí. Santiago: Editorial Los Andes, 1992. 103 p. (Serie la Otra narrativa)

Novela ganadora del primer concurso de novelistas jóvenes de Editorial Los Andes.

El trágico desenlace de las relaciones entre los primeros conquistadores del Perú es relatada por el mismo Diego de Almagro mientras espera su ajusticiamiento. Buen exponente chileno de la llamada "nueva novela histórica hispanoamericana."

3780 Gómez, Sergio. Adiós, Carlos Marx, nos vemos en el cielo. Santiago: Planeta, 1992. 150 p. (Biblioteca del sur)

Cuentos de excelente factura literaria que giran en torno al motivo del fracaso y la imposibilidad de entender circunstancias incomprensibles. Un lenguaje artísticamente muy bien construído reproduce el habla coloquial de una generación joven, confusa y desorientada. El autor se muestra como uno de los mejores narradores de la última promoción.

3781 Guerra-Cunningham, Lucía. Muñeca brava. Caracas: Monte Avila Editores Latinoamericana, 1993. 159 p. (Continentes)

Con un estilo de notable intensidad, se relata desde un punto de vista femenino la historia de tres mujeres pertenecientes al mundo de la prostitución en un Chile dominado por el régimen militar. La novela representa adecuadamente algunas de las preocupaciones de la actual literatura chilena escrita por mujeres.

3782 Gumucio, Rafael. Invierno en la torre. Santiago: Planeta, 1995. 167 p. (Biblioteca del sur)

Cuentos que tienen una ubicación común y una temática compartida: sus historias transcurren en un mismo edificio de apartamentos en Santiago y muestran la irrupción inesperada de la violencia que destruye una existencia cotidiana aparentemente inalterable e insípida. Una metáfora de la forma como muchos narradores chilenos jóvenes consideran el pasado inmediato de su país.

3783 Guzmán, Jorge. Ay mamá Inés: crónica testimonial. Santiago: Editorial Andrés Bello, 1993. 242 p.

Premio Novela Ilustre Municipalidad de Santiago 1994. Este relato junto con el de José Donoso (item **3776**) constituyen las dos mejores novelas publicadas entre 1993–95. Identificada con la tendencia de la "nueva novela histórica" (ver también items **3779** and **3785**) su narrador mira la realidad desde la perspectiva de Inés de Suárez, compañera del conquistador español Pedro de Valdivia, quien fundara Santiago a mediados del siglo XVI. Gracias a dicho recurso narrativo, el texto ofrece una descanonificación de los discursos históricos tradicionales y, a la vez, instaura una nueva manera de interpretar los cimientos de una psicología nacional.

3784 Harris, Tomás. Historia personal del miedo. Santiago: Planeta, 1994. 187 p.

Excelente volumen de cuentos cuya característica común es la creación de una atmósfera inusual donde los personajes viven situaciones límites y delirantes. Es un buen ejemplo de los esfuerzos que llevan a cabo los narradores jóvenes para ensayar novedosas perspectivas sobre la realidad nacional.

Jodorowsky, Alexandro. Sombras al mediodía. See item **3497.**

3785 Labarca Goddard, Eduardo. Butamalón. Madrid: Anaya & M. Muchnik, 1994. 417 p. (Analectas)

El proceso de traducir un libro sobre Juan Barba, misionero de la época de Felipe II, permite que se introduzca un segundo nivel temporal donde se desarrolla una visión compleja y riquísima de la conquista española a través de un excelente lenguaje narrativo.

3786 López-Aliaga Roncagliolo, Luis. Cuestión de astronomía. Santiago: Grijalbo Mondadori, 1995. 154 p. (Literatura Mondadori)

Premio Consejo Nacional del Libro, 1995, Cuentos Inéditos. Volumen que anuncia la aparición de un narrador de excelentes posibilidades. Todos los cuentos giran en torno a motivos de soledad, fracaso, incomunicación, destino funesto. Sus narradores, no obstante, vencen a la derrota mediante un lenguaje cuyo optimismo vital se traduce en ironía y parodia de las experiencias negativas.

3787 Marchant, Reinaldo Edmundo et al. Jóvenes narradores chilenos: antología. Recopilación y prólogo de Luis R. Gutiérrez Infante. Santiago: Red Internacional del Libro, 1992. 130 p.

Interesante selección de cuentos escritos por narradores y narradoras nacidos en la década de los años 50.

3788 Marín, Germán. Círculo vicioso. Santiago: Planeta, 1994. 385 p.: bibl. (Biblioteca del sur. Historia de una absolución familiar)

Primer volumen de la trilogía *Historia de una absolución familiar.* Relato de fuerte experimentalismo narrativo donde se enmarcan diferentes niveles discursivos para proponer una visión dinámica del destino de dos familias, chilena una e italiana otra, marcadas por fuertes motivaciones dramáticas. Debe ser considerada entre las mejores novelas publicadas después de 1993. Veáse también item **3789.**

3789 Marín, Germán. El Palacio de la Risa. Santiago: Planeta, 1995. 198 p. (Biblioteca del sur)

Formado por dos relatos que indagan y dramáticamente sacan a luz aspectos de la violencia vivida en Chile durante los últimos 20 años. Veáse también **3788.**

3790 Matamala, Tito. Hoy recuerdo la tarde en que le vendí mi alma al diablo (era miércoles y llovía elefantes). Santiago: Mondadori; Grijalbo Mondadori, 1995. 132 p.: ill. (Literatura Mondadori)

Premio de Novela 1995 "Revista de Libros El Mercurio." Relato breve y entretenido cuya historia parodia los grandes viajes míticos occidentales, narrada en un lenguaje que permanentemente estimula la atención del lector con imágenes desusadas, novedosas las más de ellas, todas de excelente factura literaria. Anuncia a su autor como una figura que puede llegar a ser importante en la narrativa chilena futura.

3791 Maturana, Andrea. (Des)encuentros (des)esperados. Santiago: Editorial Los Andes, 1992. 98 p. (Serie La Otra narrativa)

Relatos de asunto erótico inusuales por el tono y la pasión que comunican sus voces narrativas. Giran en torno al motivo que se anuncia en el título: fracasados y dolorosos esfuerzos por establecer vínculos sentimentales con el otro. Volumen que muestra bien uno de los propósitos de las escritoras chilenas actuales: una alternativa a la manera como la relación hombre-mujer ha sido literariamente representada por la mirada masculina.

3792 Oses, Darío. Machos tristes. Santiago: Planeta, 1992. 260 p. (Biblioteca del sur)

El autor utiliza la técnica narrativa del "monogatari," donde narrador y lector se confunden entre sí y con sus personajes, para relatar la historia de dos individuos que pudieran ser sólo dos aspectos de una misma personalidad escindida, cuyas ideologías constituyen los extremos de la realidad chilena actual. Se crea así una imagen proteica de la sociedad donde desorientación y confusión son sus notas más características.

3793 Oses, Darío. El viaducto. Santiago: Planeta, 1994. 282 p. (Biblioteca del sur)
Premio Academia Chilena de la Lengua 1995. La historia de la existencia frustrada de un individuo permite recrear dos tiempos paralelos: la década de los años 70 y la presidencia de José Manuel Balmaceda que culminó con la revolución de 1891 y la muerte del mandatario. Se descubre así la homología entre ambos tiempos como épocas de expectativas frustradas, dolor y desgarro.

3794 Parra, Marco Antonio de la. La pérdida del tiempo. Santiago: Editorial Sudamericana, 1994. 155 p.
El proceso de escribir una novela conduce al narrador a reflexionar sobre la novela chilena actual a través de un discurso en que se ensayan diferentes modalidades narrativas. Es un texto interesante para conocer la percepción que uno de los más populares narradores actuales tiene sobre las posibilidades del género en Chile.

3795 Rivera Letelier, Hernán. La Reina Isabel cantaba rancheras. Santiago: Planeta, 1994. 231 p. (Biblioteca del sur)
Premio de Novela 1994 del Consejo Nacional del Libro y la Lectura. Extraordinaria visión del mundo de la pampa salitrera contemplada desde una perspectiva eminentemente artística que establece un contrapunto con la forma en que la novela social había considerado este tema.

3796 Sepúlveda, Luis. Nombre de torero. Barcelona: Tusquets Editores, 1994. 223 p. (Col. Andanzas; 220)
El autor utiliza la forma de la novela de persecución y suspenso (*thriller*) para relatar la historia de un acoso cuyos orígenes se encuentran en la Alemania nazi y cuyo desenlace tiene lugar en la Patagonia chilena. Esta novela ofrece una estructura narrativa que se ha ensayado esporádicamente en la literatura nacional.

3797 Serrano, Marcela. Antigua vida mía. México: Alfaguara, 1995. 371 p.
Utilizando los escritos de una amiga, la narradora cuenta una historia que viene a ser la suya propia. A partir de esta situación, su discurso transparenta otras voces femeninas que contribuyen a configurar la imagen de los conflictos de la mujer en el mundo contemporáneo, mostrándolos también como expresión de la experiencia femenina a través del tiempo. Este relato confirma a su autora como una de las más importantes novelistas chilenas actuales.

3798 Tejeda, Guillermo. La gente no me gusta. Santiago: Editorial Los Andes, 1994? 269 p. (Serie La otra narrativa)
Relato donde el protagonista busca sus raíces y con ellas su lugar en el mundo. Representa una de las tendencia narrativas características de la actual novela chilena, especialmente de las escritas por autores más jóvenes: el reencuentro consigo mismo.

3799 Urbina, José Leandro. Cobro revertido. Santiago: Planeta, 1992. 200 p. (Biblioteca del sur)
La historia de un refugiado político chileno en Canadá permite que el narrador interprete el exilio como expresión actualizada de la condición trágica universal. El discurso adquiere fundamentos míticos y se desarrolla circularmente. El reiterado tema del exilio adquiere aquí una imagen novedosa e inusual.

3800 Vásquez, Ana. Mi amiga Chantal. Barcelona: Editorial Lumen, 1991. 271 p. (Palabra menor; 85)
El recuerdo de su amistad con Chantal, una singularísima profesora francesa que trabaja en Santiago durante los años previos a 1973, y de la apasionada relación destructiva entre ésta y su alumno Edgardo, permiten a la narradora desarrollar un discurso de forma testimonial que actualiza las tensiones y conflictos que se vivieron durante ese período.

LITERARY CRITICISM AND HISTORY

3801 Alegría, Fernando. La novela chilena del exilio interior. (*Rev. Chil. Lit.*, 42, 1993, p. 13–17)
Observaciones críticas sobre tres novelistas chilenos: Sergio Marras, Ana Vásquez y Antonio Montero Abt.

3802 Barraza, Eduardo. El discurso paratextual en la narrativa neorrealista de Chile. (*Estud. Filol.*, 28, 1993, p. 33–43)

Análisis de las principales técnicas narrativas con que los autores de la generación chilena de 1938 disfrazaban el carácter ficticio de su discurso, dándole la apariencia de un texto documental.

3803 Cánovas, Rodrigo. Siete ciudades, siete destinos: apuntes sobre la novela chilena actual. (*Acta Lit.*, 19, 1994, p. 17–37)

Análisis de la manera como la ciudad de Santiago es percibida y configurada en novelas representativas de José Donoso, Jorge Edwards y cinco narradores pertenecientes a promociones posteriores. El autor plantea que existe una continuidad circular entre temas y formas retóricas. Lenguaje, sujeto y ciudad constituyen así una *figura diagramática*.

3804 Díaz Arrieta, Hernán. Alone y los Premios Nacionales de Literatura. Recopilación y selección de Pedro Pablo Zegers B. Santiago: Dirección de Bibliotecas, Archivos y Museos, Centro de Investigaciones Diego Barros Arana, 1992. 338 p.: bibl., ill. (Escritores de Chile; 1)

Conjunto de artículos críticos sobre autores chilenos que han recibido el Premio Nacional de Literatura, publicados en el periódico *El Mercurio* por el más famoso crítico literario chileno, Hernán Díaz Arrieta (Alone). Contiene varios artículos sobre José Donoso, Enrique Campos Menéndez, Marcela Paz, Edgardo Garrido Merino, Francisco Coloane y otros narradores anteriores.

3805 Edwards, Jorge. El whisky de los poetas. Santiago: Editorial Universitaria, 1994. 262 p. (Col. Letras de América)

Conjunto de amenísimas crónicas que giran en torno a diferentes temas, pero destacándose siempre el interés por conceptualizar la función de la literatura actual, la responsabilidad del autor y la relación entre la literatura y su contexto extraliterario.

3806 Fernández Fraile, Maximino. Historia de la literatura chilena. v. 1–2. Santiago: Editorial Salesiana, 1994. 2 v. (752 p.): bibl., ill., indexes, maps.

Obra importante de ser considerada porque desde que el escritor Manuel Rojas publicó su *Historia breve de la literatura chilena* (Santiago: Zig-Zag, 1964), nadie se había

preocupado de escribir una historia actualizada de las letras nacionales. En sus capítulos dedicados a la narrativa chilena contemporánea ofrece útiles panoramas y buena información sobre narradores actuales.

3807 Lértora, Juan Carlos. Una poética de literatura menor: la narrativa de Diamela Eltit. Santiago: Para Textos/Editorial Cuarto Propio, 1993. 195 p.: bibl. (Serie Ensayo)

Conjunto interesante y útil de ensayos y artículos críticos sobre la narrativa de Diamela Eltit.

3808 Magnarelli, Sharon. Understanding José Donoso. Columbia: Univ. of South Carolina Press, 1993. 192 p.: bibl., index. (Understanding modern European and Latin American literature)

Interesante y bien presentada introducción a la narrativa de José Donoso.

3809 Promis Ojeda, José. La novela chilena del último siglo. Santiago: Editorial La Noria, 1993. 273 p.: bibl.

En 14 capítulos se analizan los vínculos entre relato y referente y se recorre cronológicamente la trayectoria de la ficción chilena en este siglo. [M.L. Bastos]

3810 Promis Ojeda, José. Programas narrativos de la novela chilena en el siglo XX. (*Rev. Iberoam.*, 60:168/169, enero/julio 1994, p. 925–933)

Estudio sobre los diversos programas narrativos que se han sucedido en Chile durante el siglo XX y que originan las distintas estructuras históricas que ha asumido el género "novela" durante este período.

3811 Román-Lagunas, Jorge. The Chilean novel: a critical study of its secondary sources and a bibliography. Metuchen, N.J.: Scarecrow Press, 1994. 561 p.: bibl., index.

La bibliografía más ambiciosa e importante publicada sobre la novela chilena en los últimos años. En tres partes: 1) análisis crítico de los estudios generales sobre la novela chilena: bibliografías anteriores, libros, estudios colectivos, tesis doctorales y artículos críticos; 2) fuentes de referencia sobre las generaciones de 1842, 1938 y 1950; y 3) bibliografías críticas sobre los principales novelistas chilenos de los siglos XIX y XX. Un libro indispensable para los estudiosos del tema.

River Plate Countries

MARIA LUISA BASTOS, *Professor of Spanish, Lehman College and the Graduate School, City University of New York*

MAGDALENA GARCIA PINTO, *Associate Professor of Spanish and Director of Women's Studies, University of Missouri*

MARIA CRISTINA GUIÑAZU, *Associate Professor of Spanish, Lehman College, City University of New York*

ARGENTINA

EN ESTE VOLUMEN se reseñan relatos publicados entre los años finales de la década de 1980 y la de 1994. Superada la era del terror institucionalizado, a diferencia de las narraciones del período anterior, la ficción de este lapso se puede permitir una actitud menos documental, *prima facie* más puramente literaria por así decirlo. Perduran aún aquellas tendencias en *El Dock* de Matilde Sánchez (item **3844**) y en *Redondeces* de Norberto Firpo (item **3827**), novelas que acusan el terrorismo de Estado. Por otra parte, las novelas de Sergio Chejfec (item **3823**), Osvaldo Soriano (items **3845** y **3846**) y Jorge Torres Zavaleta (item **3847**) notan la inestabilidad actual y cuestionan la falta de pautas tanto políticas como sociales con miras al futuro. Pertenecen a otra categoría las novelas de Noé Jitrik (item **3832**) y Luisa Peluffo (item **3839**). Ambas narrativas reflexionan sobre el proceso de la escritura y exploran las relaciones entre texto, voz narrativa y autor/a.

Entre los libros recibidos, predominan los cuentos, más o menos breves, por sobre una producción relativamente escasa de novelas. Merecen destacarse, por la estructura cuidada, la imaginación y el sentido del equilibrio del relato los textos de Vlady Kociancich (item **3833**) y César Aira (items **3814, 3812, 3815** y **3813**). En otra tónica, el volumen de Luisa Valenzuela recoge una colección de parodias concebidas con ironía y talento narrativo (item **3849**). También hay que notar por su economía expresiva, diversidad y coherencia los relatos de carácter intimista de Marta Nos (item **3838**) y de Sylvia Iparraguirre (item **3831**).

Se podría afirmar, simplificando, que la democratización de este fin de siglo está ampliamente representada en la ficción. O, expresado de otra manera: es como si finalmente hubiese cuajado, para expandirse, la renovación iniciada por Roberto Arlt y perfeccionada por Cortázar, Bioy y Puig. Esto significa que los personajes de la pequeña clase media no funcionan como meros elementos circunstanciales, guiños al lector, sino como datos inmediatos, funcionales, de la trama. Es decir: por pintorescos, extravagantes o vulnerables que sean, los personajes son tomados en serio. Con todo, esa naturalidad, por así llamarla, a veces se puede atribuir a una especie de alarde, o impostación, comparable al que tradicionalmente se atribuye a la literatura de minorías: es decir, la ficción va dirigida a quienes entienden el alcance de matices y alusiones. En el otro extremo, también se tiene la impresión de que algunos autores no tienen en cuenta que el texto escrito no es, no puede ser, una mera transposición de lo oral porque la fluidez narrativa tiene sus exigencias propias, tan diferentes de las de la conversación como de las de la exposición formal o académica. Sería quizás posible atribuir a ese desajuste las notorias y abundantes incorrecciones de sintaxis; más desconcertantes resultan los errores de ortografía a los que se agregan las numerosas erratas. En todo caso, se trata de índices perturbadores de una paradoja: el empobrecimiento (en más de un sentido) de la hipertrofiada industria literaria argentina. [MLB and MCG]

PARAGUAY

Con *Contravida* y *El Fiscal* (items **3855** y **3856**), la narrativa de Roa Bastos encabeza la producción de este bienio en la producción literaria del Paraguay. Notamos marcado interés por la indagación histórica en la elaboración de la narrativa paraguaya. En particular, debemos destacar una nueva edición de los cuentos de Helio Vera, titulado *Angola y otros cuentos* (item **3858**), que representa una búsqueda del ancestro africano en este país sudamericano. [MGP]

URUGUAY

Este período fue testigo de la desaparición del gran uruguayo Juan Carlos Onetti el 30 de mayo de 1994, quien hizo conocer la literatura de su país en el dominio internacional. Recordemos que su obra comenzó a ser conocida fuera del Uruguay a principios de la década del 70, cuando las editoriales Monte Avila de Caracas y Corregidor de Buenos Aires publicaron sus *Novelas cortas* y sus *Cuentos completos* respectivamente. Posteriormente, la editorial española Aguilar publicó sus *Obras completas* en México. En 1974 fue arrestado por el gobierno uruguayo a raíz de haber aceptado ser jurado de un concurso de cuentos patrocinado por el semanario *Marcha*, con el cual había declarado su discrepancia públicamente. Fue encarcelado varios meses en una celda y después internado en el Hospital Etchepare para enfermos mentales de siniestra reputación. Posteriormente pudo llegar a España, donde fue tratado con generosidad. Allí vivió 20 años en sosiego, calma, y seguridad; allí se le concedió el prestigioso Premio Cervantes. No volvió nunca más a su país ni cuando fue ganador del Premio Nacional de Letras ni en muchas otras ocasiones en que fue invitado por sus compatriotas. Su visión del ser humano en fracaso casi diríamos profetizó la catastrófica situación de su país y de muchos otros en el continente americano. En su exilio español este escritor no comprometido con la política ejerció significativa gravitación en las letras hispanas.

En este mismo año de 1994, el 8 de marzo, el Uruguay y las letras continentales también perdieron a otra grande creadora, Armonía Somers. Sin embargo, la escritura de ficción en el Uruguay continúa produciendo obras interesantes. Destacamos a propósito de la obra de Onetti, el estudio de Elena M. Martínez, *Onetti: estrategias textuales y operaciones del lector* (item **3887**). En este período, el siempre prolífico Mario Benedetti ha publicado *Despistes y franquezas* (item **3861**) y *Perplejidades de fin de siglo* (item **3863**) a cargo de la Editorial Alfaguara y *Cuentos completos: 1947–1994* (item **3860**) a cargo de Seix Barral. [MGP]

PROSE FICTION
Argentina

3812 Aira, César. El bautismo: novela. Buenos Aires: Grupo Editor Latinoamericano, 1991. 154 p. (Col. Escritura de hoy)

En un refugio precario en medio del campo, una tormenta como de juicio final reúne a un sacerdote compulsivamente especulativo con un joven a quien había bautizado 30 años atrás. El protagonista, en sostenido y paradójico alarde de lucidez, postula el predominio del azar sobre los recursos del intelecto. [MLB]

3813 Aira, César. La costurera y el viento. Rosario, Argentina: B. Viterbo Editora, 1994. 127 p. (Ficciones)

Relato vertiginoso en que el viento, transformado en personaje, es metáfora del olvido. El subtexto abunda en alusiones y referencias a la presumiblemente innata superficialidad de la mujer. [MLB]

3814 Aira, César. Embalse. Buenos Aires: Emecé Editores, 1992. 272 p. (Escritores argentinos)

La novela que en sus comienzos explora lo extraño y lo absurdo derivados de situaciones cotidianas cambia de tono y se transforma en un relato de ciencia ficción que culmina en el horror. Alude a gran variedad de temas que no logran desarrollo. [MCG]

3815 Aira, César. La guerra de los gimnasios. Buenos Aires: Emecé Editores, 1993. 177 p. (Escritores argentinos)

La rivalidad entre instituciones similares se alimenta de las mitologías y las mezquindades de jóvenes de la pequeña burguesía en un barrio popular de Buenos Aires. La escritura, rigurosa, articulada y sin resquicios, da cuenta del impulso de lo irracional. Es refrescante el tono de burla por el celo deportivo. [MLB]

3816 Arcidiácono, Carlos. La vidente no tenía nada que ver. Buenos Aires: Editorial Atlántida, 1993. 309 p. (Voces del Plata)

Dos registros narrativos estructuran la novela: la narración de la primera parte y la larga serie de "Referencias" de la segunda. El diálogo que se establece entre ambas sugiere reflexiones heteróclitas—sobre literatura, erotismo, tecnología e historia, así como comentarios humorísticos. Las observaciones agudas pierden a veces fuerza en el collage resultante. [MCG]

3817 Arlt, Roberto. El jorobadito; Aguafuertes porteñas; El criador de gorilas: selección. Buenos Aires: Ediciones Colihue, 1993. 156 p.: ill. (Col. literaria LYC—leer y crear; 103)

Antología de relatos cortos anteriormente publicados útil para cursos de iniciación a los estudios literarios. Incluye una introducción con datos biográficos sobre el autor y ejercicios prácticos preparados por María C. Arostegui y Ofelia Mindlin. [MCG]

3818 Azcona Cranwell, Elizabeth. La mordedura. Buenos Aires: Editorial Atlántida, 1993. 205 p. (Voces del Plata)

Once cuentos, cuyos protagonistas notablemente especulativos consiguen desentrañar sus motivaciones infraconcientes. Los temas van desde la angustia existencial hasta la imposibilidad, o el tabú, del idilio entre un preadolescente y una mujer madura. [MLB]

3819 Brailovsky, Antonio Elio. Esta maldita lujuria. Buenos Aires: Planeta, 1992. 188 p. (Biblioteca del sur)

Supuestas cartas de un colonizador de la Patagonia al Virrey, obviamente respalda-das en una minuciosa investigación y en un detallado trabajo de "reconstrucción." Este texto, extremadamente artificial, escrito en un español que ni es el nuestro ni reproduce o imita el del siglo XVIII, recibió el premio Casa de las Américas. [MLB]

3820 Calvetti, Jorge. Escrito en la tierra. Buenos Aires: Grupo Editor Latinoamericano; Distribuidor exclusivo, Emecé Editores, 1993. 139 p. (Col. Escritura de hoy)

Relatos breves de tono autobiográfico, que tienen como escenario el noroeste argentino. [MLB]

3821 Caparrós, Martín. Larga distancia. Buenos Aires: Planeta, 1992. 254 p. (Biblioteca del sur. Crónicas)

Recopilación de crónicas y relatos de viaje. Saludablemente, personajes y lugares son vistos sin reverencia convencional. [MLB]

3822 Catania, Carlos. La mutiladora. Santa Fe, Argentina: Ediciones Colmegna, 1993. 121 p.

Diez relatos muy originales. Catania crea situaciones fantásticas en las que la perversidad, el delirio, el misterio y la culpa desafían prejuicios de toda índole. [MCG]

3823 Chejfec, Sergio. El aire. Buenos Aires: Aguilar, Altea Taurus, Alfaguara, S.A., 1992. 196 p. (Alfaguara literaturas)

En esta novela al narrador articula con precisión las lucubraciones de un protagonista que, dominado por la abulia y rodeado por una sociedad en decadencia, se limita a observar el deterioro progresivo. [MCG]

3824 Costa, Norberto. Los duros nunca ríen. Montevideo: Editorial Graffiti, 1993? 157 p. (Col. de narrativa El Cuarto sello)

Premio Dashiell Hammet 1992 de Novela Policial del Río de la Plata. Excelente manejo de la parodia y de la ironía en la exploración de este popular género. [MGP]

3825 Diaconú, Alina. Los devorados. Buenos Aires: Editorial Atlántida, 1992. 289 p. (Voces del Plata)

Novela muy bien narrada. Las historias de tres personajes pertenecientes a clases socio-económicas diferentes se entrecruzan y sugieren la falta de comunicación en una sociedad acartonada. [MCG]

3826 Fernández Moreno, Inés. La vida en la cornisa. Buenos Aires: Emecé Editores, 1993. 206 p. (Escritores argentinos)

La ironía entre la voz narrativa—aparentemente inocente—y los conflictos, inseguridades y sufrimientos que cuenta realza la significación e interés de escenas cotidianas que se vuelven situaciones límite. [MCG]

3827 Firpo, Norberto. Redondeces. Buenos Aires: Editorial Sudamericana, 1992. 169 p. (Col. Narrativas argentinas)

La novela elabora una sátira policial sobre el régimen de terror de comienzos de los 80. El recurso al melodrama—si bien de intención paródica—le resta eficacia. [MCG]

3828 Fogwill, Rodolfo Enrique. Restos diurnos. Buenos Aires: Editorial Sudamericana, 1993. 155 p. (Col. Narrativas argentinas)

Con técnicas diferentes, seis relatos de valor variado desarrollan situaciones que abarcan desde la sexualidad hasta lo fantástico. [MCG]

3829 Fresán, Rodrigo. Historia argentina. Barcelona: Anagrama, 1993. 240 p. (Narrativas hispánicas; 148)

Primer libro de ficción de un autor de 28 años. En 13 relatos—en que hay ironía, autocrítica, imaginación narrativa—se plantea "la imposibilidad de cambiar la historia y el relativo consuelo de poder contarla de otra manera." [MLB]

3830 Gandolfo, Elvio E. Parece mentira. Montevideo: Editorial Fin de Siglo, 1993. 113 p.: bibl. (Col. Deletras)

Reúne seis textos compilados en dos partes que combinan la literatura con el periodismo. La primera está dedicada a Montevideo: Mario Benedetti, Onetti y el sexo en Montevideo. La segunda parte incluye tres relatos que mezclan "la vida y obra de autores del 'mundo desarrollado:'" H.G. Wells, S. Sontag y W. Gombrowicz. [MGP]

3831 Iparraguirre, Sylvia. Probables lluvias por la noche. Buenos Aires: Emecé Editores, 1993. 150 p. (Escritores argentinos)

Nueve cuentos muy bien logrados. A partir de situaciones cotidianas construye dramas personales en que la angustia, el misterio y el medio traducen el malestar de personajes cuyas relaciones quedan truncas. [MCG]

3832 Jitrik, Noé. Citas de un día. Buenos Aires: Aguilar, Altea, Taurus, Alfaguara, 1992. 175 p. (Alfaguara literaturas)

La novela se estructura en torno a enigmas de carácter policial que intenta resolver. Narrada con gran lucidez, constituye una meditación crítica sobre el proceso de la escritura y la práctica del género novelesco. [MCG]

3833 Kociancich, Vlady. Todos los caminos. Madrid: Espasa Calpe, 1991. 183 p. (Calpe narrativa)

En siete relatos excelentes, de factura y escenarios diversos, se desarrolla el tema del desencuentro, de la oportunidad perdida, que se suelen llamar destino. [MLB]

3834 Lamborghini, Leónidas C. Un amor como pocos. Buenos Aires: Aguilar, Altea, Taurus, Alfaguara, 1993. 127 p. (Alfaguara literaturas)

Parodia poco convincente de relato pastoril, supuestamente escrita por alguien a quien la protagonista, una prostituta, contó la historia de su idilio imposible con un pastor en la Patagonia. [MLB]

Latbook: libros y revistas argentinas en Internet. See item 40.

3835 Llinás, Julio. De eso no se habla. Buenos Aires: Editorial Atlántida, 1993. 229 p. (Voces del Plata)

Diez relatos componen este primer libro de cuentos del autor. Cabe destacar aquéllos que, ambientados en medios rurales, asocian sentimientos personales, humor y político local sin caer en la formulación de críticas fáciles. El relato que titula a la colección fue llevado al cine por María Luisa Bemberg con título homónimo. [MCG]

3836 Manara, Alejandro. Tigre Hotel. Buenos Aires: Planeta, 1993. 196 p. (Biblioteca del sur)

El título es el nombre de un viejo hotel de un pueblo cercano a Buenos Aires donde la burguesía acomodada veraneaba a principios del siglo XX, donde ninguno de estos 18 relatos, o anécdotas, está localizado. [MLB]

3837 Masetto, Antonio dal. Reventando corbatas. Buenos Aires: Torres Agüero Editor, 1989. 203 p.

Cuarenta y ocho narraciones muy breves, con ambiente y personajes de la baja clase media de Buenos Aires. A veces, la voz narrativa se contamina de los tics de los personajes en detrimento de la "corrección" sintáctica, imprescindible en el texto escrito. [MLB]

3838 Nos, Marta. Mata, Yocasta, mata y otros cuentos. Buenos Aires: Grupo Editor Latinoamericano; Distribuidor exclusivo, Emecé Editores, 1993. 167 p. (Col. Escritura de hoy)

La diversidad de técnicas y de situaciones de estos 24 relatos no amenaza su gran coherencia. Con precisión, la autora crea procesos mentales concientes o semi-concientes por medio de los cuales los personajes enfrentan sus propias vidas. Los últimos cuatro relatos combinan el humor y la parodia para cuestionar el orden patriarcal. [MCG]

3839 Peluffo, Luisa. La doble vida. Buenos Aires: Editorial Atlántida, 1993. 215 p. (Voces del Plata)

Novela bien articulada que reflexiona sobre la relación entre ficción y realidad. La narradora—una escritora que compone una novela en base a personajes que conoce a medias—entreteje relatos múltiples en los que incluye el suyo propio. Los diferentes niveles narrativos dan como resultado la historia de la novela misma. [MCG]

3840 Posse, Abel. Los bogavantes. Ed. revisada y corregida por el autor. Buenos Aires: Editorial Atlántida, 1992. 324 p. (Voces del Plata)

Reedición de la novela publicada en los 70, se añade un prólogo en el que el autor relaciona a sus personajes, ambientados en la década crítica del 60, con la época actual. Diferentes procedimientos narrativos—diario, relatos en primera y tercera persona—trazan las diversas propuestas de los personajes en su búsqueda por hallar sentido a sus vidas. [MCG]

3841 Posse, Abel. El largo atardecer del caminante. Buenos Aires: Emecé Editores, 1992. 261 p. (Escritores argentinos)

Novela histórica. El diestro manejo de la forma autobiográfica en esta novela histórica facilita la verosimilitud de los hechos narrados. Alvar Núñez Cabeza de Vaca reescribe su crónica y revela los secretos de su vida íntima. Ofrece una visión crítica de la conquista pero el final melodramático debilita la tensión narrativa. [MCG]

3842 Sábato, Matilde. El conjuro. Buenos Aires: Torres Agüero Editor, 1992. 79 p.

Con gran economía doce relatos evocan situaciones fantásticas en las que predominan elementos mágicos, lúgubres premoniciones y cuadros de fantasía y horror. [MCG]

3843 Sáenz, Dalmiro. Los bebedores de agua. Buenos Aires: Editorial Atlántida, 1994. 264 p. (Voces del Plata)

Novela intrincada, armada con el contrapunto entre la reconstrucción de los pasos de un crimen y las elucubraciones sobre la lógica *sui generis* que impulsó al criminal. [MLB]

3844 Sánchez, Matilde. El Dock. Buenos Aires: Planeta, 1993. 301 p. (Biblioteca del sur)

Desde una perspectiva intimista, esta novela presenta las consecuencias emocionales que una muerte trágica—rememoración de las luchas internas de los 70—tiene sobre quienes se relacionaban con la víctima. [MCG]

3845 Soriano, Osvaldo. Cuentos de los años felices. 3. ed. Buenos Aires: Editorial Sudamericana, 1994. 245 p.

Colección de cuentos muy dispares organizados en tres partes: 1) "En Nombre del Padre" reúne 17 relatos nostálgicos sobre recuerdos de infancia y juventud; 2) "Otra Historia" agrupa 10 "crónicas sobre la Independencia [que] a veces contradicen la historia oficial y también la de los revisionistas;" y 3) "Pensar con los Pies" reedita seis cuentos en torno a la pasión del fútbol. [MCG]

3846 Soriano, Osvaldo. El ojo de la patria. 2. ed. Buenos Aires: Editorial Sudamericana, 1992. 286 p. (Col. Narrativas argentinas)

Parodia del género policial, la novela incorpora recursos del neobarroco—el disfraz, la máscara y el humor—para cuestionar las posibilidades políticas de un país sudamericano en la situación actual. [MCG]

3847 Torres Zavaleta, Jorge. La casa de la llanura. Buenos Aires: Editorial Atlántida, 1993. 222 p. (Voces del Plata)

En búsqueda de la reconstrucción de la biografía de un escritor, el narrador incursiona en un pasado no muy lejano del que recupera relatos fragmentarios sobre otros personajes. Surge el contraste con el presente de la narración en que reina la decadencia. [MCG]

3848 Ulla, Noemí. El ramito. Buenos Aires: Ediciones Ultimo Reino, 1990. 45 p.

Breve memoria de una etapa de la infancia, que combina visión y lenguaje adultos para rescatar recuerdos. [MLB]

3849 Valenzuela, Luisa. Simetrías. Buenos Aires: Editorial Sudamericana, 1993. 191 p. (Col. Narrativas argentinas)

Con ironía, y acaso con nostalgia, la autora reescribe fábulas o situaciones convencionales de la literatura, y aun de la tradición popular. [MLB]

3850 Walsh, Rodolfo J. Cuentos. Introducción de Horacio Verbitsky. Buenos Aires: Página 12, 1993? 60 p. (Biblioteca Página 12)

Antología que reúne tres cuentos publicados que pertenecen a la serie "Irlandeses." Incluye datos biográficos sobre el autor y la introducción explica la relación entre la obra y la militancia política de Walsh. [MCG]

Paraguay

3851 Halley Mora, Gerardo. El talismán: novela. Asunción?: Ediciones El Lector, 1992. 242 p.

La novela se sitúa en Asunción en 1935 durante la Guerra del Chaco. Explora las posibilidades narrativas de una leyenda local, "San La Muerte." [MGP]

3852 Halley Mora, Mario. Ocho mujeres y los demás: novela. Asunción: El Lector, 1994. 137 p.

El autor es un reconocido dramaturgo que se ha propuesto explorar el campo de la ficción. Su primera novela presenta una visión del mundo a través de la óptica de una galería de personajes femeninos en el continuo y diario quehacer. [MGP]

3853 Karlik, Sara. Preludio con fuga. Buenos Aires: Grupo Editor Latinoamericano; Distribuidor exclusivo, Emecé Editores, 1992. 152 p. (Col. Escritura de hoy)

Esta escritora paraguaya que vive en Chile ha publicado cuatro colecciones de cuentos: *La oscuridad de afuera* (1987), *Entre ánimas y sueños* (1987), *Demasiada historia* (1988) y *Efectos especiales* (1989) y dos novelas, *Los fantasmas no son como antes* (1989) y *Juicio a la memoria* que recibió el Premio Planeta de Novela 1990. Este volumen de cuentos está dividido en cuatro partes, constituidas por ocho relatos, que exploran la libertad, la identidad, el tiempo y la soledad en el quehacer diario de la vida. [MGP]

3854 Roa Bastos, Augusto Antonio. El baldío. Madrid: Alfaguara, 1992. 237 p. (Alfaguara/bolsillo)

Del gran novelista paraguayo nos llega esta colección de cuentos sobre los devenires de los seres humanos en la trayectoria vital. Este volumen incluye "El Baldío," "Contar un Cuento," "Encuentro con el Traidor," "Juegos Nocturnos," "La Rebelión," "El Aserradero," "Borrador del Informe," "La Tijera," "Hermanos," "La Flecha y la Manzana," "El y el Otro," "Kurupí," y "El Pájaro Mosca." [MGP]

3855 Roa Bastos, Augusto Antonio. Contravida. Asunción: El Lector, 1994. 261 p. (Col. literaria; 23)

Al decir de su autor, esta novela cierra el ciclo de su obra narrativa cuando publicó su primer volumen de cuentos (see *HLAS 23:5008*). Narración en primera persona del único sobreviviente de una matanza colectiva. [MGP]

3856 Roa Bastos, Augusto Antonio. El fiscal. Madrid: Alfaguara, 1993. 352 p. (Alfaguara hispánica; 108)

El autor advierte que "con *Hijo de hombre* y *Yo El Supremo, El fiscal* compone la trilogía sobre el "monoteísmo" del poder, uno de los ejes temáticos de mi obra narrativa." Esta obra surge de las "cenizas" de una primera versión, y después de haber desaparecido "una de las dictaduras más largas y feroces de América Latina." De indispensable lectura para el estudio sobre la "novela del dictador." [MGP]

3857 Rodríguez Alcalá, Guido. Caballero rey. Asunción: RP Ediciones, 1988? 187 p.: maps.

Poeta, ensayista, crítico y novelista, el autor continúa explorando la novela histórica en la figura del general de división don Bernardino Caballero de Añazco, el Centauro de Ybicuí, durante la terrible humanamente costosa Guerra Grande. [MGP]

3858 Vera, Helio. Angola y otros cuentos. Prólogo de la primera edición de Osvaldo González Real. Prólogo de la segunda edición de Ramiro Domínguez. 2. ed., corr. y aum. Asunción: Arandurã, 1994. 143 p.

Volumen de cuentos en los que se rastrea los orígenes del afrocubanía y el encuentro de americanos y africanos. De gran interés para los estudiosos de la literatura afrohispana en América del Sur. [MGP]

Uruguay

3859 Benedetti, Mario. Articulario: desexilio y perplejidades; reflexiones desde el sur. Madrid: El País; Aguilar, 1994. 391 p. (El viaje interior)

Volumen en dos partes: 1) "El Desexilio y otras Conjeturas (1982–84) y "Perplejidades de Fin de Siglo" (1990–93). Selección de artículos, en su mayoría publicados en el periódico El País (Madrid) sobre temas diversos de esta importante figura de la cultura latinoamericana. [MGP]

3860 Benedetti, Mario. Cuentos completos. Madrid: Santillana, 1994. 615 p. (Alfaguara)

Edición reciente prologada por José Emilio Pacheco como homenaje a los 50 años de escritor que inaugura la generación uruguaya de 1945, identificada con Marcha, según designación de Angel Rama, incluye Esta mañana, Montevideanos, La muerte y otras sorpresas, Con y sin nostalgia, Geografías y Despistes y franquezas. Pacheco anota que Benedetti ha trabajado durante medio siglo "como habitante natural en todos los géneros con una fidelidad inexpugnable a las más diversas manifestaciones del cuento." [MGP]

3861 Benedetti, Mario. Despistes y franquezas. 2a ed. Madrid: Alfaguara, 1993. 252 p. (Alfaguara/bolsillo)

Este prolífico y admirado escritor describe este volumen como "un entrevero: cuentos realistas, viñetas de humor, enigmas policíacos, relatos fantásticos. Fragmentos autobiográficos, poemas, parodias, graffiti." Un ejemplo del género entrevero sería La vuelta al día en ochenta mundos de Julio Cortázar o Miramar de Oswald de Andrade. Para los interesados en Benedetti, la lectura de este libro es indispensable puesto que está presentado como un homenaje a los lectores que lo han acompañado durante su trayectoria dentro y fuera del Uruguay. [MGP]

3862 Benedetti, Mario et al. La muerte hace buena letra. Coordinación de Omar Prego. Montevideo: Ediciones Trilce, 1993. 214 p.: bibl.

Novela colectiva en 23 capítulos. Colaboraron 11 autores destacados de las letras contemporáneas: Mario Benedetti, Hugo Bourel, Miguel Angel Campodónico, Enrique Estrázulas, Milton Fornaro, Suleika Ibáñez, Sylvia Lago, Juan Carlos Mondragón, Teresa Porzecanski, Omar Prego Gadea y Elvio Rodríguez Bilari. Experimento textual en el que cada uno escribió dos capítulos en dos vueltas, por riguroso órden alfabético. No acordaron en desarrollar un argumento ni obedecer reglas preestablecidas. El último capítulo fue planificado por todos los participantes. [MGP]

3863 Benedetti, Mario. Perplejidades de fin de siglo. Montevideo: Cal y Canto, 1993. 195 p.

Este volumen recopila textos de conferencias y artículos publicados en periódicos de Madrid, Barcelona, Montevideo, Buenos Aires, Ciudad de México, Managua, Santiago de Chile y en Nuevo Texto Crítico, escritos entre 1987–93 sobre temas diversos que enfocan la realidad latinoamericana. [MGP]

3864 Butazzoni, Fernando. El príncipe de la muerte. Montevideo: Editorial Graffiti, 1993. 431 p. (Col. de narrativa los centauros del sol)

Espléndida novela histórica que recorre el turbulento siglo XIX situada en la disputada zona que hoy es el Uruguay, Paraguay ante las aspiraciones imperialistas del Brasil, y protagonizada por un cuchillero montevideano. Sus otras obras incluyen Los días de nuestra sangre, La noche abierta, Nicaragua: noticias de la guerra, El tigre y la nieve y La danza de los perdidos. Esta obra ha recibido el prestigioso premio "Casa de las Américas." [MGP]

3865 Campodónico, Miguel Angel. La rebelión de los sordos. Montevideo: Editorial Fin de Siglo, 1993. 153 p. (Col. Deletras)

Nueva novela de este autor que satiriza algunos hábitos y construcciones cotidianas de popularidad vacua, tales como los programas de radio, la ubicuidad del mate uruguayo, la religiosidad postmoderna y otros productos de la cultura finisecular. [MGP]

3866 Chavarría, Daniel. El ojo dindymenio. Montevideo: Editorial Graffiti, 1993. 367 p. (Col. de narrativa los centauros del sol)

Premio Planeta 1993, que sitúa su acción en la Grecia de Pericles, uno de sus personajes. Aspasia, Sócrates, Alcibíades y otras figuras de la época son los protagonistas de esta historia de intrigas políticas y de prosperidad de aquella idealizada Atenas. Sus obras pertenecen al género de la novela de aventuras y de espionaje. [MGP]

3867 Cuentos de ajustar cuentas. Recopilación de Sylvia Lago. Montevideo: Ediciones Trilce, 1990. 132 p.

Interesante colección o "recopilación mostrativa" en la que participan 17 escritoras uruguayas que reúnen textos que replican un juguete llamado *juego de ajustar cuentas*, esparcimiento "de entrecasa" destinado a entretener o desarrollar las "inclinaciones lúdicas femeninas." Estas narradoras representan la actividad creativa del Uruguay contemporáneo. Los temas son diversos: testimonio del pasado, develación de conflictos dentro de un marco de enfrentamiento psicológico y el desenmascaramiento de una realidad sofocante son señalados en el prólogo por Sylvia Lago. Entre las participantes se encuentran Cristina Peri Rossi, Suleika Ibáñez, Teresa Porzecanski, Rita Perdomo, Alicia Migdal, Armonía Somers e Idea Vilariño. Podría incluirse en un curso de literatura femenina latinoamericana. [MGP]

3868 Estrázulas, Enrique. Soledades pobladas de mujeres. Buenos Aires: Legasa, 1993. 148 p. (Nueva literatura)

Con esta colección de cuentos dedicada a Enrique Pezzoni, este destacado poeta y narrador ofrece dos grupos de textos. Uno de ellos consiste en cuentos en su acepción mas canónica y el segundo grupo, titulado "Galerías," reúne estampas de un carácter o un hecho al margen de la historia, como los "homenajes" a Shakespeare, Esquilo o a Borges. [MGP]

3869 Galeano, Eduardo H. Las palabras andantes. Con grabados de J. Borges. Madrid: Siglo Veintiuno de España Editores, 1993. 316 p.: ill. (La Creación literaria)

Volumen en colaboración de historias de "espanto y encanto," junto a historias orales recogidas durante sus viajes del autor y otros relatos ilustrados con grabados del poeta y artista de cordel del Nordeste de Brasil, José Francisco Borges. [MGP]

3870 Hernández, Felisberto. Narraciones fundamentales. Prólogo de Ana María Hernández de Elena. Cronología anotada, bibliografía activa y *Felisberto Hernández, mi amigo* por Walter Rela. Montevideo: Editorial Relieve, 1993. 210 p.: bibl.

Nueva edición de ocho cuentos de Felisberto Hernández prologada por su hija. Incluye "El Caballo Perdido," "El Balcón,"

"Nadie Encendía las Lámparas," "La Mujer Parecida a Mí," "El Cocodrilo," "Lucrecia" y "La Casa Inundada." Incluye una cronología realizada por Walter Rela, y una bibliografía extensa. [MGP]

3871 Migdal, Alicia. Historia quieta. Montevideo: Ediciones Trilce, 1993. 61 p. (Col. Pandora)

Esta destacada narradora ha escrito *Mascarones* (1981), una colección de poemas, *Historia de cuerpos*, (1986) y la novela, *La casa de enfrente* (1988). Esta novela breve y original inscribe la voz de un sujeto femenino articulada en tercera persona sobre la experiencia del deseo y del desamor, o que superpone el espacio del cuerpo en el espacio del relato. [MGP]

3872 Mondragón, Juan Carlos. Mariposas bajo anestesia. Montevideo: Ediciones Trilce, 1993. 163 p.

Diez cuentos que incluyen el titulado "Nocturno Tenue por Libertad Lamarque," que recibió Mención especial del Premio Juan Rulfo 1990. [MGP]

3873 Montserrat, María de. Los juegos: relatos. Montevideo: Ediciones de la Banda Oriental, 1993. 67 p.

La obra de esta narradora incluye *Cuentos mínimos* (1953); *Con motivo de vivir* (1962), *Los lugares* (1965), *Los habitantes* (1968), *El país secreto* (1977); *El sonido blanco* (1979); *La casa quinta* (1982); *Grandes sueños* (1982); *Los musicantes* (1985) y *El caballo Azul* (1991). Estos relatos centrados en el tema de los juegos infantiles exploran la conexión entre el presente y el avatar de la memoria colectiva. [MGP]

3874 Mujeres de mucha monta: cuentos. 3a. ed. Montevideo: Arca, 1992. 142 p.

Colección de 21 cuentos eróticos femeninos de Teresa Porzecanski, Armonía Somers, Amanda Berenguer, Marosa Di Giorgio, Suleika Ibáñez, entre otras. [MGP]

3875 Onetti, Juan Carlos. Cuentos completos. Madrid: Santillana, 1994. 468 p.: bibl. (Alfaguara)

Edición precedida de un prólogo iluminador de Antonio García Muñoz, con un análisis inteligente de la obra de Onetti en el contexto de la literatura hispanoamericana. Incluye 37 cuentos publicados entre 1933–93. [MGP]

3876 **Polleri Sierra, Felipe.** Colores. Montevideo: Arca, 1991. 85 p. (Col. deúltima; 1)

Escrito por el autor de *Carnaval de 1990*, la novela breve que aquí anotamos está en apariencia fragmentada por la brevedad de sus capítulos que, sin embargo, contribuyen a una estructura narrativa compleja, innovadora tanto de la concepción de la novela como del lenguaje creado para articular dicha concepción. [MGP]

3877 **Rosencof, Mauricio.** El bataraz. Montevideo: Arca, 1992. 138 p.

La obra de este autor y militante político (dirigente del Movimiento de Liberación Nacional-Tupamaros del Uruguay) incluye obras de teatro, poesía, literatura infantil, crónica, testimonio y novela. Dedicada a uno de sus compañeros, Raúl Sendic, esta novela es una narración que se sustenta sobre la experiencia de la cárcel y de la tortura. [MGP]

3878 **Sclavo, Jorge** and **Fidel Sclavo.** Almanario. Montevideo: Editorial Relieve, 1993. 82 p.: ill.

Una desusada asociación de Jorge Sclavo—alias literario Cuque—con su sobrino, Fidel Sclavo, pintor y diseñador gráfico, en una empresa conjunta que dio como resultado textos poemático-narrativos de gran calidad y fino humor escritos por Jorge, el narrador, e ilustrado por Fidel, el artista, tales como "Para Cuando Mary Shelley se Quede sin Monstruos," "Indicación para Evitar el Exito," o "Consejo Práctico para Volver a Casa." [MGP]

3879 **Solari, Ana.** Cuentos de diez minutos. Prólogo de Hugo Achugar. Montevideo: Arca, 1992. 78 p. (Col. deúltima; 2)

Figura original de la nueva narrativa femenina uruguaya. Consiste de una introducción de Hugo Achugar, seis cuentos y 10 preguntas a la autora. El prologuista caracteriza estos textos como hiperrealistas por explosionar "los objetos, los paisajes, las situaciones y los personajes hasta volverlos irreconocibles en su amplificada presencia." Escritura innovadora, violenta, sin dejos de sentimentalismo, y en la cual el tiempo de la escritura se entrelaza con el tiempo presente. [MGP]

3880 **Somers, Armonía.** Viaje al corazón del día: elegía por un secreto amor. Montevideo: Arca, 1986. 144 p.

De la gran narradora recientemente fallecida, esta novela relata historias de amores secretos y prohibidos. [MGP]

3881 **Valdés, Ana Luisa.** El navegante. Montevideo: Ediciones Trilce, 1993. 116 p. (Col. Pandora)

Este quinto libro de la autora, es una excelente colección de 12 cuentos en los que el tiempo y el espacio se conciben más allá de las fronteras habituales. La oficina del sujeto narrador masculino está en un museo de muy diversos objetos que quieren detener el tiempo futilmente al haber sido transformados en unas líneas de enciclopedia o en el armario mental de los que saben cosas innecesarias en "La Paz de los Muertos" o el dormitorio transformado en barco con las velas desplegadas de "El Navegante." [MGP]

3882 **Varela, Julio C.** Vieja es la noche. Montevideo: Arca, 1993. 144 p. (Col. deúltima)

Primera novela de Varela, premiada por el Ministerio de Educación y Cultura en 1987. Sus otras obras son *Los cuernos de la liebre* (1989) y *Costumbres de Anita* (1991). De raigambre onettiana, cuatro personajes viajan por una ciudad, Megalópolis, a través de la noche. En el transcurso del viaje se reflexiona acerca de la configuración de este universo cerrado y caótico que agobia y asfixia a los personajes. [MGP]

LITERARY CRITICISM AND HISTORY
Paraguay

3883 **Tovar, Paco.** Augusto Roa Bastos. Lleida: Pagès Editors, 1993. 172 p.: bibl. (Col. El Fil d'Ariadna; 14. Sèrie Literatura)

Estudio sobre la vida y obra del maestro paraguayo. Incluye bibliografía muy completa de y sobre Roa Bastos. [MGP]

Uruguay

3884 **Adolfo Bioy Casares en Uruguay: de la amistad y otras coincidencias.** Coordinación de Lisa Block de Behar Isidra Solari de Muró. Salto, Uruguay: Centro Cultural Internacional de Salto, 1993. 228 p.: bibl., ill. (some col.).

Colección de comunicaciones que celebran la adjudicación del Premio Miguel de Cervantes al distinguido escritor argentino en 1991. [MGP]

3885 Ainsa, Fernando. Nuevas fronteras de la narrativa uruguaya, 1960–1993. Montevideo: Ediciones Trilce, 1993. 151 p.: bibl., index.

Estudio en dos partes del conocido crítico sobre una de las narrativas más productivas del continente: 1) especulación acerca de la producción literaria a partir de los 60 incluye reflexiones sobre los "nuevos" géneros: el testimonio, la crónica, la historia ficcionalizada y el cuento; y 2) se concentra en la literatura de la primera mitad del siglo XX. [MGP]

Gandolfo, Elvio E. Parece mentira. See item **3830.**

3886 *Letterature d'America.* Vol. 13, 1993. Roma: Facoltà di Lettere e Filosofia dell'Univ. di Roma.

Este número titulado "La letteratura uruguayana di fine secolo" está dedicado a presentar una muestra muy parcial de un siglo de literatura uruguaya según apunta Hugo Achugar, el editor invitado. Está constituido por siete trabajos: Hugo Achugar, "Sueños y Fracturas: Narrativa Uruguaya de Fin de Siglo;" Gustavo Verdesio, "Escritura e Identidad Cultural en los Discursos Coloniales;" Magdalena García Pinto, "Delmira Agustini Frente a los Letrados Uruguayos del 900;" Amir Hamed, "Un Cuerpo para Brausen entre las Tumbas de Onetti;" Sylvia Lago, "El Enmascaramiento en el Discurso Poético Femenino: Sara de Ibáñez y el 'Antifaz de Hielo;'" Martha Canfield, "La Isotopía del Agua en la Poesía de Juana de Ibarbourou;" Rosa María Grillo, "Il 'Portuñol' da Spazio Fronterizo a Spazio Letterario." [MGP]

3887 Martínez, Elena M. Onetti: estrategias textuales y operaciones del lector. Madrid: Editorial Verbum, 1992. 177 p.: bibl. (Verbum ensayo)

Excelente estudio—provocado por la idea borgeana de que un libro es una relación o el eje de innumerables relaciones, en "Notas sobre (Hacia) Bernard Shaw"—sobre las estrategias narrativas a partir de la perspectiva del lector propuesta por Robert Jauss y Wolfgang Iser, entre las que figuran la metaficción, la intertextualidad, el narrador y el personaje. [MGP]

3888 Panesi, Jorge. Felisberto Hernández. Rosario: Beatriz Viterbo Editora, 1993. 112 p.: bibl. (Tesis)

Aporte crítico al estudio de la ficción de Felisberto, enfocado a dilucidar la representación del consumo y recepción artística en su narrativa. [MGP]

3889 Silva Vila, María Inés. Cuarenta y cinco por uno: 45 x 1. Prólogo de Mario Benedetti. Montevideo: Editorial Fin de Siglo, 1993. 131 p. (Col. 45)

Narradora contemporánea de Cortázar y con el cual tiene afinidades señaladas por Mario Benedetti en el prólogo a este nuevo libro. Su primera colección de siete cuentos se tituló *La mano de nieve* (1951, el año de *Bestiario*), su segundo libro *Felicidad y otras tristezas* (1964, colección que reúne los siete anteriores y 10 relatos más). Es también autora de una novela, *Salto Cancán* (1969). Este volumen incluye 27 textos, publicados en el semanario *Jaque* entre mayo y agosto 1985, que hilvanan anécdotas diversas sobre los debates intelectuales entre los escritores y periodistas de esa década, que solían reunirse en el Café Metro. Una especie de historia literaria anecdótica. Entre los personajes que circulan por este volumen figuran Onetti, Felisberto Hernández, Isabel Gilbert, Angel Rama, Ida Vitale, Amanda Berenguer, José Pedro Díaz, y muchos otros uruguayos y no uruguayos. [MGP]

Poetry

FRANCISCO CABANILLAS, *Associate Professor of Spanish, Bowling Green State University*
MIGUEL GOMES, *Assistant Professor of Spanish, University of Connecticut*
PEDRO LASTRA, *Professor Emeritus, State University of New York at Stony Brook*
ELIZABETH MONASTERIOS, *Assistant Professor of Spanish, State University of New York, Stony Brook*
JOSE MIGUEL OVIEDO, *Trustee Professor of Spanish, University of Pennsylvania*
OSCAR RIVERA-RODAS, *Professor of Spanish, University of Tennessee, Knoxville*
JACOBO SEFAMI, *Associate Professor of Spanish, University of California, Irvine*
LILIAN URIBE, *Associate Professor of Spanish, Central Connecticut State University,*

GENERAL

ADEMAS DE LOS LIBROS y autores destacados en los resúmenes que siguen, en estos años aparecieron obras sobre aspectos más generales del quehacer poético, que deben recomendarse por su carácter provocativo y estimulante. Muy considerable en este sentido es la *Antología de la poesía hispanoamericana moderna*, coordinada por G. Sucre y en la que trabajó un equipo de notable competencia (item **3912**). Más allá de las aprobaciones o desacuerdos que este libro suscite, es preciso reconocer que tanto la formulación como la ejecución del proyecto son muy meritorios: el resultado obtenido ayudará no sólo al especialista sino a todo lector de poesía.

También es novedoso el libro que J. Fernández dedica al poema en prosa (item **3900**), un tema poco atendido, o tratado con vaguedad por la crítica. Junto a esta importante contribución hay que mencionar el estudio sobre el género en México, de L.I. Helguera (item **3892**).

Entre las obras de comentario y análisis, sobresale la lectura del proceso poético contemporáneo realizada por A. Ferrari (item **4116**). La propuesta de Ferrari sugiere otras posibilidades críticas e invita a nuevas reflexiones.

La décima fue objeto de oportunos estudios y antologías en la República Dominicana (items **3898** y **3908**). Con respecto a trabajos de carácter más específico—movimientos, temas o ediciones—hubo aportes muy significativos, como los libros sobre Los Contemporáneos de L. Maristany (item **3901**) y de R. Olea Franco y A. Stanton (item **4113**), la meritoria antología de poesía femenina de Nicaragua (item **3905**), la dedicada a la poesía amorosa colombiana (item **3914**) y la reedición de *Canto kechwa*, de J.M. Arguedas (item **4157**). Un proyecto mayor puesto en marcha en este período fue la publicación de las *Obras completas de Octavio Paz*, de las cuales ya han aparecido 11 volúmenes (items **4161**).

El interés de los estudiosos de la poesía hispanoamericana se concentró en C. Vallejo (items **4134, 4137, 340, 4143** y **4151**), V. Huidobro (items **4153** y **4130**), G. Mistral (item **4140**), N. Guillén (item **4142**), N. Parra (item **4128**), P.A. Cuadra (item **4129**), G. Rojas (item **4148**), A. Mutis (item **4145**), C. Dávila Andrade (item **4146**), J.E. Pacheco (item **4139**), P. de Rokha y P. Neruda (item **4147**). [PL]

MEXICO

Con el apoyo del Consejo Nacional para la Cultura y las Artes (México), continúan publicándose antologías voluminosas de diferentes estados de la República. En ambas fronteras, tanto el norte como el sur (casi parangonando lo que sucede en el terreno político), hay una dimensión muy rica de la poesía actual (items **3893, 3903** y **3915**), que de algún modo intenta descentralizar la focalización en la capital. Sin embargo, el panorama nacional se rige aún en el centro.

En este período han aparecido antologías y recopilaciones de escritores ya maduros (items **3946, 3956, 3998** y **4074**), además de la reedición de poetas que necesitan revalorarse, como M.J. Othón (item **4053**) y A. Reyes (item **4073**).

La poesía mexicana sigue brindando una cantidad inconmensurable de nuevas voces y una multiplicidad de variantes expresivas. Ademas de poéticas reconocidas internacionalmente, como la de J.E. Pacheco (item **4055**), en este período predominan los escritores nacidos en los 40 y 50, aunque se anotan libros de ciertos novísimos nacidos en los 60 y 70 (items **3923, 3931** y **4020**). La línea que acude a la poesía de la selva o la exuberancia natural está representada por J. Bañuelos, H.E. Bartolomé, J.M. Pintado y J.L. Rivas (items **3929, 3933, 4061** y **4074**); los juegos con el lenguaje y la escritura en L. Amara, G. Deniz, I. Palacios y C. Bracho, A. Paredes y L.R. Vera (items **3923, 3969, 4056, 4057** y **4100**); la parodia o la socarronería coloquial en C. Benítez Torres, R. Castillo y, en menor medida, en R. Vargas (items **3945, 3956** y **4095**); la liturgia, el mito y la rememoración sagrada en M. Baranda, A. Blanco, E. Cross y M. Moscona (items **3931, 3946, 3963** y **4040**).

Es encomiable la labor de las series *El Ala del Tigre* (UNAM), *Margen de Poesía* (Revista *Casa del Tiempo*, UAM), *Luzazul* (CONACULTA), además de la nueva serie, *Los Cincuenta*, editada por escritores nacidos en esa década y también publicada por CONACULTA.

En cuanto a la crítica literaria, continúa el interés por la poesía de O. Paz (item **4149**), cuyas *Obras completas* están en curso de publicación (item **4161**); la vigencia del grupo Los Contemporáneos (item **4113**) es indudable; por igual, con la recopilación crítica sobre su obra, A. Chumacero recibió el reconocimiento que merece (item **4132**). Hay que agregar, además, la excelente reedición del libro de H.J. Verani sobre J.E. Pacheco (item **4139**). [JS]

CENTROAMERICA

Sin duda las publicaciones que más destacan en este período corresponden a figuras notables de la tradición poética centroamericana: *Los ovnis de oro: poemas indios*, de E. Cardenal (item **4158**); *Pól-la d'anánta katánta paránta*, de J. Coronel Urtecho (item **3962**); *Tres amores*, de M. Cuadra (item **3965**); y *Salomón de la Selva: antología mayor*, de J. Valle-Castillo (item **4084**). Asimismo, se debe mencionar la aparición de *Antología de la poesía hondureña* preparada por J.L. Oviedo (item **3891**) y el surgimiento de poesía nueva y fresca, como la de G. Martínez (item **4035**) y O. Sauma (item **4083**). El período ha producido también algunos estudios críticos indispensables para el conocimiento de estas literaturas. Me refiero fundamentalmente a dos textos de J.E. Arellano, *Entre la tradición y la modernidad: el movimiento nicaragüense de vanguardia* (item **4111**) y *Pablo Antonio Cuadra: aproximaciones a su vida y obra* (item **4129**). También destacable es el artículo de P.A. Cuadra, titulado "El Espectro del Cisne" (item **4135**). [EM]

EL CARIBE

Más que una propuesta de ruptura o de innovación, la poesía del Caribe se inscribe, en estos últimos años, en un espacio de continuidad, que no necesariamente implica una permanencia inalterada; hay nuevas voces pero predomina la tradición. Tiempo de silencio, quizás, pero no de inactividad; los poetas escriben sin hacer mucho ruido y la poesía se mantiene dentro de sus definiciones.

Entre los poetas consagrados, se destaca el poemario de C. Vitier (item **4102**), tributo a la tradición origenista. Después, en la próxima esfera de reconocimiento, la de los poetas establecidos, está el poemario de V. López Suria (item **4030**), como una articulación del sujeto poético con la cultura letrada y popular. Dos poemarios de poetas en proceso de establecerse son: desde el exilio cubano, el brevísimo poemario de J. Kozer (item **4024**); y, como constancia del movimiento dominicano de La Poesía Sorprendida, el de F. Gatón Arce (item **3994**). Hay que señalar también, como publicación importante de un escritor más novelista que poeta, el poemario de S. Sarduy (item **4082**), que reúne dos libros anteriormente publicados por separado.

En el trabajo antológico, sobresalen las colecciones dedicadas a D.M. Loynaz, ganadora del Premio Cervantes en 1992. Tres publicaciones le rinden tributo a la poeta cubana; una que acentúa el carácter lírico de toda literatura de Loynaz, ya en verso o en prosa (item **4031**); otra que presenta la poesía según la época en que fueron escritos los poemas, independientemente de la fecha de publicación (item **4032**); y, finalmente, un homenaje que, además de antología, incluye estudios y opiniones sobre la vida y obra de Loynaz (item **4144**). Cabe también señalar la antología de la literatura puertorriqueña de E. Barradas, cuya recopilación de poemas persigue una iluminación de la trayectoria histórico-cultural de Puerto Rico (item **3909**), y, como proyecto de marcada inclusividad, la muestra de poesía de España y las Américas preparada por M. de la Puebla, donde el lector tiene acceso, entre otras, a la poesía quechua, guaraní y maya (item **3917**).

Entre las reediciones destacables, cabe mencionar dos de la *Biblioteca de Clásicos Dominicanos:* la poesía romántica de F. Fiallo (item **3982**) y la poesía indigenista de J.J. Pérez (item **4059**). Entre los estudios, dos merecen mención: uno sobre la presencia del indio en la poesía puertorriqueña, de C. Corchado Juarbe (item **3895**), y otro, de Marcos Reyes Dávila, sobre la poesía social y política que se escribió en torno a la revista *Guajana* de Puerto Rico (item **3902**). Especial atención debe recibir el intento de rescatar la décima en la República Dominicana, materializado en una colección de décimas premiadas en 1992 (item **3898**), al igual que en un estudio panorámico de L. Beiro Alvarez (item **3908**). [FC]

COLOMBIA Y VENEZUELA

Dos antologías de conocidos autores venezolanos se descatan en el período: una selección de la obra poética y ensayística de J. Liscano editada por la Biblioteca Ayacucho (item **4026**) y una concisa muestra de la poesía de J. Calzadilla preparada por A. López Ortega (item **3948**). También aparecieron un intenso libro elegíaco de V. Gerbasi (item **3997**) y un diario poético de C. Ovalles, que ilustra un recorrido por diversos países (item **4054**). Entre los escritores más jóvenes sobresale la atractiva poesía amorosa de M. James, quien procesa con ingenio variadas modalidades expresivas consagradas por la tradición (item **4016**). Algunos estudios y trabajos deben señalarse como contribuciones estimables: J. Barroeta analiza la imagen del padre en la poesía venezolana (item **4114**) y J.C. Santaella recopila manifiestos literarios de 13 grupos que se expresaron a través de revistas, desde 1894–1961 (item **4120**).

Con respecto a Colombia, se cumplieron tareas importantes de rescate y difusión de obras poéticas que merecen, desde hace tiempo, un mayor reconocimiento internacional. Tal es el caso de la poesía de A. Arturo y L. de Greiff, publicada en Madrid por Cultura Hispánica y por Visor, respectivamente (items **3927** y **4003**). También deben celebrarse las nuevas ediciones españolas de autores más familiares para ese público y para el de Hispanoamérica, como F. Charry Lara y A. Mutis (items **3958** y **4042**).

Otras antologías necesarias son la de G. Quessep, aparecida en Bogotá (item **4068**), y la de D. Jaramillo Agudelo, publicada por Monte Avila, en Caracas (item **4018**). Libros que también sobresalen en este panorama son los de W. Ospina, *El país del viento* (item **4052**), y P. Bonnett, *De círculo y ceniza* (item **3947**).

Un interesante y provocativo estudio de O. Torres Duque, sobre el sentido de lo clásico en la poesía colombiana, fue editado por Colcultura (item **4126**). No menor interés tiene una notable antología de la poesía amorosa colombiana, dispuesta por D. Jaramillo Agudelo e ingeniosamente titulada *Sentimentario* (item **3914**). De los trabajos dedicados a un autor, es muy recomendable el volumen de conversaciones de F. Quiroz con A. Mutis (item **4145**), presentado de manera ejemplar. [PL]

BOLIVIA Y ECUADOR

En el panorama editorial de la poesía boliviana de los años recientes destacan, como rasgo sobresaliente, los libros de autores nacidos en la década de 1940 y que afloraron en la actividad literaria en los años de 1960. Tales libros representan a una generación, en general, muy activa, que ofrece pautas y orienta el quehacer poético nacional. Como ejemplo, citamos la obra completa de S.M. Avila (item **3928**) y los nuevos volúmenes de J. Urzagasti (item **4091**), B. Garnica (item **3993**), M. Casazola (item **3954**) y J. Mansilla (item **4034**), este último muy conocido también con el pseudónimo de Coco Manto por sus epigramas que aparecen en periódicos y revistas de la Ciudad de México, donde actualmente reside. Por otra parte, en el panorama de la poesía boliviana reciente se registró asimismo el surgimiento de un número considerable de jóvenes y nuevos autores que tratan de ofrecer productos renovados mediante la experimentación formal y de contenido. Entre esos nuevos nombres cabe señalar un grupo importante de poetas mujeres, de las que se destacan especialmente S.M. Vázquez Rivero (item **4097**) y R. Quiroga de Urquieta (item **4070**).

La actividad poética del Ecuador de los últimos años ha registrado una producción editorial considerable y continua. Lo más notable de esa producción puede ser señalado por tres tendencias. Por una parte, ha habido una difusión de textos de autores afroecuatorianos que descubren nuevas áreas de diversidad en un país conocido tradicionalmente como andino. Así, se ha realizado la edición crítica de un libro de A. Preciado (item **4066**) y la publicación de nuevos libros de N. Estupiñán Bass (item **3978**) y L.A. Chiriboga (item **3959**). Por otra parte, es también notable la aparición de un número considerable de poetas mujeres con una expresión femenina muy definida y de calidad, como las colecciones de C. Váscones (item **4096**), A. Galindo Palomeque (item **3989**) y J. Londoño (item **4028**). Asimismo, cobra relieve la publicación de volúmenes que reúnen la poesía de valores consagrados, como la de J.E. Adoum (item **3920**) y E. Granda (item **4002**), o ensayos críticos sobre poesía, como el libro dedicado al estudio de la obra de C. Dávila Andrade (item **4146**). [ORR]

PERU

Las fechas de 1988 y 1992, que marcaron respectivamente los 50 años de la muerte de C. Vallejo y los 100 de su nacimiento, fueron conmemoradas con varios simposios y homenajes. Estos actos y fechas dieron como resultado un buen número de volúmenes críticos colectivos (items **4137** y **4131**) y algunos libros individuales (items **4143** y **4151**) que contribuyeron a engrosar la ya vasta bibliografía vallejiana, a veces con revisiones y valoraciones novedosas. Estos trabajos pueden considerarse entre los aportes más importantes al estudio de la poesía peruana contemporánea que se hayan producido en el período. La aparición de la primera edición crítica de la obra poética de Vallejo (item **4092**) confirma la privilegiada atención que el poeta ha recibido en esta ocasión desde diversas partes del mundo.

Hay que descatar también varias antologías y recopilaciones de la obra personal de otros notables poetas de este siglo: J.M. Eguren, E.A. Westphalen, C.G. Belli y B. Varela (items **3975, 4105, 3937** y **4094**); el hecho de que todas esas recopilaciones hayan aparecido en España aseguran—a parte de un merecido reconocimiento—un nuevo público lector para autores poco conocidos en ese ámbito. Dos libros actualizan la faceta poética del novelista J.M. Arguedas, como recopilador (item **4157**) y como creador él mismo (item **4141**). Varios poetas vivos y activos han publicado importantes nuevos libros: entre ellos, pueden mencionarse los de J. Sologuren (item **4085**), B. Varela (item **4093**), C.G. Belli (item **3936**), W. Delgado (item **3968**) y A. Cisneros (item **3961**). Y en el campo de la nueva poesía femenina, cabe destacar la reedición de *Noches de adrenalina* de C. Ollé (item **4049**) y un nuevo libro de R. Di Paolo (item **3970**), que representan bien las distintas direcciones que sigue ese sector de la poesía peruana actual. [JMO]

CHILE

En este período destacan cuatro títulos de poetas no consagrados: *Territorios secretos* de E. Toro Leontic (item **4088**), *Los invitados de tu memoria* de C. Casanova (item **3953**), *Noche de brujas y otros hechos de sangre* de T. Harris (item **4009**) y *The Boston Evening Transcript* de R. Jacob (item **4015**). Los dos primeros confirman la solidez de una tradición lírica nacional que sepulta de una vez el encasillamiento intimista de lo femenino y concilia la construcción de mundos interiores con el retrato amargo de un orbe político confuso y amenazante. El breve poemario de Harris, por su parte, explota la imaginería cinematográfica con un sabio y poco usual humor negro. La obra de Jacob, finalmente, es un descubrimiento en todo el sentido de la palabra: un primer libro que delata una madurez poética sorprendente lograda tras muchos años de trabajo silencioso.

En lo concerniente a reediciones y a obras de autores que ya ocupan un lugar indiscutible en la historia poética chilena, debe mencionarse, en primer lugar, la cuidadosa edición de poemas póstumos de G. Mistral bajo el título de *Lagar II* (item **4038**). Tampoco debe olvidarse la reimpresión de *Maremoto* de P. Neruda (item **4046**), una breve colección de poemas hasta ahora escasamente difundidos. La poesía completa del recientemente fallecido E. Anguita vuelve a aparecer, con valiosos inéditos y añadidos de sus críticos (item **3924**).

En el área de las antologías merece destacarse la labor de J. Ortega, que ha escogido los *Poemas para combatir la calvicie* de N. Parra (item **4058**), muestra que abarca varios poemarios completos publicados desde los 1950 e incluye textos inéditos y el discurso (en verso) leído en la recepción del Premio Juan Rulfo. También ha de prestarse atención a *Las hermosas*, una selección de la poesía erótica de G. Rojas (item **4077**), cuyo prestigio internacional se afianza cada vez más; este volumen, sin duda, recoge lo más luminoso y vivaz de su obra. P. de Rokha, asimismo, es objeto de un merecido redescubrimiento por parte de editoriales extranjeras (item **4078**).

En cuanto a testimonios sobre poesía chilena lo más memorable es *Huidobro, la marcha infinita* (item **4153**), libro con el que V. Teitelboim cierra una trilogía biográfica cuyo valor literario intrínseco sobrepasa el esperable de fuentes bibliográficas secundarias. Curiosamente, también ha sido dedicado al autor de *Altazor* el mejor volumen de crítica literaria aquí reseñado; se trata de *Vicente Huidobro y el cubismo*, de S. Benko (item **4130**), cuya experiencia en el campo de la pintura le permite examinar paralelismos de estética y técnica entre dos expresiones del arte de vanguardia, la verbal y la visual, no siempre convincentemente asociadann s por los estudiosos. [MG]

ARGENTINA, URUGUAY Y PARAGUAY

Las obras de A. Pizarnik y J. Gelman continúan siendo objeto de interés crítico y editorial. De la primera destacamos la reedición corregida y ampliada de la *Obra completa* (item **4063**). Gelman ha publicado *Salarios del impío* (item **3996**), poemario caracterizado por su radicalidad, sobriedad e intensidad expresiva. También O. Orozco da muestra de su magisterio poético a través de *Mutaciones de la realidad* (item **4051**). De especial interés resulta además la selección antológica de la obra de R. González Tuñón (item **4001**). En la joven poesía argentina sigue predominando la tendencia neorromántica.

De la producción poética paraguaya sobresale la voz de L. Cardozo (item **3952**), cuyos aciertos poéticos auspician una promisora voz dentro de la joven poesía paraguaya. De este período merece mencionarse también el nuevo poemario de S. Delgado (item **3967**).

La nota más constante de la joven poesía uruguaya es la búsqueda de racionalización de la realidad circundante. Hay un notorio desencantamiento y desesperanza que se suma a la pérdida de otras utopías a nivel continental y mundial. La publicación de *A pesar de la muerte y otros poemas* (item **3944**) de H. Benítez Casco pone a disposición de los lectores toda la obra édita de este importante y casi desconocido poeta uruguayo. También la amplia selección antológica de la obra de I. Gutiérrez (item **4008**) constituye un aporte editorial relevante. Dos importantes poetas del 900 fueron objeto de publicación de sus obras completas: D. Agustini (item **3921**) y J. de Ibarbourou (item **4013**). En ambos casos, las ediciones han sido enriquecidas con valiosos aportes críticos. [LU]

ANTHOLOGIES

3890 Un ángulo del mundo: muestra antológica de los poetas invitados al Encuentro Iberoamericano de Poesía Centenario del Natalicio de Vicente Huidobro. Edición de Andrés Morales. Santiago: Red Internacional del Libro, 1993. 232 p.: bibl.

Registra la participación de 46 poetas de Chile y de Iberoamérica en los actos conmemorativos del centenario de Huidobro. Incluye un solo texto—y no siempre representativo de cada autor. Muy modesta como antología, interesa como testimonio de un acontecimiento cultural importante. [PL]

3891 Antología de la poesía hondureña. v. 1. Recopilación de Jorge Luis Oviedo. Prólogo de Juan Antonio Medina Durón. Tegucigalpa: Editorial Higueras, 1993. 1 v.: bibl.

Para J.L. Oviedo, antologador de este volumen, el género antología todavía tiene el mérito de satisfacer necesidades culturales y de llenar los vacíos que impone la dependencia económica. El trabajo quiere, por tanto, reivindicar una literatura nacional y, hasta cierto punto, cumplir una labor pedagógica. El volumen que ahora se reseña es el primero de una serie de dos e incluye autores del siglo XIX y XX. [EM]

3892 Antología del poema en prosa en México. Estudio preliminar, selección y notas de Luis Ignacio Helguera. México:

Fondo de Cultura Económica, 1993. 479 p. (Letras mexicanas)

Comenzando con Othón (1858–1906) y terminando con C. Leñero (n. 1959), cubre un siglo de promociones literarias en México. Es la primera antología de este tipo. Está muy bien organizada y diseñada. Aunque el propio Helguera reconoce que es difícil llegar a una definición precisa del campo, el volumen es espléndido en su selección de textos. Incluye también escritores comúnmente identificados como narradores. [JS]

3893 Un camino de hallazgos: poetas bajacalifornianos del siglo veinte. Recopilación de Gabriel Trujillo Muñoz. Mexicali, Mexico: Univ. Autónoma de Baja California, 1992. 2 v.: bibl., ill. (Serie Literatura)

Extensa y útil introducción de G. Trujillo. La antología se agrupa bajo diferentes generaciones: bohemio-periodística, de medio siglo, de la californidad, de la ruptura y de fin de milenio. Quizá el compilador debió restringirse a un número más limitado de escritores, puesto que con 135 poetas (la mayoría de ellos de las últimas dos generaciones) se impide la posibilidad de una selección más amplia de poemas y un mejor conocimiento de los escritores incluidos. [JS]

3894 Cervantes y el Quijote en la poesía venezolana. Recopilación de Mario Briceño Perozo. Caracas: Academia Nacional de la Historia, 1992. 201 p.: bibl., ill., index.

Selección poética sobre temas y personajes cervantinos, publicada como parte del homenaje a España por los 500 años del Descubrimiento de América. Incluye textos de 66 autores de los siglos XIX y XX. Aunque el mérito de los poemas es discreto, interesa como antología temática. [PL]

3895 Corchado Juarbe, Carmen. El indio en la poesía puertorriqueña desde 1847 hasta la generación del sesenta: antología. Río Piedras, P.R.: Esmaco Printers Corp., 1993. 352 p.: bibl.

Rastreo y contextualización histórico-literaria, esta antología cuenta con una excelente introducción y con numerosas acotaciones críticas que explican la presencia del indio en cuatro momentos de la literatura puertorriqueña: 1) en el siglo XIX; 2) en la poesía modernista; 3) en las generaciones del 30–40; 4) en las generaciones del 50–60. [FC]

3896 Daneri, Juan José et al. Retaguardia de la vanguardia. Viña del Mar, Chile: Altazor, 1992. 80 p.

Muestra poética de Daneri, Alex von Bischhoffshausen, Mauricio Barrientos y Sergio Madrid Sielfeld, grupo de poetas nacidos hacia 1967. Pese al título, la mejor tradición vanguardista sigue viva en este volumen, como lo delatan las citas de Breton, Pessoa y las alusiones a un neovanguardista, Juan Luis Martínez, cuya presencia en las letras chilenas apenas ha empezado a estimarse. [MG]

3897 La décima escrita en la República Dominicana: antología histórica. Recopilación de Luis Beiro Alvarez y Huchi Lora. Santo Domingo: Fundación Barceló Pro Cultura, 1994. 203 p.: bibl.

Como primera antología de la décima dominicana, ésta recoge una muestra panorámica de la producción escrita a partir del siglo XVI hasta el siglo XX sin por eso convertirse en un estudio, una valoración o una historia. Se persigue el ordenamiento, el establecimiento y la ubicación en el tiempo y el espacio. En la breve introducción, se definen las características del género y se comenta la particularidad de la décima dominicana, cuyo desarrollo es ajeno a la música. [FC]

3898 Décimas premiadas: Concurso Nacional de Décimas por el Autodescubrimiento Cultural Dominicano. Santo Domingo: Ediciones CEDEE; Librería Caribe—CEDEE, 1993. 78 p. (Investigación e identidad)

Se recogen en esta compilación, publicada por el Centro Dominicano de Estudios de la Educación, las décimas ganadoras del concurso celebrado en 1992, cuyo primer premio lo obtuvo César Sánchez Beras, como parte de un proyecto encaminado al rescate y la recuperación histórica de los valores de la cultura dominicana. [FC]

3899 Encuentro con la Poesía Hispanoamericana, Lima, 1994. El uso de la palabra: Encuentro con la Poesía Hispanoamericana, del 7 al 10 de junio '94. Lima: Univ. de Lima, Vice-Rectorado, 1994. 426 p.

Antología de 93 participantes en el Encuentro realizado en Lima en 1994. Buena muestra del estado poético actual, por la presencia de escritores muy representativos: J.E. Pacheco, J. Gelman, R. Juarroz, F. Charry Lara, G. Rojas, O. Hahn, I. Vilariño, J. Hierro, R. Zurita, E.A. Westphalen, C.G. Belli, B. Varela, A. Cisneros, etc. Incluye 66 autores peruanos, un panorama bastante completo de ese país. Aunque la disposición alfabética de autores es funcional, la falta de índices entorpece su consulta. [PL]

3900 Fernández, Jesse. El poema en prosa en Hispanoamérica: del modernismo a la vanguardia; estudio crítico y antología. Madrid: Hiperión, 1994. 247 p.: bibl. (Poesía Hiperión; 225 [i.e. 227])

Una breve historia del poema en prosa y atendibles consideraciones sobre los aspectos formales y estilísticos que lo caracterizan, fundamentan la investigación de J. Fernández, que concluye con un acucioso estudio del proceso de esta manifestación en Hispanoamérica. La generosa antología incluye textos de J. del Casal, R. Darío, P. Prado, G. Mistral, J. de Ibarbourou, R. López Velarde, J. Torri, V. Huidobro, C. Vallejo y P. Neruda. Muy destacable también la bibliografía activa y pasiva (p. 85–94). Libro atractivo para el lector de poesía y de gran utilidad para el especialista. [PL]

3901 Gorostiza, José et al. Poesías: Contemporáneos. Edición de Luis Maristany. Malaga, Spain?: Anaya & M. Muchnik; Ayuntamiento de Málaga, 1992. 256 p.: bibl., ill. (Escritores de América; 4)

Excelente edición de textos representativos del grupo "Contemporáneos." La introducción de L. Maristany es muestra ejemplar de precisión crítica, que cumple el propósito de situar a los autores y describir y valorar adecuadamente su estética. Entre sus méritos antológicos debe señalarse la inclusión completa de los poemas extensos de J. Gorostiza, X. Villaurrutia, J. Cuesta y G. Owen. Un libro esencial, cuyo único punto discutible podría ser la presencia de S. Novo, prescindible en este contexto. [PL]

3902 Guajana: tres décadas de poesía 1962–1992. Selección e introducción de Marcos F. Reyes Dávila. San Juan: Editorial Guajana, 1992. 485 p.: bibl., ill. (Col. Guajana)

Correspondiente a la década de los 60, la revista *Guajana* agrupó a los poetas de izquierda que, bajo la euforia del momento, asumieron un compromiso político y social desde la poesía puertorriqueña. En la introducción, Reyes Dávila contextualiza el aporte literario de *Guajana* en los 60 a la vez que contrasta esta poesía con la de los años 80. [FC]

3903 Inventario de voces: visión retrospectiva de la literatura sonorense. Coordinación de Gerardo Cornejo Murrieta *et al.* Hermosillo, Mexico: Editorial UniSon, 1992. 555 p.: bibl.

Compila crónica, poesía, cuento, novela, teatro y ensayo. Abarca obras del siglo XVIII al XX. Es parte del proyecto nacional de publicación de antologías literarias de los diferentes estados de México. Aunque tenga utilidad mayor para los especialistas, el libro sirve también como recurso para investigar peculiaridades de la literatura norteña de México. [JS]

3904 Morelos, literatura bajo el volcán: poesía y narrativa, 1871–1990. Selección, prólogo y notas de Lorena Careaga Viliesid. México: Consejo Nacional para la Cultura y las Artes, 1991. 295 p. (Letras de la República)

A pesar de ser tierra de inspiración nacional e internacional, Morelos no cuenta con escritores reconocidos. La antología no precisa el criterio de selección de sus autores (algunos nacen en Morelos, otros son residentes). De todos modos, el volumen es valioso porque pone en circulación nuevos nombres. [JS]

3905 La mujer nicaragüense en la poesía: antología. Recopilación de Daisy Zamora. Managua: Editorial Nueva Nicaragua, 1992. 479 p.: bibl.

Con este volumen aparece, por primera vez en Nicaragua, una muestra de poesía escrita por mujeres. A los legendarios nombres de R. Darío, J. Coronel Urtecho, M. Cuadra, P. Antonio Cuadra, A. Cortés, S. de la Selva . . . , se suman ahora el de Ana Ilce, Gioconda Belli, Vidaluz Meneses, Rosario Murillo, Michele Najlis, Marianela Corriols, Daisy Zamora y muchos otros. Y, como caso especial, Claribel Alegría, siempre considerada como escritora salvadoreña. [EM]

3906 Noche insular: antología de poesía cubana. Recopilación, selección e introducción de Mihály Dés. Barcelona: Editorial Lumen, 1993. 408 p.: bibl. (Poesía; 79)

De M. de Zequeira y Arango (1746–1846) a M. Díaz Martínez (n. 1936), esta antología recoge lo imprescindible de la poesía cubana consagrada. Sin embargo, la guía el deseo de destacar, junto a los poetas y a los poemas más reconocidos, el papel de otros poetas menos conocidos al igual que de otros poemas menos emblemáticos. [FC]

3907 Nombres para una espada. Selección, introducción y notas de Roberto Sosa. Tegucigalpa?: Centro Editorial, 1992? 83 p.: bibl., ill.

Este volumne rinde homenaje poético a la figura clave de la política centroamericana del siglo XIX: el hondureño Francisco Morazán. Con precisión, Roberto Sosa ha reunido una interesante colección de poemas dedicados a la memoria de Morazán y escritos por poetas de la talla de R. Darío, R. Dalton, P. Neruda y F. Gavidia. [EM]

3908 Panorama de la décima: apuntes para su historia, 1430–1975. Recopilación de Luis Beiro Alvarez. La Vega, República Dominicana: Univ. Tecnológica del Cibao, 1990. 152 p.

Como la estrofa más popular en la historia de la poesía de habla española, la décima tiene dos versiones inconfundibles: la escrita, que es literatura, y la oral, que es actuación. Los apuntes históricos y la selección de décimas aquí incluidos conjugan las aportaciones españolas e hispanoamericanas a partir del siglo XVI. En el siglo XX, Cuba asume el liderazgo de la décima en América. [FC]

3909 Para entendernos: inventario poético puertorriqueño; siglos XIX y XX. Recopilación de Efraín Barradas. San Juan: Instituto de Cultura Puertorriqueña, 1992. 458 p.

Un inventario—recopilación e interpretación—de la poesía puertorriqueña que tiene como objetivo incidir en el desarrollo histórico y cultural de la isla. Incluye, a partir de 1970, a J.M. Lima, R. Ferré, J.L. Vega, P. Pietri y J. Melendes. P. Barradas, la poesía ofrece un conocimiento de la sociedad que no se circunscribe únicamente a la temática. [FC]

3910 El poema venezolano en prosa. Prólogo y selección de Pedro Pablo Paredes. Caracas: Contraloría General de la República, 1989. 117 p. (Col. Medio siglo de la Contraloría General de la República. Serie Letra viva)

Título prometedor y resultado decepcionante. El brevísimo prólogo (p. 7–9) no avanza ninguna caracterización del poema en prosa y la selección acumula muestras de 58 autores, desde Bolívar (1783) a Mariela Arvelo (1949), sin indicar procedencia de las piezas o fragmentos. Un contraste flagrante con investigaciones acuciosas sobre esta forma, como la de J. Fernández (item **3900**). [PL]

3911 Poesía chilena contemporánea: breve antología crítica. Recopilación de Naín Nómez. Santiago: Fondo de Cultura Económica; Editorial Andrés Bello, 1992. 352 p.: bibl. (Col. V centenario Chile)

Notable trabajo antológico en todos sus aspectos: la introducción traza líneas definitorias de la poesía chilena desde el modernismo hasta hoy; cada sección va precedida de notas que sintetizan lecturas críticas acerca de los poetas; se imprimen pasajes donde éstos reflexionan acerca de sus principios; la mayoría de los nombres que figuran en la lista son claves. [MG]

3912 Re, Ana María del et al. Antología de la poesía hispanoamericana moderna. v. 1–2. Coordinación de Guillermo Sucre. 1. ed. en M.A., corr. y aum. Caracas: Monte Avila Editores Latinoamericana; Baruta: USB-Equinoccio, 1993. 2 v. (Altazor)

El competente equipo que trabajó con G. Sucre ha dado fin a una tarea emprendida hace más de 10 años (vol. 1, que ahora se reedita, apareció en 1982). Propuesta antológica ejemplar, producto de investigaciones compartidas y de diálogos críticos que han permitido a los autores sortear o reducir el grado de arbitrariedad, frecuente en obras de su especie. Vol. 1 incluye 31 poetas representativos del modernismo y de los movimientos iniciales de vanguardia desde J. Martí a H. Díaz-Casanueva. Vol. 2, sin duda más expuesto a la polémica, es una muestra de 40 poetas desde J. Lezama Lima a A. Oliveros. La generosa selección de textos y su atinada disposición permite seguir el proceso de escritura en cada caso. Notas introductorias precisas e informadas bibliografías acrecientan el mérito de esta obra estimulante y de consulta indispensable. [PL]

3913 Roca, Juan Manuel et al. Diez años Premio Nacional de Poesía Universidad de Antioquia. Medellín, Colombia: Editorial Univ. de Antioquia, 1990. 395 p.: ill. (Col. Premio Nacional de Poesía)

Muestra de los autores premiados en los concursos de Antioquia (1979–89). Selección interesante, pero omite informaciones sobre ese evento. Sólo en la solapa del libro aparecen datos de los premios acordados cada año: J.M. Roca, V. Gaviria, R. Vélez (1979); R. Vélez, A. Torres, J.A. Vélez (1980); A. Miranda, S. Jaramillo, J.A. Vélez (1981); A. Vélez, L. Mejía (1982); J. Jaramillo Escobar, O. Gallo (1983); F. Herrera (1985); D. Jiménez, M. Arias (1987); S. Jaramillo (1988); G. Moseley-Williams (1989). [PL]

3914 Sentimentario: antología de la poesía amorosa colombiana. Recopilación de Darío Jaramillo Agudelo. Bogotá: Editorial Oveja Negra, 1987? 172 p. (Biblioteca de literatura colombiana; 99)

En un prólogo muy ingenioso, D. Jaramillo puntualiza su intención de disponer un libro útil para "la vida de los amantes." El resultado supera ese propósito, por sus buenas páginas iniciales y por la notable y amplia selección de poemas. Atractiva antología, que logra innovar en esta trajinada materia. [PL]

3915 Tiempo vegetal: poetas y narradores de la frontera sur. Prólogo, selección y notas de María José Rodilla. Tuxtla Gutiérrez, Mexico: Gobierno del Estado de Chiapas, Consejo Estatal de Fomento a la Investigación y Difusión de la Cultura, DIF-Chiapas, Instituto Chiapaneco de Cultura, 1993. 747 p.: ill.

Esta antología compila obra de escritores de Chiapas, Tabasco, Campeche, Yucatán y Quintana Roo. Esta región ha nutrido mucha de la mejor literatura mexicana: C. Pellicer, J. Gorostiza, J.C. Becerra, R. Castellanos, J. García Ponce, J. Sabines y E. Zepeda, por sólo mencionar algunos. El grueso volumen introduce, además, una buena cantidad de escritores menos conocidos. En total, se reúnen 59 poetas y 38 narradores. El libro es una alternativa para aquellos cansados de la literatura urbana de la Ciudad de México. [JS]

3916 Universidad de El Salvador. Quizás tu nombre salve: antología bilingüe de la poesía salvadoreña = Et si ton nom sauvait: anthologie bilingue de la poésie salvadorienne. Textos escogidos y traducidos por María Poumier-Tuquechel. Prefacio de Matilde Elena López. Prólogo de Roberto Armijo. San Salvador?: Editorial Universitaria, Univ. de El Salvador, 1992. 452 p.: index. (Col. obras representativas. Serie Latinoamérica)

Esta antología bilingüe de la poesía salvadoreña tiene el mérito de dar a conocer la importante contribución de este país a la tradición literaria latinoamericana. La nota de originalidad está dada por el abandono de criterios cronológicos para presentar a los 47 antologados, que aparecen—y reaparecen—a la señal de un motivo o de un verso. [EM]

3917 Ventana al mar: muestra de poesía de España y las Américas. Edición de Manuel de la Puebla. San Juan: Ediciones Mairena, 1992. 293 p.: bibl., ill.

Surge esta muestra de poesía como un proyecto "puro de amistad" y como una necesidad de dar a conocer el trabajo de los poetas del mundo hispánico y de todo el continente americano, por lo cual se incluyen poetas de Canadá y los Estados Unidos, el Caribe anglo y francés, la poesía aymara de Bolivia, la quechua de Bolivia y Perú, la guaraní del Paraguay y la maya de México. [FC]

BOOKS OF VERSE

3918 Achugar, Hugo. Orfeo en el salón de la memoria. Montevideo: Ediciones de Uno, 1991. 148 p. (Col. de poesía/Ediciones de Uno; 41)

Los siete núcleos temáticos en que se divide el libro están unificados por la constante puesta a prueba de las virtualidades de la palabra al destacar con libertad las muchas asociaciones fónicas y semánticas que esas palabras evocan en el poeta. Escritura que se autocorrige sin invalidar ni excluir las formas escriturales que le preceden. [LU]

3919 Acosta, Leonardo. El sueño del samurai. La Habana: Editorial Letras Cubanas, 1989. 135 p. (Giraldilla. Poesía)

Más investigador que poeta, sin embargo, Acosta reúne aquí una colección de poemas y "minitextos," escritos o esbozados entre 1962–85, donde el tiempo, la filosofía zen, la historia, la muerte, la música, la literatura dan lugar a la reflexión, a la paradoja, al comentario, al poema y a la prosa que vienen, como el verbo, despúes—y nunca antes—de la creación. [FC]

3920 Adoum, Jorge Enrique. El amor desenterrado y otros poemas. Quito: Editorial El Conejo, 1993. 97 p. (Col. Ecuador/letras)

Integrado por cuatro textos largos: "El Amor Desenterrado," "Tras la Pólvora, Manuela," "Postales del Trópico con Mujeres" y "Sobre la Inutilidad de la Semiología." Los textos mantienen el mismo nivel de calidad de este poeta ecuatoriano, cuya obra se caracteriza por la densidad de la reflexión poética que articula símbolos complejos y herméticos con notable grado de subjetividad e irracionalismo. [ORR]

3921 Agustini, Delmira. Poesías completas. Edición de Magdalena García Pinto. Madrid: Cátedra, 1993. 356 p.: bibl., ill. (Letras hispánicas; 372)

Cuidada edición de la obra de esta importante poeta uruguaya del 900 a cargo de Magdalena García Pinto. La valiosa introducción se detiene en el contexto cultural de la poeta y destaca la perspectiva marginalizante con que ciertos críticos han analizado la obra de D. Agustini. Las numerosas advertencias y notas agregan valor e interés a esta edición. [LU]

3922 Alvarez, Mario Rubén. La sangre insurrecta. Asunción: Editorial Don Bosco, 1992. 100 p.

Testimonio poético de las injusticias sufridas por nuestros indios a la llegada de los españoles. El poeta ve en la viva presencia del guaraní, el único gesto de insurrección triunfal frente a tanta destrucción y muerte. Epicidad y lirismo se aúnan en este poemario. [LU]

3923 Amara, Luigi. El decir y la mancha. México: Univ. Autónoma Metropolitana, Unidad Xochimilco, 1994. 61 p. (Mantícora)

En este primer libro de Amara (n. México, 1971) hay una concepción de la escritura como borrones de tinta sobre el papel. Un verso de David Huerta ("El Mundo es una Mancha en el Espejo") parece permear el volumen. La voz es un eco que rebota y desaparece; las letras deambulan por la página en blanco ("¿Cómo Atrapar en Sílabas la Nube?"); todo parece perderse en un haz de luz difuminado. [JS]

3924 Anguita, Eduardo. Poesía entera: obra poética completa. Santiago: Editorial Universitaria, 1994. 219 p.: bibl. (El poliedro y el mar)

Necesaria reedición de la obra poética completa de quien mejor ha sintetizado, sin dejarse poseer por ellas, algunas de las principales tendencias líricas de su país en el siglo XX: creacionismo, surrealismo, antipoesía e, incluso, religiosidad tradicional. De sumo valor resultan los ensayos y testimonios de Pedro Lastra y Cristián Warnken incluidos en el volumen. [MG]

3925 Antezana, René. La flecha del tiempo. La Paz: Ediciones Casa de la Cultura, Alcaldía Municipal, 1993. 104 p.

Este volumen obtuvo el Premio Unico de Poesía del XXII Concurso Anual de Literatura Franz Tamayo, de la Municipalidad de La Paz. Estructuras yuxtapuestas y enumerativas caracterizan a estos textos, en los que se observan asimismo cierta dubitación que le impide realizar plenamente su expresión. [ORR]

3926 Arteche, Miguel. Tercera antología. Buenos Aires: Corregidor, 1991. 138 p.

Esta selección abarca textos escritos entre 1952–91 e ilustra las principales tendencias de la obra de Arteche, formalmente conservadora pero temáticamente excéntrica: después de todo, constituye un verdadero reto y una provocación a la norma moderna el proyecto de someter a nuevas variaciones la milenaria imaginería cristiana. [MG]

3927 Arturo, Aurelio. Morada al sur y otros poemas. Madrid: Ediciones de Cultura Hispánica, 1992. 92 p.: bibl. (Col. Poesía)

Importante reedición de la singular obra de A. Arturo (1906–74), cuyo reconocimiento recién empieza a manifestarse en trabajos críticos y en ediciones como ésta, que incorpora sus versiones de poetas ingleses contemporáneos, publicadas póstumamente. Poesía del asombro y de la memoria es descripción que conviene a esta escritura de intenso lirismo y de rara perfección. [PL]

3928 Avila Villanueva, Silvia Mercedes. Obra poética. Edición de Guido Orías. Prólogo de Julio de la Vega. La Paz: La Palabra, 1993. 237 p.: ill.

Obra completa póstuma de esta poeta boliviana (1940–92), preparada por otro poeta, Guido Orías. La autora es una de las integrantes más destacadas de la generación de poetas y escritores bolivianos que aparecieron en la década del 60. El volumen está precedido por un "Prólogo" del poeta y crítico Julio de la Vega, quien destaca el estilo unitario que caracteriza a la obra poética. [ORR]

3929 Bañuelos, Juan. Estelas de los confines. México: Univ. Autónoma Metropolitana, Casa del Tiempo, 1994. 56 p. (Margen de poesía; 37)

En la poesía de Bañuelos (n. Tuxtla Gutiérrez, México, 1932) hay una triple articulación de su tierra natal: el espacio selvático, la recuperación de cierta mitología maya y, en irrupción infeliz, la injusticia y la destrucción. En el poema que da título al libro se combinan descripciones pormenorizadas del cañón de El Sumidero (en Chiapas) con un paulatino ingreso del terror, del abuso y de la pobreza. Hay, por lo demás, una vuelta a la tradición indígena y un rescate de la antigua civilización maya. [JS]

3930 Barahona Riera, Macarena. Atlántico. San José?: Ediciones Guayacán, 1991? 60 leaves.

En este poemario la costarricense M. Barahona Riera hurga en los mundos femeninos hasta vislumbrar una posibilidad de mujer que responda a sus ansiedades y deseos. La mujer que le interesa a Barahona Riera está vinculada al mágico Caribe y es distinta porque lleva en sí misma el mar, le siguen la tierra, la luna, las estrellas, un calor que huele a patria y sexo. [EM]

3931 Baranda, María. Ficción de cielo. México: Univ. Autónoma Metropolitana, Casa del Tiempo, 1993. 42 p. (Margen de poesía; 38)

Entre las poetas jóvenes mexicanas, M. Baranda (pseudónimo de Alicia Meza, n. 1962) destaca por su fuerza evocadora. Recuerda un poco a Olga Orozco, por la dimensión mítica y gravedad de las imágenes. Baranda hace de las situaciones más banales episodios mayores en que se vislumbran los conflictos más arraigados del hombre. Por este libro pasan el origen, el exilio, el regreso a casa, la muerte y el canto órfico. [JS]

3932 Barros, Manoel de. O encantador de palavras: poemas escolhidos de Manoel de Barros. Ilustrações de Siron Franco. Rio de Janeiro: Sociedade de Bibliófilos do Brasil, 1996. 131 p.: bibl., ill. (some col.)

In this valuable and unique creation, the Brazilian Society of Bibliophiles' first publication, poems of *matogrossense* Manoel de Barros are lovingly illustrated by *goiano* Siron Franco. Heavily influenced by the sounds and images of the Pantanal, this limited edition (165 numbered copies) reproduces the selected work of Barros, who, in the words of Brazil's premier bibliophile José Mindlin, "if he did not exist, would have to be invented." [I. Siqueira Wiarda]

3933 Bartolomé, Efraín. Corazón del monte. México: Coordinación Nacional de Descentralización; Saltillo, Mexico: Instituto Coahuilense de Cultura, 1995. 90 p. (Los cincuenta)

En estos poemas con cierto matiz ecologista, Bartolomé (n. Ocosingo, México, 1950) defiende la selva chiapaneca. Pero lo hace con un discurso indirecto, sugerente, que evoca los espacios naturales, los recupera y advierte su destrucción. Véase, en particular, el último poema del libro, "Audiencia de los Confines," que convoca innumerables voces del pasado y del presente, una amalgama colectiva que presencia el dinamitaje de su tierra. [JS]

3934 Baytelman, Shlomit. Escritos para un amor inconcluso. Prólogo de Nicanor Parra. Dibujos de Roser Bru. Santiago: Hachette, 1992. 119 p.: col. ill.

Poemario en el que se cataloga concienzudamente la imaginería del amante fantasma; la remisión directa a María Luisa Bombal no debe hacernos perder de vista una tradición mucho más antigua en la que Sor Juana constituye un precedente insoslayable. [MG]

3935 Bellessi, Diana. El jardín. Rosario, Argentina: Bajo la Luna Nueva, 1992. 128 p.

El jardín es el espacio donde la creación tiene lugar. Como árboles y plantas, las palabras cumplen su ciclo vital. La poeta contempla ese jardín-lenguaje; de su ciclo vital participa, descubre e ilumina el universo de seres que lo pueblan y dan vida. Hay un rescate de

la belleza natural del mundo. Destacamos el poema "Cada Fragmento de Mí." [LU]

3936 Belli, Carlos Germán. Acción de gracias. Trujillo, Peru: Municipalidad Provincial de Trujillo; Casa del Artista, 1992. 52 p. (Col. Homenaje al centenario de César Vallejo; 16)

La insólita voz poética de Belli—quizá la más extraña después de Vallejo—se ha ido serenando con el tiempo, aunque sin perder su don para reelaborar una imagen del mundo contemporáneo mediante un lenguaje arcaico y formas tradicionales de versificación. En esta colección el modelo parece ser la poesía neoclásica, afín a su resignada certeza de que ha alcanzado en la paz del hogar una forma modesta del paraíso. [JMO]

3937 Belli, Carlos Germán. Los talleres del tiempo: poemas escogidos. Edición de Paul W. Borgeson, Jr. Madrid: Visor, 1992. 267 p.: bibl. (Col. Visor de poesía; 284)

Amplia y muy ilustrativa selección de la obra del autor—la cuarta que publica—desde *Poemas* (1958) hasta *En el restante tiempo terrenal* (1988, 1990). Ofrece una visión sintética de su evolución poética y la forma cómo se han reiterado y renovado sus motivos, obsesiones y modelos. [JMO]

3938 Bellinghausen, Hermann. De una vez. Xoco, Mexico: Consejo Nacional para la Cultura y las Artes, 1992. 121 p. (Luzazul)

Poesía amorosa; recurre a diferentes códigos del amor para inventar el propio. Bellinghausen (n. México, 1953) utiliza descripciones minuciosas que, en ocasiones, tienen que acudir al lenguaje cultista o especializado: "Pero no hay sol más reverdecido/que el de mi gubia presa/en su pasión de cisne." [JS]

3939 Benavides, Wáshington. Lección de exorcista. Montevideo: Ediciones de la Banda Oriental, 1991. 51 p. (Ediciones de la Banda Oriental; 145)

La reflexión sobre la escritura y el escritor predomina en estos textos. El libre juego intertextual enriquece este poemario de notables aciertos poéticos. [LU]

3940 Benavides, Wáshington. Tía Cloniche. Montevideo: Ediciones de la Banda Oriental, 1990. 68 p. (Poetas uruguayos; 25)

Poesía que ilustra las formas cotidianas del amor, la muerte, los deseos y otras vivencias de importancia para los anónimos personajes que pueblan este poemario. Poesía de indudable estilo narrativo atenta a las realizaciones del habla popular. [LU]

3941 Benedetti, Mario. Antología poética. Prólogo de J.M. Caballero Bonald. Selección del autor. 1. ed. en México. México: Editorial Nueva Imagen, 1986. 195 p.

El prólogo de Caballero Bonald destaca la coherencia interna de la obra crítica y artística del autor y especialmente las conexiones entre la obra poética y narrativa. Sugiere vínculos entre Benedetti y "ciertos exponentes de nuestro grupo poético del 50, y más concretamente con la de Angel González." En cuanto a la temática destaca los siguientes "espacios temáticos:" "el del amor como programación solidaria de la vida y el de la historia como experiencia moral, con el capítulo del exilio al fondo." Desde el punto de vista del lenguaje, el prologuista destaca la sensación de empecinada libertad expresiva, de soltura verbal enraizada en un fértil mestizaje lingüístico." [LU]

3942 Benedetti, Mario. Canciones del más acá. Montevideo: Cal y Canto, 1993. 151 p.: ill.

El volumen reúne letras de canciones y poemas del autor que han sido musicalizados. [LU]

3943 Benedetti, Mario. Las soledades de Babel. Montevideo: Arca, 1991. 155 p.

Frente a las distintas formas de la "extranjería," el lenguaje se presenta como refugio y morada. El lenguaje aparece como—quizás—el único vehículo que posibilite el regreso. Es la seña de identidad desde la cual se reflexiona sobre el país de fin de siglo. Los más importantes núcleos temáticos del libro—lenguaje, tiempo y exilio—están unificados, traspasados por un mismo sentimiento de soledad. [LU]

3944 Benítez Casco, Humberto. A pesar de la muerte y otros poemas. Diseño de la carátula e ilustraciones de Alvaro Pemper. Exordio de Ricardi Pallares. Montevideo: Edinor-Comunidad del Sur, 1992. 101 p.: ill.

Solitario y abandonado, Benítez Casco es uno de los poetas más originales y valiosos de la actual poesía uruguaya. Se reúnen aquí los tres libros anteriores publicados, todos ellos caracterizados por un profundo clasicismo y rigor formal. En gran parte de esta poesía predomina la reflexión sobre la soledad y Dios. [LU]

3945 Benítez Torres, César. Juegos de dados. México: Univ. Nacional Autónoma de México, 1994. 100 p. (El ala del tigre)

Benítez Torres (n. Amacuzac, México, 1958) desciende de la veta irónica, coloquial, de un Efraín Huerta, Jaime Sabines o Ricardo Castillo. Este libro mereció el Premio Nacional de Poesía "Manuel José Othón" en 1992. Lo peculiar es la incursión sarcástica de ciertos símbolos mexicanos. "Mala Sangre" es un excelente ejemplo: "Canto a pelo y con mariachi," dice en un verso autoburlón. En "Vuelo en Papalote," el sujeto es una especie de Altazor mexicanizado, que hace un recorrido de sí mismo a través de los terrenos de la infancia. [JS]

3946 Blanco, Alberto. Amanecer de los sentidos: antología personal. Presentación de Alvaro Mutis. México: Consejo Nacional para la Cultura y las Artes, 1993. 220 p. (Lecturas mexicanas, tercera serie; 79)

Primera antología de Blanco (n. México, 1951). Libro necesario, puesto que el autor ha publicado ya 10 libros de poesía y muchos de ellos son inencontrables. El libro está bien balanceado, excepto que la selección de *Antes de nacer* (1983) es demasiado escueta y, dada la importancia de ese libro, merecería mayor espacio. De todos modos, el libro es una excelente introducción a este poeta, quien se destaca por sus exploraciones de lo sagrado en los terrenos de lo cotidiano, además de su vínculo con la pintura y su elocuencia verbal. El volumen no recopila poesía de *Cuenta de los guías* (1992) y *Triángulo amoroso* (1992). [JS]

3947 Bonnett, Piedad. De círculo y ceniza. Prólogo de Ramón de Zubiría. Bogotá: Ediciones Uniandes, 1989. 59 p.

En una iluminadora Carta-Prólogo, Ramón de Zubiría puntualiza las características esenciales del libro, cuyos temas (el tiempo, la nostalgia, el sueño) giran en torno a un centro primordial: el amor asumido como una experiencia de plenitud. Nota sobresaliente de esta cuidadosa escritura poética es la alianza eficaz de naturalidad y rigor expresivos. [PL]

3948 Calzadilla, Juan. Antología paralela. Introducción y selección de Antonio López Ortega. Caracas: Fundarte, 1988. 87 p. (Col. Delta; 17)

Antología necesaria de un poeta significativo del movimiento "El Techo de la Ballena," surgido en Venezuela en la década del 60. López Ortega describe bien el proceso de esta poesía, desde iniciales preferencias simbolistas, algo divagatorias, a una expresión sentenciosa, precisa, capaz de condensar imágenes, formulaciones o situaciones insólitas, con destellos de estirpe surrealista (ver también *HLAS 48:5778* y *HLAS 52:4030*). [PL]

3949 Camarillo, Baudelio. En memoria del reino. México: Editorial Joaquín Mortiz, 1994. 94 p. (Premios bellas artes de literatura)

Este libro obtuvo el Premio Nacional de Poesía de Aguascalientes en 1993. La poesía de Camarillo (n. Tamaulipas, México, 1959) usa un lenguaje simple, en combinación con motivos clásicos (la luna, el agua, el sueño, la poesía misma) que sirven como pretexto para explorar el pasado y el presente del hablante. [JS]

3950 Cancel Negrón, Ramón. Socialidades y politicadas. San Juan: Ediciones Abonuco, 1992. 125 p.: ill.

Poesía satírica y conversacional inscrita como comentario ante la realidad social, política y cultural de Puerto Rico, donde todo parece estar al revés. Ante la farsa insular, el poeta escéptico quiere enderezar el mundo. [FC]

3951 Canese, Jorge. Paloma blanca, paloma negra. 2. ed. Asunción: Intercontinental Editora; Ediciones Ñandutí, 1989. 80 p. (Ñandutí vive)

Reedición de interesante poemario cuya primera edición fuera censurada por Stroessner en 1982. La mirada desencantada y desesperanzada del yo lírico se expresa a través de un lenguaje irreverente con permanentes giros humorísticos y un marcado coloquialismo. Destacamos "Primavera de Película" y "¿Quién Soy Yo para Decirte Tantas Cosas?." [LU]

3952 Cardozo, Lisandro. Poemas de fin de siglo. Asunción?: Editora Taller, 1992. 113 p. (Col. Cabichu'i 2. Serie Poesía)

Estos poemas son el pretexto para revisar la historia: las miserias del hombre y los errores que se repiten a lo largo de ella. Hay desencanto y desesperanza en la voz de Cardozo. Poemario en tres partes: 1) el poeta reflexiona sobre las obsesiones que acompañan la historia de la humanidad; 2) el centro de atención lo ocupa el fin de siglo y el tono se hace más irónico; y 3) se hace más intimista:

no las circunstancias del hombre sino las de un hombre forman eje temático. Cardozo es una de las voces más interesantes de la actual poesía paraguaya. [LU]

3953 Casanova, Cecilia. Los invitados de tu memoria. Chile: Casa Doce, 1993. 65 p.

Una de las voces más destacables de la poesía chilena actual. Los detalles íntimos, cotidianos, incluso insignificantes—la brevedad material de las composiciones confirma esa voluntad de atenerse a lo "menor"—se mezclan con la alusión política para crear efectos dramáticos que, no obstante, jamás llegan a lo tremebundo. [MG]

3954 Casazola Mendoza, Matilde. Tierra de estatuas desteñidas: poemas, 1973–1975. La Paz: Ediciones Gráficas, 1992. 137 p.

Cuarto volumen y el mejor de esta poeta boliviana ya consagrada. Reúne la producción escrita entre 1973–75. Sobresale la reflexión serena sobre aspectos cotidianos de la realidad, descubiertos en su profundidad gracias a la percepción trascendente de la autora, por la cual descubre poesía en lo habitual. [ORR]

3955 Castelvecchi, Gladys. Claroscuro. Montevideo: Ediciones de la Banda Oriental, 1993. 60 p.

A través de la imagen recurrente de la sombra, la autora recorre nuevas fascetas de lo real en poemas breves que no pretenden, sin embargo, ofrecer una idea acabada del mundo. [LU]

3956 Castillo, Ricardo. Islario. México: Consejo Nacional para la Cultura y las Artes, Instituto Coahuilense de Cultura, 1995. 100 p. (Los cincuenta)

Ricardo Castillo (n. Guadalajara, México, 1954) hace una selección y reordenamiento de sus siete poemarios. Castillo llamó la atención de la crítica con *El pobrecito señor X* (1976), libro afín al espíritu burlón y soez de la antipoesía de Parra. *Islario* se agrupa en cuatro archipiélagos o secciones, que no siguen un orden cronológico. Ofrece la oportunidad de conocer diversos registros y tener una visión de conjunto del poeta. [JS]

3957 Cea, José Roberto. La guerra nacional. San Salvador: Canoa Editores, 1992. 173 p.: ill.

La guerra nacional forma parte de trilogía poéticacuyos otros dos títulos son *Los herederos de Farabundo* (1981) y *Los pies sobre la tierra de Preseas* (1984). El autor, integrante del Círculo Literario Universitario, explora las posibilidades más originales del testimonio, el relato oral y el humor, para poetizar una historia colectiva cargada de desastres y violencias. [EM]

3958 Charry Lara, Fernando. Llama de amor viva. Madrid: Ediciones de Cultura Hispánica, 1989. 116 p. (Col. Poesía)

Excelente suma de una obra de tanta intensidad y transparencia como de singular afinamiento expresivo. La invocación a San Juan de la Cruz que es su título constituye homenaje y programa, que los poemas corroboran cumplidamente. Los textos proceden de *Nocturnos y otros sueños* (1949), *Los adioses* (1963) y *Pensamientos del amante* (1981). El prólogo del autor (p. 9–20) es pieza de antología, como relación autobiográfica y como reflexión poética. [PL]

3959 Chiriboga, Luz Argentina. La contraportada del deseo. Quito?: s.n., 1992. 117 leaves.

Este es el primer poemario de una escritora afro-ecuatoriana conocida hasta ahora como novelista. Tres preocupaciones sobresalen en la temática de estos textos: la condición de la mujer, la identidad cultural africana y el erotismo, expuestos en una variedad de motivos de la vida diaria. [ORR]

3960 Choque Mata, Jaime. Antología del ensueño: selección de poemas, 1966 a 1988. La Paz: Producciones Cima, 1991. 134 p.: ill.

Selección que el propio autor ha hecho de su poesía escrita entre 1966–88. Sus poemas se caracterizan por su tono épico y preocupaciones telúricas suscitadas por motivos de las dos culturas mayores pre-hispánicas de Bolivia: Tiwanaku e Inca. Sin embargo, no marginan motivos actuales de la realidad boliviana y latinoamericana en general. [ORR]

3961 Cisneros, Antonio. Las inmensas preguntas celestes. Madrid: Visor, 1992. 74 p. (Col. Visor de poesía; 288)

Las conocidas virtudes—ironía, distancia crítica, originales síntesis históricas o culturales—de este poeta, la figura más visible de su generación, se confirman en el presente libro. Es evidente también su afección por los paisajes marinos y la herencia precolombina. Pero nada en el breve volumen supera la sutil belleza del primer poema: "Un Puerto en el Pacífico," un texto digno de cualquier antología. [JMO]

3962 Coronel Urtecho, José. Pól-la d'anánta katánta paránta, dedójmia t'élson: imitaciones y traducciones. Managua: Nueva Nicaragua, 1993. 356 p.: ill.

Con este volumen, Coronel Urtecho se integra a la tradición de "reescritura" de poemas que, en rigor, más que una reescritura de textos ya publicados, interpreta una propuesta estética que descansa en la idea de que no existe el poema terminado sino más bien el proceso, la obra en curso. El volumen viene acompañado por un "Prólogo Conversado" (entre el autor y Luis Rocha) que es imprescindible para situar al poeta, a la obra y a la poesía nicaragüense. [EM]

3963 Cross, Elsa. Poemas desde la India. México: Univ. Autónoma Metropolitana, Casa del Tiempo, 1993. 24 p. (Margen de poesía; 18)

Cross (n. México, 1946) es heredera de la faceta oriental de la poesía de Octavio Paz, especialmente la derivada de *Ladera este* y *El mono gramático*. Este breve libro se compone de cinco poemas, que parten de reflexiones de sitios específicos en la India, y que se refieren a ciertos mitos asociados con una situación particular de la hablante. [JS]

3964 Cuadra, Angel. Angel Cuadra: the poet in socialist Cuba. Edited by Warren Hampton. Gainesville: Univ. Press of Florida, 1994. 158 p.: ill.

Traducidos al inglés, aparecen ensayos y poemas de Cuadra, destacado opositor de Fidel Castro. El material aquí incluido circuló en su momento en la clandestinidad como parte de la propaganda anticastrista del grupo Unidad Nacional Revolucionaria que Cuadra capitaneaba con la pluma. [FC]

3965 Cuadra, Manolo. Tres amores. Edición y prólogo de Julio Valle-Castillo. Epílogo de Mario Cajina-Vega. Managua: Editorial Nueva Nicaragua, 1992. 209 p.: bibl., ill.

Desde 1955 (fecha en que se publicó por primera vez *Tres amores*,) no se había producido ninguna reedición de este poemario. Su aparición es pues importante, ya que aporta al conocimiento de uno de los poetas más representativos de la Vanguardia poética nicaragüense. [EM]

3966 Degiovanangelo, Guillermo. Poemas de amor contra Albertina y otras lluvias. Montevideo: Ediciones del Mirador, 1991. 53 p.: ill. (Col. Libros del Mirador)

Segundo poemario del autor (n. Canelones, Uruguay, 1956). Predominan en sus textos el tono ligero, la claridad en la escritura y el humor. Destacamos los siguientes poemas: "Poema sin Albertina," "Poema sin Lluvia," "Otoño," "Opus 74" y "Pirexia II." [LU]

3967 Delgado, Susy. El patio de los duendes. Asunción: Arandurã Editorial, 1991. 79 p.: ill.

Predomina el tono íntimo y de suave erotismo. La quinta y última parte del libro está compuesta por un poema—"Yataity"—escrito en español y guaraní. El fuerte elemento dialógico y la libertad en el uso de ambas lenguas da un atractivo singular a este poema. [LU]

3968 Delgado, Wáshington. Historia de Artidoro. Lima: Seglusa Editores; Editorial Colmillo Blanco, 1994. 61 p.: ill.

La gran novedad de este notable conjunto de poemas es que su autor se los atribuye a un personaje de su invención, *alter ego* que sintetiza su amargura y desconsuelo ante la época de violencia y tragedia que vivió recientemente el Perú. La pulcritud formal y las graves cadencias del verso le dan un perfil muy sugestivo a la colección, una de las mejores del autor. [JMO]

3969 Deniz, Gerardo. Op. cit. México: Univ. Autónoma Metropolitana, Casa del Tiempo, 1992. 52 p. (Margen de poesía; 12)

Deniz (pseudónimo de Juan Almela, n. España, 1934) es uno de los poetas mexicanos más leídos por las nuevas generaciones. Su poesía está en contra del uso pomposo de lo "literario;" acude, en cambio, a discursos importados de variadas disciplinas: el científico, el de la música, etc., con múltiples referencias librescas. Cito, como ejemplo, esta parodia de anuncio de periódico: "APROVECHE, Soneto 1962. Excelente estado de conservación. Muy heterotónico. Filosófico. Audaz. Chute remarquable. Buen precio. Informes 5 36 22 82 tardes." [JS]

3970 Di Paolo, Rossella. Piel alzada. Lima: Editorial Colmillo Blanco, 1993. 53 p.: ill. (Col. de arena)

Tercer libro de la autora (n. Lima, 1960) que ofrece su versión personal del trance de ser mujer y escritora. Como tantas otras poetas feministas, habla como alguien que ha tomado conciencia de los poderes y flaquezas de su cuerpo. Un rasgo característico de su poesía es el uso de citas y textos clásicos o modernos para hacerlos significar otra cosa. [JMO]

3971 Díaz Casanueva, Humberto. Vox tatuada. Santiago: Editorial Universitaria, 1991. 94 p. (Col. Los Contemporáneos)

Uno de los últimos volúmenes publicados por un autor cuya valoración ha suscitado posiciones extremas por parte del público. Este poemario probablemente aporte argumentos a quienes cuestionan el sitial que ciertos premios y editoriales de prestigio dieron a Díaz-Casanueva. El empleo no siempre justificado de jerga filosófica, la arbitrariedad de sus imágenes, el prosaísmo de sus versos pesados y solemnes se intensifican en estas páginas. [MG]

3972 Diego, Eliseo. Poesía y prosa selectas. Selección, prólogo, cronología y bibliografía de Aramís Quintero. Caracas: Biblioteca Ayacucho, 1991. 376 p.: bibl. (Biblioteca Ayacucho; 161)

Reconocido como uno de los poetas cubanos más importantes de este siglo, la obra de Diego—"un continuo penetrar en el silencio"—constituye un intento de hallar el sentido trágico de la vida. Tanto en la prosa como en la poesía, Diego antepone lo poético como actividad de reconstrucción, y asume el tiempo y el vacío como resistencia que el poeta trata de vencer. [FC]

3973 Duverrán, Carlos Rafael. Tal vez en dura tierra: obra recobrada,1953–1989. Selección y prólogo de Antidio Cabal. San José: Editorial de la Univ. de Costa Rica, 1992. 282 p.: ill.

Más que una antología, el organizador de este volumen ha querido entregar al lector una obra. En ella, puede apreciarse el desarrollo del pensamiento poético del costarricense C. Duverrán. [EM]

3974 Egüez, Iván. El Olvidador. Quito: Abrapalabra Editores, 1992. 92 p.

Una nueva colección de un poeta ecuatoriano ya conocido. El título del volumen corresponde a una composición larga, compuesta por 37 textos breves. Esta unidad es, sin embargo, aparente, pues la segmentación es también dispersión de motivos. La brevedad de los textos se condiciona hacia un efecto final con el que el autor desea sorprender al lector. [ORR]

3975 Eguren, Jose María. De Simbólicas a Rondinelas. Edición de Gema Areta Marigó. Madrid: Visor, 1992. 189 p. (Col. Visor de poesía; 277)

Cuidada edición de la obra del singular poeta generalmente asociado con el modernismo, pero, en realidad, un introductor de la poesía contemporánea en el Perú. La recopilación permite comprobar su actualidad y es una rara ocasión que los lectores de España, donde apenas si ha sido antes publicada, tienen de conocerla directamente. [JMO]

3976 Escalante, Evodio. Cadencias de amor y neciedumbre. México: Univ. Autónoma Metropolitana, Casa del Tiempo, 1994. 44 p. (Margen de poesía; 30)

Aunque Escalante (n. Durango, México, 1946) es mejor conocido como crítico, también es autor de varios libros de poesía. Este volumen se centra en el amor. El hablante no parece enfocarse en una sola mujer; los textos varían en extensión, lenguaje y aproximación al tema. Van desde la metaforización clásica de la amada como centro de gravitación y vida hasta el relato semiconfesional de historias amorosas específicas. [JS]

3977 Espada, Joaquín. Anfora inexhausta. Cochabamba, Bolivia: Imprenta Veloz, 1991. 72 p.

Esta colección de textos tiene como tema principal el amor, sobre el cual reflexiona su autor desde diversas perspectivas y en circunstancias diversas. El lenguaje, que todavía conserva reminiscencias modernistas, logra un equilibrio entre representaciones ideales y el goce de una delicada sensualidad. En el año de publicación del volumen, su autor cumplía 93 años. [ORR]

3978 Estupiñán Bass, Nelson. Esta goleta llamada poesía. Quito: Editorial Casa de la Cultura Ecuatoriana, 1991. 177 p.

Este volumen reúne una selección de la obra del poeta afroecuatoriano más destacado. Los textos elegidos representan 50 años (1934–84) de una producción poética de indiscutible calidad, cuya característica es su sensibilidad ante los cambios históricos y sociales de su medio social. El material está ordenado de acuerdo a tres temas, según las secciones tituladas: 1) "Poesía Negrista;" 2) "Poesía Corozonal;" y 3) Poesía Comprometida." [ORR]

3979 Fernández, Macedonio. Poesías completas. Edición de Carmen de Mora Valcárcel. Madrid: Visor, 1991. 74 p.: bibl. (Col. Visor de poesía; 265)

La introducción de Mora Valcárcel expone con claridad la trayectoria creativa y las principales características de la obra de este singular poeta. [LU]

3980 Fernández Moreno, César. Ambages completos. Buenos Aires: Ediciones de la Flor, 1992. 208 p.

Esta edición reúne los textos breves de tono sarcástico y humorístico que el autor ha llamado "ambages" y que habían aparecido en diversas publicaciones anteriores. [LU]

3981 Ferrer de Arréllaga, Renée. El acantilado y el mar. Asunción: Arandurã Editorial, 1992. 74 p.: ill.

Nuevo poemario de esta poeta paraguaya. Su voz, de delicado lirismo, reflexiona sobre el hombre, el tiempo y el amor. Destacamos el poema "Las Declinaciones del Mar." [LU]

3982 Fiallo, Fabio. La canción de una vida. Prólogo y notas de José Enrique García. Santo Domingo: Ediciones de la Fundación Corripio, 1992. 365 p.: ill. (1 col.). (Biblioteca de clásicos dominicanos; 12)

Se recoge en esta antología la poesía de Fiallo (1866–1942) como una aportación raigal al romanticismo dominicano. Poesía intimista y amorosa, dada al "galanteo" y al "requiebro," la de Fiallo es también un rechazo del modernismo y la vanguardia. [FC]

3983 Fierro, Enrique. La clave, el tono: 1978–1979. México?: Ediciones de la Feria, 1991. 51 p.

Se abre con una serie de breves poemas cuyo tema es el cuestionamiento de lo temporal o la convivencia de los distintos tiempos y formas de lo real. El poema "Espíritu, no Letra: Pero" (1981) reflexiona sobre la imposibilidad del regreso, el tiempo que pasa y cambia la realidad de lo que fuimos anulando así como la re-unión con lo vivido. [LU]

3984 Fierro, Enrique. Homenajes: 1980–1984. Montevideo?: Vinten Editor, 1991. 52 p.

Poemas de homenaje a Onetti, Alí

Chumacero, Jesualdo, Neruda y Carlos Real de Azúa. Destacamos el tercero y el cuarto. [LU]

3985 Flores, Marco Antonio. Persistencia de la memoria. Guatemala: Ministerio de Cultura y Deportes, 1992. 97 p.: ill. (Col. Poesía guatemalteca siglo XX; 5. Serie Rafael Landívar)

Este colección de poemas narrativos cuenta una historia personal que funciona, al mismo tiempo, como una historia colectiva. Detrás del relato de una vida individual se esconden los rostros de un país—Guatemala—y de un exilio. [EM]

3986 Franco Oppenheimer, Félix. Ser: sonetario. San Juan: Editorial Yaurel, 1992. 99 p.: ill.

Uno de los fundadores del Movimiento Trascendentalista de los años 50 en Puerto Rico, el autor hace de la poesía un espacio para la meditación del ser, acompañada siempre de angustia pero también de una religiosidad consoladora donde se descifra, mediante el conocimiento propio, el sentido apocalíptico de la realidad. [FC]

3987 Fressia, Alfredo. Cuarenta poemas. Montevideo?: Ediciones de Uno, 1989. 64 p.

Lo exiliar como experiencia que afecta todas las zonas de realización del individuo unifica el poemario de este valioso poeta uruguayo. Destacamos los poemas "El Miedo, Padre," "Retrato" y "El Enamorado." [LU]

3988 Fuentes Montenegro, Luis. Contra el silencio. Panamá: INAC; Editorial Mariano Arosemena, 1991. 55 p. (Col. Letrabierta; 18)

Cada uno de los poemas que conforma este volumen recuerdan al ser humano su condición mortal, la inmensidad de la nada que lo determina y la radical incertidumbre de la existencia. Heideggeriana de pensamiento y latinoamericana de expresión, la poesía de este poeta es intensa y provocadoramente original. [EM]

3989 Galindo Palomeque, Axa. Axa: desde el fondo de mí—. Ilustraciones de Carlos Iturralde. Puyo, Ecuador: Editorial La Gente, 1990. 69 p.: ill.

Poesía femenina vigorosa que se enfrenta al tema de amor no sólo como motivo de su escritura sino como condición existencial. Desde esa perspectiva, la experiencia amorosa es percibida y manifestada desde múltiples variantes emocionales de la cotidianidad, ante la cual, sin embargo, se abre una dimensión poética en la que el amor es visto como dolor. La autora es ecuatoriana. [ORR]

3990 Gangotena, Alfredo. Tempestad secreta: poema. Prólogo de Claude Couffon (Traducción de Filoteo Samaniego). 1a. Ed. bilingüe español-francés. Traducción de Margarita Guarderas de Jijón. Quito: Ediciones Libri Mundi; Servicio Cultural de la Embajada de Francia, 1992. 109 p.: ill.

Edición póstuma bilingüe de un volumen aparecido orginalmente en 1940 por un poeta ecuatoriano vanguardista original. Gangotena (1904–44) es poco conocido en el contexto del vanguardismo latinoamericano debido a su permanencia en Francia y la publicación de su primer libro en francés (*Orogenia*, Edición Gallimard, 1928). Pese a estos antecedentes, no se justifica del todo la traducción al francés de la edición póstuma de *Tempestad secreta*.

3991 García Morales, Luis. Poesía. Prólogo de Francisco Pérez Perdomo. Caracas: Monte Avila Editores, 1992. 93 p. (Altazor)

Reúne *Lo real y la memoria* (1962) y *El río siempre* (1983), que constituyen la breve pero significativa obra de un poeta de activa participación en el conocido grupo "Sardio." El tiempo es motivo central en estos poemas, cuyo fraseo moroso y envolvente intensifica las impresiones de su fugacidad y pérdida. [PL]

3992 García Ramos, Reinaldo. Caverna fiel. Madrid: Editorial Verbum, 1993. 52 p. (Verbum poesía)

Poemas del exilio cubano, éstos de García Ramos son además una depuración lírica de esa experiencia, contenida en la palabra justa y en la imagen sobria pero también sugerente. Más que una rememoración nostálgica, aquí se asume el presente desde una extranjeridad a veces marcada por la impersonalidad, pero también—como en "Baladita del Crack"—por la empatía. [FC]

3993 Garnica, Blanca. Siempre el amor. Prólogo de Gaby Vallejo de Bolívar. Cochabamba, Bolivia?: Ediciones Puente, 1993. 109 p.: ill. (Col. Poesía)

Textos poéticos que ratifican el estilo delicado de una de las poetas bolivianas actuales más destacadas. Mantienen una reflexión siempre serena sobre el amor, a través de una expresión que selecciona imágenes tenues y propias. Este volumen lleva una presentación de otra prestigiosa escritora boliviana, Gaby Vallejo de Bolívar, quien señala que una de las imágenes constantes en esta poesía sobre el amor es la luz. [ORR]

3994 Gatón Arce, Freddy. La moneda del príncipe. Santo Domingo: Ediciones La Poesía Sorprendida, 1993. 98 p.

Dividido en dos partes, este poemario enlaza citas bíblicas con referencias, constantes en su obra, a la pobreza, la justicia, la muerte, el amor, la amistad y la poesía—vista siempre como llave de acceso: "La Poesía Está." Se incluye en la segunda parte un diálogo entre poemas de Gatón Arce, Manuel Rueda y José Enrique García. [FC]

3995 Gelman, Juan. Juan Gelman: antología personal. Buenos Aires: Ediciones Instituto Movilizador de Fondos Cooperativos, 1993. 128 p. (Desde la gente)

Primera selección antológica, hecha por el autor, de los libros aparecidos entre 1962–88, con la exclusión de *Bajo la lluvia ajena* y *Com/posiciones.* [LU]

3996 Gelman, Juan. Salarios del impío: París, Ginebra, México, Nueva York, 1984–1992. Buenos Aires: Libros de Tierra Firme, 1993. 60 p.: ill. (Col. de poesía Todos bailan; 136)

En este poemario—cuya brevedad, intensidad, fecha y lugar de gestación se emparentan con *Carta a mi madre* (1989)—el tema del exilio aparece como exilio de sí mismo. La memoria como único y tal vez último vínculo, la recurrencia a un particular bestiario, el constante uso de imágenes y expresiones oximorónicas, todo ello en el marco de una poesía desprovista de los énfasis de su producción anterior, dan a este nuevo texto la radicalidad, sobriedad e intensidad que lo singulariza. [LU]

3997 Gerbasi, Vicente. Diamante fúnebre. Caracas: Editorial Binev, 1991. 75 p.: ill. (Encantamientos para encantados)

Uno de los libros más intensos y conmovedores de Gerbasi (1913–92). La escritura elegíaca, desencadenada por la muerte de la esposa, alcanza particular profundidad en el proceso reflexivo de un hablante que enfrenta ahora su existir como "vacío." A partir de esa

comprobación, la palabra poética suele asumir dimensiones de exorcismo o conjuro: acto de fe en los poderes salvadores de la naturaleza y la memoria (ver *HLAS 52:4080*). [PL]

3998 Gervitz, Gloria. Migraciones. México: Fondo de Cultura Económica, 1991. 124 p. (Letras mexicanas)

Este libro es una nueva versión de tres libros anteriores: *Shajarit* (1979), *Fragmento de ventana* (1986) y *Yiskor* (1987). En la poesía de Gervitz (n. México, 1943) hay ciertas resonancias de la argentina Alejandra Pizarnik, especialmente por el lenguaje fragmentado y angustiante. Sin embargo, Gervitz recurre con mayor fuerza a la liturgia judía. El libro explora una sola línea argumental: el discurso dirigido a un tú femenino que se desvanece, un monólogo elegíaco que repite insistentemente su frustración: "¿me escuchas?" Las palabras se revierten sobre sí mismas: sólo encuentran su eco. [JS]

3999 Girri, Alberto. Juegos alegóricos. Buenos Aires: Editorial Fraterna, 1993. 74 p.

La alegoría impone una nueva perspectiva del mundo desde la que el poeta interroga o reflexiona. Mirada transgresora que invierte los órdenes de lo real y elimina las tradicionales dicotomías por las que nos guiamos. Este cuestionamiento de lo real afecta también la poesía como se advierte en el poema que cierra el libro: "El Poema Durante su Borrador." Poemario de singular sintaxis. [LU]

4000 González, Natalicio. Obra poética completa: 1925–1966. Asunción: Editorial Cuadernos Republicanos, 1993. 308 p.: bibl., ill. (1 col.).

El autor (1897–1966) fue el fundador de la revista *Guarania*. Su poesía, de vinculación modernista, se caracteriza por el rigor formal y amplia temática. González conceptualiza la poesía como "arte intelectual." Se incluyen en esta edición todos los libros éditos del autor y otros trabajos inéditos como el poemario *Laudes de Eva*, el poema "Infancia" y una serie de traducciones. El libro se cierra con una útil noticia bio-bibliográfica. [LU]

4001 González Tuñón, Raúl. Antología poética. Edición y prólogo de Héctor Yánover. Madrid: Visor, 1989. 161 p. (Col. Visor de poesía; 235)

El prólogo destaca cómo el itinerario vital del autor está también trazado en su poesía en cuanto a sus preocupaciones centrales: la injusticia, las luchas sociales, lo cotidiano, la ciudad y los pintorescos personajes que la habitan, el tango. Valiosa edición de este importante poeta que tanta influencia ha tenido, fundamentalmente, sobre la llamada "generación del 60" argentina. [LU]

4002   Granda, Euler. Poemas con piel de oveja. Quito: Casa de la Cultura Ecuatoriana Benjamín Carrión, 1993. 113 p.: ill. (Col. Pachacamac)

Nueva colección de textos de uno de los poetas mayores del Ecuador. Este volumen presenta algunas novedades respecto a la poesía anterior del mismo autor. El discurso entra en juego con el lenguaje, con las estructuras sintácticas de su escritura y con su propio sentido. Esta reflexividad muestra el afán de renovar su expresión. [ORR]

4003   Greiff, León de. Antología poética. Edición y prólogo de Fernando Charry Lara. Madrid: Visor, 1992. 270 p. (Col. Visor de poesía; 276)

Importante selección, realizada por un poeta y ensayista sobresaliente. El prólogo es una pieza de consulta indispensable para la cabal inteligencia de la poética de De Greiff. Después de demostrar su filiación simbolista, el estudioso avanza la tesis, sin duda correcta y bien fundada, de que su vanguardismo fue otro beneficio que le dejó el temprano acercamiento a esa tendencia. Antología ejemplar de la vasta y singular poesía del autor (ver también item **4004**, *HLAS 46:5713* y *HLAS 50:3617*). [PL]

4004   Greiff, León de. Sonetos. Selección y prólogo de Hjalmar de Greiff. Bogotá: El Ancora Editores, 1992. 156 p.

Estos 140 sonetos muestran la sorprendente facultad verbal y constructiva de De Greiff, quien abordó esta forma, según dice el antólogo, como desafío y como marco específico de su mundo poético. Los escribió en diversos metros, a veces con ingeniosos estrambotes, y en todos resaltan las notas de inconformismo, humor y audacia imaginativa (ver también item **4003**, *HLAS 46:5713* y *HLAS 50:3617*). [PL]

4005   Gruss, Irene. La calma. Buenos Aires: Libros de Tierra Firme, 1990. 62 p. (Col. de poesía Todos bailan; 122)

Tercer poemario de la autora (n. Buenos Aires, 1950). Poesía que se detiene en el ab-surdo de las situaciones cotidianas exhibe un gran coloquialismo. Hay un diálogo "irreverente" con textos, personajes y autores de la tradición cultural. Intento de apropiación de un lenguaje que se percibe como falso, engañoso, ficticio. Constante uso de la ironía como aproximación a la realidad. [LU]

4006   Guerra, Silvia. Replicantes astrales. Montevideo: División Cultura, Intendencia Municipal de Montevideo, 1993. 43 p. (Col. Los Premios: Primera serie)

Tercer poemario de esta valiosa poeta uruguaya (n. 1961). El yo lírico contempla sin asombro la cambiante y evasiva realidad a la que la recurrente imagen del agua simboliza. [LU]

4007   Guerrero Pou, Wenceslao. Un silencio reacio a desnudarse: 1986–1987. Santo Domingo: ONAP, 1990. 85 p.

Tras motivos de variada procedencia (la música, los colores, las secuencias numéricas), estos poemas se inscriben y se incrustan en la lírica dominicana de "La Poesía Sorprendida," a cuyo movimiento Guerrero Pou contribuyó con *Donde nos mira el día*. La poesía aquí es siempre una aproximación consciente de las imágenes y de las fragmentaciones lúcidas que patrocinan juegos paradojales. [FC]

4008   Gutiérrez, Ibero. Antología. v. 1–2. Investigación, selección y clasificación de Laura Oreggioni de Infantozzi y Luis Bravo. Prólogo y notas de Luis Bravo. Montevideo: Arca, 1992. 2 v.

Amplia selección que muestra cabalmente los valores de este poeta célebre, aunque prácticamente inédito hasta ahora. El vol. 2 se cierra con una útil cronología, cuadro sinóptico y clasificación de la obra del autor. [LU]

4009   Harris, Tomás. Noche de brujas y otros hechos de sangre. Santiago: Mosquito Editores, 1993. 39 p. (La Estocada sorpresiva)

La obra de Harris gana cada vez más público y este poemario puede aclararnos por qué: a un decir preciso y seguro, apto para la ironía, se agrega un novedoso ejercicio intertextual—en este caso, de referentes cinematográficos, hasta ahora muy explotados en narrativa pero rara vez en poesía. [MG]

4010   Hernández Matos, Gilberto. De los nombres del poeta. San Juan?: s.n., 1990. 81 p.

Bajo la tutela de Joserramón Melendes—cuya grafía es ya una marca en la poesía puertorriqueña—Hernández Matos hace un inventario de "los nombres del poeta" para dar con la poesía de siempre; esa que nombra el "caos real" de la permanencia en la diversidad, esa que está detrás de los nombres (B. de Otero, V. Aleixandre, C. Vallejo, J.R. Jiménez) como un reflejo de vida. [FC]

4011 Huidobro, Vicente. Vicente Huidobro: textos inéditos y dispersos. Recopilación, selección e introducción de José Alberto de la Fuente A. Santiago: Dirección de Bibliotecas, Archivos y Museos, Centro de Investigaciones Diego Barros Arana, 1993. 254 p.: bibl., ill. (Escritores de Chile; 3)

Necesaria compilación en volumen de textos poéticos, ensayísticos, periodísticos y epistolares, algunos de ellos inéditos y la mayoría de difícil acceso en múltiples periódicos y revistas. Destacan los 18 poemas escasamente divulgados y los facsímiles de *Ombligo* y *Vital*, virulentas revistas de vanguardia editadas por Huidobro. [MG]

4012 Hurtado, Gerardo César. La faena inextinguible. Ilustraciones de Virginia Trejos. San José: Editorial Costa Rica, 1991. 145 p.: ill.

Inspirados por las culturas pre-hispánicas que habitaban Costa Rica antes de 1492 y atentos al acontecer cotidiano y a las provocaciones que suscita la metáfora, los poemas de esta colección son retablos de una tierra natal, de su historia, su memoria y sus gentes. [EM]

4013 Ibarbourou, Juana de. Obras: Acervo del Estado. v. 1–5. Edición prologada, anotada y dirigida por Jorge Arbeleche. Montevideo: Instituto Nacional de Libro; Signos, 1992. 5 v.: bibl., ill.

El vol. 1 se abre con un prólogo de Arbeleche que destaca los múltiples y variados alcances de la poesía de Juana y propone una legítima valoración de su obra última. Varios trabajos estudian el tratamiento de la crítica y sus consecuencias. Análisis de la obra incluyen enfoques globales (destacamos el de Pallares), aproximaciones parciales y estudios comparativos de su poesía y la de otros poetas coetáneos. "Testimonios" incorpora el recuerdo que de Juana guardan autoras como Gladys Castelvecchi, Marosa di Giorgio, Circe Maia. Se cierra con dos piezas creativas de Amanda Berenguer y Sylvia Lago. [LU]

4014 Islas, Maya. Merla. Traducción al inglés de Edgar Soberon. Ilustraciones de Edgar Soberón Torchia Madrid: Editorial BETANIA, 1991. 112 p.: ill. (Col. Betania de poesía)

Incluida en varias antologías de la poesía cubana en Nueva York, Islas aborda en este poemario una poesía metafísica que, como alegoría de la luz, parte de un diálogo con la ciencia, la física cuántica. La poesía, como una imagen hipotética del universo, se llena de voces que van sucediéndose: la vida y la muerte; la sabiduría y la oscuridad; y, claro, la voz del poeta que va preparándose para abrir la última puerta. [FC]

4015 Jacob, Rubén. The Boston evening transcript: variaciones sobre un poema de T.S. Eliot y coda sobre un texto de J.L. Borges. Santiago: Carpe Diem, 1993. 92 p.

Primer libro de poemas de su autor y, ciertamente, revelación de un talento excepcional. Las variaciones construidas sobre textos de Eliot y J.L. Borges sorprenden por su riqueza inventiva y por la sabia conjunción de referencias literarias y musicales. [MG]

4016 James, Miguel. Albanela, Tuttifrutti, Blanca y las otras. Caracas: FUNDARTE, Alcaldía del Municipal Libertador, 1990. 55 p. (Cuadernos de difusión; 143)

Atractiva poesía amorosa, en la que se asumen con desenfado y propiedad las lecciones del pasado: salmos, cantares, fábulas, situaciones cinematográficas. Como un trovador moderno, el poeta venezolano (n. Trinidad, 1953) procesa libremente esos subtextos, con notable musicalidad y gracia. Igual desenvoltura tienen sus logrados poemas en prosa. [PL]

4017 Jara, Marcelo. Las venas dan al mar. Santiago: Ediciones Delenero, 1990? 21 p.

Bajo el mediocre discurso de amores juveniles, se insinúa en estos versos la presencia de mundos opresivos, estados de sitio, violencia silenciosa y dictatorial. La influencia de los *Epigramas* de Cardenal es por supuesto obvia, pero ha sido asimilada discretamente. [MG]

4018 Jaramillo Agudelo, Darío. Antología poética. Prólogo de Rafael Arráiz Lucca. 1a. ed. en M.A. Caracas: Monte Avila Editores, 1991. 79 p. (Altazor)

Intertextualidad, narrativa y lenguaje conversacional inscriben esta poesía en un plano literario muy actual en Hispanoamérica, pero a diferencia de otros autores, en Jaramillo Agudelo estos recursos son siempre funcionales y no desvirtúan la intensidad de una percepción corrosiva o escéptica del contorno, y del hablante mismo en su relación con el mundo. [PL]

4019 Jaramillo Levi, Enrique. Siluetas y clamores: hibridario poético de momentos disímiles. Panamá: Fundación Editorial Signos, 1993. 83 p.

El volumen consta de un poema extenso ("Las Hondas Escrituras," 334 versos) más cuatro secciones, cada una con número diferente de composiciones. En la tradición de la poesía conversacional, el discurso va conformándose a manera de *collage.* Es evidente sin embargo la primacía de ciertos motivos: el desarraigo de la patria y la denuncia política y social. [EM]

4020 Juanes Sevilla, Jorge. La siniestra cúpula del pterodáctilo. Querétaro, Mexico?: Joan Boldó i Climent, 1992. 87 p.: ill.

A Juanes Sevilla (n. México, 1971) le preocupa poco el control y el cuidado de los versos. En este primer libro lo consume la necesidad de recrear ambientes turbios, en donde conviven viejos monstruos con alucinaciones cibernéticas (realidad virtual). Aunque en ocasiones caiga en el cliché de la megalópolis, el libro atrae por su intensa querella rebelde. [JS]

4021 Juarroz, Roberto. Duodécima poesía vertical. Buenos Aires: Ediciones C. Lohlé, 1991. 106 p.

Nuevo poemario que continúa los lineamientos de su poesía anterior: cuestionamiento sobre la temporalidad y la muerte, reflexión sobre el hombre y el lenguaje, aspiración a lo trascendente. [LU]

4022 Juarroz, Roberto. Poesía vertical: antología. Edición y selección de Francisco José Cruz Pérez. Madrid: Visor, 1991. 289 p.: bibl. (Col. Visor poesía; 275)

Representativa muestra antológica que da cuenta de las principales características de la obra de Juarroz: poesía metafísica que reflexiona sobre la existencia y sus vacíos, la muerte, el fenómeno del lenguaje, lo sagrado, el misterio. [LU]

4023 Kowii, Ariruma. Tsaitsik: poemas para construir el futuro. Ibarra, Ecuador: Centro de Ediciones Culturales de Imbabura, 1993. 128 p.

La novedad de estos textos de un poeta quechua procede de su escritura bilingüe en quechua y castellano. Esa característica formal es a la vez expresión de una reflexión sobre la pérdida del contexto original del pensamiento y la cultura que implicaba el idioma quechua prehispánico. De ahí que esta poesía sea un lamento por tal pérdida esencial para el conocimiento y expresión de la propia identidad. [ORR]

4024 Kozer, José. Nueve láminas (glorieta) y otros poemas. Iztapalapa, Mexico: Sección de Publicaciones, Unidad Iztapalapa, Univ. Autónoma Metropolitana, 1984. 31 p. (Correo menor)

Considerado uno de los mejores poetas cubanos de la diáspora, la poesía de Kozer está marcada por la necesidad de no olvidar, la necesidad de escribir, desde Nueva York, en español. En este breve poemario, Kozer se desplaza por el espacio de las semejanzas geométricas y de los tiempos remotos hasta alcanzar una proximidad con el recuerdo que espera la plentitud. [FC]

4025 Lindo, Hugo. Desmesura. Prólogo de Francisco Andrés Escobar. San Salvador: UCA Editores, 1992. 325 p. (Col. Gavidia: Serie menor; 39)

Extenso poema autobiográfico que sobrepasa los 9000 versos. En opinión de F.A. Escobar, su prologador y crítico, se trata del "poema lírico e intimista más largo, hermoso y profundo escrito hasta ahora en la literatura salvadoreña." [EM]

4026 Liscano, Juan. Fundaciones, vencimientos y contiendas. Selección, prólogo, notas, cronología y bibliografía de Oscar Rodríguez Ortiz. Caracas: Biblioteca Ayacucho, 1991. 278 p.: bibl. (Biblioteca Ayacucho; 166)

Muestra de la vasta producción poética y ensayística del autor, dispuesta con estimable criterio selectivo. En poesía resaltan la dimensión épico-elegíaca de *Nuevo mundo orinoco* (1959) y la erótica de *Cármenes* (1966). Cinco ensayos sobre literatura dan la medida del trabajo de Liscano en ese género, confiriéndole al volumen especial interés. "Experiencia Borgeana y el Horror por la Historia" es lectura particularmente provocativa e iluminadora. [PL]

4027 Llanos Guzmán, Fernando. Pabellones del caracol: poemario, La Paz, 1992. La Paz: Carrera de Literatura, 1993. 1 v. (unpaged).: ill.

Textos primerizos de un joven poeta boliviano, ganador del concurso literario auspiciado por la Carrera de Literatura de la Univ. Mayor de San Andrés de La Paz. Lenguaje coloquial, aunque con referentes ajenos a lo cotidiano, el discurso de esta poesía es sometido a frecuentes rupturas. Una de sus preocupaciones principales es la reflexividad discursiva por la cual el propio lenguaje es sometido a observación. [ORR]

4028 Londoño, Jenny. De nostalgias y sueños. Quito: Instituto Andino de Artes Populares del Convenio Andrés Bello, 1992. 222 p.

Poesía enérgicamente femenina alerta sobre la condición de la mujer en la sociedad contemporánea. Acude con frecuencia a la crítica del papel tradicional de la mujer y a la protesta por su mantenimiento en la actualidad. Consciente de sus propósitos, estos textos buscan el efecto de alentar a la participación igualitaria de la mujer y del hombre en la vida pública. [ORR]

4029 López Mills, T. Segunda persona. México: Univ. Autónoma Metropolitana, Casa del Tiempo, 1994. 48 p. (Margen de poesía; 34)

La T es una letra que abstrae el nombre (Tedi), le borra su género (femenino), lo neutraliza. En ese sentido, la primera persona cede su dominio en el lugar lírico a la *segunda persona*, al interlocutor(a) que, entonces, aparece reflejado(a) en la obra. Esa segunda persona se convierte en una aspiración constante, una búsqueda de identidad en donde el yo quisiera verse retratado: "tú eres quien quise ser." [JS]

4030 López Suria, Violeta. Polvorín de Santa Elena. Hato Rey, P.R.: Esmaco Printers Corp., 1992. 63 p.: ill.

Una de las figuras más destacadas de la generación del 50 en la literatura puertorriqueña, en su poesía López Suria reconstruye el pasado personal sin por eso desvincularse de lo social. En este poemario, figuras como Celia Cruz, Zenobia, Aurora de Albornoz, Isabel Allende, Nilita, María Cervantes y otras—convertidas en poemas—establecen el vínculo entre lo personal y lo colectivo. [FC]

4031 Loynaz, Dulce María. Antología lírica. Edición de María Asunción Mateo. Madrid: Espasa Calpe, 1993. 261 p.: bibl. (Col. Austral; 316. Literatura)

Precedida de una introducción sustanciosa que enlaza vida y obra, esta antología enfatiza la naturaleza poética de toda la producción literaria de Loynaz, por lo cual incluye, además de la poesía, fragmentos de la novela *Jardín* (1951) y del libro de viajes, *Un verano en Tenerife* (1951), al igual que la "Carta de Amor al Rey Tut-Ank-Amen" (1953). [FC]

4032 Loynaz, Dulce María. Poemas escogidos: selección de Pedro Simón. Madrid: Visor, 1993. 203 p. (Col. Visor de poesía; 305)

A diferencia de otras antologías, ésta ordena los poemarios según "la época aproximada" en que fueron escritos en vez de ceñirse a la fecha de publicación. Así, por ejemplo, un poemario como *Bestiarium*, publicado en 1991 pero escrito en los años 20, cobra una relevancia inusitada pues incide en la poesía vanguardista cubana con la que no dialogó explícitamente. [FC]

4033 Madrid, Edwin. Caballos e iguanas. Quito: Editorial Casa de la Cultura Ecuatoriana, 1993. 87 p.

Otro aporte de uno de los jóvenes poetas ecuatorianos. Su carácter principal es el juego y la ironía con símbolos y mitos culturales. Destaca la parodia de textos de la historiografía colonial hispanoamericana escrita por españoles, de los que no sólo toma las modalidades de escritura sino los temas más graves para invertirlos y lograr un efecto sorprendente, del que no se sustrae la crítica ideológica. [ORR]

4034 Mansilla Torres, Jorge. Con premeditación y poesía. La Paz: Ediciones Casa de la Cultura, Alcaldía Municipal, 1993. 189 p.: ill.

Genuina identificación con las clases sociales menos favorecidas, empeño por cultivar una poesía con lenguaje popular y actitud crítica a través del humor y la ironía son las características más notables de este poeta boliviano que reside desde su exilio en México. De actitud pragmática permanente, esta poesía se construye sin prescindir de su relación con un interlocutor implícito y su efecto en el lector. Premio Nacional de Poesía Franz Tamayo (1980) de su país; así como el Premio Nacional Ramón López Velarde, de México, entre otros reconocimientos. [ORR]

4035 Martínez, Gerson. Pequeño David: confesiones desde el ánima de un fusil. San Salvador: Editorial Sombrero Azul, 1993. 112 p.: ill.

Testimonio poético que recoge la tragedia nacional de El Salvador. Este legítimo continuador de Oswaldo Escobar Velado y Roque Dalton enriquece la tradición poética salvadoreña con un libro que cumple los más altos rigores de la creación poética: imaginación, creatividad, y sobre todo, riesgo. En conjunto, poetiza 12 años de guerra y el horror de 75.000 muertos. José Coronel Urtecho consideró que con este libro G. Martínez "dio en el blanco." Ilustran el volumen dibujos pertenecientes a diferentes artistas plásticos, entre ellos el mismo autor. [EM]

4036 Martínez, Luis María. Días de vida: 1958–1959. Asunción: Editorial Arandurã, 1993. 187 p.

Testimonio poético de ciertos hechos políticos que conmovieron a América Latina y al poeta en particular durante los años de escritura de este "diario:" la caída de la dictadura militar de Pérez Jiménez en Venezuela; el viaje de Nixon por América Latina; las atroces consecuencias de los experimentos nucleares; el triunfo de la revolución cubana. Sujeto lírico en evidente solidaridad frente al dolor y la injusticia que padecen los marginados sociales. [LU]

4037 Migdal, Alicia. Historias de cuerpos. Montevideo: Arca, 1986. 59 p. (Col. Maremagnum)

Segundo poemario de la autora (n. Uruguay, 1947). Poesía de la realidad inapresable, de la inherente soledad del ser humano y del amor como imposible. El tono intenso y descarnado de los primeros poemas se va perdiendo hacia el final. [LU]

4038 Mistral, Gabriela. Lagar II. Edición de Pedro Pablo Zegers B. Santiago: Dirección de Bibliotecas, Archivos y Museos, Biblioteca Nacional, 1991. 172 p.

Rigurosa labor de transcripción y cotejo de originales y variantes realizada por Pedro Pablo Zegers, con el apoyo de varios expertos. Algunos de estos poemas póstumos se cuentan entre los mejores de la autora. El inacabamiento de otros o el hecho de haber sido desechados puede servir a la crítica para explorar a fondo la poética y las técnicas mistralianas. [MG]

4039 Morales-Valkenberg, Desirée. Con el espejo del alma; & Fine print. Hato Rey, P.R.: Esmaco Printers, 1990. 126 p.: ill.

Poeta puertorriqueña que, entre Puerto Rico, Nueva York y Curazao, le escribe un canto a la vida y al amor tanto en español como en inglés. Entre la celebración de la vida y el misterio del amor—también el gozo encendido del cuerpo—están el tiempo, la memoria y el humor. [FC]

4040 Moscona, Myriam. El árbol de los nombres. Guadalajara, Mexico: Secretaría de Cultura, Gobierno de Jalisco, 1992. 50 p. (Cuarto menguante)

Poema de amor, dividido en nueve secciones. Moscona (n. México, 1955) transita por la órbita de lo sagrado, a partir del árbol que funda y que crea mundos. No obstante, allí también está la corrosión del tiempo. La voz poética habla desde un "nosotros," el relato de una pareja en tránsito, con sus liturgias y mitología. [JS]

4041 Mutis, Alvaro. Obra poética. Bogotá: Arango Editores, 1993. 284 p.

Reproduce el contenido de *Suma de Maqroll de Gaviero* (ver item **4042**), menos el prólogo de Rafael Conte. [PL]

4042 Mutis, Alvaro. Summa de Maqroll, el Gaviero: poesía 1948–1988. Prólogo de Rafael Conte. Madrid: Visor, 1992. 271 p. (Col. Visor de poesía; 285)

Se reedita en España esta obra fundamental. Como la anterior edición mexicana (Fondo de Cultura Económica, 1990), incluye toda la producción poética de Mutis. Interesante introducción de R. Conte que sin duda apreciarán los nuevos lectores y estudiosos españoles de esta poesía (ver también item **4041**). [PL]

4043 Nájera, Francisco. Sujeto de la letra *a*. Guatemala: Impresos D&M, 1991. 104 p.

Con esta colección de poemas la poesía guatemalteca gana una expresión poética propia. Largo discurrir/filosofar sobre el sentido y el valor de la poesía. Se indaga su ser en tanto lenguaje, palabra, hasta llegar al vértigo de la provocación: la poesía percibida como disolución hacia la muerte y como invitación a los profundos misterios que se esconden más allá de lo conocido. [EM]

4044 Negroni, María. Per/canta. Buenos Aires: Libros de Tierra Firme, 1989. 53 p. (Col. de poesía Todos bailan; 80)

El poemario se divide en tres partes: 1) predominan poemas de una gran fragmentación; 2) contiene poemas que parten de motivaciones intelectuales, sobre todo relacionados con la plástica; y 3) incluye poemas de un mayor intimismo en la parte más lograda. [LU]

4045 Neruda, Pablo. Canto general. Edición de Enrico Mario Santí. Madrid: Cátedra, 1990. 655 p.: bibl., ill., index. (Letras hispánicas; 318)

Es urgente, sin duda, la edición crítica y comentada de la obra maestra de Neruda, síntesis y reelaboración de la historia continental y, por tanto, de registros casi enciclopédicos. El lúcido y valiosísimo prólogo de este volumen, sin embargo, se ve disminuido por múltiples inexactitudes de las notas al pie de página. [MG]

4046 Neruda, Pablo. Maremoto. Ilustraciones de Carin Oldfelt. Santiago: Pehuén, 1991. 1 v. (unpaged): col. ill. (Pehuén poesía)

En 1970 aparecieron por primera vez estos poemas en edición limitada de 110 ejemplares, por lo que la presente reimpresión constituye un valioso aporte a la bibliografía nerudiana. Los despojos dejados por el mar (estrellas, conchas, langostinos, anémonas, etc.) sirven de marco, una vez más, al autorretrato de un hablante heroico dividido entre su añoranza de la naturaleza ("pertenezco a la arena:/volveré al mar redondo") y sus obligaciones cívicas ("me acechan: las mujeres/y los hombres/quieren mi amor, piden mi compañía/¡los niños [. . .]/quieren jugar también con el poeta!"). [MG]

4047 Nina, Diógenes. Metamorfosis del silencio: prólogo y edición de Odalís Pérez. Santo Domingo: Taller, 1989. 66 p.

Uno de los poetas importantes de la poesía dominicana en los EE.UU., Nina propone en este poemario—que se suma a tres publicaciones anteriores, *Hora de la araña* (1974), *República permutable* (1979) y *Apriscina bestia del paraíso* (1987)—un mundo anterior a la imagen hecha, al concepto estable y

al lenguaje convencionalizado para indagar en la paradojas y dualidades del ser, visto como unidad y multiplicidad. [FC]

4048 Nogueras, Luis Rogelio. Nada del otro mundo. Edición de Eliana Dávila. La Habana: Editorial Letras Cubanas, 1988. 137 p. (Poesía. Giradilla)

Antología personal que reúne, entre otros, títulos premiados por Casa de la Américas (*Imitación de la vida,* 1981), al igual que material inédito ("La Forma de las Cosas que Vendrán"). La precisión de la palabra, incluso cuando se deforma, la parodia literaria, el trabajo preciso y, a veces, minimalista de la forma, la presencia de la poesía universal y la conciencia del poeta cubano legitiman el mundo imaginario y real de Nogueras, atestado de referencias literarias. [FC]

4049 Ollé, Carmen. Noches de adrenalina. 2a ed. Buenos Aires: Libros de Tierra Firme, 1994. 51 p. (Col. de poesía Personæ)

Publicado por primera vez en 1981 y desde entonces visto como un hito de la nueva escritura femenina en el Perú, de lo que dan testimonio esta reedición y su edición bilingüe (inglés-español) en California. En un estilo agitado y tenso, más cercano a la prosa que al verso, la autora hace una confesión descarnada de sus años europeos, marcados por el desorden vital, sus crisis y el descubrimiento de su identidad. Cabe considerar a estos poemas como fragmentos de un diario alucinante. [JMO]

4050 Oñate, Iván. El fulgor de los desollados: poemas. Quito: Ediciones Libri Mundi E. Grosse-Luemern, 1992. 213 p.

Consiste de cuatro colecciones escritas en casi 15 años: "En Casa del Ahorcado" (1977); "El Angel Ajeno" (1983); "Anatomía del Vacío" (1988) y "El Fulgor de los Desollados" (1988). Hay un tono común en estos textos, en los que el discurso se expresa grave, escéptico, insatisfecho y desencantado, pero de indudable efecto poético. [ORR]

4051 Orozco, Olga. Mutaciones de la realidad. Madrid: Ediciones Rialp, 1992. 69 p. (Adonais; 496)

Desea fijar lo real a pesar de la conciencia del sujeto lírico de que "la realidad es errante." En esa realidad mutante se encuentra la poesía tal como puede verse en el poema "Densos Velos Te Cubren, Poesía." Personajes distintos—no siempre identificables—invaden ese espacio, casa-morada-guarida del sujeto poético. Lo nocturno es la atmósfera privilegiada de esta poesía caracterizada también por la recurrencia a la imagen de la estatua de sal, la utilización del versículo y el uso de un lenguaje siempre metafórico. Bellísimo el poema dedicado a Alejandra Pizarnik. [LU]

4052 Ospina, William. El país del viento. Bogotá: Colcultura, 1992. 66 p. (Premios nacionales '92. Literatura)

Feliz realización imaginativa de escritura poética, mediante los recursos a la narratividad y a la máscara. Hablantes de diversos lugares y épocas (un mongol, un jefe *sioux*, un *viking*, Rodrigo de Triana, Lope de Aguirre, Walt Whitman, Lucila Godoy, *et al.*) cuentan sus versiones de una historia posible, comunal o individual. Libro muy atractivo por su material y por la eficacia de su lenguaje. [PL]

4053 Othón, Manuel José. Poesías completas. Recopilación, prólogo y notas de Joaquín Antonio Peñalosa. 2. ed. San Luis Potosí, México: Comité Organizador San Luis 400, 1992. 526 p.: ill. (Col. Cuatro siglos. Serie Obras escogidas de autores potosinos; 5)

Othón (San Luis Potosí, México, 1858–1906) tiene su lugar en la historia de la poesía hispanoamericana moderna. Se le conoce sobre todo por sus *Poemas rústicos* (1902). Aunque se le suele asociar con el modernismo, Othón se opuso a la innovación de las formas métricas y a la artificialización de las imágenes. De todos modos, su musicalidad, vocabulario y rigor formal están empapados de la estética modernista. Casi toda su poesía tiene que ver con el paisaje: el de fuera que emerge también dentro, como melodía mental. Othón es antecedente claro de Ramón López Velarde e, indudablemente, uno de los mejores poetas de México. [JS]

4054 Ovalles, Caupolicán. Convertido en pez viví enamorado del desierto. Caracas: Dirección de Cultura, Univ. Central de Venezuela, 1989. 143 p. (Col. Letras de Venezuela; 92. Serie Poesía.)

Diario poético sobre ciudades de Rusia, Checoeslovaquia, Bulgaria e Irak (1986–87). El viaje suscita una escritura imaginativa, ágil y desplegada, que produce una doble impresión: el disfuminado dibujo de lugares es también el del sujeto que los interioriza y los transforma caprichosamente en materia de reflexión o vía de autoconocimiento. [PL]

4055 Pacheco, José Emilio. El silencio de la luna: poemas 1985–1993. México: Ediciones Era, 1994. 175 p. (Biblioteca Era)

Pacheco (n. México, 1939) es uno de los poetas mexicanos más conocidos a nivel internacional. Desde su legendario *No me preguntes cómo pasa el tiempo* (1969), estableció una voz inconfundible en nuestro panorama literario. Este libro continúa sus diferentes vetas poéticas: el cuestionamiento moral en torno a un mundo perdido y añorado, el azoro frente a las innovaciones tecnológicas y científicas, la ironía breve, mordaz, y la reflexión acerca del entorno actual. Se destaca la sección "Circo de Noche," con 12 poemas sobre diferentes personajes del espectáculo. [JS]

4056 Palacios, Irma and **Coral Bracho.** Tierra de entraña ardiente. México: Galería López Quiroga, 1992. 96 p.: ill.

Arte de Palacios y poemas de Bracho (n. México, 1951) en edición de excelente calidad. Bracho está en plena madurez y debe contarse entre los mejores poetas actuales de México. Su escritura destaca por mostrar rasgos inusitados en la tradición mexicana: una sintaxis inventada, que asigna nuevas funciones a los paréntesis, a los guiones, a los dos puntos; un vocabulario excéntrico, barroco, aglutinante, pormenorizador; imágenes hiladas a base de quiebres, reencuentros por paronomasias. Su visión acude a las "entrañas" de los objetos; en el trasfondo de las ventiscas, las selvas, las rocas o la espesura, hay un resplandor que destella en los resquicios, la luz que se asoma en la maraña. [JS]

4057 Paredes, Alberto. Derelictos. México: J. Mortiz, 1992. 87 p.: ill. (Serie del volador)

Reúne poemas, reflexiones, relatos breves y apuntes. El hilo conductor del volumen es su afán por preguntarse acerca de la escritura y el lenguaje. Los derelictos son los papeles abandonados a su suerte, el naufragio de la escritura en altamar. A pesar de concebirse como "inacabados," algunos de los poemas muestran el amplio repertorio metafórico de Paredes (n. Pachuca, México, 1956), mejor conocido como reseñista y crítico. [JS]

4058 Parra, Nicanor. Poemas para combatir la calvicie: muestra de antipoesía. Recopilación de Julio Ortega. México: Consejo Nacional para la Cultura y las Artes; Univ. de Guadalajara; Fondo de Cultura Económica, 1993. 382 p.: bibl., ill. (Col. Tierra firme)

La más atinada de las antologías de Parra. Además de selecciones de diversos poemarios, se recogen íntegramente *Poemas y antipoemas, La cueca larga, Sermones y prédicas del Cristo de Elqui* y *Nuevos sermones y prédicas* . . . Se añaden textos inéditos y se cierra el volumen con *Mai mai peñi: discurso de Guadalajara,* decisión oportuna que acompaña la consagración que supone el otorgamiento del Premio Juan Rulfo. [MG]

4059 Pérez, José Joaquín. Fantasías indígenas y otros poemas. Prólogo y notas de José Alcántara Almánzar. Santo Domingo: Fundación Corripio, 1989. 361 p.: ill. (Biblioteca de clásicos dominicanos; 6)

Publicado originalmente en 1877, esta nueva edición de la Biblioteca de Clásicos Dominicanos le rinde tributo al más logrado poeta del siglo XIX dominicano: "el más alto representante del indigenismo antillano." Contiene, además de los poemas indigenistas, una muestra de "la poesía hogareña," de recogimiento religioso, al igual que poemas de corte neoclásico y modernista. [FC]

4060 Pichardo, Tony. —antes y después del fuego. Santo Domingo: Ediciones CEDEE, 1992. 105 p.: ill.

Poemas de solidaridad, poesía de voces culturales e históricas. Pichardo le escribe a la africanía de Haití en creole y en español desde una insularidad compartida, La Hispaniola. Antes y después de la esclavitud, una energía vital se plantea como constancia de lo haitiano. [FC]

4061 Pintado, José Manuel. Conversatorio de Yaxilán. Tlalpan, Mexico: Ediciones Toledo, 1991. 92 p.

Como se advierte por el título, el libro se sitúa en la antigua ciudad maya, junto al Río Usumacinta, en la frontera con Guatemala. Se divide en tres secciones: 1) poemas asociados con el origen y el mito del mundo antiguo; 2) poema de amor dividido en 29 partes; y 3) que se sitúa la acidez del tiempo. Pintado (n. México, 1948) recoge el sabor de lo selvático, de lo pristino, y ofrece un libro con un fuerte poder de la naturaleza. [JS]

4062 Pizarnik, Alejandra. La extracción de la piedra de locura [y] otros poemas. Madrid: Visor Libros, 1993. 120 p. (Col. Visor de poesía; 292)

Muestra representativa de los principales libros de poemas de la autora y otros textos en prosa de los que se destaca *La condesa sangrienta* (1965). De *Arbol de Diana* no se incluye el texto de Octavio Paz y faltan los poemas 13 y 16. De *Los trabajos y las noches* falta el poema "Revelaciones." [LU]

4063 Pizarnik, Alejandra. Obras completas: poesía completa y prosa selecta. Edición de Cristina Piña. Nueva versión corr. y aum. Buenos Aires: Corregidor, 1993. 431 p.

Reedición de *Obras completas* aparecidas en 1991 con importantes adiciones que completan el corpus poético y mejoras como el ordenamiento cronológico de los libros, lo cual facilita el seguimiento de sus obsesiones. Los textos en prosa son altamente reveladores de sus preferencias y afinidades literarias; ellos evidencian la agudeza crítica de A.P. a vez que se convierten en documentos claves de su propia concepción estética. [LU]

4064 Pizarnik, Alejandra. Obras selectas. Selección y compilación de Gustavo Zuluaga. Medellín, Colombia: Ediciones Holderlin, 1992. 227 p.: bibl., ill.

Incluye poemas recogidos en libros y otros aparecidos en publicaciones periódicas. Ante la edición de Cristina Piña de las *Obras completas* (item **4063**) o de antologías, como la de Frank Graziano, ésta no parece agregar otros valores. Carecen de rigor crítico las referencias bibliográficas. [LU]

4065 Posternak, Dora. Y—el bosque. Panama: Instituto Nacional de Cultura, Dirección Nacional de Publicación y Comunicación, Editorial Mariano Arosemena, 1992. 60 p. (Col. Letrabierta; 22)

En la tradición de la poesía conversacional, Posternak ha producido un poemario que capta la realidad latinoamericana desde la compleja perspectiva del inmigrante que tiene que aprender a vivir lejos del sitio de origen. Judía, nacida uruguaya, y panameña por afinidad de sentimiento, la persona misma de la autora expresa la situación de *collage* que permea su obra. [EM]

4066 Preciado, Antonio. De sol a sol: antología. Estudio introductorio y notas de Esther Bermejo de Crespo. Quito: Libresa, 1992. 255 p.: bibl. (Col. Antares; 86)

Edición crítica de un libro aparecido originalmente en 1979 y cuyo autor es uno de los poetas afroecuatorianos de mayor consagración. Precedida por un nuevo estudio de Esther Bermejo de Crespo. La poesía de Preciado se caracteriza por su preocupación universal (crítica y denuncia) por las condiciones de los sectores sociales menos favorecidos de los pueblos. [ORR]

4067 Puig, Salvador. Si tuviera que apostar y otros poemas. Montevideo: Arca, 1992. 136 p.

Recoge 23 nuevos poemas cuya nota más singular es el marcado tono irónico. Incorpora además textos de poemarios anteriores en orden cronológico inverso: *Lugar a dudas* (1984), *Apalabrar* (1980), *La luz entre nosotros* (1963). Aparece también el poema "Ernesto 'Che' Guevara," recogido anteriormente en el No. 46 de la *Revista Casa de las Américas* y en *Antología de la Poesía Rebelde Hispanoamericana* (1967) de Enrique Fierro. [LU]

4068 Quessep, Giovanni. Antología poética. Prólogo de Hernán Reyes Peñaranda. Bogotá: Instituto Caro y Cuervo, 1993. 154 p.: ill. (Serie La Granada entreabierta; 63)

G. Quessep ha creado una mitología poética personal que lo singulariza en la actual literatura colombiana. En sus poemas discurren personajes de leyenda o se despliegan situaciones líricas que manifiestan una concepción de la poesía como posibilidad de plenitud: "vive el poeta a solas y su canto es su cielo," se lee en un verso definitorio de esta empresa. La antología incluye textos de seis libros (1968–85), y la precede un buen estudio de H. Reyes Peñaranda, que hace justicia a esta escritura precisa y transparente. [PL]

4069 Quiroga, Juan Carlos Ramiro. Eco de Kámara: Ariana de pozo el. La Paz: Ediciones Espanto del Los Mancos, 1992. 46 leaves: ill.

La lectura de este libro obliga a invertir los órdenes habituales de la lectura. La última página es la primera, a partir de la cual se debe leer el volumen. Asimismo, en cada poema los versos han sido escritos a la inversa (de derecha a izquierda) y algunos poemas pueden leerse también de abajo hacia arriba. A pesar de estos experimentos que, sin duda, obstaculizan la lectura sin ofrecer a cambio efecto o novedad, los textos conforman una poesía de calidad. [ORR]

4070 Quiroga de Urquieta, Rosario. Aquí la grieta. Cochabamba, Bolivia?: Ediciones Vialva, 1993. 92 p.: ill.

Esta colección presenta a una joven poeta boliviana de indudable calidad. Una actitud de interrogación y búsqueda constantes, al mismo tiempo que una nostalgia de insatisfacción por anhelos no alcanzados, están presentes en estos textos. No obstante, la esperanza de la respuesta o del hallazgo alimentan el afán de la escritura y la reflexión. [ORR]

4071 Quiroz Escobar, Francisco. Noche de trompos. Santiago: Ediciones La Piel, 1993. 1 v. (unpaged).

El impacto causado por la obra de Oscar Hahn en las nuevas generaciones de poetas chilenos podría medirse a través de este volumen. No obstante, la reiteración de símbolos escatológicos e imaginería surreal no se encuentra aquí acompañada ni de instinto lúdico ni de ingenio. [MG]

4072 Rentas Lucas, Eugenio. Decir de luz amanecida: poemas. Prólogo por Francisco Lluch Mora. Ilustraciones de Ernesto Alvarez. San Juan: Editorial Yaurel, 1990. 115 p.: bibl., ill.

Uno de los fundadores del Movimiento Trascendentalista de los años 50 en Puerto Rico, Rentas Lucas incide nuevamente en la propuesta de una espiritualidad vital, atenta y fiel al mundo interior del poeta cuya religiosidad—un diálogo entre el ser y Dios—busca en la palabra un vehículo de comunicación. [FC]

4073 Reyes, Alfonso. Una ventana inmensa: antología poética. Selección y coda de Gerardo Deniz. Prólogo de Octavio Paz. México: Editorial Vuelta, 1993. 277 p. (El gabinete literario)

Antología que vuelve a poner en el terreno de la discusión la poesía de Reyes (1889–1959). Según Deniz, el mejor Reyes es el poeta y no, como se suele pensar, el ensayista. Paz afirma que *Ifigenia cruel* (poema capital del autor) es "una de las obras más perfectas y complejas de la poesía moderna hispanoamericana;" la traslación del mito helénico a las circunstancias personales de Reyes, en vínculo con la Revolución Mexicana, además de la erudición, lucidez y gracia, hacen de este poema y, con ello, de la antología entera, un volumen altamente recomendable. [JS]

4074 Rivas, José Luis. Raz de marea: obra poética, 1975–1992. México: Fondo de Cultura Económica, 1993. 339 p. (Letras mexicanas)

Excepto *Luz de mar abierto* (1992), este volumen reúne la poesía completa de Rivas (n. Tuxpan, México, 1950). El libro consagra a uno de los poetas más imponentes de los últimos años. Rivas es conocido principalmente por "Tierra nativa," poema que recrea su infancia en Veracruz. La versatilidad del lenguaje (desde la brevedad del *haiku* hasta la amplitud del versículo y la prosa), el poder evocador y la riqueza verbal hacen de la recopilación una obra fundamental en la poesía mexicana actual. [JS]

4075 Rodas Morales, Hugo. Palabras de una vez. La Paz?: s.n., 1993. 105 p.

Resultado de los experimentos de un joven poeta, quien busca con sus textos provocar el suspenso y el efecto inesperado en el lector, que pueden alcanzar calidad. De ahí que se advierta con frecuencia el juego con el contenido de la expresión, en un afán de refutar concepciones tradicionales. [ORR]

4076 Rojas, Gonzalo. Cinco visiones: selección de poemas de Gonzalo Rojas. Prólogo de Carmen Ruiz Barrionuevo. Salamanca, Spain: Ediciones Univ. de Salamanca; Patrimonio Nacional, 1992. 241 p., 1 p. of plates: bibl., ill. (Biblioteca de América; 1)

Antología publicada a raíz de recibir el autor el I Premio Reina Sofía de Poesía Iberoamericana. Los poemas se redistribuyen en cinco partes que reafirman la complejidad de una poética en la que lo lúdico y lo místico, lo erótico y lo experimental tienen cabida. Es de destacar el prólogo, que logra dar una valiosa visión de conjunto de las creencias y técnicas de Rojas. [MG]

4077 Rojas, Gonzalo. Las hermosas: poesías de amor. Selección de Hilda R. May. Madrid: Ediciones Hiperión, 1991. 142 p. (Poesía Hiperión; 190)

Dentro del reciente y merecido redescubrimiento internacional de Rojas, esta antología cumple un papel necesario al enfatizar el erotismo como clave de su obra. La experiencia de la mujer se revela en el contexto de un viaje por distintos países que da a la reflexión del hablante el aire de búsqueda mística. No son secundarios en esta empresa, desde luego, el humorismo y la ironía de raigambre surrealista. [MG]

4078 Rokha, Pablo de. Antología. Edición de Rita Gnutzmann. Madrid: Visor, 1992. 315 p.: bibl. (Col. Visor de poesía; 278)

Volumen que será imprescindible para la divulgación de un poeta injustamente desconocido fuera de su país, cuya obra ofrece una rica variedad de estilos y tendencias: desde el modernismo residual, cargado de desafiantes estridencias, hasta el realismo de denuncia política, pasando por el surrealismo, que tan honda huella ha dejado en Chile. [MG]

Rosencof, Mauricio. El bataraz. See item **3877.**

4079 Sacoto Arias, Augusto. Obras completas. Estudio introductorio y recopilación de Filoteo Samaniego Salazar. Quito: Banco Central del Ecuador, 1993. 480 p.: ill. (Biblioteca de la revista Cultura; 9)

Reunión de la obra literaria de un autor (1907–79) que inició su carrera en 1931, bajo los efectos de la experiencia vanguardista, sello que caracteriza a su obra. Aunque escribió dos textos dramáticos en verso, así como ensayo, Sacoto fue fundamentalmente poeta. Su obra es breve y los últimos textos que se le conocen son anteriores a 1950. Ya sus primeros críticos señalaron en su estilo cierta influencia de García Lorca. [ORR]

4080 Salas, Horacio. Antología personal. Madrid: Ediciones de Cultura Hispánica, 1992. 131 p. (Col. Poesía)

Util selección de este poeta y crítico integrante de la generación argentina del 60. El coloquialismo y la combinatoria de discursos de distinto valor (tangos, slogans publicitarios y políticos, versos de Neruda, titulares de la prensa, clichés de la escritura, etc.) constituyen lo más destacado de su estilo poético. [LU]

4081 Sánchez Beras, César. Travesía a la quinta estación. Santo Domingo?: s.n., 1994. 46 p.: ill.

Dos veces ganador en concursos nacionales de la décima dominicana, Sánchez Beras busca aquí un conocimiento que esté más allá del lenguaje organizado a partir de la razón—un conocimiento como el del ángel "en el minuto mágico de saberse posible." La quinta estación es, por supuesto, el viaje a lo poético. [FC]

4082 Sarduy, Severo. Un testigo perenne y delatado: precedido de un testigo fugaz y disfrazado. Madrid: Hiperión, 1993. 109 p.: ill. (Poesía Hiperión; 209)

Entre sonetos y décimas, estos poemas constituyen un tributo a las formas cerradas. Sin embargo, no se trata únicamente de una consagración formal; la temática aquí propuesta es también un reclamo poético. Entre sonetos y décimas se conjuga lo culto y lo popular; la metafísica de la vida en la muerte; la homoerótica y el dolor; la cubanía y el exilio; lo efímero y lo perenne. [FC]

4083 Sauma, Osvaldo. Asabis. Presentación de Jorge Boccanera. San José: Editorial Lunes, 1993. 126 p. (Col. Caimán)

Asabis, que en árabe significa "solidaridad de la sangre," contribuye a la excelencia de la poesía costarricense contemporánea. Con maestría de poeta que sabe su oficio, Sauma recrea el pensamiento oriental y al mismo tiempo crea vínculos poéticos con la poesía y el arte universal. Jorge Boccanera hace las presentaciones y se refiere al autor como a un "nacido en Costa Rica que viaja en un camello y con el desierto a cuestas." [EM]

4084 Selva, Salomón de la. Salomón de la Selva: antología mayor. Acroasis y selección de Julio Valle-Castillo. Managua: Nueva Nicaragua, 1993. 457 p.: bibl.

Publicada para conmemorar el primer centenario del nacimiento del poeta (20 marzo 1893), incluye la obra poética aparecida desde su muerte (1959) hasta 1993. Complementa el volumen un ensayo crítico del antologador, indispensable para apreciar el desarrollo de la poesía nicaragüense y la influencia de S. de la Selva. [EM]

4085 Sologuren, Javier. Un trino en la ventana vacía. Trujillo, Peru: Ediciones SEA; Casa del Artista, 1993. 44 p. (Col. Homenaje al centenario César Vallejo; 21)

Uno de los mayores poetas peruanos del siglo, con más de 50 años de persistente producción, presenta aquí poemas que, siendo reconocibles por la habitual destreza formal y la serenidad de la visión, ofrecen algunos rasgos nuevos, signos de que su larga búsqueda de la perfección continúa. [JMO]

4086 Teillier, Jorge. El molino y la higuera. Santiago: Ediciones del Azafrán, 1993. 54 p.

La elaborada simplicidad de Teiller se combina aquí con cierto humor mágico. El hablante aprovecha una y otra vez las posibilidades líricas de la anécdota, sin incurrir por ello en los excesos y la agresividad de lo anti-poético; el resultado del conjunto es, así, una punzante ironía que juega a ser ingenua. [MG]

4087 Terán Cavero, Antonio. Ahora que es entonces. La Paz?: Fundaciones Simón I. Patiño & Pro Bolivia, 1993. 86 p.

Con este volumen reaparece un poeta boliviano (n. 1932) que pertenece a la conocida segunda generación de "Gesta Bárbara." La colección que presenta ahora constituye sin duda lo mejor que este autor ha publicado. Una reflexión constante sobre motivos trascendentales a través de un discurso breve que logra llevar la palabra coloquial a un nivel poético logrado. [ORR]

4088 Toro, Emilia. Territorios secretos por Sarajevo. Santiago: LOM Ediciones, 1992. 1 v. (unpaged).

Poemas que retratan el desaliento de un nuevo fin de milenio; con todo, la reiteración abrumadora de imágenes de la guerra en los Balcanes se mezcla con la reconstrucción de la "urbe" nebulosa de la intimidad, en un contrapunto cuyo resultado es la individuación paulatina pero efectiva de una voz poética esperanzada. [MG]

4089 Torres, Angel Luis. Ira lira. San Juan: Instituto de Cultura Puertorriqueña, 1989. 171 p.: index.

En esta propuesta antológica, Torres le da cuerpo a una poesía que, desde los años 70, viene inscribiéndose en la literatura puertorriqueña como conciencia crítica de la realidad, vista siempre desde una antillanía latinoamericanizante. Además de la poesía con temática social, son constantes las alusiones al paisaje, la literatura, la ciudad y el campo. [FC]

4090 Torres, Jorge. Poemas encontrados y otros pre-textos. Valdivia, Chile: Paginadura Ediciones, 1991. 1 v. (unpaged): ill.

El autor, a partir de recortes periodísticos y materiales afines, elabora un *collage* que aprovecha sugerencias líricas de múltiples voces. Elemento unificador es la crítica del régimen de Pinochet. Este volumen, a fines del siglo XX, confirma el arraigo latinoamericano del espíritu lúdico de las vanguardias, en tantas otras latitudes superado. [MG]

4091 Urzagasti, Jesús. De la ventana al parque. La Paz: OFAVIM, 1992. 101 p.

Textos de uno de los poetas bolivianos más originales de la actualidad. Su escritura ha trasvasado los géneros de la poesía y la narrativa, para lograr una poesía narrativa. Mediante una crónica testimonial aparente, su discurso acude a la memoria para reelaborar e inventar los hechos de la realidad y crear una atmósfera poética de gran efecto. El relato se transforma así en una reflexión poética que no prescinde de recursos narrativos en primera persona. [ORR]

4092 Vallejo, César. Obra poética. Edición crítico coordinado por Américo Ferrari. 1. ed. argentina. Buenos Aires: Fondo de Cultura Económica, 1992. 753 p.: bibl., ill., index. (Col. Archivos; 4)

Esta edición crítica, bajo la coordinación general de Américo Ferrari, es una obra fundamental y de consulta indispensable para todo estudioso vallejiano. Siguiendo los lineamientos generales de la colección, un equipo internacional de investigadores abordan los complejos problemas textuales que presenta el poeta y ofrecen un copioso aparato crítico que guía al lector interesado.

4093 Varela, Blanca. Ejercicios materiales. Lima: Jaime Campodónico, 1993. 50 p. (Col. del sol blanco)

Trece intensos nuevos poemas de esta notable poeta peruana, que confirman la originalidad de su voz y la hondura desgarrada de su visión. Todos giran alrededor de su tema de siempre—el misterio, el horror y la belleza de la vida y el amor humanos—, pero la depuración del lenguaje y el impacto emocional que producen son todavía mayores que antes. [JMO]

4094 Varela, Blanca. Poesía escogida 1949–1991. Barcelona: Icaria, 1993. 108 p. (Bagdad; 9)

Valiosa recopilación—la primera de su tipo—de más de 40 años de creación de la autora, permite una lectura o una revisión de un corpus poético de gran belleza y concentración, en el que se perciben las huellas del surrealismo y del existencialismo. Es de esperar que esta edición contribuya a difundir un nombre que merece ser mejor conocido en América. [JMO]

4095 Vargas, Rafael. Signos de paso. México: Consejo Nacional para la Cultura y las Artes, Instituto Coahuilense de Cultura, 1995. 148 p. (Los cincuenta)

Vargas (n. México, 1954) selecciona, reordena, revisa y amplia sus poemarios an-

teriores, dándole consistencia y magnitud a su obra. El libro tiene resonancias de Enrique Molina y Gonzalo Rojas; el asombro (y la familiaridad) ante el entorno, aunado a un lenguaje simple (a veces coloquial) que, en ocasiones, se ve inmerso en una espesa savia surrealista. Da gusto releer "Susana San Juan," uno de los mejores poemas, o los textos autorreflexivos de la última sección. [JS]

4096 Váscones, Carmen. Con/fabulaciones. Quito: Editorial El Conejo, 1992. 88 p. (Col. Metáfora)

Con esta colección se presenta una nueva poeta ecuatoriana. Su poesía, asediada por interrogantes y el desconocimiento, habita la realidad como un espacio poco iluminado y misterioso. Acude al diálogo constante con su interlocutor para advertir con gravedad de las urgencias cotidianas que descubre. De ese modo ofrece una nueva percepción, aunque angustiada a veces, de la realidad. [ORR]

4097 Vázquez Rivero, Sara María. La sombra que me habita. Cochabamba, Bolivia: Oficialía Mayor de Cultura, H. Municipalidad de Cochabamba, 1993. 119 p.

Este volumen recibió el segundo premio en el Concurso Nacional de Poesía 1991, convocado por la Municipalidad de Cochabamba. Su autora es uno de los nuevos valores de la poesía de su país y ha recibido ya el reconocimiento público. En versos bien logrados, testimonia la percepción de hechos sutiles y delicados en plena agitación y rutina cotidianas. [ORR]

4098 Vechtas, Joseph. Cosmoagónicas: selección de poesías, antología. Montevideo: Ediciones de la Banda Oriental, 1992. 51 p. (Poetas uruguayos de hoy; 39)

El sujeto poético existe y se reconoce en los objetos y oficios sencillos y cotidianos. Cierto tono nerudiano—del de las odas—recorre el poemario. De las distintas vivencias sentidas como "cosmogonías" es sin duda el tiempo la que el sujeto lírico percibe como más angustiante. Poesía en permanente diálogo con la tradición poética en lengua española. [LU]

4099 Veiravé, Alfredo. Palabra cazada al vuelo. Entre Ríos, Argentina: Editorial de Entre Ríos, 1992. 118 p.: ill. (Col. Homenajes)

Reedición de los textos anteriormente incluidos en: *Historia natural* (1980), textos caracterizados por el deseo de describir la flora, fauna y ciencia del presente con el tamiz textual del pasado, en cuanto al estilo y aún al lenguaje; *Radar en la tormenta* (1985) cuyo eje temático es el horror y el absurdo de la guerra de Malvinas; y *Laboratorio Central* (1991) en el que predomina la reflexión metapoética. [LU]

4100 Vera, Luis Roberto. Clerestoria. México: Univ. Nacional Autónoma de México, 1992. 60 p. (El Ala del tigre)

Ya por el título, el lector puede anticipar el tono de este libro: versos medidos y bien cuidados, música de la imagen, vocabulario exquisito (grisalla, cinosura, glicinas, grumos, etc.). La mayor parte de los poemas fueron escritos durante viajes; en ellos hay una fijación de ciertas escenas o instantes (por ejemplo: "Llovizna hecha tamiz / sus escamas plateadas / bajo la verde fronda del follaje," en un poema alusivo a una pintura de Monet). El rigor poético de Vera (n. Chile, 1947; residente en México) lo hace uno de los escritores más interesantes de las últimas generaciones. [JS]

4101 Verón de Astrada, Manuel. Cantos liberados. Asunción: Ediciones Intento, 1990? 58 p.

Poeta que escribió desde la prisión y el exilio exuberantes y tradicionales poemas a su país. [M. García Pinto]

4102 Vitier, Cintio. Versos de la nueva casa: 1991–1992. Caracas: Pomaire, 1993. 103 p. (Col. La diosa; 3)

Con este poemario Vitier reafirma sus filiaciones origenistas; aparecen transformados en objetos de la memoria, en deseos de la poesía, Fina García Marruz, Lezama Lima, Eliseo Diego, Fidelio Ponce, Víctor Manuel. Pero también asoma el presente, a veces envuelto en la cotidianidad ("Tercetillos para un Flan"), en lo autobiográfico ("Suite") y en la esperanza ("La Nueva Casa"). Para Vitier, la poesía continúa siendo ese otro lugar posible. [FC]

4103 Volpe Mossoti, Enrique. Crónica del adelantado. Santiago: Primera Edición, 1990. 112 p.: ill.

Poema que homenajea el decir cronístico colonial y, por tanto, ejemplo de un género típicamente latinoamericano. En este caso, la persona lírica, Diego de Almagro, reflexiona sobre sus hechos y la geografía chilena. La discursividad de Volpe, por parecerse a la de varias epopeyas coloniales, le otorga verosimilitud literaria a su escrito. [MG]

4104 Watanabe, José. Historia natural. Lima: PEISA, 1994. 91 p.: ill. (Alma matinal)

El título del nuevo libro de este poeta de la generación de los 70 es exacto: es un nostálgico retorno a la tierra natal, a los paisajes y humildes rincones de la costa norte peruana, con retratos de tipos populares y *anónimos*. No se puede decir, sin embargo, que éste sea el mejor libro del autor: el lenguaje luce sin mayor tensión y las imágenes resultan con frecuencia borrosas. [JMO]

4105 Westphalen, Emilio Adolfo. Bajo zarpas de la quimera: poemas, 1930–1988. Presentación de José Angel Valente. Madrid: Alianza Editorial, 1991. 261 p. (Alianza tres; 256)

Importante recopilación de la obra poética de una figura clave del movimiento surrealista en Hispanoamérica, cuyas obras, inaccesibles para la mayoría, contribuyeron a convertirlo en una figura casi mítica de la poesía continental. El volumen cubre su producción de 1930–88 y tiene un valioso prólogo de Angel Valente; en una breve nota, el autor hace aclaraciones sobre su silencio creador de varias décadas. [JMO]

4106 Wiethüchter, Blanca. El verde no es un color. La Paz: Ediciones del Hombrecito Sentado, 1992. 63 p.: ill.

Esta colección de poemas se define por una actitud contemplativa en un esfuerzo por reconocer un sentido no manifiesto en la realidad, para describir a ésta en condiciones habitualmente no conocidas. Como resultado de esa actitud, se percibe la descripción subjetiva—con notable carga irracional y surrealista—de un mundo propio y apenas entrevisto. [ORR]

4107 Zárate, Milton. Confesiones de olvido. San José: Editorial Universitaria Centroamericana, 1991. 61 p. (Col. Séptimo día)

Conjuntamente con *La isla de piedra*, de Mario Matarrita Ruiz, este poemario ha sido ganador del Premio Poesía en el Certamen Latinoamericano "Valle Inclán" 1990. Estéticamente vinculado a principios propuestos por los manifiestos trascendentalistas, *Confesiones de olvido* es poesía interior, consciente de que "volver las cosas a su mundo es trazar rutas en la soledad." [EM]

4108 Zurita, Raúl. Selección de poemas. Temuco, Chile: Univ. de la Frontera, Facultad de Educación y Humanidades, Depto. de Lenguas y Literatura, 1990. 140 p.: ill.

Colección de textos inéditos elaborados durante la estadía del autor en la Univ. de La Frontera. El onirismo y la reutilización de material paisajístico con propósitos expresionistas son dos prácticas usuales de Zurita que reaparecen en estos poemas, que podrían considerarse por ello muy representativos de su obra. [MG]

4109 Zurita, Raúl. La vida nueva. Santiago: Editorial Universitaria, 1994. 519 p.: ill. (some col.). (Col. Fuera de serie)

Voluminosa síntesis de la poesía de Zurita que, por su magnitud, añade a la ya característica oscuridad de su estilo una monumentalidad titánica, un notorio desequilibrio que—guardando las distancias, por supuesto—desciende más del Pound de los *Cantos* que de Dante Alighieri. [MG]

GENERAL STUDIES

4110 Alonso, María Nieves; Mario Rodríguez y Gilberto Triviños. Cuatro poetas chilenos: Gonzalo Rojas, Floridor Pérez, Omar Lara, Jaime Quezada. Concepción, Chile: LAR, 1992. 203 p.: bibl. (Col. Estudios, tesis y monografías)

Colección de trabajos críticos en torno a G. Rojas, F. Pérez, O. Lara y J. Quezada. Valiosos *close readings* de algunos poemas. [MG]

4111 Arellano, Jorge Eduardo. Entre la tradición y la modernidad: el movimiento nicaragüense de vanguardia. San José: Libro Libre, 1992. 198 p.: bibl., ill. (Serie Literaria)

Estudia el significativo aporte nicaragüense a la vanguardia hispanoamericana. Nicaragua es presentada como un país de intensa producción poética, creadora de una vanguardia distinta a las otras porque surge de realidades y problemas otros, que atañen a la realidad centroamericana misma. Continuadora de Darío, esta vanguardia se funda más en los aportes de la *New American Poetry* que en los movimientos vanguardistas sudamericanos. [EM]

4112 Arganãraz, Nicteroy Nazareth. Poesía latinoamericana de vanguardia: de la poesía concreta a la poesía inobjetal. Montevideo: Ediciones O Dos, 1992. 107 p.: bibl., ill. (some col).

Contribución al estudio de la poesía concreta en Brasil y en el Río de la Plata, que incluye "el poema/proceso," "la poesía para y/o a realizar" (Argentina) y "La poesía inobjetal" uruguaya. [M. García Pinto]

4113 Barriga Villanueva, Rebeca; Luis Mario Schneider; and Guillermo Sheridan. Los Contemporáneos en el laberinto de la crítica. Edición de Rafael Olea Franco y Anthony Stanton. México: Colegio de México, Centro de Estudios Lingüísticos y Literarios, 1994. 461 p.: bibl. (Serie Literatura mexicana Cátedra Jaime Torres Bodet; 2)

Excelente recopilación de las actas del Congreso sobre Contemporáneos, en homenaje a Torres Bodet, (Colegio de México, marzo 1992). El grupo sigue atrayendo la atención de numerosos estudiosos y lectores. Se recogen una sesión de testimonios y 39 ponencias que exploran, entre otros temas poco trabajados por la crítica, la narrativa, las artes plásticas, el cine, las relaciones con los estridentistas, y sus resonancias en otras literaturas; además de estudios sobre la poesía propia. El volumen cuenta con ensayistas de prestigio y ofrece una amplia gama de perspectivas críticas. [JS]

4114 Barroeta, José. El padre, imagen y retorno. Caracas: Monte Avila Editores, 1992. 170 p.: bibl. (Estudios)

Analiza la presencia de la imagen paterna en la poesía venezolana contemporánea, y su sentido en relación con el afán de definir una identidad individual y colectiva. Comenta, con irregular eficacia, numerosos textos centrados en esta temática, pero el libro es útil como registro de una constante en la que sobresalen poemas de A. Arráiz, E. Arvelo Larriva, V. Gerbasi, R. Palomares y C. Ovalles. [PL]

4115 Carrera, Arturo. Nacen los otros. Rosario, Argentina: B. Viterbo Editora, 1993. 108 p. (El Escribiente; 3)

Aparecen aquí cuatro ensayos sobre "secreto y misterio en la poesía argentina:" 1) se intenta hacer una distinción entre misterio y secreto; 2) examina las conexiones que ambos conceptos han mantenido con la poesía; 3) se detiene en las variaciones de secreto y misterio en los poemas de Pizarnik, Orozco y Girri; y 4) analiza la obra de M. Fernández, F. Madariaga, E. Molina, O. Lamborghini, O. Girondo y N. Perlongher. [LU]

4116 Ferrari, Américo. El bosque y sus caminos: estudios sobre poesía y poética hispanoamericanas. Valencia, Spain: Pre-Textos, 1993. 220 p.: bibl. (Pre-textos; 167)

Estudia la evolución de la poesía moderna desde una perspectiva novedosa y enriquecedora, que pone el acento en "la creación del objeto poético en Hispanoamérica." Esa apertura permite considerar, junto a figuras como R. Darío, J. Herrera y Reissig, J.M. Eguren, O. Girondo, C. Vallejo y E.A. Westphalen, las interpenetraciones genéricas de lo lírico en textos narrativos, desde las obras de Ramos Sucre y M. Fernández a *Pedro Páramo* y *Cien años de soledad.* Son muy notables la libertad del enfoque crítico, la solvencia de su fundamentación y la elegancia expositiva. Un libro ejemplar y necesario, que gratificará igualmente al lector de poesía y al especialista. [PL]

4117 Gordon, Samuel. Notas sobre la vanguardia en México. (*Cuad. Hispanoam.*, 524, feb. 1994, p. 57–69)

En este ensayo, Gordon reseña el surgimiento de los dos grupos preponderantes de la vanguardia en México: los Estridentistas y los Contemporáneos. El objetivo principal de Gordon es documentar el antagonismo entre los dos grupos, a través de ataques provocados por la aparición de ciertas antologías. [JS]

4118 Higgins, James. Hitos de la poesía peruana. Edición e ilustración de Carlos Milla Batres. Lima: Editorial Milla Batres, 1993. 241 p.: bibl., ill.

Excelente estudio sobre la poesía peruana contemporánea. Abarca gran parte de la producción poética en el Perú durante el presente siglo.Tras discutir la tradición moderna inaugurada por J.M. Eguren, el autor hace una lectura por décadas de las diversas generaciones posteriores y sus figuras más representativas. Estas incluyen la Vanguardia de la década del 20 y del 30 (C. Vallejo, E.A. Westphalen); la década del 40 y 50 (M. Adán, C.G. Belli, B. Varela); la generación del 60 (A. Cisneros, R.Hinostroza, entre otros); y la década del 70 (el grupo "Hora Zero," E. Verástegui y A. Sánchez León). Se incluye una amplia bibliografía sobre cada poeta. [C. Ferreira]

4119 Literatura mexicana/Mexican literature. Philadelphia: Univ. of Pennsylvania, 1993. 200 p.

Este libro recoge las actas del congreso homónimo, celebrado en 1992. Se compilan 12 ponencias, de las cuales tres versan sobre E. Poniatowska y cuatro sobre J.E. Pacheco, ya que estos escritores fueron los invitados especiales del congreso. También se recoge la conferencia "Ser un Escritor en México," de Poniatowska, y nueve poemas de Pacheco, que aparecerían después en su último libro. [JS]

4120 Manifiestos literarios venezolanos. Recopilación y prólogo de Juan Carlos Santaella. 1a ed., ampliada, en M.A. Caracas: Monte Avila Editores, 1992. 115 p. (Documentos)

Reúne textos programáticos de 13 grupos que se expresaron principalmente a través de revistas, desde *Cosmópolis* (1984) hasta *Tráfico* (1981). Sobresalen los idearios de momentos significativos de la historia literaria venezolana: *La Alborada* (1909), *Válvula* (1928), *Revista Nacional de Cultura* y *Viernes* (1938), *Sardio* (1958) y *El Techo de la Ballena* (1961). [PL]

Medina, José Ramón. Noventa años de literatura venezolana, 1900–1990. See item **3650.**

4121 Melendes, Joserramón. Postemporáneos. Río Piedras, P.R.: QueAse, 1994. 134 p.: ill.

Written in his distinctive orthographic style, this brief collection of lectures and articles is aimed at characterizing the work of Puerto Rican poets from the mid-1960s to the 1980s. [E. Acosta-Belén]

4122 Mitologías del estridentismo. (*Memoria/CEMOS*, 79:3/4, julio 1995, p. 3–4, 37–54)

Número de la revista *Memoria*, dedicado casi por completo a los estridentistas, con artículos de A. Aquino Casas, E. Escalante, L. de la Peña Martínez, C. López, A. Miguel, C. Laguna y J.A. Leyva. Ya que el estridentismo ha sido menospreciado en México, se intenta corregir la idea de que este movimiento fue tan solo una calca del futurismo. Escalante, por ejemplo, analiza la contradicción entre el sujeto individual y el colectivo en *Urbe* de M. Maples Arce, para concluir que se trata de "uno de los textos capitales de la literatura mexicana." [JS]

4123 Núñez, Estuardo. Panorama actual de la poesía peruana. 2. ed. corr. y con dos addendas. Trujillo, Peru: Comisión Centenario de César Vallejo U.N.M.S.M; Municipalidad Provincial de Trujillo; Ediciones S. Aguilar; Univ. Nacional de Trujillo, 1994. 139 p. (Col. Homenaje al centenario de César Vallejo: Serie mayor; 1)

Reedición de un trabajo crítico pionero que conserva buena parte de su valor más de medio siglo después de haber sido publicado por primera vez. El autor le ha agregado tres apéndices: uno autocrítico y complementario, otro sobre la época "trílcica" de Vallejo, y el tercero sobre Chocano. [JMO]

4124 Oviedo, José Miguel. Padres pródigos e hijos fecundos. (*Cuad. Hispanoam.*, 532, oct. 1994, p. 53–67, bibl., photo)

Examina la poesía peruana de las últimas décadas, a partir de una reflexión sobre la persistencia de la actividad creadora en una sociedad en estado de emergencia. Excelente lectura de la obra de J. Sologuren, J.E. Eielson, C.G. Belli, E. Verástegui y A. Cisneros. Trabajo ejemplar, que ilustra las posibilidades de un análisis que relacionía adecuadamente las condiciones de producción cultural y el resultado literario. [PL]

4125 Quirarte, Vicente. Peces del aire altísimo: poesía y poetas en México. México: UNAM; Ediciones del Equilibrista, 1993. 322 p. (Serie Manatí)

Además de poeta reconocido (recibió el Premio Villaurrutia), Quirarte (n. México, 1954) es autor de varios libros de ensayos. Aquí reúne artículos sobre R. López Velarde, A. Reyes, C. Pellicer, G. Owen, el estridentismo, O. Paz, E. Huerta, A. Chumacero, R. Bonifaz Nuño, J. Sabines, E. Lizalde, J.E. Pacheco y otros más jóvenes. Por el amplio conocimiento del tema y la versatilidad crítica, el volumen debe atraer la atención de los estudiosos y aficionados. [JS]

4126 Torres Duque, Oscar. La poesía como idilio: la poesía clásica en Colombia. Bogotá: Colcultura, 1992. 74 p.: bibl. (Premios nacionales '92: Literatura)

Explora relaciones estéticas fundamentales en algunos poetas, a la luz de ciertas constantes: "una común localización fuera del ámbito de la historia," como consecuencia de la atención prestada al origen. Sugestiva lectura del carácter arquetípico de la poesía de Silva, A. Arturo, T. Vargas Osorio, A. Mutis, G. Quessep, A. Rodríguez y M. Jursich. [PL]

4127 Villegas Morales, Juan. El discurso lírico de la mujer en Chile en el período 1973–1990. Santiago: Mosquito Editores, 1993. 209 p.: bibl. (Biblioteca setenta & 3)

Necesaria incursión en un tema poco explorado. Aporta un rico bagaje informativo e intenta vertebrar un corpus a partir de circunstancias históricas: los sucesos de 1973, el período pinochetista y el exilio de numerosas intelectuales. El texto recurre a terminologías y métodos críticos de gran difusión en los EEUU cuya aplicación a Latinoamérica ha de considerarse tentativa. [MG]

SPECIAL STUDIES

4128 Aproximaciones a la poesía de Nicanor Parra. Recopilación, revisión de textos y notas de Angel Flores y Dante Medina. Guadalajara, Mexico: EDUG, 1991. 201 p.: bibl.

Util recopilación de textos críticos. Incluye entrevistas, lo que permite confrontar puntos de vista del autor y sus estudiosos. De especial importancia son las selecciones de Goić, Schopf, Rodríguez Fernández y Lihn; se echan de menos, sin embargo, páginas imprescindibles como las escritas, entre otros, por Escobar, Sucre o De Costa. [MG]

4129 Arellano, Jorge Eduardo. Pablo Antonio Cuadra: aproximaciones a su vida y obra. Managua: Ministerio de Educación, Instituto Nicaragüense de Cultura, 1991. 112 p.: bibl., ill.

Se trata éste de un libro-homenaje al poeta P.A. Cuadra en ocasión de su 79 aniversario. Esquemáticamente, el libro da cuenta de la vida y la obra de este importante vanguardista nicaragüense, que junto a J. Coronel Urtecho, L.A. Cabrales, M. Cuadra y J. Pasos, ha contribuído a la excelencia de la literatura centroamericana. [EM]

4130 Benko, Susana. Vicente Huidobro y el cubismo. Caracas: Monte Avila Editores Latinoamericana; Fondo de Cultura Económica; Banco Provincial, 1993. 225 p.: bibl., ill. (some col.). (Estudios)

Cotejándola con la crítica de los últimos decenios, podría afirmarse sin lugar a duda que estamos ante la visión de conjunto más original y rigurosa de la labor huidobriana. Sopesa detalladamente las deudas del poeta con las vanguardias europeas y su contribución a ellas. Componente importantísimo del trabajo de Benko es el examen de relaciones entre la poesía de Huidobro y el arte más experimental de principios del siglo XX: la pintura. [MG]

4131 César Vallejo: vida y obra. Edición de Roland Forgues. Lima: Amaru Editores, 1994. 211 p.: bibl., ill.

Fruto de un simposio organizado por la Univ. de Grenoble, Francia, en 1988 en homenaje al poeta en el 50 aniversario de su muerte, el volumen recoge contribuciones de críticos y estudiosos hispanoamericanos y europeos. Como de costumbre en este tipo de recopilaciones, el material es de muy diversa calidad y significación. [JMO]

4132 Chumacero, Alí. Retrato crítico. Recopilación de Evodio Escalante y Marco Antonio Campos. México: Univ. Nacional Autónoma de México, 1995. 478 p.

Excelente recopilación crítica sobre uno de los poetas más importantes de México. Merecido reconocimiento que ojalá tenga repercusiones en la difusión de este escritor. El volumen contiene cinco secciones: un discurso del propio Chumacero (n. México, 1918); ensayos y artículos; estudios; reseñas o notas breves; y bibliografía. Aunque no siempre es posible, hubiera sido oportuno pedir ensayos inéditos para la recopilación (y hacer traducir el ensayo de Frank Dauster). El libro, de todos modos, ya es indispensable para cualquier estudioso del poeta. [JS]

4133 Coloma González, Fidel. Introducción al estudio de *Azul.* Managua: Editorial Manolo Morales, 1988. 208 p.: bibl.

Well documented and useful study by noted specialist on Rubén Darío. The poet's omnivorous penchant for imitation is amply discussed as are his many linguistic, stylistic, and thematic innovations. Includes a chronology of Daríos's years in Chile and a short bibliography. [R. Prieto]

4134 Coloquio Internacional César Vallejo, su Tiempo, su Obra, *Lima, 1992.* Vallejo: su tiempo y su obra; actas. Lima: Univ. de Lima, Vice-Rectorado, 1994. 2 v.: bibl.

El coloquio internacional organizado por la Univ. de Lima en homenaje a Vallejo, fue seguramente el más concurrido de todos. Más de 40 ponencias de ese acto se publican en el presente volumen y cubren casi todos los aspectos posibles, desde la vida del poeta hasta análisis de poemas específicos y la crítica de la crítica vallejana. [JMO]

4135 Cuadra, Pablo Antonio. El espectro del Cisne. (*Rev. Pensam. Centroam.*, 43: 198, enero/marzo 1988, p. 33–37, ill.)

Escrito en ocasión del centenario de *Azul* (1988), en este artículo Cuadra se refiere a *Azul* como a un texto que marca la independencia literaria de América. Al mismo tiempo redime la figura autorial de Darío de la etiqueta que le diera Rodó (Darío no es el poeta de América), advirtiendo que en tanto prevalezca una interpretación ideológica en Nicaragua, habrá menos lugar para él y para su obra. [EM]

4136 Elías, Eduardo F. and **Jorge H. Valdés.** Entrevista: Ernesto Cardenal. (*Hispamérica/Gaithersburg*, 16:48, 1987, p. 39–50)

Se trata ésta de una entrevista reveladora que permite situar y conocer el proyecto poético del último Cardenal. En la dialéctica pregunta-respuesta ve el lector la posición de este poeta frente a la tradición poética latinoamericana. [EM]

4137 Encuentro con Vallejo: coloquio internacional en el centenario de César Vallejo, 1892–1992. Lima: Comisión Conmemorativa del Centenario del Nacimiento de César Vallejo, Univ. Nacional Mayor de San Marcos, 1993. 226 p.: bibl., ill.

Otro volumen colectivo resultante de un coloquio realizado en Lima con ocasión del centenario del nacimiento de Vallejo. Dedicado a la memoria de Julio Vélez, el vallejista español tempranamente desaparecido, el volumen contiene contribuciones—algunas de fondo, otras meramente circunstanciales— de críticos peruanos, latinoamericanos y europeos. [JMO]

Escobar, Eduardo. Nadaísmo crónico y demás epidemias. See item **3614.**

4138 González Trujillo, Alejandro. Neruda: su carácter a través de sus versos. Santiago?: Tall. Gráf. CET, 1992. 135 p.: bibl., col. ill.

Pocas aportaciones críticas encontrará el lector en estas páginas. No obstante, un texto que habla del "héroe letrado" siempre podrá ser de valor a quienes estudien procesos de mitologización romántica de autores a fines del siglo XX. [MG]

4139 La hoguera y el viento: José Emilio Pacheco ante la crítica. Selección y prólogo de Hugo J. Verani. 1. ed., corr. y aum. en Biblioteca Era. México: Coordinación de Difusión Cultural, Dirección de Literatura, Univ. Nacional Autónoma de México; Ediciones Era, 1993. 341 p.: bibl. (Biblioteca Era)

Recopilación de artículos sobre la poesía y la narrativa de Pacheco, además de una excelente y amplísima bibliografía de fuentes primarias y secundarias, hecha por Verani. Esta edición (la primera es de 1987) agrega nueve artículos (entre ellos, un homenaje-crónica de E. Poniatowska). El volumen recoge ensayos claves de Oviedo, Debicki, Soto y otros. Dada la difusión internacional de la obra de Pacheco, el libro es de suma utilidad e interés. [JS]

4140 Horan, Elizabeth. Gabriela Mistral: an artist and her people. Washington: Organization of American States, 1994. 216 p.: bibl., ill., index. (INTERAMER; 33. Cultural series)

Acertada exploración de las circunstancias sociohistóricas de la poesía mistraliana, sobre todo en lo concerniente a su identidad de mujer chilena. Se comentan con detenimiento las reacciones de sus primeros críticos y "descubridores." El cap. 3 es particularmente valioso para lectores interesados en rastrear vaivenes en la recepción de esta poesía. [MG]

4141 Huamán, Miguel Angel. Poesía y utopía andina. Lima: DESCO, 1988. 142 p.: bibl.

El título no indica realmente cuál es su tema específico: la obra poética en quechua de José María Arguedas. El autor, conocido indigenista y poeta vernacular él mismo, hace una revisión de los aspectos que esa poesía plantea (sincretismo, nacionalidad y cultura andina, la cuestión del quechua como instrumento poético, etc.). El esfuerzo que resulta algo convencional pero que, al menos, tiene el mérito de enfocar un aspecto poco tratado en la obra de Arguedas. [JMO]

4142 Irish, J.A. George. Nicolás Guillén: growth of a revolutionary consciousness. New York: Caribbean Research Center, Medgar Evers College, City Univ. of New York, 1990. 144 p.: bibl.

Se estudia la poesía de Guillén desde su faceta modernista de 1922, hasta la poesía más emblemática de factura social y política de 1972, donde se circunscribe lo racial. La simplicidad y accesibilidad estilística—el romance, la décima, la letrilla, la silva, la canción, la redondilla, el son y otros—y la diversidad de los modos satíricos e intereses temáticos fundamentan, según Irish, la conciencia revolucionaria del poeta. [FC]

4143 Lambie, George. El pensamiento político de César Vallejo y la Guerra Civil Española. Edición de Carlos Milla Batres. Lima?: Editorial Milla Batres, 1993. 301 p.: bibl., ill.

Basado en una tesis universitaria presentada en la Univ. de Warwick, Inglaterra, este trabajo rechaza tanto la interpretación crítica que su autor llama "humanista" (en realidad, la que analiza los poemas como emanaciones del espíritu vallejiano) y la "estructuralista," que desprende los textos de toda referencia externa. Propone, en cambio, una perspectiva decididamente historicista e ideológica, con abundante acopio de materiales y documentos poco conocidos. La carencia de un índice general hace algo incómoda la consulta del libro. [JMO]

4144 Loynaz, Dulce María. Homenaje a Dulce María Loynaz: obra literaria, poesía y prosa, estudios y comentarios. Edición de Ana Rosa Núñez. Miami: Ediciones Universal, 1993. 415 p.: bibl., ill. (Col. Clásicos cubanos)

Además de contener los poemarios más importantes de Loynaz, se incluye una versión manuscrita de *Poemas sin nombre* de gran utilidad para el investigador. Se incluyen trabajos en prosa al igual que estudios y opiniones sobre la literatura de la poeta (entre otros, de G. Baquero, J.R. Jiménez, E. Ballagas, J. de Ibarbourou y G. Mistral). [FC]

Melendes, Joserramón. Secretum. See item **3570.**

4145 Mutis, Alvaro. El reino que estaba para mí: conversaciones con Alvaro Mutis. Entrevistado por Fernando Quiroz. Barcelona, Spain: Grupo Editorial Norma, 1993. 116 p.: ill. (Col. Biografías y documentos)

Interesantísimo trabajo que recoge y ordena momentos significativos de la vida de Mutis, narrados en primera persona. Hábilmente, Quiroz ha suprimido las preguntas que suscitan el relato de su personaje: el resultado es un libro fascinante y revelador sobre un autor fundamental, que puede leerse también como una animada autobiografía (ver también items **4041** y **4042**). [PL]

4146 Noboa Arízaga, Enrique et al. César Dávila Andrade, 25 años—. Quito: Editorial Casa de la Cultura Ecuatoriana, 1993. 95 p.: ill.

Reunión de ocho ensayos, entre biográficos y aproximaciones críticas, a la personalidad y obra del escritor ecuatoriano C. Dávila Andrade (1919–67). Llevan la firma de F. Samaniego, D. Araujo Sánchez, G.A. Jácome, M.R. Crespo, E. Cárdenas, H. Rodríguez Castelo, E. Noboa Arizada y H. Vacas Gómez. Esta publicación se realizó con motivo de los 25 años de la muerte del escritor en Caracas. [ORR]

4147 Nómez, Naín and **Manuel Alcides Jofré.** Pablo de Rokha y Pablo Neruda: la escritura total. Santiago: Ediciones Documentas; Ottawa, Canada: Ediciones Cordillera, 1992. 214 p.: bibl.

Estudio comparado de la obra de los dos poetas. La motivación inicial simplemente biográfica pronto queda desplazada por certeros análisis textuales que permiten, mediante el examen de dos carreras individuales, la comprensión del panorama poético de todo Chile durante el siglo XX. [MG]

4148 Poesía y poética de Gonzalo Rojas. Edición de Enrique Giordano con la colaboración de Jaime Giordano, Pedro Lastra y Enrique Andrade. Santiago: Instituto Profesional del Pacífico; New York: Ediciones del Maitén, 1987. 219 p.: bibl. (Monografías del maitén; 6)

Compilación insustituible para reconstruir la recepción que ha tenido uno de los poetas chilenos de mayor proyección internacional de los últimos decenios. Reconocidos nombres (Gullón, Sucre, Earle, Pope, Hozven, Jaime y Enrique Giordano, etc.) garantizan al lector una considerable variedad de aproximaciones y métodos críticos. Se incluye una sección de entrevistas. [MG]

4149 *Revista Canadiense de Estudios Hispánicos*, Vol. 16, No. 3, primavera 1992, Leyendo a Paz. Toronto, Canada: Asociación Canadiense de Hispanistas; Univ. of Toronto.

Número dedicado a la poesía de Paz. Salvo el ensayo teórico de M.J. Valdés (director de la revista), todos los análisis siguen la misma norma: reproducción de un poema concreto (predominan los breves) de Paz y lectura atenta del mismo. En su mayor parte, los colaboradores provienen de El Colegio de México y de las universidades de Toronto y Calgary. Acompañan *collages* de Ludwig Zeller. [JS]

4150 Roballo, Alba. Alba Roballo: pregón por el tiempo nuevo. Entrevistas de Guillermo Chifflet. Montevideo: Ediciones TAE, 1992. 216 p. (Cuadernos de un militante socialista; 2)

Diálogo-entrevista con esta mujer del interior uruguayo que destaca por su vocación por la justicia. Fue abogada, parlamentaria, pública, poeta y militante socialista. [M. García Pinto]

4151 Sobrevilla, David. César Vallejo, poeta nacional y universal, y otros trabajos vallejianos. Lima: Amaru Editores, 1994. 335 p.: bibl.

El autor, un hombre que pasó de la filosofía a la crítica literaria y estética, ha dedicado, a lo largo de los años, numerosos trabajos al estudio de diversos aspectos de la obra vallejiana. En este volumen recoge seis de ellos. Son de lectura muy recomendable, especialmente las páginas que tratan la filiación marxista de Vallejo y su visión del pasado incaico. [JMO]

4152 Suárez, Eulogio. Neruda total. Chile: Ediciones Systhema, 1991. 426 p.: bibl.

Primera edición chilena de un libro ya aparecido en Grecia (1987) y en Colombia (1988). Aunque sus aportaciones al entendimiento crítico de la obra nerudiana no son incisivas ni originales, la labor de Suárez resulta, en cambio, estimulante para el interesado en reconstruir la historia textual de cada libro de Neruda. [MG]

4153 Teitelboim, Volodia. Huidobro: la marcha infinita. Santiago: Ediciones BAT, 1993. 303 p.: bibl., ill.

Este título completa una trilogía de libros biográficos de Teitelboim, quien ya antes se había ocupado de Mistral y Neruda. Como los anteriores, este volumen constituye una fuente esencial de información acerca del poeta que retrata. Por la agilidad de su prosa, el lirismo y los aciertos narrativos de muchos pasajes, resulta una lectura placentera independizable de todo interés documental. [MG]

4154 Varas, José Miguel. Aquellos anchos días: Neruda, el Oriental. Montevideo: Monte Sexto, 1991. 125 p.: ill.

Aporte importante a la amplia bibliografía del poeta chileno sobre sus varias visitas al Uruguay. Recoge el testimonio de la amistad de Alberto y Olga Mántaras Rogé y el propio con Neruda. [M. García Pinto]

4155 Varas, José Miguel. Neruda y el huevo de Damocles. Santiago: Editorial Los Andes, 1991. 142 p.: ill. (Serie Personajes)

Nueva aportación a la abrumadora lista de biografías de Neruda. Se trata de un anecdotario especializado en los aspectos humorísticos o excéntricos de la personalidad del poeta, trabajo oportuno si se tiene en cuenta la solemnidad dominante en las semblanzas de quien, en vida, era ya considerado un clásico. [MG]

4156 Zapata Gacitúa, Juan. Enrique Lihn: la imaginación en su escritura críticoreflexiva. Santiago?: Editorial la Noria, 1994. 264 p. (Col. Aguas firmes)

Valiéndose de teorías estructuralistas, semióticas y posestructuralistas, el autor emprende un análisis ambicioso y detallado de la poética lihneana, es decir, de su concepción del arte proyectada tanto en la lírica como en textos críticos. Especialmente cuidadosas son las relecturas de conversaciones, entrevistas y ensayos publicados por Lihn. [MG]

MISCELLANEOUS

4157 Arguedas, José María. Canto kechwa: con un ensayo sobre la capacidad de creación artística del pueblo indio y mestizo. Lima: Editorial Horizonte, 1989. 73 p.: ill. (Poesía; 4)

Reedición de un clásico trabajo antropológico sobre el folklore indígena peruano, que el autor conocía de modo directo y con la pasión de quien había sido criado en ella desde niño. Las bellas traducciones que hizo de estas expresiones quechuas son una de sus tempranas contribuciones al redescubrimiento de la literatura andina. [JMO]

4158 Cardenal, Ernesto. Los ovnis de oro: poemas indios. Madrid: Visor, 1992. 242 p. (Col. Visor de poesía; 287)

Anunciada por el mismo Cardenal como el vol. 2 de Poemas Indios, esta colección es el producto de años de lecturas e investigaciones sobre las antiguas culturas americanas. Uno a uno los poemas van recreando los aspectos más secretos y misteriosos de la antigüedad americana, y luego son reactualizados de acuerdo a las urgencias de nuestros tiempos. [EM]

Epistolario: catálogo electrónico del epistolario de Nicolás Guillén. See item **11.**

Latbook: libros y revistas argentinas en Internet. See item **40.**

4159 Mistral, Gabriela. Pasiones del vivir. Selección y prólogo de Juan Antonio Massone. Ed. especial. Santiago: Editorial Los Andes, 1992. 140 p. (Col. V centenario Chile)

La presente selección de ensayos de Mistral constituye un esfuerzo que prolonga algunos, muy afortunados, de antólogos anteriores como A. Calderón o R.E. Scarpa. La tensión rítmica y tropológica de estos textos es notable, pero ello no los convierte en meros apéndices a la poesía de la autora; de hecho, por la efervescencia americanista, convendría leerlos en el marco de su época e integrarlos al movimiento mundonovista, junto a ensayos de Reyes, Picón-Salas, Vasconcelos y otros ilustres representantes del género. [MG]

4160 Navarrete Araya, Micaela. Balmaceda en la poesía popular, 1886–1896. Santiago: Dirección de Bibliotecas, Archivos y Museos, Centro de Investigaciones Diego Barros Arana, 1993. 126 p.: bibl., ill. (Col. Sociedad y cultura; 3)

Estudio metodológicamente impecable que ilustra la relación del acontecer político y la forja de identidades colectivas en el ámbito del folklore. La lectura de poetas menores o anónimos permite rehacer un cuadro social de la época y da pie para ver en la poesía una manifestación fidedigna de la "conciencia histórica" de una nación. [MG]

Obras completas de José Martí: iconografía, cronología. See item **19.**

4161 Paz, Octavio. Obras completas de Octavio Paz. v. 1–11. Ed. del autor, 2. ed. Barcelona: Círculo de Lectores; México: Fondo de Cultura Económica, 1994–1997. 11 v.: bibl., ill. (some col.), indexes. (Letras mexicanas)

Obra de suma importancia en las letras de este siglo. La división obedece a un esquema temático. Los primeros cinco tomos recogen sus ensayos sobre literatura: 1) sobre poesía (*El arco y la lira, Los hijos del Limo, La otra voz*); 2) literatura extranjera; 3) literatura en lengua española; 4) literatura mexicana; y 5) Sor Juana. Vol. 6 reúne sus ensayos sobre arte universal, Vol. 7 sobre México, Vols. 8–10 sobre historia, política, ideas y costumbres y Vol. 11–12 compilan su obra poética. Vol. 13 recogerá sus primeros escritos y vol. 14 se dedicará a las entrevistas y últimos escritos. Paz escribe prólogos a cada uno de los tomos; además, revisa y altera las ediciones originales. (Vols. 12–14 están en prensa.) [JS]

4162 Romero Rojas, Francisco José et al.
Bibliografía de la poesía colombiana, 1970–1992. Bogotá: Instituto Caro y Cuervo, 1993. 286 p.: index. (Publicaciones del Instituto Caro y Cuervo: Serie bibliográfica; 14)
Continúa y complementa el trabajo de H. Orjuela, publicado por el mismo instituto (1971). Además de la completa bibliografía de autores, incluye entradas analíticas de revistas extranjeras. Instrumento utilísimo para

los estudiosos de ese período. [PL]

4163 Zalamea, Jorge. Erótica y poética del siglo XX. Presentación y edición de Carlos Vásquez Zawadzki. Cali, Colombia: Ediciones Univ. del Valle, 1992. 208 p.: bibl. (Col. Ensayo iberoamericano)
Reúne las conferencias del seminario que J. Zalamea dictó en la Univ. del Valle en 1969. A partir de importantes poemas contemporáneos, desarrolla un amplio temario. Notas algo adjetivales, pero valiosa selección de piezas fundamentales de Eliot, Pasternak, Desnos, S.J. Perse, Prevert, Huidobro, Block, S. de la Selva, Cendrars, Mutis, Neruda y otros autores. [PL]

Drama

MARIO A. ROJAS, *Associate Professor of Modern Languages, Catholic University of America*

LA INFLUENCIA QUE EJERCE la televisión y los videos en el mundo latinoamericano contemporáneo es cada vez mayor; sin embargo, esto no ha impedido que los espectáculos teatrales se mantengan vivos, no sólo en salas privadas, sino también en representaciones desplegadas en los espacios abiertos de parques, plazas y calles de pueblos y ciudades. No es sorprendente, por tanto, que hayan surgido nuevos dramaturgos y que los establecidos prosigan su fecunda labor escritural. No sólo subsiste el interés por el espectáculo propiamente tal, sino también por el texto dramático o literario, razón por la cual se continúan editando o reeditando autores destacados como Argüelles, Chocrón, Galich, C. Gorostiza, J. Hernández, Maggi, Méndez Ballester, Mosquera, Pavlovsky, Vodánovic, y que se abra el espacio editorial a dramaturgos jóvenes, como N. Caballero, R. Rodríguez, Escofet. En el ámbito latinoamericano, el teatro didáctico, de contenido social-realista, sigue vigente como un instrumento de auscultamiento y reflexión de los problemas sociales o individuales que se perciben en contextos locales, nacionales o internacionales. Sin embargo, la norma ya no es la adhesión incondicional a la convención realista puramente mimética que privilegiaba la función ideológica de concientización reformadora.

La mayoría de los dramaturgos jóvenes siguen reflexionando con la misma intensidad sobre su entorno, pero con una sensibilidad y profesionalismo literario más refinado, atento a los recursos o a las convenciones literarias y teatrales que el siglo XX les ha enseñado. Hay textos de contenido filosófico que nagevan por la diacronía de la historia de la cultura, de la literatura y del teatro para establecer relaciones intertextuales que nos invitan a mirar hacia el pasado, y detenernos en figuras históricas o ficticias que el canon cultural las señala como parte integral de nuestro cuerpo cultural, figuras que han sido glorificadas por el mito o que, por el contrario, a pesar de su valor señero, no son incluidas en la historia cultural oficial (items **4177, 4190, 4232, 4259, 4243, 4200** y **4228**). Hay dramaturgos que ficcionalizan figuras históricas no sólo para recrear su perdida e irrecuperable vida privada, sino por sobre todo, para inventar verosímiles alternativas del pasado que se vieron truncadas por ideologías y poderes. De este modo, la conjetura (lo que pudo ser) relativiza la historia o se yergue sin timidez paralela a ella (items **4194, 4221** y **4250**). Hay obras que abordan problemas concretos del mundo contemporáneo, que no sólo afectan al mundo latinoamericano sino que son de universal preocupación, como es el caso del SIDA que es tratado por tres dramaturgos (items **4186, 4238** y **4244**).

Algunas editoriales latinoamericanas dedicadas especialmente a la publicación de textos dramáticos, como es el caso de GIROL en Canadá y Galerna en Argentina, siguen enriqueciendo el campo teatral con la publicación de antologías y de estudios críticos. Otras editoriales han iniciado la publicación de esmeradas colecciones de obras representativas de países latinoamericanos. Tal es el caso de Fondo de Cultura Económica y de Escenografía, ambas de México (items **4263, 4264, 4265, 4265, 4266, 4268, 4269** y **4271**). Otras iniciativas editoriales están contribuyendo al registro de la historia del teatro latinoamericano con reediciones de obras agotadas o que nunca fueron publicadas (items **4197, 4212, 4208, 4198, 4175, 4216** y **4246**). Merece especial atención la publicación de obras que han sido pensadas para estudiantes secundarios o universitarios (items **4187, 4193, 4209, 4210** y **4270**).

En un recuento general es posible advertir que la producción dramática todavía proviene en su mayor parte de la pluma masculina. Es de notar, sin embargo, que a los nombres de autoras conocidas como Isidora Aguirre, Josefina Hernández y Maruxa Vilalta se han agregado los de autoras más jóvenes que tienen a su haber obras de excelente calidad (items **4175, 4180, 4196** y **4261**). Los países que producen más textos dramáticos son Argentina y México, que ostentan una rica tradición teatral permanentemente estimulada por organismos nacionales o regionales. Aunque en países como Chile y Uruguay se mantiene una dramaturgia de calidad, es preciso señalar que, en las últimas décadas, los dramaturgos venezolanos son los que más se han destacado por la gran calidad de sus obras, como las de Caballero, Cabrujas, Chocrón, Martínez, Santana, Rodríguez Romano, Romero y muchos más. Otros países como Costa Rica están igualmente desarrollando una dramaturgia con valiosos talentos locales que, unido a jóvenes de otros lugares, ayudan a la configuración de una rica tradición teatral en nuestro continente.

PLAYS

4164 Agüero, Luis. *Desengaño cruel.* La Habana: Unión de Escritores y Artistas de Cuba, 1989. 79 p.

Obra en dos actos cuyo protagonista, después de una prolongada ausencia, regresa de los EE.UU. a Cuba, para recuperar su identidad escindida y honrar a sus muertos. A través de la memoria del protagonista se evocan violentos hechos pre-revolucionarios. No demanda grandes recursos de montaje.

4165 Aguirre, Isidora. *Los libertadores, Bolívar y Miranda:* teatro. Santiago: Ediciones LAR, 1993. 70 p.

Obra de carácter histórico, en dos partes, que presenta a Bolívar al borde de su muerte junto a su ayudante José. En su delirio postrero, van surgiendo las figuras de Miranda y Manuela Sáenz y de otros personajes relacionados con la vida personal del Libertador.

4166 Ahunchaín, Alvaro. *Hijo del rigor.* Prólogo de Rubén Castillo. Montevideo: Ministerio de Educación y Cultura, Instituto Nacional del Libro, 1991. 58 p. (Col. Teatro uruguayo; 10)

Obra con tres protagonistas que tiene como espacio escénico un ring de boxeo. En ella se intercalan escenas dramáticas con los rounds de una pelea. La ingeniosa propuesta de montaje y el ritmo e intensidad dramáticos hacen de ésta una excelente obra.

4167 Aranzazu Arboleda, Elías. *Sebastián de las Gracias* y otras obras: teatro. Medellín, Colombia: Editorial Lealón, 1991. 234 p.

El volumen tiene seis obras dramáticas

de carácter costumbrista, que presentan situaciones y personajes típicos y un registro fidedigno de sociolectos regionales. Incluye además tres piezas de teatro infantil.

4168 Argudín, Antonio. Teatro de Antonio Argudín. Xalapa, Mexico: Gobierno del Estado de Veracruz-Llave, 1994. 200 p.

Se agrupan nueve obras en un acto, en que se emplean distintas convenciones teatrales, la farsa, el género revisteril, la pastorela. La más conocida en el ambiente nacional es la pastorela *Las peripecias de un costal o la corona de hierro* que tiene como intertexto un cuento de Gogol. La mejor lograda es *La sirena azul.*

4169 Argüelles, Hugo. *La tarántula art noveau de la calle del oro:* una comedia gráfica en dos actos; *El cerco de la cabra dorada:* pieza en dos actos, cada uno dividido en dos cuadros. México: Univ. Autónoma Metropolitana, Unidad Iztapalapa, 1991. 188 p. (Col. Taller de teatro mexicano; 2)

Dos obras recientes de excelente calidad, con personajes que revelan sin aspavientos su malévola naturaleza, sus pasiones y su capacidad (auto)destructiva.

4170 Argüelles, Hugo. Teatro de Hugo Argüelles: antología de comedias, tragicomedias y farsas. v. 1–2. Jalapa Enríquez, Mexico: Gobierno del Estado de Veracruz, 1992. 2 v.: ill. (Veracruz en la cultura)

Los dos volúmenes antologan varias piezas teatrales del autor. Desde una amplia visión humanista, matizada con humor negro, un tono satírico y visos de realismo mágico, el autor codifica patrones culturales de las sociedades mexicana y latinoamericana. La introducción de Gonzalo Valdés Medellín es notable.

4171 Argüelles, Hugo. Trilogía colonial. México: Plaza y Valdés, 1992. 365 p.: ill. (Cinco centenarios)

En las tres obras, *Aguila Real, La dama de la luna rosa* y *La ronda de la hechizada,* los *dramatis personae* que propulsan la acción dramática son los típicos personajes que perfilan el mundo colonial. A través de las figuras del indio, mestizo, criollo y español, se van presentando distintas versiones/visiones del Nuevo Mundo.

4172 Argüelles, Hugo. Trilogía mestiza. México: Plaza y Valdés Editores, 1994. 431 p.: bibl., ill. (Cinco centenarios)

Las tres obras comparten como motivo dramático conductor el mestizaje. La fusión de lo indígena y lo español se dramatizan hasta límites extremos. La más celebrada de las tres obras es *Los gallos salvajes* en que el machismo exacerbado, paternal y filial, desencadena la tragedia. Excelentes textos.

4173 Balla, Andrés. *Viana.* Buenos Aires: Torres Agüero Editor, 1994. 67 p. (Col. Cuarta pared; 20)

Drama histórico que tiene como protagonista una figura del siglo XV, el príncipe de Viana, cuyos ideales filosóficos, éticos y políticos son destacados y propuestos como aún persistentes paradigmas en la cultura contemporánea.

4174 Barbery Suárez, Oscar. *Tu nombre en palo escrito.* Santa Cruz, Bolivia: Casa de la Cultura Raúl Otero Reiche, 1992. 75 p.: ill. (Col. Teatro)

La acción dramática se establece mediante el diálogo contrapuntual de voces interiores, sintomáticas de la conducta de personajes motivados por fuerzas ambientales convencionales y por el egoísmo personal. Obra bien construida, una de las mejores del teatro boliviano actual.

4175 Berman, Sabina. *Entre Villa y una mujer desnuda; Muerte súbita; El suplicio del placer.* México: Grupo Editorial Gaceta; DDF, Secretaría General de Desarrollo Social, 1994. 219 p. (Teatro mexicano contemporáneo: Col. Escenología/drama; 10)

Obras de excelente calidad. En la más reciente, *Entre Villa y una mujer desnuda,* la autora, con humor y seriedad, se centra en las figuras de Pancho Villa y su biógrafo para relativizar la pretendida omnisciencia cientificista de la historia.

4176 Caballero, Néstor. Con una pequeña ayuda de mis amigos. Prólogo Orlando Rodriguez B. Caracas: Monte Avila Editores, 1990. 227 p. (Col. Teatro)

Contiene tres obras de alto nivel estético. En una atmósfera alucinante, se recoge el pasado, los sueños irrealizados y frustraciones de generaciones para demitificar figuras patrióticas, o desconstruir mitos culturales.

4177 Caballero, Néstor and **César Rojas.** *Desiertos del paraíso* [de] Néstor Caballero; *El regreso:* teatro [de] César Rojas. Caracas: Fundarte, Alcaldía de Caracas; Teatro Nacional Juvenil, 1993. 95 p. (Cuadernos de difusión; 194)

En *Desiertos del Paraíso,* la pasión literaria y la vital se trasvasan en un espacio escénico que representa la casa del poeta Lezama Lima. *El regreso,* insuflada de humor absurdista, se sitúa en los 50, y su conflicto dramático gira en torno a un asesinato que va desovillando un convulsionado mundo.

4178 Carballido, Emilio. Querétaro imperial. Querétaro, Mexico: H. Ayuntamiento de Querétaro, Coordinación de Publicaciones, 1994. 92 p.

Contiene nueve piezas breves que presentan aquellos acontecimientos históricos o cotidianos que marcaron hito en la historia del pueblo colonial de Querétaro. Entre las obras se encuentra *Paredón,* que tiene como personaje central al Emperador Maximiliano.

4179 Carballido, Emilio. Teatro de Emilio Carballido. v. 1–2. Jalapa?: Gobierno del Estado de Veracruz, 1992. 2 v.: ill. (Veracruz en la cultura)

En una excelente edición se recogen 21 obras del destacado dramaturgo mexicano. Además de los textos se incluyen fotos de puestas. Entre las obras más famosas se encuentran *Te juro, Juana, que tengo ganas, Las cartas de Mozart, Yo también hablo de la rosa* y *Felicidad.*

4180 Castagnino, Lucrecia. Mosaico urbano. Rosario, Argentina: Dirección de Publicaciones UNR, 1992. 98 p.: ill.

Contiene ocho obras breves, de argumentos bien trazados, en que se combinan armoniosamente diálogo, poesía y música. En todas ellas los personajes femeninos constituyen el eje estructural del conflicto planteado.

4181 Castagnino, Lucrecia. Veraneo y tormentas. Rosario, Argentina: Impresiones Módulo, 1992. 66 p.

Tetralogía que tiene como protagonistas a mujeres que reflexionan sobre de sí y su circunstancia y que sueñan con mundos utópicos destilados de los valores negativos que las agobian. Como es característico en las obras de Castagnino, las puestas requieren de complementos visuales y sonoros.

4182 Castillo, Andrés. *Metastasio.* Prólogo de Eduardo Schinca. Montevideo: Ministerio de Educación y Cultura, Instituto Nacional del Libro, 1991. 68 p. (Col. Teatro uruguayo; 9)

Los protagonistas son dos payasos y el espacio escénico, una pista de circo. El espectáculo cirsense y el micromundo circundado por la carpa se convierte en una metáfora de la violencia y del poder que generan el desamor y el fracaso.

4183 Castillo Alva, Arturo. *El gran poder de Dios.* Ciudad Victoria, Mexico: Instituto Tamaulipeco de Cultura, 1990. 84 p.

Obra basada en un hecho histórico sucedido en las postrimerías del siglo XIX en la sierra de Sonora y Chihuahua. La violencia militar-gubernamental que agobió a un pueblo se insinúa como resonando todavía en muchos lugares de México y Latinoamérica.

4184 Castillo Bautista, Víctor Manuel. *Nuño de Guzmán o la espada de Dios:* obra en un acto. Guadalajara, Mexico: Univ. de Guadalajara, 1994. 63 p.

Obra que dramatiza un episodio de la conquista en que realza la victimización de los indios y la avaricia de los conquistadores. La figura intermediaria de un bufón al tiempo que modula la acción se yergue como una voz que evalúa éticamente los hechos presentados.

4185 Chalbaud, Román. Teatro. v. 1–3. Prólogo de Marita King. Caracas: Monte Avila Editores, 1991–92. 3 v. (Col. Teatro)

Se recogen nueve obras, todas de buena calidad, en que lo cotidiano se amalgama con la magia poética y en que el referente local adquiere una trascendencia universal.

4186 Chocrón, Isaac E. *Escrito y sellado:* pieza en dos partes y ocho escenas. Caracas: Centro Cultural Consolidado, 1993. 70 p.: ill.

El SIDA y el necesario sostén de la fe son las dos líneas isotópicas que configuran la acción dramática de esta nueva obra. A través de ingeniosos recursos escénicos se cala en la naturaleza de las relaciones humanas y se explicitan los flagelos físicos y espirituales contemporáneos.

4187 Los clásicos del teatro hispanoamericano. v. 1–2. Selección, introducciones, notas y bibliografías de Gerardo Luzuriaga y Richard Reeve. 2. ed. ampliada. México: Fondo de Cultura Económica, 1994. 2 v.: bibl. (Tezontle)

Reedición corregida y ampliada. Ordena las obras generacionales marcando el desarrollo del teatro hispanoamericano desde sus orígenes hasta 1950. Recomendable como texto básico para universitarios. Aunque bastante completa, puede complementarse con textos individuales.

4188 Cosío Osuna, José Joaquín. *Tomóchic: el día que se acabó el mundo.* Chihuahua: Ediciones del Gobierno del Estado de Chihuahua, 1993. iv, 34 p. (Col. Divisadero)

Drama histórico que refiere a un episodio ocurrido en 1892 en el pueblo de Tomóchic, el cual fue violentamente arrasado por tropas federales mientras se resistía épicamente a la dominación hegemónica del gobierno de Porfirio Díaz.

4189 Cuadra, Pablo Antonio. El coro y la máscara: tres obras escénicas. San José: Libro Libre, 1991. 77 p.: ill. (Obra poética completa; 9)

Se incluyen tres textos: dos obras en un acto y un breve episodio escénico que protagoniza el filibustero Walker. La presencia de la escritura de Cuadra se hace evidente en la calidad literaria de estos textos.

4190 Cuatro, Augusto. Una poquita de tierra. Caracas: Monte Avila Editores, 1992. 68 p. (Col. Teatro)

La obra se estructura en torno a la vida de la escritora Teresa de la Parra, mujer de letras y precursora de los movimientos feministas actuales. Requiere de cuatro actrices que representan distintos momentos de su vida.

4191 Del patricidio a la utopía: el teatro argentino actual en 4 claves mayores. Estudio preliminar por Osvaldo Pellettieri. Dirigida por Miguel Angel Giella y Peter Roster. Ottawa, Canada: GIROL Books Inc., 1993. 195 p. (Col. Telón)

Selección apta para estudiantes universitarios interesados en el teatro latinoamericano actual. Contiene *Una noche con Magnus e hijos* de Ricardo Monti, *Miembros del jurado* de Roberto Perinelli, *Cuarteto* de Eduardo Rovner y *Salto al cielo* de Mauricio Kartun.

4192 Dimayuga, José. *Afectuosamente, su comadre.* México: Consejo Nacional para la Cultura y las Artes, 1993. 70 p. (Fondo editorial tierra adentro; 79)

Excelente obra que relata el encuentro accidental de un joven travestí con una maestra de edad madura. Ambas figuras, alejadas y contrastantes en un comienzo, van paulatinamente encontrando el espacio común del afecto y la solidaridad.

4193 Dragún, Osvaldo. Osvaldo Dragún: su teatro. Selección, presentación y entrevistas de John F. Garganigo. Medellín, Colombia: Ediciones Otras Palabras, 1993. 307 p.: bibl. (Col. de narrativa y teatro; 4)

Se seleccionan cuatro obras conocidas del autor: *Historias para ser contadas, Los de la mesa 10, El amasijo* y *¡Arriba Corazón!* Una acuciosa introducción que pone en perspectiva toda la labor dramática del autor es complementada con dos entrevistas en que Dragún habla extensamente de su obra.

4194 Endara, Ernesto. *Sir Henry, el pirata.* Panamá: Editorial Mariano Arosemena del Instituto Nacional de Cultura, 1993. 191 p. (Col. Ricardo Miró: Premio teatro; 1992)

Obra de carácter histórico. Desde las últimas horas de vida del legendario pirata inglés, Henry Morgan, se revive en *flashbacks* retrospectivos su agitado y tormentoso pasado. El texto se acompaña de música y canciones.

4195 Engel, José Luis. *Puesta en escena.* Aguascalientes, Mexico: Instituto Cultural de Aguascalientes, 1992. 22 p. (Voces abiertas)

En esta obra de corte posmodernista se dramatiza lúdicamente el trasvasamiento de géneros literarios, como también la relación autor-personaje-receptor a nivel del texto literario y del espectacular.

4196 Escofet, Cristina. Teatro completo. v. 1. Buenos Aires: Torres Agüero Editor, 1994. 1 v. (Col. Telón abierto; 5)

Obras de excelente calidad que conllevan como tema esencial la identidad femenina. Humorísticamente se desmontan las distintas formas de poder que signan culturalmente a la mujer.

4197 Esteve, Patricio. *La gran histeria nacional; Palabras calientes.* Buenos Aires: Editorial Plus Ultra, 1992. 92 p.: bibl.

Dos textos satírico-paródicos que carnavalescamente cuestionan la verticalidad, el autoritarismo y los cánones estéticos del discurso hegemónico nacional argentino que rigió la década de los 70. La intencionalidad referencial no menoscaba la calidad teatral de ambos textos.

4198 Fernández Guardia, Ricardo. *Magdalena.* Introducción, bibliografía y notas de Alvaro Quesada Soto. San José: Editorial de la Univ. de Costa Rica, 1993. 98 p. (Col. Retorno)

Obra costumbrista escrita en 1902 que constituye una de las primeras manifestaciones del género dramático costarricense. En ella se critica la sociedad burguesa de la época.

4199 Freidel, José Manuel. Teatro. Prólogo de Joe Broderick. Medellín, Colombia: Ediciones Autores Antioqueños, 1993. 492 p.: ill. (Col. Autores antioqueños; 83)

Contiene 16 piezas teatrales de este importante dramaturgo colombiano y tres estudios críticos sobre su obra. Entre las obras antologadas se destacan *Amantina o la historia de un desamor, Los infortunios de la bella Otero* y *Las tardes de Manuela* en que la protagonista es Manuela Sáenz.

4200 Fundora, Carlos. *La última obra del bardo inmortal.* Santa Clara, Cuba: Ediciones Capiro, 1992. 39 p. (Teatro)

Obra farsesca que, en un contrapunto intertextual paródico, alterna personajes de Shakespeare con otros de la época actual. La acción dramática se configura en función del encadenamiento de situaciones dramáticas sorpresivas.

4201 Galich, Manuel. La obra dramática del doctor Manuel Francisco Galich López. v. 2. Recopilación de Víctor Hugo Cruz. Guatemala: Univ. de San Carlos de Guatemala, Dirección General de Extensión, Consejo Editorial, 1989–91. 1 v.: ill. (Col. Editorial Universitaria; 2)

Contiene nueve piezas teatrales escritas entre 1938–53. Se incluyen tres entrevistas, una introducción y otros documentos que ayudan a mejor comprensión de la motivación escritural de Galish y el carácter socio-referencial y didáctico de sus obras.

4202 García, Carlos Jesús. *Jugando a si mismo:* teatro. Holguín, Cuba: Dirección Municipal de Cultura Holguín, 1989. 57 p.

Metateatro en que los niveles ficcionales y temporales y la delimitación del es-pacio dramático y del espectador se entremezclan.

4203 García del Toro, Antonio. *La primera dama:* drama en dos actos. Coral Gables, Fla.: Iberian Studies Institute, North-South Center, Univ. of Miami, 1992. 78 p. (Letras de oro)

El poder de un innominado dictador, prototípico de los muchos que han gobernado Latinoamérica, es confrontado por su mujer, la primera dama, después que el mismo hijo del dictador es condenado a muerte por su padre.

García Márquez, Gabriel. Diatriba de amor contra un hombre sentado: monólogo en un acto. See item **3670.**

4204 Gariano, Carmelo. *El último trovador:* comedia en tres actos. Miami, Fla.: Ediciones Universal, 1991. 80 p. (Col. Teatro)

Obra de ambientación trovadoresca cuya acción sucede en la Provenza de 1239–41. Su trama se estructura alrededor de un triángulo amoroso que se resuelve positivamente cuando una joven supera los obstáculos familiares y sociales para unirse con su verdadero amor.

4205 Gavlovski E., Johnny. *Los puentes rotos; Más allá de la vida:* teatro. Caracas: Fundarte, Alcaldía del Municipio Libertador, 1991. 102 p. (Cuadernos de difusión; 148)

Se plantean situaciones límites, conflictos humanos de gran intensidad originados y causados por diferencias generacionales.

4206 Germano, Antonio. Teatro. Santa Fe, Argentina: Centro de Publicaciones de la Univ. Nacional del Litoral, 1992. 92 p.

Dos obras de sólida estructura dramática. Aunque ostentan claros referentes político-sociales, no adoptan enteramente la modalidad teatral realista. El mito de Icaro en *Vuelo circular* se reelabora dándosele un sentido metafórico contestatario.

4207 Gil, Rubén Darío and **César Rojas.** *La curiosidad mató al gato.* Rubén Darío Gil. *Los alfareros* [y] *Las puntas del triángulo* [de] César Rojas. Caracas: Fundarte, Alcaldía de Caracas; Centro de Directores para el Nuevo Teatro, 1993. 98 p. (Cuadernos de difusión; 192)

Ambos dramaturgos son también directores, lo cual se refleja en sus interesantes propuestas de montaje. Se trata de obras cuya tensión dramática se produce por la transgresión de códigos religiosos y sociales cuyo efecto se suaviza con la incorporación de elementos lúdicos.

4208 González Castillo, José. *Los invertidos.* Buenos Aires: Puntosur Editores, 1991. 101 p. (Col. Repertorio)

Es uno de los primeros dramaturgos hispanoamericanos que usa explícitamente la homosexualidad para dar forma al conflicto dramático. Escrita a comienzos del siglo XX, la obra registra el cruce de varios códigos literario-teatrales: realismo, naturalismo, sainete y melodrama.

4209 Gorostiza, Carlos. *El pan de la locura.* Buenos Aires: Ediciones Colihue, 1993. 132 p.: ill. (Col. literaria LYC—leer y crear; 101)

Obra de carácter didáctico-social que intenta concientizar al receptor y desarrollar en él un espíritu solidario. Se acompaña de un valioso material pedagógico que estimula al estudiante a adoptar una postura crítica.

4210 Gorostiza, Carlos. *El puente.* Buenos Aires: Ediciones Colihue, 1993. 148 p.: ill. (Col. literaria LYC—leer y crear; 106)

Estrenada en 1949, es una obra representativa de la producción dramática del autor. En ella se representan *calle/casa* como dos espacios contrastantes para reflejar la crisis de la clase media argentina del momento. Como item **4209** es un texto preparado con fines pedagógicos.

4211 Gorostiza, Carlos. Teatro. v. 2. Prólogo de Osvaldo Pellettieri. Buenos Aires: Ediciones de la Flor, 1992? 1 v.

Contiene cinco obras del autor, quien por su afán de superar la convención teatral realista de hace 40 años, se considera como fundador del teatro contemporáneo argentino. El prólogo es de gran utilidad por sus lúcidos comentarios sobre la escritura dramática del autor.

4212 Gorostiza, Manuel Eduardo de. *Contigo pan y cebolla.* Edición, introducción y notas de John Dowling. Valencia, Spain: Albatros Hispanófila, 1992. 116 p. (Clásicos Albatros; 11)

Farsa decimonónica en que se parodia las convenciones literarias románticas. Como Don Quijote, la protagonista se sumerge en el mundo ficcional de sus lecturas para emular

inverosímiles personajes. Excelente obra con resonancias neoclásicas.

4213 Griffero S., Ramón. Tres obras. Prólogo de Alfonso de Toro. Santiago: IITCTL/ Neptuno Editores, 1992. 174 p.: ill.

Griffero es considerado uno de los directores más importantes del Chile de las últimas décadas. De carácter postmoderno, las piezas reunidas fueron escenificadas durante la dictadura militar a que se alude abierta o metafóricamente.

4214 Heredia, Juan Franklin. *¿Qué cara tienen los cornudos?* y otras obras. Buenos Aires: Ediciones Filofalsía, 1989. 43 p. (Col. Teatro)

Contiene cuatro piezas teatrales breves de las que se destacan *¿Qué cara tienen los cornudos?* y *Los homosexuales se divierten* por los equívocos que llevan a una seria reflexión o a divertidas situaciones.

4215 Hernández, Leopoldo M. Piezas cortas. Honolulu, Hawaii: Editorial Persona, 1990. 114 p. (Serie Teatro)

Se recogen nueve piezas de este autor cubano en el exilio. Escritas a lo largo de 22 años muestran una evolución tanto en el plano temático como en sus recursos dramáticos. La alienación, marginación y hostilidad que permea el mundo ficcional estampan la huella del teatro absurdista.

4216 Hernández, Luisa Josefina. *La paz ficticia; Popol Vuh; La fiesta del mulato; Quetzalcoatl.* México: Grupo Editorial Gaceta; DDF, Secretaría General de Desarrollo Social, 1994. 229 p. (Teatro mexicano contemporáneo: Col. Escenología/drama; 4)

Estas obras de carácter didáctico y de compleja estructura forman la tetralogía *Los nacimientos de México.* Escritas en los 60s y 70s, en sus personajes simbólicos se busca una sociedad utópica en que los valores humanos sublimes son lo más importante.

Inventario de voces: visión retrospectiva de la literatura sonorense. See item **3903.**

4217 Jiménez, José Alfredo. *Las manos del minero y el muñeco:* drama en tres actos. Oruro, Bolivia: Editorial Universitaria UTO, 1991. 64 p.

Obra de carácter social que denuncia las precarias condiciones sociales del minero boliviano. Aunque el dialogante principal es un muñeco, el texto sigue los principios de la dramatización realista.

4218 Kartun, Mauricio. Teatro. Estudio preliminar de Osvaldo Pellettieri. Buenos Aires: Ediciones Corregidor, 1993. 287 p.: bibl. (Col. Dramaturgos argentinos contemporáneos; 6)

Se incluyen seis piezas del autor, entre ellas las que han tenido un mayor éxito escénico, *Cumbia morena cumbia, Pericones* y *El partener.* En ellas se combinan intertexto histórico y literario para reflexionar sobre el presente argentino con la mirada puesta a un utópico futuro.

4219 Leal Carretero, Silvia. *Xurawe, o, La ruta de los muertos:* mito huichol en tres actos. Guadalajara, Mexico: Editorial Univ. de Guadalajara, 1992. 204 p.: ill. (Col. Fundamentos)

En esta obra se vierte el resultado de una investigación sobre un mito huichol que describe la ruta seguida por el espíritu después de abandonar el cuerpo. En este viaje hay tres etapas, que coinciden con los tres actos. Tiene más valor antropológico que teatral.

4220 Leñero, Vicente. *Compañero.* 3. ed. Guadalajara, Mexico: Editorial Agata, 1992. 86 p.: ill. (Teatro completo; 4)

Obra estrenada en 1970, dos años después del asesinato del Che Guevara, presenta una semblanza psicológica y política del famoso guerrillero quien aparece rodeado de figuras históricas no identificadas, pero reconocibles, que compartieron su lucha y sus ideales revolucionarios.

4221 Leñero, Vicente. *La noche de Hernán Cortés:* obra en un acto. Prólogo de José Luis Martínez. Introducción de Luis de Tavira. México: Ediciones El Milagro, 1994. 118 p.: bibl., ill. (Teatro)

Situado en la última noche de vida de Cortés, Leñero recrea la figura del conquistador conforme a la composición de la metahistoria en que historia y ficción, tiempo y espacio se confunden en planos simultáneos. En esta obra, lo factual cede el paso a lo probable.

4222 Magaña, Sergio. *La dama de las camelias:* un acto; ejercicio para estudiantes de teatro. México: Instituto Michoacano de Cultura; J. Boldó i Climent, 1993. 18 p. (Cuadernos de teatro)

Obra con tres protagonistas jóvenes especialmente diseñadas para la práctica actoral.

4223 Magaña, Sergio. *La última Diana:* farsa en un acto. Mexico: Instituto Michoacano de Cultura; J. Boldó i Climent, 1993. 28 p. (Cuadernos de teatro)

En esta obra breve, la tensión dramática se genera a partir de la contradictoria conducta que crea el ejercicio abusivo del poder tanto en víctimas como victimarios.

4224 Maggi, Carlos and **Eduardo Sarlós.** Teatro uruguayo: premios Florencio; texto de autor nacional 1985, 1986, 1987. Montevideo: ACTU; Signos, 1991. 141 p.

Se recogen dos obras de Maggi (*Frutos,* 1985), cuyo protagonista es un héroe nacional desmitificado y *El patio de la torcaza,* 1986, que combina el sainete y grotesco con una compleja simbología y una de Sarlós (*La pecera,* 1987), que tiene lugar en un asilo de ancianos. Excelentes textos.

4225 Martínez, Carlota. *Que Dios la tenga en la gloria; Ultima recta final.* Caracas: FUNDARTE, Alcaldía de Caracas, 1994. 111 p. (Col. Cuadernos de difusión; 221. Teatro)

Que Dios la tenga en la gloria tiene dos mujeres de diferentes edades que defienden los valores éticos de generación. En *Ultima recta final,* el protagonista es un jubilado agobiado por su pobreza y mala suerte. Buen teatro.

4226 Mejía Ricart, Gustavo Adolfo. *María de Toledo.* 2. ed. Santo Domingo: Fundación Mejía Ricart-Guzmán Boom, 1990. 145 p.: ill. (Col. literaria; 1)

Basado en la novela *Un blazón colonial* del mismo autor, este drama histórico tiene como escenario el Santo Domingo de las primeras décadas del siglo XVI. Todos los sucesos convergen alrededor de la Virreina Doña María de Toledo.

4227 Méndez Ballester, Manuel. Teatro de Manuel Méndez Ballester, 1930–1988: medio siglo de teatro puertorriqueño. v. 1–2. San Juan: Instituto de Cultura Puertorriqueña, División de Publicaciones, 1991. 2 v.: ill.

Buena selección de obras del dramaturgo puertorriqueño más importante de la generación de los 30. En la trayectoria de su escritura dramatúrgica, el autor explora distintas temáticas y formas de expresión teatral: realismo social, poético, el grotesco y el absurdo.

4228 Mendoza, Héctor. *Hamlet, por ejemplo:* discusión en un acto con algunos momentos de William Shakespeare. Introducción de Fernando de Ita. México: Ediciones El Milagro, 1992. 95 p.: ill. (Teatro)

Excelente metateatro sobre tres actores que aspiran a conseguir el papel de Hamlet. El comentario y la improvisación que cada uno hace de pasajes de la obra de Shakespeare permiten ahondar en las posibles interpretaciones del personaje, su contexto y el proceso mismo de su teatralización.

4229 Mendoza, Héctor. *Juicio suspendido; Del día que murió el señor Bernal dejándonos desamparados; Noche decisiva en la vida sentimental de Eva Iriarte.* Introducción de David Olguín. México: Ediciones El Milagro; Instituto Nacional de Bellas Artes, 1994. 247 p.: ill. (Teatro)

Aunque presentadas en el marco de la convención realista, las obras incluidas traspasan lo cotidiano para entrar en una realidad transmutada por el deseo. Excelentes obras con bien delineados personajes femeninos que son los principales motores de la acción dramática.

4230 Mera, Fernando. *El otro Cristóbal Colón:* drama en tres actos. Quito: Poly Color, 1991. 57 p.

Obra breve que representa episodios de la vida del Almirante. La brevedad del texto y la amplitud del tiempo que se abarca son obstáculos para una buena construcción dramática y un mayor ahondamiento en la figura del descubridor.

4231 Moncada, Luis Mario. *El motel de los destinos cruzados:* histeria introspectiva basada en textos e ideas de Calvino, Wenders, Bulgákov, Capote, Borges, *et al.* México: Consejo Nacional para la Cultura y las Artes, 1993. 69 p. (Fondo editorial tierra adentro; 82)

Obra posmodernista que se aparta del diseño lógico-cronológico de los acontecimientos, pero sin que se sacrifique la coherencia interna. De excelente calidad literaria. En ella se asume creativamente una intertextualidad en que se refleja la escritura de conocidos autores del siglo XX.

4232 Mosquera, Beatriz. Teatro. v. 1. Buenos Aires: Torres Agüero Editor, 1992. 1 v. (Col. Telón abierto)

Se incluyen seis nuevas obras inéditas de la autora, quien con diversas modalidades escénicas se dirige críticamente a referentes sociales y políticos de su país y de Latinoamérica. La negatividad contextual se contrarresta con el vigor de señeras figuras, como es el caso de Violeta Parra.

4233 Natali, Franco. Teatro y realidad. v. 1–2. Dibujos de José María Troncoso. Buenos Aires: Ediciones La Máscara, 1990–93. 2 v.: ill.

Los dos volúmenes contienen cuatro obras en que, mediante personajes arquetípicos, se recrean hechos políticos y sociales de la Argentina en los últimos 30 años. La obra más sobresaliente del conjunto es *Sin patente.*

4234 Núñez, Jorge. *Lo que mata es la humedad.* Buenos Aires: Corregidor, 1992. 127 p.

Inspirada en la tradición del sainete argentino se representan con mucha verosimilitud situaciones y personajes típicos del mundo rioplatense.

4235 Núñez, José Gabriel. *Noches de satén rígido; María Cristina me quiere governá; Bromelia madrigal; Soliloquio en negro tenaz; El llamado de la sangre:* teatro. Caracas: FUNDARTE/Alcaldía del Municipio Libertador, 1991. 170 p. (Cuadernos de difusión; 157)

Se recogen las obras más significativas del autor. *María Cristina me quiere gobernar, Bromelia Madrigal* y *Soliloquio* son protagonizadas por bien delineados personajes femeninos. En *El llamado de la sangre* se parodia la radio-novela.

4236 Núñez, José Gabriel. *Soliloquio en rojo empecinado* y otras piezas. Caracas: Fundarte, Alcaldía de Caracas, 1993. 133 p. (Cuadernos de difusión; 197. Teatro)

Se reúnen cinco obras bien escritas, de breve extensión, en que a través de la ironía, sátira, humor y sarcasmo se profundiza en personajes bien delineados psicológicamente.

4237 Olguín, David. *Bajo tierra.* México: Coordinación de Difusión Cultural, Dirección de Literatura/UNAM, 1992. 95 p.: ill. (Textos de difusión cultural: Serie La Carpa)

Excelente obra. Aunque se ubica en México entre 1906–13 y contiene personajes históricos como Porfirio Díaz, Francisco Madero y Victoriano Huerta, no es una obra histórica tradicional. Mito e historia, ficción y realidad se confunden para dar forma a un mundo ambivalente y circular.

4238 Osorio, David. *El último brunch de la década:* pieza en dos actos. Caracas: Fundarte, Alcaldía de Caracas, 1993. 70 p. (Cuadernos de difusión; 207. Teatro)

Pieza realista en torno al SIDA y sus devastadores efectos en la juventud.

4239 País, Carlos and **Américo Alfredo Torchelli.** *El hombrecito.* Buenos Aires: Torres Agüero Editor, 1992. 52 p. (Col. Cuarta pared)

Dos hombres de físico y condición social contrastantes descubren paulatinamente la humanidad que los une. Elementos de cultura popular, como el tango y el bolero, están perfectamente integrados en la composición dramática.

4240 Pantin, Yolanda. *La otredad y el vampiro.* Caracas: FUNDARTE, Alcaldía de Caracas, 1994. 45 p. (Col. Cuadernos de difusión; 220. Teatro)

Obra teatral de gótica atmósfera que tiene como protagonistas dos personajes mitológicos, un ángel y un vampiro los cuales experimentan un proceso de recíproca transmutación.

4241 Pavlovsky, Eduardo A. *El cardenal.* Buenos Aires: Ediciones Búsqueda, 1992. 62 p. (Col. Literatura de hoy)

Obra que tematiza la llamada "condición posmodernista" y sus antiparadigmas, entre ellos la relativización de verdades científicas, el desenmascaramiento de mecanismos represivos automatizados y el cuestionamiento de la objetividad científica.

4242 Pirela, Marvin. *Anastasia, la esclava del santo.* Maracaibo, Venezuela: Univ. del Zulia, Rectorado, 1991. 81 p.

La acción se sitúa en Maracaibo en las postrimerías del período colonial. En la obra se destaca el papel que jugó la mujer en la lucha contra la esclavitud. Se incorporan en ella la música y lo mágico-religioso como elementos inherentes del mestizaje venezolano.

4243 Plaza Noblía, Héctor. *Ecce homo.* Madrid: Instituto de Cooperación Iberoamericana, Ediciones de Cultura Hispánica, 1992. 147 p.

Obra de carácter histórico se centra en

la figura de García Lorca. Desde los momentos previos a su muerte se proyecta el contexto histórico y social de España durante la guerra civil. Excelente texto.

4244 Prieto, Ricardo. Teatro. Montevideo: Proyección, 1993. 180 p.

La tensión dramática surge del subterráneo y complejo mundo interior de personajes degradados que son incapaces de sobreponerse a las limitaciones que ejerce sobre ellos el poder social. *Pecados mínimos* versa sobre el SIDA.

4245 Quintana, Germana. Teatro dominicano: 3 obras de un acto. Santo Domingo?: s.n., 1993. 112 p.

Obras de carácter realista que tienen como protagonistas a mujeres que se afanan por lograr una identidad propia mientras luchan con los prejuicios y patrones de conducta familiares o sociales que obstaculizan sus anhelos.

4246 Rascón Banda, Víctor Hugo. *Manos arriba; Sabor de engaño; La banca.* México: Grupo Editorial Gaceta; DDF, Secretaría General de Desarrollo Social, 1994. 251 p. (Teatro mexicano contemporáneo: Col. Escenología/drama; 11)

En estas obras el dramaturgo recupera la convención teatral realista para, sin ambages, reflejar fidedignamente hechos cotidianos en que se revelan problemas del hombre contemporáneo. Excelentes obras.

4247 Rechani Agrait, Luis. Teatro de Luis Rechani Agrait. v. 1–2. San Juan: Instituto de Cultura Puertorriqueña, 1991. 2 v.: bibl.

Siete obras de corte realista en que se recrean situaciones familiares y sociales arquetípicas. Una actitud satírica y fustigante traspasa casi todos los textos. De especial interés es el drama histórico *Llora en el atardecer la fuente,* que tiene a Juan Ponce de León como protagonista.

4248 Reyes, Candelario. *Siete muecas:* teatro. Santa Bárbara, Honduras: Ediciones Centro Cultural Hibueras, 1991. 144 p.

Piezas breves, especialmente construidas para grupos comunitarios hondureños. Con las situaciones dramáticas planteadas se propone llamar la atención sobre el estado precario de los campesinos. Su fin es el de concientización social.

4249 Reyes, Carlos José. *Dentro y fuera.* Medellín, Colombia: Editorial Univ. de Antioquia, Depto. de Publicaciones, Univ. de Antioquia, 1992. 421 p.: bibl., ill. (Col. Teatro; 4)

Contiene siete obras del autor, en su mayoría obras de carácter realista en que, desde un enfoque existencialista y usando el humor negro, se presentan personajes reificados o deshumanizados. *Recorrido en redondo* se destaca por su bien lograda construcción dramática.

4250 Rial, José Antonio. *Cipango; Panamá; Darién; Contraluz de un hereje.* Caracas: Monte Avila Editores, 1992. 349 p. (Col. Teatro)

En esta obra, las figuras de Colón y Vasco Núñez de Balboa y sus utópicos mundos son puntos de arranque para meditar sobre el mundo actual en que los valores humanitarios y las utopías sociales están a punto de convertirse en materiales de desecho.

4251 Rodríguez, Romano. *Los amantes del Imperio; Vía Benetton; La vecina de enfrente* (teatro clip). Caracas: FUNDARTE, Alcaldía de Caracas, 1991. 90 p. (Cuadernos de difusión; 166)

Excelente teatro, innovador tanto en la concepción del texto dramático como en su propuesta de escenificación. En ellas hay niveles de ficción y referentes que se intersectan.

4252 Rodríguez Muñoz, Alberto. *Una catedral gótica; Nadie debe morir.* Buenos Aires: Editorial Plus Ultra, 1992. 139 p.

Textos metateatrales y reflexivos tienen como autoreferente el proceso teatral mismo.

Rosencof, Mauricio. El bataraz. See item **3877.**

4253 Rovner, Eduardo. *Cuarteto.* Buenos Aires: Torres Agüero Editor, 1992. 51 p. (Col. Cuarta pared)

A través de un lenguaje metafórico y el empleo del grotesco y del humor negro, el autor moraliza sobre los efectos destructores y deshumanizantes el personalismo. Excelente obra.

4254 Sáenz, Guido. *La llamada del tiempo:* teatro. San José: Editorial Costa Rica, 1992. 102 p.: ill.

El conflicto dramático surge a partir de un viejo violinista que pierde su puesto en una orquesta. Su frustración y desesperanza contrasta con la firme voluntad de su hijo músico, que pese a las circunstancias adversas decide continuar sus estudios y la ruta de su padre.

4255 Sáenz Andrade, Bruno. Comedia del cuerpo: 1974–1989. Ed. rev. y ampliada. Quito?: Editora Nacional, Secretaría Nacional de Comunicación Social, 1992? 127 p.

Recoge siete obras, todas breves y de carácter episódico. La de mayor extensión y más relevante es *Crónica de los incas sin incario*, que trata de la guerrilla campesina.

4256 Santaliz Avila, Pedro. Teatro. San Juan: Instituto de Cultura Puertorriqueña, 1992. 272 p.

Selección de cuatro obras de tipo realista costumbrista, con personajes típicos y lenguaje popular. *El castillo interior de Medea Camuñas* es una adaptación libre de la tragedia de Eurípides.

4257 Santana, Rodolfo. *Mirando al tendido:* y otras obras de Rodolfo Santana. Caracas: Banco Central de Venezuela, 1992. 255 p. (Col. Cincuentenaria)

Contiene cinco de las obras más recientes del autor, todas de gran profundidad filosófica. A través de un lenguaje metafórico o de un directo referente político-social se reflexiona sobre fenómenos de carácter mundial.

4258 Sarlós, Eduardo. *Los ecos del silencio* y otras obras de teatro. Montevideo: Caiguá Editores, 1992. 209 p.: ill.

Contiene cuatro obras del autor. Se destaca *Los ecos del silencio*, en que a través de la yuxtaposición de espacio interior/exterior y de narración/diálogo se recrean episodios de los movimientos anarquistas de los 20. *Perdóname Sábato* intenta una continuación de la historia de *El túnel* de Sábato.

4259 Schmidhuber de la Mora, Guillermo. *El día que Mona Lisa dejó de sonreír.* México: Editorial Oasis, 1987. 67 p. (Col. Lecturas del milenio; 21)

Drama que recrea los acontecimientos sucedidos en Francia, en mayo de 1519, cuando muere Leonardo da Vinci. Del diálogo de los discípulos que lo acompañan en su agonía, se recrea fragmentariamente la vida del maestro. En la obra la conjetura hace flaquear la factualidad de la historia.

4260 Sieveking, Alejandro. *Ingenuas palomas* y otras obras de teatro. Santiago: Editorial Universitaria, 1994. 208 p. (Col. Los contemporáneos)

Tres obras que trazan el camino recorrido por la dramaturgia del autor. *La remolienda*, muy popular en el ambiente chileno, es considerada prototípica del realismo folklórico poético vigente en los 60 en Chile. En *Ingenuas palomas*, la obra más reciente, se combina diestramente la parodia, del grotesco y el esperpento.

4261 Sosa Llano, Ana Teresa. *Corazón de fuego:* teatro. Caracas: Fundarte, Alcaldía de Caracas, 1992? 59 p. (Cuadernos de difusión; 183)

A través de los recuerdos de tres viejas abandonadas en la soledad de un asilo de ancianos, se rememoran momentos de sus pasados, de sus ilusiones y amores frustrados.

4262 Taboada, Carlos Enrique. *Alboíno:* tragedia en tres actos y seis cuadros. México: Univ. Autónoma Metropolitana, Unidad Xochimilco, 1988. 111 p. (Col. de teatro mexicano. Serie DAME EL PIE; 9)

Historia y ficción se confunden en esta obra que tiene como protagonistas a Alboíno, fundador del reino de Lombardía en Italia, y Rosamunda, la reina de los gépidos. Excelente texto dramático.

4263 Teatro argentino contemporáneo: antología. Coordinación de Gerardo Fernández. Madrid: Sociedad Estatal Quinto Centenario; Fondo de Cultura Económica; Centro de Documentación Teatral, 1992. 1205 p. (Teatro iberoamericano contemporáneo)

Con una introducción de Gerardo Fernández, se reúnen 15 obras que han sido destacadas por la crítica como de excelente calidad. Hay textos desde Carlos Gorostiza hasta Mauricio Kartun. A través de estas obras pasan las distintas tendencias teatrales del país y los referentes histórico-culturales reflejados en ellas.

4264 Teatro chileno contemporáneo: antología. Coordinación de Juan Andrés Piña. Madrid: Quinto Centenario; Fondo de Cultura Económica; Centro de Documentación Tea-

tral, 1992. 1251 p.: bibl. (Teatro iberoamericano contemporáneo)

Muy buena selección que agrupa 15 piezas de teatro chileno (1950–90), desde *Mama Rosa* de Fernando Debesa, estrenada en 1957, hasta *Cinema Utoppia* de Ramón Griffero.

4265 Teatro colombiano contemporáneo: antología. Coordinación de Fernando González Cajiao. Madrid: Sociedad Estatal Quinto Centenario; Fondo de Cultura Económica; Centro de Documentación Teatral, 1992. 995 p. (Teatro iberoamericano contemporáneo)

Se incluyen 15 obras representativas del país, unas de creación colectiva como *El paso* de La Candelaria, otras que reflejan la sociedad colombiana como *Los burgueses*, o aquellas que son de carácter histórico como *El grito de los ahorcados* de Martínez Arango, *Un réquiem por el padre Las Casas* de Buenaventura y *I took Panama* de Luis Alberto García.

4266 Teatro cubano contemporáneo: antología. Coordinación de Carlos Espinosa Domínguez. Madrid: Sociedad Estatal Quinto Centenario; Fondo de Cultura Económica; Centro de Documentación Teatral, 1992. 1508 p. (Teatro iberoamericano contemporáneo)

Selección de 16 obras no sólo de la Cuba revolucionaria, sino también de dramaturgos en el exilio, como Montes Huidobro, José Triana y René Alomá. Las obras reflejan una amplia temática que va desde mitos universales hasta costumbres y creencias típicas de la cultura cubana.

4267 Teatro dieciochesco de Nueva España. Edición, introducción, notas y apéndices de Germán Viveros. México: Univ. Nacional Autónoma de México, Coordinación de Humanidades, 1990. ciii, 258 p.: bibl. (Biblioteca del estudiante universitario; 111)

Se incluyen fragmentos ("jornadas") de tres piezas del siglo XVIII, dos de Juan Manuel de San Vicente y otra anónima. La trama, visión de mundo y versificación siguen los preceptos dramáticos y éticos del neoclasicismo. Aunque incompletos, son textos de importancia para la historia teatral mexicana.

4268 Teatro mexicano contemporáneo: antología. Coordinación de Fernando de Ita. Madrid: Sociedad Estatal Quinto Centenario; Fondo de Cultura Económica; Centro de Documentación Teatral; Sociedad General de Escritores de México, 1991. 1527 p. (Teatro iberoamericano contemporáneo)

Los 16 títulos que recoge esta antología exponen los distintos estilos teatrales de 40 años, desde *Debiera haber obispas* de Solana hasta *Playa azul* de Rascón Banda que, si bien manifiestan distintas modalidades dramatúrgicas, tienen en común un interés por el contexto social y político del país.

4269 Teatro uruguayo contemporáneo: antología. Coordinación de Roger Mirza. Madrid: Sociedad Estatal Quinto Centenario; Fondo de Cultura Económica; Centro de Documentación Teatral, 1992. 1111 p. (Teatro iberoamericano contemporáneo)

Contiene 16 títulos de los dramaturgos más destacados del país. Sin disminuir la excelente calidad de los autores que les precedieron (Rosencof por ejemplo) merecen especial atención las obras de jóvenes dramaturgos como Varela, Prieto, Ahunchain y Magnabosco.

4270 Teatro uruguayo contemporáneo: antología. Selección, introducción, notas y propuestas de trabajo de María Nélida Riccetto. Buenos Aires: Ediciones Colihue, 1993. 235 p.: bibl. (Col. literaria LYC—leer y crear; 112)

Se antologan tres obras: *Doña Ramona* de Leites; *El herrero y la muerte* de Rein y Curi; y *. . . Y nuestros caballos serán blancos* de Rosencof. Edición especialmente preparada para secundarios o universitarios incluye una documentación que ayuda a la lectura de los textos y a la comprensión del contexto sociohistórico.

4271 Teatro venezolano contemporáneo: antología. Coordinación de Orlando Rodríguez B. Madrid: Sociedad Estatal Quinto Centenario; Fondo de Cultura Económica; Centro de Documentación Teatral, 1991. 1181 p.: bibl. (Teatro iberoamericano contemporáneo)

Excelente antología en que se recoge lo mejor del teatro venezolano del siglo XX, como *Clipper* de Chocrón, *El día que me quieras* de Cabrujas, *Encuentro en el parque peligroso* de Santana, *El juego* de Romero, *Con una pequeña ayuda de mis amigos* de Caballero y *Hembra fatal de los mares del trópico* de Oscar Garaycochea.

4272 Tovar, Franklin. *Una boda y parte de otra; Había una vez—no hubo nada.* Caracas: FUNDARTE, Alcaldía de Caracas, 1994. 59 p. (Col. Cuadernos de difusión; 217. Teatro)

Contiene dos obras breves. En la primera el dramaturgo crea situaciones dramáticas con la ayuda del grotesco, humor negro y del uso de máscaras. La segunda es una obra para niños, muy bien lograda, que trata sobre la creatividad literaria.

4273 Trejo Zaragoza, Oscar. *¿Qué pasa aquí?* 2. ed. Guadalajara, Mexico: Editorial Ágata, 1992. 143 p.: ill., ports. (Col. Teatro)

Drama compuesto de acuerdo a los códigos del drama realista. En él se exponen problemas familiares, en especial la relación entre padres e hijos. Obra bien estructurada dramáticamente que se destaca especialmente por la facilidad del diálogo y fluidez de la acción dramática.

4274 Triana, José. *Medea en el espejo; La noche de los asesinos; Palabras comunes.* Madrid: Editorial Verbum, 1991. 257 p. (Teatro)

Se incluyen las obras más conocidas del autor. En ellas se funden mitos clásico y vernaculares, el conflicto sicológico con el contexto social, la metáfora con el referente inmediato. De especial mención es su reciente obra *Palabras comunes,* cuya protagonista es una mujer.

4275 Vacarezza, Alberto. Teatro. v. 1, Los escrushantes. Edición y estudio preliminar de Osvaldo Pellettieri. Buenos Aires: Corregidor, 1993. 1 v.: bibl. (Col. Clásicos del teatro argentino; 1)

Se recogen aquí cinco de los mejores sainetes del autor publicados entre 1911–29. Vacarezza es un fiel exponente del sainete criollo argentino. En sus obras se aprecia un claro distanciamiento del sainete costumbrista español en boga en ese tiempo en boga.

4276 Vargas Llosa, Mario. *El loco de los balcones:* teatro. Barcelona: Seix Barral, 1993. 117 p. (Biblioteca breve)

Excelente obra en que mediante *flashbacks* se imbrican presente y pasado para presentar la historia de un excéntrico viejo profesor que quiere salvar los balcones coloniales limeños amenazados por la ominosa figura de un constructor de rascacielos. Al revés del planteo de *Romeo y Julieta*, la hija del quijotesco profesor se casa con el hijo del constructor.

4277 Veronese, Daniel. *Crónica de la caída de uno de los hombres de ella; Del maravilloso mundo de los animales: los corderos.* Buenos Aires: CELCIT, 1993. 36 p.: ill. (Teatro CELCIT. Dramática latinoamericana; 2)

Hay en estas obras extrañas y ambiguas relaciones que van suscitando tensiones y conflictos con desenlaces igualmente irresolutos.

4278 Vidal, Javier. *Mojiganga clásica:* teatro. Caracas: FUNDARTE, Alcaldía de Caracas, 1993. 53 p. (Cuadernos de difusión; 198)

Drama metaficcional cuyas protagonistas, una compañía de comediantes, se debaten en el dilema de si deben mantenerse firmes en la defensa de los principios estéticos de su arte o de someterse a la censura gubernamental.

4279 Vieyra, Jaime Julio. *Hijo de la tierra: vida de José Hernández;* dos actos divididos en cinco cuadros. Argentina: Ediciones Ocruxaves, 1992. 68 p.

Obra de tipo costumbrista basada en el autor de *Martín Fierro.* A través de la figura de Hernández se recrean escenas de la pampa y se alude a figuras históricas del siglo pasado.

4280 Vilalta, Maruxa. *Francisco de Asís:* obra en 14 cuadros. México: Fondo de Cultura Económica, 1993. 142 p.: bibl. (Col. popular; 492)

En 14 cuadros bien ensamblados, se relatan los hechos más sobresalientes de la vida del santo. Obra poética y didáctica que al mismo tiempo que humaniza la vida del santo, la glorifica.

4281 Vivas, José Miguel. *Pequeños disturbios.* Caracas: FUNDARTE, Alcaldía de Caracas, 1994. 63 p. (Col. Cuadernos de difusión; 225. Teatro)

Se incluyen siete piezas que aunque muy breves son bien elaboradas. Sus personajes son puestos en situaciones límites en que revelan su precariedad e incapacidad para enfrentarse a la vida.

4282 Vodánovic, Sergio. *Deja que los perros ladren; Viña.* Santiago: Pehuén, 1990. 160 p.: ill. (Teatro Pehuén; 6)

Reúne cinco obras del autor. En tono serio o jocoso se critica la sociedad chilena mediante la exposición de motivaciones individualistas, de intereses de clase, de engaños institucionalizados.

THEATER CRITICISM AND HISTORY

Castro, Donald S. "Entre bueyes no hay cornadas" = Among equals there are no disagreements; the Argentine popular theater as a source for the historian. See item **2990.**

4283 Cea, José Roberto. Teatro en y de una comarca centroamericana: ensayo histórico-crítico. San Salvador: Canoa, 1993. 274 p.: bibl., ill.

Historia del teatro salvadoreño en que se incluyen desde manifestaciones dramáticas populares de origen colonial, como "Las historias de Moros y Cristianos" hasta el teatro actual. Contiene importante información sobre las distintas tendencias teatrales, de los grupos teatrales y actores más destacados del país.

4284 Dauster, Frank. Perfil generacional del teatro hispanoamericano, 1894–1924: Chile, México, el Río de la Plata. Edición de Miguel Angel Giella y Peter Roster. Ottawa: GIROL Books, 1993. 249 p. (Col. Telón)

Utilizando con flexibilidad el conocido marco taxonómico generacional de Arrom, después de exponer el transfondo histórico a partir de 1894, el autor se concentra en la Generación del 1924, cuya acción innovadora se dio especialmente en México, Chile y en el Río de la Plata (Argentina-Uruguay).

4285 Escritoras chilenas. v. 1, Teatro y ensayo. Edición de Benjamín Rojas Piña y Patricia Pinto Villarroel. Santiago: Editorial Cuarto Propio, 1994-. 1 v.: bibl. (Serie Ensayo)

Una valiosa introducción para el estudio de la vida y obra de ocho dramaturgas chilenas del siglo XX, entre otras, Isidora Aguirre, Magdalena Petit, María Asunción Requena y Gabriela Roepke.

4286 Giella, Miguel Angel. De dramaturgos: teatro latinoamericano actual. Edición de Osvaldo Pellettieri. Buenos Aires: Ediciones Corregidor, 1994. 283 p. (Col. dramaturgos argentinos contemporáneos.)

Colección de ensayos sobre teatro latinoamericano con entrevistas a dramaturgos y críticos latinoamericano y españoles. Contiene ensayos de Roberto Cossa, Jorge Díaz y Eduardo Pavlovsky. Entre los entrevistados figuran Rodolfo Santana, Fermín Cabal y Eduardo Rovner.

4287 Guerrero del Río, Eduardo. Conversaciones: el teatro nuestro de cada Díaz. Santiago: REISS Producciones; Red Internacional del Libro, 1993. 125 p.

Entrevistas bien conducidas y muy informativas en que Jorge Díaz habla de su vida personal y su escritura dramatúrgica. En el diálogo se intersectan texto y contexto, acto creativo y recepción. Se agregan breves entrevistas a personajes del mundo teatral del autor.

Harris, Max. The dialogical theatre: dramatizations of the conquest of Mexico and the question of the other. See item **459.**

4288 Hurtado, María de la Luz. Memorias teatrales: el teatro de la Universidad Católica en su cincuentenario, 1978–1993. Santiago: Pontificia Univ. Católica de Chile, 1993. 226 p.: bibl., ill.

Recensión de las actividades teatrales realizadas por la Escuela de Teatro de la Univ. Católica de Chile (1978–93). De especial interés son los datos relacionados con las puestas de obras chilenas, sobre todo las de dramaturgos y directores jóvenes. Hermosa edición con abundantes ilustraciones.

4289 Martorell de Laconi, Susana. Estudios y ensayos sobre la narrativa y el teatro de Juan Carlos Dávalos. Salta, Argentina: Instituto Salteño de Investigaciones, 1991. 145 p.: bibl., ill.

Comparada con su narrativa, la producción teatral de Dávalos es mínima. Martorell le dedica algunas páginas a la obra más destacada del autor, *La tierra en armas*, en que se destaca el importante papel que tuvo el gaucho en la guerra de la independencia del norte argentino.

4290 Monasterios, Rubén. Rómulo Gallegos, dramaturgo. Caracas: Monte Avila Editores Latinoamericana, 1993. 60 p.: bibl. (Estudios)

El autor destaca el interés de Gallegos por el teatro y el cine, de que es testimonio 14 textos de piezas teatrales o guiones cinematográficos. El análisis temático-estructural de los textos dramáticos disponibles se realiza en función de su entorno sociocultural.

4291 Ordaz, Luis. Aproximaciones a la trayectoria de la dramática argentina. Edición de Miguel Angel Giella y Peter Roster. Ottawa: GIROL Books, 1992. 124 p. (Col. Telón)

Breve historia del teatro argentino desde sus orígenes hasta la época actual. Hay ensayos dedicados a cada uno de los períodos o tendencias teatrales consignados por el autor. Se ordenan y ponen en perspectiva importantes datos, básicos para estudios posteriores.

4292 Palabra viva. v. 4, Dramaturgos. Entrevistas de Roland Forgues. Lima?: Librería Studium Ediciones, 1991. 1 v.: ill.

Diálogo del autor con damaturgos peruanos contemporáneos que hablan de su labor creativa y su relación con el mundo teatral. Entre los entrevistados figuran Julio Ramón Ribeyro, Aureo Soleto, Alonso Alegría y Miguel Rubio, el coordinador del Yuyachkani, uno de los grupos del país más conocido.

4293 Quiles Ferrer, Edgar Heriberto. Teatro puertorriqueño en acción: dramaturgia y escenificación, 1982–1989. San Juan, P.R.: Ateneo Puertorriqueño, 1990. 299 p. (Cuadernos del Ateneo; 2. Serie de teatro; 2)

Contiene reseñas y ensayos sobre la actividad teatral puertorriqueña de casi toda la década de los 80. Se comentan producciones independientes y subvencionadas. Contiene ensayos breves sobre dramaturgos contemporáneos como Myrna Casas, Roberto Ramos-Perea, Luis Ramos Escobar y Antonio García del Toro.

4294 Rapp, Siegfried. "Wir erinnern uns an die Zukunft": das "Teatro Popular" in Nicaragua, oder, Der mühevolle Weg eines Entwicklungslandes zu authentischem Theater. Egelsbach, Germany; New York: Hänsel-Hohenhausen, 1992. 111 p.: bibl., ill. (Deutsche Hochschulschriften; 417)

Examines impetus for and development of popular theater in Nicaragua and its contribution to cultural identity and integration. Author spent four extended periods in

Nicaragua (1977–87), and emphasizes process of maturation of an authentic Nicaraguan theater during 1985–87. [C.K. Converse]

4295 Río, Marcela del. Perfil del teatro de la Revolución Mexicana. New York: P. Lang, 1993. 278 p.: bibl., index. (American university studies: Series XXII, Latin American literature; 17)

La autora considera autores, nacidos desde fines de siglo XIX hasta 1915, para estudiar sus textos en relación a los procesos revolucionarios mexicanos acaecidos entre 1900–40. Su interés principal es la descodificación de la ideología tanto de texto dramático-espectacular como de su recepción crítica.

4296 Rosell, Rosendo. Vida y milagros de la farándula de Cuba. v. 1–2. Santa Domingo: Taller, 1990–1992. 2 v.: ill., index.

Contiene información sobre artistas cubanos en los EE.UU., especialmente de Miami, matizada con comentarios personales y vivencias del autor. Debido a su carácter general e informativo, no hay un estudio sistemático de textos.

4297 Sáenz, Andrés. ¡Dispárenle al crítico!: aproximación al teatro en Costa Rica, 1984–1991. San José: Editorial de la Univ. de Costa Rica, 1993. 467 p.: ill., index.

Recensiones teatrales publicadas en *La Nación* de obras nacionales y extranjeras estrenadas en Costa Rica. Pocas son las puestas que se salvan del disparo crítico del autor, cuyo patrón de mirada eurocentrista hace que se le escapen muchas virtudes de la escena local, que serían mejor apreciadas por una visión más contextualizada.

4298 Teatro latinoamericano, siglo XX: selección de lecturas. Recopilación de Ileana Azor. La Habana: Editorial Pueblo y Educación, 1989. 298 p.: bibl.

Colección de ensayos agrupados en tres etapas que marcan la evolución del teatro latinoamericano desde comienzo del siglo XX hasta la época actual. En la última etapa, que empieza a partir de los 60, colaboran Augusto Boal, Enrique Buenaventura y Santiago García.

4299 Teatros de México. Fotografía de Eduardo del Conde Arton. Coordinación editorial de Armando Díaz de Léon de

Alba. Coordinación y seleccíon de textos de Héctor Azar. México: Banamex, 1991. 269 p.: bibl., col. ill.

Una historia visual ampliamente documentada de los espacios teatrales que desde la época colonial surgieron en distintas ciudades de México. De especial relevancia son los comentarios sobre el valor estético y funcional de la arquitectura de los teatros más importantes.

4300 Vega, Roberto. El teatro en la comunidad: instrumento de descolonización cultural; de la acción a la reflexión. Buenos Aires?: Espacio Editorial, 1993. 143 p.: bibl. (Col. ciencias sociales)

El autor presenta los fundamentos, objetivos, metodología y ejemplificación de lo que llama "juegos teatrales," teatro concebido para educadores de niños, adolescentes y adultos.

4301 Versényi, Adam. Theatre in Latin America: religion, politics, and culture from Cortés to the 1980s. Cambridge, England; Cambridge Univ. Press, 1993. 229 p.: bibl., index.

El autor examina el teatro latinoamericano y su relación con la religión y la política, y su primordial función como un medio de edificación político-social. Una forma contemporánea de este teatro de concientización social es el llamado "teatro de la liberación."

4302 Weiss, Judith A. *et al.* Latin American popular theatre: the first five centuries. Albuquerque: Univ. of New Mexico Press, 1993. 269 p.: bibl., ill., index.

Un estudio interdisciplinario y diacrónico de las distintas manifestaciones del teatro popular latinoamericano, analizadas en el contexto histórico e ideológico que las condicionaron. El libro culmina con el llamado Nuevo Teatro Popular.

4303 Zedillo Castillo, Antonio. El Teatro de la Ciudad de México, Esperanza Iris: lustros, lustres, experiencias y esperanzas. México: Sociocultur D.D.F., 1989. 139 p.: bibl., ill.

Historia del *Teatro de la Ciudad de México,* donde por más de un siglo se dieron las mejores temporadas de las artes escénicas del país y donde se vivió una intensa actividad artística. Bien documentada con fotografías.

BRAZIL
Novels

REGINA IGEL, *Associate Professor, Department of Spanish and Portuguese, University of Maryland, College Park*

IN 1995, NÉLIDA PIÑON, the subject of an in-depth study by Moniz (item **4328**), was awarded Mexico's international Premio Juan Rulfo, becoming the first Brazilian author to receive that important literary recognition. Another of the accomplished studies on a Brazilian woman writer is Gotlib's critical biographical volume, *Clarice: uma vida que se conta* (item **4321**). Two books of literary criticism include Brazil in their comprehensive studies of Latin American literature: Payne and Fitz focus on Clarice Lispector, Osman Lins, and Guimarães Rosa as part of a comparative analysis (item **4335**) and Jorge Schwartz includes an analysis of Brazilian *modernismo* in his voluminous study on vanguardism in South America (item **4340**).

It may seem a curious coincidence, but among the female characters who have most challenged critics, the famous character "Capitu" of Machado de Assis' *Dom Casmurro* reemerges in two fictional works: in Sabino's *O bom ladrão* (item **4338**), in which the protagonist falls in love and marries a woman because of her resemblance to the Capitu of his imagination, and in Sá's *Capitu conta Capitu* (item **4337**), in which the novelist gives the celebrated character an opportunity to respond to (and confirm) her reputation as an adulteress. In another attempt to clarify history, Ferreira's *Os rios turvos* (item **4318**), which was awarded the 1992 Prêmio Joaquim Nabuco for biography from the Brazilian Academy of Letters, presents Felipa Raposa, the vilified wife of colonial poet Bento Teixeira, as a woman whose youth, intelligence, and attractive appearance, combined with her husband's neglect, lead her to extraconjugal involvements. These women, pioneers in terms of controlling their own destinies, were followed chronologically by Teresa Margarida da Silva e Orta, an 18th-century rebellious Brazilian writer and daughter of austere Portuguese nobles who spent most of her life in Portugal. Her writings are gathered in *Obra reunida* (item **4333**).

In contrast to these women who seem to control their destinies, others were dragged into a life of degradation, prostitution, and despair, as portrayed in Monteiro's *Maria de todos os rios* (item **4329**), narrated by a woman who has navigated many ignoble rivers during her life; in Largman's *Jovens polacas* (item **4323**), a composite of voices belonging to young Jewish women who were lured across the Atlantic Ocean only to find a wicked fate; and in Chiavenato's *As meninas do Belo Monte* (item **4311**), which reveals the well-kept secret of the selling and exploitation of young girls captured by government forces after the defeat of Canudos in the 19th century.

The military coup of 1964 still casts its shadow on literary writings, as can be seen in Cabral's *Xambioá: guerrilha no Araguaia*, which portrays the bloody assassinations carried out regularly by police forces during 1970–72 in Araguaia, state of Pará (item **4307**). Awarded the second Prêmio Osvaldo Orico by the Brazilian Academy of Letters in 1991, Leal's *Dia Santo* portrays rebellions that started a decade earlier through a tale of a priest caught between the dogmas of his Church and his hope for a future molded by members of the "guerrillas" (item **4324**). Existential ponderings occupy the mind of an ex-priest and ex-communist, the central subject of

Elias Netto's *Isto é o meu corpo* (item **4316**), while Albergaria's *Em nome do filho* induces an allegory ("in the name of the son") to expose a father facing a child with AIDS (item **4304**). This disease is also the subject of Campos' *O massacre*, set in a prison where prisoners accelerate the death of AIDS-infected fellow inmates through foul means (item **4309**).

This introductory essay should end with a joyful celebration, in spite of the somber aspects of some of the narratives reviewed. A deserved interlude comes with the 84th birthday of Jorge Amado (b. 1912), an event celebrated in Bahia, throughout the rest of Brazil, and around the world. Among the many reference books on Jorge Amado being published in several languages is Rubim and Carneiro's *Jorge Amado, 80 anos de vida e obra: subsídios para pesquisa* (item **4322**), which collects the most important writings published on the most universally recognized Brazilian author. A long and healthy life for Jorge Amado!

4304 Albergaria, Lino de. Em nome do filho. Belo Horizonte, Brazil: Editora Lê, 1993. 95 p. (Os Narradores)

Theme is relationship between father and son before and during son's struggles with AIDS. Narrative makes strong appeal for understanding the terminally-ill AIDS patients and the difficulties their families face.

4305 Amaral, Maria Adelaide Santos do. Aos meus amigos: romance. São Paulo: Editora Siciliano, 1992. 310 p.

Narrative is set mostly in the few hours preceding the burial of Leo, who committed suicide shortly after reaching age 50. The gathering of his friends affords them an opportunity for self-examination and evaluation of their activities in the 1960s. In the process, they admit that the reasons for the defeat of their ideas and quixotic campaigns lie with both the repressive military regime and their own lack of direction and coherence. Novel is loosely based on the life and death of Décio Bar of São Paulo, a journalist, poet, and advertising professional to whom the book is dedicated.

4306 Buarque, Cristovam. Os deuses subterrâneos. Rio de Janeiro: Editora Record, 1994. 205 p.

Science fiction, surrealistic characters, political intrigue, and scholarly pursuits converge in this tale of a group of explorers somewhere in South America. Allegory plays a definite role in the portrayal of an American and a Brazilian president who might have been programmed and controlled by non-natural forces to hold their offices.

4307 Cabral, Pedro Corrêa. Xambioá: guerrilha no Araguaia. Rio de Janeiro: Editora Record, 1993. 252 p.: map.

Semi-fictional account of actions of the Brazilian Army and military police against rebels in southern Pará in early 1970s. Rebels were mostly students, blue-collar workers, and peasants from the backlands who, guided by the Partido Comunista Brasileiro and assisted by socialist governments, intended to inaugurate a new social order in Brazil. Labeling them as "guerrillas," "communists." "enemies of the people," etc., the government set out to incarcerate and/or eliminate them. Story includes excerpts from military archives and newspapers concerning police activities.

4308 Campello, Myriam. São Sebastião blues. São Paulo: Editora Brasiliense, 1993. 243 p.

Novel is presented as an extensive dialogue, without dashes or quotation marks to indicate voice exchanges. Emotional boredom, traumas, and mystical revelations are experienced and reported by a female writer who lives in São Sebastião do Rio de Janeiro (better known by the three last words of its name), giving the book its title.

4309 Campos, Cândido de. O massacre. Rio de Janeiro: Bertrand Brasil, 1993. 141 p.

Presents detailed, crude description of harsh life of incarcerated men in contemporary Brazil. Narrative discloses how death of AIDS victims is hastened by their cell companions. Prison staff is corrupted through their connivance with the oppressors on the outside and the bribery system operating inside the penitentiary walls where drugs are common currency. Novel's social realism portrays the formation of rebellions and the legal system's method of resolving the problem through massacres of prisoners.

4310 Cardoso, Lúcio. Crônica da casa assassinada. Coordenação de Mario Carelli. Ed. crítica. Nanterre, France: ALLCA XX, Univ. Paris X, Centre de recherches latino-américaines, 1991. 810 p.: bibl., ill. (Col. Arquivos; 18)

The uniqueness of Lúcio Cardoso's literary work and the originality of his personal life were little understood or accepted by his contemporaries. Writing from self-imposed isolation, author reached the height of his creativity with the novel *Crônica da casa assassinada* (see *HLAS 22:5488*), the focus of this extraordinary volume of critical essays. Articles by outstanding personages from the fields of fiction, literary criticism, comparative literature, and psychoanalysis—among them Alfredo Bosi, Júlio Castañon Guimarães, Eduardo Portella, Octavio de Faria, Sônia Brayner, Guy Besançon, Teresa de Almeida, Hélio Pellegrino, and Clarice Lispector—are included in this book.

4311 Chiavenato, Júlio José. As meninas do Belo Monte. São Paulo: Scritta Editorial, 1993. 197 p.

Following the catastrophic defeat of Canudos, thousands of children were taken prisoner by the Brazilian Army. This historical novel relates the rape of girls by soldiers who sold them as prostitutes to bordellos throughout Brazil, and the secret, informal pact drawn up by generals and soldiers on the treatment of young female "prisoners of war."

4312 Costa, Flávio Moreira da. Avenida Atlântica: romance policial. Rio de Janeiro: Rio Fundo Editora, 1992. 158 p. (Col. Polar)

A kind of detective story, novel focuses on an American journalist employed by a New York newspaper reporting on violence in Rio de Janeiro. A love interest permeates his adventures, which involve him with drug dealers, police, businessmen, and diplomats. Discourse reflects a film script that the narrator intended to write, which contains descriptions of scenes and terse dialogues among the few characters.

4313 Coutinho, Edilberto. Piguara, senhor do caminho: a saga do defensor dos índios e pioneiro das comunicações. Belo Horizonte, Brazil: Editora Lê, 1993. 231 p.: ill. (Romances da história)

Fictional narrative focuses on life and work of Marshall Mariano Rondon, the Brazilian pioneer dedicated to establishing peaceful communication with indigenous peoples. Author's enthusiasm for him and his cause is rooted in an interview he conducted with the ecologist and environmentalist in 1957, a few months before Rondon's death. (The Brazilian state of Rondônia is named after him.)

4314 Dourado, Autran. Um cavaleiro de antigamente: romance. São Paulo: Editora Siciliano, 1992. 226 p.

The last volume of a trilogy on the financial and moral decadence of some members of the Minas Gerais oligarchy, novel was preceded by *Ópera dos Mortos* (Rio de Janeiro: Civilização Brasileira, 1967—for English translation see *HLAS 46:6477*) and *Lucas Procópio* (Rio de Janeiro: Editora Record, 1985). Shows how, despite social changes ensuing from the proclamation of the Republic, landowners retained old values and resisted change. Those who were guilty of corruption, injustice, and abuse of power were glorified by their descendants and other family members who aimed to secure good, honest reputations for their ancestors.

4315 Drummond, Roberto. Inês é morta: romance. 2a. ed. São Paulo: Geração Editorial, 1993. 240 p. (Série Histórias do Brasil; 1)

A parody of political novels, the focus of this good-humored narrative is a "stunt man" who plays the double of a past Brazilian president-dictator.

4316 Elias Netto, Cecílio. Isto é o meu corpo: romance. São Paulo: Ars Poetica, 1993. 191 p. (Col. Ficção. Série Modernos; 3)

Protagonist is a man who never found answers to his many existential questions. Having been a Communist and a priest, he left the Church, got married, and had children. He was harassed by the military as a Communist priest and then by the Church as a dissident priest. He interprets the Church and the military as very similar with respect to their hierarchical structure and oppressive role. His questions concern dogma, the manipulative power of encyclicals, and the commercialization of human nature. Allegory of the Church as Jesus' self-centered, domineering, and temperamental lover permeates the work, suggesting that by not allowing marriage for her followers, the Church intends to remain the only bride in men's hearts. Novel is an obvious attack on Catholic dogma and an exaltation of Communist doctrine.

4317 Euclides Neto. Os magros: romance. 2a ed. São Paulo: G&B Editores, 1992? 164 p.: ill.

Poignant narrative contrasts startling poverty of a peasant family with luxurious lifestyle of farm owners. The Bahian cocoa plantations are the background for a sequence of tragedies ranging from infant deaths to a high mortality among adults to the indifference of the monied elite. Novel of social criticism, work owes much of its style and theme to the first phase of Jorge Amado's literary career.

4318 Ferreira, Luzilá Gonçalves. Os rios turvos. Rio de Janeiro: Rocco, 1993. 211 p.

Fictional biography of the much neglected Felipa Raposa, wife of colonial poet Bento Teixeira. Novel relates her extraconjugal affairs, and her sensitivity, intelligence, and patience with her husband's follies. Story focuses on the atmosphere of terror prevailing during the Inquisition, the poet's disturbed personality, and the mutual demands on their marriage that neither were able to meet. History (and the novel) leaves unclear the reason for Teixeira's murder of his wife; it was caused either by her liaisons or her denouncement of him to the Holy Office as a "judaizer," or possibly by his weariness from the pressures of his life.

4319 Fião, José Antonio do Vale Caldre e. A divina pastora: romance. Ensaio crítico, notas e fixação do texto por Flávio Loureiro Chaves. Ensaio biográfico por Carlos Reverbel. 2a. ed. Porto Alegre, Brazil: RBS, 1992. 260 p.: bibl., ill.

Published first as a *folhetim* over 100 years ago, narrative focuses on the Revolution of 1835 led by Bento Gonçalves in Rio Grande do Sul, with the goal of installing an independent territory, the República Piratini. Against a background of military operations, story involves EEdiléia, also known as "The Divine Shepherdess," and her love for one of the revolutionaries. The novel itself has its own story: after publication of individual chapters, work disappeared without a trace until the surprising discovery in Uruguay of a book with this title relating the story first published in installments. A reading of the fore-

word by Flávio Loureiro Chaves is required for understanding the vocabulary, structure, and subject matter of the novel.

4320 Freire, Paulo de Oliveira. Zé Quinha e Zé Cão: vai ouvindo—. Rio de Janeiro: Editora Guanabara, 1993. 169 p.

Attempts to communicate a characteristic of orality, in the best tradition of storytellers of the Brazilian backlands. Narrator tells, to an invisible listener, the life story of two country singers who are twin brothers. In a language typical of an interior region of Minas Gerais, storyteller reveals region's rich folklore, describing celebrations related to Christian feasts such as Folias de Reis. Author's musical background shines forth in this versatile novel that mingles descriptions of local customs, transcriptions of popular and folkloric songs, and cowboys' perspectives on local social issues. The twin brothers' past interest in the same woman keeps the course of the story within dramatic margins.

4321 Gotlib, Nádia Battella. Clarice: uma vida que se conta. São Paulo: Editora Ática, 1995. 493 p.: bibl., ill.

Biography of Clarice Lispector (1925–77) is a comprehensive introduction to the life and work of one of the most innovative of Brazilian writers. Work covers her arrival in Brazil with her displaced family when she was two months old to her burial in the Jewish Caju Cemetery of Rio de Janeiro. The stages of Lispector's life, her travels, and her personal observations lie at the core of this extensive work, the result of 10 years of intense research and interviews with her family, friends, and others who offer various perspectives on Clarice. Gotlib provides a description that reveals the person underneath the writer, then the opposite, and finally the complex merging of both sides of the author's nature, which Clarice herself was unable to distinguish or separate. The descriptive approach to Lispector's works should be of interest primarily to an emerging generation of new readers who will find here a sure guide to the writings of one of Brazil's preeminent authors. A voluminous family album and other memorabilia are included in this resourceful biography of Lispector.

4322 Jorge Amado, 80 anos de vida e obra: subsídios para pesquisa. Organização, texto e pesquisa de Rosane Rubim e Maried

Carneiro. Salvador, Brazil: Fundação Casa de Jorge Amado, 1992. 179 p.: bibl. (Casa de palavras. Acervo Jorge Amado)

Published in celebration of Jorge Amado's 80th birthday, substantial collection of essays includes a gracious, though short, introduction by Zélia Gattai, the novelist's' wife who is also an author. Anthology is also introduced by Amado himself, where he discloses, tongue-in-check, his likes, dislikes, and other personal information. The core of the volume includes a chronology of the main events in the author's life, a genealogical chart of the Amado family, an extensive bibliography of works by and about him (up to 1992), and a list of translations of his books. Based on sources preserved in the Fundação Casa de Jorge Amado, in Salvador, Bahia.

4323 Largman, Esther. Jovens polacas. Rio de Janeiro: Editora Rosa dos Tempos, 1993. 284 p.: bibl.

Semi-fictional narrative depicts tribulations of a few Jewish women, called "young Polish females" although they actually came from Russia and other countries, who migrated to South America. Naive, misled, and unprotected, the young women were lured to Rio de Janeiro and Buenos Aires and forced to engage in prostitution. Resistance was punished by mutilation or death. Novel relates attempts to escape, cruelty of the prostitutes' bosses (men and women), life of descendants, and other aspects of the underworld, based on newspaper accounts, published research, and memories of those directly involved with this phase of Jewish immigration which lasted from the turn-of-the-century to after World War I. Preface is written by Moacyr Scliar, author of *O ciclo das águas* (see *HLAS 42: 6106*), whose novel also treats the theme of Jewish involvement with prostitution.

4324 Leal, Humberto Batista. Dia Santo. 2a. ed. São Paulo: Maltese, 1992. 158 p.

This prize-winning novel depicts Brazilian Amazon rainforest as a place that accommodates the differences among indigenous witchcraft, Catholicism, and the guerrilla movements of the 1960s. Protagonist is a priest who, endowed with a liberal view of the world, confronts witches and protects displaced people. The latter are viewed as heroes for their attempts to survive in spite of the hunger pervasive in the rainforest, the devouring nature of established institutions, and the discrepancies inherent in different ideals and illusions.

4325 Leite, Maria Cecília Álvares. Conto como fomos: juventude de chumbo.

Following the military coup of 1964, many Brazilian university students organized themselves into groups fomenting rebellion. One of these groups was comprised of students from the prestigious Faculdade de Direito de São Francisco of the Univ. de São Paulo. Narrative alternates between descriptions of their urban rebellion and that of another group that engaged in slower-paced activities in a small town. Both groups, however, faced similar challenges, including ruthless persecution by the military government. Semi-autobiographic story, work may foster respect for the unknown citizens, mainly young students and factory workers, who tried, through the spoken and written word, to hold off the rolling tanks, and who endured the jets of water, beatings, and imprisonment that finally overcame them.

4326 Mainardi, Diogo. Arquipélago. São Paulo: Companhia das Letras, 1992. 113 p.: maps.

A few survivors of a cataclysmic flood, perched on the top of a church extending out of the water, create a utopian system of life. They ponder their situation and that of other survivors who, down through the centuries and throughout the world, also endured disasters and lived on islands. Novel is rich in archetypical images, while narrative abounds in erudite and lofty quotations sustained by an imagery based on selected periods of the history of humankind. Author conveys precariousness and persistence as opposite elements inherent to the human race.

Malta, Maria Helena. A intentona de vovó Mariana. See item **3330**.

4327 Miranda, Ana Maria. Sem pecado: romance. São Paulo: Companhia das Letras, 1993. 254 p.

Entertaining reading focuses on Bambi, a destitute 13-year-old northeastern girl who moves to Rio de Janeiro determined to become an actress. Controlled by much older men who play the role of protectors, she in turn manipulates them in order to achieve her main goal. Bambi is also endowed with some attributes recognizable in other characters such as Macabea, in Lispector's *A hora da estrela* (see *HLAS 40:7417*), and "Annie," the orphan portrayed in the North American musical and movie. Trivial and light as the story is, narrative still manages to convey a threat of assassination against the heroine, who survives to tell her story.

4328 Moniz, Naomi Hoki. As viagens de Nélida, a escritora. Campinas, Brazil: Editora da Unicamp, 1993. 216 p.: bibl. (Col. Viagens da voz)

Moniz offers a scholarly and pedagogically-oriented study of Piñon's fiction, examining such topics as the epic style of her novel (*Fundador* (Rio de Janeiro: J. Alvaro, 1969); the lyrical aspects of *A casa da paixão* (see *HLAS 38:7327*); the carnivalesque tone of *Tebas do meu coração* (Rio de Janeiro: J. Olympio, 1974); the burlesque vein of *A força do destino* (see *HLAS 42:6104*); and the psychological, social, and political aspects of a family saga in *A república dos sonhos* (see *HLAS 48:6148*). Author examines Piñon's method of communication that is at once feminist, spiritual, and erotic. The novelist's social concerns are observed in light of political conditions in Brazil at the time the novels were written. Study is an in-depth and comprehensive examination of Piñon's major literary accomplishments.

4329 Monteiro, Benedicto. Maria de todos os rios. Belém, Brazil: Edições Cejup, 1992. 144 p.

Female narrator addresses an invisible listener/interviewer, describing her life as a prostitute. Author's attempts to define and interpret women's viewpoints on sexuality, race, and politics are generally not successful. The narrative voice in this novel—a male author represented by a female narrator—is not convincing.

4330 Montello, Josué. O baile da despedida. Rio de Janeiro: Editora Nova Fronteira, 1992. 390 p.

In 1889, a few days before the fall of the Brazilian Empire, the Emperor offered a banquet and dance for the Luso-Brazilian nobility, local society, and dignitaries from many countries. The event, held on Guanabara Bay's tiny Ilha Fiscal, still remains in the Brazilian collective memory. Narrator is a journalist who interviews an elderly woman who may, or may not, have witnessed the gala occasion. In relating her recollections of the ball, novel portrays the splendor of a turn-of-

the-century event and the confusion in the mind of a woman who spent 11 years of her life in a mental institution in the period following the ball.

4331 Nascimento, Esdras do. A dança dos olhares: romance. Rio de Janeiro: Bertrand Brasil, 1993. 390 p.

Diaries, dreams, and dialogues are the fabric of this novel with multiple narrative voices. Characters are residents of present-day Rio de Janeiro, who are seemingly devoid of economic concerns. As if sealed in a bottle, characters immerse themselves in self-analysis, scrutinizing their ambitions, frustrations, delusions, and perceptions of reality. Author seems to indulge the behavior of some of the characters by either explaining or subtly justifying their behavior as rooted in experiences of their childhood or recent past.

4332 Noll, João Gilberto. Harmada. São Paulo: Companhia das Letras, 1993. 126 p.

Protagonist remains anonymous throughout the novel, which concerns episodes of his life as an actor and theater artistic director. Story reveals main character's anguished quests, partially resolved when he opens a shelter for the homeless and lives among them. Silent children emerge in the narrative as allegorical punctuations to significant passages of the man's life. The story features subtleties and innuendos about the lifestyle chosen by the middle class.

4333 Orta, Teresa Margarida da Silva e. Obra reunida. Introdução, pesquisa bibliográfica e notas de Ceila Montez. Rio de Janeiro: Graphia, 1993. 244 p.: bibl., ill. (Série Revisões)

Born in São Paulo in 1711, Teresa Margarida was raised in Portugal amid the atmosphere of change prevailing in the court of King João V. She became known as the *enfant terrible* in a family that was both politically and financially well-endowed. The sister of philosopher and author Matias Aires, she is considered the first female writer of fiction born in Brazil. After many years of neglect by both Portuguese and Brazilian literary historians, present study appraises her literary contribution as exceeding the parameters established for women of her time. Many aspects of her personal life, such as her early marriage contracted against her father's wishes, are examined. Her attitude of rebellion resulted in her exclusion from her father's will, and other expressions of her independent mind cost her seven years of incarceration in an isolated Portuguese convent by order of the Marquis of Pombal. This valuable volume includes Teresa Margarida's fictional and poetic works, and many of her other writings.

4334 Paiva, Marcelo Rubens. Bala na agulha. São Paulo: Editora Siciliano, 1992. 203 p.

Novel structured around the underworld of the golden youth of Brazil's rich families. These youth are portrayed as having questionable international connections, dealing in illegal drugs, associating with murderers, and trading in prostitution. Corruption among politicians is also part of the scenario, which spans New York to Miami to Brasília.

4335 Payne, Judith A. and **Earl E. Fitz.** Ambiguity and gender in the new novel of Brazil and Spanish America: a comparative assessment. Iowa City: Univ. of Iowa Press, 1993. 225 p.: bibl., index.

In their successful attempt to cover a broad geographical area, authors examine and compare major aspects of the treatment of ambiguities and gender in selected works by seven novelists: three Brazilian (Clarice Lispector, João Guimarães Rosa, and Osman Lins); and four Spanish-American (Julio Cortázar, Gabriel García Márquez, Carlos Fuentes, and Mario Vargas Llosa). Authors contend that Brazilian novelists were committed as early as their Spanish-American colleagues to the formidable tasks of reconstructing the process of writing, shedding traditional procedures, and creating a new mode of literary craft by focusing anew on representation of the ambiguities of the male and female roles in fiction. Two books, both of which came out in 1944, would have meaningful implications in the development of a new novel in South America: Jorge Luis Borges' *Ficciones* (Buenos Aires: Sur) and Clarice Lispector's *Perto do coração selvagem* (Rio de Janeiro: A Noite). Both works are available in English (see *HLAS 42:6551* and *HLAS 52:5040*). The scholars' contribution to their analysis and comparison is paramount for understanding differences and similarities in these works that created new fictional modes in the literatures of South America.

4336 Pinheiro, Mauro. Cemitério de navios. Rio de Janeiro: Rocco, 1993. 159 p.

Revisiting topic of mythical search, narrator travels through several Brazilian cities looking for a friend. Descriptions of his own adventures alternate with episodes related to the friend's peripatetic and unfortunate destiny. Brazilian social structure is represented by a variety of characters. Narrative style echos Rubem Fonseca's novels, particularly *Bufo & Spallanzani* (see *HLAS 52: 4543*).

4337 Sá, Adísia. Capitu conta Capitu. Fortaleza, Brazil: Multigraf Editora, 1992? 104 p.

An airy "diary" attributed to the enigmatic Capitu, the controversial female character of *Dom Casmurro* by Machado de Assis. Author gives the woman a chance to tell her side of the story, which, surprisingly, reaffirms her husband's subtle accusation of adultery.

4338 Sabino, Fernando Tavares. O bom ladrão. São Paulo: Editora Ática, 1992. 62 p.: ill. (Série Rosa dos ventos)

Obsessed with the image of Capitu, the presumably coy and cynical character of Machado de Assis' *Dom Casmurro*, narrator finds himself married to Isabel, who physically resembles that character. A kleptomaniac and a liar, his wife gets away with petty and serious crimes ranging from shoplifting to incriminating her honest and law-abiding husband for her misconduct. Narrative conveys author's typical humor and irony, a hallmark of his *crónicas*, some of which he has stretched skillfully into novels.

4339 Sales, Herberto. Rio dos Morcegos: romance. Rio de Janeiro: Civilização Brasileira, 1993. 570 p.

Renowned author of *Cascalho* (see *HLAS 10:3891*) and *Além dos Marimbus* (see *HLAS 25:4683*)—among many other novels, *crónicas*, short stories, and collected folk narratives—returns to the hinterland through the construct of protagonist's recollections. Character's obsession with death paradoxically leads him to a life filled with new and strange experiences. Narrative is left in suspension, concluded by his sister.

4340 Schwartz, Jorge. Vanguardas latino-americanas: polêmicas, manifestos e textos críticos. São Paulo: EDUSP; Iluminuras; FAPESP, 1995. 639 p.: bibl., ill.

In the foreword to this dense study, Alfredo Bosi emphasizes Jorge Schwartz's inclusion of the history of Brazilian Vanguardism (known as *Modernismo*) as part of the vast and multifaceted movement that changed the Latin American literary scene. Bosi also notes the connection Schwartz makes between history and criticism in this comparative study of the ideas that stormed thorough the artistic circles of South and Central America between the two World Wars. The book, divided into two parts, treats the theoretical aspects of *Modernismo* as well as its representative writings. Drawing upon many of the manifestoes, magazines, and anthologies of the movement, the author notes the beginnings of Latin American Vanguardism in Chile, then focuses on its development in Brazil, Mexico, Peru, Puerto Rico, Venezuela, and Nicaragua. Characterizing these facets as "-ismos" (as in *futurismo, construtivismo, expressionismo,* and *surrealismo*), he uncovers and comments on texts authored by Rubén Darío, Vicente Huidobro, Mário de Andrade, César Vallejo, Joaquín Torres-García, and José Carlos Mariátegui. The author directs the reader through the maze of "tensões ideológicas" found in the writings of Jorge Luis Borges, Roberto Ortelli, Serafín Delmar, Oswald de Andrade, Diego Rivera, Menotti del Picchia, José Vasconcelos, Sérgio Buarque de Holanda, Nicolás Guillén, and Guillermo de Torre, among many others. A significant contribution to the knowledge and understanding of this monumental stage in South American literary and cultural history.

4341 Wilheim, Jorge. Fax: mensagens de um futuro próximo. São Paulo: Paz e Terra, 1994. 127 p.

An epistolary and cybernetic novel, work is composed mostly of faxes exchanged between a terrestrial being and an alien, beginning in the present and continuing to the coming millenium. Novel's theme is that Brazil will have a pivotal role to play in the future, when science fiction will evolve from virtual to living reality, with many benefits for the populations of contemporary Third World countries.

Short Stories

MARIA ANGELICA GUIMARÃES LOPES, *Associate Professor, Department of Spanish, Italian, and Portuguese, University of South Carolina, Columbia*

THE WORKS REVIEWED FOR *HLAS* 56 include mainly short story collections published between 1993–95 and a few published earlier. Of the 200 or so works examined for this volume, one-quarter were of sufficient literary interest and value for review. Established authors continue to publish works of note (items **4367, 4395, 4396,** and **4403**). Given the passage of time, the social denunciations of some writers have mellowed, as discussed in *HLAS 54.* Other authors, including journalists making the transition to fiction, present their first published works (items **4355, 4356, 4385, 4348, 4379** and **4381**).

Another sign of the decline of fiction as denunciation are the new lyrical voices of established writers such as Fonseca, Giudice, and to some extent Sant'Anna, a trend first noted in the last volume (see *HLAS 54:4775, HLAS 54:4777,* and *HLAS 54:4798*). It must be remembered that when these authors wrote during the repressive decades of the 1960s-70s, they were subject to censorship, with all its attendant dangers and problems. At first prophetic in their denunciations and clamorings for justice, their voices were eventually muffled or silenced until the relaxing of literary censorship in Dec. 1978. Some were journalists who resorted to the allegory as a literary disguise of sorts. Others, most notably Rubem Fonseca, however, continued on their outspoken paths. As a case in point, Fonseca, a lawyer, sued the federal government when his *Feliz ano novo* (see *HLAS 38:7361*) was banned.

Although some authors returned to journalism proper, many persisted in writing fiction, to the readers' good fortune. Among recent efforts is a superb collection by Lygia Fagundes Telles (item **4403**), the doyenne of women writers. Rubem Fonseca has also produced an impressive work (item **4362**), as have Sabino (item **4395**), Giudice (item **4367**), and Callado (item **4350**). Todt, who started publishing in the 1980s, has written yet another remarkable collection (item **4404**). As expected, these mature writers often use official and unofficial historical incidents as topics for their stories. Younger writers demonstrate the same interest in contemporary historical, philosophical, and literary currents.

Among new writers with outstanding collections are Becker (item **4348**), A.C. Carvalho (item **4354**), B. Carvalho (item **4355**), Carrascoza (item **4355**), Castro (item **4356**), Neubarth (item **4385**), and Oliveira (item **4387**). Each of these authors exhibits an individual style, yet their works are recognizable as belonging to that of a specific generation. Their concerns encompass a wide range of topics, from material desires to spiritual needs. In contrast to the previous biennium, 1993–95 has not brought forth more black or gay short fiction, two important trends in the literature of the Americas.

Although the women authors examined here are diverse in their styles and topics, most deal with issues of general interest from the vantage point of the female consciousness. Some follow a traditional path (items **4351** and **4378**), but the majority employ daring techniques, producing more valuable and stimulating fiction. Becker (item **4348**), Calage (item **4349**), A.C. Carvalho (item **4354**), and Telles (item **4403**) generated the most distinguished collections. The focus of these authors is perceived through their tales, although in her preface Pio explicitly and earnestly reminds readers about a "woman's fight to become herself" (item **4390**). Given the substantial role women journalists and fiction writers have played in the last 100 years of Brazilian literature, and given that Brazil's population consists of more women than men, one hesitates to classify short fiction by women as a marginal area. Unfortunately, for the general public in Brazil, women are still associated with affairs of the heart rather than with literature. One need only turn to the Sunday pages of a prestigious newspaper such as *O Estado de São Paulo* and its women's pages or "Caderno Feminino" to find the same topics as 100 years ago: romance, children, clothes, and food, all still regarded as the female province.

As expected, authors reviewed here are mostly from the southeast. The great majority of publishing houses are located in Rio, São Paulo, and Porto Alegre, and editorial houses in Santa Catarina have published many good collections during this biennium.

In stories that can be classified as regionalist, the geographic setting is as significant as are the characters and story line. Amazonian Manaus is the theme for Souza's collection (item **4402**), as Northeastern Recife is for Oliveira's superb collection (item **4387**). In the latter, allusion and allegory weave an intricate and effective design. Also in the north, São Luiz do Maranhão becomes nocturnal and dangerous. The southeastern metropolises appear in their usual guises: Rio is lively and beach-strewn, while São Paulo is relentlessly consumed by business and industry. Rio is the acknowledged setting for stories by Callado (item **4350**), B. Carvalho (item **4355**), Giudice (item **4367**), and Sabino (item **4395**), whereas Campanário (item **4351**) and Rheda (item **4392**) focus on São Paulo. In the south, Santa Catarina inspires several fine writers as a motif and setting: Athanazio (item **4347**), Pereira (item **4388**), Ribas (item **4393**), and Todt (item **4404**). Napp employs Porto Alegre both as a geographical and an allegorical setting (item **4384**). From the Center-West (Brazil's "Far West"), we have on the one hand Ibanhes' optimistic frontier tales (item **4372**), and on the other, Jorge's ironic collection featuring Brasília as the site of political power (item **4373**).

4342 Alcântara, Maria Beatriz Rosário de. Daquém e dalém-mar: contos. São Paulo: M. Ohno-R. Gadelha, 1993. 86 p.: ill.

Title points to both sides of the Atlantic Ocean (*além-mar*=overseas). Four stories are set in Portugal and the other 12 in Brazil. In this varied but uneven collection, the best stories are well-written, inventive, and humorous.

4343 Almada, Roberto. Faces de seda: contos. Vitória, Brazil: UFES, Secretaria Cultural, 1993. 61 p.

Perceptive, concise, and sensitive, these tales reveal the poet's eye and hand. Award-winning collection by Minas Gerais poet who has resided in Espírito Santo for 30 years.

4344 Alves, Hamilton. Três cisnes de vidro. Florianópolis, Brazil: FCC Edições, 1992. 73 p.

In this collection, author of three *crônicas* volumes has ably managed the transition from writing newspaper columns to stories. The best of these highly readable tales show author's ease with language, psychological powers, sense of direction, and gentle irony. Literary characters James Joyce and Emma Bovary are treated in an erudite but amusing fashion. Other stories present solitude and other everyday experiences of ordinary characters.

4345 Aquino, Marçal. Miss Danúbio. São Paulo: Scritta, 1994. 124 p. (Brasilis)

First-rate collection by prize-winning poet and novelist offers varied stories in which narrative relies on observation and imagination conveyed through significant details. A lot is left unsaid, but readers read between lines and get to know reserved, sensitive protagonists and their milieux, often in dramatic episodes.

4346 Aragão, Adrino. Tigre no espelho. Brasília: Da Anta Casa Editora, 1993. 115 p.: bibl.

Well-crafted stories by Amazonas author focus on writing as a profession and are most entertaining. Some have magic realist themes (Jorge Luis Borges meets another Jorge Luis Borges; typewriter writes only erotic fiction to owner's despair; characters exchange roles with their author; housemaid poses as foreign noblewoman at autograph cocktail party).

4347 Athanázio, Enéas. O aparecido de Ituy: causos do mato e da vila; contos. Blumenau, Brazil: Fundação Casa Dr. Blumenau, 1991. 77 p.

Solid stories by literary critic make for good reading with their able characterization and plots dealing with everyday occurrences. A few are fantastic.

4348 Becker, Maria Aparecida. A navalha dos deuses: contos. Porto Alegre, Brazil: Movimento, 1992. 77 p. (Col. Rio Grande; 106)

Stories in this collection represent successful portraits of individualists (often isolated, old eccentrics lost in their own dreams), with author's gentle sense of humanity revealed in the characterization. An impressive book pervaded by humor that is never low or cowardly and always exact. Notable for use of language, work is one of the best collections of *contos* published over the past three years.

4349 Calage, Eloí. Bernardo, Raquel e Sarah: com participação especial de Marilda; contos. 2a. ed. Campinas, Brazil: Gráf. e Editora São Paulo, 1990. 83 p.: ill.

Six versatile stories exhibit narrative skills: lively language and believable, engaging characters in dramatic situations that are, however, lightly handled. Introduction by distinguished story writer J.J. Veiga is proof of excellence of this collection.

4350 Callado, Antônio. O homem cordial e outras histórias. São Paulo: Editora Atica, 1993. 84 p.: ill. (Série Rosa dos ventos)

Five stories by celebrated novelist, journalist, and playwright. Ironic title refers to modernist era's concern with Brazilian essence, i.e., "cordial man." Callado does not spare self-indulgent characters such as the quasi-leftist intellectuals and eccentrics in Rio's south side. A few stories recreate historical characters and events. Book offers interview with author in lieu of preface. In this work author reveals his finely modulated powers of invention, psychological acuity, and journalistic pragmatism.

4351 Campanário, Mildes. Palavra vaí, palavra vem—. Capa e ilustrações de Fernando Fernandes. São Paulo: M. Ohno Editor, 1991. 91 p.: ill.

Competent, light, and varied stories examine life from different perspectives: children, old people, eccentrics, and young lovers. Written by a poet whose humor is often wry and cryptic. Some stories deal with specific issues in the modern Brazilian metropolis (in this case, São Paulo); others focus on country lives.

4352 Carneiro, Flávio. Da matriz ao beco e depois. Rio de Janeiro: Rocco, 1994. 121 p.

Well-written, enigmatic fables offer surprising insights and remind reader of Borges.

4353 Carrascoza, João Anzanello. Hotel Solidão. Curitiba, Brazil: Governo do Paraná, Secretaria de Estado da Cultura, 1993. 104 p.: ill.

Winner in prestigious Concurso Nacional de Contos de Paraná in 1992, *Hotel Solidão* is a marvelous book. Intelligent and poetical, stories bring forth the mystery in everyday life, including occasional tragedy. Thus a young boy wonders about the making of glass, and a baker bakes bread at night while his wife perishes in a house fire. Author has won previous awards for children's literature.

4354 Carvalho, Ana Cecília. Uma mulher, outra mulher. Belo Horizonte, Brazil: Editora Lê, 1993. 79 p. (Os Narradores)

Beautifully modulated stories revealing female consciousness make for first class reading. Awarded the National Literature Prize from the Fundação Cultural do Distrito Federal, collection deals with ontological questions.

4355 Carvalho, Bernardo. Aberração. São Paulo: Companhia das Letras, 1993. 171 p.: ill.

With Rio de Janeiro's Flamengo Beach in front cover foreground and the Christ the Redeemer statue in the background, the geographical reference seems clear. However, some stories are set in other cities and countries. Imaginative and elegant stories develop around nucleus that is an "aberration:" sexual depredation, racism, kidnapping, life in underground prison. Leit-motif is inescapable human loneliness and return to the past. *Aberração* is the first published fiction by this young São Paulo journalist.

4356 Castro, Jorge Viveiros de. De todas as únicas maneiras. Rio de Janeiro: Diadorim, 1993. 102 p.

Expressive and paradoxical title suggests wit, profundity, and versatility of short pieces that touch upon the pain resulting from the absence of one's beloved. Other stories represent childhood memories embedded with swatches of other people's memories, in a cinematic technique. Some are exquisitely wrought, with a sad, even elegiac touch. Impressive and professional collection by very young journalist.

4357 Cruz, Euler. A máquina do mundo. Belo Horizonte, Brazil: Mazza Edições, 1993. 216 p.

With famous Drummond de Andrade poem title reminiscent of Renaissance Neoplatonism, Cruz offers reader an erudite, carefully wrought, and exciting puzzle. Connecting tales echo Borges, Cortázar, and Calvino.

4358 Dinossauria tropicalia. São Paulo: Edições GRD, 1994. 141 p. (Ficção científica GRD. Nova sér., 18)

Anthology will be of interest to paleontologists, science fiction aficionados, and general public. Competent stories lean toward expository (in the Jules Verne tradition) rather than current elliptic or neo-baroque aesthetic literary direction.

4359 Eça, Othon d'. Homens e algas. 3. ed. Florianópolis, Brazil: FCC Edições; Fundação Banco do Brasil; Editora DAUFSC, 1992. 182 p.: ill.

The title's "human beings and marine algae" refer to fishermen and other coastal dwellers in southern Santa Catarina state. Eça is sensitive to and appreciative of both fishermen's courage and endurance and the majesty of the surrounding nature. Scholarly edition celebrates 100th anniversary of author's birth. Collection was first published in 1957.

4360 Erótica: contos eróticos escritos por mulheres. Organização de Bebéti do Amaral Gurgel. 2a ed. São Paulo: Editora Brasiliense, 1994. 230 p.

Most of these stories by São Paulo-based female authors are competent and make for good reading. Stories deal with sundry aspects of female eroticism in tones ranging from farcical to tragic.

4361 Farias, Herculano. O tambor: contos. Brasília: Thesaurus, 1992. 89 p.

Forceful, agile, and well-written stories

present unusual characters in various situations. Prize-winning title story concerns an odd couple whose lives change when they find a drum in a garbage dump. Versatile author uses different approaches and styles for characters, making for very satisfying reading.

4362 Fonseca, Rubem. O buraco na parede: contos. São Paulo: Companhia das Letras, 1995. 159 p.

Misdemeanors and crimes ranging from fraudulent ghostwriting and other forms of cheating, stealing, kidnapping, and murder abound in these stories thematically connected to author's past as chief of police and criminal lawyer. In Fonseca's colloquial, lively carioca style, they are often infused with suspense. Superb story is "Orgulho" (Pride), a stream-of-consciousness monologue by character fighting against and winning over death.

4363 Fontes, Luis Olavo. Ócio do ofício: contos. Rio de Janeiro: Editora Objetiva, 1993. 114 p.

Book's title is a double pun: "ossos do ofício" (bones, difficulties of one's profession) becomes "ócio" (i.e., spare time). Collection is a bazaar with its varied fare: cosmopolitan drug-taking hippies stranded in Goa; playful ghosts at a seance; flasher in front of convent school; werewolf dying of pneumonia, etc. An engaging book.

4364 Freire, Roberto. Histórias curtas & grossas. v. 1. Rio de Janeiro: Guanabara Koogan, 1991. 1 v.

Competent and lengthy, these "short and gross/thick stories" purport to shock the reader but not to determine the line between the erotic and the pornographic—that is the reader's business. D.H. Lawrence's quotation on the salubriousness of indecency appears as an epigraph. Theme is developed into various sexual permutations—a different one for each story.

4365 Galdino, Luiz. A noite do enforcado: contos. São Paulo: Carthago & Forte, 1994. 92 p.

These forceful and somber stories present social vignettes from period during and after "the [1964] coup which in those dark days was called a 'revolution.'" The fantastic is deftly used as a major ingredient in the

shape of Kafkaesque metamorphoses. Inventive and varied, these very fine stories have varied plots, settings, characters, and even narrative styles.

4366 Garcia, Alfredo. O homem pelo avesso. Belém, Brazil: Secretaria de Estado da Cultura, 1993. 90 p.: ill.

Sensitive and poetical stories focus on children's experiences and erotic aspects of life in northernmost state of Pará.

4367 Giudice, Victor. O Museu Darbot e outros mistérios. Rio de Janeiro: Leviatã, 1994. 151 p.

Seven stories exhibit author's narrative aplomb and fantastic invention powers. Here, unlike author's earlier fiction, the bizarre goes beyond symbol or stylistic device; rather, it is a very real component of life in present-day Rio. Characters such as the middle-aged intellectual man in love with a flighty young woman, and the married lovers, witness and participate in prodigies. In contrast to his previous collection (see *HLAS 54: 4777*), here Giudice exhibits mellowness and distances himself from his trademark: farce. The dedication shows the power of sentiment acting upon mature writer: the book is dedicated to his father and to four childhood friends.

4368 Gomes, Duílio. Deus dos abismos. Belo Horizonte, Brazil: Editora Lê, 1993. 78 p. (Os Narradores)

Powerful stories by prize-winning author examine human foibles and passions including hatred, fear, and unusual sexual hunger and practices. Lucid and acerbic, Gomes casts some of his stories in magic realist mold. A fine collection by experienced author who has not lost his vigor.

4369 Gouvêa Filho, Helvídio. Contos de 4a. dimensão. São Paulo: Editora Ateniense, 1992? 127 p.: ill.

Poet and novelist presents in clear syntax and vocabulary science fiction tales in which colors and light play an important role. "Logic is no more," explains narrator, as people walk on air and through concrete. Peace and tranquility of characters, and their gentle sense of humor, enchant the reader. However, exposition is too detailed and pace is sometimes slower than accustomed by the modern reader.

4370 Gusmão, Oswaldo. Festa das almas. Rio de Janeiro: Imago Editora, 1992. 291 p. (Série Diversos)

Consists of four novellas, the first of which is the title one. Subtle text and clever plot add to interest provided by complex characters.

4371 Hass, Haelmo. Sonhar é preciso: contos. Belém, Brazil: Edições CEJUP, 1993. 192 p.

Carefully written stories set in northern Pará tell of dreams often shattered by disasters. Characters are mainly hardworking proletarians whose family relations set in an Amazonian background engage the reader's interest.

4372 Ibanhes, Brígido. Che ru (Chirú): contos mestiços às margens do Rio Apa. Campo Grande, Brazil: Gráf. Edit. Alvorada, 1990. 87 p.: appendix.

Autobiographical chapters—each a separate story—tell of young boy's life from his birth in a small Brazilian/Paraguayan frontier town. There, near the Apa River, inhabitants are bilingual and bicultural. Book conveys child's perspective accompanied by adult's respectful humor. Charming and well-written, with appendix of cultural explanations and Guarani glossary.

4373 Jorge, Miguel. A descida da rampa: contos. São Paulo: Estação Liberdade, 1993. 235 p.

Author creates dense and hermetic world with imprecise borders between dream and awakened states, and between characters and author/narrator. Carefully constructed background and episodes make for mysterious events in which atmosphere is paramount. Title refers primarily to ex-President Collor's weekly press conferences and, metaphorically, to his impeachment/resignation.

4374 Lazzaro, Agostino. A árvore do verão. Vitória, Brazil: Depto. Estadual Cultura; Secretaria Cultural, UFES, 1993. 69 p.: ill. . (Col. Cultura UFES; 16)

Although story titles are in Italian and theme focuses on life of author's ancestors before or after migrating to Espírito Santo, work is decidedly Brazilian, rendered in superb Portuguese. Illustrated with impressive and moving old photographs. Author of this prize-winning collection is an actor, playwright, and researcher of Italian immigration in his state.

4375 Leuzinger, Audemir. Branca. Rio de Janeiro: Diadorim, 1993. 134 p.

Half of these stories have women's names as titles and are more impressions than narratives. In these well-written and engaging stories, oneiric perspective and situations convey unusual circumstances centered around nostalgia, drugs, or lack of voice.

4376 Lima, Geraldo França de. Folhas ao léu: contos. Rio de Janeiro: J. Olympio Editora, 1992. 207 p.: ill.

Written by established novelist and member of the Academia Brasileira de Letras, these tales gently mock social and intellectual pretensions as they honor goodness and the scent of the earth in small towns and country. Last story, however, is tragic: young love destroyed during repressive military regime of 1964–84.

4377 Lopes Neto, João Simões. Novos textos simonianos. Organização de Adão Fernando Monquelat, Mário Osório Magalhães, e Carlos F. Sica Diniz. Pelotas, Brazil: Confraria Cultural e Científica Prometheu; Livraria Lobo da Costa, 1991. 86 p.: bibl. (Série Letras pelotenses; 3)

Scholarly, though slight, volume unites recently-found work (three poems and three stories) by Simões Lopes Neto, pre-modernist from Rio Grande do Sul. Organizers contribute critical preface and primary and secondary Simões Neto bibliography. Of interest to literary scholars and Simões Neto aficionados.

4378 Malta, Teomirtes de Barros. As três meninas do parque: e outros contos. Maceió, Brazil: Serviços Gráficos de Alagoas, 1992. 123 p.

Well-made stories focusing on memory trying to reclaim misty past are laced with nostalgia and disillusion often caused by betrayal. Narrators and protagonists are generally female. Good treatment of oneiric matter informs setting and climate as perceived by characters' and narrators' consciousness.

4379 Mambrini, Miriam. O baile das feias. Rio de Janeiro: Obra Aberta, 1994. 122 p.

Successful, humorous, and versatile collection offers a representation of life that brings forth daily reality in which fantastic elements are solidly embedded. Mambrini is a born storyteller and this book is a must. There is a small mystery, however: in the collection that includes the title "Crime Perfeito," the story "Sorte," although listed in table of contents, is not printed.

4380 Martins, Fran. A análise. Rio de Janeiro: Editora Revan, 1989. 86 p.

Strong collection by well-known, precocious author who started as a modernist. After long hiatus following 1966 novel, during which he worked as a legal writer, Martins brought out this fine work. Here, lively plots match language often exceptional in its orality. The quotidian examined by Martins is made up of seemingly inconsequential events, but his "laser beam" reaches hidden comedy and tragedy.

4381 Marun, Bete. O olhar do macaco. São Paulo: Art Editora, 1994. 133 p.

Some of these well-written tales are reflexive sketches conveying and combining characters' wishes, dreams, and memories that recreate states of mind rather than tell stories. However, pieces such as mystery novella "As Faces de Eva" do have a story line. Marun deals with mosaic of modern corporate life in São Paulo and environs (workaholic businessman, female bank clerk, young girls on beach) from modern woman's consciousness.

4382 Mautner, Jorge Henrique. Miséria dourada. São Paulo: Maltese, 1993. 97 p.: ill.

A musician and entertainer in 1950s, Mautner was chronologically Brazil's first "beatnik." He still amazes readers with his surreal and political mixture. With epigraphs by Jesus Christ and Mautner himself, stories exude enormous breadth and invention. In denunciatory tone, they blend fact and fiction as they cover 30 years of Brazilian history. Touching, heavy, baroque, brutal, and poetical, stories are entertaining but often strike like bullets.

4383 Minas de liberdade. Organização de Angelo Oswaldo de Araújo Santos, Eneida Maria de Souza, e Wander Melo Miranda. Belo Horizonte, Brazil: Assembléia Legislativa do Estado de Minas Gerais; Secretaria de Estado da Cultura de Minas Gerais, 1992. 119 p.: bibl., ill.

Written and illustrated by Minas Gerais writers, this handsome volume marks 200th anniversary of death of Tiradentes, martyr and precursor of Brazilian independence. Work also celebrates Minas Gerais state, famous for its literature, baroque splendor, political vigor, and pursuit of freedom. This thematic, multi-genre offering includes poems, essays, and stories by present-day authors (Sabino, Villela, Drummond, Angelo, *et al.*). Additional noteworthy entries are unpublished poems by Henriqueta Lisboa and Murilo Rubião's notes for his short stories.

4384 Napp, Sérgio. Para voar na boca da noite. Porto Alegre, Brazil: Tchê!, 1987. 119 p.

Poet, musician, and engineer Napp achieves concentration associated with poetry in order to show varied characters and situations—dramatic, lyrical, ironic, and farcical—in his inventive tales. With his ear for dialogue it is no surprise that he is the recipient of song, poem, and story awards. A valuable and exciting book.

4385 Neubarth, Fernando. Olhos de guia. Porto Alegre, Brazil: Instituto Estadual do Livro; Tchê; Cachoeirinha, Brazil: Igel, 1993. 106 p. (Col. Noventa)

These "guiding eyes" are written by young prize-winning author and medical doctor who introduces reader to his own German-Brazilian world. Stories recreate cast of relatives in small family group, and some also touch on Rio Grande do Sul's frontier history. Introspective, even melancholy, characters catch reader's attention and interest. A gentle, thorough collection.

4386 Nunes, Pedro José. Vilarejo e outras histórias. 2a. ed. Vitória, Brazil: Edições Você, 1993. 132 p. (Col. Cultura UFES; 18)

"Vilarejo" novella and accompanying short stories evince strong narrative skills and whet reader's curiosity. In the regionalist tradition, stories evoke mystery of evil which shapes and dominates tales of Espírito Santo. One is about a pig ("O Porco"), a trademark of Brazilian regional literature (two others are ghosts and snakes).

4387 Oliveira, Silvio Roberto de. Saveiro do inferno. Recife, Brazil: Fundação de Cultura Cidade do Recife; São Paulo: Iluminuras, 1993. 94 p.

Title story is a felicitous representative of, and descendent of, medieval morality plays, specifically the great Gil Vicente's trilogy *Auto das barcas.* This excellent collection is symmetrically constructed in two parts, each preceded by a "boat of hell" story in which modern-day Recife's buildings, rivers, marshes, beaches, and mangroves burn. Collection shows keen powers of observation by geologist who is also prize-winning poet and playwright.

4388 Pereira, Francisco José. Desterro de meus amores. Florianópolis, Brazil: FCC Edições; Editora Lunardelli, 1993? 120 p.: ill.

In first part of collection, Pereira recalls Florianópolis (previously named *desterro*) in his memoir of a young law student and soap opera author. Other stories are much shorter and examine plight of the poor and powerless in Santa Catarina with concern, sensitivity, and gentleness. Author was political exile of 1964–84 military regime. Well done.

4389 Pericás, Luiz Bernardo. A risada. Rio de Janeiro: Editora Index, 1993. 72 p.

Demanding readers should appreciate wry irony and minimalist style in these imaginative and melancholy stories. Characters are introspective, alienated by timidity that may have led some to madness ("A Risada," "A Doença," "A Amada," "O Violinista," "O Homem que Achava Conhecer Gogol"). Other pieces are historical, surrealistic, and equally successful.

4390 Pio, Djanira. Seres humanos: contos. São Paulo: Clip Editora, 1991. 68 p.

Collection is dedicated "to woman . . . who has fought against the grain in order to achieve her dimension as a human being." Narratives work psychologically as they center on misunderstandings between family members, children and adults, teachers and students. Restrained though ironic, author is observant as she practices a concerned but non-judgmental attitude.

4391 Proença Filho, Domício. Breves estórias de Vera Cruz das Almas. Rio de Janeiro: Fractal Editora, 1991. 134 p.: ill., index.

Pieces about fictional village are couched as poems or chapters in a book. The latter are clever pastiches: the art of literary criticism by local litterati, including some found in old chest. Other stories consist of lists or glossaries. Wry, clever pieces accumulate as they build up the town of Vera Cruz with its "souls" and their lives. An imaginative collection.

4392 Rheda, Regina. Arca sem Noé: histórias do Edifício Copan. São Paulo: Editora Paulicéia, 1994. 182 p.

Perceptive, clever, satirical, and very entertaining, these tales about the fictional inhabitants of a "Noah-less Ark" refer to downtown São Paulo's Edifício Copan, simultaneously both prestigious and decadent. Farce tinges these stories, which may read like extended jokes but are actually carefully crafted pieces.

4393 Ribas Júnior, Salomão. O velho da Praia Vermelha e outros contos. Florianópolis, Brazil: Editora Lunardelli, 1993? 112 p.

Sensitive, dramatic, and humorous stories are set on an island off the Santa Catarina coast. Written between 1973–93 and previously published in literary reviews, this fine collection is by a state representative and journalist.

4394 Rodrigues, Francisco Assis. Fabiano não matou Baleia: contos. Brasília: Edições Pindorama, 1991. 99 p.

Dramatic, dense situations are presented as if in slow motion—during which characters' feelings and actions are focused. Natural scenery is almost physical presence as it conspires to aid or hinder characters. And sometimes Nature is synonymous with Fate. Title refers to fabled characters in Graciliano Ramos' 1938 classic novel *Vidas secas* (see *HLAS 13:2332* and *HLAS 28:2536*), the peasant Fabiano and the family dog Baleia. Unfortunately, typos and grammatical errors mar this otherwise admirable book.

4395 Sabino, Fernando Tavares. Aqui estamos todos nus. Rio de Janeiro: Editora Record, 1993. 201 p.

Written by celebrated novelist and dean of Brazilian *cronistas*, these three long stories, starting with their titles, develop themes of naked bodies and death. With his flawless, flowing narrative, Sabino evokes tragedy in "Um Corpo de Mulher" and tragicomedy in "Os Restos Mortais." In the middle novella, "A Nudez da Verdade," he enlarges his famous *crônica, O homem nu* (see

HLAS 25 : 4753), with episodes and commentaries, without sacrificing story's zany pace. An accomplished, humane, and entertaining book.

4396   Sant'Anna, Sérgio. O monstro: três histórias de amor. São Paulo: Companhia das Letras, 1994. 146 p.

Three novellas deal with eroticism, art, and the intellect. "O monstro" is a professor who inexplicably rapes and murders an acquaintance. "As Cartas Não Mentem Jamais" unites in a Chicago hotel a touring world-famous pianist, a French scientist and his teen-aged Lolita, and an American psychoanalyst—all concerned with or obsessed by sex. The third story, "Uma Carta," is by far the best. It tells of an apparently arbitrary seduction of a female engineer in the provinces. Although competent, this collection lacks the literary distinction of much of the prestigious author's previous short fiction.

4397   Santos, Walmor. O ventre da terra: contos. Porto Alegre, Brazil: Movimento, 1994. 124 p.: ill. (Col. Rio Grande; 115)

Exuding undeniable impact, these "earth womb" tales propel characters into the throes of passion: prostitute nurturing unconscious priest; character trying to seduce friend who is in love with first character's wife; older man murdering young mistress; etc. Melodramatic indeed, but sustained as narrative, these stories received first prize in the prestigious Concurso Nacional de Contos, Prêmio Paraná, in 1991.

4398   Santos Filho, Cunha. Pesadelo. São Luís, Brazil: SIOGE, 1993. 88 p.

Title is apt for collection in which characters live/move by night in São Luís do Maranhão. Each protagonist has an interlocutor, and the "prisoner of memory" protagonist talks to a mouse. Dense atmosphere successfully carries and emphasizes gloomy thoughts, many of which appear to be the result of author's antipathy towards machines and pessimistic prognosis for 21st century.

4399   Scliar, Moacyr. Contos reunidos. São Paulo: Companhia das Letras, 1995. 437 p.

Deservedly one of Brazil's most popular and translated fiction writers, Scliar deals with Jewish life in the South, although he is not limited by an exclusive, ethnic perspec-

tive. His selected stories offer a generous sample of his wit, compassion, and skill.

4400   Silva, Osório Peixoto. O Ururau da Lapa e outras estórias. 4a. ed. Rio de Janeiro: Imago Editora, 1991. 132 p. (Série Ficção e experiência interior)

Witty, learned, spontaneous, these stories relate legends from two cities in the southeast. Narrative strategy employs centenarian ex-slave who recites traditional *livretos de cordel*, interspersed with an erudite narrator's historical reports on 16th- and 17th-century Portuguese invasion and conquest. Collection makes for delightful reading. This is 4th, augmented printing.

4401   Soares, Iaponan. Sob a pele do sono: contos. Florianópolis, Brazil: Letras Contemporâneas, 1993. 70 p.

The majority of these tales—very brief, evocative, and often powerful—deal with episodes from Santa Catarina's history, which are presented as "flashes."

4402   Souza, Márcio. A caligrafia de Deus. São Paulo: Marco Zero, 1994. 159 p.: ill.

Five Amazonian tales written between 1976–94 are thematically linked by Manaus, as is the epigraph: "a city where the urban tissue has been destroyed . . . hit, raped, and . . . robbed by her lovers." Migrants from the countryside are unable to adapt to urban life. The collection, Souza's 18th book, is marked by his usual forcefulness bordering on hyperbole.

4403   Telles, Lygia Fagundes. A noite escura e mais eu: contos. Rio de Janeiro: Editora Nova Fronteira, 1995. 205 p.

Superb collection by doyenne of Brazilian short fiction continues her previous themes: childhood in rural São Paulo; premeditated and unpremeditated crimes; anthropomorphic animals and objects (possessed of consciousness and perhaps narrative powers); troubled family relationships, especially serious misunderstanding between parents and children. Title's "dark night and me," from Cecília Meireles' poem, envelops these melancholy and very intelligent stories.

4404   Todt, Erwin. A cabaretista. Florianópolis, Brazil: FCC Edições, 1990. 65 p.

With a few deft touches, these award-winning stories exert undeniable impact on reader. The mystery of everyday life molds these characters and their quiet surroundings. Written by one of the finest story writers in present-day Brazil and winner of several literary prizes.

4405 Trevisan, Dalton. Dinorá: novos mistérios. Rio de Janeiro: Editora Record, 1994. 141 p.: ill.

Work is not a collecton of stories, but rather of miscellany: stories, essays, literary criticism of sorts, and two or three pieces as eulogy of faithful dog Topi—narrator's only true friend. Still, Trevisan's characteristically acerbic, lively style makes for good reading. *Dinorá* was one of the two finalists for the prestigious Jabuti Fiction Prize, more for author's well-deserved reputation than for its own literary merits.

4406 Zeitel, Amália. Morangos com chantilly: e outros contos. São Paulo: Editora Perspectiva, 1992. 139 p. (Col. Paralelos)

Female consciousness examines protagonist named Alice who feels uncomfortable in various roles: wife, mother, daughter, lover. Witty and inventive, each story reflects or refracts "pieces of female condition which reader must compose mentally at end of book" (from postface). "Strawberries and cream" is a favorite dessert in Brazil. Book is part of a series by Jewish authors, Brazilian and foreign.

4407 Zide Neto, Gabriel. O segundo par de olhos. Rio de Janeiro: Litteris Editora, 1993. 157 p.

Satirical tales propose philosophical inquiry into several situations as seen through "second pair of eyes."

Crônicas

CHARLES A. PERRONE, *Professor of Portuguese and Luso-Brazilian Culture, Unversity of Florida*

THE MAIN ISSUE EXAMINED IN STUDIES of the *crônica*—for which there is no adequate English translation—continues to be its very definition. Scope and depth have concerned all those who want to characterize the genre. Agrippino Grieco, for example, noted that in contrast to the novelist who swims seas, the *cronista* swims in swimming pools (see quote by Viana in item **4432**, p. 6). The space of the *crônica* may be fiction or history, but it moves in a day-to-day realm, ranging from intimate confessions of family life to reactions to current affairs. The genre continues to evolve and expand, as authors and publishers (as well as catalogers) stretch concepts of the *crônica* and its practical applications in order to embrace a spectrum of short prose phenomena. This mixed type of literature comprises more than ever a fluid category with hazy lines of demarcation, ranging from a sketch of manners and the loose forms of a journal column to memoirs in short segments and poetic prose.

The current primary and secondary bibliographies are as varied as ever in terms of authors' states of origin, chronology of titles, style, and subject matter. The corpus reviewed for this volume includes materials ranging from 1920s reprints (item **4409**) to an anthology honoring a recognized master of the genre (item **4412**). Significant new critical studies, such as those by Antonio Candido (item **4411**), consider the historical roots of the genre, its birth in 19th-century periodicals, and its consolidation in the Modernist decade of the 1930s. Following the recent deaths of "classical" exponents of the 1950s-60s *crônica*—Carlos Drummond de Andrade (1902–87), Rubem Braga (1913–90), and Paulo Mendes Campos (1922–91)—there is a trend towards diversification, as Preto-Rodas has emphasized in a retrospective of the past quarter century's production (item **4413**).

Constantly challenging the cultural hegemony of Rio de Janeiro, authors in (or from) many different states are asserting their presence. Settings and frames of reference are local, regional, national, and sometimes international. Realistic content (social problems, decadence, etc.), related commentary, and more serious tones are increasingly evident, constituting counterweights to the conventions of humor and levity in the genre. Opinion-giving in *crônicas* is on the rise, often overshadowing the tradition of evocation. Attempts to convey forward-looking attitudes may be found in articles about eco-politics and the changing role of women in society (e.g., item **4419**). National self-examination—with the advent of the New Republic, and the disastrous Collor Administration—and self-questioning were commonplace during the preceding decade (item **4430**).

In publishing terms, *crônicas* in the 1990s continue to be popular and relatively widely consumed works. All manner of producers and publishers—established houses, small presses, government printers, self-producers, and so on—issue new editions. There are many reprints and republications of living (e.g., item **4421**) and deceased writers (e.g., items **4420** and **4409**), both of earlier books and of material gathered in periodical literature (e.g., items **4427, 4425,** and **4410**). Numerous "specialty items" have appeared, such as business chronicles (item **4430**), soccer commentaries (item **4428**), crime pages (item **4409**), and biographical notes (item **4425**).

Meta-literary manifestations in recent production are significant. In addition to frequent allusions to the art and craft of the *crônica,* there have been numerous compositions about the genre itself (items **4429** and **4419**). Several studies in Candido *et al.* (item **4411**) refer to writers who tried to define the genre, notably Mário de Andrade. In a preface to his own collection in the 1940s, the "pope" of *modernismo* wrote that the *crônica* is a short free text, neither an article nor fiction, not requiring exhaustive artfulness nor informational rigor, yet inventive (see *Os filhos da Candinha,* São Paulo: Livraria Martins, 1943, p. 7).

If, in comparison to the most admired authors of the *crônica* of previous decades, the linguistic art of today's authors has been questioned, there is no doubt that many still seek originality. With so many competitors, it is not surprising to find authors of *crônicas* seeking a mark of distinction, a signature procedure, to distinguish themselves as writers. The best example of this effort in the current body of reviewed works is Viana. His approach, what he calls diagnostic "sessions," all conclude with linguistic shorts—puns, witticisms, aphorisms, pseudo-proverbs, microdramas, etc. In one instance he writes: "Man is a domestic animal who gets bored at home" (item **4432**). And in the domain of readership, what better remedy for such tedium than the compelling contemporary *crônicas?* The editor gratefully acknowledges Barbara Domcekova for her assistance in preparing this section.

4408 Alencar, Marcos. Adoráveis peruas. Espírito Santo, Brazil: Gráfica Espírito Santo, 1990. 117 p.

Contains recent prose by a journalist in Vitória, whose urban rhythms concern the author. He also offers perspective on national themes. Several quite sarcastic pieces ridicule the public presence of the very ostentatious "tacky" women alluded to in the title.

4409 Barbosa, Orestes. Bambambã! 2a. ed. Rio de Janeiro: Prefeitura da Cidade do Rio de Janeiro, Secretaria Municipal de Cultura, Depto. Geral de Documentação e Informação Cultural, Divisão de Editoração, 1993. 134 p.: bibl. (Col. Biblioteca carioca; 26. Série Literatura)

This re-edition of early 1920s pieces by the noted *carioca* poet-journalist constitutes a personal reading of a marginal Rio, the unofficial "mysterious" city: back streets, *bas-fonds*, sites of popular culture. Of the 32 titles, about half concern jail and the encarcerated; others observe "deviant" social types: gamblers, prostitutes, hustlers. The sparse, quick-attack style makes for a dramatic, urban mosaic.

4410 Braga, Rubem. Uma fada no front. Seleção de Carlos Reverbel. Ilustrações de Joaquim da Fonseca. Porto Alegre, Brazil: Artes e Ofícios, 1994. 154 p.: ill.

Includes 40 of the almost 100 *crônicas* Braga composed in 1939 during one of his first jobs. While most pieces concern local themes, this is an important collection for studying early career of one of the most significant of all Brazilian *cronistas*.

4411 A crônica: o gênero, sua fixação e suas transformações no Brasil. Organização de Setor de Filologia da Fundação Casa de Rui Barbosa. Introdução de Antonio Candido. Campinas, Brazil: Editora da Unicamp; Rio de Janeiro: Fundação Casa de Rui Barbosa, 1992. 551 p.: bibl., ill.

Collection of 30 useful studies is divided into five categories: origins and definitions; the early practitioners' art of leading; specific varieties (humor, theater, daily); Machado de Assis; and visual documentation. Only the introduction by Antonio Candido is fully relevant to current manifestations; the others address issues of emergence and development of the genre from mid-19th century to 1930s. This is the most important publication about the history of this genre in many years.

4412 Crônicas brasileiras: fim de século. Prefácio de Germano Machado. Organização e comentário de Graciela Santos. Salvador, Brazil: Editorão CEPA, 1991. 114 p.: ill.

Sixteen different authors of diverse age, origin, and levels of literary experience offer titles of irregular quality and interest. One of the intentions of anthology is to give an idea of the end-of-the-century status of the genre. Thus it is interesting to note in several titles a nostalgia for days gone by, of perceived greater social order, morality, and literacy. Collection pays homage to legacy of Rubem Braga and his engaging observations of urban life.

4413 Crônicas brasileiras: nova fase. Edited by Richard A. Preto-Rodas, Alfred Hower, and Charles A. Perrone. 2nd ed. Gainesville: Univ. Press of Florida, 1994. 329 p.: bibl., ill., map.

Updated and expanded edition of widely-used university reader (1st ed.: Gainesville, Fla.: 1971) includes refurbished pedagogical material, many new and more recent titles, and a concluding essay re-situating *crônicas* in 1990s. Useful both as teaching tool and as anthology of the genre since about 1960.

4414 Falabella, Miguel. Pequenas alegrias. Rio de Janeiro: Editora Objetiva, 1993. 122 p.

This first collection of a successful actor-director turned *cronista* has a sensitive, but hardly critical, approach. He shows preferences for urban *carioca* scenes and sentimental themes, with much retrospection on adolescence and personal experience.

4415 Faraco, Sérgio. A lua com sede. Porto Alegre, Brazil: L&PM Editores, 1993. 86 p.

In the sharp style of a short-story writer, these 19 pieces alternate between *crônicas* about contemporary Brazilian life and reflections on international historical themes from a Brazilian, at times openly comparative, perspective.

4416 Golin, Cida. Luís Fernando Veríssimo: a crônica como um jazz-improviso. (*Brasil/Porto Alegre*, 6:10, 1993, p. 101–112)

A free-flowing exchange with the leading present-day exponent of the humorous *crônica* is achieved in an interview conducted by Cida Golin.

4417 Konder, Rodolfo. Palavras aladas. São Paulo: J. Scortecci Editora, 1992. 133 p.

While self-catalogued as *crônicas*, these urgent pieces by a former political prisoner clearly tend more toward acrid political commentary than social portraits. Among the pressing topics of concern are abuse of power, torture, and amnesty.

4418 Paiva, Marcelo Rubens. As fêmeas. São Paulo: Editora Siciliano, 1994. 170 p.

This author of best-selling fiction himself selected the short *crônicas* in this provocative collection. As the title suggests, his principal preoccupation is images of women—stereotypes, media projections, vanity, etc.—but, in a very modern urban vein, he also demonstrates a general concern with relationships, sexuality, star figures, and "difference" (homosexual community, the handicapped, outsiders). Author's frank approach to cosmopolitan life in the age of AIDS has brought him wide readership.

4419 Paoliello, Lindolfo. Banquete dos mendigos: aventuras no cotidiano brasileiro. Belo Horizonte, Brazil: Oficina de Livros, 1992. 150 p. (Col. Saco de gatos)

Author's prose is rather straightforward and sometimes flat, but he has a good eye for engrossing current events and contemporary themes. In tragi-comical contrasts of utopian and dystopian elements, he varies between the anecdotal and the philosophical, and the local and the universal. While keen to real problems, he tends to seek notes of idealism or happiness.

4420 Porto, Sérgio. Tia Zulmira e eu. 8a. ed. Rio de Janeiro: Civilização Brasileira, 1994. 205 p.: ill.

This is a reprint edition of short works by this celebrated *cronista* known for portraying with critical intelligence comical and farcical aspects of national life. Original dates are not given, but prose remains fresh for the most part.

4421 Queiroz, Rachel de. Mapinguari: crônicas. Rio de Janeiro: José Olympio Editora, 1989. 189 p.

Volume includes reprints (from 1963 and 1976) of two of author's six books of *crônicas*, as well as some new material that further diversifies the many Brazilian settings in titles judged to be relevant to the 1990s.

4422 Queiroz, Rachel de. As terras ásperas. São Paulo: Editora Siciliano, 1993. 205 p.

Title refers to the longest piece, which deals with the Northeast. Regional and racial identities are among the varied national themes, news commentaries, and observations of people and events of 1988–92. In these 96 titles one gets the stylistically dry perspectives of an opinionated writer in her seventh decade of public life.

4423 Queiroz, Valdemar. Os olhos de dentro. Brasília: Thesaurus, 1993. 86 p. (Col. Itiquira)

Contains series of very short pieces in a lyrical prose-poetry vein of almost diary-like entries. These collected pieces of an academic essayist are unusual in editorial terms because they have not previously appeared in periodical form.

4424 Resende, Otto Lara. Bom dia para nascer: crônicas. São Paulo: Companhia das Letras, 1993. 213 p.

In this diverse collection about life in Rio de Janeiro in 1991–92, pieces are uniformly short and tend to favor people—including numerous writers—over places or issues.

4425 Resende, Otto Lara. O príncipe e o sabiá e outros perfis. Organização de Ana Maria Miranda. Poços de Caldas, Brazil: Instituto Moreira Salles, Casa de Cultura de Poços de Caldas; São Paulo: Companhia das Letras, 1994. 331 p.: index.

These 60 *crônicas* (almost all dating from 1977–83) comprise sketches, portraits, or profiles of leading political or cultural figures (including Rubem Braga) in a straightforward journalistic style. These insightful accounts are based largely on personal encounters or friendships.

4426 Ribeiro, Mário. Vícios impressos. Belo Horizonte, Brazil: Editora Itatiaia, 1991. 159 p. (Col. Crônicas de ontem e de hoje; 7)

Author complements a long and respected career in journalism with this volume. His sympathies are evident: he is concerned largely with contrasts between an idyllic past and a present replete with social ills and different behaviors. The better segments are those "mood" pieces that lyrically capture difficult human situations.

4427 Rodrigues, Nelson. O óbvio ululante: primeiras confissões; crônicas. Seleção de Ruy Castro. São Paulo: Companhia das Letras, 1993. 303 p.: index. (Col. das obras de Nelson Rodrigues; 3.)

Work is one of two books of *crônicas* in posthumous re-edition of complete works of this noted dramatist. These self-christened "confessions" originally appeared in 1967–68. Whether anecdotal or philosophical, writings are very involved in the life of Rio de Janeiro, and informed by literature and popular culture alike.

4428 Rodrigues, Nelson. A sombra das chuteiras imortais: crônicas de futebol. Seleção e notas de Ruy Castro. São Paulo: Companhia das Letras, 1993. 197 p.: index. (Col. das obras de Nelson Rodrigues; 4)

This fourth volume of author's complete works brings together 70 commentaries on memorable soccer matches, from 1955 to Brazil's third World Cup victory in 1970. Metaphor-laden prose takes these "chronicles of sport" to a literary plane and offers a window on the soul of the Brazilian people through one of their national passions.

4429 Sant'Anna, Affonso Romano de. Mistérios gozosos. Rio de Janeiro: Rocco, 1994. 236 p.

With this fifth collection of *crônicas*, this most active author continues to establish his name as one of the prominent practitioners of the genre in last decades of the century. Here he organizes recent titles under thematic rubrics: sentiment, language, personalities, daily life, and history. Within these divisions there remains notable diversity, from local details and personages to universal concepts. Sant'Anna frequently uses literary topics and allusions.

4430 Semler, Ricardo. Embrulhando o peixe. Ilustrações de Glauco. São Paulo: Editora Best Seller, 1992. 167 p.: ill.

This literate CEO is author of a bestseller on business. His columns are never fictional and rarely anecdotal; rather, they largely concern current events and affairs of state. The social and political commentary speaks against government and industry corruption, inefficiency, and hypocrisy. This outspoken "bad boy" of the bourgeosie displays a humorous, unabashed, direct style. His "corporate" approach, where editorial meets opinionated whimsical judgment, offers an interesting new face to the genre.

4431 Silva, Carmen Novoa. Trilhos de prata. Manaus, Brazil: s.n., 1992. 158 p.: ill.

This is a good example of the genre in non-metropolitan circumstances. Items were published during 1988–89 in provincial periodicals. Pieces include nostalgic evocations of Manaus and its customs, discussions of attitudes in the old city before the free trade zone, and complaints about current urban violence and social crises. Naive poetic style aims at elegance, but instead offers a curious contrast with more urban approaches.

Veríssimo, Luís Fernando. Chronicles. See item **4627.**

4432 Viana, Chico. Astronauta sem luar: crônicas. Rio de Janeiro: Presença, 1992. 98 p.

Pieces are organized in four alternating groups: explorations of change and passage of time; current events and public life; personal and domestic life; and strong expressions of opinion (his own or others'). Under these rubrics, one sees the natural variety of the genre in mixes of history, quotidian narrative, lyrical moments, and speculative commentary. A home (interior)/away (exterior) dialectic structures this often humorous and consistently insightful prose.

Poetry

NAOMI HOKI MONIZ, *Associate Professor of Portuguese, Georgetown University*

POETRY IN BRAZIL TODAY is distinguished by its diversity and its distance from a clearly identifiable programmatic theory. In 1995, the "Generation of '45" commemorated its 50th anniversary and the neo-vanguardists of the 1950s concretism movement have also left their mark on the Brazilian poetic landscape, but since then poets have been producing works that do not belong to any identifiable "school" or "current." This independence is seen among consecrated poets such as Ferreira Gullar, Mário Faustino, and José Paulo Paes. In contrast to the Centros Populares de Cultura of the 1960s, today's literary manifestoes or its collective desire for a social role for literature does not translate into a trend reconciling and unifying diverse poets engaged in a common poetic voice and vision. In fact, with the return to democracy, marginalized social groups, such as peoples from the Amazon forest, landless peasants of the Northeast, and Afro-Brazilians, are now expressing their own voices both politically and poetically. Others outside the traditional Luso-African-Indian groups, such as the *nisei* (Brazilian-born descendants of Japanese immigrants) and Lebanese are also translating their unique Brazilian experiences into lyric form.

Among mainstream authors, currently there is a strong desire to work with language and poetry as a craft, paying particular attention to poetics, meter, and even rhyme. For many young Brazilian poets, this desire takes the form of translating well-known Western poets as a training ground, even before publishing their own work. Among the diverse techniques and theories, modernism, concretism, and even some "parnasianisms," formalistic concerns are revisited. The practice of haiku poetry is still popular, as demonstrated by the number of publications of this literary form.

Aside from the groups influenced by "traditional" movements, other active groups include women, Afro-Brazilians, and descendants of immigrants. The celebration of the 300th anniversary of Zumbi's death in 1995 has renewed and reinvigorated the Afro-Brazilian community, and we expect to see further development of Négritude as a significant aesthetic and cultural movement. Finally, the publication of biographies of two of the best-known and most beloved poets in Brazil—Carlos Drummond de Andrade and Vinícius de Moraes—is a sign of an editorial trend favoring this genre, alas, rather than an indication of the popularity of poetry.

4433 Antologia de poesia nikkey. Apresentação de Haquira Osakabe. São Paulo: Estação Liberdade; Aliança Cultural Brasil-pão, 1993. 124 p.:

"Nikkey" is a collection of poems by—as the title indicates—the second generation of Japanese in Brazil, who are Brazilian and write in Portuguese. In a good introduction, Haquira Osakabe points out that, although one should not expect to find direct Japanese influences in this poetry, there is a thread of the "poetics of cultural survival," or the poetics of "transition:" "o olhar da cultura de origem se perdeu num horizonte menos palpável."

4434 As aves que aqui gorjeiam: vozes femininas na poesia maranhense. Estudo e antologia por Clóvis Ramos. São Luís, Brazil: SIOGE, 1993. 180 p.: bibl.

Taking for its title the verse from Gonçalves Dias' most famous poem, the "birds" that sing are the women poets of Maranhão. Historical anthology begins with Romanticism and ends with post-modernists.

4435 Barbosa, Frederico. Nada feito nada. São Paulo: Editora Perspectiva, 1993. 84 p. (Col. Signos; 15)

Elegant and careful edition of a new poet in the line of concretism (neo-concret-ism) in the aftermath of post-modern. Author experiments with language and meaning, playing with words that are visually and aually pregnant with rich and ambiguous meanings: "do sem/ sentido intenso/ se faz/ um tudo atento/ feito a palavra/ em/ cantada."

4436 Barbosa, José Túlio. O corpo sentido: poesia. Porto Alegre, Brazil: Movimento, 1992. 88 p. (Col. Poesiasul; 70)

The poems by this *gaucho* poet have two major themes. The first, indicated in the title, is the "corpo sentido," reclaiming the body from the traditional classic Judeo-Christianilosophical tradition. The second is his commitment to and empathy with the oppressed, marginalized, landless, but especially those of the "corpos negros/ são libertos mas trazem marcas/ de sobreviventes."

4437 Batista, Otacílio. Poemas escolhidos. João Pessoa, Brazil: Boa Impressão—Gráfica e Editora, 1993. 151 p.

Otacílio Batista, a popular *cantador* from Paraíba, has published many books, recorded many songs, and made many *livretos de cordel* (books on a string). In the way of the troubadours of the Northeast, he talks about traditional nationalist themes ("As Três Raças," "A Bandeira Brasileira") and a variety of contemporary social and political issues such as the impeachment and corruption of the president.

4438 Bernis, Yeda Prates. O rosto do silêncio. Belo Horizonte, Brazil: Edições Cuatiara, 1992. 42 p.

As the title suggests, these poems are like "grains of rice" in their contained, concise, simple, and elegant style that manages to blend Western classic *topoi* with the minimalism of a *haiku* practitioner.

4439 Braga, Rubem. Livro de versos. Projeto gráfico de Scliar. Ilustraçãoes de Jaguar e Scliar. Rio de Janeiro: Editora Record, 1993. 53 p.: ill.

Edition celebrates Braga's 80th birthday. Known mostly for his *crônicas*, this is his only book of poems. Affonso Romano de Sant'Anna, in his preface, likens them to the poems in *Viola de bolso* by Carlos Drummond de Andrade (see *HLAS 18:2785*) or *Mafuá do malungo* by Manuel Bandeira (see *HLAS 14:3057*).

4440 Camargo, Milton. O caminho do cais e outros caminhos: poesia. Belém, Brazil: Cultural CEJUP, 1991. 272 p. (Col. Verso & reverso; 1)

Title ("The dock's road and other roads") illustrates Camargo's poetical and geographical journey from the port city of Santos, where he was born, to Belém, the big Amazon River port. Ports and ships of his dreams take him back to his childhood or reflect his new life in the north. This new life he praises in the manner of Manuel Bandeira, with the freshness of Cora Coralina, the mystical tone of Adélia Prado, the love of music of Murillo Mendes, and a bitter-sweetness that pays hommage to Carlos Drummond de Andrade.

4441 Cançado, José Maria. Os sapatos de Orfeu: biografia de Carlos Drummond de Andrade. São Paulo: Scritta Editorial, 1993. 371 p.: bibl., ill., index.

First biography of Carlos Drummond de Andrade, one of the greatest Brazilian poets of all time and a contemporary of all the important cultural, literary, and political figures of this century.

4442 Castello, José. Vinícius de Morais: o poeta da paixão; uma biografia. São Paulo: Companhia das Letras, 1994. 452 p.: ill., index.

Biography of Vinícius de Moraes, the multifaceted composer, poet, and Brazilian cultural icon. Organized around two themes: his love life, involving nine women, and his friends, including school friends, friends from his diplomatic life, artists, other poets, and bohemian companions. In Drummond de Andrade's envious words, he "was the only one who lived his life as a poet."

4443 Castro, Sílvio. Viver em Malabase. Rio de Janeiro: Nórdica, 1993. 66 p.

"Malabase" becomes this Brazilian poet's Pasárgada of the 1990s, a long journey that seems to be an end in itself and is reflected in his two "Cantos do Exílio" from his exile in Venice where he has lived since 1962. "Malabase" stands for "alto" and "base": "no alto da montanha sendo vale plano sempre base."

4444 Chamie, Mário. Natureza da coisa. São Paulo: Maltese, 1993. 117 p.

This latest collection of poems by Mário Chamie, pioneer and main theorist of the "Praxis" poetic movement, reflects Gilberto Freyre's observation that Latin American art is a reconciliation of the "extremely cultural and the very primitive," as well as offering a New World voice that reintegrates past Western *topoi* and metaphors in a contemporary and refreshing manner.

4445 Colasanti, Marina and **Affonso Romano de Sant'Anna.** O imaginário a dois: textos escolhidos. Ilustrações de Augusto Rodrigues. Rio de Janeiro: Art Bureau, 1987. 158 p.: ill.

Illustrated book of poems by Mariana and Affonso, both of whom are poets, essayists, writers, and jounalists. Divided in eight parts, each poet alternates in a "dialogue" of groups of poems.

4446 Correia, Lepê. Caxinguelê. Recife, Brazil: Sambaxé Consultoria, 1993. 70 p.: ill.

Dedicating his book to Solano Trinidade, another black poet from Pernambuco, Correia declares that he himself is "a black man with a black soul," inverting the popular Brazilian saying of a "good black man with a white soul." Thus his poems present this type of deconstruction of the "white myths," replacing them with black legends, values, and experiences. "Boi da Cara Branca" and "Fadas Negras Nordestinas" recall legends from West Africa as well as black heroes resisting slavery in Brazil. His poem "Mana Dete" is a soul brother response to Jorge de Lima's "Nega Fulô," and "Bença Marcelino" is his black version of Manuel Bandeira's "Evoca, Ão do Recife" that recalls the sugar plantation aristocrats' children.

4447 Cunha, José Guilherme da. Canudos: a luta. Salvador, Brazil: Editora Pé de Bode, 1991. 198 p.: ill. (some col.), maps.

Poem celebrates Canudos' epic battle as a way of protesting the lack of agrarian reform despite the promises of the first Plano Nacional de Reforma Agrária of 1985. Takes Antônio Conselheiro as inspiration and symbol for the "sem-terras."

4448 Dias, Marcos Antônio. Rebelamentos: das absconsas áfricas da minha diáspora; poemAfros. Belo Horizonte, Brazil: Mazza Edições, 1990. 44 p.

Work is divided into three parts: 1) "Rebelamentos e Cismas;" 2) "Quizomba (Batuque Menor Para Atabaques & Terreiros);" and 3) "De Púlpito & Música Para Suláfrica." These "poemAfros" are poems of solidarity with Africans suffering in the diaspora and under apartheid in South Africa.

4449 Duncan, Silvio. Paisagem xucra = Paisaje chucaro. Versión en español de Héctor Báez. Porto Alegre, Brazil: Instituto Estadual do Livro; Tchê, 1993. 97 p. (Col. pampeana)

Neo-regionalist poems celebrate customs, traditions, and culture of the *gaucho* and the pampas.

4450 Em busca de Thargélia: poesia escrita por mulheres em Pernambuco no segundo oitocentismo, 1870–1920. v. 1. Organização de Luzilá Gonçalves Ferreira. Recife, Brazil: Fundação do Patrimônio Histórico e Artístico de Pernambuco, Secretaria de Educação, Cultura e Esportes de Pernambuco, 1991. 1 v.: ill. (Oficina Espaço Pasárgada; 17)

Very useful anthology of poems written by women from Pernambuco between 1870–1920. Includes iconography and biographical notes on 37 poets. Introduction by Luzilá Gonçalves Ferreira. Title comes from name of one of the poets who was the daughter of the philosopher Tobias Barreto.

4451 Faustino, Mário. Evolução da poesia brasileira. Salvador, Brazil: Fundação Casa de Jorge Amado, 1993. 170 p. (Col. Casa de palavras)

Originally published in Sunday supplements of *Jornal do Brasil* in 1958, work is a very useful anthology of the development of Brazilian poetry in colonial times.

4452 Freitas Filho, Armando. Números anônimos, 1990–1993. Rio de Janeiro: Editora Nova Fronteira, 1994. 96 p. (Poesia brasileira)

Poems about the quotidian. The heavy silence of endless summer days in Rio is presented in the desperately quiet, elegant tradition of the classics.

4453 Gontijo, Elizabeth. De cor. 2a. ed. Belo Horizonte, Brazil: Mazza Edições, 1992. 49 p.

Poems are at heart *mineiro,* as title suggests. Poet has an interesting blend of baroque passion and style in her "cor" (which is purple), but with the restraint and bittersweet feeling of Drummond de Andrade's poetic overtones, this heart is not of "iron" but of "poeira vermelha/pedras/túneis/morro."

4454 Grande Otelo. Bom dia, manhã: poemas. Organização e seleção de Luiz Carlos Prestes Filho. Rio de Janeiro: Topbooks, 1993. 153 p.

Sebastião Bernardes de Souza Prata is the name of this poet and famous, beloved black actor known as "Grande Othelo." Actor, musician, and poet, he wrote lyrics for many songs. This collection includes poems with themes from his childhood in Minas Gerais to his life in Rio as a performer in radio, movies, and television.

4455 Gullar, Ferreira. Toda poesia, 1950–1987. 5a. ed., rev. e aum. Rio de Janeiro: J. Olympio Editora, 1991. 375 p.

Collection includes all Gullar's poems from 1950–87. Very useful volume for becoming acquainted with his work and observing his aesthetic and stylistic development.

4456 Haicaístas brasilienses. Organização de Delores Pires. São Paulo: M. Ohno Editor; Aliança Cultural Brasil-Japão, 1992. 54 p.: bibl., ill.

The *haiku* is a form introduced in Brazil as early as 1917 by Afranio Peixoto. Form now has many adept practitioners; this anthology of 13 poets is the result of a 1991 workshop held in Brasília.

4457 Lobo, Luiza. O haikai e a crise da metafísica. Rio de Janeiro: Numen Editora, 1993. 78 p.: bibl.

The popularity of *haiku* in Brazil is examined by this critic in the context of the world crisis of capitalism and metaphysics. For her, the road to *haiku* is a search for a more tactile and sensorial universe. She examines the origins of *haiku* in Brazil and its metamorphosis since Symbolism. The short poem—anti-discursive, humoristic—is the answer to the exhaustion of the Western philosophical discourse.

4458 Losekann, Maria Sandra. Entre mentes, o amor e os semblantes. Porto Alegre, Brazil: IEL; Tchê, 1992. 65 p. (Estado interior)

This poet is among the new female voices in Brazilian poetry. Her themes are expressed in the pun of the title of this collection—"entre mentes, o amor"—that also reiterates her belief that "é pela alma que se chega ao corpo."

4459 Machado, Gilka. Poesias completas. Nova ed. Rio de Janeiro: L. Christiano Editorial, 1992. 447 p.: bibl.

Second edition of the complete poems celebrating the centenary of the birth of Gilka Machado, an important feminine voice in Latin American poetry.

4460 Martins, Max. Não para consolar: poemas reunidos, 1952–1992. Belém, Brazil: Edições CEJUP, 1992. 351 p.: ill. . (Col. Verso & reverso; 2)

A collection of poems written over a 40-year period by Martins, a member of the "modernos" from Pará. Good introduction by Benedito Nunes, who analyzes Martins' aesthetic periods from his early affiliation with Drummond de Andrade, to his discovery of the French Symbolists and, later, English-language poets such as Hopkins and Dylan Thomas.

4461 Marupiara: antologia de novos poetas do Amazonas. Organização e colaboração de Aníbal Beça e André Gatti. Manaus, Brazil: Superintendência Cultural do Amazonas, Edições Governo do Estado, 1988. 260 p.

Marupiara is a Tupi word used in the Amazon region to describe a person lucky in fishing or hunting, love, or business. According to Aníbal Beça, the word is an appropriate metaphor for poets—hunters and fishers of words and impossible love. Collection includes works of 34 poets from movements that came after the Movimento do Clube da

Madrugada (1954): the "Geração Pós-Madrugada" and the "Novíssima Geração."

4462 Míccolis, Leila. O bom filho a casa torra. São Paulo: EDICON; Rio de Janeiro: BLOCOS, 1992. 64 p.

The pun in the title—the good son who *torra* (burns) the house instead of *torna* (returning) to it—sets the tone. Presents penetrating view of the quotidian lives of men and women—passions, petty desires, rape, AIDS, feminism, machismo, materialistic society—in realistic language that portrays loneliness, alienation, and violence.

4463 Monteiro, Ierecê Barbosa. Sabor ZF. São Paulo: J. Scortecci Editora, 1992. 55 p.

ZF stands for the free trade zone in Manaus. Series of poems with universal themes of love is set in a primeval world confronting modern consumerist society: "O boto cor-derosa usa Ray Ban/Surubim tem antenas parabólicas/Capivara usa Crest/Pacu desfila de Reebok."

4464 Moraes, Vinícius de. Jardim noturno: poemas inéditos. Organização e seleção de Ana Maria Miranda. São Paulo: Companhia das Letras, 1993. 196 p.:

Collection contains poems by Moraes that were not published previously. Includes 107 poems from different periods of his work, organized thematically rather than chronologically.

4465 Moraes, Vinícius de. Roteiro lírico e sentimental da cidade do Rio de Janeiro e outros lugares por onde passou e se encantou o poeta. Fotos de Márcia Ramalho. Apresentação e textos adicionais de José Castello. São Paulo: Companhia das Letras, 1992. 143 p.: ill.

Lovely guide to Rio de Janeiro. The *cariocas* and their spirit are celebrated by one of the city's beloved poets, himself the quintessential *carioca*. According to Moraes, "Carioca é um sujeito que/por princípio acorda tarde/e chateado." Includes poems of other places visited by him.

4466 Moraes Neto, Geneton. O dossiê Drummond. São Paulo: Editora Globo, 1994. 287 p.: ill., index.

Transcribes last interview granted by the poet. Also includes 45 interviews with people who knew him.

4467 Naveira, Raquel. Sob os cedros do Senhor. São Paulo: J. Scortecci Editora, 1994. 101 p.: bibl.

Poems were inspired by Arab and Armenian immigrants in Mato Grosso do Sul. Themes include Lebanese and Armenian exile from their homeland and their settlement in the New World.

4468 Neder, Cristiane. Revolution. São Paulo: M. Ohno Editor, 1992. 77 p.: ill.

Poems by a young woman perplexed by São Paulo and by the people who live on the fringes of this hard, unrelenting, business-oriented metropolis. Dedicated to "bêbados, aos negros, aos ateus, aos homossexuais, aos débeis mentais e prostitutas."

4469 Pacheco, Alvaro. A geometria dos ventos. Rio de Janeiro: Editora Record, 1992. 173 p.: bibl.

Senator form Piauí and former journalist, Pacheco writes philosophical meditations in the humanist tradition that characterizes many Northeastern poets. Divided in three parts: 1) *A janela*, short, impersonal poems; 2) *O palco*, 243 long poems focusing on contemporary cultural myths (Hitler, Marx, Tancredo Neves, among others); and 3) *O pátio interno*, 32 more personal and intimate poems.

4470 Pinto, José Alcides. O sol nasce no Acre. Fortaleza, Brazil: s.n., 1991. 55 p.: ill.

Book of three poems ("O Sol Nasce no Acre," "Poema de Chico," and "Do 'Empate' à Via Crucis") was written in honor of Chico Mendes, the hero and martyr-symbol of Amazon rainforest preservation groups such as Aliança dos Povos da Floresta, Sindicato dos Trabalhadores Rurais de Xapuri, Empate, and the literacy movement Cartilha Elementar.

4471 Poesia negra brasileira: antologia. Organização de Zilá Bernd. Prefácio de Domício Proença Filho. Porto Alegre, Brazil: Age Editora; Instituto Estadual do Livro; Cachoeirinha, Brazil: IGEL, 1992. 153 p.: bibl., index.

Very useful chronological anthology of poems representative of the black experience in Brazil, from pre-abolitionists to contemporary groups such as Quilombhoje, Negrícia, and poets from Bahia. Selection of authors was based on their ethnic background: ". . . seus autores são reconhecidamente negros e mestiços de negro e por força de configurarem a assunção de singularidade cultural que os identifica e com a qual se identificam."

4472 Sant'Anna, Affonso Romano de. O lado esquerdo do meu peito: livro de aprendizagens. Rio de Janeiro: Rocco, 1992. 212 p.

This work is poet's contemplation of the decade following the long period of dictatorship—the period of transition to democracy in Brazil, of the "end of communism," and of what some label the "end of history." Also includes a series of erotic poems.

4473 Silva, Renato Ignácio da. Alma verde. São Paulo: RENIG-Editora e Assessoria Publicitária, 1990. 140 p.: map, photos. (Série Horizonte de encantos)

The theme of this collection of poems is the beauty of the Amazon rainforest and the looming environmental disaster that threatens the area. Part of author's collection "Os Melhores sobre Ecologia-Amazônica." Photos are by the author.

4474 Souza, Expedito Ribeiro de. O canto negro da Amazônia. Belém, Brazil: Falangola Editora, 1991. 71 p.

This poet was "poor, a farmer, religious, a communist, a migrant workers' union leader," and a poet who lived in Pará and was murdered in the Amazon southern region. These *cordel* poems talk about the disputes and conflicts faced by the landless peasants who moved to the Amazon region with promises of land grants during the Médici government. Includes the last interview with the author before his death.

4475 Teixeira, Gervásio and Dalva Lazaroni. Réquiem para a floresta:canção para Chico Mendes. Desenho de Gervásio Teixeira. Poesia de Dalva Lazaroni. Introdução de René Capriles. Rio de Janeiro: Tricontinental Editora, 1992. 80 p.: ill. (some col.).

Work is a "requiem" for the Amazon rainforest and for the internationally renowned Chico Mendes who became the hero of the "Saga do Seringal." Poems alternate with drawings.

4476 Teles, Gilberto Mendonça. Os melhores poemas. Seleção de Luiz Busatto. São Paulo: Global, 1993. 189 p.: bibl., ill. (Melhores poemas; 27)

Anthology of poems dating from 1955–93, from author's 12 books. Also includes some previously unpublished poems.

4477 Ventura, Adão. Texturaafro. Belo Horizonte, Brazil: Editora Lê, 1992. 1 v.

Ventura's most recent poetic work preserves his previous concern with racial and political issues, here joined with an aesthetic and formal invention. Themes include life on the plantation, children of the *favela*.

4478 Vieira, Oldegar Franco. Gravuras no vento. São Paulo: M. Ohno Editor, 1994. 70 p.: ill.

This poet was one of the first in Brazil to publish a book of poems in the *haiku* style (*Folhas de chá*; see *HLAS 42:6346*).

Vinholes, Luiz Carlos. Intercâmbio cultural e artístico nas relações Brasil-Japão. See *HLAS 55:4391*.

4479 Vitorino, Diniz. Lírios do canto. Recife, Brazil: Governo do Estado de Pernambuco, Secretaria de Turismo, Cultura e Esportes/FUNDARPE, 1989. 106 p. (Oficina Espaço Pasárgada; 1)

Diniz Vitorino was born in Paraíba and has lived exclusively from his profession as a "poeta-repentista" (oral troubadour). He has recorded LPs, and has written many *folhetos de cordel* and poems dealing with historical, social, and political issues. In this book he talks about the plight of the landless peasants.

Drama

SEVERINO JOÃO ALBUQUERQUE, *Associate Professor of Portuguese, University of Wisconsin, Madison*

THEATER IN BRAZIL IN THE FIRST HALF of the 1990s has been dominated by *encenadores*, "multi-faceted individuals who assume the roles of director, set designer, and scriptwriter and who took to the stages in the early eighties while national dramatists active during the 1960s-70s tried to respond to the new working conditions" (item **4501**). *Encenadores* favor adaptations of Greek tragedies, Shakespeare, and more recent European classics; the only Brazilian dramatists to have merited their attention are proven masters like Nelson Rodrigues and Jorge Andrade. The work of Antunes Filho and Gerald Thomas, the most distinguished of these practitioners, displays a wide range of interests and influences, from myth and *carnaval* (Antunes) to minimalist opera (Thomas), but little concern or support for the work of younger Brazilian playwrights. Staging of new plays has been thwarted by an additional trend, prevalent since the early 1980s—the theatrical adaptation of works from other genres and art forms. As a consequence, theater has been thriving in Brazil while national drama has languished, as the scarcity of good original plays seems to indicate.

Of note among published texts is the continuation of *Palco Iluminado*, Editora Scipione's new drama series, with new titles by Edson d'Santana (item **4486**) and Edla van Steen (item **4487**). The only major playwright to publish an important new play has been Plínio Marcos, whose *A mancha roxa*—published privately by the author—portrays a group of HIV-positive women in a state penitentiary (item **4482**).

Other titles reflect efforts in community theater (item **4484**), historical drama (item **4481**), and denunciation of torture (item **4480**), all of which point to a continuation—new sensibilities notwithstanding—of Brazil's rich tradition of politically committed theater. Yet another earlier trend, "teatro besteirol," is represented here by what playwright Ricardo Pérsio calls "teatro cretino," light theater strongly influenced by improv, stand-up comedy, and television sitcoms (item **4485**).

Criticism has begun to reflect the shift to an *encenador*-oriented theater, with Antunes Filho as the focus of important works such as those by David George (item **4494**) and Sebastião Milaré (item **4500**). Older critics have stayed away from the topic, opting instead for compilations of articles and essays, most of which have been previously published in newspapers and other venues. In this vein, Décio de Almeida Prado examines colonial and 19th-century theater (item **4504**) and selected actors, directors, and trends of early- and mid-20th-century Brazilian theater (item **4503**). Two other critical compilations pay homage to seminal critics Jacó Guinsburg (item **4496**) and, posthumously, Anatol Rosenfeld (item **4507**).

A welcome resurgence of critical studies of 19th-century theater includes, in addition to sections in Prado's collected writings (item **4504**), books on movements (Faria on Realist drama, item **4491,** and Fraga on Symbolist theater, item **4492**), genres (two works on *teatro de revista,* by Ruiz, item **4508,** and Neyde Veneziano, item **4513**), and playwrights (Huppes on Gonçalves de Magalhães, item **4497**). Equally welcome is the continued appearance in printed form of otherwise difficult to locate records of mainstream companies (item **4488**), State-supported ensembles (item **4499**), experimental groups (item **4511**), and general documentation on the theater scene away from the traditional centers (items **4509, 4510,** and **4502**).

Authored by members of a younger generation of critics working in Brazil and the US, two books deserve special mention for scholarship and insight: Elza de Vincenzo's *Um teatro da mulher* surveys women's theater in contemporary Brazil (item **4514**) and Leslie Damasceno's *Espaço cultural e convenções teatrais na obra de Oduvaldo Vianna Filho* uses cultural and political theory to approach the work of a key playwright (item **4490**).

Brazilian theater in the mid-1990s continues to be receptive to all forms, themes, and styles. As David George writes, "the vitality of the theatre as an institution, its diversity and unflagging energy put to rest any notion that it is an art form on the wane. And if 'serious' Brazilian playwrights are quiet these days, they are waiting in the wings and they will soon be heard from again" (item **4493**).

ORIGINAL PLAYS

4480 Concurso Nacional de Dramaturgia.
Porto Alegre, Brazil: Prefeitura Municipal de Porto Alegre, Secretaria Municipal da Cultura, 1991. 273 p.

Contains the three winning plays of a national playwriting contest. First-prize winner, *Tortura não é brinquedo,* takes up the formidable challenge of combining satire and torture and almost succeeds. *Pierrô saiu à francesa* combines vaudeville and suspense to represent a criminal investigation set against the backdrop of Vargas' repressive regime. *O dia da caça* depicts victim and victimizer as pawns in the hands of rich power-wielders.

4481 García-Guillén, Mario. *Palmares: a epopéia do negro do Brasil. Hoje: ensaio geral.* São Paulo: Edições Loyola, 1992. 60 p.

Dramatizes the African-Brazilian struggle for freedom by juxtaposing the colonial episode of Palmares with a youth theater group as they rehearse a new play set in contemporary Brazil.

4482 Marcos, Plínio. *A mancha roxa.* São Paulo: Marcos Plínio, 1989? 1 v.

Best play by Marcos since his heyday of 1960s–early 1970s. A group of HIV-positive women inmates wallow in fear, hatred, and ignorance in a ruthless state penitentiary.

4483 Moreyra, Alvaro. *Adão, Eva e outros membros da família.* 4a. ed. Porto Alegre, Brazil: Instituto Estadual do Livro, 1990. 134 p.

New edition of the long out-of-print cornerstone of Moreyra's Teatro de Brinquedo. Two men (named simply "Um" and

"Outro") interact with each other and a number of supporting characters in an exploration of class perceptions as seen through the biased eyes of the press and theater establishments.

4484 Orsolin, Constantino. *Canelinha, morte e vida.* Porto Alegre, Brazil: IGEL; Instituto Estadual do Livro, 1990. 68 p.: ill. (Teatro, textos & roteiros; 9)

Play produced by an amateur group in a small town in Rio Grande do Sul to celebrate their identity and unity, and to dramatize their daily life and struggles. Community involvement in play selection, casting, and production is detailed in the preface by the playwright, a former farm hand and teacher.

4485 Pérsio, Ricardo Paulinelli. Micropeças cretinas. Belo Horizonte, Brazil: Mazza Edições, 1992. 77 p.

Four short texts show influence of *besteirol* and sitcoms. Flippant, unpretentious, deliberately inconsequential, Pérsio's *micropeças* reflect feelings and attitudes of contemporary middle-class youth in urban Brazil.

4486 Santana, Edson d'. *Ao mar!* São Paulo: Editora Scipione, 1991. 40 p. (Col. Palco iluminado; 3)

A fisherman and four washerwomen are visited by folk myths (Saci, Iara, Negrinho do Pastoreio) as they face both dreams and harsh reality on the margins of the Rio São Francisco in Minas Gerais. First published text by director and playwright Santana, a veteran of political theater.

4487 Steen, Edla van. *O último encontro.* São Paulo: Editora Scipione, 1991. 47 p. (Col. Palco iluminado; 4)

This first play by the well-known novelist portrays love, betrayal, an elusive inheritance, and other family complications set against the decline of German influence in southern Brazil.

HISTORY AND CRITICISM

4488 Almeida, Maria Inez Barros de. Panorama visto do Rio: Cia. Tônia-Celi-Autran. Rio de Janeiro: Ministério da Cultura, Instituto Nacional de Artes Cênicas, 1987. 115 p.: bibl., ports. (Col. Ensaios)

Traces history of the best of the professional theater groups spawned by the Teatro Brasileiro de Comédia in the 1950s. Includes analysis and photographs of the plays staged

by the company led by actors Tonia Carrero and Paulo Autran and actor-director Adolfo Celi.

4489 Castro, Ruy. O anjo pornográfico: a vida de Nelson Rodrigues. São Paulo: Companhia das Letras, 1992. 457 p.: bibl., ill., index.

Much-acclaimed study of the life, times, and theater of Brazil's foremost playwright is carefully researched and well documented. Information on the writing and stagings of Nelson's 17 plays blends neatly with biographical and historical material. Likely to be the definitive biography of Nelson Rodrigues for a long time.

4490 Damasceno, Leslie Hawkins. Espaço cultural e convenções teatrais na obra de Oduvaldo Vianna Filho. Tradução de Iná Camargo Costa. Campinas, Brazil: Editora da Unicamp, 1994. 334 p.: bibl., ill. (Col. Repertórios)

Combines textual analysis and cultural production studies to trace the career of one of the major political and aesthetic voices of the 1960s-70s. Best critical study to date of the theater of Oduvaldo Vianna Filho.

4491 Faria, João Roberto. O teatro realista no Brasil, 1855–1865. São Paulo: Edusp; Editora Perspectiva, 1993. 273 p.: bibl., ill. (Estudos; 136. Teatro)

Solid scholarship from author of earlier book on theater of José de Alencar. Provides substantial background on influence of French drama on Brazilian realist theater. Studies major names (Alencar and Joaquim Manuel de Macedo) but also includes invaluable information on lesser-known figures of the period (e.g., Aquiles Varejão and Maria Angélica Ribeiro).

4492 Fraga, Eudinyr. O simbolismo no teatro brasileiro. São Paulo: Art & Tec Editora, 1992. 193 p.: bibl.

Survey of unjustly neglected period of Brazilian theater. As Sábato Magaldi writes in preface, Brazil's Symbolist drama includes a surprising number of major works, most of which are studied here. Particularly strong sections on Goulart de Andrade, João do Rio and Roberto Gomes.

4493 George, David Sanderson. Brazil's Festival de Teatro de Curitiba II: the healthy state of the art. (*Lat. Am. Theatre Rev.*, 27:2, Spring 1994, p. 139–144)

Informative account of the state of Brazilian theater in first half of 1990s stresses vitality of the theater as an institution despite scarcity of new plays.

4494 George, David Sanderson. Grupo Macunaíma: carnavalização e mito. São Paulo: Editora Perspectiva: Editora da Univ. de São Paulo, 1990. 153 p.: bibl., ill. (Debates; 230. Teatro)

Pioneer monograph on work of Antunes Filho and Grupo Macunaíma. Studies group's stagings in light of Bakhtin's carnivalization, Jung's archetypes, Eliade's eternal return, and Grotowski's poor theater. Examines in detail three of Grupo Macunaíma's key productions (*Macunaíma, Nelson 2 Rodrigues, Augusto Matraga*).

4495 Guidarini, Mário. Os pícaros e os trapaceiros de Ariano Suassuna. São Paulo: Ateniense, 1992? 93 p.: bibl.

Short study of role of clowns and tricksters in Suassuna's theater focuses on his five best-known plays (*Auto da compadecida, A pena e a lei, Farsa da boa preguiça, O santo e a porca, O casamento suspeitoso*).

4496 Guinsburg, J. Diálogos sobre teatro. Organização de Armando Sérgio da Silva. São Paulo: Edusp; COM ARTE, 1992. 262 p.: bibl.

Writings on the theater by respected critic and professor. All but two of the 15 essays are co-authored by other critics and former students of Guinsburg. Covers a wide range of topics, from theater history and theory to contemporary groups and performance art.

4497 Huppes, Ivete. Gonçalves de Magalhães e o teatro do primeiro Romantismo. Lajeado, Brazil: Fundação Alto Taquari de Ensino Superior; Porto Alegre, Brazil: Movimento, 1993. 223 p.: bibl. (Col. Ensaios; 45)

Best book to date on the theater of Magalhães, the author of Brazil's first Romantic play, examines his work in light of the theater scene of the early Romantic period. Excellent bibliography and chronologies.

4498 Martuscello, Carmine. O teatro de Nelson Rodrigues: uma leitura psicanalítica. São Paulo: Editora Siciliano, 1993. 260 p.: bibl.

Plays are grouped under eight headings and explicated in close readings from a strictly Freudian perspective. Strong sections on *Beijo no asfalto* and *Toda nudez será castigada.*

4499 Michalski, Yan and **Rosyane Trotta.** Teatro e estado: as companhias oficiais de teatro no Brasil; história e polêmica. São Paulo: Editora Hucitec; Rio de Janeiro: Instituto Brasileiro de Arte e Cultura, 1992. 235 p.: ill. (Teatro; 21)

Posthumous publication by a leading theater critic; co-author Trotta completed the project after Michalski's death. Originally planned as a volume in the discontinued series on theater groups published by the journal *Dionysos,* work provides important documentation on three State-supported theater companies (Comédia Brasileira, Companhia Dramática Nacional, Teatro Nacional de Comédia).

4500 Milaré, Sebastião. Antunes Filho e a dimensão utópica. São Paulo: Editora Perspectiva, 1994. 287 p.: bibl., ill. (Col. Estudos; 140. Teatro)

Traces career of Brazil's leading director. Excellent scholarly work includes valuable new information on the pre-Grupo Macunaíma period of Antunes' work. Bibliography and illustrations.

4501 Milleret, Margo. An update on theatre in Brazil. (*Lat. Am. Theatre Rev.,* 28:2, Spring 1995, p. 123–131)

Draws on personal interviews with leading playwrights and critics to survey current state of Brazilian theater. Presents two opposing views: 1) that the aesthetic differences between *encenadores* and national dramatists are irreconcilable; and 2) that Brazilian playwrights have potential audiences but have yet to find a dramatic voice to suit the times.

4502 Peixoto, Fernando. Um teatro fora do eixo: Porto Alegre, 1953–1963. São Paulo: Editora Hucitec; Porto Alegre, Brazil: Prefeitura Municipal de Porto Alegre, 1993. 362 £. (Teatro; 22)

Third in a series, following *Teatro em pedaços* (see *HLAS 44:6156*) and *Teatro em movimento* (see *HLAS 50:4090*), of substantial collections of pieces written by the distinguished actor, director, and critic. This volume focuses on the Porto Alegre theater scene during Peixoto's formative period (1953–63), before his move to São Paulo and Teatro Oficina.

4503 Prado, Décio de Almeida. Peças, pessoas, personagens: o teatro brasileiro de Procópio Ferreira a Cacilda Becker. São Paulo: Companhia das Letras, 1993. 173 p.: bibl., ill.

Collection of essays, prefaces, and posthumous homages written at different moments in the career of the doyen of Brazilian theater criticism. The essay on Procópio Ferreira is an excellent account of the celebrated actor's career. Other chapters provide important insights on the relationship between theater and censorship, modernism, and *antropofagia*.

4504 Prado, Décio de Almeida. Teatro de Anchieta a Alencar. São Paulo: Editora Perspectiva, 1993. 346 p.: bibl. (Col. Debates; 261. Teatro)

Collected writings on colonial and 19th-century Brazilian theater. Pt. 1 contains substantial essays on Jesuit theater and the early Romantic theater, while Pt. 2 examines specific plays and authors including a seminal study of Gonçalves Dias' *Leonor de Mendonça*.

4505 Reis, Roberto. "Escracha! eu sou batata, entende?": família e autoritarismo no moderno teatro brasileiro. (*Lat. Am. Theatre Rev.*, 28:1, Fall 1994, p. 49–66)

Questions the popular orientation usually ascribed to major plays and posits that even the most politically committed Brazilian drama speaks from an authoritarian stance. Close examination of *Pagador de promessas*, *Eles não usam black-tie*, and *O beijo no asfalto*, with additional references to other important plays.

4506 *Revista USP.* Vol. 14, junho/agosto 1992. São Paulo: Univ. de São Paulo, Coordenadoria de Atividades Culturais.

Contemporary Brazilian theater is the focus of this special issue of the prestigious scholarly journal. Several of the essays point to the schism between drama and theater in the 1980s. Contributors include some of Brazil's top theater critics (Sábato Magaldi, Alberto Guzik, Mariângela Alves de Lima).

4507 Rosenfeld, Anatol. Prismas do teatro. Campinas, Brazil: Editora da UNICAMP; São Paulo: Edusp; Editora Perspectiva, 1993. 257 p.: bibl. (Col. Debates; 256. Teatro)

A new collection of pieces unpublished at the time of critic's death in 1973. Pt. 1 contains essays on dramatic theory and Pt. 2 reviews plays staged in São Paulo during a difficult yet highly energized decade (1964–73).

4508 Ruiz, Roberto. Teatro de revista no Brasil. v. 1., Do início à I Guerra Mundial. Introdução de Tânia Brandão. Pesquisa de Tânia Brandão e Roberto Ruiz. Rio de Janeiro: Ministério da Cultura, Instituto Nacional de Artes Cênicas, 1988. 1 v: bibl., ill. (Col. Memória)

History and analysis of one of the mainstays of Brazilian theater includes rare stills of *revistas* and excellent chronologies. See also item **4513.**

4509 Silva, Erotilde Honório. O fazer teatral: forma de resistência. Fortaleza, Brazil: EUFC, 1992. 229 p.:

Extended study of Ceará's Grupo Independente de Teatro Amador (GRITA) affords a rare look at experimental theater outside the Rio de Janeiro/São Paulo area in the 1970s–80s.

4510 Silva, José Armando Pereira da. O teatro em Santo André, 1944–1978. Santo André, Brazil: Prefeitura Municipal de Santo André, 1991. 140 p.: bibl., ill. (Memórias da cidade; 3)

History and documentation of the theater scene in the heart of São Paulo state's industrial belt.

4511 Teatro SESC Anchieta. São Paulo: Serviço Social do Comércio, Administração Regional no Estado de São Paulo, 1989. 193 p.: ill.

Abundantly documented and illustrated history of São Paulo's Anchieta, the theater supported by the city's business community. Provides strong background on years before and after Antunes Filho assumed artistic direction.

4512 Vassallo, Lígia. O sertão medieval: origens européias do teatro de Ariano Suassuna. Rio de Janeiro: F. Alves, 1993. 180 p.: bibl., ill.

Sound scholarly work studies Suassuna's theater in light of medieval tradition. Relies on Bakhtinian carnivalization to trace survival of genres ("autos" and farces) and types (tricksters) in cultural context of Brazil's Northeast, with particular attention to *cordel*, *folguedos*, and *teoria armorial*.

4513 Veneziano, Neyde. O teatro de revista no Brasil: dramaturgia e convenções. Campinas, Brazil: Editora da UNICAMP; Pontes, 1991. 194 p.: bibl., ill.

Study of *teatro de revista* with less focus on history than on form and structure.

Includes abundant quotes from dialogue and songs from key revues. Excellent bibliography and illustrations. Nicely complements Ruiz's work (see item **4508**).

4514 Vincenzo, Elza Cunha de. Um teatro da mulher: dramaturgia feminina no palco brasileiro contemporâneo. São Paulo:

Edusp; Editora Perspectiva, 1992. 296 p. (Col. Estudos; 127. Teatro)

Best book to date on women's theater in Brazil. Concentrates on period from 1969 to mid-1980s, but also refers to earlier efforts. Includes useful footnotes but lacks a bibliography.

TRANSLATIONS INTO ENGLISH FROM THE SPANISH AND PORTUGUESE

CAROL MAIER, *Professor of Spanish, Kent State University, Ohio*
DAPHNE PATAI, *Professor of Portuguese, University of Massachusetts, Amherst*
KATHLEEN ROSS, *Associate Professor of Spanish, New York University*
MAUREEN AHERN, *Professor of Spanish, Ohio State University*

TRANSLATIONS FROM THE SPANISH

READERS WILL NOTE changes in the section's authorship and in the focus of its individual reviews. First, editors Carol Maier and Kathleen Ross have been joined by Maureen Ahern. She has reviewed many of the titles in fiction; in future volumes she will also be involved with the other genres and will begin to review significant translations of work published in Latin America before 1900. Editors Maier and Ross have shared the other sections equally, with the exception of "Essays, Interviews, and Reportage," which has been prepared by Ross, and "Bibliography, Theory, and Practice," which has been prepared by Maier. The reviews include titles received between July 1, 1993 and June 30, 1995; authorship is indicated by the reviewer's initials.

The second change concerns the evaluation of the titles reviewed. In previous volumes, reviews primarily offered brief evaluations of the "quality" or "success" of the English versions. This focus was shifted slightly in *HLAS 54*, when editors Maier and Ross endeavored to "provide information . . . most helpful to teachers and scholars." In the present volume it has been altered more definitively. Aware that users of the *Handbook* constitute a highly specialized readership whose members are not primarily literary scholars and critics, the editors decided that conventional (principally literary) evaluative criteria are not appropriate for most of the *Handbook's* readers. That decision was based on their experience as practitioners, evaluators, and readers of translations and on discussion occasioned by a session they organized, "Translation as a Scholarly Resource," at the 1995 Latin American Studies Association (LASA) meeting, which occurred shortly after the biennium had ended. In view of the extent to which *Handbook* readers rely on the introductions, afterwords, glossaries, indexes, notes, and bibliographies that frequently accompany translations used in libraries, studies, and classrooms, the editors decided to emphasize the use of such apparata in the definition of "excellence."

Accordingly, the reviews in this section will note accuracy and omissions only if necessary. The "readability," so important for a translation's appeal to a wide, general readership, will be discussed only when more pertinent than research and classroom needs, when it directly impinges on those needs, or when it is clearly inseparable from them. Even when questions of style and elegance of language are of utmost importance (in the case of poetry and fiction, for instance), the reviews will often focus on what might be termed questions of content and presentation. Given the extreme brevity of the reviews, the three editors believe that it is more important to indicate which works are contained in a collection of poetry or an anthology of short stories, whether or not the edition is bilingual, and which works offer introductions, rather than to comment summarily on the "value" of the translations as works of literature—much less advise readers which translation is the "best" selection available (as did the *Bloomsbury Review* of Ken Krabbenhoft's translation of Pablo Neruda's *Odes to common things,* item **4545**). As with "good," "best" often depends principally on a reader's interests and needs. For example, the new critical edition of *Men of maize* (item **4570**) would no doubt overwhelm the general reader, but the foreword in the new translation of *Pedro Páramo* (item **4594**) might seem inadequate to teachers. And Debra A. Castillo's long introduction about "borderlining" (item **4555**) has been found more valuable by some readers than others. In the case of anthologies, which often contain works by many translators or varied works by a single translator who may excel in one genre or piece but not in others, short reviews are not only inadequate but unjust.

By reorienting the reviews, the editors believe they will better perform a professional service to the field of Latin American studies as a whole. The reviews should also serve to encourage publishers to take a chance on projects they might consider a "luxury" (Herbert R. Lottman, "The Notable Trade Imbalance: The Buying of Book Translations," *Publishers Weekly* June 5, 1995, p. 12). Furthermore, they should reinforce translators' requests to include useful supporting materials, making literature from Latin America not merely available, but truly accessible. This is especially important when a writer's work has not been published previously in English. The editors' hope that the reviews, despite their brevity, will prompt translators, publishers, and readers to consider the question Jean Franco asks in only a slightly different context at the conclusion of her foreword to the translation of Pedro Mir's *Countersong to Walt Whitman* (item **4542**): "[How] can the translation of such a poem do more than offer us a missing element of Latin America's past?"

Both this question and our shift in focus correspond to a trend in the translation of works to English noted in *HLAS 52*—an increased interest in the principles that guide translation practice. This trend has continued throughout the biennium on the part of scholars, critics, and translators. It can be seen clearly in both the preparation of the translations themselves and the support of ancillary materials that accompany them (e.g., David Bowen and Juan A. Ascencio's *Pyramids of Glass,* item **4526,** and Debra A. Castillo's translation of *Tijuana,* item **4555**). It is also evident in commentary by translation scholars and critics, some of whom analyze a particular aspect of translation from Latin America in detail (e.g., Johnny Payne, item **4634,** and Lawrence Venuti, item **4637**). And it is evidenced by the more and more numerous sessions devoted to translation at national conferences, the considerable growth of the American Translators Association's Literary Division, which now publishes a newsletter entitled *Source,* and the formation of a new Translation Discussion Group within the Modern Language Association or MLA.

Other trends, noted in random order, include the continued translation and retranslation of work by canonical writers such as Neruda (items **4543, 4544,** and **4545**) and García Márquez (items **4558** and **4580**) and the continued absence or near absence of translations of drama. In genres other than drama, there has also been continued attention to significant writers whose work has been long overdue for publication beyond Spanish or whose work in English has received limited distribution or gone out of print. Examples below include Teresa de la Parra (item **4590**), María Luisa Bombal (item **4572**), and Miguel Angel Asturias (item **4570**).

The translation of work by women writers has also continued to increase. Outstanding examples include Alicia Borinsky's *Mina cruel* (item **4573**), Daisy Zamora's *Clean slate* (item **4552**), Marjorie Agosin's *These are not sweet girls* (item **4528**), and the *Secret Weavers* series Agosin edits for White Pine Press. Translation of work from Mexico, Chile, and Argentina has also remained consistent.

New trends, albeit rather general ones, include a relative decline in the translation of work from Central America, although there are exceptions in each genre, especially in poetry. There has been a marked increase, however, in the translation of work from the Caribbean, particularly from Puerto Rico, which often provides a translator specific challenges because of the strong presence of English and the mainland. Examples include Magali García Ramís' *Happy days, Uncle Sergio* (item **4582**), Ana Lydia Vega's *True and false romances* (item **4567**), Giannina Braschi's *Empire of dreams* (item **4574**), and Emilio Díaz Valcárcel's *Hot soles in Harlem* (item **4575**). Translator Andrew Hurley is particularly successful with Puerto Rican literature, especially with dialogue. Walsh and Cohen's translation of Pedro Mir's work (item **4542**) and Margarite Fernández Olmos and Lizabeth Paravisini-Gebert's anthology of stories from the Hispanic Caribbean (item **4524**) reflect the broader interest in this region.

Finally, it is discouraging to note that not only many commercial presses, but also small presses and university presses—despite their continued willingness to support "unprofitable" translations—continue to highlight aspects of a title that might have market appeal, exoticizing or stressing a work's violent or titillating aspects while providing little or no information about the work or author. One example of this is the cover descriptions and illustration for Alfonso Quijada Urías' *The better to see you* (item **4563**).

Numerous anthologies appeared during the biennium, and they form a heterogeneous group with respect to focus, inclusions, and appropriateness for research and teaching needs. Volumes that stand out include *TriQuarterly's* special issue on Chiapas (item **4531**); the *livre d'artiste* published by Yolla Bolly Press (item **4517**); *Poetry like bread* from Curbstone, a Pan-American volume of "poets of the political persuasion" (item **4525**); and Ilan Stavans's *Tropical synagogues* (item **4530**).

In poetry, notable titles include Krabbenhoft's work with Neruda's *Odes to common things* (item **4545**), Jonathan Cohen's version of Mir's *Countersong to Walt Whitman* (item **4542**), and Renata Treitel's translation of Susana Thénon's *Distancias/distances* (item **4549**). The total or near absence of supporting information in a volume such as Krabbenhoft's, however, leads one to ask if Neruda has truly become so well known in English that readers need no orientation whatsoever to his work. Here, John Lyons' work on Ernesto Cardenal deserves special mention, particularly *The doubtful strait* (item **4538**).

The single item published in theater was not available until the reviews for this volume had been completed, and it will be reviewed in volume 58. The items in brief fiction, like those in anthologies, are highly varied. Highlights include *Piano stories*, by Felisberto Hernández, translated by Luis Harss (item **4560**); Andrew Hurley's translation of Ana Lydia Vega's *True and false romances*, despite its lack of supporting materials (item **4567**); and *Selected stories*, by Adolfo Bioy Casares, translated by Suzanne Jill Levine (item **4554**).

Among the new titles in fiction, Mexico and Argentina are well represented—Argentina with works by Ricardo Piglia (item **4591**), Juan José Saer (items **4595** and **4596**) and others, and Mexico by novels such as a new translation of *Pedro Páramo* (item **4594**), Sergio Galindo's *Otila's body* (item **4578**), García Ponce's *House on the beach* (item **4581**), and several novels by Taibo (items **4601, 4600,** and **4599**). Jesús Urzagasti's *In the land of silence* (item **4603**) continues the line started by translator Kay Pritchett (see *HLAS 54:5034*). Other translations of note include Edith Grossman's version of Alvaro Mutis' short novels (item **4586**), Charles Philip Thomas' rendering of Marco Antonio de la Parra's *The secret holy war of Santiago de Chile* (item **4589**), and Peter Bush's translation of *The old man who read love stories* (item **4598**). Many of the fiction titles carry little or no annotation or supplementary information, especially those published by commercial presses. A happy exception to novels that lack such materials is Daniel Balderston's translation of Piglia's *Artifical respiration* (item **4591**).

Essays in translation published during the biennium show a clear emphasis on the memoir, narrated through the various media of letters, chronicles, collage, testimony, biography and autobiography. Two well-known Cuban authors—Reinaldo Arenas (item **4607**) and Guillermo Cabrera Infante (item **4608**)—are represented in this area, as are the Chileans Isabel Allende (item **4606**) and Marjorie Agosin (items **4605** and **4532**). From Mexico, we have three books from past eras, all narrated in the first person: Sor Juana Inés de la Cruz's famous 17th-century *Respuesta* (item **4611**), the 1918 letters of Olga Beatriz Torres written on the Texas border (item **4614**), and the personal/political recollections of Benita Galeana, Communist militant from the 1930s-40s (item **4609**). In addition, Elena Poniatowska's reconstruction of the aftermath of the 1985 Mexico City earthquakes carries a strong personal component (item **4613**), as does Eduardo Galeano's collection of journalistic chronicles (item **4610**). Lynn Stephen's edition of the story of María Teresa Tula, a Salvadoran human rights activist (item **4615**), contributes to the growing number of published *testimonios* narrated by women. Indeed, across the board, a majority of the essays reviewed this biennium were written by women, including the only book of traditional literary criticism, Sylvia Molloy's *Signs of Borges* (item **4612**).

No bibliographic work, strictly speaking, about Latin American literature has appeared in English translation during the biennium, although there has been a gradual increase in the annotation and critical evaluation of translation. In 1995, for example, *Translation Review* (item **4636**) began to publish a special *Annotated Books Received Supplement*, which includes a section devoted to translation from Spanish. In addition, a slow but steady increase in attention has been paid to the quality of translations, in both newspapers and journals; Jason Wilson's essay illustrates this trend well (item **4638**). As mentioned above, not only have more scholars and critics addressed translation issues, translators and anthologists themselves have shown more concern for questions of practice that traditionally many translators have considered too "theoretical."

It is also important to note an increase in what might be referred to as the history of translation theory and practice. Although this work appears most often under the rubric of anthropology, cultural studies, history, or literary theory, it also fits within translation studies. Walter Mignolo's chapters on "The Colonization of Languages" in colonial Latin America offer an outstanding example (see Pt. 1 of *The darker side of the Renaissance*, item **4633**). The appearance of several studies about translation history and practice in Latin America must also be noted, in particular, Víctor Díaz Arciniega's essay on translation's role in the Fondo de Cultura Económica (item **4631**) and Frances R. Aparicio's *Versiones, interpretaciones y creaciones* (item **4628**). This work discusses translation into Spanish, but it also offers a necessary complement to the study of Latin American literature in English translation; there has been frequent interaction between Latin American and North American writers, and an understanding of translation theory and practice can hardly be achieved by studying one of the traditions in isolation.

In conclusion, it seems fitting to note what the editors hope will become a trend in the translation of literature: an increased recognition of the contribution made by translators. It is a pleasure to close the section with congratulation to several translators of work from Latin America whose awards have come to our attention. Helen R. Lane received the Gregory Kolovakos prize and Carolyn Wright was awarded a 1994 Outstanding Translation Award from the American Literary Translators Association for Jorge Teillier's *In order to talk with the dead* (see *HLAS 54: 4985*). [CM, with MA and KR]

TRANSLATIONS FROM THE PORTUGUESE

For the second biennium in a row, the number of translations from Brazilian literature has declined. *HLAS 54* included 17 translations, down from *HLAS 52*, which had 22 translations. This *HLAS* volume, which covers the period 1993–95, saw a mere 12 literary works from Brazil being published in English translation. However, several new and talented translators have appeared, and it is to be hoped that their continuing activities will help reverse this downward trend. Especially to be noted is Adria Frizzi, who tackled two difficult works by Osman Lins (1924–78) with great skill and care (items **4619** and **4622**). Irene Matthews' translation of *The women of Tijucopapo* introduces North American readers to a new and quirky Brazilian literary voice, that of Marilene Felinto (item **4620**). Established translators such as Clifford Landers (item **4625**), Margaret Neves (item **4624**), and Ellen Watson (item **4621**) continue to make important contributions to the dissemination of Brazilian literature in the English-speaking world. The range of publishers bringing out works from Brazil in translation has also expanded, with Dalkey Archives and Sun and Moon Press branching into this field.

The translations of fiction in this biennium's crop are all highly readable and enjoyable. It is only when comparisons are made with the originals that careless errors (usually signalled by awkward phrasing and syntax) are revealed. All of these should, of course, have caught the eye of a diligent editor. A perennial problem continues to be the pull between an extremely literal rendition on the one hand, and an overly free handling of the Portuguese language, on the other. Some translators still seem inclined to double as editors of their authors, deciding which phrases are superfluous and hence should be omitted. In my view, such decisions almost invariably damage the original work, which should not be presumed to be in need of improvement.

Translations of poetry are, not surprisingly, more problematic still, and most of the translators reviewed here have opted for overly literal versions, especially unfortunate when confronting a poet of the caliber of João Cabral de Melo Neto. As others have noted, too, it is not necessarily the case that poets produce the best translations of other poets.

Nevertheless, the willingness of publishers to bring out works by younger Brazilian writers is encouraging. One hopes they will be convinced, as well, to take a chance on more of the Brazilian classics, many of which have never been translated into English or exist only in dated or out-of-print translations.

Meanwhile, the Brazilian government has initiated a grant program for supporting the translation of works by Brazilian authors. Applications may be made once a work is under contract. For further information, write to: Fundação Biblioteca Nacional, Departamento Nacional do Livro, Seção de Divulgação Internacional, Av. Rio Branco 219 / 40 andar, 20040–008, Rio de Janeiro, RJ, Brazil, or FAX (021) 220-4173 or E-mail bndnlsdi@ars.bn.br.

The world of translation lost a major figure on Feb. 10, 1996, with the death of Giovanni Pontiero at the age of 62. The Scottish-born Pontiero was not only a scholar in his own right but an untiring and prize-winning translator, with many volumes to his credit, including, in particular, works by Clarice Lispector and José Saramago. His translation of Lya Luft's *Exílio* is reviewed below (item **4623**). [DP]

ANTHOLOGIES

4515 Armand, Octavio. Refractions. Translated by Carol Maier. New York: SITES/Lumen Books, 1994. 232 p.: bibl., ill.

Includes 11 essays and 11 poems chosen by author and translator, as well as an introduction by the translator. Named "Outstanding Translation of the Year" (1994) by American Literary Translators Association. [CM]

4516 Barnstone, Willis. Six masters of the Spanish sonnet: essays and translations. Carbondale: Southern Illinois Univ. Press, 1993. 311 p.: bibl., ill., index.

In addition to four Peninsular poets, Barnstone has included Sor Juana Inés de la Cruz and Jorge Luis Borges. Some of his translation decisions and comments—particularly those about Sor Juana—will not please all readers (or translators), but work offers valuable readings of two Latin American writers whose work can now be read in an increasing number of English-language versions. *En face.* [CM]

4517 The bread of days = El pan de los días. Edited by Octavio Paz. Translated by Samuel Beckett. Illustrated by Enrique Chagoya. Introduction by Eliot Weinberger. Covelo, Calif.: The Yolla Bolly Press, 1994. 1 v.

A *livre d'artiste* reprints 12 selections from 11 poets included in Octavio Paz's *Anthology of Mexican poetry* (Bloomington: Indiana Univ. Press, 1958). Chagoya's etchings, the introduction by Eliot Weinberger, and the inclusion of a 1994 interview of Paz by Weinberger about the preparation of the original anthology make this limited edition (141 copies) well worth consulting. [CM]

4518 Contemporary short stories from Central America. Edited by Enrique Jaramillo Levi and Leland H. Chambers. Translations coordinated by Leland H. Chambers. Austin: Univ. of Texas Press, 1994. 275 p. (Translations from Latin America series)

Collection of 51 stories (five by women) from six countries, all written between 1963–88. Editors' introduction places work in both Spanish and Central American literary contexts. Wide variety of styles represented. Chambers, Elizabeth Gamble Miller, Pamela Carmell and others attain a generally high level of work. [KR]

4519 *International Quarterly.* Vol. 1, No. 4, 1994, Faces of the Americas. Edited by Van K. Brock. Tallahassee, Fla.: International Quarterly, Inc.

Widely varied selection of material from "the present inhabitants of the continents and archipelagos" of the Americas includes translations from the Spanish of fiction and poetry by Carmen Naranjo, Alicia Borinsky, Edgar Bayley, and others; several are excellent. Introduction by editor Van K. Brock is thought-provoking. [CM]

4520 Light from a nearby window: contemporary Mexican poetry. Edited by Juvenal Acosta Hernández. San Francisco: City Lights Books, 1993. 231 p.: bibl.

Valuable collection of works by 21 poets, including nine women, all born after 1945 in different regions of Mexico. *En face* edition includes work by 11 translators. Varied topics and poetic styles; translations are generally literal. Short introduction and biblio-biographical notes by Acosta Hernández place poets in Mexican and world literary tradition. For poetry specialist's comment see *HLAS 54:4270.* [KR]

4521 Miketen, Antonio Roberval *et al.* Paths of integration: an anthology of poetry. Brasília: Thesaurus, 1993. 220 p.: ill.

This unusual book, in need of proper editing, is a trilingual edition of four Spanish-American and four Brazilian poets, with Spanish and Portuguese versions side-by-side in one half, English translations in the other, and the table of contents in between. The four Brazilian poets are Antonio Roberval Miketen, Anderson Braga Horta, Antonio Miranda (all three translated rather literally and with some errors of English, by Asta-Rose Alcaide), and José Santiago Naud (translated by author himself). The Spanish-American poets represented are Mabel Cháneton, Manila Cháneton, Sofía Vivo, and Trina Quiñones. [DP]

4522 Northern Cronopios: Chilean novelists and short story writers in Canada; anthology. Edited with an introduction by Jorge Etcheverry. Ottawa: Split Quotation, 1993. 138 p.

Despite some less-than-accomplished translations, work is a valuable anthology for English-language readers unfamiliar with prose written by Chilean authors in Canada. Quality of translation of the 15 stories varies. Etcheverry's brief but informative introduction profiles the writers and Chilean literary activity in Canada, and it places their work within the context of Latin Americans writing in other countries. [CM]

4523 Novo, Salvador. The war of the fatties and other stories from Aztec history, as told by Salvador Novo. Translated by Michael Alderson. Austin: Univ. of Texas Press, 1994. 232 p.: appendices, bibl., maps. (The Texas Pan American series)

In addition to the title comedy (*In Pipilzintzin* [Los niñitos] o *La guerra de las gordas: comedia en dos actos*, 1963), this generous collection contains selections of both drama and prose, including two essays and a chapter from the unpublished *Historia de Coyoacán*. Also contains a lengthy introduction about Salvador Novo, a glossary of Nahuatl terms, and an extensive bibliography of work by and about Novo. [CM]

4524 Pleasure in the word: erotic writings by Latin American women. Edited by Margarite Fernández Olmos and Lizabeth

Paravisini-Gebert. Fredonia, N.Y.: White Pine Press, 1993. 284 p.: bibl.

Collection of poetry and prose by 20th-century writers from all over the region celebrates both hetero- and homosexual pleasure. Translators include Suzanne Jill Levine, Magda Bogin, the editors, and others. Works range from best-sellers (Isabel Allende) to lesser-known poems. Short introduction and brief biographical notes on the authors. [KR]

4525 Poetry like bread: poets of the political imagination from Curbstone Press. Ed- ited by Martín Espada. Willimantic, Conn.: Curbstone Press; East Haven, Conn.: InBook, 1994. 282 p.

Unusual, strong collection of poems from across the Americas, all by authors previously published by Curbstone, deals with multiple facets of political life. Translations from Spanish and French (for 16 of the 37 authors included) presented *en face*. Includes short, explanatory introduction by Espada and biographical notes. [KR]

4526 Pyramids of glass: short fiction from modern Mexico. Edited by Joshua David Bowen and Juan Antonio Ascencio. Introduction by Ilan Stavans. San Antonio, Tex.: Corona Pub. Co.; Dallas, Tex.: Taylor Pub. Co., 1994. 244 p.

Heterogeous collection of stories by 27 contemporary authors born between 1915–59 is introduced by Ilan Stavans' comprehensive, if somewhat schematic introduction to the Mexican short story. Quality of translations (by 20 translators) varies; some are excellent. Several translators have participated in an intriguing experiment to "punctuate English in Spanish." Brief paragraphs about authors and translators. [CM]

4527 Remaking a lost harmony: stories from the Hispanic Caribbean. Edited by Margarite Fernández Olmos and Lizabeth Paravisini-Gebert. Fredonia, N.Y.: White Pine Press, 1995. 249 p.: (Dispatches)

Includes 25 stories by authors born between 1918–54 in Cuba, Puerto Rico, or the Dominican Republic. Introduction surveys recent history and contemporary society of the Hispanic Caribbean, and notes criteria for selecting and translating stories that "allow for convincing and authentic translations." Further explanation (and more information about the writers) would have been welcome. Translations, by six translators, are uneven. [CM]

4528 These are not sweet girls: Latin American women poets. Edited by Marjorie Agosin. Fredonia, N.Y.: White Pine Press, 1994. 368 p. (Secret weavers series; 7)

Highly personal, unorthodox selection and arrangement of poems that "view the world from a woman's perspective" includes authors such as Storni and Mistral alongside younger poets from all over the region. Useful introduction by Agosín. Afterword by Celeste Kostopulos-Cooperman reflects on translation practice. English text only. [KR]

4529 *Translation.* Vol. 21, 1994, Venezuelan Feature Issue. Edited by Lyda Zacklin. New York: Columbia Univ., The Translation Center.

Special issue on Venezuela includes translations of poetry, short stories, and selections from three novels, drawn from work by authors representing several generations of Venezuelan writers and "classic" as well as more recent writing. Zacklin's brief but comprehensive introduction surveys contemporary Venezuelan literature, offering specific examples. Many of the translators are highly accomplished. [CM]

4530 Tropical synagogues: short stories. Edited and with an introduction by Ilan Stavans. New York: Holmes & Meier, 1994. 239 p.: bibl.

Interesting stories from six countries (including Brazil) and exceptional translations make this volume particularly useful. Many stories collected here were previously published in other volumes and journals. Long introduction by Stavans provides background. Extensive bibliography. Includes three stories by Borges with Jewish themes. [KR]

4531 Voices from Chiapas. (*Tri-Quarterly/ Evanston*, 91, Fall 1994, p. 87–158)

Selections from this rich anthology emphasize rural life and augment dramatically the information about Chiapas available to English-language readers. Texts include translations of work by well-known writers from or identified with Chiapas (e.g., Jaime Sabines, Rosario Castellanos), folktales from indigenous languages, letters from the EZLN guerrilla movement's Subcomandante Mar-

cos, and material from Ambar Past's Taller Leñateros (her workshop in Chiapas). [CM]

TRANSLATIONS FROM THE SPANISH
Poetry

4532 Agosin, Marjorie. Dear Anne Frank. Translated by Richard Schaaf. Washington, D.C.: Azul Editions, 1994. 1 v.

Short poems and prose treating themes of adolescent emotion, antisemitism, human cruelty and goodness, and historical memory reflect Agosin's identification and interior dialogue with Anne Frank. Lucid translation. Agosin's introduction explains book's genesis and resonance of Frank's story with contemporary events in Latin America. [KR]

4533 Agosin, Marjorie. Hogueras = Bonfires. Translated by Naomi Lindstrom. Critical introduction by Juan Villegas. Tempe, Ariz.: Bilingual Press/Editorial Bilingüe, 1990. 143 p.

Marjorie Agosin's eroticism and her "rewriting" of love poetry by men present special challenges to a translator. Some of Lindstrom's lines seem wordy and clichéd, but many of her images are surprising and effective and her English closely parallels Agosin's work. Juan Villegas discusses the development he finds in Agosin's writing, placing it in the context of Hispanic, particularly Chilean, poetry. *En face.* [CM]

4534 Agosin, Marjorie. Sargasso. Translated by Cola Franzen. Fredonia, N.Y.: White Pine Press, 1993. 91 p.

Lyrical poems of nature, the body, and love all share sea and water imagery. Bilingual edition. Volume stresses simplicity of language, elemental passion, and experience. Fine translation by Franzen. Includes cover notes, but no introduction. [KR]

4535 Alegría, Claribel. Fugues. Translated by Darwin J. Flakoll. Willimantic, Conn.: Curbstone Press; East Haven, Conn.: InBook, 1993. 143 p.

In new poems Alegría explores the "flight"—death, separation, aging, flux—at the root of "fugue." Translations work more adequately with this topic than with the complexity of the poems. No annotation; readers unfamiliar with Alegría's work will not be alerted to the departure this collection represents for her as a writer. *En face.* [CM]

4536 Cabrera, Fernando. El arbol = The tree. Translated by Charlene S. Santos. Santo Domingo: Casa de Teatro, 1993. 168 p.: ill.

Prize-winning poem by a young (b. 1964) Dominican, in bilingual edition. Derivative of T.S. Eliot in style and theme, poem departs from an apocalyptic Biblical passage to reflect on the human condition and fall from grace. Translation does a creditable job with heavy, sometimes leaden poetry. [KR]

4537 Cardenal, Ernesto. Cosmic canticle. Translated by John Lyons. Willimantic, Conn.: Curbstone Press; East Haven, Conn.: InBook, 1993. 490 p.

This huge narrative epic poem is divided into 43 *cantigas.* Five centuries of Latin American history are presented in a universal frame ranging from the sub-atomic to the Sandinistas. Excellent translation by Lyons. No supporting materials, notes, or introduction; many references will be difficult for the uninitiated reader. In English only. [KR]

4538 Cardenal, Ernesto. The doubtful strait = El estrecho dudoso. Translated by John Lyons. Introduction and glossary by Tamara R. Williams. Bloomington: Indiana Univ. Press, 1995. 189 p.: bibl.

Book-length, epic poem (first published 1966—see *HLAS 32:4179* and *HLAS 36: 6521*) narrates both European conquest and colonization of Central America, and recent Nicaraguan history. Cardenal builds poem incorporating verbatim excerpts from Spanish chronicles. Excellent presentation by Williams. Bilingual; Spanish text edited by Lyons in collaboration with Cardenal. This monumental project makes an important contribution. [KR]

Cuadra, Angel. Angel Cuadra: the poet in socialist Cuba. See item **3964.**

4539 García, Carlos Ernesto. Even rage will rot. Merrick, N.Y.: Cross-Cultural Communications, 1994. 48 p.: bibl.

Translation of Salvadoran author's first volume, which was published in 1987 in Spain. Bilingual edition. Themes of youthful confusion, European exile, memory. Capable translation by Gamble Miller. Biblio-

graphical note on García (b. 1960). [KR]

4540 Guillén, Nicolás. New love poetry: in some springtime place; elegy. Edited, translated, and with a commentary by Keith Ellis = Nueva poesía de amor: en algún sitio de la primavera; elegía. Edición, traducción y comentario de Keith Ellis. Toronto; Buffalo, N.Y.: Univ. of Toronto Press, 1994. 159 p.: bibl., ill., index.

This unusual and intriguing totally bilingual book, which contains drawings created for the project by Ernesto García Peña, offers the translation of Nicolás Guillén's previously unpublished poetry written to Sara Casal, his "confidant" and assistant at the Unión de Escritores y Artistas de Cuba. Keith Ellis accomplishes well his goal of presenting both the poems and their "story" as an integral work. [CM]

Islas, Maya. Merla. See item **4014.**

4541 López Velarde, Ramón. Song of the heart: selected poems. Translated by Margaret Sayers Peden. Art by Juan Soriano. Austin: Univ. of Texas Press, 1995. 104 p.: ill. (some col.).

A doubly bilingual volume in two languages and two media, since Juan Soriano's drawings were created for this edition. Peden's afterword summarizes the challenges she encountered as a translator. She is unnecessarily apologetic, however, for she manages to achieve a good balance between what she terms her "license" and the work's "integrity." [CM]

Miketen, Antonio Roberval *et al.* Paths of integration: an anthology of poetry. See item **4521.**

4542 Mir, Pedro. Countersong to Walt Whitman: song of ourselves. Translated by Donald D. Walsh and Jonathan Cohen. Washington: Azul Editions, 1993. 179 p.: bibl.

These eight selections provide an excellent introduction to Mir's poetry. Silvio Torres-Salvat's brief essay includes minimal information about Mir and his work, although Jean Franco presents the *Contracanto a Walt Whitman* more fully. Selected bibliography. Translations by Donald D. Walsh offer "a fair [accurate] paraphrase"; Jonathan Cohen's "lyric paraphrase" achieves a more complex version. *En face.* [CM]

4543 Neruda, Pablo. Maremoto = Seaquake; poems. Translated by Maria Jacketti and Dennis Maloney. Fredonia, N.Y.: White Pine Press, 1993. 64 p.

First English edition of 1969 work that was rediscovered at Neruda's house in Chile and published in 1991 (see item **4046**). Short poems, inspired by sea creatures of Isla Negra, employ typically direct, deceptively simple Nerudian language. Bilingual edition. Literal translations occasionally miss subtle passages. [KR]

4544 Neruda, Pablo. Neruda's garden: an anthology of odes. Selected and translated by Maria Jacketti. Pittsburgh, Pa.: Latin American Literary Review Press, 1995. 253 p.

Jacketti's selection from all four volumes of Pablo Neruda's *Odas* affords English-language readers a welcome opportunity to experience the full range of these poems. Her translations, however, would likely be more satisfying if she had tackled fewer poems. Some poems, and parts of many others, are both effective and affective; but the whole here is less than the sum of its translations. *En face.* [CM]

4545 Neruda, Pablo. Odes to common things. Selected and illustrated by Ferris Cook. Translated by Kenneth Krabbenhoft. Boston: Little, Brown, 1994. 147 p.: ill.

A beautiful, provocative book. Krabbenhoft's highly accomplished versions of 26 *odas* and Cook's drawings translate—activate—in a new way the poems' dynamic tension between "thingness" and poetry. They also focus on a single theme of the odes. This is instructive, but it may also be deceptive, especially since volume lacks any annotation. *En face.* [CM]

4546 Pacheco, José Emilio. An ark for the next millennium: poems. Drawings by Francisco Toledo. Translated by Margaret Sayers Peden. Selected by Jorge Esquinca. Austin: Univ. of Texas Press, 1993. 147 p.: ill.

Bilingual selections from Pacheco's 1991 *Album de zoología* (Guadalajara: Cuarto Menguante Editores, 1985) are illustrated by Toledo's fine, somewhat threatening drawings. Poems focus on animals of land, sea, and sky to reflect on both their strangeness and their relation to human beings. Peden's elegant, polished translations sometimes mask Pacheco's colloquial, ironic tone. Sparse trans-

lator's notes; no other supporting material. [KR]

4547 Peri Rossi, Cristina. Evohé: erotic poems. Translated by Diana P. Decker. Washington: AZUL Editions, 1994. 1 v.: bibl.

Peri Rossi's brief introduction (written for this edition) provides helpful commentary on the erotic poems in *Evohé* (1971), but readers unfamiliar with her and her work may wish for a more general introduction. Translation seems prosaic for a voice crying out "against the expression of desire." Short selected bibliography. *En face.* [CM]

4548 Sosa, Roberto. The common grief: poems. Translated by Jo Anne Engelbert. Willimantic, Conn.: Curbstone Press, 1994. 109 p.

Volume combines Honduran poet's "El Llanto de las Cosas" and "Máscara Suelta" (written 1982–87), works treating love in its selfless and erotic forms. *En face* bilingual edition. Engelbert's translation is thoughtful and strong, projecting this poetry's mature voice of experience, joy, and suffering. Short, informative introduction by translator. [KR]

4549 Thénon, Susana. Distancias = Distances. Translated by Renata Treitel. Los Angeles: Sun and Moon, 1994. 118 p.

A fine, "complete" translation of *Distancias* (Buenos Aires: Torres Agüero, 1984). Treitel has not only worked creatively with poetry described by Thénon herself as "difficult," but has introduced it eloquently and straightforwardly. Her afterword provides an unusually clear discussion of a translator's purpose and practice. Ana María Barrenechea's epilogue offers a brief critical reading of Thénon's poetics. *En face.* [CM]

4550 Trujillo Muñoz, Gabriel. Permanent work: poems, 1981–1992. Translated by Patricia Irby, Robert L. Jones, and Gustavo V. Segade, with author. San Diego: San Diego State Univ. Press, 1993. 96 p.: ill. (Baja California literature in translation)

Interesting volume of translations of poems by Trujillo (b. 1958), one of Baja California's most prolific contemporary figures in literature. Volume suffers from lack of Spanish text. Translations capture a young, lyrical voice reflecting on phenomena of nature and on historical events and personages. Occasional footnotes. Short, informative introductory essay by Humberto Félix Berumen. [KR]

4551 Vallejo, César. The black heralds = Los heraldos negros. Translated by Barry Fogden. East Sussex, England: Allardyce, Barnett; Berkeley, Calif.: SPD Inc., 1995. 108 p.: ill.

This monolingual volume illustrates well the difficulty in presenting *Los heraldos negros* (Lima: 1918) without providing any orientation. Fogden is clearly a careful, informed reader of Vallejo, and sometimes the poems are striking; but the translations cannot "stand alone" in English and at times they seem less provocative than confusing. For annotation of 1959 edition of *Los heraldos negros*, see *HLAS 24:5463*. [CM]

4552 Zamora, Daisy. Clean slate: new & selected poems. Translated by Margaret Randall and Elinor Randall. Willimantic, Conn.: Curbstone Press; East Haven, Conn.: InBook, 1993. 1 v.

A wide selection from Daisy Zamora's two collections (1981, 1988) and new poems (1993). The translations, especially of the poems, are highly successful. In most cases the "mother [Elinor] and daughter [Margaret] team" of translators has achieved the balance they sought between Zamora as a "poet's poet" and a "people's poet." Brief but informative translator's note. *En face.* [CM]

Brief Fiction and Theater

4553 Agosin, Marjorie. Happiness: stories. Translated by Elizabeth Horan. Fredonia, N.Y.: White Pine Press, 1993. 238 p.

Collection of translations of very short (some one-page) stories, all told through women's voices and treating various subjects: love, death, Jewishness, immigration. Translator's introduction is notable for its reflections on questions of class, feminism, and complex North-South American experience of the author. Stories range greatly in style from lyric to fantastic. [KR]

4554 Bioy Casares, Adolfo. Selected stories. Translated, with an introduction, by Suzanne Jill Levine. New York: New Directions, 1994. 176 p.

Collection of 15 stories from the mid-1950s to late 1980s is divided according to broad topics of love and the fantastic. Levine's lucid introduction locates author and work; also discusses her experience translating Bioy.

Selection reflects Bioy's cosmopolitan concerns and fascination with the surreal. Highly polished volume. [KR]

4555 Campbell, Federico. Tijuana: stories on the border. Translated and introduced by Debra A. Castillo. Berkeley: Univ. of California Press, 1995. 167 p.: bibl.

Castillo has been criticized for the long "academic" introduction to her translation of *Tijuanenses* (see *HLAS 52:3472*); however, scholars, teachers, and students will find it informative and useful, even though "borderlining" has been developed at the expense of other important aspects of the stories. A translator's statement, for example, might have accounted for spots that seem overly literal. [CM]

4556 Conde, Rosina. Women on the road—. San Diego, Calif.: San Diego State Univ. Press, 1994. 146 p.: port. (Baja California literature in translation)

Ten different translators have translated these stories from *Arrieras somos* into English, but they all followed the "theoretical principles" discussed by Gustavo Segade in his prologue. Those principles include "a conscious effort to preserve . . . 'foreignness.'" Includes introduction to Rosina Conde and her work by Sergio D. Elizondo. Spanish edition was not available to consult. [CM]

4557 Denevi, Marco. The redemption of the cannibal woman, and other stories. Translated by Alberto Manguel. Toronto: Coach House Press, 1993. 143 p.

Four stories of loneliness, desire, and mystery are set in Buenos Aires: one never before collected in a book; three from the volumes *Hierba del cielo* (see *HLAS 54:4095*) and *Reunión de desaparecidos* (Buenos Aires: Macondo Ediciones, 1977). Creative translation by Manguel of some difficult colloquial language. Short biographical afterword on Denevi. Well-crafted collection. [KR]

4558 García Márquez, Gabriel. Strange pilgrims: twelve stories. Translated by Edith Grossman. New York: Knopf, 1993. 188 p.

Stories with Latin American protagonists set in Barcelona and other European cities were written on and off by García Márquez over 18 years. Amusing introduction by the author explains the book's title (*Doce cuentos peregrinos* in the original: Madrid:

Mondadori, 1992) and evolution. Elegant translation by Grossman. [KR]

4559 Heker, Liliana. The stolen party: and other stories. Translated by Alberto Manguel. Toronto: Coach House Press, 1994. 135 p. (Passport books; 4)

Six stories are selected from Liliana Heker's *Los que vieron la zarza* (Buenos Aires: Editorial J. Alvarez, 1966, see *HLAS 30:3394*), *Acuario* (Buenos Aires: Centro Editor de América Latina, 1972), and *Las peras del mal* (Buenos Aires: Editorial de Belgrano, 1982), the last of which includes the title story ("La Fiesta Ajena"). Alberto Manguel's translations present Heker well, although his afterword to her work and its context is brief. [CM]

4560 Hernández, Felisberto. Piano stories. Translated by Luis Harss. New York: Marsilio Publishers, 1993. 260 p. (Eridanos library)

Harss' work probably will not please all translators, but he has served English-language readers well by presenting Hernández's brief fiction as a "genre" and offering them the opportunity to read more than an anthologized sample. Collection includes stories from *Nadie encendía las lámparas* (Barcelona: Editorial Lumen, 1982, see *HLAS 46:5559*), *Las hortensias* (Montevideo: Arca, 1966), *La casa inundada* (Montevideo: Editorial Alfa, 1960), *El caballo perdido* (Montevideo: González Panizza hnos., 1943) and *Explicación falsa de mis cuentos* (1955). Translator's note and Italo Calvino's preface introduce Hernández briefly but adequately. [CM]

4561 Jaramillo Levi, Enrique. Duplications, and other stories. Translated by Leland H. Chambers. Pittsburgh, Pa.: Latin American Literary Review Press, 1994. 188 p. (Series Discoveries)

Contains 45 very short stories (most 3–7 pages), 40 of which made up Panamanian author's original work *Duplicaciones* (México: J. Mortiz, 1973, see *HLAS 44:5268*). Stories center on the abnormal and strange, and are grouped loosely by theme. Many explore interior thoughts and situations without explicit geographical setting. Consistent voice is achieved by Chambers' translation. Includes a biographical note on cover, but no other supporting materials. [KR]

4562 Ortega, Julio. Ayacucho, goodbye. Translated by Edith Grossman. [and] Moscow's gold. Translated by Alita Kelley. Pittsburgh, Pa.: Latin American Literary Review Press, 1994. 103 p. (Series Discoveries)

"Two novellas on Peruvian politics and violence" (cover notes). *Ayacucho Goodbye* (59 p.), a translation of *Adios Ayacucho* (Philadelphia: Institute for the Study of Human Issues, 1986), presents allegorical tale of disappeared corpse seeking to recover his bones for Christian burial. *Moscow's Gold* (28 p.) treats adolescents living during the Cold War. Colloquial and humorous language; skillful translations. Includes many Peruvian political, historical, and literary references; lacks explanatory materials. [KR]

4563 Quijada Urías, Alfonso. The better to see you. Translated by Hugh Hazelton. Dunvegan, Canada: Cormorant Books, 1993. 93 p.

Hazelton's translation of *Para mirarte mejor* (Tegucigalpa: Editorial Guaymas, 1987) plunges readers effectively into the horror and repression of a broad spectrum of Salvadoran "official history." However, the book offers no orientation, a need for many North American readers. Brief cover description stresses Salvadoran suffering and the impact of these 16 stories. [CM]

4564 Ribeyro, Julio Ramón. Marginal voices: selected stories. Translated by Dianne Douglas. Foreword by Dick Gerdes. Austin: Univ. of Texas Press, 1993. 137 p. (The Texas Pan American series)

Includes translations of 15 stories by the Peruvian author from *La palabra del mudo*, written between 1952–75. (For annotation of vols. 1–2 of this work, see *HLAS 40: 6782*; for vol. 3 see *HLAS 42:5364*.) Translator's note explains her selection as "crossing borders," treating culturally diverse marginal voices. Foreword by Gerdes positions Ribeyro in literary context. Translation works well, with a few exceptions; occasional explanatory footnotes provided. [KR]

4565 Samperio, Guillermo. Beatle dreams and other stories. Translated by Russell M. Cluff and L. Howard Quackenbush. Pittsburgh, Pa.: Latin American Literary Review Press, 1994. 169 p. (Discoveries)

Contains translations of 38 stories and micro-stories by the prolific Mexican story writer, collected from various volumes published between 1974–90. Short translators' introduction provides background on work. Many stories with Mexican or Mexico City settings. Various themes include contemporary mores and culture; often ironic tone. Well-executed translations. [KR]

4566 Vallbona, Rima de. Flowering inferno: tales of sinking hearts. Translated by Lillian Tagle. Pittsburgh, Pa.: Latin American Literary Review Press, 1994. 92 p. (Discoveries)

Unfortunately, *Los infiernos de la mujer y algo más* (Madrid: Torremozas, 1992) has not been well served here. No information is provided about Rima de Vallbona or her work except for a biographical note on the cover. Nor does the English do justice to Vallbona's use of language; idiomatic expressions ring true, but descriptive, lyrical passages are frequently awkward and labored. [CM]

4567 Vega, Ana Lydia. True and false romances: stories and a novella. Translated by Andrew Hurley. London; New York: Serpent's Tail, 1994. 261 p. (Masks)

Hurley offers appropriately idiomatic translations of nine pieces from three collections (1983, 1987, 1991). The book itself, though, which includes no introductory materials, raises provocative questions about the extent to which English-language readers are familiar with Puerto Rican society and language, and about their comprehension of Spanish expressions embedded in the text. [CM]

Novels

4568 Alegría, Fernando. The Maypole warriors. Translated by Carlos Lozano. Pittsburgh, Pa.: Latin American Literary Review Press, 1993. 192 p. (Discoveries)

Interesting novel *Mañana los guerreros* (see *HLAS 28:2012*), set in 1938 Santiago, treats rising Chilean Nazism, leftist youth, and the situation of the old bourgeoisie. Translation is clear and readable, if sometimes a bit plodding. No accompanying materials or preface. [KR]

4569 Arenas, Reinaldo. The assault. Translated by Andrew Hurley. New York: Viking, 1994. 145 p.

El asalto (see *HLAS 54:3817*), the last novel in Arenas' five-novel series *Pentagonia* treating Cuba and his own life, is given excel-

lent and creative translation by Hurley. Orwellian, violent, and surreal narration of life in a controlled society, told from the point of view of a government torturer. [KR]

4570 Asturias, Miguel Angel. Men of maize. Translated by Gerald Martin. Critical ed. Pittsburgh, Pa.: Univ. of Pittsburgh Press, 1993. 466 p.: bibl. (Col. Archivos. The Pittsburgh editions of Latin American literature.)

Rich critical edition of *Hombres de maíz* (see *HLAS 15:2281*) contains Gerald Martin's revision of his 1975 translation (see *HLAS 40:7882*), with an introduction, translator's note, glossary, extensive notes, and bibliography. Also reprints essays by Ariel Dorfman, Ronald Christ, and Mario Vargas Llosa; Nobel Peace Prize Address by Rigoberta Menchu; and an account of an interview with Asturias by Luis Harss and Barbara Dohmann from their work *Into the mainstream* (see *HLAS 30:2916*). [CM]

4571 Belli, Gioconda. The inhabited woman. Translated by Kathleen N. March. Willamantic, Conn.: Curbstone Press; East Haven, Conn.: InBook, 1994. 412 p.

March's adequate translation of the Nicaraguan poet's first novel *La mujer habitada* (see item **3529**) counted on creative assistance from the author. Yet their work does not gloss over the excessive revolutionary rhetoric or stereotyped characters in this double-voiced feminist fable of political and sexual awakening that shadows Belli's earlier Sandinista militancy. [MA]

4572 Bombal, María Luisa. House of mist [and] The shrouded woman: two novels. Translated by the author. Foreword by Naomi Lindstrom. Austin: Univ. of Texas Press, 1995. 259 p.: bibl. (The Texas Pan American series)

Important re-publication of two innovative novels about women's experiences by the Chilean writer, whose English version (see *HLAS 14:2741*) of *La última niebla* (Santiago?: 1935) contains significant revisions and entirely new segments. Her own translation (see *HLAS 14:2843*) of *La amortajada* (see *HLAS 4:3939*) is adequate, although "faintly old-fashioned" (*Chicago Tribune*). Lindstrom supplies welcome context. [MA]

4573 Borinsky, Alicia. Mean woman. Translated and with an introduction by Cola Franzen. Lincoln: Univ. of Nebraska Press, 1993. 179 p. (Latin American women writers)

Cola Franzen's suggestive English title for *Mina cruel* (Buenos Aires: Corregidor, 1989) reflects the wit and subtlety that informs her translation. Her introduction is valuable, too. Both direct and academic in the best senses, Franzen discusses Borinsky's work, their collaboration, the novel's context and composition, and—all too briefly—her own work as a translator. [CM]

4574 Braschi, Giannina. Empire of dreams. Translated by Tess O'Dwyer. Introduction by Alicia Ostriker. New Haven, Conn.: Yale Univ. Press, 1994. 219 p.

"I traded in my voice," Tess O'Dwyer writes in a provocative translator's note, inviting readers to reflect on the relationship between the "license" she has exercised and her "faithful" approach to *Imperio de los sueños* (Barcelona: Anthropos, 1988). Her lucid sense of language complements Braschi well. Ostriker's laudatory introduction replaces Francisco José Ramos' highly academic "Postfacio," and seems equally inappropriate. [CM]

4575 Díaz Valcárcel, Emilio. Hot soles in Harlem. Translated by Tanya T. Fayen. Pittsburgh, Pa.: Latin American Literary Review Press, 1993. 203 p. (Series Discoveries)

The challenge of translating this verbal tour of greater Harlem demands idiomatic English as brashly strident as the cacophony of immigrant voices that created it. Fayen's version of *Harlem todos los dias* (see *HLAS 42: 5298*) is overly cautious, sometimes stiff or missing nuances. Lacks needed introduction. [MA]

4576 Domecq, Brianda. Eleven days. Translated by Kay S. García. Albuquerque: Univ. of New Mexico Press, 1995. 226 p.

Once días, y algo más (Xalapa, Mexico: UV Editorial, 1979), a semi-fictional account of the Mexican author's own 1978 kidnapping, provides an absorbing story with a view of different sectors of Mexico City society. García's translation neutralizes or Anglicizes many cultural aspects of the text, and introductory material other than cover notes is lacking. [KR]

4577 Fuentes, Carlos. The orange tree. Translated by Alfred J. Mac Adam. New York: Farrar, Straus, and Giroux, 1994. 229 p.

Adequate translation of alternating narrative voices, as *El naranjo* (Madrid: San-

tanilla, 1993) meditates on language as link or barrier between conflicting cultures in American and Iberian history. Occasional awkward syntax and cognates, or deletion of final sentences of paragraphs. Received mixed reviews in North American press (*Bloomsbury Review, Atlanta Journal and Constitution, New Statesman*). [MA]

4578 Galindo, Sergio. Otilia's body: a novel. Translated by Carolyn and John Brushwood. Austin: Univ. of Texas Press, 1994. 225 p.: ill. (Texas Pan American series)

Otilia Rauda (México: Grijalbo, 1986), winner of Mexico's Villarrutia prize, reads very smoothly in translation by distinguished scholar-translators of Mexican narrative. Readers unfamiliar with Galindo's novels or their settings in provincial Veracruz of 1910–40 would have appreciated a more substantial introduction to this drama of a sexually liberated woman. [MA]

4579 García Aguilar, Eduardo. Boulevard of heroes. Translated by Jay Anthony Miskowiec. Introduction by Gregory Rabassa. Pittsburgh, Pa.: Latin American Literary Review Press, 1993. 192 p. (Discoveries)

Bulevar de los héroes (see *HLAS 52: 3736*), a 1987 Colombian novel in the tradition of García Márquez, is set in Paris and the Andean region. Miskowiec's translation does a good job with sometimes dense prose and varied cultural references. Helpful short introduction by Gregory Rabassa locates work in the context of the Boom and magic realism. [KR]

4580 García Márquez, Gabriel. Of love and other demons. Translated by Edith Grossman. New York: Knopf; Random House, 1995. 147 p.

Grossman accomplishes excellent translation of *Del amor y otros demonios* (see item **3669**), author's latest work. Short novel based on a legend of Colombia's coastal region regarding 18th-century aristocrats is told in masterful Marquesian style. Translation handles cultural details such as the patois of slaves with aplomb. [KR]

4581 García Ponce, Juan. The house on the beach: a novel. Translated by Margarita Vargas and Juan Bruce-Novoa. Austin: Univ. of Texas Press, 1994. 201 p.: bibl. (The Texas Pan American series)

Superb translation of *La casa en la playa* (see *HLAS 30: 3168*), a Mexican intellectual's exploration of "the inner world of experience" of a professional woman rendered in elegant scenes and intimate conversations. Bruce-Novoa's "Juan García Ponce in Context" provides valuable introduction to aesthetics in Mexico at mid-century. [MA]

4582 García Ramis, Magali. Happy days, Uncle Sergio. Translated by Carmen C. Esteves. Fredonia, N.Y.: White Pine Press, 1995. 175 p. (The secret weavers series; 8)

In her afterword, Esteves situates *Felices días, Tío Sergio* (see *HLAS 50:3219*) in recent Puerto Rican "historical discourse," a term that also suggests her own approach as a translator. She has paid close attention to historical context and spoken language, endeavoring to make them both accessible and spontaneous in English. Afterword hovers uneasily between undergraduate needs and those of the general reader, but the translation is more successful. [CM]

4583 Jacobs, Bárbara. The dead leaves. Translated by David Unger. Willimantic, Conn.: Curbstone Press; East Haven, Conn.: INBOOK, 1993. 126 p.

No doubt Jacobs' first-person narrator presented the principal challenge to translator Unger, but he has worked well with this aspect of *Las hojas muertas* (México: Ediciones Era, 1987). This is the first English-language translation of any work by Jacobs, which makes it particularly unfortunate that not even the cover provides information about her or clearly suggests the book's rich cross-cultural dimension. [CM]

4584 Marchant, Reinaldo Edmundo. Varona en el jardín: novela. Santiago?: Editorial Nowadays, 1993? 111 p.

The English translation of this work by an unknown translator is unusually disappointing and riddled with typographical errors. It fails to convey the sense of Marchant's narrative, much less the richness of his images or his innovative use of language. *En face.* [CM]

4585 Martínez, Guillermo, Regarding Roderer. Translated by Laura C. Dail. New York: St. Martin's Press, 1994. 90 p.

Readers who do not have the dust jacket may wish for a word about Guillermo Martínez (b. 1962), a mathematician whose previous work has won awards in his native Argentina. *Acerca de Roderer* (Buenos Aires: Planeta, 1992), his first novel, has been translated competently, although greater consistency in the register would have made the narrative more compelling. [CM]

4586 Mutis, Alvaro. The adventures of Maqroll: four novellas. Translated by Edith Grossman. New York: HarperCollins Publishers, 1995. 369 p.

Second volume of translation of Columbian-born Mutis' novellas about a seafarer whose "only true wealth is life" (*The Washington Post*). Includes translations of four works originally published separately: *Amirbar* (Madrid: Ediciones Siruela, 1990); *La última escala del Tramp Steamer* (see *HLAS 52:3740*); *Abdul Bashur, soñador de navíos* (Madrid: Ediciones Siruela, 1991); and *Tríptico de mar y tierra* (Barcelona: Grupo Editorial Norma, 1993). Grossman's splendid translation renders powerful storytelling into English, "as natural as it is noble" (*Atlanta Journal and Constitution*). [MA]

4587 Onetti, Juan Carlos. No man's land. Translated by Peter Bush. London: Quartet Books, 1994. 277 p.

Might the limited readership Juan Carlos Onetti has found in English owe to an inadequate presentation of his work, as well as to the lack of critical interest, Onetti's style, and the bleakness of his "outdated" world (*TLS, The Times Literary Supplement*, 30 December 1994)? In this translation of *Tierra de nadie* (Madrid, Editorial Debate, 1992), Peter Bush conveys both style and world well. Biographical paragraph and plot summary on dust jacket provide the only "introduction." [CM]

4588 Pacheco, José Emilio. You will die in a distant land. Translated by Elizabeth Umlas. Coral Gables, Fla.: North-South Center, Univ. of Miami, 1991. 175 p. (Letras de oro)

This translation of *Morirás lejos* (first published in 1967) won the 1988–89 Letras de Oro prize. Includes a very brief translator's note and a set of annotations on selected historical references, terms, and texts incorporated or evoked in the novel. Umlas' work is careful but uneven with respect to register and syntax. (For annotation of 2nd, revised edition of original work, see *HLAS 42:5202*.) [CM]

4589 Parra, Marco Antonio de la. The secret holy war of Santiago de Chile: a novel. Translated by Charles Philip Thomas. New York: Interlink Books, 1994. 319 p. (Emerging voices)

Creative colloquial response to challenge of translating a romping parody of politics and psyche in a Chile that is "almost a country . . ." However, this translation of *La secreta guerra santa de Santiago de Chile* (Santiago: Planeta, 1989), a bestseller by a playwright censored under Pinochet, lacks an introduction to bring full dimensions of satire and slapstick within reader's grasp. [MA]

4590 Parra, Teresa de la. Iphigenia: the diary of a young lady who wrote because she was bored. Translation by Bertie Acker. Introduction by Naomi Lindstrom. Austin: Univ. of Texas Press, 1993. 354 p.: bibl. (The Texas Pan American series)

Acker successfully recreates the intimate, chatty, "hyper-feminine" orality of a young woman in search of herself in stifling Caracas society of the 1920s. This first English version of *Ifigenia; diario de una señorita que escribió porque se fastidiaba* (Paris: Bendelac, 1928), based on translator's composite of several editions, includes informative essay by Lindstrom. [MA]

4591 Piglia, Ricardo. Artificial respiration. Translated by Daniel Balderston. Durham, N.C.: Duke Univ. Press, 1994. 229 p.: bibl. (Latin America in translation/en traducción/em tradução)

Outstanding translation of *Respiración artificial* (Buenos Aires: Pomaire, 1982), a complex and important novel published during the Argentine military dictatorship that focuses on the violence, history, and literature of that country. Short introduction and ample notes by Balderston accompany the text, making it particularly good for classroom use. [KR]

4592 Ponce de León, N. Baccino. Five black ships: a novel of the discoverers. Translated by Nick Caistor. New York: Harcourt Brace, 1994. 347 p.

Translation of *Maluco* (Barcelona: Seix Barral, 1990), 1989 winner of Casa de las Américas prize. Fictionalized account of Magellan's voyage to the Spice Islands is in the form of a letter sent by Magellan's buffoon to the Emperor Carlos V. Excellent translation

by Caistor captures archaic language in readable flow. No locating materials or information; possibly difficult for uninitiated readers to follow. [KR]

4593 Prado, Pedro. Alsino. Translated by Guillermo I. Castillo-Feliú. New York: P. Lang, 1994. 191 p. (American university studies. Series XXII. Latin American literature, 0895–0490; 21)

This first English version of *Alsino* (Santiago: Nascimento, 1928), a 1920 Chilean allegory, needs thorough revision. Castillo-Feliú adheres so closely to Prado's syntax and lexicon that English becomes difficult and unnatural in its heavy reliance on cognates and retention of untranslated words. Typographical and format problems also detract. Not recommended for classroom use. [MA]

4594 Rulfo, Juan. Pedro Páramo. Translated by Margaret Sayers Peden. Foreword by Susan Sontag. Evanston, Ill.: Northwestern Univ. Press, 1992. 1 v.

Peden has been praised highly by most reviewers for conveying the lyricism and complex simplicity of *Pedro Páramo* (see *HLAS 19:4938*), and for restoring the omissions in Lysander Kemp's translation (New York: Grove Press, 1959). Susan Sontag's foreword provides minimal introductory information and is no doubt appropriate for the general public; scholars, students, and teachers may still have need for a critical edition of this novel in English. [CM]

4595 Saer, Juan José. The event. Translated by Helen R. Lane. London; New York: Serpent's Tail, 1995. 196 p.

La ocasión (see *HLAS 52:3865*) poeticizes the ebb of consciousness, memory, and perspective as a magician migrates to the *pampas.* Lane's fine translation captures the sweep and tension of the layered syntax that is the hallmark of this Argentine-born author's haunting allegories, although this work received mixed reviews (*The Washington Post, Kirkus Reviews*). [MA]

4596 Saer, Juan José. Nobody nothing never. Translated by Helen R. Lane. London: Serpent's Tail, 1994. 218 p.

Translation of *Nadie nada nunca* (México: Siglo XXI Editores, 1980), a haunting novel of violence and sensuality in the Argentine countryside by one of that country's most important contemporary authors.

Lane's beautiful translation captures the sultry, slow-moving atmosphere of summer on the Paraná River as well as Saer's lyrical prose style. No notes or introduction. [KR]

4597 Scorza, Manuel. Garabombo, the Invisible. Translated by Ana-Marie Aldaz. New York: P. Lang, 1994. 230 p. (American university studies. Series XXII. Latin American literature, 0895–0490; 22)

Translation of *Garabombo, el Invisible* (Barcelona: Monte Avila, 1978), a novel that fictionalizes the true story of an uprising of Andean peasants, by important, insufficiently translated Peruvian writer. Useful locating introduction and glossary by the translator explain local terminology; translation does a good job in preserving cultural context. [KR]

4598 Sepúlveda, Luis. The old man who read love stories. Translated by Peter Bush. New York: Harcourt Brace, 1994. 131 p.

The felicitous blend of story-telling and finely-wrought prose found in *Un viejo que leía novelas de amor* (see *HLAS 54:4058*) has been well translated here. However, contains no supplementary material, introduction, or annotations, and omits original prologue by Juan Benito Argüelles. Named "Outstanding Translation of the Year" (1994) by American Literary Translators Association. [CM]

4599 Taibo, Paco Ignacio. Four hands. Translated by Laura C. Dail. New York: St. Martin's Press, 1994. 378 p.

In *Cuatro manos* (Managua: Editorial Vanguardia, 1990), Taibo's protagonist, like Taibo himself, presents a translator with two main challenges. One, a highly idiomatic, journalistic prose, Dail has met well. The other, which she has met far less successfully, is a narrative sprinkled with instances of "lingusitic imperialism," in which English turns up frequently and significantly in the Spanish. The omission of Taibo's brief author's note in the original is regrettable. [CM]

4600 Taibo, Paco Ignacio. Life itself. Translated by Beth Henson. New York: Mysterious Press, 1994. 209 p.

Translation of *La vida misma* (México: Planeta, 1987), an entertaining work by the well-known writer of detective novels. Au-

thor combines political satire of Mexico's government with a plot involving a writer much like himself. Henson's deft translation successfully communicates the Mexican context, aided by author's explanatory notes directed to the non-Mexican reader. [KR]

4601 Taibo, Paco Ignacio. No happy ending. Translated by William I. Neuman. New York: Mysterious Press, 1993. 175 p.

Neuman's inventive, idiomatic translation of *No habrá final feliz* (México: Planeta, 1989) includes neither notes nor introduction, but would provide fine reading for courses in literature and the social sciences. Bits of explanatory information have been worked into the translation, which also contains fragments of Spanish that make contemporary Mexico accessible in its own words. [CM]

4602 Tizón, Héctor. The man who came to a village. Translated by Miriam Frank. London: Quartet Books, 1993. 120 p.

El hombre que llegó a un pueblo (Buenos Aires: Legasa, 1988), a short novel set in the northern provinces of Argentina in the early decades of this century, has a storytelling-like tone of detachment. Skillfully translated into Frank's British English, but with no accompanying materials to explain context and historical references contained in author's notes. [KR]

4603 Urzagasti, Jesús. In the land of silence. Translated by Kay Pritchett. Fayetteville: Univ. of Arkansas Press, 1994. 366 p.

Pritchett briefly introduces her competent rendition of *En el país del silencio* (La Paz: Hisbol, 1987), a work cast in three alternating narrative personae. However, the obtuse denseness of the original style sorely tries the reader's endurance of such heavy prose by this Bolivian author from the Gran Chaco region. [MA]

4604 Valenzuela, Luisa. Bedside manners. Translated by Margaret Jull Costa. London; New York: High Risk Books/Serpent's Tail, 1995. 121 p.

Excellent translation of the Argentine Valenzuela's *Realidad nacional desde la cama* (see *HLAS 54:4160*), a short, somewhat absurdist novel dealing with the persistance of military dominance in a newly democratic country. Translator does a very good job with local details and dialect. Text is unaccompanied by any supporting material other than a short explicatory note on the flap. [KR]

Essays, Interviews, and Reportage

4605 Agosin, Marjorie. A cross and a star: memoirs of a Jewish girl in Chile. Translated by Celeste Kostopulos-Cooperman. Albuquerque: Univ. of New Mexico Press, 1995. 179 p.: ill.

Translation of *Sagrada memoria* (Santiago: Editorial Cuarto Propio, 1994), in which Agosin assumes the voice of a young girl to narrate the story of her mother's childhood and youth in southern Chile. Family pictures enhance the text, which treats Chilean antisemitism before, during, and after World War II. Translation is absorbing despite occasional awkwardness. Useful translator's locating introduction. For historian's comment see item **2868**. [KR].

4606 Allende, Isabel. Paula. Translated by Margaret Sayers Peden. New York: HarperCollins Publishers, 1995. 330 p.

Translation of best-selling account (see item **3768**) of the illness, coma, and death of author's daughter during 1992, presented as an autobiographical retelling of the Allende family's history. Author also discusses writing and the inspiration for her novels. Distinct "magical" cast to a text that is gripping, though long. Well-translated by Peden. [KR]

4607 Arenas, Reinaldo. Before night falls. Translated by Dolores M. Koch. New York: Viking, 1993. 317 p.

Arenas' memoir *Antes que anochezca* (see *HLAS 54:3849*) was begun before he left Cuba from Mariel and finished shortly before his death in 1990. Emphasizes political, literary, and sexual themes; narration often verges on the hyperbolic but is always compelling. Koch's generally good translation inserts occasional bracketed notes into the text. [KR]

4608 Cabrera Infante, Guillermo. Mea Cuba. Translated by Kenneth Hall with the author. New York: Farrar, Straus, Giroux, 1994. 503 p.: index.

Translation of collection of articles originally published between 1968–72 (see *HLAS 54:3821*) treating Cuban author's political views of his homeland and experiences living in exile. Written with Cabrera Infante's trademark wordplay and wit; well translated

to capture his humor. Occasional footnotes and index are helpful. [KR]

4609 Galeana, Benita. Benita. Translated by Amy Diane Prince. Pittsburgh, Pa.: Latin American Literary Review Press, 1994. 175 p. (Discoveries)

Translation of memoirs written in 1940 (see *HLAS 6:4139*) by a legendary Mexican Communist born in 1907. Fragmentary story is rich with details of political and cultural life of early decades of this century. Effective translation does a good job with frequent colloquial dialogue. Edition includes anecdotal introduction by Elena Poniatowska. [KR]

4610 Galeano, Eduardo H. We say no: chronicles, 1963–1991. Translated by Mark Fried *et al.* New York: Norton, 1992. 317 p.

Translation of *Nosotros decimos no* (Madrid: Siglo Veintiuno de España, 1989), work includes 33 essays ranging from five to 25 pages in length, arranged chronologically. Topics concern all of Latin America, focusing especially on human rights and cultural issues. Excellent translations from Cedric Belfrage, Asa Zatz, and others. Occasional notes help explain political and historical references. [KR]

4611 Juana Inés de la Cruz, Sor. The answer: including a selection of poems = La respuesta. Critical edition and translation by Electa Arenal and Amanda Powell. New York: Feminist Press at the City Univ. of New York, 1994. 196 p.: bibl., index.

Bilingual, annotated edition of 17th-century Mexican writer's famous 1691 letter to the Bishop of Puebla. Extensive introduction and notes provide historical background. Translators' gendered approach to the text and their polemical stance on its interpretation are clearly explained. Includes selection of Sor Juana's poetry. [KR]

4612 Molloy, Sylvia. Signs of Borges. Translated and adapted by Oscar Montero in collaboration with the author. Durham, N.C.: Duke Univ. Press, 1994. 142 p.: bibl., index. (Latin America in translation/en traducción/ em tradução. Post-contemporary interventions.)

Originally published as *Las letras de Borges* (see *HLAS 42:5599*), Molloy's book is one of the best-regarded critical studies ever written on the Argentine author. A brilliant consideration of the tensions present in a wide variety of Borges' texts. Excellent, lucid translation; brief footnotes, index. [KR]

4613 Poniatowska, Elena. Nothing, nobody: the voices of the Mexico City earthquake. Translated, with a foreword, by Aurora Camacho de Schmidt and Arthur Schmidt. Philadelphia: Temple Univ. Press, 1995. 327 p.: ill., index, map. (Voices of Latin American life)

Translation of *Nada, nadie: las voces del temblor* (see *HLAS 52:3495*), testimony compiled by the author in the aftermath of the 1985 earthquake, offers an emotional, panoramic view of Mexico City and its inhabitants. Translation generally succeeds, with occasional awkwardness. Historical preface, maps, and glossary make text especially suitable for classroom use. [KR]

4614 Torres, Olga Beatriz. Memorias de mi viaje = Recollections of my trip. Translated by Juanita Luna-Lawhn. Albuquerque: Univ. of New Mexico Press, 1994. 142 p.: bibl., map.

Unusual bilingual edition of letters written by a 13-year-old Mexican girl to her aunt, published in 1918 in *El Paso del Norte*, a newspaper for Mexicans living in Texas. Luna-Lawhn's translation preserves Torres' own bilingualism developing during her trip and reflecting the border experience. Useful locating introduction and bibliography. [KR]

4615 Tula, María Teresa. Hear my testimony: María Teresa Tula, human rights activist of El Salvador. Translated and edited by Lynn Stephen. Boston: South End Press, 1994. 240 p.: bibl., ill., map.

Moving, courageous story told by activist organizer living in Washington, DC since 1987. Editor follows with several chapters on Salvadoran context. Also provides essay reflecting on the politics of *testimonio* production. Very good for classroom use. [KR]

TRANSLATIONS FROM THE PORTUGUESE
Poetry

4616 Cabral de Melo Neto, João. Selected poetry, 1937–1990. Edited by Djelal Kadir. Translated by Elizabeth Bishop *et al.* Hanover, N.H.: Univ. Press of New England;

Wesleyan Univ. Press, 1994. 200 p. (Wesleyan poetry)

At last, a comprehensive bilingual edition representing all stages of Cabral de Melo's poetry, with translations (varying considerably in quality) by Elizabeth Bishop, Djelal Kadir, Galway Kinnell, W.S. Merwin, Alastair Reid, Ricardo Sternberg, Richard Zenith, and others. Work draws on the translations of Cabral de Melo's poems in Elizabeth Bishop's and Emanuel Brasil's coedited *An anthology of twentieth-century Brazilian poetry* (Middletown, Conn.: Wesleyan Univ. Press, 1972, see *HLAS 40:7830*). The selection, however, is debatable, especially in its failure to include in their entirety some of Cabral de Melo's most famous long poems. [DP]

4617 Enfim—nós: escritoras negras brasileiras contemporâneas = Finally—us: contemporary black Brazilian women writers. Portuguese language texts selected and edited by Miriam Alves. English language texts edited and translated by Carolyn Richardson Durham. Colorado Springs, Colo.: Three Continents Press, 1995. 258 p.: bibl., ill.

Bilingual edition represents work of 17 contemporary poet-activists including editor Miriam Alves. The selection of texts by these little-known poets stresses Afro-Brazilian identity; introduction emphasizes the struggle to document black women's literary contributions. Translations are for the most part readable and accurate, but the quality of the poems themselves is very uneven. [DP]

Miketen, Antonio Roberval *et al.* Paths of integration: an anthology of poetry. See item **4521.**

Brief Fiction and Theater

4618 Coutinho, Edilberto. Bye, bye soccer. Translated by Wilson Loria. Introduction by Elzbieta Szoka. Edited by Joe W. Bratcher. Austin, Tex.: Host Pub., 1994. 123 p.

Coutinho's prize-winning 1980 collection *Maracanã, adeus* (La Habana: Casa de las Américas, 1980, see *HLAS 44:6018*), 11 tales of soccer and politics, is at last available in English. Translated in a humorous and aggressive style that conveys the considerable bite of the original and nicely captures its flavor and energy, but Loria also takes some extraordinary and inexplicable liberties with the original. [DP]

4619 Lins, Osman. Nine, novena. Translated and with an introduction by Adria Frizzi. Los Angeles: Sun & Moon Press, 1995. 276 p. (Sun & Moon classics; 104)

Frizzi's excellent introduction helps orient the reader to Lins' complex and innovative fiction. Her considerable skills as a translator are apparent in these nine challenging stories, a collection originally published as *Nove, novena* (see *HLAS 32:4743*). The translations are in every respect worthy of the original, faithful but also creative and eminently readable. [DP]

Novels

4620 Felinto, Marilene. The women of Tijucopapo. Translated and with an afterword by Irene Matthews. Lincoln: Univ. of Nebraska Press, 1994. 132 p.: bibl. (Latin American women writers)

Matthews' illuminating commentary on the problems of translating *As mulheres de Tijucopapo* (see *HLAS 50:4171*), author's first novel, precedes the text, and an insightful short essay follows it. Translation succeeds in capturing the raw, often awkward, always striking tone of the novel, which is part Bildungsroman, part stream-of-consciousness meditation. [DP]

4621 Hatoum, Milton. The tree of the seventh heaven. Translated by Ellen Watson. New York: Atheneum; Toronto: Maxwell Macmillan Canada; New York: Maxwell Macmillan International, 1994. 210 p.

Hatoum's prize-winning 1989 novel, originally titled *Relato de um certo oriente* (São Paulo: Companhia das Letras, 1989), is a lyrical story of a family of Lebanese immigrants in Manaus, told by multiple narrators. Watson's eloquent translation is faithful to the mood and tone of the original. A fascinating work, evocative and multilayered, beautifully rendered in English. [DP]

4622 Lins, Osman. The queen of the prisons of Greece. Translated by Adria Frizzi. Normal, Ill.: Dalkey Archive Press, 1995. 186 p.: bibl., ill. (World literature series)

This translation of *A rainha dos cárceres da Grécia* (see *HLAS 40:7416*), Lins' last novel, published two years before his

death, is the second work by Lins that translator Adria Frizzi brought out in 1995. A complex and difficult novel written in a postmodernist spirit, reminiscent of Nabokov's *Pale fire* in its untiring self-reflexivity, work is excellently translated in Frizzi's inventive yet faithful rendition. [DP]

4623 Luft, Lya Fett. The red house. Translated by Giovanni Pontiero. Manchester, England: Carcanet Press, 1994. 182 p.

Luft's novel *Exílio* (see *HLAS 52:4552*), a haunting and surrealist exploration by an unidentified woman narrator, is movingly translated by the late Giovanni Pontiero. Luft's prose—incisive, poetic, and cruel—is compellingly recreated by Pontiero, whose English version is faithful to the evocative hues and rhythms of the original. [DP]

4624 Ribeiro, Edgard Telles. I would have loved him if I had not killed him. Translated by Margaret A. Neves. New York: St. Martin's Press, 1994. 199 p.

O criado-mudo (São Paulo: Editora Brasiliense, 1991) is a fascinating, multilayered novel of past and present, of love and revenge. Neves' translation, sensationally retitled, reads beautifully; but in fact she has taken some surprising editorial liberties with the original, omitting phrases and passages and adding explanations. [DP]

4625 Ribeiro, João Ubaldo. The lizard's smile. Translated by Clifford E. Landers. New York: Atheneum; Toronto: Maxwell Macmillan Canada; New York: Maxwell Macmillan International, 1994. 355 p.

A very fluent, readable, and faithful translation of *O sorriso do lagarto* (Rio de Janeiro: Editora Nova Fronteira, 1989), a funny, clever, and sexy novel. Ribeiro's reputation abroad is growing, not surprisingly given the exuberance and inventiveness of his prose, ably captured by Landers, a talented translator. [DP]

4626 Santiago, Silviano. Stella Manhattan. Translated by George Yúdice. Durham, N.C.: Duke Univ. Press, 1994. 212 p.

A readable but at times careless English rendition of Santiago's melodramatic novel *Stella Manhattan* (Rio de Janeiro: Editora Nova Fronteira, 1985), which treats gay life and political passions in New York's community of Brazilian exiles during the dictatorship. The special characteristics of the Portuguese (e.g., subject-less verbs, which better capture the sexual ambiguity of the novel's title character) are valiantly dealt with in the English. [DP]

Essays, Interviews, and Reportage

4627 Veríssimo, Luís Fernando. Chronicles. Translated by Nelson Vieira. (*Brasil/ Porto Alegre*, 7:11, 1994, p. 93–97)
Translations of two *crônicas* from his work *O gigolô das palavras* (see *HLAS 50: 4002*) illustrate well the style and subject matter of this leading author. [C. Perrone]

BIBLIOGRAPHY, THEORY, AND PRACTICE

4628 Aparicio, Frances R. Versiones, interpretaciones, creaciones: instancias de la traducción literaria en Hispanoamérica en el siglo veinte. Gaithersburg, Md. Ediciones Hispamérica, 1991. 193 p.: bibl.
Four essays provide a thorough, insightful introduction to literary translation in contemporary Spanish America. Principal topics: translation practice during *El Modernismo*; translation as an activity integral to the aesthetics of Octavio Paz, Jorge Luis Borges, and Julio Cortázar; Spanish-American translations of European and North American literature. [CM]

4629 Barnstone, Willis. The poetics of translation: history, theory, practice. New Haven, Conn.: Yale Univ. Press, 1993. 302 p.: bibl., index.
A translator well known to readers of Latin American literature in English translation for his work with Jorge Luis Borges and others, Barnstone has written an extensive commentary on the "basic principles and problems of translation." His examples are drawn mainly from two "paradigms:" Biblical translation and the translation of classical literature. [CM]

Brotherston, Gordon. Book of the fourth world: reading the Native Americas through their literature. See item **401.**

4630 Coloquio Chileno-Argentino de Traducción Literaria, 1st, Santiago, 1988? Sobre la traducción literaria en Hispanoamérica: actas. Edición de Patricia Hörmann Villagrán y M. Isabel Diéguez Morales. San-

tiago: Pontifica Univ. Católica de Chile, Facultad de Letras, Instituto de Letras, Depto. de Traducción, 1988. 104 p.: bibl.
Proceedings contain 11 articles. Topics include translation in general (such as Valentín García Yebra's "Sobre la Traducción Literaria") and individual translation projects. A joint piece, "El Escritor y el Traductor," by Chilean poet Raúl Zurita and Jack Schmitt, his North American translator, is of particular interest; their comments deal with preparation of the translation of *Anteparaíso* (see *HLAS 50:4262*). [CM]

4631 Díaz Arciniega, Víctor. Oficio y beneficio: traductores y editores en el FCE. (*Relaciones/Zamora*, 14:56, otoño 1993, p. 75–121)
In this printing of a chapter from his book *Historia de la Casa: el Fondo de Cultura Económica, 1934–1994* (México: FCE, 1994), Víctor Díaz Arciniega surveys and describes in depth translation's role in the Fondo de Cultura Económica. In so doing, he chronicles the history of translation theory and practice in Mexico, and provides a thorough commentary and documentary. [CM]

4632 Frost, Elsa Cecilia. De la humildad y el esplendor de la traducción: don Agustín Millares Carlo, 1893–1978. (*Relaciones/Zamora*, 14:56, otoño 1993, p. 9–25)
Augustín Millares Carlo exemplifies well the valuable role played in Mexico by Spanish intellectuals after the Spanish Civil War. Soon after his arrival, this philologist, historian, paleographer, librarian, and translator was teaching Latin, publishing new editions of his writings, and preparing numerous translations. Frost catalogs these translations, evaluating some. [CM]

4633 Mignolo, Walter. The darker side of the Renaissance: literacy, territoriality, and colonization. Ann Arbor: Univ. of Michigan Press, 1995. 426 p.: bibl., ill., index, maps.
Although Mignolo works with colonial texts, his work represents a significant contribution to contemporary translation theory and practice. This is particularly true in the case of Latin America, where the colonial past is continually present in all literary genres. [CM]

4634 Payne, Johnny. Conquest of the new word: experimental fiction and translation in the Americas. Austin: Univ. of Texas

Press, 1993. 292 p.: bibl., index. (The Texas Pan American series)

Although translation practice or product as conventionally defined is only one of Johnny Payne's concerns here, his effort to redefine translation within a "broader cultural emphasis" yields a provocative study of recent fiction in the US and Latin America. Moreover, the introduction and first chapter offer incisive comments about the Boom writers in English-language translations. [CM]

4635 Pérez Martínez, Herón. Alfonso Reyes y la traducción en México. (*Relaciones/Zamora*, 14:56, otoño 1993, p. 27–74)

Offers comprehensive discussion of Alfonso Reyes' extensive work as a translation critic, theorist, and practitioner. Pérez Martínez describes Reyes' translation activities; examines his methods with respect to those of other theorists, particularly E.A. Nida, Ch.R. Taber, and José Gaos; and analyzes Reyes' translations in the context of Reyes' own theories, [CM]

4636 *Translation Review*. Richardson: Univ. of Texas at Dallas.

Translation Review often contains essays, reviews, and interviews that will interest translators, scholars, teachers, and readers of Latin American literature. For example, interviews with Edith Grossman (No. 41) and Helen Lane (No. 47) have appeared in recent issues. [CM]

4637 Venuti, Lawrence. The translator's invisibility: a history of translation. London; New York: Routledge, 1995. 353 p.: bibl., index. (Translation studies)

Many of Venuti's comments about theories and practices that enable a translator to "counter the [prevailing] strategy of fluency" are relevant to the translation of Latin American literature. Venuti also works with some specific examples from Latin America, in particular the fiction of Julio Cortázar and the reception it received in North America. [CM]

4638 Wilson, Jason. Literal translations: recent Spanish American and Spanish poetry in English translation. (*in* Periplus: poetry in translation. Delhi, India: Oxford Univ. Press, 1993, p. 176–189)

Wilson's comments—brief but refreshingly candid—focus on several poets rela-

tively well known in English, among them Ariel Dorfman, Ernesto Cardenal, and César Vallejo. Wilson also offers some evaluations (for example, of Eliot Weinberger's work with César Vallejo, and of Myralyn Allgood's translations of Rosario Castellanos as compared with those of Maureen Ahern). [CM]

JOURNAL ABBREVIATIONS

Acta Lit. Acta Literaria. Instituto de Lenguas, Univ. de Concepción. Concepción, Chile.

Am. Anthropol. American Anthropologist. American Anthropological Assn., Washington.

Bol. Inst. Riva-Agüero. Boletín del Instituto Riva-Agüero. Pontificia Univ. Católica del Perú. Lima.

Brasil/Porto Alegre. Brasil = Brazil. Pontifícia Univ. Católica do Rio Grande do Sul. Porto Alegre, Brazil.

Colon. Lat. Am. Rev. Colonial Latin American Review. Simon H. Rifkind Center for the Humanities, Dept. of Romance Languages, City College of New York. New York.

Cuad. Hispanoam. Cuadernos Hispanoamericanos. Instituto de Cultura Hispánica. Madrid.

Cuba. Stud. Cuban Studies. Univ. of Pittsburgh, Center for Latin American Studies. Pittsburgh, Penn.

Estud. Filol. Estudios Filológicos. Univ. Austral de Chile, Facultad de Filosofía y Humanidades. Valdivia, Chile.

Fénix/Lima. Fénix: Revista de la Biblioteca Nacional del Perú. Biblioteca Nacional. Lima.

Folk/Copenhagen. Folk: Journal of the Danish Ethnographic Society. Danish Ethnographic Society. Copenhagen.

Hispamérica/Gaithersburg. Hispamérica. Gaithersburg, Md.

Histórica/Lima. Histórica. Pontificia Univ. Católica del Perú, Depto. de Humanidades. Lima.

Int. Q. International Quarterly. International Quarterly, Inc. Tallahassee, Fla.

Invest. Ens. Investigaciones y Ensayos. Academia Nacional de la Historia. Buenos Aires.

LARR. Latin American Research Review. Latin American Research Review Board. Univ. of New Mexico, Albuquerque, N.M.

Lat. Am. Theatre Rev. Latin American Theatre Review. Univ. of Kansas, Center of Latin American Studies. Lawrence, Kan.

Lat. Rev. Books. The Latino Review of Books. State Univ. of New York at Albany (SUNY), Center for Latino, Latin American, and Caribbean Studies (CELAC). Albany, N.Y.

Lett. Am./Rome. Letterature d'America. Dipartimento di Studi Americani, Univ. di Roma; Bulzoni Editore. Rome.

Memoria/CEMOS. Memoria: Boletín de CEMOS. Centro de Estudios del Movimiento Obrero y Socialista. México.

MLN/Baltimore. MLN. Modern Language Notes. Johns Hopkins Univ. Press. Baltimore, Md.

NWIG. New West Indian Guide/Nieuwe West Indische Gids. KITLV Press. Leiden, The Netherlands.

Quad. Ibero-Am. Quaderni Ibero-Americani. Associazione per i Rapporti Culturali con la Spagna, il Portogallo e l'America Latina. Torino, Italy.

Relaciones/Zamora. Relaciones. El Colegio de Michoacán. Zamora, Mexico.

Rev. Can. Estud. Hisp. Revista Canadiense de Estudios Hispánicos. Asociación Canadiense de Hispanistas; Univ. of Toronto. Toronto, Canada.

Rev. Chil. Lit. Revista Chilena de Literatura. Univ. de Chile, Depto. de Literatura. Santiago.

Rev. Crít. Lit. Latinoam. Revista de Crítica Literaria Latinoamericana. Latinoamericana Editores. Lima.

Rev. Hist. Am. Revista de Historia de América. Instituto Panamericano de Geografía e Historia, Comisión de Historia. México.

Rev. Iberoam. Revista Iberoamericana. Instituto Internacional de Literatura Iberoamericana; Univ. de Pittsburgh. Pittsburgh, Penn.

Rev. Pensam. Centroam. Revista del Pensamiento Centroamericano. Centro de Investigaciones y Actividades Culturales. Managua.

Rev. USP. Revista USP. Coordenadoria de Comunicação Social (CCS), Univ. de São Paulo.

Transl. Rev. Translation Review. Univ. of Texas at Dallas. Richardson.

Translation/Columbia. Translation. The Translation Center, Columbia Univ., New York.

Tri-Quarterly/Evanston. Tri-Quarterly. Northwestern Univ., Evanston, Ill.

MUSIC

ROBERT STEVENSON, *Professor of Music, University of California, Los Angeles*

CROWNING THE BIENNIUM are three music encyclopedias, each of which devotes generous space to Latin American persons and topics: *The New Grove Dictionary of Opera*, 1992, *The New Grove Dictionary of Women Composers*, 1994 (published in the US in 1995 as the *Norton/Grove Dictionary of Women Composers*), and the first two Sachteil volumes of what is to become eventually a "new" 20-volume lexicon, *Die Musik in Geschichte und Gegenwart*. Impossible though it be for encyclopedia articles to carry authority unless they are based on cogent research articles, still it cannot be gainsaid that musician and layman alike begin their investigation (or even acquaintance) with most Latin American topics by consulting a dictionary. Both the 1992 and 1994 *New Grove* dictionaries contained so many Latin American entries that not even the present *HLAS* Music Section can begin to include them all. Nonetheless, the lexicon that will outdistance all other relevant encyclopedias will be the forthcoming multi-volume *Diccionario de la música española e hispanoamericana*, edited by Emilio Casares Rodicio (item **4643**), Ismael Fernández de la Cuesta (item **4656**), and José López-Calo (see *HLAS 54:5255*).

As for monumental publications, Aurelio Tello's 1994 edition of the Manuel de Zumaya=Sumaya's vernacular delights that are stored in the Oaxaca Cathedral music archive stirred universal admiration of both the music and the edition (item **4770**). The Gulbenkian Foundation's issue in 1990 of Robert Snow's edition of Gaspar Fernandes' Latin works (item **4777**) was similarly luxurious. Piotr Nawrot heaped honors on the 18th-century Latin repertory now stored at Concepción, Bolivia with his incandescent edition of vespers music sung and played by Indian musicians in the Jesuit reductions (item **4682**). Edited by Seoane and Eichmann, *Lírica colonial boliviana* (item **4685**) contained what may well be the earliest extant example of a Sor Juana Inés de la Cruz villancico set by a South American composer. The Mexican and Bolivian cultural authorities who financed the Tello, Seoane, and Nawrot editions—always the most altruistic of outlays—deserve warmest thanks and praise.

Nineteenth-century Latin American musicology benefited from the protracted investigations of the career of Chile's paramount touring virtuoso (by the editor of *Revista Musical Chilena*, Luis Merino Montero, item **4746**) and of Cuba's foremost African-descended celebrity (by Cristina Magaldi, item **4708**). Samuel Claro Valdés' posthumous "Chile" article in the second Sachteil volume of *Die Musik in Geschichte und Gegenwart* does his nation great honor (item **4741**). Published the year before his death, a biography of Rosita Renard (item **4742**) invites equally persuasive traversals of the triumphant careers of such other Latin American star performers as Guiomar Novaes, Angélica Morales, Bidú Sayão, and Fanny Anitúa.

Esperanza Pulido (d. 1991), founder-editor of *Heterofonía*, reaped the deserved tribute of an issue dedicated to her memory by Juan José Escorza, her distinguished successor in editing Mexico's longest running musical journal. In it, her *La mujer mexicana en la música* reached a second deserved edition (item **4788**). Only too surely does the Anglo-Saxon world need frequent reminding that not merely Mexican, but also Argentine, Brazilian, Chilean (Magdalena Vicuña Lyon leading the procession), and Venezuelan women (with Isabel Aretz and Teresa Carreño in the ascendant), shine among the brightest luminaries in their pantheons. In 1995, *Revista Musical Chilena* broke new ground with an issue entirely devoted to a woman folklorist (items **4750** and **4751**).

Succeeding Luis Jaime Cortez as director of the Mexican Centro Nacional de la Investigación, Documentación e Información, José Antonio Robles Cahero drew to his side as second in authority Ricardo Miranda, whose London doctoral dissertation (item **4652**) gave rise to the first volume of a long-needed biography of Jalisco's José Rolón. As valuable as is the article by the world's leading Carlos Chávez authority, former University of Miami dean Robert Parker (item **4786**), no less salutary have been biographies of such unfairly neglected Mexican figures as Vicente Teódulo Mendoza (item **4782**) and Eduardo Hernández Moncada (item **4774**). In Brazil, Vasco Mariz added to his lengthy publications list a biography of Cláudio Santoro (item **4711**). In his panegyric published in *Inter-American Music Review* (Vol. 14, No. 2, Winter/Spring 1995), he welcomes the biography of Brazil's most transcendent composer, Heitor Villa-Lobos (item **4697**), by Gerard Béhague—who continues editing *Revista Latinoamericana de Música/Latin American Music Review*, the one music periodical published in several languages that takes the whole domain of Latin America, past and present, as its rightful territory.

The Congress of the International Musicological Society (15th, Madrid, 1992) generated a body of papers published in two successive issues of *Revista de Musicología* (Madrid, Vol. 16, Nos. 1/2, 1993) under the superintendence of Spanish Musicological Society president Ismael Fernández de la Cuesta (e.g., items **4649** and **4703**). Two relevant US periodicals being published in English remained active during the biennium, *Inter-American Music Review* and *Ars Musica Denver*, the latter edited by Paul Laird. Barbara G. Valk continued as general editor of the *Hispanic American Periodicals Index (HAPI)*, a University of California, Los Angeles publication that annually lists more articles than can be annotated in *HLAS*.

The first half of the 1990s proved a particularly propitious period for not only the publication of a variety of relevant printed materials, but also for the launching of several best-selling commercial recordings (item **4678**). Previously, the Roger Wagner Chorale had pioneered with five LPs of Latin American classic polyphony— beginning in 1966 with the Angel album titled *Salve Regina*. Lustrous as were the Latin-texted beauties rescued by Roger Wagner (item **4664**), his albums lacked the marketing expertise that ensures lavish sales. This problem evanesced when not only the Latin repertory, but, much more cogently, the Spanish- and Portuguese-text enticements composed during the viceroyalties began being recorded on compact discs in America, in England, and on the Continent. The first-class production of *La púrpura de la rosa* (Lima, 1701) at the 1994 national meeting of the American Musicological Society in Minneapolis (item **4809**) at last awoke opinion-makers in the US to the magnificence of the earliest extant opera composed in the Western Hemisphere (item **4810**).

GENERAL

4639 Aviñoa, Xosé. Presència musical catalana a Amèrica. (*in* Jornades d'Estudis Catalano-Americans, *4th, Barcelona, Spain,* 1990. Actes. Barcelona: Generalitat de Catalunya, Comissió Amèrica i Catalunya, 1992, p. 157–164)

The national anthems of both Mexico and Chile were composed by Catalonians.

The most notable chapelmaster of colonial Chile was a Catalonian. A brilliant array of named Catalonians (to the present) includes some of the most noted figures in Latin American musical history. Their dates and chief activities are listed in chronological order.

4640 Béhague, Gerard. Amerika. (*in* Die Musik in Geschichte und Gegenwart. Kassel, Germany: Bärenreiter, 1994, Sachteil 1, columns 548- 567)

With his accustomed mastery, the author traverses the Western Hemisphere areas now comprising Latin America. After sections on pre-1492 musics, colonial vocal expressions, and folk musics influenced by aboriginal, Iberian, and African traditions, the article contains surveys of art-music through the 20th century, and concludes with an aperçu of distinctive Latin popular genres.

4641 Compositores de las Américas: datos biográficos y catálogos de sus obras. Edición de Efraín Paesky. Washington: Secretaria General, Organización de los Estados Americanos, 1993. 132 p.: music facsims., portraits.

Again possessing all the admirable qualities that distinguished the previous 19 volumes (bilingual text, composers' portraits, manuscript or printed musical excerpts), vol. 20 in the Composers of the Americas series (initiated in 1955), boasts several useful innovations, among them, information on recordings, list of abbreviations, and composers' addresses (when authorized). The 17 composers represent Argentina (1), Brazil (2), Chile (5), El Salvador (1), Mexico (2), Peru (3), Uruguay (1), Venezuela (1), and Puerto Rico (1).

4642 García Muñoz, Carmen. Códices coloniales con música. (*Rev. Inst. Invest. Musicol. Carlos Vega,* 11 : 1, 1990, p. 199–218)

The distinguished *directora* of this journal analyzes three collections of South American origin: 1) Fray Gregorio de Zuola's 500-page *Libro de varias curiosidades. Tesoro de diversas materias* housed in the Ricardo Rojas museum at Buenos Aires; 2) a tome containing 19 pieces of music sent to Madrid from Trujillo, Peru, by Baltasar Jaime Martínez Compañón y Bujanda who ruled Trujillo diocese 1779–89; and 3) a collection now held in the Archivo General de Indias at Seville containing nine vocal selections (AGI, Mapas, Planos, 200–201) composed by three Moxos

Indians in what is now the Bolivian Department of Beni and dispatched to Madrid by their governor Lázaro de Ribera in 1790. The latter collection was first described and facsimiles of its musical contents published in the Buenos Aires journal *Historia,* No. 15, in 1958. A synopsis of the present article appeared in *Inter-American Music Review* (Vol. 13, No. 1, Fall/Winter 1992, p. 115–116).

4643 García Muñoz, Carmen. La musicología hispanoamericana hoy. (*Rev. Inst. Invest. Musicol. Carlos Vega,* 12, 1992, p. 153–154)

Emilio Casares Rodicio, chief editor of the *Diccionario de la música española e hispanoamericana,* obtained the collaboration of 700 contributors. His gigantic enterprise rises without parallel in Spanish and Spanish-American lexicography.

4644 Hickmann, Ellen. Altamerika. (*in* Die Musik in Geschichte und Gegenwart. Kassel, Germany: Bärenreiter, 1994, Sachteil 1, columns 483–506, bibl., ill.)

The three areas in South America that have yielded the most organological information are southern Peru (Paracas/Nasca/Chincha cultures), northern Peru (Vicus/Moche/Chimu/Lambayeque cultures), and the Ecuadorian coast. Archaeological instruments found in Colombia include a profusion of vessel flutes with a mouthpiece and two to four fingerholes (Tairona culture). Among melodic instruments, Nasca panpipes 10cm to 1.30m in length, some with as many as 13 tubes, have often turned up in graves or on sacrificial altars. No giant panpipes resting on the ground have been found in Ecuador, but musicians in precious clothing played them. Huge straight trumpets decorated with menacing figures served the Nasca, straight and coiled trumpets with animal heads at the bell joints were used by the Moche. In Ecuadorian sites, no trumpets whatsoever have appeared. This dense article continues with descriptions of archaeological instruments found in Middle American sites.

4645 Hickmann, Ellen. Musik aus dem Altertum der Neuen Welt: archäologische Dokumente des Musizierens in präkolumbischen Kulturen Perus, Ekuadors und Kolumbiens. Frankfurt am Main; New York: P. Lang, 1990. 491 p.: bibl., ill., map.

In his 1653 *Historia del Nuevo Mundo* (modern edition, Biblioteca de Autores Españoles, 91–92 [1956], p. 270), Bernabé Cabo (1580–1657) commented on the Peruvian Indians' great variety of musical instruments played during their *taquis* (dances and songs performed equally on joyous and lugubrious occasions). Since no one practiced assiduously any of the instruments played at the *taquis*, their sound—said Cobo—betrayed no artistry. According to him, their drums (*huáncar*) came in large, medium, and small sizes. Made of a hollow log covered at both ends with thin, dried llama skin, the biggest was the size of a Spanish war drum and the least was the size of a small box. Despite quoting Cobo in an endnote (p. 467), Hickmann places little faith in European missionaries' accounts, no matter how lengthy and intimate their contacts with American indigenous populations. She intersperses photos of archaeological instruments, grouped in Hornbostel-Sachs order, with data on their places of origin, present habitat, materials used (clay, metal, bone), cultural contexts, coloration, and previous descriptive literature. Pitches when given in staff notations are modified by diacritics (plus- and minus-signs). She analyzes the sound spectrum of selected pitched instruments. Because so many archaeological instruments have fled to European museums and organological expertise such as Hickmann's costs a lifetime of specialized training in privileged institutions, a book such as hers can scarcely be written by stay-at-home native Andeans.

Iberian and Latin American Music Online. See item **44.**

4646 Katz, Israel J. In memoriam: Carleton Sprague Smith, 1905–1994. (*Inter-Am. Music Rev.*, 14:2, Winter/Spring 1995. p. 115–120, bibl.)

Smith, one of the chief musicologists and librarians of his epoch, profoundly intervened in Latin American music developments. Unlike Charles Seeger, who exalted only folk music south of the border, and rated all art music before Villa-Lobos, Chávez, and Ginastera as piddling and contemptible, Smith welcomed all phases of Western Hemisphere historic music as worthy of respect and frequently as deserving of admiration.

4647 Koegel, John. Recent recordings of Latin American colonial music. (*Newsl. Int. Hisp. Study Group*, 1:2, Winter 1995, p. 9–14)

With his unmatched sovereignty, the author (member of the Nebraska Wesleyan Univ. faculty in 1995) describes and evaluates the contents of four CDs: 1) *Masterpieces of Mexican polyphony* (Westminster Cathedral Choir, James O'Donnell, director, Hyperion CDA66330 [1990]); 2) *Nueva España: close encounters in the New World 1590–1690* (Boston Camerata, Joel Cohen, director, Erato CD2292-45977-2 [1993]); 3) *Música virreinal mexicana: siglos XVI y XVII* (Conjunto Vocal de Musica Antigua Ars Nova, Magda Zalles, director [1993]); and 4) *Mexican Baroque* (Chanticleer and Chanticleer Sinfonia, Joseph Jennings, director, Teldec 4509-96353-2 [1994]). The first CD contains works in Latin by Hernando Franco (1532–85), Juan Gutiérrez de Padilla (ca. 1592–1664), Francisco López Capillas (ca.1605–74), and Antonio de Salazar (ca. 1650–1715) as well as excellent notes by Bruno Turner, London proprietor and chief editor of the Mapa Mundi Performing editions. The less satisfactory notes accompanying the second CD betray nescience of recent scholarship. Both Zalles' and Cohen's groups availed themselves almost exclusively of vernacular festive works published in *Inter-American Music Review*, 7:1 (1985), an indebtedness suggesting the need for exploration of other archives than those at Mexico City, Oaxaca, and Puebla cathedrals. The fourth CD raises the problem of royalties desired by possessors of the music sources. *The Los Angeles Times* (Feb. 28, 1994) carried Abigail Goldman's story on Joseph Jennings and Louis Botto, Chanticleer's Conductor and Artistic Director, respectively.

4648 Kubik, Gerhard and **Tiago de Oliveira Pinto.** Afroamerikanische Musik. (*in* Die Musik in Geschichte und Gegenwart. Kassel, Germany: Bärenreiter, 1994, Sachteil 1, columns 194–262, bibl., photos)

Sections IV (South America), V (Caribbean), and VI (Central America) contain invaluable summaries organized under geographic units. Kubik's nonpareil domination of African modalities enabled him to identify what is distinctively African in the heritages of Brazil, Venezuela, Suriname, Guyana, the Antilles, and Guatemala. On an island like Martinique, for example, Kubik discovers the Arada as originating in west coast Dahomey (whence came their martial dances such as the *laghia*); the *calenda* bespoken by Jean-Baptiste Labat (1725) originated on the

Guinea coast. He reveals that an illustrated xylophone obtained by Isabel Aretz's now defunct Instituto Interamericano de Etnomusicología y Folklore at Caracas was obtained in 1975 from *negros de la costa* at Esmeraldas in Ecuador. Oliveira Pinto, a chief contributor to the Brazilian section, is copiously represented in the bibliography, his most recent article having appeared in 1992, "La musique dans le rite et la musique comme rite dans le condomblé brésilien" (in *Cahiers de Musiques Traditionelles 5: Musiques Rituelles*, Ateliers d'ethnomusicologie, p. 53–76).

4649 Kuss, Malena. The "invention" of America: encounter settings on the Latin American lyric stage. (*Rev. Musicol./ Madrid*, 16:1, 1993, p. 185–204, bibl., music)

Framed within illuminating discourse on Edmundo O'Gorman's *The invention of America* (Bloomington: Indiana Univ. Press, 1961) and Alejo Carpentier's novella, *Concierto barroco* (1974), Kuss concludes with an excerpt from the José Montes-Baguer film released by Westdeutscher Rundfunk Köln, SWF, SRG, and UNITEL in 1982, *Concierto barroco-Montezuma*. Kuss' two music examples derive from Aniceto Ortega del Villar's *episodio lirico, Guatimotzín* (premiered Sept. 13, 1871 with Enrico Tamberlick and Angela Peralta heading the cast), the first of which— the *tzotopizahuac* quoted in Ortega's "Danza Tlaxcalteca"—had bemused Otto Mayer-Serra in his *Música y músicos de Latinoamérica* (México: Editorial Atlante, 1947), p. 714.

Latin American Music Center, Indiana Univ. See item **45.**

Latin Music Online. See item **46.**

4650 Maehder, Jürgen. The representation of the "Discovery" on the opera stage. (*in* Musical repercussions of 1492. Edited by Carol E. Roberston. Washington: Smithsonian Institution Press, 1992, p. 257–287, bibl.)

Ending with a list of stage works (ca. 1600–1992)—not all performed and not all with assured music—this essay treats primarily of text. According to the author, all works for the musical stage produced before 1992 set librettos adopting a "Eurocentric viewpoint." Distortions of history ranged from the unintentional to the malevolent.

4651 Medina Alvarez, Angel. Perfil biobibliográfico del professor Emilio Casares. (*Inter-Am. Music Rev.*, 14:1, Spring/ Summer 1994, p. 141–147, bibl.)

Primus inter pares, Emilio Casares Rodicio (b. Vega de Espinareda, León province, Spain, Feb. 28, 1943) edits the multivolume *Diccionario de la música española e hispanoamericana* that has set Latin American musicology on a new high pitch. His journeys from Mexico to Chile have stimulated research that promises a dictionary of epochal value. His other formidable accomplishments gave rise to this biobibliographical article by his successor in the professorship of music history at Oviedo Univ.

4652 Moore, Robin. Directory of Latin American and Caribbean music theses and dissertations since 1988. (*Lat. Am. Music Rev.*, 14:1, Spring/Summer 1993, p. 145–171)

Each entry includes author's name, address, academic status, univ. dept., date of degree received (or expected), title, summary, and list of publications (if any). As samples of extremely valuable entries: Victoria Eli Rodríguez received her PhD at Humboldt Univ., Berlin, June 1987, with a thesis titled "La creación musical en Cuba después del triunfo de la Revolución (1959–1986);" Ricardo Miranda anticipated his PhD from City Univ., London, England, Oct. 1992, with a dissertation titled "A Mexican Voice from Zapotlán: the music of José Rolón."

4653 Moreno Chá, Ercilia. Bibliografía: centros de investigación y archivos sonoros de música tradicional en Latinoamérica. (*Lat. Am. Music Rev.*, 12:1, Spring/Summer 1991, p. 42–64.)

Expanded from "Research Centers and Sound Archives of Traditional Music in Latin America" (in *Fontes artis musicae*, Vol. 37, No. 2, April-June 1990, p. 179–191, a paper originally presented to the Bibliography Commission at a meeting of the International Association of Music Librarians Conference in Tokyo, Sept. 1988), this article is the fruit of a specially designed questionnaire sent to 83 centers of musical research throughout Latin America requesting information about their activities and locales.

4654 Moreno Chá, Ercilia. New research generated by the UMH Project: chordophones of traditional use in continental Latin America. (*Rev. Musicol./Madrid*, 16:2, 1993, p. 1095–1102)

Valuable, densely documented essay, superseding previously relevant scholarship.

4655 Pelinski, Ramón. "Yo es otro:" reflexiones sobre el encuentro musical entre Europa y América. (*Rev. Musicol./Madrid*, 16:1, 1993, p. 287–297, bibl.)

The Quincentennial of Columbus' first transatlantic voyage stimulated diverse evaluations: Todorov (1982) popularized the term "encounter," Lévi-Strauss (1990) called the voyage and its successors an "invasion," Galeano (1992) named it "murder of others." Musically, European modalities still reign supreme wherever anything of the art-music category prevails. Pelinski's thoughtful discourse includes abundant bibliographic references to Carpentier, Comte, Kuss, Maehden, and others.

4656 Rey García, Emilio. Ismael Fernández de la Cuesta: músico y maestro. (*Inter-Am. Music Rev.*, 13:1, Fall/Winter 1992, p. 99–107)

One of the supreme musicologists of the century, Fernández de la Cuesta has notably stimulated Latin American scholarship.

4657 Starr, S. Frederick. Bamboula!: the life and times of Louis Moreau Gottschalk. New York: Oxford Univ. Press, 1995. 564 p.: bibl., ill., index.

Diverging from previous biographies, the author gives proportionate space to Gottschalk's nine years in the Caribbean and South America. Fermin Moras, the mulatto amateur violinist picked up in Martinique who traveled everywhere as Gottschalk's bosom companion and valet during his last decade, was (according to the author) a blackguard, thief, and blackmailer. Gottschalk's slave-owning Jewish father kept a mulatto mistress by whom he had children before and after marrying Aimée Bruslé.

4658 Stevenson, Robert. Amerindian music. (*in* The Cambridge Encyclopedia of Latin America. Cambridge, England: Cambridge Univ. Press, 1992, p. 404–405, bibl., ill.)

Survey article emphasizes indigenous expressions in Mexico, Peru, and Brazil.

4659 Stevenson, Robert. Eleanor Hague, 1875–1954: pioneer Latin Americanist. (*Inter-Am. Music Rev.*, 14:1, Spring/Summer 1994, p. 57–66)

Biobibliography of the first scholar to publish a general history of Latin American music (Santa Ana, Calif.: The Fine Arts Press, 1934). A still valuable work.

4660 Stevenson, Robert. Ethnological impulses in the Baroque villancico. (*Inter-Am. Music Rev.*, 14:1, Spring/Summer 1994, p. 67–106, music)

Standard histories of the epoch, such as Manfred Bukofzer's *Music in the Baroque Era*, falsely label Iberian world 17th- and 18th-century works as retrogressive and archaic. This mistake arises from ignorance of the vernacular repertory. Musical examples appended to this article reveal the richness in Latin America of *villancicos* influenced by African and indigenous musical traditions.

4661 Stevenson, Robert. Gilbert Chase: 1906–1992. (*Inter-Am. Music Rev.*, 12: 2, Spring/Summer 1992, p. 121–122)

Born at Havana, Cuba, Sept. 4, 1906, Chase married Danish writer Kathleen Barentzen Dec. 27, 1929, and died Feb. 22, 1992 at Chapel Hill after many years as a victim of Alzheimer's disease. He was survived by his wife and three sons. From 1963–67 Chase served as music section contributor to the *Handbook of Latin American Studies.* A paramount bibliographer and polished prose writer, he began his lengthy publication career as a poet.

4662 Stevenson, Robert. Music. (*in* The Cambridge History of Latin America. Cambridge, England: Cambridge Univ. Press, 1994, vol. 11, p. 160–163)

Bibliographical essay itemizing publications dealing chiefly with the colonial period.

4663 Stevenson, Robert. Nicolas Slonimsky: centenarian lexicographer and musicologist. (*Inter-Am. Music Rev.*, 14:1, Spring/Summer 1994, p. 149–155.)

Gilbert Chase's acerbic review of Slonimsky's epochal *Music of Latin America* (1945) in the *Musical Quarterly* (Vol. 22, No. 1, Jan. 1946, p. 140–143), began thus: "The book is divided into three parts. The first might be described as a bureau of general misinformation, flamboyantly decorated with colorful but irrelevant examples of the author's rampant exhibitionism." This judgment, typical of Chase, has not countervailed the work's translation into Spanish, reprintings, a facsimile Da Capo Press issue in 1972, its continued presence in all public libraries, and its honored use in Latin American college and university courses.

4664 Stevenson, Robert. Roger Wagner: 1914–1992. (*Inter-Am. Music Rev.*, 12 : 2, Spring/Summer 1992, p. 125.)

Born at Le Puy, France, Jan. 16, 1914, Wagner died at Dijon, France (his mother's birthplace) Sept. 17, 1992. An incomparable conductor of Renaissance polyphony, Wagner directed the Roger Wagner Chorale and Sinfonietta in five LP's, beginning in 1966 with *Salve Regina: choral music of the Spanish New World* (Angel S36008) that for the first time in modern history exposed the sublime music created in Mexico and South America before 1800. Knighted by Paul VI in 1966, Wagner's inestimable services to Latin American historic music were magisterially reviewed and catalogued by Lester D. Brothers in *Latin American Music Review*, Vol. 5, No. 2, Fall/Winter 1984, p. 293–305.

ARGENTINA

4665 Arzruni, Sahan. Terzian, Alicia. (*in* New Grove Dictionary of Women Composers. New York: W.W. Norton, 1994, p. 458–459, bibl.)

Among the most widely traveled of Argentine notables, Terzian was born at Córdoba July 1, 1934 (not 1936 as stated in Rodolfo Arizaga's *Enciclopedia de la música argentina*, 1971, and in the *Dizionario enciclopedico universale della musica e dei musicisti*, Turin, 1988, vol. 8). Her activities as composer, musicologist, and conductor have brought her renown shared by few of her musical compatriots.

4666 Béhague, Gerard. Argentinien. (*in* Die Musik in Geschichte und Gegenwart. Kassel, Germany: Bärenreiter, 1994, Sachteil 1, columns 768–783; 793–804, bibl., music)

After a summary of Argentine political history by Juan Pedro Franze, the article surveys indigenous music in the Tierra del Fuego, Chaco, and northwest regions, and next turns to folk music of criollos and mestizos, their musical instruments, folk genres, folk dances, and African influence, in the Río de la Plata area. Juan Pedro Franze returns with a ten-column history of art music to 1850, Béhague ending the article with events to the present (including *Rock nacional*). The great length and detail in this article augur well for anticipated entries of other Organization of American States nations.

4667 Bra, Gererdo. ¿Dónde nació Carlos Gardel? (*Todo es Hist.*, 329, dic. 1994, p. 84–92, bibl., photo)

Despite enormous effort to make him an Uruguayan born in 1887, the author accepts the singer's birth date as Dec. 11, 1890 at Toulouse, his mother and eventual heir being Berthe Gardes, and his birth name being Charles Romuald Gardes. Whatever his circumstances of birth, he died, still unmarried, June 24, 1945 at Medellín, Colombia, victim of an air disaster.

4668 Chase, Gilbert and **Lionel Salter.** Ginastera, Alberto. (*in* New Grove Dictionary of Opera. New York: Grove's Dictionaries of Music, 1992, v. 2, p. 420–421, appendix, bibl.)

Argentina's most world-renowned composer left three operas: *Don Rodrigo* (Colón, July 24, 1964); *Bomarzo* (Washington, Lisner Auditorium, May 19, 1967); and *Beatrix Cenci* (Washington, Kennedy Center, Sept. 10, 1971). At his death in Geneva June 25, 1983, he was reportedly composing a fourth opera, *Barabbas*, begun in 1977.

4669 Franze, Juan Pedro. Buenos Aires. (*in* Die Musik in Geschichte und Gegenwart. Kassel, Germany: Bärenreiter, 1995, Sachteil 2, columns 235–239, bibl.)

For lack of assigned space, or for any other reason, this article lacks the impact expected from an author of Franze's stature. The bibliography omits crucial literature.

4670 Frega, Ana Lucía. Mujeres de la música. Buenos Aires: Planeta, 1994. 140 p., 8 p. of plates: bibl., ill., music. (Mujeres argentinas)

Profiles of 25 Argentine singers, 11 instrumentalists, 8 promoters, and 11 educators by a renowned lecturer, administrator, and pedagogue who from 1990–92 belonged to the Board of Directors of the International Society for Music Education. Some of the women are listed in more than one category, but all are deceased.

4671 García Brunelli, Omar. La obra de Astor Piazzolla y su relación con el tango como especie de música popular urbana. (*Rev. Inst. Invest. Musicol. Carlos Vega*, 12, 1992, p. 155–221, bibl., music)

Born at Mar del Plata, March 11, 1921, Piazzolla died at Buenos Aires July 6, 1992. Prepared in 1988, this report begins with a chronology that includes the following data: from 1925–30 and 1932–36 his family lived in New York City. From 1940–46 he studied composition, orchestration, and counterpoint with Ginastera, and in 1955 was a pupil of Nadia Boulanger in Paris. He resided in New York City from 1958–60 and in Europe in 1973. Despite these absences, he made the *bandoneón* his virtuoso vehicle, and presented himself as a tango composer. In 1951 he recorded the tangos *Chiqué, Triste, La comparsita,* and the vals *Dedé.* The author continues with analyses, ending with a paragraph on his "harvest time" decade of world touring.

4672 García Muñoz, Carmen. Juan José Castro. (*Rev. Inst. Invest. Musicol. Carlos Vega,* 12, 1992, p. 137–152, bibl.)

With her usual accuracy and comprehensiveness the author classifies Castro's 78 compositions (not counting unfinished works, tangos, school songs, juvenilia) under the following headings: 4 operas, 2 ballets, 1 score of incidental music for a stage work, 2 for films, 14 orchestral works, 8 chamber compositions, 17 piano pieces, 1 *bandoneón* work (*Sonatina campestre,* 1948, in 3 movements dedicated to Alejandro Barletta), 19 songs with piano accompaniment, 2 unaccompanied choral works (written in New York on Spanish popular themes in 1941), 1 choral work for basses, harp, and piano (*Tenèbres,* 1947, Paul Claudel text). Aided by composer's widow, Raquel Aguirre de Castro, author also itemizes 5 articles and 18 poems published in *Ars.*

García Muñoz, Carmen. Lauro Ayestarán (Montevideo, 9-VII-1913; 22-VII-1966). See item **4814.**

4673 Goyena, Héctor Luis. Los instrumentos musicales arqueológicos del Museo Dr. Eduardo Casanova de Tilcara, Jujuy. (*Rev. Inst. Invest. Musicol. Carlos Vega,* 12, 1992, p. 111–135, bibl., table, ill.)

In 1987 the Organization of American States joined the Argentine Instituto Nacional de Musicología in a project devoted to the assessment of musical instruments in the museums of Argentina, Paraguay, and Uruguay. Goyena's visit to Tilcara in the far north of Argentina netted his catalogue of idiophones and aerophones classified according to the Hornbostel-Sachs scheme. The larger of the two Nasca syrinxes yields the series f#, a#, c1#, d1#, f1#, a1, c2#, d2#, f2#, g2, a2#, and c3 (the latter sounding three octaves above middle C). Each tube was independently fashioned before being joined to its neighbors in a clay covering. The stone four-tube syrinx found at the Tilcara pre-Columbian fort belongs to the Humahuaca culture horizon.

4674 Kuri, Carlos. Piazzolla, la música límite. Buenos Aires: Corregidor, 1992. 229 p.: bibl.

Although concerned chiefly with such controversial issues as the degree of jazz infiltration and the place of Nadia Boulanger in Piazzolla's development, the author begins with a chronology (years, not day or month) and ends with a discography (both only partially useful).

4675 Kuss, Malena and **Lionel Salter.** Bomarzo. (*in* New Grove Dictionary of Opera. New York: Grove's Dictionaries of Music, 1992, v. 1, p. 534–535, ill.)

Premiered at Washington on May 19, 1967, *Bomarzo* (two acts, 15 scenes) created a sensation at its premiere, but was banned in Buenos Aires until five years later. Kuss magisterially reacts to both the composer's musical language and the opera's structure.

4676 Kuss, Malena. Castro, Juan José. (*in* New Grove Dictionary of Opera. New York: Grove's Dictionaries of Music, 1992, v. 1, p. 768, bibl.)

Authoritative account of Argentine composer and conductor's career by a paramount scholar. The 3-act *Proserpina y el extranjero* won the Verdi Prize in 1951 and was performed in Spanish at Milan's La Scala and again there the year after in Italian translation.

4677 Piazzolla, Astor. Astor Piazzolla: a manera de memorias. Coordinación de Natalio Gorin. Buenos Aires: Editorial Atlántida, 1990. 224 p.: bibl., ill.

Taped during March and April 1990, these memories include details of his two marriages interluded by six years with Amelita Baltar, a series of 13 vignettes ranging from his opinions of Gershwin to recollections of a fugitive encounter with Stravinsky, a chapter devoted to his reactions to rock musicians from the Beatles to Charly García, another on his instrument, the *bandoneón*. He did all his composing at the piano (p. 128).

4678 Salzman, Eric. Astor Piazzolla: concierto para bandoneón; tres tangos for bandoneón and orchestra. [sound recording] Bajo la dirección de Lalo Schifrin. New York: Elektra/Asylum/Nonesuch Records, 1988. 1 sound recording.

Admirable exposition of Piazzolla's unique place in the history of the tango. The three-movement *Concierto para bandoneón* was commissioned by the Banco Provincia de Buenos Aires for a 1989 radio broadcast. *Tres tangos* "is to the Argentine tango what Ravel's *La valse* is to the old Viennese waltz or what the Gershwin concerto is to piano blues." The recording was done Sept. 1987 at Richardson Auditorium in Alexander Hall, Princeton, N.J.

4679 Schwartz, Deborah. Gaito, Constantino. (*in* New Grove Dictionary of Opera. New York: Grove's Dictionaries of Music, 1992, v. 2, p. 325–326, bibl.)

Recognized as a foremost Buenos Aires native-born opera composer, Gaito is also remembered for his ballets and incidental music.

4680 Stevenson, Robert. Efraín Paesky. (*Inter-Am. Music Rev.*, 12:2, Spring/Summer 1992, p. 3–4)

Born at Resistencia, capital of Chaco prov., Argentina, Oct. 29, 1931, Paesky, has headed the Organization of American States' Music and Folklore (later Performing Arts) Division since 1974. His colossal achievements (congresses, recordings, catalogs, commissions, prizes, and musicological publications fomented by him, frequently with the collaboration of his wife, Dr. Emma Garmendia de Paesky) place him in the front rank of Latin American musical promoters in any generation. A sample commission: Astor Piazzolla's *Gran Tango para Violoncello* premiered April 27, 1990 at the Gusman Cultural Center in Miami by Mstislav Rostropovich.

4681 Velo, Yolanda M. Carta abierta al Prof. Carlos Vega. (*Rev. Inst. Invest. Musicol. Carlos Vega*, 12, 1992, p. 3–4)

Ninetieth-birthday tribute to the pioneer Argentine ethnomusicologist (1898–1966) who in 1931 became head of the Instituto de Musicología in Buenos Aires and in

1966 *miembro de número* of the Academia Nacional de Bellas Artes.

BOLIVIA

4682 Archivo Musical Chiquitos (Concepción, Bolivia) Musica vesperarum in Chiquitorum reductionibus Boliviæ, 1691–1767 = Música de vísperas en las reducciones de Chiquitos-Bolivia, 1691–1767: opera Domenici Zipoli ac anonymorum magistrorum jesuitarum et indigenarum. Transcripción y edición de Piotr Nawrot. Concepción, Bolivia: Archivo Musical Chiquitos, 1994. 1 score (xxxii, 334 p.) + 4 parts.

This supremely important anthology of 18th-century Latin polyphony produced in the Jesuit reductions does highest credit to the transcriber and to the authorities who made possible so lustrous a publication. In particular, Dr. Alberto K. Bailey Gutiérrez, Bolivian National Secretary of Culture, and Lic. Jorge Velarde Chávez, subsecretary of the Cultural Patrimony, fomented and encouraged the publication. Both Nawrot and Carlos Seoane Urioste signed the bilingual introduction, which contains performance suggestions and designates the source manuscripts, mostly vocal and instrumental partbooks. Originating in the San Rafael and Sant'Ana mission churches, the source materials now reside in the Episcopal Archives at Concepción de Ñuflo de Chávez in eastern Bolivia. The published music contents start with 15 items constituting Vespers of a Confessor. Zipoli's works in the Archivo Musical Chiquitos [AMCh] 141, 184, 106, 003, 008, 007, here transcribed as items 1–3, 5, and 18–19 in the anthology, are outnumbered by the anonymous items; but many of these might have been his. Bright major keys with less than four accidentals in the key signature prevail throughout the entire anthology. All works include continuo, figured or unfigured; one or two violins are the rule, never winds. Nawrot's continuo realizations are a model of sobriety and propriety. Partbooks for violins and continuo join the published score.

4683 Axel Roldán, Waldemar. Catálogo de los manuscritos de música colonial de los archivos de San Ignacio y Concepción (Moxos y Chiquitos) de Bolivia. (*Rev. Inst. Invest. Musicol. Carlos Vega*, 11:11, 1990, p. 225–478)

Rivaling in length his *Catálogo de manuscritos de música colonial de la Biblioteca Nacional de Bolivia* (Lima, UNESCO, 1986), this catalog now establishes Bolivia as the nation possessing the most profuse collections of 17th- and 18th-century music manuscripts anywhere to be found in South America.

4684 Baumann, Max Peter. Bolivien. (*in* Die Musik in Geschichte und Gegenwart. Kassel, Germany: Bärenreiter, 1995, Sachteil 2, columns 7–23, bibl, ill.)

In the second section, the much published author divides his survey of traditional indigenous music expressions between Highland groups (Aymaras, Quechuas, Callawas, Chipayas) and Lowland entities (Moxos, Morés, Sirionés, Chimanes). Less versed in historical sources, he would have avoided errors had he consulted Gerard Béhague's article on Bolivia in the *New Grove Dictionary*, 1980, v. 2, p. 671–672. His bibliography in particular lists outmoded and faulty historical literature, but the ethnological section includes six of his own definitive articles in addition to a vast array by others published between 1925–93.

García Muñoz, Carmen. Lauro Ayestarán (Montevideo, 9-VII-1913; 22-VII-1966). See item **4814.**

4685 Seoane Urioste, Carlos and **Andrés Eichmann.** Lírica colonial boliviana. La Paz: Editorial Quipus, 1993. 167 p.: bibl, ill. (some col.).

In her perceptive prologue, Gisbert aptly characterized as a true breakthrough the present anthology of 31 mostly festive texts in Spanish, nine of which are supplemented with exquisitely copied music transcriptions. Of the nine transcriptions, five are instrumentally accompanied duets, and the rest are accompanied solos. The editors divide the 31 texts among four *cantadas*, 10 *villancicos*, two *jácaras*, and 15 *otros*. Although all are obviously baroque poetry, only 11 of the 31 original copies carry dates from 1718–1803. Antonio Durán de la Mota, *maestro de capilla* at the *matriz* in Potosí ca. 1720–40 and composer of the music for five of the texts printed in the literary portion of this anthology, composed the "8th tone" duo in the musical supplement, *Dios y José apuestan*, the lyrics of which were written by Sor Juana Inés

de la Cruz for performance with music by Miguel Matheo de Dallo y Lana during the San José *maitines* celebrated in Puebla Cathedral in 1690. For other revelations see the review in *Inter-American Music Review*, Vol. 14, No. 2, Winter/Spring 1995, p. 105–106. All sources of texts and music are presently housed in the Bolivian National Library at Sucre.

4686 Villalpando, Alberto. Reflexiones sobre la historia de la música contemporánea de Bolivia. (*in* Encuentro de Estudios Bolivianos, 2nd, Cochabamba, Bolivia, 1984. La cultura del 52: documento final. Coordinación de Juan José Alba *et al*. Cochabamba, Bolivia: Centro Portales, 1984, p. 2–7)

The Bolivian Orquesta Sinfónica Nacional, founded in 1945 through the impetus of José María Velasco Maidana and Mario Estenssoro, suffered a pause during 1952–64 when the Movimiento Nacionalista Revolucionario tolerated only music for the masses. Even after Melba Zárate took a folkloric ballet to Mexico, the artistic success of the group abroad counted for naught on their return. In 1965 the funding of the OSN at last took a swing upward and the national conservatory began teaching the needed orchestral instruments. Author, a leading composer, raises this question: "Why prepare musicians for whom no viable careers are open to Bolivian nationals?"

4687 Waisman, Leonardo Julio. Los "Salve Regina" del Archivo Musical de Chiquitos: una prueba piloto para la exploración del repertorio. (*Rev. Inst. Invest. Musicol. Carlos Vega*, 12, 1992, p. 69–85, music)

Author of an extensive 1988 Univ. of Chicago PhD dissertation entitled "The Ferrarese madrigal in the mid-sixteenth century," Waisman (b. Dec. 22, 1947) brings nonpareil musicological expertise to this inspection of the Marian antiphon repertory in the Concepción (Bolivia) archive. His privileged background includes intensive study with Edward E. Lowinsky and Howard Mayer Brown, time in Italy as awardee of a Martha Baird Rockefeller Fund for Music grant, and further sponsorship by the Argentine Consejo Nacional de Investigaciones Científicas y Técnicas. For the tentative identification of Bartolomé Massa=Mazza as composer ca. 1761–65 of the Salves cataloged Am11 and Am12 a and b, he credits his exceptional protégé Bernardo Illari. With what thoroughness was possible in the absence of the professional calligrapher requested but not provided by CONICET, Waisman devises a chronology for the Salve copies Am05 to Am18. This brilliant article, an outgrowth of a paper presented at the Jornadas Argentinas de Musicología (5th, Buenos Aires, 1990) comprehends not only stylistic analyses, suggestions of composers (Martin Schmid in Chiquitos territory, 1730–67, and Anton Mesner there, 1743–67, possibly composed Salves Am05 and Am06), and identification of concordant versions in the Archivo de San Ignacio de Moxos (Am08 and Am09), but also suggestions concerning the use to which the Salves were put in San Rafael and Santa Ana indigenous communities.

BRAZIL

4688 Antônio, Irati and Cristina Magaldi. Camêu (de Cordoville), Helza. (*in* New Grove Dictionary of Women Composers. New York: W.W. Norton, 1994, p. 100, bibl.)

Prior to publishing her landmark *Introdução ao estudo da música indígena brasileira* (Rio de Janeiro: Conselho Federal de Cultura, 1977) Camêu had composed extensively. She added to her scientific reputation with *Instrumentos musicais dos indígenas brasileiros: catálogo da exposição* (Rio de Janeiro: Biblioteca Nacional, 1979).

4689 Antônio, Irati and John M. Schechter. Carvalho, Dinorá (Gontijo). (*in* New Grove Dictionary of Women Composers. New York: W.W. Norton, 1994, p. 107–108, bibl.)

With the aid of the catalog of her works published at Brasília in 1977, Antônio exceeds the one listed source in the bibliography, the *Enciclopédia da música brasileira* (São Paulo, 1977, p. 163–164). Dinorá Carvalho (1904–80) founded the first women's orchestra in South America and was the first woman elected to the Academia Brasileira de Música.

4690 Antônio, Irati. Sodré, Joanidia (Núñez). (*in* New Grove Dictionary of Women Composers. New York: W.W. Norton, 1994, p. 433)

With slight omissions, the São Paulo author of this article concerning one of Brazil's most important women composers (b. Porto Alegre, Dec. 22, 1903, d. Rio de Janeiro, Sept. 7, 1975; directed the Escola Nacional de Música at Rio, 1946–67) provides a word-for-word translation of the Sodré article in the *Enciclopédia da música brasileira: erudita, folclórica, popular* (São Paulo, Art Editora, 1977, p. 730).

4691 Antunes, Jorge. Interlúdio No. 1 para Olga: um *new folder* para Wagner. (*Rev. Soc. Bras. Mús. Contemp.*, 1 : 1, 1994, p. 37–58, facsims., ill., music, photo)

A pioneer electronic composer in Brazil, Antunes (b. Rio de Janeiro, April 23, 1942) spent Nov. 4, 1992 to July 31, 1993 in Paris researching data concerning the revolutionary Olga Benário who died on his own birthdate. She and her lover Luís Carlos Prestes paralleled somewhat Tristan and Isolde. In 1935 Prestes tried to lead a communist revolt in Brazil. Antunes explains the structure of his opera, the timing of the interludes, and his transformation of the "Tristan" chord (FBd#g#).

4692 Araújo, Vitor Gabriel de. A crítica musical paulista no século XIX: Ulrico Zwingli. (*ARTEunesp*, 7, 1991, p. 59–63)

Using a pseudonym, either academician Ferreira Braga or Vicente Xavier de Toledo published in the *Correio Paulistano* between July 25 and Aug. 11, 1867 a series of nine articles devoted to "Literatura Musical." Derogating from the universal custom of flooding concerts with operatic fantasies, "Zwingli" calls for musical expressions reflecting Brazil's soul. While admiring the virtuosity of visiting instrumentalists Ricardo de Carvalho and Rafael J. Croner, he decries their program content. He animadverts against Rousseau and Fétis, whose definitions do not coincide with the Brazilian reality.

4693 Balzi, Beatriz. Breve resenha da história do piano no Brasil. (*ARTEunesp*, 7, 1991, p. 1–12, bibl.)

Between approximately 1820–50 Antônio Venâncio Teixeira constructed verticals at Itu. However, imports dominated the 19th-century. Formerly a technician in the Bechstein piano manufacturing firm, Florian Essenfelder emigrated to Buenos Aires where he initiated his firm that, after uprights, exhibited its first grand in 1898. In 1902, with his six children and two specialists, he moved to

Porto Alegre and in 1904 to Pelotas, where he began teaching his sons Floriano and Frederico to succeed him. In 1911 Frederico took Essenfelder pianos—now made at Curitiba—to an international exposition at Turin, where they won first prizes. In 1924 the firm began selling concert grands. In 1991 the firm employed 240 workers, but made concert grands only on commission and added the middle sustaining pedal solely on request. In São Paulo, a firm started May 13, 1950, now sells pianos with trade name of Fritz Dobbert.

4694 Barbieri, Domenico. Pestana: suas polcas, su tutor e Machado de Assis. (*Rev. Soc. Bras. Mús. Contemp.*, 1:1, 1994, p. 25–35, music)

Strong evidence supports the identification of Miguel Emídio Pestana's tutor in Machado de Assis' tale "Um homem célebre" as having been modeled on José Maurício Nunes Garcia. Pestana, composer of *modinhas A Casa branca da serra* and *Bem-te-vi*, also ranked in Machado de Assis' opinion as the best Brazilian composer of *polcas.* Introduced at Rio de Janeiro July 3, 1845 in the Teatro São Pedro, the *polca* took Brazilian society by storm. The Brazilian composer whose *polcas* survive include Henrique Alves de Mesquita (1830–1906), Francisca Edwiges Neves (Chiquinha), Gonzaga (1847–1935), Joaquim Antônio de Silva Calado (1848–80), Pattapio Silva (1881–1907), Ernesto Nazareth (1863–1934), Anacleto de Medeiros (1866–1907), and Irineu de Almeida (1890–1916).

4695 Béhague, Gerard. Brasilien. (*in* Die Musik in Geschichte und Gegenwart. Kassel, Germany: Bärenreiter, 1995, Sachteil 2, columns 100–129, bibl., music)

Especially notable in this fine article is the section on *Afrobrasilianische Volkmusik*, a subject to which the learned author has devoted a lifetime of study *in situ*.

4696 Béhague, Gerard. Gomes, (António) Carlos. (*in* New Grove Dictionary of Opera. New York: Grove's Dictionaries of Music, 1992, v. 2, p. 483–484, bibl.)

Although Brazilian, Gomes after 1866 spent "most of the rest of his life in Italy, and his compositional ideals became so thoroughly Italianized that his output has frequently been considered within the history of Italian opera." Béhague's four articles on Gomes' operas *Fosca, Il Guarany, Maria Tudor,* *Salvator Rosa,* and *Lo Schiavo* are all of highest value, and provide splendid insights into Gomes' operas premiered in Italy. For him, *Lo Schiavo* exceeds any of the others; *Salvator Rosa* succeeded partly because its subject matter flattered Genoa, where it was premiered. *Maria Tudor's* failure may have been exacerbated by the negative characterization of the one Italian in the cast, Fabiano.

4697 Béhague, Gerard. Heitor Villa-Lobos: the search for Brazil's musical soul. Austin: Institute of Latin American Studies, Univ. of Texas at Austin, 1994. 202 p.: bibl., index, music, photos. (ILAS special publication)

This invaluable work by the most noted corresponding member of the Academia Brasileira de Música, founded in 1954 by Villa-Lobos, was definitively reviewed by José Maria Neves of the same Academy, in *Latin American Music Review* (Vol. 16, No. 1, Spring/Summer 1995, p. 95–105) and by Vasco Mariz in *Inter-American Music Review* (Vol. 14, No. 2, Winter-Spring 1995, p. 108–109).

4698 Béhague, Gerard. Luiz Heitor Corrêa de Azevedo: 13 December 1905—10 November 1992. (*Lat. Am. Music Rev.*, 14:1, Spring/Summer 1993, p. iii-vi, ill.)

Counted among the most illustrious disciples of "the foremost Brazilian musicologist of his generation," Béhague offers a most moving and informed obituary.

4699 Borges, Urquiza Maria. Josefina deve ou não tocar em público? (*ARTEunesp,* 7, 1991, p. 173–185, bibl., ill.)

Gabriel Giraudon, leading São Paulo piano teacher, advertised a concert programmed Oct. 22, 1862 in the Theatro that included performances by two of his pupils, one of whom—adolescent Josefina Porfirio de Lima—was listed to play a *Norma* transcription with her teacher. Adverse criticisms in the press obliged Giraudon to withdraw her name from the printed program. Three years later no objection was launched when she returned to participate in a patriotic concert designed to aid soldiers in the war with Paraguay.

4700 Câmara, Marcos. Microcosmos: 1) Sobre os Grupos de Música Antigua; 2) Uma Nota; 3) Opera Selvagem; 4) Imaterialidade da Música; 5) Andamento e Compasso.

(*Rev. Soc. Bras. Mús. Contemp.*, 1:1, 1994, p. 59–69)

In the first of the short essays, São Paulo composer Câmara bursts the bubble of baroque enthusiasts who vainly imagine that "early music" enactments demand a 415 vps A; in the second he agrees with the hypnotic effect of repeated notes, but he demands changing background and harmony for a *Sambinha feita numa nota só*; in the third he complains of the expense required to keep the Teatro Amazonas in Manaus habitable for the production of *Aida, Die Meistersinger,* and *Carmen,* rather than Brazilian works; in the last he distinguishes between pulse rate and periodicity of accents.

4701 Carpentier, Alejo. Un gran compositor Latinoamericano Héctor [i.e., Heitor] Villa-Lobos. (*Gac. Mus./México*, 1:7/8, 1994, p. 6–13)

In this panegyric, Carpentier praises to the skies the Choros Nos. 2, 3, 4, 7, 8, and the *Nonetto, Rudepoema,* and a suite of *Sirandas.* He closes with a description of a typical Sunday evening salon in Villa-Lobos' studio filled to suffocation with notables. Their entertainment ranged from Mozart to Falla, and culminated with Villa-Lobos' formidable music.

4702 Collins, William J. Gomes, Antonio Carlos. (*in* International Dictionary of Opera. Detroit: St. James Press, 1993, p. 535–536, bibl.)

Marred by incorrect spellings, accentuations, and titles, this enthusiastic but misguided article contains such statements as these: "one of his grandmothers had been a fullblooded Guarani Indian"—a "fact" that assisted Gomes in choosing "Alencar's embodiment of the cutting-edge intellectual preoccupation of the time, *indianismo.*" Nonetheless the closing statement carries conviction: Gomes' "dramatic sensibility, his thoroughly professional and often astonishing orchestration, and his considerable melodic gifts have not yet occasioned a merited reappraisal by opera companies or critics." No other 19th-century Western Hemisphere composer eclipsed Gomes or even perhaps equaled him.

4703 Conati, Marcello. Fortuna e aspetti del "Guarany" di Gomes. (*Rev. Musicol./Madrid*, 16:1, 1993, p. 205–264)

The prodigious worldwide success of *Il Guarany,* premiered at Milan's La Scala March 19, 1870, involved later productions in 117 cities (Alfred Loewenberg's *Annals of Opera, 1597–1940,* 2nd ed., Geneva, Societas Bibliographica, 1955, column 1013, lists only 15 cities). The La Scala run beginning Sept. 25, 1881 yielded 19 nights; the Genoa run initiated Feb. 17, 1872 continued 17 nights and the run begun Jan. 8, 1879 lasted for 19 nights; the Naples run that commenced Jan. 24, 1877 reached 17 nights. The author reprints 32 criticisms (in Italian), some extremely lengthy, nearly all extolling *Il Guarany* in highest terms.

4704 Galvão, Cláudio Augusto Pinto. Modinhas baianas do século XIX no Rio Grande do Norte. (*ARTEunesp*, 7, 1991, p. 153–172, music, table)

Thanks to the cooperation of singing teacher Fátima Brito, the author publishes a single-line transcription of 14 19th-century *modinhas* learned at Bahia in her youth by Raimunda Amalia da Motta Bittencourt (1869–1959), who after marriage moved with her physician-husband to Natal in 1889. She there taught them to her daughter Consuela who served as the author's informant. The originators of both lyrics and music have not yet been determined, but their stylistic characteristics place them firmly around the 1880s.

4705 Golin, Cida *et al.* Theatro São Pedro: palco da cultura, 1858–1988. Porto Alegre, Brazil: Instituto Estadual do Livro, 1989. 215 p.: bibl., ill.

Luiz Roberto Lopez's "A música no theatro" (p. 139–155) is followed by a chronological list of operas, operettas, ballets, orchestral concerts, and recitals given in the Theatro São Pedro 1860–1988 (with their program contents, p. 159–215), making his section an indispensable source for the history of art music in Porto Alegre.

4706 Graham, Richard. Technology and culture change: the development of the *berimbau* in colonial Brazil. (*Lat. Am. Music Rev.*, 12:1, Spring/Summer 1991, p. 1–20, bibl.)

In the conclusion to this documented history, the author states that "Today the *berimbau*—having survived 25 years as a percussive novelty in popular music—occupies a similar social office as the banjo in the United States, that is, one divorced from its ultimate African origins."

4707 Lopes, Nei. O negro no Rio de Janeiro e sua tradição musical: partido-alto, calango, chula e outras cantorias. Rio de Janeiro: Pallas, 1992. 149 p.: bibl., ill., maps. (Série Raízes; 1)

After definitions of *batuque, calereté, coco, capoeira,* and other terms, including two types of samba (reinforced with citations from authorities), the author contrasts "modernidade versus tradição," "tradição e recriação." In his *anexos,* he transcribes taped interviews with seven artists, concluding with Geraldo Babão and Catone.

4708 Magaldi, Cristina. José White in Brazil, 1879–1888. (*Inter-Am. Music Rev.,* 14: 2, Winter/Spring 1995, p. 1–19, bibl., facsims., ill., music)

This landmark essay covering White's decade at Rio de Janeiro corrects the prolific errors that have infested every previous account. All documentation appears in English in the text and in its original Portuguese in the footnotes. Serving as a model for future research articles on Cuba's supreme African-descended concert artist, this splendid essay is buttressed by meticulous traversal of the contemporary ambiance at the imperial capital.

4709 Magaldi, Cristina. Music for the elite: musical societies in Imperial Rio de Janeiro. (*Lat. Am. Music Rev.,* 16:1, Spring/ Summer 1995, p. 1–41)

This splendid essay opens new windows on concert life in the most active South American 19th-century capital. Embellished with 97 bibliographic end notes, this authoritative account singles out for extended discussion—from a list of 27 music societies requiring membership—the activities of the Club Mozart (concerts/balls, 1867–89) and Club Beethoven (concerts, 1882–90). The Sociedade de Concertos Clássicos founded in 1883 by the Cuban violinist José White (1836–1918) and the Portuguese pianist Arthur Napoleão (1843–1925) sponsored mostly symphonic and chamber music by respected German composers; its advertised events were open to both sexes and required ticket purchase.

4710 Mariz, Vasco. César Guerra-Peixe, 1914–1993. (*Inter-Am. Music Rev.,* 14:1, Spring/Summer 1994, p. 169–170)

Born March 18, 1914 at Petrópolis, Guerra-Peixe died at Rio, Nov. 23, 1993. Heavily restricted by allegiance to Koellreutter during his early stages, the composer in him blossomed when he embraced Mário de Andrade's philosophy of what Brazilian music should be. His Symphony No. 2 subtitled *Brasília* (1960), written to celebrate the inauguration of the new capital, confirmed his reputation as a foremost Brazilian composer.

4711 Mariz, Vasco. Cláudio Santoro. Rio de Janeiro: Civilização Brasileira, 1994. 155 p.: bibl., ill.

Originally intended as a 70th-birthday tribute (Nov. 23, 1989), this monograph is dedicated to one of Brazil's most prolific and prominent composers (d. Brasília March 27, 1989) and adds another jewel to the crown of Rio's most eminent living music encyclopedist and historian. See Cristina Magaldi's review in *Inter-American Music Review* (Vol. 14, No. 2, Winter/Spring 1995, p. 112–113).

4712 Mendonça, Belkiss Spenzièri Carneiro de. Apresentação. (*Rev. Soc. Bras. Mús. Contemp.,* 1:1, 1994, p. 9)

Elected president of the Brazilian Section of the International Society for Contemporary Music on Dec. 12, 1993, Mendonça took office Jan. 1, 1994. Her predecessors included Edino Krieger, Luiz Augusto Milanesi, and Paulo Affonso de Moura Ferreira. The president of the Banco de Estado de Goiás, Dr. Aires Neto Campos Ferreira, guaranteed the costs of the first issue of the *Revista da Sociedade Brasileira de Música Contemporânea.* Born at Goiás on Feb. 25, 1928, Mendonça founded the Conservatório Goiano de Música in 1956 (now the Instituto de Artes da Univ. Federal de Goiás).

4713 Menezes Bastos, Rafael José de. Musicologia no Brasil, hoje. (*ANPOCS BIB,* 30, segundo semestre 1990, p. 56–71, bibl.)

Before 1960 Brazilian musicologists flourished in conservatories and schools of music, thereafter in university faculties. The author helpfully names leading representatives of each group, in each instance identifying their specific focus.

4714 Nogueira, Lenita Waldige. Manoel José Gomes em Campinas. (*ARTEunesp,* 7, 1991, p. 103–124, ill., music)

Born in 1792 at historic Parnaíba, the father of Brazil's most famous 19th-century composer counted as his parents Antonia Maria de Jesus and José Pedroso de Morais Lara. Well-trained musically by Lara and literate in an epoch when ability to read and write was usually a middle- or upperclass acquirement, Manuel José settled in 1815 at what is now Campinas (then São Carlos), a village counting in that year 4,099 inhabitants, of whom 1,855 were slaves. With admirable meticulousness, the author traces the family and professional career of Manoel José through 1840, four years after the birth of António Carlos. This extremely important article deserves universal attention.

4715 Segato, Rita Laura. Okarilé: Yemoja's icon tune. (*Lat. Am. Music Rev.*, 14:1, Spring/Summer 1993, p. 1–19, bibl., music)

Deriving data concerning traditional Nagô (Yoruba) religious practices at Recife from 18 months of research, the Argentine author teaching anthropology at the Univ. de Brasília, whose 1984 PhD dissertation, *A Folk Theory of Personality Types: Gods and their Symbolic Representation by Members of the Sango Cult in Recife, Brazil*, (Queens Univ., Belfast), touched on some of the same material, stresses "the value of anthropological contributions in the understanding of music." John Blacking commented on the Okarilé tune in his last book (1987): "The irregular meter of the song called 'Gege of seven strokes' was intended to portray the falseness and tricky character of the deity Yemoja," goddess of the sea.

4716 Silva, Leonardo Dantas. O piano em Pernambuco. Recife, Brasil: Governo de Pernambuco, Secretaria de Turismo, Cultura e Esportes, Fundação do Patrimônio Histórico e Artístico de Pernambuco, Diretoria de Assuntos Culturais, 1987. 119 p.: bibl., ill. (Col. pernambucana; 2a. fase, vol. 33)

More than a history of the piano (its repertory and local composers, its sales representatives, its teachers, its recital locales, its tuners and movers), this admirable local chronicle documents all phases of musical life in Recife from Aug. 1810 (in which year this most active port city in Brazil boasted some 20,000 inhabitants).

Stevenson, Robert. Amerindian music. See item **4658.**

4717 Stevenson, Robert. Gomes de Araújo, João. (*in* New Grove Dictionary of Opera. New York: Grove's Dictionaries of Music, 1992, v. 2, p. 484–485, bibl.)

Bibliographical article dealing with a paramount São Paulo composer who died there aged 97 on Sept. 8, 1943.

4718 Stevenson, Robert. Periódicos musicais brasileiros: sua história. (*Rev. Bras. Mús.*, 19, 1991, p. 1–13)

History of Brazilian music periodicals, followed by translations of Gilbert Chase's annotations on articles published in *Revista Brasileira de Música*, 1934–1940.

4719 Tacuchian, Ricardo. Pesquisa musicológica e vida contemporânea. (*Rev. Soc. Bras. Mús. Contemp.*, 1:1, 1994, p. 93–108, bibl.)

Eminent composer and conductor and 1995 president of the Academia Brasileira de Música confronts the enmity in governmental circles against concert music, called incorrectly "elitist activity." In this valuable article, Tacuchian treats Brazilian concert music instead as a national treasure, surveys its historiography, and itemizes current Brazilian publications that contain relevant articles.

4720 Wehrs, Carlos. Neukomm e A. Maersch, músicos, e De Simoni, libretista, precursores do nacionalismo musical brasileiro. (*Not. Bibliogr. Hist.*, 23:143, julho/set. 1991, p. 264–278, bibl.)

Sigismund Neukomm (1778–1858), in Brazil from May 30, 1816 to April 15, 1821, has been profiled in every lexicon. Not so Adolf Maersch, who resided at Rio de Janeiro from 1849–58, teaching voice, piano, and composition at three locations signaled in the Laemmert *Almanak* of 1850, 1854, 1858, and in the *Jornal do Commercio* of Nov. 24, Dec. 11, and Dec. 21, 1857. During that decade he published at Rio at least 22 works with Portuguese titles, 14 of which are for piano (Wehrs provides an exact list). At Rio he represented himself as being the son of the orchestra director at Stettin and called himself a graduate of the Berlin Akademie der Kunste music department (headed 1832–69 by August Wilhelm Bach). An 1846 member of the court theater at Gotha, he perhaps left Germany during the 1848 political upheaval. Maersch succeeded Joaquim José Lodi as music instructor at the imperial Instituto dos Meninos Cegos (Blind Children's Institute) from Dec. 1, 1855 to Sept. 1, 1858. Upon returning to Germany immediately thereafter, he sang in opera houses at Leipzig, Coburg, and Frankfurt-am-Main, meantime continuing to compose. He died at Karlsruhe Feb. 17, 1863. His opera, *Marília de Itamaracá ou a Donzela da Mangueira,* composed in 1854 to a libretto by Luis Vicente De Simoni failed of staging, but excerpts were published in 1854. His choral fantasia-sinfonia entitled *Confederação dos tamoios,* which like his opera glorifies a Brazilian subject, was performed at the Teatro Lírico Fluminense on Dec. 12, 1857. He qualifies as a precursor of Brazilian nationalism.

THE CARIBBEAN (except Cuba)

Allen, Rose Mary. *Muzik di ingles tambe a bira di nos:* an overview of the Calypso on Curaçao in the period of its popularity. See *HLAS 55:775.*

4721 Averill, Gage. *Aranje* to *Angaje:* carnival politics and music in Haiti. (*Ethnomusicology/Society,* 38:2, Spring/Summer 1994, p. 217–247, bibl.)
  In this scintillating chronicle, the widely published author, who carried out research for this paper in Haiti and in Haitian communities in Miami and New York City between 1987–93, traces the political implications of Haitian carnival music from 1924–92. End note five contains valuable etymologies.

Birth, Kevin K. Bakrnal: coup, carnival, and calypso in Trinidad. See *HLAS 55:781.*

4722 Boxill, Ian. The two faces of Caribbean music. (*Soc. Econ. Stud.,* 43:2, June 1994, p. 33–56, bibl.)
  Based chiefly on experiences in Barbados, Jamaica, and Trinidad and Tobago, author argues that protest calypso and reggae nonetheless reinforce capitalist concepts: the oppressed idealize the material goods owned by the oppressor.

Cooper, Carolyn. Noises in the blood: orality, gender, and the "vulgar" body of Jamaican popular culture. See *HLAS 55:785.*

Davis, Martha Ellen. Music and black ethnicity in the Dominican Republic. See *HLAS 55:789.*

4723 Gilard, Jacques. "Ricas mieles y buen café:" le café dans la chanson populaire du pourtour caraïbe. (*Caravelle/Toulouse,* 61, 1993, p. 27–48)
  A musicologist's account of the celebration of coffee in popular songs of Cuba, Puerto Rico, Colombia, and Venezuela, starting with the 1927 song *Nina Rita* by Cuban composer Eliseo Grenet. [B. Aguirre-López]

4724 Lewin, Olive. The UMH contribution to the English, French, and Dutch-speaking Caribbean. (*Rev. Musicol./Madrid,* 16:2, 1993, p. 1081–1082, bibl.)
  UMH is the acronym for *The Universe of Music: A History,* formerly known as *Music in the Life of Man,* a multi-volume project initiated and fomented by Barry S. Brook. The present article offers no new facts and the text is not accompanied by an adequate bibliography.

4725 Malavet Vega, Pedro. Historia de la canción popular en Puerto Rico, 1493–1898. Ponce, Puerto Rico: P. Malavet Vega; Santo Domingo: Editora Corripio, 1992. 607 p.: bibl., ill., index.
  More an encyclopedia boasting first-class indexes of persons, subjects, and titles than a history, this extremely handsome, beautifully illustrated volume tantalizes the reader on nearly every page. Musical excerpts are cut short and sources of widely varying authenticity are treated as equally relevant. The author, an attorney who has specialized in what is loosely called music for the masses, deserves special thanks for his voluminous treatment of post-1850 events in Ponce. Donald Thompson's review in *Latin American Music Review* (Vol. 14, No. 2, Fall/Winter 1993, p. 288–293) carries great weight.

4726 Manuel, Peter. Puerto Rican music and cultural identity: creative appropriation of Cuban sources from *danza* to *salsa.* (*Ethnomusicology/Society,* 38:2, Spring/Summer 1994, p. 249–280, bibl.)
  According to the prolific, New York-based author, "the Cuban *son/guaracha/rumba* complex continues to provide the basis for most aspects of salsa style, including rhythm, formal structure, orchestration, and individual instrumental styles. This continuity is of course the case for senior artists like Celia Cruz and Tito Puente" (p. 269). Manuel's arguments cannot be encapsulated in a mere two sentences, but inevitably tread on Puerto Rican sensitivities.

4727 McDaniel, Lorna. Memory spirtuals of the liberated American soldiers in Trinidad's "company villages." (*Caribb. Q.*, 40:1, March 1994, p. 38–58)

The "Trumpet Songs" transcribed in the early 1950s by Andrew Pearse, director of Research in the Extra-Mural Dept. of the Univ. of the West Indies at St. Augustine, Trinidad, are here shown to have been brought to Trinidad by resettled, freed American slaves who had joined British forces during the War of 1812.

4728 Quintero-Rivera, Angel G. The camouflaged drum: melodization of rhythms and maroonaged ethnicity in Caribbean peasant music. (*Caribb. Q.*, 40:1, March 1994, p. 27–37)

The author concludes thus: "With a sound so radically different from the drums, a brillant metallic sound, the *cuatro* camouflaged in our contradictory plantation world the African presence. No one could imagine (except those loving these rhythms) that jibaro music was full of (camouflaged) drums."

4729 Rodríguez, Victoria Eli. El Caribe: unidad y diversidad de su cultura musical. (*Rev. Musicol./Madrid*, 16:2, 1993, p. 1087–1094)

In two of the three footnotes the author cites Argeliers León's publications, in the other an unpublished book by Zoila Gómez and herself, *Música latinoamericana y caribeña* (1991). This platitudinous paper does not address a scholarly audience.

4730 Stevenson, Robert. Port-au-Prince. (*in* New Grove Dictionary of Opera. New York: Grove's Dictionaries of Music, 1992, v. 3, p. 1071–1072, bibl.)

During the latter half of the 18th century Saint-Domingue's riches permitted an exemplary operatic life that included 23 Grétry presentations: from *Le huron* (1769), *Silvain* (1770), and *Zémire et Azor* (1772) to *Richard Coeur-de-lion* (1786), and *Panurge dans l'île des lanternes*, Operas by Monsigny, Gossec, Piccinni, and Gluck (*Orphée et Eurydice*, 1779; *Iphigénie en Aulide*, 1789) were heard. From 1764–90 blacks in Saint-Domingue played violin, French horn, trumpets, drums, and mandolin in opera orchestras. Minette and Lise were two mulatto sisters who sang in numerous operas throughout the 1780s. Two local composers saw their operas produced: Dufresne (*Laurette*, Oct. 28, 1775) and Bisséry (*Le sourd dupé*, June 21,

1771; *Bouquet disputé*, June 18, 1783). In Jan. 1782 François Mesplès, resident in Port-au-Prince from 1766, completed a theater seating 750, the best in the island until it burned down in Nov. 1791.

4731 Thompson, Donald. The *Cronistas de Indias* revisited: historical reports, archeological evidence, and literary and artistic traces of indigenous music and dance in the Greater Antilles at the time of the *Conquista*. (*Lat. Am. Music Rev.*, 14:2, Fall/Winter 1993, p. 181–201)

This welcome examination by a prime authority of the evidence mentioned in the title reveals that archaeological bone flutes have been found (although these are not mentioned by the *cronistas*). No idealized picture emerges. Among the *cronistas* discussed here, only Gonzalo Fernández de Oviedo (1478–1557) boasted any musical training. According to Toribio de Motolonía (1490?-1565) the rustic dancing and singing in the islands witnessed by him in 1524 on his way to Mexico could not compare with the exquisite and refined equivalents encountered among the Aztecs. He knew that the word *areito* was of island origin.

CENTRAL AMERICA

4732 Acevedo Vargas, Jorge Luis. Sánz, Rocío. (*in* New Grove Dictionary of Women Composers. New York: W.W. Norton, 1994, p. 405, bibl.)

Born Jan. 28, 1933 at San José, Sanz died April 14, 1993 at Mexico City, where from 1953 she established her base, studied with three leading composers, and wrote most of her music.

4733 Boggs, Stanley Harding. Apuntes sobre instrumentos de viento pre-colombinos de El Salvador. San Salvador: Ministerio de Educación, Dirección de Publicaciones e Impresos, 1990? 111 p.: bibl., ill. (Col. Antropología e historia; 19. Arqueología)

In this bilingual report on 310 Salvadoran wind instruments, 275 of which were examined for the present project, the author divides them into two types: tubular and globular (segmented resonating chamber, single resonating chamber, two resonating chambers). "The Popol Vuh refers at least nine times to piping and flute playing," states Boggs, but "if less than one-fifth of pre-Columbian wind instruments can be assigned to the flute category . . . we must conclude that they were anciently less popular than believed, or that the archaeological evidence is too scanty to be taken seriously." He assigns most instruments examined to the Late Classic Period, and agrees on the ceremonial or religious significance routinely accorded most precolumbian musical instruments.

4734 Delgadillo, Luis A. Del folklore musical de Nicaragua. (*Gac. Mus./México,* 1:9, 1994, p. 23–25)

Briefly describes instruments favored by the indigenous peoples, including the *xul, jucos,* and *quijongo.* Among other instruments, Delgadillo catalogues the *marimba india* encompassing three to four octaves, reed flutes with five finger holes (sometimes six), and the violin made of *talalate* wood, but he does not claim that Nicaraguan folk music echoes the aboriginal past. The cultivation of art music is hampered by lack of a national music academy and eternal preoccupation of elite classes with *política de parroquia.*

4735 Stevenson, Robert. Martín de Montesdoca: Spain's first publisher of Sacred Polyphony (1550's); *chantre* in Guatemala Cathedral (1570's). (*Inter-Am. Music Rev.,* 12:2, Spring/summer 1992, p. 3–16)

After publishing Miguel de Fuenllana's *Orphénica lyra* (1554), Francisco Guerrero's *Sacrae cantiones* (1555), and Juan Vásquez's *Agenda defunctorum,* Martín de Montesdoca (b. at Utrera, near Sevilla, in 1525 or 1526) emigrated in 1561 to Honduras. He served first as a vicar at Tuxtla pueblo while learning indigenous languages, and from 1570 to about 1585 as *chantre* of Guatemala Cathedral, where his term overlapped with that of *maestro de capilla* Hernando Franco (1532–85), the most noted composer in North America before 1600.

4736 Tánchez, J. Eduardo. La música en Guatemala: algunos músicos y compositores. Guatemala: Impresos Industriales, 1987. 243 p.: bibl., ill., index.

This welcome textbook contains 169 short biographies of Guatemalan musicians, all but 4 of whom were born after 1800 (José Castañeda is prominent among those omitted). Although Guatemala's proud colonial past goes begging, sections on the history of the national conservatory, of the Orquesta Sinfónica Nacional, and of various music education entities, are compensations.

CHILE

4737 Benjamin, Gerald R. "Dramma per Musica" en las obras de Juan Orrego-Salas, opera 76–106. (*Rev. Music. Chil.,* 48:182, julio/dic. 1994, 44–100, music)

Sympathetic analyses of works composed between 1979–92, written by the Trinity Univ. (San Antonio, Texas) professor responsible for the Orrego-Salas articles in *The New Grove Dictionary* (1980, v. 13, p. 892), *The New Grove Dictionary of American Music* (1986, v. 3, p. 453), and *The New Grove Dictionary of Opera,* (1992, v. 3, p. 779). Forty-two music examples accompany the text.

4738 Bustos Valderrama, Raquel. Alexander (Pollack), Leni. (*in* New Grove Dictionary of Women Composers. New York: W.W. Norton, 1994, p. 8, bibl.)

Born at Breslau (now Wrocław), June 8, 1924, she came to Chile in 1939 and became a Chilean citizen in 1951.

4739 Bustos Valderrama, Raquel. Canales (Pizarro), Marta. (*in* New Grove Dictionary of Women Composers. New York: W.W. Norton, 1994, p. 101, bibl.)

Born at Santiago July 17, 1893, Canales died there Dec. 6, 1986. Her main works involve chorus, unaccompanied or with orchestra.

4740 Catálogo de la obra musical de Juan Orrego-Salas, 1984–1992. (*Rev. Music. Chil.,* 48:182, julio/dic. 1994, p. 101–104)

The Windows— opera in nine scenes lasting 160 minutes, composed 1987–90, with the composer's libretto based on Ariel Dorfman's novel, *Viudas*— takes for its locale a third world village a year after a democratically elected government is deposed.

Ciencia y cultura en Chile. See item **5.**

4741 Claro Valdés, Samuel. Chile. (*in* Die Musik in Geschichte und Gegenwart. Kassel, Germany: Bärenreiter, 1995, Sachteil 2, columns 671–695, bibl., ill., music)

Authoritative survey by the leading specialist in Chilean music history.

4742 Claro Valdés, Samuel. Rosita Renard, pianista chilena. Santiago: A. Bello, 1993. 318 p.: bibl., facsims., ill.

Born at Santiago Feb. 8, 1894, Rosita Renard died there May 24, 1949. She first toured the US in 1917 and played her last Carnegie Hall, New York City recital Jan. 19, 1949 (Bach, Partita BWV 825; Mozart Sonata K300d=310; Mendelssohn *Variations Sérieuses*; Chopin Mazurka, 6 Études; Ravel *Valses nobles et sentimentales*; Debussy *Danse*).

4743 Ernst F., Raymundo and **Enrique Valdés.** Orquesta Sinfónica de Chile: 50 años, 1941–1991. Santiago?: Univ. de Chile, Centro de Extensión Artística y Cultural, 1991. 50 p.: ill.

Documented history from the inaugural concert in the Teatro Municipal at Santiago Jan. 7, 1941, led by the founder and first Director Titular, Armando Carvajal. The competing Orquesta Filarmónica Municipal was born in 1955, causing the OSC to move to the Teatro Astor. Finally in 1987 a 20-year contract was signed with the Teatro Baquedano, assuring uncontested space for musical groups sponsored by the Univ. of Chile. Victor Tevah, Director Titular from 1947–57 and 1977–86, assured performance of more than 20 symphonic and orchestrally accompanied choral works by Chileans during his fruitful tenure.

4744 Fabela, Isidro. Claudio Arrau. (*Gac. Mus./México*, 1:6, 1994, p. 17–20)

At 23, Arrau "is one of the entire world's ten greatest virtuosos." For him the world's most musical country still remains Germany; the most eminent composer alive is Stravinsky; next to him Prokofiev. But other composers whom he names include insignificant Auric, Sauget, Jarnach. Conforming with his later *desprecio*, he names no compatriot composers, nor for that matter any Latin American.

4745 Merino, Luis. Samuel Claro Valdés, musicólogo por sobretodo. (*Rev. Music. Chil.*, 48:182, julio/dic. 1994, p. 105–115)

Claro Valdés' death at Santiago on Oct. 10, 1994, after a long bout with cancer, removed one of Chile's supreme musical scholars. Merino traces the illustrious steps of his admired friend's musicological advance.

4746 Merino, Luis. Tradición y modernidad en la creación musical: la experiencia de Federico Guzmán en el Chile independiente. Santiago: Univ. de Chile, Facultad de Artes, 1993. 148 p.: appendices, bibl., ill., music, tables.

Without cavil the supreme monograph

thus far published concerning any 19th-century composer-performer born in the Spanish-speaking Americas, this palmary publication on Guzmán (1836–85) adds another to the already towering achievements of Chile's foremost living musicologist. See the extended review published in *Inter-American Music Review* (Vol. 14, No. 2, Winter/Spring 1995, p. 103–105).

4747 Orrego-Salas, Juan. Altazar y la Missa in tempore discordiae: reciprocidad de palabra y música. (*Rev. Music. Chil.*, 48:182, julio/dic. 1994, p. 14–43, music)

Completed in about six months after Jan. 18, 1969, Orrego-Salas' Opus 64 for tenor soloist, mixed chorus, and orchestra juxtaposes sections of Vicente Huidobro's lengthy poem *Altazor*, published at Madrid in 1919, with the Latin text of the Ordinarium. The composer's analysis is fortified with 13 music examples.

4748 Orrego-Salas, Juan. Discurso de aceptación del Premio Nacional de Arte, 1992. (*Rev. Music. Chil.*, 48:182, julio/dic. 1994, p. 11–13)

Despite settling in the US in 1961 to direct the Latin American Music Center at Indiana Univ. and remaining in the Bloomington area as professor of composition until retirement, Orrego-Salas (b. Santiago, Jan. 18, 1919) has never forsaken his roots.

4749 Peña Fuenzalida, Carmen. Bibliografía selectiva de publicaciones de Samuel Claro Valdés. (*Rev. Music. Chil.*, 48:182, julio/dic. 1994, 116–120)

The 79 items in this bibliography of articles, scholarly monographs, books, and scores published from 1963–94 (including 31 contributions to *Revista Musical Chilena*) document a 30-year devotion to South American—and more especially Chilean—music history, never to be sufficiently extolled.

4750 Ruiz Zamora, Agustín. Conversando con Margot Loyola. (*Rev. Music. Chil.*, 49:183, enero/junio 1995, p. 11–41, ill.)

Question-and-answer review of the career of Chile's 1994 Premio Nacional de Arte en Música. Loyola's reflections on Carlos Vega, Isabel Aretz, and Ercilia Moreno Chá throw valuable light. The latter lived three years in Chile and accompanied Loyola during a northern trip in search of *cachimbo* data. Loyola's first published article, "Danzas Criollas Tradicionales de Chile," appeared in *Cultura: Chile* (Moscow: Editorial Ciencias, Academia de Ciencias de la URSS, 1968, p. 186–200). Her second article published outside Chile was titled "Como Aprendo e Interpreto, Canto y Danza: Apéndice de mi Trabajo; El cachimbo" appeared in *1a Muestra de Bailes Folklóricos por Pareja*, (Bogotá, April 1993, p. 99–118).

4751 Ruiz Zamora, Agustín. Discografía de Margot Loyola. (*Rev. Music. Chil.*, 49: 183, enero/junio 1995, p. 42–58)

From the vantage point of sound quality and fidelity, the two LPs recorded in the USSR by Mezhdunarodmaya Kniga (MEK) in 1957 and 1961, the latter of songs collected by her in Easter Island, exceed all other recordings dated 1940–92 by Margot Loyola Palacios. *Danzas Tradicionales de Chile* (Alerce, Chile, 35-minute cassette ALCE 806; CDAE 0211.DDD), sponsored by FONDART (Fondo Nacional para el Desarrollo del Arte y la Cultura del Ministerio de Educación), was made cooperatively in 1993 with her husband of the last quadrennium, Osvaldo Cádiz Valenzuela. A 70-minute video with the same title, contents, and sponsorship provides visualizations of the ten traditional Chilean dances included in the cassette and CD: *seguidilla, chocolate, cachimbo* (2 versions), *paloma, cañaveral, cielito, balambito* (2 versions), and *cueca del pavo*. The video is enriched with descriptive commentary giving all desirable data on ambience and performance groups.

COLOMBIA

4752 Friedmann, Susana. Nova (Sondag), Jaqueline. (*in* New Grove Dictionary of Women Composers. New York: W.W. Norton, 1994, p. 348)

The most prominent Colombian woman composer of her time, Nova was born at Ghent on Jan. 6, 1935 and died at Bogotá on June 13, 1975. In 1967 she gained a two-year scholarship for study with Ginastera at the Instituto Torcuato Di Tella in Buenos Aires, where performance of several of her avant-garde works brought her talents to international attention.

Gilard, Jacques. "Ricas mieles y buen café:" le café dans la chanson populaire du pourtour caraïbe. See item **4723.**

Hickmann, Ellen. Musik aus dem Altertum der Neuen Welt: archäologische Dokumente des Musizierens in präkolumbischen Kulturen Perus, Ekuadors und Kolumbiens. See item **4645.**

4753 Stevenson, Robert. Bogotá. (*in* New Grove Dictionary of Opera. New York: Grove's Dictionaries of Music, 1992, v. 1, p. 515, bibl.)

Between 1848–1978 Bogotá hosted visits by 13 touring companies who mounted some 72 operas by 35 composers. The venues were the Coliseo Maldonado, from 1840, and then the Teatro de Colón inaugurated March 24, 1885. Oreste Sindici (1837–1904), member of the Egisto Petrelli visiting troupe, sang the Duke in the local premiere of *Rigoletto* on July 20, 1865. Marrying a Bogotá resident, he remained in Colombia and in 1887 composed the Colombian national anthem. José María Ponce de León (1846–82) was the first native of Colombia to have his operas sung by visiting Italian companies.

4754 Stevenson, Robert. Ponce de León, José María. (*in* New Grove Dictionary of Opera. New York: Grove's Dictionaries of Music, 1992, v. 3, p. 1056, bibl.)

Born at Bogotá on Feb. 16, 1846, Ponce de León died there Sept. 21, 1882. Of his four stage works (premiered at Bogotá Dec. 17, 1863, July 2, 1874, April 27, 1876, and Nov. 22, 1880), the last, four-act *Florinda*, dealing with the betrayal of Count Julian's daughter by the Visigothic ruler, Don Rodrigo, won him a gold medal and ecstatic approval by his fellow townspeople.

CUBA

4755 Alén, Olavo. De lo afrocubano a la salsa: géneros musicales de Cuba. Hato Rey, Puerto Rico: Cubanacán, 1992. 122 pages: bibl., photos, 2 audio cassettes.

Designed for the broad public rather than the scientist, this study of the *son, rumba, canción cubana, danzón,* and *punto guajiro* heavily stresses African precedents of each genre. According to Jorge Duany (*Latin American Music Review*, 16:1, Spring/Summer 1995, p. 94) "the author's wide-ranging coverage inevitably glosses over key issues in Cuba's musical history, such as the question of Hispanic (as opposed to African) antecedents or the mutual influence between American jazz and Afro-Cuban music." Duany also considers the title a misnomer.

4756 Esquenazi Pérez, Martha. Representación cartográfica de la música popular tradicional en Holguín. (*Anu. Etnol./Habana,* 1988, p. 148–174, bibl., maps)

Inventory of different varieties of traditional song current in the various urban and rural localities of eastern Holguín province. Descendants of Haitian and Jamaican sugarcane cutters contracted early in the century preserve some of their own traditions.

4757 Fernández, Raúl A. The course of U.S. Cuban music: margin and mainstream. (*Cuba. Stud.,* 24, 1994, p. 105–122)

Reviews impact of Cuban musical traditions on salsa and Latino music in the US. Includes sections on Cuban dance forms in the US, the impact of salsa on ethnic identity of Latinos, and marketing issues. [B. Aguirre-López]

Gilard, Jacques. "Ricas mieles y buen café:" le café dans la chanson populaire du pourtour caraïbe. See item **4723.**

4758 González, Jorge Antonio. Sánchez Ferrer, Roberto. (*in* New Grove Dictionary of Opera. New York: Grove's Dictionaries of Music, 1992, v. 4, p. 162)

Born at Havana Dec. 31, 1927, Sánchez Ferrer went to Paris in 1961 with the Cuban Modern Dance Company as orchestral conductor. After study in 1962 at Leipzig Conservatory, he returned to conduct the Cuban National Opera. His three-act opera to his own libretto, based on Alejo Carpentier's tale *Ecue-Yamba-O,* reached production at the Gran Teatro in Havana on Dec. 25, 1986.

4759 González, José Antonio. Sánchez de Fuentes, Eduardo. (*in* New Grove Dictionary of Opera. New York: Grove's Dictionaries of Music, 1992, v. 4, p. 162, bibl., list of works)

Six of the composer's stage works were premiered at Havana between 1898 and 1942.

4760 Lezcano, José Manuel. African-derived rhythmical and metrical elements in selected songs of Alejandro García Caturla and Amadeo Roldán. (*Lat. Am. Music Rev.,* 12:2, Fall/Winter 1991, p. 173–186, bibl., music)

Roldán's *Negro Bembón* and *Mulata* and García Caturla's *Mari-Sabel* and *Mulata,*

all involving accompanied voice, are the musical examples with which the author makes his points.

Magaldi, Cristina. José White in Brazil, 1879–1888. See item **4708.**

Manuel, Peter. Puerto Rican music and cultural identity: creative appropriation of Cuban sources from *danza* to *salsa.* See item **4726.**

4761 Rodríguez, Victoria Eli and **Zoila Gómez García.** Haciendo música cubana. La Habana: Editorial Pueblo y Educación, 1989. 147 p.: bibl., ill.

In this textbook of Cuban music history designed for seventh-grade teachers, the authors delay consideration of concert music until the last chapter. Chaps. 3–7 successively review congeners of *punto, rumba, danzón, son,* and *canción.* The authors presuppose advanced music reading ability.

4762 Stevenson, Robert. Havana. (*in* New Grove Dictionary of Opera. New York: Grove's Dictionaries of Music, 1992, v. 2, p. 669–670, bibl.)

During the 19th century, Havana advantageously competed with every other western hemisphere capital as a preeminent operatic center. Mozart's *Don Giovanni* was sung at the Teatro Principal on Nov. 3, 1818. Rossini, Bellini, Donizetti, and Verdi in rapid succession dominated the boards. The first world premiere at the Teatro Tacón (seating for 2,287, with standing room for 700; opened Feb. 28, 1838) was Giovanni Bottesini's *Cristoforo Columbo* sung for his benefit under his own direction on Jan. 31, 1848. The most prolific Cuban composer of operas was Eduardo Sánchez de Fuentes (1874–1944), with five Havana premieres to his credit.

4763 Stevenson, Robert. Musical silhouettes drawn by José Martí. (*Inter-Am. Music Rev.,* 14:2, Winter/Spring 1995, p. 21–37)

No other independence hero came close to Martí's cultural supremacy. His musical reportage reveals surpassing critical ability. Nicolás Ruiz Espadero's *Sur la tombe de L.M. Gottschalk* (New York: Wm. Hall & Son, 1870) serves as a 12-page musical annex.

4764 Valdés Cantero, Alicia. Lecuona Casadó, Ernestina. (*in* New Grove Dictionary of Women Composers. New York: W.W. Norton, 1994, p. 272)

Sister of Ernesto Lecuona (1896–1963) and grandmother of Leo Brouwer, Ernestina was born at Matanzas on Jan. 16, 1882 and died at Havana on Sept. 3, 1951. In 1937 she founded the Orquesta Feminina de Concierto. A pianist, she composed songs, some of the more popular of which are itemized in Helio Orovio's *Diccionario de la música cubana biográfico y técnico* (Havana: Editorial Letras Cubanas, 1981, p. 232).

ECUADOR

4765 Archivos de arte y literatura: fichero de autores y de agrupaciones. v. 2, La música. Coordinación e investigación de Pablo Guerrero Gutiérrez. Investigación de Raúl Levoyer, Paulina de Ponce y Milton Castañeda. Quito: Casa de la Cultura Ecuatoriana Benjamín Carrión, 1992? 1 v.

All praise is due this one-volume encyclopedia. Anyone cognizant of the difficulties engendered in making a national music dictionary will laud this extremely useful compendium, replete with alphabetized names of individuals and organizations. Information sources conclude most articles. Lists of compositions abound. Exact dates and places are specified to the degree possible.

4766 Banning, Peter. El sanjuanito o sanjuán en Otavalo: análisis de caso. (*Sarance/Otavalo*, 16, agosto 1992, p. 131–150, music, tables)

Harmonic and melodic analyses of three versions sung in Quechua of the instrumentally accompanied courtship sanjuanito called chimbaloma. According to this author from Amsterdam Univ., chimbaloma means an "over there" place where a woman awaits her suitor. She wears on her shoulders a mantle that she throws off at the moment of a desired encounter.

Hickmann, Ellen. Altamerika. See item **4644.**

Hickmann, Ellen. Musik aus dem Altertum der Neuen Welt: archäologische Dokumente des Musizierens in präkolumbischen Kulturen Perus, Ekuadors und Kolumbiens. See item **4645.**

4767 Stevenson, Robert. Ecuador. (*in* Die Musik in Geschichte und Gegenwart. Kassel, Germany: Bärenreiter, 1995, Sachteil 2, columns 1640–1649, bibl.)

Historical survey begins with a synopsis of yields from archaeological sites.

MEXICO

4768 Aharomián, Cariún. La muerte de Manuel Enríquez. (*Rev. Music. Chil.*, 48:182, julio/dic. 1994, p. 121–126)

Enríquez's death on April 26, 1994 at Mexico City removed a cardinal composer of his generation. The list of his works since 1969 (in which year *Compositores de América*, No. 15, Organization of American States, included his works list to that date) and a selective discography concludes the present obituary.

4769 Alvarez Coral, Juan. Compositores mexicanos. 6. ed., aumentada. México: EDAMEX, 1993. 373 p.: bibl., ill.

The author (b. Cozumel, Quintana Roo, May 22, 1943) published the first edition of this valuable anthology of biographies in 1971. The added entries in this edition include: Alicia Colmenares Vargas (1918–87); Víctor Cordero Aurrecochea (1914–83); Claudio Estrada Báez (1910–84); Salvador Flores Rivera (1920–87); Blas Galindo Dimas (1910–93); José Guízar Morfín (1912–80); and Miguel Prado Paz (1905–80). As in previous editions, only deceased musicians are profiled. Always the maternal name is added, and a portrait and a sample page of composition are included.

4770 Archivo musical de la Catedral de Oaxaca: cantadas y villancicos de Manuel de Sumaya; revisión, estudio y transcripción. Edición de Aurelio Tello. México: Centro Nacional de Investigación, Documentación e Información Musical Carlos Chávez, 1994. 336 p.: bibl., ill., facsims., index, music. (Tesoro de la música polifónica en México; 7)

This exemplary edition (conforming with the most exalted standards) initiates a series of three volumes dedicated to the works of Manuel Sumaya=Zumaya conserved in the music archive of the Oaxaca Cathedral. Among the 27 pieces deominnated *cantatas* or *villancicos*, Tello here publishes the 18 that survive with a complete or reasonably complete number of parts. In the literary introduction all 24 members of the cathedral music establishment active during the Oaxaca chapelmastership of Sumaya from Jan. 1, 1745 to his death there Dec. 21, 1755 are profiled to the extent that cathedral capitular acts and payment records permit. In the introduction, lyrics are printed with the original orthography; in the music, transcriptions wear modern spellings. With the exception of the 1719 *villancico a 4, Pedro es el maestro que sabe* (originally in high clefs, transcribed at p. 198–206 a fourth lower), all 18 pieces are transcribed at original pitches. Tello's continuo realizations are throughout impeccable. In all respects, his edition cannot be overpraised, his abettors and patrons equally deserving warmest plaudits. Best of all, the music everywhere declares Sumaya to have been a composer who worthily competes with his best contemporaries anywhere in Europe.

4771 La Armonía: Organo de la Sociedad Filarmónica Mexicana. T. 1, Año 1, Nos. 1–13, 10. de nov. de 1866–10 de mayo de 1867. Facsimile ed. México: Consejo Nacional para la Cultura y las Artes; Instituto Nacional de Bellas Artes; Centro Nacional de Investigación, Documentación e Información Musical Carlos Chávez (CENIDIM), 1991. 104 p.

Prefaced by Juan José Escorza's illuminating history of the Mexican Philharmonic Society, founded 1865, this facsimile reprint of the 13 issues of *La Armonía* (published in 1866–67) contains a mother lode of valuable information, ranging from Luis F. Muñoz Ledo's articles on Luis Baca and Joaquín Beristáin to data on the Mexico City music publishers "Juan M. Rivera e hijo" and the "Sres. Wagner y Ca." that preceded A. Wagner y Levien. See the review in *Inter-American Music Review* (Vol. 12, No. 2, Spring/Summer 1992, p. 115–116) for a summary of *La Armonía's* contents and identifications of its founders.

4772 Brenner, Helmut. La obra de Juventino Rosas: un acercamiento musicológico. (*Lat. Am. Music Rev.*, 16:1, Spring/Summer, 1995, p. 58–77, bibl., music)

This pathbreaking article by a member of the Institute for Ethnomusicology of the School of Music and Performing Arts in Graz, Austria, effectively inaugurates a scientific study of Rosas' oeuvre, which includes 17 valses; seven each of danzas, mazurkas, and schottisches; five polkas, two marchas, and one *danzón*. After establishing a chronology, Brenner compares *Sobre las olas*, containing four melodic themes, with *Amelia, Aurora,*

Carmen, Ensueño Seductor, Flores de margarita, and *Ilusiones juveniles,* each of which contains eight melodic themes.

4773 Campos, Rubén M. Las danzas aztecas. (*Gac. Mus./México,* 1:1, 1994, p. 6–14; 1:3, 1994, p. 19–24, music)

Extracted from Campos' *El folklore y la música mexicana: investigación acerca de la cultura musical en México: 1525–1925* (México: Secretaría de Educación Pública, 1928), a work saluted by Ralph S. Boggs in the Folklore section of HLAS (see *HLAS 3: 1487*), this article came from the first of three still influential "folklore" books by Campos (b. Ciudad Manuel Doblado, Guanajuato, April 25, 1876; d. Coyoacán, D.F., June 7, 1945), whose definition of "folklore" set its boundaries in Mexico. Campos was an extremely prolific, persuasive, and skilled writer. His musical excerpts, supplied him by Mariano Rojas of Tepoxtlán (*Danza de la peregrinación de Aztlán*) and by Daniel Brinton (*Danza de la Malinche*), share the spuriosity of Má Teadora's song (see *HLAS 38:9126*).

4774 Contreras Soto, Eduardo. Eduardo Hernández Moncada: ensayo biográfico, catálogo de obras y antología de textos. México: Centro Nacional de Investigación, Documentación e Información Musical Carlos Chávez, 1993. 179 p., 16 p. of plates: bibl., photos.

Among the most versatile of conductors, pianists, and composers of his generation, Hernández Moncada (b. Xalapa, Veracruz, Sept. 24, 1899, the same year as Carlos Chávez) gains an entry in the leading English-language, German, and Italian music lexicons but still remains insufficiently known. The present splendid traversal of his crowned career and record of his compositions additionally contains Hernández Moncada's truly insightful appraisals and comments on Ricardo Castro, Silvestre Revueltas, Chávez, and numerous others. His own succinct autobiography is a welcome bonus.

4775 Correa, Fabio. Quitarse la ropa y cantando al sexo: Gloria Trevi y la trampa rockera de la juventud mexicana. (*Lat. Am. Music Rev.*, 16:1, Spring/Summer 1995, p. 78–92, bibl.)

Aspiring to emulate Madonna, Gloria de los Angeles Treviño Ruiz, native of Monterrey, Mexico, has become at 22 a commercialized product, whose song-texts tread the outer limits of the socially permissible. This article by a graduate research assistant in the Dept. of Languages and Literature at Arizona State Univ. in Tempe offers no hint of musical analysis, but includes lines from five identified lyrics.

4776 Drewes, Michael. El órgano de la parroquia "La Purísima Concepción" de Real de Catorce, S.L.P. (*An. Inst. Invest. Estét.*, 61, 1990, p. 81–83, photos)

One of the few extant organs made in Mexico during early independence years, the one-manual instrument in the parish church at Real de Catorce, San Potosí state, has 54 keys extending from C_1 below the bass clef to f^2 above the treble clef. José Tomás Tello de Orosco made it in 1834. Approximately ten months of intensive labor would restore it. Twenty photographs show all aspects of its present interior and exterior condition.

4777 Fernandes, Gaspar. Obras sacras. Transcrição e estudo de Robert J. Snow. Lisboa: Fundação Calouste Gulbenkian, Serviço de Música, 1990. 1 score (lx, 140 p.). (Portugaliae musica; 49)

Some 14 of the Latin-text works in this edition derive from the Oaxaca Codex discovered in 1967 by Robert Stevenson and first inventoried in his *Renaissance and Baroque Musical Sources in the Americas* (Washington: General Secretariat, Organization of American States, 1970, p. 194–204). Stevenson's suggestion that Fernandes=Fernández was of Portuguese birth needs confirmation from discovery of the composer's will.

4778 Gomezanda, Antonio. Música moderna en la capital de México. (*Gac. Mus./México*, 1:4, 1994, p. 36–37)

In 1896 Luis G. Saloma (1866–1956) founded the first professional string quartet in Mexico and in 1920 organized the first *Orquesta Femenina* in Mexico. Eclectic in his tastes, he ranged as soloist from Corelli to Hubay; and in 1928 he actively propagandized on behalf of Stravinsky and Milhaud.

4779 Gomezanda, Antonio. Notas mexicanas. (*Gac. Mus./México*, 1:10/12, 1994, p. 42–43)

While awaiting completion of the Palacio de Bellas Artes (not ready for inauguration until Sept. 29, 1934, although projected as early as 1905), the Teatro Esperanza Iris at Donceles núm. 36, inaugurated May 21, 1918 during Venustiano Carranza's presidency, served as locale for Sunday presentations of opera (*Aida*), alternating with *zarzuela* (*El Gato Montés*, by Penella). Carlos Chávez conducted the first concert of the Orquesta Sinfónica Mexicana in the same theater on Sept. 2, 1928. His program included the *Sonata Trágica* for violin and orchestra by long-time professor of composition at the Conservatorio Nacional, Rafael J. Tello (1872–1946).

4780 Lannert, John. 20 million albums and counting . . . international superstar Juan Gabriel brings the sounds of Mexico to the world. (*ASCAP Playback*, 2:4, July/Aug. 1995, p. 6, ill.)

Born Alberto Aguilera Valadez in 1951, Juan Gabriel grew up in Michoacán, where he started writing songs at age 13 and changed his name to Adam Luna. Performing in a local nightclub called El Noa Noa, its name became the title of one of his first hits. From age 20 Mexico City became his base, where between 1971–85, under the name of Juan Gabriel, he recorded a variety of musical styles from mariachi to soft pop in over 20 best-selling albums. By 1994 his catalog included some 450 songs. In 1995 he joined ASCAP.

4781 Meierovich, Clara. Alternativas de interpretación sobre la fortuna de la primera biografía dedicada a Carlos Chávez. (*An. Inst. Invest. Estét.*, 63, 1992, p. 141–150, appendix)

Without acknowledging Vicente T. Mendoza's never published *Carlos Chávez y la música mexicana* as his source for many details of Chávez's life up to 1928, Roberto Garcia Morillo profited from it greatly in *Carlos Chávez vida y obra* (México: Fondo de Cultura Económica, 1960). Contrary to the Gilbert Chase article in *The New Grove Dictionary* (1980), Chávez came from a propertied, wholly European-derived family based at Aguascalientes, of which state his grandfather, José María Chávez, was interim governor in the Juárez epoch. Everything written about Chávez by Mendoza, including "Técnica de Carlos Chávez compositor" in *Anales del Instituto de Investigaciones Estéticas*, tomo 2, núm. 3, 1939, poured incense on Chávez's altar.

4782 Meierovich, Clara. Vicente T. Mendoza: artista y primer folclorólogo musical. México: Univ. Nacional Autónoma de México, 1995. 257 p.: bibl., plates, facsim.

Unjustly neglected by biographers until publication of this superior book, Vicente Teódulo Mendoza Gutiérrez (b. Cholula, Puebla, Jan. 27, 1894; d. Mexico City, Oct. 27, 1964) instigated the birth of the Sociedad Folklórica de México in Aug. 1938. Not disagreeing with any of the biographical data published in *Die Musik in Geschichte und Gegenwart*, Vol. 16, 1979, columns 1266–1267 (the *New Grove Dictionary*, vol. 12, p. 160–161, article is faulty), the author now does Mendoza's memory a salutary service by fleshing out all aspects of his multi-faceted career. Not least problematical among these are his late-blooming love affairs, poetic bathos, his adulation of Chávez, the polemic caused by his derivation of the *corrido* from the romance, and his field transcription methods.

4783 Morales, Olga. Una "Misa a 4" anónima del período colonial mexicano y un "Benedictus qui venit" de Manuel de Sumaya. (*Herencia/San José*, 5:1, 1993, p. 29–34, bibl., music)

According to Aurelio Tello, Zumaya = Sumaya died at Oaxaca, Dec. 21, 1755. Not the first Mexico City chapelmaster born in Mexico, Zumaya was preceded in that post from 1654–74 by Francisco López Capillas, whose will certifies that he was born at Mexico City.

4784 Olmstead, Andrea. Montezuma. (*in* International Dictionary of Opera. Detroit: St. James Press, 1993, p. 896–897, bibl.)

Composed by Roger Sessions to a libretto by Giuseppe Antonio Borgese, the three-act *Montezuma* gained a favorable reception at its premiere April 19, 1964 in West Berlin (Deutsche Oper), but only a mixed critical reaction when mounted at Boston in 1967. As in all prior Montezuma operas, history is twisted to the purposes of the librettist. In this version, Montezuma praises Malinche as the builder of a new race. For his pains at ending strife Montezuma is stoned to death by his own Aztec subjects.

4785 Páramo, José Alfredo. Miguel Bernal Jiménez: he nacido para cantar tus alabanzas. México: Comisión Editorial del Partido Acción Nacional (PAN), 1992. 99 p.: ill. (Col. Semblanzas)

The first stage work by a Mexican composer to be mounted in Spain was Bernal Jiménez's opera *Tato Vasco*, Feb. 20, 1948, at Madrid. His other stage works include the ballets *El chueco* (México, Palacio de Bellas Artes, Oct. 1951), and *Los tres galanes de Juana* (same locale, Sept. 9, 1952). One of Mexico's culminating and best trained musical geniuses, he was appointed dean of the Music Faculty, Loyola Univ., New Orleans, Feb. 12, 1954, but died of a heart attack as a result of overwork on July 26, 1956 at León, Guanajuato, aged 46. Both his religious and political stance kept him distanced from Mexican officialdom during his comparatively short life.

4786 Parker, Robert L. A recurring melodic cell in the music of Carlos Chávez. (*Lat. Am. Music Rev.*, 12:2, Fall/Winter 1991, p. 160–172, music)

With his usual perspicacity, the leading Chávez authority identifies a four-note motive (descending third, ascending fourth, descending second, descending third) as endemic in nine different compositions "encompassing a broad range of genres and media" that date from 1926–76.

4787 Prieto, Carlos. De la URSS a Rusia: tres décadas de experiencias y observaciones de un testigo. Prólogo de Isabel Turrent. México: Fondo de Cultura Económica, 1993. 325 p.: ill., index. (Vida y pensamiento de México)

Limitations of space in *HLAS* prohibit the paragraph upon paragraph of praise that this book merits. No less nonpareil a writer than he is a violoncellist, Prieto provides a vivid chronicle that deserves universal dissemination and encomium.

4788 Pulido, Esperanza. La mujer mexicana en la música. Edición de Juan José Escorza. (*Heterofonía/México*, 22:104/105, Jan./Dec. 1991, p. 5–99, bibl, ill.)

First published in 1958 (Mexico City: Ediciones de la Revista Bellas Artes), this monograph covers all aspects of Mexican women's musical contributions. Beginning with information concerning Aztec women, gathered from Diego Durán, Sahagún, and Torquemada, Pulido continues with chapters devoted to colonial figures and institutions, and the 19th and 20th centuries. Reviews of the 1958 publication reprinted from newspapers (*Excelsior, Novedades*) and from *Carnet Musical* (April and Oct. 1959) accompany this second edition of her pioneering study. The review in *Inter-American Music Review* (Vol.

14, No. 2, Winter/Spring 1995, p. 89–94) is interleaved with two of Pulido's compositions.

4789 Revista Musical de México. Nos. 1–12, 1919–1920. México: Instituto Nacional de Bellas Artes; Centro Nacional de Investigación, Documentación e Información Musical Carlos Chávez, 1991.

In all 12 issues, the *Crónica Mexicana* section gives a valuable résumé of happenings during the preceeding four weeks. While in Mexico, Arthur Rubenstein played Ricardo Castro's *Himno Nacional,* Felipe Villanueva's *Vals poético,* and Ponce's *Balada Mexicana* (no. 5, p. 27). In *My Many Years* (New York: Alfred A. Knopf, 1980, p. 64), Rubinstein recalled having played as the only Mexican work during his 26 concerts "a dreadful arrangement of the overlong Mexican anthem by Manuel Ponce," a wrong statement on every account, typical of the unjust disdain that he poured on every Latin American composer except Villa-Lobos.

Royce, Anya Peterson. Music, dance, and fiesta: definitions of Isthmus Zapotec community. See *HLAS* 55:760.

4790 Russell, Craig H. The Eleanor Hague Manuscript: a sampler of musical life in eighteenth-century Mexico. (*Inter-Am. Music Rev.,* 14:2, Winter/Spring 1995, p. 59–62, facsim.)

Box four under "Ms203 Eleanor Hague" at the Braun Research Library of the Southwest Museum in Los Angeles contains a highly eclectic collection of nearly 300 popular dance tunes (especially minuets) assembled by Joseph María García to whom the collection belonged in 1772. Joseph Mateo González Mexía bought it from the García estate Nov. 16, 1790 for two pesos. Lacking composer attributions, and strewn with titles in corrupt Castilian, English, French, and Náhuatl, dances range from single-line adaptations of works by Lully, Campra, and six other French composers identifiable from correspondences, to tunes drawn from John Playford's *The Dancing Master* and *Apollo's Banquet* and three Robert Bremner anthologies. Spanish sources include collections by Bartolomé Ferriol y Boxeráus (1745), Pablo Minguet y Yrol, and Antonio Martín y Coll. Santiago Murcia's *Al verde Retamar* (No. 95) and *Las Penas* (No. 101) were possibly composed during his putative sojourn in Mexico. The only stated attributions in the manuscript

choose José Herrando (1720/21–1763), Spanish violin virtuoso, and Luis Misón (1727–1766), Royal Chapel oboist, and prolific composer for the Madrid stage. This manuscript provides further evidence of the vibrant and multifarious culture that flourished in Mexico's colonial past.

Stevenson, Robert. Amerindian music. See item **4658.**

4791 Stevenson, Robert. Grever, María (La Portilla y Torres, María Joaquina de). (*in* New Grove Dictionary of Women Composers. New York: W.W. Norton, 1994, p. 197, bibl.)

ASCAP Biographical Dictionary, 4th ed. (New York and London: R.R. Bowker Co., 1980, p. 201), incorrectly cites her date and place of birth as Aug. 15, 1894, Mexico City. She was born Aug. 15 or 16, 1885 at León, Guanajuato, and died at New York City on Dec. 15, 1951 (obituary in the *New York Times,* Dec. 16, 1951). Her three greatest commercial triumphs were *Magic in the Moonlight* (Te quiero dijiste, 1929), sung in the film *Nancy goes to Rio* (1950), *What a Diff'rence a Day Made* (Cuando vuelvo a tu lado, 1934), revived in 1959 as a best-seller for Dinah Washington, and Ti-Pi-Tin (1938). She was the first Mexican woman to join the American Society of Composers, Authors and Publishers (ASCAP) in 1935.

4792 Stevenson, Robert. Manuel Enríquez, 1926–1994. (*Inter-Am. Music Rev.,* 14:1, Spring/Summer 1994, p. 171–172)

Universally recognized as one of Mexico's most signal composers and music administrators after Chávez, Enríquez (d. Mexico City, April 26, 1994) abandoned the nationalist philosophy that accounted for Revueltas' major successes, and instead allied himself with Darmstadt and Donaueschingen outlooks. After two years as a visiting faculty member at the Univ. he was appointed professor of music at the Univ. of California, Los Angeles in 1993, but declined the invitation that year to become chair of the dept.

4793 Stevenson, Robert. Mexico. (*in* New Grove Dictionary of Opera. New York: Grove's Dictionaries of Music, 1992, v. 3, p. 363–364, bibl.)

Mexico's first opera, *La Partenope,* with music by Manuel de Zumaya (ca. 1678–1755), a Mexico City native, was sung in the viceregal palace on Philip V's name-day, May 1, 1711, at the expense of Fernando de Alencastre Noroña y Silva, Duke of Linares. During the 19th century, Italian opera dominated the musical scene everywhere from Mexico City to Mazatlán, where Angela Peralta, the nation's internationally acclaimed diva, died on Aug. 30, 1882. She sang in the Mexican premieres of the nation's most prolific opera composer, Melesio Morales. Plácido Domingo (b. Jan. 21, 1941), who reached Mexico at the age of nine, sang leading roles in *La traviata* at Monterrey in May 1961, in *Madama Butterfly* with Monserrat Caballé at Puebla in 1965, and appeared in 1966 at Guadalajara in *Lucia* and *Il Barbiere di Siviglia*, Most of Mexico's leading native opera singers have been women: Fanny Anitúa, María Romero, Irma González, and Oralia Domínguez, for example. But Mexico's operatic century was the 19th, headed by Angela Peralta, soprano; and with Cenobio Paniagua, Melesio Morales, and Ricardo Castro, composers of still viable operas.

4794 Stevenson, Robert. Mexico City. (*in* New Grove Dictionary of Opera. New York: Grove's Dictionaries of Music, 1992, v. 3, p. 364–365, bibl.)

Public opera performance at the Coliseo Nuevo (opened 1753, rebuilt in 1806) awaited the first decade of the 19th century, during which Italian works by Cimarosa and Paisiello were given in Spanish. Beginning with *Il Barbiere di Siviglia*, the first Italian opera sung in the original tongue (Teatro de los Gallos, June 29, 1817), Manuel García opened the floodgates that overflowed the rest of the century. Four operas by Mexico City native Melesio Morales were premiered there 1863–91, but always in Italian by visiting companies. During the Porfirian heyday, 1885–1910, Mexico City heard all the Italian novelties of the epoch. German opera arrived in the decade of the 1890s. Mexicans Ricardo Castro and Gustavo E. Campa saw their operas produced in the capital, but the Palacio de Bellas Artes (capacity 3,500, opened Sept. 29, 1934), the city's leading opera venue, has not up to the present housed a stable Mexican opera company.

4795 Stevenson, Robert. Mulata de Córdoba, La. (*in* New Grove Dictionary of Opera. New York: Grove's Dictionaries of Music, 1992, v. 3, p. 508)

In no sense reminiscent of the jollities of *Huapango*, José Pablo Moncayo's one-act opera, with libretto by Xavier Villaurrutia and Agustín Lazo, debuted at Mexico City's Palacio de Bellas Artes on Oct. 23, 1948.

4796 Stevenson, Robert. Ortega del Villar, Aniceto. (*in* New Grove Dictionary of Opera. New York: Grove's Dictionaries of Music, 1992, v. 3, p. 780)

Born at Tulancingo, Hidalgo in 1825, the obstetrician and composer of the *episodio lírico, Guatimotzín*, on the life and death of Cuauhtemoc (Mexico City, Gran Teatro Nacional, Sept. 13, 1871, with Angela Peralta and Enrico Tamberlik in leading roles) died at Mexico City on Nov. 17, 1875.

4797 Stevenson, Robert. Peralta, Angela. (*in* New Grove Dictionary of Opera. New York: Grove's Dictionaries of Music, 1992, v. 3, p. 948–949, bibl.)

Born at Puebla on July 6, 1843, Mexico's paramount diva died at Mazatlán on Aug. 30, 1883, during a tour with her own opera company. Her triumphant international appearances took her to Milan, Havana, New York, and numerous other centers. In Mexico she sang *Lucia* 166 times and *La sonnambula* 122 times.

4798 Stevenson, Robert. Urreta [Urreta] (Arroyo), Alicia. (*in* New Grove Dictionary of Women Composers. New York: W.W. Norton, 1994, p. 467, bibl.)

Contrary to her birthdate given in *Baker's Biographical Dictionary* (8th ed., 1992, p. 1925), Urreta was born at Veracruz on Oct. 12, 1933 (not 1935). *Baker's* does correctly state that she died at Mexico City on Dec. 20, 1986 (not 1987). A brief obituary and notice of a memorial concert at which was performed her *Homenaje a cuatro* (Schoenberg, Ravel, Bartók, Bizet) appeared in *Heterofonía* (No. 95, oct./nov./dic. 1986, p. 56).

4799 Stevenson, Robert. Zubeldia, Emiliana de [Bydwealth, Emily]. (*in* New Grove Dictionary of Women Composers. New York: W.W. Norton, 1994, p. 513–514, bibl.)

Born at Salinas de Oro, Navarra on Dec. 6, 1888, Zubeldia died at Hermosillo, Sonora on May 26, 1987. A Mexican citizen from 1942, she taught 40 years at Hermosillo, where she was invited in 1947 to join the university faculty. Esperanza Pulido dedicated an issue of *Heterofonía* (Vol. 11, No. 5) to her prodigious teaching, composing, and conducting career.

4800 Tapia Colman, Simón. Música y músicos en México. México: Panorama Editorial, 1991. 262 p.

Read with discretion, this anthology of biographical vignettes and miscellaneous data can prove especially useful in searches for information concerning figures not yet in encyclopedias. The author (b. March 24, 1906 at Aguaridón, Zaragoza province, northeastern Spain) emigrated to Mexico City on July 7, 1936, where he quickly ascended to heights—directing the Conservatorio Nacional from Jan. 1971-Sept. 1972. He offers more data concerning himself, his daughter, and son (separate entries each) than about any other musicians of comparable stature. But despite awarding Adolfo Salazar a mere 17 lines, himself 159 lines, and his daughter 40, this compendium belongs in every large library.

4801 Turrent, Lourdes. La conquista musical de México. México: Fondo de Cultura Económica, 1993. 210 p.: bibl. (Sección de obras de historia)

Turrent (b. Mexico City, 1951) studied sociology in the Univ. Nacional Autónoma, music in the Conservatorio Nacional, and is a specialist in bassoon (Escuela Vida y Movimiento). Despite the all-inclusive title, she takes into account only precontact activity in the Valley of Mexico (p. 46-108) and the Franciscan evangelization enterprise in the same area (p. 115-176). As Andrés Lira González, her assessor, states in the *prólogo:* "Este estudio circunscrito al valle de México en el siglo XVI, es punto de partida para adentrarse en otros lugares de nuestro país." Even with this geographic limitation the author frequently fails to convince because of dependence on outmoded secondary material (only two items among 106 in the bibliography bear a later publication date than 1978; most bear much earlier dates). Lacks an analytic index.

4802 Varela-Ruiz, Leticia T. Maestra maitea. Hermosillo, Mexico: Pro Música de Hermosillo, 1992. 336 p.: bibl., ill.

After tours that included Paris, New York, and Latin America, Emiliana Zubeldia settled at Mexico City. During Zubeldia's last four decades in Hermosillo, the author of this splendid biography (summarized in the *New Grove Dictionary of Women Composers* article) was her most eminent disciple.

4803 Velazco, Jorge. Antonio Gomezanda y el nacionalismo romántico mexicano. (*Lat. Am. Music Rev.*, 12:1, Spring/Summer 1991, p. 65-73)

In this splendid article, Velazco traces the career of "one of the highest summits of Mexican romantic nationalism," Antonio Gomezanda (1894-1961). Before Carlos Chávez, only Ricardo Castro and he enjoyed professional publication of their works in Europe. Among Gomezanda's masterpieces, Velazco learnedly discusses his *Fantasía mexicana* (piano and orchestra), *Xiuhzitzquilo* (*La fiesta del fuego*, ballet-pantomime), *Seis danzas mexicanas* (piano and orchestra), and *Lagos* (symphonic poem for violoncello, piano, and orchestra, named after the place in Jalisco where he was born on Sept. 3, 1894; see *Riemann Musik Lexikon, Ergänzungsband Personenteil*, A-K, 1972, p. 442).

4804 Velazco, Jorge. Elisa Osorio Bolio de Saldívar, 1906-1993. (*Inter-Am. Music Rev.*, 14:1, Spring/Summer 1994, p. 165)

Born at Palencia, Hidalgo on Feb. 22, 1906, Elisa Osorio Bolio died at Mexico City on Nov. 4, 1993. In 1936 she married Gabriel Saldívar y Silva (1909-80), two years after the publication of his epochal *Historia de la música en México*. A true partner in this history, she edited his two posthumous publications, *Refranero musical mexicano* (1984) and *Bibliografía mexicana de musicología y musicografía* (2 vols., 1991, 1993). On her own, she published eight valuable children's music instruction books. No praise can surpass her valuable contributions to Mexican musicology and bibliography.

PARAGUAY

4805 Ferreira Pérez, Saturnino. Agustín Barrios: su entorno, su época y su drama. Asunción: Ediciones Comuneros, 1990. 116 p.

Born May 5, 1885 in Villa Florida, Paraguay, the preeminent guitar-touring virtuoso Agustín Pio Barrios died at San Salvador, El Salvador on Aug. 7, 1994. Literary works by his brother Francisco Martín (b. March 19, 1893), dramatist and poet, often interlarded his concerts. His repertoire leaned heavily on transcriptions but even more so on his original compositions bearing such titles as *Gran jota, Serenata española, Mazurka appassionata, Marcha heroica, Danza mora, Leyenda guaraní,* and *Leyenda de España.*

PERU

4806 Béclard d'Harcourt, Marguerite. ¿Existe una música incaica? (*Gac. Mus. / México*, 1 : 2, 1994, p. 21–28)

Replying to critics of *La musique des incas et ses survivances* (1925), she contends that since Spaniards did not introduce pentaphony, its survival strongly argues for its Andean indigenous origins.

4807 Castro Pinto, Ricardo. Villancicos cusqueños. (*Bol. Lima*, 15 : 89, sept. 1993, p. 33–48, music)

Of the 15 Christmas season items transcribed in this pleasant article, seven are songs with Quechua words. In addition, minor mode *Gloria a Dios* includes the 4-3-1 scale degree cadence characteristic of the Quechua-text songs. Vocal melodies predominantly in thirds are accompanied by formula bass patterns (eighth, two sixteenths, for instance).

4808 Gruszczyńska-Ziółkowska, Anna and **Jan Szemiński.** La importancia de la *Crónica* del Inca Garcilaso de la Vega para las investigaciones sobre la cultura musical contemporánea. De Manqu Qhapaq Inka según el Inca Garcilaso de la Vega, 1609. Varsovia, Poland: Centro de Estudios Latinoamericanos, Univ. de Varsovia, 1992. 16 p.: bibl., tables. (Documentos de trabajo; 2)

According to Garcilaso, Andean cane syrinxes came in four sizes, corresponding to soprano, alto, tenor, bass. They answered each other antiphonally in single-line melodies that consisted solely of equal-duration pitches. Flutes (*quenas*) played *tonadas* that differed from each other. A lover could summon his beloved with his own individual *tonada*. Two separate essays.

Hickmann, Ellen. Altamerika. See item **4644.**

Hickmann, Ellen. Musik aus dem Altertum der Neuen Welt: archäologische Dokumente des Musizierens in präkolumbischen Kulturen Perus, Ekuadors und Kolumbiens. See item **4645.**

4809 Russell, Craig H. Ex Machina's Productions of Torrejón y Velasco's *La Púrpura de la Rosa.* (*Newsl. Int. Hisp. Study Group*, 1 : 2, Winter 1995, p. 5–9)

Produced elegantly from Oct. 28–30, 1994 by baroque opera company Ex Machina in the Aveda Institute at Minneapolis, Torrejón y Velasco's 1701 opera owed its stunning impact to director/designer James Middleton's attention to all details from scenery, costumes, dance, orchestration, blocking, and acting to phrasing. Russell draws attention to the two extant scores for Torrejón's opera, one without music in the Bodleian Library at Oxford (MS.Add.A.143, folios 170–193), the other with music in the Biblioteca Nacional at Lima (MS C1469).

4810 Stein, Louise K. Tomás de Torrejón y Velasco's *La Púrpura de la Rosa* in the early history of opera. (*Inter-Am. Music Rev.*, 14 : 2, Winter/Spring, p. 79–82)

Originating as explanatory material published in the form of a program note for the first US production of the earliest extant Western Hemisphere opera (Lima, 1701), given by Ex Machina Baroque Opera Ensemble (artistic director James Middleton) at the 1994 annual meeting of the American Musicological Society, this article profits from the author's paramount command of all aspects of 17th-century Spanish stage music history.

Stevenson, Robert. Amerindian music. See item **4658.**

4811 Stevenson, Robert. Cuzco. (*in* Die Musik in Geschichte und Gegenwart. Kassel, Germany: Bärenreiter, 1995, Sachteil 2, columns 1047–1051, bibl.)

History of musical activity in 3,490 m. high former capital of the Incas, with emphasis on cathedral music in the colonial epoch.

4812 Stevenson, Robert. Rodolfo Holzmann, 1910–1992. (*Inter-Am. Music Rev.*, 13 : 1, Fall/Winter 1992, p. 123–125)

Holzmann's death at Lima on April 4, 1992 brought to a close the career of a notable scholar, teacher, and performer.

Turino, Thomas. Moving away from silence: music of the Peruvian Altiplano and the experience of urban migration. See *HLAS 55 : 1068.*

4813 Valcárcel, Alberto. Suray Surita habla de Theodoro. 2. ed. aum. Lima: Instituto Nacional de Cultura, 1991. 49 p.: ill.

Born at Puno on Oct. 19, 1900, the internationally renowned composer died at Lima on March 20, 1942. Banished from official recognition during a political parenthesis, he finally in 1986 entered the pantheon of officially recognized Peruvian geniuses, when Fernando Silva Santisteban became director of the Peruvian Instituto Nacional de Cultura. More recently, Edgar Valcárcel, brother of the author of this publication, has participated in revival and publication of various proofs of Theodoro's remarkable genius.

URUGUAY

Benedetti, Mario. Canciones del más acá. See item **3942.**

4814 García Muñoz, Carmen. Lauro Ayestarán (Montevideo, 9-VII-1913; 22-VII-1966). (*Rev. Inst. Invest. Musicol. Carlos Vega*, 12, 1992, p. 5–6)

Responsible for the first modern performance in Argentina of South American colonial music July 30, 1964 at the Centro de Altos Estudios Musicales del Instituto Di Tella, Ayestarán also instigated the first performance at Buenos Aires on Nov. 14, 1965 of Zipoli's *Missa*, copied at Potosí in 1784. Discovered at Sucre Cathedral by Robert Stevenson and advertised by him in *The Music of Peru* (1960, p. 179), it was Stevenson's transcription scored from the parts that Ayestarán passed to conductor Lamberto Baldi for use at the South American premiere.

4815 Salgado, Susana. Montevideo. (*in* New Grove Dictionary of Opera. New York: Grove's Dictionaries of Music, 1992, v. 3, p. 453)

Despite listing Uruguayan opera composers in her *Breve historia de la música culta en el Uruguay* (Montevideo: Aemus, 1971), she mentions none in this article that recalls five names of Italian opera companies visiting Montevideo before 1960. Against 32 internationally famous singers' names, she lists 3 Uruguayan singers who sang in the five-tier, 2,500-seat Teatro Solis that opened on Aug. 25 1856 with Verdi's *Ernani*.

4816 Velazco, Jorge. La confluencia intelectual y académica en la formación escolástica y la obra de investigación de Francisco Curt Lange. (*An. Inst. Invest. Estét.*, 63, 1992, p. 151–172, bibl., photo)

With the formidable erudition that is uniquely the author's, Velazco delineates the careers of Erich Moritz von Hornbostel (1877–1935), Karl Montgomery Siegfried Straube (1873–1950), Arthur Nikisch (1855–1922), Adolf Sandberger (1864–1943), Paul Mies (1889–1976), Ernst Bücken (1884–1949),

Ludwig Schermair (1876–1957), Charles Jean Eugène van den Borren (1874–1966), Curt Sachs (1881–1959), Georg Schünemann (1884–1945), and Max Seiffert (1868–1948), these being the 11 leaders whom Lange told Velazco had most influenced him before his emigration to Uruguay.

VENEZUELA

Gilard, Jacques. "Ricas mieles y buen café:" le café dans la chanson populaire du pourtour caraïbe. See item **4723.**

4817 Grases, Pedro. Participació dels catalans en la música coral veneçolana. (*in* Jornades d'Estudis Catalano-Americans, *4th, Barcelona, Spain, 1990. Actes.* Barcelona: Generalitat de Catalunya, Comissió Amèrica i Catalunya, 1992, p. 249–257)

In 1941 Joan Gols i Soler founded the Coral Catalana at Caracas. After his death the group took the name of Coral Gols in 1948, his son Marçal Gols Cavagliani assuming direction in 1967. Albert Grau (b. at Vich in 1937 but reared in Venezuela) founded the Schola Cantorum de Caracas, whose US and European tours in 1971–72 elicited rave reviews.

4818 Kuss, Malena. Virginia. (*in* New Grove Dictionary of Opera. New York: Grove's Dictionaries of Music, 1992, v. 4, p. 1018)

Premiered at the Teatro Caracas on April 27, 1873, José Angel Montero's operatic masterpiece sets a libretto by Domenico Bancalari. Kuss rightly concurs with quoted critical opinion that rates Montero as the only 19th-century Latin American whose "musico-dramaturgical craftsmanship" enabled him to compete with Carlos Gomes.

4819 Marciano, Rosaria. Carreño (García de Sena y Toro, (María) Teresa (Gertrudis de Jesús). (*in* New Grove Dictionary of Women Composers. New York: W.W. Norton, 1994, p. 106–107, bibl., facsim.)

For lack of an adequate bibliography, this unsatisfactory article dwells on Carreño's marriages (she married Emile Sauret in June 1873, not 1872 [Milinowski, p. 395]), and incorrectly states that "Caracas society was outraged that the aristocratic Carreño appeared in public playing the piano." Also mistaken is the statement: "almost all her works for piano were written between the ages of six and 15." Marciano cites five of her own pedagogic works as authorities for her text, disregarding Mario Milanca Guzmán's authoritative Carreño publications, and omitting any mention of the four piano pieces reprinted in *Inter-American Music Review* (Vol. 11, No. 2, 1991), opus numbers 9, 17, 25, and 35.

4820 Milanca Guzmán, Mario. La música en *El Cojo Ilustrado, 1892–1915.* Caracas: Dirección de Cultura, Univ. Central de Venezuela (UCV), 1993. 2 v. (932 p.): bibl. (Col. Letras de Venezuela; 113. Serie Ensayo)

Qualified in 1973 by Pedro Grasses as "the best Venezuelan fortnightly heretofore published," *El Cojo Ilustrado* went through 559 numbers. Jesús María Herrera Irigoyen, editor and proprietor, favored music and musicians with mentions or articles that serve Milanca Guzmán for 2,646 entries grouped under diverse headings. By far the largest musical excerpts in *El Cojo Ilustrado* refer to foreigners. Samples of excerpts pertaining to Venezualans: Pedro Elías Gutiérrez (p. 123) and Redescal Uzcátegui (p. 501–502). The history of Venezuelan bands (p. 125–131) is extremely valuable.

4821 Milanca Guzmán, Mario. La música en el tiempo histórico de Cipriano Castro: Caracas, 1899–1908. Caracas: Biblioteca de Autores y Temas Tachirenses, 1995. 292 p.: bibl., ill., index. (Biblioteca de Autores y Temas Tachirenses; 125)

After a succinct biography of Tachira native Cipriano Castro (1858–1924) and a summary of political events in Venezuela during Castro's rulership, the author studies musical events narrated in newspapers. Dividing subject matter under 14 headings, he proceeds from theaters, bands, eminent musicians, music teachers and music stores, violinists and pianists, two violin prodigies, opera singers, Venezuelan notables abroad, operas and zarzuelas, sacred music, National Academy of Fine Arts, women musicians, dances, and composers' scores, to conclusions. An unanalyzed name index at p. 275–288 enables the reader to pinpoint names mentioned five times or less, but is less useful for names such as José Antonio Calcaño, Sebastián Díaz Peña, and Emilio J. Mauri. Serious proofreading lapses constantly recur. In the same paragraph the death in New York of

Narciso L. Salicrup, a potential rival of Teresa Carreño, is given as 1902 and 1908 (p. 69). But the enormous amount of data merits the author limitless recognition. At p. 223–226 he lists the compositions (valses, polkas) dedicated to Zoila Rosa Martínez de Castro (1868–1952), and at p. 180 lists church compositions by natives. Publication of his book was aided by Cipriano Castro's being a native of Tachira, and the dedicatee being Dr. Ramón J. Velásquez, Director of the Biblioteca de Autores y Temas Tachirenses, of which series this book is number 125.

4822 Milanca Guzmán, Mario. La música venezolana: de la colonia a la república. Caracas: Monte Avila Editores Latinoamericana, 1994. 238 p.: bibl. (Estudios)

Contains five essays, three of them previously published: "Los Pardos en la Música Colonial Venezolana," "La Música en el Centenario del Libertador: 1883," and "Ramón de la Plaza Manrique (c. 1831–86): Autor de la Primera Historia Musical Publicada en el Continente Latinoamericano." Collection is fleshed out with two hitherto unpublished essays, "La Música Colonial Venezolana, según las Actas del Cabildo Eclesiástico de Caracas, 1580–1770" and "La Música en el Tiempo Histórico de José Antonio Páez: Visión Holística, 1830-1835/1839–1843." Author begins "Los Pardos" with the complaint that in 15 years of publication, the Mexican periodical *Heterofonía* from 1968–86 published only one article having to do with blacks, Alfred Lemmon's "Los Jesuitas y la Música de los Negros" (Nov./Dec. 1977 issue, p. 5–9). Instead, there were three more, not to mention ancillary articles in Jazz and Rock: "Baile de Negros" (Vol. 3, No. 17, March/April 1971); "El Elemento Negro en los Albores de la Música del Nuevo Mundo" (Vol. 10, No. 59, March/April 1978); and "El Condombe en el Folklore Afro-Uruguayo" (Vol. 14, Nos. 74/75, July/Dec. 1981). The author avers that only one book having to do with blacks was reviewed in *Heterofonía*, but he mistakes the title, calling Jorge Velazco's book *Dos músicos esclavos* whereas the book was titled *Dos músicos eslavos* and it discussed Anton Rubinstein and Dmitri Shostakovich rather than slaves. Throughout this work, music is slighted in favor of sociology. Accuracy being less favored, the author classes José Bernardo Alcedo (wrong birth year) and Daniel Alomía[s] Robles as Peruvian "músicos aborígenes"—an incorrect racial classification. The essay title ascribing to De la Plaza "the first musical history published in the Latin American continent" errs. J. Agustín Guerrero published *La música ecuatoriana desde su origen hasta 1875* (Quito: Imprenta Nacional, 1876) seven years before De la Plaza published his *Ensayos sobre el arte en Venezuela*, and J. Sáenz Poggio published his *Historia de la música guatemalteca desde la monarquía española hasta fines del año de 1877* at Guatemala City in 1878, five years before De la Plaza's *Ensayos*. Milanca Guzmán's newly published essays in this volume begin with an arid traversal of 190 years of published Caracas cathedral capitular acts that add nothing of musical significance to an article on the same subject published in *Revista Musical Chilena* (Vol. 33, No. 145, Jan./March 1979), an article certainly known to him (his note 30) but excluded from his bibliography.

4823 Olsen, Dale Alan. Music of the Warao of Venezuela: song people of the rain forest. Gainesville: Univ. Press of Florida, 1996. 1 v.: bibl., index.

This professor of ethnomusicology and director of the Center for Music of the Americas at Florida State Univ. is editor of the *Garland Encyclopedia of World Music* volume on "The Caribbean, Middle and South America." For the Warao, who live in a habitat that remains relatively undisturbed by outside influences, most aspects of life include music; it offers diversion, stability, protection, and power. Olsen provides 58 musical examples and textual transcription of 51 song texts which are translated, explained, analyzed, and several of which are included on an enclosed compact disk. He presents detailed information about Warao musical instruments, relating them to mythology, describing them (with numerous photographs), and placing them in their Circum-Caribbean context. He also describes how he conducted his research—creating a musical-cultural rapport with the Warao as he learned their songs and taught them music from his own traditions. In time he came to know and record the voices of the most knowledgeable singers, most of whom were shamans, and ultimately he was invited to attend shamanistic curing sessions.

4824 Stevenson, Robert. Luis Felipe Ramón y Rivera. (*Inter-Am. Music Rev.*, 14:1, Spring/Summer 1994, p. 163–164, bibl.)

Life story and panegyric of the Venezuelan ethnomusicologist and folklorist, husband of Isabel Aretz. Born at San Cristóbal, Táchira, on Aug. 23, 1913, he died at Caracas on Oct. 21, 1993. His abundant publications, 23 of which are itemized, assure future generations opportunity to admire and digest the results of his indefatigable ethnological and folklore research.

4825 Stevenson, Robert. Montero, José Angel. (*in* New Grove Dictionary of Opera. New York: Grove's Dictionaries of Music, 1992, p. 444–445, bibl.)

Born at Caracas on Oct. 2, 1832, Venezuela's preeminent composer of his generation died there on Aug. 24, 1881.

JOURNAL ABBREVIATIONS

An. Inst. Invest. Estét. Anales del Instituto de Investigaciones Estéticas. Univ. Nacional Autónoma de México. México.

ANPOCS BIB. Boletim Informativo e Bibliográfico de Ciências Sociais: BIB. Associação Nacional de Pós-Graduação e Pesquisa em Ciências Sociais. Rio de Janeiro.

Anu. Etnol./Habana. Anuario de Etnología. Academia de Ciencias de Cuba; Editorial Academia. La Habana.

ARTEunesp. ARTEunesp. Univ. Estadual Paulista. São Paulo.

ASCAP Playback. ASCAP Playback. American Society of Composers, Authors & Publishers. New York.

Bol. Lima. Boletín de Lima. Revista Cultural Científica. Lima.

Caravelle/Toulouse. Caravelle. Cahiers du monde hispanique et luso-brésilien. Univ. de Toulouse, Institute d'études hispaniques, hispano-americaines et luso-brésiliennes. Toulouse, France.

Caribb. Q. Caribbean Quarterly. Univ. of the West Indies. Mona, Jamaica.

Cuba. Stud. Cuban Studies. Univ. of Pittsburgh, Center for Latin American Studies. Pittsburgh, Penn.

Ethnomusicology/Society. Ethnomusicology. Society for Ethnomusicology. Ann Arbor, Mich.

Gac. Mus./México. Gaceta Musical. Centro Nacional de Investigación, Documentación e Información Musical Carlos Chávez (CENIDIM). México.

Herencia/San José. Herencia. Programa de Rescate y Revitalización del Patrimonio Cultural. San José.

Heterofonía/México. Heterofonía. México.

Inter-Am. Music Rev. Inter-American Music Review. Robert Stevenson. Los Angeles, Calif.

Lat. Am. Music Rev. Latin American Music Review. Univ. of Texas. Austin.

Newsl. Int. Hisp. Study Group. Newsletter of the International Hispanic Study Group. Dartmouth College, Dept. of Music. Hanover, N.H.

Not. Bibliogr. Hist. Notícia Bibliográfica e Histórica. Depto. de História, Pontifícia Univ. Católica de Campinas. Campinas, Brazil.

Rev. Bras. Mús. Revista Brasileira de Música. Escola de Música da Univ. Federal do Rio de Janeiro. Rio de Janeiro.

Rev. Inst. Invest. Musicol. Carlos Vega. Revista del Instituto de Investigación Musicológica Carlos Vega. Pontifícia Univ. Católica de Argentina, Facultad de Artes y Ciencias Musicales, Instituto de Investigación Musicológica Carlos Vega. Buenos Aires.

Rev. Music. Chil. Revista Musical Chilena. Univ. de Chile, Facultad de Ciencias y Artes Musicales y de la Representación. Santiago.

Rev. Musicol./Madrid. Revista de Musicología. Sociedad Española de Musicología. Madrid.

Rev. Soc. Bras. Mús. Contemp. Revista da Sociedade Brasileira de Música Contemporânea. Sociedade Brasileira de Música Contemporânea. São Paulo.

Sarance/Otavalo. Sarance. Instituto Otavaleño de Antropología. Otavalo, Ecuador.

Soc. Econ. Stud. Social and Economic Studies. Univ. of the West Indies, Institute of Social and Economic Research. Mona, Jamaica.

Todo es Hist. Todo es Historia. Buenos Aires.

PHILOSOPHY: LATIN AMERICAN THOUGHT

JUAN CARLOS TORCHIA ESTRADA, *General Secretariat, Organization of American States*

SIGUEN SIENDO VALIDAS las observaciones generales hechas al comienzo de esta Sección en el *HLAS 54*. No se detectan grandes cambios de orientación. No ha variado mayormente la posición sobre lo que es o debe ser la filosofía latinoamericana por parte de los grupos predominantes que la entienden como algo diferente de la filosofía en general, o de la realizada en otras regiones del mundo, y le atribuyen una misión de praxis concreta vinculada a la realidad latinoamericana actual y a la posición de América Latina en el mundo. Y puede decirse también que lo que aquí se ha denominado "filosofía en general" (en sus muy diversas variantes de escuela) se sigue practicando en la región por parte de los interesados en ella, con prescindencia del sector antes mencionado, el cual podría recibir la caracterización amplia de "latinoamericanismo filosófico." Quizás uno de los puntos de encuentro tangencial (lo que no necesariamente supone diálogo) sea el tema de modernidad/postmodernidad, que interesa tanto a los filósofos académicos como a los latinoamericanistas, bien que por distintas razones. En el caso de Brasil la dicotomía señalada no parece tan visible; pero hay una notable preocupación por el pensamiento nacional, persistente a lo largo de los años. Como quiera que sea, debe afirmarse que la dedicación al pensamiento latinoamericano (tomando "pensamiento" en un sentido amplio), ya sea ella más o menos cercana al estudio formal o al juicio de valor ideológico, tiene como consecuencia una producción constante que, más allá de diferencias, cumple con una voluntad y—podría agregarse—obligación de autoconocimiento.

El resumen que sigue pretende facilitar al lector una rápida visión de algunos temas salientes de la información recogida. En los casos en que es pertinente, por el asunto o por ser menos abundante la bibliografía, remitimos a entradas que se relacionan con el mismo tema en el *HLAS 54*, sean de esta Sección o de otra.

GENERAL

Como siempre, hay trabajos que enfocan el tema de América Latina con alto grado de generalidad, amplitud o visión filosófica. En algunos casos, la amplitud está dada por la variedad de enfoques, proveniente de las contribuciones a reuniones o congresos. Entre las reuniones se encuentran, en esta entrega, dos que han tenido por tema, respectivamente: *América Latina ante la Revolución Francesa* (item **4869**), y *América Latina, el desafío del tercer milenio* (item **4827**).[1] En cuanto a congresos, se encuentran las actas del que tuvo lugar en Ciudad Juárez como Congreso Internacional de Filosofía Latinoamericana, en 1990 y con el título general de "América Latina, Identidad y Diferencia" (item **4850**).

Algunas obras generales, tanto individuales como colectivas, pueden identificarse por el tema principal: Mestizaje e Identidad (items **4828** y **4924**, y también sobre identidad, *HLAS 54:5351* y *HLAS 54: 5318*); Mestizaje y Racismo (item **4878,** y sobre mestizaje cultural, *HLAS 54:5370*); Caudillaje (item **4855**); Modernidad y Modernización (items **4876, 4895** y **4903**); Integración (items **4886** y **4897** y *HLAS 54:5336*); e Idea de Nación (items **4830** y **4888**). Entre este tipo de obras cabe señalar, por último, un oportuno trabajo sobre las relaciones entre América Latina y el Caribe de habla inglesa (item **4864**) y la obra de Ezequiel Martínez Estrada, *Diferencias y semejanzas entre los países de América Latina* (item **4879**).

El tema de la filosofía latinoamericana, como problema y como objeto de labor historiográfica, sigue interesando, cincuenta años después de sus primeras manifestaciones más sistemáticas en la década del '40: después de tan extenso período, el asunto ya está pidiendo una historia. En esta entrega, y con algún retraso, se incluye sobre el particular un valioso número de la revista *The Philosophical Forum* (item **4893**). Horacio Cerutti-Guldberg realiza una visión general del problema (item **4845**) y Raúl Fornet Betancourt incursiona en el mismo tema en dos oportunidades (items **4863** y **4862**). Arturo A. Roig, desde una perspectiva personal y recientemente relacionada con la teoría del discurso, examina la misma cuestión (item **4900**). De gran utilidad para el estudio del tema (un tema que no siempre es tratado con intención de *estudio*) son el trabajo de Iván Jaksic y Ceres Birkhead (item **4870**) y un artículo de Abelardo Villegas (item **4915**). También conviene recordar aquí la antología de Isabel Monal (véase *HLAS 54:5339*). Pueden verse también las ponencias del Congreso Internacional Extraordinario de Filosofía (item **4851**) y el volumen *Para una filosofía desde América Latina* (item **4887**). Por último, representa una posición crítica frente al latinoamericanismo filosófico actual el artículo de Javier Sasso, "El autodescubrimiento de América como tarea filosófica" (item **4905;** del mismo autor, véase *HLAS 54:5367*).

El concepto de "historia de las ideas," clave en la historiografía latinoamericanista que se practica desde (o cercanamente a) la filosofía, tiene en la presente Sección varias manifestaciones. Manuel Claps presenta una visión marxista de la disciplina (item **4847**). La concepción de José Gaos al respecto es estudiada por Estela Fernández y Adriana Arpini (item **4858;** de Estela Fernández véase también item **4933**). Posiciones no latinoamericanas sobre el tema son expuestas por F. Ferreira de Cassone (item **4860**). Arturo A. Roig concibe la historia de las ideas como instrumento de autoconciencia latinoamericana (item **4901**). Por último, Enrique Zuleta Alvarez ofrece una visión amplia de autores y ofrece conclusiones sobre el futuro de la disciplina (item **4923**).

Tanto la teología como la filosofía de la liberación siguen estando representadas, aunque tal vez la primera mantiene mayor identidad, en tanto los autores de la segunda, después de la etapa programática y de afirmación de la nueva posición filosófica, han tendido a diversificarse dentro del mismo clima intelectual o ideológico. Sobre la teología de la liberación—cuyas manifestaciones, como se ha indicado en otras oportunidades, se recogen aquí sólo selectivamente—puede verse una importante bibliografía (item **4838**) y una clara visión de conjunto (item **4871**).[2] Una posición equilibrada desde la filosofía de la liberación se expresa en un artículo de Mario Casalla (item **4842**). Sobre estos temas pueden verse, en *HLAS 54*, los items 5328, 5341, 5350, 5352, 5511.

La temática de la conquista de América y los múltiples problemas a que dio lugar en la época, en especial la cuestión del indio, obtuvo gran vigencia con motivo del Quinto Centenario, pero podría decirse que ha tomado nuevo incremento con independencia de esa celebración (o execración). El lado negativo del fenómeno esta expresado aquí en un libro de Enrique Dussel, con el estilo directo de este autor (item **4852**). Una obra de síntesis de franca utilidad, aunque no se compartan todas sus opiniones, es la de Luciano Pereña, *La idea de justicia en la conquista de América*, título con resonancias hankeanas (item **4892**). Para volúmenes colectivos sobre el tema pueden verse los items **4896** y **4907** y, en *HLAS 54*, items 5320, 5323, 5325, 5329. Las Casas es objeto de varios enfoques, destacándose especialmente el libro de Gustavo Gutiérrez (item **4866**). Sobre Vitoria se encontrará la excelente obra de Castilla Urbano (item **4843**), además de la de María Lourdes Redondo, que contiene referencias a José de Acosta y a Veracruz (item **4898**). Interesa señalar la publicación de una obra en italiano sobre el padre Clavijero (item **4877**) y otra sobre las reducciones jesuíticas en el marco de "América como utopía," de Beatriz Fernández Herrero (item **4859**).[3]

En la literatura sobre el marxismo latinoamericano encontramos reiterada la atención a las ideas de Antonio Gramsci en el trabajo de José Aricó (item **4834**) y en otro dedicado a la influencia de Gramsci en América Latina (item **4826**).[4]

Finalmente, desde varios ángulos se hace referencia a la influencia del krausismo: para el caso de Hostos, especialmente en el artículo de José Luis Abellán (item **4959**); en Brasil, con un estudio de Antonio Paim (item **5053**); y en Uruguay, items **5065** y **5070**.

MEXICO

En el caso de México se encuentran representados los diversos períodos de su pensamiento filosófico: 1) la colonia, con *Filosofía social de los pensadores novohispanos*, de Mauricio Beuchot (item **4927**);[5] 2) el siglo XIX, con trabajos sobre el liberalismo (item **4934**), el positivismo (sobre Porfirio Parra, item **4925** y también *HLAS 54: 1333*), la relación entre liberalismo y positivismo (item **4928**) y la ideología conservadora (items **4937**); y 3) el siglo XX, con dos enfoques de conjunto, el volumen colectivo *Historia de la filosofía en México: siglo XX* (item **4948**) y un artículo de Adolfo Sánchez Vázquez (item **4943**), además de la atención prestada a pensadores individuales, como Vasconcelos (especialmente la extensa obra de Claude Fell, item **4932**), Gaos (un libro de Vera Yamuni, item **4950**), Zea (Jalif de Bertranou, item **4938**) y Abelardo Villegas (un libro dedicado a este autor por Tzvi Medin, item **4939**). Hay que agregar además dos oportunas reediciones: la obra bibliográfica clásica de Valverde Téllez (item **4944**) y la de García Cantú sobre el socialismo en México (item **4935**).

AMERICA CENTRAL

Donald Hodges continúa su obra sobre Sandino (item **4953** y *HLAS 54:5402*). Para el sandinismo visto desde el cristianismo revolucionario, véase item **4952**. Resultan también muy oportunas la publicación póstuma del libro de Constantino Láscaris, *Las ideas en Centroamérica, 1838–1970* (item **4957**), y la reedición de textos de José Cecilio del Valle (item **4958**).

CARIBE INSULAR

La difusión de Hostos se ha beneficiado con un número de la revista *Cuadernos Americanos* que le dedica parte de su contenido, según se refleja en los items **4959, 4960, 4967, 4969** y **4985**. A esto se agrega un nuevo libro de Maldonado Denis (item **4970**) y un estudio de la filosofía de Hostos por parte de Carlos Rojas Osorio (item **4980**).[6] Lo que no es frecuente, se hallarán en esta entrega cinco publicaciones sobre Santo Domingo: un panorama de sus manifestaciones filosóficas (item **4963**); una obra sobre el socialismo en el país (item **4973**); otra sobre marxismo y positivismo (item **4978**); un examen de la cuestión nacional dominicana (item **4974**); y un estudio del pensamiento dominicano entre 1844 y 1861 (item **4977**). Como siempre, hay varias entradas sobre Martí, entre las que recordamos una sobre sus ideas económicas (item **4975**). En el caso de Cuba hay también una buena contribución sobre Félix Varela (item **4983**). La figura científica de Antonio Mestre es atendida en un artículo (item **4968;** véase también *HLAS 54:2082*).

VENEZUELA

Señalaremos en esta parte dos obras documentales: una sobre Miranda (item **4991;** véase también *HLAS 54:5426*) y otra sobre el pensamiento liberal en el siglo XIX (item **4986**). De Laureano Vallenilla Lanz se reedita su obra *Disgregación e integración: ensayo sobre la formación de la nacionalidad venezolana* (item **4993**). Entre los trabajos críticos recordaremos uno escrito en italiano sobre Bolívar (item **4992**) y otro sobre variados temas, del destacado crítico Pedro Grases (item **4990**).

COLOMBIA

Una vez más se incluye una excelente obra sobre el desarrollo de la filosofía en Colombia, en este caso del siglo XX: *Tendencias actuales de la filosofía en Colombia* (item **4996**).[7] También hay una buena edición de naturaleza documental sobre la influencia de Bentham (item **4998;** sobre benthamismo y antibenthamismo en Colombia, ver *HLAS 52:5371*).

ECUADOR

Un libro sobre Espinoza Pólit (item **5005**), la reedición de una obra de Belisario Quevedo (item **5009**) y una visión de conjunto sobre el ensayo ecuatoriano (item **5010**) son de obligada mención. Hay también dos entradas sobre Montalvo (items **5004** y **5007;** para un amplio libro sobre Montalvo, ver *HLAS 54:5443*).

PERU

En el caso de Perú, y habida cuenta de lo que hemos comprobado en otras oportunidades, no extrañará que abunde la literatura sobre Mariátegui. Casi la mitad de las entradas que aquí se incluyen sobre este país se ocupan total o parcialmente con el Amauta. Nos limitamos a señalar las obras de mayor extensión: un Encuentro Internacional realizado en Francia (item **5027**); un simposio llevado a cabo en Nueva York (item **5013**); una edición de escritos juveniles (item **5020**); una síntesis clara de la vida y la obra de Mariátegui (item **5012**); y un intento de interpretación fundado en el análisis del lenguaje (item **5015**). Hay también en esta subsección entradas sobre Salazar Bondy (item **5011;** ver también *HLAS 54:5461*); sobre el tema del indio (item **5016**), sobre el positivismo (item **5022**); sobre la ideología de la Independencia (item **5028**); y sobre Haya de la Torre (items **5017, 5026** y **5032**). Asimismo debe recordarse el justo y bien elaborado homenaje a Francisco Miró Quesada en *Lógica, razón y humanismo* (item **5019**).

BOLIVIA

Un libro sobre Franz Tamayo (item **5034**) es lo más saliente en la escasa producción recogida sobre este país.

CHILE

No es mucho tampoco lo que se ha incluido sobre el pensamiento chileno en esta entrega. Se destacan dos artículos sobre el liberalismo del siglo XIX: uno sobre "los girondinos chilenos" (item **5036**) y otro sobre Francisco Bilbao (item **5037**).[8]

BRASIL

En esta subsección hallamos varios trabajos sobre Gilberto Freyre, especialmente los de Vamireh Chacon (items **5044** y **5042**) y de Ricardo Vélez Rodríguez (item **5061**).[9] La Escuela de Recife continúa recibiendo atención: los items **5045** y **5048** se refieren a Tobias Barreto (el segundo es un artículo de Ubiratan Macedo), el **5050** a Tobias Barreto y Sylvio Romero, y el item **5057** es un número especial de la *Revista Brasileira de Filosofia*.[10] Temas menos frecuentados son atendidos por el citado Vamireh Chacon (sobre Lukács en Brasil, item **5043**) y Antonio Paim (sobre el krausismo lusobrasileño, item **5053**). Sobre religión en Brasil escriben Riolando Azzi (item **5039**) y Fred Gillette Sturm (item **5060**). Una obra de conjunto sobre la realidad brasileña es *A idéia de Brasil moderno*, de Octavio Ianni (item **5046**).

URUGUAY

Dos obras sólidas se encuentran entre los materiales recogidos sobre Uruguay: el libro de García Morales sobre Clarín y Rodó (item **5066**) y el de Thomas Glick sobre el darwinismo (item **5067**). Sobre historia de las ideas pueden verse items **5064** y **5071**. Con el krausismo están relacionados un libro sobre Batlle Ordóñez (item **5065**) y un artículo sobre los "krausistas belgas" (item **5070**). Interpretaciones de Vaz Ferreira aparecen en items **5069, 5068** y **5072**. Un ensayo de amplia visión sobre la historia uruguaya es la obra de Abril Trigo, item **5073**.

ARGENTINA

Entre las obras de mayor aliento dentro de esta entrega se cuentan: el volumen colectivo *La Argentina del 80 al 80* (item **5076**); *Las vetas del texto: una lectura filosófica de Alberdi, los positivistas, Juan B. Justo* (item **5088**) y *La letra gótica: recepción de Kant en la Argentina* (item **5087**), ambas de Jorge E. Dotti; un homenaje a José Luis Romero (item **5118**); un volumen colectivo sobre la recepción de la Revolución Francesa en el país (item **5094;** ver también *HLAS 54:5537*); *El nacimiento de la psicología en la Argentina* (item **5079;** ver también *HLAS 54:5502*); un homenaje a Arturo A. Roig (item **5077**); y un libro sobre Joaquín V. González (item **5117**). La obra de Juan Bautista Alberdi es un tema que se reitera. Además del libro de Dotti antes citado, se lo encuentra en *La filosofía de Alberdi*, de Olsen Ghirardi (item **5093**); en un artículo de Angel Castellán (item **5080**); y en el libro *Pensamiento argentino*, de Lucía Piossek Prebisch (item **5112**). En cuanto a recuperación de textos, puede verse: *La ciudad anarquista americana* de Pierre Quiroule (item **5095**); la edición crítica de *Radiografía de la pampa*, de Ezequiel Martínez Estrada (item **5109**); y *El pensamiento peronista* (item **5111**). Sin pretensión de exhaustividad, hay también trabajos críticos sobre: Esteban Echeverría (item **5075**), las formas de identidad en el Río de la Plata (item **5081**), Martínez Estrada (items **5082** y **5115**), Juan B. Justo (item **5090** y *HLAS 54:2895.*), Enrique Dussel (item **5091**), el humanismo platónico en la Argentina (item **5102**), Rodolfo Kusch (item **5097**), Sarmiento (items **5108** y **5125**), Carlos Octavio Bunge (item **5113**), el krausismo—que vimos antes examinado en Brasil y Uruguay—(item **5119**), Alejandro Korn (item **5121**) y Héctor P. Agosti (item **5124**).

NOTAS:

1   Sobre la Revolución Francesa y América Latina en general véase también *HLAS 54: 5310.* Para el mismo tema en relación con Brasil, véase *HLAS 54:3265;* en relación con México, *HLAS 54:1150.* Sobre Argentina, véase más adelante en esta Introducción.

2   Es interesante cómo es vista la misma corriente desde el Caribe anglófono, en item bi91–23820. Para el caso de Brasil véase más adelante, item bi90–3385.

3   Sobre el problema del indio véase también el artículo de Rolena Adorno en *HLAS*

54:3558; el libro de Pagden en *HLAS 54:5355;* y las indicaciones dadas en la Introducción a *HLAS 52.*

4   Para Gramsci en el caso particular de Colombia véase más adelante, item bi94–3225.

5   Para otros temas de filosofía en la Nueva España en *HLAS 54,* véase items 5385, 5392, 5395, 5398.

6   De este autor, sobre el mismo tema, ver *HLAS 54:5420.* Otras entradas de y sobre Hostos se encuentran en *HLAS 54,* items 1988, 5406, 5411 y 5412.

7   Obras semejantes se encuentran en *HLAS 50:4631, HLAS 50:4632, HLAS 52:5372* y *HLAS 54:5439.*

8   Sobre Chile, siglo XIX, pueden verse varias entradas en *HLAS 54,* items 5464–5470.

9   Sobre Freyre, ver también *HLAS 54:5483.*

10   En relación con Tobias Barreto, ver también *HLAS 54,* items 5474 y 5475.

GENERAL

4826   Alvarez, Federico *et al.* Gramsci en América Latina: del silencio al olvido. Caracas: Fondo Editorial Tropykos; Instituto de Filosofía, UCV, 1991. 101 p.: bibl.

Estudios y comentarios sobre la obra de Gramsci que, en su mayoría, se refieren a la aplicación que de esa obra puede hacerse a América Latina. El más explícito en ese sentido: Eduardo Quintana B., "Gramsci, el Estado y la Democracia en Venezuela."

4827   América Latina, el desafío del tercer milenio. Dirección de Adolfo Colombres. Buenos Aires: Ediciones del Sol, 1993. 306 p.: bibl., ill. (Serie antropológica)

Algunos de los temas que se reiteran en el volumen: minorías étnicas (alteridad, identidad); utopía; y modernidad y postmodernidad (aplicado a América Latina). Entre los autores figuran: Roberto Fernández Retamar, Guillermo Bonfil Batalla, Darcy Ribeiro, Eduardo Galeano, Juan G. Cobo Borda, Fernando Aínsa, Miguel León Portilla y Alfredo Colombres, quien pone al volumen un extenso prólogo y es autor de dos trabajos.

4828   Amériques latines: une altérité. Direction de Christian Descamps. Paris: Centre Georges Pompidou, 1993. 207 p.: bibl. (Espace international. Philosophie, 0989–3830)

Utilizable para el problema del mestizaje—principalmente en el sentido cultural—y consiguientemente para la cuestión de la identidad latinoamericana. Incluye ejemplos del área portuguesa. Finalmente, un artículo se refiere a Lastarria y otro a la función del filósofo latinoamericano.

4829   Amherster Kolloquium zur Deutschen Literatur, *18th, Germany, 1994.* Neue Welt—Dritte Welt: interkulturelle Beziehungen Deutschlands zu Lateinamerika und der Karibik. Edited by Sigrid Bauschinger and Susan L. Cocalis. Tübingen, Germany: Francke, 1994. 279 p.: bibl., ill., index.

Papers presented by specialists in Germany at Amherst College colloquium. Works analyze German perceptions and interpretations of Latin American and Caribbean culture, especially in art and literature. Of particular interest are German analyses of Brazilian and Caribbean syncretism, the epistemology of exoticism, and solidarity with Latin American revolutionary activities depicted in East German drama. [C.K. Converse]

4830   Anderle, Adán. El positivismo y la modernización de la identidad nacional en América Latina. (*Anu. Estud. Am.,* 45, 1988, p. 419–484)

Trabajo extenso que maneja una amplia bibliografía. Se detiene especialmente en los conceptos de nación y nacionalidad en el positivismo latinoamericano.

Arcelus-Ulibarrena, Juana Mary. La profecía de Joaquín de Fiore en el "Floreto de Sant Francisco" y su presencia en el Nuevo Mundo. See item **795.**

4831   Arciniegas, Germán. América es otra cosa. Antología y epílogo de J.G. Cobo Borda. Bogotá: Intermedio Editores; Círculo de Lectores, 1992. 245 p.: bibl.

Además de los textos antológicos, contiene una carta de Arciniegas a Cobo Borda, en la que el primero reflexiona sobre su obra.

4832   Arciniegas, Germán. América, tierra firme y otros ensayos. Prólogo de Pedro Gómez Valderrama. Cronología y bibliografía de J.G. Cobo Borda. Caracas: Biblioteca Ayacucho, 1990. 428 p.: bibl. (Biblioteca Ayacucho; 158)

Contiene: *América, Tierra Firme*

(1937); *Los alemanes en la conquista de América* (1941); y *Este pueblo de América* (1945). Como todos los libros de esta colección va precedida de un prólogo, una cronología y una bibliografía.

4833 Argumedo, Alcira. Los silencios y las voces en América Latina: notas sobre el pensamiento nacional y popular. Buenos Aires: Ediciones del Pensamiento Nacional; Ediciones Colihué, 1993. 334 p.: bibl.

En la apreciación de los problemas—especialmente los político-sociales—la obra es manifestación de la corriente que en la Argentina se ha calificado como "nacional y popular" y que no es ajena al peronismo. Además de ensayos que se ocupan de la situación mundial contemporánea y de la fundamentación de las ciencias sociales, hay artículos como los siguientes: "Las Otras Ideas en América Latina;" "La Idea de Naturaleza Humana y Sociedad en el Pensamiento Latinoamericano;" y "Algunos Conceptos de Análisis Político en la Perspectiva Nacional y Popular."

4834 Aricó, José. La cola del diablo: itinerario de Gramsci en América Latina. Buenos Aires: Puntosur Editores, 1988. 226 p.: bibl.

Es un trabajo testimonial de meditación teórico-política más que de historiografía. Importa como muestra de la gran influencia que Gramsci tuvo sobre el autor y un grupo de intelectuales marxistas argentinos, quienes fueron expulsados del Partido Comunista y fundaron la revista *Pasado y Presente.* Es de hecho también una contribución a la historia del marxismo en América Latina, que será de indudable utilidad al historiador de las ideas.

4835 Arpini de Márquez, Adriana. La concepción de la historia y la utopía en tres pensadores latinoamericanos: Alejandro Korn, Alejandro Deustua y José Vasconcelos. (*Cuyo/Mendoza*, 7:1, 1990, p. 123–152)

La concepción de la historia en los tres pensadores estudiados, y la proporción de pensamiento utópico que hay en cada uno de ellos son los ejes de la comparación que realiza el artículo.

4836 Baciero, Carlos. *Carta Magna de los indios*: ensayo de filosofía de la historia hispanoamericana. (*Relig. Cult.*, 35;170, junio/sept. 1989, p. 385–395)

Comentario al libro de Luciano Pereña, *Carta Magna de los indios* (1987). En éste se destaca la participación de los teólogos de la Escuela de Salamanca en la denuncia de los abusos de la conquista y en la legislación sobre las Indias.

4837 Baptiste, Victor N. Bartolome de Las Casas and Thomas More's *Utopia*: connections and similarities; a translation and study. Culver City, Calif.: Labyrinthos, 1990. 84 p.: bibl., ill.

Se trata de la traducción al inglés del *Memorial de remedios para las Indias* (1516) de Bartolomé de las Casas. En el estudio preliminar el autor sostiene que Thomas More conoció este escrito y lo utilizó para su *Utopía.*

4838 Birkeflet, Svein Helge and **Kjell Nordstokke.** Latin American liberation theology: a bibliography on essential writings. Oslo: Univ. of Oslo, Faculty of Theology, 1991. 122 p. (Bibliography series/Univ. of Oslo, Faculty of Theology, 0802–6556; 2)

Incluye 80 autores, además de documentos de la Iglesia. La mayor parte de las entradas se refieren a obras teológicas. El total es de casi 500. Proporciona notas biográficas de los autores, señala traducciones cuando las obras originales son en español, y recoge también trabajos en alemán e inglés cuando tratan de la teología latinoamericana de la liberación.

4839 Botero Uribe, Darío. Manifiesto del pensamiento latinoamericano / Darío Botero Uribe. 1. ed. Cali : Universidad del Valle, 1993. 63 p. ; (Colección Edición previa. Serie Ensayo)

En la tónica del lationamericanismo filosófico, una de sus insitencias es negar el carácter occidental de América Latina.

4840 Buela, Alberto E. El sentido de América: seis ensayos en busca de nuestra identidad. Prólogo de Alberto Caturelli. Buenos Aires: Distribuidora y Editora Theoría; Ediciones Nuestro Tiempo, 1990. 130 p.: bibl.

No son tanto seis ensayos en busca de una identidad, como seis ocasiones en que una identidad ya encontrada se confronta, no sin cierta pasión, con otras posiciones. Sostiene que "los principios de una conciencia nacional iberoamericana están dados por una simbiosis de lo católico y lo indigenista." América es en parte producto de Occidente, pero del Occidente anterior a la Reforma y el cartesianismo. En otros aspectos se expresan opiniones contra el liberalismo y el "social-cristianismo," y en favor del nacionalismo y del peronismo.

4841 Casa de Velázquez (Madrid). Las utopías en el mundo hispánico: actas del coloquio celebrado en la Casa de Velázquez, 24/26-XI-1988 = Les utopies dans le monde hispanique: actes du colloque tenu à la Casa de Velázquez, 24/26-XI-1988. Edición coordinada por Jean-Pierre Etienvre. Madrid: Casa de Velázquez, Univ. Complutense, 1990. 319 p.: bibl., ill.

Los artículos referentes a América Latina son dos: "Las Reducciones Jesuíticas en la Encrucijada de Dos Utopías," por Stelio Cro; y "Tensiones Utópicas en la Literatura Hispanoamericana del Siglo XX," por Luis Sainz de Medrano. El resto está dedicado a expresiones "utópicas" en España, pero todos son de interés para este tema, muy reiterado en los últimos tiempos.

4842 Casalla, Mario. Sentido y vigencia actual de la filosofía de la liberación en América Latina. (*Rev. Filos. Latinoam. Cienc. Soc.*, 4:14m, nov. 1989, p. 69–81)

Afirma el autor que la filosofía de la liberación es un "acto fundacional" del pensamiento latinoamericano. Por ella, dicho pensamiento deja de ser filosofía hecha *en* Latinoamérica, para ser filosofía *desde* Latinoamérica. Intenta también aclarar los conceptos de "liberación" y "filosofía." El artículo revela una actitud equilibrada y constructiva.

4843 Castilla Urbano, Francisco. El pensamiento de Francisco de Vitoria: filosofía política e indio americano. Barcelona: Anthropos, Editorial del Hombre; Iztapalapa, México: Univ. Autónoma Metropolitana, Unidad Iztapalapa, 1992. 378 p.: bibl., index. (Pensamiento crítico/pensamiento utópico; 69. Filosofía política)

Como lo indica el subtítulo, la obra trata dos temas interconectados: la teoría política de Vitoria y la función que sus ideas cumplieron en el debate sobre la cuestión de la Conquista. Ambos aspectos, tal como son desarrollados por el autor, son de lectura altamente recomendable. El enfoque se separa de la historiografía anterior, en la proporción en que ésta estuvo ideológicamente motivada— nacionalismo de corte imperial-franquista—o

puso el principal acento en Vitoria como creador del Derecho Internacional. El método seguido es "historicista," en el sentido de situar los textos en su momento histórico. Esto es particularmente aplicable al tratamiento de las Relecciones sobre tema americano. Dichas Relecciones son vistas no tanto en función de la cuestión de los justos títulos como en el marco del problema de la naturaleza del indio y su posible salvación religiosa. El lector encontrará bien resumido el contenido del libro en las Conclusiones. Muy buena bibliografía.

4844 Castro Leiva, Luis. The ironies of the Spanish-American revolutions. (*Int. Soc. Sci. J.*, 119, Feb. 1989, p. 53–67, facsims.)

Crítica a la función de la Ilustración— especialmente la francesa—en el pensamiento político de la Independencia, desde el punto de vista de la teoría del discurso y de la retórica. Artículo de argumentación compleja y difícil intelección. El autor lo es también de *La Gran Colombia: una ilusión ilustrada* (1984).

4845 Cerutti Guldberg, Horacio. Latin American philosophy: history and epistemological problems. Translated by John D. Kraniauskas. (*UNISA Lat. Am. Rep.*, 5:1, March 1989, p. 12–21, bibl.)

El libro está dividido en dos partes: 1) se intenta la difícil tarea de resumir en pocas páginas el proceso de cómo se ha concebido la filosofía latinoamericana desde 1930 hasta la actualidad, y lo hace con actitud objetiva; y 2) se examinan los problemas epistemológicos y metodológicos de la cuestión: el objeto de la filosofía latinoamericana, su lenguaje, las categorías historiográficas y el modo de utilización del marxismo.

4846 Cesar, Constança Marcondes. Filosofia na América Latina. São Paulo: Paulinas, 1988. 84 p. (Ensaios filosóficos)

Rápida revisión del tema. Excesivamente panorámica para el estado actual de la investigación.

4847 Claps, Manuel. Notas para una metodología de la historia de las ideas. (*Estud. Polít. Econ. Filos.*, 104, sept. 1989, p. 59–61)

Propone que la historia de las ideas sea historia de las ideologías, y que para realizarla se utilice "como marco conceptual la teoría marxista de la historia."

4848 Claro Tocornal, Regina. La Revolución Francesa y la independencia hispano-americana. (*Rev. Chil. Humanid.*, número especial, 1989, p. 73–92, bibl.)

No se refiere únicamente a la Revolución Francesa, sino en general a la influencia de ideas europeas en el movimiento de Independencia. El artículo parece influido por las tesis de Carlos Stoetzer sobre la preeminencia de las ideas escolásticas y españolas frente a las francesas. Ver *HLAS 54:1085* para el comentario del historiador.

4849 Colóquio UERJ, *4th, Rio de Janeiro, 1992.* América: descoberta ou invenção. Rio de Janeiro: Imago Editora, 1992. 391 p.: bibl. (Série Diversos)

Exposiciones centrales del coloquio: 1) José J. Brunner, "América Latina en la Encrucijada de la Modernidad;" 2) Guillermo Giucci, "A tecnologia e o Sagrado no Novo Mundo;" 3) Carlos Monsiváis, "La Vanguardia y el Proceso Revolucionario;" 4) Eulália M. Lahmeyer Lobo, "Os Límites da Dependência;" y 5) João A. Hansen, "Colonial e Barroco." Hay además comunicaciones y comentarios para cada tema del coloquio. El conjunto del material es muy variado.

4850 Congreso Internacional de Filosofía Latinoamericana, *1st, Ciudad Juárez, Mexico, 1990.* América Latina, identidad y diferencia: actas del I Congreso Internacional de Filosofía Latinoamericana. Ciudad Juárez, Chihuahua: Univ. Autónoma de Ciudad Juárez, 1992. 267 p.: bibl.

De esta extensa obra destacamos algunas ponencias: 1) Leopoldo Zea, "Filosofar desde la Realidad Americana." Señala la necesidad de una ética que norme las relaciones entre las Américas y el mundo. 2) Enrique Dussel, "Filosofía de la Liberación: Desde la Praxis de los Oprimidos." Es a la vez: historia de la filosofía de la liberación, confrontación con otras posiciones y apreciación del horizonte futuro de dicha filosofía. 3) Raúl Fornet Betancourt, "Filosofía y Teología en América Latina." Traza líneas para un diálogo entre la teología de la liberación y la filosofía de la liberación. 4) Fernando Ainsa, "Reflejos y Antinomias de la Problemática de la Identidad en el Discurso Narrativo Latinoamericano." El tema de la identidad, tan abundantemente tratado por los enfoques filosóficos, es visto aquí desde la perspectiva de la novela latino-americana. 5) Ofelia Schutte, "La Creación Cultural desde la Perspectiva de la Diferencia." Tiene por objetivo "revigorizar la crítica de izquierda en relación al ideario conservador vigente." 6) José Luis Gómez-Martínez, "Consideraciones Epistemológicas Para una Filosofía de la Liberación." Teniendo muy en cuenta la cuestión de la dependencia, propone un "discurso axiológico que sea verdadero fundamento de la filosofía latinoamericana." 7) Rosa Licata y Clara Jalif de Bertranou, "El Análisis Lingüístico y la Indagación Filosófica." 8) Tomás Mallo, "Aproximación a una Antropología Filosófica Latinoamericana." La antropología filosófica latinoamericana debería ocuparse de tres temas: el conocimiento científico-técnico, las comunicaciones y el poder. 9) Laura Mues de Schrenk, "Una de las Tareas de la Filosofía Latinoamericana." Propone que la filosofía contribuya a "una discusión racional, pública y abierta acerca de las leyes morales que las personas estén dispuestas a aceptar." 10) Enrique Arriagada, "Enjuiciamiento al Pensar Americano por una Autenticidad Sobornada." En América se debe "hacer filosofía de la miseria desde la miseria." 11) Rubén R. García Clark, "La Historiografía de las Ideas Filosóficas en Latinoamérica: la Propuesta de Arturo Andrés Roig." Es una buena exposición de lo esencial del pensamiento de Roig sobre el tema, y contiene algunas observaciones a dicho autor, muy cuidadosamente formuladas. 12) Enrique Hernández, "Función de la Filosofía y Misión del Pensamiento." Opone la función de la filosofía, que es importar paradigmas, a la misión del pensamiento, que es lograr la liberación. 13) Edgard Montiel, "Dialéctica de la Razón Americana." De acuerdo con Leopoldo Zea, distingue cuatro etapas de la conciencia filosófica latinoamericana: el estudio del pensamiento nacional; la historia de las ideas latinoamericanas; la filosofía de la historia americana; y la historia universal vista desde América Latina. 14) Jaime Rubio Angulo, "Prácticas Populares, Ficciones Narrativas y Reflexión Filosófica en América Latina." Aplica a *Cien años de soledad* reflexiones basadas en Ricoer, Lacan y la hermenéutica contemporánea. 15) Michele Pallotini, "Meditación en Cuidad Juarez." Llama la atención sobre la conveniencia de no "regionalizar" excesivamente la filosofía latinoamericana, de modo que tienda a ser válida para el resto del mundo.

4851 Congreso Internacional Extraordinario de Filosofía, *1987, Córdoba, Argentina.* Congreso Internacional Extraordinario de Filosofía: del 20 al 26 de setiembre de 1987. v. 3. Córdoba, Argentina: Univ. Nacional de Córdoba, 1988. 3 v. (1492 p.): bibl.

Destacamos los siguientes artículos de interés para esta sección: José Luis Abellán, "José Gaos y el Fundamento Filosófico de la Historia de las Ideas;" E. Demenchonok, "La Filosofía de la Liberación Latinoamericana;" Pablo Guadarrama González, "¿Por qué y para qué Filosofar en América Latina?;" Carlos Gutiérrez, "Hegel y Humboldt: Dos Visiones Antitéticas y Contemporáneas de América;" Carlos E. Paladines, "El Humanismo Histórico a la Luz de un Pensador Argentino: Rodolfo Agoglia;" Arturo A. Roig, "Civilización y Barbarie;" R. Ruibal Gutiérrez y Leticia Soler, "Sobre el Sentido de los Positivismos Latinoamericanos y los Proyectos Modernizadores en un Siglo de Historia."

Cruz Capote, Orlando. La primera conferencia de los comunistas latinoamericanos. See item **1054.**

4852 Dussel, Enrique. 1492: el encubrimiento del otro; hacia el origen del "mito de la modernidad;" conferencias de Frankfurt, octubre de 1992. Bogotá: Ediciones Antropos, 1992. 256 p.: bibl., ill., maps.

Filosóficamente argumentado, pero en la tónica de la denuncia. El "mito de la modernidad" se entiende como el mito de la modernización, es decir, el supuesto beneficio que una sociedad menos "desarrollada" recibe de una que se estima de más alto desarrollo. Este criterio se aplica a la conquista y a las argumentaciones empleadas entonces para justificar la violencia ejercida sobre las poblaciones originarias. En la segunda parte interesan comparaciones entre Sepúlveda, Mendieta y Las Casas. La tercera es una meditación del mismo fenómeno, pero desde la perspectiva del Otro, del indio.

4853 Dussel, Enrique. Teología de la Liberación y marxismo. (*Cuad. Am.*, 2:12, nov./dic. 1988, p. 138–159)

De particular interés para el conocimiento de cuándo y cómo se incorporan elementos del marxismo a la teología de la liberación en la breve trayectoria histórica de esta tendencia. También importa para el conocimiento de los orígenes de ella.

4854 Duviols, Jean-Paul and **Charles Minguet.** Humboldt: savant-citoyen du monde. Paris: Gallimard, 1994. 144 p.: bibl., ill., index.

Duviols and Minguet, two French professors of Latin American literature and civilization, have joined forces to examine the scientific impulses of the Englightenment in this vivid portrait of Alexander von Humboldt's life, voyages, and writings. The German savant appears to have espoused a confusing melange of universalist and humanitarian conceptions, reinforced by the everpresent gap between his ideals of justice, beauty, and progress, and the political conditions of his time. Pocket-book provides synthetic, useful panorama of a pioneer's extensive work. [T. Hampe-Martínez]

4855 Entrena Durán, Francisco. Interpretaciones teóricas de la inestabilidad y el caudillaje latinoamericanos. (*Rev. Int. Sociol.*, 47:1, enero/marzo 1989, p. 7–26)

El fenómeno del caudillaje es examinado en Carlos Octavio Bunge (*Nuestra América*), en Sarmiento (*Conflicto y armonías de las razas en América*) y en Leonardo Paso (*Los caudillos, historia y folklore*). El autor tiende a explicar dicho fenómeno por las condiciones económicas, políticas e institucionales que se dieron inmediatamente después de la Independencia, las cuales facilitaron a los caudillos representar cierta forma de legitimidad.

4856 España y América entre la Ilustración y el liberalismo. Edición de Joseph Pérez y Armando Romá Alberola. Madrid: Ecole des hautes études hispaniques, Casa de Velázquez; Alicante, Spain: Instituto de Cultura Juan Gil-Albert, Diputación Provincial de Alicante, 1993. 161 p.: bibl. (Col. Seminarios (mayor); 3. Col. de la Casa de Velázquez; 44)

De este libro, que se ocupa de temas de historia política y económica de España y América entre finales del siglo XVIII y las primeras décadas del XIX, deben destacarse tres artículos sobre Hispanoamérica: Joseph Pérez, "Las Luces y la Independencia de Hispanoamérica;" Mari-Laure Rieu Millán, "José Mexía Lequerica, un Americano Liberal en las Cortes de Cádiz" [Mexía fue diputado quiteño]; e Ives Aguila, "La Nueva España entre el Antiguo Régimen y el Liberalismo, 1765–1810."

4857 Fernández, Teodosio. Los géneros ensayísticos hispanoamericanos. Madrid: Taurus, 1990. 163 p.: bibl. (Historia crítica de la literatura hispánica ; 35)

Síntesis breve pero muy abarcadora en autores y obras, entendiendo el concepto de ensayo en un sentido amplio. Por esas características es de evidente utilidad.

4858 Fernández de Amicarelli, Estela and **Adriana Arpini de Márquez.** Actualidad de Gaos para nuestra historia de las ideas. (*Rev. Hist. Am.*, 107, enero/junio 1989, p. 147–158)

Examina los fundamentos filosóficos de la historia de las ideas en José Gaos, en comparación con el pensamiento que al respecto desarrolló Ortega y Gasset. Se reconocen en Gaos varios aspectos positivos para constituir la historia de las ideas en América Latina, a la vez que se le objeta que no tomó debidamente en cuenta la conflictividad social.

4859 Fernández Herrero, Beatriz. La utopía de América: teoría, leyes, experimentos. Prólogo de J.L. Abellán. Barcelona: Anthropos; Madrid: Centro de Estudios Constitucionales, 1992. 460 p.: bibl., ill., maps. (Pensamiento crítico/pensamiento utópico; 63)

Los dos grandes temas del libro son: 1) América como utopía, en general y desde el punto de vista del Derecho; y 2) la utopía específica de las reducciones jesuíticas del Paraguay. La legislación a que dio lugar la Conquista se considera como una utopía moderna. Se insiste mucho en la diferencia entre la colonización del Norte y del Sur de América, con juicios muy favorables a la segunda. La parte correspondiente a las reducciones jesuíticas es un libro en sí misma, en tanto síntesis muy detallada.

4860 Ferreira de Cassone, Florencia. Teoría y realidad histórica en América. Mendoza, Argentina: Editorial de la Facultad de Filosofía y Letras, Univ. Nacional de Cuyo, 1994. 188 p.: bibl.

La primera parte se ocupa del problema de la historia de las ideas y los distingos conceptuales que se encuentran en Lovejoy, Hayden White y otros autores contemporáneos. La segunda se compone de cuatro trabajos de tema hispanoamericano: "Historia y Política en Hispanoamérica;" "Continuidad y Crisis en el Pensamiento Político de J.M. Balmaceda;" "América e Historia en la Obra de Pedro Henríquez Ureña;" y "Arturo Uslar Pietri, una Posición Americana Frente a Nuestro Tiempo."

4861 Filippi, Alberto. Las Américas para Marx. (*Bol. Acad. Nac. Hist./Caracas*, 71:283, julio/sept. 1988, p. 663–689)

La tesis de esta larga argumentación es que no se pueden entender las afirmaciones de Marx sobre América Latina sin examinar la totalidad de los escritos en que esas opiniones se presentan; sin entender los juicios de Marx sobre otras partes del mundo no europeo; y sin comprender los supuestos de Marx y sus expectativas internacionales.

4862 Fornet-Betancourt, Raúl. Estudios de filosofía latinoamericana. México: Univ. Nacional Autónoma de México, 1992. 165 p.: bibl. (500 años después; 7)

El tema principal de los trabajos recogidos en este libro es el de la reiterada cuestión de la filosofía latinoamericana (posibilidad, autenticidad, contenido, etc.). El autor estima que una filosofía latinoamericana debe surgir de una "inculturación" y contextualización propias, superando las formas eurocéntricas y la concepción tradicional de la filosofía. Encuentra acertado, por lo tanto, el camino de la llamada filosofía de la liberación.

4863 Fornet-Betancourt, Raúl. La pregunta por la "filosofía latinoamericana" como problema filosófico. (*Rev. Filos./México*, 22:65, mayo/agosto 1989, p. 166–188)

Afirma la necesidad de eliminar la visión eurocéntrica de la filosofía. Señala los principales momentos de la conciencia latinoamericanista en filosofía. Concluye que la verdadera filosofía latinoamericana es la filosofía de la liberación. De ésta traza lo que según el autor serían sus principales características.

Gaete Avaria, Jorge. Historia de un lenguaje infortunado: Mariátegui y el marxismo. See item **5015.**

4864 Giménez Saldivia, Lulú. Caribe y América Latina. Caracas: Monte Avila Editores; Centro de Estudios Latinoamericanos Rómulo Gallegos, 1991. 239 p.: bibl. (Estudios)

La primera parte contiene útiles aclaraciones sobre las denominaciones que recibió el Continente y las islas del Caribe. La segunda, que es muy oportuno que aparezca en español, se refiere a las concepciones que el Caribe de habla inglesa ha dado de sí. La tercera muestra cómo América Latina es vista desde el Caribe. En su conjunto es una obra de lectura muy conveniente y que contribuye al mutuo entendimiento entre Latinoamérica y el Caribe anglófono.

4865 Guevara, Ernesto. Teoría y práctica revolucionaria. Havana?: Ediciones Pececap, 1988. 35 p. (El Pensamiento del Che)

Reproduce dos artículos de Ernesto Guevara, publicados en la revista *Verde Olivo:* "Táctica y Estrategia de la Revolución Latinoamericana" (aparentemente escrito en oct.–nov. 1962, pero publicado en 1968) y "Cuba: Excepción Histórica o Vanguardia en la Lucha Contra el Colonialismo?" (abril 1961).

4866 Gutiérrez, Gustavo. En busca de los pobres de Jesucristo: el pensamiento de Bartolomé de las Casas. Lima: Instituto Bartolomé dc las Casas, 1992. 700 p.: bibl., col. ill., index. (CEP; 124. Col. Bartolomé de las Casas; 3)

El lenguaje, el tono y ciertas conclusiones son los de un teólogo de la liberación actual, pero la obra fue realizada sobre la base de una amplia compulsa de fuentes y por su análisis tiene su lugar propio y muy atendible en la bibliografía sobre Las Casas.

4867 Heer, Peter Soehlke. El Nuevo Mundo en la visión de Montaigne, o, Los albores del anticolonialismo. Caracas: Univ. Simón Bolívar, Instituto de Altos Estudios de América Latina: Fundación Bicentenario de Simón Bolívar, 1993. 212 p.: bibl., ill.

Además de consideraciones generales sobre Montaigne, el libro ofrece el análisis de dos de los famosos ensayos del autor francés que tienen relación directa con el problema de América, tal como aquél podía verlo en el siglo XVI. También se refiere a las fuentes utilizadas por Montaigne: Las Casas, André Thevet, Girolamo Benzoni, Jean de Léry y Gómara. Especula el autor que los orígenes judíos de Montaigne (por el lado materno) nunca declarados o mencionados por él, habrían jugado un papel en su compasión por los oprimidos con motivo de la conquista de América.

4868 Identidades y nacionalismos: una perspectiva interdisciplinaria. Coordinación de Lilia Granillo Vázquez. México: Gernika; Univ. Autónoma Metropolitana, Unidad Azcapotzalco, 1993. 346 p.: ill. (Col. Ensayos; 39)

El volumen se originó en el propósito de realizar investigaciones interdisciplinarias sobre el fenómeno cultural en México, aunque también hay trabajos sobre América Latina en general y sobre Perú. Destacamos como ejemplos: Elsa Muñoz García, "Identidad y Cultura en México: Hacia la Conformación de un Marco Teórico Conceptual;" Rosaura Hernández Monroy, "Rasgos de Identidad Nacional en la Conciencia Novohispana;" Margarita Alegría de la Colina, "Cultura e Identidad Nacional en el Siglo XIX [México]: Reflexiones Sobre el Elemento Indígena;" Ruth Madueño Paulette, "Identidad y Nación en el Perú: Apuntes para un Análisis."

Imagination, emblems, and expressions: essays on Latin American, Caribbean, and continental culture and identity. See item 3390.

4869 International Federation of Latin American and Caribbean Studies. Congress, *4th, Paris, 1989*. América Latina ante la Revolución Francesa. Coordinación de Leopoldo Zea. México: Univ. Nacional Autónoma de México, Coordinación de Humanidades, Centro Coordinador y Difusor de Estudios Latinoamericanos, 1993. 193 p.: bibl. (Panoramas de nuestra América; 4)

Se reproducen las ponencias presentadas a una reunión de la Federación Internacional de Estudios sobre América Latina y el Caribe, realizada en París en 1989. Algunos de los artículos de interés para esta sección son: Renán Silva, "La Revolución Francesa en el *Papel Periódico* de Santa Fe de Bogotá;" Cristián Gazmuri Riveros, "Libros e Ideas Políticas Francesas en la Gestación de la Independencia de Chile;" Hugo Cancino Troncoso, "*El catecismo político cristiano* (1810), el *Catecismo de los patriotas* (1813) y el Discurso de la Revolución Francesa en Chile;" Noemí Goldman, "Morenismo y Derechos Naturales en el Río de la Plata;" Dieter Janik, "La Noción de Sociedad en el Pensamiento de Lizardi y de sus Contemporáneos;" Antonio Colomer Viadel, "La Revolución Francesa, la Independencia y el Constitucionalismo en Iberoamérica."

4870 Jaksic, Ivan. Philosophy: essay. (*in* Latin America and the Caribbean: a critical guide to research sources. Edited by Paula H. Covington. New York: Greenwood Press, 1992, p. 605–626)

Este capítulo se compone de dos partes: un ensayo de síntesis global del pensamiento filosófico latinoamericano desde la Colonia hasta la actualidad, a cargo de Iván Jaksic, y una bibliografía de fuentes para el estudio de dicho pensamiento, elaborada por Ceres B. Birkhead. Ambos intentos están muy bien logrados. El ensayo de Jaksic es particularmente valioso para ordenar la masa de datos correspondientes al siglo XX y a las opiniones vertidas sobre lo que la filosofía latinoamericana es o debería ser.

4871 Klaiber, Jeffrey. Prophets and populists: liberation theology, 1968–1988. (*Americas/Francisc.*, 46:1, July 1989, p. 1–15)

Traza sintética pero claramente los desarrollos de la teología de la liberación y es uno de los artículos más esclarecedores que conocemos sobre ese tema.

4872 Larramendi, Ignacio Hernando de. Utopía de la Nueva América: reflexiones para la edad universal. Madrid: Editorial MAPFRE, 1992. 296 p.: maps. (Col. América 92; 9. Col. MAPFRE 1492)

Partiendo de una meditación sobre las condiciones actuales de la sociedad occidental, y especialmente de Europa, España en particular y América, proyecta la "utopía" de una "Nueva América" en el contexto de un "Nuevo Orden Universal." No es simple futurología, sino afirmación de valores y obligaciones—tales como son vistos por el autor—para lograr la construcción de la utopía realizable que propone.

Latino 3. See *HLAS 55:36.*

4873 Lombardi, Angel. Sobre la unidad y la identidad latinoamericana. Caracas: Academia Nacional de la Historia, 1989. 219 p.: bibl. (El Libro menor; 162)

Podría caracterizarse como ensayo de opinión, que tiende a una interpretación general del pasado y el futuro de la región. Entiende que hay necesidad de "una historia crítica de nuestra historia de las ideas." Tal vez las páginas más animadas sean las dedicadas a los pensadores latinoamericanos del siglo XIX. Al final contiene un capítulo sobre Francisco García Calderón y otro sobre Manuel Ugarte, simpatizando mucho más con el segundo que con el primero.

4874 Löwy, Michael. Marxismo e cristianismo na América Latina. (*Lua Nova*, 19, nov. 1989, p. 5–21)

El autor, que parece partir de una posición marxista gramsciana, intenta mostrar las "afinidades" generales que hicieron posible el acercamiento entre el marxismo (o el socialismo) y el cristianismo. Luego examina la cuestión en tres casos concretos: la izquierda cristiana brasileña; la teología de la liberación; y la revolución sandinista. Véase item **4875** para la versión en español.

4875 Löwy, Michael. Marxismo y cristianismo en América Latina. (*Cuad. Sur/ Buenos Aires*, 13, dic. 1991, p. 91–106)

Trata de explicar las razones por las cuales se produjo el acercamiento entre cristianos y marxistas. Utiliza la idea de "afinidades electivas," de Max Weber. Ilustra las posiciones generales con tres casos concretos: la izquierda cristiana brasileña, la teología de la liberación y la Revolución sandinista.

4876 Mansilla, H.C.F. Los tortuosos caminos de la modernidad: América Latina entre la tradición y el postmodernismo. La Paz: CEBEM, 1992. 132 p.: bibl.

Es una intensa crítica a la modernidad y a todos los inconvenientes que habría traído al Tercer Mundo, especialmente a América Latina. Hay gran énfasis en lo ecológico. De aquella crítica no se excluye la democracia tal como se concibe y practica. De ahí la importancia que el autor atribuye a los enfoques postmodernistas para corregir los defectos de la modernidad en los países periféricos. Un último capítulo se dedica a los "Aspectos Rescatables de la Cultura Premoderna en América Latina."

4877 Marchetti, Giovanni. Cultura indígena e integración nacional: la *Historia antigua de México* de F.J. Clavijero. 1. ed. en español. Xalapa, Mexico: Univ. Veracruzana, 1986. 144 p.: bibl., index. (Biblioteca)

Amplio estudio de la *Historia antigua de México* (1780–81), que el Padre Clavijero escribió como reacción ante la despectiva imagen que Buffon y de Pauw trazaron de América. Aunque no contiene bibliografía, se encuentra gran riqueza bibliográfica en las notas de pie de página.

4878 Martínez Echazábal, Lourdes. Positivismo y racismo en el ensayo hispanoamericano. (*Cuad. Am.*, 2:9, mayo/junio 1988, p. 120–129)

El propósito del artículo es una revisión del mestizaje según se reflejó en el ensayo hispanoamericano entre 1850–1950, señalando "la influencia del pensamiento positivista . . . y la presencia de una marcada veta racista en su elaboración." También señala elementos clasistas en las opiniones estudiadas.

4879 Martínez Estrada, Ezequiel. Diferencias y semejanzas entre los países de la América Latina. Prólogo de Liliana Irene Weinberg de Magis. Cronología y bibliografía de Horacio Jorge Becco. Caracas: Biblioteca Ayacucho, 1990. 369 p.: bibl. (Biblioteca Ayacucho; 156)

La obra—ensayística y polémica, pero importante—es el resultado de un seminario dictado por el autor en México en 1959, y fue publicada originalmente por la Univ. Nacional de ese país en 1962. El prólogo es una excelente contribución a la interpretación de Martínez Estrada. Contiene una cronología y muy buena bibliografía.

4880 Merquior, José Guilherme. El otro Occidente: un poco de filosofía de la historia desde Latinoamérica. (*Cuad. Am.*, 3:13, enero/feb. 1989, p. 9–23, bibl.)

Inteligentes reflexiones de "filosofía de la historia" de América Latina. Aunque la posición del autor es definida e independiente, dialoga en su transcurso con Leopoldo Zea y Richard Morse. Una de sus conclusiones es que América Latina se inscribe en la trayectoria occidental, a la que pertenece como "el otro Occidente."

4881 Moreno Alonso, Manuel. Las "Conversaciones Americanas sobre España y sus Indias" de Blanco White. (*Anu. Estud. Am.*, 45:1, 1988, suplemento, p. 79–104)

Reproduce el texto "Conversaciones Americanas sobre España y sus Indias," escrito por Blanco White y publicado en su periódico *El Español* (Londres) en 1812. Las *Conversaciones* son un diálogo imaginario que ocurre en América entre personajes de la sociedad de entonces. La escena se supone ser desarrollada en 1808. Se expresan ideas sobre la situación española con motivo de la invasión napoleónica y sobre la independencia de América. Las consideraciones que preceden a la reproducción del texto de Blanco White son más bien de naturaleza descriptiva.

4882 Moreno Alvarez, Gloria. Hacia una conciencia de mexicanidad. (*Bol. Am.*, 31:39/40, 1989/90, p. 159–173)

A pesar del título, el objetivo es "investigar la participación de los letrados de la época [Escuela de Salamanca] en el debate sobre el Nuevo Mundo." En este sentido, el tema principal es Francisco de Vitoria. La autora encuentra en Vitoria una dualidad: "su pensamiento cristiano" y "su razonamiento aristotélico." Por este último sostiene la inmadurez del indio, de la que se deriva la necesidad de la tutela, por la cual a su vez se habría justificado la explotación mediante el régimen de la encomienda. El artículo es resumen de una tesis doctoral.

4883 Mörner, Magnus. Los indios como objetos y actores en la historia de Latinoamérica. (*Anales/Göteborg*, 1, 1989, p. 161–177)

Aunque el autor es historiador, promueve la búsqueda interdisciplinaria—especialmente la colaboración con la sociología y la antropología—para el examen de cómo los indios han sido considerados (condición de objetos) y cómo han reaccionado (condición de actores). Ofrece una periodización histórica para ese propósito. Para versión en inglés, ver *HLAS 50:691*.

4884 Navarrete Orta, Luis. Literatura e ideas en la historia hispanoamericana. Caracas: Lagoven S.A., 1991. 186 p.: bibl., ill. (some col.), index. (Cuadernos Lagoven. Serie Medio milenio)

Mezcla de ensayo y material de curso, es un panorama principalmente de la literatura, pero extendiéndose también a la "literatura de ideas." El contenido—por razones de espacio, según se explica—destaca solamente ciertos elementos de la historia que se persigue, y las ausencias se hacen más visibles en el siglo XIX y XX.

4885 Ocampo López, Javier. Los catecismos políticos en la independencia de Hispanoamérica: de la monarquía a la república. Tunja, Colombia: Publicaciones del Magister en Historia, Escuela de Posgrado de la Facultad de Educación, Univ. Pedagógica y Tecnológica de Colombia, 1988. 69 p.: bibl. (Nuevas lecturas de historia; 3)

Interesan en particular aquellos cate-cismos (sistema elemental de enseñanza por preguntas y respuestas) que tendían a difundir las ideas de independencia y su fundamenta-ción. Muestra que también los hubo que de-fendieron la autoridad del rey.

4886 Ocampo López, Javier. La integración de América Latina: historia de las ideas. 2a. ed. Bogotá: Editorial El Buho, 1991. 321 p.: bibl., ill., index.

Los capítulos más relacionados con el título de la obra son: "La Idea de la Integra-ción Regional de América Latina;" "Simón Bolívar y el Idearlo de la Hispanoamericani-dad;" y "El Nacionalismo Latinoamericano." Otros temas tratados: "Ontología Colom-biana y Latinoamericana" y "La Idea de Amé-rica en los Movimientos Populares y en el Pensamiento y Acción de los Criollos Pre-cursores." Es una guía útil para la temática elegida.

Página latinoamericana de filosofía, Montevi-deo, Uruguay. See item **47.**

4887 Para una filosofía desde América La-tina. Recopilación de Ignacio Ellacuría y Juan Carlos Scannone. Bogotá: Pontificia Univ. Javeriana, 1992. 290 p.: bibl. (Col. Uni-versitas philosophica; 4)

El volumen presenta parte de la labor teórica del Equipo Jesuita Latinoamericano de Reflexión Filosófica. La introducción señala: "El objetivo del presente libro es contribuir a la elaboración de una filosofía que, con vali-dez universal, en continuidad con lo perenne de la tradición filosófica y en diálogo con el pensamiento contemporáneo, esté pensada *desde* América Latina . . . *para responder* . . . a los acuciantes problemas teóricos y prácti-cos del Continente." En función del interés de esta sección destacamos dos documentos de trabajo: 1) "Dimensión Etica de la Filosofía Latinoamericana" y 2) "Dimensión Histórica de la Filosofía Latinoamericana;" y tres po-nencias: 1) Gerardo Remolina, "El Quehacer Filosófico en América Latina;" 2) Pedro Trigo, "Filosofía Latinoamericana. Coordenadas;" y 3) Juan Carlos Scannone, "Hacia una Filosofía a Partir de la Sabiduría Popular."

4888 Pedrosa, Damián. El concepto de "na-ción" en Latinoamérica. (*Rev. Hist. Ideas,* 10, 1990, p. 153-171)

Reconoce tres vías para encarar la cues-tión de la nación (o la identidad): la cultura-lista, la política y la historicista. En las dos últimas juega un papel central la "liberación política."

4889 Peña, Roberto I. La teoría teocrática de Fray Bartolomé de las Casas O. P. y el *Regnum Indiarum.* (*An. Univ. Chile,* 20, agosto 1989, p. 401-424)

Estudio detallado de las Casas como jurista y de su doctrina teocrática. Se toma en cuenta principalmente su *Tratado comproba-torio del imperio soberano y principado uni-versal que los reyes de Castilla y León tienen sobre las Indias* (1552).

4890 Pensadores nacionales iberoamerica-nos. v. 1-2. Recopilación, introducción y noticias de Alberto E. Buela. Buenos Aires: Biblioteca del Congreso de la Nación, 1993. 2 v.: bibl.

Esta antología ha sido preparada en Argentina, donde la expresión "pensador na-cional" puede referirse a intelectuales vincu-lados a la ideología peronista o sus antece-dentes, y no tanto al nacionalismo argentino tradicional. Esto se revela en la selección rea-lizada para el caso de la Argentina: Manuel Ugarte, José Luis Torres, Arturo Jauretche y J.J. Hernández Arregui. En el caso de otros países no difiere de criterios generalmente aceptados, como la representación de México por José Vasconcelos, Leopoldo Zea y Alfonso Reyes, por ejemplo.

4891 El pensamiento demócratacristiano. Edición de Joaquín Roy. Madrid: Insti-tuto de Cooperación Iberoamericana; Edicio-nes de Cultura Hispánica, 1991. 267 p.: bibl. (Antología del pensamiento político, social y económico de América Latina; 15)

Muy útil reunión de textos básicos de la democracia cristiana en América Latina. Hay declaraciones y manifiestos, y también escritos individuales. La introducción, con simpatía hacia la tendencia estudiada, es una presentación seria y bien elaborada, tanto desde el punto de vista histórico como en sus referencias a la situación contemporánea. Buena bibliografía.

4892 Pereña, Luciano. La idea de justicia en la conquista de América. Madrid: Editorial MAPFRE, 1992. 304 p.: bibl., ill., in-dexes. (Col. Relaciones entre España y Amé-rica; 6. Col. MAPFRE 1492)

La obra es síntesis de extendidas inves-tigaciones del autor sobre el tema, y contiene sus opiniones, en general favorables a la posición de España; pero puede cumplir los fines de una introducción a un asunto de tan vasta bibliografía. Presenta los hechos deplorables de la conquista, la legislación que se intentó, y la doctrina de Francisco de Vitoria y sus seguidores. Contiene, además: un índice de documentos representativos; un índice de protagonistas (teólogos e intelectuales representantes del pensamiento sobre la conquista); una lista de fuentes (informes y documentos); una bibliografía representativa; y una útil cronología. En el sentido apuntado la obra presta un gran servicio, se compartan o no todas las opiniones del autor.

4893 The Philosophical Forum. Vol. 20, Nos. 1/2, 1988/1989. New York: Dept. of Philosophy, Baruch College, City Univ. of New York.

Número dedicado a la filosofía latinoamericana actual. Los artículos que contiene son los siguientes: Jorge J.E. Gracia, "Introduction: Latin American Philosophy Today." Buena síntesis del desarrollo filosófico latinoamericano, especialmente en el período 1960–80. Expresa observaciones o críticas que son aprovechables se coincida totalmente con el autor o no. Así, las que se refieren a la polarización entre filósofos "académicos" y filósofos "comprometidos;" a la retórica como instrumento de convencimiento; al estilo menos argumentativo y más personal de la filosofía latinoamericana; y a la tendencia a atribuir mayor valor a priori a las filosofías europeas o norteamericanas, como expresión de inseguridad. Leopoldo Zea, "Identity: A Latin American Philosophical Problem." Expone la concepción de la identidad de América Latina a lo largo de su historia (Bolívar, Sarmiento, Rodó, Martí, etc.). También se ocupa de la historia de las ideas y de la función que ésta tuvo y puede tener para desarrollar una filosofía de la historia de Latinoamérica que sea más propia de la realidad de la región. Horacio Cerutti Guldberg, "Actual Situation and Perspectives of Latin American Philosophy for Liberation." Escrito por uno de los representantes y expositores de la filosofía de la liberación, el artículo cumple el cometido de dar una visión de conjunto de esa tendencia. Se refiere a sus comienzos y sus tesis originarias; a las diversas subcorrientes que se desarrollaron dentro de ella; y a los temas actualmente en debate. Una de las principales

conclusiones es que ya no puede hablarse de una filosofía de la liberación, sino de variados intentos teóricos que colaboran en el proceso de la liberación latinoamericana. Ofelia Schutte, "Philosophy and Feminism in Latin America: Perspectives on Gender Identity and Culture." Posiblemente la mayor contribución del ensayo resida en el destaque de la especificidad de la situación de la mujer en América Latina y su relación con los modelos conceptuales posibles para captar filosóficamente el problema femenino. Se compara con el feminismo en EE.UU. Es opinión básica de la autora que la teoría feminista no puede limitarse a los problemas de género, sin abrirse a las más amplias cuestiones económicas, políticas y culturales. David Sobrevilla, "Phenomenology and Existentialism in Latin America." Exposición panorámica bien informada. Sobresale la parte dedicada a Perú. En las conclusiones sugiere que la hora de la fenomenología y el existencialismo en América Latina ya ha pasado. A la etapa de aprovechamiento teórico ha sucedido una más reciente de exégesis profesional rigurosa. Adolfo Sánchez Vázquez, "Marxism in Latin America." Es más una discusión sobre el sentido del marxismo en América Latina que una exposición de sus manifestaciones (aunque algunas de éstas se usan para ilustrar el propósito principal). Quizás uno de los aspectos más interesantes sea el tratamiento de Mariátegui. No prescindible en la discusión sobre el marxismo en Latinoamérica. Jorge J.E. Gracia, "The Impact of Philosophical Analysis in Latin America." Muy buena exposición de los desarrollos y la situación actual del análisis filosófico en América Latina. También se refiere a la relación (o choque) con otras corrientes filosóficas latinoamericanas, como las que se proponen representar una posición eminente o exclusivamente "americana" y aportar soluciones a los problemas sociales e ideológicos de la región. Iván Jaksic, "The Sources of Latin American Philosophy." Aunque el propósito (bien logrado) es identificar las fuentes de la filosofía latinoamericana, todo el trabajo está dominado por el problema que presenta la dicotomía entre filósofos "académicos" (interesados en la filosofía per se) y los filósofos "comprometidos" (que buscan la aplicación de la filosofía a los problemas inmediatos de la sociedad). Una de las formas en que esa oposición se manifiesta es el tema, aparentemente inagotable, de la naturaleza y condiciones de la filosofía latinoamericana. En general se trata de un volumen valioso.

4894 Popescu, Oreste. Económica indiana. (*Económica/La Plata*, 35 : 1/2, 1989, p. 37–69, bibl.)

Aunque trata de la historia de las doctrinas económicas en la época colonial iberoamericana, importa para la historia de las ideas en general, especialmente en lo que concierne a "la economía indiana y la escolástica económica."

Proyecto Filosofía en Español. See item **49.**

4895 Quijano, Aníbal. Modernidad, identidad y utopía en América Latina. Quito: Editorial El Conejo, 1990. 70 p. (Col. 4 suyus)

Contiene dos trabajos: 1) "Lo Público y lo Privado: un Enfoque Latinoamericano" (intento de superar lo privado-capitalista y lo público-estatal por lo "privado-social" y las "instituciones públicas-no-estatales"). 2) "Modernidad, Identidad y Utopía en América Latina" (referencia a la polémica sobre la postmodernidad desde el punto de vista de la realidad y los intereses de Latinoamérica).

4896 Quinientos años de historia, sentido y proyección. Recopilación de Leopoldo Zea. México: Instituto Panamericano de Geografía e Historia; Fondo de Cultura Económica, 1991. 200 p.: bibl. (Col. Tierra firme)

Resultado de un simposio convocado por el Gobierno de México para conmemorar el Quinto Centenario, en 1988. Recoge 19 trabajos agrupados por temas, algunos de los cuales son: "Problemas Sociales, Políticos, Económicos y Culturales;" "Presencia Indígena y su Participación en la Historia;" "Mestizaje Racial y Cultural." Entre sus autores figuran Gregorio Weinberg, Domingo Miliani, Samuel Silva Gotay, Arturo Ardao, Manuel Maldonado-Denis, Carlos Paladines, Juan A. Ortega y Medina, Juan Oddone, Otto Morales Benítez, Abelardo Villegas y Germán Arciniegas.

4897 Recondo, Gregorio. La integración cultural latinoamericana: entre el mito y la utopía. (*Integr. Latinoam.*, 14 : 149/150, sept./oct. 1989, p. 36–52)

Fundamentos de una posible integración cultural latinoamericana y su lugar en formas más amplias de integración. Va más allá de lo declarativo y maneja variadas interpretaciones de la cultura latinoamericana.

4898 Redondo Redondo, María Lourdes. Utopía vitoriana y realidad indiana. Madrid: Fundación Universitaria Española, 1992. 372 p.: bibl. (Monografías; 56)

Uno de los puntos en que se hace mayor énfasis es la de conocer la realidad de la que partió Vitoria. De ahí que la primera parte se dedique a las "fuentes" (relatos y precedentes filosóficos, teológicos, políticos e intelectuales) que dicho teólogo manejara. Trata luego la doctrina de Vitoria sobre el indio y la conquista, y su proyección americana en Fray Alonso de la Veracruz, José de Acosta y la legislación de la Corona. En cuanto a la "utopía" vitoriana, la encuentra razonable, realizable y moderada, dentro del molde tomista.

4899 Restrepo Toro, Hernando. Ensayos sobre historia y cultura. Selección y prólogo de Mario Franco Hernández y Martha Elena Bravo de Hermelín. Semblanza por Marco Antonio Mejía T. Medellín, Colombia: Ediciones Autores Antioqueños, 1993. 320 p.: bibl., ill. (Col. Autores antioqueños; 84)

De este conjunto de trabajos destacamos: "La Filosofía del Hombre Americano," referido a Leopoldo Zea; "La Ideología de la Independencia Hasta 1830," que se refiere a México y es parte de una tesis de maestría, titulada *Impacto de las ideas modernas en dos sociedades tradicionales, México y Colombia*; "Universidad y Modernidad" y "La Universidad y las Ideas Después de la Independencia," siendo los dos últimos parte de una tesis doctoral: *La formación de la Universidad Nacional en México y Colombia.*

4900 Roig, Arturo Andrés. ¿Cómo orientarnos en nuestro pensamiento?: la filosofía latinoamericana y su problema hoy. (*Rev. Hist. Ideas*, 10, 1990, p. 189–205)

El tema de cómo enfrentar el quehacer de la filosofía latinoamericana en la actualidad es discutida en función de asunto tales como "la cuestión del discurso," "la cuestión del sujeto del discurso," la alienación, el humanismo y la conflictividad social.

4901 Roig, Arturo Andrés. La *Historia de las ideas* y la historia de nuestra cultura. (*Cuad. Am.*, 3 : 17, sept./oct. 1989, p. 9–18)

La historia de las ideas excede a una "labor historiográfica descriptiva." Es, por el contrario, "una labor constructiva y determinadamente selectiva," que debe dar "las bases para afianzarnos en una conciencia de lo propio," "porque hacer historia es también un modo de hacer política." La ordenación del "ser histórico" depende de un "deber ser histórico." La historia de las ideas es una forma de la historia social, y la sociedad se explica por su interna conflictividad.

4902 Rojas-Mix, Miguel. Los cien nombres de América: eso que descubrió Colón. Barcelona: Lumen, 1991. 410 p.: bibl., ill. (Palabra en el tiempo; 209. Ensayo)

Aunque en efecto se ocupa de historiar y comentar los orígenes y el significado de los diferentes nombres que se han dado a la región (Hispanoamérica, Iberoamérica, Indoamérica, América Latina, etc.), va asimismo más allá, como lo ilustran los capítulos sobre Martí, Mariátegui, Bilbao y la indianidad, entre otros. Es un ensayo rico en opiniones sobre temas y autores, y pertinente también para el debatido asunto de la "identidad" latinoamericana.

4903 Rojas Paz, Nerva Bordas de. Ontológia y ética en América. (*Rev. Filos. Latinoam. Cienc. Soc.*, 4:14, nov. 1989, p. 7–22)

Complejas consideraciones, de naturaleza ensayística, que concluyen en la negación del proyecto modernizador de América Latina por ser dicho proyecto contrario a lo que la autora considera la estructura ontológica de aquélla.

4904 Sabiduría popular, símbolo y filosofía: diálogo internacional en torno de una interpretación latinoamericana. Editado por Juan Carlos Scannone. Buenos Aires: Editorial Guadalupe, 1984. 222 p.: bibl.

Señalamos las ponencias de Carlos A. Cullen, "Sabiduría Popular y Fenomenología;" Juan Carlos Scannone, "Sabiduría Popular y Pensamiento Especulativo;" y Enrique Mareque, "Líneas Fundamentales del Pensamiento de Rodolfo Kusch (1922–1979)." Scannone en la introducción y Mareque en la primera ponencia explican la posición del grupo argentino en este coloquio.

4905 Sasso, Javier. El autodescubrimiento de América como tarea filosófica. (*Apunt. Filos.*, 4, 1993, p. 53–66)

De este artículo, que es un examen crítico del modo "americanista" de hacer filosofía, pueden por lo menos destacarse tres puntos: 1) no tiene validez la adopción, por el americanismo filosófico actual, de la posición

de Alberdi, frecuentemente tomada como modelo; 2) los filósofos "americanistas" no aprovechan debidamente el avance de las ciencias sociales, agotándose más bien en las fuentes que representan los "pensadores" latinoamericanos clásicos; 3) es cuestionable la concepción de la filosofía o del saber filosófico en los filósofos "americanistas."

4906 Scannone, Juan Carlos. Nuevo punto de partida en la filosofía latinoamericana. Buenos Aires: Editorial Guadalupe, 1990. 256 p.: bibl.

Desarrolla una personal concepción de la filosofía, cuyos orígenes se remontan a la génesis de la filosofía de la liberación en la Argentina. La posición tiende a basarse en la sabiduría popular latinoamericana. Se enlaza con otras obras del autor, como *Teología de la liberación y doctrina social de la Iglesia* y *Evangelización, cultura y teología.* Aunque no en forma dependiente, es cercana al pensamiento de autores como Carlos Cullen y Rodolfo Kusch.

Seminario Latinoamericano de Filosofía e Historia de las Ideas. See item **50.**

4907 Sentido y proyección de la conquista. Recopilación de Leopoldo Zea. México: Instituto Panamericano de Geografía e Historia; Fondo de Cultura Económica, 1993. 188 p.: bibl., ill. (Col. Tierra firme)

Contiene artículos de interés. Los más relacionados con la temática de esta sección son: Leopoldo Zea, "Descubrimiento de América: de la Conquista a la Reconciliación;" Fernando Aínsa, "Invención de la Utopía y Deconstrucción de la Realidad;" Elsa Cecilia Frost, "De Esclavos a Angeles: la Primera Imagen del Hombre Americano en la Conciencia Europea;" Mario Magallón Anaya, "Filosofía Política de la Conquista."

4908 Stam B., Juan. La Biblia en la teología colonialista de Juan Ginés de Sepúlveda. (*Rev. Hist./Heredia*, 25, enero/junio 1992, p. 157–164)

Proporciona el detalle del uso que Sepúlveda hizo de citas bíblicas en su polémica con Las Casas.

4909 Torre Villar, Ernesto de la. Notas para una bibliografía de la cultura colonial hispanoamericana. (*Rev. Hist. Am.*, 107, enero/junio 1989, p. 39–117, bibl.)

Buena bibliografía, con extensa introducción. Además de recoger bibliografías generales, cubre numerosos campos, entre ellos: arte, filosofía, humanismo, ciencia, religión, derecho, historia, literatura, lingüística y educación. En cada caso México recibe tratamiento especial, pero hay entradas también para los demás países.

4910 Uslar Pietri, Arturo. La creación del Nuevo Mundo. Madrid: Editorial MAPFRE, 1991. 241 p.: indexes. (Col. América 92; 1. Col. MAPFRE 1492)

Conjunto de ensayos—en general, breves—de recreación histórica y de particular valor literario, que tiene por temas a personajes y acontecimientos de la conquista y la colonización. Destacamos: "Un Juego de Espejos Deformantes," sobre la relatividad de la historiografía latinoamericana, y "Política y Pensamiento Político en América Latina," sobre el destino de las ideas occidentales en América.

4911 Uslar Pietri, Arturo. Páginas. Caracas: Instituto de Altos Estudios de América Latina, Univ. Simón Bolívar, 1992. 157 p.

Parte del contenido coincide con lo recogido en *La creación del Nuevo Mundo* (véase item **4910**). De la presente obra señalamos dos ensayos: "Lo Específico del Hombre Latinoamericano" y "La América Latina y el Pecado Original." Véase asimismo el comentario de *HLAS 54:5370.*

4912 Vargas Lozano, Gabriel. ¿Qué hacer con la filosofía en América Latina? México: Univ. Autónoma Metropolitana; Tlaxcala, Tlax.: Univ. Autónoma de Tlaxcala, 1990? 224 p.: bibl. (Materiales para la historia de la filosofía en México)

Los artículos que más interesan son: "Premisas Metodológicas para una Historia de la Filosofía en México, Siglo XX;" "Corrientes Actuales de la Filosofía en México;" "El Debate por la Filosofía del Marxismo en México;" "Marx Hoy en América Latina;" "Gramsci y América Latina;" "La Filosofía Latinoamericana en el Siglo XX." Hay también artículos sobre Aníbal Ponce, Adolfo Sánchez Vázquez y una polémica sostenida entre Leopoldo Zea y Luis Villoro. El autor aplica su posición marxista a todos esos temas.

4913 Velázquez Mejía, Manuel. Introducción a la filosofía latinoamericana. México: Centro de Investigación en Ciencias

Sociales y Humanidades, U.A.E.M., 1990. 56 leaves: bibl., ill.

Reflexiones sobre América Latina, su historia y la posibilidad de una filosofía propia, teniendo como guía la obra de Leopoldo Zea.

4914 Villegas, Abelardo. Democracia y dictadura: el destino de una idea bolivariana. México: Coordinación de Difusión Cultural, Dirección de Literatura, UNAM, 1987. 137 p.: bibl. (Textos de ciencias sociales)

Sensatas reflexiones sobre la democracia en América Latina. Además, entre otros temas, hay artículos sobre Morelos, Molina Enríquez, Antonio Caso, Ortega en México y el nacionalismo mexicano.

4915 Villegas, Abelardo. Sobre el estudio de la filosofía latinoamericana. (*Rev. Hist. Ideas,* 10, 1990, p. 207–217)

Revisa con claridad y equilibrio la situación del tema. Destaca tres aspectos: historia de las ideas, filosofía de la historia de América y ontología de América. Consideraciones muy recomendables en torno a un asunto largamente debatido.

4916 Weinberg, Gregorio. Tiempo, destiempo y contratiempo. Buenos Aires: Editorial Leviatán; Ediciones Siglo Veinte, 1993. 127 p. (Col. Vida del espíritu)

El primer ensayo, que da título al libro, es de naturaleza conceptual sobre el tema del tiempo histórico, con particular aplicación a América Latina. La segunda parte reúne trabajos sobre integración latinoamericana, especialmente la cultural, pero desde la perspectiva menos frecuente de una meditación de la realidad histórica de Latinoamérica.

4917 Zapata, Francisco. Ideología y política en América Latina. México: Colegio de México, 1990. 299 p.: bibl. (Jornadas; 115)

La primera parte presenta a Martí e Ingenieros (el antiimperialismo); a los comunistas Luis Emilio Recabarren y Julio Antonio Mella; a Mariátegui y Haya de la Torre; y al nacionalismo de la revolución mexicana. A estos autores los designa como "ideólogos de la izquierda naciente." La segunda parte trata del desarrollismo y la modernización. Se atiende a Prebisch, Medina Echavarría y Gino Germani. Dentro de esta misma etapa se exponen interpretaciones marxistas, ejemplificadas con la polémica entre André Gunder Frank y Ernesto Laclau sobre feudalismo y

capitalismo en América Latina. La última
parte se ocupa de la teoría de la dependencia,
considerándose autores como Frank; Cardoso
y Faletto; y Ruy Mauro Marini. En su conjunto es una útil exposición.

4918 Zavala, Silvio Arturo. Por la senda his-
pana de la libertad. Madrid: Editorial
Mapfre, 1992. 276 p.: bibl., indexes. (Col.
América 92; 4. Col. MAPFRE 1492)
Reproduce textos aparecidos en obras
anteriores del historiador mexicano vincula-
dos a la defensa hispánica de los indios. Los
principales autores considerados son Las
Casas, Fray Alonso de la Veracruz, Vasco de
Quiroga y Fray Jerónimo de Mendieta.

4919 Zea, Leopoldo *et al.* América Latina:
entre a realidade e a utopía. Vigo, España: Edicións Xerais de Galicia, 1992. 398 p.:
bibl. (Universitaria)
Todos los textos están presentados en
lengua gallega. Destacamos la parte correspondiente al tema: "La filosofía y América Latina," con artículos de: Leopoldo Zea (sobre
especificidad y universalidad de la filosofía
latinoamericana); Marta Harnecker (sobre
evolución y revolución); Enrique Dussel (sobre los orígenes de la filosofía de la liberación
en América Latina); O. Fernández Díaz (sobre
Mariátegui); A. Sánchez Vázquez (sobre el
aporte del exilio español en México).

4920 Zea, Leopoldo. Descubrimiento e identidad latinoamericana. México: Univ.
Nacional Autónoma de México, Coordinación de Humanidades, Centro Coordinador y
Difusor de Estudios Latinoamericanos, 1990.
155 p.: bibl. (500 años después; 1)
Contiene diversos artículos, dentro de
la familiar temática del maestro mexicano.
Algunos fueron escritos teniendo en cuenta la
proximidad del Vo. Centenario. "Latinoamérica entre la Dependencia y la Emancipación"
se refiere a las relaciones históricas entre
EE.UU. y América Latina. Otros dos artículos
se refieren al socialismo ("Liberación Nacional y Socialismo" y "El Socialismo y la Situación Espiritual de la Epoca") y están fechados
en Yugoslavia en 1987.

4921 Zea, Leopoldo. Filosofar desde la realidad latinoamericana. (*Cuyo/Mendoza,*
7:1, 1990, p. 9–25)
Destaca que la experiencia latinoamericana puede servir en la búsqueda de "normas
de conciliación del hombre con el hombre."

4922 Zea, Leopoldo. Regreso de las carabelas. México: Univ. Nacional Autónoma
de México, 1993. 231 p.: bibl. (500 años después; 16)
Destacamos los siguientes artículos:
"El Nuevo Mundo como Utopía;" "La Utopía
del Mestizaje;" "Xenofobia y Raza Cósmica;"
"De la Conquista a la Reconciliación;" y
"Sentido y Proyección del Descubrimiento."

4923 Zuleta Alvarez, Enrique. La historia de
las ideas en el marco político de la historiografía. (*Bol. Acad. Nac. Hist./Buenos
Aires,* 61, 1988, p. 109–135)
Tres aspectos de contenido caracterizan a este artículo: 1) consideraciones sobre
el concepto de historia de las ideas en varios
autores: Lovejoy, Randall, Brinton, Baumer,
I. Berlin, Q. Skinner, Groethuysen, J. Dunn, y
Francisco Romero y Arturo Ardao entre los
hispanoamericanos; 2) un repaso de numerosas obras latinoamericanas de variadas tendencias que se han ocupado de las ideas en
relación con su contexto social y político; y
3) conclusiones del autor sobre el futuro de la
disciplina.

4924 Zuleta Alvarez, Enrique. El mestizaje
en la historia de las ideas hispanoamericanas. (*Invest. Ens.,* 39, enero/dic. 1989,
p. 399–422)
Sobre las diversas formas en que el
mestizaje—racial y cultural—ha sido reconocido o apreciado desde la colonia hasta la
actualidad. El mestizaje cultural, según el
autor, es algo aceptado y se comporta como
"un elemento esencial de nuestra singulari-
dad [latinoamericana]."

MEXICO

4925 Alvarado, Lourdes. Asociación Metodófila 'Gabino Barreda:' dos ensayos representativos. (*Estud. Hist. Mod. Contemp.
Méx.,* 12, 1989, p. 211–245)
Oportuna reproducción de dos estudios
de Porfirio Parra (1854–1912), discípulo de
Gabino Barreda y representante, como éste,
del positivismo comteano en México. Los escritos se publicaron en los *Anales de la Asociación Metodófila Gabino Barreda,* en 1877.
Ellos son: la "Introducción" a los *Anales* y
"Las Causas Primeras." La edición va precedida de una introducción aclaratoria.

Alvarez Mosso, Lucía and **María Luisa González Marín.** Industria y clase obrera en México, 1950–1980. See *HLAS 55:4460.*

4926 Barreda, Horacio. El siglo XIX ante el feminismo: una interpretación positivista. Recopilación de Lourdes Alvarado. México: Univ. Nacional Autónoma de México, Coordinación de Humanidades, Centro de Estudios de la Universidad, 1991. 151 p.: bibl.

Reedición del *Estudio sobre el feminismo,* publicado por Horacio Barreda (hijo de Gabino Barreda, célebre representante del positivismo mexicano). Apareció en la *Revista Positiva,* fundada por Agustín Aragón en 1909. El escrito se opone a las manifestaciones del feminismo de la época y se basa en la doctrina de Comte, con la consiguiente pretensión de demostración "científica." La introducción expone el contenido del *Estudio* y orienta al lector sobre el tema en la época estudiada. Importa para la historia del feminismo en América Latina, pero también para el positivismo comteano en México. Util bibliografía.

4927 Beuchot, Mauricio. Filosofía social de los pensadores novohispanos: la búsqueda de la justicia social y el bien común en tiempos del Virreinato. México: Instituto Mexicano de Doctrina Social Cristiana, 1990. 139 p.: bibl. (Col. Iglesia y sociedad)

Obra de divulgación, pero seria y útil, tanto por el número de autores que trata como por atender en ellos al aspecto de "filosofía social." Con ese enfoque se exponen, 1) del siglo XVI: Zumárraga, Las Casas, Vasco de Quiroga, Veracruz, y Mercado; 2) del siglo XVII: Zapata y Sandoval, Palafox y Mendoza, y Sigüenza y Góngora; 3) del siglo XVIII: Francisco Javier Alegre, Clavijero y Fray Servando Teresa de Mier. Los artículos son, en general, breves.

4928 Boggio de Harasymowicz, Adriana. Controversias ideológicas en el siglo XIX. (*Palabra Hombre,* 70, abril/junio 1989, p. 65–86, bibl.)

Se refiere al siglo XIX mexicano. El mayor espacio lo ocupa la exposición del liberalismo. El contraste con los conservadores se sigue hasta el fin del Porfiriato, durante el cual la diferenciación entre los dos grupos se hace más tenue. Se expone también la relación entre liberalismo y positivismo. Por la posible comparación con otros países latinoamericanos interesa el parágrafo sobre la búsqueda de la identidad cultural.

4929 Bonfil Batalla, Guillermo. Pensar nuestra cultura: ensayos. México: Alianza Editorial, 1991. 172 p.: bibl. (Estudios)

Conjunto de trabajos que tienden a la reivindicación de la diversidad cultural. Aunque trata de México, mucho de lo que dice es aplicable a otras regiones latinoamericanas. La introducción señala distinciones básicas: cultura como nación (etnia); cultura nacional (al nivel del Estado moderno); y cultura en el contexto de la globalización creciente. Otros temas son: pluralismo cultural; culturas populares; civilización y proyecto nacional; culturas indias como proyecto civilizatorio, etc. El objetivo es construir una cultura de la pluralidad.

4930 Brading, David A. Manuel Gamio and official *indigenismo* in Mexico. (*Bull. Lat. Am. Res.,* 7:1, 1988, p. 75–89)

Afirma que en último análisis el indigenismo de Gamio (1883–1960) fue influido por su liberalismo, y estuvo animado por un nacionalismo modernizador que buscaba integrar las masas indígenas a la vida nacional, aun al precio de que perdieran su cultura originaria.

4931 Colchero, Carlos. La fundación de la Escuela de Filosofía y Letras de la UAP: ensayo de unas memorias. Puebla, Mexico: Univ. Autónoma de Puebla, 1990. 92 p., 16 p. of plates: ill. (Col. Crónicas y testimonios; 7)

Crónica que abarca desde la fundación de la Escuela, en 1965, hasta 1987. Se indican los cambios en los planes de estudio.

4932 Fell, Claude. José Vasconcelos: los años del águila, 1920–1925; educación, cultura e iberoamericanismo en el México postrevolucionario. México: Univ. Nacional Autónoma de México, 1989. 742 p.: bibl. (Serie Historia moderna y contemporánea; 21)

Extensa y pormenorizada monografía sobre la obra educativa de José Vasconcelos, que contiene también capítulos sobre el iberoamericanismo de este filósofo, su viaje por América del Sur en 1922 y su obra *La raza cósmica.* En el aspecto de la labor educacional es prácticamente exhaustivo. Comienza con la actuación de Vasconcelos como Rector de la Univ. de México y llega hasta 1924. Importante también para la biografía de Vasconcelos. Contiene muy valiosa bibliografía.

Ver *HLAS 54:1490* para el comentario del historiador.

4933 Fernández de Amicarelli, Estela. Lenguaje y filosofía: anotaciones sobre la lectura de un texto gaosiano. (*Rev. Hist. Am.*, 108, julio/dic. 1989, p. 159–169)

De Gaos se toman dos fuentes: 1) algunas afirmaciones de su obra *De la filosofía*, referentes a la relación entre filosofía y lenguaje, y 2) su posición sobre lo que debe ser una historia de las ideas en el caso de América Latina. De ello la autora saca consecuencias sobre la hermenéutica en general y sobre la hermenéutica aplicada a la historia de las ideas latinoamericanas. Afirma que en última instancia no hay texto (en el sentido de único y válido para todos), sino tantos textos como interpretaciones históricas posibles del texto.

4934 Galeana de Valadés, Patricia. Los liberales y la Iglesia. (*in* The Mexican and Mexican American experience in the 19th century. Edited by Jaime E. Rodriguez O. Tempe, Arizona: Bilingual Press, 1989, p. 44–54)

Visión panorámica de las reformas liberales y el poder de la Iglesia en México, desde la Independencia hasta el fin del porfiriato.

4935 García Cantú, Gastón. Idea de México. v. 2, El socialismo. México: Consejo Nacional para la Cultura y las Artes; Fondo de Cultura Económica, 1991. 6 v.: bibl., ill., indexes. (Vida y pensamiento de México)

Originalmente publicado en 1969 (véase *HLAS 36: 5085*), esta edición contiene algunos cambios. Los numerosos artículos y documentos están agrupados según las dos grandes partes del libro: las correspondientes al siglo XIX y al XX, respectivamente. Entre la figuras individuales tratadas se cuentan: Ricardo Flores Magón, José C. Valadés y, con mayor extensión, Vicente Lombardo Toledano.

4936 Gómez-Martínez, José Luis. Posición de Alfonso Reyes en el desarrollo del pensamiento mexicano. (*Nueva Rev. Filol. Hisp.*, 37:2, 1989, p. 433–463)

Visión de Alfonso Reyes como momento previo o antecedente de la filosofía de la liberación.

4937 González, María del Refugio. El pensamiento de los conservadores mexicanos. (*in* The Mexican and Mexican American experience in the 19th century. Edited by Jaime E. Rodriguez O. Tempe, Arizona: Bilingual Press, 1989, p. 55–67)

Consideraciones sobre la ideología conservadora en México, entre 1808–67, destacando la conveniencia de "analizar el pensamiento conservador a partir de los principios de la religión católica." Aunque brevemente, se comparan Clemente Mungía (*Del derecho natural en sus principios comunes . . .*, 1849), Lucas Alamán y Juan Rodríguez de San Miguel.

4938 Jalif de Bertranou, Clara Alicia. Descubrimiento e identidad latinoamericana en Leopoldo Zea. (*Cuyo/Mendoza*, 7:2, 1990, p. 277–282)

Exposición de la obra de Leopoldo Zea como filósofo de la historia de América Latina, con motivo de la aparición de *Descubrimiento e identidad latinoamericana* (1990), del maestro mexicano.

4939 Medin, Tzvi. El pensamiento de Abelardo Villegas: itinerario y esencia intelectual. México: Univ. Nacional Autónoma de México, Coordinación de Humanidades, Centro Coordinador y Difusor de Estudios Latinoamericanos, 1992. 126 p.: bibl. (Serie Nuestra América; 35)

Obra única sobre el crítico y pensador mexicano contemporáneo. Señala que su preocupación originaria fue la relación entre la universalidad de la filosofía y su inserción en la realidad histórica concreta. Sigue su trayectoria a través de tres etapas: la de la filosofía de lo mexicano (hasta 1968); la del marxismo crítico (hasta 1977); y la etapa más reciente. Los principales libros de este itinerario serían: *Filosofía de lo mexicano* (1960); *La filosofía en la historia política de México* (1966); y *Reformismo y revolución en el pensamiento político mexicano* (1972).

4940 O'Gorman, Edmundo *et al.* Cultura, ideas y mentalidades. Introducción y selección de Solange Alberro. México: Colegio de México, Centro de Estudios Históricos, 1992. 262 p.: bibl. (Lecturas de historia mexicana; 6)

Valiosa reedición de algunos de los artículos aparecidos en *Historia Mexicana*. Entre los de mayor interés para esta sección se cuentan: Edmundo O'Gorman, "La Idea Antropológica del Padre Las Casas: Edad Media y Modernidad;" Francisco López Cámara, "Los Socialistas Franceses en la Reforma Mexicana;" William D. Raat, "Los Intelectuales, el

Positivismo y la Cuestión Indígena;" Luis Villoro, "La Cultura Mexicana de 1910 a 1960."

4941 Quintanilla, Lourdes. El nacionalismo de Lucas Alamán. Guanajuato, Mexico: Gobierno del Estado de Guanajuato, 1991. 86 p. (Nuestra cultura; 1)

Es un intento de leer, en forma comprensiva (previa a toda crítica), aunque no necesariamente aprobatoria, los textos histórico-políticos de Alamán. Estima que un diálogo con él, con sus tesis (conservadoras) y con sus intenciones es necesario para comprender la historia de México. Se basa en las dos obras clásicas de Alamán: las Disertaciones sobre la historia de la República Mejicana. ., 3 vols., 1884–89, y la Historia de Méjico desde los primeros movimientos que prepararon su independencia en el año 1808, hasta la época presente, 5 vol., 1849–52, aunque los títulos completos de estas obras y sus fechas de edición nunca aparecen en este ensayo.

4942 Reyes, Alfonso. *Ultima Tule* y otros ensayos. Selección y prólogo de Rafael Gutiérrez Girardot. Cronología de Anja Maria Erdt y Rafael Gutiérrez Girardot. Bibliografía de James Willis Robb y Rafael Gutiérrez Girardot. Caracas: Biblioteca Ayacucho, 1991. 303 p.: bibl. (Biblioteca Ayacucho; 163)

Recoge parte de *Ultima Tule* y otros ensayos de las *Obras completas* de Alfonso Reyes. Como es habitual en la Biblioteca Ayacucho, contiene cronología y bibliografía. El prólogo por momentos apasionado pero imprescindible.

4943 Sánchez Vázquez, Adolfo. Vicisitudes de la filosofía contemporánea en México. (*Cuad. Am.,* 1:4, julio/agosto 1987, p. 208–221)

Rápido repaso de la filosofía en México en lo que va del siglo. Los momentos que distingue son: el Ateneo; el debate Caso-Lombardo Toledano; Samuel Ramos; los españoles exiliados; Leopoldo Zea; la filosofía analítica; el marxismo. A ésta última corriente, en la forma de lo que podría llamarse un "marxismo abierto," pertenece el autor, lo que explica algunas de sus opiniones. Sin embargo, es evidente en el artículo una considerable amplitud de juicio.

4944 Valverde Téllez, Emeterio. Bibliografía filosófica mexicana. v. 1–2. Estudio introductorio por Herón Pérez Martínez. Indices elaborados por Pilar González y Marcelo Sada. Ed. facsimilar. Zamora, Mexico: Colegio de Michoacán, 1989. 2 v.

Muy oportuna reedición de esta obra clásica de Valverde Téllez, importante fuente bibliográfica sobre la filosofía y la cultura en México. Apareció por primera vez en 1907 y la segunda edición apareció en 1913–14. De esta última se ha hecho la presente edición facsimilar. Se antepone una biobibliografía de Valverde Téllez y se incluyen también valiosos índices.

4945 Vasconcelos, José. José Vasconcelos. Edición de María Justina Sarabia Viejo. Prólogo de Antonio Lago Carballo. Madrid: Instituto de Cooperación Iberoamericana, Ediciones de Cultura Hispánica, 1989. 123 p.: bibl. (Antología del pensamiento político, social y económico de América Latina; 6)

Contiene, además de un prólogo de orientación general, pasajes tomados de *La raza cósmica, Indología y Bolivarismo y monroísmo,* entre otros. También incluye una bibliografía de y sobre Vasconcelos. Tiene la utilidad de los volúmenes de esta serie: dar lo esencial del autor, con introducción y bibliografía.

4946 Vasconcelos, José. José Vasconcelos y la universidad. Introducción y selección de Alvaro Matute. Presentación de Alfonso de María y Campos. Colaboración de Angeles Ruiz. 2a ed. México: UNAM, Coordinación de Difusión Cultural, Dirección de Literatura; IPN, Dirección de Publicaciones y Bibliotecas, 1987. 217 p.: bibl. (Textos de humanidades. Colección Educadores mexicanos)

Antología de discursos y documentos que reflejan la acción de Vasconcelos en la Universidad. También incluye "Don Gabino Barreda y las Ideas Contemporáneas," conferencia en el Ateneo de la Juventud, de 1910, y "El Movimiento Intelectual Contemporáneo en México," de 1916.

4947 Vasconcelos, José. Obra selecta. Estudio preliminar, selección, notas, cronología y bibliografía de Christopher Domínguez Michael. Caracas: Biblioteca Ayacucho, 1992. 351 p.: bibl. (Biblioteca Ayacucho; 181)

Recoge partes de *La raza cósmica* e *Indología;* fragmentos de las *Memorias* de Vasconcelos; y otros escritos, como "Don Gabino Barreda y las Ideas Contemporáneas" (1910), y "Discurso en la Universidad" (1920). El prólogo o estudio preliminar sigue la agitada vida pública de Vasconcelos y da una visión general de su significado intelectual y político en la historia reciente de México.

4948 Villegas, Abelardo *et al.* Historia de la filosofía en México, siglo XX. v. 1, Aproximaciones. Tlaxcala, Mexico: Univ. Autónoma de Tlaxcala, 1988. v. 1: bibl. (Col. Materiales para la historia de la filosofía en México)

Se trata de artículos breves, pero en general muy aprovechables: Abelardo Villegas, "Sobre el Estudio de la Filosofía Latinoamericana" (orientadoras consideraciones sobre el tema); Daysi Rivero, Pablo Guadarrama y otros, "El Positivismo y el Materialismo Científico-Natural en Latinoamérica" (15 conclusiones sobre el positivismo latinoamericano); Elsa Cecilia Frost, "Samuel Ramos y la Filosofía de lo Mexicano" (inteligente comentario a la obra de Ramos, *El perfil del hombre y la cultura en México*); Laura Benítez, "Gaos y Gallegos Rocafull en torno a *El tema de nuestro tiempo*" (útil para la idea de filosofía en Gaos, y porque Gallegos Rocafull es poco conocido fuera de su labor historiográfica); Walter Beller, "Tres Lógicos Mexicanos, un Paradigma Epistémico" (dedicado a Porfirio Parra, Francisco Larroyo y Eli de Gortari como estudiosos de la lógica); Juliana González Valenzuela, "Nicol en el Contexto de la Filosofía de México en el Siglo XX" (breve pero útil porque Nicol no ha sido estudiado como merece); Lisbeth Sagols Sales, "Humanismo y Filosofía en Ramón Xirau" (destaca las ideas centrales, pero sobre todo la *actitud* filosófica de Xirau); Mauricio Beuchot, "Esquema de la Filosofía Cristiana en México en el Siglo XX" (inventario de nombres y obras que incluye a Vasconcelos, a tomistas, suarecianos, escotistas e independientes); Gabriel Vargas Lozano, "La Filosofía Frente a la Dependencia y la Liberación de América Latina" (básicamente es una discusión con Luis Villoro, en la que el autor sostiene que la reflexión filosófica debe contribuir "a la liberación de las clases dominadas y explotadas"); Roberto Hernández Oramas, "Problemas Metodológicos de la Historia de la Filosofía" (se refiere a la historia de la filosofía en México, y específicamente a la obra de Gaos, *En torno a la filosofía mexicana*, además de atender a otros historiógrafos del siglo XX, como Samuel Ramos y Valverde Téllez).

4949 Wojcieszak, Janusz. Dependencia constitutiva y constructiva de la cultura latinoamericana: vigencia del ideario de Alfonso Reyes. (*Cuad. Am.*, 3 : 18, nov./dic. 1989, p. 90–119)

Destaca en Reyes la aspiración universalista de la cultura, por oposición a los particularismos y al exceso de énfasis en las formas culturales nacionalistas. Para Reyes, la historia se hace de "hibridismos," y América puede instalarse en la universalidad de la cultura *sumando* lo suyo a lo ajeno. O en palabras de Reyes: "No nos mutilemos voluntariamente."

4950 Yamuni Tabush, Vera. José Gaos, su filosofía. México: Facultad de Filosofía y Letras, Univ. Nacional Autónoma de México, 1989. 69 p.: bibl. (Jornadas de la Facultad de Filosofía y Letras; 4)

El tono es expositivo y aclaratorio de los textos de Gaos, que como bien afirma la autora, no siempre son de estilo llano. El contenido de la exposición es la filosofía sistemática de Gaos, dividida en cuatro grandes temas: filosofía de la filosofía; la expresión verbal, oral o escrita; la razón pura; y la razón práctica. Las principales obras tomadas en cuenta son: *Confesiones profesionales; Dos ideas de la filosofía; De la filosofía;* y *Del hombre.*

AMERICA CENTRAL

4951 Burnett, Virginia Garrat. Positivismo, liberalismo e impulso misionero: misiones protestantes en Guatemala, 1880–1920. (*Mesoamérica/Antigua*, 11 : 19, junio 1990, p. 13–31)

El objetivo del trabajo es mostrar las conexiones entre los siguientes hechos históricos: la expansión protestante en Guatemala; las doctrinas y programas liberales en ese país; las ideas del darwinismo social; y los intereses económicos de los EE.UU. Las misiones protestantes habrían sido vistas por los gobernantes liberales (Justo Rufino Barrios, Manuel Estrada Cabrera) como vehículo civilizatorio.

4952 Girardi, Giulio. Sandinismo, marxismo, cristianismo: la confluencia. 2. ed. Managua: Centro Ecuménico Antonio Valdivieso, 1987. 457 p.: bibl.

Examina extensamente las relaciones entre las ideas de Sandino y el sandinismo, el marxismo y el cristianismo. Manifiesta intensa adhesión a la teología de la liberación y al cristianismo revolucionario. Precisamente el sandinismo habría descubierto el potencial revolucionario del cristianismo. Como Sandino asimiló ideas teosóficas en México, el autor habla de la "teosofía de la liberación" en Sandino.

4953 Hodges, Donald Clark. Sandino's communism: spiritual politics for the twenty-first century. Austin: Univ. of Texas Press, 1992. 246 p.: bibl., index.

Continuación de la obra anterior del autor que se reseñó en *HLAS 54:5402.* La precisa definición de la posición de Sandino sería "comunismo," no entendido sin embargo el término en el sentido habitual que lo asocia con el marxismo. Su significado se remontaría a manifestaciones de la Revolución Francesa y se vincularía a Proudhon, el anarquismo libertario y ciertas ideas teosóficas (las que Sandino asimiló durante su estancia en México). El autor analiza la totalidad del pensamiento de Sandino, a diferencia de otros enfoques motivados políticamente, que son selectivos. La interpretación es compleja, pero la profundidad y amplitud de la búsqueda hace que no sea posible a los estudiosos de Sandino y su legado prescindir de este libro. Véase la reseña del historiador, item **1734**.

4954 Mora Rodríguez, Arnoldo. Historia del pensamiento costarricense. San José: Editorial Univ. Estatal a Distancia, 1992. 183 p.: bibl., ill., map.

Aunque tiene una estructura didáctica, es un panorama para amplio público hecho con seriedad. Se da gran amplitud a la parte colonial. En lo que corresponde a los siglos XIX y XX predomina el pensamiento vinculado a los movimientos y partidos políticos. El aspecto de ideas nunca se presenta desconectado del contexto histórico.

4955 Mora Rodríguez, Arnoldo. El ideario de don Joaquín García Monge. San José: Editorial Costa Rica, 1990. 99 p.: bibl.

Semblanza y apreciación de Joaquín García Monge, intelectual costarricense reconocido en toda América Latina por haber fundado (1919) y sostenido por largos años la revista *Repertorio Americano.*

4956 Quesada Soto, Alvaro. Transformaciones ideológicas del período 1900–1920. (*Rev. Hist./Heredia,* 17, enero/junio 1988, p. 99–130, bibl.)

Se refiere a Costa Rica. El material analizado es principalmente de literatura o "literatura de ideas." Destaca las manifestaciones de autores que pueden considerarse "socialistas" y "anarquistas," pero apreciando su significado dentro del contexto histórico del país, y no sólo por lo que aquellos rótulos sugieren en general. Trabajo muy aprovechable.

4957 *Revista de Filosofía de la Universidad de Costa Rica.* Vol. 27, No. 65, junio 1989. San José: Depto. de Filosofía de la Facultad Central de Ciencias y Letras.

Libro póstumo de Constantino Láscaris, *Las ideas en Centroamérica, 1838–1970,* concluido en 1976, que aparece como número especial. Continúa lo presentado en libro anterior del mismo autor: *Historia de las ideas en Centroamérica* (1970). Láscaris publicó también *Desarrollo de las ideas en Costa Rica* (1965).

4958 Valle, José Cecilio del. Ensayos y documentos. Introducción y selección de Carlos Meléndez Chaverri. San José: Libro Libre, 1988. 251 p.: 1 ill. (Serie Clásicos centroamericanos)

Reúne escritos de José Cecilio del Valle (1780–1834) que expresan sus ideas americanistas, económicas y políticas. La introducción divide los comentarios en función del orden de la antología. La obra había sido publicada anteriormente por la OEA.

CARIBE INSULAR

4959 Abellán, José Luis. La dimensión krauso-positivista en Eugenio María de Hostos. (*Cuad. Am.,* 3:16, julio/agosto 1989, p. 58–66)

Hostos ha sido visto como influido por el positivismo comteano y por el krausismo. La tesis del autor, que desarrolla examinando *Moral social,* es que se trata de "krauso-positivismo," una corriente de la cual da las principales características al comienzo del artículo. Considera que el reconocimiento de esta posición filosófica abre un capítulo nuevo en el estudio del pensamiento filosófico latinoamericano.

4960 Ainsa, Fernando. Hostos y la unidad de América Latina: raíces históricas de una utopía necesaria. (*Cuad. Am.,* 3:16, julio/agosto 1989, p. 67–88)

Hostos no escribió ninguna utopía en el sentido específico del género, pero el autor encuentra que en un sentido amplio es utópica su prédica por la unidad de América Latina, la cual se da junto con su defensa de la independencia de las Antillas. El artículo persigue esos temas en la "profusa obra periodística, epistolar y libresca" de Hostos.

4961 Alvarez, Nicolás Emilio. Jorge Mañach y José Martí. (*Círculo/Verona,* 18, 1989, p. 183–189)

Sobre la obra martiana de Mañach, que comenzó en 1933 con *Martí, el apóstol,* y continuó como constante dedicación hasta la muerte del autor, en 1961.

4962 Antonin, Arnold. Les idées haïtiennes et la révolution sud-américaine. Pétion-Ville, Haiti: Editions du Centre Pétion-Bolivar, 1990. 143 p., 5 leaves of plates: bibl., ill.

Interesa un breve artículo titulado "Bolívar et les principes haïtiens," que se refiere a las relaciones de Bolívar con el gobierno haitiano después de la revolución en Haití y al influjo que el Libertador pudo recibir de los principios en que se basó esa revolución.

4963 Artidiello Moreno, Mabel. Pensamiento filosófico dominicano hasta la década del 1950. (*Ecos/Santo Domingo,* 1:2, 1993, p. 129–144)

Breve pero claro panorama de la filosofía en Santo Domingo desde la colonia hasta la obra de Andrés Avelino, pasando por Pedro Varela Jiménez (1757–1833), Andrés López de Medrano (1780–1835) y Eugenio María de Hostos, entre otros. Mediante algunos juicios se intenta relacionar la filosofía con la vida económica, política y social.

4964 Febres, Laura. Pedro Henríquez Ureña: crítico de América. Caracas: Ediciones La Casa de Bello, 1989. 165 p.: bibl. (Col. Zona tórrida; 12. Letras universitarias)

Aunque centrado en la crítica, este atinado ensayo recorre de hecho toda la obra de Pedro Henríquez Ureña. El texto obtuvo mención honorífica en el Concurso propiciado por la OEA con motivo del Centenario del autor dominicano.

4965 Garza Cuarón, Beatriz. La herencia filológica de Pedro Henríquez Ureña en El Colegio de México. (*Rev. Iberoam.,* 54:142, enero/marzo 1988, p. 321–332)

Valoriza el legado de Henríquez Ureña como filólogo y contribuye a la historia institucional de El Colegio de México. (Sobre este segundo aspecto véase *HLAS 52:5336*).

4966 Gómez García, Carmen and **Ramón Rodríguez Salgado.** Algunas consideraciones acerca de la periodización de la historia de la filosofía en Cuba. (*Lateinamerika/Hamburg,* 2, 1988, p. 30–40)

Ofrece una periodización de la filosofía en Cuba basada en la expresión de las clases sociales y sus intereses. Sin embargo, critica un intento parecido, realizado por el autor soviético O.C. Ternevoi.

4967 Guerra-Cunningham, Lucía. Feminismo e ideología liberal en el pensamiento de Eugenio María de Hostos. (*Cuad. Am.,* 3:16, julio/agosto 1989, p. 139–150)

El tema es un discurso pronunciado por Hostos en Santiago de Chile en 1872 sobre "La Educación Científica de la Mujer." Destaca en dicho texto el valor reivindicador que tiene para la concepción de la mujer y su distancia con respecto a opiniones consagradas en aquella época.

Hostos, Eugenio María de. Obras completas. v. 1, Literatura: t. 2, Cuento, teatro, poesía, ensayo. See item **2032.**

4968 La Rosa Corzo, Gabino. Los hermanos Mestre y las tesis del teleologismo y del antropologismo en la segunda mitad del siglo XIX en Cuba. (*Islas/Santa Clara,* 94, sept./dic. 1989, p. 122–133, bibl.)

El propósito principal es destacar los escritos científicos, de corte positivista, de Antonio Mestre (1834–77), como parte del pensamiento progresista "pre-marxista" en Cuba. En este sentido el artículo es útil, porque estas manifestaciones cientificistas, de interés para la historia de las ideas, no han sido mayormente atendidas por la historiografía de la filosofía y merecen ser comparadas con otras semejantes en el resto de América Latina. Desde su punto de vista, el autor contrasta con intenso énfasis el valor de Antonio Mestre con el de su hermano José Manuel Mestre (uno de los antecedentes de la historiografía filosófica en Cuba), representante del espiritualismo. (Para otra crítica a José Manuel Mestre desde el punto de vista marxista véase *HLAS 50:4611*).

4969 Lipp, Solomón. Releyendo a Hostos: algunas facetas de su ideario. (*Cuad. Am.*, 3 : 16, julio/agosto 1989, p. 93–100)

Variados comentarios sobre el pensamiento de Hostos y apreciación de su figura.

4970 Maldonado-Denis, Manuel. Eugenio María de Hostos y el pensamiento social iberoamericano. México: Fondo de Cultura Económica, 1992. 186 p.: bibl. (Col. Tierra firme)

Conjunto de trabajos sobre Hostos, de parte de uno de los mejores conocedores del autor puertorriqueño. Algunos fueron publicados anteriormente, pero sólo hay datos de publicación de los aparecidos en periódicos. Los que más directamente se refieren a Hostos como pensador son: "Eugenio María de Hostos, Fundador de la Sociología Iberoamericana;" "Visión de Hostos Sobre el Descubrimiento, la Conquista y la Colonización de América;" "Eugenio María de Hostos: Maestro y Pensador del Derecho;" y "Hostos y el Pensamiento Social Iberoamericano." Contiene cronología y bibliografía selecta.

4971 Martínez Bello, Antonio. Martí: antimperialista y conocedor del imperialismo. La Habana: Editorial de Ciencias Sociales, 1986. 134 p.: bibl. (Ediciones políticas)

Se propone un paralelo entre Lenin y Martí en la cuestión del antiimperialismo. La mayor parte del libro se refiere a Martí.

4972 Mestas, Juan E. El pensamiento social de José Martí: ideología y cuestión obrera. Madrid: Editorial Pliegos, 1993. 175 p.: bibl. (Pliegos de ensayo; 84)

El autor ha extraído de la obra escrita de Martí las expresiones relacionadas con la "cuestión social." Trata de verlas en su momento histórico y sin desproporcionarlas en relación con la obra total del autor cubano. La inquietud ética de Martí lo habría llevado a una adhesión incuestionable hacia los obreros, pero sin extremismos.

4973 Moreta, Angel and **Alexis Viloria.** Introducción al pensamiento político de Adalberto Chapuseaux: las ideas pre-socialistas en la República Dominicana, 1920–1930. (*Islas/Santa Clara*, 90, mayo/agosto 1988, p. 117–128)

Examinado desde un punto de vista

marxista-leninista, el autor estudiado se considera como el primer antecedente del marxismo en la República Dominicana. Chapuseaux escribió *El porqué del bolchevismo* (1925) y *Revolución y evolución* (1929), y en su obra se encuentran elementos de marxismo (generalmente de conocimiento indirecto), del positivismo de Hostos y de cristianismo primitivo.

4974 Núñez, Manuel. El ocaso de la nación dominicana. Santo Domingo: Editora Alfa y Omega, 1990. 347 p.: bibl., ill., index.

Toda la obra está dominada por una preocupación básica: la de la "desnacionalización" o pérdida de la identidad del país. Esa identidad descansa en la cultura (y por eso no es casual que se hable de "*nación* dominicana"). Una parte considerable del peligro la ve el autor en la proximidad de Haití.

4975 Pazos, Felipe. Las ideas económicas de José Martí. (*Pensam. Iberoam.*, 10, julio/dic. 1986, p. 369–386)

Ilumina un aspecto poco frecuentado de Martí. Trata de las opiniones del clásico cubano sobre la agricultura, la propiedad de la tierra, el comercio internacional, el monopolio, el capitalismo de EE.UU., etc. El autor afirma que Martí era liberal en economía, pero reaccionaba fuertemente contra el capitalismo descarnado. Exposición clara y moderada.

4976 Pensar al Che. v. 1–2. La Habana: Centro de Estudios sobre América; Buenos Aires: Ediciones Dialéctica, 1989. 2 v.: bibl.

Contiene 18 trabajos, la mayoría de autores cubanos. Con una orientación de simpatía ideológica hacia el personaje estudiado, algunos de los temas son: las "visiones tergiversadas" del Che; el Che y la historia latinoamericana; el pensamiento económico del Che; el Che y el socialismo; la ética del Che; construcción socialista y vanguardia.

4977 Pérez Memén, Fernando. El pensamiento dominicano en la primera república, 1844–1861. Santo Domingo: Univ. Nacional Pedro Henríquez Ureña, 1993. 460 p.: bibl.

Es en realidad una historia general del período abarcado, destacando los aspectos de "ideas," tal como se perciben en un muy nutrido material documental: periódicos, constituciones, deliberaciones parlamentarias, leyes, etc. Predomina la exposición del pensamiento liberal. Se alude frecuentemente a situaciones semejantes en otras partes de América Latina. Dada la profusión de materiales utilizados, el lector hará bien en poner especial atención al resumen final de conclusiones.

4978 Pimentel, Miguel A. Marxismo y positivismo. Santo Domingo: Editora Universitaria, UASD, 1985. 304 p.: bibl. (Publicaciones de la Universidad Autónoma de Santo Domingo; vol. 373. Col. Filosofía y sociedad; 2)

Se refiere a la República Dominicana. Aunque no es obra de naturaleza académica, importa por tratar autores poco conocidos: Federico García Godoy (1857–1924); José Ramón López (*La alimentación y las razas*, 1896); Ricardo Sánchez Lustrino (*Pro-psiquis*, 1912); y A. Chapuseaux (*El porqué del bolcheviquismo*, 1925). (Sobre este último, véase item **4973**).

4979 Rojas Gómez, Miguel and Ramón Pérez Linares. La filosofía nietzscheana de Alberto Lamar Schweyer. (*Islas/Santa Clara*, 92, enero/abril 1989, p. 45–54)

Lamar Schweyer (1902–42) fue ensayista filosófico y periodista. Entre otras obras escribió *La palabra de Zaratustra* (1922) y *Biología de la democracia* (1927). Por sus inclinaciones filosóficas es juzgado severamente por los autores del artículo, desde el punto de vista que es oficial actualmente en Cuba.

4980 Rojas Osorio, Carlos. Hostos, apreciación filosófica. Humacao, Puerto Rico: Colegio Universitario de Humacao, Instituto de Cultura Puertorriqueña, 1988. 112 p.: bibl., ill.

De naturaleza expositiva pero con el mérito de tratar de cubrir todos los aspectos filosóficos de Hostos: lógica (generalmente menos atendida) y teoría del conocimiento; ética; filosofía social y política; valores; psicología; filosofía de la educación. También se examina el "naturalismo" de Hostos.

Taverna Sánchez, Cristina. Hacia una concepción de la ciencia en el siglo XIX cubano: José de la Luz y Caballero. See item **2090**.

4981 Taylor, Burchell. The theology of liberation. (*Caribb. Q.*, 37:1, March 1991, p. 19–34)

Aunque contiene una caracterización de la teología de la liberación en general, lo de mayor interés son las conclusiones desde el punto de vista del Caribe de habla inglesa. En ese sentido afirma que la mencionada teología no podría adoptarse sin agregarle énfasis que no están adecuadamente representados en el concepto de "pobreza." Entre éstos se contarían asuntos como raza, color, clase, identidad, derechos femeninos y preocupaciones ecológicas.

4982 Torres-Cuevas, Eduardo. Antidogma, conciencia y patriotismo en Félix Varela. (*Anu. Cent. Estud. Martianos*, 12, 1989, p. 73–100)

Escolástica, ideología y "patriotismo" en Varela. Algunos aspectos de la interpretación muestran una posición marxista.

4983 Torres-Cuevas, Eduardo y Félix Borges Legrá. Formación de la personalidad y de las ideas de Félix Varela y Morales. (*Rev. Bibl. Nac. José Martí*, 31:2, mayo/agosto 1989, p. 35–76)

Muy completo y útil para el conocimiento de la formación y estudios del filósofo cubano Félix Varela (1787–1853).

4984 Venegas Delgado, Hernán. El pensamiento temprano de la Ilustración Cubana como expresión de su nacionalidad: Francisco de Arango y Parreño, 1765–1837. (*Islas/Santa Clara*, 90, mayo/agosto 1988, p. 69–74)

A pesar de que Arango fue representante de la "ideología liberal burguesa" y de que, por razones de conveniencia económica, promovió la continuación de la esclavitud, aquí se destaca ante todo su contribución al fortalecimiento de la nacionalidad cubana. El interés del autor parece ser el de vincular la Revolución Socialista a las etapas anteriores de la historia de Cuba, especialmente a la "consolidación de la nacionalidad" en el siglo XIX.

4985 Zea, Leopoldo. Hostos como conciencia latinoamericana. (*Cuad. Am.*, 3:16, julio/agosto 1989, p. 49–57)

Apreciación general de Hostos en su significado para la historia de las Antillas y de América Latina en general.

VENEZUELA

4986 Bruzual, Blas et al. Pensamiento liberal del siglo XIX: antología. Selección y estudio preliminar de Inés Mercedes Quintero

Montiel. Caracas: Monte Avila Editores, 1992. 329 p.: bibl. (Biblioteca del pensamiento venezolano José Antonio Páez; 4)

Esta antología recoge escritos políticos y económicos que, aparecidos en el período 1834–46, giran en torno a las ideas y realizaciones "liberales" en ese período. Algunos temas son: los partidos políticos; la libertad de imprenta; la cuestión agraria; y la reacción de ciertos intereses económicos ante "los excesos del liberalismo." Ver item **2647** para el comentario del historiador.

4987 Carrera Damas, Germán. El dominador cautivo: ensayos sobre la configuración cultural del criollo venezolano. 1a. ed. venezolana. Caracas: Grijalbo, 1988. 260 p.: bibl. (Grijalbo/testimonios)

Destacamos tres trabajos: "El Dominador Cautivo: Ensayo Sobre la Configuración Cultural del Criollo Venezolano;" "El Análisis de los Obstáculos Puestos a la Creación Intelectual: el Pasado Histórico Como Ideología;" y—quizás el de mayor interés general— "Posible Esquema de la Dinámica del Nivel Técnico-Ideológico en Hispanoamérica: Compuesto Tomando Como Base el Caso Venezolano."

4988 Castillo Didier, Miguel. Miranda y la senda de Bello: tras las huellas de Homero, elogio de Virgilio y otros ensayos sobre el Precursor. Caracas: Ediciones de la Presidencia de la República, 1991. 163 p.: bibl., index.

Sobre el conocimiento de la cultura clásica por parte de Miranda, especialmente en el caso de Homero y Virgilio. También hay capítulos sobre el Archivo del Precursor, sobre lo "clásico" y lo "romántico" en él, y sobre la relación de Miranda con el joven Bello en Londres.

4989 Fernández Heres, Rafael. La evolución conceptual del Doctor Rafael Villavicencio. (*Bol. Acad. Nac. Hist./Caracas*, 71: 283, julio/sept. 1988, p. 615–627)

Visión general de la personalidad y las ideas de Villavicencio (1838–1920), pensador positivista venezolano.

4990 Grases, Pedro. Un paso cada día. Caracas: Editorial Seix Barral, 1993. 526 p.: index. (Obras de Pedro Grases; 19)

Continúa la ingente y valiosa obra del autor. De mayor interés para esta sección son los trabajos de la primera parte, sobre Roscio,

Bello, Picón Salas y José Toribio Medina, entre otros.

4991 Miranda, Francisco de. Miranda, la aventura de la libertad: antología. Prólogo David Ruiz Chataing. Selección y notas de David Ruiz Chataing y Edgardo Mondolfi. Bibliografía de Horacio Jorge Becco. Caracas: Monte Avila Editores, 1991. 2 v.: bibl. (Biblioteca del pensamiento venezolano José Antonio Páez; 3)

Antología basada en el *Archivo de Miranda*, pero también en otras obras documentales. El prólogo repasa la accidentada vida de Francisco de Miranda y defiende al Precursor de acusaciones que se le hicieron en su época. El segundo volumen contiene una bibliografía de y sobre Miranda.

4992 Scocozza, Antonio. Abbiamo arato il mare: l'utopia americana di Bolívar tra politica e storia. Napoli, Italia: Morano, 1990. 252 p.: bibl., index. (Nobiltà dello spirito; 27)

La primera parte consta de dos estudios (reelaboración de escritos anteriormente publicados): "Dalla Rivoluzione Independentista all'Utopia dell'Unitá Latinoamericana: l'Itinerario Político-ideologico di Simón Bolívar," e "Il Pensiero Costituzionale." La segunda parte contiene tres trabajos: "Il Bolívar di Karl Marx;" "Il Bolívar di Luigi Nascimbene" (autor de una *Storia dell'America Meridionale*, inédita); y "Morale e Política nel Pensiero del 'Primo' Bolívar." Contiene también una cronología bolivariana.

4993 Vallenilla Lanz, Laureano. *Disgregación e integración*: ensayo sobre la formación de la nacionalidad venezolana. Recopilación, comentarios y notas de Federico Brito Figueroa y de Nikita Harwich Vallenilla. Caracas: Fondo Editorial Lola de Fuenmayor, Centro de Investigaciones Históricas, Univ. Santa María, 1984. 427 p.: bibl., index, port. (Colección Clásicos del pensamiento social venezolano) (Obras completas/Laureano Vallenilla Lanz; 2)

Reproduce la obra indicada en el título, publicada por Laureano Vallenilla Lanz en 1930. Está precedida de dos estudios: Federico Brito Figueroa, "Laureano Vallenilla Lanz y la Comprensión Histórica de la Venezuela Colonial;" y Nikita Harwich Vallenilla, "La Influencia de los Viejos Conceptos o el Estudio de la Historia de Venezuela," título tomado del que lleva la introducción de Vallenilla Lanz a su obra.

COLOMBIA

4994 Antonio Gramsci y la realidad colombiana. Bogotá: Ediciones Foro Nacional por Colombia, 1991. 223 p.: bibl. (Col. Pensamiento político)

Gramsci aparece a la vista de estos autores como la modalidad marxista del momento, después de la caída del "socialismo real" y de la vuelta al juego democrático aun por parte de grupos que estaban hace poco en la lucha armada. De interés para las ideas políticas en Colombia en la actualidad.

4995 Cobo Borda, J. G. Germán Arciniegas. Bogotá: Procultura, 1992. 134 p.: bibl., ill. (Clásicos colombianos; 26)

Excelente introducción a Arciniegas. Se expone concisamente la vida y la obra del ensayista colombiano. Contiene también una parte antológica, una bibliografía de y sobre Arciniegas y una cronología.

4996 Congreso Internacional de Filosofía Latinoamericana, *4th, Bogotá, 1986.* Tendencias actuales de la filosofía en Colombia: ponencias. IV Congreso Internacional de Filosofía Latinoamericana, julio 7–11 de 1986. Bogotá: Univ. Santo Tomás, Facultad de Filosofía, Centro de Investigaciones, 1988. 615 p.: bibl. (Biblioteca colombiana de filosofía; 7)

La filosofía en Colombia es vista en este volumen desde distintos ángulos: primero en su desarrollo histórico y luego en sus aspectos contemporáneos: recepción e incidencia de la filosofía alemana, del marxismo, de la filosofía analítica, de la hermenéutica, de la filosofía española y de la propia filosofía latinoamericana. Concluye con la reproducción de lo expuesto en un "panel" sobre problemática y perspectivas de la filosofía en Colombia. Es una obra de real importancia y modelo para realizar el mismo intento en el caso de otros países latinoamericanos.

4997 Manrique, Marco Antonio and **Alvaro Ucrós M.** Apuntes sobre el pensamiento filosófico-político de José Ma. Samper. (*Franciscanum/Bogotá,* 31:93, sept./dic. 1989, p. 237–258)

Sobre los orígenes ideológicos e intelectuales de José María Samper, pero en especial sobre su participación en los debates constitucionales de 1886.

4998 Obra educativa—la querella Benthamista, 1748–1832. Recopilación de Luis Horacio López Domínguez. Prólogo de Jorge Eliécer Ruiz. Bogotá: Fundación para la Conmemoración del Bicentenario del Natalicio y el Sesquicentenario de la Muerte del General Francisco de Paula Santander, 1993. 485 p.: bibl., ill., index. (Biblioteca de la Presidencia de la República, administración Cesar Gaviria Trujillo. Col. Documentos; 72)

Significativa obra documental que refleja la influencia de Bentham en Colombia, tanto en los aspectos de aceptación de esa filosofía como en los de crítica. Además del prólogo y una nota que explica la metodología de la preparación del volumen, contiene índices onomástico, toponímico y temático, una cronología (1811–75) y una amplia bibliografía.

4999 Ocampo López, Javier. Los hombres y las ideas en Boyacá. Tunja, Colombia: Univ. Pedagógica y Tecnológica de Colombia, 1989. 347 p.: bibl., ill., index.

De este amplio panorama de la cultura en Boyacá, que se remonta a la época prehispánica, destacamos los artículos: "Diego Mendoza Pérez y el Darwinismo Social en Colombia" y "Carlos Arturo Torres y el Idealismo Latinoamericano." Tienen relación con el benthamismo y el indigenismo las páginas dedicadas a Ezequiel Rojas y Juan Climaco Hernández, respectivamente.

5000 Ocampo López, Javier. ¿Qué es el liberalismo colombiano? Bogotá: Plaza & Janés, 1990. 202 p.: bibl., ill.

Al repasar la historia del Partido Liberal contribuye a la historia política de Colombia y a la de los movimientos de ideas subyacentes a ella.

5001 Uribe Garzón, Carlos. El pensamiento social cristiano en Colombia. Bogotá: FIEL, Instituto de Estudios Sociales Juan Pablo II, 1991. 298 p.: bibl. (Col. Horizontes de solidaridad; 3)

La segunda parte de esta obra está dedicada a la exposición del pensamiento social-cristiano en Colombia hasta 1851. La tercera es antológica, y cubre desde 1851–1991. Los textos recogidos son breves, pero para cada período hay un comentario general, y para cada autor (50 en total) hay datos biográficos y bibliográficos.

5002 Valderrama Andrade, Carlos. Relación polémica de Miguel Antonio Caro con el benthamismo. (*Ideas Valores,* 80, agosto 1989, p. 121–143)

Ilustra, con numerosas citas de Miguel Antonio Caro (1843–1909), la oposición de este autor a las ideas de Bentham y a la enseñanza de ellas en Colombia. Sostiene que la argumentación de Caro se basó principalmente en "principios morales y religiosos." Valderrama Andrade es autor de *El pensamiento filosófico de Miguel Antonio Caro,* 1961.

5003 Valencia Villa, Alejandro. El pensamiento constitucional de Miguel Antonio Caro. Bogotá: Instituto Caro y Cuervo, 1992. 214 p.: bibl. (Serie La Granada entreabierta; 61)

Aunque la mayor parte del trabajo se dedica a la participación protagónica de Miguel Antonio Caro en la preparación de la Constitución colombiana de 1886, no deja de ser una visión de conjunto del pensamiento y la acción de dicho autor, incluyendo sus estudios clásicos y sus ideas filosóficas fundadas en el tradicionalismo católico.

ECUADOR

5004 Agramonte y Pichardo, Roberto Daniel. La filosofía de Montalvo. v. 1–3. Quito: Banco Central del Ecuador, 1992. 3 v. (1344 p.): bibl., ill., indexes.

Muy detallada y a ratos encomiástica obra sobre Montalvo. Parte del vol. 1 se dedica a una exhaustiva biografía. Los vols. 2 y 3 son una especie de enciclopedia de los temas que trató Montalvo. El capítulo titulado "Problemas Cardinales de la Filosofía" es una extensa consideración de lo que el autor estima como los aspectos filosóficos de la obra del clásico ecuatoriano.

5005 Bravo, Julián G. Aurelio Espinosa Pólit S.J.: apóstol de la educación católica y de la evangelización de la cultura. Quito: J.G.Bravo Santillán, 1990. 169 p.: bibl., ill.

Traductor de clásicos, Rector de la Pontificia Univ. Católica del Ecuador, fundador de la Biblioteca-Archivo de Autores y Asuntos Ecuatorianos, y autor de trabajos sobre la historia y la literatura de su país, Espinosa Pólit, SJ (1894–1961) es una gran figura de la cultura ecuatoriana. Este libro es una elogiosa exposición de su vida y su obra. Lamentablemente no ofrece la bibliografía del autor estudiado. Sobre el mismo tema véase el trabajo de Arturo A. Roig, *HLAS 44:7609.*

5006 Handelsman, Michael H. En torno al verdadero Benjamín Carrión. Quito: Editorial El Conejo, 1989. 133 p.: bibl. (Col. Ecuador/hoy)

Buen ensayo de conjunto sobre la personalidad y la obra de Benjamín Carrión (1889–1979), autor de *Mapa de América* (1930) y *El nuevo relato ecuatoriano* (1950–51).

5007 Paladines Escudero, Carlos. Aporte de Juan Montalvo al pensamiento liberal. Quito: Fundación Friedrich-Naumann, 1988. 39 p.: bibl.

Antes de examinar a Montalvo traza un cuadro esquemático del liberalismo ecuatoriano anterior. La contribución de Montalvo habría estado en la tónica combativa con que adoptó las tesis del liberalismo y en la fundamentación que dio a algunos componentes del ideario liberal en un "nuevo humanismo," secular y opuesto a la visión religiosa del hombre.

5008 Paz y Miño C., Juan J. Fray Vicente Solano y el pensamiento conservador en Ecuador. (*Procesos/Quito,* 3, segundo semestre 1992, p. 103–113)

Narra la polémica sostenida entre Fray Vicente Solano (1791–1865) y Antonio José de Irisarri (1786–1868, de origen guatemalteco, radicado en Ecuador), durante los años 1840–43. Solano defendía una posición religiosa y clerical a ultranza. Aunque no hubo mucha profundidad de pensamiento en la polémica, puede considerarse anticipo de las diferencias entre católicos y liberales que ocurren posteriormente, más avanzado el siglo XIX, en Ecuador como en otros países hispanoamericanos.

5009 Quevedo, Belisario. Ensayos sociológicos, políticos y morales. Estudio introductorio y selección de Samuel Guerra Bravo. Quito: Banco Central del Ecuador; Corporación Editora Nacional, 1981. 365 p.: bibl. (Biblioteca básica del pensamiento ecuatoriano; 10)

De Belisario Quevedo (1883–1921), quien adhirió a tesis positivistas, se recogen aquí escritos suyos publicados en revistas y en su libro póstumo, *Sociología, política y moral* (1932). La introducción tiende a destacar la relación de las ideas de Quevedo con la realidad ecuatoriana.

5010 Sacoto, Antonio. El ensayo ecuatoriano. Cuenca, Ecuador: Univ. del Azuay, 1992. 252 p.: bibl. (Serie Textos universitarios)

Los autores estudiados en capítulos individuales son: Eugenio Espejo; Fray Vicente Solano; Juan León Mera; Juan Montalvo; Manuel J. Calle; Remigio Crespo Toral. Además, hay dos estudios: "El Ensayo y la Crítica Literaria en Ecuador (1925–60)" y "El Ensayo Ecuatoriano (1960–Presente)." Contiene una "bibliografía mínima" del ensayo ecuatoriano. Señala: 1) que el ensayo en Ecuador va más allá de lo literario y trata asuntos como la identidad y aspectos políticos e ideológicos; y 2) que sus autores no parecen conscientes de que las mismas características se dan en el resto del ensayo hispanoamericano.

PERU

5011 Andrade Talledo, Rolando. Augusto Salazar Bondy, hacia una educación liberadora. Lima: Consejo Nacional de Ciencia y Tecnología, 199pp 155 p.: bibl.

De la obra de Salazar Bondy destaca principalmente sus ideas sobre educación (Salazar Bondy colaboró con la reforma educativa del gobierno del General Velasco), sobre la base de su concepto de "cultura de la dominación." Compara su posición con las de Leopoldo Zea, Darcy Ribeiro, Paulo Freire y José María Arguedas, entre otros.

5012 Casal, Juan Manuel. Mariátegui: el socialismo indoamericano. Montevideo: Proyección, 1992. 192 p.: bibl.

Es una síntesis clara, ecuánime y razonable de la vida de Mariátegui y del desarrollo de su pensamiento político. Pone énfasis en su carácter *socialista*, a distinción del aprismo y del comunismo soviético.

5013 Concha, Jaime et al. Ensayos sobre Mariátegui: simposio de Nueva York, 12 de diciembre de 1980. Edición de Víctor Berger. Lima: Biblioteca Amauta, 1987. 186 p.: bibl.

Contiene: Jaime Concha, "Mariátegui y su Crítica del Latifundio;" Antonio Melis, "Mariátegui y la Crítica de la Vida Cotidiana;" Eugenio Chang-Rodríguez, "La Superación del Anarquismo en Mariátegui;" Salvador Rodríguez del Pino, "La Influencia Ideológica de Mariátegui en el Movimiento Chicano;" Harry S. Vanden, "Mariátegui, Marxismo, Comunismo y Otras Notas Bibliográficas;" Solomon Lipp, "Releyendo a Mariátegui: Algunos Aspectos de su Mundo Literario;" David O. Wise, "*Amauta* (1926–1930): una Fuente para

la Historia Cultural Peruana;" William W. Stein, "Una Apreciación Antropológica de José Carlos Mariátegui." Los que más interesan para la historia de las ideas son los trabajos de Chang-Rodríguez, Vanden y Wise.

5014 Etica y política hoy en el Perú. Edición de Oscar Mavila Marquina, Oswaldo Medina García y Eusebio Quiroz Paz Soldán. Lima: Facultad de Teología Pontificia y Civil de Lima, Centro de Investigaciónes Teológicas, 1992. 166 p.: bibl.

Trabajos presentados a reuniones sostenidas en 1991–92 sobre la "crisis" del Perú. Los editores afirman que las aportaciones recogidas buscan el diálogo crítico, "con el Perú como marco de referencia y la Doctrina Social de la Iglesia como sustento." La comunicación de mayor extensión y más compleja elaboración es: Norberto Strotmann, MSC, "Etica y Moral Social en el Perú: El Trasfondo de la Crisis Actual."

5015 Gaete Avaria, Jorge. Historia de un lenguaje infortunado: Mariátegui y el marxismo. Caracas: Fundación Centro de Estudios Latinoamericanos Rómulo Gallegos, 1988. 211 p.: bibl., ill. (Col. La Alborada)

El autor quiere captar el "lenguaje" de Mariátegui, con el fin de "hacer inteligible el sentido con que [aquél] aprehende, expone y utiliza el marxismo." Desde este enfoque se critican varios intentos de captar el marxismo (o falta de marxismo) en Mariátegui. Rico en argumentación, es el tipo de libro que se perjudica con el resumen. Entre las fuentes del autor se encuentran J.L. Austin y Quentin Skinner, lo que da al enfoque un carácter diferente de lo que es habitual en la exégesis del autor de los *Siete ensayos.*

5016 Gonzales, Osmar. Los arielistas frente al problema indígena. (*Allpanchis*/ Cusco, 21:34, segundo semestre 1989, p. 163–205)

Trabajo interesante, que analiza la "preocupación" por el indio en intelectuales como Francisco García Calderón, Víctor Andrés Belaúnde y José de la Riva Agüero, entre otros. Concluye que esos autores tuvieron una actitud ambivalente, y que su motivación fue el problema de la unidad nacional.

5017 Hurtado Oviedo, Víctor et al. A 60 años del Antimperialismo y el APRA. Lima: CONCYTEC; Centro de Estudios e Investigación Realidad y Cambio, 1989. 122 p.

Conjunto de apreciaciones sobre el libro *El antimperialismo y el APRA* (1928), de Haya de la Torre. Los autores son, en general, parte del movimiento aprista o simpatizantes de él, y la tónica está dada por la opinión de tipo político y de análisis de la realidad del Perú contemporáneo.

5018 Ibáñez I., Alfonso. Para repensar nuestras utopías: materiales de cultura política. Lima: Sur Casa de Estudios del Socialismo; TAREA, 1993. 193 p.: bibl.

Contiene tres artículos sobre Mariátegui: "Análisis y Utopía en Mariátegui;" "*La agonía de Mariátegui* Según Alberto Flores Galindo;" y "Mariátegui, un Pedagogo Socialista." También incluye uno sobre Zea: "El Conflicto de los Proyectos Históricos en la Perspectiva de Leopoldo Zea." Los demás pueden interesar como expresión de una posición socialista de óptica reciente.

5019 Lógica, razón y humanismo: la obra filosófica de Francisco Miró Quesada C.; libro de homenaje por sus 70 años. Edición de David Sobrevilla y Domingo García Belaúnde. Lima: Univ. de Lima, 1992. 443 p.: bibl.

Justiciero homenaje a uno de los más importantes filósofos latinoamericanos contemporáneos. Con excepción de dos, todas las contribuciones se refieren a la obra de Miró Quesada. Entre los autores se cuentan: Luis Felipe Alarco, David Sobrevilla, Newton da Costa, José Ferrater Mora, Héctor Neri Castañeda, Fernando Salmerón, Ernesto Garzón Valdés y Ernesto Mayz Vallenilla. Leopoldo Zea y María Luisa Rivara de Tuesta sitúan a Miró Quesada en la filosofía latinoamericana. El homenajeado contesta a cada uno de sus expositores y críticos y antepone un bosquejo autobiográfico o autoexposición, que quizás por la brevedad no da la medida de su importancia filosófica. Cierra este volumen, oportuno y bien realizado, una bibliografía de y sobre Miró Quesada.

5020 Mariátegui, José Carlos. Escritos juveniles: la edad de piedra. v. 3, Entrevistas, crónicas y otros textos. Estudio preliminar, compilación y notas de Alberto Tauro. Lima: Biblioteca Amauta, 1987–1994. 8 v.: bibl., ports. (Obras completas de José Carlos Mariátegui. Biblioteca Amauta)

Continuación de la recopilación de escritos del Mariátegui de la primera época. La mayor parte de los materiales periodísticos recogidos se publicaron entre 1914–18 (ver *HLAS 52:5390*).

5021 Mariátegui, unidad de pensamiento y acción. v. 2. Lima: Ediciones Unidad, 1987. 2 v.: bibl.

Segundo volumen de las ponencias presentadas a un seminario internacional sobre Mariátegui promovido por el Partido Comunista Peruano.

5022 Mejía Valera, Manuel. El positivismo en Perú. (*Cuad. Am.*, 1:4, julio/agosto 1987, p. 107–125)

Expone y comenta el positivismo peruano en sus principales representantes. Entre ellos: Carlos Lisson, Federico Villarreal, Joaquín Capelo, González Prada, Mariano H. Cornejo, Prado y Ugarteche. También se consideran otros autores que no corresponden a dicha corriente.

5023 Montiel, Edgar. Mariátegui: un ensayo de lectura epistemológica. (*Cuad. Am.*, 3:14, marzo/abril 1989, p. 15–30)

El artículo está centrado en los *Siete ensayos*. Subraya que ya en su estructura ese libro responde a ideas básicas del marxismo. Con esta obra se habría producido, en las ciencias sociales latinoamericanas, una "ruptura epistemológica."

5024 Nalewajko, Malgorzata. La imagen del indio en el Perú durante los años veinte de nuestro siglo: la discusión sobre la integración nacional. (*Jahrb. Gesch.*, 26, 1989, p. 229–259)

Verdadero "catálogo" descriptivo de opiniones expresadas sobre las modalidades, características y modos de ser del indio peruano en la época estudiada. En las conclusiones se menciona cierta coincidencia en la explicación de los rasgos negativos del indio por sus condiciones de vida.

5025 Nugent, José Guillermo. El conflicto de las sensibilidades: propuesta para una interpretación y crítica del siglo XX peruano. Lima: Instituto Bartolomé de las Casas-Rímac, 1991. 183 p.: bibl.

Título excesivamente amplio. Destacamos tres trabajos: "Tipos Humanos, Mito e Identidad Individual en *El alma matinal* de José Carlos Mariátegui" (1984); "La Construcción de la Vida en el Perú como Identidad Histórica Moderna" (1987); y "Postfeudales y

Modernos: sobre las Formas del Desacuerdo en el Fin de Siglo" (1988).

5026 Ramos Alva, Alfonso. Haya de la Torre, creador y visionario. Lima?: I.D.E.A., 1990. 128 p.: bibl. (Publicación del Instituto de Estudios Antimperialistas; 3)

La exposición y apreciación de Haya de la Torre se realiza desde cinco aspectos: filosófico (su teoría del espacio-tiempo), económico, sociológico, ideológico y político.

5027 Rencontre internationale José Carlos Mariátegui et l'Europe, *Pau, France and Tarbes, France, 1992.* Encuentro Internacional José Carlos Mariátegui y Europa: el otro aspecto del descubrimiento. Lima: Empresa Editora Amauta, 1993. 383 p.: bibl., ill.

Con respecto a la persona y la obra del autor peruano se abordan principalmente temas literarios y políticos. Algunas ponencias: Antonio Melis, "La Experiencia Italiana en la Obra de Mariátegui;" Osvaldo Fernández Díaz, "Una Proposición de Lectura de *Defensa del marxismo*;" César Germaná, "Socialismo y Democracia en el Pensamiento de José Carlos Mariátegui;" Aníbal Quijano," 'Raza', 'Etnia' y 'Nación' en Mariátegui: Cuestiones Abiertas."

5028 Rivara de Tuesta, María Luisa. Ideólogos de la emancipación peruana. Prólogo de Mario Magallón Anaya. 2. ed. Toluca, México: Univ. Autónoma del Estado de México, 1988. 155 p.: bibl. (Serie Mito-utopia-ideología)

Se trata de una historia intelectual o ideológica de la Independencia peruana. Abarca, por lo tanto, el siglo XVIII y los comienzos del XIX. El tema es el pensamiento ilustrado, según se refleja: en las ideas científicas; en las críticas al sistema político, jurídico y religioso; y en el cuestionamiento de la situación económico-social. La autora estima que las ideas de la Ilustración constituyeron "la base ideológica de la emancipación." Buen trabajo de síntesis.

5029 Tur, Carlos M. La cultura hispanista y autoritaria en Perú, 1920–1945. (*Cuad. Am.,* 1:4, julio/agosto 1987, p. 126–137)

Es una crítica a la mentalidad informada—entre otros rasgos—por el hispanismo (España imperial y civilizadora de América), la simpatía por la época colonial, el antiliberalismo y la atracción del gobierno fuerte. De esta mentalidad, en la época señalada en

el título, José de la Riva Agüero habría sido el representante más elocuente, aunque no el único. Esta posición se contrasta con movimientos más sensibles a los reclamos populares.

5030 Unruh, Vicky. Mariátegui's aesthetic thought: a critical reading of the avant-gardes. (*LARR,* 23:3, 1989, p. 45–69)

La lectura que Mariátegui hizo de las vanguardias (especialmente literarias) de su tiempo se relaciona con su credo artístico, y éste con sus ideas de reforma de la sociedad peruana. Enfoque complementario del exclusivamente político, más frecuente en el análisis de Mariátegui.

5031 Vargas Llosa, Mario. El país que vendrá. (*Vuelta/México,* 14:161, abril 1990, p. 42–45)

Resumen de la posición económica, política, social y cultural de Vargas Llosa como candidato a la presidencia de su país. Importa, más allá de ser expresión de campaña electoral, como "credo" o doctrina cuya mínima caracterización sería "liberal," pero en un sentido muy amplio e inscrito en el contexto de la situación latinoamericana y mundial hacia 1989.

5032 Vida y obra de Víctor Raúl Haya de la Torre. v. 1. Lima: Instituto Cambio y Desarrollo, 1990. 1 v.: ill. ; (Col. Historia política; 1)

Resultado de un concurso sobre la acción y la obra de Haya de la Torre. Contiene: Raúl Chanamé Orbe, "Haya de la Torre y las Universidades Populares;" Pedro Planas Silva y Hugo Vallens Málaga, "Haya de la Torre en su Espacio y en su Tiempo;" y María Teresa Quiroz, "El Partido: Obra Principal de Víctor Raúl Haya de la Torre (1930–34)." Para comentario del historiador, ver item **2814.**

BOLIVIA

5033 Antezana, Luis H. *et al.* El pensamiento de Sergio Almaraz. Cochabamba, Bolivia: Centro de Investigación de Sociología, CISO, FACES-UMSS, 1993. 160 p.: bibl.

Conjunto de trabajos sobre Sergio Almaraz (1928–68), representante del pensamiento nacionalista de izquierda en Bolivia y autor de *El petróleo en Bolivia* (1958), *El poder y la caída* (1987) y *Réquiem para una república* (1970). Los dos últimos se publicaron póstumamente.

5034   Condarco Morales, Ramiro. Franz Tamayo: el pensador. La Paz: Edit. e Imp. San José, 1989. 105 p.: bibl.

Recoge artículos periodísticos. Destacamos: "Antipositivismo y Positivismo en la Obra de Tamayo" y "Herencia Filosófica de Tamayo." En otro ensayo hace una comparación entre Tamayo y Toynbee.

CHILE

5035   Araya G., Juan Gabriel. Hostos: hacia una definición ensayística de una república. (*Cuad. Am.*, 3:16, julio/agosto 1989, p. 101–117)

El tema es una memoria escrita por Hostos sobre Chile (sus condiciones naturales, políticas, sociales, industriales, etc.) con motivo de una Exposición inaugurada en 1872, cuando el maestro puertorriqueño se encontraba en ese país. El autor elogia ampliamente el mencionado texto.

5036   Jocelyn-Holt Letelier, Alfredo. *Los girondinos chilenos:* una reinterpretación. (*Mapocho/Santiago*, 29, primer semestre 1991, p. 46–55)

Tomando como punto de partida *Los girondinos chilenos,* que Vicuña Mackenna publicó en 1876, da una interpretación positiva del liberalismo chileno del siglo XIX, a pesar de que nunca habría sobrepasado el plano romántico y el ámbito de la "república de las letras."

5037   Melgar Bao, Ricardo. Francisco Bilbao y la rebelión de los igualitarios en Chile. (*Cuad. Am.*, 5:27, mayo/junio 1991, p. 52–68)

Exposición de las circunstancias que facilitaron la constitución de la Sociedad de la Igualdad, las ideas que la conformaron, su disolución por el poder político gobernante y la función de Bilbao en todo ese conjunto.

5038   Ossandón B., Carlos. Una historia de la filosofía en Chile: modernidad e institucionalidad. (*Estud. Soc./Santiago*, 77, trimestre 3, 1993, p. 9–15)

Apreciación del libro de Cecilia Sánchez, *Una disciplina de la distancia: institucionalización universitaria de los estudios*

filosóficos en Chile (1992), realizada en el contexto de la historiografía sobre el pensamiento filosófico chileno. También se trata el tema de la posibilidad de establecer dicha historiografía como una disciplina epistemológica fundamentada.

Pinedo, Javier. Reflexiones en torno al Abate Juan Ignacio Molina, la Ilustración, y el *Ensayo sobre la historia natural de Chile.* See item **2502.**

BRASIL

5039   Azzi, Riolando. Catolicismo do povo brasileiro. Brasília: SER-Editora Rumos, 1993. 158 p.: bibl.

Muy útil para mostrar la dialéctica entre catolicismo oficial y catolicismo popular, caracterizado este último por su sincretismo. Se muestran diversos momentos históricos, desde la implantación de la religión cristiana en la colonia hasta la función social que actualmente cumplen las comunidades eclesiales de base.

Borges, Dain. Brazilian social thought of the 1930s. See item **3284.**

Borges, Dain. "Puffy, ugly, slothful and inert": degeneration in Brazilian social thought, 1880–1940. See item **3285.**

5040   Campos, Fernando Arruda. O Pe. Henrique Lima Vaz S.J. e a nova antropologia tomista. (*Rev. Bras. Filos.*, 40:168, out./nov./dez. 1992, p. 404–415)

Nota apreciativa sobre la obra del filósofo brasileño contemporáneo Henrique Lima Vaz, S.J., *Antropologia filosófica*, vol. 1, São Paulo, 1991, de tendencia neotomista.

5041   Carvalho, José Murilo de. Entre a liberdade dos antigos e a dos modernos: a República no Brasil. (*Dados/Rio de Janeiro*, 32:3, 1989, p. 265–280)

Examen de los antecedentes y modelos que sirvieron para la concepción de la República en Brasil y su repercusión y adaptación según las características nacionales e históricas del país. Además de los esquemas jurídico-institucionales se consideran los aspectos de identidad y los rasgos del país como *nación*, señalando la contribución de Euclides da Cunha, Graça Aranha, Monteiro Lobato y Gilberto Freyre. Artículo de verdadero interés.

5042 Chacon, Vamireh. A antropologia filosófica de Gilberto Freyre. (*Rev. Bras. Filos.*, 39:166, abril/maio/junho 1992, p. 112–117)

Caracterización de las bases teóricas y temperamentales del enfoque de Gilberto Freyre. Reconoce como fuentes de este autor, bien que reelaboradas personalmente, dos formas de culturalismo: el etnológico angloamericano y el filosófico alemán de Rickert.

5043 Chacon, Vamireh. A descorberta de Lukács no Brasil. (*Rev. Bras. Filos.*, 409:186, out./nov./dez. 1992, p. 416–422.)

De interés para conocer la difusión y el conocimiento de Lukács en Brasil, pero también para la biografía intelectual de Vamireh Chacon, destacado autor brasileño.

5044 Chacon, Vamireh. A luz do norte: o Nordeste na história das idéias do Brasil. Recife, Brasil: Fundação Joaquim Nabuco, Editora Massangana, 1989. 165 p., 8 p. of plates: bibl., ill. (Série Monografias; 31)

El tema principal de este ensayo es la figura de Gilberto Freyre y su significación. Este habría sido, de hecho, el animador de una Segunda Escuela de Recife, después de la primera, liderada por Tobias Barreto y Silvio Romero.

5045 Coutinho, Aluízio Bezerra. A filosofia das ciências naturais na Escola do Recife. Recife, Brasil: Editora Universitária, UFPE, 1988. 84 p.: bibl.

Mira con simpatía la Escuela de Recife, tomada en un sentido amplio, y proporciona datos de interés sobre las inclinaciones naturalistas de la Escuela. No llega sin embargo a ser un tratamiento sistemático del asunto.

5046 Ianni, Octávio. A idéia de Brasil moderno. São Paulo: Editora Brasiliense, 1992. 181 p.: bibl.

Util para manejarse en la frondosa literatura brasileña sobre la realidad del país, su historia, sus características, y las opciones que resultan de esas diversas interpretaciones.

5047 Leite, Jurandyr Carvalho Ferrari. Proteção e incorporação: a questão indígena no pensamento político do positivismo ortodoxo. (*Rev. Antropol./São Paulo*, 30/31/32, 1987/88/89, p. 255–275, bibl.)

Ideas del Apostolado (Iglesia Positivista de Brasil) para la protección de los indígenas, en función del pensamiento de Comte. Debe-

ría compararse con las formas asumidas por el indigenismo hispanoamericano.

5048 Macedo, Ubiratan. A idéia de liberdade em Tobias Barreto. (*Rev. Bras. Filos.*, 38:154, abril/junho 1989, p. 127–144, bibl.)

Expone y comenta dos grandes temas en Tobias Barreto: la fundamentación del Derecho y la idea de libertad. Artículo claro y útil en un asunto que tiene amplia bibliografía.

5049 Machado, Germano. Cosmovisão e cosmovidência de Rui Barbosa: introdução ao pensamento e ação de Rui Barbosa. Salvador, Brazil: Editoração CEPA, 1992? 162 p.:

Con gran simpatía hacia Rui Barbosa (1851–1923), el pensamiento y la acción de esta figura se ponen en relación con la realidad brasileña de su época. Entre otros, se destacan dos temas: los escritos de reforma educativa y las ideas políticas y sociales.

5050 Moraes Filho, Evaristo de. Medo à utopia: o pensamento social de Tobias Barreto e Sílvio Romero. Rio de Janeiro: Editora Nova Fronteira em convênio com o Instituto Nacional do Livro, Fundação Nacional Prómemória, 1985. 284 p.: bibl.

Contiene sendos capítulos sobre Tobias Barreto y Sílvio Romero, precedidos de uno sobre la Escuela de Recife en general. La introducción se ocupa del tema de la utopía. No analiza solamente textos filosóficos en los autores estudiados, sino que además los sitúa en su biografía y en la vida política e intelectual de la época.

5051 Oliveira, Lúcia Lippi. A inteligência brasileira à luz da sociologia profética de Guerreiro Ramos. (*Dados/Rio de Janeiro*, 31:3, 1988, p. 357–371)

Expone los juicios del sociólogo Guerreiro Ramos (n. 1915) sobre la intelectualidad brasileña del siglo XX, en sus obras *A crise do poder no Brasil* (1961) y *A nova ciência das organizações* (1981).

5052 Paim, Antônio. A filosofia brasileira. Lisboa: Instituto de Cultura e Lingua Portuguesa, Ministério da Educação, 1991. 212 p.: bibl. (Biblioteca breve, 0871–5173; 123)

En la línea de su fundamental libro sobre la filosofía en Brasil (ver *HLAS 48:7634* para la 3a. edición), y acentuando los nexos con la filosofía en Portugal, se exponen, entre otros temas: el pensamiento de Silvestre Pinheiro Ferreira; el eclecticismo; el tradicionalismo; el kantismo y el krausismo; el positivismo; la Escuela de Recife; y el pensamiento contemporáneo.

5053 Paim, Antônio. O krausismo brasileiro. (*Rev. Bras. Filos.*, 38:156, out./dez. 1989, p. 292–307)

Los autores que trata son: Vicente Ferrer Neto Paiva (portugués), cuyos *Elementos de direito natural* (1844) fueron adoptados como texto en São Paulo; Galvão Bueno (1834–83), autor de *Noções de filosofia* (1877); João Teodoro Xavier de Matos (1828–78), *Teoria trascendental do direito* (1876); y Teixeira de Freitas (1816–83), *Introdução à consolidação das leis civis*. El movimiento krausista se pone en relación con el pensamiento político, especialmente del liberalismo. De particular interés para comparar con el krausismo hispanoamericano.

Paulo Freire Institute/Instituto Paulo Freire. See item **48.**

5054 Paupério, A. Machado. A obra polimórfica de Djacir Menezes e sua síntese filosófica. (*Rev. Ciênc. Polít.*/Rio de Janeiro, 32:3, maio/julho 1989, p. 94–102)

Destacando el valor y la profundidad de la obra filosófica de Djacir Menezes y su detallado conocimiento de Hegel, expone lo fundamental de su filosofía del derecho.

5055 Peritore, N. Patrick. Liberation theology in the Brazilian Catholic Church: a Q-methodology study of the diocese of Rio de Janeiro in 1985. (*Luso-Braz. Rev.*, 26:1, Summer 1989, p. 59–92)

De los resultados de una encuesta se destacan tres cuerpos de opinión: los más agresivos, los más conservadores y la posición centrista del Papa. Aunque expresa la situación tal como era en 1985, contribuye al conocimiento de: 1) la situación de la Iglesia en Brasil; 2) la función de las comunidades eclesiales de base y sus dimensiones; 3) la disputa teológico-ideológica que está en la base de las controversias.

5056 Queiroz, Maria Isaura Pereira de. Desenvolvimento das ciências sociais na América Latina e contribuição européia: o caso brasileiro. (*Ciênc. Cult.*, 41:4, abril 1989, p. 378–388)

Util por dos razones: 1) por los datos que aporta sobre la investigación en ciencias sociales en Brasil desde el siglo XIX hasta 1930; y 2) por ponerlos en relación con la capacidad propia del país para seleccionar temas y elaborarlos. Concluye que esta capacidad es mayor de lo que estima una visión pesimista de la dependencia con respecto a los países más adelantados. Es interesante también como muestra del modo en que los estudios se han vinculado a interpretaciones sobre la identidad brasileña.

5057 *Revista Brasileira de Filosofia.* Vol. 38, No. 154, abril/maio/junho 1989. São Paulo: Instituto Brasiliero de Filosofia.

Este número está dedicado al filósofo brasileño Tobias Barreto (1839–89), con motivo del centenario de su muerte. Los artículos se destacan por la autoridad de la mayoría de los autores en el tema. Contiene: Mario G. Losano, "O Germanismo de Tobias Barreto" (escrito en italiano); Antonio Paim, "A Trayetória Filosófica de Tobias Barreto;" Ubiratan Macedo, "A Idéia de Liberdade em Tobias Barreto"; Paulo Mercadante, "Tobias Barreto Enquanto Evolucionista;" Ricardo Vélez Rodríguez, "A Significação das Comemorações do Centenario de Tobias Barreto;" Nelson Saldanha, "Nota sobre a Noção de 'Monismo' em Tobias Barreto e na Escola de Recife;" Angelo Monteiro, "Tobias Barreto, Pensador Político."

5058 Severino, Antônio Joaquim. A filosofia no Brasil: catálogo sistemático do profissionais, cursos, entidades e publicações da área da filosofia no Brasil. Rio de Janeiro: Associação Nacional de Pós-Graduação em Filosofia, 1990. 1 v. (various pagings)

Registra 844 profesionales dedicados a la filosofía en el país, más una lista anotada de revistas filosóficas y de instituciones de investigación.

5059 Silva, Raul de Andrada e. Presença de Feijó na história do pensamento Brasileiro. (*Rev. Inst. Hist. Geogr. São Paulo*, 84, 1989, p. 115–119)

Breves referencias a Diogo Antonio Feijó (1784–1843), figura religiosa y política de São Paulo. Con cierta influencia del kantismo, escribió *Cadernos de Filosofia*, publicados en edición moderna por Miguel Reale en 1967.

5060 Sturm, Fred Gillette. Religion. (*in* Modern Brazil. Edited by Michael L. Conniff and Frank D. McCann. Lincoln: Univ. of Nebraska Press, 1989, p. 246–264)

Informativo, claro y sintético. Da una idea general de: 1) las manifestaciones del catolicismo (Iglesia y catolicismo popular); 2) las religiones afro-brasileñas; 3) las formas del protestantismo; 4) el espiritismo.

5061 Vélez Rodríguez, Ricardo. Gilberto Freyre, Oliveira Viana e a sociologia do patrimonialismo. (*Rev. Bras. Filos.*, 38:156, out./dez., p. 334–354)

Presenta los fundamentos desde los cuales Freyre y Oliveira Viana construyeron sus respectivas obras sociológicas. Trata de captar la contribución que esas obras hicieron a la interpretación de la realidad brasileña. Destaca como uno de los elementos fundantes la estructura patrimonialista del Brasil rural a lo largo de su historia. Artículo muy atendible.

5062 Zancanaro, Lourenço. Trajetória filosófica de Miguel Reale. (*Reflexão/São Paulo*, 14:42, sept./dez. 1988, p. 120–130)

Exposición de algunos aspectos básicos del pensamiento de Reale, uno de los principales filósofos brasileños contemporáneos.

URUGUAY

5063 Altesor, Homero. Cronología filosófica del Uruguay. Montevideo?: Indice, 1993? 123 p.: bibl.

Comienza siendo una cronología de hechos filosóficos desde la época de la colonia y concluye con una serie de estampas de intelectuales y pensadores del Ateneo de Montevideo, entre ellos: Alejandro Magariños Cervantes; Julio Herrera y Obes; José Batlle y Ordóñez; y Prudencio Vázquez y Vega.

5064 Aportes para una historia de las ideas en el Uruguay. Montevideo: Depto. de Cultura, Causa-Uruguay, 1990. 135 p.: bibl.

Destacamos los siguientes trabajos: Carlos Alberto Roca, "Influencias Ideológicas Predominantes en la Emancipación Americana: la Banda Oriental" (enfocado principalmente desde la historia del derecho, sostiene que fue Francisco Suárez, y no las ideas enciclopedistas, el factor que proporcionó las bases para la Independencia hispanoamericana); Oscar Varela Siandra, "Algunos Aspectos del Pensamiento Filosófico de Monseñor Mariano Soler" (los textos filosóficos y teológicos de Soler fueron escritos entre 1878–1910: se los comenta en función de ideas y corrientes actuales); Oscar Amorín Supparo,

"El Rol del Estado en la Concepción Democrática de José Batlle y Ordóñez" (sobre la formación filosófica de Batlle—"espiritualista y racionalista"—y su aplicación a la acción política); Héctor Patiño Gardone, "La Escuela del Ateneo" (sobre la Escuela del Ateneo, en la década del 80 del siglo pasado, y en el contexto del pensamiento filosófico de la época); Helena Costábile de Amorín, "Razón y Creencia en la Filosofía de Vaz Ferreira" (comparación del tema de razón y creencia en Vaz Ferreira y Rodó); Homero Altesor, "La Fenomenología en el Uruguay" (posiblemente las noticias más completas sobre la fenomenología en el Uruguay, exponiendo al comienzo la difusión que se debió a Ortega y Gasset y a Francisco Romero).

5065 Fernández Prando, Federico. Acercamiento a las raíces doctrinarias y filosóficas del batllismo: *Memorias y escritos, inéditos, de un íntimo colaborador de José Batlle y Ordóñez.* Montevideo: Ediciones de la Banda Oriental, 1991. 224 p.: bibl.

Después de exponer brevemente el "organicismo" de Ahrens y de Spencer y sus consecuencias para los límites de la intervención estatal, estudia el pensamiento y los escritos de Julio María Sosa (m. 1931), que perteneció al círculo de Batlle y Ordóñez. En la segunda parte se publican, del mismo Sosa, *Memorias y escritos, inéditos, de un íntimo colaborador de José Batlle y Ordóñez.*

5066 García Morales, Alfonso. Literatura y pensamiento hispánico de fin de siglo: Clarín y Rodó. Sevilla, Spain: Secretariado de Publicaciones de la Univ. de Sevilla, 1992. 102 p.: bibl. (Serie Filosofía y letras; 136)

Obra importante en la investigación sobre Rodó. Aunque el tema principal es la relación de Rodó con Leopoldo Alas (Clarín)—más cercana de lo que habitualmente se reconoce desde el campo de la historia de las ideas -, también se iluminan aspectos del autor uruguayo tales como su situación ante el modernismo hispanoamericano, las fuentes francesas del idealismo finisecular, el sentido de *Ariel* y su recepción en España.

5067 Glick, Thomas F. Darwin y el darwinismo: en el Uruguay y en América Latina. Montevideo: Univ. de la República, Facultad de Humanidades y Ciencias, Depto. de Publicaciones, 1989. 136 p.: bibl.

El autor de esta obra es una reconocida autoridad en el tema de la recepción del darwinismo en diferentes países. El libro contiene más de lo que señala su título, a saber: 1) la historiografía darwiniana después de 1970, influida por la publicación de manuscritos de Darwin no utilizados anteriormente; 2) recepción del darwinismo en Francia, Italia y España; 3) positivismo y darwinismo en América Latina (importante por los problemas que discute); 4) la recepción del darwinismo en el Uruguay, con un apéndice de "Obras de Interés Darwiniano en las Bibliotecas de Montevideo." En síntesis se trata de un libro de particular importancia para la historia del darwinismo y el positivismo en América Latina.

5068 Mato, Carlos. Pensamiento uruguayo. v. 1, La época de Carlos Vaz Ferreira. Montevideo: Roca Viva Editorial, 1991–1992. v. 1–2

Al hilo de un repaso de la edición de las *Obras completas* de Vaz Ferreira, comenta el pensamiento del filósofo uruguayo.

5069 Mato, Carlos. Pensamiento uruguayo. v. 2. Montevideo: Roca Viva Editorial, 1992? 2 v.

Es continuación de item **5068.** Tiene como prólogo una reseña de Celina Lértora Mendoza. Concluye la parte correspondiente a Vaz Ferreira (vol. 10 de las *Obras completas* en adelante) y trata a Arturo Ardao y al teólogo Juan Luis Segundo.

5070 Monreal, Susana. Influencia de los krausistas "belgas" en la redefinición de las funciones del Estado en el Uruguay 1875–1915. (*Estud. Cienc. Let.*, 22, marzo 1992, p. 12–19, port.)

Expone, en el contexto de la época, el efecto de las ideas krausistas (específicamente, Ahrens y Tiberghien) en el desarrollo del "Estado tutor" en Uruguay, por obra de Batlle y Ordóñez. Es resumen de una tesis doctoral del mismo título que, a juzgar por el artículo, convendría publicar completa.

5071 Navia, Ricardo J. and Mauricio Langón. Introducción a la historia de las ideas. Montevideo: Signos, 1989. 112 p.

Responde a la inclusión de una unidad temática sobre *Historia de las Ideas* en los programas de filosofía de la enseñanza secundaria en Uruguay. Se compone de dos trabajos: 1) introducción conceptual a la historia de las ideas como disciplina; y 2) un programa, con breves lecturas y preguntas.

5072 Romero Baró, José María. Ciencia y filosofía en el pensador Uruguayo Carlos Vaz Ferreira. (*Hoy Hist.*, 10:58, julio/agosto 1993, p. 10–14)

Sobre lógica, ciencia, filosofía y metafísica en Vaz Ferreira.

5073 Trigo, Abril. Caudillo, Estado, nación: literatura, historia e ideología en el Uruguay. Gaithersburg, Md.: Ediciones Hispamérica, 1990. 276 p.: bibl.

Ensayo interpretativo, no carente de intención literaria, de la historia de Uruguay desde la colonia hasta los años más recientes. Sus fuentes no son solamente historiográficas, sino también provenientes de la literatura, la sociología y la política. Contiene amplia bibliografía.

ARGENTINA

5074 Alconada Sempé, Raúl *et al.* Evolución y crisis de la ideología de izquierda: Seminario-taller y Segundas Jornadas sobre la cuestión ideológica en la U.C.R. organizadas por la Secretaría de Acción Doctrinaria de la Juventud Radical, Capital Federal. Recopilación de María José Lubertino Beltrán. Apéndice de Raúl R. Alfonsín. Buenos Aires: Centro Editor de América Latina, 1991. 3 v. (289 p.). (Biblioteca Política argentina; 317–319)

El primer volumen y la casi totalidad del segundo se dedican a la situación de "la izquierda" en el mundo desarrollado y en América Latina. El tercero se refiere a la Unión Cívica Radical y sus posiciones recientes, en especial frente a lo que los autores denominan "neoconservadurismo." Entre los colaboradores se cuentan: José Aricó, Luis Aznar, Eduardo Passalacqua y Juan Carlos Portantiero.

5075 Anastasía, Luis Víctor. El espíritu nuevo y Esteban Echeverría. Montevideo: Fundación Prudencio Vázquez y Vega, 1989. 106 p. (Pensamiento latinoamericano)

Extenso comentario a la obra de Echeverría (especialmente *El dogma socialista*) y a su acción político-intelectual.

5076 La Argentina del 80 al 80: balance social y cultural de un siglo. Recopilación de Arturo Andrés Roig. México: Univ. Nacional Autónoma de México, Coordinación de Humanidades, Centro Coordinador y

Difusor de Estudios Latinoamericanos, 1993. 312 p.: bibl. (Serie Nuestra América; 38)

Abarca el período 1880–1980 y cubre aspectos sociales, educativos y políticos, entre otros. De más directo interés para esta sección son: Hugo Biagini, "Algunas Posiciones Sobre la Identidad Nacional a lo Largo del Siglo;" Cristián Buchrucker, "El Proteico Nacionalismo Argentino;" y Arturo A. Roig, "Negatividad y Positividad de la 'Barbarie' en la Tradición Intelectual Argentina."

5077 Arturo Andrés Roig, filósofo e historiador de las ideas. Recopilación de Horacio Cerutti Guldberg y Manuel Rodríguez Lapuente. Guadalajara, Mexico: Univ. de Guadalajara, 1989. 347 p.: bibl.

Este justificado homenaje al filósofo e historiador de las ideas Arturo A. Roig contiene trabajos sobre su obra de los siguientes autores: Jorge J.E. Gracia, Mario Magallón Anaya, Gregor Sauerwald y Ofelia Schutte. Además, hay artículos sobre diversos temas de la historia de las ideas en América Latina, cuyos autores, entre otros, son: Fernando Ainsa, Arturo Ardao, Adriana Arpini, Hugo Biagini, Horacio Cerutti Guldberg, Alejandra Ciriza, Estela Fernández, Raúl Fornet-Betancourt, Liliana Giorgis, José L. Gómez Martínez, Clara Alicia J. de Bertranou, Günther Maihold, Oscar Martí, Jaime Rubio Angulo, Joaquín Sánchez Mac Gregor y Leopoldo Zea.

5078 Biagini, Hugo. Ruptura y estancamiento en la teoría historiográfica argentina: la década de 1980. (*Todo es Hist.*, 283, enero 1988, p. 68–71, photos)

Repasa y valoriza personalmente manifestaciones historiográficas argentinas de la década de 1980. Se refiere tanto a la teoría de la historia como al análisis de la historiografía, a trabajos históricos propiamente dichos y a meditaciones generales sobre la Argentina.

5079 Bunge, Carlos O. *et al.* El nacimiento de la psicología en la Argentina: pensamiento psicológico y positivismo. Estudio preliminar y selección de textos por Hugo Vezzetti. Buenos Aires: Puntosur, 1988. 221 p.: bibl.

Constituye una importante contribución al conocimiento de la historia de la psicología en la Argentina. Recoge textos de autores relevantes de la época positivista, en su mayoría procedentes de los primeros años del siglo XX, hasta 1911. Las expresiones reunidas se refieren a la concepción de la psicología, a la enseñanza de la disciplina y a su tratamiento en congresos. También hay antecedentes historiográficos sobre el tema (de Horacio Piñero y de José Ingenieros). La introducción de Vezzetti es de valor en sí misma para la historia a la cual el libro contribuye.

5080 Castellán, Angel. Cuando una afirmación se convierte en interrogante: ¿Vico en Alberdi?; un ensayo de metodología del pensamiento. (*Cuyo/Mendoza*, 6, 1989, p. 9–53)

No sin algún tono polémico, persigue la difusión de Vico en Francia—especialmente por medio de Michelet—para entrar a la cuestión del posible conocimiento de Vico por parte de Alberdi. Concluye que dicho conocimiento fue superficial.

5081 Chiaramonte, José Carlos. Formas de identidad en el Río de la Plata luego de 1810. (*Bol. Inst. Hist. Ravignani*, 1, primer semestre 1989, p. 71–92)

Excelente artículo que examina las distintas formas de identidad—americana, provincial y "nacional"—que se manifiestan, en el caso de Argentina, entre el comienzo de la Independencia y mediados del siglo XIX. Las fuentes son principal, pero no únicamente, textos constitucionales de las provincias y otros escritos jurídico-políticos. Muestra que el sentimiento de nación en el territorio argentino fue el resultado de un lento proceso, y de ninguna manera algo preexistente a la decisión de la Independencia. En un tema que se presta a la vaguedad retórica es un trabajo de contenido bien concreto.

5082 Ciriza, Alejandra. Martínez Estrada: las categorías de 'civilización' y 'barbarie' en el discurso de un intelectual del siglo XX. (*Rev. Hist. Ideas*, 10, 1990, p. 139–152)

Establece ciertas similitudes entre las interpretaciones de Martínez Estrada y de Sarmiento. Sostiene que las categorías interpretativas de Martínez Estrada tienen su raíz en el siglo XIX.

5083 *Cuyo.* No. 1, 1984. Mendoza, Argentina: Univ. Nacional de Cuyo, Facultad de Filosofía y Letras, Instituto de Filosofía Argentina y Americana.

Entre otros materiales, contiene: Diego

F. Pró, "El Ser de lo Americano;" Arturo García Astrada, "La Presencia del Tiempo en el Pensamiento de Nimio de Anquín;" Clara Alicia Jalif de Bertranou, "Ortega y 'El Hombre a la Defensiva';" Armando Rodríguez, "El Pensamiento Filosófico del Dr. Ismael Quiles." Hay también textos de Juan R. Sepich y Carlos Jesinghaus.

5084   Cuyo. Nos. 2/3, 1985/86. Mendoza: Univ. Nacional de Cuyo, Facultad de Filosofía y Letras, Instituto de Filosofía Argentina y Americana.

Destacamos los siguientes trabajos: Vol. 2: Arturo A. Roig, "Acotaciones para una Simbólica Latinoamericana" (Véase *HLAS 50:4575*); Rosa Licata, "La Etica Axiológica de Miguel Angel Virasoro;" Angélica Gabrielidis de Luna, "El Pensamiento Estético de Mariano Antonio Barrenechea" (1884–1949); Daniel von Matuschka, "Exposición y Crítica del Concepto de 'Estar' en Rodolfo S. Kusch." Vol. 3: Diego F. Pró, "La Filosofía que Enseñaba y Hacia Coriolano Alberini;" Juan R. Sepich, "Las Corrientes Filosófico-Espirituales en Latinoamérica, Especialmente en la Argentina;" Clara de Bertranou, "Max Scheler y los Estudios de Etica en la Argentina;" Luis Adolfo Dozo, "Nuevos Aspectos del Positivismo en la Argentina;" María Musso de Cavallaro y Norma Isabel Sánchez, "Coriolano Alberini y Waldo Frank."

5085   Cuyo. No. 4, 1987. Mendoza: Univ. Nacional de Cuyo, Facultad de Filosofía y letras, Instituto de Filosofía Argentina y Americana.

Principales artículos: Angel Castellón, "Una Crítica a los Ideales Pedagógicos del 80: el Pensamiento de Juan Agustín García;" Eduardo Peñafort, "El Pensamiento Filosófico del Doctor Miguel Angel Virasoro;" Adriana Arpini de Márquez, "La Cuestión de la Libertad en Tres Pensadores Americanos: Alejandro Korn, Alejandro Deustua, José Vasconcelos;" Clara A. Jalif de Bertranou, "Testimonios de Pensamiento Argentino: Diego Francisco Pró." El volumen contiene también textos de Coriolano Alberini y una ficha biobibliográfica de Arturo Andrés Roig.

5086   Cuyo. No. 5, 1988. Mendoza, Argentina: Univ. Nacional de Cuyo, Facultad de Filosofía y Letras, Instituto de Filosofía Argentina y Americana.

Contiene los siguientes artículos y estudios monográficos: Diego F. Pró, "Antropovisión Filosófica del Dr. Juan Dalma;" Armando Rodríguez, "El Pensamiento y la Filosofía del Dr. Juan Ramón Sepich y la Filosofía de Martín Heidegger;" Néstor Hugo Sánchez, "El Estudio de las Influencias Filosóficas en el Pensamiento Argentino: Alejandro Korn;" María del Carmen Yerga de Isaguirre, "Los Fundamentos Filosóficos de la Libertad Jurídica en la Teoría Egológica del Derecho" [Carlos Cossio]. El volumen incluye también una ficha biobibliográfica del filósofo argentino Carlos Astrada, elaborada por Matilde García Losada.

5087   Dotti, Jorge Eugenio. La letra gótica: recepción de Kant en Argentina, desde el romanticismo hasta el treinta. Buenos Aires: Facultad de Filosofía y Letras, UBA, 1992. 247 p.: bibl., index.

Unica obra especialmente dedicada a la recepción de Kant en la Argentina. Se extiende desde Alberdi hasta la fundación de la Sociedad Kantiana (1929), pasando por el "espiritualismo," el krausismo, el positivismo, la "reacción antipositivista" y aun algunas manifestaciones literarias. Con acertado criterio interesa al autor no sólo el aspecto técnico del conocimiento de Kant, sino cualquier resonancia que pudiera provenir de la recepción del filósofo alemán para la vida intelectual argentina. Libro de lectura necesaria dentro de la literatura sobre el pensamiento filosófico argentino.

5088   Dotti, Jorge Eugenio. Las vetas del texto: una lectura filosófica de Alberdi, los positivistas, Juan B. Justo. Buenos Aires: Puntosur Editores, 1990. 136 p.: bibl. (La Ideología argentina)

Contiene tres trabajos: "La Emancipación Sudamericana en el Pensamiento de Juan Bautista Alberdi;" "La Hermanas-Enemigas: Ciencia y Etica en el Positivismo del Centenario" [sobre Carlos Octavio Bunge y José Ingenieros]; "Justo [Juan B. Justo] Lector de *El Capital*." En la introducción expone los supuestos metodológicos del trabajo. Por ejemplo, explica por qué realiza una lectura "interna" de los textos. Asimismo descree de que las ideas deban comprenderse "como la mera transcripción ideológica del efecto social provocado por algún . . . condicionamiento primario;" y afirma que las debilidades de información de los pensadores latinoamericanos no anulan su "originalidad."

5089 Ferrero, Roberto A. Saúl Taborda: de la reforma universitaria a la Revolución Nacional. Córdoba, Argentina: Alción Editora, 1988. 178 p.: bibl.

No es obra monográfica sino de apreciación desde una posición política: el nacionalismo popular o populista. Taborda es seguido en su vinculación con la Reforma Universitaria de 1918; su posición en la renovación posterior al positivismo; su teoría pedagógica; y su nacionalismo federalista y "facúndico," que el autor estima antecedente de la "izquierda nacional" argentina.

5090 Franzé, Javier. El concepto de política en Juan B. Justo. v. 1–2. Buenos Aires: Centro Editor de América Latina, 1993. 2 v. (214 p.): bibl. (Biblioteca Política argentina; 395–396)

Exposición del pensamiento de Juan B. Justo (1865–1928), fundador del Partido Socialista argentino. La tesis central es que en Justo se dan, orgánicamente fundidas, las influencias del positivismo, del liberalismo y del marxismo. Consiguientemente, los errores de interpretación sobre su pensamiento se han debido a actitudes reduccionistas, que privilegian sólo una de estas facetas, desconociendo su carácter integral.

5091 Galeano A., Adolfo. La crítica del pensamiento totalizador en Enrique Dussel: para una liberación de la ideología totalizante en América Latina. (*Franciscanum/ Bogotá*, 30:89, mayo/agosto 1988, p. 123–153, bibl.)

Extensa exposición, y también crítica, de la obra de Dussel: *Para una ética de la liberación latinoamericana*. Al autor le interesa el asunto desde el punto de vista teológico. El punto de partida es que la identidad latinoamericana no ha sido descubierta porque América Latina es "una realidad en-cubierta por Europa, conquistada, colonizada y dominada por Europa."

5092 García Losada, Matilde Isabel. Inquietud metafísica en los representantes de la filosofía existencial argentina. (*Anu. Veritas*, 8, 1989, p. 5–12)

Los autores atendidos son: Carlos Astrada, Miguel Angel Virasoro, Vicente Fatone, Carlos Alberto Erro y Homero Guglielmini. La etapa considerada se extiende entre 1925 y fines de los 1940s.

5093 Ghirardi, Olsen A. La filosofía en Alberdi. Córdoba, Argentina: Academia Nacional de Derecho y Ciencias Sociales de Córdoba, 1993. 168 p.: bibl. (Ediciones de la Academia Nacional de Derecho y Ciencias Sociales de Córdoba; 9)

Continuación de una obra anterior: *El primer Alberdi*. La presente se dedica al análisis del *Fragmento preliminar al estudio del Derecho*. Examina detenidamente las fuentes francesas de Alberdi, y para este aspecto la obra es imprescindible. El resultado, de atenerse a las conclusiones del autor, es una gran dependencia de dicho autor con respecto a esas fuentes, y consiguientemente una escasa originalidad filosófica. El primer capítulo se refiere a la idea de filosofía. El segundo, a la filosofía de la historia en Alberdi. El tercero, a la filosofía en su proyecto constitucional.

5094 Goldman, Noemí *et al*. Imagen y recepción de la Revolución Francesa en la Argentina: jornadas nacionales. Palabras preliminares de Gregorio Weinberg. Comité Argentino para el Bicentenario de la Revolución Francesa. Buenos Aires: Grupo Editor Latinoamericano, 1990. 399 p.: bibl., ill. (Col. Estudios políticos y sociales)

De los artículos de este volumen que se refieren específicamente a las ideas, la mayoría se dedican al tema de la independencia argentina y a personajes que actuaron en la primera mitad del siglo XIX. Se trata de una buena contribución historiográfica.

5095 Gómez Tovar, Luis; Ramón Gutiérrez; Silvia A. Vázquez; and Pierre Quiroule. Utopías libertarias americanas. La ciudad anarquista americana. Madrid: Ediciones Tueros; Fundación Salvador Seguí, 1991. 353 p.: bibl., ill., index. (Col. Investigación y crítica; 5)

Edición de *La ciudad anarquista americana*, de Pierre Quiroule, que apareció originalmente en Buenos Aires en 1914. La edición se enriquece con varios trabajos críticos: 1) Luis Gómez Tovar, "Geografía de lo Imaginario," visión general sobre utopías y pensamiento utópico, con un apéndice sobre "Relación de Colonias y Proyectos Comunitarios Asentados en América;" Silvia A. Vázquez, "Pierre Quiroule: Historia de una Existencia Singular entre la Configuración Utópica y la Realidad," breve pero claro y muy útil para situar al autor; 3) Ramón Gutiérrez, "La Utopía

Urbana y el Imaginario de Pierre Quiroule," examen de la misma utopía desde el punto de vista urbanístico. La obra de Quiroule (pseudónimo de Joaquín Alejo Falconnet) había sido publicada anteriormente por Félix Weinberg en *Dos utopías argentinas de principios de siglo* (1976).

5096 González Gazqués, Gustavo. "Cultura" y "sujeto cultural" en el pensamiento de Rodolfo Jusch. (*Cuyo/Mendoza*, 6, 1989, p. 55–95)

Examina la problemática del sujeto cultural en Rodolfo Kusch, por considerarla "una de las vías más fecundas" para comprender la obra del autor de *América profunda* (1992).

5097 González Gazqués, Gustavo et al.
Kusch y el pensar desde América. Recopilación y prólogo de Eduardo A. Azcuy. Buenos Aires: F. García Cambeiro, 1989. 194 p.: bibl. (Col. Estudios latinoamericanos; 36)

Volumen dedicado a destacar el valor del filósofo argentino Rodolfo Kusch (1922–79), de orientación americanista. Los autores de los trabajos son: Gustavo González Gazqués, Abraham Haber, Enrique Mareque, Juan Carlos Scannone, Graciela Maturo, Mariano Juan Garreta, Nerva Bordas de Rojas Paz y Guillermo Steffen. Se incluyen dos textos del propio Kusch, sin indicación de procedencia: "El Hombre Argentino y Americano" y "El Pensamiento Popular desde el Punto de Vista Filosófico."

5098 Hernández Muñoz, María. Algunas consideraciones acerca del historicismo de Arturo Andrés Roig en la filosofía de la liberación. (*Islas/Santa Clara*, 90, mayo/agosto 1988, p. 105–109, bibl.)

Entre los rasgos que encuentra elogiables en la obra de Roig se cuentan: proponer la categoría de conflictividad social; el reconocimiento de que la filosofía tiene una función social; la advertencia de que el concepto de "pueblo" puede ocultar las contradicciones de clase; y el "situarse del lado de los oprimidos y plantearse una filosofía humanista politizada."

5099 Herrendorf, Daniel E. Carlos Cossio, iusfilósofo de la época contemporánea. (*Rev. Bras. Filos.*, 38:153, jan./fev./março 1989, p. 50–57)

Apreciación de la personalidad y la filosofía del derecho de Carlos Cossio, con motivo de su fallecimiento.

5100 Higuero, Francisco Javier. Escepticismo epistemológico en la ensayística de Borges. (*MACLAS: Lat. Am. Essays*, 2, 1990, p. 27–34)

Intenta presentar "la manera sutil e ingeniosa como Borges refuta el tiempo en general, y su progresión o regresión infinita en particular." Admite que junto con el tratamiento racional del asunto hay en Borges un fondo lúdico que lo mantiene en el plano propiamente literario.

5101 Indice de la *Revista Philosophia*. Mendoza, Argentina: Univ. Nacional de Cuyo, Facultad de Filosofía y Letras, Instituto de Filosofía, 1988. 145 p.

Contiene casi 800 entradas, cubriendo el período 1944–87. Incluye índices onomástico y de temas. Cuatro tendencias son visibles: pensamiento de fuente escolástica; fenomenología y existencialismo; marxismo y cristianismo de izquierda; y filosofía analítica y científica.

5102 Jalif de Bertranou, Clara Alicia. El humanismo platónico en el pensamiento argentino. (*Cuyo/Mendoza*, 7:1, 1990, p. 65–122)

Para ejemplificar la presencia del humanismo platónico (y neoplatónico) en el pensamiento argentino escoge cuatro autores: Luis de Tejeda (siglo XVII); José Peramás (siglo XVIII), autor de *La República de Platón y los guaraníes*; Amadeo Jacques (siglo XIX), seguido en su obra educativa; y Alberto Rougès, autor de *Las jerarquías del ser y la eternidad*, a quien se concede el tratamiento más extenso en páginas bien logradas.

5103 Jalif de Bertranou, Clara Alicia. Modernidad y posmodernidad: la visión de Roberto Follari. (*Cuyo/Mendoza*, 7:2, 1990, p. 261–279)

Sobre el libro de Roberto Follari, *Modernidad y postmodernidad: una óptica desde América Latina* (1990).

5104 Leis, Héctor Ricardo. Intelectuales y política, 1966–1973: estudio del debate intelectual. Buenos Aires: Centro Editor de América Latina, 1991. 92 p.: bibl. (Biblioteca Política argentina; 330)

El capítulo "Los Intelectuales Políticos

Ante el Autoritarismo" se refiere a la Argentina en el período indicado en el título. Hay también consideraciones sobre los intelectuales y la política en general y en América Latina. Aunque no carece de firmes posiciones, puede ayudar a clarificar el panorama abigarrado de las posiciones políticas adoptadas por los intelectuales argentinos en la época elegida para el análisis.

5105 Lértora Mendoza, Celina Ana. Filosofía rioplatense durante el período hispánico. (*Rev. Hist. Ideas,* 10, 1990, p. 67–84)
Como síntesis, es la más autorizada y confiable del período estudiado.

5106 Liebscher, Arthur F. Toward a pious republic: Argentine social Catholicism in Córdoba, 1895–1930. (*J. Church State,* 30: 3, Autumn 1988, p. 549–567)
Expone la acción de grupos católicos, interesados en el mantenimiento de los valores religiosos pero también en la asistencia a los sectores obreros más necesitados. Esta acción no pudo superar el cambio que produjo el peronismo. La información va más allá del ámbito de la Provincia de Córdoba y la base documental del trabajo es considerable.

5107 Linossi, Jorge Alberto. Ficha biobibliográfica del Dr. Nimio de Anquín. (*Cuyo/Mendoza,* 7:2, 1990, p. 321–355)
Continúa un trabajo aparecido también en este *Anuario* en 1979. Contiene, de acuerdo con su título, rasgos biográficos y una bibliografía del autor seleccionado. El mismo número de esta publicación reproduce textos filosóficos de Nimio de Anquín, 1896–1979.

5108 Martí, Oscar R. Sarmiento y el positivismo. (*Cuad. Am.,* 3:13, enero/feb. 1989, p. 142–154)
Encuentra algunas semejanzas entre ciertos aspectos del pensamiento de Sarmiento y las ideas de Comte y Spencer. Concluye que la originalidad y el valor de Sarmiento son más importantes que los antecedentes o influencias que se puedan rastrear en su obra.

5109 Martínez Estrada, Ezequiel. Radiografía de la pampa. Ed. crítica, 1. ed. Coordinación de Leo Pollmann. Nanterre, France: ALLCA XX, Univ. Paris X, Centre de recherches latino-américaines, 1991. 586 p.: bibl., ill. (Col. Archivos; 19)
Edición crítica de la famosa obra de

Martínez Estrada. Además del texto hay un conjunto de trabajos en torno al autor y el libro, entre cuyos autores se cuentan: Dinko Cvitanovic, León Sigal, Miguel A. Guérin, David Viñas, Rodolfo A. Borello, Leo Pollmann, Peter G. Earle, Liliana Weinberg de Magis, Elena M. Rojas. Hay también índices, cronología y bibliografía.

5110 Paso, Leonardo. La idea del cambio social. Buenos Aires: Centro Editor de América Latina, 1993. 140 p.: bibl. (Biblioteca Política argentina ; 399)
Contiene cuatro ensayos: sobre Mariano Moreno, José Hernández (el autor de *Martín Fierro*), Domingo F. Sarmiento y José Carlos Mariátegui (el único autor no argentino entre los seleccionados). El punto de vista del autor es marxista, pero el criterio es amplio y comprensivo.

5111 El pensamiento peronista. Edición y selección antológica por Aníbal Iturrieta. Prólogo de Jordi Borja. Madrid: Instituto de Cooperación Iberoamericana, Ediciones de Cultura Hispánica, 1990. 224 p.: bibl. (Antología del pensamiento político, social y económico de América Latina; 11)
Obra de carácter documental, y como tal, útil. Según declara el compilador, "esta selección antológica contiene discursos, conferencias, documentos y textos oficiales y político-partidarios." También hay trabajos interpretativos de autores individuales, como Guido di Tella y John William Cooke. Los textos son en general breves y van desde 1944 hasta el final de la década de 1980. Buena bibliografía.

5112 Piossek Prebisch, Lucía. Pensamiento argentino: creencias e ideas. Tucumán, Argentina: Univ. Nacional de Tucumán, Facultad de Filosofía y Letras, Instituto de Historia y Pensamiento Argentinos, 1988. 175 p.: bibl.
Casi todo el material recogido, de útil lectura, había sido previamente publicado. Entre otros, contiene artículos sobre Sarmiento y Alberdi; asimismo, sobre la "generación del ochenta" y la historia de las ideas y sobre el pensamiento en Tucumán, dedicados a Alberto Rougès y Juan B. Terán.

5113 Prada, Gloria Isabel. La formación de la conciencia moral en el positivismo argentino. v.1. Mendoza, Argentina: Univ. Nacional de Cuyo, Facultad de Filosofía y Letras,

Instituto de Filosofía Argentina y Americana, 1988. v. 1: bibl.

Trabajo expositivo sobre la "ciencia de la ética" en Bunge, que incluye las correspondientes teorías de la moral y del Derecho. Las principales obras tomadas en cuenta son: *El Derecho: ensayo de una teoría integral* y *Estudios filosóficos.* Señala al final las limitaciones del positivismo para construir una ética no relativista.

5114 Pró, Diego F. Osvaldo N. Guariglia: ficha bibliográfica, 1982. (*Cuyo/Mendoza*, 6, 1989, p. 221–245)

En lo que se refiere a la obra de Guariglia (n. 1938), el propio autor describe el contenido de los trabajos.

5115 Pucciarelli, Eugenio. Ezequiel Martínez Estrada: poesía, filosofía y realidad nacional. Buenos Aires: Centro de Estudios Filosóficos, 1986. 45 p.: bibl. (Publicaciones del Centro de Estudios Filosóficos; 6)

Se recogen aquí dos finos trabajos de Pucciarelli: "Motivos Filosóficos en la Poesía de Martínez Estrada" (1977) y "La Imagen de la Argentina en la Obra de Martínez Estrada."

5116 Rivarola, Francisco Bruno de. Religión y fidelidad argentina, 1809. Estudio preliminar por José M. Mariluz Urquijo. Buenos Aires: Instituto de Investigaciones de Historia del Derecho, 1983. 364 p.: bibl. (Edición de fuentes de derecho indiano en conmemoración del V centenario del descubrimiento de América; 1)

Se trata de la edición de una obra cuyo manuscrito es de 1809, pero que no llegó a publicarse antes. El objetivo era instruir para afianzar la religión y la fidelidad al Rey, lo que ocurría a un año de la Revolución de 1810. Mariluz Urquijo estudia la vida del autor y describe la obra. Considera a Rivarola como "reaccionario," pero de todas maneras inmerso en el siglo XVIII. Francisco Bruno de Rivarola (1752–1825) no debe confundirse con Pantaleón Rivarola.

5117 Roldán, Darío. Joaquín V. González, a propósito del pensamiento político-liberal, 1880–1920. Buenos Aires: Centro Editor de América Latina, 1993. 126 p.: bibl. (Biblioteca Política argentina; 408)

Exposición de la obra de Joaquín V. González (1863–1923), especialmente en lo que respecta a su reflexión sobre la historia argentina; la elaboración del Código Nacional del Trabajo; y la creación y orientación de la Univ. de La Plata. Resulta una introducción al pensamiento de este autor, sobre el cual no abundan las visiones de conjunto.

5118 Shuberoff, Oscar J. *et al.* Homenaje a José Luis Romero, 1909–1978. (*Cuad. Am.*, 2:10, julio/agosto 1988, p. 104–136)

Varios autores, entre ellos Norberto Rodríguez Bustamante, Ruggiero Romano y Juan Antonio Oddone destacan los valores de José Luis Romero como universitario y maestro. Publicación parcial de las intervenciones realizadas en un homenaje al historiador argentino en el décimo aniversario de su fallecimiento.

5119 Stoetzer, Carlos. Deutschland und Argentinien: der geistige Einfluss Krauses in der jüngsten argeninischen Geschichte. (*Jahrb. Gesch.*, 25, 1988, p. 635–671)

Exposición amplia, que atiende a la filosofía de Krause, el krausismo español, la influencia de Ahrens y Tieberghien y los representantes argentinos del krausismo, entre ellos Julián Barraquero (*Espíritu y práctica de la ley constitucional argentina*, 1878) y Wenceslao Escalante (*Lecciones de filosofía del derecho*, 1884).

5120 Tau Anzoátegui, Víctor. La influencia alemana en el derecho argentino: un programa para su estudio histórico. (*Jahrb. Gesch.*, 25, 1988, p. 607–634)

Buen panorama que a la vez da elementos para una mayor profundización. Trata la influencia de Savigny, Ihering y Stammler; los autores argentinos que se sintieron cercanos a las fuentes alemanas (como por ejemplo Ernesto Quesada, 1858–1934); y los campos específicos en que se refleja la influencia: el derecho natural; el historicismo o escuela histórica (Alberdi, Vicente F. López); el derecho científico o pandectismo; el krausismo; el renacimiento iusfilosófico; y las nuevas orientaciones sociológicas e históricas (Spengler, por ejemplo). El examen llega hasta la primera mitad del siglo XX.

5121 Vetter, Ulrich. Alejandro Korn: *Philosophie der Freiheit.* (*Lateinamerika/ Hamburg*, 2, 1988, p. 107–123)

Del filósofo argentino se examinan su posición ante el positivismo; su concepto de la metafísica; su axiología; y su ética. El pensamiento de Bloch (*Das Prinzip Hoffnung*) es utilizado para la interpretación.

5122 Vicente de Alvarez, Sonia. No toda metafísica es la de los ojos kantianos. (*Cuyo/Mendoza*, 7:1, 1990, p. 205–223)

Expone el concepto de la metafísica en Macedonio Fernández (1874–1952). Ver *HLAS 50:4696* sobre Macedonio Fernández de la misma autora.

5123 Virgillito, Miguel Angel. La tolerancia en el pensamiento de la Ilustración en el periodismo de Mendoza. (*Cuyo/Mendoza*, 6, 1989, p. 127–158)

Examina los conceptos de "religión" y "tolerancia" en la prensa de la época (1824–25), en el contexto de los problemas regionales. Atiende a los aspectos propios, derivados de ese contexto, frente a las fórmulas de contenido semejante que aparecen en textos europeos.

5124 Zamudio Barrios, Arturo. Las prisiones de Héctor P. Agosti. v. 1–2. Buenos Aires: Centro Editor de América Latina, 1992. 2 v. (242 p.): bibl. (Biblioteca política argentina ; 356–357)

Ensayo que es en realidad un amplio comentario—y defensa- del intelectual argentino y militante del Partido Comunista, Héctor P. Agosti.

5125 Zea, Leopoldo. El proyecto de Sarmiento y su vigencia. (*Cuad. Am.*, 3:13, enero/feb. 1989, p. 85–96)

Reflexiones sobre el proyecto modernizador de Sarmiento, desde el punto de vista de las ideas reiteradamente sostenidas por el autor, el más reconocido filósofo de la historia de América Latina.

5126 Zimmermann, Eduardo A. Los intelectuales, las ciencias sociales y el reformismo liberal: Argentina 1890–1916. (*Desarro. Econ.*, 31:124, enero/marzo 1992, p. 545–564)

Muestra que junto a la preocupación de algunos sectores católicos, y sobre todo a la acción del Partido Socialista argentino, hubo, en los primeros años del siglo, un grupo de profesionales e intelectuales (vinculados principalmente al Derecho) que expresaron gran interés en la "cuestión social," aunque sin salirse del liberalismo vigente y limitándose a promover la intervención del Estado en las cuestiones laborales. El artículo destaca un aspecto poco trabajado por la bibliografía sobre el tema en general, y por eso y por su buena elaboración es importante.

JOURNAL ABBREVIATIONS

Allpanchis/Cusco. Allpanchis. Instituto de Pastoral Andina. Cusco, Peru.

Americas/Francisc. The Americas. Academy of American Franciscan History. Washington.

An. Univ. Chile. Anales de la Universidad de Chile. Santiago.

Anales/Göteborg. Anales. Instituto Iberoamericano, Univ. de Gotemburgo. Göteborg, Sweden.

Anu. Cent. Estud. Martianos. Anuario del Centro de Estudios Martianos. Centro de Estudios Martianos. La Habana.

Anu. Estud. Am. Anuario de Estudios Americanos. Consejo Superior de Investigaciones Científicas; Univ. de Sevilla, Escuela de Estudios Hispano-Americanos. Sevilla, Spain.

Anu. Veritas. Anuario Veritas. Univ. Regiomontana, Depto. de Publicaciones. Monterrey, Mexico.

Apunt. Filos. Apuntes Filosóficos. Escuela de Filosofía, Univ. Central de Venezuela. Caracas.

Bol. Acad. Nac. Hist./Buenos Aires. Boletín de la Academia Nacional de la Historia. Buenos Aires.

Bol. Acad. Nac. Hist./Caracas. Boletín de la Academia Nacional de la Historia. Caracas.

Bol. Am. Boletín Americanista. Univ. de Barcelona, Facultad de Geografía e Historia, Depto. de Historia de América. Barcelona.

Bol. Inst. Hist. Ravignani. Boletín del Instituto de Historia Argentina y Americana Dr. Emilio Ravignani. Facultad de Filosofía y Letras, Univ. de Buenos Aires.

Bull. Lat. Am. Res. Bulletin of Latin American Research. Society for Latin American Studies. Oxford, England.

Caribb. Q. Caribbean Quarterly. Univ. of the West Indies. Mona, Jamaica.

Ciênc. Cult. Ciência e Cultura. Sociedade Brasileira para o Progresso da Ciência. São Paulo.

Círculo/Verona. Círculo: Revista de Cultura. Círculo de Cultura Panamericana. Verona, N.J.

Cuad. Am. Cuadernos Americanos. Editorial Cultura. México.

Cuad. Sur/Buenos Aires. Cuadernos del Sur. Revista Cultural de Problemas Actuales. Buenos Aires.

Cuyo/Mendoza. Cuyo: Anuario de Historia del Pensamiento Argentino. Univ. Nacional de Cuyo, Instituto de Filosofía, Sección de Historia del Pensamiento Argentino. Mendoza, Argentina.

Dados/Rio de Janeiro. Dados. Instituto Univ. de Pesquisas. Rio de Janeiro.

Desarro. Econ. Desarrollo Económico. Instituto de Desarrollo Económico y Social. Buenos Aires.

Económica/La Plata. Económica. Univ. Nacional de La Plata, Facultad de Ciencias Económicas, Instituto de Investigaciones Económicas. La Plata, Argentina.

Ecos/Santo Domingo. Ecos. Instituto de Historia, Univ. Autónoma de Santo Domingo.

Estud. Cienc. Let. Estudios de Ciencias y Letras. Instituto de Filosofía, Ciencias y Letras. Montevideo.

Estud. Hist. Mod. Contemp. Méx. Estudios de Historia Moderna y Contemporánea de México. Univ. Nacional Autónoma de México. México.

Estud. Polít. Econ. Filos. Estudios: Políticos, Económicos, Filosóficos, Culturales del Uruguay. Partido Comunista. Montevideo.

Estud. Soc./Santiago. Estudios Sociales. Corporación de Promoción Universitaria. Santiago.

Franciscanum/Bogotá. Franciscanum. Univ. de San Buenaventura. Bogotá.

Hoy Hist. Hoy es Historia: Revista Bimestral de Historia Nacional e Iberoamericana. Editorial Raíces. Montevideo.

Ideas Valores. Ideas y Valores. Instituto de Filosofía y Letras, Univ. Nacional. Bogotá.

Int. Soc. Sci. J. International Social Science Journal. Blackwell Publishers. Oxford, England.

Integr. Latinoam. Integración Latinoamericana. Instituto para la Integración de América Latina. Buenos Aires.

Invest. Ens. Investigaciones y Ensayos. Academia Nacional de la Historia. Buenos Aires.

Islas/Santa Clara. Islas. Univ. Central de Las Villas. Santa Clara, Cuba.

J. Church State. Journal of Church and State. J.M. Dawson Studies in Church and State, Baylor Univ., Waco, Tex.

Jahrb. Gesch. Jahrbuch für Geschichte von Staat, Wirtschaft und Gesellschaft Lateinamerikas. Köln, Germany.

LARR. Latin American Research Review. Latin American Research Review Board. Univ. of New Mexico, Albuquerque, N.M.

Lateinamerika/Hamburg. Lateinamerika. Institut für Iberoamerika-Kunde. Hamburg, Germany.

Lua Nova. Lua Nova. Editora Brasiliense. São Paulo.

Luso-Braz. Rev. Luso-Brazilian Review. Univ. of Wisconsin Press. Madison, Wis.

MACLAS Lat. Am. Essays. MACLAS Latin American Essays. Middle Atlantic Council of Latin American Studies. New Brunswick, N.J.

Mapocho/Santiago. Mapocho. Biblioteca Nacional. Santiago.

Mesoamérica/Antigua. Mesoamérica. Centro de Investigaciones Regionales de Mesoamérica. Antigua, Guatemala.

Nueva Rev. Filol. Hisp. Nueva Revista de Filología Hispánica. El Colegio de México. México.

Palabra Hombre. La Palabra y el Hombre. Univ. Veracruzana. Xalapa, Mexico.

Pensam. Iberoam. Pensamiento Iberoamericano. Instituto de Cooperación Iberoamericano (ICI) de España; Comisión Económica para América Latina y el Caribe (CEPAL). Madrid.

Philos. Forum. The Philosophical Forum. Dept. of Philosophy, Baruch College, City Univ. of New York. New York.

Procesos/Quito. Procesos. Corporación Editora Nacional. Quito.

Reflexão/São Paulo. Reflexão. Pontifícia Univ. Católica de Campinas. São Paulo.

Relig. Cult. Religión y Cultura. Madrid.

Rev. Antropol./São Paulo. Revista de Antropologia. Univ. de São Paulo, Faculdade de Filosofia, Letras e Ciências Humanas; Associação Brasileira de Antropologia. São Paulo.

Rev. Bibl. Nac. José Martí. Revista de la Biblioteca Nacional José Martí. La Habana.

Rev. Bras. Filos. Revista Brasileira de Filosofia. Instituto Brasileiro de Filosofia. São Paulo.

Rev. Chil. Humanid. Revista Chilena de Humanidades. Facultad de Filosofía, Humanidades y Educación, Univ. de Chile. Santiago.

Rev. Ciênc. Polít./Rio de Janeiro. Ciência Política. Fundação Getúlio Vargas. Rio de Janeiro.

Rev. Filos. Latinoam. Cienc. Soc. Revista de Filosofía Latinoamericano y Ciencias Sociales. Asociación de Filosofía Latinoamericana y Ciencias Sociales. Buenos Aires.

Rev. Filos./México. Revista de Filosofía. Univ. Iberoamericana, Depto. de Filosofía; Asociación Fray Alonso de la Veracruz. México.

Rev. Filos. Univ. Costa Rica. Revista de Filosofía de la Universidad de Costa Rica. Editorial de la Universidad de Costa Rica. San José.

Rev. Hist. Am. Revista de Historia de América. Instituto Panamericano de Geografía e Historia, Comisión de Historia. México.

Rev. Hist./Heredia. Revista de Historia. Univ. Nacional de Costa Rica, Escuela de Historia. Heredia, Costa Rica.

Rev. Hist. Ideas. Revista de Historia de las Ideas. Instituto Panamericano de Geografía e Historia; Editorial Casa de la Cultura Ecuatoriana. Quito.

Rev. Iberoam. Revista Iberoamericana. Instituto Internacional de Literatura Iberoamericana; Univ. de Pittsburgh. Pittsburgh, Penn.

Rev. Inst. Hist. Geogr. São Paulo. Revista do Instituto Histórico e Geográfico de São Paulo. São Paulo.

Rev. Int. Sociol. Revista Internacional de Sociología. Consejo Superior de Investigaciones Científicas. Instituto de Economía y Geografía Aplicadas. Madrid.

Todo es Hist. Todo es Historia. Buenos Aires.

UNISA Lat. Am. Rep. UNISA Latin American Report. Univ. of South Africa. Pretoria.

Vuelta/México. Vuelta. México.

ABBREVIATIONS AND ACRONYMS

Except for journal abbreviations which are listed: 1) at the end of each major disciplinary section (e.g., Art, History, Literature); 2) after each journal title in the *Title List of Journals Indexed* (p. 000); and 3) in the *Abbreviation List of Journals Indexed* (p. 000).

ALADI	Asociación Latinoamericana de Integración
a.	annual
ABC	Argentina, Brazil, Chile
A.C.	antes de Cristo
ACAR	Associação de Crédito e Assistência Rural, Brazil
AD	Anno Domini
A.D.	Acción Democrática, Venezuela
ADESG	Associação dos Diplomados de Escola Superior de Guerra, Brazil
AGI	Archivo General de Indias, Sevilla
AGN	Archivo General de la Nación
AID	Agency for International Development
a.k.a.	also known as
Ala.	Alabama
ALALC	Asociación Latinoamericana de Libre Comercio
ALEC	*Atlas lingüístico etnográfico de Colombia*
ANAPO	Alianza Nacional Popular, Colombia
ANCARSE	Associação Nordestina de Crédito e Assistência Rural de Sergipe, Brazil
ANCOM	Andean Common Market
ANDI	Asociación Nacional de Industriales, Colombia
ANPOCS	Associação Nacional de Pós-Graduação e Pesquisa em Ciências Sociais, São Paulo
ANUC	Asociación Nacional de Usuarios Campesinos, Colombia
ANUIES	Asociación Nacional de Universidades e Institutos de Enseñanza Superior, Mexico
AP	Acción Popular
APRA	Alianza Popular Revolucionaria Americana, Peru
ARENA	Aliança Renovadora Nacional, Brazil
Ariz.	Arizona
Ark.	Arkansas
ASA	Association of Social Anthropologists of the Commonwealth, London
ASSEPLAN	Assessoria de Planejamento e Acompanhamento, Recife
Assn.	Association
Aufl.	Auflage (edition, edición)
AUFS	American Universities Field Staff Reports, Hanover, N.H.
Aug.	August, Augustan
aum.	aumentada
b.	born (nació)
B.A.R.	British Archaeological Reports
BBE	Bibliografia Brasileira de Educação
b.c.	indicates dates obtained by radiocarbon methods

BC	Before Christ
bibl(s).	bibliography(ies)
BID	Banco Interamericano de Desarrollo
BNDE	Banco Nacional de Desenvolvimento Econômico, Brazil
BNH	Banco Nacional de Habitação, Brazil
BP	before present
b/w	black and white
C14	Carbon 14
ca.	*circa* (about)
CACM	Central American Common Market
CADE	Conferencia Anual de Ejecutivos de Empresas, Peru
CAEM	Centro de Altos Estudios Militares, Peru
Calif.	California
Cap.	Capítulo
CARC	Centro de Arte y Comunicación, Buenos Aires
CARICOM	Caribbean Common Market
CARIFTA	Caribbean Free Trade Association
CBC	Christian base communities
CBD	central business district
CBI	Caribbean Basin Initiative
CD	Christian Democrats, Chile
CDI	Conselho de Desenvolvimento Industrial, Brasília
CEB	comunidades eclesiásticas de base
CEBRAP	Centro Brasileiro de Análise e Planejamento, São Paulo
CECORA	Centro de Cooperativas de la Reforma Agraria, Colombia
CEDAL	Centro de Estudios Democráticos de América Latina, Costa Rica
CEDE	Centro de Estudios sobre Desarrollo Económico, Univ. de los Andes, Bogotá
CEDEPLAR	Centro de Desenvolvimento e Planejamento Regional, Belo Horizonte
CEDES	Centro de Estudios de Estado y Sociedad, Buenos Aires; Centro de Estudos de Educação e Sociedade, São Paulo
CEDI	Centro Ecumênico de Documentos e Informação, São Paulo
CEDLA	Centro de Estudios y Documentación Latinoamericanos, Amsterdam
CEESTEM	Centro de Estudios Económicos y Sociales del Tercer Mundo, México
CELADE	Centro Latinoamericano de Demografía
CELADEC	Comisión Evangélica Latinoamericana de Educación Cristiana
CELAM	Consejo Episcopal Latinoamericano
CEMLA	Centro de Estudios Monetarios Latinoamericanos, Mexico
CENDES	Centro de Estudios del Desarrollo, Venezuela
CENIDIM	Centro Nacional de Información, Documentación e Investigación Musicales, Mexico
CENIET	Centro Nacional de Información y Estadísticas del Trabajo, Mexico
CEPADE	Centro Paraguayo de Estudios de Desarrollo Económico y Social
CEPA-SE	Comissão Estadual de Planejamento Agrícola, Sergipe
CEPAL	Comisión Económica para América Latina y el Caribe
CEPLAES	Centro de Planificación y Estudios Sociales, Quito
CERES	Centro de Estudios de la Realidad Económica y Social, Bolivia
CES	constant elasticity of substitution
cf.	compare
CFI	Consejo Federal de Inversiones, Buenos Aires
CGE	Confederación General Económica, Argentina
CGTP	Confederación General de Trabajadores del Perú
chap(s).	chapter(s)
CHEAR	Council on Higher Education in the American Republics
Cía.	Compañía
CIA	Central Intelligence Agency

CIDA	Comité Interamericano de Desarrollo Agrícola
CIDE	Centro de Investigación y Desarrollo de la Educación, Chile; Centro de Investigación y Docencias Económicas, Mexico
CIE	Centro de Investigaciones Económicas, Buenos Aires
CIEDLA	Centro Interdisciplinario de Estudios sobre el Desarrollo Latinoamericano, Buenos Aires
CIEDUR	Centro Interdisciplinario de Estudios sobre el Desarrollo Uruguay, Montevideo
CIEPLAN	Corporación de Investigaciones Económicas para América Latina, Santiago
CIESE	Centro de Investigaciones y Estudios Socioeconómicos, Quito
CIMI	Conselho Indigenista Missionário, Brazil
CINTERFOR	Centro Interamericano de Investigación y Documentación sobre Formación Profesional
CINVE	Centro de Investigaciones Económicas, Montevideo
CIP	Conselho Interministerial de Preços, Brazil
CIPCA	Centro de Investigación y Promoción del Campesinado, Bolivia
CIPEC	Consejo Intergubernamental de Países Exportadores de Cobre, Santiago
CLACSO	Consejo Latinoamericano de Ciencias Sociales, Secretaría Ejecutiva, Buenos Aires
CLASC	Confederación Latinoamericana Sindical Cristiana
CLE	Comunidad Latinoamericana de Escritores, Mexico
cm	centimeter
CNI	Confederação Nacional da Indústria, Brazil
CNPq	Conselho Nacional de Pesquisas, Brazil
Co.	Company
COB	Central Obrera Boliviana
COBAL	Companhia Brasileira de Alimentos
Col.	Collection, Colección, Coleção
col.	colored, coloured
Colo.	Colorado
COMCORDE	Comisión Coordinadora para el Desarrollo Económico, Uruguay
comp(s).	compiler(s), compilador(es)
CONCLAT	Congresso Nacional das Classes Trabalhadoras, Brazil
CONCYTEC	Consejo Nacional de Ciencia y Tecnología (Peru)
CONDESE	Conselho de Desenvolvimento Econômico de Sergipe
Conn.	Connecticut
COPEI	Comité Organizador Pro-Elecciones Independientes, Venezuela
CORFO	Corporación de Fomento de la Producción, Chile
CORP	Corporación para el Fomento de Investigaciones Económicas, Colombia
Corp.	Corporation, Corporación
corr.	corrected, corregida
CP	Communist Party
CPDOC	Centro de Pesquisa e Documentação, Brazil
CRIC	Consejo Regional Indígena del Cauca, Colombia
CSUTCB	Confederación Sindical Unica de Trabajadores Campesinos de Bolivia
CTM	Confederación de Trabajadores de México
CUNY	City University of New York
CUT	Central Unica de Trabajadores (Mexico); Central Unica dos Trabalhadores (Brazil); Central Unitaria de Trabajadores (Chile; Colombia); Confederación Unitaria de Trabajadores (Costa Rica)
CVG	Corporación Venezolana de Guayana
d.	died (murió)
DANE	Departamento Nacional de Estadística, Colombia
DC	developed country; Demócratas Cristianos, Chile
d.C.	después de Cristo
Dec./déc.	December, décembre

Del.	Delaware
dept.	department
depto.	departamento
DESCO	Centro de Estudios y Promoción del Desarrollo, Lima
Dez./dez.	Dezember, dezembro
dic.	diciembre, dicembre
disc.	discography
DNOCS	Departamento Nacional de Obras Contra as Secas, Brazil
doc.	document, documento
Dr.	Doctor
Dra.	Doctora
DRAE	*Diccionario de la Real Academia Española*
ECLAC	UN Economic Commision for Latin America and the Caribbean, New York and Santiago
ECOSOC	UN Economic and Social Council
ed./éd.(s)	edition(s), édition(s), edición(es), editor(s), redactor(es), director(es)
EDEME	Editora Emprendimentos Educacionais, Florianópolis
Edo.	Estado
EEC	European Economic Community
EE.UU.	Estados Unidos de América
EFTA	European Free Trade Association
e.g.	*exempio gratia* (for example, por ejemplo)
ELN	Ejército de Liberación Nacional, Colombia
ENDEF	Estudo Nacional da Despesa Familiar, Brazil
ESG	Escola Superior de Guerra, Brazil
estr.	estrenado
et al.	*et alia* (and others)
ETENE	Escritório Técnico de Estudos Econômicos do Nordeste, Brazil
ETEPE	Escritório Técnico de Planejamento, Brazil
EUDEBA	Editorial Universitaria de Buenos Aires
EWG	Europaische Wirtschaftsgemeinschaft. *See* EEC.
facsim(s).	facsimile(s)
FAO	Food and Agriculture Organization of the United Nations
FDR	Frente Democrático Revolucionario, El Salvador
FEB	Força Expedicionária Brasileira
Feb./feb.	February, Februar, febrero, febbraio
FEDECAFE	Federación Nacional de Cafeteros, Colombia
fev./fév.	fevereiro, février
ff.	following
FGTS	Fundo de Garantia do Tempo de Serviço, Brazil
FGV	Fundação Getúlio Vargas
FIEL	Fundación de Investigaciones Económicas Latinoamericanas, Argentina
film.	filmography
fl.	flourished
Fla.	Florida
FLACSO	Facultad Latinoamericana de Ciencias Sociales
FMI	Fondo Monetario Internacional
FMLN	Frente Farabundo Martí de Liberación Nacional, El Salvador
fold.	folded
fol(s).	folio(s)
FRG	Federal Republic of Germany
FSLN	Frente Sandinista de Liberación Nacional, Nicaragua
ft.	foot, feet
FUAR	Frente Unido de Acción Revolucionaria, Colombia

FUCVAM	Federación Unificadora de Cooperativas de Vivienda por Ayuda Mutua, Uruguay
FUNAI	Fundação Nacional do Indio, Brazil
FUNARTE	Fundação Nacional de Arte, Brazil
FURN	Fundação Universidade Regional do Nordeste
Ga.	Georgia
GAO	General Accounting Office, Wahington
GATT	General Agreement on Tariffs and Trade
GDP	gross domestic product
GDR	German Democratic Republic
GEIDA	Grupo Executivo de Irrigação para o Desenvolvimento Agrícola, Brazil
gen.	gennaio
Gen.	General
GMT	Greenwich Mean Time
GPA	grade point average
GPO	Government Printing Office, Washington
h.	hijo
ha.	hectares, hectáreas
HLAS	*Handbook of Latin American Studies*
HMAI	*Handbook of Middle American Indians*
Hnos.	hermanos
HRAF	Human Relations Area Files, Inc., New Haven, Conn.
IBBD	Instituto Brasileiro de Bibliografia e Documentação
IBGE	Instituto Brasileiro de Geografia e Estatística, Rio de Janeiro
IBRD	International Bank for Reconstruction and Development (World Bank)
ICA	Instituto Colombiano Agropecuario
ICAIC	Instituto Cubano de Arte e Industria Cinematográfica
ICCE	Instituto Colombiano de Construcción Escolar
ICE	International Cultural Exchange
ICSS	Instituto Colombiano de Seguridad Social
ICT	Instituto de Crédito Territorial, Colombia
id.	*idem* (the same as previously mentioned or given)
IDB	Inter-American Development Bank
i.e.	*id est* (that is, o sea)
IEL	Instituto Euvaldo Lodi, Brazil
IEP	Instituto de Estudios Peruanos
IERAC	Instituto Ecuatoriano de Reforma Agraria y Colonización
IFAD	International Fund for Agricultural Development
IICA	Instituto Interamericano de Ciencias Agrícolas, San José
III	Instituto Indigenista Interamericana, Mexico
IIN	Instituto Indigenista Nacional, Guatemala
ILDIS	Instituto Latinoamericano de Investigaciones Sociales, Quito
ill.	illustration(s)
Ill.	Illinois
ILO	International Labour Organization, Geneva
IMES	Instituto Mexicano de Estudios Sociales
IMF	International Monetary Fund
Impr.	Imprenta, Imprimérie
in.	inches
INAH	Instituto Nacional de Antropología e Historia, Mexico
INBA	Instituto Nacional de Bellas Artes, Mexico
Inc.	Incorporated
INCORA	Instituto Colombiano de Reforma Agraria
Ind.	Indiana

INEP	Instituto Nacional de Estudios Pedagógicos, Brazil
INI	Instituto Nacional Indigenista, Mexico
INIT	Instituto Nacional de Industria Turística, Cuba
INPES/IPEA	Instituto de Planejamento Econômico e Social, Brazil
INTAL	Instituto para la Integración de América Latina
IPA	Instituto de Pastoral Andina, Univ. de San Antonio de Abad, Seminario de Antropología, Cusco, Peru
IPEA	Instituto de Pesquisa Econômica Aplicada, Brazil
IPES/GB	Instituto de Pesquisas e Estudos Sociais, Guanabara, Brazil
IPHAN	Instituto de Patrimônio Histórico e Artístico Nacional, Brazil
ir.	irregular
IS	Internacional Socialista
ITT	International Telephone and Telegraph
Jan./jan.	January, Januar, janeiro, janvier
JLP	Jamaican Labour Party
Jr.	Junior, Júnior
JUC	Juventude Universitária Católica, Brazil
JUCEPLAN	Junta Central de Planificación, Cuba
Kan.	Kansas
km	kilometers, kilómetros
Ky.	Kentucky
La.	Louisiana
LASA	Latin American Studies Association
LDC	less developed country(ies)
LP	long-playing record
Ltd(a).	Limited, Limitada
m	meters, metros
m.	murió (died)
M	mille, mil, thousand
M.A.	Master of Arts
MACLAS	Middle Atlantic Council of Latin American Studies
MAPU	Movimiento de Acción Popular Unitario, Chile
MARI	Middle American Research Institute, Tulane University, New Orleans
MAS	Movimiento al Socialismo, Venezuela
Mass.	Massachusetts
MCC	Mercado Común Centro-Americano
Md.	Maryland
MDB	Movimiento Democrático Brasileiro
MDC	more developed countries
Me.	Maine
MEC	Ministério de Educação e Cultura, Brazil
Mich.	Michigan
mimeo	mimeographed, mimeografiado
min.	minutes, minutos
Minn.	Minnesota
MIR	Movimiento de Izquierda Revolucionaria, Chile and Venezuela
Miss.	Mississippi
MIT	Massachusetts Institute of Technology
ml	milliliter
MLN	Movimiento de Liberación Nacional
mm.	millimeter
MNC	multinational corporation
MNI	minimum number of individuals
MNR	Movimiento Nacionalista Revolucionario, Bolivia
Mo.	Missouri

MOBRAL	Movimento Brasileiro de Alfabetização
MOIR	Movimiento Obrero Independiente y Revolucionario, Colombia
Mont.	Montana
MRL	Movimiento Revolucionario Liberal, Colombia
ms.	manuscript
M.S.	Master of Science
msl	mean sea level
n.	nació (born)
NBER	National Bureau of Economic Research, Cambridge, Massachusetts
N.C.	North Carolina
N.D.	North Dakota
NE	Northeast
Neb.	Nebraska
neubearb.	neubearbeitet (revised, corregida)
Nev.	Nevada
n.f.	neue Folge (new series)
NGO	nongovernmental organization
NGDO	nongovernmental development organization
N.H.	New Hampshire
NIEO	New International Economic Order
NIH	National Institutes of Health, Washington
N.J.	New Jersey
NJM	New Jewel Movement, Grenada
N.M.	New Mexico
no(s).	number(s), número(s)
NOEI	Nuevo Orden Económico Internacional
NOSALF	Scandinavian Committee for Research in Latin America
Nov./nov.	November, noviembre, novembre, novembro
NSF	National Science Foundation
NW	Northwest
N.Y.	New York
OAB	Ordem dos Advogados do Brasil
OAS	Organization of American States
Oct./oct.	October, octubre, octobre
ODEPLAN	Oficina de Planificación Nacional, Chile
OEA	Organización de los Estados Americanos
OIT	Organización Internacional del Trabajo
Okla.	Oklahoma
Okt.	Oktober
op.	opus
OPANAL	Organismo para la Proscripción de las Armas Nucleares en América Latina
OPEC	Organization of Petroleum Exporting Countries
OPEP	Organización de Países Exportadores de Petróleo
OPIC	Overseas Private Investment Corporation, Washington
Or.	Oregon
OREALC	Oficina Regional de Educación para América Latina y el Caribe
ORIT	Organización Regional Interamericana del Trabajo
ORSTOM	Office de la recherche scientifique et technique outre-mer (France)
ott.	ottobre
out.	outubro
p.	page(s)
Pa.	Pennsylvania
PAN	Partido Acción Nacional, Mexico
PC	Partido Comunista
PCCLAS	Pacific Coast Council on Latin American Studies

PCN	Partido de Conciliación Nacional, El Salvador
PCP	Partido Comunista del Perú
PCR	Partido Comunista Revolucionario, Chile and Argentina
PCV	Partido Comunista de Venezuela
PD	Partido Democrático
PDC	Partido Demócrata Cristiano, Chile
PDS	Partido Democrático Social, Brazil
PDT	Partido Democrático Trabalhista, Brazil
PDVSA	Petróleos de Venezuela S.A.
PEMEX	Petróleos Mexicanos
PETROBRAS	Petróleo Brasileiro
PIMES	Programa Integrado de Mestrado em Economia e Sociologia, Brazil
PIP	Partido Independiente de Puerto Rico
PLN	Partido Liberación Nacional, Costa Rica
PMDB	Partido do Movimento Democrático Brasileiro
PNAD	Pesquisa Nacional por Amostra Domiciliar, Brazil
PNC	People's National Congress, Guyana
PNM	People's National Movement, Trinidad and Tobago
PNP	People's National Party, Jamaica
pop.	population
port(s).	portrait(s)
PPP	purchasing power parities; People's Progressive Party of Guyana
PRD	Partido Revolucionario Dominicano
PREALC	Programa Regional del Empleo para América Latina y el Caribe, Organización Internacional del Trabajo, Santiago
PRI	Partido Revolucionario Institucional, Mexico
Prof.	Professor, Profesor(a)
PRONAPA	Programa Nacional de Pesquisas Arqueológicas, Brazil
prov.	province, provincia
PS	Partido Socialista, Chile
PSD	Partido Social Democrático, Brazil
pseud.	pseudonym, pseudónimo
PT	Partido dos Trabalhadores, Brazil
pt(s).	part(s), parte(s)
PTB	Partido Trabalhista Brasileiro
pub.	published, publisher
PUC	Pontifícia Universidade Católica
PURSC	Partido Unido de la Revolución Socialista de Cuba
q.	quarterly
rev.	revisada, revista, revised
R.I.	Rhode Island
s.a.	semiannual
SALALM	Seminar on the Acquisition of Latin American Library Materials
SATB	soprano, alto, tenor, bass
sd.	sound
s.d.	*sine datum* (no date, sin fecha)
S.D.	South Dakota
SDR	special drawing rights
SE	Southeast
SELA	Sistema Económico Latinoamericano
SENAC	Serviço Nacional de Aprendizagem Comercial, Rio de Janeiro
SENAI	Serviço Nacional de Aprendizagem Industrial, São Paulo
SEP	Secretaría de Educación Pública, Mexico
SEPLA	Seminario Permanente sobre Latinoamérica, Mexico
Sept./sept.	September, septiembre, septembre

SES	socioeconomic status
SESI	Serviço Social da Indústria, Brazil
set.	setembro, settembre
SI	Socialist International
SIECA	Secretaría Permanente del Tratado General de Integración Económica Centroamericana
SIL	Summer Institute of Linguistics (Instituto Lingüístico de Verano)
SINAMOS	Sistema Nacional de Apoyo a la Movilización Social, Peru
S.J.	Society of Jesus
s.l.	*sine loco* (place of publication unknown)
s.n.	*sine nomine* (publisher unknown)
SNA	Sociedad Nacional de Agricultura, Chile
SPP	Secretaría de Programación y Presupuesto, Mexico
SPVEA	Superintendência do Plano de Valorização Econômica da Amazônia, Brazil
sq.	square
SSRC	Social Sciences Research Council, New York
SUDAM	Superintendência de Desenvolvimento da Amazônia, Brazil
SUDENE	Superintendência de Desenvolvimento do Nordeste, Brazil
SUFRAMA	Superintendência da Zona Franca de Manaus, Brazil
SUNY	State University of New York
SW	Southwest
t.	tomo(s), tome(s)
TAT	Thematic Apperception Test
TB	tuberculosis
Tenn.	Tennessee
Tex.	Texas
TG	transformational generative
TL	Thermoluminescent
TNE	Transnational enterprise
TNP	Tratado de No Proliferación
trans.	translator
UABC	Universidad Autónoma de Baja California
UCA	Universidad Centroamericana José Simeón Cañas, San Salvador
UCLA	University of California, Los Angeles
UDN	União Democrática Nacional, Brazil
UFG	Universidade Federal de Goiás
UFPb	Universidade Federal de Paraíba
UFSC	Universidade Federal de Santa Catarina
UK	United Kingdom
UN	United Nations
UNAM	Universidad Nacional Autónoma de México
UNCTAD	United Nations Conference on Trade and Development
UNDP	United Nations Development Programme
UNEAC	Unión de Escritores y Artistas de Cuba
UNESCO	United Nations Educational, Scientific and Cultural Organization
UNI/UNIND	União das Nações Indígenas
UNICEF	United Nations International Children's Emergency Fund
Univ(s).	university(ies), universidad(es), universidade(s), université(s), universität(s), universitá(s)
uniw.	uniwersytet (university)
Unltd.	Unlimited
UP	Unidad Popular, Chile
URD	Unidad Revolucionaria Democrática
URSS	Unión de Repúblicas Soviéticas Socialistas
US	United States

USAID	*See* AID.
USIA	United States Information Agency
USSR	Union of Soviet Socialist Republics
UTM	Universal Transverse Mercator
UWI	Univ. of the West Indies
v.	volume(s), volumen (volúmenes)
Va.	Virginia
V.I.	Virgin Islands
viz.	*videlicet* (that is, namely)
vol(s).	volume(s), volumen (volúmenes)
vs.	versus
Vt.	Vermont
W.Va.	West Virginia
Wash.	Washington
Wis.	Wisconsin
WPA	Working People's Alliance, Guyana
WWI	World War I
WWII	World War II
Wyo.	Wyoming
yr(s).	year(s)

TITLE LIST OF JOURNALS INDEXED

For journal titles listed by abbreviation, see *Abbreviation List of Journals Indexed*

Acta Literaria. Instituto de Lenguas, Univ. de Concepción. Concepción, Chile. (Acta Lit.)

Actas Americanas. Univ. de La Serena, Facultad de Humanidades. La Serena, Chile. (Actas Am.)

Afro-Hispanic Review. Univ. of Missouri-Columbia. Columbia, Missouri. (Afro-Hisp. Rev.)

Agricultural History. Agricultural History Society. Univ. of Calif. Press. Berkeley. (Agric. Hist.)

Allpanchis. Instituto de Pastoral Andina. Cusco, Peru. (Allpanchis/Cusco)

América Indígena. Instituto Indigenista Interamericano. México. (Am. Indíg.)

América Meridional. Sociedad Regional de Ciencias Humanas. Montevideo. (Am. Merid.)

América Negra. Pontificia Univ. Javeriana. Bogotá. (Am. Negra)

American Anthropologist. American Anthropological Assn., Washington. (Am. Anthropol.)

The American Economic Review. American Economic Assn., Evanston, Ill. (Am. Econ. Rev.)

The American Historical Review. American Historical Assn., Washington. (Am. Hist. Rev.)

American Sociological Review. American Sociological Assn., Washington. (Am. Sociol. Rev.)

The Americas. Academy of American Franciscan History. Washington. (Americas/Francisc.)

Anales. Instituto Iberoamericano, Univ. de Gotemburgo. Göteborg, Sweden. (Anales/Göteborg)

Anales de Arqueología y Etnología. Univ. Nacional de Cuyo, Facultad de Filosofía y Letras. Mendoza, Argentina. (An. Arqueol. Etnol.)

Anales de Historia Contemporánea. Cátedra de Historia Contemporánea, Univ. de Murcia. Murcia, Spain. (An. Hist. Contemp.)

Anales de la Academia Nacional de Ciencias Económicas. Buenos Aires. (An. Acad. Nac. Cienc. Econ.)

Anales de la Universidad de Chile. Santiago. (An. Univ. Chile)

Anales del Instituto de Investigaciones Estéticas. Univ. Nacional Autónoma de México. México. (An. Inst. Invest. Estét.)

Anales del Museo de América. Museo de América. Madrid. (An. Mus. Am.)

Anales Valentinos: Revista de Filosofía y Teología. Facultad de Teología San Vicente Ferrer. Valencia, Spain. (An. Valent.)

Ancient Mesoamerica. Cambridge Univ. Press. Cambridge, England. (Anc. Mesoam.)

Annales. Centre national de la recherche scientifique de la VIe Section de l'Ecole pratique des hautes études. Paris. (Annales/Paris)

Annales historiques de la Révolution française. Société des Études Robespierristes; Firmin-Didot. Reims, Paris. (Ann. hist. Révolut. fr.)

Anthropological Quarterly. Catholic Univ. of America, Catholic Anthropological Conference. Washington. (Anthropol. Q.)

Anuario. Univ. Nacional de Rosario, Escuela de Historia. Argentina. (Anuario/Rosario)

Anuario. Talleres Gráficos Túpac Katari. Archivo y Biblioteca Nacionales de Bolivia. Sucre. (Anuario/Sucre)

Anuario Colombiano de Historia Social y de la Cultura. Univ. Nacional de Colombia, Facultad de Ciencias Humanas, Depto. de Historia. Bogotá. (Anu. Colomb. Hist. Soc. Cult.)

Anuario de Estudios Americanos. Consejo Superior de Investigaciones Científicas; Univ. de Sevilla, Escuela de Estudios Hispano-

Americanos. Sevilla, Spain. (Anu. Estud. Am.)

Anuario de Etnología. Academia de Ciencias de Cuba; Editorial Academia. La Habana. (Anu. Etnol./Habana)

Anuario de Historia de la Iglesia en Chile. Seminario Pontificio Mayor. Santiago. (Anu. Hist. Iglesia Chile)

Anuario del Centro de Estudios Martianos. Centro de Estudios Martianos. La Habana. (Anu. Cent. Estud. Martianos)

Anuario del Departmento de Historia. Depto. de Historia, Univ. Complutense de Madrid. (Anu. Dep. Hist./Madrid)

Anuario do Museu da Inconfidência. Museo Inconfidência. Ouro Preto, Brazil. (Anu. Mus. Inconfidência)

Anuario IEHS. Univ. Nacional del Centro de la Provincia de Buenos Aires, Instituto de Estudios Histórico-Sociales. Tandil, Argentina. (Anu. IEHS)

Anuario Veritas. Univ. Regiomontana, Depto. de Publicaciones. Monterrey, Mexico. (Anu. Veritas)

Apuntes. Univ. del Pacífico, Centro de Investigación. Lima. (Apuntes/Lima)

Apuntes Filosóficos. Escuela de Filosofía, Univ. Central de Venezuela. Caracas. (Apunt. Filos.)

Arbor. Consejo Superior de Investigaciones Científicas. Madrid. (Arbor/Madrid)

Archaeology. Archaeology Institute of America. New York. (Archaeology/New York)

Archives de sciences sociales des religions. Centre nationale de la recherche scientifique. Paris. (Arch. sci. soc. relig.)

Archivo Ibero-Americano. Revista de Estudios Históricos. Los Padres Franciscanos. Madrid. (Arch. Ibero-Am.)

Archivum Franciscanum Historicum. Collegio S. Bonaventura. Rome. (Arch. Francisc. Hist.)

Art Journal. The College Art Assn., New York. (Art J.)

ARTEunesp. Univ. Estadual Paulista. São Paulo. (ARTEunesp)

ASCAP Playback. American Society of Composers, Authors & Publishers. New York. (ASCAP Playback)

Boletim Informativo e Bibliográfico de Ciências Sociais: BIB. Associação Nacional de Pós-Graduação e Pesquisa em Ciências Sociais. Rio de Janeiro. (ANPOCS BIB)

Boletín Americanista. Univ. de Barcelona,

Facultad de Geografía e Historia, Depto. de Historia de América. Barcelona. (Bol. Am.)

Boletín Cultural y Bibliográfico. Banco de la República; Biblioteca Luis-Angel Arango. Bogotá. (Bol. Cult. Bibliogr.)

Boletín de Fuentes para la Historia Económica de México. Centro de Estudios Históricos, El Colegio de México. México. (Bol. Fuentes Hist. Econ. Méx.)

Boletín de la Academia Chilena de la Historia. Santiago. (Bol. Acad. Chil. Hist.)

Boletín de la Academia Nacional de Historia. Quito. (Bol. Acad. Nac. Hist./Quito)

Boletín de la Academia Nacional de la Historia. Buenos Aires. (Bol. Acad. Nac. Hist./Buenos Aires)

Boletín de la Academia Nacional de la Historia. Caracas. (Bol. Acad. Nac. Hist./Caracas)

Boletín de la Biblioteca Nacional. Biblioteca Nacional. Lima. (Bol. Bibl. Nac.)

Boletín de Lima. Revista Cultural Científica. Lima. (Bol. Lima)

Boletín del Archivo Nacional de Historia. Quito. (Bol. Arch. Nac. Hist.)

Boletín del Centro de Investigaciones Históricas. Facultad de Humanidades, Univ. de Puerto Rico. Río Piedras. (Bol. Cent. Invest. Hist.)

Boletín del Instituto de Historia Argentina y Americana Dr. Emilio Ravignani. Facultad de Filosofía y Letras, Univ. de Buenos Aires. (Bol. Inst. Hist. Ravignani)

Boletín del Instituto Riva-Agüero. Pontificia Univ. Católica del Perú. Lima. (Bol. Inst. Riva-Agüero)

Boletín Nicaragüense de Bibliografía y Documentación. Biblioteca, Banco Central de Nicaragua. Managua. (Bol. Nicar. Bibliogr. Doc.)

Brasil = Brazil. Pontifícia Univ. Católica do Rio Grande do Sul. Porto Alegre, Brazil. (Brasil/Porto Alegre)

Bulletin de la Société d'histoire de la Guadeloupe. Archives départementales avec le concours du Conseil général de la Guadeloupe. Basse-Terre, Guadeloupe. (Bull. Soc. hist. Guadeloupe)

Bulletin de l'Institut français d'études andines. Lima. (Bull. Inst. fr. étud. andin.)

Bulletin du Centre d'histoire des espaces atlantiques. Talence-Cedex, France. (Bull. Cent. hist. atl.)

Bulletin hispanique. Univ. de Bordeaux; Centre national de la recherche scientifique. Bordeaux, France. (Bull. hisp./Bordeaux)

Bulletin of Latin American Research. Society for Latin American Studies. Oxford, England. (Bull. Lat. Am. Res.)

Business History Review. Harvard Univ. Graduate School of Business Administration. Boston, Mass. (Bus. Hist. Rev.)

Cahiers des Amériques latines. Paris. (Cah. Am. lat.)

Les cahiers du patrimoine. Bureau du patrimoine du Conseil régional de la Martinique. Fort-de-France. (Cah. patrim.)

Canadian Journal of African Studies. Assn. of African Studies. Ottawa, Canada. (Can. J. Afr. Stud.)

Canadian Journal of History. Univ. of Saskatchewan. Saskatoon, Canada. (Can. J. Hist.)

Caravelle. Cahiers du monde hispanique et luso-brésilien. Univ. de Toulouse, Institute d'études hispaniques, hispano-americaines et luso-brésiliennes. Toulouse, France. (Caravelle/Toulouse)

Caribbean Quarterly. Univ. of the West Indies. Mona, Jamaica. (Caribb. Q.)

Caribbean Studies. Univ. of Puerto Rico, Institute of Caribbean Studies. Río Piedras. (Caribb. Stud.)

Caribena: cahiers d'études américanistes de la Caraïbe. Centre d'études et de recherches archéologiques (CERA). Martinique. (Caribena/Martinique)

Chemins critiques: revue haïtiano-caraïbéenne. Société sciences-arts-littérature. Port-au-Prince, Haiti. (Chemins crit.)

Ciência e Cultura. Sociedade Brasileira para o Progresso da Ciência. São Paulo. (Ciênc. Cult.)

Ciencia Hoy. Asociación Ciencia Hoy; Morgan Antártica. Buenos Aires. (Cienc. Hoy)

Círculo: Revista de Cultura. Círculo de Cultura Panamericana. Verona, N.J. (Círculo/Verona)

Colonial Latin American Historical Review. Spanish Colonial Research Center, Univ. of New Mexico. Albuquerque. (CLAHR/Albuquerque)

Colonial Latin American Review. Simon H. Rifkind Center for the Humanities, Dept. of Romance Languages, City College of New York. New York. (Colon. Lat. Am. Rev.)

Comparative Studies in Society and History.

Society for the Comparative Study of Society and History; Cambridge Univ. Press. London. (Comp. Stud. Soc. Hist.)

Comunicação e Sociedade. Instituto Metodista do Ensino Superior. São Paulo. (Comun. Soc.)

Conjonction. Bulletin de l'Institut français d'Haïti. Port-au-Prince. (Conjonction/Port-au-Prince)

Critique: Journal of Critical Studies of the Middle East. Center for Critical Studies of the Middle East. St. Paul, Minn. (Critique/St. Paul)

Cuadernos Americanos. Editorial Cultura. México. (Cuad. Am.)

Cuadernos de Historia. Instituto de Historia del Derecho y de las Ideas Políticas. Córdoba, Argentina. (Cuad. Hist./Córdoba)

Cuadernos de Historia. Univ. de Chile, Facultad de Humanidades y Educación, Depto. de Ciencias Históricas. Santiago. (Cuad. Hist./Santiago)

Cuadernos del CLAEH. Centro Latinoamericano de Economía Humana. Montevideo. (Cuad. CLAEH)

Cuadernos del Sur. Revista Cultural de Problemas Actuales. Buenos Aires. (Cuad. Sur/Buenos Aires)

Cuadernos Hispanoamericanos. Instituto de Cultura Hispánica. Madrid. (Cuad. Hispanoam.)

Cuadernos para la Historia de la Evangelización en América Latina: CHELA. Centro Bartolomé de las Casas. Cusco, Peru. (CHELA)

Cuban Studies. Univ. of Pittsburgh, Center for Latin American Studies. Pittsburgh, Penn. (Cuba. Stud.)

Current History. Philadelphia, Penn. (Curr. Hist.)

Cuyo: Anuario de Historia del Pensamiento Argentino. Univ. Nacional de Cuyo, Instituto de Filosofía, Sección de Historia del Pensamiento Argentino. Mendoza, Argentina. (Cuyo/Mendoza)

Dados. Instituto Univ. de Pesquisas. Rio de Janeiro. (Dados/Rio de Janeiro)

Desarrollo Económico. Instituto de Desarrollo Económico y Social. Buenos Aires. (Desarro. Econ.)

Diogenes. International Council for Philosophy and Humanistic Studies (Paris); Berg Publishers. Oxford, England. (Diogenes/Philosophy)

Economía. Depto. de Economía, Pontificia Univ. Católica del Perú. Lima. (Economía/Lima)

Economic and Social History in the Netherlands. Nederlandsch Economisch-Historisch Archief. Amsterdam. (Econ. Soc. Hist. Neth.)

Económica. Univ. Nacional de La Plata, Facultad de Ciencias Económicas, Instituto de Investigaciones Económicas. La Plata, Argentina. (Económica/La Plata)

Ecos. Instituto de Historia, Univ. Autónoma de Santo Domingo. (Ecos/Santo Domingo)

Espace Caraïbe. Maison des Pays Ibériques, Univ. M. de Montaigne, Bordeaux, France; Centre d'Études et de Recherches Caraïbéennes, Univ. des Antilles et de la Guyane, Pointe-à-Pitre, Guadeloupe. (Espace Caraïbe)

Estudios. Instituto de Investigaciones Históricas, Antropológicas, y Arqueológicas, Univ. de San Carlos de Guatemala. Guatemala. (Estudios/Guatemala)

Estudios de Ciencias y Letras. Instituto de Filosofía, Ciencias y Letras. Montevideo. (Estud. Cienc. Let.)

Estudios de Cultura Maya. Centro de Estudios Mayas, Univ. Nacional Autónoma de México. México. (Estud. Cult. Maya)

Estudios de Cultura Náhuatl. Instituto de Investigaciones Históricas, Univ. Nacional Autónoma de México. México. (Estud. Cult. Náhuatl)

Estudios de Historia Moderna y Contemporánea de México. Univ. Nacional Autónoma de México. México. (Estud. Hist. Mod. Contemp. Méx.)

Estudios de Historia Novohispana. Univ. Nacional Autónoma de México. México. (Estud. Hist. Novohisp.)

Estudios de Historia Rural. Univ. Nacional de La Plata, Centro de Estudios Histórico-Rurales. La Plata, Argentina. (Estud. Hist. Rural)

Estudios de Historia Social y Económica de América. Univ. de Alcalá de Henares. Madrid. (Estud. Hist. Soc. Econ. Am.)

Estudios Filológicos. Univ. Austral de Chile, Facultad de Filosofía y Humanidades. Valdivia, Chile. (Estud. Filol.)

Estudios Jaliscienses. Univ. de Guadalajara. Guadalajara, Mexico. (Estud. Jalisc.)

Estudios Latinoamericanos. Academia de Ciencias de Polonia, Instituto de Historia. Wrocław. (Estud. Latinoam./Poland)

Estudios: Políticos, Económicos, Filosóficos, Culturales del Uruguay. Partido Comunista. Montevideo. (Estud. Polít. Econ. Filos.)

Estudios sobre las Culturas Contemporáneas. Centro Universitario de Investigaciones Sociales, Univ. de Colima. México. (Estud. Cult. Contemp.)

Estudios Sociales. Corporación de Promoción Universitaria. Santiago. (Estud. Soc./Santiago)

Estudios Sociales. Centro de Estudios Sociales Juan Montalvo, SJ. Santo Domingo. (Estud. Soc./Santo Domingo)

Estudos Históricos. Associação de Pesquisa e Documentação Histórica. Rio de Janeiro. (Estud. Hist./Rio de Janeiro)

Estudos Ibero-Americanos. Pontifícia Univ. Católica do Rio Grande do Sul, Depto. de História. Porto Alegre, Brazil. (Estud. Ibero-Am./Porto Alegre)

Ethnohistory. American Society for Ethnohistory. Duke Univ., Durham, N.C. (Ethnohistory/Society)

Ethnohistory: the Bulletin of the Ohio Valley Historic Indian Conference. Columbus, Ohio. (Ethnohistory/Columbus)

Ethnomusicology. Society for Ethnomusicology. Ann Arbor, Mich. (Ethnomusicology/Society)

Etudes Guadeloupéennes. Association guadeloupéenne de recherches et d'études. Abymes, Guadeloupe. (Etud. Guad.)

EURE: Revista Latinoamericana de Estudios Urbanos Regionales. Centro de Desarrollo Urbano y Regional, Univ. Católica de Chile. Santiago. (EURE/Santiago)

Fénix: Revista de la Biblioteca Nacional del Perú. Biblioteca Nacional. Lima. (Fénix/Lima)

The Florida Historical Quarterly. The Florida Historical Society. Jacksonville, Fla. (Fla. Hist. Q.)

Folk: Journal of the Danish Ethnographic Society. Danish Ethnographic Society. Copenhagen. (Folk/Copenhagen)

Franciscanum. Univ. de San Buenaventura. Bogotá. (Franciscanum/Bogotá)

Gaceta Musical. Centro Nacional de Investigación, Documentación e Información Musical Carlos Chávez (CENIDIM). México. (Gac. Mus./México)

Généalogie et histoire de la Caraïbe. Assn. de

la généalogie et histoire de la Caraïbe. Le
Pecq, France. (Généal. hist. Caraïbe)
Guyana Historical Journal. History Society,
Dept. of History, Univ. of Guyana. George-
town. (Guyana Hist. J.)

Handbook of Latin American Studies CD-
ROM: HLAS/CD. Fundación MAPFRE
América, Madrid. Hispanic Division,
Library of Congress, Washington.
(HLAS/CD)
Herencia. Programa de Rescate y Revitaliza-
ción del Patrimonio Cultural. San José.
(Herencia/San José)
Heterofonía. México. (Heterofonía/México)
Hispamérica. Gaithersburg, Md. (Hispa-
mérica/Gaithersburg)
Hispania. Instituto Jerónimo Zurita, Consejo
Superior de Investigaciones Científicas.
Madrid. (Hispania/Madrid)
Hispania Sacra: Revista de Historia Eclesiás-
tica de España. Centro de Estudios Histó-
ricos, Instituto Enrique Flórez. Madrid.
(Hisp. Sacra)
Hispanic American Historical Review. Con-
ference on Latin American History of the
American Historical Assn.; Duke Univ.
Press. Durham, N.C. (HAHR)
Hispanic American Periodicals Index: HAPI
(CD-ROM). UCLA Latin American Center.
Los Angeles; National Information Ser-
vices Corporation (NISC). Baltimore, Md.
(HAPI/CD)
História. Fundação para o Desenvolvimento
da Univ. Estadual Paulista, Instituto de
Letras, História e Psicologia. São Paulo.
(História/São Paulo)
Historia. Univ. Católica de Chile. Instituto de
Historia. Santiago. (Historia/Santiago)
Historia Mexicana. Colegio de México. Mé-
xico. (Hist. Mex.)
Historia Nuestra. Concepción, Chile. (Hist.
Nuestra)
Historia y Cultura. Museo Nacional de Histo-
ria. Lima. (Hist. Cult./Lima)
Historia y Grafía. Depto. de Historia, Univ.
Iberoamericana. México. (Hist. Graf.)
Historia y Sociedad. Depto. de Historia, Univ.
de Puerto Rico. Río Piedras. (Hist. Soc./Río
Piedras)
The Historian. Phi Alpha Theta, National
Honor Society in History; Univ. of Pennsyl-
vania. Univ. Park, Penn. (Historian/Honor
Society)
Histórica. Pontificia Univ. Católica del Perú,

Depto. de Humanidades. Lima. (Histórica/
Lima)
Historical Research. Institute of Historical
Research. Oxford, England. (Hist. Res./
Oxford)
Historiografia Rioplatense. Instituto Biblio-
gráfico Antonio Zinny. Buenos Aires. (His-
toriogr. Rioplat.)
Historiografía y Bibliografía Americanista.
Escuela de Estudios Hispano-Americanos
de Sevilla. Sevilla, Spain. (Historiogr.
Bibliogr. Am.)
History Gazette. Univ. of Guyana, History
Society. Turkeyen, Guyana. (Hist. Gaz.)
History of Religions. Univ. of Chicago. Chi-
cago, Ill. (Hist. Relig.)
History Workshop. Ruskin College, Oxford
Univ., Oxford, England. (Hist. Workshop)
L'Homme. Laboratoire d'anthropologie,
Collège de France. Paris. (Homme/Paris)
Hoy es Historia: Revista Bimestral de Histo-
ria Nacional e Iberoamericana. Editorial
Raíces. Montevideo. (Hoy Hist.)

Ibero-Americana: Nordic Journal of Latin
American Studies. Institute of Latin Ameri-
can Studies, Univ. of Stockholm. (Ibero-
Am./Stockholm)
Ibero-Amerikanisches Archiv. Ibero-Amerika-
nisches Institut. Berlin. (Ibero-Am. Arch.)
Ideas y Valores. Instituto de Filosofía y Letras,
Univ. Nacional. Bogotá. (Ideas Valores)
Imago Mundi: the Journal of the International
Society for the History of Cartography.
King's College. London. (Imago Mundi/
London)
Integración Latinoamericana. Instituto para
la Integración de América Latina. Buenos
Aires. (Integr. Latinoam.)
Inter-American Music Review. Robert Steven-
son. Los Angeles, Calif. (Inter-Am. Music
Rev.)
Interciencia. Asociación Interciencia. Cara-
cas. (Interciencia/Caracas)
The International History Review. Univ. of
Toronto Press. Downsview, Ontario, Can-
ada. (Int. Hist. Rev.)
International Quarterly. International Quar-
terly, Inc. Tallahassee, Fla. (Int. Q.)
International Social Science Journal. Black-
well Publishers. Oxford, England. (Int. Soc.
Sci. J.)
Investigaciones y Ensayos. Academia Nacio-
nal de la Historia. Buenos Aires. (Invest.
Ens.)

Islas. Univ. Central de Las Villas. Santa Clara, Cuba. (Islas/Santa Clara)

Itinerario. Leiden Centre for the History of European Expansion. Leiden, The Netherlands. (Itinerario/Leiden)

Jahrbuch für Geschichte von Staat, Wirtschaft und Gesellschaft Lateinamerikas. Köln, Germany. (Jahrb. Gesch.)

The Jamaican Historical Review. The Jamaican Historical Society. Kingston. (Jam. Hist. Rev.)

Journal of African History. Cambridge Univ. Press. London. (J. Afr. Hist.)

Journal of Anthropological Research. Univ. of New Mexico. Albuquerque, N.M. (J. Anthropol. Res.)

The Journal of Caribbean History. Caribbean Univ. Press. St. Lawrence, Barbados. (J. Caribb. Hist.)

Journal of Caribbean Studies. Assn. of Caribbean Studies. Coral Gables, Fla. (J. Caribb. Stud.)

Journal of Church and State. J.M. Dawson Studies in Church and State, Baylor Univ., Waco, Tex. (J. Church State)

The Journal of Decorative and Propaganda Arts. Wolfson Foundation of Decorative and Propaganda Arts. Miami, Fla. (J. Decor. Propag. Arts)

The Journal of Economic History. Economic History Assn.; Univ. of Kansas. Lawrence. (J. Econ. Hist.)

Journal of Interamerican Studies and World Affairs. Institute of Interamerican Studies, Univ. of Miami. Coral Gables, Fla. (J. Interam. Stud. World Aff.)

The Journal of Interdisciplinary History. The MIT Press. Cambridge, Mass. (J. Interdiscip. Hist.)

Journal of Latin American Studies. Centers or Institutes of Latin American Studies at the Universities of Cambridge, Glasgow, Liverpool, London, and Oxford. Cambridge Univ. Press. London. (J. Lat. Am. Stud.)

The Journal of Mississippi History. Mississippi Historical Society; Mississippi Dept. of Archives and History. Jackson, Miss. (J. Miss. Hist.)

Journal of Social History. Carnegie Mellon Univ., Pittsburgh, Penn. (J. Soc. Hist.)

La Mei Shi Yan Jiu Tong Xun [Latin American History Newsletter]. s.n., Beijing?. (La Mei Shi Yan Jiu Tong Xun)

Laboratorio de Arte: Revista de Departmento de Historia del Arte. Univ. de Sevilla. Sevilla, Spain. (Lab. Arte)

Lateinamerika. Institut für Iberoamerika-Kunde. Hamburg, Germany. (Lateinamerika/Hamburg)

Latin American Music Review. Univ. of Texas. Austin. (Lat. Am. Music Rev.)

Latin American Perspectives. Univ. of California. Newbury Park, Calif. (Lat. Am. Perspect.)

Latin American Research Review. Latin American Research Review Board. Univ. of New Mexico, Albuquerque, N.M. (LARR)

Latin American Theatre Review. Univ. of Kansas, Center of Latin American Studies. Lawrence, Kan. (Lat. Am. Theatre Rev.)

The Latino Review of Books. State Univ. of New York at Albany (SUNY), Center for Latino, Latin American, and Caribbean Studies (CELAC). Albany, N.Y. (Lat. Rev. Books)

Letterature d'America. Dipartimento di Studi Americani, Univ. di Roma; Bulzoni Editore. Rome. (Lett. Am./Rome)

Li Shi Yan Jiu [Chinese History Research]. Renmin Zhubanshe [People's Publishing House]. Beijing. (Li Shi Yan Jiu)

Louisiana History. Louisiana Historical Assn., Lafayette, La. (La. Hist.)

Lua Nova. Editora Brasiliense. São Paulo. (Lua Nova)

Luso-Brazilian Review. Univ. of Wisconsin Press. Madison, Wis. (Luso-Braz. Rev.)

MACLAS Latin American Essays. Middle Atlantic Council of Latin American Studies. New Brunswick, N.J. (MACLAS Lat. Am. Essays)

Maguaré. Depto. de Antropología, Univ. Nacional de Colombia. Bogotá. (Maguaré/Bogotá)

Mapocho. Biblioteca Nacional. Santiago. (Mapocho/Santiago)

Mélanges de la Casa de Velázquez. Ecole des hautes études hispaniques. Paris. (Mélanges/Paris)

Mélanges de l'Ecole française de Rome: Italie et Méditerranée. L'Ecole française de Rome. Rome. (MEFRIM)

Memoria Americana. Instituto de Ciencias Antropológicas, Facultad de Filosofía y Letras, Univ. de Buenos Aires. (Mem. Am.)

Memoria: Boletín de CEMOS. Centro de Estudios del Movimiento Obrero y Socialista. México. (Memoria/CEMOS)

Memorias de la Academia Mexicana de la Historia. México. (Mem. Acad. Mex. Hist.)

Mesoamérica. Centro de Investigaciones Regionales de Mesoamérica. Antigua, Guatemala. (Mesoamérica/Antigua)

Mexican Studies/Estudios Mexicanos. Univ. of California, Berkeley. (Mex. Stud.)

MLA International Bibliography. H.W. Wilson. New York. (MLA Int. Bibliogr./CD)

MLN. Modern Language Notes. Johns Hopkins Univ. Press. Baltimore, Md. (MLN/Baltimore)

Nação e Defesa. Estudos Políticos do Gabinete de Estudos e Planeamento do Estado-Maior do Exército. Lisboa. (Nação Def.)

Nariz del Diablo. Centro de Investigaciones y Estudios Socio-Económicos. Quito. (Nariz Diablo)

National Geographic Magazine. National Geographic Society. Washington. (Natl. Geogr. Mag.)

New Mexico Historical Review. Historical Society of New Mexico; Univ. of New Mexico. Albuquerque, N.M. (N.M. Hist. Rev.)

New Scholar. Univ. of California, Committee on Hispanic Civilization and Center for Chicano Studies. Santa Barbara. (New Sch.)

New West Indian Guide/Nieuwe West Indische Gids. KITLV Press. Leiden, The Netherlands. (NWIG)

The New York Review of Books. New York. (N.Y. Rev. Books)

Newsletter of the International Hispanic Study Group. Dartmouth College, Dept. of Music. Hanover, N.H. (Newsl. Int. Hisp. Study Group)

Notas Históricas y Geográficas. Univ. de Playa Ancha. Valparaiso, Chile. (Notas Hist. Geogr.)

Notícia Bibliográfica e Histórica. Depto. de História, Pontifícia Univ. Católica de Campinas. Campinas, Brazil. (Not. Bibliogr. Hist.)

Nuestra Historia. Fundación Nuestra Historia. Buenos Aires. (Nuestra Hist./Buenos Aires)

Nuestra Historia. Litografía Litota. Caracas. (Nuestra Hist./Caracas)

Nueva Revista de Filología Hispánica. El Colegio de México. México. (Nueva Rev. Filol. Hisp.)

Op. Cit.: Boletín del Centro de Investigaciones Históricas. Depto. de Historia, Facultad de Humanidades, Univ. de Puerto Rico. Río Piedras. (Op. Cit./Río Piedras)

OSO. Stichtring Instituut ter Bevordering van de Surinamistick (IBS) te Nijmegen. Nijmegen, The Netherlands. (OSO/Netherlands)

La Palabra y el Hombre. Univ. Veracruzana. Xalapa, Mexico. (Palabra Hombre)

Past and Present. London. (Past Present)

Pensamiento Iberoamericano. Instituto de Cooperación Iberoamericano (ICI) de España; Comisión Económica para América Latina y el Caribe (CEPAL). Madrid. (Pensam. Iberoam.)

The Philosophical Forum. Dept. of Philosophy, Baruch College, City Univ. of New York. New York. (Philos. Forum)

Plantation Society in the Americas. Univ. of New Orleans. (Plant. Soc. Am.)

Plural. Excelsior Compañía Editorial. México. (Plural/México)

Procesos. Corporación Editora Nacional. Quito. (Procesos/Quito)

Publicaciones del Instituto de Estudios Iberoamericanos. Instituto de Estudios Iberamericanos. Buenos Aires. (Publ. Inst. Estud. Iberoam.)

Quaderni. Istituto Italiano di Cultura; Istituto Cultural Italo-Brasileiro. São Paulo. (Quaderni/São Paulo)

Quaderni Ibero-Americani. Associazione per i Rapporti Culturali con la Spagna, il Portogallo e l'America Latina. Torino, Italy. (Quad. Ibero-Am.)

Radical History Review. Mid-Atlantic Radical Historians' Organization. New York. (Radic. Hist. Rev.)

Razón y Fe. La Compañía de Jesús. Madrid. (Razón Fe)

Reflexão. Pontifícia Univ. Católica de Campinas. São Paulo. (Reflexão/São Paulo)

Relaciones. El Colegio de Michoacán. Zamora, Mexico. (Relaciones/Zamora)

Religión y Cultura. Madrid. (Relig. Cult.)

Res. Peabody Museum of Archaeology and Ethnology, Harvard Univ., Cambridge, Mass. (Res/Harvard)

Res Gesta. Instituto de Historia, Facultad de Derecho y Ciencias Sociales, Univ. Católica Argentina. Rosario, Argentina. (Res Gesta)

Revista Andina. Centro Bartolomé de las Casas. Cusco, Peru. (Rev. Andin.)

Revista Brasileira de Filosofia. Instituto Brasileiro de Filosofia. São Paulo. (Rev. Bras. Filos.)

Revista Brasileira de História. Associação Nacional dos Professores Universitários de História (ANPUH). São Paulo. (Rev. Bras. Hist.)

Revista Brasileira de Música. Escola de Música da Univ. Federal do Rio de Janeiro. Rio de Janeiro. (Rev. Bras. Mús.)

Revista Canadiense de Estudios Hispánicos. Asociación Canadiense de Hispanistas; Univ. of Toronto. Toronto, Canada. (Rev. Can. Estud. Hisp.)

Revista Chilena de Historia y Geografía. Sociedad Chilena de Historia y Geografía. Santiago. (Rev. Chil. Hist. Geogr.)

Revista Chilena de Humanidades. Facultad de Filosofía, Humanidades y Educación, Univ. de Chile. Santiago. (Rev. Chil. Humanid.)

Revista Chilena de Literatura. Univ. de Chile, Depto. de Literatura. Santiago. (Rev. Chil. Lit.)

Revista Ciclos en la Historia, Economía y la Sociedad. Fundación de Investigaciones Históricas, Económicas y Sociales, Facultad de Ciencias Económicas, Univ. de Buenos Aires. Buenos Aires. (Rev. Ciclos)

Revista Colombiana de Antropología. Ministerio de Educación Nacional, Instituto Colombiano de Antropología. Bogotá. (Rev. Colomb. Antropol.)

Revista Complutense de Historia de América. Facultad de Geografía e Historia, Univ. Complutense de Madrid. (Rev. Complut. Hist. Am.)

Revista Cubana de Ciencias Sociales. Centro de Estudios Filosóficos, Academia de Ciencias de Cuba. La Habana. (Rev. Cuba. Cienc. Soc.)

Revista da Sociedade Brasileira de Música Contemporânea. Sociedade Brasileira de Música Contemporânea. São Paulo. (Rev. Soc. Bras. Mús. Contemp.)

Revista de Antropologia. Univ. de São Paulo, Faculdade de Filosofia, Letras e Ciências Humanas; Associação Brasileira de Antropologia. São Paulo. (Rev. Antropol./São Paulo)

Revista de Ciência Política. Fundação Getúlio Vargas. Rio de Janeiro. (Rev. Ciênc. Polít./Rio de Janeiro)

Revista de Ciências Históricas. Univ. Portucalense. Porto, Portugal. (Rev. Ciênc. Hist.)

Revista de Ciencias Sociales. Univ. de Puerto Rico, Colegio de Ciencias Sociales. Río Piedras. (Rev. Cienc. Soc./Río Piedras)

Revista de Ciencias Sociales. Facultad de Derecho y Ciencias Sociales, Univ. de Valparaíso. Chile. (Rev. Cienc. Soc./Valparaíso)

Revista de Crítica Literaria Latinoamericana. Latinoamericana Editores. Lima. (Rev. Crít. Lit. Latinoam.)

Revista de Filosofía. Univ. Iberoamericana, Depto. de Filosofía; Asociación Fray Alonso de la Veracruz. México. (Rev. Filos./México)

Revista de Filosofía de la Universidad de Costa Rica. Editorial de la Universidad de Costa Rica. San José. (Rev. Filos. Univ. Costa Rica)

Revista de Filosofía Latinoamericano y Ciencias Sociales. Asociación de Filosofía Latinoamericana y Ciencias Sociales. Buenos Aires. (Rev. Filos. Latinoam. Cienc. Soc.)

Revista de Historia. Depto. de Ciencias Históricas y Sociales, Univ. de Concepción, Chile. (Rev. Hist./Concepción)

Revista de Historia. Univ. Nacional de Costa Rica, Escuela de Historia. Heredia, Costa Rica. (Rev. Hist./Heredia)

Revista de Historia. Instituto de Historia de Nicaragua. Managua. (Rev. Hist./Managua)

Revista de Historia Americana y Argentina. Univ. Nacional de Cuyo, Instituto de Historia. Mendoza, Argentina. (Rev. Hist. Am. Argent.)

Revista de Historia de América. Instituto Panamericano de Geografía e Historia, Comisión de Historia. México. (Rev. Hist. Am.)

Revista de Historia de las Ideas. Instituto Panamericano de Geografía e Historia; Editorial Casa de la Cultura Ecuatoriana. Quito. (Rev. Hist. Ideas)

Revista de Historia Naval. Instituto de Historia y Cultura Naval Armada Española. Madrid. (Rev. Hist. Naval)

Revista de Indias. Consejo Superior de Investigaciones Científicas, Instituto Gonzalo Fernández de Oviedo. Madrid. (Rev. Indias)

Revista de la Biblioteca Nacional José Martí. La Habana. (Rev. Bibl. Nac. José Martí)

Revista de la Junta Provincial de Historia de Córdoba. Córdoba, Argentina. (Rev. Junta Prov. Hist. Córdoba)

Revista de Musicología. Sociedad Española de Musicología. Madrid. (Rev. Musicol./Madrid)

Revista de Occidente. Madrid. (Rev. Occident.)

Revista del Archivo Nacional de Historia, Sección del Azuay. Casa de la Cultura Ecuatoriana, Núcleo del Azuay. Cuenca, Ecuador. (Rev. Arch. Nac. Hist. Azuay)

La Revista del Centro de Estudios Avanzados de Puerto Rico y el Caribe. San Juan. (Rev. Cent. Estud. Av.)

Revista del Instituto de Cultura Puertorriqueña. San Juan. (Rev. Inst. Cult. Puertorriq.)

Revista del Instituto de Investigación Musicológica Carlos Vega. Pontifícia Univ. Católica de Argentina, Facultad de Artes y Ciencias Musicales, Instituto de Investigación Musicológica Carlos Vega. Buenos Aires. (Rev. Inst. Invest. Musicol. Carlos Vega)

Revista del Pensamiento Centroamericano. Centro de Investigaciones y Actividades Culturales. Managua. (Rev. Pensam. Centroam.)

Revista do Departamento de História. Univ. Federal de Minas Gerais. Belo Horizonte, Brazil. (Rev. Dep. Hist./Belo Horizonte)

Revista do Instituto Histórico e Geográfico de São Paulo. São Paulo. (Rev. Inst. Hist. Geogr. São Paulo)

Revista do Instituto Histórico e Geográfico Paraibano. Univ. Federal da Paraiba. João Pessoa, Brazil. (Rev. Inst. Hist. Geogr. Para.)

Revista Ecuatoriana de Historia Económica. Banco Central del Ecuador, Centro de Investigación y Cultura. Quito. (Rev. Ecuat. Hist. Econ.)

Revista Española de Antropología Americana. Facultad de Geografía e Historia. Univ. Complutense de Madrid. (Rev. Esp. Antropol. Am.)

Revista Española de Estudios Norteamericanos. Centro de Estudios Norteamericanos, Univ. de Alcalá de Henares. Spain. (Rev. Esp. Estud. Norteam.)

Revista Europea de Estudios Latinoamericanos y del Caribe = European Review of Latin American and Caribbean Studies. Center for Latin American Research and Documentation; Royal Institute of Linguistics and Anthropology. Amsterdam. (Rev. Eur.)

Revista Iberoamericana. Instituto Internacional de Literatura Iberoamericana; Univ. de Pittsburgh. Pittsburgh, Penn. (Rev. Iberoam.)

Revista Internacional de Sociología. Consejo Superior de Investigaciones Científicas. Instituto de Economía y Geografía Aplicadas. Madrid. (Rev. Int. Sociol.)

Revista Jurídica de la Universidad de Puerto Rico. Escuela de Derecho, Univ. de Puerto Rico. Río Piedras. (Rev. Juríd. Univ. P.R.)

Revista Mexicana de Sociología. Instituto de Investigaciones Sociales, Univ. Nacional Autónoma de México. México. (Rev. Mex. Sociol.)

Revista Musical Chilena. Univ. de Chile, Facultad de Ciencias y Artes Musicales y de la Representación. Santiago. (Rev. Music. Chil.)

Revista Nacional. Ministerio de Instrucción Pública. Montevideo. (Rev. Nac./Montevideo)

Revista Paraguaya de Sociología. Centro Paraguayo de Estudios Sociológicos. Asunción. (Rev. Parag. Sociol.)

Revista/Review Interamericana. Inter-American Univ. Press. Hato Rey, Puerto Rico. (Rev. Rev. Interam.)

Revista UNITAS. Unión Nacional de Instituciones para el Trabajo de Acción Social. La Paz. (Rev. UNITAS)

Revista USP. Coordenadoria de Comunicação Social (CCS), Univ. de São Paulo. (Rev. USP)

Revue d'Auvergne. Société des Amis de l'Université de Clermont. Clermont-Ferrand, France. (Rev. Auvergne)

Revue de la Société haïtienne d'histoire et de géographie. Port-au-Prince. (Rev. Soc. haïti.)

Revue française d'histoire d'Outre-mer. Société de l'histoire des colonies françaises. Paris. (Rev. fr. hist. Outre-mer)

Revue historique. Presses Univ. de France. Paris. (Rev. hist./Paris)

Ruralia: Revista Argentina de Estudios Agrarios. FLACSO; Ediciones Imago Mundi. Buenos Aires. (Ruralia/Buenos Aires)

Santiago. Univ. de Oriente. Santiago, Cuba. (Santiago/Cuba)

Sarance. Instituto Otavaleño de Antropología. Otavalo, Ecuador. (Sarance/Otavalo)

SECOLAS Annals. Southeastern Conference on Latin American Studies; West Georgia College. Carrollton, Ga. (SECOLAS Ann.)

Secuencia. Instituto Mora. México. (Secuencia/México)

Sefárdica. Centro de Investigación y Difusión de la Cultura Sefardí. Buenos Aires. (Sefárdica/Buenos Aires)

Senderos. Biblioteca Nacional de Colombia. Bogotá. (Senderos/Bogotá)

Siglo XIX. Facultad de Filosofía y Letras, Univ. Autónoma de Nuevo León. Monterrey, Mexico. (Siglo XIX)

Slavery & Abolition. Frank Cass & Co., Ltd., London. (Slavery Abolit.)

Social and Economic Studies. Univ. of the West Indies, Institute of Social and Economic Research. Mona, Jamaica. (Soc. Econ. Stud.)

Social Compass. The International Catholic Institute for Social-Ecclesiastical Research. The Hague. (Soc. Compass)

Social History. Methuen. London. (Soc. Hist./London)

Southwestern Historical Quarterly. The Texas State Historical Assn., Austin, Tex. (Southwest. Hist. Q.)

Studi Emigrazione. Centro Studi Emigrazione. Rome. (Stud. Emigr.)

Studia Historica: Historia Moderna. Univ. de Salamanca. Salamanca, Spain. (Stud. Hist. Hist. Mod.)

SWI Forum voor Kunst, Kultuur en Wetenschop. De Stichting. Paramaribo, Suriname. (SWI Forum)

Tierra Firme. Caracas. (Tierra Firme)

Tijdschrift voor Geschiedenis. P. Noordhoff. Groningen, Netherlands. (Tijdschr. Geschied.)

Todo es Historia. Buenos Aires. (Todo es Hist.)

Translation. The Translation Center, Columbia Univ., New York. (Translation/Columbia)

Translation Review. Univ. of Texas at Dallas. Richardson. (Transl. Rev.)

Tri-Quarterly. Northwestern Univ., Evanston, Ill. (Tri-Quarterly/Evanston)

UCLA Historical Journal. Univ. of California, Dept. of History. Los Angeles. (UCLA Hist. J.)

UNISA Latin American Report. Univ. of South Africa. Pretoria. (UNISA Lat. Am. Rep.)

La Universidad. Univ. Nacional del Litoral. Santa Fe, Argentina. (Universidad/Santa Fe)

Universum. Univ. de Talca. Talca, Chile. (Universum/Talca)

Vuelta. México. (Vuelta/México)

Wampum. Archeologisch Centrum. Leiden, The Netherlands. (Wampum/Leiden)

Wani: Una Revista sobre la Costa Atlántica. Centro Investigaciones y Documentación de la Costa Atlántica. Managua. (Wani/Managua)

Yaxkin. Instituto Hondureño de Antropología e Historia. Tegucigalpa. (Yaxkin/Tegucigalpa)

Yearbook. Conference of Latin Americanist Geographers; Ball State Univ., Muncie, Ind. (Yearbook/CLAG)

Yumtzilob: Tijdschrift over de Americas. Archeologisch Centrum. Leiden, The Netherlands. (Yumtzilob/Leiden)

ABBREVIATION LIST OF JOURNALS INDEXED

For journal titles listed by full title, see *Title List of Journals Indexed*

Acta Lit.   Acta Literaria. Instituto de Lenguas, Univ. de Concepción. Concepción, Chile.

Actas Am.   Actas Americanas. Univ. de La Serena, Facultad de Humanidades. La Serena, Chile.

Afro-Hisp. Rev.   Afro-Hispanic Review. Univ. of Missouri-Columbia. Columbia, Missouri.

Agric. Hist.   Agricultural History. Agricultural History Society. Univ. of Calif. Press. Berkeley.

Allpanchis/Cusco.   Allpanchis. Instituto de Pastoral Andina. Cusco, Peru.

Am. Anthropol.   American Anthropologist. American Anthropological Assn., Washington.

Am. Econ. Rev.   The American Economic Review. American Economic Assn., Evanston, Ill.

Am. Hist. Rev.   The American Historical Review. American Historical Assn., Washington.

Am. Indíg.   América Indígena. Instituto Indigenista Interamericano. México.

Am. Merid.   América Meridional. Sociedad Regional de Ciencias Humanas. Montevideo.

Am. Negra.   América Negra. Pontificia Univ. Javeriana. Bogotá.

Am. Sociol. Rev.   American Sociological Review. American Sociological Assn., Washington.

Americas/Francisc.   The Americas. Academy of American Franciscan History. Washington.

An. Acad. Nac. Cienc. Econ.   Anales de la Academia Nacional de Ciencias Económicas. Buenos Aires.

An. Arqueol. Etnol.   Anales de Arqueología y Etnología. Univ. Nacional de Cuyo, Facultad de Filosofía y Letras. Mendoza, Argentina.

An. Hist. Contemp.   Anales de Historia Contemporánea. Cátedra de Historia Contemporánea, Univ. de Murcia. Murcia, Spain.

An. Inst. Invest. Estét.   Anales del Instituto de Investigaciones Estéticas. Univ. Nacional Autónoma de México. México.

An. Mus. Am.   Anales del Museo de América. Museo de América. Madrid.

An. Univ. Chile.   Anales de la Universidad de Chile. Santiago.

An. Valent.   Anales Valentinos: Revista de Filosofía y Teología. Facultad de Teología San Vicente Ferrer. Valencia, Spain.

Anales/Göteborg.   Anales. Instituto Iberoamericano, Univ. de Gotemburgo. Göteborg, Sweden.

Anc. Mesoam.   Ancient Mesoamerica. Cambridge Univ. Press. Cambridge, England.

Ann. hist. Révolut. fr.   Annales historiques de la Révolution française. Société des Études Robespierristes; Firmin-Didot. Reims, Paris.

Annales/Paris.   Annales. Centre national de la recherche scientifique de la VIe Section de l'Ecole pratique des hautes études. Paris.

ANPOCS BIB.   Boletim Informativo e Bibliográfico de Ciências Sociais: BIB. Associação Nacional de Pós-Graduação e Pesquisa em Ciências Sociais. Rio de Janeiro.

Anthropol. Q. Anthropological Quarterly. Catholic Univ. of America, Catholic Anthropological Conference. Washington.

Anu. Cent. Estud. Martianos. Anuario del Centro de Estudios Martianos. Centro de Estudios Martianos. La Habana.

Anu. Colomb. Hist. Soc. Cult. Anuario Colombiano de Historia Social y de la Cultura. Univ. Nacional de Colombia, Facultad de Ciencias Humanas, Depto. de Historia. Bogotá.

Anu. Dep. Hist./Madrid. Anuario del Departmento de Historia. Depto. de Historia, Univ. Complutense de Madrid.

Anu. Estud. Am. Anuario de Estudios Americanos. Consejo Superior de Investigaciones Científicas; Univ. de Sevilla, Escuela de Estudios Hispano-Americanos. Sevilla, Spain.

Anu. Etnol./Habana. Anuario de Etnología. Academia de Ciencias de Cuba; Editorial Academia. La Habana.

Anu. Hist. Iglesia Chile. Anuario de Historia de la Iglesia en Chile. Seminario Pontificio Mayor. Santiago.

Anu. IEHS. Anuario IEHS. Univ. Nacional del Centro de la Provincia de Buenos Aires, Instituto de Estudios Histórico-Sociales. Tandil, Argentina.

Anu. Mus. Inconfidência. Anuario do Museu da Inconfidência. Museo Inconfidência. Ouro Preto, Brazil.

Anu. Veritas. Anuario Veritas. Univ. Regiomontana, Depto. de Publicaciones. Monterrey, Mexico.

Anuario/Rosario. Anuario. Univ. Nacional de Rosario, Escuela de Historia. Argentina.

Anuario/Sucre. Anuario. Talleres Gráficos Túpac Katari. Archivo y Biblioteca Nacionales de Bolivia. Sucre.

Apunt. Filos. Apuntes Filosóficos. Escuela de Filosofía, Univ. Central de Venezuela. Caracas.

Apuntes/Lima. Apuntes. Univ. del Pacífico, Centro de Investigación. Lima.

Arbor/Madrid. Arbor. Consejo Superior de Investigaciones Científicas. Madrid.

Arch. Francisc. Hist. Archivum Franciscanum Historicum. Collegio S. Bonaventura. Rome.

Arch. Ibero-Am. Archivo Ibero-Americano. Revista de Estudios Históricos. Los Padres Franciscanos. Madrid.

Arch. sci. soc. relig. Archives de sciences sociales des religions. Centre nationale de la recherche scientifique. Paris.

Archaeology/New York. Archaeology. Archaeology Institute of America. New York.

Art J. Art Journal. The College Art Assn., New York.

ARTEunesp. ARTEunesp. Univ. Estadual Paulista. São Paulo.

ASCAP Playback. ASCAP Playback. American Society of Composers, Authors & Publishers. New York.

Bol. Acad. Chil. Hist. Boletín de la Academia Chilena de la Historia. Santiago.

Bol. Acad. Nac. Hist./Buenos Aires. Boletín de la Academia Nacional de la Historia. Buenos Aires.

Bol. Acad. Nac. Hist./Caracas. Boletín de la Academia Nacional de la Historia. Caracas.

Bol. Acad. Nac. Hist./Quito. Boletín de la Academia Nacional de Historia. Quito.

Bol. Am. Boletín Americanista. Univ. de Barcelona, Facultad de Geografía e Historia, Depto. de Historia de América. Barcelona.

Bol. Arch. Nac. Hist. Boletín del Archivo Nacional de Historia. Quito.

Bol. Bibl. Nac. Boletín de la Biblioteca Nacional. Biblioteca Nacional. Lima.

Bol. Cent. Invest. Hist. Boletín del Centro de Investigaciones Históricas. Facultad de Humanidades, Univ. de Puerto Rico. Río Piedras.

Bol. Cult. Bibliogr. Boletín Cultural y Bibliográfico. Banco de la República; Biblioteca Luis-Angel Arango. Bogotá.

Bol. Fuentes Hist. Econ. Méx. Boletín de Fuentes para la Historia Económica de México. Centro de Estudios Históricos, El Colegio de México. México.

Bol. Inst. Hist. Ravignani. Boletín del Instituto de Historia Argentina y Americana Dr. Emilio Ravignani. Facultad de Filosofía y Letras, Univ. de Buenos Aires.

Bol. Inst. Riva-Agüero. Boletín del Instituto Riva-Agüero. Pontificia Univ. Católica del Perú. Lima.

Bol. Lima. Boletín de Lima. Revista Cultural Científica. Lima.

Bol. Nicar. Bibliogr. Doc. Boletín Nicaragüense de Bibliografía y Documentación. Biblioteca, Banco Central de Nicaragua. Managua.

Brasil/Porto Alegre. Brasil = Brazil. Pontifícia Univ. Católica do Rio Grande do Sul. Porto Alegre, Brazil.

Bull. Cent. hist. atl. Bulletin du Centre d'histoire des espaces atlantiques. Talence-Cedex, France.

Bull. hisp./Bordeaux. Bulletin hispanique. Univ. de Bordeaux; Centre national de la recherche scientifique. Bordeaux, France.

Bull. Inst. fr. étud. andin. Bulletin de l'Institut français d'études andines. Lima.

Bull. Lat. Am. Res. Bulletin of Latin American Research. Society for Latin American Studies. Oxford, England.

Bull. Soc. hist. Guadeloupe. Bulletin de la Société d'histoire de la Guadeloupe. Archives départamentales avec le concours du Conseil général de la Guadeloupe. Basse-Terre, Guadeloupe.

Bus. Hist. Rev. Business History Review. Harvard Univ. Graduate School of Business Administration. Boston, Mass.

Cah. Am. lat. Cahiers des Amériques latines. Paris.

Cah. patrim. Les cahiers du patrimoine. Bureau du patrimoine du Conseil régional de la Martinique. Fort-de-France.

Can. J. Afr. Stud. Canadian Journal of African Studies. Assn. of African Studies. Ottawa, Canada.

Can. J. Hist. Canadian Journal of History. Univ. of Saskatchewan. Saskatoon, Canada.

Caravelle/Toulouse. Caravelle. Cahiers du monde hispanique et luso-brésilien. Univ. de Toulouse, Institute d'études hispaniques, hispano-americaines et luso-brésiliennes. Toulouse, France.

Caribb. Q. Caribbean Quarterly. Univ. of the West Indies. Mona, Jamaica.

Caribb. Stud. Caribbean Studies. Univ. of Puerto Rico, Institute of Caribbean Studies. Río Piedras.

Caribena/Martinique. Caribena: cahiers d'études américanistes de la Caraïbe. Centre d'études et de recherches archéologiques (CERA). Martinique.

CHELA. Cuadernos para la Historia de la Evangelización en América Latina: CHELA. Centro Bartolomé de las Casas. Cusco, Peru.

Chemins crit. Chemins critiques: revue haïtiano-caraïbéenne. Société sciences-arts-littérature. Port-au-Prince, Haiti.

Ciênc. Cult. Ciência e Cultura. Sociedade Brasileira para o Progresso da Ciência. São Paulo.

Cienc. Hoy. Ciencia Hoy. Asociación Ciencia Hoy; Morgan Antártica. Buenos Aires.

Círculo/Verona. Círculo: Revista de Cultura. Círculo de Cultura Panamericana. Verona, N.J.

CLAHR/Albuquerque. Colonial Latin American Historical Review. Spanish Colonial Research Center, Univ. of New Mexico. Albuquerque.

Colon. Lat. Am. Rev. Colonial Latin American Review. Simon H. Rifkind Center for the Humanities, Dept. of Romance Languages, City College of New York. New York.

Comp. Stud. Soc. Hist. Comparative Studies in Society and History. Society for the Comparative Study of Society and History; Cambridge Univ. Press. London.

Comun. Soc. Comunicação e Sociedade. Instituto Metodista do Ensino Superior. São Paulo.

Conjonction/Port-au-Prince. Conjonction. Bulletin de l'Institut français d'Haïti. Port-au-Prince.

Critique/St. Paul. Critique: Journal of Critical Studies of the Middle East. Center for Critical Studies of the Middle East. St. Paul, Minn.

Cuad. Am. Cuadernos Americanos. Editorial Cultura. México.

Cuad. CLAEH. Cuadernos del CLAEH. Centro Latinoamericano de Economía Humana. Montevideo.

Cuad. Hispanoam. Cuadernos Hispanoamericanos. Instituto de Cultura Hispánica. Madrid.

Cuad. Hist./Córdoba. Cuadernos de Historia. Instituto de Historia del Derecho y de las Ideas Políticas. Córdoba, Argentina.

Cuad. Hist./Santiago. Cuadernos de Historia. Univ. de Chile, Facultad de Humanidades y Educación, Depto. de Ciencias Históricas. Santiago.

Cuad. Sur/Buenos Aires. Cuadernos del Sur. Revista Cultural de Problemas Actuales. Buenos Aires.

Cuba. Stud. Cuban Studies. Univ. of Pittsburgh, Center for Latin American Studies. Pittsburgh, Penn.

Curr. Hist. Current History. Philadelphia, Penn.

Cuyo/Mendoza. Cuyo: Anuario de Historia del Pensamiento Argentino. Univ. Nacional de Cuyo, Instituto de Filosofía, Sección de Historia del Pensamiento Argentino. Mendoza, Argentina.

Dados/Rio de Janeiro. Dados. Instituto Univ. de Pesquisas. Rio de Janeiro.

Desarro. Econ. Desarrollo Económico. Instituto de Desarrollo Económico y Social. Buenos Aires.

Diogenes/Philosophy. Diogenes. International Council for Philosophy and Humanistic Studies (Paris); Berg Publishers. Oxford, England.

Econ. Soc. Hist. Neth. Economic and Social History in the Netherlands. Nederlandsch Economisch-Historisch Archief. Amsterdam.

Economía/Lima. Economía. Depto. de Economía, Pontificia Univ. Católica del Perú. Lima.

Económica/La Plata. Económica. Univ. Nacional de La Plata, Facultad de Ciencias Económicas, Instituto de Investigaciones Económicas. La Plata, Argentina.

Ecos/Santo Domingo. Ecos. Instituto de Historia, Univ. Autónoma de Santo Domingo.

Espace Caraïbe. Espace Caraïbe. Maison des Pays Ibériques, Univ. M. de Montaigne, Bordeaux, France; Centre d'Études et de Recherches Caraïbéennes, Univ. des Antilles et de la Guyane, Pointe-à-Pitre, Guadeloupe.

Estud. Cienc. Let. Estudios de Ciencias y Letras. Instituto de Filosofía, Ciencias y Letras. Montevideo.

Estud. Cult. Contemp. Estudios sobre las Culturas Contemporáneas. Centro Universitario de Investigaciones Sociales, Univ. de Colima. México.

Estud. Cult. Maya. Estudios de Cultura Maya. Centro de Estudios Mayas, Univ. Nacional Autónoma de México. México.

Estud. Cult. Náhuatl. Estudios de Cultura Náhuatl. Instituto de Investigaciones Históricas, Univ. Nacional Autónoma de México. México.

Estud. Filol. Estudios Filológicos. Univ. Austral de Chile, Facultad de Filosofía y Humanidades. Valdivia, Chile.

Estud. Hist. Mod. Contemp. Méx. Estudios de Historia Moderna y Contemporánea de México. Univ. Nacional Autónoma de México. México.

Estud. Hist. Novohisp. Estudios de Historia Novohispana. Univ. Nacional Autónoma de México. México.

Estud. Hist./Rio de Janeiro. Estudos Históricos. Associação de Pesquisa e Documentação Histórica. Rio de Janeiro.

Estud. Hist. Rural. Estudios de Historia Rural. Univ. Nacional de La Plata, Centro de Estudios Histórico-Rurales. La Plata, Argentina.

Estud. Hist. Soc. Econ. Am. Estudios de Historia Social y Económica de América. Univ. de Alcalá de Henares. Madrid.

Estud. Ibero-Am./Porto Alegre. Estudos Ibero-Americanos. Pontifícia Univ. Católica do Rio Grande do Sul, Depto. de História. Porto Alegre, Brazil.

Estud. Jalisc. Estudios Jaliscienses. Univ. de Guadalajara. Guadalajara, Mexico.

Estud. Latinoam./Poland. Estudios Latino-americanos. Academia de Ciencias de Polonia, Instituto de Historia. Wrocław.

Estud. Polít. Econ. Filos. Estudios: Políticos, Económicos, Filosóficos, Culturales del Uruguay. Partido Comunista. Montevideo.

Estud. Soc./Santiago. Estudios Sociales. Corporación de Promoción Universitaria. Santiago.

Estud. Soc./Santo Domingo. Estudios Sociales. Centro de Estudios Sociales Juan Montalvo, SJ. Santo Domingo.

Estudios/Guatemala. Estudios. Instituto de Investigaciones Históricas, Antropológicas, y Arqueológicas, Univ. de San Carlos de Guatemala. Guatemala.

Ethnohistory/Columbus. Ethnohistory: the Bulletin of the Ohio Valley Historic Indian Conference. Columbus, Ohio.

Ethnohistory/Society. Ethnohistory. American Society for Ethnohistory. Duke Univ., Durham, N.C.

Ethnomusicology/Society. Ethnomusicology. Society for Ethnomusicology. Ann Arbor, Mich.

Etud. Guad. Etudes Guadeloupéennes. Association guadeloupéenne de recherches et d'études. Abymes, Guadeloupe.

EURE/Santiago. EURE: Revista Latino-americana de Estudios Urbanos Regionales. Centro de Desarrollo Urbano y Regional, Univ. Católica de Chile. Santiago.

Fénix/Lima. Fénix: Revista de la Biblioteca Nacional del Perú. Biblioteca Nacional. Lima.

Fla. Hist. Q. The Florida Historical Quarterly. The Florida Historical Society. Jacksonville, Fla.

Folk/Copenhagen. Folk: Journal of the Danish Ethnographic Society. Danish Ethnographic Society. Copenhagen.

Franciscanum/Bogotá. Franciscanum. Univ. de San Buenaventura. Bogotá.

Gac. Mus./México. Gaceta Musical. Centro Nacional de Investigación, Documentación e Información Musical Carlos Chávez (CENIDIM). México.

Généal. hist. Caraïbe. Généalogie et histoire de la Caraïbe. Assn. de la généalogie et histoire de la Caraïbe. Le Pecq, France.

Guyana Hist. J. Guyana Historical Journal. History Society, Dept. of History, Univ. of Guyana. Georgetown.

HAHR. Hispanic American Historical Review. Conference on Latin American History of the American Historical Assn.; Duke Univ. Press. Durham, N.C.

HAPI/CD. Hispanic American Periodicals Index: HAPI (CD-ROM). UCLA Latin American Center. Los Angeles; National Information Services Corporation (NISC). Baltimore, Md.

Herencia/San José. Herencia. Programa de Rescate y Revitalización del Patrimonio Cultural. San José.

Heterofonía/México. Heterofonía. México.

Hisp. Sacra. Hispania Sacra: Revista de Historia Eclesiástica de España. Centro de Estudios Históricos, Instituto Enrique Flórez. Madrid.

Hispamérica/Gaithersburg. Hispamérica. Gaithersburg, Md.

Hispania/Madrid. Hispania. Instituto Jerónimo Zurita, Consejo Superior de Investigaciones Científicas. Madrid.

Hist. Cult./Lima. Historia y Cultura. Museo Nacional de Historia. Lima.

Hist. Gaz. History Gazette. Univ. of Guyana, History Society. Turkeyen, Guyana.

Hist. Graf. Historia y Grafía. Depto. de Historia, Univ. Iberoamericana. México.

Hist. Mex. Historia Mexicana. Colegio de México. México.

Hist. Nuestra. Historia Nuestra. Concepción, Chile.

Hist. Relig. History of Religions. Univ. of Chicago. Chicago, Ill.

Hist. Res./Oxford. Historical Research. Institute of Historical Research. Oxford, England.

Hist. Soc./Río Piedras. Historia y Sociedad. Depto. de Historia, Univ. de Puerto Rico. Río Piedras.

Hist. Workshop. History Workshop. Ruskin College, Oxford Univ., Oxford, England.

Historia/Santiago. Historia. Univ. Católica de Chile. Instituto de Historia. Santiago.

História/São Paulo. História. Fundação para o Desenvolvimento da Univ. Estadual Paulista, Instituto de Letras, História e Psicologia. São Paulo.

Historian/Honor Society. The Historian. Phi Alpha Theta, National Honor Society in History; Univ. of Pennsylvania. Univ. Park, Penn.

Histórica/Lima. Histórica. Pontificia Univ. Católica del Perú, Depto. de Humanidades. Lima.

Historiogr. Bibliogr. Am. Historiografía y Bibliografía Americanista. Escuela de Estudios Hispano-Americanos de Sevilla. Sevilla, Spain.

Historiogr. Rioplat. Historiografía Rioplatense. Instituto Bibliográfico Antonio Zinny. Buenos Aires.

HLAS/CD. Handbook of Latin American Studies CD-ROM: HLAS/CD. Fundación MAPFRE América, Madrid. Hispanic Division, Library of Congress, Washington.

Homme/Paris. L'Homme. Laboratoire d'anthropologie, Collège de France. Paris.

Hoy Hist. Hoy es Historia: Revista Bimestral de Historia Nacional e Iberoamericana. Editorial Raíces. Montevideo.

Ibero-Am. Arch. Ibero-Amerikanisches Archiv. Ibero-Amerikanisches Institut. Berlin.

Ibero-Am./Stockholm. Ibero-Americana: Nordic Journal of Latin American Studies. Institute of Latin American Studies, Univ. of Stockholm.

Ideas Valores. Ideas y Valores. Instituto de Filosofía y Letras, Univ. Nacional. Bogotá.

Imago Mundi/London. Imago Mundi: the Journal of the International Society for the History of Cartography. King's College. London.

Int. Hist. Rev. The International History Review. Univ. of Toronto Press. Downsview, Ontario, Canada.

Int. Q. International Quarterly. International Quarterly, Inc. Tallahassee, Fla.

Int. Soc. Sci. J. International Social Science Journal. Blackwell Publishers. Oxford, England.

Integr. Latinoam. Integración Latinoamericana. Instituto para la Integración de América Latina. Buenos Aires.

Inter-Am. Music Rev. Inter-American Music Review. Robert Stevenson. Los Angeles, Calif.

Interciencia/Caracas. Interciencia. Asociación Interciencia. Caracas.

Invest. Ens. Investigaciones y Ensayos. Academia Nacional de la Historia. Buenos Aires.

Islas/Santa Clara. Islas. Univ. Central de Las Villas. Santa Clara, Cuba.

Itinerario/Leiden. Itinerario. Leiden Centre for the History of European Expansion. Leiden, The Netherlands.

J. Afr. Hist. Journal of African History. Cambridge Univ. Press. London.

J. Anthropol. Res. Journal of Anthropological Research. Univ. of New Mexico. Albuquerque, N.M.

J. Caribb. Hist. The Journal of Caribbean History. Caribbean Univ. Press. St. Lawrence, Barbados.

J. Caribb. Stud. Journal of Caribbean Studies. Assn. of Caribbean Studies. Coral Gables, Fla.

J. Church State. Journal of Church and State. J.M. Dawson Studies in Church and State, Baylor Univ., Waco, Tex.

J. Decor. Propag. Arts. The Journal of Decorative and Propaganda Arts. Wolfson Foundation of Decorative and Propaganda Arts. Miami, Fla.

J. Econ. Hist. The Journal of Economic History. Economic History Assn.; Univ. of Kansas. Lawrence.

J. Interam. Stud. World Aff. Journal of Interamerican Studies and World Affairs. Institute of Interamerican Studies, Univ. of Miami. Coral Gables, Fla.

J. Interdiscip. Hist.   The Journal of Interdisciplinary History. The MIT Press. Cambridge, Mass.

J. Lat. Am. Stud.   Journal of Latin American Studies. Centers or Institutes of Latin American Studies at the Universities of Cambridge, Glasgow, Liverpool, London, and Oxford. Cambridge Univ. Press. London.

J. Miss. Hist.   The Journal of Mississippi History. Mississippi Historical Society; Mississippi Dept. of Archives and History. Jackson, Miss.

J. Soc. Hist.   Journal of Social History. Carnegie Mellon Univ., Pittsburgh, Penn.

Jahrb. Gesch.   Jahrbuch für Geschichte von Staat, Wirtschaft und Gesellschaft Lateinamerikas. Köln, Germany.

Jam. Hist. Rev.   The Jamaican Historical Review. The Jamaican Historical Society. Kingston.

La. Hist.   Louisiana History. Louisiana Historical Assn., Lafayette, La.

La Mei Shi Yan Jiu Tong Xun.   La Mei Shi Yan Jiu Tong Xun [Latin American History Newsletter]. s.n., Beijing?.

Lab. Arte.   Laboratorio de Arte: Revista de Departmento de Historia del Arte. Univ. de Sevilla. Sevilla, Spain.

LARR.   Latin American Research Review. Latin American Research Review Board. Univ. of New Mexico, Albuquerque, N.M.

Lat. Am. Music Rev.   Latin American Music Review. Univ. of Texas. Austin.

Lat. Am. Perspect.   Latin American Perspectives. Univ. of California. Newbury Park, Calif.

Lat. Am. Theatre Rev.   Latin American Theatre Review. Univ. of Kansas, Center of Latin American Studies. Lawrence, Kan.

Lat. Rev. Books.   The Latino Review of Books. State Univ. of New York at Albany (SUNY), Center for Latino, Latin American, and Caribbean Studies (CELAC). Albany, N.Y.

Lateinamerika/Hamburg.   Lateinamerika. Institut für Iberoamerika-Kunde. Hamburg, Germany.

Lett. Am./Rome.   Letterature d'America. Dipartimento di Studi Americani, Univ. di Roma; Bulzoni Editore. Rome.

Li Shi Yan Jiu.   Li Shi Yan Jiu [Chinese History Research]. Renmin Zhubanshe [People's Publishing House]. Beijing.

Lua Nova.   Lua Nova. Editora Brasiliense. São Paulo.

Luso-Braz. Rev.   Luso-Brazilian Review. Univ. of Wisconsin Press. Madison, Wis.

MACLAS Lat. Am. Essays.   MACLAS Latin American Essays. Middle Atlantic Council of Latin American Studies. New Brunswick, N.J.

Maguaré/Bogotá.   Maguaré. Depto. de Antropología, Univ. Nacional de Colombia. Bogotá.

Mapocho/Santiago.   Mapocho. Biblioteca Nacional. Santiago.

MEFRIM.   Mélanges de l'Ecole française de Rome: Italie et Méditerranée. L'Ecole française de Rome. Rome.

Mélanges/Paris.   Mélanges de la Casa de Velázquez. Ecole des hautes études hispaniques. Paris.

Mem. Acad. Mex. Hist.   Memorias de la Academia Mexicana de la Historia. México.

Mem. Am.   Memoria Americana. Instituto de Ciencias Antropológicas, Facultad de Filosofía y Letras, Univ. de Buenos Aires.

Memoria/CEMOS.   Memoria: Boletín de CEMOS. Centro de Estudios del Movimiento Obrero y Socialista. México.

Mesoamérica/Antigua.   Mesoamérica. Centro de Investigaciones Regionales de Mesoamérica. Antigua, Guatemala.

Mex. Stud.   Mexican Studies/Estudios Mexicanos. Univ. of California, Berkeley.

MLA Int. Bibliogr./CD.   MLA International Bibliography. H.W. Wilson. New York.

MLN/Baltimore.   MLN. Modern Language Notes. Johns Hopkins Univ. Press. Baltimore, Md.

N.M. Hist. Rev.   New Mexico Historical Review. Historical Society of New Mexico; Univ. of New Mexico. Albuquerque, N.M.

N.Y. Rev. Books. The New York Review of Books. New York.

Nação Def. Nação e Defesa. Estudos Políticos do Gabinete de Estudos e Planeamento do Estado-Maior do Exército. Lisboa.

Nariz Diablo. Nariz del Diablo. Centro de Investigaciones y Estudios Socio-Económicos. Quito.

Natl. Geogr. Mag. National Geographic Magazine. National Geographic Society. Washington.

New Sch. New Scholar. Univ. of California, Committee on Hispanic Civilization and Center for Chicano Studies. Santa Barbara.

Newsl. Int. Hisp. Study Group. Newsletter of the International Hispanic Study Group. Dartmouth College, Dept. of Music. Hanover, N.H.

Not. Bibliogr. Hist. Notícia Bibliográfica e Histórica. Depto. de História, Pontifícia Univ. Católica de Campinas. Campinas, Brazil.

Notas Hist. Geogr. Notas Históricas y Geográficas. Univ. de Playa Ancha. Valparaiso, Chile.

Nuestra Hist./Buenos Aires. Nuestra Historia. Fundación Nuestra Historia. Buenos Aires.

Nuestra Hist./Caracas. Nuestra Historia. Litografía Litota. Caracas.

Nueva Rev. Filol. Hisp. Nueva Revista de Filología Hispánica. El Colegio de México. México.

NWIG. New West Indian Guide/Nieuwe West Indische Gids. KITLV Press. Leiden, The Netherlands.

Op. Cit./Río Piedras. Op. Cit.: Boletín del Centro de Investigaciones Históricas. Depto. de Historia, Facultad de Humanidades, Univ. de Puerto Rico. Río Piedras.

OSO/Netherlands. OSO. Stichting Instituut ter Bevordering van de Surinamistick (IBS) te Nijmegen. Nijmegen, The Netherlands.

Palabra Hombre. La Palabra y el Hombre. Univ. Veracruzana. Xalapa, Mexico.

Past Present. Past and Present. London.

Pensam. Iberoam. Pensamiento Iberoamericano. Instituto de Cooperación Iberoamericano (ICI) de España; Comisión Económica para América Latina y el Caribe (CEPAL). Madrid.

Philos. Forum. The Philosophical Forum. Dept. of Philosophy, Baruch College, City Univ. of New York. New York.

Plant. Soc. Am. Plantation Society in the Americas. Univ. of New Orleans.

Plural/México. Plural. Excelsior Compañía Editorial. México.

Procesos/Quito. Procesos. Corporación Editora Nacional. Quito.

Publ. Inst. Estud. Iberoam. Publicaciones del Instituto de Estudios Iberoamericanos. Instituto de Estudios Iberamericanos. Buenos Aires.

Quad. Ibero-Am. Quaderni Ibero-Americani. Associazione per i Rapporti Culturali con la Spagna, il Portogallo e l'America Latina. Torino, Italy.

Quaderni/São Paulo. Quaderni. Istituto Italiano di Cultura; Istituto Cultural Italo-Brasileiro. São Paulo.

Radic. Hist. Rev. Radical History Review. Mid-Atlantic Radical Historians' Organization. New York.

Razón Fe. Razón y Fe. La Compañía de Jesús. Madrid.

Reflexão/São Paulo. Reflexão. Pontifícia Univ. Católica de Campinas. São Paulo.

Relaciones/Zamora. Relaciones. El Colegio de Michoacán. Zamora, Mexico.

Relig. Cult. Religión y Cultura. Madrid.

Res Gesta. Res Gesta. Instituto de Historia, Facultad de Derecho y Ciencias Sociales, Univ. Católica Argentina. Rosario, Argentina.

Res/Harvard. Res. Peabody Museum of Archaeology and Ethnology, Harvard Univ., Cambridge, Mass.

Rev. Andin. Revista Andina. Centro Bartolomé de las Casas. Cusco, Peru.

Rev. Antropol./São Paulo. Revista de Antropologia. Univ. de São Paulo, Faculdade de Filosofia, Letras e Ciências Humanas; Associação Brasileira de Antropologia. São Paulo.

Rev. Arch. Nac. Hist. Azuay. Revista del Archivo Nacional de Historia, Sección del Azuay. Casa de la Cultura Ecuatoriana, Núcleo del Azuay. Cuenca, Ecuador.

Rev. Auvergne. Revue d'Auvergne. Société des Amis de l'Université de Clermont. Clermont-Ferrand, France.

Rev. Bibl. Nac. José Martí. Revista de la Biblioteca Nacional José Martí. La Habana.

Rev. Bras. Filos. Revista Brasileira de Filosofia. Instituto Brasileiro de Filosofia. São Paulo.

Rev. Bras. Hist. Revista Brasileira de História. Associação Nacional dos Professores Universitários de História (ANPUH). São Paulo.

Rev. Bras. Mús. Revista Brasileira de Música. Escola de Música da Univ. Federal do Rio de Janeiro. Rio de Janeiro.

Rev. Can. Estud. Hisp. Revista Canadiense de Estudios Hispánicos. Asociación Canadiense de Hispanistas; Univ. of Toronto. Toronto, Canada.

Rev. Cent. Estud. Av. La Revista del Centro de Estudios Avanzados de Puerto Rico y el Caribe. San Juan.

Rev. Chil. Hist. Geogr. Revista Chilena de Historia y Geografía. Sociedad Chilena de Historia y Geografía. Santiago.

Rev. Chil. Humanid. Revista Chilena de Humanidades. Facultad de Filosofía, Humanidades y Educación, Univ. de Chile. Santiago.

Rev. Chil. Lit. Revista Chilena de Literatura. Univ. de Chile, Depto. de Literatura. Santiago.

Rev. Ciclos. Revista Ciclos en la Historia, Economía y la Sociedad. Fundación de Investigaciones Históricas, Económicas y Sociales, Facultad de Ciencias Económicas, Univ. de Buenos Aires. Buenos Aires.

Rev. Ciênc. Hist. Revista de Ciências Históricas. Univ. Portucalense. Porto, Portugal.

Rev. Ciênc. Polít./Rio de Janeiro. Revista de Ciência Política. Fundação Getúlio Vargas. Rio de Janeiro.

Rev. Cienc. Soc./Río Piedras. Revista de Ciencias Sociales. Univ. de Puerto Rico, Colegio de Ciencias Sociales. Río Piedras.

Rev. Cienc. Soc./Valparaíso. Revista de Ciencias Sociales. Facultad de Derecho y Ciencias Sociales, Univ. de Valparaíso. Chile.

Rev. Colomb. Antropol. Revista Colombiana de Antropología. Ministerio de Educación Nacional, Instituto Colombiano de Antropología. Bogotá.

Rev. Complut. Hist. Am. Revista Complutense de Historia de América. Facultad de Geografía e Historia, Univ. Complutense de Madrid.

Rev. Crít. Lit. Latinoam. Revista de Crítica Literaria Latinoamericana. Latinoamericana Editores. Lima.

Rev. Cuba. Cienc. Soc. Revista Cubana de Ciencias Sociales. Centro de Estudios Filosóficos, Academia de Ciencias de Cuba. La Habana.

Rev. Dep. Hist./Belo Horizonte. Revista do Departamento de História. Univ. Federal de Minas Gerais. Belo Horizonte, Brazil.

Rev. Ecuat. Hist. Econ. Revista Ecuatoriana de Historia Económica. Banco Central del Ecuador, Centro de Investigación y Cultura. Quito.

Rev. Esp. Antropol. Am. Revista Española de Antropología Americana. Facultad de Geografía e Historia. Univ. Complutense de Madrid.

Rev. Esp. Estud. Norteam. Revista Española de Estudios Norteamericanos. Centro de Estudios Norteamericanos, Univ. de Alcalá de Henares. Spain.

Rev. Eur. Revista Europea de Estudios Latinoamericanos y del Caribe = European Review of Latin American and Caribbean Studies. Center for Latin American Research and Documentation; Royal Institute of Linguistics and Anthropology. Amsterdam.

Rev. Filos. Latinoam. Cienc. Soc. Revista de Filosofía Latinoamericano y Ciencias Sociales. Asociación de Filosofía Latinoamericana y Ciencias Sociales. Buenos Aires.

Rev. Filos./México. Revista de Filosofía. Univ. Iberoamericana, Depto. de Filosofía; Asociación Fray Alonso de la Veracruz. México.

Rev. Filos. Univ. Costa Rica. Revista de Filosofía de la Universidad de Costa Rica.

Editorial de la Universidad de Costa Rica. San José.

Rev. fr. hist. Outre-mer. Revue française d'histoire d'Outre-mer. Société de l'histoire des colonies françaises. Paris.

Rev. Hist. Am. Revista de Historia de América. Instituto Panamericano de Geografía e Historia, Comisión de Historia. México.

Rev. Hist. Am. Argent. Revista de Historia Americana y Argentina. Univ. Nacional de Cuyo, Instituto de Historia. Mendoza, Argentina.

Rev. Hist./Concepción. Revista de Historia. Depto. de Ciencias Históricas y Sociales, Univ. de Concepción, Chile.

Rev. Hist./Heredia. Revista de Historia. Univ. Nacional de Costa Rica, Escuela de Historia. Heredia, Costa Rica.

Rev. Hist. Ideas. Revista de Historia de las Ideas. Instituto Panamericano de Geografía e Historia; Editorial Casa de la Cultura Ecuatoriana. Quito.

Rev. Hist./Managua. Revista de Historia. Instituto de Historia de Nicaragua. Managua.

Rev. Hist. Naval. Revista de Historia Naval. Instituto de Historia y Cultura Naval Armada Española. Madrid.

Rev. hist./Paris. Revue historique. Presses Univ. de France. Paris.

Rev. Iberoam. Revista Iberoamericana. Instituto Internacional de Literatura Iberoamericana; Univ. de Pittsburgh. Pittsburgh, Penn.

Rev. Indias. Revista de Indias. Consejo Superior de Investigaciones Científicas, Instituto Gonzalo Fernández de Oviedo. Madrid.

Rev. Inst. Cult. Puertorriq. Revista del Instituto de Cultura Puertorriqueña. San Juan.

Rev. Inst. Hist. Geogr. Para. Revista do Instituto Histórico e Geográfico Paraibano. Univ. Federal da Paraiba. João Pessoa, Brazil.

Rev. Inst. Hist. Geogr. São Paulo. Revista do Instituto Histórico e Geográfico de São Paulo. São Paulo.

Rev. Inst. Invest. Musicol. Carlos Vega. Revista del Instituto de Investigación Musicológica Carlos Vega. Pontifícia Univ. Católica de Argentina, Facultad de Artes y Ciencias Musicales, Instituto de Investigación Musicológica Carlos Vega. Buenos Aires.

Rev. Int. Sociol. Revista Internacional de Sociología. Consejo Superior de Investigaciones Científicas. Instituto de Economía y Geografía Aplicadas. Madrid.

Rev. Junta Prov. Hist. Córdoba. Revista de la Junta Provincial de Historia de Córdoba. Córdoba, Argentina.

Rev. Juríd. Univ. P.R. Revista Jurídica de la Universidad de Puerto Rico. Escuela de Derecho, Univ. de Puerto Rico. Río Piedras.

Rev. Mex. Sociol. Revista Mexicana de Sociología. Instituto de Investigaciones Sociales, Univ. Nacional Autónoma de México. México.

Rev. Music. Chil. Revista Musical Chilena. Univ. de Chile, Facultad de Ciencias y Artes Musicales y de la Representación. Santiago.

Rev. Musicol./Madrid. Revista de Musicología. Sociedad Española de Musicología. Madrid.

Rev. Nac./Montevideo. Revista Nacional. Ministerio de Instrucción Pública. Montevideo.

Rev. Occident. Revista de Occidente. Madrid.

Rev. Parag. Sociol. Revista Paraguaya de Sociología. Centro Paraguayo de Estudios Sociológicos. Asunción.

Rev. Pensam. Centroam. Revista del Pensamiento Centroamericano. Centro de Investigaciones y Actividades Culturales. Managua.

Rev. Rev. Interam. Revista/Review Interamericana. Inter-American Univ. Press. Hato Rey, Puerto Rico.

Rev. Soc. Bras. Mús. Contemp. Revista da Sociedade Brasileira de Música Contemporânea. Sociedade Brasileira de Música Contemporânea. São Paulo.

Rev. Soc. haïti. Revue de la Société haïtienne d'histoire et de géographie. Port-au-Prince.

Rev. UNITAS. Revista UNITAS. Unión Nacional de Instituciones para el Trabajo de Acción Social. La Paz.

Rev. USP. Revista USP. Coordenadoria de Comunicação Social (CCS), Univ. de São Paulo.

Ruralia/Buenos Aires. Ruralia: Revista Argentina de Estudios Agrarios. FLACSO; Ediciones Imago Mundi. Buenos Aires.

Santiago/Cuba. Santiago. Univ. de Oriente. Santiago, Cuba.

Sarance/Otavalo. Sarance. Instituto Otavaleño de Antropología. Otavalo, Ecuador.

SECOLAS Ann. SECOLAS Annals. Southeastern Conference on Latin American Studies; West Georgia College. Carrollton, Ga.

Secuencia/México. Secuencia. Instituto Mora. México.

Sefárdica/Buenos Aires. Sefárdica. Centro de Investigación y Difusión de la Cultura Sefardí. Buenos Aires.

Senderos/Bogotá. Senderos. Biblioteca Nacional de Colombia. Bogotá.

Siglo XIX. Siglo XIX. Facultad de Filosofía y Letras, Univ. Autónoma de Nuevo León. Monterrey, Mexico.

Slavery Abolit. Slavery & Abolition. Frank Cass & Co., Ltd., London.

Soc. Compass. Social Compass. The International Catholic Institute for Social-Ecclesiastical Research. The Hague.

Soc. Econ. Stud. Social and Economic Studies. Univ. of the West Indies, Institute of Social and Economic Research. Mona, Jamaica.

Soc. Hist./London. Social History. Methuen. London.

Southwest. Hist. Q. Southwestern Historical Quarterly. The Texas State Historical Assn., Austin, Tex.

Stud. Emigr. Studi Emigrazione. Centro Studi Emigrazione. Rome.

Stud. Hist. Hist. Mod. Studia Historica: Historia Moderna. Univ. de Salamanca. Salamanca, Spain.

SWI Forum. SWI Forum voor Kunst, Kultuur en Wetenschop. De Stichting. Paramaribo, Suriname.

Tierra Firme. Tierra Firme. Caracas.

Tijdschr. Geschied. Tijdschrift voor Geschiedenis. P. Noordhoff. Groningen, Netherlands.

Todo es Hist. Todo es Historia. Buenos Aires.

Transl. Rev. Translation Review. Univ. of Texas at Dallas. Richardson.

Translation/Columbia. Translation. The Translation Center, Columbia Univ., New York.

Tri-Quarterly/Evanston. Tri-Quarterly. Northwestern Univ., Evanston, Ill.

UCLA Hist. J. UCLA Historical Journal. Univ. of California, Dept. of History. Los Angeles.

UNISA Lat. Am. Rep. UNISA Latin American Report. Univ. of South Africa. Pretoria.

Universidad/Santa Fe. La Universidad. Univ. Nacional del Litoral. Santa Fe, Argentina.

Universum/Talca. Universum. Univ. de Talca. Talca, Chile.

Vuelta/México. Vuelta. México.

Wampum/Leiden. Wampum. Archeologisch Centrum. Leiden, The Netherlands.

Wani/Managua. Wani: Una Revista sobre la Costa Atlántica. Centro Investigaciones y Documentación de la Costa Atlántica. Managua.

Yaxkin/Tegucigalpa. Yaxkin. Instituto Hondureño de Antropología e Historia. Tegucigalpa.

Yearbook/CLAG. Yearbook. Conference of Latin Americanist Geographers; Ball State Univ., Muncie, Ind.

Yumtzilob/Leiden. Yumtzilob: Tijdschrift over de Americas. Archeologisch Centrum. Leiden, The Netherlands.

SUBJECT INDEX

Abad de Santillán, Diego, 1046.
Abascal, Salvador, 1419, 1597.
Abolition (slavery). Bibliography, 782. British Caribbean, 1989. Central America, 1627. Cuba, 1998, 2027, 2080, 2087. Dutch, 1953. Dutch Caribbean, 2143. France, 1905, 2035. Freemasonry, 779. French Caribbean, 1987, 2077. Guadeloupe, 1907. Puerto Rico, 1990, 2015, 2024.
Abstract Art. Andean Region, 315. Inca Influences, 315. Mexico, 251, 260, 267, 275. Venezuela, 324.
Abused Children. See Child Abuse.
Academia Brasileira de Música, 4689.
Academia Colombiana de Historia, 2734.
Acámbaro, Mexico (city). Land Reform, 1539. Land Tenure, 1539.
Acarete, du Biscay, 2224.
Acción Democrática (Venezuela), 2638–2639, 2645, 2653, 2655, 2661, 2666, 2675, 2680.
Acculturation. Argentina, 3053, 3137. Aztecs, 404, 475–476. Brazil, 3280, 3308. Central America, 1665. Chile, 614. Guarani, 607, 657. Indigenous Peoples, 455, 475, 605, 614, 622, 624, 670. Latin America, 786, 1036. Mapuche, 621. Mexico, 455, 1117. Nicaragua, 1728. Patagonia, 624. Pehuenche, 621. Peru, 567, 622, 2788. Puerto Ricans, 2144. South America, 670. Venezuela, 4993. Viceroyalty of New Spain, 392–393, 499, 1117, 1162, 1273.
Aché. See Guayaqui.
Acosta, José de, 605.
Acuña, Guido, 2637.
Adolescents. See Teenagers; Youth.
Aesthetics. Brazil, 344. Political Ideology, 331.
African Influences. Barbados Area, 1803. Bibliography, 1209. Brazil, 3223, 3237, 4695, 4706–4707, 4715, 5060. Caribbean Area, 1829. Colonial History, 980. Costa Rica, 1730. Cuba, 4755, 4760. Ecuador, 2736. Folk Dance, 4707. Folk Music, 4695, 4707. Mexico, 1209. Mortuary Customs, 3237.

Music, 4648, 4660, 4706, 4715, 4728, 4760. Panama, 1656. Religious Life and Customs, 1730, 4715. US, 2006. Viceroyalty of New Spain, 1209, 1239.
Africans. Brazil, 2084, 3223, 3368. British Guiana, 2073. Colonial History, 970, 979. Cuba, 2084. Return Migration, 2084. Venezuela, 2263.
Afro-Americans. See Africans; Blacks.
Agosin, Marjorie, 2868, 4533, 4605.
Agosti, Héctor Pablo, 5124.
Agostini, Alberto María de, 619.
Agrarian Reform. See Land Reform.
Agricultural Colonization. Argentina, 610, 668, 2999, 3031. Brazil, 3287, 3337, 3353. British Guiana, 2166. Costa Rica, 1733. Jews, 2999.
Agricultural Credit. Argentina, 2940.
Agricultural Development. Argentina, 2968, 3064. Central America, 1790. Chile, 2899. Colombia, 2283, 2300, 2701. Costa Rica, 1726. Guatemala, 1650. Mexico, 1094, 1150, 1450. Nueva Granada, 2283, 2300. Viceroyalty of New Spain, 1124.
Agricultural Development Projects. See Development Projects.
Agricultural Ecology. Mexico, 1191.
Agricultural Geography. Cuba, 2134.
Agricultural Industries. Dominican Republic, 2172. Ecuador, 2752.
Agricultural Labor. Argentina, 2945, 3000, 3056, 3108–3109, 3149. Barbados, 2119. Brazil, 3339. British Caribbean, 2041. Caribbean Area, 1964. Coffee Industry and Trade, 3372. Colonial History, 2263. Cuba, 2087. Haciendas, 1106. Indigenous Peoples, 2327. Jamaica, 2096, 2099. Labor Movement, 2096. Mexican-American Border Region, 1486. Mexico, 1106, 1111, 1298, 1446, 1486. US, 1486. Venezuela, 2263.
Agricultural Policy. Bolivia, 2477. Cuba, 2049. Dominican Republic, 2163. Puerto Rico, 2049.

Agricultural Productivity. Andean Region, 2439. Argentina, 2968, 3059, 3064. Incas, 664. Mexico, 1232, 1325, 1359, 1523. Peru, 2762. Viceroyalty of New Spain, 1232.

Agricultural Systems. Argentina, 2939, 2968, 3108–3109. Central America, 1640. Cuba, 2105. Puerto Rico, 2105. Viceroyalty of New Spain, 1124.

Agricultural Technology. Argentina, 2968. Brazil, 3302. Slaves and Slavery, 3302.

Agriculture. Argentina, 595. Guatemala, 1634. Indigenous Peoples, 595. Mayas, 519. Peru, 2762.

Agroindustry. *See* Agricultural Industries.

Aguascalientes, Mexico (state). Economic History, 1483. Historical Demography, 1483. History, 1483. Land Reform, 1483. Modernization, 1483.

Aguirre, Juan Francisco, 2548.

Aguirre, Lope de, 2233, 3433.

Ahuachapán, El Salvador (dept.). Colonial History, 1648.

Akwẽ Shavante. *See* Xavante.

ALADI. *See* Asociación Latinoamericana de Integración.

Alakaluf. *See* Alacaluf.

Alamán, Lucas, 1347.

Alas, Leopoldo, 5066.

Alberdi, Juan Bautista, 2943, 5080, 5088, 5093, 5112.

Alberti, Leon Battista, 1244.

Albizu Campos, Pedro, 2178.

Alcohol and Alcoholism. Andean Region, 644. Incas, 644. Indigenous Peoples, 644. Mexico, 1513. Peru, 2771. Religious Life and Customs, 644.

Aldama, Miguel de, 2072.

Alemán, Miguel, 1397, 1520–1521.

Alexander Pollack, Leni, 4738.

Alianza Nacional Popular (ANAPO), 2693.

Alianza Popular Revolucionaria Americana. *See* APRA (Peru).

Allende, Isabel, 4606.

Allende Family, 2616, 4606.

Almagro, Diego de, 3779, 4103.

Almaraz Paz, Sergio, 5033.

Alta Verapaz, Guatemala (dept.). Genealogy, 1789. Germans, 1789.

Altarpieces. Brazil, 337. Colombia, 173. Mexico, 78, 128.

Altazor, 4747.

Altos de Jalisco (Mexico). Cultural Identity, 1165. Social History, 1165.

Alvarado, Pedro de, 3766.

Alvarado, Salvador, 1400, 1608.

Alvarez Restrepo, Antonio, 2689.

Alzate y Ramírez, José Antonio de, 3431.

Amado, Jorge, 4322.

Amarakaeri. *See* Mashco.

Amazon Basin. Boundary Disputes, 2806. Colonial History, 630, 649. Commerce, 649. Cronistas, 630. Description and Travel, 630, 649. Discovery and Exploration, 630, 2257, 2806. Economic Development, 2807. Economic History, 2769. Foreign Investment, US, 3326. Geographical History, 2707. Historiography, 630. Human Ecology, 587. Indigenous Art, 371. Indigenous Peoples, 630, 671. Insurrections, 3433. Missionaries, 3221. Natural History, 2257. Navigation, 3334. Rubber Industry and Trade, 2769. Social History, 2807. Travelers, 649.

Amazonas, Brazil (state). Governors, 3336. Modernization, 3336. Political History, 3336. Public Works, 3336.

Amazonas, Venezuela (territory). History, 611.

American Revolution (1776–1783). British Caribbean, 1911, 1914. French Caribbean, 1932. Jamaica, 1910, 1948. Latin America, 1042. Saint Eustatius, 1939.

Americans (US). Bermuda, 1861. Brazil, 3291. Central America, 1740. Cuba, 2207. Mexico, 1299. Nicaragua, 1697.

Amiama Tió, Luis, 2151.

Anales de Cuauhtitlan, 449.

Anarchism and Anarchists. Argentina, 5095. Belize, 1747. Colombia, 2735. Costa Rica, 4956. Latin America, 1046, 5095. Mexico, 1357, 1393, 1474. Nicaragua, 1734. Uruguay, 3194, 3202.

Anchieta, José de, 3267.

Andalucía, Spain (region). Migration, 1028.

Andean Region. Abstract Art, 315. Agricultural Productivity, 2439. Alcohol and Alcoholism, 644. Art History, 315. Catholic Church, 658. Chicha, 577. Climatology, 2439. Colonial Administration, 600. Colonial History, 592, 658, 2235. Ecology, 2792. Economic Conditions, 571. Economic History, 2792. Encomiendas, 600. Ethnic Groups and Ethnicity, 633, 640, 2398. Ethnohistory, 606. Historiography, 606, 2394. History, 2220. Human Ecology, 669. Inca Conquest, 606. Independence Movements, 2235. Indigenous Literature, 551. Indigenous Peoples, 176, 571, 609. Indigenous Resistance, 658. Insurrections, 592, 654, 658, 2235. Inter-Tribal Relations, 602, 654, 669. Mestizos and Mestizaje, 633. Mita,

bean Area, 291. Central America, 280. Chile, 302–303, 306. Colombia, 309–310. Directories, 239. Ecuador, 200, 311–312. Exiles, Spanish, 215. Latin America, 216. Mexico, 33, 220, 225, 227, 229–230, 233, 238–240, 245, 250, 255–257, 260–261, 263, 267, 274, 276, 1331. Peru, 183, 314, 317, 2770. Social Movements, 270. Spain, 57. Suriname, 287. Uruguay, 318–319. Venezuela, 320, 322–324, 328, 330. Web Sites, 31, 33.

Artists, Women. Brazil, 341. Catalogs, 341.

Arze, José Antonio, 2816.

Asamblea Popular (Bolivia), 2865.

Ascuhul, Agustín, 499, 1273.

Asian Influences. Peru, 2804.

Asians. Peru, 2804.

Asociación Nacional de Mineros Medianos (Bolivia), 2827.

Assassinations. Dominican Republic, 2151. El Salvador, 1798. Guatemala, 1713. Jesuits, 1798. Mexico, 1487, 1525, 1566, 1591–1593, 1602. Nicaragua, 1690. Paraguay, 1690.

Assimilation. *See* Acculturation.

Assis, Machado de, 4694.

Association of Research Libraries (ARL), 26.

Astronomy. Aztecs, 470. Incas, 626. Mayas, 490, 519, 525.

Asturias, Spain (region). Migration, 847, 999, 2092.

Atacama Desert (Chile). Description and Travel, 2846. Historical Geography, 2846.

Atacama Desert Region (Chile). History, 2855.

Atahualpa, 596, 663, 672, 3408–3409.

Atl, Dr, 257.

Atlantic Coast (Nicaragua). *See* Mosquitia (Nicaragua and Honduras).

Audiencia of Caracas, 2255–2256.

Audiencia of Chile, 2488.

Audiencia of Guadalajara, 1124.

Audiencia of Guatemala, 1652, 1688. Indigenous Resistance, 485. Manuscripts, 485.

Audiencia of Mexico, 1124.

Audiencia of Nueva Granada. Travelers, 2685.

Audiencia of Quito, 2322, 2328. Agricultural Labor, 2326. Catholic Church, 2364. Cinchona, 2353. Clergy, 2364. Colonial Administration, 2333, 2341, 2370. Colonial Architecture, 2329. Commerce, 2375. Cults, 2357–2358. Cultural History, 2363, 2365. Economic History, 2316, 2318–2319, 2324, 2326, 2353, 2359, 2362, 2366. Economic Policy, 2315. Education, 2323.

Elites, 2355, 2369, 2377. Encomiendas, 2355. Ethnic Groups and Ethnicity, 2360. Finance, 2341, 2377. Franciscans, 2364. Higher Education, 2361. Historical Demography, 2350, 2360, 2363, 2365–2366, 2381. Historical Geography, 2371. History, 2373–2374. Indigenous Peoples, 2317, 2330, 2359, 2363–2365, 2381, 2404. Indigenous Policy, 2317, 2330. Jesuits, 2323. Land Tenure, 2330. Law and Legislation, 2317. Maps and Cartography, 2372. Mestizos and Mestizaje, 2360. Migration, 2330, 2363–2365. Minerals and Mining Industry, 2338, 2366, 2404. Mita, 2330. Myths and Mythology, 2404. Poets, 2322. Political Corruption, 2367–2368. Political Culture, 2369. Prisons, 2379. Religious Life and Customs, 2352, 2357–2358. Roads, 2371. Salt and Salt Industry, 2342. Schools, 2323. Science, 2372. Slaves and Slavery, 2336, 2339, 2380. Social History, 2318, 2351, 2355, 2359. Social Life and Customs, 2377. Social Structure, 2359. Social Welfare, 2379. Sources, 2313–2314, 2325, 2343–2346. Textiles and Textile Industry, 2375. Universities, 2361. Women, 2319.

Augustinians. Bibliography, 734. Colombia, 2276. Missionaraies, 734. Missionaries, 884. Peru, 638.

Authoritarianism. Argentina, 3112. Brazil, 3288, 3300, 3340. Chile, 2491, 2906. Peru, 2793, 2801, 5029. Uruguay, 3200. Venezuela, 2638.

Authors. Brazil, 3306. Mexico, 1385, 1388, 3524. Puerto Rico, 2032. Women, 3524, 3627.

Autobiography. Aymara, 2825. Nuns, 3442.

Automobile Industry and Trade. Argentina, 2979.

Autonomy. Mexico, 1152. Puerto Rico, 2188.

Avellaneda, Argentina (city). Social History, 2947.

Avila, Francisco de, 3434, 3455.

Avila Camacho, Manuel, 1521, 1591.

Awa. *See* Cuaiquer.

Ayacucho, Peru (dept.). Colonial History, 655, 2462. Economic History, 2779. History, 2779. Indigenous Peoples, 2462. Indigenous Resistance, 655. Political History, 2779. Social History, 2779.

Ayala, Eligio, 3158.

Aycinena, Juan Fermín de, 1646.

Aycinena Family, 757.

Ayestarán, Lauro, 4814.

Ayllus, 598.

Casado del Alisal, Carlos, 3065.
Casares, Emilio, 4651.
Casas, Bartolomé de las, 816, 823–825, 857, 876–877, 907, 976, 988, 3424, 3427, 3432, 3443, 4837, 4866, 4889, 4908.
Casasús, Joaquín Demetrio, 1607.
Castañeda y Nájera, Pedro, 3425.
Castelar, Emilio, 1000.
Castillo, Francisca Josefa de la Concepción de, 3420.
Castillo, Francisco del, 2441.
Castillo, Marcos, 329.
Castillo y Negrete, Manuel del, 879.
Castro, Fidel, 2142, 2148, 2167, 2184, 2192.
Castro, Izaque de, 3248.
Castro, Juan José, 4672, 4676.
Castro Filho, Amilcar Augusto Ferreira de, 351.
Castro Pacheco, Fernando, 233.
Castro Solórzano, Antonio, 1490.
Catalan Influences. Chile, 4639. Latin America, 683. Mexico, 4639. Musical History, 4639.
Catalans. Cuba, 2059. Musicians, 4817. Puerto Rico, 2009. Sources, 2059. Uruguay, 3206. Venezuela, 4817.
Catalogs. Archives, 716. Graphic Arts, 253. Historic Sites, 201. Mexico, 1120. Nahuas, 524. Religious Art, 114. Viceroyalty of New Spain, 1120. Votive Offerings, 114.
Cathedrals. Archives, 4770. Mexico, 4770.
Catholic Church. Amazon Basin, 3221. Andean Region, 658. Archives, 692. Argentina, 164, 2964, 5106, 5116. Audiencia of Quito, 2364. Aztecs, 404, 418. Belize, 1747. Bibliography, 1778. Bolivia, 2838, 2840. Brazil, 3295, 3307, 5039, 5055, 5060. Canary Islands, 870. Central America, 1628, 1747, 1772. Chile, 2903, 2911, 2930. Chronology, 1680. Colombia, 2694. Colonial Administration, 2494. Colonial History, 818, 895, 932. Conservatism, 4937. Costa Rica, 1680, 1705. Cuba, 1927, 1937, 2052–2053. Dominican Republic, 1927, 2026. Economic History, 1188. Ecuador, 2321, 2741. El Salvador, 1773, 1798. France, 1987. French Caribbean, 1987. Haiti, 1858. Higher Education, 2064–2065. History, 691, 745, 1032. Honduras, 1778–1779. Independence Movements, 809. Indigenous Peoples, 567, 799, 811, 813, 840, 870, 883, 932, 982, 2446. Indigenous Policy, 448, 454, 460, 541, 605, 632, 638, 643, 1686. Inquisition, 848, 949, 992. Labor Movement, 2911. Latin America, 703, 720, 1064, 4892. Manu-

scripts, 522. Mexico, 99, 412, 418, 448, 454, 458–460, 511, 1126, 1167, 1180, 1188, 1196, 1253, 1414, 1418, 1439, 1474, 1537–1538, 1555, 3457, 4934, 4937. Missionaries, 1060. Missions, 4918. Nicaragua, 1686, 1772. Paraguay, 3154. Peru, 567, 605, 2390, 2780. Political Participation, 2715. Populism, 1057. Puerto Rico, 1885–1887, 1927, 2064–2065. Slaves and Slavery, 991, 2008. Social Change, 1048. Social Movements, 5106. Sources, 691–692. Spain, 691–692. Spanish Borderlands, 1968. Spanish Conquest, 643. Symbolism, 535. Uruguay, 3186. Venezuela, 2250, 2673. Viceroyalty of New Spain, 394, 511, 522, 1126, 1161, 1168, 1178, 1182, 1187, 1253. Viceroyalty of Peru, 643, 2465. Women, 903, 969.
Catholicism. Brazil, 3307, 3312, 5060. Colonial History, 436. Indigenous Peoples, 922–923, 2438. Latin America, 1048. Liberalism, 5008. Mayas, 436. Mexico, 510. Peru, 2756. Puerto Rico, 1894. Slaves and Slavery, 3228. Symbolism, 509–510.
Cattle Raising and Trade. Argentina, 2586, 3064, 3096, 3146. Brazil, 3234. Guatemala, 1762. Mexico, 1340, 1577. Panama, 1668. Venezuela, 2265.
Cauca, Colombia (dept.). Economic Conditions, 2731. History, 2730.
Caudillos. Argentina, 2995, 3032, 3095. Latin America, 766, 1027. Mexico, 1343, 1562–1563, 1573. Peru, 2810. Political Theory, 4855. Venezuela, 2644, 2649, 2681.
Cayambe, Ecuador (town). History, 635.
Cayenne, French Guiana (city). Social History, 1959.
CBI. See Caribbean Basin Initiative.
CD-ROMs. Architecture, 3. Archives, 1, 12. Art History, 3. Bibliography, 5, 15. Colonial History, 12. Cultural History, 8. Demography, 20. Ethnohistory, 13. Film, 6. Historiography, 12. History, 4, 16. Indigenous Peoples, 13. Libraries, 8. Literature, 2, 9, 17, 19. Mexico, 1. Music, 5. Peru, 16. Photography, 3. Political Culture, 18. Portuguese Language, 10. Statistics, 20.
Ceará, Brazil (state). Theater, 4509.
Cemeteries. Barbados, 1952. Chile, 2903. Peru, 2809.
Cempoala Site (Mexico). Precolumbian Trade, 526.
Censorship. Brazil, 3338. Colonial Administration, 887. Mass Media, 1518. Mexico, 1518.

Contestado Insurrection (Brazil, 1912–1916), 3296.
Contras. *See* Counterrevolutionaries.
Contreras Soto, Eduardo, 4774.
Contumazá, Peru (prov.). Caudillos, 2810. Political Systems, 2810.
Convención de Ocaña (1828), 2704.
Convento de Huejotzingo (Mexico), 88.
Convento de Jesús María (México), 1081.
Convento de Santo Domingo (Quito), 2223.
Convents. Colonial Architecture, 88. Dominicans (religious order), 97. Latin America, 838. Mexico, 67, 87–88, 97, 838, 1081, 1235, 3442, 3454. Viceroyalty of New Spain, 67, 1235.
Conversaciones Americanas sobre España y sus Indias, 4881.
Copán Site (Honduras). Demography, 441. Environmental Degradation, 441. Households, 450. Inscriptions, 523. Kings and Rulers, 523. Social Structure, 450.
Copper Industry and Trade. Chile, 2932. Labor and Laboring Classes, 1482. Mexican-American Border Region, 1498. Mexico, 1482, 1585. Strikes and Lockouts, 1482.
Cordero Hoyos, Juan, 95.
Córdoba, Argentina (city). Automobile Industry and Trade, 2979. Cabildos, 2587. Colonial Administration, 2586–2587, 2603. Colonial History, 2609. Commerce, 2609, 2616. Economic History, 2609, 2615–2616. Encomiendas, 2603. Historical Demography, 2542. History, 2546, 2942. Indigenous-Non Indigenous Relations, 2603. Indigenous Peoples, 2603. International Trade, 2609. Labor and Laboring Classes, 2979. Labor Movement, 2979. Meat Industry, 2586. Merchants, 2609. Riots, 2942. Slaves and Slavery, 2615. Social History, 2615–2616. Students, 2973. Trade Unions, 2979.
Córdoba, Argentina (prov.). Agricultural Credit, 3077. Agricultural Productivity, 3077. Birth Rate, 2513. Catholic Church, 5106. Cattle Raising and Trade, 3077. Church Records, 2554. Colonial Administration, 2543. Colonial History, 2514, 2543. Commerce, 3006. Diseases, 2513. Economic History, 2514, 3005, 3077, 3088. Encomiendas, 2566. Federal-State Relations, 3088. Frontier and Pioneer Life, 3078. Historical Demography, 2513, 2554. History, 3078. Indigenous-Non Indigenous Relations, 3078. Indigenous Peoples, 3078. Indigenous Policy, 2543. Land Settlement, 2566. Land Tenure, 2566. Land Use, 3077.

Law and Legislation, 3004. Marriage, 2554. Merchants, 3005. Minerals and Mining Industry, 2568. Mortality, 2513. Political History, 3022. Slaves and Slavery, 2541. Social Classes, 3004, 3006. Social History, 2514, 3004, 3006. Social Movements, 5106. Social Policy, 3004. Social Structure, 3004, 3006. Spaniards, 3005.
Cordón Batres, Francisco, 1762.
Coronel, Pedro, 236.
Corporatism. Brazil, 3340.
Correa, Juan, 141.
Corrientes, Argentina (city). Historical Demography, 2970. Labor and Laboring Classes, 2970. Social History, 2970.
Corrientes, Argentina (prov.). Colonization, 2537. Economic History, 2994. Merchants, 2994. Political History, 2994. Precolumbian Civilizations, 2537. Urbanization, 2537.
Corruption. Guatemala, 1711. Mexico, 1296. Venezuela, 2273.
Corruption in Politics. *See* Political Corruption.
Corsicans. Viceroyalty of Peru, 2431.
Cortázar, Julio, 4637.
Cortés, Hernán, 399, 410, 417, 912, 1136, 1190, 1208, 1220, 1243, 1645, 3402, 3427, 4221.
Cortés y Larraz, Pedro, 1641.
Coruña, Agustín de, 2276.
Cosío Villegas, Daniel, 1521.
Cosmology. Aztecs, 513. Incas, 616, 651–652. Mexico, 1364.
Cossio, Carlos, 5099.
Cost and Standard of Living. Historical Demography, 1223. Mexico, 1223, 1531. Uruguay, 3210. Viceroyalty of New Spain, 1223.
Costa, Janete, 375.
Costa Méndez, Nicanor, 3008.
Costa Rican Development Corporation. *See* Corporación Costarricense de Desarrollo.
Costume and Adornment. Exhibitions, 133. Mexico, 133, 244.
Cotton Industry and Trade. Dutch Caribbean, 1966. Mexico, 1488. Saint Croix, 1966.
Counterinsurgency. Guatemala, 1787.
Counterrevolutionaries. Cuba, 2136.
Coups d'Etat. Argentina, 3025. Brazil, 3370. Costa Rica, 1744. Dominican Republic, 2157. Guatemala, 1729, 1737. Haiti, 2018. Mexico, 1372. Trinidad and Tobago, 2162. Venezuela, 2655, 2666, 2680.
Covarrubias, Miguel, 263.
Cowboys. Ecuador, 2737.

Dominican Republic, 4974. Ecuador, 570. Elites, 902. European Influences, 5091. French Caribbean, 1849. Guarani, 604. Guatemala, 1666. Honduras, 1716. Indigenous Peoples, 393, 475, 636, 784. Kekchi, 1799. Language and Languages, 3414. Latin America, 787, 4897, 4949. Literature, 5115. Mayas, 1667. Mexico, 86, 452, 1165, 4928–4930, 4945. Nahuas, 479, 3412. Nicaragua, 4294. Nueva Granada, 2288. Peru, 5025, 5029. Puerto Ricans, 2144. Puerto Rico, 1802, 2009, 2024, 2155, 2194, 4726. Slaves and Slavery, 3228. Venezuela, 2246. Viceroyalty of New Spain, 392. Women, 700.

Cultural Policy. Brazil, 4719. Mexico, 86, 143.

Cultural Property. Brazil, 334. Conservation and Restoration, 52, 212, 214. Dominican Republic, 153. Ecuador, 214. Mexico, 86. Peru, 212.

Cumajuncosa, Antonio, *Padre*, 2481.

Cumana (indigenous group). Venezuela, 2254.

Cumanagoto. *See* Cumana.

Cumbal, Colombia (town). Collective Memory, 636. Land Tenure, 636. Oral History, 636.

Cúpira Site (Venezuela). Excavations, 620.

Curicó, Chile (prov.). Brigands and Robbers, 2933. Crime and Criminals, 2933.

Currency. *See* Money Supply.

Cusco. *See* Cuzco.

Customs. Dutch Caribbean, 1846.

Cuzco, Peru (city). Colonial Music, 4811. History, 625. Musical History, 4811. Photography, 2765. Pictorial Works, 2765. Quechua, 188. Villancicos, 4807.

Cuzco, Peru (dept.). Anthologies, 665. Colonial Administration, 653. Description and Travel, 2757. Educational Reform, 2808. Elites, 2763. Higher Education, 2808. Historiography, 660. History, 616. Indigenismo and Indianidad, 665, 2808. Indigenous Peoples, 2763, 2808. Local History, 665. Political Culture, 2763. Precolumbian Civilizations, 616, 660, 2808. Water Rights, 653.

Cyclones. *See* Hurricanes.

Dance. Nicaragua, 1685.

Dance, Cuban. US, 4757.

Danes. Mexico, 1309.

Darío, Rubén, 4135.

Darwin, Charles, 5067.

Das Prinzip Hoffnung, 5121.

Databases. Web Sites, 28.

Dávalos, Juan Carlos, 4289.

Dávila, Pedrarias, 1644.

Dávila Andrade, César, 4146.

Dávila Vázquez, Jorge, 3691.

Davis, Daniel Gateward, 2095.

De la filosofía, 4933.

De la réhabilitation de la race noire par la République d'Haïti, 2012.

De Szyszlo, Fernando, 317.

De viajero naturalista a historiador, 2221.

Death. Mexico, 1316. Precolumbian Civilizations, 453. Religious Life and Customs, 453. Viceroyalty of Peru, 2382.

Debien, Gabriel, 1823.

Debt. *See* External Debt; Public Debt.

Debt Conversion. *See* Debt Relief.

Decentralization. Argentina, 3123. Bolivia, 2861.

Decolonization. History, 742.

Decorative Arts. Architecture, 144. Cuba, 292. Mexico, 144, 247, 249, 4299. Suriname, 1866.

Deities. Aztecs, 494, 498. Mayas, 498.

Delgado de León, Bartolomé, 1454.

Democracy. Colombia, 2687. Latin America, 1067, 4914. Nicaragua, 1792. Peru, 5018. US, 1345. Venezuela, 2642, 2666.

Democratization. El Salvador, 1796. Latin America, 1050, 1066.

Demography. Antigua, 2039. Argentina, 3074. Aztecs, 400. Brazil, 20. CD-ROMs, 20. Chile, 2927. Colonial History, 942, 1877. Ecuador, 2354. Guadeloupe, 1986. Indigenous Peoples, 556, 569, 2354. Jamaica, 1868, 2088. Labor and Laboring Classes, 942. Mayas, 441. Mexico, 1373. Peru, 569. Saint-Barthélemy, 2050. Slaves and Slavery, 899, 1933–1935. Spaniards, 891. Trinidad and Tobago, 1944.

Denevi, Marco, 4557.

Dependency. Central America, 1637. Latin America, 723. Panama, 1709. Paraguay, 3169. Uruguay, 3216.

Depressions (economic). Brazil, 3309. Chile, 2891. Latin America, 1061, 1063.

Desaparecidos. *See* Disappeared Persons; Missing Persons.

Description and Travel. Amazon Basin, 630, 649. Antigua, 2039. Bolivia, 2846, 2849. Chile, 2511, 2846, 2925, 4159. Colombia, 2685. Dominica, 1851. Dominican Republic, 1808, 1853. Ecuador, 184, 2742. Latin America, 758, 1020, 4879. Mexico, 90, 122, 268, 1362, 1556. Panama, 149. Patagonia, 619. Peru, 2511, 2757, 2798. South America, 2217, 2233, 3456. Tierra del

Divorce. Costa Rica, 1705. Río de la Plata, 3063.

Dobrizhoffer, Martin, 2517.

Documentation Centers. *See* Libraries.

Domestic Violence. *See* Family Violence.

Domínguez, Belisario, 1487.

Dominicans (people). Exiles, 2126.

Dominicans (religious order). Colonial History, 964. Convents, 97. Ecuador, 2223. Indigenous Peoples, 484, 964. Land Tenure, 1111. Mexico, 97, 484, 1111. Missions, 584. Nicaragua, 1686. Relations with Tojolabal, 484.

Donoso, José, 3803–3804, 3808.

Dorado, El. *See* El Dorado.

Dorrego, Manuel, 3084.

Drama. Brazil, 4504–4507.

Dramatists, 4286. Argentina, 4289. Brazil, 4489–4491, 4500–4501, 4514. Chile, 4285, 4287. Peru, 4292. Venezuela, 4290. Women, 4514.

Dresden Codex. *See* Codices. Dresden.

Drug Abuse. Artisans, 1761. Costa Rica, 1761. Latin America, 1056.

Drug Traffic. Latin America, 1056.

Drug Utilization. Culture, 1056. Latin America, 1056.

Drugs and Drug Trade. *See* Drug Abuse; Drug Enforcement; Drug Traffic; Drug Utilization; Pharmaceutical Industry.

Durán, Diego, 96, 540.

Durango, Mexico (state). History, 1574.

Durazno, Uruguay (dept.). History, 3203.

Durazno, Uruguay (town). History, 3203.

Dussel, Enrique, 5091.

Dutch. Abolition (slavery), 1953. British Guiana, 1949. Indigenous Policy, 1882.

Dutch Caribbean. Abolition (slavery), 2143. Architecture, 1814. Capitalism, 2143. Colonial Administration, 1804, 1846, 1884, 1908. Colonization, 1867, 1884. Constitutional History, 1804. Cotton Industry and Trade, 1966. Customs, 1846. Finance, 1965. Historiography, 1941. Indigenous Peoples, 1882. Maps and Cartography, 1938. Migration, 1835. Modernization, 2143. Political History, 1804. Slaves and Slavery, 1805, 1846, 1876, 1884, 1953, 1966. Social History, 1835. Sources, 1941. Sugar Industry and Trade, 1835.

Dwellings. Chile, 162. Ecuador, 178, 193.

Dyes and Dyeing. Central America, 1681. Mexico, 1681.

Earthquakes. Central America, 1630. Church

Architecture, 206. Guatemala, 1763. Mexico, 4613. Peru, 206.

East Indians. British Guiana, 2044–2045, 2071, 2073, 2083, 2191. Entrepreneurs, 2193. Historiography, 2071. Jamaica, 2088. Peasants, 2083. Religious Life and Customs, 2044–2045, 2093. Trinidad and Tobago, 1818, 2093, 2193, 2199. Women, 2088.

Easter Island. Ethnohistory, 578. Ethnology, 578. Folklore, 578. Social Life and Customs, 578.

Echeverría, Esteban, 5075.

Echeverría, Luis, 1594.

Echevers, Pedro Ignacio de, 1290.

ECLAC. *See* Comisión Económica para América Latina y el Caribe.

Ecological Crisis. *See* Environmental Protection.

Ecology. Andean Region, 2792. Aztecs, 470. Bolivia, 2792. Indigenous Peoples, 406. Peru, 2792. Precolumbian Civilizations, 406. Tarahumara, 465. Urubu Kaapor, 559.

Economic Anthropology. Mexico, 1586.

Economic Assistance, Spanish. Argentina, 3105.

Economic Commission for Latin America and the Caribbean. *See* Comisión Económica para América Latina y el Caribe.

Economic Conditions. Andean Region, 571. Aztecs, 431. Belize, 1696. Bolivia, 2821, 2859. Central America, 1743. Chile, 2880. Ecuador, 177, 575. Latin America, 4879. Mexico, 529, 1092. Nicaragua, 1753. Nueva Granada, 2299. Precolumbian Civilizations, 521, 529. Venezuela, 2665.

Economic Destabilization. *See* Economic Stabilization.

Economic Development. Amazon Basin, 2807. Argentina, 3058. Brazil, 3230. Central America, 1637. Dominican Republic, 2172. Ecuador, 2315, 2744. El Salvador, 1788. Elites, 3230. Jamaica, 2154. Latin America, 1007. Mexico, 1332, 1444, 1469. Nueva Granada, 2283, 2304. Peru, 2807. State, The, 776.

Economic Development Projects. *See* Development Projects.

Economic Growth. *See* Economic Development.

Economic History. Amazon Basin, 2769. Andean Region, 2792. Argentina, 610, 2959, 2967, 2971, 2983, 3011, 3039, 3115, 3146. Audiencia of Quito, 2326. Bahamas, 1816.

538. History, 7. Indigenous Languages, 538.
Otomi, 538.
Elementary Education. Argentina, 2976–
2977. Colonial History, 2079. Cuba, 2079.
Political Ideology, 2976–2977.
Elites. Audiencia of Quito, 2369, 2377. Aztecs, 383, 480. Bibliography, 1251. Bolivia,
2842, 2855. Brazil, 3230, 3234, 3367. Cak-
chikel, 518. Chile, 2896, 2924, 2937. Chinese, 772. Coffee Industry and Trade, 3347.
Colombia, 2701, 2716. Colonial History,
902, 1982. Costa Rica, 1752, 1759, 1761,
1793. Cuba, 1982, 1997, 2102, 2213. Cultural Identity, 902. Economic Development, 3230. Ecuador, 2378. El Salvador,
1788. Guatemala, 518, 1736, 1769, 1795. Indigenous Peoples, 640, 2763. Industry and
Industrialization, 1035. Mayas, 414, 436,
466, 492. Mexico, 1232, 1251, 1298, 1313,
1344, 1519, 1577, 1623. Nicaragua, 1703,
1732, 1785. Panama, 1782. Peru, 2763,
2787, 2796, 2811. Precolumbian Civilizations, 403. Social Change, 1035. Sugar Industry and Trade, 2213. Venezuela, 902,
2642, 2648–2649, 2660, 2672, 2679, 2682.
Viceroyalty of New Spain, 1199, 1232,
1290. Viceroyalty of Peru, 2419, 2421, 2451,
2456. Zapotec, 492.
Ellauri, José Eugenio, 3173.
Elliott, John Huxtable, 974.
Eltit, Diamela, 3807.
Emancipation. See Abolition.
Embassy of Mexico (Washington), 1432.
Emigrant Remittances. Basques, 710. Span-
iards, 1018.
Emigration and Immigration. See Migration.
Emociones de la guerra, 2710.
Employment. Women, 2152, 2156.
Encomiendas. Andean Region, 600. Audiencia
of Quito, 2355. Chile, 2507. Ecuador, 635,
2355. Guatemala, 1657–1658. Indigenous
Peoples, 2414, 2507. Mexico, 1140, 1158.
Nueva Granada, 2289. Paraguay, 2618.
Slaves and Slavery, 962. Viceroyalty of New
Spain, 395, 506, 1199. Viceroyalty of Peru,
634, 2452.
Encuentro de Historiadores en Puerto Rico,
1st, Río Piedras, P.R., 1990, 2129.
Encyclopedias. Aztecs, 494.
Energy Policy. Mexico, 1444. Uruguay, 3193.
Energy Sources. Uruguay, 3193.
Energy Supply. Uruguay, 3193.
Engineers. Mexico, 1485.
Englightenment. Spain, 4856.

Enlightenment. Colombia, 2306. Colonial
Literature, 3406. Discovery and Explora-
tion, 4854. Independence Movements,
4844. Latin America, 809. Nueva Granada,
2306. Peru, 3465, 5028. Wars of Indepen-
dence, 5028.
Enlightment. Colonial History, 3465.
Enríquez, Manuel, 4768, 4792.
Ensayo sobre la historia natural de Chile,
2502.
Entre Ríos, Argentina (prov.). Guarani, 3093.
Political History, 3016. Revolutions and
Revolutionary Movements, 3016, 3141.
Entrepreneurs. Central America, 1740. Chile,
2934. Colombia, 2713. East Indians, 2193.
Guatemala, 1646. Trinidad and Tobago,
2193.
Environmental Degradation. Mayas, 441.
Environmental Protection. Chile, 2922.
Epidemics. Aztecs, 497. Cultural Contact,
497.
Epístola de Amarilis a Belardo, 3441.
Erauso, Catalina de, 3445.
Ercilla y Zúñiga, Alonso de, 3430, 3443–3444,
3461.
Escobar, Eduardo, 3614.
Escobedo y Alarcón, Jorge, 2400.
Escola do Recife (Brazil), 5044–5045, 5050.
Escoto, José Augusto, 2068.
Escudero Luján, Carolina, 1466.
Escuela de Bellas Artes de Cusco (Peru), 2393.
Escuela Normal del Paraná (Argentina), 2973.
Escuintla, Guatemala (dept.). Ethnohistory,
504.
Esequiba Region. See Essequibo Region (Guy-
ana and Venezuela).
O espelho de Próspero, 3272.
Espíndola, Luis de, 209.
Espínola Gómez, Manuel, 318.
Espinosa Medrano, Juan de, 2410, 3438, 3453,
3464.
Espinosa Pólit, Aurelio, 5005.
Espionage, US, 1515.
Espírito Santo, Brazil (state). Slaves and Slav-
ery, 3219.
Esquipulas II. See Arias Peace Plan (1987).
Essays. Argentina, 5100. Chile, 5035. Ecua-
dor, 5010. Literary Criticism, 4857.
Estado Novo (Brazil), 3300, 3320, 3338, 3373.
Estancias. Mexico, 1151.
Esteban, Edgardo, 3018.
Estete, Miguel de, 3460.
Estigarribia, José Félix, 3150.
Estrada Cabrera, Manuel, 1737, 1763.

Food Industry and Trade. El Salvador, 1650. Guatemala, 1650.
Food Supply. Cities and Towns, 1156. Guatemala, 1650. Mexico, 1156. Nueva Granada, 2290. Precolumbian Civilizations, 526.
Forced Labor. Central America, 1627. Indigenous Peoples, 617, 1627. Peru, 617. Venezuela, 562. Viceroyalty of New Spain, 395.
Foreign Aid. See Economic Assistance.
Foreign Debt. See External Debt.
Foreign Exchange. See Exchange Rates.
Foreign Influences. Baroque Architecture, 102. Colonial Art, 63. Haiti, 1812. Mexico, 102, 1332, 1557.
Foreign Intervention, Brazilian. Argentina, 3121.
Foreign Intervention, British. Río de la Plata, 2574. Venezuela, 2247.
Foreign Intervention, Cuban. Dominican Republic, 2113. Vietnam, 2204.
Foreign Intervention, French. Mexico, 1399, 1581.
Foreign Intervention, US, 2211. Central America, 1423, 1735. Costa Rica, 1706, 1744, 1757. Cuba, 1455, 2142, 2187, 2195. Dominican Republic, 2110, 2206. Guatemala, 1713, 1736. Haiti, 2124, 2159. Mexico, 1455, 1462, 1532, 1603. Nicaragua, 1423, 1710, 1748, 1757. Panama, 1701, 1722, 1781.
Foreign Investment. Argentina, 3058. Chile, 2871. Costa Rica, 1704. Guatemala, 1711, 1786. Mexico, 1335, 1358, 1475. Nicaragua, 1739. Uruguay, 3190. Venezuela, 2643, 2659, 2662.
Foreign Investment, Canadian. Brazil, 3283.
Foreign Investment, US. Amazon Basin, 3326. Brazil, 3326.
Foreign Policy. Argentina, 3024, 3054–3055, 3106–3107, 3130. France, 1022. US, 1055, 1074, 1603, 1706, 1710, 1727, 1735–1736, 1738, 1766, 1781, 2067, 2110, 2132, 2137, 2145, 2184, 3054.
Foreign Policy, Spanish. Colonial History, 885.
Foreign Trade. See International Trade.
Forests and Forest Industry. Mexico, 1333, 1391. Nicaragua, 1784, 1794.
Fort-de-France, Martinique (city). Cultural History, 2117. Social History, 2117. Urban History, 2117.
Fortifications. Bermuda, 2098. Colombia, 170. Honduras, 1642. Mexico, 118. Panama, 1687.
Franciscan Influences. Mexico, 4801.

Franciscans. Bibliography, 937. Bolivia, 179, 2844–2845. California, 1259. Colonial Art, 165. Colonial History, 795, 850, 937, 961, 966, 996. Discovery and Exploration, 845. Education, 2551. Expeditions, 797, 830. Finance, 966. Haiti, 1858. Indigenous Peoples, 850. Intellectual History, 795. Land Tenure, 2571. Manuscripts, 458, 1159. Maps and Cartography, 845. Mexico, 108, 458–459, 1131, 1227, 1231, 1259, 1274. Missions, 108, 165, 458, 1227, 2828, 2844–2845. Monasteries, 183. New Mexico, US, 1274. Paraguay, 165. Peru, 183, 2788, 2805. Sources, 961. Spain, 867. Theater, 459. Viceroyalty of New Spain, 135, 407, 1131, 1159, 1182, 1194, 1227, 1231, 1271, 1274, 1282. Viceroyalty of Peru, 2418. Writing, 996.
Franco, Siron, 3932.
Free Trade. Bolivia, 2821.
Freedmen. Aruba, 1805. Barbados, 1989. Brazil, 3360, 3368. Brazilians, 3325. Cuba, 2087. French Caribbean, 2077. Jamaica, 1989, 2099. Political Development, 2099. Puerto Rico, 1990. Saint Domingue, 1932.
Freedmen, US. Music, 4727. Trinidad and Tobago, 4727.
Freemasonry. Abolition (slavery), 779. Argentina, 779, 3189. Cuba, 779. Independence Movements, 779. Mexico, 1297. Puerto Rico, 1981. Uruguay, 3186, 3189.
Freemasonry, Spanish, 779.
Frei Montalva, Eduardo, 2892.
Freire, Paulo, 48.
French. Argentina, 2951. Colonization, 1276. Haiti, 2146. Saint Domingue, 1916. Saint Martin, 1954.
French Caribbean. Abolition (slavery), 1987, 2077. Banking and Financial Institutions, 1988. Catholic Church, 1987. Colonial Administration, 1956. Colonial History, 1891–1892, 1906. Communism and Communist Parties, 2196. Cultural Identity, 1849. Economic Policy, 1956. Freedmen, 2077. Genealogy, 1857. Historians, 1823. Historiography, 1823, 1849. Indentured Servants, 1888. Mercantile System, 1956. Migrant Labor, 2076. Military History, 1932. Political Culture, 2196. Political History, 2120. Race and Race Relations, 1857. Slaves and Slavery, 1905, 1933–1934, 2008. Social History, 1960, 2008. Social Structure, 1960. World War II, 2120.
French Influences. Argentina, 5094. Brazil, 3278, 3311, 4491. Caribbean Area, 1829.

2962, 3072–3073, 3100. Brazil, 2962, 3280, 3287, 3299, 3343, 3353, 3372. Chile, 2883, 2898, 2915, 2927. Colonial Administration, 2274. Discovery and Exploration, 2274. Genealogy, 1789. Guatemala, 1789. Honduras, 1693. Latin America, 1070, 1075. Mexico, 1544, 1595. Paraguay, 2962. South America, 2962. Uruguay, 3171, 3195. Venezuela, 2274.

Gerzso, Gunther, 240.

Gibson, Percival William, 2153.

Ginastera, Alberto, 4668.

Ginés de Sepúlveda, Juan, 4908.

Girard, Rosan, 2196.

Giraudon, Gabriel, 4699.

Girón, Ecuador (town). Religious Life and Customs, 2357.

Girvan, D.T.M., 2154.

Glassware. Mexico, 107.

Gobineau, Arthur, *comte de*, 3305.

Godoy Cruz, Tomás, 3028.

Goiás, Brazil (state). Agricultural Colonization, 3287. Colonial History, 3261. Economic History, 3261. Slaves and Slavery, 3261.

Gold. Colombia, 2284, 2310. Costa Rica, 1683. Mexico, 1090. Nueva Granada, 2284, 2310.

Goldwork. Colombia, 173. Mexico, 133.

Gols i Soler, Joan, 4817.

Gomes, Antonio Carlos, 4696, 4702–4703.

Gomes, Manoel José, 4714.

Gómez, José F., 1458.

Gómez, Máximo, 2005, 2021–2022, 2047, 2062.

Gómez de Cervantes, Gonzalo, 1278.

Gómez de Lamadriz, Francisco, 485.

Gómez de Santoya, Alonso, 2533.

Gómez Nadal, Emili, 2533.

Gómez Robledo, Antonio, 1552.

Gómez Toro, Francisco, 2023.

Gómez Wangüemert, Luis Felipe, 1848.

Gomezanda, Antonio, 4803.

Góngora y Argote, Luis de, 3438.

González, Joaquín Víctor, 5117.

González, Manuel, 1314.

González, Manuel A., 321.

González Pacheco, Rodolfo, 1046.

González Videla, Gabriel, 2890.

González y González, Luis, 1571.

Good Neighbor Policy, 1074.

Gorriti, Juan Ignacio de, 2964.

Gothic Architecture. Manuscripts, 81.

Gottschalk, Louis Moreau, 4657.

Government, Resistance to. Colombia, 2688. Cuba, 2072. Guatemala, 1729. Mexico,

1317, 1387, 1452, 1537. Mosquito, 1728. Venezuela, 2641. Zapotec, 1452.

Government Publicity. Argentina, 3092. Colonial Administration, 967.

Governors. Argentina, 2967, 2987. Brazil, 3336. Mexico, 1136, 1220, 1292, 1400, 1411, 1494, 1588, 1615. Nueva Granada, 2297. Venezuela, 2273.

Grammar. Web Sites, 38.

Gramsci, Antonio, 4826, 4834, 4994.

Gran Colombia. Diplomatic History, 2733.

Granada, Nicaragua (city). Architecture, 147.

Granma (yacht), 2142.

Graphic Arts. Catalogs, 253. Mexico, 253, 263. Uruguay, 318.

Grassroots Movements. *See* Social Movements.

Grazing. Mexico, 1191.

Great Britain. Foreign Office, 2684.

Great Savannah. *See* Gran Sabana (Venezuela).

Gremio de Chauffers Mexicanos, 1589.

Grenadines. *See* Windward Islands.

Grillo, Max, 2710.

Groot, José Manuel, 307.

Grupo Independente de Teatro Amador (Brazil), 4509.

Grupo Macunaíma (Brazil), 4494.

Grupo Obrero Marxista (Argentina), 3140.

Guadalajara, Mexico (city). Colonial Architecture, 98. Economic History, 1114, 1129. Historic Sites, 98. Historical Demography, 1129. Labor and Laboring Classes, 1369. Mexican Revolution (1910–1920), 1617. Newspapers, 1617. Political History, 1114. Social History, 1114. Urban History, 1087, 1114. Women, 1369.

Guadalajara, Mexico (state). Economic History, 1170, 1225. Liberalism, 1367. Property, 1225. Slaves and Slavery, 1145. Social Life and Customs, 1367.

Guadalupe, Our Lady of, 502, 509. History, 510. Mexico, 92.

Guaithero Díaz, Genaro, 2658.

Guajira, Colombia. *See* La Guajira, Colombia (dept.).

Guajiro (indigenous group). *See* Goajiro.

Guamán Poma de Ayala, Felipe, 176, 573, 588, 2242, 2455.

Guanajuato, Mexico (state). Exhibitions, 279. Modern Art, 279. Municipal Government, 1539.

Guano Industry. Peru, 2784.

Guarani (indigenous group). Acculturation, 607, 657. Archives, 656. Argentina, 3093. Bibliography, 656, 2595. Colonial History,

Britain, 2007. Uruguay/Great Britain, 1044. Venezuela/Great Britain, 2268.
International Finance. Argentina, 3046. Cuba, 2122. Uruguay, 3190.
International Law, 4843.
International Migration. *See* Migration.
International Relations. Argentina, 2958, 3019, 3024. Argentina/Chile, 2969. Argentina/France, 2969, 3124. Argentina/Great Britain, 3036, 3124. Argentina/Middle East, 3052. Argentina/Paraguay, 3161. Argentina/Spain, 3105, 3117. Argentina/US, 3054, 3107. Barbados, 2135. Barbados/Africa, 1803. Belize/Guatemala, 1696. Belize/Mexico, 1310. Bolivia/Chile, 2926. Bolivia/Germany, 2822. Bolivia/Peru, 2796. Brazil/France, 3305. Brazil/Poland, 3329. Brazil/US, 3334. Brazil/USSR, 3371. Caribbean Area/Africa, 1803. Caribbean Area/Great Britain, 2145. Caribbean Area/US, 2145. Central America/US, 1055, 1740. Chile/France, 2874. Chile/Peru, 2797. Chile/Spain, 2893. Chile/US, 2891. Colombia, 2733. Colombia/Great Britain, 2684. Colombia/Peru, 2708, 2781. Costa Rica/Nicaragua, 1757–1758, 1772. Costa Rica/US, 1706, 1744, 1757. Cuba/Mexico, 1441. Cuba/Spain, 1997, 2014. Cuba/US, 2184, 2187. Dominican Republic, 2048. Dominican Republic/Haiti, 2108. Dominican Republic/US, 2165, 2189, 2206. Dutch Caribbean/The Netherlands, 1804. Germany/Spain, 1980. Germany/US, 1980. Guatemala/US, 4951. Haiti, 2000. Haiti/France, 2146. Haiti/US, 2124, 2159. Latin America/Europe, 1003. Latin America/France, 1022, 1077. Latin America/Germany, 1070, 1075. Latin America/Poland, 1065. Latin America/Russia, 775, 1099. Latin America/Spain, 698, 1033, 1059, 1107, 4872, 5066. Latin America/US, 1055, 1074, 1076, 4920. Mexico, 689. Mexico/Nicaragua, 1423. Mexico/Poland, 1567. Mexico/Spain, 1524. Mexico/UK, 1315. Mexico/US, 1315, 1375, 1423, 1432, 1455, 1462, 1470, 1532. Nicaragua/US, 1710, 1757, 1766. Panama/US, 1701, 1709, 1722, 1727, 1745, 1781–1782. Paraguay, 3166. Paraguay/Europe, 3167. Paraguay/France, 3160. Peru/US, 2766, 2785. Puerto Rico/US, 2140, 2150, 2188, 2194, 2216. Río de la Plata/Great Britain, 3209. Río de la Plata/US, 3209. Uruguay, 3182. Venezuela/Great Britain, 2651, 2680. Venezuela/US, 2651, 2655, 2680.

International Socialist Party, 2984.
International Trade. Argentina, 2971, 3058. Brazil, 3263. Cacao, 2248. Central America, 1021. Chile, 1021. Colonial History, 858, 868, 929, 947, 2243. Ecuador, 2316. History, 1019. Nicaragua, 1748. Spain, 868. Venezuela, 2664–2665.
International Trade Relations. Argentina/Great Britain, 3062, 3130. Argentina/US, 3127, 3130. Brazil/Uruguay, 3191. History, 1040. Latin America, 1021. Latin America/Europe, 1003. Latin America/France, 1041. Latin America/Germany, 1034. Latin America/Great Britain, 1029. Latin America/Spain, 858, 1002. Mexico/US, 1377. Panama/Spain, 1687. Río de la Plata/Canary Islands, 2632. Venezuela/Spain, 2258.
Intervention, Foreign. *See* Foreign Intervention.
Intoxicants. *See* Stimulants.
Iquique, Chile (city). Social Conflict, 2876. Strikes and Lockouts, 2876.
Ironwork. Architecture, 79. Mexico, 79.
Irrigation. Incas, 652–653. Mexico, 1368. Peru, 653.
Irving, Henry, 2043.
Isabela, Dominican Republic. *See* La Isabela, Dominican Republic (settlement).
Islamic Influences. Architecture, 60. Colonial Architecture, 51, 60, 180. Peru, 180.
Italian Influences. Argentina, 3080. Colombia, 4753. Cultural Development, 55. Latin America, 55. Opera, 4793–4794.
Italians. Argentina, 2950, 3013–3014, 3050, 3080. Brazil, 3312. Chile, 2889. Peru, 2761. Río de la Plata, 2520. Uruguay, 3181.
Iturbide, Agustín de, 757, 1392.
Itzá (indigenous group). Manuscripts, 508. Material Culture, 508. Relations with Spaniards, 458, 473. Sovereignty, 473.
Ivory Carving. Brazil, 336. Religious Art, 336.
Ixil (indigenous group). Cultural History, 514. Inheritance and Succession, 514. Neutrality, 1787. Social Conditions, 1787. Social Structure, 514.
Iza, Washington, 313.
Izalco, El Salvador (town). Spanish Conquest, 1651.
Jácome Durango, Ramiro, 313.
Jagan, Cheddi, 2145.
Jalapa, Mexico (city). Architecture, 1332. Economic Development, 1332. Foreign Influences, 1332. Modern Architecture, 1332.
Jalisco, Mexico (state). Art History, 255. Art-

ists, 255. Church-State Relations, 1588. Economic History, 1140. Ethnohistory, 407. Exhibitions, 255. Governors, 1588. Haciendas, 1146. History, 1130, 1140, 1146, 1484, 1552. Indigenous Peoples, 407, 1130. Intellectuals, 1588. Land Tenure, 1146, 1449. Latifundios, 1146. Mexican Revolution (1910–1920), 1617. Political History, 1551. Regional Development, 1348. Social Conflict, 1449. Social History, 1140. Textiles and Textile Industry, 1547.

Jamaicans. Cuba, 4756.

James, C.L.R., 2116, 2203.

Japanese. Brazil, 3312.

Japanese Influences. Brazil, 4433.

Jazz. Web Sites, 46.

Jesuits. Architecture, 65. Archives, 2267. Argentina, 604. Assassinations, 1798. Bibliography, 2595. Biography, 5005. Bolivia, 202, 2838. Brazil, 3267. California, 1262, 1269. Chile, 641, 2489. Church Architecture, 202. Colombia, 650. Colonial Architecture, 367. Colonial History, 2230. Demography, 2620. Ecuador, 2323, 2327, 5005. Education, 724, 2261. El Salvador, 1798. Guarani, 2531. Indigenous Peoples, 724, 2230, 2512, 2630. Libraries, 1272. Life Expectancy, 2620. Mexico, 65, 76, 1149, 1251, 1269, 1272. Missionaries, 683. Missions, 65, 160, 202, 568, 579, 613, 641, 1262, 1269, 1272, 2528, 2588, 2594–2595, 4859. Paraguay, 160, 568, 724, 2528, 2531, 2540, 2552, 2555, 2588, 2594, 2604, 2620, 4859. Peru, 724, 2788. Río de la Plata, 2540, 2630. Slaves and Slavery, 2239. Uruguay, 2588. Venezuela, 2261, 2267. Viceroyalty of New Spain, 1149, 1269, 1271–1272, 1283. Viceroyalty of Peru, 2402, 2441.

Jesus, Carolina Maria de, 3321–3322.

Jews. Agricultural Colonization, 2999. Argentina, 2992, 2999, 3021, 3050, 3137. Barbados, 1952. Brazil, 3238, 3248, 3299, 3318–3320. Caribbean Area, 1807. Chile, 2868, 2908, 4605. Colonial History, 848. Cuba, 1838. Curaçao, 1867. Dominican Republic, 1852. Mexico, 1245. Portuguese, 2621–2622. Río de la Plata, 2621–2622. Viceroyalty of New Spain, 1245.

Jiménez de Cisneros, Francisco, 870.

Jiménez de la Espada, Marcos, 2221.

Jiménez de Quesada, Gonzalo, 2291.

Jivaro. See Shuar.

Jolibois Fils, Joseph, 2159.

Journalism. Argentina, 3034, 5123. Brazil, 3338. Chile, 2900. Costa Rica, 1759. Do-

minican Republic, 2208. European Influences, 5123. Haiti, 1827. Latin America, 697. Mexico, 1349. Puerto Rico, 2130. Spanish-American War, 2030.

Journalists. Dominican Republic, 2208. Haiti, 1827. Mexico, 1349, 1442, 1506, 1528. Repression, 1349.

Juan de Almaraz, Fray, 2409.

Juan Lacaze, Uruguay (town). Social Conditions, 3212. Strikes and Lockouts, 3212.

Juana Inés de la Cruz, Sor, 43, 1134, 1178, 1236, 3405, 3420, 3445, 3457, 3463, 3466, 4611.

Juárez, Benito, 1334.

Juárez, Mexico. See Ciudad Juárez, Mexico.

Judicial Power. Mexico, 1291.

Judicial Process. Hispaniola, 1895. Mexico, 1349.

Jujuy, Argentina (prov.). Colonial Art, 157. Colonial History, 647. Elementary Education, 3118. Ethnic Groups and Ethnicity, 647. History, 3118. Indigenous Peoples, 647. Landowners, 3118. Religious Art, 157.

Juliaca, Peru (city). Precolumbian Civilizations, 558.

Junín, Peru (dept.). Peasants, 2790. State, The, 2790.

Junta Central Republicana de Cuba y Puerto Rico, 2072.

Juruna. See Yuruna.

Justo, Agustín Pedro, 2941, 3030, 3102.

Justo, Juan Bautista, 5088, 5090.

Juvenile Literature. See Children's Literature.

Juventud Peronista (Argentina), 2946.

Ka'apor. See Urubu.

Kagwahiv. See Parintintin.

Kahlo, Frida, 33, 227, 234, 262.

Kahlo, Guillermo, 103.

Kalapalo. See Apalakiri.

Kalinya. See Carib.

Kaminer, Saúl, 256.

Kant, Immanuel, 5087.

Karajá. See Caraja.

Kayapó. See Cayapo.

Kekchi (indigenous group). Cultural Identity, 1799. Ethnic Groups and Ethnicity, 1799. Genealogy, 1789. Religious Life and Customs, 1799.

Kennedy, John F., 2165.

Kent, Rockwell, 2194.

Kings and Rulers. Aztecs, 383, 464, 513, 553. Clothing and Dress, 383. Incas, 627, 637, 652. Mayas, 523. Mexico, 405. Mixtec, 443. Otomi, 516. Peru, 627. Precolumbian Civilizations, 406.

4856. Venezuela, 2644, 2647, 2672, 2679, 2681, 4986.

Liberation Theology. Argentina, 5098. Bibliography, 4838. Brazil, 5055. British Caribbean, 4981. Latin America, 4842, 4862–4863, 4871, 4874, 4906, 5091. Marxism, 4853. Mexico, 4936. Nicaragua, 4952. Philosophy, 4893, 4906. Sandinistas, 4952.

Libertad, Peru. *See* La Libertad, Peru (dept.).

Libraries. CD-ROMs, 8. Colombia, 2683. Cuba, 8. Jesuits, 1272. Medicince, 927. Mexico, 1113, 1272. Nueva Granada, 2306. Viceroyalty of New Spain, 1272. Web Sites, 24.

Library Catalogs. *See* Online Catalogs.

Library Resources. Ecuador, 2218, 2223.

Lienzo de Tiltepec, 457.

Lienzo of Tabaá I, 505.

Ligua, Chile. *See* La Ligua, Chile (city).

Lihn, Enrique, 4156.

Lima, Josefina Porfirio de, 4699.

Lima, Peru (city). Artists, 183. Bullfighters and Bullfighting, 2425. Cemeteries, 2809. City Planning, 207. Collective Memory, 2789. Colonial Administration, 2385. Colonial Architecture, 210. Colonial History, 2385, 2434. Elites, 2796. Family and Family Relations, 2786. Franciscans, 183. Historic Sites, 2789. Historical Demography, 2427. History, 207. Iconography, 207. Indigenous/Non-Indigenous Relations, 2796. Indigenous Peoples, 2427, 2796. Intellecuals, 2796. Monasteries, 183. Monuments, 2789. Mortuary Customs, 2809. Nationalism, 2796. Plazas, 2789. Religious Art, 183. Silverwork, 192. Slaves and Slavery, 2786. Social History, 2427. Urban History, 2397.

Limón, Costa Rica (prov.). African Influences, 1730.

Linguistics. Indigenous Peoples, 954. Missionaries, 954. Quechua, 554.

Lisbon, Portugal (city). Social History, 3251.

Lispector, Clarice, 4321.

Literacy and Illiteracy. Mexico, 1511. Nahuas, 479. Peasants, 1511. Precolumbian Civilizations, 551.

Literary Criticism, 4884, 4964. Brazil, 3293, 3304. Essays, 4857.

Literature. Bibliography, 3519, 3641, 3811. Bilbliography, 3619. CD-ROMs, 2, 9, 17, 19. Chile, 3811. Discovery and Conquest, 3460. Ecuador, 3619. Mexican Americans, 41. Mexico, 9, 3519. Peru, 3641. Venezuela, 4988. Web Sites, 40–43.

Lithics. *See* Stone Implements.

Livestock. Argentina, 3127. Viceroyalty of New Spain, 444.

Llanos Orientales Region (Colombia and Venezuela), 2721. Cattle Raising and Trade, 2269. Colonization, 2269. Economic History, 2269. Guerrillas, 2695. Insurrections, 2695. Missionaries, 2269. Social History, 2269.

Llerena, Spain (town). Migration, 872.

Lobbyists. *See* Pressure Groups.

Local Government. *See* Municipal Government.

Local History. Cuba, 1864. Mexico, 1447, 1484, 1502, 1536, 1548.

Local Transit. Argentina, 3029.

Locatelli, Aldo, 349.

Logroño, Ecuador (town), 2348.

Loja, Ecuador (prov.). Political History, 2740.

Lombardo Toledano, Vicente, 1576.

Lopes Neto, João Simões, 4377.

López, Carlos Antonio, 3167.

López, Estanislao, 2993.

López, Francisco Solano, 3156.

López, José Ramón, 2168.

López, Juan, 546.

López, Vicente Fidel, 3094.

López Albújar, Enrique, 2772.

López Arango, Emilio, 1046.

López Contreras, Eleazar, 2666.

López de Gamarra, Francisco, 3427.

López de Solís, Luis, 2321.

López Jordán, Ricardo, 3015–3016.

López Pumarejo, Alfonso, 2717, 2723.

Lorenzana, Cristóbal de, 979.

Loreto, Peru (dept.). Economic Development, 2807. History, 2807. Social History, 2807.

Los Angeles, California (city). History, 1284.

Los Angeles, Chile (city). Colonial History, 2496.

Los Toldos, Argentina (town). Local History, 580.

Louisiana, US (state). African Influences, 901. Catholic Church, 1968. Church History, 1968. Colonial History, 901. Refugees, 1928. Saint Domingans, 1928.

Lovera, Juan, 326.

Low Intensity Conflicts. Guatemala, 1776.

Loynaz, Dulce María, 4144.

Loyola, Margot, 4750–4751.

Ludwig, Daniel Keith, 3326.

Luján, Argentina (town). Migration, 3069.

Lukács, György, 5043.

Luperón, Gregorio, 2042.

Luz y Caballero, José de la, 1995, 2090.

Machiganga. *See* Machiguenga.

4778–4779. Musicians, 4778. Myths and Mythology, 464. Nuns, 1235. Opera, 4303, 4794. Painting, 113. Photography, 1404. Pictorial Works, 1404. Political History, 1304. Poor, 1137. Popular Culture, 1407. Pottery, 131. Precolumbian Civilizations, 543. Property, 1246. Public Finance, 1386. Race and Race Relations, 1137. Railroads, 1376. Religious Art, 1364. Religious Music, 4783. Sculpture, 113. Social Classes, 1372. Social Conditions, 4613. Social History, 89, 1112, 1304, 1407, 1618. Social Life and Customs, 89, 1404, 1407, 1618. Social Movements, 1410. Spanish Conquest, 543, 1164. Theater, 4303. Transportation, 1210, 1376. Urban History, 1407. Urban Sociology, 1410. Urbanization, 543. Zarzuelas, 4303.

México, Mexico (state). Bibliography, 1084. Church Architecture, 101. Governors, 1292. Historic Sites, 101. History, 1084, 1088, 1396, 1443. Indigenous Peoples, 1135. Land Reform, 1396. Pictorial Works, 1293. Political History, 1292. Political Systems, 1292. Postcards, 1293. Public Finance, 1351.

Mibclli, Celestino, 3177.

Michelena e Ibarra, Juan Manuel de, 96.

Michelena y Rojas, Francisco, 2257.

Michelet, Karl Ludwig, 5080.

Michelini, Pedro E., 3075.

Michoacán, Mexico (state). Bibliography, 1144. Brigands and Robbers, 1554. Catholic Church, 1126, 1161, 1188, 1196. Church History, 1126, 1161, 1188, 1196. Church-State Relations, 1401. Colonial Adminstration, 1254. Colonization, 1200. Confraternities, 392. Constitutional History, 1401. Crime and Criminals, 1319. Economic History, 1188. Ejidos, 1480. Encomiendas, 506. Federal-State Relations, 1590. Forests and Forest Industry, 1333. Generals, 1590. Historical Demography, 1200. History, 1161, 1200, 1484. Indigenous Peoples, 392, 515. Indigenous Policy, 1254. Land Reform, 1480. Land Settlement, 515. Land Tenure, 1142, 1449. Legislators, 1401. Minerals and Mining Industry, 1333. Nationalism, 1342. Peasants, 1480, 1619. Political Culture, 1620. Political History, 1620. Political Systems, 1619. Politicians, 1619. Railroads, 1333. Social Conflict, 1449. Social History, 1319. Sources, 1144. Violence, 1554. Water Rights, 1378. Water Supply, 1378.

Middle Classes. Colombia, 2722.

Migrant Labor. French Caribbean, 2076.

Migration. Arabs, 1723. Argentina, 2972, 3031, 3069, 3081, 3132, 3135. Basques, 1001, 1014. Bibliography, 3132, 3175. Brazil, 3312, 3318, 3320, 3337. Chile, 2916. Churumata, 631. Colonial History, 1881. Costa Rica, 1733, 1771. Diseases, 2972. Family and Family Relations, 684. Guadeloupe, 1986. Guatemala, 1789. Haiti, 4962. Historiography, 3013, 3069. Honduras, 1693, 1716. Households, 684. Incas, 581. Mayas, 456. Mexican-American Border Region, 1486. Mexico, 1313, 1373, 1409, 1421, 1445, 1459, 1486, 1572. Peru, 16, 581, 2782. Precolumbian Civilizations, 608. Saint Domingue/US, 1909. Tlaxcalans, 493. Uruguay, 3175. US, 1486. Venezuela, 4962. Viceroyalty of New Spain, 444, 493.

Migration, African. French Caribbean, 2076.

Migration, American (US). Brazil, 3291.

Migration, Armenian. Brazil, 3308.

Migration, Asturian. Latin America, 847.

Migration, Basque. Argentina, 2953, 3129. Uruguay, 2953, 3196.

Migration, Brazilian. Africa, 3325. Nigeria, 3325.

Migration, British. British Caribbean, 1878. Chile, 2909. Mexico, 274.

Migration, Canary Islander. Cuba, 1826, 1848, 2058. Latin America, 740. Santo Domingo, 1874.

Migration, Chinese. British Caribbean, 2041. British Guiana, 2037–2038. Mexico, 1409, 1616. Peru, 2812. South America, 772.

Migration, East Indian. British Caribbean, 2041, 2128. French Caribbean, 2076. Trinidad and Tobago, 1818, 2093.

Migration, European. Latin America, 748, 1003.

Migration, French. Argentina, 2951. Cuba, 1924. French Caribbean, 1888. Saint Domingue, 1916.

Migration, German. Argentina, 3072–3073. Brazil, 3343, 3353, 3372. Chile, 2898.

Migration, Haitian. Dominican Republic, 2108. Venezuela, 1806.

Migration, Italian. Argentina, 2950, 3013–3014, 3050. Chile, 2889. Peru, 2761. South America, 2950. Uruguay, 3181.

Migration, Jewish. Argentina, 3050. Brazil, 3319. Chile, 2868, 2908.

Migration, Lebanese. Mexico, 1575.

Migration, Middle Eastern. Argentina, 3052–3053.

Migration, Palestinian. Honduras, 1723.

Migration, Polish. Brazil, 3319, 3329.

479. Manuscripts, 524, 1257. Maps and Cartography, 483. Marriage, 384. Relations with Spaniards, 391, 479, 501. Religious Life and Customs, 463. Sex Roles, 384. Spanish Conquest, 391. Views of, 501. Writing, 479.

Nahuatl (language). *See* Indigenous Languages.

Names. Historiography, 4902.

Napoleanic Wars, 4881.

Napoleão, Arthur, 4709.

Naranjo Site (Guatemala). Kings and Rulers, 523.

Nariño, Colombia (dept.). Colonization, 586. Ethnohistory, 586. Land Tenure, 586. Precolumbian Land Settlement Patterns, 586.

Narváez, Pórfilo de, 3410.

Nasca. *See* Nazca.

Nascimento, Abdias do, 3223.

Natchez, Mississippi (city). British, 1973. Colonial Administration, 1971. Spaniards, 1973.

National Autonomy. *See* Autonomy.

National Characteristics. Argentina, 4840, 5081, 5109, 5115. Brazil, 5041, 5046. Chile, 2869. Colombia, 2729. Costa Rica, 1759. Honduras, 1716. Latin America, 4830, 4850, 4895, 4920. Mexico, 4868, 4882, 4896, 4929, 4945. Nicaragua, 1732. Portuguese, 3269. Puerto Rico, 3601. Venezuela, 2246, 2660, 3648, 3651.

National Defense. *See* National Security.

National Federation of Bolivian Peasant Women. *See* Federación Nacional de Mujeres Campesinas.

National Identity. *See* National Characteristics.

National Parks and Reserves. *See* Parks and Reserves.

National Patrimony. Bolivia, 2855. Mexico, 86.

National Songs. Chile, 4639. Colombia, 4753. Mexico, 4639, 4789.

Nationalism. Amazon Basin, 2707. Argentina, 2981, 3112, 4840, 5081. Blacks, 2033. Bolivia, 2861. Brazil, 3296, 3320, 4720. Caribbean Area, 2145. Central America, 1640, 1689. Costa Rica, 1632, 1707, 1749. Cuba, 1847, 2033, 4865, 4984. Dominican Republic, 4974. Ecuador, 2738. Haiti, 2012, 2182. Latin America, 1011, 4830, 4850, 4886, 4888, 4890, 4895, 4949. Mexico, 1294, 1308, 1342, 1350, 1485, 2791, 4803, 4868, 4914, 4929–4930. Musical History, 4720. Nicaragua, 1423, 1712, 1732. Peru, 1350,

2791, 2794, 2796, 2798, 5016. Puerto Rico, 2129, 2178. Río de la Plata, 3111. Trinidad and Tobago, 2199. Venezuela, 2653, 2660, 4993.

Nationalization. Chile, 2871.

Natural Disasters. Central America, 1630. Guadeloupe, 2139.

Natural History. Amazon Basin, 2257. Colombia and Venezuela, 2257.

Natural Resources. Andean Region, 640. Indigenous Peoples, 618, 640. Patagonia, 618.

Naufragios, 3449, 3458.

Nauzontla, Mexico (town). History, 482.

Naval History. Bermuda, 2098. Great Britain, 2247. Medicine, 911. Peru, 2813. Portugal, 3251. Spain, 893, 911, 2428.

Navarre, Spain (region). History, 757.

Navarro, José Gabriel, 2329.

Navas y Quevedo, Andrés de, 1652.

Navies. Argentina, 3114. Spain, 893.

Navigation. Amazon Basin, 3334. China, 739. Colonial History, 2372. Latin America, 739.

Nayarit, Mexico (state). Censorship, 1518. Mass Media, 1518.

Nazi Influences. Chile, 2883. Guatemala, 1736. Latin America, 1070.

Nee, Luis, 854.

Negritude. Brazil, 3324.

Neighborhood Associations. Argentina, 2954. Brazil, 3270.

Neoclassicism (architecture). Mexico, 1123.

Neoliberalism. Latin America, 2650. Venezuela, 2650.

Neruda, Pablo, 4138, 4147, 4152, 4154–4155.

Neukomm, Sigismund, 4720.

Neuquén, Argentina (prov.). Colonization, 3043. History, 3043.

Neutrality. Guatemala, 1713. Ixil, 1787.

New Amsterdam, Guyana (town). History, 1908.

New Mexico, US (state). Basques, 1267. Franciscans, 1274. History, 1267. Indigenous/Non-Indigenous Relations, 1265, 1274. Indigenous Peoples, 1604. Military History, 1604. Religious Life and Customs, 1265.

New Orleans, Louisiana (city). Catholic Church, 1968. Church History, 1968.

New World Order, 4872.

New York, New York (city). Puerto Ricans, 3554.

New York & Bermudez Company, 2659.

Newen Zeytung auss Presillg Landt, 2521.

Newspapers. Argentina, 3034, 3128. Brazil, 3349. Costa Rica, 1793. Elites, 3349. Haiti,

Orígenes (Cuban literary group), 3596.
Orinoco River Region (Venezuela and Colombia). Legends, 572. Myths and Mythology, 572. Oral Tradition, 572. Religion, 572.
Oro, Ecuador. *See* El Oro, Ecuador (prov.).
Orozco, Pascual, 1429.
Orozco Romero, Carlos, 264.
Orquesta Sinfónica de Chile, 4743.
Orquesta Sinfónica Nacional (Bolivia), 4686.
Orrego-Salas, Juan, 4737, 4740, 4747–4748.
Ortega del Villar, Aniceto, 4796.
Ortega y Gasset, José, 4858.
Ortega y Medina, Juan Antonio, 676.
Ortés de Velasco, Francisco, 1199.
Ortiz Rubio, Pascual, 1591.
Oruro, Bolivia (city). Colonial History, 2475, 2487. Minerals and Mining Industry, 2475, 2487. Political Culture, 2475. Social History, 2475.
Oruro, Bolivia (dept.). Historic Sites, 201. History, 2866.
Osorio Bolio, Elisa, 4804.
Otavalo, Ecuador (town). Colonial History, 645. Mortuary Customs, 645. Religious Life and Customs, 645. Inheritance and Succession, 645.
Otero Silva, Miguel, 325, 3649.
Otomi (indigenous group). Colonization, 550. Electronic Resources, 538. Kings and Rulers, 516. Manuscripts, 516. Myths and Mythology, 516. Relations with Mexica, 516. Relations with Spaniards, 516. Religious Life and Customs, 516.
Our Lady of Guadalupe. *See* Guadalupe, Our Lady of.
Ouro Preto, Brazil (city). Colonial History, 3256. Households, 3256.
Outlaws. Brazil, 3327.
Paalen, Wolfgang, 267.
Pacheco, José Emilio, 3525, 4139.
Paesky, Efraín, 4680.
Páez, José Antonio, 1027.
Pagaza, Joaquín Arcadio, 1414.
Pagden, Anthony, 907.
Painters. Bolivia, 2849. Brazil, 342, 354. Caribbean Area, 291. Chile, 303, 306. Colombia, 309–310. Diaries, 2849. Dominican Republic, 290. Ecuador, 311, 313. Guatemala, 282. Mexico, 123, 141, 227–228, 234, 242, 256, 261, 266, 276, 278. Peru, 317. Puerto Rico, 289. Suriname, 287. Uruguay, 318–319. Venezuela, 322–324, 328–330.
Painting. Argentina, 295, 300. Brazil, 343, 354. Chile, 305. Colombia, 172, 307. Cuba,

292. Ecuador, 200. Indigenous Peoples, 517. Mexico, 66, 76, 94, 109, 113, 123, 130, 141, 231, 235, 255, 263, 275, 517. Peru, 316. Suriname, 287. Venezuela, 326. Viceroyalty of New Spain, 130.
País García, Frank, 2148.
Palacio de Bellas Artes (México), 269.
Palacio de Gobierno (Morelia, Mexico), 110.
Palafox, Manuel, 1422.
Paleogeography. Venezuela, 2245.
Paleoindians. *See* Paleo-Indians.
Palestinians. Honduras, 1716, 1723.
Palma, Ricardo, 3733.
Pampa, Argentina. *See* La Pampa, Argentina (prov.).
Pampas, Argentina (region). Agricultural Labor, 3000. Historiography, 2583. Human Geography, 668. Indigenous/Non-Indigenous Relations, 668. Indigenous Peoples, 668, 2583. Labor Movement, 3000. Land Tenure, 668. Peasant Movements, 2945. Social Conflict, 2945.
Pamplona, Colombia (city). History, 757.
Pan-Americanism, 1308, 4873, 4945, 4958, 4992. Philosophy, 4960.
Panama Canal. History, 1709, 1745.
Panclasta, Biófilo, 2735.
Pantanal, Brazil (region). Pictorial Works, 3932. Poetry, 3932.
Papermaking. Mexico, 1100.
Pará, Brazil (state). Colonial History, 3266. Slaves and Slavery, 3266.
Paraguayan War (1865–1870), 3047, 3160, 3268, 3305.
Paraíba, Brazil (state). Slaves and Slavery, 3303.
Paraíso occidental, 3454.
Paraíso Site. *See* El Paraíso Site (Peru).
Paramaribo, Suriname (city). Decorative Arts, 1866.
Paraná, Argentina (city). Schools, 2973.
Pardo, Felipe, 2796.
Pardo, José Joaquín, 1672.
Pardo, Manuel, 2794.
Paredes, Antonio, 2681.
Pareja y Díez Canseco, Alfredo, 3621.
Parliamentary Systems. *See* Political Systems.
Parra, Nicanor, 4128.
Parra, Teresa de la, 4190.
Parra, Violeta, 3397.
Parroquia de Santa Catarina Virgen y Mártir de México (México), 1211.
Parti communiste guadeloupéen, 2196.
Partido Aprista Peruano. *See* APRA (Peru).

Refugees, Jewish. Brazil, 3299.
Refugees, Saint Domingan. Jamaica, 1915.
Refugees, Spanish. Mexico, 1460, 1543.
Reggae Music. Caribbean Area, 4722.
Regional Development. Colombia, 2707, 2720, 2728. Mexico, 1348, 1380.
Regional Integration. Argentina, 2960.
Regionalism. Argentina, 2960. Bolivia, 2861. Brazil, 5044. Mexico, 1317, 1380. Saint Domingue, 1936.
Regla, Pedro Ramón Romero de Terreros, 1251.
Reinafé, Francisco Isidoro, 3022.
Reinafé, Guillermo, 3022.
Reinafé, José Antonio, 3022.
Reinafé, José Vicente, 3022.
Reinafé Family, 3022.
Relación de las antigüedades deste reyno del Pirú, 3455.
Relaciones Geográficas, 2240.
Relation du voyage de la Mer du Sud aux côtes du Chily e du Perou, fait pendant les années 1712, 1713 & 1714, 2511.
Religion. Brazil, 3356, 5060. Chiriguano, 2824. Incas, 564. Indigenous Peoples, 198, 567. Orinoco River Region, 572. Peru, 198, 567. Quechua, 590. Yecuana, 572.
Religion and Politics. Colonial History, 2236. Haiti, 1858. Latin America, 682, 703, 1032, 1048, 1057, 1064. Paraguay, 3154. Trinidad and Tobago, 2158. Viceroyalty of Peru, 2388.
Religión y fidelidad argentinas, 2584.
Religious Architecture. Argentina, 161. Bolivia, 179. Peru, 180.
Religious Art. Argentina, 157, 164, 167. Bolivia, 197. Brazil, 335–337. Catalogs, 114. Colombia, 172–173, 208. Conservation and Restoration, 172. Ecuador, 208. Exhibitions, 100, 336. Flemish Influences, 172. Guadalupe, Our Lady of, 92. Ivory Carving, 336. Latin America, 58–59, 64. Mexico, 80, 92, 94, 100, 109, 114, 243, 1364. Paraguay, 165. Peru, 183, 185, 198. Portuguese Influences, 335. Viceroyalty of Peru, 185, 2393.
Religious Life and Customs. African Influences, 1730, 4715. Alcohol and Alcoholism, 644. Andean Region, 2406. Aztecs, 440, 470, 487, 489, 494–495, 498, 512, 531. Bolivia, 3654. Brazil, 3265, 3307, 3312. British Guiana, 2044–2045. Central America, 1673. Chinese, 2788. Colonial History, 795, 922–923. Costa Rica, 1730. Death, 453. East Indians, 2044–2045, 2093. Ecuador, 213, 645. Incas, 643, 646. Indigenous

Peoples, 412–413, 454–455, 632, 638, 644, 4904. Jamaica, 2153. Kekchi, 1799. Latin America, 681–682, 703, 1067. Mayas, 463, 472, 487, 490, 498. Mexico, 134, 412, 436, 455, 459, 472, 510, 1190, 1214–1215, 1308, 1582. Mixtec, 443, 463. Nahuas, 463. New Mexico, US, 1265. Nueva Granada, 2298. Otomi, 516. Peru, 2788. Pima, 499. Precolumbian Civilizations, 453, 463. Puerto Rico, 1894. South America, 4904. Suriname, 1837. Trinidad and Tobago, 2093. Uruguay, 3171. Viceroyalty of New Spain, 535, 1162, 1202, 1214–1215, 1228, 1265–1266. Zapotec, 382, 463.
Religious Music. Bolivia, 4682, 4687. Guatemala, 4735. Mexico, 4770, 4776–4777, 4783. Trinidad and Tobago, 4727.
Remesal, Antonio de, 1250.
Remittances. *See* Emigrant Remittances.
Renard, Rosita, 4742.
Repatriation. Mexico, 1486.
Repertorio Americano, 1759.
Repression. Argentina, 3026, 3135. Brazil, 3288. El Salvador, 1765, 1798. Guatemala, 1742. Journalists, 1349. Nicaragua, 1797.
Republicanism. Venezuela, 2642, 2664, 2672.
Requena, Francisco, 2349.
Rescue Archaeology. *See* Salvage Archaeology.
Research. Bolivia, 2818. Caribbean Area, 1813. Haiti, 1832. Saint Domingue, 1841, 1918.
Research Institutes. Bolivia, 2818. Colombia, 2734.
Restrepo Escovar, Pedro Antonio, 2720.
Return Migration. Africans, 2084.
Revenga, José Rafael, 2268.
Reverón, Armando, 328.
Revillagigedo, Juan Vicente Güémez Pacheco de Padilla Horcasitas y Aguayo, 1157.
Revista Brasileira de Música, 4718.
Revista de la Universidad Católica, 2756.
Revolution of the Comuneros. *See* Insurrection of the Comuneros (Paraguay, 1730–1735).
Revolutionaries. Argentina, 2964. Bolivia, 2834, 4686. Clergy, 2964. Cuba, 2021, 2047, 2103, 2148, 2173. Latin America, 696. Mexico, 1097, 1167, 1294, 1327, 1415, 1434–1435, 1443, 1457–1458, 1496–1497, 1507, 1541, 1545–1546, 1550, 1560, 1566, 1570, 1578. Women, 1545.
Revolutionaries, Cuban. Mexico, 2111.
Revolutionary Literature. Cuba, 4142. Discourse Analysis, 696. Latin America, 696.

1140, 1165, 1203, 1206–1207, 1286, 1302, 1304, 1313, 1319, 1338, 1366, 1390, 1407, 1439, 1474, 1528, 1575, 1585, 1616, 1618. Mosquito, 1784. Nicaragua, 1703. Paraguay, 2607, 3163. Peru, 16, 2430, 2779, 2798, 2806–2807. Puerto Rico, 1885–1887. Saint Barthélemy, 2050. Spain, 836. Suriname, 1825. Uruguay, 3174, 3185. Venezuela, 2253, 2649, 2652, 2656, 2671, 2682. Viceroyalty of New Spain, 1155, 1197, 1204.

Social Justice. Colombia, 2709. Costa Rica, 1714.

Social Life and Customs. Andean Region, 577. Aztecs, 430. Bolivia, 2849, 2859, 3654. Brazil, 3275, 3349, 3361, 4418. British Guiana, 2055. Chile, 2869, 2925, 4159. Chiquito, 613. Colombia, 2721, 2729. Costa Rica, 1632. Cuba, 2057. Easter Island, 578. Ecuador, 213, 570, 2737. Guatemala, 504. Honduras, 1636. Huanca, 2764. Incas, 622, 640. Indigenous Peoples, 176, 429, 434, 504, 659, 2764. Mapuche, 560. Mexico, 89, 429, 504, 1089, 1110, 1117, 1133, 1339, 1354, 1366–1367, 1404, 1407, 1454, 1618, 3483. Military, 2510. Nueva Granada, 2309. Peru, 2798. Portuguese, 2055. Precolumbian Civilizations, 669. Puerto Rico, 3612. Saint Domingue, 1916, 1945. Slaves and Slavery, 1935. Uruguay, 3171, 3198. Venezuela, 2667. Viceroyalty of New Spain, 434, 1117, 1133, 1228, 1286. Women, 434. Zapotec, 537.

Social Marginality. Brazil, 3321–3322. Chile, 2879. Colonial Literature, 3407. Historiography, 765. Puerto Rico, 1850.

Social Mobility. French Guiana, 1959. Military History, 2624.

Social Movements. Argentina, 2975, 5106. Artists, 270. Brazil, 3270. British Guiana, 2210. Catholic Church, 5106. Chile, 2888. Colombia, 2703. Ecuador, 2751. Guatemala, 1769, 1776. Latin America, 726. Mexico, 270, 1394, 1406, 1410, 1511, 1526, 1565, 1598. Nicaragua, 1712, 1718. Peru, 2888. Women, 738, 1068, 2210.

Social Organization. See Social Structure.

Social Policy. Argentina, 3135. Barbados, 2016. British Caribbean, 2016. Caribbean Area, 1993. Mexico, 1082. Puerto Rico, 2118. Venezuela, 2645.

Social Prediction. Dominican Republic, 4974.

Social Relations. See Social Life and Customs.

Social Sciences. Argentina, 5126. Brazil, 5056. Mexico, 4927. Philosophy, 4927.

Social Structure. Andean Region, 615. Argentina, 2963. Aztecs, 431, 435, 477, 480, 513, 528, 530, 549, 553. Bolivia, 2859. Brazil, 3341. Caribbean Area, 2060. Chibcha, 591. Chol, 1675. Colonial History, 936. Cuba, 2215. Dutch Caribbean, 2031. French Caribbean, 1960. French Guiana, 593, 1959. Incas, 581, 585, 615, 628, 653. Indigenous Peoples, 569, 603, 622, 1130. Ixil, 514. Latin America, 4895. Mayas, 414, 450, 478, 1653, 1675. Nueva Granada, 2288, 2304. Peru, 569. Precolumbian Civilizations, 408, 467, 602. Tarahumara, 465. Viceroyalty of New Spain, 1207. Zapotec, 537.

Social Thought. Christianity, 5001. Cuba, 4972. Puerto Rico, 4970. Peru, 5030.

Social Values. Nueva Granada, 2308.

Social Welfare. Argentina, 2997. Barbados, 2016. Chile, 2879. Ecuador, 2379. Jamaica, 2154. Viceroyalty of New Spain, 1203.

Socialism and Socialist Parties. Argentina, 2939, 2984, 3140, 5074–5075, 5090, 5126. Bolivia, 2830–2832, 2847. Chile, 2872, 2931. Colombia, 4994. Costa Rica, 4956. Dominican Republic, 4973. Guadeloupe, 2086, 2115. Mexico, 1394, 4935. Nicaragua, 1792. Peru, 5012, 5018. Philosophy, 4920. Uruguay, 3177, 3194.

Sociedad Económica de La Habana, 1902.

Sociedad Filarmónica Mexicana, 4771.

Sociedad Nacional de Agricultura (Chile), 2899.

Sociedad Rural Argentina, 3020.

Sociedade Colonizadora Hanseática (Brazil), 3353.

Sociedades Amigos de Bairros (Brazil), 3270.

Société de la morale chrétienne (France), 2035.

Sociolinguistics. Colombia, 2706.

Sociology. Colombia, 5001. Ecuador, 5009. Puerto Rico, 4970.

Soconusco, Mexico (region). Ethnohistory, 504.

Sodré, Joanidia Núñez, 4690.

Soldiers. British Caribbean, 4727. Cuba, 2075. Mexico, 1606.

Soldiers, Spanish. Cuba, 1843.

Sollér, Spain (town). Migration, 2004.

Solórzano Pereira, Juan de, 939.

Somoza, Anastasio, 1724, 1738, 1797.

Somoza Debayle, Anastasio, 1690, 1699, 1739, 1766.

Somoza Family, 1739.

Sonora, Mexico (state). Acculturation, 499, 1273. Agricultural Productivity, 1523. Archives, 1437. Capitalism, 1519. Chinese,

Policy, 2450. Elites, 2415, 2419, 2421, 2451, 2456, 2471, 2485. Encomiendas, 634, 2414, 2452. Ethnic Groups and Ethnicity, 2226, 2398. European Influences, 195. Expeditions, 2483. Family and Family Relations, 2456. Finance, 2450. Franciscans, 2396, 2418. French Revolution, 2415. Guilds, 2405. Haciendas, 2407. Historical Demography, 2414, 2479. Historical Geography, 2395. Historiography, 2459. History, 2389. Iconography, 185, 195. Indigenous/Non-Indigenous Relations, 2403, 2406, 2455, 2471, 2484. Indigenous Peoples, 588, 594, 655, 2404, 2414, 2427, 2435, 2438, 2444, 2449, 2462, 2484, 2487. Indigenous Policy, 569, 617, 2331, 2406, 2414, 2428, 2440, 2458, 2462, 2484. Inheritance and Succession, 2410. Inquisition, 2408–2409, 2412, 2453. Insurrections, 2420, 2444, 2471. Intellectual History, 2411, 2435. Intellectuals, 2435. International Relations, 2227. Interpersonal Relationships, 2382. Jesuits, 2402, 2473, 2482. Kinship, 2434. Labor Market, 2427. Land Tenure, 634, 2407, 2452, 2479, 2484. Law and Legislation, 2407, 2443, 2458. Libraries, 2408, 2411. Marriage, 2456. Merchants, 2431, 2485. Military History, 2463. Minerals and Mining Industry, 2404, 2445, 2447, 2486–2487. Missionaries, 2396, 2418, 2436. Missions, 2390, 2454, 2481–2482. Mita, 617. Monetary Policy, 2429. Money, 2429. Naval History, 2384. Newspapers, 2419. Peasants, 2479. Political Corruption, 2625. Political Culture, 2398, 2625. Political Ideology, 2415. Political Reform, 2415. Popular Culture, 2426. Popular Religion, 2423–2424, 2426. Prices, 2432. Publishers and Publishing, 2468. Race and Race Relations, 2226. Rain and Rainfall, 2439. Religion and Politics, 2388. Religious Art, 185, 2393. Religious Life and Customs, 2392, 2406, 2423–2424, 2426, 2438, 2449, 2453. Repression, 2420. Revolutions and Revolutionary Movements, 2420. Rites and Ceremonies, 2331, 2437. Rural-Urban Migration, 2427. Sculpture, 185. Sex and Sexual Relations, 2387, 2434. Silver, 2445, 2486. Silverwork, 192, 211. Slaves and Slavery, 2457, 2463. Social Change, 2487. Social Classes, 2434. Social Conditions, 2428. Social Conflict, 634, 2452, 2471. Social History, 2430, 2434, 2487. Social Life and Customs, 2387, 2423–2424, 2426, 2434, 2443, 2485. Social Structure, 2385, 2415, 2451. Sources, 2419,

2459. Spaniards, 2461. Spanish Conquest, 2454. Tombs, 195. Traditional Medicine, 2423. Universities, 2391, 2476. Urban History, 2397. Violence, 2420. Water Supply, 2395. Wine and Wine Making, 2422. Women, 2424.

Viceroyalty of Río de la Plata (1776–1810). Bibliography, 2523. Bourbon Reforms, 2613. Cabildos, 2585. Church-State Relations, 2634. Colonial Administration, 2469, 2585, 2587, 2598, 2600, 2613. Elites, 2623. Family and Family Relations, 2600, 2623. Feminism, 2584. Finance, 2626. Higher Education, 2523. Indigenous/Non-Indigenous Relations, 2603. Kinship, 2600, 2623. Mercantile System, 2600. Military, 2624. Military History, 2624. Mortuary Customs, 2631. Political Corruption, 2625. Political Culture, 2600, 2625, 2627. Race and Race Relations, 2623. Religion and Politics, 2634. Slaves and Slavery, 2581. Social Life and Customs, 2559. Social Mobility, 2624. Tobacco Use, 2515–2516. Universities, 2523. Women, 2584, 2591.

Viceroys. Mexico, 1157.

Vico, Giambattista, 5080.

Victoria, Francisco de, 3443.

Vicuña Mackenna, Benjamín, 5036.

Vidaurri, Santiago, 1317.

Viedma, Francisco de, 2481.

Vieques, Puerto Rico (island). Indigenous Peoples, 1893.

Vietnamese Conflict (1961–1975). Cuba, 2204.

Vigas, Oswaldo, 324.

Vilcabamba Site (Peru), 2454.

Villa, Pancho, 1435, 1497, 1524, 1574, 1615.

Villa-Lobos, Heitor, 4697, 4701.

Villaflor Family, 2947.

Villages. History, 755. Production (economics), 1416.

Villagrán Kramer, Francisco, 1764, 1795.

Villancicos. African Influences, 4660. Indigenous Influences, 4660. Indigenous Music, 4807. Musical History, 4660. Peru, 4807. Web Sites, 44.

Villanueva, Carlos Raúl, 323.

Villard, de Honnecourt, 81.

Villas, Cuba. See Las Villas, Cuba (prov.).

Villavicencio, Rafael, 4989.

Villegas, Abelardo, 4939.

Vindobonensis Codex. See Codices. Vindobonensis.

Violence. Andean Region, 592, 654. Colombia, 2718, 2722. Costa Rica, 1704. Guate-

AUTHOR INDEX

Etcheverry, Jorge, 4522
Ethnohistory: the Bulletin of the Ohio Valley Historic Indian Conference, 434
Etica y política hoy en el Perú, 5014
Etienvre, Jean-Pierre, 4841
Euclides Neto, 4317
Euraque, Darío, 1716
Evans, Susan T., 435
Evans, Walker, 2138
Exil in Brasilien: die deutschsprachige Emigration, 1933–1945; eine Ausstellung des Deutschen Exilarchivs 1933–1945, die Deutsche Bibliothek, Frankfurt am Main, 3299
La Expedición Malaspina, 1789–1794, 854–855
La explotación del éxito colombino: con el sistema de viajes de "descubrimiento y rescate.", 856
Exposición Barroco Latinoamericano, 53
Exposición Universal de 1991 (Sevilla, Spain). Pabellón del Perú, 187
Exposiciones, 1989–1994, 245
Ezquerra Abadia, Ramón, 1012
Ezquerra de la Colina, José Luis, 246

Fabela, Isidro, 4744
Fabre, F., 2139
Fábregas Puig, Andrés, 1469
Fabrés y su tiempo, 1854–1938, 247
Fadanelli, Guillermo J., 3486
Falabella, Miguel, 4414
Falcón, Romana, 1312
Falconnet, Joaquín Alejo, 5095
Faraco, Sérgio, 4415
Farago, Claire J., 63
Faria, João Roberto, 4491
Farias, Herculano, 4361
Farriss, Nancy, 436
Faustino, Mário, 4451
Favre, Henri, 1313
Fayen, Tanya T., 4575
Fe, riqueza y poder: antología crítica de documentos para la historia de Honduras, 1649
Febres, Laura, 4964
Federalismos latinoamericanos: México, Brasil, Argentina, 1013
Fedorova, I.K., 578
Feierstein, Ricardo, 3021
O feixe e o prisma: uma revisão do Estado Novo, 3300
Feldman, Lawrence H., 1630
Felinto, Marilene, 4620
Fell, Claude, 4932
Ferlini, Vera Lucia Amaral, 3242

Fermandois, Joaquín, 2891
Fernandes, Gaspar, 4777
Fernández, Alejandro, 54
Fernández, Ariosto, 2551
Fernández, Aurea Matilde, 2014
Fernández, Gerardo, 4263
Fernández, Jesse, 3900
Fernández, Juan Patricio, 579, 2552
Fernández, Macedonio, 3979
Fernández, María del Carmen, 3701
Fernández, Miguel Angel, 2604
Fernández, Raúl A., 4757
Fernández, Rodolfo, 1145–1146
Fernandez, Ronald, 2140
Fernández, Teodosio, 4857
Fernández Alexander de Schorr, Adela, 2553
Fernández Alonso, Serena, 2399–2400, 2777
Fernández Buey, Francisco, 726, 857
Fernández Cabrelli, Alfonso, 3185–3186
Fernández Canales, Consuelo, 2015
Fernández de Amicarelli, Estela, 4858, 4933
Fernández de Pinedo, Emiliano, 1014
Fernández Fernández, José, 2069
Fernández Fraile, Maximino, 3806
Fernández García, Angel Valentín, 1927
Fernández García, Martha, 93
Fernández González, Alvaro, 1717
Fernández González, Francisco, 1015
Fernández Gordián, Osvaldo, 3561
Fernández Guardia, Ricardo, 4198
Fernández Heres, Rafael, 4989
Fernández Herrero, Beatriz, 4859
Fernández Martín, Luis, 2401
Fernández Molina, José Antonio, 1650
Fernández Moreno, César, 3980
Fernández Moreno, Inés, 3826
Fernández Olmos, Margarite, 4524, 4527
Fernández Perera, Manuel, 3487
Fernández Poncela, Anna M., 1718
Fernández Prando, Federico, 5065
Fernández Rueda, Sonia, 2329
Fernández Ruiz, Consuelo, 248
Fernández Valledor, Roberto, 1927
Fernández Valverde, Juan, 835
Fernández Vial, Ignacio, 831
Fernlund, Kevin J., 1470
Ferrari, Américo, 4092, 4116
Ferrari, Marcela P., 3003
Ferraz, Marcelo Carvalho, 363
Ferré, Luis Alberto, 2141
Ferré, Rosario, 2141, 3562–3563
Ferreira, César, 3636
Ferreira, Luzilá Gonçalves, 4318, 4450
Ferreira, Marieta de Moraes, 3298
Ferreira de Cassone, Florencia, 4860

Pérez, Francisco Javier, 2991
Pérez, José Joaquín, 4059
Pérez, Joseph, 4856
Pérez, Louis A., 2187
Pérez, Odalís, 4047
Pérez, Osvaldo, 2602
Pérez Acevedo, Martín, 1371
Pérez Bertruy, Ramona Isabel, 1563
Pérez Brignoli, Héctor, 1765, 1790
Pérez Bustamante, Ciriaco, 906
Pérez Correa, Hernán, 629
Pérez González, María Luisa, 1675
Pérez Guzmán, Francisco, 2070
Pérez Herrero, Pedro, 951, 1059
Pérez Jiménez, Marcos, 2670
Pérez Ledesma, Manuel, 726
Pérez Linares, Ramón, 4979
Pérez Martínez, Herón, 4635, 4944
Pérez Memén, Fernando, 4977
Pérez Mota, Luis Enrique, 1564
Pérez Olivares, Porfirio, 1565
Pérez-Prendes y Muñoz de Arracó, José Manuel, 1017
Pérez-Rocha, Emma, 84, 1209
Pérez Salazar, Francisco, 123
Pérez Toledo, Sonia, 1372
Pérez Tomás, Eduardo E., 952
Pérez Torres, Raúl, 3619, 3696
Pérez Torrico, Alexis, 2855
Peri Rossi, Cristina, 4547
Pericás, Luiz Bernardo, 4389
Perissinotto, Renato Monseff, 3347
Peritore, N. Patrick, 5055
Perón, Juan Domingo, 3075, 3089
Pérotin-Dumon, Anne, 1849, 1926, 1955
Perrone, Charles A., 4413
Perry, Richard D., 124
Persaud, Walter H., 2071
Pérsio, Ricardo Paulinelli, 4485
El Perú emergente: la nación de la mil interpretaciones, 2798
Perú, hombre e historia, 2799
Perusse, Roland I., 2188
Pesavento, Sandra Jatahy, 3348–3349
Pescador, Juan Javier, 1210–1211
Peset Reig, José Luis, 698
Pesoa, Manuel, 3165
Peterson, Jeanette Favrot, 509
Petit Muñoz, Eugenio, 3204
Petitjean-Roger, Henri, 1873
Petrocelli, Héctor B., 953
Peynado, Francisco José, 2189
Pezzullo, Lawrence, 1766
Pezzullo, Ralph, 1766

Pfeiffer, Erna, 3524
Phillips, George Harwood, 1275
The Philosophical Forum, 4893
Piana de Cuestas, Josefina, 2603
Piazzolla, Astor, 4677
Picado, Miguel, 1680
Picazo I Muntaner, Antoni, 1276
Piccagli, Américo E., 3090
Pichardo, Tony, 4060
Pickens, Buford, 108
Picó, Fernando, 1850
Piel, Jean, 760, 1073
Pietschmann, Horst, 1034, 1212
Piglia, Ricardo, 4591
Pignatelli, Adrián, 3091
Pike, Fredrick B., 1074
Pimentel, Miguel A., 4978
Pimentel, Thaïs Velloso Cougo, 3350
Piña, Cristina, 4063
Piña, Juan Andrés, 4264
Piña Chán, Román, 274
Piña Homs, Román, 701
Pinacoteca do Estado de São Paulo, 376
Pinckert Justiniano, Guillermo, 2829
Pinedo, Javier, 2502
Piñero, Eugenio, 2264–2265
Pinheiro, Mauro, 4336
Pino Iturrieta, Elías, 2636, 2671–2673
Pinochet de la Barra, Oscar, 956
Piñón Flores, Iraís, 1254
Pintado, José Manuel, 4061
Pinto, José Alcides, 4470
Pinto, Julieta, 3540–3541
Pinto, Tiago de Oliveira, 4648
Pinto Rodríguez, Jorge, 954
Pinto Vallejos, Julio, 2919–2920
Pinto Villarroel, Patricia, 4285
Pintura peruana: década de los 90; homenaje a Juan Acha, 316
Pinzón de Lewin, Patricia, 2719
Pio, Djanira, 4390
Piossek Prebisch, Lucía, 5112
Pirela, Marvin, 4242
Pires, Delores, 4456
Pisarello Virasoro, Roberto Gustavo, 2948
Pitol, Sergio, 3507
Pivel Devoto, Juan E., 3182, 3205
Pizarnik, Alejandra, 4062–4064
Pizarro, Ana, 3406
Pizzurno Gelós, Patricia, 1643, 1692
Plá, Josefina, 2604
El Plan de Pitic de 1789 y las nuevas poblaciones proyectadas en las Provincias Internas de la Nueva España, 1277

Wasserman, Mark, 1622–1623
Watanabe, José, 4104
Waters, Mary-Alice, 2834
Watson, Ellen, 4621
We people here: Nahuatl accounts of the conquest of Mexico, 547
Weaver, Frederick Stirton, 1639
Weber, David J., 786
Webmuseo de Latinoamérica, 34
Webre, Stephen, 1688
Weckmann, Luis, 3269
Wedovoy, Enrique, 3146
Weeks, John M., 548
Wehrs, Carlos, 4720
Weinberg, Gregorio, 4916
Weinberger, Eliot, 4517
Weiss, Judith A., 4302
Wells, Alan, 1507
Wende, Frank, 3299
Westphalen, Emilio Adolfo, 4105
Where cultures meet: frontiers in Latin American history, 786
Whigham, Thomas, 3170
Whitehead, Laurence, 2867
Whitehead, Neil L., 670–671
Whitfield, Teresa, 1798
Wiegert, Jutta, 295
Wieser, Lothar, 3343
Wiethüchter, Blanca, 4106
Wilheim, Jorge, 4341
Wilkie, James Wallace, 1468
Williams, Eduardo, 426
Williams, Edward J., 1624
Williams, Eric Eustace, 2212
Williams, Gayle, 32
Williams, Jerry M., 3465
Williams, Patrick, 3377
Williams, Philip J., 1796
Williams, Robert Gregory, 1640
Williams, Tamara R., 4538
Willock, Roger, 2098
Wilmot, Swithin R., 2099
Wilson, Jason, 4638
Wilson, Patricia Ann, 1625
Wilson, Richard, 787, 1799
Winfield Capitaine, Fernando, 1119
Winn, Peter, 788
Winocur, Marcos, 2213
Wobeser, Gisela von, 1092, 1252–1253
Wojcieszak, Janusz, 4949
Wolfe, Joel, 3373
Wonen in Suriname [Housing in Suriname], 1866
Wood, Stephanie, 471, 549
Woodward, Ralph Lee, 1800

Woolford, Hazel M., 2100, 2214
The world out of which Canudos came, 3374
Wright, A.D., 995
Wright Carr, David Charles, 550
Writing without words: alternative literacies in Mesoamerica and the Andes, 551
Wuffarden, Luis Eduardo, 2767
Wünderich, Volker, 1801

Xin Shijiede Zhendang: Lading Meichou Duli Yundong [New World tremblings: the Independence Movement of Latin America], 1045
Xul Solar, Alejandro, 300

"Y por mí visto—" : mandamientos, ordenanzas, licencias y otras disposiciones virreinales del siglo XVI., 1254
Yacou, Alain, 1873, 2101
Yampolsky, Mariana, 145, 1404
Yamuni Tabush, Vera, 4950
Yáñez, Mirta, 3560
Yánez Cossío, Alicia, 3710
Yáñez Díaz, Gonzalo, 1255
Yánover, Héctor, 4001
Yarrington, Doug, 2682
Ycaza Cortez, Patricio, 2752
Yeager, Gertrude Matyoka, 700
Yoneda, Keiko, 146
Yúdice, George, 4626

Zabala Ruiz, Manuel, 3699
Zacklin, Lyda, 4529
Zagarra, Margarita, 2815
Zago, Manrique, 160, 3100
Zalamea, Jorge, 4163
Zamalloa Armejo, Raúl, 2468
Zamora, Bladimir, 2023
Zamora, Daisy, 3905, 4552
Zamora, Hermenegildo, 996
Zamudio Barrios, Arturo, 5124
Zamudio Espinosa, Guadalupe Yolanda, 1256
Zancanaro, Lourenço, 5062
Zanetti Lecuona, Oscar, 2215
Zantwijk, Rudolf van, 552
Zapata, Alfredo, 3517
Zapata, Francisco, 4917
Zapata, Luis, 3518
Zapata Gacitúa, Juan, 4156
Zapata Olivella, Manuel, 3686
Zapata Oliveras, Carlos R., 2216
Zapico, Hilda Raquel, 2635
Zárate, Milton, 4107
Zárate Toscano, Verónica, 1392
Zarzar, Alonso, 672